A gift from

Marin Association of
Life Underwriters, Inc.
Jun

D0553963

LIFE INSURANCE
Theory and Practice

LIFE INSURANCE
THEORY AND PRACTICE

Robert I. Mehr

Professor of Finance
University of Illinois at Urbana-Champaign

1970
BUSINESS PUBLICATIONS, INC.
Dallas, Texas   75224

Irwin-Dorsey Limited, Georgetown, Ontario

FIRST PRINTING, JUNE, 1970
SECOND PRINTING, APRIL, 1972

Library of Congress Catalog Card No. 79–112834

Printed in the United States of America

To CIRILO A. McSWEEN

Of all my eminently successful students, I have the greatest admiration for Cirilo A. McSween, not only for his success as a professional life insurance man (he has made the Million Dollar Round Table each year since leaving the University in 1956), but, more importantly, for his dedication to making a better life for his race through his total commitment to Operation Breadbasket and devotion to the duties of his office of Treasurer of the Southern Christian Leadership Conference.

R. I. M.

Preface

An English philosopher once said, "When a new book comes out I read an old one." I suppose that this philosophy is based on the belief that "books, like proverbs, receive their chief value from the stamp and esteem of the ages through which they have passed." But adherence to this philosophy creates a problem if one is seeking a fresh textbook for use in an up-to-date course, unless he is willing to settle for a new "old book." *Life Insurance: Theory and Practice* is precisely that: a new "old book."

This book is what might have been the fourth edition of *Modern Life Insurance* by Robert I. Mehr and Robert W. Osler, a work first published in 1949, with revised editions appearing in 1956 and in 1961. Not long after preparation began for the fourth edition, other interests forced R. W. Osler to request termination of the joint project. Those contributions of his to *Modern Life Insurance* that have been salvaged for *Life Insurance: Theory and Practice* are acknowledged with genuine gratitude. Furthermore, Chapter 20 of this text is dedicated to him in recognition of his pioneering efforts in integrated programming of life and health insurance.

What else is old? Of course, there is the author who joined the human race in June, 1917, and the rat race some years later. Then there is the name of the publisher, Business Publications, Inc., the original name of its parent company, Richard D. Irwin, Inc., a company that for years has specialized in the publication of books in business and economics. Also old are the basic organization, writing style, objectivity, and emphasis found in its prior work, *Modern Life Insurance*. And finally, there is Professor William T. Beadles, editor of the *Journal of Risk and Insurance*, who has been the mainstay of the work throughout all three editions and who again read every line, dot, and comma of the manuscript and caught many loose, and sometimes ridiculous, statements that otherwise would have gone into print to haunt the author forever. Fortunately the author, in reading Professor Beadles' sometimes caustic comments, was not enslaved by the notion put forth in Cervantes' observation that "no fathers or mothers think their own children ugly; and this self-deceit is yet stronger with respect to the offspring of the mind." Professor Beadles caused the author the greatest hangup on Chapter 27, requiring him days of rethinking and rewriting.

Therefore, Chapter 27 of this book is dedicated to Professor William T. Beadles for his insistence on clarity and precision despite the feeling of some academicians that "clear writers, like clear fountains, do not seem so deep as they are; the turbid seem the most profound."

What is new? *Life Insurance: Theory and Practice* integrates the new theories and practices developed in the decade of the sixties. It approaches the subject of life and health insurance as a risk management device and develops the framework for this approach in Chapters 2 and 3. Attention is given to the concepts of the fair mathematical bet and the expected value of the game and how they may be used in insurance purchase decisions. The discussion of the concept of risk is designed to focus attention on how the concept is used in disciplines other than insurance in order to provide a perspective for an operational definition of risk for the study of life and health insurance, and to examine in some detail the various measurements of risk.

The life insurance business continues to be an exciting one. New issues arise as old ones are either solved or forgotten. Among the major issues of the 1960's were the wide disparity in the prices charged for credit life insurance, the problem of dual regulation of the issuers of variable annuities, the conflict-of-interest problems created by the tie-in between life insurers and mutual funds, the regulatory problems created by life insurers becoming a part of holding companies and conglomerates, the question of disclosure of life insurance price information, the problem of effectively regulating mail-order insurance companies, the problem of selection against the insurer in policy loans, the need to adjust medical care insurance coverage to the medicare provisions of the Social Security Act, the problem of replacement of policies and its effect on insureds and insurers, the problem of improving the competitive position of insurers as funding agencies for pension plans, the need for legislation to improve the standard of security offered employees covered under private pension plans, the problems created by the expanding birthrate of new life insurers, and the problem of developing life insurance products that adjust to an economy characterized by inflation and growth.

The past decade has brought with it important revolutionary trends in the life insurance business, principally the introduction of equity products and the movement toward widening the financial services offered to the public by finance-related holding companies formed principally by insurance interests to serve the total financial needs of clients, and to meet the competition of other financial institutions.

The decade just completed witnessed the genesis of an industry-wide awareness that self-interest dictates responsiveness not only to customer interests, competitive forces, and regulatory forces, but also to environmental changes taking place in the urban society in which insurers largely operate. For survival, insurers are dependent on social stability. They cannot operate successfully in an environment in which the probability of anarchy and rebellion is high. Some enlightened insurers recognize the healthy economic implications of upgrading the skills and managerial talents of minority races in the United States, and of providing them the opportunity to contribute more, and therefore share more, of the fruits of the economy. These insurers are giving embryonic responses to the need for social stability by accepting some degree of responsibility for commitments to urban planning; investments in projects designed to provide those in the inner cities better housing and better employment opportunities; upgrading minority employment including those at management levels; and working with the coalition of business, governmental, and voluntary organizations on problems which are too large for any one sector alone. Their motivation is not a part of a moral crusade but rather of a well-conceived sound business policy.

In the sixties a notable trend was the growing spirit of mutual understanding and cooperation between life insurance companies and the government. The public and private sectors moved closer together in the handling of three major problems of financial security: Federal Government Employees' Group Life and Group Health Insurance issued by private insurers, Servicemen's Group Life Insurance underwritten by private insurers through a contract with the Veterans' Administration, and the role of private insurers in helping to administer benefits under medicare.

The sixties witnessed the expansion of health insurance covers and of health insurance purveyors. About 30 percent of all life insurance company premiums were generated by health insurance at the end of the decade, compared with about 23 percent at the beginning of the decade. Health insurance is treated in this text not only through integrated discussions with life insurance at various points throughout the text, but also through segregated discussions in three separate chapters: one devoted to health insurance covers generally, another handling individual policies primarily, and the third dealing with group insurance exclusively.

The sixties also experienced a major thrust not only in the introduction and expansion of employee benefits plans in the American economy, but also in the use of life insurers as funding agencies for these plans. About 40 percent of the life insurance in force in the United States at the end of the decade was in group insurance compared with less than 30 percent at the beginning of the decade. And more than 67 percent of the health insurance premiums written in this country at the end of the decade were group premiums compared with less than 62 percent at the beginning of the decade. Furthermore, about 25 percent of the assets of life insurers at the end of the decade was attributable to pension business compared with about 15 percent at the beginning of the decade. More than 42 percent of all life insurance premium income at the end of the decade was attributable to group insurance and pension plans compared to about 33 percent at the beginning of the decade. Because of the importance of insurance in employee benefit plans, five chapters are given to this subject.

The sixties found debate and discussion of the question of price competition in the life insurance business stimulated by the scholarly writings of Indiana University Professor Joseph M. Belth. The materials in this text that draw on Professor Belth's works are found in Chapters 8, 28, 29, and appended to Chapters 25 and 26. Professor Belth graciously read the manuscript for these chapters and appendixes and offered thoughtful suggestions that proved valuable to the author in polishing the final draft of the manuscript. In recognition of Joseph Belth's outstanding contributions to the literature on life insurance companies and their variations, Chapter 28 of this text is dedicated to him.

The compelling desire of the author to discuss all of these new ideas and practices without economizing in the treatment of essential basic topics has resulted in a book longer than other life insurance textbooks. If the professor and student attempt to cover this book in a one-semester, three-hour, undergraduate course, then, to paraphrase Bacon, parts of the book are simply to be tasted, other parts are solely to be swallowed, and only a small part is to be chewed and digested. It is up to the professor, after determining where individual interests lie, to order the portions in quantities that satisfy the tastes and appetites of his students.

For a more structured one-semester course, several combinations of chapters are appropriate, depending on whether a previous course in insurance has been taken, what other insurance courses will follow, and the emphasis desired for the course. Each chapter is self-contained so that whole chapters may be omitted without affecting the student's ability to understand those chapters assigned.

In addition to the basic life insurance course, this book may be used in a course in employee benefit plans by assigning parts of Chapters 13, 14, and 29, and all of Chapters 6, 15, 16, 17, 18, and 19, plus cases and problems relating to employee benefit plans. It may be used also in a course in life insurance planning by assigning parts of Chapters 8, 9, 13, 14, and 28, and all of Chapters 10, 20, 21, and 22, plus a series of programming and estate planning problems and cases.

All mathematical and statistical explanations have been appended to the appropriate chapters rather than included in the body of the chapters, so as not to complicate these chapters for those students not interested in mathematical complexities. Footnotes have been used extensively for some detailed explanations and for appropriate comments. Questions for each chapter are appended to the end of the book.

That the length of the book is an advantage rather than a limitation should be quickly recognized by insurance teachers and their students because a close parallel exists between textbook content and insurance. It is true for both that it is better to have it and not need it, than to need it and not have it.

In addition to those already thanked in this preface, the author acknowledges the help of four graduate assistants in Finance at the University of

Illinois, Urbana: Mark Dorfman, William Kessner, David Klock, and Keith McVicker. Also, the author wishes to thank his conscientious and competent typist, Barbara Foil, and to express appreciation to Jane Fetrow, Finance departmental secretary, for showing genuine interest in the progress of the members of the department and deep concern for their frustrations.

The author congratulates those readers who find errors of substance in the text, and accepts full credit for providing them with this additional exhilarating intellectual experience.

"There are three difficulties in authorship—to write anything worth publishing—to find honest men to publish it—and to get sensible men to read it." The author is confident that he is home free with his publisher. Beyond that there is only hope for all concerned that the other difficulties have been overcome.

Champaign, Illinois   ROBERT I. MEHR
May, 1970

Contents

xiii

manent Life Insurance: *The Unit Purchase Plan. The Level Premium Plan.*
7. Wholesale (Franchise) Life Insurance. 8. Group Credit Life Insurance:
Group Credit Life Insurance and Public Policy.

ministrative Regulation. Self-Regulation. 4. What is Regulated? *Organization of New Companies. Company Finance. Product Regulation. Group Insurance Regulation. Regulation of Marketing Activities.* 5. Taxation of Life Insurance Companies. *The Federal Income Tax. State Taxes.*

1

What Life Insurance Is All About

Life insurance, one of the largest and most important industries in America, is a business with far-reaching social and economic implications. Its first concern is with people's lives. It provides men and women with an institution through which they can systematically create financial security for their families and businesses. It also serves the economy as an important channel through which capital is made available to business and industry. It is a business that affects everyone, directly or indirectly. Thus it is an important field of study that merits the thoughtful attention of all who would consider themselves knowledgeable in business, economics, or finance. Fortunately, it is also an interesting business.

1. INTERDEPENDENCE OF SUBJECT MATTER

The subject of life insurance is one that nearly everyone will discuss sooner or later. Nearly everybody knows something about it, but unfortunately many who buy it and some who sell it have only a superficial knowledge. Even those who legislate controls or propose reforms for the business are not always sufficiently informed.

What does one need to know to become adequately informed about life insurance? It is essential that he know a few basic principles of contract and agency law, accounting, economics, marketing, finance, business management, actuarial mathematics, government, and the behavioral sciences—all as they apply to life insurance. Although this seems like a rather large order, it is not, because everything is logical, and the pattern as a whole fits quite neatly.

However, in gaining a life insurance education, one problem does present itself. Although the pieces fit together snugly, it is not easy to determine the order in which the pieces should be developed. For example, to understand types of policies thoroughly one should know something about methods of premium computation. But to comprehend premium computations adequately, one must know something about types of policies. This interdependence applies with equal force to other aspects of knowledge about the field.

Thus, since it is necessary to know something of the whole to understand and appreciate the parts, the basic question is where to begin. The bright young man will say, "With Chapter 1, of course," but that does not solve the problem of Chapter 1 for the author. Perhaps the best beginning is to give a bird's-eye view of life insurance—a sort of short summary in advance. In other words, it seems that a full understanding of life insurance can be developed best by mapping the forest before beginning a study of the trees. In this way, there is less likelihood of becoming lost in what might appear to be a wild, uncultivated waste.

2. WHY LIFE INSURANCE?

In the great majority of family units, the principal source of income is compensation for work performed by the family head. If this source of income were to be cut off, the family would find it necessary to make economic and social adjustments which might result in serious physical or psychological harm. The mother might have to take outside employment at the expense of her homemaking responsibilities; the children might have to go to work at the expense of their formal education; the family members might have to accept charity from relatives, friends, or social agencies at the expense of their independence and self-respect; and the family standard of living might have to be reduced to a level below that essential for health and happiness.

Illness, death, unemployment, and retirement are four basic threats to the continuation of income from wages or salaries. The first three of these can strike any time during a man's life; and when they do, it is essential that a replacement for the lost income be available if the family is to be spared the hardships of unsatisfactory economic adjustment.

The level of earnings of a business is dependent upon the effectiveness of its management. Disability and death of key personnel can adversely affect a firm's net profit. When they do, it is essential that adequate resources be available if the business is to regain its profit position.

Successful financial management requires that effective before-the-loss arrangements be made to provide after-the-loss resources needed to preserve the operating efficiency of the family or business unit. Life insurance is one of the techniques available for this purpose. Through the use of life insurance a man can plan for the continuation of an income if death, disability, or old age destroys his ability to earn a living, and a business can plan for the resources to offset potential losses if a key man becomes disabled or dies. Life insurance is used here in its generic meaning to include all forms of insurance designed to protect against loss of income arising from inability to work, whether this be caused by death, accidental injury, sickness, or old age.

In its narrow or specific meaning, life insurance implies financial protection in the event of death only. Protection in event of accidental injury or sickness is covered by health insurance and retirement income is provided through annuities. Perhaps a better generic term for the broader field is income insurance; but unfortunately, even this term has its limitations, for it does not imply expense coverage. Dying costs money, and illnesses are expensive. Bills from tax collectors, funeral directors, doctors, druggists, nurses, and hospitals mount quickly. Life and health insurance are used to help pay these expenses.

3. HUMAN LIFE VALUES

The concept of the human life value has been developed to measure the economic value of a life. It is an important concept in the economics of litigation involving wrongful deaths and injuries.

Measure of Human Life Value. The two basic sources of income are capital and labor, or money at work and men at work. Money at work earns interest, rent, or dividends. Men at work earn wages, salaries, fees, or commissions.

If, for example, the owner of the building which houses the campus drugstore earns $10,000 a year rent, net after taxes, depreciation, and the cost of insurance, the building would be worth $100,000, assuming a 10 percent capitalization rate. An individual with an earning power of $10,000 a year, net after taxes, also has an economic value measurable in terms of dollars.

A man's economic value is a direct linear function of his expected annual earnings and his work life expectancy and an inverse linear function of his expected income tax liability and his expected personal maintenance expenses. Assume that a 35-year-old man is earning $16,000 annually and expects his earnings to remain at this level,[1] that he has a work life expectancy of 28.6 years;[2] that his expected annual income tax liability is $2,000,[3] and that his expected annual personal maintenance expenses are

---

[1] Because of inflation, growth, and natural progression, it is unrealistic to assume that a man now earning $16,000 a year will continue to earn at this rate throughout his life expectancy. However, this assumption is made for the purpose of simplifying the illustration.

[2] Stuart Garfinkle, "Table of Working Life for Men, 1960," *Monthly Labor Review*, July, 1963, p. 822.

[3] A person's income tax liability is a function of a number of variables aside from earnings. Even if earnings remain the same as is assumed here, it cannot be assumed that the income tax liability also will remain the same. Tax rates change, the number of dependents vary, investment and other income may not be stable and the dollar amount of deductions fluctuate. For this reason the courts have avoided dealing specifically with deductions for taxes in establishing damages for wrongful injury or death. Nevertheless, for simplicity, the assumption is made here that the income tax liability will remain at its current level.

and will continue to be $4,000, 25 percent of his gross earnings. Based on these assumptions, this man's family can expect to gain $10,000 a year for 28.6 years from this man's continued life, computed as follows:

Gross Income		$16,000
Less: Income Tax Liability	$2,000	
Personal Expenses	4,000	
		− 6,000
Net Income to Family		$10,000

The $10,000 annually is expected to continue for 28.6 years, the work life expectancy of the working male, age 35 as computed by the Bureau of Labor Statistics.[4] The measure of the life value of this man would be that amount which at the appropriate interest rate will provide $10,000 annually received in 12 monthly payments for 28.6 years. Tables showing the present value at various interest rates of one per annum payable in 12 equal monthly installments are published for use in making computations.[5] Assuming 5 percent to be appropriate, the present value of one per annum payable in 12 equal monthly installments for 28.6 years is 15.38. The present value of $10,000 per year would then be 15.38 × $10,000 or $153,800, the human life value of the man in question.

Life Insurance and Human Life Value.   The amount of the human life value is irrelevant to the study of life insurance as will soon become apparent. With respect to human life value, life insurance has two functions: (1) to contribute toward its conservation and (2) to protect against financial losses resulting from its destruction.

Life Conservation.   Life insurance companies are concerned not only with people's lives but also with situations that affect the value of those lives. Just as fire insurance companies are interested in fire prevention, so life insurance companies are interested in the prevention of accident, disease, and death.

Life insurance has fostered and maintained medical research and health conservation activities directed toward preserving human life value. The Life Insurance Medical Research Fund, cooperatively supported by many United States and Canadian companies, is one example. It offers fellowships and grants-in-aid for research.

---

[4] The work life expectancy reflects the separations from the labor force due to all causes including death, disability, and retirement. Work life expectancy, the average number of remaining years of labor force participation, obviously would be less than life expectancy, the average number of remaining years of life. For the 35-year-old male, life expectancy, using the same set of data, is 35.7 years.

[5] The quantity tabulated is as follows:

$$\frac{1 - (1 + i)^{-n}}{p[(1 + i)^{1/p} - 1]}$$

where i is the interest rate, n is the number of years over which payments are to be made, and p is the number of payments per year.

Life insurance companies have been active in the promotion of public health legislation, using their facilities for the distribution of information pertaining to the need for such legislation. The collection and dissemination of information regarding the extra accident and health hazard in certain occupations has tended to emphasize the need for corrective measures. A number of life insurance companies prepare and distribute to the public, health booklets which are designed to promote life conservation. One major company devotes most of its media advertising to health conservation themes. Another advertises widely that it gives lower rates to nonsmokers.

Protection against Financial Loss. It is through its service of providing protection against financial losses resulting from the destruction of human life value that life insurance is best known. However, a great deal of folk-lore has been developed that relates the appropriate amount of life insurance to be purchased to the concept of human life value.[6] This folklore suggests that the appropriate amount of life insurance needed is the present value of future net earnings. Another lore may be developing that relates the appropriate amount of life insurance to be purchased to a concept of insurable value, defined as the amount of income forfeited in the event of death before planned retirement.[7] But neither the concepts of human life value or insurable value are useful in determining the amounts of life insurance to be purchased because insuring full value generally is not necessary. The amount of life insurance needed is not a linear function of the amount of earned income exposed to loss.

Potential intelligent purchasers of life insurance are seeking an efficient predeath arrangement for an effective postdeath balance between resources that will be needed and resources that will be available. They are not seeking compensation per se for earnings lost as a result of death or disability. The efficiency and effectiveness of life insurance as an instrument in financial planning are discussed in Chapters 20, 21, and 22.

---

[6] Authors who write about human life value are not in agreement as to the precise way in which this value should be measured. In this text, the measurement is the present value of projected net earnings for the work life expectancy, net earnings being defined as gross earnings minus personal maintenance expenses and income tax liability. Other measurements for human life value are (1) the present value of projected net earnings as defined for a period to anticipated retirement age and (2) the present value of projected net earnings to anticipated retirement age discounted for mortality as well as for interest. Assuming the foregoing net earning figures, and the retirement age to be 65, the human life value computed under the first of these methods would be $157,215, the present value of $10,000 annually, paid in equal monthly installments for 30 years using 5 percent interest. Recognizing that the $10,000 would be earned only for each year that the individual survives between age 35 and age 65, the second method would produce a human life value of only $154,900, the present value of a 30-year temporary life annuity of $10,000 at age 35, using 5 percent interest and an appropriate annuity mortality table. (The formula for this latter computation is discussed in Chapter 25.)

[7] J. B. Aponte and H. S. Denenberg, "A New Concept of the Economics of Life Value and the Human Life Value: A Rationale for Term Insurance as the Cornerstone of Insurance Marketing," *Journal of Risk and Insurance,* Vol. XXXV (September, 1968), pp. 337–56. Note that the concept of insurable value of a life is equivalent to the concept of human life value as defined in measurement (1) in footnote 6 above but different from the concept of human life value as used in this text and in measurement (2) in footnote 6.

4. LIFE INSURANCE AS A SAVINGS MEDIUM

Health insurance has confined its function to protection both from loss of income and from the burden of expenses arising out of accidents or sickness. On the other hand, life insurance has extended its services to offer a medium for accumulating savings. The invasion of the field of savings institutions, however, was purely accidental. It developed as a by-product of the method of financing the cost of life insurance. This by-product has taken an important place in the sales presentations of most life insurance plans. It is a means by which assets may be accumulated by the policyholder to finance the education of his children and to build a retirement program for himself and his wife. That the amount of predeath benefits paid to the policyholders themselves as cash surrender values, matured endowment claims, and annuity benefits equals about 80 percent of the amount paid in postdeath benefits to beneficiaries indicates the importance of the "savings" accumulation feature of life insurance in the purchase plans of American policyholders.

Relationship between the Policy Terms and Its Cost.   The cost of a life insurance policy is a function of what the insurance company has obligated itself to do under the terms of the contract. The company may obligate itself to pay a death claim only if the insured dies within 1 year; or it may agree to pay the claim if the insured dies within an extended period of 5, 10, or 20 years or before he reaches age 60, 65, or 70. These types of contracts are called term insurance. The company may even agree to pay a death claim no matter when that death occurs, setting no time limit. These policies are called whole life insurance. Some contracts provide for payment of a claim not only if the insured dies within a given period but also if he survives to the end of that period. This latter type of contract is called endowment insurance.

Naturally, the more liberal the promise of the company, the more the insured will have to pay for his insurance. Contracts limiting the payment of claims to death that occurs within one year are the least expensive type of life insurance. As the term of coverage lengthens, the cost of the insurance increases, reaching its highest cost when the time restriction is eliminated entirely. When a benefit also is promised to those who survive the period for which death protection is provided, the company must charge extra for that additional benefit. For endowment policies, the shorter the term, the higher will be the cost. Why this is true will be seen presently.

Term Insurance.   The point that has already been made that the one-year term policy is the least expensive form of life insurance. The reason is as simple as it is obvious. Assume that 9,575,636 people, aged 25, purchased $1,000 of insurance for 1 year. This rather unlikely number of people is selected since it conforms with the number of people assumed to be alive at age 25 in the Commissioners 1958 Standard Ordinary Mortality Table. According to this table (1958 CSO), 18,481 of the group will die during the year.[8] If the reasonable assumption is made that these deaths are spread evenly throughout the year, then the total contributions from members of the group, to pay for the cost of insurance, can be assumed to be invested for an average period of six months. At an assumed interest rate of $2\frac{1}{2}$ percent, a deposit of $18,254,238 is necessary to accumulate in 6 months to $18,481,000, the amount needed to pay $1,000 each to the beneficiaries of the unfortunate 18,481 who die.[9] Each member's share of the mortality cost would be $1.91, which does not include any contribution for the expenses of operating the company. If the policy ran for two years, it would cost more because funds would have to be provided to pay the additional 18,732 death claims that would occur throughout the second year. The added burden of $18,732,000 discounted for $1\frac{1}{2}$ years would result in an additional $1.89 for each participant, bringing the total net single premium to $3.80. Each year added to the term of the policy, of course, adds another year for a possible death claim, and increases the cost of insurance accordingly.

If the term restrictions were eliminated altogether and the policy extended over the entire life of every member of the group, funds would have to be available to pay death claims over a 75-year period. This is true because under the 1958 CSO Mortality Table, not until age 100 will all the 9,575,636 who enter at age 25 be assumed to be dead. The last 6,415 live to age 99 and then die in that year. To be prepared to meet all claims when they mature, the group must collect $3,252,364,768, assuming an investment return of $2\frac{1}{2}$ percent.[10] The single premium mortality cost to each member would be $339.65.

Therefore, at age 25, the pure cost of $1,000 of life insurance (the cost without the expense loading and on a single premium basis) will run from $1.91, on a 1-year basis, to $339.65 on a whole life basis.

Endowment Insurance. Suppose these 9,575,636 people, age 25, purchase $1,000 life insurance policies for a 10-year period with the provision that those who survive the period also would be paid $1,000. In one respect this contract is similar to the life insurance policy written without time limit: both policies are certain to result in a claim. Since all 9,575,636

---

[8] The basic data underlying the Commissioners 1958 Standard Ordinary Mortality Table cover the combined mortality experience of 15 large life insurance companies that contribute to the annual mortality studies of the Society of Actuaries. These data cover mortality experience during the period between 1950 and 1954 anniversaries, and are loaded to allow a safety margin. In the aggregate, the average safety margin for all ages combined is about 20 percent, which means that about 20 percent more deaths per 1,000 are assumed than were reported. For a reproduction of the Commissioners 1958 Standard Ordinary Mortality Table and a discussion of mortality tables generally, see Chapter 24.

[9] As this is written, an interest assumption of $2\frac{1}{2}$ percent is low, since life insurance companies are now earning more than 5 percent net on their investment portfolios. Yet some prominent insurers still are using a $2\frac{1}{2}$ percent interest assumption. This low interest assumption gives an added safety cushion to that already built into the mortality table, and the two together create surpluses from which policyholders in participating companies receive dividends. For nonparticipating policies, insurers are using interest assumptions in the 3 to $3\frac{1}{2}$ percent range.

[10] How this figure is computed is discussed in Chapter 25.

policies will mature for $1,000 claims (to those who are alive at the end of the period and for those who die during the period), enough money must be collected from each policyholder to equal a fund which when invested at 2½ percent will be sufficient to pay claims amounting to $9,575,-636,000. In the whole life contract, interest will make up a larger part of the contribution than it will in the 10-year endowment contract because a longer interest period is involved: 75 years rather than 10 years. The amount needed in advance to fund the 9,575,636 whole life policies for the group was computed earlier and was found to be $3,252,364,768. This amount provides only about 34 percent of the total money needed. Investment earnings make up the other 66 percent. The money needed to fund the 9,575,636, 10-year endowment insurance contracts amounts to $7,498,-594,000, about 78 percent of the total money needed. Investment earnings provide the other 22 percent. If the endowment period were increased to 20 years, the money needed to fund the benefits would be only $5,907,968,-000, with investment income providing the other 38 percent.

Reduced to an individual basis, the 10-year endowment insurance contract would cost each person $783.08 at age 25. The 20-year endowment would cost $616.98. These compare with $339.65 for a whole life policy. These costs include only enough to pay policy benefits and do not provide any margin for expenses. Additional investment income, made possible by longer periods in which to earn interest, accounts for the reduction in cost as the term of the endowment increases.

The following graph shows pictorially the effect of the term of a life insurance policy upon its cost. The graph is not drawn to exact scale because its purpose is to indicate direction, not magnitude.

FIGURE 1-1

Effect of the Term upon the Cost of Insurance

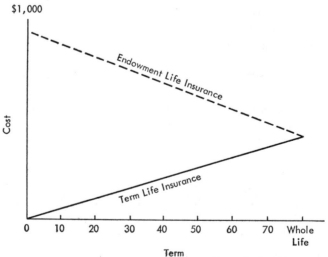

Three important observations are to be made from this graph.

1. The cost of life insurance *increases* with its term.

2. The cost of endowment insurance *decreases* with its term.

3. Whole life insurance is the most expensive form of term life insurance, and the cheapest form of endowment life insurance.

The first two of these observations already have been explained. The third one, at first glance, seems contradictory. How can one policy be both endowment and term insurance?

Conceptually, whole life insurance can be viewed either term to age 100 or endowment at age 100. When a whole life policyholder reaches age 100, he is considered to be dead because the mortality table shows all policyholders dead by that age. The rare policyholder who outlives the mortality table is given the face amount of the policy upon completing his first century. What is this payment? Is it a survivorship benefit or is it a death benefit? The facts suggest that it is a hybrid. The funds paid to the 100-year-old policyholder are funds which had been earmarked to pay a death benefit on behalf of the policyholder had he obliged by dying during his 99th year, as was expected of him. These payments, therefore, are mortality payments to survivors who, according to the mortality table, should be dead.

If the above seems confusing, do not worry. Just remember that, figured *actuarially*, a whole life policy is term insurance to age 100, since its cost includes death benefits only. Death benefits will have to be paid to all participants, the last of whom is expected to die at age 100. No endowment benefits are figured because no one is expected to survive the period. Viewed *functionally*, however, a whole life policy is an endowment at age 100 because benefits are paid not only to those who die before age 100 but also to those who survive to age 100. Except for this seeming contradiction in terms, the observation that a whole life policy is the most expensive form of term life insurance and the cheapest form of endowment insurance already has been explained.

Source of Savings Accumulations to Policyholders. It should be clear now that in all but the short-term policies, investment earnings play a significant role in the cost of life insurance. Earlier it was pointed out that the savings accumulations in life insurance policies are developed as a by-product of the method of financing the premium. Three premium plans are available: the natural premium, the single premium, and the level premium. The natural premium is the only one of the three that offers no *savings accumulations* to the living policyholder. The natural premium is that charged for yearly renewable term insurance.

Yearly Renewable Term Insurance. A buyer of life insurance who wants coverage throughout his lifetime theoretically has the choice of buying a term insurance contract and renewing it as the period expires,[11] or of

---

[11] The choice is theoretical because insurance companies place a limit on the number of times or the age at which the policyholder may renew his contract. The reason for this limitation is explained later.

buying a whole life policy. If he buys the one-year term policy and renews it each year until he dies, no savings accumulations are involved in the policy. The full premium paid each year is used to pay the cost of the insurance for that year. The renewal premium increases each year, of course, to reflect the annual increase in the death rate as age advances. Table 1–1

TABLE 1-1

Pure Cost of $1,000 1-Year Term Policies*

(1958 CSO 2½%)

Age	Cost	Age	Cost	Age	Cost
25	$1.91	41	$ 3.79	57	$ 15.35
26	1.94	42	4.12	58	16.79
27	1.97	43	4.47	59	18.36
28	2.01	44	4.86	60	20.09
29	2.05	45	5.28	61	21.97
30	2.10	46	5.76	62	24.01
31	2.16	47	6.28	63	26.24
32	2.22	48	6.86	64	28.68
33	2.29	49	7.51	65	31.36
34	2.37	50	8.22	70	49.18
35	2.48	51	9.00	75	72.47
36	2.61	52	9.84	80	108.63
37	2.77	53	10.76	85	159.16
38	2.97	54	11.75	90	225.34
39	3.21	55	12.84	95	346.93
40	3.49	56	14.04	99	987.73

* No additions have been made for the cost of doing business, and, therefore, these premiums will not be representative of those appearing in company rate manuals.

shows the mortality cost of successive one-year term policies for $1,000 starting at age 25, computed on the basis of 1958 CSO at 2½ percent. Thus, the pure premium begins at $1.91 (without the expense loading), and increases each year, reaching $3.49 in 15 years, $12.84 in 30 years, $49.18 in 45 years, and $159.16 in 60 years. The rate of increase is slow during the early years, but picks up later when the year-to-year increases in the death rate become more significant. Figure 1–2 shows graphically the trend in the net yearly renewable term rate.

Whole Life Insurance—Single Premium. The other method of obtaining coverage for the whole of life is through a policy issued without time limit. The pure premium for this policy at age 25, as shown earlier, is $339.65 for each $1,000 of coverage. This amount, when increased by an expense loading, pays for the contract in full, and is therefore called a single premium.[12]

Unlike the yearly renewable term policy, the single premium whole life

[12] Each premium for the successive one-year term contracts is also a single premium, for it pays in full for the coverage involved. Thus, the single premium for a whole life policy issued at age 99 would be the same as the premium for a 1-year term policy issued at age 99, since only 1 year of coverage is involved in either case.

FIGURE 1–2

Premiums for $1,000 Whole Life Insurance Written
under Various Plans at Age 25; 1958 CSO 2½% net

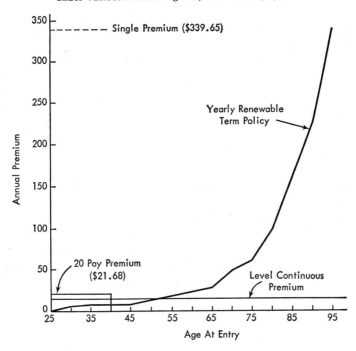

policy contains savings accumulations for the policyholder. These accumulations arise from the advance payment of the full premium for coverage
written for an extended period, in this case for life. The savings accumulations grow each year from two sources: interest earnings and survivorship
benefits. Interest earnings are produced by the investment of the advance
premium. Survivorship benefits are from the release of the savings accumulations in the policies of those who fail to survive the period. When a
policyholder dies, the savings accumulations in his policy are released and
distributed among the surviving policyholders to increase the savings
accumulations in their policies. A death benefit is paid on behalf of those
who die, a pro rata share of which is charged against all policies in force.
Since in the single premium whole life policy, interest earnings and survivorship benefits always exceed the cost of the insurance benefit, accumulations will grow each year. For the first five years, the growth is as follows:

Attained Age	Growth of Accumulations
26	$346.87
27	354.27
28	361.86
29	369.63
30	377.57

A policyholder who purchases a $1,000 single premium whole life policy at age 25 for $339.65 therefore can cash it in at age 30 for $377.57 and have a gain of $37.92.[13] It should be pointed out that this gain is understated by $9.99, which is the value of the life insurance protection the policyholder has enjoyed during the 5-year period that this whole life insurance was in force.

An Illustration. An example is helpful in reviewing how savings accumulations are generated in life insurance policies. For the sake of simplicity, the illustration assumes no loading for expenses, no penalty for early policy surrender, and the payment of all death claims at the end of the policy year in which they become due.[14] The actuarial assumptions are 1958 CSO at 2½ percent which produce a net single premium of $339.65 for $1,000 of insurance issued at age 25.

At age 25 the policyholder pays a single premium of $339.65 which at 2½ percent interest accumulates in 1 year to $348.14. Since the 1958 CSO death rate at age 25 is 1.93 per thousand, the fund is decreased at the end of the year by an insurance charge of $1.93, leaving a total of $346.21. Note that this amount falls $0.66 short of the $346.87 accumulation indicated at age 26 in the foregoing tabulation of the growth of accumulations. Since $346.87 is needed to fund $1,000 of whole life insurance at age 26, an additional $0.66 must be provided from some other source. That source is the survivorship benefit, a concept which needs careful explanation.

Referring to the 1958 CSO Mortality Table,[15] it is assumed that out of a group of 9,575,636 people alive at age 25, a total of 18,481 will be dead at age 26, leaving 9,557,155 survivors. Each of the initial 9,575,636 people pays $339.65 at the beginning of the year, earns $8.49 interest for the year, and is charged $1.93 for his portion of the $18,481,000 paid in death claims, leaving a net balance of $346.21. For those who die during the year, a death claim of $1,000 is paid on their behalf, but their claim to the $346.21 in savings accumulations is relinquished. Since 18,481 claims to $346.21 are released, a fund of $6,398,307 (18,481 × $346.21) becomes available for the 9,557,155 survivors, making a total of $0.66 for each survivor ($6,398,307 ÷ 9,557,155).

Table 1–2 shows the way in which the savings accumulations in the policy grow and indicates the sources of these accumulations year by year. Note the increasing importance of the survivorship benefit with the passing of time. By the time the insured reaches age 63, the survivorship benefit becomes more important than interest earnings as a contributor to the growth of savings accumulations. The increasing importance of the sur-

---

[13] These are figured at *net* rates based on 1958 CSO at 2½ percent, with no allowance for expenses. The absence of an expense allowance prevents these figures from being comparable to those published by the companies in their rate manuals, but does no harm to the theory.

[14] More realism is injected into the picture in Chapter 27. Nothing is lost, however, by ignoring these complications at this point.

[15] Reproduced in Chapter 24.

TABLE 1-2

Savings Accumulations: Single Premium Life Insurance Policy*†
(1958 CSO at 2½%)

(1) Age	(2) Fund at Beginning of Year	(3) Interest	(4) Mortality Cost	(5) Survivor Benefit	(6) Fund at End of Year	(7) Total Premiums Paid
25	$339.65	$ 8.49	$ 1.93	$ 0.66	$346.87	$339.65
26	346.87	8.67	1.96	0.69	354.27	339.65
27	354.27	8.85	1.99	0.72	361.86	339.65
28	361.86	9.04	2.03	0.75	369.63	339.65
29	369.63	9.24	2.08	0.78	377.57	339.65
30	377.57	9.43	2.13	0.82	385.70	339.65
31	385.70	9.64	2.19	0.86	394.01	339.65
32	394.01	9.85	2.25	0.90	402.51	339.65
33	402.51	10.06	2.32	0.95	411.20	339.65
34	411.20	10.28	2.40	1.00	420.08	339.65
35	420.08	10.50	2.51	1.07	429.14	339.65
36	429.14	10.72	2.64	1.15	438.38	339.65
37	438.38	10.96	2.80	1.25	447.79	339.65
38	447.79	11.19	3.01	1.37	457.34	339.65
39	457.34	11.43	3.25	1.51	467.03	339.65
40	467.03	11.67	3.53	1.68	476.86	339.65
41	476.86	11.92	3.84	1.86	486.80	339.65
42	486.80	12.17	4.17	2.07	496.87	339.65
43	496.87	12.42	4.53	2.29	507.05	339.65
44	507.05	12.65	4.92	2.53	517.32	339.65
45	517.32	12.93	5.35	2.82	527.72	339.65
46	527.72	13.19	5.83	3.13	538.21	339.65
47	538.21	13.45	6.36	3.49	548.80	339.65
48	548.80	13.72	6.95	3.88	559.45	339.65
49	559.45	13.98	7.60	4.33	570.17	339.65
50	570.17	14.25	8.32	4.83	580.93	339.65
51	580.93	14.52	9.11	5.44	591.78	339.65
52	591.78	14.79	9.96	6.00	602.61	339.65
53	602.61	15.06	10.89	6.68	613.47	339.65
54	613.47	15.33	11.90	7.43	624.33	339.65
55	624.33	15.61	13.00	8.25	635.19	339.65
56	635.19	15.88	14.21	9.18	646.04	339.65
57	646.04	16.15	15.54	10.20	656.85	339.65
58	656.85	16.42	17.00	11.35	667.61	339.65
59	667.61	16.69	18.59	12.61	678.31	339.65
60	678.31	16.96	20.34	14.01	688.94	339.65
61	688.94	17.22	22.24	15.55	699.47	339.65
62	699.47	17.48	24.31	17.26	709.90	339.65
63	709.90	17.75	26.57	19.13	720.21	339.65
64	720.21	18.00	29.04	21.21	730.39	339.65
65	730.39	18.26	31.75	23.51	740.40	339.65
66	740.40	18.51	34.74	26.06	750.23	339.65
67	750.23	18.75	38.04	28.90	759.85	339.65
68	759.85	18.99	41.68	32.06	769.23	339.65
69	769.23	19.23	45.61	35.50	778.35	339.65
70	778.35	19.46	49.79	39.20	787.21	339.65
71	787.21	19.68	54.15	43.10	795.83	339.65
72	795.83	19.89	58.65	47.17	804.24	339.65
73	804.24	20.11	63.26	51.40	812.48	339.65

* These computations have been rounded off and therefore will not be accurate to the exact penny.
† Age of issue—25; face amount—$1,000.

TABLE 1-2 (cont.)

(1) Age	(2) Fund at Beginning of Year	(3) Interest	(4) Mortality Cost	(5) Survivor Benefit	(6) Fund at End of Year	(7) Total Premiums Paid
74	812.48	20.31	68.12	55.90	820.56	339.65
75	820.56	20.51	73.37	60.80	828.48	339.65
76	828.48	20.71	79.18	66.23	836.22	339.65
77	836.22	20.91	85.70	72.33	843.73	339.65
78	843.73	21.10	93.06	79.21	850.94	339.65
79	850.94	21.28	101.19	86.83	857.82	339.65
80	857.82	21.45	109.98	95.10	864.35	339.65

vivorship benefit is explained by the decreasing rate of survivorships at each advancing age level. Note that a simple subtraction of the figure in column 7 from that in column 6 will produce the amount of gain upon surrender of the contract in the year considered.

The Annual Level Premium Whole Life. Two methods of purchasing insurance coverage for the full span of life have been discussed; yearly renewable term insurance and single premium whole life insurance. The first plan offers no savings accumulations (no cash values) whereas the second offers a substantial amount of savings accumulations (large cash values increasing each year). However, neither of these plans enjoys much popularity. Yearly renewable term insurance is unpopular because people dislike an increasing premium burden, and because they fear losing their protection by the inability to pay the high premium at a later date when the premium jumps out of reach. The single premium whole life policy is unpopular because few people believe that they can afford the large advance premium it requires and those who can afford it often prefer other investment media for their free capital.[16] What people want is the opportunity to buy their whole life insurance on the installment plan, just as they purchase their homes, automobiles, heavy appliances, and other large capital items. For example, instead of paying a single premium of $339.65 for a $1,000 whole life policy, the 25-year-old buyer normally would prefer to pay a series of equal annual payments, either for life or for a limited number of years.

Life insurance was among the first products marketed on the installment plan. The installment arrangement as applied to life insurance is known as the level premium plan. Under this plan, a man aged 25 can purchase a $1,000 whole life policy for a pure premium of $12.55 a year, payable for life, or $21.68, payable for 20 years or until death—whichever occurs first.[17]

---

[16] Inflation fears have reduced the attractiveness of fixed dollar savings plans thus decreasing the popularity of life insurance plans with heavy emphasis on savings accumulations.

[17] These premium charges are based on 1958 CSO at 2½ percent, and since they do not include an expense loading they will not be comparable to the premiums quoted in the rate manuals of the various companies. How they are computed is explained in Chapter 25.

The level premium for life plan is known technically in the business as "straight life" or "ordinary life," or, as will be used in this book, "continuous premium whole life." The level premium for 20 years plan is called simply 20-pay life. Other limited payment plans are written to spread the premiums over periods longer or shorter than 20 years. As will be seen, the shorter the period over which the premium on a whole life policy is to be paid, the greater is the emphasis on accumulating savings (cash values) in the contract.

Figure 1–2 (page 11) reviews some of the premium plans available to the 25-year-old who seeks to purchase coverage for the full span of life. Several other plans are available which, although differing slightly, follow the same general pattern. For example, a whole life paid up at age 65 would take a premium lower than the 20-pay but higher than the continuous premium. Some plans, known as "modified life," are written under arrangements whereby the cost is distributed by charging a premium lower than the level continuous premium during the first few years of the contract and a premium slightly higher thereafter. All these premium plans, except the yearly renewable term plan, involve accumulations for the policyholder.

The 20-Payment Whole Life. The rate of growth of accumulations in the 20-pay whole life policy and the amounts contributed by each of the growth factors can be observed in Table 1–3. The column labeled *Fund at*

TABLE 1–3

Savings Accumulations in the 20-Payment Whole Life Policy*†
(1958 CSO at 2½%)

(1)	(2)	(3) Fund at Beginning of Year	(4)	(5)	(6)	(7) Fund at End of Year	(8) Total Premiums Paid
Age	Premium		Interest	Mortality Cost	Survivor Benefit		
25	$21.68	$ 21.68	$ 0.54	$ 1.93	$ 0.03	$ 20.32	$ 21.68
26	21.68	42.00	1.05	1.96	0.08	41.17	43.36
27	21.68	62.85	1.57	1.99	0.12	62.55	65.04
28	21.68	84.23	2.10	2.03	0.17	84.48	86.72
29	21.68	106.16	2.65	2.08	0.22	106.95	108.40
30	21.68	128.63	3.21	2.13	0.27	129.99	130.08
31	21.68	151.67	3.79	2.19	0.33	153.60	151.76
32	21.68	175.28	4.38	2.25	0.40	177.81	173.44
33	21.68	199.49	4.98	2.32	0.47	202.63	195.12
34	21.68	224.31	5.60	2.40	0.54	228.06	216.80
35	21.68	249.74	6.24	2.51	0.63	254.10	238.48
36	21.68	275.78	6.89	2.64	0.74	280.77	260.16
37	21.68	302.45	7.56	2.80	0.86	308.07	281.84
38	21.68	329.75	8.24	3.01	1.01	335.99	303.52
39	21.68	357.67	8.94	3.25	1.18	364.54	325.20
40	21.68	386.22	9.65	3.53	1.38	393.73	346.88
41	21.68	415.41	10.38	3.84	1.62	423.58	368.56
42	21.68	445.26	11.13	4.17	1.89	454.11	390.24
43	21.68	475.79	11.89	4.53	2.19	485.34	411.92
44	21.68	507.02	12.67	4.92	2.54	517.32	433.60
45	—	517.32	12.93	5.35	2.82	527.72	433.60

* These computations have been rounded off and therefore will not be accurate to the exact penny.
† Age of issue—25; face amount—$1,000.

TABLE 1–3 (cont.)

(1)	(2)	(3) Fund at Beginning of Year	(4) Interest	(5) Mortality Cost	(6) Survivor Benefit	(7) Fund at End of Year	(8) Total Premiums Paid
Age	Premium						
46	—	527.72	13.19	5.83	3.13	538.21	433.60
47	—	538.21	13.45	6.36	3.49	548.80	433.60
48	—	548.80	13.72	6.95	3.88	559.45	433.60
49	—	559.45	13.98	7.60	4.33	570.17	433.60
50	—	570.17	14.25	8.32	4.83	580.93	433.60
51	—	580.93	14.52	9.11	5.44	591.78	433.60
52	—	591.78	14.79	9.96	6.00	602.61	433.60
53	—	602.61	15.06	10.89	6.68	613.47	433.60
54	—	613.47	15.33	11.90	7.42	624.33	433.60
55	—	624.33	15.60	13.00	8.25	635.19	433.60
56	—	635.19	15.88	14.21	9.18	646.04	433.60
57	—	646.04	16.15	15.54	10.20	656.85	433.60
58	—	656.85	16.42	17.00	11.34	667.61	433.60
59	—	667.61	16.69	18.59	12.60	678.31	433.60
60	—	678.31	16.95	20.34	14.01	688.94	433.60
61	—	688.94	17.22	22.24	15.55	699.47	433.60
62	—	699.47	17.48	24.31	17.25	709.90	433.60
63	—	709.90	17.74	26.57	19.13	720.21	433.60
64	—	720.21	18.00	29.04	21.21	730.39	433.60
65	—	730.39	18.26	31.75	23.50	740.40	433.60
66	—	740.40	18.51	34.74	26.06	750.23	433.60
67	—	750.23	18.75	38.04	28.90	759.85	433.60
68	—	759.85	18.99	41.68	32.06	769.23	433.60
69	—	769.23	19.23	45.61	35.50	778.35	433.60
70	—	778.35	19.45	49.79	39.19	787.21	433.60
71	—	787.21	19.68	54.15	43.09	795.83	433.60
72	—	795.83	19.89	58.65	47.16	804.24	433.60
73	—	804.24	20.10	63.26	51.39	812.48	433.60
74	—	812.48	20.31	68.12	55.89	820.56	433.60
75	—	820.56	20.51	73.37	60.78	828.48	433.60
76	—	828.48	20.71	79.18	66.21	836.22	433.60
77	—	836.22	20.90	85.70	72.30	843.73	433.60
78	—	843.73	21.09	93.06	79.18	850.94	433.60
79	—	850.94	21.27	101.19	86.80	857.82	433.60
80	—	857.82	21.44	109.98	95.06	864.35	433.60

Beginning of Year is the value of the policy at the end of the previous year increased by the payment of the annual level premium for the current year. The actuarial assumptions used in preparing this illustration are the same as those used in the preparation of Table 1–2.

Note in this illustration (Table 1–3) that the pure cost of insurance (mortality costs) exceeds the total of interest and survivorship benefits for each of the first three policy years. It takes three more years to recoup these losses so that the policy will show no net gain until the seventh year.[18]

The Continuous Premium Whole Life. Table 1–4 indicates the rate of

---

[18] Actually, there are no real losses during the first years since the policyholder has the benefit of insurance which is worth more than the indicated loss.

TABLE 1–4

Savings Accumulations in the Continuous Premium Whole Life Policy*†

(1958 CSO 2½%)

(1)	(2)	(3) Fund at Beginning of Year	(4) Interest	(5) Mortality Cost	(6) Survivor Benefit	(7) Fund at End of Year	(8) Total Premiums Paid
Age	Premium						
25	$12.55	$ 12.55	$ 0.31	$ 1.93	$ 0.02	$ 10.95	$ 12.55
26	12.55	23.50	0.58	1.96	0.04	22.17	25.10
27	12.55	34.72	0.86	1.99	0.06	33.66	37.65
28	12.55	46.21	1.15	2.03	0.09	45.43	50.20
29	12.55	57.98	1.45	2.08	0.11	57.46	62.75
30	12.55	70.01	1.75	2.13	0.14	69.77	75.30
31	12.55	82.32	2.05	2.19	0.18	82.37	87.85
32	12.55	94.92	2.37	2.25	0.21	95.25	100.40
33	12.55	107.80	2.69	2.32	0.25	108.43	112.95
34	12.55	120.98	3.02	2.40	0.29	121.89	125.50
35	12.55	134.44	3.36	2.51	0.34	135.63	138.05
36	12.55	148.18	3.70	2.64	0.39	149.63	150.60
37	12.55	162.18	4.05	2.80	0.45	163.88	163.15
38	12.55	176.43	4.41	3.01	0.53	178.36	175.70
39	12.55	190.91	4.77	3.25	0.62	193.05	188.25
40	12.55	205.60	5.14	3.53	0.73	207.94	200.80
41	12.55	220.49	5.51	3.84	0.85	223.01	213.35
42	12.55	235.56	5.88	4.17	0.99	238.27	225.90
43	12.55	250.82	6.27	4.53	1.14	253.70	238.45
44	12.55	266.25	6.65	4.92	1.32	269.31	251.00
45	12.55	281.86	7.04	5.35	1.52	285.08	263.55
46	12.55	297.63	7.44	5.83	1.75	300.99	276.10
47	12.55	313.54	7.83	6.36	2.01	317.03	288.65
48	12.55	329.58	8.24	6.95	2.31	333.18	301.20
49	12.55	345.73	8.64	7.60	2.65	349.42	313.75
50	12.55	361.97	9.04	8.32	3.04	365.74	326.30
51	12.55	378.29	9.45	9.11	3.51	382.15	338.85
52	12.55	394.70	9.86	9.96	3.96	398.57	351.40
53	12.55	411.12	10.27	10.89	4.51	415.02	363.95
54	12.55	427.57	10.68	11.90	5.13	431.49	376.50
55	12.55	444.04	11.10	13.00	5.82	447.96	389.05
56	12.55	460.51	11.51	14.21	6.59	464.40	401.60
57	12.55	476.95	11.92	15.54	7.47	480.80	414.15
58	12.55	493.35	12.33	17.00	8.45	497.13	426.70
59	12.55	509.68	12.74	18.59	9.54	513.37	439.25
60	12.55	525.92	13.14	20.34	10.77	529.50	451.80
61	12.55	542.05	13.55	22.24	12.13	545.49	464.35
62	12.55	558.04	13.95	24.31	13.64	561.32	476.90
63	12.55	573.87	14.34	26.57	15.32	576.97	489.45
64	12.55	589.52	14.73	29.04	17.20	592.42	502.00
65	12.55	604.97	15.12	31.75	19.29	607.63	514.55
66	12.55	620.18	15.50	34.74	21.62	622.56	527.10
67	12.55	635.11	15.87	38.04	24.23	637.18	539.65
68	12.55	649.73	16.24	41.68	27.15	651.44	552.20
69	12.55	663.99	16.60	45.61	30.34	665.32	564.75
70	12.55	677.87	16.94	49.79	33.79	678.82	577.30
71	12.55	691.37	17.28	54.15	37.47	691.97	589.85
72	12.55	704.52	17.61	58.65	41.33	704.81	602.40
73	12.55	717.36	17.93	63.26	45.38	717.41	614.95

* These computations have been rounded off and therefore will not be accurate to the exact penny.
† Age of issue—25; face amount—$1,000.

TABLE 1-4 (cont.)

(1)	(2)	(3) Fund at Beginning of Year	(4)	(5) Mortality Cost	(6) Survivor Benefit	(7) Fund at End of Year	(8) Total Premiums Paid
Age	Premium		Interest				
74	12.55	729.96	18.24	68.12	49.71	729.80	627.50
75	12.55	742.35	18.55	73.37	54.43	741.97	640.05
76	12.55	754.52	18.86	79.18	59.69	753.89	652.60
77	12.55	766.44	19.16	85.70	65.60	765.50	665.15
78	12.55	778.05	19.45	93.06	72.28	776.72	677.70
79	12.55	789.27	19.73	101.19	79.68	787.49	690.25
80	12.55	800.04	20.00	109.98	87.74	797.80	702.80

growth of savings accumulations in the continuous premium whole life policy. In this contract the pure cost of insurance exceeds the combined total of interest and survivorship benefits during each of the first six years. It takes the next six years to recoup the losses so that the policy does not show a net gain until the 13th year.[19]

It should be emphasized at this point that this policy actually yields gains each year. In the early years, these gains are used to pay part of the cost of insurance. Since interest earnings and survivorship benefits together increase at a faster rate than the cost of insurance, a point will be reached when the annual gain will exceed the cost of insurance for the year. At this point the fund at the end of the policy year will increase faster than total premiums paid. And before too many years, the savings accumulations will become greater than the total premium paid. When this final stage is reached, the policy is said to produce a net gain. But investment gains are achieved at any point. For example, assume that the policy in Table 1–4 is terminated at the end of the fourth year. A loss of $4.77 is indicated. But since the policyholder has had four years of insurance protection worth a total of $7.91 ($1.93 + $1.96 + $1.99 + $2.03), he has had, in effect, a net gain of $3.14.

The Decreasing Protection, Increasing Accumulations Concept. Some authorities prefer to ignore the survivorship benefit in explaining accumulations in life insurance policies. Instead, they choose to couch their explanation in terms of a decreasing amount of protection coupled with an increasing amount of accumulations. Under this concept the amount at risk decreases each year with the accumulation of the values in the policy.[20] For

---

[19] Remember these are net figures only and do not include an expense loading. Therefore, they are not comparable with rates and values shown in company premium manuals.

[20] The amount at risk is the difference between the face amount of the policy and its savings accumulations. It is the amount by which death will increase the value of the policy. The amount at risk on a $1,000 policy having a savings accumulations, technically known as cash value, of $300 would be $700. (To be technically correct, the policy reserve rather than its cash value should be used, but for purposes of the discussion at this point, use of the cash value is sufficient. The difference between the cash value and policy reserve is discussed in Chapter 27.)

example, in the $1,000 single premium whole life policy issued at age 25, the initial accumulations value is its single premium of $339.65. The amount at risk would then be $660.35 ($1,000 — $339.65). At 2½ percent, $339.65 accumulates in one year to $348.14. At the rate of $1.93 a thousand, the cost of insuring the $660.35 at a risk would be $1.27 which, when charged against the policy, will produce a value of $346.87 at the end of the first year, the value shown in Table 1–2. Reference is made to Table 1–4 for another illustration of the concept. At age 35, the fund at the beginning of the year is $134.45. Invested at 2½ percent, this yields $3.36 for the year. The amount at risk for that year is the face of the policy ($1,000) less the fund at the beginning of the year ($134.44), or a total of $865.56. At a rate of $2.51 per $1,000, the insurance cost for the $865.56 at risk under this policy would be $2.17. Adding the $3.36 interest to the $134.44 fund at the beginning of the year and subtracting the mortality cost of $2.17, the fund at the end of the year is $135.63 ($135.63 = $134.44 + $3.36 — $2.17). Although arrived at differently, this is the same figure shown in Table 1–4 for the fund at the end of the year at age 35. Under the survivorship concept, the figure was reached by adding both the interest earnings and the survivorship benefits to the fund at the beginning of the year and then subtracting the cost of $1,000 of insurance: $134.44 + (3.36 + .34) — 2.51 = $135.63.

The principal difference between the breakdown of figures produced under the decreasing term, increasing accumulations concept and that produced under the survivorship concept is that what one method shows as a survivorship benefit, the other shows as a reduction in mortality cost. Naturally, the interest earnings will be identical. Under the survivorship concept, it is assumed that the amount of life insurance protection in force is a level $1,000 throughout the life of the contract. When a policyholder dies, his beneficiaries are paid the $1,000 from company "mortality funds." The predeath cash value of the policy is terminated when the policy matures as a death claim. The cash values of the policies held by the surviving policyholders are increased as a group by the amount released by the deceased policyholders. Under the decreasing protection concept, it is assumed that the amount of life insurance protection decreases each year throughout the life of the contract to the same degree that the cash value increases. When a policyholder dies, his beneficiaries are paid $1,000, part of which comes from mortality funds and the remainder from the predeath cash value of the policy.

Although the decreasing protection concept is a useful tool for explaining the savings accumulation feature of a life insurance policy, the survivorship concept is technically the correct one. The decreasing protection concept has the psychological advantage of not making it appear that when a policyholder dies he forfeits his predeath cash values. And for the individual policyholder, the concept is quite logical. If his $1,000 policy has a cash value of $339.65, he is worth only $660.35 more dead than alive.

Thus he finds it easy to reason that his death protection is not $1,000, but only $660.35.

Termination or Transfer of Cash Value upon Insured's Death. The assumption, however, that death claims are paid in part from cash values and in part from mortality funds has led to confused thinking and conflicting court opinions. The policyholder has a right to either the cash value before death or the face amount at death, but never both. Cash values die with the policyholder, and along with them so should any rights, actual or potential, held by anyone else in these cash values. The beneficiary is paid entirely from mortality funds, no part of which represents any predeath interests of the policyholder. And, therefore, when the beneficiary is other than the insured or his estate, no part of the death benefits should be available to meet the insured's predeath obligations.

Failure of the Commissioner of Internal Revenue to adopt this view has led him, in a number of cases, to demand that the beneficiaries pay from life insurance proceeds any income tax deficiencies existing when an insolvent insured dies. The Commissioner, arguing that these beneficiaries are liable as transferees of the entire death proceeds, has been successful in convincing the tax courts of the logic of his position, but has been less successful in the United States Courts of Appeals. The Second Circuit in *Rowan* v. *Commissioner*[21] went along with the Commissioner on his contention that the beneficiary was a transferee but only for an amount equal to the predeath cash surrender values. The Courts of Appeals for the Third, Fifth, and Seventh Circuits have agreed with the Second Circuit on this interpretation.[22] The Third Circuit in the Bess case had this to say: "It is therefore not realistic here . . . to view Bess's death as wiping out the loan or surrender values. Bess's death was merely a condition on the occurrence of which the loan or surrender values of the policies no longer were payable to him but became merged in the larger values which the insurance companies were obligated to pay Mrs. Bess."

But the Sixth Circuit took issue with this view. In *Stern* v. *Commissioner*[23] the court said: ". . . it appears to us that, upon the death of the insured, the cash surrender values no longer existed. To say that the cash surrender values on the death of the insured become merged with the proceeds of the policies paid to the widow is figurative. . . . The cash surrender values were not part of the proceeds of the insurance policies paid to the widow, and to hold otherwise would seem to transform plain language to the advantage of the tax-gathering authority, and to the loss of the widow."

The United States Supreme Court in reviewing the Bess case[24] attempted

---

[21] 215F. (2nd) 641.

[22] *U.S.* v. *Bess* 243F. (2nd) 675; *U.S.* v. *Trucex*, C. A.-5, 223F. (2nd) 229; and *U.S.* v. *New*, C. A.-7, 217F. (2nd) 166.

[23] 242F. (2nd) 322.

[24] *U.S.* v. *Bess*, 357 U.S. 51.

to clear up the confusion by making a distinction between what it considers to be the technical relationship among the parties and what it considers to be the practical relationship for certain economic purposes. On this point it concluded: "Thus in economic reality, the insurer pays the beneficiary the insured's fund, plus another amount sufficient to perform the insurer's promise to pay the proceeds on the insured's death. Therefore, we hold that . . . there was a transfer of property from the insured to Mrs. Bess."[25]

This decision of the Supreme Court tends to favor the decreasing protection, increasing accumulations concept as a logical economic explanation of life insurance cash values while at the same time recognizing the technical accuracy of the survivorship concept.

The Problem of Invidious Comparisons. Viewing cash value life insurance as decreasing protection and increasing savings has led to invidious comparisons between the products of life insurance companies on the one hand and the products of savings and investment institutions on the other. Numerous articles, scholarly and otherwise, have appeared in professional and trade journals on the subject of the rate of return on the savings element in cash value life insurance. Some of these articles report the results of dispassionate research designed to find the "truth" whereas others are written either in defense of or as an attack upon life insurance as an investment.

The insurance industry accepts the "credit" or "blame" for the widespread public "notion that a contract of ordinary life insurance should be regarded as a two part contract—one part a declining account of pure insurance and the other a rising account of investments or savings."[26] The president of the Institute of Life Insurance, the public relations arm of the life insurance business, observed that "we in our own business sent that idea out into the world when we sought a convenient sales handle on the product at the expense of a careful, precise explanation. Now we find this so-called 'savings account' being invidiously compared to the performance of true savings and investment media, coupled to the inevitable advice—'Buy term and invest difference.' "[27] The Chairman of the Institute of Life Insurance recognized publicly that ". . . using the concept of a divided account, partially protection and partially savings . . . does not do justice to the concept of the level premium and of protection for the whole of life, however long it may be."[28]

---

[25] A discussion of creditors' rights is found in Chapter 9. The purpose of the present discussion is to indicate the confusion as to source of funds for the payment of claims.

[26] Blake T. Newton, Jr., "The Sovereign Power of Public Opinion," an address before the 1968 Annual Meeting of the Institute of Life Insurance. See *Annual Meeting and Staff Reports—Institute of Life Insurance 1968* (annual; New York: Institute of Life Insurance) p. 57.

[27] *Ibid.* The question of buy term and invest the difference and related issues are discussed in Chapters 4 and 8 of this text.

[28] John S. Pillsbury, Jr., "The Institute 1968," *Annual Meeting and Staff Reports, ibid.* p. 11.

Cash Values as a Fund. It might appear from a reading of these pages that the savings accumulations or cash value of a life insurance policy is a specific fund belonging to the policyholder and held in trust for him by the insurance company. However, such an appearance is only illusory. A life insurance policy is a contract between the insured and the insurer under which the insurer agrees to make payments under certain stipulated conditions. Thus, the insurance company agrees to pay a cash surrender value to the policyholder in lieu of paying the face amount of the policy to his beneficiaries after his death. To compel the insurer to pay him the cash surrender value, the insured must only surrender the policy. Until this condition is fulfilled and payment is made to the policyholder, all funds held by the company are company funds. None of these assets belongs to the policyholder. Of course, the company must report these conditional promises as liabilities and evaluate them properly on its financial statement.[29]

Since the policyholder can borrow against, assign, or pledge his right to collect the cash value, this right must be considered by him as a part of his assets. However, the policyholder's asset is not a pro rata share in his company's funds as is so often loosely suggested. Instead, it is the right to collect funds from the company upon giving up the right to have the full face amount of the policy paid at his death. That this distinction is subtle is illustrated by the words of the United States Supreme Court.[30] "But the courts have long recognized that the surplus of paid premiums accumulated to make up the cash surrender value should be treated for some purposes as though in fact a 'fund' held by the insurer for the benefit of the insured." *In re McKinney,*[31] a case cited by the United States Supreme Court, the judge stated: "Though this excess of premiums paid is legally the sole property of the company, still in practical effect, though not in law, it is the moneys of the assured deposited with the company in advance to make up the deficiency in later premiums. . . . So long as the policy remains in force, the company has not practically any beneficial interest in it, except as its custodian, with the obligation to maintain it unimpaired and suitably invested for the benefit of the insured. This is the practical, though not the legal, relation of the company to this fund."

Thus, although the courts recognize that life insurance cash values are not funds held in trust by the companies for the policyholders, they have found it helpful to view them as such.

Policy Dividends. Earlier, in figuring the cost of life insurance, two assumptions were made: (1) Mortality will conform to the 1958 CSO Table and (2) interest will be earned at the rate of $2\frac{1}{2}$ percent. Both of these assumptions are conservative. A margin is built into this mortality

29 See Chapter 27 for a discussion of the problems of evaluating liabilities.
30 *U.S.* v. *Bess,* 357 U.S. 51.
31 15 Fed. 535, 537.

table so that there will be fewer deaths than projected. For example, at age 25 the basic data underlying the 1958 CSO Table indicate only 0.93 deaths per 1,000 whereas the mortality table shows 1.93 deaths per 1,000, a margin of 107.5 percent.[32] And history shows that only five times since the turn of the century have the life insurance companies as a group earned interest, net before federal income taxes, at a rate of less than 3 percent a year.[33] Never during this period have they earned less than 2.88 percent. During the 1920's the average rate of interest earned was 5.07 percent; for the 1930's, 4.10 percent; for the 1940's, 3.18 percent, for the 1950's, 3.51 percent; and for the 1960's about 4.65 percent.

When an insurance company experiences a lower death rate and a higher interest rate than it assumes in calculating its premium, the effect is an increase in its surplus. An expense allowance is added to the pure premium to produce the premium charged the policyholder. If expenses turn out to be less than those allowed in computing the premium, the difference is reflected in the surplus. This surplus is available for dividends. Over two thirds of the life insurance in force in United States companies is written on a participating basis, which means that the policyholder participates in the surplus of the company through an annual policy dividend. More than 23 percent of the payments made under life insurance and annuity policies are for policy dividends. Under the terms of his contract, the participating policyholder has several optional methods by which he may take his dividend. These options are discussed in Chapter 11.

5. SOCIAL AND ECONOMIC VALUES

In addition to contributing to the economy by preserving human life values and protecting against the financial consequences of their loss, life insurance also aids in financing business, industry, and government.

Expanding production is necessary to the maintenance of full employment and a healthy economy. Capital is required to finance a growing economy.

Life insurance companies, by investing funds that flow to them from their many policyholders, have become a principal source of capital for the economy. They make available to industry the savings of those people who would not or could not invest directly in business. Further, by creative selling, life insurance companies encourage many to save who would not do so in any other form.

In effect, life insurance forms a huge investment pool of the combined savings of 130 million Americans, a pool to which business and industry can turn for money to aid in expansion.

---

[32] The percentage margin varies from age to age. It is highest at age 10, where it is 236.4 percent and lowest at age 0, where it is 11.8 percent. From age 64 to 93 it remains at 15 percent. See Chapter 24 for a further discussion of mortality margins.

[33] 1946; 1947; 1948.

In addition to supplying capital funds to business and industry, life insurance is an important source of financing in a number of other important economic activities. The life insurance industry has about $4½ billion invested in United States government securities and about $5½ billion in securities of other governmental units. Its total investment in mortgages is $75 billion. More than one sixth of the mortgage debt in the United States is held by life insurance companies. These mortgage loans finance homes, farms, and business properties. They have helped to revitalize deteriorating metropolitan centers by financing many new downtown office buildings, hotels, and apartment houses. Life insurance companies have about $5.5 billion invested directly in real estate including shopping centers, factories, department stores, office buildings, and residential properties.

Life insurers pledged $1 billion for investment in the inner city areas in late 1967 and virtually all of it had been committed by early 1969 when another $1 billion was pledged. The funds were invested in housing and job-creating projects designed to help meet the problems of the urban core. Some of the funds were used to develop minority business enterprises in the central city.

2

The Nature of Risk

Insurance is a device for reducing some of the risks inherent in the economy. It operates by combining a sufficient number of homogeneous exposure units to make losses predictable within an acceptable range. By definition, therefore, risk is a condition precedent to insurance. Consequently, an understanding of the nature and meaning of risk (and of certain matters closely related to it) is necessary to an understanding of insurance.

Each field of knowledge has its own terminology. Insurance is no exception. Certain terms have several connotations outside the field, and are subject to varying usage even within it. Such variations in usage may not be particularly confusing to one well acquainted with the field; but to the beginning student they can be both a bother and also an unending source of misunderstanding. Therefore, it will help in the understanding of risk and its relation to life insurance if the terms "chance of loss," "risk," "peril," "hazard," and "loss" as used in this text are carefully defined and differentiated.

1. CHANCE OF LOSS

The chance of loss is an important concept for the understanding of the nature of risk and risk management.

Definition. Chance of loss is the long-run relative frequency of a loss. It is measured numerically by the percentage of exposures to loss which result in actual loss. For example, if, in the long run, 10 losses result out of 1,000 exposures to loss, the chance of loss is 1 percent. However, to clear the way for a simple illustration it is useful to consider chance of loss as the fraction obtained by dividing the probable number of unfavorable events (losses) by the total number of possible events. To illustrate: A coin has two sides. Tossed in the air, it will come down either heads or tails. Assume that the appearance of tails is an unfavorable event; then the probable number of unfavorable events is one, whereas the total number of possible events is two. As a percentage, the probability of an unfavorable event (tails) is 50 percent. As a fraction, it is $\frac{1}{2}$. As a fair mathematical bet, it is even money—one to one. If $10 is the amount bet on the toss, the expected value of winning is $10 $\times$ 0.50, or $5. The expected value of losing also is $10 $\times$ 0.50, or $5. The concept of the expected value of gains and losses is a useful concept for the study of insurance as will become apparent later in this discussion.

Suppose 3 people each were to toss a coin and the odd man wins $10 from each of the 2 losers. What is the chance of loss and the chance of gain for each player? Eight combinations are possible, but since two of them (all heads and all tails) call for another toss only six combinations affect the outcome of the bet. Of these six outcomes, four can cause loss and two can cause gain. Therefore, the chance of loss is $\frac{4}{6}$, or 66$\frac{2}{3}$ percent and the chance of gain is $\frac{2}{6}$, or 33$\frac{1}{3}$ percent. The expected value of the loss is $6.67 ($10 $\times$ 0.667), and the expected value of the gain also is $6.67 ($20 $\times$ 0.333). The game just described with the odds 2 to 1, the chance of winning $20 against the chance of losing $10 produces a fair mathematical bet.

Suppose two of the coin flippers have already shown their coins, and both are heads. What is the chance of loss for the third one who is about to reveal his coin? If his coin is tails, he wins, but if his coin is heads the coins must all be flipped again. There is a 50 percent chance that his coin is heads and that all coins will have to be tossed again. When all coins are flipped again his chance of loss will be 66$\frac{2}{3}$ percent. Therefore the revelation that the other two coins are heads has reduced his chance of loss to 33$\frac{1}{3}$ percent ($\frac{1}{2} \times \frac{4}{6}$). Since there is also a 50 percent chance of gain on the first toss and a 33$\frac{1}{3}$ percent chance of gain on the second toss, he now has a 66$\frac{2}{3}$ percent chance of winning ($\frac{1}{2} + [\frac{1}{2} \times \frac{2}{6}]$). The expected value of his loss has been reduced to $3.33 ($10 $\times$ 0.333) whereas the expected value of his gain has been increased to $13.33 ($20 $\times$ 0.667).

The other players now have an 83$\frac{1}{3}$ percent chance of loss ($\frac{1}{2} + [\frac{1}{2} \times \frac{4}{6}]$) and a 16$\frac{2}{3}$ percent chance of gain ($\frac{1}{2} \times \frac{1}{3}$). The expected value of their loss has now risen to $8.33 ($10 $\times$ 0.833) and the expected value of their gain has dropped to $3.33 ($20 $\times$ 0.167).

The Expected Value of the Game.   Before the revelation of the two coins, the expected value of the game to each player was zero: the sum of the expected values of the gain and the loss ($6.67 — $6.67). But now that the faces of two of the three coins have been uncovered and are heads, the expected value of the new game is $ + 10 ($13.33 — $3.33) for the third tosser and —$5 ($3.33 — $8.33) for the first and second tossers. Mathematically, before revealing his coin, the third tosser should be willing to sell his stake in the game for $10. And the first and second tosser each should be willing to pay $5 to be excused from the game.

The concept of the *expected value of the game* is useful in making consumer decisions about life insurance, annuities, and health insurance contracts and will be discussed in this context later.

Empirical Probabilities.   In illustrations based on tossed coins, it is simple to measure the chance of loss (which is the reason such illustrations were used). In them, the probability is based on logic. Supposedly, there is no need to experiment by flipping the coins thousands of times to confirm the conclusions reached by simple mathematics. Probabilities arrived at in this manner are called a priori probabilities, and, unless the coins to be tossed are irregular, these probabilities can be accepted.

But what about the probability that a man now 21 will die before he reaches age 22—or the probability that he will die before reaching 65? What are the probabilities involved in loss by premature death, old age, accident, or sickness? It is not possible to use logic to determine these probabilities a priori. Instead, they must be determined from observation of statistical data. Probabilities determined in this manner are called empirical or a posteriori probabilities.

To determine the probable number of persons in any given group who will die or become disabled at any age, statistics on a large number of lives have to be collected and formulated into tables—"tables of mortality" in the case of life insurance, "tables of morbidity" in the case of health insurance. By observing the number of deaths out of a sizable group at a given age, the probability of death at that age can be ascertained. Thus, on a mortality table widely used in the United States at the present time, the probable number of persons aged 21 who will die before 22 is 17,655 out of 9,647,694, and the probable number dying before 65 is 2,847,163 out of 9,647,694 alive at 21; hence the probability of death during age 21 is 17,655/9,647,694 or 0.183 percent, and the probability of death during the 44-year period from 21 to 65 is 2,847,163/9,647,694 or 29.5 percent.

These are the probabilities based on just one mortality table, the 1958 Commissioners Standard Ordinary Mortality Table, a table used in connection with individual life insurance policies as distinguished from group policies. Based on the 1960 Commissioners Standard Group Mortality Table, the probability of death during age 21 is 20,517/9,587,223 or 0.214 percent. The probability of death during the 44-year period from age 21 to 65 is 3,118,625/9,587,223 or 32.6 percent.

Mortality tables are discussed in some detail in Chapter 24. It is sufficient to mention here that the stated probabilities of death at any given age will vary among mortality tables, and that mortality tables differ in accordance with the data from which they are compiled, the margins added for safety, and the purposes for which the tables are used.[1]

---

[1] Mortality tables are used for many different purposes: constructing premium rates for ordinary life insurance, establishing premiums for industrial life insurance, computing premiums for group life insurance, fixing minimum required legal reserves for ordinary life insurance, determining the values under the "extended term" nonforfeiture option, setting minimum guarantees under life income settlement options, constructing premiums for individual annuity contracts, and making minimum guarantees under group annuity policies, to name a few. For example, mortality tables used in computing annuity rates will show lower probabilities of death at each age than will mortality tables used for compiling life insurance premiums. Mortality tables used in setting premiums for ordinary life insurance may show lower probabilities of death at most ages than will mortality tables used in computing reserve liabilities under these policies.

Reliability of Probabilities.   Probabilities which must be arrived at a posteriori are not as reliable as those that can be arrived at a priori. One can have full confidence that the probability of toss heads on the next flip of an unloaded coin is 50 percent even though heads came up on the last 9 consecutive tosses of this coin. The basis for this confidence is the physical nature of the coin which allows one to predict only two possible outcomes, each of which is equally likely. It does not matter that the probability of tossing 10 consecutive heads is only 0.098 percent.[2] It must be admitted, however, that if heads continues to come up uninterruptedly time after time one would be inclined to question his assumption that in this particular instance *two equally likely* outcomes are possible. Perhaps the coin is really not perfect or the tosser has developed a technique for turning up heads which he has learned to apply successfully.

The reliability of empirical probabilities depends upon the degree of homogeneity between the sample and the population from which it is drawn and upon the stability of the experience of that population.

The base for measuring the chance of death in any particular year or the chance of survival over a given number of years is a mortality table which has been constructed from a mortality study. Suppose the study (1) is limited to those persons who have ordinary life insurance at standard rates in 15 large United States companies, (2) includes only the experience under these policies for the years falling between the policies' 1950 and 1954 anniversaries, (3) excludes Korean war deaths, (4) ignores the experience for the first five years of all recently issued policies, and (5) does not separate male and female experience.[3] What can be said about the comparability between that base and the exposure for which the chance of loss is being measured? Suppose the data show that the chance of death for the year at age 20 is 0.084 percent.[4] What could one say about the chances of survival of 20-year-olds in Vietnam? Certainly one would need a sample drawn from a more comparable population than that which produced a death rate of 0.084 percent.[5]

Empirical probability estimates frequently have to be adjusted to allow for the lack of homogeneity in the sample. For example, when legislation was adopted making the 1958 CSO Table the official mortality table for

---

[2] Cf. Appendix 1 (2) to this chapter.

[3] These five features describe the study upon which the 1958 Commissioners Standard Ordinary Table was constructed.

[4] The 1958 CSO Table shows the chance of death to be 0.179 percent but this table has been "enriched" with a safety margin to make its use more than safe for companies whose experience is not as good as the average of the 15 companies.

[5] Death rates are not solely a function of age as the 1958 CSO Table presents them. They are also a function of sex, race, national origin, place of residence, level of income, marital status, physical condition, occupation, habits, and hobbies. The fact that the 1958 CSO Table does not reflect variables other than age is of no consequence if age is the only variable to be considered in predicting death rates for the population with which it is concerned and if the exposure to which the table is to be applied is comparable in mass to the exposure from which the data for the table were collected.

establishing minimum reserve liabilities on ordinary life insurance policies, an adjustment was allowed for the lower mortality rates among women by permitting insurers to use ages up to three years younger than the actual ages of their female policyholders.

How stable is the experience of the population from which the samples are taken for mortality studies? Is there any reason to believe that past death rates are unlikely to be repeated? Is mortality experience static? Do dynamic factors affect the rates of mortality to the extent that the death rates of one decade do not accurately indicate the death rates of another decade? The answers to these questions are important in appraising the reliability of a mortality table.

Progress in the medical arts and sciences, programs to improve the living standards of the disadvantaged people, and broader education in health and safety have kept alive people who according to yesterday's mortality tables should be dead. Continued efforts along these lines hopefully will keep alive tomorrow people who according to today's mortality tables should be dead.

The National Office of Vital Statistics prepares mortality tables from their not entirely accurate census data. These tables show that based on the 1939–41 census data the chance of death for the year at age 20 was 0.217 percent. Based on the 1949–51 data, the chance had reduced to 0.135 percent, and again to 0.115 percent, based on the 1959–61 data. Similar improvement is found at other ages, 0.524 percent, 0.368 percent, and 0.300 percent at age 40, for example.

Actuaries make an attempt at estimating rates of improvements in mortality experience and present these estimates through what are known as projection scales to be applied to various mortality tables. To the extent that there is a predictable rate of improvement in mortality experience, the use of these scales increases the reliability of probability estimates of mortality.

Fair Mathematical Bets. Earlier in this section the phrase "fair mathematical bet" was used in discussing the tossing of coins. It was said that on the toss of one coin, a fair mathematical bet was one to one because the chance of loss and the chance of gain were equal. In the odd man example, where three coins were flipped, a fair mathematical bet was considered to be two to one because the chance of loss was twice the chance of gain. And in both examples, with the odds as stated, the expected value of the game was said to be zero because the expected value of the gain was exactly offset by the expected value of the loss. Using only these illustrations of the concept of a fair mathematical bet, one would be led to conclude that a fair mathematical bet is one in which the expected value of the game is zero. If the expected value of the game to one player is greater than zero, then the expected value of the game to another must be less than zero, that is, the game cannot have a positive expected value to all players. That such a conclusion is incorrect suggests that there is more to the concept of a fair mathematical bet than these simple illustrations reveal.

If the only expected benefits and expected costs involved in a coin matching game were the dollar amounts to be transferred from the loser to the winner, then if the odds were mathematically fair the expected value of the game would be zero. There would be no reason for anyone to enter a game that had no positive expected value for him. But people do gamble, and they gamble in the casinos where the expected value of the gain in dollars bet is actually less than the expected value of the loss in dollars bet. Does this mean that the expected value of the game of roulette at the casino is negative? The flourishing business of the gambling casinos would seem to indicate that for some people the answer is no.

What about the expected value of the game when one enters into an insurance contract? If the probability of death during the year for a man age 50 is 0.671 percent,[6] then the expected value of the gain on the purchase of $100,000 of one-year term life insurance for a premium of $1,100 would be $100,000 × 0.00671, or $671. The expected value of the loss would be the $1,100 premium. Computed in this way, the expected value of the insurance would be minus $429. There would be no reason for anyone to purchase insurance that had no positive expected value to him. But people do buy insurance, and in practically every case, the expected value of the gain in dollars of insurance proceeds is less than the expected value of the loss in dollars of premium charged for the insurance.

Economic and Psychological Considerations.   To make the concept of a fair mathematical bet sophisticated and useful in insurance decision making, additional items must be included in estimating the expected values of gains and losses. Take first the coin tossing game. Even though both the chance of loss and the chance of gain are equal at 50 percent, an even-money bet to some people is not a fair mathematical bet. The higher the stakes, the fewer are the number of people who would find such a bet fair mathematically. For example, a man is asked to flip a coin: heads his $30,000 mortgage debt is canceled; tails his $30,000 mortgage debt is doubled. What is the expected value of the game to him? He reasons as follows: the utility to be gained by elimination of a $30,000 debt is worth less to me than the utility to be lost by increasing my debt by $30,000. Assume that he assigns twice the weight to the loss than he does to the gain. Assigning the integer 100 to the gain and 200 to the loss, he finds the expected value of the gain to be 0.50 × 100, or 50, and the expected value of the loss to be 0.50 × 200, or 100. The expected value of the game becomes 50 — 100, or —50, clearly not a fair mathematical bet for him.

Suppose the law of diminishing utility does not affect him in any measurable quantity and he puts equal values on the elimination of a $30,000 debt and the doubling of a $30,000 debt. He does, however, have a strong psychological aversion to gambling with such high stakes. He reasons that he

---

[6] Based on the 1958 CSO Mortality Table without safety margins. This table is an ultimate table, that is it excludes recently selected lives so that if the man is insurable, the probability of his death during the year is actually less than 0.671 percent.

would require $1,000 to offset this aversion.[7] What then is the expected value of the game? The expected value of the gain is $30,000 × 0.50 or $15,000, and the expected value of the loss is ($30,000 ×0.50) + $1,000, or $16,000. The expected value of the game is $15,000 — $16,000 or minus $1,000, again clearly not a fair mathematical bet for him.

Suppose this man is asked by another person to flip a coin. Heads he wins $10; tails he loses $10. What is the expected value of this game to him? He reasons as follows: "The amount involved is of no serious consequence to me so the principle of diminishing utility has no effect on the evaluation process. Also, while I have a strong aversion to gambling with large stakes, I find that I get a thrill out of gambling when the stakes are low. In fact, I believe that I would get a utility value of one dollar from the game."

What then is the expected value of the game? The expected value of the gain is ($10 × 0.50) + $1 or $6. The expected value of the loss is $10 × 0.50, or $5. The expected value of the game is then $6 — $5, or plus $1, clearly a fair mathematical bet for him. Since his friend invited him into the game, presumably the friend also had the "gambling bug" so that an even-money bet would also produce for him a game with a positive expected value.

Assume that the man had a dislike for gambling even though the stakes are low and, therefore, would not enter into the game for even money. Suppose his friend knew this, wanted to gamble, and had no one else to ask. The friend might suggest that three coins be tossed, the friend would toss one coin and would allow the reluctant gambler to toss two coins. The person who turns up the coin face that does not match the other two would win $10 from the loser. Under these arrangements, the winning odds would be two to one against the friend and two to one in favor of the reluctant gambler. The friend's craving for the game was so strong that he had put a utility value of $4 on its enjoyment. The reluctant gambler's aversion to the game had a disutility of $2. Under these game arrangements and with these assigned utility and disutility values, the expected value of the proposed game to both parties may be measured as follows:

For the Friend

Expected value of the gain ($10 × 0.333) + $4 or	$7.33
Less Expected value of the loss (−$10 × 0.667), or	−6.67
Expected value of the game	$0.66

For the Reluctant Gambler

Expected value of the gain ($10 × 0.667) or	$6.67
Less Expected value of the loss −([$10 × 0.333] + $2) or	−5.33
Expected value of the game	$1.34

---

[7] In an insurance purchase decision, the question is not one of how much he would require to offset his aversion to gambling, but one of whether he would be willing to pay $X to get out of the gambling situation in which he finds himself when he does not purchase insurance.

With these odds, the proposed game is a fair mathematical bet for both parties.

Net gambling gains are reportable as income for federal tax purposes whereas *net* gambling losses are not a tax deductible item. For honest taxpayers, tax considerations call for further adjustments in the expected value of the game by affecting the expected value of the gain. What might be a fair mathematical bet in one man's tax bracket might not be so in another man's tax bracket. Income and death tax considerations play an important role in a number of decisions involving the purchase of life insurance, annuities, and health insurance.

Expected Value of the Game---Purchase Decisions. The use of the concept of the expected value of the game in making decisions relative to the purchase and use of life insurance, annuities, and health insurance is the subject of central interest here. A few paragraphs earlier it was stated that when a 50-year-old man is asked to pay $1,100 for a $100,000 1-year term life insurance policy, the value of the game is minus $429 if the only important consideration in the transaction is the absolute dollars involved in it. What considerations in the purchase of life insurance, annuities, and health insurance transform into fair mathematical bets what appear on the surface, at least, to be unfair mathematical bets insofar as the prospective insured is concerned?[8]

Assume that the 50-year-old man has a wife, also age 50, and that his objective in purchasing the $100,000 of life insurance is to provide his wife with a lifetime income of about $450 a month should he die during the policy year. In purchasing the insurance, he reasons that the monthly utility to be gained from a lifetime payment of about $450 a month to his wife is worth much more than 5 times the monthly utility to be lost by the payment of a $90-a-month premium. His reasoning is based on the principle of diminishing utility in that the $90 a month premium will be paid from predeath earnings and calls for a financial sacrifice of a low order. The $450 a month income will be received after the family income has been drastically reduced by his death and the financial sacrifices it will prevent will be of a high order.

Suppose for each dollar to be paid in the event of his death he assigns a utility value five times that he assigns to each dollar he pays in premiums. What would be the expected value of the game? The expected value of the gain would be $500,000 $\times$ 0.00671 or $3,355. The expected value of the loss would be the $1,100 premium. The expected

---

[8] The author's use of the terms "bet" and "game" in referring to the purchase of life insurance is not intended to mean that the author considers the purchase of insurance a gambling transaction. In fact, quite the opposite is true. When a person enters into a gambling transaction, he is creating a risk that did not exist before the transaction took place. But when a person enters into an insurance contract, he has reduced a risk that had existed before the transaction was made. Gambling creates risk; insurance reduces risk.

value of the insurance, therefore, would be $3,355 — $1,100, or $2,255, a fair mathematical bet.

The higher utility assigned to after-the-loss dollars relative to before-the-loss dollars is not the only consideration that makes the expected value of a particular insurance transaction positive for the insured in face of premiums loaded for expenses and contingencies. Elimination of the worry about, and the fear of, the financial consequences following a possible major illness, for example, is worth something. When the plus values for the psychological benefits of insurance are added to the expected value of the gain, a tentative negative game value may become positive. If it were worth $429 to the 50-year-old man to eliminate his worry about (or his wife's fear of) the adverse financial effect that his death would have on his wife, he would purchase the insurance even though the relative utility values of the predeath and postdeath dollars were equal.

Suppose the 50-year-old man had a premonition that he would die within the year. Although this premonition came through a dream (really a nightmare) he gave considerable weight to it so that his estimate of the chance of his death during the year was well in excess of 1.10 percent. In this context, the concept of chance of loss is different from that used by insurance companies in computing their premium rates. It is an expression of a degree of rational belief rather than a long-run relative frequency, and is, therefore, personal or subjective rather than objective. It is not necessary in insurance purchase decisions to measure subjective chance of loss precisely. Indeed there is always some vagueness about exactly where on the scale between 0 and 1 a subjective chance of loss falls. Subjective appraisals of the chance of loss will vary among individuals in accordance with their experience, knowledge, emotion, and cultural background.

In an insurance purchase decision it is necessary only that the decision makers have feelings definite and strong enough to say that the chance of loss for them is in excess of some given point on the scale between zero and one. Presumably the feelings are based on something more than intuition and have a foundation based on understanding, knowledge, and logic. But to the decision maker a subjective chance of loss based on intuition is just as real as, if not in fact more real than, one based on long-run relative frequencies and can be used in precisely the same way in the decision-making process.

Now back to the 50-year-old man who estimates the chance of his death during the year to be in excess of 1.10 percent. Were he to purchase $100,000 of one-year term life insurance at the above said premium of $1,100 and the chance of his death were 1.10 percent, the value of the game would be zero if no other considerations were involved. Since he considers the chance of his death well in excess of 1.10 percent, his expected value of gain exceeds his expected value of loss. The game, therefore, has a positive expected value to him, even assuming that the postloss and preloss dollar utility values are equal and that there are no financial worries or fears.[9]

Importance of Chance of Loss Estimates in Insurance.   Life and health insurance companies use chance of loss estimates to establish a basis for premium computations. A workable measure of probability is essential if the companies are to set a rate that will produce a net gain in expected values. In the writing of life insurance and annuities, insurers are interested in loss probabilities that measure loss frequency only. Once an insured or annuitant dies, insurers are not concerned with the question of how long he will be dead.[10] In the writing of health insurance, the companies seek probability estimates that measure not only loss frequency but also loss severity rates. When an insured becomes sick, the insurer wants to know the expected duration of his illness and the expected amount of his medical expenses.

The importance of chance of loss to insurance should now be patent: For the prospective buyer, it is a tool for measuring expected benefits associated with the purchase; for the insurer its importance is as a basis for developing rate structures and as a basis for accepting or rejecting an application for coverage.

2. RISK

The concept of risk has several meanings, depending on whether its use is technical or nontechnical. When used nontechnically, the term means the taking of a chance or the exposure to danger or adversity. When novelists, poets, moralists, and dramatists use the word risk in their writings, the reader can tell without difficulty what the word means. No one would question what the British poet John Gay meant in "The Elephant and the Bookseller" when he wrote:

> When we risk no contradiction,
> It prompts the tongue to deal in fiction.

---

[9] The author has purchased several thousand dollars of term life insurance under a university employee pay-all group franchise plan even though he has no worries about the financial security of his wife in the event of his death. He has sufficient postloss resources from other sources. The relative values of the utilities of the predeath and postdeath dollars involved were of no importance in making the decision to purchase the insurance. The decision was based on the author's appraisal of the odds. Because he is uninsurable under nongroup type contracts (for physical not moral reasons) he suspects the financial odds are in his favor (or, more realistically, in his wife's favor). Also, getting insurance at a lower price knowing that it is unavailable even at a much higher price *outside* the university plan has its satisfying overtones.

[10] Wide publicity has been given to cases involving the death of patients who have been brought back to life by skilled physicians. The author does not know if the questions were raised whether these persons' life insurance became payable or their annuity incomes terminated upon their first death. The author does know that scientists have been reexamining their definition of death. Advances in medical science may require that a definition of death be written into life insurance and annuity contracts—perhaps requiring that death be permanent.

The British novelist Jane Austin in *Persuasion* was undoubtedly understood when she wrote of men: "You have difficulties, and privations, and dangers enough to struggle with. You are always labouring and toiling, exposed to every risk and hardship." And the French philosopher Voltaire made himself clear in *Zadig* when he observed, "It is better to risk saving a guilty person than to condemn an innocent one."

As a scientific concept, the meaning of risk depends upon the discipline in which it is used. A definition that is useful in solving problems in one field might not be equally as useful in solving the problems of another field.

Mathematics and Risk.   In dealing with risk, mathematicians are interested in the behavior of phenomena. They define risk as the degree of dispersion of values in a distribution around a central position (the average or expected value) which occurs in random, chance patterns. The larger the degree of dispersion, the greater is the risk. About four decades ago, a distinguished pioneer in the theory of risk wrote: "The object of the theory of risk is to give a mathematical analysis of the random fluctuations in an insurance business, and to discuss the various means of protection against their inconvenient effect."[11]

While mathematical models have been used to solve problems in the life insurance business for many years, such models involving the theory of risk are now being used in solving problems in other businesses. For the business manager using risk theory in his decision-making process, risk is defined as the probability that the profitability of an undertaking will not be as forecast at the time the decision is made. Risk viewed in this way can produce more profit than anticipated if the results are better than those predicted, or less profit than anticipated if the results are not as good as those predicted. Risks that can produce either profits or losses are called speculative risk.

In the context of the mathematical definition of risk, a distinction is drawn between the concept of risk and the concept of uncertainty. To the extent that a decision maker lacks confidence in the reliability of the projected probability distribution, he is faced not only with risk but, also, with uncertainty. The greater the degree of confidence he has about the accuracy of the probability distribution, the less is the uncertainty. Risk, however, is independent of the decision maker's confidence in the probability distribution. It is a function only of the degree of dispersion in the probability distribution. The 17th-century English poet George Herbert, in speaking of uncertainty, observed, "Be not too presumptuously sure in any business, for things of this world depend on such a train of unseen chances that if it were in man's hand to set the table, still he would not be certain to win the game." Yet decisions must be made on the basis of probability, and managements in dealing with their staff

---

[11] Harald Cremér, "On the Mathematical Theory of Risk," *Skandia Jubilee Volume,* Stockholm, 1930, p. 7.

technicians find comfort in the attitude so well expressed by the German philosopher Johann Wolfgang von Goethe: "Give me the benefits of your conviction, if you have any, but keep your doubts to yourself, for I have enough of my own."

Behavioral Scientist and Risk.   In dealing with risk, behavioral scientists are interested in human behavior in reaction to the behavior of phenomena. They rarely define risk because they use it to mean different things. The meaning of the term must be interpreted by the reader or listener from the context in which it is used.

One economist writes, "Risk exists when each alternative will lead to one of a set of possible outcomes and there is a known probability of each outcome. Uncertainty exists when the probabilities of these outcomes are . . . unknown."[12] He goes on to say that if the chance is only one out of ten that a particular action will prove successful, the conditions are risky, but that if the chance of success "is unknown, or partially known, the conditions are uncertain as well as risky." Thus, here he is using risk as a function of the chance of loss, and uncertainty as a function of the ability to measure the chance of loss (or gain). Later he uses the mathematical concepts of risk and uncertainty relating them to the dispersion in a probability distribution and the degree of confidence in its correctness.[13]

In his basic textbook, another economist has a chapter on "Risk in Economic Activity." Although he does not define risk, he uses it to mean exposure to loss. He writes, "In its ordinary operation, a business firm is beset by numerous risks. . . . Some of these risks have troubled business firms for a long time. . . . An effort is usually made to reduce or eliminate risks or to transfer them to professional risk-bearers. . . ."[14]

In discussing the necessity of making decisions, he uses the words "uncertainty" and "risk." He writes, "And in the case of each decision, there exists a degree of uncertainty as to the proper course to be followed and a risk that the decision may produce results which will be unfavorable to the firm."[15] It appears that he has assigned no technical meaning to the word uncertainty and that he is using the word risk to mean chance regardless of the ability to measure it.

Risk and the Discipline of Insurance.   Precise definitions of basic con-

---

[12] Norman N. Barish, *Economic Analysis* (New York: McGraw-Hill Book Company, 1962), p. 8. Like many other authors writing in the area of economic theory, Barish uses the 50-year-old analysis offered by Frank H. Knight in *Risk, Uncertainty and Profit* (Boston: Houghton Mifflin Co., 1921). According to Knight whenever a rate of loss can be measured, "it is possible to get rid of any real uncertainty by the expedient grouping or 'consolidating' instances!" This is the characteristic which Knight argued distinguishes risk from uncertainty.

[13] *Ibid.*, p. 307.

[14] Ralph H. Blodgett, *Our Expanding Economy* (New York: Rinehart and Company, 1955), p. 200.

[15] *Ibid.*, p. 183.

cepts used in any discipline are important in order to facilitate both communication and analysis. Because authorities in the discipline of insurance cannot agree on a definition of risk, the term could be discarded in favor of phrases that precisely communicate the various concepts which have been defined as risk. Terms such as exposure to adversity, average loss expectancy, nonmeasurable uncertainty, variance, and the like can be used if the word risk is likely to cause confusion in the mind of the reader.

The Committee on General Terminology of the Commission on Insurance Terminology of the American Risk and Insurance Association has approved two definitions of risk: (1) "Uncertainty as to the outcome of an event when two or more possibilities exist" and (2) "a person or thing insured." The Committee apparently is not fully satisfied with either definition.[16] Neither one has analytical values for insurance and only the second one has communicative value and then only because it is already widely used by insurance practitioners.

The interest here is in an operational definition of risk for the study of insurance. The definition of risk that both facilitates communication and analysis in the discipline of insurance is a simple one: *Risk is uncertainty concerning loss.*[17] This definition contains two concepts: uncertainty and loss. While both concepts are important to insurance, risk represents the uncertainty and not the loss, the chance of loss, or the cause of the loss. The basic function of insurance is to deal with risk, and risk defined in this manner makes it possible to consider effectively the question of how insurance is supposed to deal with risk. It limits the attention to pure risk as distinguished from speculative risk, that is, it confines itself to risk that can produce loss only.

Life insurance and annuities are concerned with life spans. Individuals may die during the productive years of their lives, or they may live far beyond these years. In either event, loss can result if death comes too soon or too late. Where business interests or large estates are involved, the death of their owners can result in loss regardless of when death occurs. The life risk, therefore, is the uncertainty concerning the time of death. Although some people act as though they believe they are immortal, everyone knows he will die sooner or later. If he knew exactly when, there would be no risk even though his death could cause loss.

Health insurance is concerned with physical and mental conditions that interrupt the productive capacities of living persons during their produc-

---

[16] Bulletin of the Commission of Insurance Terminology, American Risk and Insurance Association, Vol. II, No. 1 (March, 1966), p. 4.

[17] The Committee on General Insurance Terminology originally approved as a definition of risk "uncertainty as to loss" (*Ibid.,* p. 3). Students with an overall interest in a given field and its related disciplines can well disagree on the analytical values of different definitions. The elimination of "loss" from the definition of risk makes it less useful in the study of insurance, and the retention of "uncertainty" makes it less useful when a mathematical definition of risk is desired.

tive years, and with accidents and illnesses that required medical attention at any time. Accidents and illnesses are not certainties; therefore, the risk involved is not only *when* they will occur but also *whether* they will occur. How long disabilities will last, whether they will be partial or total, and how much medical expense will be incurred are also uncertainties, and, hence, risks.

The purpose of life and health insurance is to eliminate these risks for the individuals, and to reduce them for the economy. The insured, by paying the insurer a small, *certain* cost (the insurance premium) that he can budget, is able to shift to the insurer an *uncertain* but potentially large loss (the amount of the insurance) that he cannot budget. How the insurers reduce the risks shifted to them is discussed in Chapter 3.

Degree of Risk. The accuracy with which the occurrence of losses can be predicted is the measure of the degree of risk. In some situations it is difficult, if not impossible, to measure the degree of risk. For example, what will be the purchasing power per dollar of monthly income under retirement annuities 25 years from now? What will be the purchasing power of annuity payments linked to the market value of the insurer's investment portfolio?[18] Can these values be predicted over a 25-year period? The purchasing power risk (the risk of a decline in the value of a dollar) and the market risk (the risk of a decline in the value of an investment portfolio) are not subject to objective measurement. Informed people may speculate but their guesses are subjective. Equally sophisticated, intelligent, and knowledgeable persons likely will come up with different results.

Life and health insurers deal in those risks which they believe they can measure accurately enough for their purposes by using the mathematics of probability. They are content to leave to their insureds the purchasing power risk associated with fixed-dollar contracts and the financial and market risks associated with "variable contracts."

The Measurement of Risk. Through the mathematics of probability, the degree of uncertainty in loss prediction can be expressed quantitatively. Assume that in any 12-month period, the chance of illness causing appreciable loss of time from employment in a given occupation is one in 100 (1 percent). If an employer has only one employee, he is faced with the possibility that his one employee, his entire staff, may be the one in 100 who becomes ill. If the loss produced by an ill employee (as defined) is $1,000, then his expected loss is $10 ($1,000 $\times$ 0.01). But what is the probability that his actual loss will equal his expected loss? If his employee becomes ill, his loss is $1,000. If his employee escapes illness, his loss is zero. Under no circumstances would his loss be $10. Thus, he is faced with a 1 percent chance that his loss will be $1,000, a 99 percent

---

18 Annuity payouts that vary with the fluctuations in the market value of the insurer's investment portfolio are called variable annuities and are discussed in Chapter 6.

chance that it will be 0, and a 0 percent chance that his actual loss will equal his expected loss.

If the employer has 100 employees, then his expected loss is 1 employee illness or $1,000. What is the probability that his actual loss will equal his expected loss? Assuming a binomial probability distribution, there is a 36.7 percent probability that the loss will be 0, a 37 percent probability that the loss will be $1,000, an 18.5 percent probability that the loss will be $2,000, a 6.1 percent probability that the loss will be $3,000, a 1.4 percent probability that the loss will be $4,000, a 0.3 percent probability that the loss will be $5,000, a 0.05 percent probability that the loss will be $6,000, a 0.01 percent probability that the loss will be $7,000, and a nearly 0 probability that the loss will be in excess of $7,000.[19] Thus he is faced with a 37 percent probability that his actual loss will equal his expected loss, a 73.7 percent probability that his actual loss will not exceed his expected loss, a 92.2 percent chance that his actual loss will not exceed twice his expected loss, and a 98.3 percent probability that his actual loss will not be more than three times his expected loss.

With 1,000 employees the loss predictive qualities are improved. The expected number of employee illnesses with 1,000 employees is $1,000 \times 0.01$, or 10, and the expected loss is $1,000 \times 10$ or $10,000. If a normal probability distribution approximation is used, then with 1,000 employees there is a 73.6 percent probability that his actual losses will not exceed his expected losses by more than 20 percent, a 94.4 percent probability that his actual losses will not exceed his expected losses by more than 50 percent, and a 99.9 percent probability that his actual losses will not be more than twice his expected losses.[20]

If the employer has 10,000 people working for him, the accuracy with whch he can predict his losses becomes relatively attractive. Although the probability that his actual losses will be within 5 percent of expected losses is only 69.2 percent, the probability that they will be within 15 percent of expected losses will be 93.4 percent. If he increases the range of his prediction to within a 25 percent deviation from the average expected losses and forecasts that not more than 125 employees nor less than 75 employees will become sick enough during the year to cause an appreciable loss of time from employment, that prediction would have a 99.4 percent chance of being correct.

An employer with 100,000 employees would have even greater ability to predict his losses arising from employee illnesses. If the 1 percent chance of loss figure is indeed correct, the loss predictive qualities of so large a number of exposures would be nearly ideal if no epidemics or other catastrophes upset the underlying probability, and if employee illnesses are random, that is, for example, no attractive health insurance

---

[19] Cf. Appendix 2 (19) to this chapter.
[20] Cf. Appendix 3 (20) to this chapter.

plan is installed during the year which would encourage a wave of employees to submit to surgery that should already have been performed. With 100,000 employees, the probability that not more than 1,050 nor less than 950 of them will become ill (as defined) is 94.4 percent. If he increases his range from within 5 percent to within 10 percent of the central tendency (average expected losses) his prediction would have a 99.9 percent chance of being correct. Thus, excluding catastrophic and nonrandom losses, the employer can forecast with nearly complete confidence that not less than 900 employees nor more than 1,100 employees will become ill during the year.[21]

However, the risk of random and noncatastrophic losses is not entirely eliminated. Given that losses will fall between 900 and 1,100, there is the uncertainty of whether the number will be closer to 900 or 1,100. Furthermore, there is a 0.1 percent probability that the losses will not stay within the predicted range. Also, there is no assurance that the underlying probability upon which the prediction is based, was, is, or will remain a completely accurate estimate. And finally, because the distribution is only an approximation of a normal distribution, another element of risk is added.

Summary Observations. The degree of risk is measured by the probable percentage variation of actual losses from expected losses. The lower the probable percentage of variation, the smaller is the degree of risk. As the number of exposures to a peril increases, the less will be the probable percentage by which actual losses will vary from the long-run relative frequency of a loss. The absolute amount of the variation will increase, of course, but the extent of the increase is limited to the square root of the multiple by which exposures are increased.[22]

To illustrate: The chance of illness causing appreciable loss of time from employment in a particular occupation was assumed to be one out of 100. If an employer has 10,000 employees, his expected loss will be 100 ill employees. The actual number of illnesses, however, will equal the expected number only by coincidence. In some years there will be more than 100; in others, fewer. Assuming a normal probability distribution approximation, there is a 99.99+ percent probability that the number of employee illnesses will be within 50 percent of the expected number, that is that not more than 150 employees nor less than 50 employees will become ill. The employer can be just about certain that 9,850 of his employees will escape illness and that 50 will be ill. The range of uncertainty is the 100 employees between the probable maximum number of illnesses and the probable minimum number of illnesses, or 1 percent of the number of employees.

If the number of employees is increased 100-fold to 1 million, the expected number of illnesses would be 10,000. The probable variation

---

[21] Cf. Appendix 4 (21) to this chapter
[22] Cf. Appendix 5 (22) to this chapter.

of the actual number from the expected number will also increase, but not by 100-fold. Instead, it will increase only 10-fold, 10 being the square root of 100. Assuming a normal probability distribution approximation, there would be a 99.99+ percent probability that the number of employee illnesses will be within 5 percent of the expected number, that is that not more than 10,500 nor less than 9,500 will become ill. The employer can be just about certain that 989,500 of his employees will escape illness and that 9,500 will be ill. The range of uncertainty is the 1,000 employees between the probable maximum number of illnesses and the probable minimum number of illnesses; or 0.1 percent of the number of employees.

Thus, given a 1 percent chance of employee illness, a 100-fold increase in the number of employees from 10,000 to 1 million reduces the range of uncertainty from 1 percent to 0.1 percent of the number of employees, a 90 percent reduction in the degree of risk while retaining a 99.99+ percent probability that the number of employee illnesses will fall within the predicted range.

Two summary observations can now be made about the degree of risk. (1) Given the range of uncertainty, the reliability of the prediction increases directly with the number of exposure units. For example, using a normal distribution approximation, with a 1 percent chance of loss, the probability that actual losses will not vary more than 5 percent from expected losses is 56.3 percent when there are 1,000 exposures, 69.2 percent when there are 10,000 exposures, 94.4 percent when there are 100,000 exposures, and 99.9 percent when there are 1 million exposures.

(2) Given the probability of success in a prediction, the range of uncertainty decreases as the number of exposure units increases. For example, again using a normal distribution approximation, with a 1 percent chance of loss and a 99.99+ percent chance of success in prediction, the range of uncertainty is 50 percent about the mean when there are 10,000 exposures and 5 percent about the mean when there are 1 million exposures. As the number of exposure units approaches infinity, the range of uncertainty narrows and the probability of successful prediction increases to the point where, theoretically, one can predict with 100 percent accuracy that the loss will be exactly the expected loss. Thus, as one randomly tosses a perfect coin from here to eternity, he could predict with 100 percent accuracy that he will throw heads 50 percent of the time.

The degree to which losses can be accurately predicted is the measure of risk. As losses become more predictable, risk is reduced, irrespective of the chance of loss. Thus, even though the chance of loss remained at 1 percent in each of the earlier illustrations in this section, risk was reduced as the number of exposures increased.[23] This fundamental observation

---

[23] As mentioned earlier in this chapter, there is wide disagreement among insurance scholars as to how risk is best defined for the study of insurance. It has been argued forcibly

fits well with the concept of risk as discussed in this text where risk itself is defined as uncertainty concerning loss and the degree of risk (its measurement) is defined in terms of the accuracy (range about the mean and the probability of a correct forecast) with which losses can be predicted. The greater the probability of a correct forecast within a given range about the mean or the smaller the range about the mean with a given probability of a successful forecast the lower is the degree of risk.

Chance of Loss and Degree of Risk. Chance of loss affects the degree of risk in two ways. *First,* if the chance of loss for a given exposure (the underlying probability) is incorrectly measured, the probability of success in a particular prediction of not less than x number nor more than y number of losses also would be incorrectly measured. For example, assume that the number of exposures is 100 and that the chance of loss is given as 30 percent. According to a table of binomial probability functions, a prediction that losses will not deviate by more than 20 percent from the expected loss (not more than 36 nor less than 24) would have about an 84 percent probability of being correct. Suppose it was found that the chance of loss was incorrectly stated and that it is, in fact, 40 percent. With a 40 percent chance of loss, a prediction of not less than 24 nor more than 36 losses would have only a 24 percent probability of being correct.

Second, assuming a given number of exposure units, the higher the chance of loss the lower is the degree of risk. If in the foregoing illustration had the chance of loss originally been given correctly as 40 percent, the expected loss with 100 exposures would have been 40. A prediction that the losses would not deviate by more than 20 percent (not more than 48 nor less than 32) would have had a 92 percent chance of being correct, compared with the 84 percent probability with a 30 percent chance of loss. To achieve a 92 percent probability of a correct prediction with a 30 percent chance of loss, the range of uncertainty would have to be increased from within 20 percent to within 26 percent of the average expected loss.

Importance of Risk and Its Measurement. An understanding of the nature and measurement of risk is important to its management. It provides a key to the operation of the insurance principle as discussed in Chapter 3, and is an important element in the formulas used to establish premiums for group life and health insurance coverage as discussed in Chapters 15 and 16. Furthermore, it is a variable that employee benefit plan managers consider in reaching decisions regarding insurance or risk retention as discussed in Chapters 3 and 19.

The Formulas and Their Proof. The mathematical formulas applied in the foregoing presentation of probabilities are described in the ap-

---

that risk should be defined "as the objective probability that the actual outcome of an event will differ significantly from the expected outcome." See George L. Head, "An Alternative to Defining Risk as Uncertainty," *The Journal of Risk and Insurance,* Vol. XXXIV, No. 2 (June, 1967), pp. 205–14.

pendix of this chapter. However, the logic used by the mathematicians in the proof of these formulas is ignored. The interest here is in identifying the measure of risk, not in explaining the tools used for this purpose. Interested readers should look to textbooks on probability and statistics for detailed discussions of the tools and techniques of actuaries and statisticians. In today's world where such emphasis is placed on quantitative analysis, detailed discussions of probability and statistics are not confined to textbooks on these subjects but are found in textbooks on economics, marketing, psychology, and just about everything else. The practice of "mathmanship" has been increasing at such a pace that it is losing its value as a status symbol. In his delightful essay on *Mathmanship,* Nicholas Vanserg defines the art as follows:[24]

Above and beyond the now-familiar recourse of writing some language that looks like English but isn't, such as Geologese, Biologese, or, perhaps most successful of all, Educationalese, is the further refinement of writing everything possible in mathematical symbols. This has but one disadvantage; namely, that some designing skunk equally proficient in this low form of cunning may be able to follow the reasoning and discover its hidden simplicity. Fortunately, however, any such nefarious design can be thwarted by a modification of the well-known art of gamesmanship.

The object of this technique, which may, by analogy, be termed *Mathmanship,* is to place unsuspected obstacles in the way of the pursuer until he is obliged, by a series of delays and frustrations, to give up the chase and concede his mental inferiority to the author.

3. PERIL, HAZARD, AND LOSS

Three terms closely related to risk are peril, hazard, and loss.

Peril.   A peril may be defined as the cause of a loss. Examples of perils which can cause loss of life values are economic aberrations, bodily injuries, physical and mental illnesses, premature death, and superannuation. Causes of loss (bodily injuries, sickness, premature death, old age) often are loosely called risks. Correctly, *risk* is the uncertainty about the happening of an event that can create loss, whereas *peril* is the cause of the loss.

Students of insurance need to understand the concept of a peril because insurance policies nearly always limit the perils from which loss is covered. Life insurance usually is written to cover death from any cause except a suicide that occurs within one or two years after the policy is issued. Health insurance policies sometimes restrict coverage to losses caused by particular named accidents or illnesses. More frequently, they cover losses caused by any accident or illness except those specifically excluded.[25] Annuities have no peril restrictions. As long as the insured is alive, for whatever reason, his annuity income continues.

---

[24] Nicholas Vanserg, "Mathmanship," *American Scientist,* Vol. 46, No. 3 (June, 1958).

[25] For a discussion of the limitations on perils in health insurance policies, see Chapter 14.

Hazard. Hazard is a condition that increases the chances of a loss arising from a peril. For example, an accident may be the cause of a permanent and total disability. The cause of the accident may have been faulty driving attributable to carelessness, poor eyesight, liquor; it may have been a faulty vehicle, with bad brakes, poor lights, defective tires; or it may be bad driving conditions such as icy roads, glaring sun, poorly marked highways. These conditions are hazards and must not be confused with perils. Illness, for example, is a peril creating loss of income and medical expenses, but it is also a hazard increasing the chance of loss by death.

For insurance purposes two types of hazard may be distinguished: physical and moral.

Physical hazard is an objective characteristic increasing the chance of loss from a given peril. For a simple example: coal mining and metal grinding are hazardous occupations because they increase the chance of illness by exposing workers to inhalation of mineral dusts. Race car driving and window washing in tall buildings are two examples of hazardous occupations that increase the chance of death by accidents. Poor health is a physical hazard that increases the chance of death by natural causes.

Moral hazard is a subjective characteristic of the insured which increases the chance of loss by reason of intention or lack of responsibility of the insured.[26] It is found in the insured's habits, financial practices, or lack of integrity. In life and health insurance, moral hazards are present in criminals, people who associate with criminals, those who skirt the edges of the law, people with unsavory moral reputations generally, alcoholics, dope addicts, and philanderers. A problem relating to moral hazard in health insurance, not found in life insurance, is claim exaggeration either through outright false statements or through malingering (that is extending their hospital stays beyond the time needed for recovery, or by staying away from their jobs longer than is necessary).

Possession of insurance may itself create a moral hazard. For instance, possession of hospital insurance increases the incidence of hospitalization.[27] Life insurance, however, produces little incidence of moral hazard arising out of indifference to loss. There is no evidence that an individual becomes careless of life simply because he is insured.

A study of hazards is important to the understanding of insurance. Insurance companies must review the hazards involved when an applica-

---

[26] Some textbook writers, but not insurers, draw a careful distinction between hazards that produce intentional loss and those that produce loss that arises from a lack of responsibility of the insured. They reserve the term moral hazard for the former and use the term morale or personal hazard to identify the latter. These writers insist that the distinction has a useful analytical value in separating the crooks from the careless.

[27] The hazard is not always wholly subjective here. Hospital insurance frequently results in more people taking advantage of hospital-needed diagnoses. However, when insurance results in unneeded hospitalization (either upon the insured's insistence or the physician's insistence because he knows the patient is insured), the loss is a result of a moral hazard.

tion for insurance is submitted. If the hazards are unusually significant, the company must either charge a higher premium, restrict the coverage, or deny the insurance.[28] Insurance buyers must review their policies to be aware of the hazardous exposures not covered by their insurance so that they know what hazards to handle through some other before-the-loss arrangement.

Loss. Loss is the detriment resulting from a decline in or disappearance of values arising from a contingency.

The major types of losses insured against through a life insurance contract are those produced by expenses and interruption of income associated with death. For the typical family, loss of income resulting from the death of its breadwinner is the more serious of the two; however, the final expenses of any family member can be a problem in those families operating on a close budget. For the wealthy family, death taxes and the cost of probating the estate could be the more serious loss. Loss of income, although large, might be of only secondary importance, especially in view of the high tax rates applicable to that income.

Accident and sickness also involve both expenses and income losses. Medical, surgical, and hospital expenses can amount to large sums. Disability resulting from accident or sickness can cause loss of income for lengthy periods, sometimes permanently. For the typical family, both types of losses can be serious, and they require efficient before-the-loss arrangements for an effective after-the-loss balance between resources needed and resources available. What is an efficient before-the-loss arrangement and what is an effective after-the-loss balance between available and needed resources will vary from family to family because decisions in these matters are personal and are governed by one's own set of values. However, some procedures for use in analyzing the problem and in reaching decisions on these matters have been developed and they are discussed later in the text.

Appendix to Chapter 2
Formulas for Risk Measurement

This appendix sets forth the formulas used in computing the figures developed as illustrations of the points made in the text. It is divided into five parts with each part having two identifying numbers. The first number represents the ordering of the appendix, and the second number,

---

[28] Cf. Chapter 10 (hazard restrictions in life insurance), Chapter 14 (hazard restrictions in health insurance), and Chapter 23 (underwriting of extra hazardous life and health exposures).

the one in parenthesis, refers to the footnote in the text where the ordered number is cited.

$$1\,(2)$$

The probability of tossing 10 consecutive "heads" can be determined from the formula

$$f_b(r;\,p,\,n) = \frac{n\,!}{r\,!\,(n-r)\,!}\,p^r(1-p)^{n-r}$$

where f_b is the probability that the event will occur r times out of n trials and p is the probability that the event will occur in a single trial. The symbol ! means factorial and is computed by multiplying together all the integers from one to the number preceding the factorial sign. For example, 4 ! means $4 \times 3 \times 2 \times 1$. Zero factorial by definition is assigned the value of one. Working out the formula,

$$P(10;\,0.50,\,10) = \frac{10\,!}{10\,!\,0\,!}\,(0.50)^{10}(0.50)^0 =$$

$$\frac{3{,}628{,}800}{3{,}628{,}800}\;(0.0009765625)\quad(1)\qquad =$$

0.0009765625, the probability of tossing 10 consecutive heads is approximately 0.098 percent. Published tables of values for n ! are available, but more useful is the table of values for the equation for binomial probability mass functions. A binomial probability distribution is a discrete probability distribution in which only two different outcomes are noted, heads or tails, for example, and the outcomes are independent, that is, neither outcome on any trial is influenced by or influences the outcome of any other trial. However, the available tables of binomial probability functions commonly published in basic statistics textbooks usually do not go beyond $n = 25$, 20, or even 10 because of the difficulty in tabulating binomial distributions conveniently. The equation involves two parameters (p and n) and there are $n + 1$ values of r for each combination of an entire range of values for p and n. Thus, a table of binomial values that would cover the range of values of n and p that might be of interest would require far too many pages for publication in a textbook on basic statistics or on probability. For example, a table of binomial mass functions (the probability of exactly r successes in n independent binomial trials with probability of success on a single trial equal to p) and a table of cumulative binomial functions (stated $P(X \geqq r) = \sum_{x=r}^{n} \binom{n}{x} p^x (1-p)^{n-x}$, the probability of r or more successes in n independent binomial trials with probability of success on a single trial equal to p) fill 92 pages $8\frac{1}{2}''$ by $11''$ of small type with the range of values for n from 1 to 100, and the range of values for p from 0.01 to 0.50 in Bracken and Christenson, *Tables for Use in Analyzing Business Decisions* (Homewood, Ill.: Richard D. Irwin, Inc., 1965), pp. 141–233.

On a binomial probability mass function table carried to 3 decimal places, the value of $P(10; 0.050, 10) = 0.001$.

A method for approximating the values of a binomial distribution is described in 3 (20) of this Appendix.

2 (19)

The equation for the binomial probability mass function is described in 1 (2) of this appendix. Working out the equations for the desired functions, the values are defined as follows:

$$f_b(0; 0.01, 100) = \frac{100\,!}{0\,!\,(100-0)\,!} \qquad 0.01^0(1-0.01)^{100-0} = 0.367$$

$$f_b(1; 0.01, 100) = \frac{100\,!}{1\,!\,(100-1)\,!} \qquad 0.01^1(1-0.01)^{100-1} = 0.370$$

$$f_b(2; 0.01, 100) = \frac{100\,!}{2\,!\,(100-2)\,!} \qquad 0.01^2(1-0.01)^{100-2} = 0.185$$

$$f_b(3; 0.01, 100) = \frac{100\,!}{3\,!\,(100-3)\,!} \qquad 0.01^3(1-0.01)^{100-3} = 0.061$$

$$f_b(4; 0.01, 100) = \frac{100\,!}{4\,!\,(100-4)\,!} \qquad 0.01^4(1-0.01)^{100-4} = 0.014$$

$$f_b(5; 0.01, 100) = \frac{100\,!}{5\,!\,(100-5)\,!} \qquad 0.01^5(1-0.01)^{100-5} = 0.003$$

$$f_b(6; 0.01, 100) = \frac{100\,!}{6\,!\,(100-6)\,!} \qquad 0.01^6(1-0.01)^{100-6} = 0.0005$$

$$f_b(7; 0.01, 100) = \frac{100\,!}{7\,!\,(100-7)\,!} \qquad 0.01^7(1-0.01)^{100-7} = 0.0001$$

$$f_b(8; 0.01, 100) = \frac{100\,!}{8\,!\,(100-8)\,!} \qquad 0.01^8(1-0.01)^{100-8} = 0.0000$$

3 (20)

A normal probability distribution is a set of continuous frequency distributions that are symmetric about their mean, with the values of the mean, mode, and median being identical. The probable values in the distribution are apportioned through a curve with a bell-shaped appearance known as a normal curve. Given the mean (μ) and the standard deviation (σ) of a frequency distribution, a continuous random variable (x) is normally distributed if its curve is represented by

$$n\,(x;\,\mu,\,\sigma) = \frac{1}{\sigma\sqrt{2\pi}}\,e^{-(x-u)^2/2\sigma^2}\,.$$

The foregoing equation for the normal curve, called the normal density function, has two parameters: the mean (μ) which determines the peak of the curve and the standard deviation (σ) which determines the spread of the curve. The equation also includes two well-known irrational numbers: 3.14159, the ratio between the circumference and the diameter of a circle (π); and 2.71828, the numerical value of the base of the "natural" or "napierian" logarithmic system (e). The random variable (x) can be any real number, large or small, extending from $-\infty$ to $+\infty$.

Standardized tables have been prepared and published for making computations using a normal probability distribution approximation. With the values of μ and σ in the distribution given as zero and one respectively, the equation for a standardized normal distribution, called the standardized normal density function, can be written with the variable t:

$$f(t;\,0,\,1) = \frac{1}{\sqrt{2\pi}}\,e^{-t^2/2}$$

$$\text{where } t = \frac{x-\mu}{\sigma}\,.$$

This equation establishes the coordinates of points on the standard normal curve for t and $f(t;\,0,\,1)$. For example, it will show values as follows:

t	$f(t;\,0,\,1)$	t	$f(t;\,0,\,1)$	t	$f(t;\,0,\,1)$
0.00	0.3989	±1.50	0.1295	±3.00	0.0044
±0.25	0.3867	±1.75	0.0863	±3.25	0.0020
±0.50	0.3521	±2.00	0.0540	±3.50	0.0009
±0.75	0.3011	±2.25	0.0317	±3.75	0.0004
±1.00	0.2420	±2.50	0.0175	±4.00	0.0001
±1.25	0.1826	±2.75	0.0091		

A curve drawn through the foregoing points plotted on a graph would produce a normal curve.

An important characteristic of the normal distribution is the fixed relationship between the mean, the standard deviation, and the percentiles. The mean, being the median, is always the 50th percentile, and the mean plus or minus a given number of standard deviations always indicates the same percentile.

Using a cumulative standard normal distribution table,

$$F(t; 0, 1) = \int_{-\infty}^{t} \frac{1}{\sqrt{2\pi}} e^{-\frac{z^2}{2}} dz$$

usually found in textbooks on statistics, the mean plus three standard deviations indicates the 99.87th percentile mark. The mean plus 2 standard deviations indicates the 97.72nd percentile mark, and the mean plus 1 standard deviation indicates the 84.13th percentile mark. One standard deviation below and above the mean covers a range from the 15.87th to the 84.13th percentile marks, the central 68.26 percent of the distribution.

By the central limit theorem, as the sample size increases, the mean of that sample approaches that of a normal distribution, irrespective of the shape of the distribution from which the sample is drawn. This means, for example, that if the number of employees is 1,000 rather than 10, a standardized normal distribution table could be used more effectively in answering such questions as what is the probability that the actual number of employee illnesses will not exceed the expected number of employee illnesses by more than some such figure as 20 percent, 40 percent, or 100 percent, given that the probability of an employee illness (p) is 0.01.

The probability function for a discrete probability distribution in which only two outcomes are noted, for example, an employee becomes ill or he escapes illness is, of course, a binomial rather than a normal distribution. However, where the numbers are large it is simpler to use the values of a normal distribution to approximate those of a binomial distribution. For example, given 1,000 employees and a 0.01 probability of illness, a cumulative standard normal distribution table can be used to approximate the probability that actual losses will not exceed expected losses by more than 20 percent $(x \leqq 12)$. To use the table, it is necessary to obtain the values for the normally distributed variable (t) by the formula

$$t = (x - \mu)/\sigma$$

where x is 12, the maximum limit of losses $[10 + (0.20 \times 10)]$; μ is 10, the mean of this binomial distribution $(0.01 \times 1,000)$; and σ is 3.15, the standard deviation of this binomial distribution $\sqrt{1,000 \times 0.01 \times 0.99}$ (cf. 5 (22) of this appendix). Using these values in the formula, t is computed to be 0.63,

$$t = [(12 - 10)/3.15] \text{ or } 0.63.$$

For a t value of 0.63, the cumulative standard normal distribution table shows a probability of 73.6 percent, which is the probability that not more than 12 employees will be ill.

4 (21)

Assuming a normal probability distribution approximation, the number of employees needed for the degree of confidence sought in a prediction that the actual number of employee illnesses will not exceed the expected number of employee illnesses by more than 15 percent when the probability of employee illness is 0.01 may be computed as follows:

Define events A and B as

$$A: \quad x \leqq np + 0.15np$$
$$B: \quad x \leqq np + 3\sqrt{np(1-p)}$$

Since the probability of event B is 0.999 (using the normal approximation), the probability of event A also will be 0.999 if, and only if, the following equation holds:

$$0.15np = 3\sqrt{np(1-p)}$$

Squaring both sides,

$$(0.15)^2 n^2 p^2 = 9np(1-p)$$

and solving for n,

$$n = \frac{9(1-p)}{(0.15)^2 np} = \frac{9(0.99)}{(0.15)^2(0.01)} = 39{,}600$$

So 39,600 employees are needed to have a 99.99 percent probability that the number of employee illnesses will not exceed the average number of illnesses (μ) by more than 15 percent.

5 (22)

The formula for variance (σ^2) in a binomial probability distribution is

$$\sigma^2 = r/pn = np(1-p)$$

where

σ^2 is the variance (the squares of the differences between the values in a distribution and the mean of the distribution)

r is the number of employees who become ill

p is the probability of illness for each employee

n is the number of employees

Assume that the probability of illness for each employee is 0.01, and that there are 10,000 employees. The variance would be computed as follows:

$$\sigma^2 = (10{,}000 \times 0.01)(0.99) = 99$$

Now assume that the number of employees increased 100-fold and that there are 1 million employees. The variance would be computed as follows:

$$\sigma^2 = (1,000,000 \times 0.01)(0.99) = 9900$$

The standard deviation, another measure of dispersion, is computed by taking the square root of the variance. Note that the standard deviation of the distribution when there are 10,000 employees is $\sqrt{99} = 9.95$. When the number of employees is increased 100-fold to 1,000,000 employees the standard deviation increases only 10-fold, $\sqrt{9900} = 99.5$. A statistic often used as a measure of risk is the coefficient of variation which is the percentage obtained by dividing the standard deviation by the mean $\left(\dfrac{\sigma}{\mu}\right)$. The lower the coefficient of variation in a probability distribution the less is the degree of risk. With 10,000 employees, the mean is 100 and the standard deviation is 9.95 producing a coefficient of variation of 0.0995. With 1 million employees, the mean is 10,000 and the standard deviation is 99.5 producing a coefficient of variation of only 0.00995. Thus, the risk with 1 million employees is only 10 percent of the risk with 10,000 employees.

3

The Management of Risk

Management is the judicious use of means to accomplish an end. The end to be accomplished in the management of risk is an efficient before-the-loss arrangement for an effective after-the-loss balance between available and needed resources. The means to accomplish this end are the tools of risk management.

1. THE RISK MANAGEMENT PROCESS

In the risk management decision-making process, the first step is to identify loss exposures. The next step is to analyze the characteristics of potential losses from these exposures to determine the amount of resources needed after the loss and the period over which these resources will be needed. The management problem is to decide what (if anything) should be done to reduce the potential resources needed (loss prevention and control) and what resources should be relied upon to offset the losses that occur. The techniques selected for loss prevention and control and for providing reliable after-the-loss resources should be those that offer the most favorable balance between benefits and costs.

Loss Exposures. The process of risk management requires that loss exposures be identified and that loss potential from these exposures be measured. The concern in the text is with the exposure to loss caused by the perils of disability, death, and old age. Important questions are: Whose death causes loss, to whom, and how much? Whose disability causes loss, to whom, and how much? Whose retirement causes loss, to whom, and how much?

How does one systematically approach the twin problem of (1) identifying loss exposures and (2) measuring the loss potential from death, disability, and old age? Useful techniques are those of family life and health insurance programming, business life and health insurance planning, and estate planning. These techniques are discussed in some detail in Chapters 20 through 22. They involve a process of determining what resources will be needed after disability, death, or retirement to fulfill the plans made for such a contingency. It is possible that there will be no need for additional resources or that the additional resources needed will be small. On the other hand, there could be a need for large additional resources. Whether there is a loss exposure and the amount of such exposure depends upon the relationship between the amount of resources required after the contingency occurs and the amount of resources available following the contingency.

The death of a small child may produce no financial loss to anyone except for the expense of burial. Adequate family resources may be available to handle these expenses without a serious burden on family finances. Burial expenses also would be the only financial loss resulting from the death of an unmarried college senior with no one to support—unless he is in debt or unless his prospective employer has financed his education. Sickness of any member of the family creates the need for resources to pay medical bills. The illness of the husband-father may result in the loss of needed family income and the disability of the wife-mother can create additional expenses for family management. The continued survival of a dependent parent causes financial loss to the family providing the support. The death of a financially wealthy person (active or retired) can create a need for liquid resources to pay death taxes and estate administration expenses.

The disability or death of a business partner or co-stockholder may create the need for liquid resources to allow the surviving (active) partner or stockholder to purchase the deceased (disabled) partner's or stockholder's interest in the business under a binding buy-and-sell agreement. When an employee cannot be replaced without a loss to the business, a life value exposure is present which needs identifying and measuring. When an employee has been retired under a pension, the continued life of that employee causes loss to the business and is therefore a life value exposure. Other business life value exposures are those inherent in employee benefit plans involving death benefits, disability income benefits, and medical care benefits.

Some of the resources needed to offset life value losses may be needed within a short time following death. For example, the resources needed to pay death expenses or to finance the purchase of a partnership interest are needed as a capital sum. Resources needed to offset loss of income because of disability or death are not needed all at once but can be spread over the period of disability or the period of dependent survivorship.

The characteristics of a loss situation are an important consideration in selecting the risk management devices to use. A resource such as the ability of the wife to earn a living can be used in the event of the death or disability of the husband to provide an income stream, but it cannot be used directly to provide a liquid capital sum to pay death expenses. Credit resources may be useful to provide a liquid capital sum but not to provide a stream of income to replace that lost by the death or disability of the breadwinner.

Risk Management Techniques.   Several methods of handling risk are commonly used. With some of these methods the technique is to deal with risk by attempting to reduce the quantity of after-the-loss resources needed. With others, the technique is to provide a source of supply for needed after-the-loss resources. The methods of handling risk can be broadly grouped into six classes: (1) risk avoidance, (2) risk assumption, (3) risk transfer, (4) risk reduction, (5) loss prevention, and (6) loss control. These broadly classed methods are not mutually exclusive in dealing with any given risk. For example, the employer, by applying techniques involving probability and statistics, may reduce the risk involved in his employee disability income benefit program. He may retain the reduced risk and transfer to an insurance company that part of the risk that he cannot reduce to a size that he considers to be manageable. He may also try to control losses by requiring his employees to take annual physical examinations.

Risk Avoidance.   Some risks can be avoided. For example, a man with no dependents can avoid the risk of financial loss from premature death by remaining a bachelor. He can avoid the risk of loss of income resulting from disability or old age by marrying a rich widow and joining the idle rich. An employer that offers no employee benefits for disability, death, or retirement has avoided the risks associated with these plans. But risk avoidance is not always possible, and when it is, it is not always desirable. Those risks that either cannot or should not be avoided will have to be handled by other risk management devices.

Risk Assumption.   Inherent in a risk is uncertainty and potential loss. In some situations, the best method of handling risk is to assume it, but when this is done, the risk bearer must be able to absorb the cost of both the uncertainty and the loss.

Sometimes risk assumption is passive and done unconsciously. For example, when a family man does not transfer the risk of loss of income in the event of his premature death to a life insurance company, his wife and children are forced to assume the risk. Sometimes this risk is assumed by the husband's or wife's parents who will feel the responsibility of caring for the widow and children. If the widow and children and the concerned grandparents are unaware of the risk to which they are exposed, the risk will be costless should the husband survive to retirement. However, if the husband dies prematurely, there is a measurable cost of risk in addition to the cost of the loss. The cost of the risk is that amount by which the cost of an unprepared for loss exceeds that of a loss for which preparations had been made. For example, had the wife prepared herself for employment in the event of the premature death of her husband, the cost of the loss would have been less because the widow would have been ready to go to work to replace part of the income.

If the wife and family were aware of the risk, and the husband survived to retirement, the risk might not have been costless. The cost could be anxiety or the disutility involved in being exposed to uncertainty concerning loss. Any costs asociated with the preparation for a loss that is not certain to happen is also a cost of risk (the cost of the wife's preparation for a job if one is needed, for example). The lack of preparation for a potential loss might impair the family's credit standing, and this would be a cost of risk.

Frequently risk assumption is active and done consciously. A person may decide to assume the risk of incurring medical expenses of *relatively* small amounts or the risk of the loss of income from illnesses lasting for *relatively* short periods.[1] He decides that he can assume the risk and forget it. It will cause no worry and the loss, if it occurs, will be no greater without than with preparation for it. The cost of risk is zero regardless of whether or not there is a loss, and consequently he sees no need to do anything but assume it. Surely he would not be acting logically to pay to have the risk transferred to an insurance company. For this reason, many intelligent purchasers of health insurance, for example, include deductibles in their medical care coverage and waiting periods in their disability income coverage.

Although risk assumption is sometimes good business, frequently it is the path of least resistance in meeting risk. Failure to take any action is automatic assumption of the risk.

Often when risk is assumed there is an attempt to build a fund to offset possible losses. Even with the use of funds, risk assumption might prove unwise. Specifically, it requires time to accumulate a fund large enough to meet heavy losses. If the loss is one which comes on slowly at a predictable rate—loss of income at retirement, for example—the building of a fund can be an effective risk management device. The certainty of the date of loss makes it posible to calculate the rate of deposits needed. But if the date or amount of the loss cannot be predicted in the individual case, then it is impossible to calculate the rate at which deposits to the fund should be made. For example, a proposed $100,000 fund to be accumulated to offset the loss of income to a family occasioned by the death or disability of its breadwinner may stand at only $10,000 when that death or disability occurs. In this type of situation the building of a fund can be an effective risk management tool when used in combination with risk transfer. As the fund grows, more and more of the risk and loss can be assumed and less and less transferred. For example, the family head who wishes to build a fund of $100,000 to protect his family in the event of his premature death could transfer the risk to an insurer by purchasing life insurance each year for an amount equal to $100,000 minus the size of the growing fund. In effect, this is what he does when he buys cash value life insurance, so argue those who view cash value life insurance as decreasing protection coupled with increasing savings.

---

[1] The use of the word *relatively* refers to the size of the loss compared to his financial strength, including liquidity as well as net worth.

Loss Prevention   Steps may be taken to reduce the hazard—i.e., to reduce the chance of loss. Loss prevention is socially desirable, particularly so with respect to the preservation of life values. The federal government has taken an interest in the research reports of a positive relationship between cigarette smoking and cancer and has forced cigarette manufacturers to label packages with a warning that cigarette smoking may be hazardous to health. The federal government has taken an active interest in establishing safety standards in the manufacturing of automobiles. Safety standards are imposed on rail, air, highway, and sea transportation. State and local governments are also actively engaged in public health and safety activities. If current trends are a key to the future, these activities can be expected to expand.

Private capital in search of profit and nonprofit research foundations supported by private capital have contributed much to the preservation of life values. For instance, the development of wonder drugs has materially reduced the hazard of premature death or prolonged disability from certain diseases such as pneumonia. Other modern drugs have kept alive and actively at work people who not too long ago would have been either totally disabled or dead. The development of effective vaccines has reduced the hazard of disability or death from a number of diseases.

Individuals usually can reduce the hazard of loss by disability or premature death by submitting to regular periodic medical checkups, following an approved diet, restricting or extending physical activity as prescribed by physicians, learning to manage emotions, pursuing a safe and healthy occupation, knowing how to relax, engaging in only healthy and safe hobbies, and in general living by the book of health. However, the benefits of loss prevention may not be worth the cost. Some may think they prefer a shorter but exciting life to a longer but dull one—if a choice is available.

Loss Control.   Loss prevention has as its objective a reduction in loss frequency. Loss control has as its objective a reduction in loss severity. Obviously loss control is not an effective substitute for loss prevention. However, no loss prevention program is perfect. The apple-a-day man does get sick, and the safest drivers in the safest cars on the safest highway driving at the safest speed during the safest weather and under the safest of road conditions during daylight do become victims of fatal accidents. Loss control requires that activities be arranged so as to reduce the severity of a loss should it occur.

The mother who is prepared to take a job to support the children following the disability or death of her husband is of no help to the children if she is seriously injured or killed in the same accident that takes her husband's life. Some married couples with dependent children try to control loss by not traveling together in the same vehicle (train, plane, ship, or automobile). A plane carrying a large number of one company's prize-winning sales distributors crashed in Tokyo bay. Aside from the adverse effects of the disaster on the families of those who had won their last prize and on the corporation that had awarded the trip as a prize for outstanding sales performances, the accident shocked others into realizing the catastrophic exposure involved in group travel on regularly scheduled or chartered flights. Are the benefits of group travel worth their cost? Groups that fly together may die together.

Predeath funeral arrangements made without emotional considerations often can reduce funeral expenses. The bereaved and sometimes repentant family is not given the opportunity to spend recklessly as a final token of affection and respect for the dearly beloved departed.

After-the-loss controls also may be possible. Hospital utilization committees of physicians are appointed by doctors in various hospitals to see that patients are not kept hospitalized by their doctors longer than is necessary. Medical boards hear complaints on alleged excessive fees charged by physicians. As the cost of medical care continues to rise, more attention and effort can be expected to be given to the problem of controlling these costs.

There may be some interacting between loss prevention and loss control. For example, while periodic medical examinations may not lessen the hazard of cardiovascular disturbance, they can often catch the trouble in its initial stages and so lessen the severity of the affliction. Further, the findings of such examinations may suggest medical treatment that will also reduce the hazard.

Loss prevention and loss control have some effect on the degree of risk. Loss *frequency* affects the predictability of losses. It is pointed out in Chapter 2 that, with a given number of exposure units, as the chance of loss decreases (1) the lower is the probability of a correct prediction that losses will not vary more than X percent from expected losses, or (2) the wider must be the range by which losses can vary from expected losses to have a Y percent probability of being correct. Furthermore, a change in the underlying probability of loss by effective loss prevention devices reduces the reliability of a probability forecast until the new underlying probability is known. A higher risk involving fewer losses, however, cannot be viewed as an unattractive development.

The employer who installs an employee benefits program for his employees will find less risk associated with hospital and medical care benefits than with survivor benefits, and less risk associated with short-term disability income benefits than with long-term disability income benefits. The reason is the higher frequency of hospital and medical care benefits than of death claims, and the higher frequency of short-term disability income claims than of long-term disability income claims. These conclusions assume equal reliability of underlying probabilities, and a sufficient number of employees to make a reasonable prediction.

Successful efforts to reduce the frequency of short-term disabilities and medical treatment will increase the employer's risk not only by reducing the loss predictive qualities arising out of lower frequency rates but also by reducing the reliability of the underlying probability. However, the risk will become less undesirable. Assuming a binomial probability distribution, a 2 percent chance of loss, and 100 employees, the probability that losses will not exceed twice the expected loss is 94.9 percent. If loss prevention techniques succeed in reducing the chance of loss to 1 percent, the probability that losses will not exceed twice the expected loss is reduced to 92 percent.

It is important to note that in terms of absolute numbers of losses the predictability is improved. Before the reduction in the chance of loss a prediction of not more than two losses would have had only a 67.7 percent chance of success compared with a 92 percent chance after the hazard is reduced. And a prediction of not more than four losses would have had only a 94.9 percent chance of success compared with a 99.7 percent chance following the reduction of the hazard.

Risk may be reduced by effective control over loss severity. For example, suppose an employer encourages his employees to submit to annual physical examinations. Through these examinations illnesses are uncovered in their initial stages and can be controlled promptly. The result is a reduction in the number of large medical bills incurred by employees, and a tendency to keep the annual bills for each patient within a narrow range. The predictability of employee medical expenses as a group is improved and the risk for the employer who pays these expenses for his employees under an employee benefit plan is reduced.

Risk Transfer. Risk may be transferred through a valid contract made between the transferor and the transferee, through an informal or implicit understanding between two or more people, or it may be shifted by one person to another without that person's approval or knowledge. And through the social security law people are required to transfer some of their life value risk to a tax-supported government plan.

Several transfer devices are available for handling the risks associated with life values. Some old people turn over their property to retirement homes in exchange for care until death. As an estate planning technique some parents may sell property to their children, asking as a purchase price a life annuity payable by the children to the parents. Large numbers of people enter into prepaid hospital and medical care contracts with hospitals and doctors through Blue Cross, Blue Shield, and similar associations. Millions of people handle their life value risks by transferring them to insurance companies, and a large and increasing number of workers at all levels of employment are shifting their life value risk to their employers through negotiated or employer-offered employee benefit plans. Much of this risk is passed on to insurance companies by the employers.

Risk shifting is a common practice in meeting the perils of premature death, disability, and old age. A man may refuse to buy life insurance and thus automatically shift the risk of loss resulting from his premature death to his widow and children, or other members of society (taxpayers or private charity). He may refuse to plan for income in old age and shift the risk of loss to his children. He may refuse to insure against disability and shift the risk of this loss to relatives, friends, and charity. In the family society that characterizes the economy, most risks that are left uncovered by one member of the family are automatically shifted to other members— usually the more provident ones, sometimes merely the ones with the least resistance.

Risk Reduction   Risk is reduced when the accuracy of a loss forecast is improved. Several measures of the accuracy of a loss forecast can be used.[2] The one used in this text relates to the probability that actual losses will fall within a given range of expected losses. Under this standard, the accuracy of the forecast is improved (1) when the probability of a correct prediction is increased over a given range of losses, that is, for example, when the probability that actual losses will fall within 15 percent of expected losses is increased, say, from 50 percent to 95 percent, or (2) when the range over which a given probability of a successful prediction is decreased, that is, for example, when the range of losses over which a 95 percent probability of a successful prediction is reduced, say, from 15 percent to 5 percent of expected losses.

Employers of large numbers of people can use probability theory to reduce the risk inherent in financing employee benefit plans. The probability of an occurrence of a loss can be stated as follows: $p = \dfrac{\lim}{n \to \infty} \dfrac{m}{n}$ which means that as the number of exposure units approaches infinity, the ratio of losses (m) to exposures (n) will approach $\dfrac{m}{n}$.[3] Assume that an employer has promised his employees $100 a week for a maximum of 26 weeks following a 3-day waiting period in the event of total disability. Morbidity tables tell him that the chance of loss under this benefit structure is 3 percent, that is $3 for every $100 exposed to the loss. With 1 employee his exposure is $2,600 ($100 a week times 26 weeks); with 100 employees his exposure is $260,000; and with 10,000 employees, his exposure is $26 million. A 3 percent chance of loss does not tell the employer that his loss with 1 employee will be exactly $78 ($2,600 × 0.03), or that it will be exactly $7,800 with 100 employees or exactly $780,000 with 10,000 employees. It tells him only that if he has to make a prediction of his losses,

---

[2] See Robert I. Mehr and Bob A. Hedges, *Risk Management in the Business Enterprise* (Homewood, Illinois: Richard D. Irwin, Inc., 1963), chap. 4.

[3] The probability (p) of the occurrence of some chance event (m) is the number of times that the outcome m appears in n trials. The equation reads: the probability (p) of m is the limit of the relative frequency as n becomes infinitely large. Because man can experiment with only a finite number of trials, and the equation cannot be interpreted with mathematical precision without introducing the abstraction of probability, the equation does not provide a rigorous definition of probability but does provide a useful conceptual interpretation of the basic idea of probability.

these figures would be the best prediction possible. However, probability theory does tell him that as his exposures increase the ratio of losses to exposures will approach 3/100.

Risk reduction for the small employer usually can be accomplished only through transferring the risk to an insurer who will combine the exposures of a large number of small employers, thus reducing the risk, just as the large employer could do alone. The insurance company would charge the small employer $78 per employee plus a loading for contingencies, expenses, taxes, and profits. An employer with a large enough number of employees to predict his losses within limits that he considers to be reasonable might assume part of the risk and transfer some of it to an insurer by insuring against all losses that exceed a given number of dollars a year. The insurer reduces an individual employer's catastrophic risk by combining his excess loss exposures with that of a large number of other employers.

Selecting Risk Management Techniques.   It was stated earlier that the objective of risk management is to make an efficient before-the-loss arrangement for an effective after-the-loss balance between needed and available resources and that the goal in risk management is to select the methods of dealing with risk that offer the most favorable balance between benefits and cost. Loss exposures must be identified and evaluated. If these exposures are to be dealt with efficiently and effectively, attention must be focused on two basic questions: (1) What can be done to reduce the amount of after-the-loss resources needed and (2) What are the most efficient arrangements that can be made to provide the postloss resources needed?

In weighing the merits of alternative solutions to risk management problems, the decision maker must consider the relative benefits and costs of each solution as they affect him. For a simple example, one solution to a risk problem is to transfer the risk to an insurance company and pay the insurer for its services. To answer the question of whether the services of the insurer is worth its cost to the insured, it is necessary that all services and all costs be identified. One cost is *regret* and represents the loss that could have been avoided were it possible for the risk management decision to have been made under conditions of certainty, that is ex post rather than ex ante. Assume that the amount of insurance necessary to cover the potential loss is $10,000 and that the premium is $100. If there is no loss, and insurance had been purchased, the $100 premium is regretted. If there is a loss and no insurance had been purchased, the $9,900 opportunity loss ($10,000 — $100) is regretted. While a $100 regret of having purchased the insurance is a much more likely outcome than a $9,900 regret of not having purchased the insurance, the potential pain of a possible $9,900 regret may be sufficient to cause the decision maker to purchase the coverage. The potential $100 regret is one of the costs of purchasing the insurance and the potential $9,900 regret is one of the costs of risk retention. The importance of the utility associated with minimizing the potential regret is one of the factors that the decision maker must consider in choosing among risk management devices. The concept of minimizing potential regret gives rise to the often heard platitude that it is better to have insurance and not suffer a loss than to suffer a loss and not have insurance. But sophisticated decision makers know that costs other than *potential* regret must be weighed against the benefits offered by each risk management tool.

The Use of Loss Prevention and Control Techniques.   Many people put a greater value on the utility derived from smoking than they do on the disutility implied in the caution that cigarette smoking may be a health hazard. Many married couples with dependent children put a greater value on the utility of traveling together than on the disutility of exposing themselves to a common disaster. The disutility of submitting to regular periodic medical examinations is greater for some people than the disutility of the potential hazard involved in the failure to be examined regularly. Decisions made on loss prevention and loss control activity might be different with some people if they could look at the risk problem objectively and had adequate information before making a decision. But there is some utility (at least in the form of psychic income) gained from indulging in subjectivity or from engaging in wishful thinking, and there are some costs involved in getting the information necessary to make an "informed" decision. These benefits and costs must be put on the scale in the balancing process.

Sources of Available Resources.   Before deciding how to provide the needed after-the-loss resources, a study has to be made of the sources of available resources. Several types of basic resources are available to offset loss: (1) the loss bearer's own resources, (2) credit resources, and (3) claims arising out of the loss.

The loss bearer's own resources include not only the capital he has accumulated but also his ability to earn income. In planning the family budget, the wife may choose not to budget funds for life insurance and instead rely on her ability to earn a living. She reasons that the value gained by "living it up" now with her husband exceeds the cost of having to take a job if her husband dies prematurely. In fact, she may reason that the possibility of having to take a job is not a cost because she will want to go to work if she becomes a widow "before her time." Of course, other women will view the choice differently and will not want to be left to their own resources. Even when there are large amounts of assets accumulated that can be used to offset losses caused by death, the choice might be to rely on some other resource. The cost of keeping capital liquid or of liquidating nonliquid capital might be greater than the cost of using life insurance as a resource to offset the loss.

For many families that use credit extensively for a before-the-loss resource, the use of credit as an after-the-loss resource might be severely restricted. Also for some types of losses, retirement income, for example, credit resources would be inappropriate. Credit can be a useful source for funds to finance buy-and-sell agreements involving business interests or to pay the settlement cost of estates composed of nonliquid earning assets.

In many cases, claims arising out of the loss are the preferred source for after-the-loss resources. The loss itself creates the offsetting resource; no loss, no resource, and no need for the resource. Insurance, private and social, is the principal vehicle through which arrangements can be made with third parties for obtaining after-the-loss resources for life value losses. Life and health insurance and federal old age, survivors, disability and health insurance ("social security") are important in the risk management plans of millions of families. Also important are "claims" against employers under employee welfare and retirement plans.

When a disability or death is judged to be the fault of another person, that person may be held liable for damages under tort law giving the plaintiff a claim against the defendant and a source of an after-the-loss resource if the defendant can honor the claim. Of course, this resource cannot be considered in life value risk management plans because obviously it is unrealistic to plan as though all life value losses will be the result of the negligence of well-heeled tort-feasors or of tort-feasors who have adequate insurance against obligations to pay bodily injury claims. (While the mentioning of the ineligibility of tort liability claims against others as a planned after-the-loss resource for life value risk management seems completely unnecessary because of its obviousness, after-the-loss resources that have equally obvious limitations are used in life value risk management plans. Some families, for example, purchase limited accident insurance policies that provide after-the-loss resources only if the loss is caused by particular kinds of accidents.)

Criteria for Measuring Utility of Resources. A preplanned after-the-loss resource must meet several criteria to be useful as a risk management device. *First,* the resource must be *adequate,* that is it must provide the amount of money needed. The loss bearer's own resources may be adequate to pay small medical and hospital bills but inadequate for major medical expenses. The wife's earning power may be adequate to support herself but inadequate to support a family. The estate assets may be substantial but still not enough to replace the amount of income needed for family support. The amount of life insurance may be adequate to support the family at today's price levels but inadequate at price levels 5 or 10 years later.

Second, the resource must be *reliable;* that is, one must be able to count on the resource to provide the funds after the loss. The wife who will go to work after the disability or death of her husband must be able to go to work, that is she must be well enough to work, and she must be able to find a job. The insurer that promises after-the loss resources must be able and willing to pay the hospital and medical bills, and to continue the disability income payments according to the before-the-loss agreements. (When an insurer promises a guaranteed income, the insured must realize that the insurer is guaranteeing its *own* obligation, a kind of meaningless concept of a guaranty.)

A *third* criterion is *cost*. What are the relative costs of the various risk management devices? Costs must be measured in terms of benefits only, not on any independent scale. Furthermore, the most favorable balance between benefits and costs might be achieved by one combination of risk management techniques for one person and by an entirely different set for another. Life insurance agents, of course, are well armed with convincing arguments why the use of life and health insurance is the best solution to all life value risk management problems, and are trained to present these arguments vigorously.

As between the use of insurance and the reliance upon credit, one would suspect that insurance would be the least expensive and credit the most expensive method of arranging for after-the-loss resources if a loss occurs, and that credit would be the least expensive and insurance the most expensive method of arranging for after-the-loss resources if a loss does not occur. Such a suspicion would not be true, and even if it were, it would be of no help in decision making because the decision has to be made before the loss.

Insurance offers relief from worry about the possibility of financial loss and from the need to borrow postloss resources, a service which may be worth more than the premium charged for the insurance. The cost of worry when added to the expected value of the loss could make the reliance on credit resources more expensive than insurance even though no loss occurs.

As mentioned in Chapter 2, another consideration that could make insurance attractive in a comparison among risk management devices is that the marginal utility of before-the-loss dollars spent on insurance premiums is likely to be far less than marginal utility of after-the-loss dollars paid under the policy.[4] Also income taxes may be an important consideration favoring one risk management device over another. For example, employer financed employee benefit plans providing medical care, disability income, survivorship, and retirement income benefits have a tax advantage over other arrangements for providing these benefits.[5]

The cost of keeping capital resources liquid is a factor to consider in weighing relative costs of using one's own capital resources as an after-the-loss resource. The advantages of an improved credit standing arising from the purchase of insurance may be an important consideration in weighing the net benefits of insurance as a risk management technique.

---

[4] Although one might be inclined to risk a little for a lot even at unfavorable odds, he is not inclined to risk a lot for a little even if the odds are favorable. For example, one is not as ready to risk $10,000 for the chance of a $50 gain when the probability of gain is 99.8 percent as he is to risk $50 for the chance of a $10,000 gain when the probability of gain is 0.4 percent. By abstaining from the purchase of insurance he risks a lot (the insurance proceeds) for a little (the insurance premium). Even at odds that must favor the insurer (premiums have to be loaded for expenses and contingencies) he often is willing to purchase insurance because he may see no net gain in exposing himself to a large loss to save the insurance premiums.

[5] These tax advantages are discussed in Chapters 15, 16, and 17.

In summary, the anticipated values of the benefits from each eligible and available risk management device must be compared with their anticipated costs, and those that maximize "the expected value of the game" are the ones to use in solving the risk management problem. Both the contingent and noncontingent benefits and costs must be considered in the equation. A common error is to overlook some of the benefits and some of the costs in making the appraisal.

2. INSURANCE AS A METHOD OF DEALING WITH RISK

For the remainder of this text, the attention is directed toward life and health insurance as a means of handling the life value risk. The Committee on General Terminology of the Commission on Insurance Terminology has had as much trouble in reaching an agreement on a definition of insurance as it has in defining risk, and about as little success.[6] The concept of insurance, as viewed by the committee, appears to be one of risk transfer, but not all risk transfer, just those transferred to an insurer, and the committee's concept of an insurer is the party to whom the risk is transferred under an insurance arrangement. Of course this is a lot of gobbledegook as one would expect when a compromise definition is developed for a concept involving disagreements that "have been and continue to be a basis of philosophical debate among insurance teachers, researchers, legal technicians, and insurance practitioners."[7]

A "transfer of risk" definition of insurance does not show precisely how insurance is supposed to deal with risk as distinguished from any other risk transfer technique, nor does it allow for the concept of self-insurance. The interest here is in an operational definition of insurance for the study of risk management, one that will facilitate both communication and analysis. Those who have other interests or objectives in a definition of insurance should feel free to define the concept in terms of its most useful application.

Definition of Insurance.   For the purposes of this text, a useful definition of insurance must include either the building of a fund or a transfer of risk *and* a combination of similar exposure units into an interrelated group. The combination of exposure units can be made by insurers who have accepted risks transferred to them by insureds, or it can be accomplished by the insured himself if he has enough of his own discrete exposure units to manage a self-insurance operation. Under a self-insurance operation, a fund is necessary to provide after-the-loss resources when needed, otherwise the risk management technique is not an insurance operation. The purpose of a combination of exposure units is to achieve a workable measure of loss predictability.

---

[6] Commission on Insurance Terminology, American Risk and Insurance Association, *Bulletin,* Vol. 1, No. 4 (October, 1965), p. 1.
[7] *Ibid.*

Insurance may be defined as a device for reducing risk by combining a sufficient number of exposure units to make their individual losses collectively predictable. The loss is then shared proportionately by all units in the combination.

This definition implies *both* that uncertainty is reduced and that losses are shared. These are the important aspects of insurance. Uncertainty and loss are the important aspects of risk also as that concept is defined in this text. Thus insurance as a risk management tool attacks both aspects of risk: it reduces uncertainty and it distributes losses.

The Mathematical Foundation of Insurance.   Insurance is based on mathematics; specifically, on that branch of mathematics known as the theory of probabilities. In that branch of mathematics, insurance is concerned primarily with the law of large numbers (or the law of averages, as it is commonly called).

The law of large numbers is based on the regularity of the occurrence of events. Therefore, what seems random occurrence in the individual happening seems so only because of an insufficient or incomplete knowledge of what may be expected to occur. For all practical purposes, the law may be stated thus:

The greater the number of exposures, the more closely will the actual results obtained approach the probable results expected from an infinite number of exposures. To illustrate: Happenings that, in the individual appearance, seem to be the result of pure chance occur with increasing regularity as the instances observed become more numerous. Crossing a downtown corner, you are struck and injured by a motorist. To you, the event seems wholly unpredictable. Had you started from home a minute later, had you been delayed along the route a second more, had you walked less rapidly, there might have been no accident for you. It seems no formula could have predicted the accident.

Yet to the National Safety Council, prediction is not nearly so impossible. That organization can tell you with a fair degree of accuracy just how many drivers will be involved in accidents this season. If you should ask the council to give you the statistics on a yearly basis, it could tell you even more accurately; and should you ask for the information on the basis of several years, the accuracy of the prediction would lead you to believe that the council has "second sight."

The council's accuracy in predicting the number of accidents increases, not because of the varying time period for which you asked for a prediction, but because the greater the elapsed time, the greater the number of pedestrians and drivers exposed to the peril. *The greater the number of exposures to a peril, the nearer will the loss results approach the underlying probability, that is the long-run relative frequency of loss.*

Just so, an insurer, with statistics on millions of exposures, can tell with reasonable accuracy the probable number of people who will be killed, maimed, and injured in automobile accidents between now and next Sunday.

Such accuracy, as in the case of the National Safety Council, seems uncanny unless it is held in mind that *as the number of exposures increases, the nearer will be the actual results to the underlying probability.*

Thus, the law of large numbers becomes the basis of insurance. Under the operation of this law, the impossibility of predicting a happening in an individual case gives way to demonstrable ability to do so when a successive number of exposures is considered. Applying these observations to life and health insurance, it is possible to predict on an annual basis within narrow limits the frequency and severity of personal accidents and illnesses and the number of deaths in each age group. Given a large group of exposures, prediction becomes, not guesswork, but mathematical calculation.

However, loss prediction is not perfectly accurate for three reasons. Since the number of exposures never reaches infinity, there will always be a deviation from the average expected loss; that is, losses will not correspond exactly to the average loss as indicated by statistical evidence but will have a measurable probability of falling within a given range of the average. In the second place, the statistics on which predictions are made are subject to error. They are based on sampling techniques and do not always measure accurately what took place in the total population from which the sample was selected. Furthermore, successful loss prediction depends upon the ability to forecast trends, a feat which no one can accomplish with perfection. When mortality and morbidity rates are changing, adjustments need to be made in mortality and morbidity projections to reflect these changes. Since these adjustments are to some extent guesswork, insurance companies cannot predict losses exactly. Therefore, insurers cannot eliminate their risk completely. However, they can reduce it to manageable levels.

3. ESSENTIALS OF AN INSURABLE RISK

Not all risks are insurable. Certain tests must be met. The requisites of insurability are, broadly:

1. The rate of loss must be predictable.
2. The loss must be unlikely to happen to the majority of the insureds simultaneously.
3. The loss must be definite.
4. The specific loss must be fortuitous.
5. The insurance must be economically feasible.

A Predictable Rate of Loss. For a loss to be predictable, there must be (1) a large group of exposure units, (2) a base for prediction, and (3) comparability between that base and the exposure units.

A large number of exposure units is necessary to make possible the functioning of the law of large numbers. A life insurer, for instance, would find it risky to operate on the basis of 10 or 20 lives. The number of exposure units would be so small that the actual losses might greatly exceed the predicted losses. Insurance is not practical when the probable deviation from predictable losses is so large that premiums must be heavily loaded to take care of the risk. Losses must be predictable within a narrow range.

The base for prediction is the observation of experience and the assumption that the future will duplicate the past. If the chance of loss cannot be determined a priori or from history, it is not mathematically calculable, and the peril is uninsurable.[8] This is one of the reasons why unemployment is sometimes said to be uninsurable commercially. The point is that the probability can neither be calculated by logic nor determined from history since unemployment does not occur with predictable regularity. However, regardless of this point one prominent United States insurance company once developed rates for unemployment insurance but never marketed the coverage.

The group to which a prediction is applied and the base from which that prediction is made must be homogeneous. This means that there must be comparability between the base and the exposure units. Monkey mortality experience, for example, cannot be used to predict death rates among human beings. And the mortality experience of central African tribesmen cannot be used to predict the mortality experience of New Englanders. An insurer that insures a heterogeneous collection of persons in unknown combinations of ages, states of health, and dangers of occupation could not predict how many deaths would result even though it insured a large number of people. There would be no base for prediction. Predictions are possible only with groups consisting of large known combinations as to age, health, and occupation.

For insurance to be possible, the collection of persons to be insured must be classified in accordance with the base from which the loss prediction is made. For example, if the rate of death among a group of persons all of whom are aged 22, in good health, and in nonhazardous occupations is established as a base for prediction, then an insurer can apply this rate to such a collection of persons if it has a large enough number of them. However, insurance classifications must be few enough in number so that there will be a great many exposures in each of the classifications used. For

---

[8] The tests of a large number of exposure units and a measurable probability may seem to be violated by insurance on the fingers of a pianist, voice of an opera star, anatomy of a burlesque queen, and the like. Such coverage is known as special risk insurance, and is not true insurance as defined in this text. It involves a transfer of risk from the insured to the insurer but not a combination of a sufficient number of exposure units to make their individual losses collectively predictable. Insurers are able to write the coverage because buyers place a high expected loss on the exposure and therefore, in the absence of competitive or comparative rates, are willing to pay a high premium for coverage. Furthermore, the loss is parceled among a number of insurers, each taking a fragment small enough to handle without financial strain. The insurer in effect becomes a speculator, since, like the speculator, he has calculated his chance of loss subjectively rather than from statistics. Sometimes on a new exposure an insurer must rely largely on guesswork. However, these transactions are not gambling, since the risk in gambling is created by the transaction itself, whereas here the risk exists apart from the transaction and continues regardless of the transaction.

example, age group classifications in life insurance are on the basis of full years rather than exact ages down to the month. The number of classifications for health and occupation also are limited. Thus, a category of male retail sales managers, all with moderately good health, all 42 and 7/12 years old and all living in the open country would be much too narrow to yield enough exposures to produce a reliably predictable death rate.

Unlikelihood of Producing Loss to Majority Simultaneously. If loss is likely to occur to the majority of the exposure units simultaneously, then the peril is usually uninsurable. Insurance operates on the principle that the few who suffer loss will be compensated by the many who escape it. If the *many* suffer the loss, then the *few* left to compensate them would have to pay a premium that would not attract enough insureds for the law of large numbers to function.

The chance of the perils of disability or death producing catastrophic losses is unlikely, assuming, of course, proper underwriting distribution. For protection against catastrophic exposures, life insurance companies, for example, during war emergencies might insert in their policies a clause excluding death as a result of war, declared or undeclared.

Definite Loss. The loss must be clearly observable and difficult to feign. The amount of the loss also must be clear. Indefinite losses can be a thorny problem to insurance companies because the promise to pay claims is conditioned upon the occurrence of some particular event. An objective method of determining what this event is and how much the insurer must pay is necessary to make an insurance contract feasible.

Death is nearly impossible to feign, at least in most civilized countries, but measuring the amount of loss caused by death is a problem. Therefore, rather than try to measure the amount of loss at death, the insurer agrees with the insured when the policy is written to pay a specified amount following the death of the person upon whom the insurance is written. The maximum amount of insurance that the insurer will write for the applicant is determined by the rules of its underwriting department.[9]

Disability is easily counterfeited. Consequently, the moral hazard involved with each application for health insurance must be checked.

What constitutes disability is not always a simple determination. For example, a professor who chose to publish rather than to perish has just finished a manuscript on which he has worked long and hard and at a damaging pace over the past three years. He is exhausted, and his doctor recommends a long sea voyage for needed rest and relaxation. He follows his doctor's advice and books passage for a six-month trip around the world. Is the professor disabled? Is he entitled to collect benefits under his disability income insurance policy? Questions of this type bother health insurance companies.

In health insurance, claims problems arise not only from an indefinite

---

[9] Cf. Chapter 23.

loss but also from an indefinite cause of loss. The nature of these problems is discussed in Chapter 14.

The amount of loss payable under a health insurance policy is fixed in the policy just as in life insurance with the underwriters limiting the amount of coverage to a figure which has some relationship to earned income, subject to an overall maximum amount. Medical care benefits usually are limited to the actual charges subject to some schedule or blanket maximums.[10]

A Fortuitous Loss.   The loss must happen by chance and not be caused intentionally by persons who are exposed to it. The time of death is usually a matter of chance and not individually foreseeable. Suicides are not insurable until after a life insurance policy has been in force for one or two years during the lifetime of the insured. Suicides occurring beyond one or two years from the inception of the policy are not foreseeable, and are considered to be by chance. There is a chance that anyone not now entertaining the thought of suicide might eventually think of suicide as an attractive solution to an unattractive problem. Furthermore, the loss resulting from suicide is not caused intentionally by the persons exposed to the loss. Presumably, a dead man cannot lose anything. Randomness is required to establish comparability between the insured for whom losses are being predicted and the base experience from which premiums are computed. By including suicides in the base experience, suicides need not be excluded from coverage as long as the policy keeps the deck from being stacked against the insurer by excluding death by suicide in the first year or two after the policy is effective.

Losses caused by accident, sickness, and old age (the continuation of of life beyond the earning span) are occasioned by chance and are not individually foreseeable. Are medical expenses associated with a normal childbirth insurable? Most insurers have chosen to write maternity coverage in their hospital, surgical, and medical expense policies without limiting the coverage to expenses resulting from accidental pregnancies. Self-inflicted injuries, however, generally are excluded in health insurance. Insurers usually are not interested in charging premiums which would allow them to cover these nonrandom losses. The moral hazard is too great. Furthermore, competing companies could draw the more desirable insureds at lower premiums. Insurers that stray too far from the "fortuitous" loss requirement of insurability are likely to be forced to play with marked cards.[11]

---

[10] *Ibid.*

[11] On two qualifications (definiteness and accidental nature), disability comes near the borderline of insurability. Even such extremes as loss of limb or sight have occurred under circumstances which have at least given rise to doubt that they were accidental. And when is a man capable of earning and when not? Physical impairment can be observed and measured; there are also psychological states that can render a man disabled but which are difficult to measure. Assume you are a physician to whom a patient comes for certification of disability. The patient is unable to find employment; his family is literally starving;

Economically Feasible.   When a person suffers a loss he would like his insurance to offset it, regardless of its severity or frequency. But when he is asked to pay an annual premium of $20 for a disability income insurance policy under which he would collect $3 a day for a maximum of 1 week in the event of his total disability, he most likely will have second thoughts on what he wants his insurance to do for him. The benefits of insurance cannot be considered independently of costs. The cost of insurance must be low enough to be economically feasible. The condition necessary for a favorable relationship between benefits and costs is a combination of a large potential loss and a small chance of loss.

The size of the potential loss must be large enough to represent a financial strain or economic hardship to the persons exposed to it. It costs money to operate an insurance company, and since net premiums must be "loaded" to cover the insured's share of this cost, the premiums for insuring small losses tend to be uneconomically high in relation to the amount of the exposure. For example, a life insurance policy with a face amount of $50 could be written for 1 year, but the cost of writing and administering the contract would tend to price it out of the market. At age 60, the loss cost of the coverage would be about $1.02 because the assumed chance of death during that year is 2.03 percent.[12] The cost of issuing the policy, handling the records, and paying a selling commission to the agent could easily amount to $12.97, bringing the total cost of the transaction to $15. In effect, such a contract, if sold at cost, would require a gross premium of 30 percent to cover a 2.03 percent chance of loss, not an attractive arrangement. Better odds can be found at the race track. Therefore, small losses can be more efficiently handled through risk assumption.

On the other hand, the premium for a $1,000, 1-year policy at age 60 is quoted in one rate book at $31.12. This represents a premium of slightly over 3.1 percent to cover a 2.03 percent chance of loss, certainly not a bad proposition for a man who cannot afford the loss. The premium for $5,000 of 1-year term insurance in this same company is quoted at $130.60, about 2.61 percent to cover a 2.03 percent chance of loss. For $10,000 of insurance, the premium is quoted at $216.20, about 2.16 percent to cover a

you know that unless he can obtain income from disability insurance, he will commit suicide in order to obtain funds for his family from his life insurance. Since a suicide drive is said to be a psychopathic condition, can you say this man is *not* mentally unfit to earn a living and hence *not* disabled? From such situations arises the need for clear definitions of what should be considered disability for the purpose of the insurance and for restrictions and limitations on benefits that render disability financially unattractive while still protecting against economic catastrophe. Unfortunately, the result of these limitations and restrictions too often renders not only disability itself unattractive but also renders disability insurance unattractive in the eyes of some individuals who need this important personal insurance coverage.

[12] This figure is based on the 1958 CSO Mortality Table. The CSO Table without safety margins, that is the table based on the raw data, shows the chance of death to be 1.76 percent.

2.03 percent chance of loss. As the size of the potential loss increases, insurance becomes more attractive as a risk management tool.

If the potential loss is large enough to cause severe economic stress, insurance against it is worth the cost even though the premium has to be loaded for expenses. The determination of what constitutes a potential loss large enough to be economically insurable depends on each individual's circumstances. A hospital bill in excess of $250 might be economically disturbing to one man, and, therefore, a loss against which he should insure. For another, a hospital bill under $1,000 might not be financially disturbing, and, therefore, in the absence of other considerations would be uneconomical to insure.

The size of the potential loss to a man's family resulting from his disability or premature death and the hardship created when a man outlives his earning ability usually is large enough for the life value risk to meet this test of insurability.

It is not economically sound to insure against perils which produce a high chance of loss. Even though all other factors about them permit the calculation of a safe rate, such a rate is usually economically impractical. A life insurance rate could be calculated for a man aged 98, but no one would be likely to pay it. The probability of death among a group of individuals aged 98 (on the 1958 CSO Mortality Table) is about 668 out of 1,000 alive at the beginning of the year. Disregarding interest calculations, the pure premium for $1,000 1-year term insurance at age 98 would be $668. When the cost of doing business is added to the loss cost, the total premium comes close to, or is even in excess of, the face amount of the insurance, an obviously uneconomic rate.

The chance of major income loss from death (at most ages) or from disability is small enough to make the premium for insuring against each of them economically feasible, assuming the coverage is written for large enough amounts, and with deductibles in health insurance to eliminate small losses.

Although the chance of reaching retirement age is high and the potential amount of funds needed for old age indemnification is large, the cost of insurance protection for this risk is within the reach of most people: (1) the person who starts his retirement planning early has a large number of years over which to prepare for old age; (2) some will never reach retirement age, and their contributions toward a retirement insurance fund can be shared by those who do; and (3) of those who reach retirement age, some will not live long, thereby releasing funds to finance those who enjoy a long period of retirement.

The test of economic feasibility includes the feasibility of the cost of rating and underwriting. For example, separating the good from the bad moral hazard within certain occupations or groups is so difficult that the whole group may be listed as uninsurable. This is especially true in health insurance. The cost of the investigation necessary to determine the acceptable applicants within an otherwise undesirable class can be prohibitive.

Adherence to the Principles. Although the five essentials just discussed are considered requisites for insurability, they are not always adhered to by companies writing life and health insurance contracts. Some policies are written for low amounts; others are written where a high chance of loss exists; and still others are written where a chance of loss is not predictable. Thus, surgical schedules covering amounts as low as $10 are found; maternity benefits are written for young married women; and major medical insurance is written providing coverage for nearly all medical expenses in excess of a very small deductible amount at premiums guaranteed to age 65.

4

Term and Endowment Contracts

Functionally,[1] there are three basic types of life insurance policies: *term, endowment,* and *whole life.* In addition, there is the annuity contract, sometimes called "life insurance in reverse." The purpose of this chapter is to discuss the nature and uses of term and endowment contracts.

1. TERM INSURANCE

Definition of Term Insurance. A term policy is a contract which offers financial protection against the occurrence of death within the given period of time stated in the policy. It offers no protection or values in case of survival beyond the specified period.

Term insurance is comparable to most forms of property insurance contracts. For instance, an automobile insurance policy offers financial protection against the perils named in it for a period of one year. It may be renewed, but it then becomes a new contract. Fire insurance is often written for periods of one, three, or five years and expires without value. If the protection is to be continued, a new policy must be obtained or the old one must be renewed.

A policyholder who takes five-year term life insurance has protection against the financial consequences of death within that period but not be-

---

[1] Actuarially, when insurance is written to the limiting age of the mortality table (age 100 on the tables being used today), there is only one type of life insurance policy, because there is practically no distinction between a whole life policy, a term to age 100, or an endowment at age 100. If the net premiums and reserves for the three of them are calculated, it will be found that the differences are *de minimis.* While this is true for policies written to the limiting age on the mortality table, it is not true of policies written for shorter durations. Policies, for example, issued at age 25 for a 20-year period may be either term, in which case the insurance is payable only on the death of the insured within the 20 years, or endowment, in which case the insurance is payable on the death of the insured in the event of his death prior to age 45 and fully payable to him if he is surviving at age 45. But based on usage and general understanding, it is convenient to classify policies into the three basic types described in this and the next chapter.

yond. If the policy is renewable, he may extend it for another term period at the premium rate applying to the new age; or he may, if it is not renewable, take a new policy, provided he is still insurable. Health insurance is written for a term period, sometimes to age 65 or longer, but at the end of the term, it expires without value.[2]

The principal appeal of term life insurance is its low premium. For example, a man aged 25 can purchase a $10,000, 10-year term policy for an annual premium of about $50. The cheapest form of permanent insurance would require an annual premium of about $135.

A principal deterrent to the purchase of term insurance is its lack of cash values available for emergency or retirement income.[3] Quite often an insurance buyer objects to the purchase of term insurance because he does not want to "pay all those premiums and get nothing back."[4] In the foregoing example, at the end of 10 years, the 10-year term policy will expire without value, whereas the permanent policy will have a cash value of $960.[5] Viewing these figures, it might be argued that because the average yearly cost for the 10-year period under a term policy is $50 whereas the average yearly cost for the same period under a permanent policy is only $39 ($135 × 10 − 960 ÷ 10), term insurance is more expensive than permanent insurance. If the fallacy of this argument is not already obvious, it will become patent after it is considered in Chapter 28. Term insurance may be more expensive than permanent insurance but the reason is not directly related to the absence of cash values in term insurance. Mortality assumptions used in computing term insurance premiums are likely to project higher death rates than those projected by tables used in computing premiums for permanent insurance because "experience shows a higher rate of mortality among term insureds than for those who have permanent insurance."[6] The reason frequently given to explain the higher mortality

---

[2] Some term life insurance policies may be changed to a permanent form of life insurance without medical examination or other underwriting scrutiny, within a given time before the end of the term period. See discussion of convertible term insurance later in this chapter. Some few health policies continue after some given age, 65, for example on a paid-up basis.

[3] While the short-term policy has no cash values, the long-term policy is an exception. For example, in one company, a $1,000 term to age 65 issued at age 25 will have $1 in cash values in 3 years, $30 in 10 years, $61 in 15 years, $91 in 20 years, and $80 at age 60, reducing to 0 at age 65.

[4] He does not feel this way about his automobile insurance premiums because automobile insurance is sold as protection only. However, the savings accumulation feature is often emphasized in the sale of a life insurance policy.

[5] All rates and values quoted in this chapter are based on nonparticipating policies unless otherwise noted. Were the rates and values based on participating plans (plans under which dividends are paid to policyholders) they would be higher. For example, the annual gross premium for the permanent plan in the foregoing illustration if written on a participating basis would be about $176 and the cash value at the end of 10 years would be $1,120. Rates and values vary widely among companies. Cf. Chapter 27.

[6] William T. Beadles, "Contracts-Term Insurance" in Davis W. Gregg (ed.), *Life and Health Insurance Handbook* (rev. ed.; Homewood, Illinois: Richard D. Irwin, Inc., 1964), p. 44. Professor Beadles points out that "an actuarial report from one large

under term insurance is adverse selection against the insurer, that is, applicants on the low end of the insurability scale are likely to buy term insurance initially because of its lower premium and are likely to keep this insurance in force on a term basis if and when they become uninsurable if these contracts are renewable at the insured's option.

Another deterrent to the purchase of term life insurance might be the sales presentation of the life insurance agent. The life insurance agent has been trained to present the virtues of cash value life insurance and might be inclined to overlook the virtues of term insurance in some of those situations where term insurance best solves the immediate life insurance problem of the insured. The system of compensating life insurance agents encourages them to tread lightly on recommending term insurance. Most insurers pay a lower rate of commission on term insurance, and in every case the premium on term insurance is lower, thus yielding fewer commission dollars.

Uses of Term Insurance. Term insurance will serve the policyholder adequately when the protection need will expire simultaneously with the expiration of the term period. For example, a young mechanic borrows $20,000 to finance the purchase of machinery and tools to equip his shop. He believes that if he lives five years, he will be able to pay back the loan out of business profits. However, should he die before the end of that time, his family will have to bear the burden of the indebtedness. Therefore, his need is for a $20,000 term insurance policy written for 5 years. If his death occurs while the loan is still outstanding, the proceeds of the insurance will extinguish the debt and his family will be left an unencumbered estate. Frequently, lenders will request, sometimes even require, that their borrowers purchase life insurance protection.

Other examples of life insurance needs for which term insurance can be used advantageously may be cited:

A father who depends on his current earning power to finance his son's education can insure this earning power for the duration of the college period.

A business engaged in research in which one man is absolutely vital can insure its investment in this research by insuring the life of the key man for the duration of the project.

A young businessman embarking on a new venture can insure his investment of time and money in the enterprise by insuring his life during the development stages of the business. It is usually several years before the new business will be of any value itself, apart from the owner.

A family man with a mortgage on his home may desire to insure his

---

company states that 'the mortality under term policies of large amounts was nearly half again as great as that under life and endowment insurance,' " and that another study which "compared the term mortality experience with the entire experience of the company," found "18 percent higher mortality by amounts of insurance for those who were insured under five-year term, and 11 percent higher for the first five years of those insured under ten-year term."

life for the decreasing amount of the mortgage debt for the period of its amortization so that in the event of his death he will be able to leave his family a home free of debt.

These are by no means all the situations in which term insurance may be used properly; however, they illustrate the point that term insurance is to be used wherever there will be a loss if the policyholder dies before the end of a specified period but where there will be no loss if he dies after that period.

Term insurance is also widely used by young people who have only a small amount of money to budget for insurance but who, on the other hand, have a large protection need. In these cases term insurance is used, not because of a temporary need, but because of a temporary financial condition. In many cases the policyholder plans to convert the term into a permanent policy form—perhaps little by little—as he has more money available for premiums.[7] For the same premium outlay, term will provide more adequate, although temporary, protection than will any permanent policy form.

Term insurance is attractive to students in professional fields, particularly those working for advanced degrees, and therefore having many years before they will be able to afford permanent insurance sufficient to cover their protection needs. Normally, a young man starting out in a profession —medical, legal, or any type where his earnings depend upon building up a clientele—may not have a sufficient income during the initial years to pay for adequate protection through permanent insurance. He can afford sufficient protection only by using term insurance.

College students planning marriage and facing military service might find term insurance appropriate. They can obtain adequate protection through term insurance while postponing the purchase of permanent insurance until such time as they establish themselves permanently in civilian life.

Term insurance, if it is convertible, will protect the policyholder's insurability for the minimum cost since, at the low term rates, a large amount of insurance can be purchased for a small amount of money. This large amount of protection can be continued on a permanent basis later if the policyholder chooses to convert it, irrespective of changes in physical condition and occupational hazards.

Many established people need more death protection than they can afford to purchase on a permanent plan. They are people who are willing to sacrifice, in whole or in part, old age protection for themselves in order to obtain adequate premature death protection for their families. They look to term insurance in such cases, not because it fits their need, but because it fits their pocketbooks. Term insurance gives the most for the premium dollar in premature death benefits but offers no cash value for financing an income at retirement or to offset interim emergencies.

---

[7] Term insurance is convertible if it may be changed to a permanent policy form without evidence of insurability.

Some people prefer term insurance to permanent insurance even though (1) they can afford the premiums for adequate permanent insurance coverage, (2) their need to arrange for resources to offset losses caused by death is not restricted to a specified term period, and (3) they must plan for old age security. They choose to limit their use of life insurance to its pristine function—the creation of an estate at death. They accumulate their savings and investments independently of their life insurance and adjust their life insurance coverage to meet their needs for postdeath resources. Some term insurance plans are written to tie in specifically with mutual fund accumulations. The fear of inflation and the desire to share in an expanding economy have encouraged people to seek capital growth through ownership of shares in business corporations rather than through the accumulative powers of compound interest.[8]

Limitations of Term Insurance. Every policy form has limitations when compared with any other policy. A caution in selecting a policy form is to avoid using one to fulfill a need for which it is not designed. If term insurance is used where the need calls for permanent insurance, term insurance has certain clear-cut disadvantages. However, term insurance is offered with various modifications, soon to be discussed, that offset some of these limitations. In the meantime the limitations of straight term insurance are as follows:

1. The need for life insurance protection may extend beyond the period of the policy. The policyholder may be uninsurable at the expiration of the term period, and therefore unable to buy a new policy. For example, a five-year term policy taken to insure the life of a research chemist during a major project will expire before the project is completed if the chemist is faced with an unforeseen difficulty and requires more time than the original five-year estimate. If the chemist loses his insurability during this period, insurance protection will be denied those who have invested heavily in the project, assuming that the term policy is neither renewable nor convertible.

2. When term insurance is used for a permanent and continuing need, the premium will increase at each renewal date and will become prohibitive in later years.[9] Table 4–1 shows the increased rate required at each renewal

---

[8] Sophisticated long-term investors usually are attuned to intermittent downside movements in the market prices of their securities or of their mutual fund shares. With their eyes focused on their long-term objective, they are only slightly annoyed with backtracking, especially if they do not have the cash position to take advantage of a good buying opportunity. If they do have a good cash position, a downside movement might be welcomed as an opportunity to acquire additional securities at favorable prices.

[9] This is true unless the total premium can be held within a narrow range of the initial premium by reducing the face amount of the policy on each successive renewal date. If under a 5-year renewable term policy the face amount of insurance is decreased each 5-year period by an amount sufficient to offset the increase in the premium per $1,000, total premiums will not advance. For example, the $49.90 annual premium charged for $10,000 of 5-year term at age 25 will purchase, roughly, only $9,300 of 5-year term at age 30; $7,600 at age 35; $6,300 at age 40, $4,700 at age 45; $3,300 at age 50; $2,200 at age 55; and $1,500 at age 60. If the amount of life insurance needed

TABLE 4–1

Annual Rates at Five-Year Intervals
Representative Five-Year Term, Nonparticipating*

Age	Rate per $1,000
25	$ 4.99
30	5.37
35	6.30
40	7.98
45	10.73
50	15.21
55	22.18
60	33.10
65	47.68

* Premiums shown are for minimum policies of $10,000; for other amounts subtract $0.80, multiply by number of thousands, and add $4 per thousand with a maximum of $8. Rates for females are the same as for males three years younger.

period of a 5-year term policy. For example, the rate at age 25 is $4.99 per thousand. The lowest premium, permanent policy (continuous premium whole life) at that age and in the same company is quoted at $13.45—well over 2½ times the rate for the 5-year term policy. Therefore, it is easy to see how a young man aged 25 might be tempted to take term insurance instead of continuous premium whole life insurance to meet his insurance needs. Assuming, however, that the portion of the insurable need which he is covering with term insurance is a permanent one continuing throughout his life, he will find that his term insurance at age 65 (which is, by the way, the last age at which this particular company will renew 5-year term) will cost him $47.68 a thousand, or more than 3½ times the level premium he would still be paying had he bought continuous premium whole life when he was age 25.

Should he reach 70, he would be unable to continue his term insurance in this company. Assuming again that his need is a continuing one, such as the need for a burial fund, he would find not only that term insurance would grow prohibitively expensive in the later years but also that there would come a time when despite the need for protection, he would be unable to buy it. He might, of course, convert to a permanent policy form during the convertible period without evidence of insurability. In the company used here for illustration, he would have to convert at age 65—the expiration date of the conversion option.[10]

---

also reduces each five-year period by these amounts then the premium can be kept level. However, few people own enough life insurance to justify reducing their coverage as they advance in age except during those later years when the children are no longer dependent on parental support.

[10] The current trend is to allow term insurance to continue to age 65 or even longer, but the practice in the industry is for companies to set some upper age limit beyond which they will not renew term insurance contracts and beyond which term insurance contracts are not convertible into permanent insurance.

The annual premium for continuous premium whole life insurance at age 65 would be $68.67 per thousand, more than 5 times the level premium at age 25. However, a man aged 65 might need less death protection than would a man aged 25.[11] Therefore, it might be possible for him to own adequate death protection at that age on a permanent policy basis, without unduly increasing premium outlay, by sharply decreasing his insurance coverage. If he continues to pay the same premium that he paid after his renewal at age 60, he could convert his term insurance to permanent insurance for an amount slightly less than 50 percent of the amount of the term policy.

3. Life insurance is sold as a vehicle for accumulating funds for emergencies and for liquidation as a lifetime income for old age. Term insurance, having no cash value, cannot be used for these purposes. Some advocates of term insurance contend that life insurance should be used solely to protect against the economic consequences of premature death and that other forms of saving and investment should be used to create values for emergencies and old age. Statistical illustrations can be constructed to show that other forms of saving and investment can build more for old age than will savings tied in with life insurance. In answer, those who advocate life insurance as a savings medium point out that there is a difference between what can be done using statistical compilations and hindsight, and what actually will be accomplished. Specifically, their argument is based on six hypotheses.

a) The typical person is unable to save over an extended period of years unless faced with some compulsion or penalty. A savings plan combined with life insurance compels a man to save at a time when he might skip a deposit under other plans. The company sends the policyholder a premium notice, the life insurance agent urges him to pay his premium, and the policyholder himself looks upon his life insurance premium payments as an expense and budgets for them accordingly. The penalty for not paying the premium is the lapsing of the policy—something which the typical policyholder will try to avoid.

b) Not only is the typical person unable to save regularly each year, but also he has difficulty keeping intact what he does save. He does not feel the same degree of restraint in drawing savings from a savings account or liquidating a government bond or corporate security to raise money to buy a luxury as he does in cashing in his life insurance policies. Many policyholders will not surrender their policies before retirement for anything

---

[11] Usually a man of 65 has only one dependent, his wife; and in all probability she will be at an age that would require less insurance to provide a lifetime income than would be needed to provide a lifetime income for a younger man's wife. For example, it takes more than $126,000 insurance to provide a widow aged 40 a life income of $500 a month, whereas at age 65 this income can be provided with less than $80,000 of insurance. Of course, if there is a large estate subject to a high liability for death taxes and estate administration expenses, the amount of life insurance needed by the estate owner would not likely be less at age 65 than at age 25 or 35.

short of an emergency.[12] The result is that the retirement fund is more nearly certain to be there at age 65 if it is tied up with life insurance.

c) Savings tied to life insurance policies earn a competitive rate of return considering the absence of any market or financial risk and the presence of guaranteed lifetime interest rates. Cash values in life insurance are contractually unaffected by market conditions, and the minimum retirement income to be paid is specified in the policy.[13] Rates of return on savings accumulations in life insurance policies are discussed in Chapter 8.

d) Currently interest and dividend returns on the usual investments are subject to federal income taxes in the year earned, whereas the annual interest increments on life insurance cash values are not subject to the federal income tax unless and until these values are paid out during the lifetime of the insured. At this point, the taxable income is the excess of the amount received from the policy over the total amount paid in premiums. For example, assume that an insured age 45 owns a $10,000 participating permanent life insurance policy which he bought 20 years ago for an annual premium of $175. He now decides to surrender the policy for its cash value to help finance his son's college education. The cash value of the policy is $2,693. The sum of the premiums paid during the 20 years that the policy was in force amounts to $3,500 less $918 returned to him as dividends making a net payment of $2,582. The difference between the $2,693 collected from the insurer and the $2,582 net amount paid to the insurer is $111, the amount subject to income taxes as ordinary income.

This method of taxing cash value accumulations is an advantage to the insured. He pays taxes on only $111. An addition of the first 20 figures in column 4 of Table 4, Chapter 1 will show that even at the low 2½ percent assumed rate of interest, the total interest earned would amount to $649.70. Part of the $918 paid to the insured in policy dividends comes from the insurer's investment earnings in excess of 2½ percent. The insured, therefore, receives tax-free interest income of $649.70 — $111 or $538.70 plus whatever portion of his policy dividends is attributable to allocated investment earnings in excess of 2½ percent. In addition he receives a tax-free survivorship income. An addition of the first 20 figures in column 6 of Table 4, Chapter 1 will show that the survivor benefit at assumed mortality rates is $87.50. This tax-free income (interest and survivor benefit) was used to pay for the cost of the $10,000 of life insurance

---

[12] A theoretical advantage of buying term insurance and putting the premium difference between term insurance and permanent insurance in other forms of savings or investments is that in an emergency, savings can be withdrawn or securities liquidated without lowering the amount of life insurance protection. However, such withdrawal reduces the total estate to the same extent as if a policy loan had been effected.

[13] The guaranteed interest and the guaranteed cash value are contractual pledges of the insurer to pay no less than a given minimum rate of interest over the lifetime of the policy and to pay the stated cash value upon surrender of the policy. However, these guarantees do not imply any pledge of security as surety for the fulfillment of the insurer's obligation.

in force over the 20-year period prior to the surrender of the policy. At the assumed mortality rates, this coverage is worth $554.80 (column 5 of Table 4, Chapter 1) plus an allowance for the insurer's expenses of doing business.[14]

e) Few men are able to accumulate sufficient resources at retirement to live off investment income alone. The typical person must liquidate his capital in order to have an income high enough to finance his retirement. For example, a man who is fortunate enough to accumulate $50,000 by age 65 will be able to earn an investment income of about $200 a month from this fund, assuming a 5 percent return, net after taxes. This is hardly enough to provide for the cost of living even for a man content to sit at home in a rocking chair. The $200 a month needs to be increased by supplementing it with a part of the principal every month. The principal must be used to purchase an annuity if income is to be guaranteed as long as the annuitant lives.[15]

The growth of employee retirement benefit plans and the rising level of old age benefits under social security have reduced the number of people who find it necessary to liquidate capital accumulations for a livable retirement income. If, however, it is granted that liquidation of capital accumulations will be necessary for an adequate retirement income, there might be an advantage in making these accumulations through a life insurance contract. Currently, $50,000 accumulated in cash values in a life insurance policy can be liquidated as an annuity for a male at age 65 under contract settlement provisions paying $391 a month—$11 more than could be purchased by a similar investment in a single-premium life annuity. In addition to paying more in annuity income, there may be another advantage of accumulating retirement funds through a life insurance policy. Annuity income rates are guaranteed in the life insurance contract. This might be an important guarantee, since mortality rates can decrease with further advancement in medical science. A decrease in the mortality rate at higher ages would be reflected in a reduction in the amount of annuity income per thousand dollars of principal. These guarantees have proved valuable to those who purchased whole life insurance contracts over 30 years ago. Today, these policies can be cashed in at age 65 for annuity benefits that are much higher than could be purchased in annuity contracts with accumulated savings.

For example, a cash value of $50,000 in one of these old policies could be liquidated as an annuity of $415 a month—$35 more than the $50,000

---

[14] The tax shelter provided for cash values in life insurance (or for any other savings accumulated under a tax shelter) is particularly attractive to those persons who withdraw the funds from the shelter at retirement: Not only will their earned income have dropped but also their personal income tax exemption will be doubled at age 65, and they may be given a retirement income tax credit. Thus, if the values in the shelter are paid out over the period of retirement, the amount subject to income tax in any one year could be small.

[15] An annuity is a form of insurance contract under which the policyholder is paid an income, either for a stated period or for life. See Chapter 6 for a discussion of annuities.

would buy as a single premium annuity at today's rates. This advantage assumes that the terminal fund will be $50,000 regardless of the type of investment medium used, an assumption which, more than likely, will not hold true. Investment losses and withdrawals might reduce the accumulations in separate investments to a figure below the $50,000. Conversely, capital gains might increase the figure to more than $50,000.

f) When an investment or savings program is initiated to build a fund to provide a retirement income, additions to this fund must be made periodically or the fund will fall short of its goal. An advantage of building the retirement (or emergency) fund through permanent life insurance is the opportunity to protect the program with a waiver-of-premium clause under which premium payments are waived if the insured becomes totally and permanently disabled. The cash value will continue to grow as if premiums were paid by the insured. The savings program can be protected against interruption through disability by tying it with life insurance.[16]

Types of Term Policies. Term insurance is written in a variety of ways, each designed to meet a particular type of need. These variations among term policies tend to offset some of the limitations of term insurance. For example, long-term level premium policies tend to offset the disadvantage of higher premiums as the age of the insured advances. Premiums for long-term policies at younger ages, however, are considerably higher than for short-term policies. At age 25, for example, the premium for $10,000 of term to age 65 is about $85 a year compared with $50 a year for 10-year term and $135 for the cheapest form of permanent insurance. Renewable and convertible term (to be explained later) can offset the disadvantage of expiring protection.

Briefly, term policies may be classified as follows:

Straight term policies are written for a specific number of years and automatically terminate at the end of the period. Most companies write 5-year term, 10-year term, 15-year term, and 20-year term on a level premium basis.

Long-term policies written by many companies take several forms. The usual form is term to some specified age, most commonly to age 65 but sometimes to age 60 or to age 70. In some companies, term is written to the end of the insured's life expectancy at the age he takes out the policy. Based on the 1958 CSO Mortality Table, this will be to age 71 for a 25-year-old man, and age 73 for a man age 45 when the policy is issued. Frequently these policies give the insured the right to convert to a permanent form of life insurance before age 65. For a man aged 25, the premium for a $10,000 term to expectancy policy would be about $95 annually. If the policy is converted at age 65, the premium cost would jump to $687 if the same amount of insurance were to be kept in force, or the amount of

---

[16] Several other qualities that make life insurance merit consideration as a savings medium are discussed in Chapter 8.

insurance would be reduced to just under $1,400 if the same premium were to be paid.[17]

Renewable term policies are those which may be renewed at expiration for additional periods without evidence of insurability. However, the renewal premium will be charged at the rate for the attained age at the time of renewal. For example, a man 25 years old who takes out a $10,000, 5-year renewable term policy will pay an annual level premium of about $47.50 for 5 years. Then, if he renews the contract at age 30, he must pay an annual level premium of about $49, which is the 5-year term rate at that age. The comparable premium for a 5-year nonrenewable term policy would be $44.50 at age 25 and $46 at age 30.

Most of the companies write some form of renewable term insurance, although (except under group insurance plans) only a limited number of them will write *yearly* renewable term—i.e., term policies written for a period of one year and renewable at the end of each year for a given number of years or up to an attained age, 65 for example. More common are 5-, 10-, 15-, or 20-year renewable term. The period over which policies may be renewed is usually limited. Two common types of limitations are: (1) a limitation on the number of times renewals may be made; (2) a limitation on the age at which the insured may make his last renewal.[18] Companies restrict the number of renewals in order to reduce adverse selection in later years. Policyholders in good health will be less likely to exercise their renewal privileges at advanced ages because of the higher premium, whereas those in poor health will be more inclined to continue their insurance in force as long as they are allowed to do so. The net result of unlimited renewal could be a higher mortality rate among policyholders, and consequently an increase in cost.

Convertible term gives the insured the right to convert to any permanent or endowment form of insurance without evidence of insurability within a given period of time before the expiration of the term of the contract. For example, a 5-year term policy may be convertible any time before maturity or, in some cases, any time within the first 3 years; a 10-year term policy may be convertible any time before maturity, or, in some companies, any time within the first 8 years. Term to 65 and expectancy term are usually convertible up to any time 5 years prior to their expiration date.

The convertible term plan is especially advantageous for a young man who is establishing a family but who is unable to afford the premium

---

[17] Long-term policies are sometimes assigned "brand" names by insurance companies. For example, one company calls its life expectancy policy the "emancipator" policy, while calling its term to 65 the "select economy" plan. The trade name given to the policy rarely will indicate its true nature; however, most insurance regulatory jurisdictions require that the exact descriptive name of the policy be stated somewhere on the face, usually in a footnote line at the bottom. The New York Insurance Department, for example, places a great deal of importance on the use of policy names that are descriptive.

[18] Yearly renewable term insurance usually restricts the number of renewals and the age at which the last renewal is allowed.

required to give adequate protection under a permanent policy form. He can use a convertible term policy, which permits him to acquire a large amount of protection at a relatively small annual premium. Then, as his income increases, he can convert the term insurance to a permanent contract.[19] For example, a young family man age 25 can purchase $25,000, 6-year convertible term for an annual premium of $106.75. He can convert this policy into a continuous premium whole life at age 30 by increasing the annual premium to $394.75, an additional $288.[20]

Automatically convertible term policies are those which are converted into continuous premium whole life or some other plan of permanent insurance at the end of a given number of years without action on the part of the insured. They may also be converted earlier if the insured so elects. The plan is said to be psychologically attractive because it takes the decision to convert out of the hands of the often reluctant policyholder, and conversion is made for him by the company at the time agreed upon when the contract is issued.

Decreasing term is another common form of term insurance. Under this type of policy, the amount of insurance is reduced monthly or yearly while the premium remains level throughout the premium paying period.

An important use of decreasing term is to provide protection against the death of the breadwinner during the child dependency period, especially when the budget available demands strict economy in the use of insurance premiums. For example, a man aged 25 can purchase term insurance starting with $50,000 and decreasing monthly to 0 over a 20-year period for a premium of $172 paid annually for 18 years. The policy will provide a monthly income of $290 for 19 years if the insured dies at the end of the first policy year. Should he die in subsequent years, the policy could be arranged to pay as follows, thus guaranteeing a fixed-dollar income during the 20-year child dependency period:

Year of Death	*Monthly Family Income*
5th year	$314 for 15 years
10th year	$345 for 10 years
15th year	$390 for 5 years

---

[19] Convertible term policies contain a provision that they may, within a stated period of years prior to expiry, be converted into a permanent policy form without evidence of insurability either by (1) paying in an amount equal to what the reserve would now be on the permanent policy had it been taken as of the date the term policy was issued, or (2) dating the permanent policy as of the date of conversion. In the first case, the premium on the converted policy will be at the rate for the age at which the term was issued. In the second case, it will be at the rate for the attained age.

[20] He might wish to make the conversions gradually over the period of the contract. For example, he can convert $5,000 at age 26 by paying an additional premium of $48.10. At age 27, by raising his premium $50.35 he can convert another $5,000. At age 28, he can convert another $5,000 increasing his annual premium $52.65. At age 29, he can convert another $5,000 by paying an additional $55.05 and the final $5,000 can be converted at age 30 with an additional premium of $57.70. In this way, the increase in premiums is gradual, with total premiums stepping up as follows: $106.75, $154.85, $205.20, $257.75, $332.80, and $390.40.

A rate of decrease in the amount of insurance may be arranged that would provide the same monthly income during the dependency period regardless of when the insured dies.

Decreasing term insurance is written most often in combination with permanent policy forms under special plans discussed in Chapter 7.

Nearly 30 percent of all ordinary life insurance in force in the United States is term insurance, an increase from about 25 percent five years ago. Currently more than 40 percent of new ordinary life insurance purchases is term insurance (regular, decreasing, and in combination with permanent policy forms). The trend is toward the greater use of term insurance in life insurance programs.[21]

More than 99 percent of all group life insurance in force is term insurance and about 7 percent of the weekly premium insurance (industrial life insurance) is term insurance.

Statistics on term insurance are interesting. Contrary to what one would expect, level term insurance seems to be purchased largely by people in high-income and high-age groups, including executives, managers, proprietors, and professional workers. The younger and low-income groups are not as heavy buyers of term insurance. For some unexplainable reason, they prefer endowment and high-premium permanent insurance forms. Perhaps it is because the concept of life insurance as a systematic method of accumulating savings has greater appeal to them. The high-income and high-age groups emphasize the concept of life insurance as a method of providing needed resources in the event of their death and see term insurance as the most efficient way of arranging for these resources.

2. ENDOWMENT INSURANCE

The endowment policy offers insurance protection against death for a specified period of time. If the insured lives to the end of the endowment period, the policy pays the face amount, either in a lump sum or, if elected by the insured, in installments. If he dies prior to endowment date, the face amount is paid to his beneficiary. Thus a $10,000, 20-year endowment policy promises to pay $10,000 in event of the insured's death before the expiration of the 20th year, or $10,000 to the insured himself, if he survives the period.

---

[21] The upward trend in the prices of common stocks and rising interest rates have increased the appeal of stock investments, bank savings accounts, and savings and loan shares. Because of the greater attractiveness of these investment and savings alternatives, it is believed that some potential life insurance buyers are allocating less cash to insurance by purchasing term insurance. Because term insurance does not provide as much money as permanent insurance for the insurers to invest, this trend, if it continues, could affect the position of the life insurance industry in the capital market. It has led the life insurance industry to develop new products to enable it to compete more favorably with other financial institutions for investable funds.

The endowment policy might be viewed as a savings fund protected by term insurance. Suppose a man aged 25 wants to accumulate a fund sufficient to put his newly born son through college 20 years from now. He figures that $10,000 will be the basic minimum necessary for this purpose. The father wants to be sure that this fund will be available for his son regardless of whether the father lives or dies. So he buys a 20-year endowment insurance contract for an annual premium of about $435.[22] By the time the father reaches age 30, he will have accumulated in his policy a savings fund of $1,750 (known in technical language as the cash surrender value). Should he die during the next year, this amount, coupled with $8,250 in insurance benefits, would make up the $10,000 then payable to his son for later use in college. Should he survive to age 40, the policy will have a value of $6,810. Death at that time would require $3,190 in insurance proceeds to complete the savings plan. At the end of 20 years the policy will be worth $10,000 and death at that time would produce no additional values. During the 20 years, the endowment policy has provided a decreasing amount of insurance protection while the savings fund was gradually accumulated. The total deposits made amounted to $8,700. Interest on these deposits was enough to pay for the cost of the decreasing term insurance and still leave a gain of $1,300.[23]

Uses of Endowment.   Endowment insurance is useful as a savings vehicle for those who are in a financial position to save but who would not adhere to a savings plan without the semicompulsive features offered through a life insurance contract. This use of the endowment policy assumes that death protection is not of major importance; however, if it is of no importance whatsoever, other methods of saving might prove more economical if the saver can save without compulsion.

Endowment insurance may be used to accumulate funds for a specific purpose. For example, an endowment can be used to build a dowry for a daughter or a capital fund to help a son get a start in business. These are, of course, "luxury" uses of life insurance and should be ignored, except by families whose death protection needs are adequately covered. Also, unless there are tax problems to be solved through life insurance, other methods of building these special funds might prove more economical. They can be built without the expense of unneeded death protection.

Perhaps the most important use of endowments is to provide retirement income. Endowments at ages 60 and 65 are primarily intended to provide

---

[22] Don't jump to the conclusion that this is the policy he should buy. Defer your judgment until you have read Chapter 8.

[23] While this is a useful illustration to explain the concept of endowment insurance, it is not technically correct as actuaries view it. Technically minded, as opposed to sales minded, actuaries hold the survivorship concept of cash value life insurance rather than the decreasing protection, increasing savings concept. Both concepts were discussed in Chapter 1.

funds for old age. Purchased at relatively early ages, they offer a reasonably large amount of death protection per premium dollar, while accumulating a retirement fund that may be taken as cash or as an annuity income. A man age 25 can purchase $30,000 of endowment at age 65 for an annual premium of $530. At age 65, the endowment policy will provide a minimum guaranteed retirement income of $210 a month for life.[24]

A special form of the endowment policy is retirement income insurance, also called "special retirement endowment," "guaranteed life income," "income endowment," "insurance income at age 65," and many other names. The contract usually provides $10 a month lifetime retirement, 120 months certain per $1,000 of life insurance. At age 65, it takes a great deal more than $1,000 to finance a lifetime income of $10 a month, 120 months certain. For example, in one company, $1,000 will provide a minimum guaranteed lifetime income of $6.09 a month at age 65, male, 120 months certain. Consequently retirement income policies must provide for cash values at age 65 in excess of the face amount of the contract in order to pay $10 per month per $1,000 of insurance. The cash value at age 65 of an age 65 retirement income policy in one company is $1,643 per $1,000 of insurance. (An age 60 retirement income policy would have a cash value of $1,864 at age 60.) Therefore, the premium per $1,000 of insurance is much higher for an age 65 retirement income policy than for an endowment at age 65. To illustrate, in one company, for a $10,000 age 65 retirement income policy, male aged 25, the annual level premium is $265, whereas it is $182.50 for an endowment at age 65.[25]

If the policy becomes a claim prior to retirement age, the face amount or the cash value, whichever is the greater at that point, is paid. For example, if the man in the foregoing illustration dies at age 60, his beneficiary will collect the cash value of the policy rather than its face amount because by that time the cash value will be $13,050, exceeding the face amount by $3,050. On the other hand, if he dies at age 45, his estate will collect the $10,000 face amount, for at that age the cash value of the policy is only $5,590.

Limitations of Endowments. The temptation of a large sum of cash to be received at the end of a given number of years might lead some people to purchase endowment insurance when their greater need is for premature death protection. Life insurance protection under an endowment

---

[24] Wait until after you have read Chapter 8 before you decide whether the endowment at age 65 is the appropriate policy to use for combining death protection with retirement income protection in the same policy.

[25] For women, the premiums for retirement income policies are higher because of the greater life expectancy of women. In the foregoing company the premium for a $10,000 age 65 retirement income policy would be $291 for a female age 25 compared to the $265 quoted for the male. The premium for an endowment at age 65 for a female would be less than that for a male because the female mortality rate is lower than the male mortality rate. For example, the annual level-premium for a $10,000 endowment at age 65 would be $175.60 for a female compared with the $182.50 quoted for males.

policy terminates when the policy matures at the end of the endowment period, leaving the insured without death protection beyond that date.[26]

Technically, the limitations of the endowment policy are two: *expiring protection* and *low death protection value*. Only when there is a limited and expiring premature death protection need plus a valid need for a specific cash fund at a given date does the endowment policy find its proper application. The premiums spent for endowment forms usually can be used more effectively to purchase insurance with higher face amounts.

Endowment policies often appeal to people as a way to "win—live or die." But viewed in this manner, one is just as certain to "lose" as he is to "win"[27] with the endowment policy. Conceptually, an endowment policy is made up of two types of insurance policies: term and pure endowment.[28] When a man dies, he wins on the term portion. When he lives, he wins on the endowment portion. However, whichever happens he has paid not only for the portion that has matured as a claim but also for the portion of the policy on which no claim has matured: the term, if he lives; the pure endowment, if he dies. If he dies, he would have been better off with pure term insurance. If he lives, he would have been better off with a pure endowment. However, because no one can know whether he will live or die within a stated period, he must prepare for whatever financial contingencies seem important to him and his family: death, survival, or both—and he must do this using the risk management techniques that produce the most favorable balance between benefits and costs.

Endowment is not so popular as term. Endowment life insurance forms make up about 0.2 percent of all group life insurance in force in the United States, about 10 percent of all industrial life insurance, and about 7 percent of all ordinary insurance in force. Endowment insurance is becoming less popular. Ten years ago endowment insurance equaled about 13 percent of all ordinary insurance in force. Currently less than 6 percent of new ordinary life insurance purchased is endowment insurance. Endowment policies seem to be purchased largely by people in low income groups and in groups under age 30.

---

[26] The policy, however, may include options other than immediate and full cash settlement: the insured may accept a paid-up policy at an *increased* amount in lieu of cash payment; or he may accept a paid-up policy for the original face amount plus a cash payment of the difference between the cash value of the new policy and the face amount of the endowment. Normally, these options are conditional: the policyholder must show evidence of insurability to exercise either one of them.

[27] The "win or lose" concept of insurance is erroneous because contracts of insurance are not wagers. In insurance, as in other businesses, one is not likely to receive more than he is charged.

[28] Pure endowment pays nothing if the insured dies before reaching the end of the endowment period but pays the face amount if he survives the period.

5

The Whole Life Contract

Confusion in nomenclature exists in the use of the term "whole life." Sometimes the term is used interchangeably with "ordinary life." Ordinary has two very different connotations. It is generally applied to that class of insurance written for a minimum of $1,000 on an annual premium basis.[1] The word ordinary is used to distinguish this type of insurance from "group insurance" and from "industrial" insurance—a form of weekly premium insurance usually of less than $1,000.[2] In an entirely different connotation, ordinary life is used to indicate that type of policy in which protection is furnished for the whole of life and upon which premiums are payable continuously throughout the lifetime of the insured. It is in its latter connotation that ordinary life is used interchangeably with whole life.[3]

Whole life insurance is a broader term than ordinary life. It is insurance that furnishes protection for the whole of life regardless of how many years premiums are to be paid. Premiums may be paid over a limited period, such as 20 or 30 years, or they may be paid in one lump sum at the inception of the policy. When premiums are to be continuous throughout the lifetime of the insured, the policy is most commonly referred to as an ordinary life policy. In this sense, ordinary life is simply a type of whole life insurance and does not include all whole life forms. A more descriptive term for such a policy is "continuous premium whole life," as contrasted to "limited payment whole life" and "single premium whole life."

Uses of Whole Life. Although the amount of postdeath resources needed from life insurance should decrease as the family matures and as predeath resources are accumulated, few people ever outlive the usefulness of life insurance as an estate asset. Death at any age costs money. Frequently

---

[1] There has been a tendency in recent years to raise the minimum amount of ordinary policies above the traditional $1,000. Also, nearly all companies will accept semiannual, quarterly, or even monthly premiums on ordinary; however, usually there is a "handling charge" when premium payment frequency is more often than annual—although not always.

[2] Cf. Chapter 12.

[3] The Committee on Life Insurance Terminology of the American Risk and Insurance Association on Insurance Terminology recommends the use of the term "straight life" instead of "whole life" or "ordinary life."

the use of life insurance to provide the postdeath resources for estate clearance is the most efficient method of arranging for these resources because it eliminates the need for (and cost of) maintaining liquid predeath resources. Consequently, there is nearly always a use for life insurance regardless of the age of the individual.

The whole life policy contains an accumulating cash value which permits the individual to protect simultaneously against the twin perils of premature death and of loss of income through old age. A whole life policy taken at a reasonably early age will have, at age 65, a substantial cash value per $1,000 of insurance which can be withdrawn in the form of periodic payments for life if the insured so desires.[4] A whole life policy, therefore, taken at an early age, makes it possible for the insured to obtain a relatively high amount of protection against premature death per dollar of premium during his family years when he needs this amount of protection most, and yet, automatically and at the same time, accumulate funds for his old age. Moreover, he will have a yearly increasing emergency fund on which he can draw for a loan if necessary.

Limitations of Whole Life.   Perhaps the principal limitation of whole life insurance, when compared with term insurance, is its higher annual premium. The primary insurance need for most families is income for the wife and children in the event of the premature death of the breadwinner. If only a small amount of money can be budgeted by the family for life insurance premiums, the purchase of whole life insurance may mean sacrificing some needed death protection in order to build up cash values for emergency or retirement.

The principal limitation of whole life insurance, when compared with endowment insurance, is its lower survivorship benefit per dollar of premium, assuming premium payment periods of equal duration. This limitation is important only when higher survival benefits are worth the cost of lower death benefits.

Although the preceding paragraphs discuss the uses and limitations of whole life insurance, they do so only broadly. It is more realistic to discuss the uses and limitations of the various types of whole life policies, for their differences are significant.

1. TYPES OF WHOLE LIFE POLICIES

Whole life polices are classified according to the method of distributing premium payments. The most common is a level premium over the lifetime of the insured. Other methods are a level premium over a limited

---

[4] Cf. Chapter 6 for a discussion of annuities. The policy should be checked to see whether the right to withdraw cash values in the form of an annuity is included as a contractual provision. It is safer to rely on a contractual provision than on a statement that "It is our policy to allow it."

number of years, a single premium, or an escalating premium for the first few years of the contract with a level premium thereafter for life.

Continuous Premium Whole Life Policies. Continuous premium or straight life policies are contracts that provide death protection for the whole of life, with premiums payable continuously until death.[5] The insured pays the premiums at each due date as long as he lives; when he dies, the proceeds go to his beneficiaries. Premiums are usually payable annually, semiannually, quarterly, or monthly. A growing number of companies permit monthly payment of ordinary insurance premiums, since monthly payments seem to be the most convenient method of paying for nearly every big-tag item a man buys. Payment at intervals other than annually usually increases the premium slightly. For example, in one company the annual premium is multiplied by 0.52 for the semiannual premium, 0.265 for the quarterly premium, and 0.092 for the monthly premium. In another company the factors are 0.505, 0.255, and 0.085.

Three reasons account for higher fractional premiums: (1) If the full annual premium is not available at the beginning of the premium year, the company will earn less interest. The policyholder must make up this loss. (2) Also, and more important, he must make up the extra expense involved in handling the premium more than once during the year—the mail room and bookkeeping costs, for example. (3) Many companies do not require payment of the unpaid portion of the annual premium should a policyholder die after paying, say, only a semi-annual premium. The loss of the other semiannual premium also must be considered in setting fractional premium rates. This latter reason does not apply to those companies that refund the unearned portion of the annual premium at death. For example, if death occurs 1 month after the annual premium is paid, the death claim is increased by some companies by $11/12$ of the annual premium.

Use of the Continuous Premium Whole Life Policy. The continuous premium whole life policy furnishes the maximum amount of *permanent* death protection at the lowest level annual premium. For instance, at age 25, a premium of $134.50 will purchase $10,000 continuous premium whole life insurance on a nonparticipating basis from one company; at the same age and in the same company, that amount of money will purchase only about $8,500 of whole life paid up at age 65; and just a little over $6,000 of 20-payment whole life. About $14,000 of life expectancy term could be purchased with the premium for $10,000 of continuous premium whole life insurance. Those seeking *permanent* life insurance protection with its accompanying cash value will find that they can use the continuous premium whole life plan with the minimum of sacrifice in the amount of insurance per premium dollar committed.

Limitations of the Continuous Premium Whole Life Policy. The limitations of the continuous premium whole life policy form are few for those

---

[5] Or until age 100 (age 96 on the older policies issued on the American Experience Mortality Table) when the policy automatically matures as a claim.

who want to cover their life insurance needs with a permanent life insurance plan. An objection to the continuous premium form sometimes heard is that its cash values at age 65 for retirement income seem low when compared to those of endowment at 65 or whole life paid up at 65. However, this may not be a valid objection. To illustrate:

Early in life, every individual faces a twin peril, the peril of premature death and the peril of the destruction of earning power brought about by old age.[6] He has no way of knowing which of these perils may occur. The continuous premium whole life policy gives in one policy protection against both of them, sacrificing some of the death protection available under term insurance and some of the retirement protection available under endowment insurance. If the insured outlives the period requiring large amounts of death protection, the indemnity offered by the continuous premium whole life policy against old age is not as satisfactory as that afforded by a policy designed particularly for retirement. However, if he dies during the critical family years, the indemnity payable to his family will be more satisfactory than it would have been under a policy designed principally for retirement. For example, with a $500 annual premium a man aged 25 can purchase about $37,000 of continuous premium whole life, whereas he can buy only about $27,500 of endowment at age 65. The cash value at age 65 of the $37,000 continuous premium whole life will be about $21,000. The cash value at age 65 of the endowment is its face amount of $27,500. Therefore in this case, when a policyholder selects a continuous premium whole life instead of an endowment at 65, he is getting approximately $9,500 more in premature death protection and giving up approximately $6,500 of old age protection—a reasonable exchange if the expected value of $9,500 in postdeath resources exceeds the expected value of $6,500 in postretirement resources.

Another objection to the continuous premium whole life policy is that premiums must be paid throughout life. Many people like the idea of a termination date for premium payments. This objection overlooks that after the early years, payment of premiums may be discontinued at any time without forfeiting the cash value accumulated under the policy. If for any reason the insured can no longer pay premiums, he may, if he still needs the insurance, take either a reduced amount of permanent insurance as paid-up insurance or retain the full amount of insurance as term insurance for a period of years. Both the reduced amount of permanent insurance and the period over which the full amount of insurance will be extended are stated in the policy as nonforfeiture values.[7] If, for example, an insured who owns a $25,000 continuous premium whole life policy taken at age 35 were to find at age 55 that he no longer wanted to pay the premium, he could exercise his right to take the paid-up insurance amount

---

[6] He also faces a third peril of disability. Cf. Chapters 13 and 14.

[7] Nonforfeiture options are discussed in Chapter 11.

in the policy, about $14,000, for example. In other words, he could discontinue all premium payments and still have life insurance protection in the amount of $14,000 for the rest of his life. If he needed more protection than $14,000, he might decide to take the extended term option, which, without payment of premiums, would keep his policy in force at its full amount ($25,000) for approximately 15 years.

The limitations of the continuous premium whole life policy become apparent only when the contract is used to fill a need for which it is not designed. For instance, if it is applied to a temporary need for protection, it does not give as much face amount of insurance per premium dollar as does one of the term insurance forms. Limitations also will appear when the continuous premium whole life policy is used to cover what is more of a retirement than premature death protection need. However, for the typical individual, whose need is primarily for protection for his family in case of his premature death and only secondarily for protection against old age, the continuous premium whole life policy provides what a large number of buyers and sellers believe to be a good balance between premature death protection and cash value for retirement or emergencies.

Nearly one half of all ordinary life insurance in force in the United States is continuous premium whole life insurance, and about one fourth of that is written in combination with term insurance under special policy plans discussed in Chapter 7. About 40 percent of the current purchase of ordinary life insurance is continuous premium whole life, of which about 37 percent is bought in combination with term insurance. About 9 percent of weekly premium (industrial) and 0.7 percent of group insurance is continuous premium whole life insurance.

Limited Payment Life Policies.   Limited payment policies are those on which the premiums are payable for a stated period: 10 years, 20 years, 30 years, or until the insured reaches a given age, 60 or 65, for example. Several companies, instead of issuing a continuous premium whole life policy, issue a policy paid up at age 85, 90, or 95 or some similar advanced age. These advanced-age, paid-up plans, for all practical purposes, are continuous premium plans, and should be viewed as such by the buyer.[8]

Under the limited payment plans, the insured pays a level annual premium during the premium paying years. With the payment of the last premium, the policy is paid up in the sense that no more premiums are required from the insured even though the full face amount of the policy will remain in force for the rest of his life. This means that the policy values are large enough so that in each of the remaining years the interest earned on them plus the survivorship benefits accruing (explained in

---

[8] Advanced-age, paid-up plans or endowments (some companies write endowments at age 90) are written to offer higher cash and loan values than are customary with the traditional continuous premium whole life plan. They were introduced also to offer a special class of policy on more attractive terms than the simple continuous premium whole life policy in order to appeal to certain types of buyers. "Specials" are discussed later in this chapter.

Chapter 1) are sufficient to enable the company (1) to pay the cost of insurance and (2) to continue to increase the values in accordance with actuarial principles.[9]

The limited payment policy must not be confused with an endowment policy. With the payment of the last premium, a limited payment policy is fully *paid up,* but it is not *matured.* A matured policy is one under which the face amount is paid either by reason of death or by reason of the survival of the insured to the end of a given period. A paid-up policy does not mature when it is paid up. The insured simply is relieved of the payment of any more premiums.

As illustrated, the limited payment life policy offers less protection for the same premium dollar than does the continuous premium form. The reason is roughly, the shorter the premium payment period, the larger must be each premium.[10]

Uses of the Limited Payment Whole Life Policy. Often it is suggested that limited payment whole life policies are properly used in a life situation in which the most productive years are limited to a relatively short span of time. A baseball player, for instance, knows that his earning period as far as his profession goes will be limited to, say, 15 years. Therefore, it is argued, he may properly buy a 15-pay policy in order to adjust his premium payments to the most productive period of his life. For example, suppose a 25-year-old baseball player estimates he has 10 years of professional life ahead of him. He decides he can budget $1,000 a year for life insurance to protect against loss of this earning power by death. He reasons that it would be wise to have the policy fully paid at the end of his productive years; so he buys $25,000 of 10-pay life. When he reaches age 35, the policy is paid up. But suppose that when he retires from baseball, he finds a high-paying job. He might be just as capable now of paying $1,000 a year for insurance as he has been over the past 15 years. But if he is uninsurable, he will be unable to purchase another policy.

Suppose, on the other hand, he had put this $1,000 a year into a continuous premium whole life policy. He could have purchased about $73,-000 of insurance, nearly three times as much as under the 10-pay plan. If circumstances are such that he cannot continue his premium payments at age 35 he can take a paid-up policy of about $18,000, $7,000 less than the amount of insurance available under the 10-pay life plan with the same premium. If he can continue the premium, he may keep the full $73,000

---

[9] To say that a policy is paid up does not mean that it costs the policyholder nothing to keep the policy in force. He could surrender the policy, take the cash value, invest it, and pocket the income earned, net after taxes. The cost of keeping a paid-up policy in force is the loss of the use of the funds tied up in the insurance policy.

[10] The nonparticipating premium for $10,000 of 20-pay life at age 25 in one company is $224.10 and for 10-pay life is $399.60. Interest and mortality factors are important in distributing the premium among any given number of years, otherwise the cost of 10-pay would be exactly twice the cost of 20-pay. See Chapter 25 for a technical explanation of this point.

in force as long as he wishes. The continuous premium whole life plan, therefore, offers the policyholder more flexibility at the end of the 10-year period. Just as important as its flexibility is the fact that it offers $48,000 more death protection during the crucial 10-year period when his children are young. The expected value of the gain of $48,000 of death protection from age 25 to 35 is likely to be greater than the expected value of the loss of $7,000 of death protection beyond age 35. This is to say that the expected value of the combination of $73,000 of death protection from age 25 to 35 and $17,000 for life thereafter is likely to be higher than the expected value of a level $25,000 of death protection for life, especially when the expectation that some or all of the $1,000 annual premiums can be continued beyond age 35 is considered. Some other combination of benefit levels might yield an even greater expected value from the $1,000 annual premium to be spent. The process of selecting and arranging policies to produce the maximum expected benefit from premiums paid is called programming and is discussed in Chapter 20.

Highly paid professional athletes might be able to put as much as $10,-000 a year into life insurance premiums. At age 25, this amount will purchase over $250,000 of 10-pay life insurance—an amount which the athlete considers adequate to settle his estate and protect his family. In this case, the 10-pay might be an attractive policy in that it would build up large cash values. The interest earned each year during the accumulation will not be taxable, resulting in an effective yield better than that earned on equally safe and liquid fixed dollar investments. If at age 35 he continues to earn a high salary and is insurable, he can purchase more insurance on a high premium plan. If he is not insurable, the present paid-up policy for $250,-000 should be adequate if he has done a competent job of estate planning.

The individual who plans to retire at age 60 or 65 and has arranged reasonable protection for his family in case of his premature death may properly use a paid-up at age 60 or 65 policy to provide the necessary cash to pay the cost of funeral and death taxes. He then will not be burdened with the obligation to pay premiums out of his retirement income when he retires.[11]

The limited payment life policy is used in special situations. For example, a father or grandfather who wishes to make a gift of paid-up life insurance to his child or grandchild may purchase the insurance on a limited payment form so as to complete the payments over a short period of time. Limited pay will often prove useful in estate planning where income, gift, and estate tax considerations are involved. Discussion of this latter point is deferred to Chapter 21.

The limited payment life policy is useful for the person who wishes to accumulate more cash value per $1,000 of death benefit than is available under continuous premium whole life. Table 5–1 shows the difference in

---

[11] Remember, too, that the insured can discontinue paying premiums on a continuous premium whole life policy at age 60 or 65 and accept a paid-up policy of a reduced amount.

the amount of cash value accumulated in continuous premium, limited premium, and endowment forms.

TABLE 5–1

Comparison of Premiums and Values for $10,000 Continuous Pay,
Limited Pay, and Endowment
(issue age 25, nonpar rates)

Policy Form	Premium	End of 10th Year	End of 20th Year	At Age 65
Continuous-premium whole life	$134.00	$ 940.00	$ 2,490.00	$ 5,700.00
Life paid-up 65	153.00	1,080.00	2,830.00	6,900.00
Endowment at age 65	183.00	1,440.00	3,690.00	10,000.00
20-pay life	220.00	1,820.00	4,590.00	6,900.00
20-year endowment	438.00	4,070.00	10,000.00	—

Limitations of the Limited Payment Whole Life Policy. The larger savings element in limited pay forms and the anticipation of completing premium payments at some time in the future often lead to a misuse of these forms. If a man's need is primarily for protection for his family in case of his premature death, the savings or cash value should be a secondary consideration.

It must be remembered that although the cash value for each $1,000 under a continuous premium form is lower, it is possible to buy more units of protection with a given premium than is the case with the limited pay or endowment form. Thus, with a given premium budget the difference in the total cash value that a policyholder has available at any given time will be less than the per $10,000 differences shown in Table 5–1. For example, the total cash value available in the continuous premium whole life policy at the end of 20 years, assuming the same amount of premium is spent in each case, would not be too far below that obtained under a 20-pay plan. For instance, the cash value per $1,000 at the end of 20 years according to Table 5–1 is about 1.84 times higher for 20-pay life than for continuous premium whole life. However, per dollar of premium paid, the cash value of the 20-pay plan is only 1.12 times higher.

Nevertheless, the difference in the cash value per $1,000 might tempt the buyer to take the 20-pay life plan when his premature death needs indicate he should purchase the continuous premium plan. A man age 25 who has $500 a year to spend for life insurance can buy about $37,000 of insurance under the continuous premium plan but only about $22,000 under the 20-pay life plan. This means that if he dies before his family is grown, his dependents will receive about $15,000 less under 20-pay life plan than under a continuous premium whole life plan, a deficiency which could prove serious. For example, $37,000 will provide a $300 a month income for approximately 13 years, whereas $22,000 will provide this income for less than 7 years. Income for this extra six years could mean independence for the family while the children finish high school.

Another significant factor in this particular illustration is that continuous premium whole life will provide higher retirement benefits at age 65. The reason is that premiums on the $22,000, 20-pay life will be paid until age 45 only, whereas premiums on the $37,000 continuous premium whole life will continue beyond that time. At age 45 the cash value of the 20-pay life policy is $10,098 whereas the cash value of the continuous premium whole life policy is only $9,213. From then on, the cash value of the continuous premium whole life policy will gain on the 20-pay policy by reason of the continued premium payments. By age 60 the cash value of the 20-pay will be $13,904 whereas the cash value of continuous premium whole life will have grown to $18,093. At age 65 the 20-pay policy will have only $15,-180 available for retirement benefits. The continuous premium whole life policy will have a cash value of $21,090 at age 65.

The decision as to which policy to buy depends on whether the need of the buyer (and especially of his family) is more for cash values or more for protection against both the peril of living too long and the peril of dying too soon.

The greatest error in the use of limited payment life forms is made by people who should place the emphasis in their insurance program upon premature death protection rather than on savings.

Limited payment life insurance policies are most popular with the weekly premium (industrial) insurance policyholders. About 70 percent of all industrial insurance in force is on a limited payment form. In ordinary insurance, limited payment life is more popular than endowment but less popular than continuous premium whole life and term. About 10 percent of all ordinary life insurance in force in the United States is limited payment life and about 9 percent of the insurance currently being purchased is written on a limited payment form. Contrary to what would be expected on the basis of sound insurance buying theory, limited pay life policies are purchased largely by low-income groups and those under age 30.

Single Premium Life Policies.   Single premium policies are contracts issued in exchange for the payment of the entire cost in advance through one lump-sum premium. For example, a $30,000 nonparticipating single-premium whole life policy can be purchased in one company at age 25 for $8,986.50. Once this premium is paid, no more premiums are required during the life of the policy.

Single premium policies must not be confused with policies under which premiums have been discounted in advance. Many companies will accept a given number or amount of annual premiums in advance of their due date at various interest rates. For example, the company writing the foregoing single premium policy will discount annual premiums currently at the following rates: premiums due the first 10 years, 4.5 percent, premiums due thereafter, 4 percent. The maximum amount of premiums discounted in advanced is $500,000. Unearned premiums may be withdrawn at a discount rate 0.5 percent higher than that given by the company. The premium discount schedules, the maximum amounts, and the withdrawal arrangements vary among companies, and companies change these schedules, amounts, and withdrawal arrangements on new deposits from time to time. Another company, for example, uses 5.5 percent for the first 5 years, 5 percent for the next 5 years, 4.5 percent for the next 10 years, and 3.5 percent thereafter. This insurer allows a maximum of $100,000 of premiums to be discounted in advance for any one individual. No withdrawals are permitted. Refund on death or surrender is made without penalty. The foregoing $30,-000 whole life contract can be purchased on the 20-pay plan for an annual premium of $655.80. The insured, by depositing a lump sum of $9,139.23 with the company can discount these 20 annual premiums and, in effect, own a paid-up policy.[12]

Although both policies will require no more premium payments, the two contracts are quite different. The 20-pay contract with premiums discounted in advance costs $152.73 more in premiums than the single premium policy. The cost differential is more than justified by the higher death benefit payable under the prepaid 20-pay life policy during the first 20 years it is in force. The small size of the differential is explained by the relatively high interest rates used in the discounting process. If these interest rates were lower, as they have been, the differential would be larger. On the other hand, a higher advance premium discount schedule could make the 20-payment life policy with discounted premiums cheaper than the single premium policy. For example, if all 19 advance premiums were discounted at 4.5 percent, as is done by several companies, the difference in the initial deposit for the two policies would favor the 20-payment life by $72.01. If the interest rate at which advance premiums are discounted is 5 percent, the 20-pay life policy would require an advance premium of $405.16 less than the single premium policy.

As to death benefits, the two policies function in this manner: When a single premium policyholder dies, his beneficiary is paid only the face amount of the contract. But upon the death of an insured whose premiums have been discounted, his beneficiary is paid the face amount of the policy plus a refund of the present value of unearned premuims. For example, if the insured dies at age 35, $30,000 will be paid under the single premium policy, whereas under the discounted premium policy $34,747.17 will be paid. This figure includes the value of the nine discounted unearned annual premiums. (The unearned portion of the 10th annual premium will also be refunded.)

The redemption values of the discounted policy also are higher during the first 20 years, since the present value (or a percentage thereof) of the unearned premiums is refundable along with the cash values of the policy.

---

[12] Only 19 premiums are discounted, since the first-year premium is paid in advance. Ten are discounted at 4.5 percent and 9 at 4 percent.

For example, at the end of the 10th year, the discounted policy has a cash value of $5,370 plus $5,403 of unearned premium or a total of $10,773. The single-premium policy has a cash value of $10,491.

At the 20th year, when the advance premiums have been exhausted and all premiums are paid, the death benefits and cash values of the two contracts are identical. They both will pay $30,000 at death, and at the end of the year they will have a cash value of $13,740. From then on, the increases in cash values will be the same in the two contracts.

Until mid-1965, interest earned on discounted premiums was not subject to income taxes. But the general rule now is that increments in the value of premium deposit funds must be reported as income in the year they are used to pay premiums or are made available for withdrawal. The taxability of the increments in premium deposit funds tends to give an advantage to single premium policies in a comparison with a fully discounted 20-payment life policy, except in periods of high interest rates.

Uses of the Single Premium Life Policy. At first blush, one would wonder why anyone would want to purchase life insurance on a single premium basis. Admittedly, the idea of paying the entire premium in one lump sum would never occur to the typical person. Such a premium paying arrangement would be neither desirable nor practical in most instances. Nevertheless, there are several legitimate uses for single premium insurance. For example:

1. Since life insurance has some attributes desirable to persons interested in an investment, the single premium policy might be an attractive purchase for some investors.[13]

2. The single premium plan sometimes is used to purchase life insurance to offset death taxes and the costs of distributing an estate.[14] The purpose of single premium insurance in this case is to put the maximum liquidity into an existing estate. Funds for the payment of single premiums often are obtained through the conversion of other investments. Such changes in the character of investment accounts might well be warranted. One of the primary requisites of an investment earmarked to pay estate taxes is liquidity. Liquidity is defined as the ability of an asset to be converted into cash without delay and without loss in value. Life insurance more than meets this liquidity test, for not only does it automatically convert into cash at death when the cash is needed, but also it does so with an increase in value. Obviously a life insurance policy is always worth more at death than immediately preceding it.

3. Single premium life insurance is used as a gift medium, particularly for gifts to children. At young ages, large amounts of life insurance can be obtained for a relatively small premium. For instance, in one company

---

[13] Cf. Chapter 8 for a discussion of the investment features of life insurance.

[14] Annual premium insurance also can be used for this purpose; but the single premium plan requires no further premiums, sometimes an advantage in particular estate arrangements. (Cf. Chapter 21.)

$25,000 of nonparticipating single premium whole life insurance can be purchased for infants under age 6 months for a premium of $4,264.26, male, or $3,956.50, female. In other words, a paid-up life insurance estate can be purchased for an infant for about $.16 or $.17 on the dollar. Moreover, the policy will provide cash values for emergencies that might arise during the child's life.

Limitations of the Single Premium Life Policy.[15]   Single premium insurance as an investment medium has the same limitations as other fixed-dollar investments (bonds, mortgages, savings and loan shares, and so on). It leaves the investor exposed to the perils of inflation and does not give him the opportunity to share in an expanding economy. On the other hand, it does eliminate the market risk and the financial risk, and where guaranteed minimum dollar amounts are important to a person's financial plans, the single premium whole life policy can be an attractive place to put large sums of money.

2. PREFERRED RISK AND SPECIALS

Until the 1950's life insurers generally charged persons of the same age who met similar insurability standards the same rate per $1,000. However, policies offering a reduced rate have been available to certain applicants since the early 1900's. For the most part, these policies were limited to persons who met insurability standards above the average range, and were known as preferred risk policies.

The term "standard" is applied to those policies written on applicants whose health, habits, and occupations conform to the norms used in the base for predicting mortality experience. It has long been the practice to charge an extra premium to those who fail to meet the standards. Insurance written on applicants not acceptable at standard premiums is called substandard or extra-risk insurance. The term "preferred risk" is applied to those policies written on applicants whose health, habits, and occupations are better than standard. Preferred risk policies are written at premiums lower than standard.

A preferred risk is a *special* policy, i.e., not the "regular" policy issued by the company. However, under the impetus of a price merchandising wave which started in the 1950's, companies began issuing special policies at reduced rates, the amount of reduction being affected by any factor or combination of factors in addition to or other than the superior health, habits, or occupation of the applicant. In fact many "specials" (as the term is now used) are even issued as substandard policies at premiums lower than normal for extra risk policies.

The Nature of Specials.   The special is usually a policy offered in a high minimum amount, carrying a premium sharply reduced over a similar, or

---

[15] This discussion assumes that the typical individual will use level premium policies in his effort gradually to build his life insurance program to acceptable levels.

the same, form issued on a regular basis, and showing a more favorable net cost,[16] especially at periods common for such comparisons—at the end of 10 and 20 years.

Table 5–2 illustrates the premiums for a life paid up at 95, a special issued only in a minimum of $25,000 and not requiring that the applicant meet better than standard underwriting requirements. The table also shows the premium for a regular life paid up at 95 in another company issued in a minimum of $3,000. Both sets of premiums are on a nonparticipating basis and are for $25,000 of insurance.

TABLE 5–2

Comparison of Premium for $25,000 of Insurance
(life paid up at 95, $25,000 minimum special, and
regular life paid up at 95, both nonpar basis)

Age of Issue	Special (Company A)	Regular (Company B)
25	$285.25	$326.75
35	416.50	475.75
45	632.25	721.75

Basis for Reducing Premiums.   A reduction in the premium rate for the special is accomplished in one or more ways.

1. *A high minimum amount will be issued,* thus spreading the fixed costs of acquisition (clerical and so on) over a greater number of units.

2. *Commissions to agents are reduced.*[17]

3. *A reduced gross premium on a participating plan* is charged by reducing the amount allowed for expenses. (This procedure, however, might lead to a lower policy dividend.)

4. *Cash values are reduced.*

5. *Less attractive settlement options are written into the policy.* In some policies, settlement options are omitted from the contract altogether. The policy provides, instead, that if an installment settlement is desired, whatever tables are currently in use by the company will apply.[18] Other specials reduce the number of settlement options offered in the policy in order to reduce the cost of handling the policy. The minimums guaranteed under the settlement options in specials may be less than those guaranteed by the company in its regular policy.

---

[16] Total premiums paid, minus total dividends, if any, minus cash value at the time selected for making the illustration.

[17] Reporting on a survey of 134 companies, the Life Insurance Agency Management Association stated that commission rates were reduced on specials by 42 percent of the companies with $1 billion or more of insurance in force, 60 percent of those with $150 million to $1 billion, and 65 percent of those with less than $150 million.

[18] This prevents the possibility that improved mortality or deteriorating interest rates will make the options in use at the time of issue unrealistic 25 years or more in the future when the policy matures.

6. A settlement dividend (also called a terminal dividend) is paid. This dividend is paid only if the policy is surrendered at the end of a specified number of years or at maturity or death.[19] Such a dividend will produce a particularly favorable net cost illustration if it is made available at the end of the number of years (10 and 20) at which net cost illustrations are commonly constructed.

7. Premiums are required to be paid annually.

8. Allowance is made for a lower lapse rate.[20]

Gradation of Premiums. It was not too great a step from the reduction of premiums for specials by reason of size to the gradation of premiums by size for all policy forms. This latter development, a practice long established in Europe, followed quickly on the heels of the specials in the second half of the 1950's.[21] The gradation of premiums was approved by the National Association of Insurance Commissioners in May, 1956, following some confusion as to whether, for example, a higher charge per $1,000 for a $5,000 policy than for a $10,000 policy would violate state statutes prohibiting discrimination in the premiums charged like individuals. The NAIC considered policy size a basis for a premium classification.

The practice of reducing premiums as the size of the policy increases has become widespread.[22] Several methods are in use:

1. Gradation may be by minimum size as in the special that offers a lower rate per thousand for, say, $25,000 than for reasonably comparable coverage for amounts under $25,000.

2. "Band" gradation is possible, under which reductions are made by "brackets": say one rate applying for any given policy issued in an amount under $5,000, another for policies in amounts from $5,000 to $9,999, another from $10,000 to $24,999, and so on.[23]

3. Under "across-the-board" or "per $1,000" gradation, rates are reduced on each subsequent $1,000 of face amount issued. For example, a quantity discount such as $1 times the amount of insurance in excess of $10,000 may be allowed.

4. A flat charge per policy may be made, under which a fixed dollar factor or charge is added to each application. Thus, if the application is for

---

19 The payment of such a dividend after death should not be confused with a post mortem dividend, which is (roughly put) the deceased policyholder's pro-rata share of the policy dividend he would have received had he been alive at the end of the policy year.

20 How lapse rates affect the cost of insurance is discussed in Chapter 24.

21 All such dates as these are "in general." It may be possible to find some few companies instituting a practice before the given date.

22 This is akin to the practice of mercantile "quantity discounts," but is not related to the practice of reduction of premiums by size in many phases of property insurance. For instance, the premium for the first $10,000 of personal liability insurance is more than for, say, the second $10,000, but this is not a quantity discount. The reduction is based on the statistical observation that more claims in amounts up to $10,000 will be paid than claims in amounts of over $10,000. However, in life insurance the frequency rate of occurrence of a $1,000 death claim is the same as that for a $100,000 death claim.

23 Bands mentioned here are illustrative only, not intended to represent typical practice.

$2,000, the per-policy charge is less per $1,000 than if it is for $3,000. For instance, if the issue charge (frequently called policy fee) is $10, it is $5 per $1,000 on a $2,000 policy but only $2 per $1,000 for a $5,000 policy and only $0.20 per $1,000 on a $50,000 policy.

Gradation of premiums is now the custom in the life insurance business. Because discounts can be given for policies of large size without devising a separate class of policies such as paid up at age 95, specials are not as important as they once were.

6

The Annuity Policy

The annuity has become an important instrument in the planning of financial security for old age. The increasing emphasis placed by labor and management on industrial pensions has accounted for much of the growth in annuities over the past three decades.

About 10 million individual annuities and group annuity certificates are in force representing more than $5 billion of annual income of which about $1.5 billion is being paid currently. Nearly 75 percent of the total benefits under annuity contracts is provided under group annuities.

Group annuities have had a steady and rapid increase both in numbers and amounts over the past 35 years. A decline in both numbers and amounts of individual annuities began in 1955 and continued through 1961. The 1954 level of benefits payable was not surpassed until 1965, a year that saw a 4 percent increase in the number of individual annuities outstanding and a more than 10 percent increase in benefits payable under individual annuities. The annual rates of growth in numbers and amounts of individual annuities since 1965 have exceeded the 4 percent and 10 percent levels accomplished in 1965.

The increase that began in 1962 was sparked by legislation making annuities a tax shelter for employees of public schools and of nonprofit organizations, and for the self-employed. The activities of the insurers and their agents in developing and selling annuities to employees of Section 501 (C) (3) organizations and of public schools and to self-employed individuals taking advantage of the Keogh-Smathers Act have revived interest in individual annuities.[1] Aside from some renewed interest in single premium individual annuities growing out of their lower cost in response to the higher interest rates in the latter part of the 1960's the interest in individual annuities is limited to the tax-sheltered market.

---

[1] Cf. Chapter 17 for a discussion of the Keogh-Smathers Act and of tax-sheltered annuities plans written for employees of Section 501 (C) (3) organizations and of public schools.

1. THE NATURE OF ANNUITIES

The annuity has been called the "upside-down application of the life insurance principle." The description is apt. Whereas the purpose of a life insurance contract is the systematic accumulation of an estate, the purpose of an annuity contract is the scientific liquidation of an estate.

When a person purchases a life insurance contract, he agrees to pay the insurer a series of payments in return for which the insurer promises to pay his beneficiaries the face amount of the policy at his death. When he purchases an annuity contract, he pays the insurer a specified capital sum in return for a promise from the insurer to make him a series of payments as long as he lives.[2] Thus, under a life insurance contract the insurer *starts* paying upon the death of the insured, whereas under an annuity contract the insurer *stops* paying upon the death of the insured.

Just as in life insurance, the annuity is a risk-sharing plan based upon a group the individual members of which are all the same age. Individually, these people could not draw upon principal without fear of outliving it. Under a risk-sharing plan, the funds of those who die early can be used to offset the excess withdrawn by those who live long after their principal is spent. While the insurer does not know how long any one given individual member of the annuity group will live, it does know how to apply the law of large numbers to the experience of a specific group of annuitants so as to approximate the actual result for that group. Therefore, when the savings or investments of a large number of individuals are combined, each member can be paid an annual or monthly amount, actuarially calculated to assure that no one will outlive his capital or income. Thus, uncertainty is reduced, and losses (the costs of "living too long") are shared.

The amount of periodic income drawn by each member of the group is determined not only by his contribution but also by his age, sex, type of annuity selected, and sometimes by his health. The older a person is when he begins to receive his annuity income, the greater will be his periodic payments per dollar of contribution. The periodic payments per dollar of contributions are higher for a man than for a woman of the same age. If the annuitant is willing to have his payments terminated at his death, he will receive a higher periodic income than if he insists on a

---

[2] Obviously this is a simplification for the sake of illustrating the concept. The life insurance premium may be paid in one payment as well as in a series of payments; the life insurance policy may provide for payment of a lump sum at the end of an endowment period if the insured survives the period; and the payments to the insured or his beneficiary may be made in installments instead of a lump sum. The annuity premium may be paid in installments or in a lump sum; some types of annuities pay benefits for a limited period only, expiring regardless of whether the annuitant is still alive; and some annuities continue payments for the life of a surviving beneficiary.

guaranteed minimum number of payments. And in some annuity plans, more will be paid to the unhealthy annuitant than to the healthy one.

Annuity Income.   The periodic income collected under an annuity contract is composed of three parts: principal, investment income, and a survivorship or insurance benefit. The amount attributable to each part from any given periodic payment may be computed easily. To illustrate, assume an annuity of $1,000 a year issued to a man aged 65, with the first payment due 1 year from date of issue. The cost of the annuity would be $11,013 figured on the basis of 3 percent interest and the 1949 Annuity Table. If the annuity were purchased 1 year later (at age 66), the net single premium would be $10,611. Thus, in the first year $402 of the original capital has been liquidated.

Segregation of the first $1,000 periodic payment into principal, interest, and survivorship benefit would be figured as follows:

Initial investment (net)	$11,013.00
Interest assumed (3%) .... +	330.39
Total amount available	$11,343.39
Annuity payment .... −	1,000.00
Amount remaining without survivorship benefit ..	$10,343.39

Note that the net cost of the annuity at age 66 would be $10,611 but that only $10,343.39 is available. How is the deficiency of $267.61 replenished? Not all of the 65-year-old annuitants will survive the 1-year period to collect their $1,000. Those who die will release their investment to be spread among the survivors. Each survivor's share will amount to $267.61 which is the deficiency in the fund available at the beginning of the second year.

Thus, the first annuity payment of $1,000 is divided as follows:

Interest income	$ 330.39	($11,013.00 at 3%)
Capital liquidation	402.00	($11,013.00 − $10,611.00)
Survivorship benefit	267.61	($10,611.00 − $10,343.39)
Total	$1,000.00	

Each successive year, the survivorship benefit will increase, and the interest income and amount of capital liquidation will decrease. For example, the annuity payment for the second year will consist of:

Interest income	$ 318.33	($10,611.00 at 3%)
Capital liquidation	401.00	($10,611.00 − $10,210.00*)
Survivorship benefit	280.67	($10,210.00 − $ 9,929.33**)
Total	$1,000.00	

* $10,210.00 is the cost of the annuity at age 67.
** $9,929.33 is the amount remaining from the initial fund plus interest after the $1,000 payment is made.

The division of payment for each successive year can be worked out using the foregoing method. The formulas for each part are as follows:

Interest Income = Net Single Premium at the beginning of the year multiplied by the interest rate assumed.

Capital Liquidation = Net Single Premium at the beginning of the year less the Net Single Premium one year later.

Survivorship Benefit = Net Single Premium one year later less the Net Single Premium at the beginning of the year plus assumed interest minus assumed annuity payment.

The Objective of an Annuity. The purpose of an annuity is to assure a person an income he cannot outlive and one which is well in excess of the income he could derive from investing the cost of the annuity in safe, interest bearing or dividend yielding securities.

The periodic income under the annuity is larger than that provided under direct investments because the annuity principle involves the gradual consumption of the invested capital. The differential between the annuity income and income from direct investments is slight at young ages because if the annuity payments are to last through the insured's lifetime, only a small part of the capital can be consumed each year. Also at the young ages the survivorship benefit will be insufficient to increase the annuity payment much in excess of interest income. For these reasons, an annuity cannot be considered a suitable investment for a young person. At older ages, especially at the retirement age of, say, 65 when life expectancy is lower, the differential is more pronounced. For example, $40,000 would purchase an immediate life annuity of about $300 a month for a man aged 65 as contrasted to about $200 a month if the purchase is made at age 50. If the annuity is purchased at age 40, the income would be only about $165 a month. A conservative 5 percent investment would yield this much while keeping the principal intact. While the $135 monthly difference between the annuity income available at age 65 and the straight investment income may be large enough to warrant the systematic liquidation of capital through an annuity, a difference of $35 monthly at age 50 may provide insufficient motivation.[3]

2. ANNUITY CLASSIFICATIONS

Up to this point the discussion has been concerned with the annuity in its simplest form, the single premium life annuity contract. Under this contract the insurer promises to pay a given amount each period (monthly, semiannually, and so on) to the annuitant during his lifetime, in exchange for a single premium that immediately becomes the property of the com-

---

[3] The annuity rates used in this chapter are nonparticipating rates, and they vary among companies, depending upon the interest and mortality assumptions used in their computations and upon the expense loadings used.

pany, no part of which is returnable following the death of the annuitant, whenever that occurs.

However, the single premium life annuity contract does not meet the economic or psychological needs of most annuity purchasers. Some buyers want to pay for their retirement annuities through a series of level annual premiums during their preretirement years. Some do not like the idea of having no part of their premiums returned to their estate in the event of early death following retirement. A few purchasers would like to have annuity payments contingent upon the lives of more than one person. Still others would like to have the amount of each annuity payment measured by units which fluctuate in dollar values. Because of the variety of interests among annuity customers, a number of variations in annuity forms has developed.

Anyone viewing the wide variety of annuities available could become baffled without a systematic method of classifying them. Annuities may be classified on at least five different bases: the method of paying premiums, the disposition of proceeds, the date when benefits begin, the number of lives covered, and the units in which payout benefits are expressed. These classifications, however, are not mutually exclusive, since every annuity will fall in all five classes. Figure 6–1 offers a useful chart for viewing annuities as a unit.

Method of Paying Premiums.   Annuities may be purchased either with a single premium or through a series of installment premiums.

Single-Premium Annuities.   An annuity purchased by one lump sum is known as a single-premium annuity. Frequently life insurance cash values or death proceeds are distributed under a settlement option, in the form of an annuity. Here the lump sum is used, in effect, to purchase a single premium annuity at net rates. For example, instead of a lump-sum settlement, $25,000 of life insurance proceeds could be paid to a 55-year-old widow as a $123 monthly income for life. A 65-year-old man could have his $25,000 of life insurance cash or endowment values paid to him as a $182 monthly life annuity.

The single premium annuity is frequently used in pension and profit-sharing plans. It may be used to fund retirement benefits at the time an employee retires. For example, an employer can fund a retirement pension of $200 a month for a male employee aged 65 for a single premium of about $26,500. Single premium annuities also can be used to fund a series of fully paid benefits deferred to age 65, financed from annual contributions made by employers and employees. For example, a single premium of $171 paid on behalf of a male employee aged 35 would purchase a fully paid annuity of $4 monthly commencing at age 65. For a male employee aged 55, a $171 single premium would purchase a fully paid life annuity of only about $1.87 monthly, deferred to age 65.

Single premium annuities compose by far the larger share of annuities in force Nearly all group annuities are single premium annuities and

FIGURE 6–1

Basis for Annuity Classification

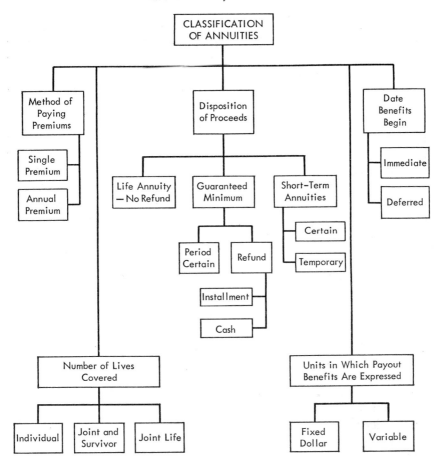

many individual annuities are acquired through cash values or maturity values of life insurance policies.

Annual Premium Annuities. Annual premium annuities are popular with purchasers of individual annuities when the annual amount budgeted for annuity premiums[4] is too small for the purchaser to qualify for single premium deferred annuities, or when the purchaser values the lifetime interest and mortality guarantees written into annual premium annuity

---

[4] Annuity rate structures favor single-premium deferred annuities over annual premium annuities. Thus, a series of single premium deferred annuities purchased at age 50 for a premium of $1,000 each year for 15 years would produce a retirement income at age 65 in excess of that produced by an annual premium annuity requiring a premium of $1,000 a year for 15 years if the rates on single premium annuities are not increased during the 15-year period.

contracts.[5] Under annual premium forms, the premiums are paid in periodic installments over the years prior to the date on which the annuity income begins.

The annual premium deferred annuity is a flexible instrument. It is usually written without forfeitures either at death or surrender during the deferred period. Consequently, there are no benefits for surviving the period. If the annuitant wishes to terminate his obligation to pay premiums, he may select a paid-up annuity for a reduced amount or withdraw the surrender value in cash. If he should die before the contract passes from the accumulation to the liquidation period, his beneficiaries are entitled to a death benefit equal to the cash value of the contract or the amount of premiums paid in, whichever is higher. The contract has one other feature giving it further flexibility: usually the annuitant may elect to have his income payments start earlier or postponed until later, with the necessary actuarial adjustment downward or upward in the amount of the benefit.

The annual premium annuity appeals to annuity purchasers who want the opportunity to purchase their full retirement annuity at today's rate. This opportunity could prove to be valuable if a medical breakthrough occurs that extends life expectancy beyond that projected in the mortality tables upon which this rate is computed, or if interest rates are allowed to fall and remain low over a long period.

A retirement annuity of $100 a month commencing at age 65 would cost a man aged 25 about $195 a year when written on a nonparticipating basis.

Disposition of Proceeds.   Annuities may be classified further on the basis of when the benefits stop. Under this classification are four types of annuities: the life annuity, no refund; the guaranteed minimum annuity; the annuity certain; and the temporary life annuity.

The Life Annuity, No Refund.   The life annuity, no refund frequently is called a straight life annuity. Under the straight life annuity the annuitant is paid an income throughout his lifetime, regardless of how long that may be. At his death, there is no further equity in the contract regardless of how few benefit payments might have been received. The straight life annuity is the purest form of annuity and offers the annuitant the largest income payment per dollar of purchase price.

The straight life annuity is used frequently in group plans but not often in individual annuity plans where the annuitant and his heirs might not understand how the insurance principle operates in annuities—failure to understand that some of the funds received as premiums from those who do not reach their life expectancy are used to pay incomes to those who live beyond their expectancy. The annuitant stands the chance of falling

---

[5] Insurance agents prefer to sell the annual premium annuity, not only because of their respect for guarantees, but also because commission rates paid on annual premium annuities are higher than on single premium annuities.

into either one of these classes. If he is willing to sacrifice his unused principal for the benefit of those annuitants who survive him, he, in turn, will benefit from the release of funds by those annuitants whom he survives. Thus the benefit of survival is greatest in the straight life annuity. Nevertheless, few annuitants want their principal fully dissipated in the event that death occurs soon after retirement.

Guaranteed Minimum Annuities. To meet the psychological and economic objections to the straight life annuity, two forms of guaranteed minimum annuities have been developed: period certain and refund. Refund annuities may be divided further into installment refund and cash refund.

Under a *life annuity, period certain contract,* the annuitant is promised an income for life but a minimum number of payments is guaranteed. For example, under a life annuity, 10 years certain contract, at least 120 payments (if written on a monthly basis) are paid regardless of whether the annuitant survives the guaranteed period. If the annuitant survives the guaranteed period, the annuity payments are continued until his death. If the annuitant dies during the guaranteed period the remaining number of guaranteed payments will be made to his beneficiary. Thus, under such an annuity, if the annuitant himself were to die at the end of the eighth year, the monthly benefits would be continued to his beneficiary for two more years, or the beneficiary may elect to take the commuted value of these payments in advance.[6] But if the annuitant lives for 20 years, payments will continue for that length of time. Upon his death after the period certain, all benefits and values terminate. The cost of this guarantee depends upon the age of the annuitant when benefits commence. For example, a 120-month guarantee for a female aged 65 would cost about 4.5 percent more than a no-refund annuity for the same monthly benefit. At age 55 the guarantee would cost about 1.2 percent more, whereas at age 45 the difference would be about 0.7 percent.

A *refund annuity* may be either an installment refund or a cash refund annuity. Under an *installment refund annuity* contract, the insurer promises to continue the periodic payments after the death of the annuitant until the combined benefits paid to the annuitant and his beneficiary have equaled the purchase price of the annuity. Under the *cash refund annuity* contract, the insurer agrees upon the death of the annuitant to return in cash the difference between benefits received and the purchase price paid. In either case, if the annuitant himself lives long enough to collect the purchase price in annuity income, payments continue as long as he lives, but upon his death all benefits and values terminate.

For example, a $100 a month installment refund annuity would cost

---

[6] To compute the commuted value the 24 monthly payments are discounted at the interest rate established by the company.

about $16,500 for a woman aged 65.[7] If she died after having received 100 installments, her beneficiary would be entitled to 65 more installments, making the total payout $16,500 which is the purchase price of the annuity. Instead of 65 monthly payments of $100 each, the beneficiary may elect to receive a lump-sum cash settlement equal to the present value of 65 monthly payments discounted at the interest rate set by the insurance company. If this were a cash refund annuity, the cost would be about $16,865.[8] In the event of the annuitant's death after having received 100 payments her beneficiary would be entitled to collect $6,865 in cash, thus completing the total payout of $16,865.

Life annuities certain and refund annuities often carry cash values equal, as a rule, to the discounted amount of the unpaid, guaranteed installments or cash refund.

The choice between a guaranteed minimum annuity and a life annuity, no refund depends upon two considerations: (1) the age at which the annuity payments are to start and (2) whether there is a need to provide for dependents in the event of the early death of the annuitant. The difference between the cost of a guaranteed minimum annuity and a straight life annuity is insignificant for annuities commencing at early ages. However, at later ages, the straight life annuity has significant cost advantages and should be given consideration unless there is a need for a refund to provide for dependents in the event of early death.

The Annuity Certain. The annuity certain is a contract which provides the annuitant with a given income for a specified number of years, independently of his life or death. Upon the termination of these years, the payments cease. Survival is not a factor. Therefore, if the annuitant should die before the expiry of the years indicated, the payments continue to the end of the stipulated period. This form of annuity is commonly used as a method of paying life insurance proceeds to a beneficiary under the fixed period or fixed amount settlement options.[9] For example, instead of having the proceeds of a $30,000 life insurance policy paid to the beneficiary in a lump sum, the insured could direct that a series of monthly payments of about $300 each be paid for 10 years. In this way, he can assure his beneficiary an income over a fixed period of years, perhaps long enough to cover the critical child development period or to allow the widow to make a less abrupt adjustment to a lower standard of living. If the beneficiary dies before she has received the income for the 10-year period, the payments are continued to a secondary beneficiary until the end of the 10-year period. The discounted value of these payments often is the settle-

---

[7] If this were a life annuity, no refund, the cost would have been only about $15,350. If this were a life annuity, 10 years certain, the cost would have been about $16,000.

[8] When the refund is made in cash instead of installments, interest on the monthly decreasing principal not yet paid is sacrificed by the company. Therefore, the cash refund is more expensive than the installment refund annuity.

[9] Cf. Chapter 11 for discussion of settlement options.

ment made with the secondary beneficiary. If the primary beneficiary survives the 10-year period, the payments are discontinued at that time.

Temporary Life Annuities. Temporary life annuities are similar to the annuity certain except that payments will cease upon the death of the annuitant. A 10-year temporary life annuity will provide monthly payments for 10 years or until the prior death of the annuitant, if earlier. These annuities are not popular, and, therefore, are rarely written. Their uses are limited. One use is to provide an income to fill a gap until an income from another source becomes available. For example, a widow aged 45 with no dependent children might purchase a 15-year temporary life annuity to provide herself with an income until her full social security benefits start at age 60, 15 years later.

The Date That Benefits Begin. Benefits may be payable immediately after the contract is purchased, or they may be deferred until a number of years later.

The Immediate Annuity. The immediate annuity is purchased with a single premium, and benefits begin at the end of the first income period. For example, a man aged 65 could purchase a nonparticipating, no-refund immediate annuity of $200 a month for about $26,000. The monthly benefit will begin one month after purchase. If benefits are to start at the beginning of the first income period, the annuity is called an *annuity due.* The annuity due is used when life insurance proceeds or cash values are distributed under settlement options. With the exception of settlement options under life insurance contracts, few immediate annuities are written on an individual basis. However, on a group basis, immediate annuities are used in connection with deposit administration plans in pension administration.[10]

Many companies writing immediate annuities establish a minimum age at which they will be written. These minimums range between age 1 to age 45. The most common minimum ages are 20 and 30. Sometimes a company will set a minimum age limit five years higher for women than for men.

When written as a straight life annuity, the immediate annuity is the simplest form of annuity contract. It provides for a regular payment throughout the lifetime of the annuitant, either annually, quarterly, or monthly. The first payment is made one year, three months, or one month after the date of purchase. Usually no proportionate payment is made for the fraction of a period from the date of the last regular payment to the date of death. There are no cash surrender values.

The Deferred Annuity. Under the deferred annuity which may be purchased with either a single premium or installment premiums, the benefit payments begin at the end of a given number of years or at optional ages established in the contract. Thus, for example, a man aged 44

---

[10] Cf. Chapter 19 for discussion of deposit administration plans in pension administration.

could purchase a $100 monthly installment refund annuity to begin at age 65 either with a single premium of $9,200 or a series of 21 annual premiums of slightly more than $600. Usually the deferred period is elected to correspond with the end of the annuitant's anticipated income-producing period. Unless the annuity is a pure deferred annuity (i.e., no payments if death occurs during the deferral period), the annuitant may shorten the deferred period, if he wishes, by accepting a smaller annuity. Thus, instead of $100 monthly at age 65, he can elect to take $59 a month at age 55 if he had purchased a single premium deferred annuity or $36 a month if he had purchased an annual premium deferred annuity. An age 50 starting date would reduce the annuities from the original $100 a month to about $47 and $16, respectively. The deferred period may also be lengthened under some deferred annuity contract, but usually only to a given maximum number of years beyond the maturity date, or to some maximum age. In annual premium annuities, if an extension is allowed, the contract usually provides that no premiums shall be payable on or after the maturity date. An extension of the deferred period, of course, produces a higher annuity payment. For example, an extension of the deferred period until the annuitant is age 70 would increase his annuity payment from $100 to about $113 monthly.

Under the annual-premium deferred annuity, if the annuitant wishes to discontinue his premium payments before the annuity matures, he may do so by agreeing to accept a smaller annuity at age 65. To illustrate, if the annuitant discontinues premium payments at age 54 he can elect to take a paid-up deferred annuity of about $55 a month commencing at age 65. If he discontinues premium payments at age 59, his paid-up annuity would amount to about $77 a month.

Deferred annuities have two periods: the deferred period and the liquidation or payout period. Minimum guarantees can be made available in one of these periods, in both, or in neither. For example, assume a single premium deferred annuity of $100 a month commencing at age 65 issued at age 25, male. The premium for this annuity would be only about $3,500 if it were written without any guaranteed minimums; that is, if no death benefits were payable during either the deferred period or the period of liquidation. If the annuity guaranteed a return of the premium or cash value, if greater, upon death during the deferred period but was written on a life income only, no refund basis during the period of liquidation, the premium would be about $4,500. But if the annuity not only guaranteed a return of premium or cash value at death or withdrawal during the deferred period but also guaranteed a minimum of 120 payments during the period of liquidation, the premium would be about $4,900. It is customary in writing deferred annuities on an individual basis to guarantee a refund at death or withdrawal during the deferred period.

However, it is common to find group annuities written with no death or withdrawal benefits before retirement. In both individual and group annuities, the choices of whether there is to be any guaranteed minimum during the period of liquidation and the nature of any such guarantees are left to the discretion of the annuitant. The annuity contract frequently allows the annuitant to make his choice on the question of guarantees during the period of liquidation any time before the annuity payout commences. Of course, the higher the guaranteed minimum selected, the lower will be the amount of each annuity payment.

Number of Lives Covered.   The usual annuity covers only one life. However, in some situations it is desirable to make annuity payments contingent upon several lives.

Joint and Last Survivor Annuity.   The most popular annuity covering more than one life is the joint and last survivor annuity. Under this contract, income is payable throughout the joint lifetimes of two or more annuitants and continues until the death of the last survivor. For example, a joint and last survivor annuity in the amount of $100 a month covering a man age 65 and his wife age 61 would cost about $19,750. This contract will pay $100 a month as long as either of them lives. In some contracts a provision is made for a reduction in income payments upon the death of the first annuitant, say a one-third reduction, with two thirds continuing to the survivor. Thus, if the adage that two can live as cheaply as one is rejected, the couple could arrange to have $114 a month paid during their joint lifetime and $76 a month during the lifetime of the survivor, instead of the level $100 a month as long as either of them is alive. The joint and last survivor annuity option is frequently offered in employee pension plans. It is also used as a method of receiving cash values or endowment proceeds of life insurance policies to provide husband and wife a guaranteed retirement income to both as long as either may live.

The Joint Life Annuity.   A type of annuity, not frequently written, is the joint life annuity which provides for payments that continue throughout the joint lifetimes of two people but cease upon the death of the first. No benefits are paid to the survivors. This type of annuity may be appropriate when there is an independent income sufficient to support one member of the family but insufficient to support both.

Units in Which Payout Benefits Are Expressed.   Annuities may be expressed in dollars or some other unit. When the annuity is expressed in dollars, it is called a fixed annuity. When it is expressed in units other than the dollar it is called a variable annuity.

The Fixed-Dollar Annuity.   Under the fixed-dollar annuity, commonly called a conventional annuity, the annuitant is guaranteed a fixed minimum number of dollars for each payout period. For example, a fixed-dollar annuity of $200 a month will pay $200 a month regardless of the value of these dollars.[11] No attempt is made to adjust the number of

---

[11] If the annuity is written on a participating basis, the amount of each payment might be higher than the guaranteed minimum amount.

dollars at each periodic payment to maintain an annuity of constant purchasing power. The fixed-dollar annuity is attractive to those who are willing to accept the risk of decreasing purchasing power brought on by inflation in return for a guaranteed fixed-dollar income for life.

The Variable Annuity. A growing number of people fear that the fixed-dollar annuity as a vehicle for building and liquidating a retirement income has become technically obsolete in view of what seems to them to be an economy geared to continued inflation. They ask how a 35-year-old man can determine today how many dollars he will need for a minimum retirement income 30 years from now? They point out that even a 65-year-old man would not find it easy to determine how many dollars he will need over his period of retirement. Realistic planning for financial security in the later years, they contend, requires a full appreciation of the need to provide a satisfactory income in terms of its purchasing power at the time it is to be spent.

When a contract seems to a large number of people to fall short of performing the function for which it has been designed, efforts will be made to develop one that will meet expectations. In 1952 the College Retirement Equities Fund (CREF) was created by a special act of the New York Legislature[12] as a nonprofit educational corporation to write variable annuities for employees of colleges and universities. The variable annuity was to be the new type of contract to supplement the fixed-dollar annuity as an instrument for financing retirement pensions. CREF's basic tenet is that, since equities tend in the long run to fluctuate with price levels, an annuity from which the payments are geared to the performance of common stocks is likely to be a useful vehicle for funding retirement plans, especially when combined with a fixed-dollar annuity.[13] And since retirement planning is a long-range operation, intermittent fluctuations in business activity have little significance because the long-run trend is toward a continued erosion of dollar values with each cyclical business peak higher than the last one.[14]

---

[12] *Laws New York 1952*, c. 124. CREF is subject to Arts. 1, 3, and 16 and Secs. 59, 66, 78, and 214 of the New York Insurance Law. CREF was organized by and is a subsidiary of the similarly nonprofit "TIAA," Teachers' Insurance and Annuity Association.

[13] The premise that benefit payments under a variable annuity will tend to vary directly with cost of living is derived from historical studies relating to "long-term" correlations in the movement of average prices of selected common stocks and cost-of-living indexes (see William C. Greenough, *A New Approach to Retirement Income* [New York: Teachers' Insurance and Annuity Association of America, 1951]). For a discussion of some strong economic arguments against the variable annuity see William A. Berridge, "Economic Facts Bearing on Some 'Variable Annuity' Arguments," *Journal of Insurance*, Vol. XXIV, No. 2 (November, 1957). For an appraisal of the pros and cons of the variable annuity see Robert I. Mehr, "The Erosion of Annuity Values," *Current Economic Comment*, Vol. XIX, No. 1 (February, 1957) (Bureau of Economic and Business Research, University of Illinois).

[14] Robert J. Meyers, chief actuary of the Social Security Administration, in commenting upon the CREF philosophy of combining the fixed and variable annuity to provide some hedge against both inflation and deflation, states: "While the combination method does have

In addition to the foregoing types of annuities, one more is available: the group annuity discussed in Chapter 19.

The various types of annuities described in this chapter are not mutually exclusive. Every annuity will have characteristics from each class. Thus, there can be a single premium, immediate, joint and last survivorship, refund, fixed-dollar annuity, or an annual premium, deferred life annuity, no refund, variable annuity.

Several other types of annuities or annuity combinations may be found. There are at least several companies that will write nearly any annuity combination anyone would want.

3. THE VARIABLE ANNUITY

The variable annuity seems to have become of age in 1966, at least as far as the Institute of Life Insurance is concerned. The Institute of Life Insurance is an organization of legal reserve life insurance companies serving the public as a central source of information about life insurance. The variable annuity had not been mentioned by the Institute in its annual *Fact Book* until its 1966 edition.

The Variable Annuity Principle. The variable annuity principle is based on the assumption that common stock prices and the cost of living will move in the same direction over the long run thus giving the annuitant a fairly stable amount of purchasing power. However, economic studies indicate that changes in the market prices of common stocks and changes in the cost of living are not perfectly correlated. The stock market is much more volatile than are price levels. For example, during the 5-year period 1961–1965, the *total* rise in consumer prices according to the Bureau of Labor Statistics was about 5.5 percent whereas the Standard and Poor's index of 500 common stocks rose about 52 percent. However, during the first 6 months of 1966 when consumer prices rose at an annual rate of 3.5 percent, the Standard and Poor's index of common stocks fell over 8.3 percent. And in 1969 during the 10-week period from the middle of May to the end of July, the Standard and Poor's index of 500 stocks fell nearly 16 percent while consumer prices were rising at an annual rate of nearly 7 percent. In the 1945–1948 period stocks fell about 7 percent while consumer prices rose about 3.3 percent and from 1948–1950 consumer prices were relatively stable but stock prices rose over 30 percent. In 1969, consumer prices rose 6.1 percent, the most inflationary year since 1951, but the S&P index of 500 stocks fell about 12.9 percent. Economic and financial history is full of similar examples. Because

some advantages in producing stability, the historical experience indicates that this was of relatively minor importance in comparison with the great advantage that the [variable] annuity would have had in keeping up with the cost of living." (*Transactions of the Society of Actuaries* [1952], IV, 772.)

of the volatility of common stocks some promoters of the variable annuity warn against committing all retirement funds to the variable annuity.

The argument for the variable annuity rests on the claim of a substantial long-term correlation between common stock averages and the cost of living and not upon any claim of a short-run correlation. Although both the cost of living and common stock values are affected by basic underlying economic factors, short-run swings in the market prices of common stocks are influenced by the market psychology of the time, and often are the work of short-term traders and of the excesses in the optimism or pessimism of emotional investors. The stock market is highly sensitive to economic and political news. Economic policies geared to restrain the upward movement in the cost of living often exert downward pressures on the level of common stock prices. For example, short-run swings in the prices of stocks are influenced by conditions in the money markets. When a tight money policy is followed many investors turn their attention away from the stock market to the bond market to take advantage of attractive current yields offered on high-grade bonds.

In the long run the stock market is responsive principally to anticipated changes in corporate profits and profit margins and not simply to the prospects of inflation. So when investors fear that rising costs, including wages, will reduce profit margins, the effect is likely to be a declining stock market in face of rising prices. Thus, if the inflation is of the cost push type rather than of the demand pull type, the investor, being uncertain of its final effect on corporate earnings, is likely to stay on the sidelines while his funds earn attractive yields elsewhere and wait for the picture to become clear or for stock prices to drop to levels he considers attractive. Those that conceived and developed the idea of the variable annuity have never offered the concept that common stocks can provide a quick hedge against sudden inflation. Viewing common stock averages from the long-term perspective, it is interesting to note that the Standard and Poor's index of 500 stocks could have dropped more than 43 percent in 1966 before reaching its June 26, 1962, low. While that 1962 low was nearly 39 percent below the December 12, 1961, high, it was more than 13 percent above the average levels of 1958. And when the Standard and Poor's index of 500 stocks reached 52.32 in late 1958, it was a new high, and more than 76 percent higher than the average levels four years earlier.

The concern for an annuity income that relates to a rising cost of living is not the only reason for interest in the variable annuity. Even were prices to remain stable, interest in the variable annuity would persist. Retired people may believe that they have a legitimate right to share in increased productivity, and, therefore, seek to have their annuity incomes relate to a rising standard of living. According to the United States Total Population Mortality tables, the life expectancy at age 65 is more than 14 years, and nearly 18 years at age 60. The standard of living in the United States has been improving. If price levels were to be stabilized, the purchasing power of a fixed dollar annuity will not be eroded but the annuitant's standard of living will be frozen to the level of his retirement income while the standard of living of productive workers gradually improves. For the 20-year period following World War II, *real* disposable income per capita increased at an average annual rate of about 1.5 percent, *real* personal consumption expenditures per capita rose at an average annual rate of about 2 percent, and the *real* average weekly earnings of production workers in manufacturing plants grew at an average annual rate of more than 1.7 percent.

Because consumer price levels rose at an average annual rate of more than 2.8 percent during this period, a person who retired in 1945 would have required an average annual increase of nearly 5 percent in his annuity income to keep pace with both the rising cost of living and the rising standard of living. The Standard and Poor's index of 500 stocks rose at an average annual rate of more than 9.4 percent over this period, rising at the average annual rate of 10.3 percent during the first 10 years and about 8.5 percent during the last 10 years. These increases are in addition to the dividends paid on these stocks during the period. Thus, the long-term performance of the stock market has produced gains sufficient to offset the erosion in purchasing power and to allow equity shareholders to participate in rising living standards.

Mechanics of the Variable Annuity.   The variable annuity contract is expressed in terms of units rather than in terms of fixed dollars. Two types of units are used: accumulation units and annuity units. When the annuitant pays his monthly premium he is credited with a number of accumulation units, the amount to be determined by the then current value of one unit. For example, if the monthly net premium is $50 and the current value of a unit is $10, he is credited with five units. If the current value of a unit is $9.52 when he pays his next $50 premium, he is credited with 5¼ accumulation units. If the value of the unit is $10.42 when he pays his third premium, he is credited with 4⅘ units. The method of establishing the value of the accumulation unit is fixed in the contract.[15]

When the annuitant reaches retirement age, annuity units are substi-

---

[15] The accumulation unit was valued initially at $10 by CREF. Over its first 18 years, the dollar value of the CREF accumulation unit fluctuated as follows:

Year	High	Low	Year	High	Low
1952	$10.52	$ 9.59	1961	$32.45	$28.54
1953	10.37	9.35	1962	30.67	22.53
1954	14.85	10.74	1963	30.83	26.80
1955	18.06	14.79	1964	33.96	31.55
1956	20.83	17.30	1965	39.08	34.83
1957	20.50	17.50	1966	39.68	33.80
1958	24.36	17.92	1967	43.78	38.55
1959	27.11	24.84	1968	47.67	39.34
1960	27.24	24.84	1969	45.25	40.19

tuted for accumulation units. The number of annuity units into which the accumulation units are converted is a function of the assumptions made with respect to mortality and investment return. Just as it is possible to use actuarial principles to determine that $13,000 of cash value accumulated under a conventional deferred annuity will pay a 65-year-old man a life annuity of $100 a month, it is also possible to use the same principles to determine that 13,000 units of something else—francs, trading stamps, bushels of corn, or simply abstract units as represented by the accumulations described here—will pay a man 65 years old a life annuity of 100 units a month. As with the accumulation unit, the method establishing the value of the annuity unit is a matter of contract.

The Accumulation Unit.   The accumulation unit is used as a statistical device to inform policyholders of the investment experience of the company and to report the nonforfeiture values of their policies.[16] However, significant differences exist among insurers as to the method to be used in establishing the value of the unit. The dollar value of the CREF accumulation unit varies monthly according to realized and unrealized capital gains and losses and to chargeable operation expenses.[17] It is computed by dividing the market value of the assets allocated to accumulation units by the number of accumulation units outstanding.[18] Income earned on the investment portfolio is reinvested and apportioned to the participants at the end of the fiscal year as additional accumulation units.[19]

---

[16] In order to assure that the policy will be used to provide retirement benefits, CREF does not allow cash or loan values in its contract. However, death benefits and paid-up retirement benefits are allowed in an amount equal to the value of the total number of units accumulated. Just as with the conventional fixed-dollar annual premium retirement annuity, the variable annuity contract issued by insurers other than CREF may be surrendered for its cash value before retirement. It also may provide for payment of the cash value in event of death before retirement and include the usual loan provision.

[17] A management contract with Teachers Insurance and Annuity Association (TIAA) currently fixes a charge for operating expenses at 1 percent of premiums. In renegotiation, this charge can be either raised or lowered, thus affecting the value of the accumulation unit. There is also a monthly charge to cover investment expenses. This charge is also subject to renegotiation. In 1968, for example, this charge was 0.07 percent of the first $500 million of the monthly mean assets plus 0.06 percent of the next $500 million of the monthly mean assets plus 0.03 percent of the monthly mean assets over $1 billion. The 1968 charge which amounted to 0.063 percent of mean monthly assets exceeded that produced by the 1967 and 1966 schedule of 0.07 percent of the first $250 million plus 0.04 percent of the next $250 million plus 0.03 percent of the excess of the monthly mean assets over $500 million. This latter schedule produced a charge of 0.05 percent of monthly mean assets in 1966 compared with the flat 0.07 percent charge in effect in 1965.

[18] This description is an oversimplified statement of the CREF accumulation unit valuation formula. For a technical discussion of the formula see Robert M. Duncan, "A Retirement System Granting Unit Annuities and Investing in Equities," *Transactions of the Society of Actuaries,* Vol. IV (1952), pp. 332–37.

[19] The usual practice is to include income earned on the investment portfolio in the unit valuation formula rather than apportion it to participants as additional accumulation units as does CREF. The advantage of reflecting portfolio investment earnings in the value of the unit is the illusion it gives of better performance than would appear if these earnings

The dollar value of the accumulation unit in most variable annuity plans varies weekly according to the net investment experience of the company. The usual plan is participating only as to investment performance, so unlike in CREF operating expenses do not enter into valuation formulas.

How the dollar value of the accumulation unit is computed in a typical plan is illustrated by the following formula:

$$CUV = PUV \; [1.000 + (d + c) - e] \, ,$$

where

CUV is the current unit value,

PUV is the previous unit value

d is the net interest and dividends earned per 1.000 at the beginning of the month after allowance for income taxes

c is the net capital gains (or losses) per 1.000 at the beginning of the month after allowing for income taxes, and

e is the investment expenses.

In determining the value of the current accumulation unit (CUV), the previous unit value (PUV) is multiplied by the net investment factor $[1.000 + (d + c) - e]$ for the valuation period which may be a day, week, or month. The net investment factor is 1.000 plus the adjusted gross investment rate ($d + c$) less an investment expense allowance (e). Assume a monthly valuation period. If capital losses caused the adjusted gross investment rate for the month to be minus 0.01, and the investment expense allowance is 0.0005 (i.e., one half of 1 percent monthly), the net investment rate would be ($-0.01 - 0.0005$) or minus 0.0105, and the net investment factor 1.000 — 0105, or 0.9895. If at the beginning of the month the value of the accumulation unit were $1, the value at the beginning of the next month would be $1 $\times$ 0.9895, or 98.95 cents. If the adjusted gross investment rate for this next month is plus 0.01, then the net investment rate becomes (0.0100 — 0.0005) or 0.0095 (assuming the same 0.0005 investment expense allowance), and the net investment factor (1.000 + 0.0005) or 1.0095. The value of the accumulation

were distributed as additional units. Declines in the market value of the investment portfolio are partially offset by investment earnings and gains in the market value are enhanced by investment earnings making the accumulation unit show the best value possible at all times. To the sophisticated purchaser it makes no difference how income earned on the investment portfolio is reflected. The concept of the accumulation unit is itself unnecessary since dollar values could be reported to the participants directly rather than through units. However, the unit concept is consistent with investment terminology (mutual fund shares, for example), and provides a useful handle for measuring performance.

unit for the following month would then be ($0.9895 × 1.0095) or 99.89 cents.

The Annuity Unit. When the participant reaches retirement age, two factors determine his dollar income: (1) the number of annuity units to which he is entitled and (2) the dollar value of each unit. The number of annuity units, once determined, remains the same throughout the annuity payout period, but the dollar value of each unit fluctuates by reflecting the investment performance of the portfolio supporting the annuity, and in some cases by reflecting mortality and expense experience.

The number of annuity units to which the participant is entitled is determined by dividing the dollar value of his accumulation units at retirement by the single premium for a life annuity in a monthly amount equal to the current dollar value of the annuity unit. For example, if the total cash value of the annuitant's accumulation units is $30,000, and the dollar value of each annuity unit is currently set at $9, a male annuitant at age 65 would receive a straight life annuity of 22.7 units computed as follows: The single premium for a straight life annuity of $9 a month beginning at male age 65 is $1,321.50 (Annuity Table for 1949, Projection Scale B, at 3½ percent).[20] This figure divided into $30,000 yields 22.7, which becomes the number of annuity units this annuitant has for the rest of his lifetime.[21] The income he receives in any given month will be 22.7 times the value of one annuity unit when that month arrives.

The value of an annuity unit, like that of an accumulation unit, initially is set arbitrarily. This value is changed periodically according to the terms of the contract. In 1952 CREF established the initial value of the annuity

---

[20] The Annuity Table for 1949, Projection Scale B, based on annuity mortality experience of insurance companies under individual contracts, projects mortality rates for each year after 1949, using the assumption that mortality rates at attained ages will decrease at a constant rate. The interest assumption of 3½ percent produces more annuity units of less value each than would a 3 percent assumption, and less units of more value each than would a 4 percent assumption. Thus, if the insurer had used a 3 percent assumption, the current value of the annuity would have been more than $9, but the annuitant would have received fewer units; if it had used a 4 percent assumption, the current annuity value would have been less than $9, but the annuitant would have received more units. Because the variable annuity fully participates in investment earnings it makes little difference to the participant, except for his initial payment, whether his insurer assumes 3 percent, 3½ percent, or 4 percent. The higher the assumed investment return, the higher will be the initial payment to the annuitant, and the higher must be the realized investment return to cause an increase in the unit value of the annuity. After the initial payment under the annuity the unit value will change to reflect the difference between the assumed investment return and the experienced rate of return.

[21] Some variable annuity contracts fix the amount of the first monthly payment to the annuitant by reference to what is simply a table of annuity values. Suppose that the table shows that $1,000 will provide a male annuitant aged 65 with $6.81 per month under a straight life annuity. The annuitant whose accumulation units are worth $30,000 will be entitled to $204.30 (30 × $6.81); and that would be his first month's payment. If the current value of 1 annuity unit at that time were $9, as was assumed above, the $204.30 would equal (204.30 ÷ 9) or 22.7 annuity units.

unit at $10.[22] The value has been changed on May 1 of each year to reflect changes as of March 31 in the market prices of the investments held by CREF, the dividend rates earned on these investments, the ratio of mortality experienced to mortality expected, and the ratio of expenses incurred to expenses expected.[23] The valuation formula for the annuity unit may be analyzed as follows:[24]

$$CA = PA \frac{(1 + d' + c')}{(1 + d)} \frac{(1 - q)}{(1 - q')} \frac{(E)}{(E')} ,$$

where

CA is the current annuity unit value,

PA is the previous annuity unit value,

d' is the investment income in terms of the annual rate,

c' is the capital gains (or losses) in terms of the annual rate

d is the assumed interest[25]

q is the death rate assumed for the past year[26]

q' is the actual death rate experienced for the past year,

E is the expenses assumed for the year, and

E' is the expenses incurred for the year.

Thus, for example, if the value of the annuity unit last year was $11, the dividend received 5 percent, the capital gain 10 percent, the death rate assumed 4 percent, the death rate incurred 6 percent, and expenses as

---

[22] The annuity year (May through April) value of the CREF annuity unit has been as follows:

1952	$10.00	1961–62	$26.25
1953–54	9.46	1962–63	26.13
1954–55	10.74	1963–64	22.68
1955–56	14.11	1964–65	26.48
1956–57	18.51	1965–66	28.21
1957–58	16.88	1966–67	30.43
1958–59	16.71	1967–68	31.92
1959–60	22.03	1968–69	29.90
1960–61	22.18	1969–70	32.50
		1970–71	28.91

[23] CREF contracts to pay TIAA 1.3 percent of each annuity payment as an expense charge. This fee is subject to change on renegotiation.

[24] One factor in the CREF operations has been eliminated from this formula for purposes of simplification. Since annuity unit values are changed only once a year, whereas investment results change throughout the year, it is necessary at the end of the year to make adjustments in the formula to give effect to the result experienced by maintaining a constant unit value throughout the year (see R. Duncan, *op. cit.*, pp. 338–39).

[25] CREF uses a 4 percent interest assumption.

[26] CREF uses the Annuity Table for 1949, Projection Scale B discussed in Footnote 20 above, and in Chapter 24.

projected, the current value of the annuity unit would be $12.42 computed as follows:

$$CA = \$11 \frac{(1 + 0.05 + 0.10)}{(1 + 0.04)} \frac{(1 - 0.04)}{(1 - 0.06)} (1) \text{ or } \$12.42.$$

The annuitant who holds 10 annuity units would then collect $124.20 a month for the next 12 months. If during these months CREF earns less than 4 percent, incurs a net capital loss, and experiences less mortality than projected, the value of the annuity unit for the following year will fall,[27] and the annuitant's dollar income will be less than $124.20 for the following year.

In contrast to CREF, under most variable annuity plans the value of the annuity unit is computed weekly, and in some plans monthly, rather than annually. Also mortality rates and expense rates are guaranteed in the annuity contract so that the value of the annuity unit fluctuates only to the extent that the net investment rate deviates from the rate of interest assumed in computing the annuity values.[28] When the annuity unit is valued in this manner, the formula is as follows:

$$CA = PA \frac{(1 + d' + c' - e').[29]}{(1 + d)}$$

Note that this formula considers only the net investment experience of the company and does not concern itself with either mortality or expense experience. If the assumed rate of interest is 3.5 percent annually or its monthly equivalent of 0.29 percent, the monthly determined value of an annuity unit would be computed by multiplying the value of the annuity unit at the end of the preceding month by the product of 0.9971 and the net investment factor.[30]

---

[27] Of course, a combination of circumstances involving greater dividend earnings than expected, a net capital loss, and greater mortality than expected would either increase or decrease the annuity unit value, depending on the predominating factor or factors.

[28] To guarantee mortality means to pay survivorship benefits equal to at least those produced under the specified mortality table. To guarantee expenses means to charge the annuitant no more for expenses than the guaranteed maximum. When the insurer guarantees mortality and expenses, it uses conservative mortality and expense assumptions. The common mortality table used is the Progressive Annuity Table which is based on the Annuity Table for 1949, Projection Scale B, from which a generation table was developed to reflect progressive mortality improvements from generation to generation (Cf. Chapter 24). Normally the ages are set back 1 year for each 25 to allow for mortality improvements among generations, however, a number of insurers seeking additional conservatism (or additional profits) set back the table 1 year for each 10 or 15.

[29] The code of translation for these symbols is the equivalent of those used in describing the CREF valuation formula. The symbol e' is investment expenses.

[30] The use of the factor 0.9971 allows for the 0.29 percent monthly equivalent of the 3.5 percent annual rate assumed in the actuarial computation of the annuity value. The value of the annuity unit fluctuates only if the net investment factor is greater or less than 0.29 percent.

Why the Variable Annuity?   The variable annuity is aimed at meeting two objectives: (1) to give the annuitant an income which will relate, at least to some extent, to variations in the cost of living; and (2) to give the annuitant an opportunity to share in the expected growth of living standards.

Studies have shown that in a growing economy, investments in common stocks have yielded returns over the long run higher than those produced by investments in fixed-dollar securities.[31] The record shows that the cost of living (depreciation in the purchasing power of the dollar) and the standard of living (the amount of goods and services that an employee can purchase with his after-tax earned income) also have been rising.

The case for the variable annuity rests upon affirmative answers to two questions: (1) is it reasonable to expect common stock investments over the long-run future to continue to outperform investments in fixed-dollar securities; and (2) can inflation and rising standards of living, one or both, be expected to continue into the long-term future?

Common Stocks versus Fixed-Dollar Investments.   Dr. William Greenough, chairman of TIAA–CREF believes "that . . . while production, profits, and prices will continue to fluctuate, economic growth, not decline, will continue to characterize the long-term trend of American economic life. And . . . the country's economic growth will be reflected in the investment experience of a diversified portfolio of common stocks of companies with prospects of effectively shaping and adapting to future changes in technology and demand."[32]

However, some students of investments question whether the financial climate will continue to favor common stocks over the long run to the degree that it has in the recent past. Some money market analysts expect sophisticated lenders to demand and receive a premium for the purchasing power risk that they must take in making fixed-dollar commitments in an economy where inflation appears to be becoming institutionalized.

If this proves to be the case, the fixed-dollar investment might perform relatively better in the future than in the past, when compared with the performance of common stocks. In such an event, when annuity pricing reflects these financial changes, through the use of higher interest assumptions in developing annuity purchase rates, the fixed-dollar annuity with its principal and interest guarantees might regain some of its lost appeal as an instrument for funding retirement income. Some of those who recently have been more fearful of the probable long-term upward fluctuation in the price level than of any possible long-term downward fluctuation

---

[31] See, for example, two works of William C. Greenough, *A New Approach to Retirement Income, op. cit.,* and "CREF and the Variable Annuity's First Fifteen Years" in *Pension and Welfare News,* August, 1967, pp. 17–20. There are, of course, numerous other studies of the performance of common stocks. For example, see Sylvan C. Coleman, "Inflation and the Stock Market in the Past 50 Years Here and Abroad," the *Commercial and Financial,* November 3, 1966.

[32] *Pension and Welfare News, op. cit.,* p. 20.

in the movement of common stock prices might reappraise the relative risks involved between the purchase of variable annuities and fixed-dollar annuities. They might decide that the higher guaranteed return on fixed-dollar annuities is sufficient to compensate for the purchasing power risk involved in its ownership and that the reduced differential anticipated between returns on common stock investments and fixed-dollar investments is insufficient to compensate for the financial risk involved in the ownership of variable annuities.

But for the present, at least, an increasing number of annuity buyers see in the variable annuity an opportunity to share in a growing economy and to protect themselves against the erosion of annuity values throughout both the accumulation and liquidation period of the annuity contract. They base their judgment on the performance of variable annuities over the past few years. Using the experience of CREF as an example, a person investing $100 a month from January 1, 1953, through December 31, 1968, would have earned an average annual rate of return of 9.04 percent. During this same period, consumer prices rose at an average annual rate of 2.2 percent, and per capita personal consumption expenditures expressed in constant dollars (1957–59 dollars), a good measure of the standard of living, increased at an average annual rate of about 4 percent.[33] Thus, participants in CREF have enjoyed full protection against inflation and a full stake in the growth in living standards with a significant margin to spare as an additional investment return. Of course, different starting dates and ending dates yield different results, but figures for any long-term period would produce highly acceptable results.[34]

The CREF Annuity Unit had an initial value in 1952–53 of $10, and by 1968–69 it had increased to $29.90, an average annual increase of about 7 percent. However, the growth of the value of CREF Annuity Unit has not been steady. For example, in 1956–57, it was $18.51, but fell to $16.88 in 1957–58, and to $16.71 in 1958–59. In 1961–62, it was $26.25, but fell to $26.13 in 1962–63, and to $22.68 in 1963–64. It was $31.92 in 1967–68 but fell to $29.90 in 1968–69. One might ask, did the cost of living move down in the years 1957–59, 1962–64, and 1968–69? On the contrary, prices rose by about 5 percent between 1957 and 1959, just under 2 percent between 1962 and 1964, and about 4.5 percent from 1967–68 to 1968–69, as measured by the consumer price index. Do these counter movements damage the case for the variable annuity? The low of 1958–59 was well above the high of $14.11 in 1955–56, the low of 1963–64 was above the $22.18 high of 1960–61, and the 1968–69 low was above the 1965–66 high of $28.21. The amount of a fixed-dollar

---

[33] U.S. Department of Labor, Bureau of Labor Statistics, *Consumer Price Index* published in the Monthly Labor Review, and *Employment and Earnings* Monthly with Annual Supplement. Calculations were made by the author.

[34] Cf. *1968 Annual Report,* TIAA-CREF, p. 22.

annuity based on long-term accumulations and liquidations would have been very much lower than the lows produced by any of these setbacks.

In musing about the record of CREF (and other variable annuity plans) the question of whether the past is a key to the future is likely to arise. Reflecting on this issue, Dr. Greenough, after 15 years of experience with CREF, observed:

When TIAA proposed the formation of CREF back in 1952, some people said the idea was good but the timing bad. Common stock prices had more than doubled in the preceding ten years and the market was just "too high" to start out on the CREF venture. We didn't agree. And we wouldn't agree if we were starting CREF now when common stock prices are 3½ times their 1952 levels. What the "prices are too high" argument overlooks is that when funds are being invested regularly over many years, the level of prices at any one point in time is quite unimportant. As the individual's funds are invested at many prices, the effect of fluctuations are ironed out; the return credited to him over the years reflects primarily the earnings record and prospects of the companies in which his funds are invested.[35]

Inflation, Growth, and the Future. Is it logical to expect inflation to continue into the long-run future? As to the desirability of a gently rising price level, distinguished economists are to be found on either side of the issue, some arguing that rising prices are essential to the maintenance of full employment and others arguing, in defense of a policy of price stability, that rising prices do increasing harm to the economy.[36] Regardless of the widespread differences in opinion among economists as to what ought to be the government's policy toward price levels, there appears to be more of a consensus among economists that the economy has built-in inflationary biases that are not likely to falter.

Barring major wars, there seems no reason to expect that the American economy will experience enough excess demand to produce "serious inflation." The prospect is rather that our price level will rise a bit during each prosperity period, level off during recession, and rise once more during the next boom. . . . Its result is a gradual upward drift of prices over the long run.[37]

However, the case for the variable annuity does not rest solely on the need for a hedge against inflation. The trend in living standards is also fundamental to the consideration of the variable annuity. Is it reasonable to expect significant increases in standards of living in the long-term future? In their book *Toward the Year 2,000: A Framework for Speculation,* Herman Kahn and Anthony Wiener project per capita personal

---

[35] *Pension and Welfare News, op. cit.,* p. 20.

[36] See, for example, Alvin H. Hansen, "The Case for High-Pressure Economics," and Henry C. Wallich, "The Case Against High-Pressure Economics" in E. S. Phelps, B. Balassa *et al.* (eds.), *Problems of the Modern Economy* (New York: W. W. Norton and Company, Inc., 1966).

[37] Lloyd G. Reynolds, *Economics* (Homewood, Illinois: Richard D. Irwin, Inc., 1966), p. 600.

consumption expenditures through the year 2020.[38] Starting with a per capita personal consumption expenditure in 1965 of $2,220, these expenditures, based on 1965 dollars, are projected as follows:

Per Capita Personal Consumption Expenditure

	1975	1985	2000	2020
Low	$2,600	$3,150	$4,400	$ 6,400
High	3,000	4,250	7,000	13,600

Starting with $3,500 in 1965, these writers project per capita GNP in 1965 dollars as follows:

Per Capita GNP

	1975	1985	2000	2020
Low	$4,150	$5,000	$ 6,850	$ 9,550
High	4,800	6,650	11,550	21,250

And they project an increase in mean after-tax family income rising from $7,580 in 1965 to the following figures for the year 2000 (in 1965 dollars).

Low	$14,510
Medium	$19,360
High	$24,190

Kahn and Wiener's projections are based upon what they consider to be reasonable assumptions relating to total hours worked and the amount of GNP generated by each hour of work. In their projections they assume that productivity will rise 2.5 percent a year in their low forecast and at 4 percent a year in their high forecast. They project the total population for each year, the percent of the population employed, and the number of hours in a work year. For the year 2,000, for example, the population was estimated at 318 million, the work force at 38 percent, and the work year at 1,600 hours. Even the low projections indicate significant future increases in living standards.

Assuming long-term growth in the prices of common stocks, a rising consumer price level, and a steady increase in living standards, variable annuities have become an acceptable financial instrument for those who seek to maintain the purchasing power of their savings and to assure themselves of a stake in a growing economy, if they are willing to accept the financial risks involved in an equity investment.

---

[38] New York, N.Y., Macmillan Company, 1967.

Drawbacks of the Variable Annuity.   There are at least two sets of drawbacks to the variable annuity, one economic and the other psychological.

An economic objection is that the cost of living of any one individual will not necessarily fluctuate directly with the Consumer Price Index. The Consumer Price Index is based on averages while the cost of living of any given person is based on his personal expenses, which may not contain in the same proportion each of the items used in computing the Consumer Price Index. For instance, the housing cost of a person who purchased a home during a period of depressed prices will not rise exactly with the CPI in which housing costs are figured at the "going rate." Similarly, the cost of living of an individual who bought a home in times of high prices will not drop exactly with the CPI. He still has his fixed monthly mortgage payments to meet. Thus, the variable annuity, even if it exactly followed the CPI, could never exactly keep pace with the cost of living of any particular individual. Also, a variable annuitant with heavy fixed-dollar obligations acquired in times of high prices could be left with a serious deficit if his income fell directly with price averages. Another economic objection is the unwillingness of some people to expose their retirement funds to the financial risks inherent in equity investments.

A psychological objection to the variable annuity is displayed in the attitude of people toward the fluctuating dollar. A man who invests $1,000 and gets back $1,500 over a period when prices rise by more than 50 percent is far less disturbed than if he had invested $1,000 and got back only $800 over a period when prices fell by 25 percent. Although he would be happier in the former case because he is better adjusted to it psychologically, in the latter case he might be better off economically. Since the variable annuity is designed to provide more dollars for retirement income when prices are high, at the risk of reducing the number of dollars when stock prices fall, its purchasers must be psychologically attuned to the idea of a downward movement in their dollar incomes.

In the final analysis the question of whether the variable annuity should be purchased is an individual matter. If the annuitant wishes a guaranteed fixed-dollar income and is willing to accept the risk of decreased purchasing power brought on by inflation, then he will purchase the fixed-dollar annuity. If he does not want to rely on the stability of the dollar and is willing to have his money income fluctuate in the hope that, as a result, his real income will increase he will purchase a variable annuity. If he wishes to achieve the advantages of both the fixed-dollar and the variable annuity (and is willing to accept the disadvantages of both) he will purchase some of each in the proportion that he feels gives him the greatest security. During the first 14 years of CREF, participants were not permitted to allocate more than 50 percent of their annuity premiums to the variable annuity: at least 50 percent had to be paid to TIAA for a fixed-dollar annuity. However, beginning January 1, 1967, CREF permitted an allocation of 75 percent of retirement annuity premiums to be made to the variable annuity. The purpose of the change in rules was to allow greater flexibility. It was "not to urge . . . members to increase their allocation to CREF. The fixed-dollar annuity and the variable annuity complement each other and work well together."[39] Other writers of the variable annuity do not require that the variable annuity be purchased in combination with a fixed-dollar annuity.

4. USES OF ANNUITIES

When a man reaches that stage in life when he can no longer earn his living and if he wishes to be financially independent, he must live on earnings he has accumulated from the past. Unless that fund is large enough to provide a sufficient income from interest and dividends alone, it will have to be liquidated to supplement the periodic income. As the principal is reduced, income will decline making it necessary to liquidate the fund at an increasing rate if a steady periodic payment is to be maintained. The fund eventually will expire. If the liquidator expires before the fund, there will be no financial problem. However, there is the possibility that the fund will expire before the liquidator, leaving an old man without an income. It is the function of the annuity to protect against this peril.

To Fund a Retirement Income.   The fundamental purpose of an annuity is to provide a vehicle for the scientific liquidation of capital over the years of retirement. It is to assure a person an income he cannot outlive as well as an income in excess of that to be derived from investing the cost of the annuity in high-grade interest bearing or dividend yielding securities. The application of the annuity principle can be used to liquidate an estate created through life insurance contracts, investments in stocks and bonds, savings accounts, real estate, or through the annuity contract itself. As long as there is a fund available the annuity principle may be used as an instrument for its liquidation. Because of high prices, high taxes, and the strong desire to live it up, more people than ever are faced with the problem of capital creation, not with the idea of preserving it for their heirs, but to finance a livable income for their old age by liquidating it systematically through the annuity principle.

To Liberate Funds for Immediate Use.   Even when a fortune large enough to provide a livable income from investment return alone has been accumulated, its owner might find a use for the annuity. The substitution of an annuity income for a direct investment income can free some capital for other uses without reducing the amount of income. For example, it takes a capital sum of $100,000 invested at 6 percent to provide an income of $500 a month. However, an income of $500 a month can be provided

---

[39] 1966 Annual Report TIAA-CREF, p. 19.

for a man aged 65 through a single premium life annuity for about $65,000, releasing $35,000 for other purposes. Some or all of the released capital can be used by the annuitant to finance a philanthropic interest or to pass on to heirs at a time when the money might do them the most good. The one problem is the possibility that inflation might make inroads on the purchasing power of this fixed income, as it will on any other fixed-income investment. However, the variable annuity can be used if the annuitant prefers to reduce the purchasing power risk at the expense of giving up the fixed-dollar guarantees and accepting the financial and market risk.

Although under the annuity plan coupled with living gifts, the annuitant's philanthropic interests and heirs will not receive as much money as they would receive if he were to pass the total $100,000 on at his death, they will receive the money earlier. Moreover, the annuitant will be absolutely certain that his money will go where he wants it to go, something he might not be sure of if it is left to be distributed under a will. Investment default might destroy the capital, and wills often are attacked by relatives. Outright gifts by the individual during his lifetime rarely can be contested. Also, there may be tax advantages of making living gifts as distinguished from transfers at death.[40]

Tax Appeals. Because only a part of the annuity payments received each year is subject to income taxation, the annuity has appeal to some investors. In order to determine the amount of annuity income to be reported for federal income tax purposes, an exclusion ratio first must be found. The exclusion ratio is determined by dividing the investment in the contract at the annuity starting date by the expected return under the contract. This "expected return" is based on what the Treasury Department judges to be the life expectancy of the annuitant at the time the annuity begins. It is found by multiplying the annual return by a multiple obtained from tables established by Treasury regulation. The exclusion ratio is applied to the total annuity income received during the taxable year. All annuity income in excess of this amount must be included as gross taxable income.

Assume that the investor referred to above purchases the $500 monthly annuity at age 65. How will these payments be taxed? According to the annuity tables put out by the United States Treasury Department, the life expectancy of a male aged 65 is 15 years. This makes the expected return $90,000 (15 × $6,000). The purchase price of $65,000 represents 72.22 percent of the $90,000 expected return. Therefore, 72.22 percent of each year's annuity income is viewed by the Internal Revenue Service as a return of invested capital and 27.78 percent is considered taxable income.

---

[40] Gift tax rates are lower than estate tax rates, and a liberal amount can be given away tax free. Also, since the gift tax rates and the estate tax rates are progressive, a taxable gift takes property from high estate tax brackets and places it in lower gift tax brackets. Cf. Chapter 21 for a discussion of estate and gift taxes.

Thus, in this example only $1,667 a year is reportable as income, whereas the entire $6,000 is subject to income taxation under the direct investment plan. Where the investor is in high surtax brackets, the annuity can offer an income tax advantage.[41]

Purchase of the annuity for $65,000 also reduces the gross estate for estate tax purposes. If the *taxable* estate before the annuity was purchased had a value of $200,000, the federal estate tax would amount to $50,700 under present tax rates. The purchase of the $65,000 annuity would reduce the taxable estate to $135,000 and reduce the federal estate tax liability to $31,200. The resulting tax saving is $19,500. There may be additional savings in state death taxes.[42]

The deferred annuity also has income tax advantages during the period of accumulation. The investment earnings are not reportable as income during the year earned. Instead, they are used to reduce the purchase price of the annuity in calculating the income tax exclusion ratio at the time of distribution. The effect is to postpone the tax until the period of retirement when income is likely to be lower, the retirement credit may be available, and the double exemption is allowed.

5. LIMITATIONS OF ANNUITIES

While annuities have a number of legitimate uses, they are not without their limitations. For a number of people these limitations outweigh the benefits.

Expenditure of Capital. For psychological and sometimes economic reasons, old people may not like to use up their capital in providing themselves with a retirement income. Some are content to live on an income well below that available with an annuity in order that they may conserve their estates.

Entire Risk Not Shifted. In any discussion of the limitations of annuities there must be a clear separation between the fixed-dollar annuity and the variable annuity. Unfortunately, the purchaser of an annuity cannot shift the entire retirement risk to which he is exposed. If he buys the fixed-dollar annuity he assumes the purchasing power risk. If he purchases the variable annuity, he assumes the financial risk—the risk of adverse investment results. While this risk might well be minimized by the insurance company, through a well-managed diversified investment portfolio, it cannot be eliminated entirely. In addition, even with the purchase of the variable annuity, the annuitant has no protection against

---

[41] That the three elements of annuity income are investment income, capital liquidation, and survivorship benefit was explained early in the chapter. The taxing authorities prefer to view investment income as a level amount and lump capital and survivorship as the expected return.

[42] Chapter 21 discusses the gift tax implications involved if a living transfer of $35,000 is made according to the illustration presented in the previous section.

the short-run purchasing power risk and no guarantee of protection against the long-term purchasing power risk. However, he does have a high expectation of long-term protection not only against the purchasing power risk but also against the failure of his standard of living to keep pace with the economic growth of the country.

7

Special Purpose Policy Plans

While functionally there are only three types of life insurance policies (term, whole life, and endowment), these basic forms can be combined or modified in a variety of ways to produce special purpose policy forms.[1]

Nearly every life insurance company offers several types of special purpose plans. Some of these plans are designed to meet a particular life insurance need; unfortunately others seem to have as their purpose some peculiar sales gimmick not at all related to life insurance needs. To attempt to discuss this latter type of policy is beyond the scope of this book; there are literally hundreds of them. Only the common special purpose plans are discussed in this chapter.

1. SPECIAL PURPOSE ADULT POLICIES

Family Income Policy. One of the most widely offered special purpose plans is the family income policy. Under this policy the beneficiary is paid a fixed monthly income upon the death of the insured until the end of a specified period that began when the policy was issued. Although the names family income policy and family income rider are widely used, some companies select trade names for their family income plans, calling them "income protector," "income security," "family security," and the like. However, it cannot be assumed that all policies named family security, for example, are family income policies.

The family income period is usually 10, 15, or 20 years. If a man aged 25 purchases a 20-year family income policy and dies at age 28, his beneficiaries will receive a monthly income for 17 years, the balance of the 20-year family income period. If he buys a 15-year family income policy and dies at age 39, his beneficiary will receive a monthly income for 1 year, the balance of the 15-year family income period.

Types of Family Income Protection. If a man wants to arrange for a monthly income to be paid to his family for a period starting with his death and ending on a specified date, he has three ways in which he can

---

[1] The annuity also is combined with life insurance to offer some special policy plans.

accomplish the objective through life insurance: the family income policy, the family income rider, and the monthly decreasing term insurance policy.

The traditional family income policy is an integrated package policy composed of an indivisible combination of continuous premium whole life insurance with monthly decreasing term insurance. A family income rider is monthly decreasing term insurance designed to be added to any form of permanent insurance.[2] And, monthly decreasing term insurance can be purchased as a separate policy to provide the desired family income protection.

Under the traditional family income package policy or the basic policy–rider combination, when the insured dies during the family income period the proceeds of the permanent insurance are held at interest until the end of the family income period, at which time they will be paid in one sum or distributed under one of the settlement options available under the policy. In the meantime the interest on these proceeds provides part of the family income payments and the proceeds from the decreasing term insurance provide the rest. The amount of the family income payable in the package or combination policy is usually expressed as a percentage of the face amount of the permanent insurance, usually 1 percent; although family incomes up to 5 percent of the face amount of the permanent insurance are available.[3] A 1 percent $10,000 family income policy will pay $100 a month for the family income period remaining after the death of the insured.

Unlike the traditional family income policy, in some plans the interest on the face amount of the permanent insurance is not programmed to provide part of the family income payments. When the family income payments are independent of the proceeds of the permanent insurance, these proceeds become payable to the beneficiary immediately upon the death of the insured as a cash sum or under one of the settlement options. However, the traditional form requires a higher premium.

For example, in one insurer the annual premium for a traditional $10,-000, 1 percent 20-year family income policy issued at age 25 is quoted at $160.70. Under the policy, if the insured is alive at the end of the 20-year family income period, the premium is reduced by $31.40.[4] If the insured dies during the family income period, $100 a month is payable until the end of the period then the $10,000 of permanent insurance becomes pay-

---

[2] Usually the family income rider may be used with any permanent policy form of longer premium payment duration than the family income period. Some companies will allow the use of the family income rider with a level term form of longer duration than the decreasing term. When family income is written as one integrated package policy, the basic insurance is usually continuous premium whole life or some practical equivalent, such as paid up at 85.

[3] Increasing the monthly income written with the permanent insurance simply is a matter of raising the amount of decreasing term insurance written with the plan.

[4] In a number of companies, the premium for the decreasing term rider or term portion of the integrated package is for a period shorter than the family income period. For example, in one company the premium for a 20-year 1 percent $10,000 traditional family income policy issued at age 25 is quoted at $172.60 payable annually for 16 years at which time the premium is reduced by $37.90 annually for the life of the policy.

able. Each $100 monthly payment is made up of $20.60 interest at 2½ percent on the $10,000 of permanent insurance held by the insurer until the end of the family income period, and $79.40 from the proceeds at decreasing term insurance liquidated as an annuity certain. In another company, the annual premium for a nontraditional $10,000 1 percent 20-year family income policy issued at age 25 is quoted at $178.60. If the insured is alive at the end of the 20-year family income period, the premium is reduced by $44.20. If the insured dies during the family income period, $100 a month is payable to his family until the end of the period but the $10,000 of permanent insurance is payable immediately upon the death of the insured. The full $100 monthly is paid from the proceeds of the decreasing term insurance settled as an annuity certain. Because the traditional family income package requires less term insurance it can be written at a lower premium. The term insurance has to provide only $79.40 a month.

In the traditional family income policy where the payment of the proceeds of the permanent insurance is deferred until the end of the income period, in some policies the beneficiary is given the option to take the permanent insurance in cash at the death of the insured, but such election will reduce the monthly income.[5] Under many family income plans, the beneficiary is allowed to collect the commutation amount of all income together with the basic proceeds at the time of death of the insured.[6]

While it is customary for the family income to be arranged through the traditional family income policy combining indivisible (and invisible) continuous premium whole life insurance and monthly decreasing term insurance or through the use of a family income rider added to a form of whole life or endowment insurance, it is possible to purchase family income protection in some companies as simply monthly decreasing term insurance involving no permanent coverage. In one company, for example, the annual premium for a 20-year monthly decreasing term policy issued at age 25 providing a monthly income of $100 is $49.70.[7] If the insured outlives the family income period, the monthly decreasing term insurance expires without value. In some companies the premiums are payable for the full 20 years whereas in other companies they are payable for only 16 years.

---

[5] As an example, in one specific $10,000 basic family income plan with a 1 percent income clause or rider, if the $10,000 is taken in a lump sum at the death of the insured, the monthly income will be reduced from $100 to $79.40.

[6] For a typical example: If the insured should die at the end of five years after taking a $10,000, 20-year family income plan, the beneficiary who commutes and takes a lump sum will receive $23,000 instead of $100 a month for 15 years and $10,000 at the end of that time. Usually the policy provides that either withdrawal of the basic sum or commutation of the term portion can be elected by a beneficiary only if the insured has, during his lifetime, given the beneficiary the right to elect that option or options in the policy. Some family income policies provide a small cash benefit at death and then the permanent insurance benefit at the expiration of the family income period.

[7] Some companies call this monthly decreasing term policy a family income policy and sell it in units, usually of $10 of monthly benefits with a minimum number of units to be sold fixed at, say, five units. This is like Alice, for after all, a decreasing term policy could be called a rainbow policy. But regardless of how its proceeds are used, it is still nothing but plain simple monthly decreasing term insurance.

Under some family income plans, the term insurance portion of the coverage is convertible to whole life or endowment insurance. However, the amount that can be converted is restricted to the amount of decreasing term still in force at the conversion date.

Uses of Family Income Insurance. The family income plan is designed primarily to produce a high level of income for a moderate cost during the years when the children are growing up. The cost of providing the same income with permanent insurance alone might be prohibitive for some families. It takes about $21,600 of proceeds to produce an income of $120 a month for 20 years. On a continuous premium whole life plan this amount of insurance in one company would require an annual non par[8] premium at age 25 of $289.74.[9]

On the other hand, in the same company, a traditional 1 percent $12,000 family income policy issued at age 25 would cost $192.84 annually. Under this policy, the insurer will pay the beneficiary $120 a month from the date of the death of the insured until the end of the 20 years from the date the policy is issued. In addition, the face amount of the permanent insurance will be paid to the beneficiary at the end of this period. If the wife is the beneficiary and she is 45 at the time the family income payments stop, the $12,000 proceeds of the permanent insurance will provide her a minimum guaranteed monthly income of $82.44 until her social security benefits start.

If the $120 a month family income is provided with a 3 percent family income rider added to $4,000 of continuous premium whole life insurance, the plan could be purchased at age 25 in one company for an annual premium of $113.04.[10] The $4,000 of permanent insurance payable at the end of the family income period would provide the 45-year-old widow only $27.48 a month until her social security benefits start.

If the $120 a month family income is provided with 12 units of a simple monthly decreasing term policy paying $10 per unit until the end of the family income period, the cost would be $59.64 annually at age 25. Of course there will be nothing payable under this plan at the end of the family income period to provide the widow an income until her social security benefits start.

The principal use of a family income plan as a risk management device is the opportunity these plans offer the insured to purchase at the lowest possible cost the protection he needs against income loss caused by premature death for the period that this income is most likely to have its greatest utility. Which type of plan, the simple monthly decreasing term

---

[8] Nonpar is used to simplify the figures. If participating rates are used, it then becomes necessary to point out that dividends can be expected to reduce the premium in future years.

[9] This figure is taken from the rate book of a company which grades premiums by use of a flat per policy addition of $9. The premium per $1,000 would be $13.09 exclusive of the flat per policy addition.

[10] The flat per policy addition used by this company is $10 and the premium per $1,000 of continuous premium whole life is $12.40 exclusive of the policy fee. The cost of the $30 rider is $13.36 per unit.

policy, the integrated traditional family income policy, the nontraditional family income policy in which the family income benefits are independent of the permanent insurance, or one of the family income riders added to a whole life or endowment policy offers the best balance between benefits and costs depends upon what after-the-loss resources he wishes to arrange for in addition to an income during the family period. For family income alone, the simple monthly decreasing term form will suffice but for cash needs at death or other income needs, including retirement, one of the combination forms is needed with emphasis placed on that basic policy which supplies the resources at the time and for the amounts planned.

Limitations of the Family Income Policy.   In the scale of division between death benefits and retirement benefits, the family income policy places the greater emphasis on death benefits. The degree of this greater emphasis depends upon how much decreasing term insurance is involved in the plan and the kind of basic policy used with the plan. The limitations of the family income policy are its reduced cash and loan values per dollar of initial insurance and its reducing amount of death protection over what is likely to be an increasingly productive period of life.

It will be recalled that a man aged 25 can provide insurance of $120 a month over a 20-year family income period for $61.92 a year if he uses simple monthly decreasing term insurance. The use of this policy would trade off cash and loan values as well as the permanent protection but such a trade off might well be warranted in those families where available premium dollars would not otherwise provide adequate family income protection. Accumulations for retirement can be postponed until the immediate obligations of providing for the family are satisfactorily met.

The $21,600 of continuous premium whole life insurance necessary to cover the family income period would provide an $85-a-month lifetime retirement income for the policyholder at age 65. The $12,000 continuous premium whole life insurance used in combination with the family income rider would provide a retirement income of $47 a month. If the basic policy were endowment at age 65, the retirement income provided would be $73. A compromise between the 1 percent family income policy and the pure decreasing term policy may be made through the purchase of a 2 percent or a 3 percent family income policy. The effect would be to acquire more death protection per premium dollar than that offered under the 1 percent family income policy without having to trade off all cash values and permanent insurance.

Family Maintenance Policy.   Somewhat akin to the family income policy is the family maintenance policy.[11] Insurance companies usually have

---

[11] Terminology has become much confused by the rise in popularity in the mid-1950's of a type of coverage which includes all members of the family as insured persons. For this form, to be discussed next, all kinds of names have been developed by the various companies —family plan, family protection, family insurance, family policy, and so on, some of which names are closely akin to names used for the form under discussion here.

their own trade name for these policies, and in many cases they use names exactly like those used by other companies for their family income plans. It is impossible to tell what a policy with a name like family provider or family security is without a careful look at it first.

The traditional family maintenance policy consists of a basic policy, usually a permanent form, plus level (instead of decreasing) term, either within the policy itself or as a rider. The term portion will provide income for a stated number of years after the death of the insured if the insured dies within the family maintenance period. Thus, if under a 20-year family maintenance policy, the insured dies at the end of the 19th year, the beneficiary receives the income for 20 years, not for just one year as under the family income plan.

As in the family income policy, the family maintenance policy usually pays a monthly income equal to a percentage of the face amount of the basic policy, 1 percent being common. The income under the traditional family maintenance policy is a combination of the term insurance proceeds paid out in monthly installments of a fixed amount over, say, 20 years, plus the interest from the basic policy's proceeds which the company holds until the end of the income period. For a $100 a month 20-year family maintenance policy issued at age 25, combining level term with $10,000 continuous premium whole life insurance, the premium in one company is about $210 a year when the $10,000 of proceeds from the basic policy is held until the end of the income period and the interest earned on it is to be applied to the $100 of monthly income.

Under a competitive form of the family maintenance policy, the monthly income may be independent of the proceeds of the basic policy. For a $100-a-month, 20-year family maintenance policy issued at age 25, combining level term with $10,000 continuous premium whole life insurance, the premium is about $265 a year if the income is independent of the basic policy.

The same rules apply in general to the family maintenance plan as to the family income plan with respect to the types of policies to which riders may be attached, the conversion privileges of the term insurance, the right to have the income payments commuted, and so forth.

Uses and Limitations of Family Maintenance. The legitimate uses of the family maintenance plan are much more restricted than those of the family income policy, because the years over which an extra income is needed are reduced as the insured grows older. The principal limitation of the family maintenance contract is its use of level term to meet what is typically a decreasing need for family protection. Therefore, in the majority of cases, the family income policy is to be preferred over the family maintenance policy. For those who want term insurance written in combination with permanent insurance, a multiple protection policy is available. This policy, as explained later, generally has greater flexibility than the family maintenance contract.

Family Policy. The family policy (called by various names such as family plan, family circle, family protection) offers coverage on all members of the family group in one package. Usually sold in "units," its simplest form is $5,000 of permanent insurance, such as continuous premium whole life, on the father, with $1,000 of term insurance to the husband's age 65 on the mother if she is the same age as her husband, and $1,000 of term insurance to some specified age (usually more than 20 and less than 26)[12] on each child. In no event will the term insurance on the children continue beyond the father's age 65. The term insurance on the wife is convertible to permanent insurance for its full amount and the term insurance on the children is convertible usually to five times its amount. In the event of the death of the husband-father, the insurance on the wife and children usually becomes paid up for its unexpired term.

The premium for the family policy is usually determined solely by the age of the husband. If the wife is older or younger than her husband the amount of her term coverage will be reduced or increased. The "package" premium remains the same. Some companies offer family coverage as a rider to a basic policy and the premium is determined by the age of the wife. While there is a charge for the term insurance on the lives of the children, this charge is not based on either their ages or their number. Moreover, additional children born to or adopted by the family are automatically covered without an increase in the premium. In computing the premium, assumptions are made as to the average ages and number of children in a typical family.[13]

Family policies have cash surrender values but the usual nonforfeiture options apply only to the permanent portion of the coverage. Waiver of premium in event of the death or disability of the husband is frequently offered. In event of the death of the wife, the premium may be reduced or it may remain level, with the coverage on the husband being increased by $1,000 of term insurance per unit.

While a package of so much whole life insurance on the husband with one fifth or one fourth of that amount written as term insurance on other family members is what might be called the basic form of the family policy, innumerable variations have been introduced—too many for discussion here. Some plans offer permanent insurance on the wife as well as on the husband. Some forms use long-term endowment as the permanent coverage on the husband. It is even possible to find a package made up entirely of term insurance. Many companies also offer a one-parent family policy for

---

[12] Variations are found among family plans in the relationship among the amounts of insurance written on the husband, wife, and children. Some companies offer more insurance on the wife than on the children. For example, a company may offer $5,000 on the husband, $1,000 on the children, and $1,500 on the wife. As in all special purpose policy plans, each plan has to be studied to determine the benefits it offers.

[13] Except for infant mortality, the death rate in the ages for children covered under the family policy is so low that it has little aggregate effect on the flat rate charged in the policy for children collectively. The "waiting period," usually 15 days, before coverage becomes effective on a newborn child eliminates most of the infant mortality problem.

use in cases in which the other parent is deceased or uninsurable, or where the parents are divorced.

Uses of the Family Policy. The family policy recognizes that there is a need for insurance, at least for final expenses, on every member of the family, but concentrates the bulk of the protection on the breadwinner. It can be a useful form of coverage for the young or very large family with limited premium money. An important advantage of the family policy is that it allows those parents who insist on insuring the lives of their children an opportunity to do so at the lowest possible cost.[14] Companies as a rule do not write term insurance separately on the lives of children. Frequently, parents buy high-premium policies on children, a practice which in many family insurance programs represents an unwise use of premium money. With the children insured under the family policy, fewer mistakes are apt to be made in the purchase of juvenile coverage.

Another use of the family policy is to protect the insurability of the children. This is accomplished through the liberal convertible privilege offered with the term coverage. The insurability of the wife is also protected since her term insurance is also convertible. Furthermore, the plan has the advantage of giving the wife paid-up insurance to age 65 on her life in the event that she survives her husband. All of these advantages are offered at a low premium. The expenses involved in issuing and administering the coverage are absorbed in the premium for the husband's insurance. For five units of family insurance offering $25,000 continuous premium whole life insurance on a 25-year-old husband, $5,000 term to husband's age 65 on a 25-year-old wife, and $5,000 term to age 22 (or father's age 65 if earlier) on each child, the annual premium would be $442, nonpar. The term insurance on the wife and children becomes paid up in the event of the death of the father, and the insurance on the children is convertible to five times its amount. In this same company, $25,000 of continuous premium whole life insurance at age 25 would cost $324.25 a year for coverage on the father alone. The additional family coverage costs $117.75. The cash values of the family policy and the continuous premium whole life insurance on the father are equal at the father's age 65.

Limitations of the Family Policy. A limitation of the family policy is that because of its low premium it tempts families to spend money on insurance coverage on family members that might be better spent on coverage on the breadwinner. The additional $117.75 cost of the family policy in the foregoing illustration could purchase more than $10,000 additional life insurance on the father and increase the retirement benefits available at age 65 by more than $40 a month.

While the family policy offers an inexpensive way to insure the lives of the wife and children, it usually requires a basic amount of permanent insurance on the life of the father. The cost of this permanent protection

---

[14] The question of the advisability of insuring the lives of children is examined later in this chapter when special juvenile forms are discussed.

might be prohibitive to a family with a small insurance budget and a large family income protection need. Such a family might need to put all its available premium dollars into term insurance on the life of the breadwinner, postponing a permanent insurance program until later, when either the family income has increased or the family obligations have decreased. A family policy with $10,000 permanent insurance on the husband's life would require an annual premium of $181.80 at age 25. If put into a 20-year family income policy of the monthly decreasing term variety (no permanent insurance) this amount of money would purchase a monthly income of more than $354.

As with all policies, the limitations of the family policy are the limitations of misuse. However, it may be true that the family policy, like the limited payment policy and the endowment policy, presents a greater temptation to misuse than some other forms.

Multiple Protection.   Multiple protection policies are sometimes called added protection, additional protection, or some other special name coined by the issuing company. Multiple protection policies provide a specified amount of insurance until a given age or for some specified period, after which the amount is reduced. For example, one common form is $2,000 or $3,000 of insurance to age 60 or 65, or to life expectancy, and $1,000 thereafter. Another is $2,000 or $3,000 of insurance for 15 or 20 years, and $1,000 thereafter. Multiple protection may be issued either as a policy or as a rider to be attached to some permanent policy form. The most common multiple policy forms are double protection and triple protection, but even quadruple protection policies and riders can be found.

In structure, the policy is a permanent policy form (usually continuous premium whole life) plus an added amount of level term for the multiple protection period. For example, double protection to 65 is $1,000 of, say, continuous premium whole life plus $1,000 of term to 65. When multiple protection is written as a rider, the premium drops at the end of the additional protection period to that for the basic policy. When it is written as a single policy, the premium may drop at the end of the multiple protection period, or it may remain level throughout the life of the policy. For example, a $20,000 double protection policy can be purchased at age 25 in one company for an annual nonpar premium of $205 until age 65, at which time coverage is reduced to $10,000, and the premium falls to $122. In another company this policy can be purchased at age 25 for a level nonpar premium of $196, which remains the same for the life of the policy.[15] The cash value under the lifetime level premium plan is lower than under the step-down plan.

---

[15] In comparing the premium of one multiple protection policy with that of another, it is necessary to be especially careful to find out if the contracts are comparable. Not only do premium plans vary but also the types of basic policies. Some might be endowment at 85, others might be whole life paid up at 65 and still others might be continuous premium whole life. In addition, some might provide the extra protection for a shorter period than others. There are still other ways in which the policies may vary.

Uses of Multiple Protection. The use of the multiple protection policy is the same as that of the family maintenance form: extra protection during a period when it is needed. The multiple protection package policy is cheaper than separate, continuous premium whole life and term bought independently of one another. The reason is that the premium on the basic policy is sufficient to cover the major portion of the expenses involved in writing the policy; therefore, the added term needs to have but little loading for expenses. Also higher mortality assumptions are used in computing premiums for term insurance separately purchased. In one company the saving at age 25 arising out of the combination plan is $12 a year for a $10,-000, 15-year double protection policy; in another it is $22 a year for a $10,000, 20-year triple protection policy.[16]

The principal advantage of multiple protection coverage is that it offers a way of getting term insurance in combination with whole life insurance at premiums less than the usual market rates for separate coverages.

Limitations of Multiple Protection. The multiple protection policy can be easily misunderstood. Buyers may be attracted by the low premium—low in comparison to the same face amount in the form of continuous-premium whole life. They fail to understand (or remember in later years) that the premium is lower because the whole life policy provides the same amount of protection until death, whenever that may be, whereas the multiple protection policy reduces the amount of protection by half or more at the end of some period, such as 20 years, or upon the attainment of some age, such as 65. Moreover, a whole life policy for an amount equal to the amount of multiple protection will provide much higher cash values throughout the life of the policy. These values may be particularly important if, at age 65, the policyholder wants to use cash values for retirement income.

That the multiple protection policy provides level term rather than decreasing term can be a disadvantage of the policy when it is used by families that must struggle to meet the premiums required for the bare minimum amount of insurance necessary to bring the children to maturity. Other things remaining the same, the need for insurance decreases gradually as the children grow older rather than decreasing all at once at some period 20 years or so in the future. A decreasing 20-year term rider can be purchased at less than two thirds of the premium for a 20-year, level term rider.

On the other hand, for the family that can afford the higher premium, level insurance has certain advantages. As a person grows older, other things are not likely to remain the same. Any number of developments could cause a need for more insurance. He may have additional children. His income may increase and along with it his standard of living. This

---

[16] A $10,000, 15-year double protection policy provides $20,000 of protection during the first 15 years and $10,000 thereafter. A $10,000, 20-year triple protection policy provides $30,000 of insurance for the first 20 years and $10,000 thereafter. The premiums on the policies used as illustrations are reduced at the end of 15 and 20 years to that for a continuous premium whole life policy for $10,000 issued at age 25.

could cause him to reevaluate the income needs of his family in the event of his death. Also, as he grows older, he may accumulate property which could increase his death tax liability. Finally, inflation is likely to reduce the real value of his present insurance, creating a need for additional protection. Many families, therefore, may find that decreasing insurance is far from a realistic solution to their insurance problems.

Mortgage Protection.   Any policy purchased with the primary purpose of retiring the mortgage in event of the death of the head of the family is mortgage protection. Many companies, however, issue a special policy form under the name mortgage protection, mortgage redemption, home protector, or some such descriptive title. These policies are written on a decreasing term basis for the period of the mortgage. They are arranged so as to provide enough funds to retire the debt if the insured dies before the expiration of the policy. If the policyholder lives to pay off the mortgage himself, the policy usually expires without value, although some mortgage policies are written to reduce to a minimum amount, $1,500 for example, where it remains for the life of the insured.

The rate for the special mortgage protection policy, as for all decreasing term policies, is low. For instance, for a 20-year, 18-pay nonpar policy issued at age 25, one company charges an annual premium of $131.40 to protect $30,000 of initial debt. The policy is written to provide the necessary funds to pay off the balance due on a 6 percent amortized mortgage in the event of the death of the insured during the 20-year amortization period.[17]

Modified Life.   A modified life contract is a continuous premium whole life contract under which premiums are redistributed. They are lower than the regular premium for continuous premium whole life insurance during the first 3, 5, or 10 years of the policy and higher than the regular premium thereafter. The premium for a modified five may be constructed so that it doubles at the end of the first five years. For example, one company's nonpar rate at age 25 for $10,000 of a modified 5 is $77.40 for the first 5 years and then $154.80 thereafter. Its level nonpar premium for $10,000 continuous premium whole life insurance at age 25 is $137.20. All companies, however, do not redistribute their premiums in this way. A company may prefer to charge a little higher premium in the beginning so that the increase at the end of the five years will not be so large. As an example of this type of premium distribution, one company charges $85.11 for the first 5 years and 162.70 thereafter. Another company may prefer to charge an even smaller premium at the beginning with an even larger increase at the end of five years. For example, one company starts out with a very low initial premium and triples it after five years. For a $10,000 modified 10, one company charges $89.80 nonpar for the first 10 years and then doubles the premium to $179.60 thereafter, whereas another company charges $98

---

[17] The insured should check to see if prepayment is allowed without a prohibitive penalty before he makes the settlement arrangements for his mortgage protection.

nonpar for the first 10 years and increases the premium to $150.80 thereafter.

Variations also exist among the premium distribution formulas used with various other modified life policies. Some companies write a modified 3-10 under which the premium starts out low and increases at the end of 3 years and again at the end of 10 years. Others write a modified 5-10.

Dividend payments on participating modified life policies will pay all or at least part of the increased premium. For example, the third-year dividend on a $10,000 modified 3 purchased at age 25 for $165.30 is $29.70, which will more than pay the $28.70 increase in the fourth-year premium. In another company the third-year dividend on a $10,000 modified 3 purchased at age 25 for $150.40 is $33.50, which is more than the $26.50 increase in the fourth-year premium. However, for a modified 5 the premium in one company for $10,000 at age 25 is $92.70. The dividend for the fifth year is $29, which is $63.70 less than the increase in premium at that time.

Some companies write modified long-term contracts such as a modified 2, 10-year term policy or a modified term to age 65.

Uses of Modified Life. The modified life policy is particularly helpful to the young family man whose income is insufficient at the present time to enable him to buy enough insurance on a continuous premium whole life plan but is sufficient to enable him to purchase something more than term insurance. Modified life enables him to finance the purchase of permanent life insurance at lower premiums for several years until his income increases than would be required for the purchase of continuous premium whole life insurance.

When a company does not write a modified life contract, it may offer, as an alternative, automatically convertible term. The difference between the two policies is in premiums and cash values. The automatically convertible term will have a lower initial premium than the modified life but will carry a higher premium at conversion. Also the modified life policy will have cash values during the modified premium period, but the automatically convertible term will have no cash values until after conversion. The choice between the two plans is basically a personal budget problem.

Limitations of Modified Life. A limitation of the modified life policy is in that cash values are smaller in the earlier years, since they do not become appreciable until the end of the initial 3-5 or 10-year period. For example, a comparison of cash values of a given modified 10 and a given continuous premium whole life shows that at the end of the 10th year a modified 10 has a cash value of $370 per $10,000 of insurance when issued at age 25, whereas the continuous premium whole life issued at the same age and for the same amount has a cash value of $930. This difference, however, decreases as the policies become older, so that by the time the insured reaches 65, the difference in these illustrative contracts will be only $260. The cash value of the continuous premium whole life at age 65 is $5,700, whereas the cash value of the modified 10 is $5,440. Comparisons drawn between other modified policies and continuous premium whole life contracts, while not yielding identical results, will show related results.

In the final analysis most policies are purchased, for death or old-age protection. The death protection afforded by the two policies is identical, and the difference in the retirement protection is small. Modified life is a good policy for the young man who wants permanent protection but cannot afford it immediately.

Another type of modified life contract is one in which the coverage rather than the premium is modified. Some companies write what they call modified 65 and modified 70 contracts, under which the face amount of insurance is reduced by 50 percent when the insured reaches the age of modification. One company quotes a nonpar annual premium of $103.30 for $10,000 of modified 65 issued at age 25, whereas another company quotes a premium of $111.10 for $10,000 of modified 70 issued at age 25.

Graded Premium Life. A variation of the modified life is the graded premium life. In this contract, premiums advance each year for the first few years (usually five) and then remain level throughout the life of the policy. For example, in one company the nonpar graded premium for $10,000 of whole life insurance issued at age 25 begins at $59.40 and increases each year, reaching $145.40 for the fifth year and thereafter. This compares with a continuous premium of $130.50 if issued level premium at age 25. The advantages and limitations of the graded premium life are the same as those of the modified life.

Cost-of-Living Policy. An increasing number of insurers are writing a cost-of-living rider which automatically increases coverage in line with increases in the consumer price index (CPI). The rider provides for term insurance in addition to the face amount of the permanent policy to which the rider is attached. The amount of coverage varies up or down in accordance with changes in the CPI. For example, if the rider is attached to a permanent policy of $100,000 and the CPI advances 4 percent during the year, $4,000 of 1-year term insurance automatically is written for the following year and the insured is billed for the additional coverage in his premium notice. No evidence of insurability is required for the additional term insurance. In the event that the CPI declines, the amount of insurance will never be decreased below the amount of the permanent insurance. The cost-of-living rider can affect only the amount of the one-year term insurance.

Cost-of-living annuities also are now being introduced under which the income payable to the annuitant can increase up to as much as, say, 3 percent a year over the initial amount of the annuity income or the amount by which the CPI changes, whichever is the smaller. Thus, a cost-of-living annuity of $1,000 a month would be increased to $1,030 a month if the CPI rises 3 percent or more. If it rises 3 percent or more the following year, the annuity would be increased to $1,060 monthly. If the CPI falls the next year, the amount of the annuity also will fall but never below its original amount of $1,000 monthly.

Life Sustaining Policy.   With the introduction of successful transplants, some insurers are beginning to write policies under which 50 percent of the face of the policy will be paid to help finance a potentially life saving transplant. If the transplant is successful, the insurer gains the use of 50 percent of the policy proceeds which otherwise would have had to be paid out as a death claim. Also, if the patient recovers, the insurer will continue to collect premiums which otherwise would never have been paid.

Return of Premium and Face Amount Plus Cash Value Policies.   In an appeal to those people who do not understand the mathematical or the economic concept of life insurance, some companies issue policies or riders that provide that in the event of death within an initial number of years, say 20, the face amount of the policy will be increased by an amount equal to the gross annual premiums paid to date. At age 35 a 20-year return of premium rider for a $10,000 endowment at 85 in one insurer amounts to $32.50 annually for 20 years. At the end of 20 years, when the rider expires, the premium will be reduced to the gross premium of the basic policy.

In structure, the return of premium is an amount of increasing term insurance which is always equal to the total of premiums paid to that point. For example, during the first policy year, the amount of term insurance in the rider attached to a policy with an annual premium of $20 will need to be only $20 and during the second policy year, $40.

The rider has the benefit of increasing the protection on a policyholder's life for a period of years, and that period often corresponds to the time during which he has the greatest need for that protection. However, the family's insurance program might be better balanced if the additional premiums spent for the rider were used to purchase decreasing term insurance instead. For example, the $32.50 needed to purchase a 20-year return of premium rider at age 35 for a $10,000 endowment at age 85 could purchase a 20-year monthly reducing term policy starting at $8,000 and leveling off at $1,600 for the last 4 years.

Some companies write life insurance plans or riders that provide for the payment of an amount of insurance equal to the cash value of the policy in addition to the face amount of the policy. The plan offers the unknowledgeable life insurance buyer who believes the insurance company unfairly retains the predeath cash value of his policy upon his death the opportunity to right a wrong by paying for what he believes is his due. It also provides the gimmick which in some cases persuades a person to buy life insurance who otherwise might not do so.

While the return of premium and the face amount plus cash value benefits are illogical benefits, they are mathematically sound.

Guaranteed Investment or Coupon Policy.   The guaranteed investment or coupon policy is offered by some companies writing nonparticipating policies. The purpose of the plan is to make a nonparticipating plan competitive with participating plans. Most commonly, the guaranteed investment or coupon policy is a variation of the 20- or 25-pay life policy, to which are attached coupons redeemable in cash at the end of each policy year. Usually the coupons compare favorably with participating policy dividends, because they are designed to meet dividend competition; but they have a sales advantage over dividends in that they are guaranteed. Structurally, the coupons are a series of pure endowment contracts for varying periods.

Commonly, the first coupon in such a policy is due at the end of the first policy year, contingent upon the payment of the next annual premium. Each coupon attached to the policy will be paid to the insured in cash upon surrender on its due date, provided the insured is then living and provided all current premiums have been paid in full. Unused, matured coupons may be payable on presentation, with compound interest for each full year after their due date. In the event of the death of the insured, matured coupons will be paid the beneficiary in addition to the amount otherwise payable.

The coupon policy places greater emphasis on savings than on protection. The rate per $1,000 for the coupon policy is simply an amount sufficient to buy the insurance values in the contract, plus an amount which, together with interest, will equal the amount of the guaranteed coupon when they fall due. However, if adequate life insurance protection is not owned, the funds used to purchase coupons could be used more advantageously to purchase additional life insurance, which, in the event of premature death, would far exceed the value of the coupons.

The guaranteed investment or coupon policy often is written in combination with the return of premium provision. In one company the annual premium for a 25-pay, 24-coupon policy for the amount of $10,000 is $281. In addition to the face amount of the policy, the plan offers to return the premiums paid if death occurs during the 25-year premium payment period. The policy has 24 $50 coupons, 1 due at the end of each year for 24 years. The $50 may be taken as a dividend when it becomes payable or it may be left with the company to accumulate at 3½ percent a year.[18] One suspects that the $281 premium can be better spent on a life insurance program that concentrates on needs rather than frills.

Joint Policies. *Joint life* policies are contracts written with more than one person named as the insured. Most commonly, the joint life policy is issued to two persons, with the face amount payable upon the first death only. The premium for a joint whole life policy (both persons the same age) will be about one third more than the premium for a single whole life policy. Occasionally, they may be issued payable upon the first death among more than two persons named as insured.

---

[18] To call the $50 a dividend is misleading because theoretically life insurance policy dividends are distributions of the insurer's earnings and are not fixed in advance or guaranteed for the full life of the policy.

Last survivor policies are a variation of joint life policies. They pay the face amount upon the death of the last of two or more named as the insured.

The uses to which these two policies might be put are highly specialized, and they are not widely written. In fact, the demand for them is so small that companies do not normally include them in the rate manuals issued to agents.

Deferred Life Policies. Under the deferred life policy, the company agrees to pay the face amount only if the insured (usually a juvenile) dies after surviving an initial period. The purpose of the policy is the preservation of the insurability of the policyholder. An allowance is made in the premium rate for the deferred life policy to reflect the reduced liability of the company. Usually, the only liability the company has if death should occur during the deferred period is a return of premiums plus interest. It follows naturally that the longer the deferred period, the lower the premium at any given age. During the period of deferral, the deferred life policy is, then, principally insurance against becoming uninsurable. This policy is not widely issued outside Europe.

Guaranteed Insurability. A policy rider that achieves the same effect as the deferred life policy has become quite widespread in the United States and Canada in recent years. Given various names, its most descriptive is "guaranteed insurability." Added to a basic policy, it provides that the insured may, at various stated times, ages, or family developments in the future, purchase fractions or multiples of the face amount of the basic policy without evidence of insurability. If an option is not exercised when it matures, that option expires but the later options are still good. Maximum additional amounts of insurance are usually set, both at each purchase period and in the aggregate. Although the terms of the options vary among companies, a common pattern is a series of options to purchase $10,000 to $15,000 of insurance at 3-year intervals from ages 25 to 40. Usually the rider is restricted to policies of at least $5,000 and to whole life or endowment policies with premiums payable to at least age 40 or for 20 years.

The coverage requires an additional premium set to develop a fund in an amount estimated to equal the extra premium needed for those who become uninsurable or who become insurable only at premiums higher than standard before taking all the additional coverage guaranteed by the rider. The annual cost of a guaranteed insurability rider added to a $10,000 whole life or endowment policy in one typical company is $13.50 at age 25.

Reversionary or Survivorship Policy. The reversionary or survivorship policy (often called a survivorship annuity) has a named insured and a named beneficiary. If the beneficiary survives the insured, he or she receives the proceeds of the policy as a life income. However, if the insured outlives the beneficiary, the policy expires without cash values or other benefits.

This type of policy offers a young person an inexpensive way to provide an income for an older beneficiary. In effect, the reversionary or survivorship policy is decreasing term insurance to the date of the death of the beneficiary. The premium is based upon both the age of the insured and the age of the beneficiary and the policy is written on a level premium basis. When written with a young insured and an old beneficiary, the premium is low, since the beneficiary is likely to die before the insured. For example, for a premium of $95 a year a 30-year-old man could arrange to have an income of $100 a month paid to his 60-year-old mother should he predecease her. A 1-year renewable term policy taken for this same purpose would take an initial premium of nearly $100.

The survivorship policy is not widely written.

2. JUVENILE POLICIES

Juvenile life insurance is insurance written on the lives of children, usually those under age 15. Ages classed as juvenile vary from company to company, commonly running from 0 through 9 or 0 through 14. There are a few cases of juvenile policies running from 0 to 4 and from 0 to 15.

Because the insured under a juvenile policy is a minor, the applicant is an adult—usually a parent—in whom control of the policy is vested. This control is conferred either (1) by making the applicant the absolute owner of the policy or (2) by use of a special provision conferring control on the applicant during his or her lifetime and on the insured when he reaches age 21. In this latter provision, control is also conferred on the insured upon the death of the applicant or upon prior release of control by the applicant. The special control provision is generally preferred. Where the policy is a gift to the child the ownership may be vested immediately in the insured or in a trustee.

Plans Available. Juvenile insurance is usually issued on one of the following plans: Life paid up at 65; 20-pay life; 30-pay life; 20-year endowment; endowment at 85; 20-pay endowment at 85; endowment at ages 16, 17, 18, 19, 20, 21. The death rate during the first year of life is higher than at any age until age 65.[19] Consequently, to hold down the cost of juvenile policies, a few companies restrict the coverage during the first year of life to a fraction of the face amount of the policy. Other companies will not accept applications for insurance on the lives of children under some age such as two weeks.

Jumping Juvenile. A type of juvenile policy, known in the trade as jumping juvenile is popular. It is called junior estate builder, junior accumulator, guaranteed estate, or some other name by the various companies issuing it. In its most common form it is sold in units which provide $1,000 of protection to some age such as 21, automatically increasing to $5,000 at that time with no evidence of insurability and with no increase in premium. The basic policy is usually endowment at 65, life paid up at 65, or continuous premium whole life. Its purpose is to protect the insurability of the child, provide protection for the parents against expenses resulting from the death of the child prior to 21, and give the young man or woman

---

[19] United States Total Population (1959–61) mortality figures show the death rate at age 0 to be 25.93 per thousand and 26.22 per thousand at age 65.

a larger amount of insurance coverage at the age when the need for it will be greater by reason of increased (or soon to be increased) responsibilities.

The nonpar premium for a $5,000 jumping juvenile policy issued at age 1 on a life paid up at age 65 plan is $150.20 a year in one company. For a $5,000 jumping juvenile policy issued at age 1 on an endowment at age 65 plan, the nonpar premium would be $190.60 a year.[20]

Uses of Juvenile Policies.   A number of arguments are used in the sale of juvenile insurance. These arguments appear to be more effective in making the sale than in solving the buyer's problems. For example, one sales argument for juvenile insurance is to establish a fund to pay the cost of final illness. Hospital and medical expense insurance provide the more logical solution to that problem. Another sales argument is that a fund can be accumulated through a juvenile endowment at age 18 to finance a college education for the child. Insurance on the life of the parent combined with growth investments appear to offer a better approach to that objective. Still another argument is that the juvenile policy has the advantage of starting a permanent insurance program for a child at a lower annual premium or that a part of the child's insurance program will be paid up at a relatively early age. For example, the annual nonpar premium for a $10,000 life paid up at age 65 issued at age 5 would be $73 in contrast to $152.90 if issued at age 25. The annual nonpar premium for a $10,000, 20-pay life issued when the child is under 6 months will be $115.10 and will give the insured $10,000 of paid-up insurance before he reaches age 21. Of course, juvenile insurance will accomplish these objectives, but can these premiums be used more effectively in an insurance program designed to solve more pressing risk management problems? Or could these funds be used more efficiently by building a diversified investment program for the child?

A use of juvenile insurance is to arrange for the resources necessary to pay the cost of the funeral in the event of the death of a child. The family policy discussed earlier in this chapter provides the best solution to this problem. The cost of the coverage on the child is low because it is written on a term insurance basis and the administrative cost of the coverage is borne principally by the insurance on the father.

Perhaps the fundamental use of juvenile insurance is to guarantee that the child will always have some life insurance even if he later becomes uninsurable. Individual juvenile policies offer the opportunity to purchase coverage in excess of and in addition to that available under the family policy.[21]

In Chapter 20 attention will be given to another important use of the juvenile policy: its use as a gift medium to implement estate plans.

---

[20] This policy will endow for $25,000 at age 65.

[21] Both the life and health insurance business have done a poor job to date in devising plans to insure the insurability of children. Perhaps a rider should be written on the policies covering the lives of the parents giving the children the option to purchase life and health insurance at some future time.

Limitations in the Use of Juvenile Insurance.   Juvenile insurance often absorbs premium dollars which should be used for protection on the life of a parent. In theory, at least, most companies will not consider an application for juvenile insurance (except in special circumstances, such as the uninsurability of the father) unless a "substantial" amount of insurance is carried by that parent himself. However, the rate book of one conservative company defines substantial as an amount "at least twice the ultimate amount of insurance in force and applied for on the lives of all of the father's children." This would seem to mean that a parent with only $6,000 in force on his own life could apply for and receive $3,000 on the life of a child. It is hard to conceive of any case in which $6,000 on the life of the father is adequate protection for his family. The death of a child will cause hardship in many families, and for at least that reason there should be insurance on the life of the child; yet it does seem that the death of the child would cause far less hardship than would the death of the father.

The college fund endowment policy is particularly expensive. The annual premium for a $10,000 endowment at age 18 issued on the life of a child under age six months is $472 in a typical company. This amount of money will purchase more than $35,000 of continuous premium whole life insurance on the life of the father, assuming he is age 25. If the father purchases $35,000 of whole life insurance on himself rather than $10,000 endowment at age 18 on his child, enough funds will be available to see his son through grade school, high school, and college should the father die before his son reaches school age. If the father is still living when his child reaches age 18, the cash value of the $35,000 of life insurance on the father will be available to help finance the son's college education. The cash value of this policy will be about $7,600, only $2,400 less than the face amount of the proposed endowment at age 18 on the life of the son. It would appear that in most cases the better use of the premium dollars would be for the purchase of insurance on the life of the father rather than the purchase of the college endowment on the life of the child.

Payor Benefits.   The payor agreement provides that if the owner of a juvenile policy (usually a parent) dies or becomes totally and permanently disabled before the policy anniversary nearest a given age of the insured (usually 21 or 25), the company will waive subsequent premiums on the policy up to that age. Most payor benefits as well as the juvenile policies themselves are written nonmedically. Various underwriting rules relating to maximum and minimum ages of the payor and of the insured, and to minimum age differences, may be applied. The annual premium for the benefit depends upon the age of the insured, age of the payor, and type of plan. For example, in one company the annual premium for a payor benefit covering disability and death of the payor issued with a $10,000, 25-pay life policy is $10.30 when the insured is age 5 and the payor is age 35. For a $10,000 endowment at age 18, the payor benefit covering disability and death would require a premium of $46.20 a year assuming the insured is age 5 and the payor is age 35.

8

The "Best" Policy[1]

Frequently the author is asked to give advice as to whether or not a particular policy is a good buy. In the spring of 1970 during a lull in campus demonstrations, the author was approached by a student for such advice. One of his fraternity brothers, who was working his way through engineering school by selling life insurance, had offered him a policy. The student had in hand a beautifully decorated proposal form filled out in somewhat illegible handwriting. "My fraternity brother," the naïve student reported, "said it was the best policy on the market. What about it?"

It took no more than an hour's study of the proposal form to deduce that this was a 20-pay modified convertible life sustaining endowment at 65 with triple protection to age 50, predeath cash values paid as an additional death benefit, a 15-year family income rider, 19 guaranteed coupons, double indemnity in case of death by accidental means, $100 monthly indemnity for 10 years and lifetime waiver of premiums in event of total and permanent disability, a return of premium rider, a guaranteed insurability rider, and a cost-of-living rider.

"Whether or not this is the 'best' policy on the market would be difficult to say," the student was told. "However, I will say that without a doubt it is the most nearly complete dictionary of life insurance terms I have ever encountered in one policy. But, before I can advise you as to its purchase, I will need to know whether you are (1) buying insurance or (2) collecting policies. If you are collecting policies, I urge you to buy this one, because it is one of the rarest I have ever seen. I have no doubt but that in years to come it will become a collectors' item. On the other hand, if you are buying life insurance, then no one can look at a policy and tell you what policy is 'best.' He must, instead, look at you."

Determining the best policy for any individual buyer starts, not with an analysis of any given policy, but with an analysis of the buyer. It is necessary, first, to determine what problems the purchaser intends to solve with his life insurance, and whether life insurance provides him the most effective solution to these problems. If it does, the next step is to help the

---

[1] This chapter is designed to serve as a summary of the four preceding chapters.

buyer find the most efficient life insurance solution. Sometimes it is necessary to guide the buyer into reconsidering whether what he wants his life
insurance to accomplish for him is indeed what he should be seeking to
accomplish through his life insurance. The life insurance buyer might be
unaware of the opportunities to gain efficiency in the use of budgeted life
insurance premium dollars by effectively trading off among desired objectives.[2]

1. THE MEANING OF THE TERM "BEST."

The term "best" has meaning only when it is used in comparisons.
Therefore, there is no best policy in an absolute sense. Until there is an
answer to the question "Best for what need?" it is impossible to say what
type of policy is the best policy. The best policy is the one that is the most
suitable for accomplishing the desired objective.

Several observations about life insurance policies in relation to buyer
objectives are useful in an appraisal of the appropriateness of various policy forms. If the objective is to fill a need for temporary protection against
premature death and there is no desire to combine savings with life insurance protection then the appropriate (best) policy is term insurance. If
the objective is to fill a need which is largely for savings and only partly
for temporary premature death protection, then endowment insurance is
the best policy. If the objective is to fill a need for permanent death protection while at the same time building cash values, the best policy is the
whole life policy that gives the desired balance between protection and
savings. It may be continuous premium or one of the limited payment whole
life forms. If the objective is to satisfy the need for income at retirement without any death protection, then an annuity is the best policy.

Given the sole purchase objective as lifetime death protection, the suitability of one particular policy form over another involves a consideration
of the differentials among the annual premiums charged for the various
whole life plans. For example, assume that the nonpar annual level premiums at age 50, male, for $10,000 of whole life insurance issued under
the following plans are as follows:

Continuous premium whole life	$348.30
20-payment whole life	448.70
15-payment whole life	563.00
(Life paid up at age 65)	

Given the insured's sole purchase objective and the foregoing array of
premium rates, which of these whole life plans is the least expensive, and
therefore the most appropriate? The annual premium for continuous
premium whole life is the lowest and the annual premium for 15-payment

---

[2] Cf. Chapter 20 for a discussion of the process of life insurance programming.

whole life is the highest, but this in itself does not mean that continuous premium whole life will be the least expensive or that 15-payment whole life will be the most expensive.

Using a 5 percent interest assumption, the present values of the maximum premiums that can be paid under these policies are shown in Table 8–1.

TABLE 8–1

The Present Value of the Maximum Premiums That Can Be Paid under Three Plans, Age 50, Male, $10,000, Nonparticipating

Plan of Insurance	Annual Premium for $10,000 of Insurance	Maximum Years Payable	Present Value Factor, 5 Percent (Premium Paid at Beginning of Each Year)	Present Value of Maximum Premiums
Continuous premium whole life	$348.30	50	19.256	$6,707
20-payment whole life	448.70	20	13.085	5,871
15-payment whole life (Life paid up at age 65)	563.00	15	10.8986	6,142

Note that the premiums to be paid if the policyholder survives the premium payment periods (50 years or to age 100 with continuous premium, 20 years or to age 70 with 20-payment, and 15 years or to age 65 with 15-payment whole life) are discounted for interest (5 percent) but not for the probability of the survival of the policyholder to pay each premium as it comes due. Based on these figures, the continuous premium whole life plan is the most expensive and the 20-payment life plan is the least expensive. But this conclusion requires the unrealistic assumption of a 100 percent probability that the insured will live throughout the maximum premium payment period.

A realistic comparison of the relative premiums charged for the foregoing policies requires the use of the expected value concept discussed in Chapter 2. By using an appropriate mortality table, the expected value of each premium payment can be determined by computing the probability that the policyholder will survive to make the payments. These expected values when discounted at the appropriate interest rate provide a basis for making a comparison of the relative premiums charged for the three policies. Table 8–2 shows the present expected values of premiums that will be paid under three plans, using 5 percent interest and an appropriate mortality table.

Based on the present expected value of premiums to be paid, the continuous premium whole life plan is the least expensive, the life paid up at

TABLE 8–2

The Present Expected Value of Premiums That Will Be Paid under
Three Plans, Age 50, Male, $10,000 Nonparticipating

Plan of Insurance	Annual Premium for $10,000 of Insurance	Present Value of Expected Premiums of 1.00, 5 percent Interest, Using Appropriate Mortality Assumptions	Present Value of Expected Premiums
Continuous premium whole life	$348.30	14.349	$4,998
20-payment whole life	448.70	11.980	5,375
15-Payment whole life (Life paid up at age 65)	563.00	10.273	5,784

age 65 is the most expensive, and the 20-payment life is in the middle. For whole life insurance, the probable total cost of the plan varies inversely with the length of the premium payment period, assuming that the insurance is purchased for death protection only and that the protection is wanted for the whole of life.

TABLE 8–3

The Present Expected Value of Premiums That Will Be Paid under
Three Plans, Age 25, Male, $10,000 Nonparticipating

Plan of Insurance	Annual Premium for $10,000 of Insurance	Present Value of Expected Premiums of 1.00, 4.5 Percent and Appropriate Mortality Assumptions	Present Value of Expected Premiums
Continuous premium whole life	$134.00	20.242	$2,712
20-payment whole life	220.00	13.192	2,902
40-payment whole life (Life paid up at age 65)	153.00	18.731	2,866

The foregoing illustrations are based on one set of plans at the nonpar premium rates quoted by one company at one given age, and using one set of interest and mortality assumptions. Table 8–3 shows the present values of expected premium payments on these plans when issued at age 25, male, and using the nonpar rates of another insurer. A different set of interest and mortality assumptions is used, this time a less conservative mortality table at 4.5 percent interest. Note that the differentials are much smaller but that the plan with the lowest expected cost is still the one with the longest premium paying period.

Varying results would be obtained by using other ages, other insurers, other interest and mortality assumptions, and by including other plans, such as, for example, renewable convertible term and modified life plans. However, the conclusion will still hold that, given the sole purchase objective as death protection for life, the suitability of one particular policy form over another involves, among other considerations, an appraisal of the differentials among the present expected values of the annual premiums charged for the various whole life plans.

The foregoing illustrations reflect only the present values of a series of premium payments discounted for interest and mortality, ignoring the subjective evaluation of the premium payer's desires with respect to the scheduling of his premium obligations. While the expected value of premiums as shown in Table 8–3 is higher for life paid up at age 65 than for continuous premium whole life, the insured might consider the benefits of satisfying his desire to complete premium payments during his productive years to be worth the additional cost. And, if the expected value of premiums for a renewable, convertible term plan is higher than the expected value of premiums for a continuous premium whole life plan, the additional utility to be derived by the insured through paying lower premiums when he can least afford them and deferring the higher premiums until he can most afford them could more than offset the higher expected value of the premiums.

If the purchase objective is dual, that is, for death protection and savings accumulations, then it is not appropriate in the purchase decision to consider differentials among the annual premiums charged for various plans. To do so would be to compare prices of unlike products. For example, while under a given set of assumptions a renewable, convertible term plan might produce the lowest probable cost for permanent death protection, it might not meet the insured's objective of savings accumulation either before or after conversion. And, while a modified life plan might show the lowest probable cost for death protection and still build some cash values, these values might fall short of a purchase objective that emphasizes savings.

Higher annual premiums for the same amount of whole life insurance under different plans are reflected in higher cash values, and the insured must select that plan which gives him the combination of savings and protection that will accomplish his objectives. However, when the opportunity to accumulate a savings fund is an important factor in the purchase of a life insurance plan, the buyer should be prepared to examine alternative outlets for his savings, and to consider the advice: "Buy term and invest the difference." Then, only when he satisfies himself that a life insurance contract is the appropriate financial instrument through which to accumulate savings should he make his decision as to which type of plan gives him the combination of savings and protection that will best accomplish his objectives.[3]

2. DETERMINING THE BEST POLICY

Most people buy life insurance for one or more of three basic reasons: (1) to pay the cost arising from death and to provide an income for surviving dependents, (2) to provide cash or income for old age, and (3) to utilize the semicompulsion features of the life insurance plan to build a savings fund. In order to determine the best policy for any individual buyer, it is necessary to know the order of importance to him of these three objectives. The best policy is the one which gives the policyholder what he finally decides he wants, regardless of whether someone else agrees that what the buyer wants is best for him.[4]

All this means that in order to determine the best policy, it is necessary to know what each policy offers with respect to three basic purchase objectives. Table 8–4 illustrates what a number of popular policy forms have to offer in terms of these objectives. Since most people think of retiring at 65, that age is used in the table to illustrate retirement values. The 20-year point has been selected arbitrarily to illustrate savings values.

If the Need Is for Death Protection. Note in Table 8–4 that initially one of the term insurance plans provides the most death protection for the

---

[3] For a different approach to making price comparisons between two plans of insurance see Joseph M. Belth, *The Retail Price Structure in American Life Insurance* (Bloomington, Indiana: Bureau of Business Research, Graduate School of Business, Indiana University, 1966), pp. 81–100. Professor Belth in computing prices of life insurance insists that price be distinguished from premium "because a part of the premium for a cash value policy is allocated to the savings element of the policy." The notion that a buyer of cash value life insurance may be seeking a level amount of protection for the whole of life under a premium payment plan most efficient for him has no place in Professor Belth's analysis. According to Professor Belth, if a buyer seeks level protection for life, and feels that a level premium would be the most appropriate payment arrangement for him, he would get his level premium if he buys a continuous premium whole life policy, but he would *not* get level protection. Instead, he would get decreasing protection and an increasing savings account. Further, he would get an arrangement under which the *price* per $1,000 of protection tends to increase year by year (after a relatively high price to reflect the front-end load). To measure life insurance prices, Professor Belth applies a technique which he calls the level price method. Under this method a set of yearly prices is determined for the declining amounts of insurance protection for each year under study, and then a level price per $1,000 of insurance is computed using an appropriate set of interest, mortality, and lapse assumptions (Cf. pp. 35–44). After much detailed analysis, Professor Belth, using his level price method, concludes: "Despite the problems involved in comparisons of markedly different policies [among the policies studied], twenty-payment life prices were found, on the average, to exceed straight life prices" (p. 232).

[4] For example, if the prospective insured has a wife and three children and refuses to budget more than $200 a year for insurance, term might be the most sensible type of policy for him to buy. But if he wants to accumulate a savings fund for an emergency and is interested in having the largest fund possible at age 65 with a minimum of death protection, then the best policy for these objectives might be an endowment at age 65 or a retirement income policy.

TABLE 8–4

Death, Savings, and Retirement Values of Popular Policies
Based on Annual Premium Outlay of $100 Issue, Age 25

(nonpar rates based on CSO 3%)

Type of Policy	Age	Death Protection	Savings (Cash Value) End of 20 Years	Cash Value at 65	Monthly Income at 65 (10 years) Certain and Life
Yearly renewable term	25	$18,726	0	0	0
	40	14,025	0	0	0
	50	8,382	0	0	0
	60	3,828	0	0	0
10-year renewable and convertible term	25	17,620	0	0	0
	35	14,493	0	0	0
	45	8,757	0	0	0
	55	4,198	0	0	0
Convertible term to 65		11,862	$1,079	0	0
Continuous premium whole life		7,231	1,801	$4,212	$25.27
Whole life paid up at 65		6,395	1,810	4,413	26.48
Endowment at 65		5,180	1,911	5,180	31.08
Retirement income at 65 (male)		3,251*	1,899	5,430	32.51
20-pay life		4,357	2,000	3,006	18.04
20-year endowment		2,397	2,397	0	0

* Or the cash value when it exceeds the face amount of insurance.

$100 annual premium. If death protection is the sole reason for buying life insurance to the complete exclusion of savings or retirement,[5] then one of the term forms may be appropriate if (1) the death protection need is not for the whole of life or (2) the death protection is for the whole of life, but the premium payer expects that it would be less burdensome for him to pay lower premiums now and higher premiums later upon converting the term to whole life insurance. When term insurance with later conversion to cash value insurance is planned, the insured must guard against allowing himself to put off conversion beyond the time that he can afford it, and against letting the final conversion date expire without action on his part.

---

[5] Death protection may be the sole reason for buying when life insurance is purchased solely to cover a debt, when the number of dollars available for premiums is so small the buyer must ignore the other needs, or when the buyer prefers to buy term insurance and invest the difference in equities in an attempt to protect against long-term inflation and acquire an interest in what he believes to be a long-term growth situation.

If the Need Is for Savings Accumulations. If the need is for savings accumulations with no need for death protection, then no insurance plan is the best policy unless for some reason one needs the discipline of the semicompulsory thrift feature so often argued as an important psychological by-product of life insurance. A savings or investment plan independent of life insurance would appear to be in order. However, if the need is predominantly for savings with little need for death protection, then a limited period endowment policy may be the best policy. The term of the endowment policy should be made to correspond with the desired savings period. If, for example, the period is 20 years, then, according to Table 8–4, at age 25 a $100 annual premium will purchase $2,397 of 20-year death protection and a savings account of $2,397 to be completed in 20 years should the insured survive the endowment period.

One of the limited payment whole life forms also may be a good contract to use when emphasis is on a savings plan rather than on protection against death or old age. For example, as indicated in Table 8–4, on a 20-pay life form a $100 annual premium will buy only $4,357 of death protection and $3,006 of cash values for retirement as compared with $7,231 of death and $4,212 of retirement values under the continuous premium form. But at the end of 20 years, $2,000 will have been accumulated in cash values under the 20-pay contract, whereas only $1,801 will be available under the continuous premium policy.

If the Need Is Retirement Income. One of the most common reasons for savings is to build a fund for retirement. If the need is to provide for retirement income to the exclusion of death protection, then the best policy is an annual premium retirement deferred annuity with neither death benefits nor cash values.[6] If the need is for some death protection but largely for retirement income, then the retirement income policy is the best policy. If there is a moderate need for death protection but retirement values are still the predominant reason for buying, then the endowment at 65 with the right to take the proceeds under income options might be best.

If the Need Is for Both Death and Old-Age Protection. If the need of the buyer is for a moderate amount of death protection and a moderate amount of retirement values then the continuous premium whole life form is likely to be the best policy. If purchased prior to approximately age 40, the whole life form has a cash value at age 65 of more than half of the face amount of the policy. Table 8–5 shows the cash values and amount of income at age 65, male, for a $1,000 continuous premium

---

[6] If the deferred life annuity is written with death benefits and cash values equal to premiums paid, then its premium is nearly as high as for retirement income insurance, especially at older ages. Nevertheless, most individual deferred annuities are written with cash values equal to premiums paid. Group deferred annuities, however, are written without refund.

whole life policy and a limited payment whole life policy at various ages of entry.

The life paid up at 65 policy, or any policy paid up before age 65 in the company used in the foregoing illustration will have a cash value of $690 per $1,000 and will pay $4.83 a month retirement income for each $1,000 of face amount of life insurance regardless of the insured's age at purchase. It should be emphasized that these figures and those in Table 8–5 are those of only one company. The figures for other companies might be quite different.

TABLE 8–5

Cash and Life Income Values per $1,000 at Age 65

(1958 CSO 3%; life income only, male)

Age of Purchase	Continuous Premium		Paid Up at 65	
	Cash	Monthly Income	Cash	Monthly Income
20	$588	$4.12	$690	$4.83
25	570	3.99	690	4.83
30	546	3.82	690	4.83
35	516	3.61	690	4.83
40	477	3.34	690	4.83
45	427	2.99	690	4.83
50	351	2.46	690	4.83

The choice between a limited pay life and continuous premium whole life policy is dependent on how predominant the retirement or cash value need is compared to the death protection need.

3. CHARACTERISTICS OF LIFE INSURANCE THAT QUALIFY IT FOR CONSIDERATION AS A SAVINGS MEDIUM

When the opportunity to accumulate a savings fund is an important factor in the purchase of a life insurance plan, it is appropriate that the characteristics of life insurance that qualify it as a savings medium be considered, and that life insurance be compared with alternative media.

Safety of Principal. Safety of the dollar value of principal is an important requirement in the savings plans of most people. No financial institution can boast of a better record than the institution of life insurance has compiled during the past half century. Life insurance has a reputation for dependable solvency that cannot be successfully challenged. Both the basic nature of the life insurance product and the method of merchandising it contribute to financial stability of the life insurance industry.

In the first place, nearly all policies are purchased on an annual (as contrasted to single) premium basis. The buyer undertakes a long-term obligation, and generally strives to keep up his premium payments despite financial difficulties for himself or the economy.

In the second place, life insurance companies use an aggressive merchandising system. Through their agents, they aggressively solicit new business and strongly encourage existing policyholders to continue their premium payments. The agent's income is directly dependent on both the new policies he sells and the old ones that stay in force. Therefore, he puts time and effort into bringing in new business and conserving old business.

While periods of economic depression markedly decrease the flow of money into nearly all other enterprises, the basic nature of the life insurance, plus the activity of the agent, maintains the flow of money into life insurance. For instance, the premium income of life insurance in 1929, before the depression, was $3,350, 367, 354; while in 1933, in the depths of the depression, it was still $3,321,797,924. This continuous inflow of new money enables companies to meet cash calls in times of depression without the necessity of liquidating securities at distressed prices. Table 8–6 shows that during the worst years of the depression, despite the heavy demands for cash and loan values, the total income of the business each year was sufficient to meet all cash calls.

Table 8–6
Premium Income, Total Income, and Total Disbursements, 1930–37

Year	Premium Income	Total Income	Total Disbursements
1930	$3,524,326,635	$4,593,973,110	$3,198,537,056
1931	3,661,105,385	4,850,375,950	3,537,704,954
1932	3,504,255,574	4,653,395,656	3,997,698,360
1933	3,321,797,924	4,622,291,932	3,917,431,410
1934	3,520,984,136	4,785,984,654	3,661,718,746
1935	3,692,127,637	5,072,095,267	3,592,956,321
1936	3,683,487,169	5,180,225,071	3,518,026,585
1937	3,761,745,196	5,257,048,795	3,610,343,044

However, these figures tell only part of the story. To meet the test of solvency, a life insurer's admitted assets (measured in accordance with state regulation) must exceed its statutory liabilities (measured in accordance with state regulation) by an amount determined by the Commissioner in accordance with state law. A number of insurers would not have been able to meet the test of solvency during the Great Depression had they not been bailed out by certain asset valuation procedures. For example, the Valuation Committee of what is now called the National Association of Insurance Commissioners approved the use of the market values of stocks and bonds as of June 30 as a substitute for December 31 for purposes of the 1931 annual statement values. On June 30, 1931, the Dow-Jones Industrial Average was 150.18 compared with 77.9 on December

31. The bond averages fell from 95.31 on June 30 to 77.77 on December 31. The bail-out effect of this ruling should be obvious. The June 30, 1931, values were permitted again in 1932, but in 1933 the June 30, 1931, values had to be averaged with the November 1, 1933, values.[7] For some insurers, efforts to keep them afloat did not succeed, and they fell into receivership.

In comparing the degree of safety afforded holders of life insurance cash values with that afforded holders of savings deposits in banks or holders of shares in savings and loan associations, it should be pointed out that life insurance policyholders do not have the benefit of having their savings insured through an agency such as the Federal Deposit Insurance Corporation or the Federal Savings and Loan Insurance Corporation.

Liquidity. Liquidity also is a desirable quality in a savings plan. Emergencies arise which call for immediate cash. The cash values of life insurance normally are completely liquid, available to the policyholder within a few hours or a few days.[8] Moreover, cash values are stated in the contract and do not fluctuate with changes in interest rates. They are similar in this respect to savings and loan shares, savings deposits, and United States Government Savings Bonds.

Avoidance of Managerial Care. The opportunity to shift managerial responsibility to someone else often is desirable in a savings plan. With life insurance, there are no rents to collect, no repairs to look after, no markets to watch, no competition to worry about, no coupons to clip, and no watching to see if bonds are called before maturity. In this respect, savings through life insurance are similar to savings accounts, savings and loan shares, and mutual fund shares. While it is important to consider the value of the utility to be gained by freedom from managerial responsibility, some savers look upon investment as a participation rather than spectator sport and enjoy the managerial activity associated with it. In this event avoidance of managerial care is a cost and not a utility.

Freedom from Reinvestment. The task of reinvestment, if not performed efficiently, is conducive to loss of interest. For the lay investor there is nearly always a time lag between the maturity of an investment and the reinvestment of the proceeds and between the receipt of interest or dividends and their reinvestment. Furthermore, reinvestment is conducive to dissipation of funds. When an investment matures, or dividends and interest are paid, there may be a temptation to spend at least part of

---

[7] For an interesting and informative discussion of the problems of the life insurance business in the Great Depression, see R. Carlyle Buley, *The American Life Convention* (New York: Appleton-Century-Crofts, Inc., 1953), pp. 681–877.

[8] Insurers are required to include a clause in their policies permitting the deferment of the payment of cash or loan values for six months, except for use to pay premiums. The clause is precautionary and resulted from the Great Depression of the 1930's when it appeared that there might be a run on cash values as there was on many banks. However, such deferment causes are rarely, if ever, invoked.

the maturity value or dividends and interest rather than to reinvest them immediately. For those savers who need the discipline of having their money reinvested for them, a life insurance plan or some similar plan such as mutual funds, passbook savings accounts, and saving and loan shares may be important to the successful completion of any long-term savings accumulation program.

Rate of Return. A competitive rate of return is an important consideration in any savings plan. Several techniques have been developed for measuring the rate of return on the cash value of a life insurance policy. These techniques all involve separating the life insurance premium into two components—the protection portion and the savings portion. Scholars attempting to determine rates of return on the savings element of a life insurance policy recognize that they must first perform a theoretical decomposition of each annual premium into that part going for protection and that part going for savings. They do not delude themselves into thinking that this decomposition is explicit.

The most popular technique for determining the interest return on the savings element in a life insurance policy is that developed in the 1930's by M. Albert Linton.[9] Mr. Linton was seeking a defense for life insurance against a particular line of attack taken by certain insurance advisers at that time. These advisers were urging policyholders to surrender their cash value insurance, use part of the surrender value to buy term insurance, and use the remainder to build a savings or investment account separate from life insurance.[10]

The Linton Technique. The Linton technique seeks to determine the average annual compound rate of interest that must be earned by a separate investment fund to equal the surrender value of a cash value life insurance policy at the end of a specified period. The amount that is assumed to go into the investment fund each year is computed as follows:[11]

1. The cash value of the policy for each year is subtracted from the face amount of the policy to determine the amount of protection being purchased each year.
2. The selected renewable term insurance rate for each year is applied to the amount of protection purchased each year to determine the yearly cost of protection.

---

[9] M. Albert Linton, *Life Insurance Speaks for Itself* (New York: Harper & Bros., 1937).

[10] Perhaps one of the most widely known books at that time offering such advice was Mort and E. Albert Gilbert, *Life Insurance, a Legalized Racket* (Philadelphia: Marlowe Publishing Co., 1936). Since then, there has been a parade of such books, all with catchy titles.

[11] What follows is an adequate general explanation of the concepts involved. For a precise reproduction of the Linton technique, including all its "nuts and bolts," see Joseph M. Belth, "The Rate of Return on the Savings Element in Cash-Value Life Insurance," *Journal of Risk and Insurance,* Vol. XXXV, No. 4 (December, 1968), pp. 569–81.

3. The yearly cost of protection is subtracted from the annual premium to determine the investment portion of each annual premium.

The Linton technique assumes that both the predeath and postdeath estates of the insured under the cash value life insurance plan and under the alternative decreasing term insurance, separate fund plan will be kept equivalent. Under the cash value insurance plan the predeath estate will be the cash value of the policy and the postdeath estate will be the face amount of the insurance. Under the alternative decreasing term insurance, separate fund plan, the predeath estate will be the value of the accumulations in the fund and the postdeath estate will be the face amount of the decreasing term insurance in force plus the accumulations in the fund. The question is what average annual compound rate of return must the savings portion of the premium earn each year under a term insurance, separate fund plan to maintain this equivalence. That rate of return is the rate of return assumed to be earned by the savings portion under the equivalent cash value insurance plan.

The calculations require a great deal of arithmetic, and are done on the basis of trial and error—that is, various rates of return are tried until the rate is found that creates equivalence between the assumed accumulated fund and the guaranteed cash value of the policy at the end of the time period selected. Mr. Linton observed: "The procedure is complicated but is greatly facilitated by the use of electronic computers."[12]

Based on the 1963 dividend scales, premium rates, and cash value schedules of 10 mutual life insurers, and using fairly low renewable term insurance rates, Linton found that the imputed composite rate of return earned under continuous premium whole life policies of $10,000 issued by these insurers would be 4.78 percent if the policies were issued at age 35 and terminated at age 55, and 6.37 percent if issued at age 55 and terminated at age 75.[13]

When the Linton "technique is applied to the policies issued by many companies a substantial variation is found among the policies in their rates of return . . . large enough to suggest that it is difficult . . . to generalize about the rate of return on the savings element in cash-value life insurance."[14] Rates of return on a sample of 88 insurers issuing $10,000 participating whole life policies in 1962 to males, aged 35 and computed on the basis of 20 years, varied from a high of over 5 percent to a low of under 1 percent with a mean of 4.11 percent, a standard devia-

---

[12] M. Albert Linton, "Life Insurance as an Investment" in Davis W. Gregg (ed.), *Life and Health Insurance Handbook* (2d ed.: Homewood, Illinois: Richard D. Irwin, Inc., 1964), p. 242.

[13] *Ibid.* For policies issued at ages 25 and 45 and terminated at ages 45 and 65 respectively, the imputed composite rates of return would be 4.80 percent and 5.17 percent. Does it seem strange that the imputed rate of return on a policy issued to an older man is higher than that issued to a younger man?

[14] Joseph M. Belth, "The Rate of Return on the Savings Element in Cash-Value Life Insurance," *op. cit.*, p. 580.

tion of 0.80 percent, and a coefficient of variation of 19.5 percent. For 60 insurers issuing $10,000 nonparticipating whole life policies, the variation was from a high of over 4 percent to a low of under 3 percent with a mean of 3.44 percent, a standard deviation of 0.43 percent, and a coefficient of variation of 12.5 percent.[15]

Rates of return vary not only among the ages of issue and among insurers but also among types of policies. For example, the mean rate of return on 20-payment policies issued at age 35 on a participating basis by 54 insurers in 1962 was 2.95 percent, and for nonparticipating policies issued by 39 insurers it was 2.10 percent. In none of the insurers studied did the rate of return reach 4 percent for 20-payment plans issued at age 35.[16]

Furthermore the rates of return vary with the duration over which they are computed. The composite rate of return of 4.78 percent computed by Linton for a 20-year period would have shown annual rates of return of minus 5.23 percent for a duration of 3 years, 3.54 percent for 6 years, 4.09 percent for 9 years, 4.37 percent for 12 years, 4.54 percent for 15 years, and 4.75 percent for 18 years.[17]

In addition to other variables, the imputed rate of return is a direct function of the level of term insurance rates used in computing the rate of return: the higher the schedule of term insurance rates used, the higher is the imputed rate of return to the cash values of life insurance policies. "When each of the term insurance rates is reduced by 25 percent, the annual rate of return is 3.57 percent" rather than 4.78 percent, and when each of the term insurance rates is increased by 25 percent, the annual rate of return is 6.12 percent.[18]

Thus it is evident that when making decisions about the purchase of particular policies, the life insurance buyer cannot rely on general statements about the levels of imputed rates of return on life insurance cash values. He will have to make his own calculations, complicated as they are, and usually without the aid of an electronic computer. Furthermore, it is unlikely that he will have the information necessary to enable him to make precise determinations of rates of return.

Protection from Creditors' Claims.   Protection of the savings fund from the claims of creditors may be an important consideration in a savings plan. In many states,[19] this protection, under certain conditions, is accorded to proceeds and often to cash values of life insurance policies by law. Also in many states, the payment of life insurance proceeds may be arranged in such a way as to protect not only against the creditors of the insured but also against creditors of the beneficiaries.

---

15 *Ibid.*, p. 573.
16 *Ibid.*, p. 574.
17 *Ibid.*, p. 578.
18 *Ibid.*, p. 577.
19 Cf. Chapter 9.

Favorable Tax Treatment. Tax considerations may be important in selecting a suitable savings plan. Life insurance cash values and proceeds are accorded favorable tax treatment. Interest earned on and added to cash values is not subject to federal income tax in the year earned. If the policy is surrendered for its cash value or matures as an endowment, that amount received in excess of premiums paid is taxable as ordinary income. If the policy matures as a death claim, generally no part of the proceeds is taxable as income.[20] Taxation of installment proceeds under settlement options is discussed in Chapter 21.

Facility of Estate Settlement. A quality that might be desired in a savings plan is ease of settlement. If so, life insurance merits serious consideration. Life insurance proceeds made payable to named beneficiaries can be settled directly without the time and expense involved in the probate of a will. They can also be made payable to the beneficiary as a life income, giving her the benefit of planned settlements without the expense involved in the creation and administration of a trust. Finally, a beneficiary under a life insurance policy, unlike a devisee under a will or testament, is not subject to the possibilities of delay or loss resulting from contention. Especially where major philanthropic interests are involved, relatives have been known to attack wills.

Protection against Disability. When a savings program is initiated to build a fund to provide a retirement income, additions to this fund must be made periodically or the fund will fall short of its goal. An advantage of building the retirement fund through cash value life insurance is the opportunity to make use of the protection offered under the waiver of premium clause. If the saver becomes totally disabled, his life insurance premiums will be waived. However, the fund will continue to grow as though the deposits were made, thus protecting his retirement savings plans against interruption through disability.

---

[20] Cf. Chapter 21 for a more extensive discussion of the taxation of benefits payable under life insurance policies.

9

Insurance and the Law

The fundamental principle of life insurance is mathematical; its application is financial; and its interpretation is legal. For the layman to understand the life insurance principle, he need not be an actuary; to understand its application to financial problems, he need not be an expert in finance; and to understand its legal ramifications, he need not be a lawyer.

The subject of insurance law covers a vast array of topics. This and the next two chapters are concerned primarily with these topics. The discussion, however, is not intended as a comprehensive survey of insurance law; instead it is directed to the general student of life insurance. It is designed primarily to provide the legal background fundamental to a practical, everyday understanding of policies and the rights and obligations of parties to them.

1. THE POLICY AS A CONTRACT

A life insurance policy establishes the legal rights and obligations of the insurer and the insured. If the document is to have value in the insured's plans for handling the financial security of his family, there must be no doubt of its validity. It must be enforceable in courts as a valid agreement. Thus, life insurance policies are legal contracts which, in general, are subject to the law of contracts,[1] although general contract law is often so modified in its application to life insurance as to be almost unrecognizable.[2]

The formation of a life insurance contract is subject to the same requirements governing the formation of any other valid contract: mutual assent

---

[1] While a few states have contract codes, these codes are only general rules. Much depends on their interpretation. The law of contracts is found chiefly in what is known as case or decisional law, which is made when an appellate court renders a decision. Such decisions have the force of law since they will generally be followed by other courts in rendering decisions.

[2] Woodruff, in his *Selection of Cases on the Law of Insurance* (1924), inserted the following significant statement in his preface: "What do they know of the law of insurance who only the law of contract know?" He goes on to say that general contract law has "in various instances been badly warped if not broken in order that insurance law may accommodate itself to the 'actuality of facts.'"

by competent parties for performance of a legal act for a valuable consideration.

Mutual Assent. Mutual assent requires that there be an offer by one party and an acceptance by another within a reasonable time. An offer is defined as "an act on the part of one person whereby he gives to another the legal power of creating the obligation called a contract. An offer, as an element of a contract, is a proposal to make a contract."[3] An acceptance is defined as the "compliance by offeree with the terms and conditions of the offer."[4]

Who makes the offer and who accepts it in the formation of a life insurance contract depends upon the circumstances of the transaction. A completed application for life insurance may be an offer, an acceptance of an offer, or an invitation to the insurer to make an offer.

An application submitted without the payment of the first premium is not an offer, but an invitation to the company to make an offer. In this case the offer is made by the insurer by approving the application, issuing the policy, and delivering it to the applicant. The offer is accepted by the applicant upon payment of the first premium.

Usually when the application is accompanied by the payment of the first premium, the company issues the applicant a conditional receipt and by this action makes a conditional offer to insure the applicant if he meets the requirements of insurability established by the company under the plan, at the premium, and for the amount requested.[5] When the applicant gives the insurance agent a check with the completed application he is accepting the conditional offer of the insurer. If the insurer later issues a policy other than the one applied for in the application, the issuance of the altered policy becomes a counteroffer by the insurer and payment of the additional premium by the applicant constitutes acceptance of the counteroffer.[6]

Occasionally, the applicant pays the premium with his application but is not given a conditional receipt. In this event, the offer is made by the applicant and accepted by the insurer when the insurer determines that the applicant is insurable.

Although there have been exceptions, the majority rule is that unreasonable delay on the part of the insurer in processing applications accompanied by the first premium does not constitute acceptance of the offer. However, some courts have held the insurer liable in tort for negligent

---

[3] Henry Black, *Black's Law Dictionary* (rev. 4th ed.; St. Paul, Minn.: West Publishing Company, 1968), p. 1233.

[4] *Ibid.*, p. 27.

[5] The *conditional* receipt often is referred to as a *binding* receipt. It is binding only *if* certain conditions precedent or subsequent are met. The use of the word "if" completely destroys the meaning of the term "binding." See 63 Yale L.J. No. 4, *Comment, Life Insurance Receipts: The Mystery of the Non-Binding Binder.*

[6] If the applicant because of poor health or a hazardous occupation is not insurable at standard rates, the insurer may issue the policy with a larger premium than quoted, or it may issue a different type of policy.

delay in acting on the application. The conditional receipt, if properly worded, should eliminate any confusion as to the insurer's responsibility for delay. For example, some insurers include a provision in their conditional receipt specifying that a delay of a given period, 60 days, for example, in issuing the policy is to be construed as a rejection.

EFFECTIVE DATE OF THE POLICY. When the premium is not paid with the application, the contract is not in full force until the policy is issued and the agent has delivered it and has accepted the first premium, all while the applicant is still in good health. The delivery of the policy is the offer; the payment of the premium constitutes its acceptance. After both acts are accomplished, the contract is completed and the insurance is in force.

When the premium is paid with the application but no conditional receipt is issued, the contract is not in force until the policy is delivered to the applicant.[7] The payment of the premium with the application constitutes the offer; the delivery of the policy is its acceptance.[8] The completion of both acts is necessary before the contract is effective and the insurance can be in force.

What constitutes delivery of a policy has been the subject of dispute among the contracting parties. Must there be physical delivery, or is constructive delivery sufficient? The answer depends largely on the wording of the application. Unless the application makes it absolutely clear that physical delivery is required, the general rule is that constructive delivery is sufficient.[9] Constructive delivery usually is considered to have been effected if the company has intentionally and unconditionally given up control over the policy. Thus, a policy placed in the mail to the applicant constitutes constructive delivery. Also, a policy placed in the mail to the agent by the company has been constructively delivered if the agent is free to deliver it to the applicant without restriction.

Possession of a policy itself does not establish delivery if all conditions have not been filled. For instance, a policy might be left with the applicant for inspection, but this does not establish delivery if the premium has not been paid.[10] On the other hand, the policyholder does not have to produce

---

[7] The applicant in this case may withdraw his offer any time before acceptance and has a legally enforceable right to a refund of the premium. On the other hand, when a conditional receipt has been issued, the applicant is not legally entitled to a refund of premium should he change his mind before the policy is issued, although in practice companies may grant this refund.

[8] Whether the issuance of the policy or its delivery to the applicant constitutes acceptance depends largely on the agreement between the insurer and insured. Delivery of a policy is not necessary to its validity or enforceability unless there is an agreement between the contracting parties requiring that delivery be made. However, most life insurance contracts specify delivery as a condition precedent.

[9] There are decisions to the contrary, holding that delivery is a condition precedent to putting the contract into force and cannot be met by constructive delivery. Conflicting decisions are the normal thing in law and are to be found on nearly every point in this discussion.

[10] This is commonly done; but it is usual to require a receipt from the applicant which shows the policy has been handed to him for inspection only and not as legal delivery.

the policy to prove it was delivered. The right to possession rather than physical possession is the controlling factor.

THE CONDITIONAL RECEIPT. Regardless of how the offer is accomplished, the necessities of the insurance business require that the life insurers perform some form of risk selection before making a genuine offer or accepting the offer of an applicant. So that insurance can be in force at the earliest date, yet still allow the insurer the processes of risk selection, the technique of the conditional receipt was developed. When the premium is paid with the application and a conditional receipt is issued, the effective date of the contract depends upon the provisions of the conditional receipt.

Conditional receipts may be broadly classified as condition precedent or condition subsequent. The condition precedent forms require that insurability be established before the policy becomes effective. As will soon become apparent, the weakest of the condition precedent types is the approval form used by a number of life insurance companies. Under this form coverage begins with the date that the application is approved by the company at its home office. The applicant does not have coverage for the period elapsing between the date that the application is sent to the insurer and the date that the application is approved by the company. The advantage that this type of receipt has for the insured is that he is given protection when the policy is approved rather than having to wait for the delivery of the policy. This limited advantage might not provide the applicant sufficient incentive to forward the first premium payment with his application.

The condition subsequent form is the strongest type of "conditional receipt." Under this form the company binds the insurance from the date of the application until the policy is issued or the application is rejected. Note the term conditional is put in quotation marks to suggest that although the insurer binds the coverage, it does not bind itself for the full duration of the applied-for policy. Thus, the coverage is immediately in force but the policy is subject to cancellation. Companies using this type of receipt place a time limit on the binder, usually 30 to 60 days. This truly binding receipt is the most desirable one for the applicant because he becomes insured from the time the application is filed until it is acted upon, even though the ultimate action is rejection. This form of receipt is not widely used.

The most common conditional receipt is a less strict type of condition precedent form. Under this form, the insurance becomes effective as of the date of the application or medical examination, whichever is the later, provided the applicant is found insurable as of that time. A claim arising after this date will be paid even if the application papers have not yet reached the home office, provided, of course, that the facts on the application and the results of the medical examination are such that the company would have accepted the application had the applicant lived. The payment

---

Such a receipt is probably not a legal necessity if it can be clearly shown he has not fulfilled all the conditions precedent, but it is a wise precaution and will prevent misunderstanding with the beneficiary should the applicant die before he pays the premium.

of claims even though no policy has been issued is by no means rare. Also, if the health of the applicant changes after the medical examination or if other changes in insurability occur, the policy will be issued as long as the applicant was insurable at the time of application or medical examination.

While the advantage to the applicant of this customary form of conditional receipt is clear, not so obvious is the advantage to the company. The cost of processing an application and issuing a policy is not insignificant. If the applicant refuses a policy after these expenses are incurred, there is no way in which the company can be reimbursed. Collection of the premium in advance under a conditional receipt helps to solve the declination problem.

OPERATIVE DATE OF THE POLICY.   Interesting questions arise with respect to applications without conditional receipts and those that have been antedated to gain the advantage of lower rates. If the application has one date, the policy another, and delivery still another, which date governs (1) subsequent payment of due premiums, (2) the incontestable period, (3) the suicide period, and (4) the inception of the term under the extended term, nonforfeiture option.[11]

The policy becomes effective when the offer has been accepted. When no conditional receipt is issued, this will be the actual or constructive delivery date of the contract after the first full premium is paid. However, the policy is not dated as of the time of delivery. The policy date is usually the date of the application, or the date the policy is written. In either case, it is a date earlier than the delivery date. The courts generally have held that the policy date, known as the date of issue, determines when premiums are due even though in the absence of a conditional receipt this means that the insured receives less than one full year of protection for the first premium. For the suicide and incontestable clauses, the operative date also is usually held to be the date on the policy. This is true even when the policy is antedated to take advantage of a lower premium.[12] If the suicide and incontestable clauses themselves state the operative dates, then these dates are usually held to apply. If the insured fails to pay a premium and the policy is placed on an extended term basis, the terms begin with the due date of the defaulted premium even though this is earlier than the anniversary of the effective date of the policy.

Consideration.   For a contract to be valid, there must be a valuable consideration—i.e., each party must give or promise something of value. In an insurance contract the value exchanged by the insurance company is its promise as defined in the contract. The consideration given by the insured for this promise is the statements made in the application and the payment of the first premium.

---

[11] Cf. Chapter 10 for a discussion of incontestability and suicide and Chapter 11 for a discussion of nonforfeiture options.

[12] A person aged 26 years and 8 months, for example, may be issued a policy dated back 2 months so that he will be charged the premium for age 26 rather than the higher premium for age 27 when the premium is based on age at nearest birthday rather than, as with some insurers, age at last birthday.

Legal Capacity. For an agreement to be binding on all parties, the parties involved must have the legal capacity to enter into a contract. With respect to the insurer, if the company is organized and empowered to solicit life and health insurance under the insurance code and under its charter, its capacity to contract in that state is clear.

With respect to the insured, the requirements are the same as for any other contracting party: he must be of legal age and of sound mind. Thus, two problems arise: minors and the mentally incompetent. In the absence of contrary state statutes, contracts made by minors are voidable except for the reasonable value of necessaries.[13]

The legal majority in most states is 21. In some states the legal age for females is 18. However, a large number of states have special statutes reducing the legal age for making life insurance contracts. These reduced legal ages range from $14\frac{1}{2}$ to 16 years. In New York, for instance, the legal age for a minor making a contract for insurance on his own life is over $14\frac{1}{2}$ (insurance age 15). This recognizes the fact that, although life insurance is not necessary, it has important values to the insured and his family, regardless of the legal age requirement.

Because a contract made with an underage applicant may be held unenforceable if the minor decides to repudiate it at a later date, "reduced-age" statutes protect the insurer rather than the minor insured. A minor is capable of entering into a contract, and it is not illegal to make a contract with a minor. The insurer is bound by the contract as long as the underage minor wishes to continue it in force. Furthermore, if the underage minor repudiates his contract, the law may allow him a refund of *all* premiums paid (although a few courts will allow a deduction for the cost of protection received). The practice of issuing an insurance contract to an underage applicant is not infrequent despite the danger of repudiation. No question of legal capacity is involved, however, if the application for insurance on a minor is made by a competent adult.

Insanity or mental incompetence precludes the making of a valid insurance contract if a guardian has been appointed. Such contracts are void. If no guardian has been appointed, a contract made by the insane or incompetent is voidable and is handled in the same manner as are contracts made by minors.[14]

A person who is too intoxicated to understand the nature of the contract he is about to make also does not have the legal capacity to contract.[15] He may repudiate the contract when he becomes sober.

Public Policy. To be valid, a contract must be for a legal purpose and

---

[13] A distinction should be made between the terms void and voidable. An agreement which is prohibited by law and held to be an invalid contract is called void. If a contract is held to be valid but one party has the right to rescind the contract on the grounds of incompetency, fraud, or duress, the contract is called voidable.

[14] The standard of mental competence is very low and includes all but the feebleminded.

[15] The ability to understand the nature of the transaction in which a person is about to enter is interpreted very broadly; otherwise, most life insurance contracts made by the soberest of men would be voidable.

not contrary to public policy. Although in the early history of the life insurance business, some courts did hold the life insurance policy to be a contract for illegal purposes, today no such question is involved.[16] However, there are several instances in which insurance contracts will be held to be against public policy. The first of these involves the absence of an insurable interest.

1. *Insurable Interest.* The applicant for life insurance must have an insurable interest in the life of the person on whose life the policy is to be written; that is, he must have a reasonable expectation of loss arising from the death of the insured. Without an insurable interest, an insurance policy becomes a gambling contract and, as such, is unenforceable at law. Usually the person on whom the insurance is to be issued and the applicant are one and the same. In this case, insurable interest is held to exist without question or to be immaterial to the contract.[17] Furthermore, the insured has the legal right to name anyone he wishes as his beneficiary without regard to insurable interest. This latter right is guaranteed by statutes in some states and is established by court decisions in others. But insurers also have the right to refuse to accept an application calling for a beneficiary which might create a hazard the insurer is not willing to accept.[18]

However, if the application for the insurance is made by a party other than the person whose life is insured and that applicant is to be the beneficiary under the policy, he must have an insurable interest in that life.[19] An insurable interest is a reasonable expectation of financial benefit from the continued life of the subject or an expectation of loss if the subject dies.

---

[16] During the Elizabethan period, life insurance was widely used as a gambling device. By the end of the 17th century, several countries had outlawed life insurance but later amended their laws to allow life insurance where a pecuniary interest existed.

[17] Vance, in his work on insurance law, argues that a person does not have an insurable interest in his own life since, in effect, he does not live to suffer a financial loss by his death. He concludes that the better reasoning is that insurable interest is not material when a person has insured his own life. Patterson, in his *Essentials of Insurance Law* (2d ed.; New York: McGraw-Hill Book Co., 1957), agrees with this contention.

[18] Regardless of the legal rights possessed by the insured, the naming of an unrelated beneficiary for other than a valuable consideration, for example, might be considered by a company's underwriting department as a possible indication of moral hazard and by its legal department as a possible source of litigation over the payment of proceeds.

[19] Aside from the insurance company, three additional parties are involved in an insurance transaction: the *subject*, the *owner*, and the *beneficiary*. The subject is the person upon whose life the insurance is written. He is usually referred to as the insured. The owner is the person who retains all the rights in the policy (technically known as "incidences of ownership"), such as the right to surrender the policy for its cash value, the right to effect a policy loan, the right to receive policy dividends, and the like. The beneficiary is the person who has the right to receive the proceeds of the policy in the event of the death of the subject. When a person insures his own life and names his estate as beneficiary, all three parties are the same person. But when one person applies for a policy on the life of another and names still another as the beneficiary, all three parties are separate and distinct as long as the applicant retains the incidences of ownership. If a person insures his own life, retaining incidences of ownership, and names another as beneficiary, the owner and subject are the same, but the beneficiary is a separate party. If a person insures the life of another, retains the incidences of ownership, and names himself as beneficiary, the owner and beneficiary are the same, but the subject is a different party.

For instance, a parent has a clear insurable interest in the life of a minor child, since he is entitled to the services and earnings of that child. A person also has a clear insurable interest in the life of his or her spouse—the wife because of her husband's legal obligation to support her and the husband because of the value of his wife's services. The relationship between husband and wife carries a sufficient presumption of insurable interest without requiring proof of close financial ties. In several jurisdictions, courts and some statutes have held close ties of blood or marriage sufficient to establish insurable interest, such as ties between brother and sister, parent and child, and even grandparent and grandchild. The court decisions in these cases seem to have based the insurable interest either on a presumptive financial relationship or on *love* and *affection*. When love and affection have been held to establish an insurable interest, the resulting loss is construed to be an emotional rather than a pecuniary one. However, such rulings are in the minority since the majority rule is that in the absence of a pecuniary interest, love and affection, even when backed by family ties, do not establish an insurable interest.

Several examples of insurable interest that do not involve family relationships may be cited. An unsecured creditor has an insurable interest in the life of a debtor.[20] A business has an insurable interest in the life of a key employee or part owner. A surety has an insurable interest in the life of the principal.[21] Anyone being supported by another has an insurable interest in that person's life, and a woman has an insurable interest in the life of her fiancé. These last two illustrations point up the general rule that insurable interest need not be based on an obligation legally enforceable by law or even on a moral obligation. An expectation is sufficient.

A general rule subject to exceptions noted below is that even though an insurable interest exists, one person may not insure the life of another without his consent. As a matter of practice, insurance companies usually require the subject to sign the application for the policy. New York has a specific statute which rules void all life and health policies procured without the consent of the subject. Certain exceptions are made. For example, a wife may insure the life of her husband without his consent;[22] an employer does not have to obtain the consent of his employees in establishing a group insurance program for them; a father does not need the consent of his minor child to effect juvenile insurance.[23] The *consent* rule is a precautionary measure taken against the moral hazard. If sufficient insurance is taken

---

[20] A creditor who is *fully* and *completely* secured in connection with his debt would not seem to have an insurable interest in the life of his debtor, since there obviously could be no financial loss by the creditor at the death of the debtor.

[21] That is, someone who has guaranteed the performance of another has an insurable interest in the life of the person for whose nonperformance he will be liable.

[22] This is an exception in the New York statute. In other jurisdictions courts may require consent.

[23] In some states statutory limits are placed on the amount of life insurance which a parent may take on a minor child.

by an applicant-beneficiary to make the subject worth more to him dead than alive, the subject might be placed in a precarious position even though the applicant-beneficiary has the necessary insurable interest.

It is generally held that the insurable interest need exist only when the policy is purchased. The courts usually do not inquire into the status of the interest as of the time the policy becomes a claim.[24] Thus, a business can continue a life insurance policy on the life of a key man or part owner who is no longer associated with the firm or company. A creditor may continue a policy on a debtor after the debt has been paid.[25]

The amount of insurable interest is not a matter of concern for the courts.[26] It is invariably held that the life insurance contract is not a contract of indemnity. Therefore, the beneficiary does not have to establish the amount of his loss in order to receive the entire proceeds of the policy following the death of the insured. If insurable interest exists at all, it is presumed to be the amount of the policy. The one exception is insurance taken by a creditor upon the life of a debtor. The courts generally require a reasonable relationship between the amount of insurance proceeds payable to the creditor and the amount of the indebtedness. A creditor cannot collect, say, $5,000 when the debt is only $150. Such a transaction would be viewed as a gambling contract, and therefore against public policy. Courts, however, have upheld insurance payments to creditors for as much as $6,500 when the debt was only $1,000. The amount of the allowable discrepancy between the amount of the insurance payable to the creditors and the amount of the debt is a matter for the court to decide in each disputed case. The courts generally have been liberal in establishing their standards of reasonableness. The amount of insurance payments in any event should be enough to repay the premiums for the insurance, the interest thereon, and the unpaid balance of the debt.

The insurable interest requirement is not solely for the safeguard of the insurer. The insurer should use reasonable care when issuing a policy to a party other than the insured. This fact was made clear the hard way to an insurer that issued life policies totalling over $6,500 to an aunt-in-law on the life of her deceased husband's niece. To obtain the policy, the aunt-in-law misrepresented the relationship between herself and the minor. The "loving" aunt-in-law, after receiving the insurance policy, proceeded to poison the niece. However, the maxim that crime does not pay proved true, and the aunt-in-law was convicted of murder and suffered the penalty of death. The

---

[24] An exception is found in Texas. Unless the subject purchases the policy and designates the beneficiary, the courts of Texas insist that an insurable interest exists as a precondition to receiving the death benefits.

[25] Some courts have held that, in a debtor–creditor relationship, an insurable interest is required at the time of the death of the insured. This is a minority view.

[26] It is a matter of concern, however, for the underwriting departments of insurance companies. Underwriters look upon excessive amounts of insurance with suspicion. They are concerned not only with excesses in relation to the amount of insurable interest involved, but also in relation to the ability of the applicant to pay for the coverage.

bereaved father sued the life company on the grounds that its wrongful and negligent act of issuing the insurance policy on his daughter created a motive for the murder. The jury granted an award of $75,000, which was supported by the Alabama Supreme Court.[27]

The lack of insurable interest may make the policy something other than an insurance contract. The proceeds of a life insurance policy paid by reason of the death of the insured usually are not taxable under the federal income tax, but if it can be proven that the contract is other than one of insurance, the proceeds may be taxable. The Internal Revenue was successful in one case in proving that a life policy taken out by an employer on an employee truckdriver was a wagering contract rather than an insurance contract. The inability of the employer to prove an insurable interest allowed the Internal Revenue Service to tax the death proceeds of the policy.[28]

The New York law states that if a party receives benefits from a contract made in violation of the insurable interest requirement, the estate of the insured may take action to recover such benefits.

2. *Enemy Aliens.* A contract with an enemy alien is held to be against public policy, and hence void. There is no question on that point. However, questions do arise when a contract has been made with an alien friend who later becomes an enemy. Usually conditions make it impossible for the alien or the company, or both, to carry out the terms of the contract. The disposition of life insurance contracts made under such conditions has been subject to diverse court decisions. In general, it has been held that the policy terminates and the reserve as of the date of failure to comply with its terms (usually to pay the premium) becomes payable to the owner of the policy. The nonforfeiture provisions apply just as in the case of any other lapse. In some cases it has been held that the policy is suspended but may be reinstated later.

3. *When the Beneficiary Murders the Insured.* Payment of life insurance proceeds to a beneficiary who has murdered the insured is considered against public policy. Where the purpose of the murder was simply to collect the insurance, the court unquestionably will not allow the beneficiary to collect. A man is not entitled to profit by his own wrongdoing. If the murder was not insurance induced, but, for example, was maritally induced the courts also will deny the murdering beneficiary the right to collect. But if the beneficiary should kill the insured in self-defense, or while the beneficiary is insane, the courts will award him or her the proceeds of the policy.

Homicides are not always murders; they may be manslaughters—i.e., they may represent the unlawful killing of a human being without malice expressed or implied. The attitude of the courts in manslaughter cases is not unanimous as in murder cases, although the general view is that the

---

[27] *Liberty National Life Insurance Company* v. *Weldon,* 267 Ala. 171, 100 S. (2d) 696.
[28] *Atlantic Oil Company* v. *Patterson,* C.A. 5, 2/23/64.

beneficiary may collect life insurance proceeds if he commits involuntary manslaughter.[29]

When the murderer-beneficiary is not allowed to collect the proceeds of the policy, the proceeds are paid to the estate of the insured. Where the murderer-beneficiary is also an heir to the estate of the insured, some courts have held that the beneficiary may receive all the estate to which he is entitled under the will or laws of descent. Other courts have ruled that the estate is to be divided among the innocent heirs. This latter ruling seems more in line with the spirit of the law.

Finally, when the insurer can prove that the policy was taken with murder in mind, it can have the policy voided on the grounds of concealment. Premiums paid usually are refunded to the estate of the murderer, his heirs, or as otherwise directed by the court.

4. *When the Insured Is Executed for a Crime.* Although some courts, on the grounds of public policy, have denied the right of a beneficiary to collect the proceeds of a life insurance policy if the subject has been executed for a crime, the general rule is to allow recovery. In most states a constitutional provision requires that no conviction be allowed to work a forfeiture of the estate of the convicted party. On the basis of these provisions, which most courts hold as expressing a public policy, life insurance policies are not held to be defeated if the insured meets his death by execution for a crime; it is felt that the innocent parties (the beneficiaries) should not be penalized for the crime of another person whose life has been insured.

Distinguishing Characteristics of Life Insurance Contracts. Although requiring the same elements that are required by all types of contracts, the life insurance contract has a number of distinguishing characteristics. It is a contract of *utmost* good faith, a *unilateral* contract, a *conditional* contract, a *valued* contract, a contract of *adhesion,* and an *aleatory* contract.

Utmost Good Faith (Uberrimae Fidei). Most contracts are good faith contracts. However, in the insurance contract each party has the right to depend on the utmost good faith of the other party regarding the nature of the risk to be assumed. Neither "buyer beware" nor "seller beware" has any place in insurance dealings. A level of good faith above that in the usual commercial transaction is required. It is upon this principle that doctrines of warranty, representation, and concealment are based.

A life insurance company does not have to insure all applicants. It can and does select among them. In the process of selection, the company relies in part on information furnished by the applicant. If this information is false or incomplete, the company may be in a position to void the contract by resorting to legal action.

---

[29] Several states have statutes which prevent a beneficiary from collecting proceeds of insurance policies if he unlawfully kills the insured. Patterson suggests, however, that the courts might interpret such statutes to apply to murders only. Cf. Patterson, *op. cit.,* pp. 166–67.

Warranty. A warranty in insurance is a statement or condition incorporated in the contract relating to the risk, which the applicant presents as true and upon which it is presumed that the insurer relied in issuing the contract. Marine insurance, the first branch of insurance to develop commercially, evolved the doctrine of warranty as it applies to insurance. The marine underwriter was usually called upon to underwrite a hull and cargo which he had no chance to inspect. In fact, it might be lying in a port 10,000 miles away. Therefore, he had to depend entirely upon the word of the person seeking the insurance. Hence, all information in the application for the insurance was warranted to be absolutely exact. If it turned out to be untrue in any way the insurance was voidable whether the misstatement was intentional or unintentional, material to the loss or immaterial. Literally, if the captain's wife were warranted to be a redhead and she turned out to be a blonde, the policy could be voided. The strict warranty rule still prevails in marine insurance. Thus the materiality of all statements is established in advance by contract and thereby is taken out of the hands of judicial interpretation.

The doctrine of warranty carried over into the field of life insurance in its early days. Answers to questions in the application had to be literally true, and the policy could be voided for any misstatement, intentional or unintentional, material or immaterial.

However necessary in marine insurance, it soon became apparent that the doctrine of warranty was too harsh for life and health insurance. Public opinion, enlightened companies, and, finally, legislation were factors in outlawing the application of the doctrine of warranty to life and health insurance. The effect is to revert to the common law rules of misrepresentation and concealment. This makes it necessary once again to rely upon a jury or the court[30] rather than upon a contractual arrangement for the determination of the materiality of misrepresented or concealed facts.

Representation. A representation in insurance is a statement made to the insurer by the applicant or his representative before the contract is made as an inducement to the formation of the contract. Technically a representation is not a part of the contract. But most states have passed *entire contract statutes* which provide, or require the policy to state, that the policy and the application attached to it constitute the entire contract between the parties. Thus, if the insurer intends to rely on statements in the application a copy of that application must be attached to the policy. However, the attachment of the application to the policy technically converts the statements of the application into warranties. Because warranties are more strictly interpreted than representations, the entire contract statutes could work against the insured even though they were enacted for his protection. To remedy this situation, states either have a statute or prescribe a mandatory policy provision which declares that all statements made by the insured in his application shall be deemed representations and not warranties.

---

[30] The jury, if evidence is conflicting; the judge, if it is not.

The doctrine of representations holds that a policy is voidable by the insurer in the event of a misrepresentation of a fact material to the risk—i.e., one which would have led the company to deny the insurance or ask for better terms had the matter been correctly stated on the application.[31] The general rule is that the policy is voidable even though the misrepresentation is nonfraudulent, that is made innocently with no intention to deceive.

However, an honest statement of *opinion,* even though it proves in error, cannot be cause to rescind a contract. Whether a statement is to be interpreted as one of *opinion* or *fact* is up to the court. On a number of questions asked in the application, the applicant obviously can be expected to give only an opinion. Examples are questions involving ancient family history, contemplated changes in occupation, contemplated trips to foreign lands, and whether he is an excessive drinker. In other cases it is obvious that the applicant is expected to present facts. Examples of these are questions involving the applicant's occupation (past and present), whether he has been refused insurance by other companies, and the amount of life insurance he owns on his life. Less obvious situations require the court to sift the evidence carefully. For example, although the applicant's answers to questions about his health usually are a matter of fact, they can under certain circumstances be a matter of opinion.

Another general rule is that a fraudulent misrepresentation of a *nonmaterial* fact will not provide sufficient grounds for avoidance. The purpose of the doctrine of representation is to protect the insurer, not to punish a dishonest insured. If the insurer is not harmed, he should not be allowed to rescind the contract under this doctrine.

Concealment. Concealment also may be grounds for rescission. A concealment is the failure to disclose a material fact; i.e, remaining silent when there is an obligation to speak. In life insurance, in order to void a policy, a concealment must be both *material* and *intentional.* It may be difficult to distinguish between an intentional and an innocent concealment. The test of fraud (intentional deception) usually applied is whether the facts are *obviously* material. If they do not seem obviously material to the judge, the insurer must show him why the insured should have been aware of their materiality.

It is the duty of the applicant to reveal all details or information asked for in the application. An incorrect answer is misrepresentation. A partial answer is concealment. Assume that the applicant is asked if he has ever had a pain in the chest, and although he has one at the time the application

---

[31] Four states (Kansas, Missouri, Oklahoma, and Rhode Island) restrict misrepresentation even beyond the question of materiality, for they require by statute that before a contract may be voided, the loss itself must result from the fact misrepresented. In these jurisdictions, death by an automobile accident may require payment of the proceeds of a life insurance policy even though the insured misrepresented his health. This type of statute excuses the court from ruling on materiality in such cases and relieves it of the task of achieving expertness in the art of underwriting (risk selection).

is being completed, he says no. He would be guilty of a misrepresentation. Assume on the other hand that the applicant is asked if he has consulted a physician in the past four years and, if so, for what purpose. He reports that he consulted one for a common cold but fails to report that he has consulted one concerning the pain in his chest. In this case he would be guilty of concealment. If, after the application is signed, but before the policy is issued, changes occur which would alter any of the answers given, the applicant must reveal these changes if they are obviously *material;* otherwise he may be guilty of concealment. Of course, if the first premium has been paid with the application and a conditional receipt issued, a subsequent change in the insurability of the applicant is *not* material to the risk because the company has agreed to accept or reject the application on the basis of the insurability of the applicant at the time the application is made or at the time the medical examination is taken, whichever is later.

As a rule, the applicant has no responsibility to reveal information not asked for on the application, since it is assumed that if it is not asked for it is not important, nor does the applicant have a responsibility to reveal information that reasonably can be presumed to be known to the company. Further, if a question on the application is not answered and the policy is issued anyway, the company will be deemed to have waived the requirement for an answer.[32]

It should be pointed out that while courts seem inclined to lean over backward in interpreting the doctrines of warranty, representation, and concealment in favor of the policyholder, they are also inclined to take a serious view of obvious fraud. The best advice to the applicant for a life insurance policy is not to rely on the penchant of the courts, and especially juries, for deciding in favor of the individual as against the "soulless corporation," but to answer each question with a clear conscience and reveal any information that he thinks might make a difference.[33]

A UNILATERAL CONTRACT.   A distinction is also drawn between *bilateral* and *unilateral* contracts. In the bilateral contract, each party to the contract makes promises to the other, each in consideration for the promise of the other. In the unilateral contract, only one of the contracting parties makes legally enforceable promises. A life insurance policy is a unilateral contract.[34] Only the insurer makes any legally enforceable promises. The insured does not even promise to pay premiums. It is impossible for him to be held for breach of contract. Payment of premiums after the first one is simply a condition precedent for the continuation of the promise of the

---

[32] Waiver is discussed in sec. 4 of this chapter.

[33] Uniquely among contracts, life insurance and a growing number of health insurance contracts contain clauses rendering them incontestable after a specified period of years, usually one or two. If the misrepresentation or concealment is not discovered by the company prior to the expiration of the period of contestability, it cannot be used to void the policy or as a defense against a claim. The incontestable clause is discussed in the next chapter.

[34] The assessment policy is an exception.

insurer in its present form. Not only is the insurer not able to force the policyholder to pay premiums, but it cannot even void the contract if premiums are not paid. The contract may remain in effect as to the non-forfeiture provisions and the right to reinstate.[35] On the other hand, the insurer is forced to accept premium payments from the insured, and to keep the contract in force in accordance with its terms.

A CONDITIONAL CONTRACT.   The obligations or promises of the insurer as set forth in the policy contract are conditional—i.e., they are conditioned on the performance of certain acts by the insured or beneficiary. For example, they are conditioned on periodic payment of a stipulated premium, furnishing proofs of death or disability and the like. Performance on the company's part is also conditioned upon the occurrence of the event insured against, for example, death or disability resulting from causes other than ones that are excluded in the policy.[36]

A VALUED CONTRACT.   Most property insurance contracts are contracts of indemnity: They agree to pay no more than the actual cash value of the loss the insured has suffered. For instance, a $10,000 fire insurance policy will not automatically pay $10,000 for a total loss by fire. It will pay only the actual cash value of the damage suffered up to a maximum of $10,000. Health insurance policies may have some indemnity provisions. For example, they may agree to pay the cost of medical or hospital care, or of surgical procedures up to a maximum limit; but if the actual cost is not the maximum limit, then they will pay only the actual cost. Health insurance policies are not contracts of indemnity but stated value contracts with respect to accidental death, dismemberment, and loss of time benefits.

However, the life insurance policy is never a contract of indemnity.[37] It is an agreement to pay a given sum of money upon the occurrence of a stated contingency (death, or survival in case of endowment). It may also pay additional amounts in event of disability or of death by accidental means, but these, too, are stated values, not indemnities. They do not measure payment by the actual cash value of the loss. Formulas for measuring human life values notwithstanding, who can place a dollar value on a life?

Furthermore, the usual physical damage, property insurance contract calls for subrogation to the insurer of any rights or claims he may have against

---

[35] These policy provisions are discussed in Chapter 10.

[36] Restrictions were once much more common. In the earlier days of life insurance in America, for example, policies were often filled with restrictions regarding travel abroad, travel below or above certain latitudes, travel in Indian country, and so forth. The present-day policy has dropped almost all such prohibitions, the latest, airplane travel, gradually being dropped from more and more policies. Special restrictions such as war clauses come and go, depending on the imminence of war or nearness to a past war. Cf. Chapters 10 and 14. Chapter 14 deals with health insurance exclusions.

[37] Even in cases of credit life insurance the contract is not one of indemnity to the insurers. The insurer must pay out the value agreed upon in the insurance contract. The creditor can take that part of the proceeds which the court allows him, and any amount of the proceeds remaining would pass to the insured's estate.

anyone else for indemnification for that same loss.[38] The doctrine of subrogation does not apply in life and health insurance. An injured person (or the dependents of a person killed) may both collect the benefits of a health (or life) insurance policy, and retain any damages the court orders paid by the party whose negligence caused the injury (or death).

A CONTRACT OF ADHESION. In some contracts, the parties involved bargain for the terms. In life and disability insurance contracts, the terms are stipulated by the insurer and must be accepted or rejected *in toto* by the applicant.[39]

But as will become apparent in the next chapter, insurance companies do not have complete control over the terms of the contract. Standard provision laws, reduction of warranties to representations, and entire contract statutes have seriously restricted the insurer in drawing up contracts.[40]

Nevertheless the law does leave the insurer some freedom in construction of the contract. However, in cases of ambiguity in contract terms the courts hold to the principle that the policy will be strongly constructed against the insurer. It is the insurer's responsibility to make the terms clear.

AN ALEATORY CONTRACT. Most contracts are commutative—i.e., each party gives up property or services of equivalent monetary values. In the sale of a secondhand textbook, for example, the buyer gets the book and the seller gets its equivalent value in cash. However, the life insurance contract is aleatory. The contracting parties realize that the number of dollars given up by each may not be equal. There is an element of chance insofar as the individual policyholder is concerned. While there is a mutual exchange of equivalent expected values, one party is likely to give up more dollar values than the other: the insured if the policy does not result in a claim, the insurer if it does result in a claim.

Aleatory contracts are of several types: gambling, speculative, and insurance. A *gambling* contract usually is illegal. It creates the risk from which the chance of gain or loss stems. The *speculative* contract is legal. It shifts an existing economic risk from those less prepared to assume it to those more prepared (or willing) to do so. The *insurance* contract, also

---

[38] To illustrate: If an automobile on which there is collision coverage is struck by another automobile, the insurer will be obligated to indemnify the owner of the struck car for the loss. When the owner accepts that indemnification from his insurance company, he hands over to it (subrogates) his right to sue the owner of the car which struck him. If his collision insurer elects to prosecute the claim, and if it subsequently collects, it retains the sum collected up to the amount it paid, turning the excess, if any, over to the policyholder. However, if the passenger in the death seat is killed, his life insurance company is not entitled to subrogation rights against the careless driver. The estate of the deceased may collect both from his insurance company and from the guilty party (or the liability insurance company involved).

[39] Except that some riders and supplemental agreements may be accepted or rejected without affecting the basic coverage. However, in such cases the rider or supplemental agreement must be accepted or rejected *in toto* with no bargaining for its terms.

[40] On occasions when the question as to whether an insurance policy is a contract or a statute (especially with respect to standard policies and provisions) has been put up to the courts, the discussion generally has been circular in nature.

legal, reduces an existing financial risk in society. The insurer accomplishes this by taking advantage of the law of large numbers to reduce risk by predicting losses. Because the insurer is expected to receive enough in premiums to pay all claims and expenses, its total business is no more aleatory than that of any other business, although it specializes in aleatory contracts.

In Summary.   An insurance policy is a contract. For a policy to be valid, it must meet the essentials of all contracts: there must be mutual assent by competent parties for the performance of a legal act for a valuable consideration. A life insurance contract has certain special characteristics, most important of which are its unilateral, adhesive, and aleatory nature.

2. CREDITORS' RIGHTS IN LIFE INSURANCE

The primary purpose of life insurance is to protect the dependent family in the event of the insured's death. If insurance benefits were limited to those who survived a solvent insured, protection for beneficiaries might in some cases be lacking when most needed. For at least this reason rights of creditors to the cash values and proceeds of life insurance policies have been restricted. The creditors' rights to values in a life insurance policy are governed by: (1) common law, (2) federal regulation, and (3) state statutes.

Any discussion of the rights of creditors to the values in a life insurance policy should explore all possible variables—i.e., the rights of the insured's creditors and the rights of the beneficiaries' creditors to the predeath cash values of the policy and to the postdeath face amount of the policy.

Common Law.   The nature of the life insurance contract raises important questions under common law concerning the rights of the creditors of the insured and of the beneficiary in the predeath and postdeath values of the policy. If the notion is accepted that the cash value of the life insurance policy is not the property of the insured unless and until he elects a settlement option or requests a policy loan, then the rights of the beneficiary's creditor and the insured's creditor would be severely restricted. A creditor of the insured is unable to reach what is technically not the insured's.[41]

Furthermore, if the concept is accepted that the particular funds which the beneficiary receives are in no way connected to the funds contributed by the insured to the insurance company, then the rights of the creditors of the insured in the death benefits also are restricted. The death benefits are paid from a pool of all premium payments made by a large group of insureds, only one of whom was this particular insured. A claim by the insured's creditors that part of the proceeds are the debtor's predeath assets may not be upheld in court.[42]

---

[41] While the courts recognize that cash surrender values are not held in trust by the insured, they have found it useful to so view them. Cf. Chapter 1.

[42] Court conclusions in this area have not been consistent. Cf. Chapter 1.

When the courts have been called upon to determine the issues involving creditor rights, it has generally been held that the rights of the insured's or beneficiaries' creditors in life insurance proceeds and life insurance cash values depend upon how the beneficiary is named in the policy.

WHEN INSURED'S ESTATE IS NAMED AS BENEFICIARY. If the insured's estate is designated as beneficiary, the proceeds of the policy are considered a part of the general assets of his estate, and as such can be reached to satisfy a judgment obtained by the creditor against the insured. Although the availability of cash values to meet claims of creditors of the insured is unclear, the general rule is that where the insured is named as beneficiary a policy containing a cash value can be attached before maturity. Whether or not the creditors can collect the cash value of the policy appears to depend upon the policy provisions. These provisions are of two broad types. If delivery of the policy to the company for cancellation is a sufficient condition of payment, the courts usually will allow creditors to obtain the cash values by effecting the delivery. If the right to have the cash values paid is an option to be exercised by the insured, the insurer is under no obligation to pay these values until the insured elects the option. The attaching creditors cannot make the election for him.

THIRD PARTY AS BENEFICIARY. If the beneficiary is a third party, the proceeds of the policy paid to the beneficiary upon the death of the insured are held to belong to the beneficiary and may not be reached by the insured's creditors. However, the proceeds are subject to the claims of the beneficiary's creditors.

The cash values of the policy also are held to be judgment-proof from the insured's creditors on the principle that the beneficiary's right cannot be defeated by the insured's creditors. It appears to make no difference whether the vesting in the beneficiary is absolute, conditional, or qualified.[43] This rule generally is followed in cases involving both irrevocable and revocable beneficiary designations, for if the insured has reserved the right to change the beneficiary, the courts ordinarily will not require him to do so to satisfy a creditor's judgment. As for the creditors of the beneficiary, the cash values of a policy may be reached only if the beneficiary has been named irrevocably and has an absolute and unconditional vested interest.

Federal Statutes. Under federal statutes designed to protect veterans' benefits the values of life insurance issued by the government are protected from the claims of both the insured's and the beneficiaries' creditors. Furthermore, this protection extends to the values before and after maturity of the policy.

BANKRUPTCY. When an insured becomes bankrupt, the Federal Bankruptcy Act determines how life insurance policies shall be treated. Under bankruptcy procedures all assets normally pass to a trustee for his impartial distribution to creditors. Section 6 of this act provides a means of exempt-

---

[43] Cf. Chapter 10 for discussion of beneficiary designations.

ing life insurance funds from the normal distribution procedures. Section 6 states:

This Title shall not affect the allowances to bankrupts of the exemptions which are prescribed by the state laws in force at the time of the filing of the petition in bankruptcy. . . .[44]

As a result, policies which come under the state exemption statutes discussed later are not subject to bankruptcy proceedings. In the absence of state exemptions under Section 6, the Bankruptcy Act, under Section 70a, dictates the rights which creditors may have to the values in the life insurance policies of the bankrupt. Section 70a states that only the cash surrender value of a life policy may pass to the trustee for distribution to the creditors. Since policies payable to an irrevocable beneficiary give the beneficiary a vested property right, the trustee will have no right to these policies. However, the trustee may take the net cash values of all policies under which the insured has reserved the right to change the beneficiary.

A surrender of life insurance policies to obtain the cash values, however, might cause the insured and his beneficiary undue hardship. The policy might be an unusually favorable one with preferred settlement options, or the insured might no longer be insurable. Recognizing a possible hardship, Section 70a adds:

When any bankrupt who is a natural person shall have any insurance policy which has a cash surrender value . . . he may, within 30 days after the cash surrender value has been ascertained and stated to the trustee, . . . pay or secure to the trustee the sum so ascertained and stated and continue such policy free from the claims of the creditors. . . .

Under this provision, the insured can continue the policy in force by paying to the trustee an amount equal to the cash surrender value of the policy. A possible source of funds for use in complying with this provision, of course, is a loan secured by the cash values of the policy.

Should the insured die while in bankruptcy proceedings, the trustee may hold only the amount of the cash surrender value as of the filing date of the bankruptcy. The remaining funds must be directed to the beneficiaries. Remember that all of the foregoing bankruptcy provisions are subject to statutory exemptions.

As dictated by court decisions, insurers have a responsibility not to pay to a bankrupt insured any part of the cash surrender value. In the decision of *Lake* v. *New York Life Insurance Company*[45] the court ruled that the trustees of a bankrupt insured may hold the insurer liable for all funds paid to the bankrupt in settlement options or policy loans after notice of bankruptcy. The trustees' action in taking control of the assets on adjudication of bankruptcy is considered notice to all concerned parties that proceedings

[44] Although this provision does not mention life insurance, it was established in *Holden* v. *Stratton,* 198 S.S. 202 (1905), that policies exempt under state law are excluded from the bankruptcy irrespective of Section 70a, explained below.
[45] 218 Fed. (2d) 394 (C.A. Md. 1955), Cert. denied 75s. Ct. 606.

in bankruptcy have commenced. An insurer not acting in a meticulous manner may be forced to pay the cash surrender value twice.

FEDERAL TAX LIENS. Under federal statute, the federal government can reach the cash values of a life policy for the purpose of satisfying a tax claim. Section 6321 of the Internal Revenue Code allows for the attachment of a lien upon the life insurance policy of a delinquent taxpayer. The provision takes precedence over all other rules, including state exemption laws. To collect the taxes owed, the law allows the government to proceed directly against the insurer. After the government places a lien upon the cash value of the policy, the delinquent taxpayer has 90 days to meet his obligations. If in that waiting period the insured fails to meet his tax debt, the insurer must pay to the federal government the amount of the tax lien or the total cash value, whichever is less. Policy loans made prior to actual notice of the lien do not affect the insurer's status as a creditor of the insured, but any loan transacted after notice of the lien will have secondary status to the government's claims. Furthermore, the tax lien does not take effect over automatic premium loans unless the lien was attached prior to the completion of the automatic premium loan provision of the insurance contract.[46]

Failure of the government to attach a tax lien prior to the insured's death may eliminate its ability to reach the proceeds received by a beneficiary. This is one of the few cases in which the state exemption laws take precedence over tax law.

At the death of the insured, the tax authorities may not collect under a tax lien an amount in excess of the cash surrender value of the policy at the time of the insured's death. However, if a joint husband-wife tax return was filed and the spouse of the insured is the beneficiary, the government may reach the proceeds to collect delinquent taxes.

Following the foregoing principles, the federal government can attach a lien on disability payments or on annuity benefits of a delinquent taxpayer. In the case of *Schwarz* v. *U.S.*[47] the insurer was ordered to make annuity payments directly to the federal government.

Prior to the passage of the 1966 Federal Tax Lien Law some confusion existed as to the effect of a federal tax lien on an insurance policy. The government's position was clarified in several court cases, but the statutory action of 1966 put into law what had previously been only court precedent.

State Statutes. The states have enacted statutory provisions exempting values of life insurance policies from the claims of the insured's and beneficiaries' creditors. In the words of a New York court, these exemption laws were enacted for

. . . the humane purpose of preserving to the unfortunate or improvident debtor or his family the means of obtaining a livelihood, and preventing them from becoming a charge upon the public.[48]

---

[46] Cf. Chapter 10 for discussion of automatic premium loan.

[47] 191 Fed. (2d) 618.

[48] *Crossman Co.* v. *Rancb,* 263, N.Y. 264, 188 N.E. 748.

The laws vary from state to state, and thus the rights of creditors in life insurance depend largely upon the state statutes that apply. The statutes not only are different in themselves but also are subject to even further variation by the effect of court decisions. The rights of a creditor in any state can be ascertained only by a close study of the laws and court decisions in the state involved. However, a general summary may be given under four headings: (1) rights of the insured's creditors in the proceeds of the policy; (2) rights of the beneficiary's creditors in the proceeds; (3) rights of the insured's creditors in the cash values; (4) rights of the beneficiary's creditors in the cash values.

RIGHTS OF THE INSURED'S CREDITORS IN THE PROCEEDS. The rights of a creditor of the insured in the proceeds of a life insurance policy are usually severely restricted.

In some states the entire proceeds may be exempt. In others, there may be a limitation. The statutes in some jurisdictions limit protection to proceeds payable to the insured's wife or children. Others protect proceeds payable to any dependent relative. A number of statutes exempt proceeds payable to any beneficiary other than one who is himself the insured, without regard to relationship or dependency.[49]

Proceeds paid to a trustee for the benefit of a given beneficiary have the same protection from creditors' claims as if they were paid directly to that beneficiary. This rule is well established by case and by statutory law.

The rights of creditors in disability income benefits payable to the insured are not usually restricted by exemption laws in the same manner as are life insurance proceeds. However, a number of states including New York do grant limited exemption to such benefits, such limit being with variations, either a fixed total amount monthly or a monthly amount equal to that purchased by a maximum annual premium.

The State of New York extends exemptions to a maximum of $400 per month of disability income benefits and further exempts all lump-sum disability payments.

New York, along with several other states, also extends its creditor exemption statute to cover annuity payments even if the purchaser is the annuitant. In New York, the amount of this exemption is dictated by the courts after due regard for the personal and family requirements of the debtor. A number of additional states have statutes exempting proceeds of annuities when a person other than the annuitant purchases the policy. In the absence of a specific statutory provision, an annuity ordinarily can be reached by the creditors of the annuitant. The right of creditors to the proceeds of an endowment policy is exempt by several states.

RIGHTS OF THE CREDITORS OF THE BENEFICIARY IN THE PROCEEDS. Generally, the statutes exempt the proceeds from the claims of the insured's

---

[49] Such broad exemption would seem a perversion of the original purpose of such exemptions and not be a protection of dependents but merely a means of avoiding the just claims of creditors. These broad exemptions have been widely criticized.

creditors only, although in a few states the law extends to the claims of the beneficiary's creditors as well. If the statute does not extend to the beneficiary's creditors, the insured may make this protection possible by including in the policy settlement agreement a *spendthrift trust clause* which states that the benefits payable to any beneficiary hereunder after the death of the insured shall not be assignable or transferable nor subject to commutation, incumbrance, legal process, execution, garnishment, or attachment proceeding.[50] To take advantage of the clause, policy proceeds have to be made payable to the beneficiary under one of the installment settlement options, and the payment arrangement usually has to be set up by the insured. The funds so held by the company for distribution are not attachable when there is a spendthrift trust clause. The clause protects only the money held by the company for the beneficiary. As soon as the beneficiary receives the money, creditors may take action for recovery against her.

More than half the states have statutes recognizing spendthrift trusts. In the majority of those states where no statutes exist, courts have upheld spendthrift trust clauses. This leaves only a few states where these clauses are held to be against public policy and are disallowed. In these states, proceeds may be protected from the claims of the creditors of the beneficiary by creating a discretionary trust and making the trustee the beneficiary under the policy. Under the discretionary trust, the corpus of the trust cannot be encumbered. The beneficiary is entitled to collect from the trust only that amount periodically that the trustee in his own discretion cares to give her.

RIGHTS OF THE CREDITORS OF THE INSURED IN THE CASH VALUES. In most states, the wording of the laws granting exemption from claims of the creditors of the insured is broad enough to exempt cash values as well as proceeds. Where the statutes are not clear on the subject, court opinion has been divided. Usually, the use of the term "proceeds" in the statute without the addition of "avails" or "cash values" is held to restrict the protection to death proceeds only. Some courts, however, have held that whatever protection is afforded against the claims of the creditors of the insured in the proceeds extends also to the cash values. Actually, much depends upon the language of the statute involved.

RIGHTS OF THE CREDITORS OF THE BENEFICIARY IN THE CASH VALUES. Most state statutes do not provide for protection against the claims of the creditors of the beneficiary. As for cash values, not much of a problem is created since the beneficiary does not have an absolute vested right in these values unless named irrevocably. Even then, many courts hold that the

---

[50] Reference to the term "trust" in the exemption statutes and court decisions is a careless use of nomenclature because no trust actually is involved. The funds used to pay the principal and interest under life insurance settlement options are mingled with the general assets of the insurer and the relationship between the insurer and the beneficiary is one of debtor–creditor only.

beneficiary cannot cash in the policy without the consent of the insured. Under this line of decisions, the beneficiary's creditors would have no rights without the consent of the insured because it is impossible for the creditors to exercise rights in the debtor's property that the debtor himself cannot exercise.

EXCEPTIONS. In addition to federal tax liens, other broad exceptions are made to the exemptions under state statutes. Creditors of the insured may attach the proceeds or cash values of a life insurance contract regardless of how the policy is set up if (1) the premiums are paid from embezzled funds, (2) premiums are paid while the insured is insolvent, and (3) premiums are paid in fraud of creditors. The burden of proof in each case is on the creditor, and is not easily established.

In the event that life insurance is purchased with embezzled funds and thereafter becomes a claim, the general rule is that the victim of the embezzlement is entitled to recover that part of the proceeds of the policy which has been purchased by these funds, i.e., the percentage of the proceeds which equals the percentage that the embezzled funds bear to the total premiums paid. Contrary opinion requires simply a return of the embezzled funds with interest.

An insolvent debtor can pay premiums for a reasonable amount of life insurance to protect his family without prejudicing the insurance to the rights of his creditors. This is the law in the absence of fraudulent intent. If fraud is established, the creditors may recover from the proceeds of the policy up to the extent of the premiums paid plus interest.

THE ILLINOIS STATUTE. To this point the discussion of necessity has been general. For a quick reference to the laws of any given state, see the *Digest of Insurance Exemption Laws,* published by Research and Review in its *Advanced Underwriting Service*,[51] or look directly into the state statutes involved.

For illustrative purposes, the following is a digest of the Illinois law relating to both life insurance exemptions and spendthrift trusts.

Life Insurance. The statute provides that all proceeds payable because of the death of the insured, and the aggregate cash value of any or all life and endowment policies and annuity contracts payable to a wife or a husband of the insured, or to a child, parent or other person dependent upon the insured, whether or not the right to change the beneficiary is reserved, and whether or not the insured or his estate is a contingent benficiary, shall be exempt from execution, attachment, garnishment or other process for the debts and liabilities of the insured, except as to premiums paid in fraud of creditors.

Spendthrift Trusts. The statute provides that any domestic life company may hold the proceeds of any policy issued by it with such exemptions from claims of creditors of beneficiaries other than the policyholder as shall have been agreed to in writing by such company and the policyholder. The same rule applies to a foreign or alien company when authorized by its charter or laws of its domicile.

---

[51] The Research and Review Service of America, Inc., 1720 East 38th Street, Indianapolis, Indiana.

3. POWER OF AGENCY

Life and health insurance operate through a system of agents. Companies grant to selected individuals the power of agency. The power of agency is much broader than the power of attorney: the power of attorney is power to act *for* the company in legal matters, but the power of agency is the power to act *as* the company for one or more specific purposes. The agent's knowledge is presumed to be the company's knowledge, and the company's knowledge is presumed to be the agent's knowledge.[52]

Types of Agents. Two types of agents may be distinguished: general agents and special agents. A general agent is empowered to act as the company in all matters. A special agent is empowered to act in specified matters only.

Unfortunately, confusion exists in the insurance business between legal terms and common usage of the word "agent." It is common to use the term "general agent" to describe an agent who is empowered to appoint subagents in a given territory. However, he is not a "general" agent because he is authorized by his agency contract to act for the company only in specified matters: appointment of subagents in his territory, solicitation of new business, collection of premiums, and related matters. He cannot bind the company on other matters reserved for executive officers. Executive officers are the only true *general agents* of the company. What is commonly called a general agent in life and health insurance is actually a special agent; the man who is usually called an agent is actually a subagent.[53]

In a discussion of the legal aspects of agency in insurance distribution, four matters need consideration: presumption of agency; authority of agents; limitation of the powers of agency; and the responsibility of principals for acts of agents.

Presumption of Agency. If a company has supplied an individual with forms and other materials which make it logical for a reasonable person to presume that such individual is an agent of the company, it is likely that a court would hold that a presumption of agency exists. Under these conditions the company would be bound by the acts of this individual as though he had been give the express authority presumed in this case. For instance, if a former agent is allowed to retain materials which could lead the public to assume that he is still an agent, he would probably be held to have a presumptive power of agency.

However, there is no reason to assume that a man is an agent for a company merely because he represents himself as an agent. He must be so

---

[52] This is a very broad generalization to which there are many exceptions. For a collection of interesting cases on agency in life and health insurance, see Barry Oakes, *Principal, Agent, and the Public*, Conference on Insurance, University of Chicago Law School Conference Series Number 14, 1954.

[53] A subagent who has the authority to appoint other subagents often is called a district agent.

equipped or so presented by the company as to raise a reasonable presumption on the part of the public that he is so empowered.

Authority of Agents. The authority of the insurance agent is set forth in his agency contract. For the soliciting agent, that stipulated authority usually includes soliciting and taking applications for new business, arranging medical examinations, collecting the first year's premium, and, in some instances, accepting renewal premiums in exchange for renewal receipts properly signed by the company. Rights usually specifically excluded are to make, alter, or discharge any contract; to waive any forfeiture; to waive payment in cash; to extend the time of payment for any premium, or to accept payment of a past-due premium; to approve evidence of good health; or to accept any money due the company other than premiums, as described.

IMPLIED AUTHORITY. In addition to the express authority granted by contract, the agent is held in common law to have certain implied authority. For example, any authority which the public may reasonably assume an agent to have is implied as long as the public has not been notified to the contrary. It arises from the realization that it is unreasonable to expect the public to scrutinize the agency contract before dealing with the agent.

However, the doctrine of implied power does not mean that the public can assume that an agent has the power to do whatever he pleases. For the presumption to exist, there must be an action or lack of action on the part of the company that (1) gives the impression that its agent has the authority in question or (2) fails to correct the impression that an agent does not actually have the express authority for the disputed act. For instance, it is well-established practice for an agent to accept the first premium. If a company were to deny this power in an agent's contract, it almost certainly would be held that the agent had this power under the doctrine of implied authority, assuming, of course, that the third party did not know of this restriction. On the other hand, it is not a common practice among companies to empower soliciting agents to commit the company to mortgage loans. Therefore, the action of an agent in making such a commitment for the company is not likely to be held within the scope of implied authority.

APPARENT AUTHORITY. Again, while the agent's contract expressly states that he does not have authority to accept a past-due premium, the court probably would hold that the agent had that power if he had frequently accepted such premiums in the past without protest from the company. The policyholder from whom he had accepted past-due premiums would have the right to assume that such acceptance was within the scope of his agency powers. This is the doctrine of apparent authority.

Limitations of the Power of Agency. Limitations of the power of agency must be properly communicated to the public. Announcements of such limitations contained in application forms and in the policy meet this requirement.[54] Policies contain a provision to the effect that only certain

---

[54] The requirement also can be met by an oral or written communication which is not a part of the policy or the application.

designated officers of the company have the power to make or modify any contract of insurance, or to extend the time for paying a premium, and that the company shall not be bound by any promise or representation "heretofore or hereafter given by any agent or person other than the above."[55] This clause serves as proper communication to the public of the limitations on the power of both special agents and company officers. Company officers not named obviously do not have the power.[56]

Responsibility of Principals.   Since an agent is a principal within the scope of his power of agency, granted and apparent, the company is responsible for his acts. In fact, in the eyes of the law the acts of the agent and the acts of the company are one and the same. Further, limitations on the agent's authority must be in conformity with the general rules of law. A company cannot disclaim responsibility for any actions of the agent which are reasonable and necessary in the pursuit of his duties as an agent. To a limited extent, the company is even responsible for the misstatements and misrepresentations of its agents, even if fraudulent in nature. In event of misrepresentations or fraudulent promises on the part of the agent, the applicant can demand and receive a refund of premiums paid. Usually, however, the company cannot be forced to live up to these misrepresentations or fraudulent promises.

Since knowledge of the agent is assumed to be the knowledge of the company, if the agent knows a material fact related to the application, the applicant has a right to presume that he has given that information to the company. The agent's failure to communicate the information to the company is no defense for the company. Assume that in answer to a question on the application, the applicant gives information to the agent that the agent knows would cause the company to "rate up" or reject the application. Assume further that the agent fails to record the answer or the adverse part of it. Should the company discover the information after the policy is issued, it cannot invoke the doctrines of concealment or misrepresentation to void the policy, since legally, when that information was given to the agent, the company had it.

The responsibility of the company, when an agent erroneously interprets

---

[55] Oddly enough, this clause does not always give the company the protection it desires. For example, in *West* v. *National Casualty Company,* 112 N.E. 115, the court accepted the principle that the agent can waive the clause which restricts his power to alter or modify the policy. The reasoning in the case was that an agent operating within his actual or apparent authority may waive any clause beneficial to the insurer since he is the insurer. Thus, the agent can waive the clause which prohibits him from waiving clauses, and, after that, waive whatever clause he wishes that is in the company's favor. However, when the restrictions are put in the application, the insured is on notice before the contract becomes effective, thus largely negating the situation which occurred in this particular case.

[56] In general, any limitation on the powers of general agents (that is, company officers) contained in the company's charter is effective. A charter is assumed to be public knowledge. However, restrictions in the bylaws would not be effective—unless properly communicated —because bylaws are not public knowledge. In general, the public has the right to assume, unless otherwise notified, that general agents (company officers) have all powers necessary to carry out the contracts of the company.

a policy provision to an applicant or policyholder, depends on the provision involved and the jurisdiction in which the dispute is heard. In some jurisdictions, if the clause is ambiguous in wording, it will be held that the agent's interpretation is valid. If, on the other hand, the wording is so clear that any reasonable person could see by reading it that the agent was misinterpreting the clause, the company would not be held to the misinterpretation. In other jurisdictions the agent's opinion is given no weight.

While conducting the medical examination, the examining physician is the agent of the company. His concealment of or failure to report any facts found by him or revealed to him by the applicant is the responsibility of the company.

Brokers as Agents.   In most jurisdictions a difference exists between the relationship among insured, broker, and company and that existing among insured, agent, and company. In general, the broker is the agent of the *insured,* not of the *company.* Technically, the insured, or prospective insured, empowers the broker to act for him as his agent in obtaining insurance. Consequently, the actions of the broker are not held to be binding upon the company. However, in insurance law, there are exceptions. Some states have statutes which make anyone who solicits insurance for persons other than himself the agent of the *insurer* on all policies arising out of the solicitation. Some states make the broker the agent of the company only for delivering the policy and collecting the premium. Therefore, it becomes necessary to look to state law to determine whether or not a statutory agency has been created out of the operations of the broker. If so, the statutes must be examined further to determine whether the agency is created for *all* or just *some* of the broker's operations.

4. REMEDIES

Although statutes and litigation have clarified the responsibilities of all parties to a life insurance contract, disputes and problems related to the terms of the contract may develop. To deal with these contingencies certain remedies have been developed by statute or legal precedent.

Interpleader.   It is not uncommon for an insurance company to be faced with conflicting claims to the proceeds of an insurance policy. Over the years that a policy is in force beneficiaries may come and go. As a result, questions may arise upon the death of the insured concerning the rights of beneficiaries. In cases involving conflicting claims to the proceeds of a life insurance policy, the insurer may use the remedy of interpleader,[57] assuming that there is no remedy in law. This technique allows the court to settle the conflict and eliminates the need for several simultaneous suits. Under this remedy, the insurer pays the proceeds directly to the court and

---

[57] This remedy is based upon the Federal Interpleader Act first passed in 1917 and revised in 1926, 1936, and in 1948. Furthermore, most states have statutes covering the use of interpleader.

leaves to the court the problem of determining who gets what. The insurer fulfills its obligation to pay the proceeds and eliminates the possibility of having to pay the claim more than once. The use of interpleader is common in cases where the insured fails to name a beneficiary, where the insured has been divorced several times, or where the insured had given positive indication that he desires to change his beneficiary.

In all of these cases questions could possibly arise concerning the distribution of the proceeds. For example, in one case a son had named his father as beneficiary of a life policy. However, the insured had given verbal intentions of changing the beneficiary to his wife. At the insured's death the wife sued to recover the proceeds. The insurer deposited the proceeds with the court for its disposition. Since the insured had taken no affirmative actions to change the beneficiary, the father's claim to the death benefits was supported by the court.[58]

Reformation. Reformation, as is also true with interpleader, is a remedy which is brought before a court of equity.[59] Reformation is a technique used to correct the unintentional clerical errors that may develop in the process of formulating the life insurance contract. Reformation allows for the contract to be corrected so as to show the original intentions of the contracting parties. It is not the purposes of reformation to construct a new contract. In order to qualify for reformation, the mistake must be mutual. However, there are two circumstances under which nonmutual mistakes can receive the benefits of reformation: (1) where there is fraud on the part of one of the contracting parties or (2) where one of the parties is guilty of unnecessary neglect to act on a known mistake (laches). The majority of courts have held that the incontestability clause does not stop reformation as a remedy for clerical errors. In addition, the parol evidence rule (see p. 196) does not apply in suits of reformation.

In cases of typographical errors similar to those found in this text, the court would reform the contract. Thus, if an insurance policy was supposed to have death benefits of $1,000, but the policy mistakenly was typed to show death benefits of $10,000, the court in all probability would allow the contract to be rewritten to show the intended amount of $1,000. The insurer would have to bear the burden of proving the error.

Waiver and Estoppel. Through the common law remedies of waiver and estoppel the insurer may be estopped from using misrepresentation or concealment as a defense against fulfillment of its obligation under the contract. By its action, the insurer may give up the right to use what are under normal circumstances acceptable defenses. Since the agent is the party who usually deals directly with the insured, it is the agent's activities which frequently create situations that bring about the use of waiver and estoppel.

---

[58] *Collins* v. *Collins,* 378 Fed. (2d) 1020; 7 Life Cases (2d) 734 (4 Cir. 1966).

[59] "Courts of equity use maxims instead of rules of law. Strictly speaking, there are no legal rights in equity, for the decision is to be based on moral rights and natural justice." Robert Corley and Robert Black, *The Legal Environment of Business* (New York: McGraw-Hill Book Co., Inc., 1963), p. 156.

A waiver is generally defined as the intentional relinquishment of a known right. Thus, the company has a right to demand an answer to the question not answered. If it does not, it has intentionally ignored the right to the answer. Closely related to waiver is estoppel. Estoppel comes about when one party to a contract, by his action or inaction, induces the other to change his position to the disadvantage of the first party. Whereas one court might hold that failure to demand an answer to an unanswered question constituted *waiver* of the right to make the demand, another might hold the company was *estopped* from demanding the answer. Waiver and estoppel are alternative methods of being placed in the same situation. Whether a given result is reached by waiver or estoppel, the effect is essentially the same. The dividing line between the two concepts is decidedly blurred.

That applicants put great reliance on the statements and actions of agents is given legal recognition through the doctrines of waiver and estoppel. However, the parol evidence rule places limitations on the processes of waiver and estoppel. Parol evidence bars any evidence from being introduced which tries to prove that the terms of the contract are other than those written in the contract.

An example of how an insurer may give up certain rights should help to remove confusion surrounding the concepts of waiver and estoppel. An insured had received a policy which did not allow him to make any beneficiary changes, but at a later date the insurer allowed such a change. At the insured's death the original beneficiary and the new beneficiary both sued for the proceeds. A request for interpleader was denied. The courts upheld both suits. The courts ruled that the old beneficiary had vested rights at the issuance of the policy, and the insurer was estopped from not paying the claims. In the case of the new beneficiary the courts ruled that the insurer had waived its rights to invoke the no change in beneficiary clause when it allowed the beneficiary change. Since the insurer had represented to the insured that it would recognize the beneficiary change, it must also pay the new beneficiary. Thus, the insurer was forced by the courts to pay the proceeds twice.[60]

---

[60] *Phillips* v. *Continental Assurance Co.*, 210 Pa. Super 178, 231 A (2d) 422, 7 Life Cases (2d) 742 (1967).

10

General Policy Provisions

It is perhaps a tribute to the insurance business and the regulation of it that an insurance contract can be called the nation's least read best seller. Nearly everyone believes in life insurance, and the majority of people buy it; yet few policyholders ever read a life insurance contract all the way through with any attempt to understand its various provisions. This is sometimes unfortunate, for policyholders frequently have the most garbled impression of what any particular policy promises.

A life insurance policy is a legal contract, its validity as such having been established in the United States since 1815.[1] As a contract, it contains provisions setting forth the rights and duties of the policyholder and the company. Although it is necessary to look beyond the policy into statutes or court decisions for the interpretation and full effect of policy provisions, these provisions nevertheless are the basis of the agreement between the company and the policyholder (and the beneficiary, estate, heirs, or assigns of the policyholder, in fact).

1. STATUTORY LAW RELATING TO POLICY CONTRACT

The provisions of the policy contract are closely regulated by statutory law. Most state insurance codes provide for certain (1) mandatory provisions, (2) prohibited provisions, and (3) permissible provisions.

Mandatory Provisions. While in life insurance there are no "standard policies"[2] such as may be found in fire insurance, nearly all states require the inclusion of several fundamental provisions in every policy issued in

---

[1] *Lord* v. *Ball,* 12 Mass. 115 (1815).

[2] Standard policies were attempted in New York following the Armstrong investigation in 1906. Four other states passed similar legislation in 1907. Standard policies were abandoned in 1909. (For a discussion of reasons, cf. Krueger and Waggoner (eds.), *The Life Insurance Policy Contract* (Boston: Little, Brown & Co., 1953), pp. 339 ff.) In lieu of the standard policy, New York adopted a set of provisions required in substance. These provisions are the basis of the mandatory or "standard" provisions now required in almost all states. They should not be confused with the 1912 Standard Provisions for health policies or the Uniform Provisions for health policies discussed in Chapter 14.

their jurisdiction. The law sets forth the substance of these provisions, which form the minimum requirement. Other wording of the mandatory provisions, if more favorable to the policyowner, may be substituted. If a mandatory provision is left out of a policy, the courts will interpret the contract as though it contained the required provision.

With some variation among the states, mandatory provisions usually cover (1) a grace period; (2) incontestability; (3) entire contract; (4) misstatement of age; (5) policy dividend distribution in the case of participating contracts; (6) options available in event of default in payment of premium; (7) loans and table of loan values; (8) table of installment payments under available settlement options; (9) reinstatement; (10) dividend options; (11) nonforfeiture provisions and tables of their values; (12) deferment of loan and cash value payments.

Each of these provisions will be discussed either later in this chapter or in Chapter 11.

Because there is no standard policy in life insurance, and the mandatory provisions specify only minimum requirements, companies may draw up policy contracts more liberal than the law requires. Therefore, competition produces some variations among policy forms and provisions.

Prohibited Provisions.   In addition to requiring minimum provisions, the laws also prohibit the inclusion of certain other clauses. Examples of prohibited provisions are (1) forfeiture because of failure to repay a loan while indebtedness under a policy is less than its cash value; (2) limiting the time in which an action in law or equity may be commenced to fewer than two years after the cause of the action; (3) backdating a policy for more than a specific period (commonly six months) before the original application was made; (4) requiring warranties in the application; (5) providing that the rights and obligations of the policy shall be governed by the laws of a state other than that in which the policy was issued; (6) excluding or restricting liability for death caused in a specified manner except certain permissible exclusions; (7) a provision for any mode of settlement at maturity of less value than the amount insured by the policy;[3] (8) assessable clause (New York); (9) a clause which attempts to make the life insurance agent the agent of the insured. If a prohibited provision is inserted in a contract, the courts will interpret the policy as though the provision did not appear.

Permissible Provisions.   The law requires the inclusion of some provisions, it prohibits the inclusion of others, and it allows but does not require another set of provisions. The permissible provisions apply to the exclusion of coverage in event of (1) death from military service in wartime;

---

[3] The latter restriction would prohibit a company from settling a $12,000 policy by paying $100 a month for 10 years. It must express the face in terms of its present or principal value (known as the commuted value) where a series of periodic payments is concerned. The present value of a series of payments of $100 a month for 10 years is worth less than $12,000, assuming an interest rate in excess of 0 percent.

(2) death within five years as a result of war while traveling outside the United States, its possessions, or Canada; (3) suicide within two years from the policy's date of issue; (4) death resulting from certain types of aviation; (5) death resulting from certain hazardous occupations, if it occurs within two years from the date of issue. Other permissible provisions include ownership provisions, change of plan provisions, and assignment provisions.

The provisions of a life insurance policy may be classified under the headings of *insuring agreement, general provisions, nonforfeiture options, settlement options,* and—in the case of participating polices—*dividend options.* This chapter will consider the insuring and general provisions. Nonforfeiture, settlement, and dividend provisions will be discussed in Chapter 11.

2. INSURING CLAUSE AND CONSIDERATION

The insuring agreement and the consideration clause are usually (but not always)[4] found on the face of the contract as the opening statement.

Insuring Agreement. In the insuring clause, the company agrees to pay the face amount of the policy immediately upon receipt in writing of due proof of the death of the insured, provided premiums have been duly paid, the policy is in force, and is then surrendered or properly released. The agreement is subject to all the conditions, benefits, and privileges described in the policy pages, which are made a part of the contract.

The insuring clause varies slightly according to the type of policy. The clause as detailed above applies to whole life contracts.

Consideration Clause. In some clauses the consideration is the advance payment of the first premium or an installment thereon. In others, the consideration includes both the premium payment and the application.[5] Payment of subsequent premiums is a condition precedent to the promise of the company to keep the policy in force.

There is confusion in law as to what constitutes payment of the premium. Does it have to be in cash? Can it be by check? Will a promissory note be sufficient?

Checks are customarily considered cash equivalents and therefore fulfill the cash payment condition. What if the check is no good? If the company agrees to accept the check as absolute payment rather than conditional

---

[4] A survey of the policies of 12 companies in the portfolio of one policyholder reveals that 8 carry the consideration clause on the face and 4 carry it elsewhere. This is no implication that the ratio would hold if the policies of all companies were surveyed, but only that there is variation in the location of the clause among policies of different companies.

[5] The same survey mentioned in footnote 4 revealed that five companies make the premium the only consideration, while 7 make the consideration both the premium and the application. It is felt in these latter companies that including the application as part of the consideration emphasizes the fact that the application is a part of the policy contract.

payment, then acceptance of a check for the full first premium binds the contract even if the check is no good. In this case the insurer has the right only to court action for recovery of the amount of the check. However, most checks are accepted as conditional payment. In these cases the courts rule that the debt is unpaid if the check is not honored. Thus, the first full premium is not considered paid, and the contract is not in force. Companies usually include a condition in the contract to the effect that "no check or bank draft accepted in exchange for this receipt shall be considered as cash unless payment is received upon presentation to the proper bank."

Many companies do not consider a promissory note the equivalent of cash. A note, therefore, is not adequate consideration for the issuance of a conditional receipt. However, if the company has granted the agent authority to deal in promissory notes, the cash payment clause is waived, and the note becomes adequate consideration for the issuance of a conditional receipt. What happens if the note is not honored when it matures? The general rule is that unless the note, premium receipt, or policy (one or the other depending upon the jurisdiction) contains a stipulation that the policy will be repudiated if the note is not honored at maturity, the premium is considered paid and the action of the company is limited to its rights on the note. Thus, once a note is unconditionally accepted in payment of a premium by an agent who has the authority to accept it, the premium is considered paid, and the policy becomes independent of the note.[6]

3. GENERAL PROVISIONS

The general provisions of the policy usually consist of the mandatory provisions plus various permissible and miscellaneous provisions. Each of these will be discussed briefly.[7]

Ownership Clause.   The person in whom the ownership privileges of the policy are vested is named. He may be the subject of the insurance (commonly called the insured) or he may be the beneficiary. He may even be someone other than the subject or the beneficiary. Ownership privileges are the right before the death of the insured to assign, transfer, or agree to any modification of the policy; without the consent of any beneficiary, to change the beneficiary at will; and to receive every benefit and exercise every option, right, and privilege provided in the policy or

---

[6] Some agents who are not authorized to extend credit on behalf of their companies independently extend credit to their policyholders by paying the premium for them. If the policyholder fails to reimburse the agent for the premium when the debt falls due, the policy is unaffected since the financing transaction is independent of the policy contract.

[7] It is beyond the scope of this book to give a definitive analysis of each provision or to go into the various case law ramifications. These details are interesting and in fact sometimes amusing but have educational value only for those specializing in the law. If interested and time is available, see Krueger and Waggoner, *op. cit.*

allowed by the company to the owner. Thus, the policy owner has the right to receive cash values, loans, dividends (if any), and other benefits accruing under the policy. The term "owner" means the named owner, his successor or transferee. Upon the death of the insured, ownership of the policy becomes vested in the beneficiary.

Entire Contract. The policy and the attached application are made the entire contract between the company and the insured or policy owner. No statement made by the insured or on his behalf shall void the policy or be used in defense to a claim under the policy unless it is contained in the written application. This clause is statutory in most states, and one of its purposes is to prevent the company from making its bylaws, charter, or any other instrument not in the contract a part of the policy. At one time, the practice of making the charter and bylaws of the company a part of the insurance contract was prevalent. This worked a hardship on the policyholder. In the first place, the policyholder rarely knew what was in the company bylaws and charter. In the second place, a change in these instruments would change his contract of insurance, probably without his knowledge.

Actually, the policy, application, and amendments are not the entire contract, despite the statement to that effect in every policy. Statutory law is also a part of every contract, as is judicial or case law. The policyholder and company cannot waive the benefits of the law even by mutual agreement. However, due to the existing system of state by state regulation and varying common law interpretations, it is not always clear which is the governing law. Consider the following situation: The policy has been issued in one state by a company domiciled in another. The policyholder has moved to a third state. He has several co-beneficiaries who reside in still different states. Laws often vary from state to state, and court decisions may vary by jurisdictions. Which law applies has been the subject of conflicting court decisions in the past.

The majority rule is that the validity and interpretation of the policy depend on the law of the state in which the last act creating the contract took place. Thus, if the first premium is collected when the policy is delivered, the state law governing will be that of the domicile of the policyholder. However, when the premium is paid in advance with the application, and a conditional receipt has been issued, the last act creating the contract is the acceptance by the company. Under these conditions, the law of the state of domicile of the company applies. This is known as the "contact" or "place-of-making" rule.

While the trend is toward the contact rule, other rules have been applied because of the varying court philosophies. Some courts, for example, have held that the laws of the state of domicile of the insured always govern; whereas other courts have held that the laws of the state of domicile of the company always control.

When there is a conflict of law, the rule used in resolving the conflict is that of the state in which the case is being tried. When the trial court determines which law governs, it must apply its own interpretation of that law even though that law happens to be one of another state. The Supreme Court of the United States has held[8] that federal courts also must follow the conflict of law rules prevailing in the state in which the case is heard. Finally, even though the policy contains a clause specifying the state law that is to govern the validity and interpretation of the contract, it appears that only the insured or his beneficiary is allowed the benefits of this clause. If its enforcement would favor the insurer, the clause is disallowed.[9]

Still other factors make it necessary to look beyond the policy despite the entire contract clause. Often, as mentioned, the conditional receipt, issued with the policy when settlement is made, contains provisions that are a part of the agreement between the policyholder and company. The law of most states does not require that an application for reinstatement of the policy after a lapse be attached to the policy; yet such an application is usually held to be a part of the contract since the company can contest settlement if there has been misrepresentation in connection with reinstatement. Riders are a part of the contract if attached to the policy and made a part of it by reference, but courts have held that such riders need not be signed by both the policyholder and the company to be effective. A few courts have held that even advertising material is a part of the policy contract. Some courts have held that the entire contract requirement does not preclude the use of subsequent agreements, since the requirement and provision refer only to the contract at the time it is first issued.

In other words, while the entire contract clause does prevent the company from making its charter or bylaws a part of the contract, and prevents the company from using statements made by the insured or on his behalf as a defense against a claim unless they are written in the application, it does not in every case prevent the necessity for looking outside the policy for the whole contract.[10]

Premium Payment.   The policy acknowledges receipt of the first premium and states the date on which subsequent premiums will be due. In ordinary policies, the basic period of premium payment is usually annual; however, the policyholder may, upon agreement with the company, pay premiums semiannually, quarterly, or sometimes monthly. Premiums are payable at the home office, agency office, or to an agent. Formerly it was the practice to issue a formal receipt signed by the company registrar or similar official and countersigned by a cashier. The statutes generally re-

---

[8] *Griffith* v. *McCoach,* 313 U.S. 549 (1941), and *Klaxon* v. *Stentor Electric,* 313 U.S. 487 (1941).

[9] If this discussion sounds inconclusive and confusing, the simple fact is that it is inconclusive and confusing. Blame the courts, not the author!

[10] For an interesting discussion of this point see Daniel J. Reidy, *Trends in Life Insurance,* in the Insurance Lecture Series, University of Connecticut, Spring, 1953.

quire that policies contain a provision for delivery of a receipt signed by a company officer and countersigned by the agent when premiums are paid to agents, but in the interest of economy, most companies no longer issue receipts unless they are specifically requested. Where the premium is paid by check, the check is sufficient receipt. Failure of an agent to give a receipt does not violate the provisions of the contract since such receipts have been held for the protection of the company. The company can, of course, "waive its rights."

Commonly, but not always, calculation of the net premium is based on the assumption that it will be paid in advance. If this assumption is used, premiums paid more frequently than annually are merely installments of an annual premium. In event of death before the full annual premium has been paid, the unpaid installments can be properly deducted from the proceeds. However, the practice of deducting unpaid premium installments has been subject to public misunderstanding. Therefore, it has become the predominant practice to waive unpaid fractional premiums due after the date of death. Moreover, some companies make a provision for refund of a proportionate amount of any premium paid beyond the date of death, whether the premium is paid annually or fractionally. The effect of these practices is to increase the cost of insurance. The added expense of premium refunds can be handled by loading the premium for it.

Some companies incorporate a premium deposit provision in the contract under which money may be deposited in advance, at interest, and used to pay premiums as they fall due. According to company practice or contract provision, the fund may or may not be withdrawable, a minimum rate of interest may or may not be guaranteed, and the deposit fund upon death of the insured may or may not become a part of the policy proceeds to be distributed under one of the settlement options to be discussed in the next chapter.

The Grace Period. Most states require companies to include in their policies a "period of grace" after the premium due date, during which period the policy remains in full force even though the premium has not been paid. The period is usually stated as 1 month, 1 month but not fewer than 31 days, or merely 31 days. The law usually permits a provision for an interest charge from the due date to the date of payment on any premium paid during the grace period, but few, if any, companies require the charge. If death occurs during the grace period and before the premium has been paid, the amount of the premium due is deducted from the proceeds.

A relatively few states require the sending of premium notices,[11] usually not less than 15 days nor more than 45 days before premiums are due. The typical law in these few states prohibits the company from lapsing a policy

---

[11] A second premium notice is rarely required. Companies formerly made a practice of sending a second notice. In the interest of economy, they have generally discontinued this plan.

within one year after default if it fails to comply with the notice provision. Therefore, in such states, failure to give a premium notice has the effect of extending the grace period to one year.

Reinstatement. If the premium is not paid within the grace period, the policy lapses if it has no surrender value; otherwise, it is placed on one of the nonforfeiture options.[12] However, the policy usually provides for reinstatement under certain conditions if applied for in a stated period after nonpayment. Although reinstatement clauses are required by only half the states, they are nearly universally used. In those states requiring a reinstatement provision the minimum period allowed is three years; but the policy may offer a more liberal provision, and periods up to five or more years are found.[13] Reinstatement clauses were voluntarily inserted into policies by a number of insurance companies long before they were required to do so. These clauses were first used before the advent of nonforfeiture provisions. They were designed to correct the inequity of making defaulting policyholders forfeit their interest in the policy completely and forever.

Reinstatement means that the policy is revived and the relationship between the policyholder and the company becomes the same as it was before the default in the payment of the premium. Reinstatement revives the old policy; it does not create a new policy. Reinstatement usually requires evidence of insurability satisfactory to the company and payment of all premiums in arrears with interest thereon at a specified rate. Naturally, the policy must not already have been surrendered to the company for cash.

Evidence of insurability, in case of reinstatement, is required to prevent selection against the company.[14] If the premium default has been recent, the company usually requires only a statement from the policyholder certifying he is in good health. If the default is not recent, a medical examination may be required. Insurability means not only good health but also good habits, good morals, an acceptable occupation, and general conformance with the underwriting standard of the company. If the policyholder no longer meets these standards, his policy will not be reinstated.

Every life insurance policy contains a clause making it incontestable after a given period. What happens to the contestability of a reinstated policy? The majority rule seems to be that a reinstated policy again be-

---

[12] Except that if the policy contains a provision for, and the policy holder has elected to take advantage of, an automatic premium loan, the loan value up to the amount of the premium due will be used to pay the premium. If there is no automatic loan provision in effect, then any cash value may be used to keep the policy in force under one of the nonforfeiture benefits discussed in the next chapter.

[13] A survey of policies reveals some containing provisions which place no time limit at all on reinstatement.

[14] Selection against the company means, in this instance, that parties with loss probabilities significantly in excess of those allowed for in the premium charged will purchase the insurance in order to take advantage of a condition adverse to the insurer. Thus, for example, there could be a tendency for people who find their health impaired after lapsation to reinstate, whereas fewer of those who have no health impairment will take action to reinstate.

comes contestable for the period provided but only as to the statements made by the applicant in applying for the reinstatement.[15] The passage of statutes supporting the majority opinion has resolved the question in many states. Nearly every policy contains a suicide clause which limits the liability of the company to a return of premiums paid if the policyholder commits suicide within one or two years. Majority opinion holds that reinstatement does not reopen the suicide clause because the policy is not a new contract but a resumption of the old one.

For three reasons it is better for defaulting policyholders to reinstate old policies than take new ones. First, many old policies have more liberal settlement options, or they may have other desired provisions which no longer are available. Second, another acquisition cost would be charged against the values of a new policy and reflected in the increments in its cash value. Reinstating old policies rather than purchasing new ones is usually the more economical way of reestablishing a given amount of insurance unless unusual circumstances are involved. Third, the investment value of a policy grows as the policy grows older, especially if the nonforfeiture values remain intact.

Incontestability. The incontestability clause in a life insurance policy makes it impossible for the company after a period of time (usually two years) to contest any statements made in the application or any concealment of material facts in order to avoid payment of the proceeds. The clause is usually a simple statement announcing that, except for nonpayment of premium, the policy is incontestable after a specified period of time. Thus, after the contestable period, the company cannot seek to set aside the policy on the grounds that it was obtained by misrepresentation or concealment.

The incontestability clause as found in life insurance contracts is an anomaly among contract provisions. The law of contracts holds that a contract involving fraud is voidable at the option of the aggrieved party. The innocent party may rescind the contract any time within the statute of limitations. The time limit allowed by the statute begins when the fraud is discovered and not when the contract is made. Further, the law usually holds that an agreement to disregard fraud is a violation of public policy and hence void.[16] Although it was not the intention of the incon-

---

[15] Among contrary opinions (all a small minority) are three theories: (1) A few courts have held that fraud in the application for reinstatement vitiates that application and therefore leaves the policy as it was—lapsed. It follows, therefore, according to this view, that reinstatement is not a contract but instead waiver of a lapse. (2) Other courts have held that reinstatement does not reopen the incontestability clause in the original policy but does subject the reinstated policy to contestability based on the reinstatement agreement which is of itself a new contract governed by all the common law principles relating to fraud. (3) Still other courts have held that the original contestable period applies. If it has expired by the time the policy is reinstated, the reinstated policy can not be contested.

[16] When the clause makes the policy incontestable from the beginning, the courts will usually honor it in cases of simple misrepresentation and concealments but not in cases of fraud.

testability clause to protect the beneficiary from fraud on the part of the insured, but to protect him only against innocent material misrepresentations,[17] the courts have interpreted the clause more broadly than expected. They have allowed it to become an agreement to disregard fraud in the life insurance contract after a specified period. The clause has been in use since the 1860's, is required by many states, and has been held to apply in the most flagrant cases of fraud. Although there is social and economic justification for incontestability in life insurance, there is no generally accepted legal explanation for the incontestability provision or for the decisions upholding it.[18] It is a clause peculiar to life insurance contracts.[19]

The incontestability clause is designed to protect the policy owner and beneficiary against any attempt to set the policy aside. However, it does not prevent a claim from being contested on the grounds that it is excluded from coverage under the terms of the contract. A defense against a claim is a suit to enforce contract provisions, not to set the contract aside. Similarly, it does not prohibit suits over construction of the policy or over its terms; nor does it bar a defense that the policy never went into force.

Since the incontestability clause is a provision of the contract, it has no force until there is a contract. If the contract legally never goes into effect, the clause is inoperative. For example, if an impersonator makes the application and takes the physical examination, or answers the health statements, the policy can be set aside even after the contestable period. In such circumstances it is held that because there was never mutual assent, as required for a valid contract, no contract ever existed.

As the clause itself is an anomaly among contract provisions, so is the inclusion of the wording, "except for nonpayment of premiums." The incontestability clause prevents setting aside the policy as of the beginning of the contract. Nonpayment of premiums does not set aside the policy from the beginning. The lapsing insured still has rights under the policy: reinstatement and nonforfeiture, for example. The wording seems to be a remnant of earlier days when some policies provided that in the event

---

[17] Some of the earlier incontestability clauses included the phrase, *except for fraud.*

[18] Horne and Mansfield in *The Life Insurance Contract* (2d ed.; New York, Life Office Management Association, 1948) refer to the incontestability clause as "something in the nature of a private contractual 'statute of limitations' to modify the statutory limitation." These authors quote the decision in *Clements* v. *Life Ins. Co. of Va.,* 155 N.C. 57, 70 S.E. 1076 (1911) to the effect that the "courts will not aid those who sleep on their rights, but only those who are vigilant." A legal right must be asserted within a proper time or not at all, and with respect to the incontestability clause the proper time is the time fixed in the policy.

[19] Lest this discussion create a one-sided impression, it should be pointed out that while it is true that the courts have interpreted factual situations which appear to be fraudulent in such a way that they are considered simply misrepresentations of material facts and within the protection of the incontestability clause, no court, to the knowledge of the author, has construed a set of facts as fraudulent and then stated that once the contestable period has run, the company may not defend against a claim the payment of which would be against public policy. In fact, in the event of a gross fraud that would outrage public policy, the incontestability clause has been set aside. Thus, when a policy is taken out with the intent to murder the insured, the incontestability clause cannot be used to prevent the company from denying liability on the grounds of fraud.

the premium was not paid, the policy would become void, thus voiding the policy from its beginning. The inclusion of the wording is now so well established that its omission might be looked upon by some courts as something different, and therefore subject to new rules of interpretation.

As has been pointed out, a defense against a claim on the grounds that it is improper or not covered is not a suit to avoid the policy but to enforce the conditions of the contract. However, enough courts have mistakenly held otherwise in the case of the disability and double indemnity provisions that the usual wording of some incontestability clauses has been altered to state an exception in the case of those provisions. Such a clause might read:

This policy shall be incontestable after it has been in force during the lifetime of the insured for two years except for nonpayment of premiums and except for the restrictions and provisions applying to the double indemnity and disability benefits provided.

Other policies will seek to meet the problem by providing, in the riders adding disability and double indemnity, that the incontestability provisions of the policy do not apply to these riders.

The incontestable clause has undergone several changes in wording in order to improve the probability that the courts will interpret the clause as intended by the insurer. The original incontestable clause stated that the policy shall be incontestable after two years from the date of issue. In interpreting this clause the majority court opinion in early cases held that if the insured should die during the contestable period, the incontestable period continues for two years. The reasoning seemed to be that since the clause is for the protection of the beneficiary as well as the insured, all terms of it also should apply to the beneficiary. For beneficiaries who feared the existence of evidence that might give grounds for contesting the policy, this ruling gave encouragement to postpone filing claims until the expiration of the two-year contestable period. These beneficiaries could then expect to be successful in their efforts to collect life insurance proceeds.

This interpretation led some companies to change the wording of the incontestability clause on new policies to read that the policy should be incontestable after having been in force for a given period. This attempt to prevent beneficiaries from obtaining the protection of the incontestability clause by withholding claim until the expiry of two years did not work according to expectations. Courts held that the policy was still in force after the death of the insured because the policy is for the benefit of the beneficiary.

In another and successful attempt to clarify their intentions insurers have reworded the clause to provide that the policy shall be incontestable after having been in force for the period specified during the lifetime of the insured. This wording has been held by virtually all courts to mean that upon the death of the insured during the contestable period, the policy can never become incontestable. This latter wording is the most common among incontestability clauses and has been adopted as part of the required policy provision laws in a number of states.

The practice of allowing parties to a life insurance contract to fix by stipulation the length of time after which fraud can be used as a defense is justified. The impracticability of assembling evidence and witnesses many years after issuance of the policy is clear. Defense against fraud is especially difficult if it must be made by a beneficiary after the death of the accused insured. The incontestability clause is particularly valuable to the beneficiary in preventing delayed settlement resulting from long, tedious, and costly court action. While it is true that the clause may allow some unscrupulous people to take unfair advantage of the insurer, the protection it gives the rank-and-file policyholder outweighs this limitation.

Misstatement of Age and Sex.   Most state laws require that life insurance policies include a provision that if the age of the insured has been misstated, the amount of the insurance will be what the premium paid would have purchased at the correct age according to the company's published rate at the date the policy was issued. For example, if a person aged 30 gives his age incorrectly as 25 when he purchases a $10,000 nonpar continuous premium whole life policy for $165.60, his coverage will be adjusted downward to about $8,670 when his correct age becomes known. The published rates at the time the policy is issued for the company from which the above illustration is drawn are $19.10 at age 30 and $16.56 at age 25. At $19.10 per $1,000, $165.60 will purchase $8,670 of insurance. The clause also applies in event the age is incorrectly overstated. If the applicant mistakenly gives his age as 30 when it is 25, a $10,000 continuous premium whole life policy purchased for $191 will be adjusted to about $11,530 when the mistake in age is rectified.

Adjustment of the proceeds by reason of misstatement of age is not blocked by the incontestability clause. The adjustment is not a contest of the policy but an operation of a policy provision. However, a misstatement of age discovered during the contestable period can give the insurer the right to rescind the contract if the underwriting rules of the company would not have permitted it to write the policy had the correct age been known. The effect of age on underwriting is discussed in Chapter 23.

Since the premium charged for females is usually less than that charged males, any misstatement of sex may also be grounds for adjustments in the proceeds. The insurer would pay proceeds based on what the insured could have purchased with his premium dollar had the sex been properly stated. To students on the college campuses at the end of the decade of the 1960's, a misstatement of sex clause in his (her or its) policy would come as no surprise. It is possible to misstate sex in those insurance situations in which the underwriters do not require a physical examination.[20]

---

[20] Cf. Chapter 23.

Unlike a misstatement of age clause, a misstatement of sex clause is not a mandatory policy provision although such a clause will be found in a number of recently issued policies.

The mandatory inclusion of age clauses and the commonly used phrasing of these clauses have come under criticism. This criticism is primarily based on the observation that the age clause works an unnecessary hardship on beneficiaries. Although the age clause protects the beneficiary from forfeiting all proceeds, it does create the possibility for the beneficiary to incur losses due to settlement delays and litigation expenses. It has been suggested that the inclusion of the presently worded age clauses works against the goal which the incontestability clause seeks to achieve, that is assurance to the beneficiary that the face amount of the policy will be readily available when the insured dies. One researcher suggests the following: (1) extend the protection of the incontestable clause to age statements and (2) eliminate the age clause as a required life insurance clause.[21] In most cases in which the beneficiaries are offered proceeds less than the face amount of the policy due to a contested age, the burden of proof is on the beneficiary to show that the insured's age is other than that used by the insurance company. This can work a hardship on the beneficiary since for many people proof of age does not exist. Furthermore, if the beneficiary wishes to contest the insurer's allegation, he must incur the costs of court action and the inconvenience and expense of delays without reimbursement.

Although debate on various policy provisions can be expected from time to time, such debate emphasizes the need for continued reappraisal of policy provisions.

Suicide. Nearly every policy contains a provision restricting the liability of the company in event of suicide. A typical clause reads, "If, within two years from date of issue hereof, the Insured shall die by his own act, whether sane or insane at the time, the company shall be liable for only an amount equal to the premiums paid hereon, without interest." In some policies the time limit is only one year. The clause developed as a result of (1) conflicting court decisions regarding the right of the beneficiary in the absence of such a clause to recover when the insured commits suicide and (2) the attitude that while the insured should be spared the higher cost which would result if claims were paid on policies purchased in contemplation of self-destruction, such costs should not be controlled at the expense of the innocent beneficiary.[22]

---

[21] Oscar R. Goodman, "Public Policy and the Age and Incontestable Clauses in Life Insurance Contracts," *Journal of Risk and Insurance,* Vol. XXXV (December, 1968), pp. 515–35. Professor Goodman apparently does not object to the misstatement of sex clause because the burden of proof here would present no special difficulty to the beneficiary.

[22] Some courts have held, in the absence of suicide clauses, that inasmuch as the charge for insurance is based on mortality statistics which include deaths from all causes, coverage of suicide is not an undue cost burden on other policyholders. Cf., for one

The one- or two-year exclusion of coverage offers the insurer some protection against the insured who fraudulently takes out a policy in contemplation of suicide. The innocent beneficiary is given some protection by allowing him to recover if suicide does not occur until the end of that period. The majority opinion of the courts today is that "suicide while sane or insane" can be properly excluded from coverage for a given period of years as in the standard suicide clause if the contract so provides and if there is no state statutory prohibition against the suicide defense.[23]

Inasmuch as suicide is an exclusion of coverage by terms of the contract, most courts hold that it is not affected by the incontestability clause. Denial of a claim on the grounds of suicide under the suicide exclusion is not a contest of the policy but a suit to enforce a policy provision. Conflicts between the suicide and the incontestability clauses arise only when the suicide exclusion runs for a longer period than the incontestability clause.[24] Since the type of incontestability clause now most widely used ceases to run upon the death of the insured, there is little possibility of conflict arising where the suicide period is less than or equal to the incontestable period.

Where suicide is suspected within the exclusion period, the burden of proof is on the defendant (the insurance company) to establish that the insured took his own life. Because of the instinct of self-preservation, where there is doubt the court always assumes that the death is unintentional rather than intentional. While the plaintiff has the benefit of the legalistic assumption that a sane man will not commit suicide, the presumption stands only until satisfactory evidence is introduced to the contrary.

Loan Value. The company will make loans on the sole security of the policy at any time while it is in force except when the policy is under the extended term nonforfeiture option.[25] The loan may be for any amount

---

example, *Campbell* v. *Supreme Conclave,* I.O.H., 66 N.J.L. 274, 49 Atl. 550, 54 L.R.A. 576 (Ct. Err. & App. 1901). In an earlier case, the U.S. Supreme Court held (*Ritter* v. *Mutual Life Insurance Co.,* 169 U.S. 139 [1898]) that the policy does not cover suicide if the policy remains silent on the subject because to do so would be against the public interest, and would not be carrying out the intentions of the contracting parties. This, however, is not the current view. The limited-duration exclusion of the modern suicide clause theoretically protects against the fraud involved in taking out a policy in contemplation of suicide while adhering to the theory that all deaths should be covered in the absence of fraud.

[23] A Missouri statute (*Mo. Rev. Stat. Ann.,* paragraph 5851) makes the suicide defense available only where it can be shown that the insured took out the policy in contemplation of self-destruction. In New York State the suicide clause cannot contain the words, "sane or insane." In order for the clause to come into operation, it is necessary to establish that the insured was sane.

[24] This might be the case in Virginia, for example, where a two-year suicide period but only a one-year incontestable period is allowed.

[25] The extended term nonforfeiture option is a provision under which the net cash value of the policy is used to purchase paid-up term insurance in an amount equal to the face amount of the policy extended for a period determined by applying the applicable premium rates to the values available. For detailed explanation, cf. Chapter 11.

which, with interest as specified in the contract, shall not exceed the cash value of the policy (and of any paid-up additions purchased with the policy dividends) at the end of the policy year in which the loan is made. Existing indebtedness to the company on the policy, including due and accrued interest and any unpaid premium for the year in which the loan is made, is deducted from the loan value. The granting of any loan, other than to pay premiums on the policy, usually may be deferred by the company for a period of not more than six months from the date of the loan application.[26]

Loans are made at an interest rate stated in the policy, usually 5 percent or 6 percent, and the statutes require that the rate be level throughout the duration of the loan. Interest is payable at dates specified in the loan agreement, usually in advance on the anniversary date of the policy at the time the premium falls due. Interest not paid when due is added to the amount of the loan and bears interest.[27] Loans may be repaid only while the policy is in force during the lifetime of the insured, but not if the policy has been placed on the extended term, nonforfeiture provision. Failure to repay a loan or to pay interest will not terminate the insurance unless the total indebtedness equals or exceeds the loan value, and then not until 31 days after notice has been mailed to the last known address of the insured and any assignee of record.

Courts have held that a policy loan is not a loan under any condition but merely an advance payment by the insurer of funds which are, or will be, payable under the policy to, or at the direction of, the policyholder either as cash values, matured endowments, or death benefits. The estate of the insured, therefore, is not liable for unpaid policy loans. The recourse of the insurer is to deduct any unpaid balance from the policy proceeds. For example, if an insured dies with a $3,000 policy loan outstanding on a $15,000 policy, the company will pay $12,000 to the beneficiary. The beneficiary cannot recover the other $3,000 from the insured's general estate because the loan is not a legal obligation of this estate.

Where there is an irrevocable beneficiary designation, the beneficiary must join the insured or owner in the request for the loan and in the loan agreement unless the policy states otherwise. In juvenile policies, the applicant, who is usually the parent, has the sole right to execute policy loan agreements until the child reaches maturity. If the law gives a juvenile the right to contract for life insurance in his own name at an age prior to legal majority,[28] the juvenile is then the owner of the policy and may exercise the loan rights contained in it. Where a juvenile or mental in-

---

[26] The deferment provision was added to policies generally after 1934 when the closing of banks led to fears of "runs" on cash values. However, some companies included deferment clauses in their policies prior to that time but often for periods less than six months.

[27] If the interest is paid by adding it to the loan rather than in cash it is not deductible for federal income tax purposes.

[28] As in New York, where a juvenile has the power to contract for insurance at age 15.

competent has a court-appointed guardian, the guardian may exercise the borrowing privilege under court approval. However, it has been held that if the insurer has no notice of mental incompetence, then a loan made upon application of the policy owner is made in good faith. The exclusive right of an assignee to borrow on the policy is clearly set forth in the standard assignment form developed by the American Bankers' Association and the Association of Life Insurance Legal Counsel, which has been accepted by the companies and which is discussed later in this chapter.

When the company makes a policy loan it usually requires that a proper loan agreement be sent to the company's home office. It has been held unnecessary for the company to have physical possession of the policy since it can prove the validity of the loan through the separate loan agreement, which in addition to the policy provision itself also sets forth the terms of the loan. Should the insured subsequently borrow from another lender on an unendorsed policy, representing to the lender that the policy is unencumbered, the insured is guilty of fraud. The lender probably would be held to have been negligent in making the loan since no assignment is binding on the company until the company is notified. If the lender had duly notified the company in advance of the loan, he would have learned of the existing policy loan. No lender who would do otherwise could be considered prudent.

The status of an insurer who makes a policy loan to a bankrupt insured depends on whether or not the insurer has received notice of the bankruptcy. As discussed in Chapter 9, when the insurer receives notice the company is under an obligation not to pay the value in the life insurance policy to the insured. However, if the company has not received notice and it pays the cash value or makes a policy loan to the insured, the federal bankruptcy statutes protect the insurer from being forced to pay these values twice.

The loan privilege in the life insurance contract is a valuable provision, because it enables a policyholder to draw upon cash values to meet a temporary financial reverse without forcing him to surrender his policy and lose his insurance.[29] If the policyholder has become uninsurable, the loan privilege is even more important to him. The danger of the loan privilege is its possible abuse. When a policyholder borrows on a policy, he must remember that he is borrowing on his family's future financial security, or, as it is sometimes put, he may be borrowing from his widow.

The question is often raised, "Why do you charge me interest to borrow my own money?"

This question arises from a misunderstanding of life insurance finance. When a policyholder borrows on the security of his policy, he is not borrowing his own money, but money which belongs to all policyholders

---

[29] Subject to the provisions of the deferment clause, previously mentioned and to be discussed more fully later.

as a group and money which must be invested at interest in order to support the premium structure of the company. The policyholder's equity in the company still continues to earn interest for him even though he has taken the money out by a loan.

This explanation inspires still another question: "Then why do you charge me 5 percent to borrow while you are paying me only $2\frac{1}{2}$ percent on my accumulated cash value?"[30]

The net return on a policy loan is less than the 5 percent charged to the policyholder. It costs money to make and service policy loans, much more money than it costs to handle the typical investment in the company's portfolio. Furthermore, the insurer incurs a cost by having to maintain sufficient liquidity to meet anticipated demands for loans. And if the insurer miscalculates its cash flows and cash demands, it might have to borrow money at the banks at rates in excess of 5 percent to be able to honor its contractual loan obligations to its policyholders.

Policy loans make up a sizable share of an insurer's assets. The percentage of assets of insurers in policy loans is a function of the state of the economy, more particularly whether there is full employment and whether money is readily available. In periods of economic expansion and stability in the money markets, such as in the first half of the 1960's, life insurance policy loans fluctuated within a narrow range above and below 4.5 percent of assets.

Policy loans increase substantially during depressions. For example, in the depression of the 1930's life insurance policy loans reached 18.3 percent of assets. Policy loans also increase during periods of tight money. By the end of 1968, when the prime rate charged by banks to their most creditworthy customers was at 7 percent, policy loans had climbed to 6 percent of insurance company assets. And by the end of the second quarter of 1969 when the prime rate had soared to 8.5 percent, policy loans had jumped 74 percent over that of the second quarter of 1968. The rise in loan requests was attributed to rapid jumps in the prime lending rate in early 1969 and to the limited supply of funds available through normal channels as the government took action to quell inflation.[31]

Policyholders seek policy loans not only when no other sources of funds are available but also to take advantage of the differential between the interest rate charged for policy loans and the interest rate at which the

---

[30] The $2\frac{1}{2}$ percent is the guaranteed rate of interest. Under participating policies, earnings in excess of $2\frac{1}{2}$ percent may be used by the insurer to pay policy dividends. It matters not whether the policy has a loan outstanding; it will be paid its full dividend.

[31] To halt the rapid drain of funds during periods of high interest rates, some insurers are investigating the possibility of fostering a change in legislation which would permit a sliding scale of interest rates for policy loans, such as one tied to an index based on government bonds, treasury notes, or the prime rate. Several insurers introduced a variable policy loan interest rate on all policies issued after November 1, 1969, effective in all states except New York where a statutory limit of 5 percent applies. The rate was set at 6 percent with the provision that a lower rate may be established for any period during which a policy loan is outstanding.

borrowed funds can be invested. As the decade of the 1960's drew to a close, funds could be invested in United States Treasury bills at an attractive rate differential without any sacrifice of the safety of principal. There appeared to be only one possible drawback. If the insured should die while these funds are invested outside the insurance policy, the funds would be distributed according to the insured's will rather than in accordance with the policy's beneficiary arrangements. Thus, the estate planning advantages associated with the payment of life insurance proceeds would not be available to those funds withdrawn from the insurer.

AUTOMATIC PREMIUM LOAN. Some policies include an automatic premium loan clause. In case of the policyholder's failure to pay a premium when due, it is paid out of the policy loan value. The typical clause states that it shall be operative if requested in the policy application or if a later written request is filed at the home office. The amount of loan value applied on the premium due is charged against the policy subject to the same terms and conditions as cash loans in respect to interest, failure to repay, and voiding of the policy. Thus, through the use of the automatic premium loan provision, a policyholder can guarantee his policy against lapse if he fails to pay a specific premium as long as the policy has sufficient loan value to cover the payment.

In most companies, automatic premium loan provisions are not included in the policy but are written as an endorsement upon request of the policyholder. In other companies, automatic premium loans are not generally made available either in the policy or as an endorsement, except in Rhode Island and Montana where the provision is required by state law. In these states, the clause is automatic unless the policyholder specifically "elects out" by selecting extended term insurance or reduced paid-up insurance as the automatic option in the event of premium default. Outside of Montana and Rhode Island, when an automatic premium loan clause is available, it is usually of the "elect-in" type; i.e., it applies only if the policyholder specifically requests in advance that it be made operative. Automatic premium loan provisions are the rule with Canadian companies. Where the provision is available, the policyholder should insist upon making it operative in his contract,[32] for it is possible to overlook the payment of a premium. However, the automatic premium loan provision must not be abused by frequent reliance upon it. It should be treated only as protection against an oversight in paying the premium, or perhaps temporary inability to meet the premium when it falls due.

Assignment. In a number of circumstances, a policy owner might wish to assign his interest in a life insurance contract. Life insurance policies frequently are used as collateral for debts and are often transferred between people with or without consideration. Contrary to the rule in fire insurance where the contract is personal in nature, the owner of a life

---

[32] Many agents make it a practice to have the clause inserted for all applicants without asking the applicant.

insurance policy has the right to assign the contract without the consent of the insurer as long as the assignment does not defeat the vested rights of others, such as, for example, an irrevocable beneficiary. The right of assignment in life insurance is so well established that no permissive clause is necessary in the policy. An assignment provision does appear in the contract, but it is concerned only with explaining the position of the company relative to an assignment.

The typical assignment clause declares (1) that the company shall not be bound by any assignment until written notice (usually in the form of the original or a duplicate of the assignment document) has been filed with the company, (2) that the assignment shall be subject to any indebtedness to the company (thus giving the company a prior right over any assignee), and (3) that the company accepts no responsibility for the validity or effect of the assignment.

This clause does not mean that an assignment of which the company has no notice is void. It means only that the company has no obligation to an unrecorded assignee if it pays the cash values or proceeds to someone else before the assignee presents a claim. In the case of a contested assignment after a policy has become a death claim, the company would seek to pay the proceeds into court, thus discharging its contractual obligation and allowing the distribution of the proceeds to be decided by legal process.[33]

Several problems can arise in connection with an assignment.

DUPLICATE ASSIGNMENTS. A situation can develop where more than one assignment has been given, the second having been made before the company was notified of the first. The majority rule is that the first assignee has the prior assignment, but an exception is made to this rule if the assignee fails to take proper precautions to protect his rights by requiring delivery of the policy and a notation of the assignment thereon. This is the so-called American Rule. The English Rule is that the first assignee to give notice to the debtor prevails. The English Rule is in force in a number of states, although these states represent a minority.[34] Controversies over the priority of assignments, however, are not matters in which the insurer needs to be arbitrator. As mentioned above, the practice of the companies is to pay the proceeds into court in case of disputes, and then let the court decide which assignee has the prior claim. If, however, the company pays the proceeds of the policy to a bona fide assignee who turns out not to be the preferred assignee, that assignee is allowed to retain the proceeds as long as no fraud is involved. Thus the preferred assignee must notify the company of his claim before the proceeds are paid to someone else in order to preserve his preferred position.

FAILURE TO REVOKE THE BENEFICIARY. The beneficiary might not be

---

[33] The procedure called interpleader is discussed in Chapter 9.

[34] See Krueger and Waggoner, *op. cit.,* for the specific states in which each rule is applied.

revoked before the assignment is made.[35] In situations where the beneficiary is revocable and there has been no revocation, the courts generally have held that the assignee has the prior claim on the ground that a revocable beneficiary has no present interest but only a future expectation.[36] Therefore, if the assignee has established his interest at any time before the proceeds have been paid to the beneficiary, the assignee is entitled to recover. Also, when an absolute assignment (a form in which the ownership of the policy is to be fully and permanently transferred, as in a gift or a sale) rather than a collateral assignment (a form used when the policy is pledged as security for a loan) is intended, the assignment itself has been held to be notice of intention to change the beneficiary and has been interpreted by the courts as a change. This interpretation cannot be applied in collateral assignments because the beneficiary is entitled to collect any proceeds in excess of the assignee's claim. Since in the past there has been a body of decisions upholding the revocable beneficiary's rights over those of the assignee where the beneficiary did not consent to or acknowledge the assignment, it would be a wise precaution for the assignee to obtain evidence of the consent of the named beneficiary at the time of the assignment or, even better, for the assignee to request that the beneficiary be changed to the insured's estate before the assignment is made. While this protection is not necessary under a majority opinion, courts do have a way of springing unhappy surprises. Although such precaution also serves as protection against possible litigation brought on by beneficiaries,[37] it creates a new danger in the case of collateral assignments: the insured may fail to reinstate the original beneficiary and settlement options when the assignment is terminated. However, this danger can be avoided by using a clause which states in essence that the beneficiary in force immediately preceding the assignment is restored subsequent to that assignment.

The problem takes on a different character when the beneficiary designation is irrevocable. Here the beneficiary must join in the assignment before it can be effective. An assignee of a policy containing an irrevocable beneficiary can exercise no rights in the policy unless the beneficiary consents.

In using a life insurance policy as collateral for a loan, conditional assignment is to be preferred to a change of beneficiary. If the beneficiary is changed to the lender, he then has the right to collect the full amount of

---

[35] If the policy contains the following clause (as some do), then no problem is created by failure to change the beneficiary: "Whenever an assignment is executed by an owner of a policy who has the reserved right to change the beneficiary, the effect of such assignment shall be to destroy the rights of any named beneficiary in favor of the assignee." Cf. Robert Dechert, "Assignments of Life Insurance Policies" in *The Beneficiary in Life Insurance* (Philadelphia: University of Pennsylvania Press, 1948), p. 28.

[36] The minority view, held in Colorado, Massachusetts, and New Jersey, is that the owner cannot assign the policy without the consent of the beneficiary unless he revokes the beneficiary designation.

[37] This procedure is required by companies in assignments involving policy loans if the policy does not take care of the problem through the contract provision itself.

the death benefits; if assignment is made, his right can be restricted to his interest "as it may appear." For example, assume that a $5,000 life insurance policy is to be used by the lender as security for a loan in the event of the death of the debtor-insured prior to debt repayment. It would seem at first glance that the simplest arrangement, in view of the confusion which exists over the rights of the beneficiary in assignments, would be to change the beneficiary on the policy to the creditor. But if the loan should be partially repaid before the death of the insured, then the contingent beneficiary will have to depend on the creditor for a refund of the difference between the proceeds and the amount still owed. This might involve the expense and delay of litigation. Where family relationships are involved, proof that the change in beneficiary was for the purpose of securing the debt might not be easily obtained. On the other hand, an assignment of the policy proceeds to the creditor as his interest may appear would automatically pay the beneficiary the difference between the $5,000 proceeds and the amount of the debt still outstanding at the time of the death of the insured. But even here, where family relationships are involved, there might be litigation over the interest of the assignee at the time of the insured's death.

FAILURE TO FOLLOW ASSIGNMENT PROCEDURE. Most courts, again, will hold that this failure can defeat the assignee's claim. However, the company can, if it wishes, waive the notice requirement and pay the proceeds to the assignee; or it can ignore the assignment and pay the proceeds to the named beneficiary.

ASSIGNMENT BY INCOMPETENT OWNER. The general rule is that unless the company has notice of incompetence, it has no liability for merely having accepted the assignment. The company takes care of this problem by including a statement in the assignment clause to the effect that the insurer accepts no responsibility for the validity of any assignment.[38]

THE ASSIGNEE HAS NO INSURABLE INTEREST. The general rule is that a life insurance policy may be assigned to a person who has no insurable interest. However, if the assignment arises from a debtor-creditor relationship, the creditor may collect under the policy only to the extent of his insurable interest. On the other hand, it has been held [39] that an absolute assignment made in exchange for a valuable consideration (a bona fide sale) can be effected to someone who has no insurable interest. This is the majority rule and is held in all except a few states.

TYPES OF ASSIGNMENTS. The two basic types of assignments are absolute and collateral assignments. The absolute assignment, designed to transfer ownership, gives the assignee all rights under the policy both be-

---

[38] If the company were to accept any responsibility for the validity of assignments, such acceptance might be held to lend weight to the assignment, whereas the company should have no standing as a judge of such validities.

[39] The leading case is *A. H. Grigsby, Petitioner,* v. *R. L. Russell and Lillie Burchard, Administrators of John Burchard, Deceased,* 222 U.S. 149 (1911).

fore and at its maturity, subject of course to any limitations in the policy.[40]

The collateral asignment, designed to serve as security for a debt, restricts the rights of the assignee to the amount of the debt, interest thereon, and premiums paid on the policy. When the original owner fulfills all his obligations to the collateral assignee, the rights in the policy are transferred back to the assignor. Under the collateral assignment, the assignor may transfer a part or all of the ownership rights in the contract.

THE ABA ASSIGNMENT FORM. Creditors prefer the absolute assignment because the collateral assignment restricts their actions with respect to the policy. A compromise has resulted in the development of the American Bankers Association's standard assignment form, which gives the assignee the rights he needs for complete freedom and security while at the same time granting the assignor the protection he needs in arranging his insurance. This assignment form was prepared by the American Bankers Association and the Association of Life Insurance Counsel. It gives the assignee bank "all claims, options, privileges, rights, titles, and interest" in the policy and all riders or supplemental contracts in connection with it, including:

1. The right to collect the net proceeds.
2. The right to surrender the policy for its cash value.
3. The right to borrow on the policy.
4. The right to receive dividends.
5. The right to exercise the nonforfeiture rights.

Under the ABA form the assignee agrees to the following: (1) that he will turn over to the beneficiary the difference between the proceeds collected and the unpaid balance of the debt, (2) that he will not surrender or borrow on the policy unless there has been default in the loan or in the payment of premiums by the assignor—and then not until after giving the assignor 20 days' notice, and (3) that he will not prevent the assignor from changing the beneficiary, from electing any optional form of settlement, or from collecting disability benefits as long as such collection does not reduce the amount of insurance. The ABA form also specifies that the assignee shall assume no obligation to pay premiums, principal, or interest on policy loans. If he does pay these items they are added to the debt and draw interest until paid at an annual rate not exceeding 10 percent.

ASSIGNMENT BY THE BENEFICIARY. Unless blocked by the contract or by state law, the beneficiary may assign whatever interest he has in a policy. The value of the beneficiary's interest before the maturity of the policy depends upon the beneficiary designation. If the beneficiary is named revocably he has no rights or values in the policy since the policy owner can at any time make a change in the beneficiary designation. Obviously, a revocable beneficiary cannot assign an interest that he does not

---

[40] For example, some policies prohibit assignees from electing settlement options and may also exclude the transfer of beneficial interest.

hold. However, an irrevocable beneficiary has a valuable interest to transfer. The worth of this interest depends upon whether the beneficiary has to survive the insured to collect or whether the beneficiary can pass on his interest to his estate if he dies before the insured.

The value of the beneficiary's interest at maturity of the policy depends upon how the proceeds of the policy are to be settled. If they are to be paid in a lump sum, then the beneficiary is free to assign the whole amount, but if they are to be paid under a settlement option, the assignment must not defeat the rights of any contingent beneficiary. It will be recalled that spendthrift trust clauses and the laws of certain states designed to protect insurance proceeds from the beneficiary's creditors also limit the right of assignment by the beneficiary.

The Deferment Clause. Insurers are required to include in their policies a clause declaring that the company has the right to defer the payment of the cash value or the making of a cash loan for a period not exceeding six months from the date of the application for such payment or for such loan. When the loan application is for the purpose of paying renewal premiums on policies in the company, the deferment does not apply. The deferment clause sometimes applies also to withdrawal of proceeds retained at interest or commutation of guaranteed payments under settlement options. Although the clause itself is often required by statute, and therefore must be in the policy, the companies may use their own discretion in invoking it. The deferment clause is in line with a similar provision introduced into bank accounts as a result of experiences during the early 1930's when bank depositors demanded funds, not because these funds were needed, but simply because the depositors were afraid of the safety of these funds.

The Beneficiary Clause. In life insurance policies the owner usually names a beneficiary, i.e., the person who is to receive the proceeds of the policy upon receipt of due proof of the death of the insured. In fact, he may name several successive beneficiaries in the order in which they are to take priority should the primary beneficiary not survive the insured or not live to collect the full amount of the proceeds guaranteed under a settlement option. These successive beneficiaries are known as contingent or secondary, tertiary, and so forth. The beneficiaries and their relationship to the insured appear on the face of the policy.

Sometimes rather than a third party, the insured's estate is named as beneficiary. As will be explained in Chapter 21, a third party beneficiary usually is more preferable than the estate. In endowment policies the owner-insured usually designates himself to receive the proceeds in the event of his survival, and a third party to receive the proceeds if death occurs during the endowment period. When the owner of the policy is not the subject of the insurance, as when an employer insures the life of a key employee, the owner-applicant usually names himself as the beneficiary.

Third party beneficiaries may be named either revocably or irrevocably. If the insured has reserved the right to change the beneficiary, he may at any time make a change without the beneficiary's permission upon conforming with the procedure for change as set forth in the policy. This procedure, in general, requires written notice to the company, with the change becoming effective only if endorsed on the policy.[41] The rights of any beneficiary usually are made subject to the rights of an assignee under any assignment by the owner. The beneficiary clause usually states that the right to revoke and change the beneficiary designation is reserved to the owner unless otherwise specified.

If the beneficiary has been named without reserving the right to change, the designation is called irrevocable and the person so named, an irrevocable beneficiary. An irrevocable beneficiary designation can be changed only with the beneficiary's written consent.

An irrevocable beneficiary designation may be absolute or reversionary. Under an *absolute* designation, the beneficiary has an unconditional vested interest in the policy and may exercise all rights in it independently of the insured. In this type of beneficiary arrangement, the policy will be a part of the beneficiary's estate should he predecease the insured, to be disposed of according to the beneficiary's will.

A *reversionary* irrevocable beneficiary designation specifies that in the event that the beneficiary predeceases the insured, all rights in the policy revert to the insured. In this type of beneficiary designation, the beneficiary's interest is conditional rather than absolute because his death prior to that of the insured will defeat this interest. Since the insured retains a reversionary interest in the policy, the exercise of any rights under the contract will require the joint action of both the insured and the beneficiary unless the policy states otherwise.[42] As is true with all forms that limit the ability of the policy owner to make beneficiary changes, the absolute and reversionary irrevocable beneficiary designations are not common.

If the contract does not state the nature of the disposition should the irrevocable beneficiary die before the insured, the majority of courts hold that the rights of the beneficiary pass on to his heirs. A substantial number of courts, however, hold that where the beneficiary is a donee or gratuitous beneficiary (i.e., not a creditor or purchaser for value), his rights terminate with his death and revert to the insured. This latter interpretation seems more in line with the intentions of the insured.

If the beneficiary is named revocably, he has no vested rights in the policy until the death of the insured.[43] The rights of the revocable bene-

---

[41] The modern trend is not to require beneficiary changes to be endorsed on the policy, because of the expense involved in handling the endorsements. The beneficiary clause in these policies simply states that the beneficiary may be changed by filing at the home office a written beneficiary designation in a form satisfactory to the company.

[42] Some policies are written in which the insured retains all the rights in the policy except the right to change the beneficiary.

[43] Horne and Mansfield, *op. cit.*, point out several cases in which courts have held a revocable designation to have the same legal effect as an irrevocable one. For example, delivery of the policy to the insured's wife in consideration of marriage gave her a vested interest which the insured could not defeat by naming another beneficiary.

ficiary become fixed upon the maturity of an endowment, unless the contract provides otherwise.

Cases arise in which, after the death of the insured, the beneficiary wishes to name his own beneficiary to receive the balance of any proceeds still payable. If this "beneficiary's beneficiary" is named irrevocably, no problem exists. However, if he is named revocably, controversy arises over whether the designation is testamentary in character—i.e., in the nature of a will rather than of a beneficiary designation. Insufficient litigation has involved the question to state a "majority opinion," although a number of able writers on the subject argue that it is not testamentary in nature, and New York has passed legislation to the effect that the rights of a beneficiary's beneficiary are not to be voided on the grounds of noncompliance with the laws of wills and intestacies.

If no beneficiary is named in the policy, or if no beneficiary survives the insured, the proceeds unless otherwise provided are paid to the insured's estate, and their distribution becomes a matter of his will, or, if he has no will, of the laws of descent.[44]

The beneficiary clause is the one provision the policy owner writes himself. It is his instruction for the disposition of the property (the proceeds). In that sense, it corresponds to a will, *but only in that sense.* A beneficiary designation is not a testamentary distribution of property. It is distribution by contract. It does not have to be drawn or witnessed with the formalities required for a will, and it does not have to be admitted to probate. In paying the proceeds, the company is not, in a legal sense, distributing the insured's property but is merely paying a stated amount from its own funds not traceable to any funds received from the policyholder, and usually in an amount in excess of that paid by the policyholder.[45]

NAMING THE BENEFICIARY. The designation of the beneficiary should be drawn so that there can be no doubt as to the exact person intended. For instance, proceeds might go to the "wrong" wife where there is both a wife and an ex-wife and the beneficiary designation was merely "wife" without indicating her name. The same situation arose when the beneficiary was designated as "Mrs. H. M. Case" rather than by her given and maiden name.[46] The accepted practice is to designate a spouse by her given

---

[44] Some policies provide that where there is no surviving beneficiary, the proceeds are payable to the person or persons who, upon proof of affidavit or other written evidence satisfactory to the company, appear to be the then living, lawful, bodily and legally adopted child or children of the insured. The proceeds are to be divided equally among two or more such persons; if there is none, they are payable to the executors or administrators of the estate of the insured.

[45] This may seem to be a contradiction, since it is obvious that, in an actuarial sense, there is a direct connection between the premiums paid by the policyholder and the amount of the policy proceeds; but here reference is made in terms of the legal agreement involved. A life insurance policy is not an agreement by the company to take money from the policyholder and later pay it back to his heirs. It is simply a contract with the policyholder stating that in consideration of the payment of the premium, it will pay a specified sum to his beneficiary at death.

[46] *Day* v. *Case* 43 Hun. 79 (1887).

and maiden name followed by her relationship with the insured, such as "Margaret Cochrun Jones, wife of the insured." "Wife of the insured" is held to be merely a description of the status of Margaret Cochrun Jones at the time of the designation and will have no effect on her right to the proceeds if she is not the wife of the insured at the time of his death.

Extreme care should be taken when children are designated as beneficiaries. If the children are designated by name, such as James Lawrence Jones and Evaline Caroline Jones, children born after the designation was made will be excluded. For children, it is better to use a class designation, with the class being described as precisely as possible to avoid questions of interpretation. The general rule is that a class designation such as "children of the insured" includes all children at the time of death, but the more precise designation, "children who survive the insured," is better because it is clear that it also means a posthumous child. While this type of designation probably will be held to include adopted children, a safer designation is to state, "children of the insured, including those legally adopted" or some statement to the effect that "children" shall be defined to include adopted children. The designation, "my children," will exclude those of a spouse by a previous marriage, while "Margaret Cochrun Jones, wife of the insured, and our children" or "children of the union" will exclude all children of either spouse by a previous marriage.

In naming a class beneficiary, the owner should indicate how the proceeds are to be paid if a member of the class predeceases the insured. Suppose, for example, the insured has two children and the class beneficiary designation is "children of the insured." If one of the children dies before the insured, how are the proceeds of his policy to be distributed? In the absence of a specific policy provision to the contrary, the majority of courts hold that the surviving child is entitled to the entire proceeds since he remains as the only living member of the class.[47] Rather than leave the distribution of the insurance to the will of the court, the insured may state specifically how he wants the proceeds distributed. For example, he may name his beneficiary as follows: "The surviving children of the insured in equal shares, and to the surviving children of any deceased children of the insured, per stirpes."[48]

These examples of the effect of various wordings of beneficiary designations indicate the necessity for careful consideration in naming the beneficiary.

MINOR BENEFICIARIES. Problems can develop when a minor is named as beneficiary, particularly if the designation is irrevocable, because a

---

[47] A large number of courts have held that the heirs of the deceased child would be entitled to his one-half interest in the proceeds of the policy.

[48] The use of the term "per stirpes" means that the equal share of the deceased beneficiary will be divided among his children. The surviving beneficiary receives one half in this case, and the other one half is distributed equally to the children of the deceased beneficiary. If he has two children, each will receive one fourth of the proceeds. If, instead of per stirpes, the designation read per capita, each child of the deceased beneficiary would share equally with the surviving beneficiary and each would collect one third of the proceeds.

minor does not have the legal capacity to consent to a beneficiary change, a surrender of the policy for its cash value, the assignment of the policy for a loan, or the exercise of the policy loan provision or any other rights contained in the policy. Of course, a guardian can be appointed by the court to act for the minor but since the guardian must act in the interest of the minor he might not be permitted to consent to an action desired by the insured.

Another problem is that of the payment of the insurance proceeds directly to a minor since, in general, he is not legally competent to accept payment and to issue receipts for them. To pay funds directly to a minor might subject the company to double payment. At majority, the beneficiary might bring suit to recover proceeds for which the company has no valid receipts. Thus, where there are minor beneficiaries, a guardian might have to be appointed to accept the proceeds.[49]

A number of states permit waiver of guardianship and allow payments to be made to an adult (usually the parent or someone acting as parent) for the benefit of the minor. The amount of such payments is limited, usually to less than $500.

Minors who have reached the age of 18 are permitted by statute in some states to legally receive and give a binding receipt for policy proceeds up to some such amount as $2,000 or $3,000 annually if the policy provides for direct payment to the minor.[50]

Another solution to the problem is for the proceeds to be held by the company, accumulated at interest until the majority of the child, and distributed at that time. While most companies will agree to this settlement plan, money left to an orphaned child in most instances is needed currently for support and education and should not be left on deposit with the company. It may be desirable to name a trustee to collect the proceeds of a policy where the beneficiary would otherwise be a minor.[51]

LIMITATIONS ON ABILITY TO CHANGE BENEFICIARY. The right of the policy owner to make beneficiary changes may be limited by several conditions. First, the owner may be prohibited from making a beneficiary change. The use of the irrevocable beneficiary designation will make it difficult, if not impossible, for the owner to initiate unilateral beneficiary changes. Second, the owner may waive his right to make a beneficiary change even in cases where a revocable beneficiary is named. Just as an insurer may waive his right to enforce a policy provision[52] the owner of

---

[49] A surviving parent is not automatically the guardian of the estate of a minor. To act in that capacity, he or she must be legally appointed as guardian by the court. Pennsylvania has a statute that allows the insured to designate a guardian in a life insurance policy to receive funds for a minor beneficiary.

[50] For example, New York permits an 18-year-old beneficiary legally to receive from a life insurance company and to give a binding receipt for up to $3,000 a year, payable by reason of death or the maturity of the policy as an endowment, if the insurer has not received written notice of the existence of a qualified guardian.

[51] Life insurance trusts are discussed in Chapter 21.

[52] Waiver and estoppel are discussed in Chapter 9.

the policy also may take an action which could cause him to waive any right to change the beneficiary. The separation agreement in a divorce may create a legal promise by the husband to maintain his former wife as the beneficiary in a specific life insurance policy, thus relinquishing any right to change the beneficiary. Third, the ability of a minor to make beneficiary changes is severely limited in most states. Many states have specific regulations as to whom the insured minor can name as a beneficiary. The laws of New York require that a minor name as beneficiary one of the following: father, mother, husband, wife, brother, sister, child, or grandparent. Fourth, those adjudicated as mentally incompetent are not allowed by law to make any changes in the beneficiary designations of their life insurance policies. In addition, most states extend this inability to make changes to the guardians of the incompetent individual.

DISTRIBUTION OF PROCEEDS TO THE BENEFICIARIES. The owner of a life insurance policy may select from among the following ways of having the death benefits distributed: (1) lump-sum settlement direct to the beneficiary, (2) lump sum paid to a trust, and (3) an optional settlement plan offered by the insurer. A lump-sum payment to a beneficiary has the advantage of making the total insurance fund available for the immediate use of the beneficiary, but if she is incapable of effectively managing the fund this option may hold many dangers. Through poor judgment the insurance fund could be quickly dissipated. The second and third selections offer professional management. While the insurer can guarantee both the safety of proceeds and a minimum earnings rate under an optional settlement plan, the trustee cannot make these guarantees. However, the use of a trust affords greater opportunity for flexibility and higher potential earnings than can be obtained through an insurance company.[53]

The life insurance trust can be established by one of two means. The trustee simply may be named as the beneficiary or the policy may be assigned to a trustee-beneficiary. When the trustee is simply named beneficiary the insured does not give up the ownership rights in the policy. However, where there is an assignment to the trustee-beneficiary he has the ownership rights in the contract. Where the trust is solely for the management of death benefits, beneficiary designation should suffice, but where the trustee must perform duties relating to the policy during the lifetime of the insured the assignment method seems appropriate.

Since the assignment technique eliminates the insured's incidence of ownership in the policy, absolute assignment has estate tax advantages.[54]

Because delays could be incurred in the settlement procedure where a trust is named without executing the necessary trust agreement, life insurers demand that proof of the trust's formation be presented as a precondition to naming a trust as beneficiary. This formality can be accomplished by presenting to the insurance company a copy of the trust

---

[53] The possibilities under settlement options are described in Chapter 11.
[54] Cf. Chapter 21.

agreement. Furthermore, the insurer, through its contract, accepts no responsibility for the fulfillment of the terms found in the trust agreement.

An important question in naming a trustee as beneficiary is whether this action runs counter to the concept that life insurance proceeds payable to a named beneficiary pass outside a will. When this question has been brought up, the rulings have clearly been that life insurance proceeds payable into a trust do not enter the probate estate but pass outside the will. Attempts by creditors of insolvent estates to reach the proceeds paid into a trust have been unsuccessful.

The trust arrangement may be appropriate with life insurance contracts used to fund business interest buy-out agreements to assure completion of the desired results of the partners.[55]

COMMON DISASTER. A common disaster occurs when both the insured and the beneficiary die in the same accident. In such cases it may be difficult, if not impossible, to determine which party died first. If the insured died first, the beneficiary's estate would receive the benefits; and if the beneficiary died first, the proceeds would go to the contingent beneficiary or the insured's estate. Thus, there could be confusion as to the distribution of the proceeds. Neither common law nor the various state laws had resolved the problem. The states placed the burden of proof on either the beneficiary's estate or the insured's estate, depending on their interpretation of whether or not the beneficiary's rights were vested. If the state concluded that the beneficiary had a vested right, the burden was on the insured's estate to prove that the beneficiary died first. If the beneficiary had no vested rights, then the burden was on the beneficiary's estate to prove that the beneficiary survived the insured.

The inconsistencies surrounding this issue have been partially resolved with the passage in most states of the Uniform Simultaneous Death Act.

This law provides that if there is no evidence as to whether the insured or beneficiary died first, the policy will be settled as though the insured survived the beneficiary. The proceeds, then, would be paid to the secondary beneficiary or, in the absence of any, to the estate of the insured.

The Uniform Simultaneous Death law provides a solution (though not necessarily a desired one) in situations where reasonable doubt exists as to which party died first. However, the law does not affect the distribution of proceeds in situations where the beneficiary clearly survives the insured and then dies shortly thereafter. In this latter event, the proceeds will go to the beneficiary's estate, a settlement which may or may not be desirable.

One method of improving the chances that the proceeds of the policy will be paid in accordance with the insured's wishes is for the policy owner to have a common disaster clause inserted in the policy. The common disaster clause states that if the insured and the beneficiary perish in a common accident, the presumption will be that the beneficiary died first.

---

[55] Cf. Chapter 22.

Such a clause can have unwanted estate tax implications so it is usually modified to state that, upon the death of the insured, the proceeds shall be held by the insurer at interest for a specified period (such as 30 days) and then paid to the primary beneficiary if surviving, otherwise to the secondary beneficiary.

However, a far better arrangement can be made through the proper selection of settlement options (discussed in Chapter 11). Settlement options offer the only method by which the insured can be guaranteed that the proceeds will be distributed as he had intended. For example, if the insured designates an installment settlement arrangement, the primary beneficiary will receive periodic payments until the proceeds are exhausted, for as long as she survives the insured whether it be one day, a year, or five years. Upon the death of the primary beneficiary the payments can be continued to the secondary beneficiary. No time limit for survival need be set as must be done when the modified common disaster clause is used.

Beneficiary designations have become exceedingly complex, but the complexity is steadily reducing litigation involving them. Today the amount of such litigation is insignificant.

4. MISCELLANEOUS PROVISIONS

In addition to the above provisions, a number of others will be found in most policies.

Policy Change. The policy may contain a provision to the effect that the insured may at any time change the policy to another form. The provision may specify the forms to which the policy may be changed. Usually change to forms requiring higher premiums and consequently higher reserve liabilities may be made without evidence of insurability; change to forms requiring lower premiums and lower reserve liabilities is subject to evidence of insurability[56] because of the possibility of adverse selection.

Policy Year. A typical clause reads, "The policy year referred to herein is the year beginning on the _____ of _____, 19__, or any anniversary thereof." Its purpose is to define clearly the actual meaning of the term policy year, so that this term will be clear when it is referred to elsewhere in the policy.

Basis of Computation. A provision in the policy sets forth the basis of reserve value, which in ordinary policies issued today is the 1958 CSO table with an interest assumption ranging between 2 percent and 3 percent, commonly $2\frac{1}{2}$ to 3 percent. Additional benefits in event of accidental death or permanent and total disability are excluded from the computation. The basis of the cash value calculation also must be stated.

---

[56] Change to a lower reserve form means the company will be increasing the amount at risk; i.e., there will be an increase in pure insurance which is defined as the difference between the face of the policy and the reserve liability charged against that policy. Hence, the insured with a health problem indicating a shortened life expectancy will be inclined to shift to a form giving him more pure insurance per premium dollar.

Modifications and Agreements.   Any modification or changes in the policy and all agreements in connection with it must be endorsed on or attached to the policy in writing, and over the signature of a specified officer or officers, such as the president, vice president, secretary, assistant secretary, treasurer, or assistant treasurer. No other person has authority to make changes and agreements, to waive provisions, or to extend the time for premium payment. Some modification clauses also declare specifically that no agent has authority to make changes, waivers, or the like.

The purpose of the clause is, of course, to clarify both to the policyholder and to the courts just who has authority to alter a printed policy.

Representations and Warranties.   All statements in the application shall be deemed representations and not warranties unless fraud is involved; and it is provided that no statement may be used to contest the policy or a claim unless it is in writing on the application attached to the policy. The subject of warranties and representations was discussed in Chapter 9.

5. HAZARD RESTRICTIONS

Two exclusions or restrictions[57] occasionally found in policies seem to merit separate discussion. One relates to aviation and the other to war.

Aviation Restriction.   The aviation hazard at one time was either excluded from coverage or subject to an extra premium. Improved safety records in aviation resulting from new techniques and greater skills have changed the attitudes of underwriters so that now travel as a passenger in any type of aircraft, except military aircraft, is no longer considered an extra hazard. In addition, insurers write policies without restrictions and at standard rates for commercial pilots and crew members who fly on regularly scheduled commercial airlines. Private pilots who can meet specific standards of flight experience, average flight time per year, and age are issued life insurance without restrictions and at standard rates. Pilots who do not meet these standards will be charged a higher premium or have an aviation exclusion rider attached to the policy. Restrictions usually can be eliminated if the insured is willing to pay an extra premium. The exclusion clauses are used only when the applicant is unwilling to pay the extra cost or where the type of aviation in which he is engaged is subject to a hazard on which the company has insufficient statistics for use in computing a rate.

Most insurers are ignoring aviation restrictions previously written into existing policies if the insured would currently qualify under the new underwriting rules. Thus, even if a policy contains an aviation restriction, the insurer may elect to pay claims that are excluded by the contract.

While there was considerable litigation over the validity of aviation ex-

---

[57] Actually, they are restrictions more than exclusions since they do cover *some* types of deaths from the so-called excluded hazards.

clusions when they were first used, all jurisdictions now permit at least some restriction. The question of whether exclusions in the restriction were in conflict with the incontestable clause has arisen, but this point now seems clearly settled. Just as in the case of the suicide exclusion, denial of a claim for an excluded hazard is not a contest of the policy but an enforcement of a policy provision. Litigation involving military aviation deaths has been undertaken on the grounds that aviation exclusions were meant to exclude only civil aviation. Courts, as a rule, have not gone along with this line of reasoning. On the other hand, the aviation exclusion was held not to apply in cases where the insured was killed by gunfire while in flight, under the interpretation that the immediate cause of the death was gunfire, not aviation. The doctrine of proximate cause (i.e., the efficient cause, the one that necessarily sets the other causes in operation), however, has been invoked to exclude deaths resulting indirectly from flying, such as drowning after a plane crash.

Some states seek to limit the extent of restrictions. However, attempts of states to outlaw all restrictions or to limit them severely can result in the denial of insurance in that jurisdiction to anyone participating in aviation.[58]

ASTROPOLICY. The advances being made in space travel may lead to changes in the structure of future life insurance policies. Policies issued on the lives of astronauts Armstrong, Aldrin, and Collins may give some clues as to how life insurance will be applied to space travelers. The policy covered "loss of life or dissappearance in space and permanent total disability of the insured astronauts." In addition, the policy provided for the following special space risks: "(a) Aggression by extraterrestrial or human beings in space. (b) Suicide or attempted suicide committed while of sound or unsound mind. (c) War of any nature, waged on Earth or in space." However, the policy restricted from coverage (1) "the case in which the insured astronauts, under favorable conditions of survival in space, should for any reason refuse to return to earth, deliberately, and contrary to NASA's instructions" and (2) "the case of the insured astronauts' kidnapping by extraterrestrial or human beings, and their detention, alive, either on or away from earth, for a minimum of three years."

The policies were issued by the Tambouras Organization of Greece and were for 900 drachmae ($10,000) each.[59] The face amount of $10,000 was selected since this figure was believed to be the average size of all policies issued to applicants in the United States. The policy went into

---

[58] This happened in Nebraska after *State* ex rel. *Republic National Life* v. *Smrha*, 138 Neb. 484, 293, N.W. 373 (1940). It was necessary to pass legislation permitting exclusion of certain aviation hazards in order to eliminate the problem.

[59] The premiums (which were paid by the Tambouras Organization) were set at 1.7 percent of the insured amounts. The premiums were based on the insurer's belief that the margin of safety on the flight was 98.3 percent (as compared to NASA's declared safety margin of 99.96 percent). This, of course, is a prime illustration of premium calculation based on subjective probabilities.

effect on the boarding of the spacecraft and expired on the completion of the quarantine period. The Tambouras Organization named the astronauts' wives and children as beneficiaries, but each astronaut was free to make any beneficiary change he desired. The policy was issued in both Greek and English, but in cases of ambiguity the Greek text took precedence over the English.

As advances in technology allow more earth inhabitants to venture further into space, it will be interesting to see how life insurers deal with the changing contingencies.

War Restriction. In wartime, companies usually insert restrictions in their contracts, generally referred to as "war clauses." These restrictions are usually contained in policies written during periods of impending war, and especially in those policies issued to young men of draft age. The clauses generally provide for a return of the premium with interest or a refund equal to the reserve valuation of the policy in event death occurs under conditions excluded in the policy.

War-caused death is a hazard not calculated in rating life insurance policies. Premiums are based on a mortality table that covers peacetime deaths only. There is no way to calculate the added mortality rate during warfare until after the war is over. Each war to date has created its own mortality rate. Further, issuance of policies without a war exclusion in time of war would result in drastic antiselection: those going into military service would be inclined to buy larger policies than they would have purchased in peacetime.[60]

War clauses usually are canceled at the end of the hostilities.

Courts universally recognize that it is impossible for a private insurer to assume the added hazard of war at ordinary rates. Therefore, virtually no legal questions arise over the validity of war clauses.

In general, there are two types of war clauses, usually known as the "status" type and the "result" type. One is a "while" clause and the other is an "if" clause. Under the status clause, liability of the company for the death of the insured is excluded *while* the insured is in military service, regardless of the cause of his death. Often this clause is liberalized to exclude only death outside the home area, as defined in the clause. The home area is usually defined as the 50 states, the District of Columbia, and Canada. Under the result clause, liability is excluded *if* the death is a re-

---

[60] After both World Wars I and II, many companies found they could have covered the war hazard without extra premium, and therefore paid war death claims retroactively despite the war exclusion clauses. The practice of paying war-incurred death has been debated on actuarial grounds. The fact that companies have found that they could have covered the hazard, however, does not mean they would have been able to do so had they issued policies without the exclusion. The exclusion tended to restrict the amount at risk to a figure small enough so that the effect of war deaths did not disturb overall mortality experience. Had policies been issued without the restriction, antiselection might have increased the proportion of insurance on military personnel to the degree that mortality might have jumped to the point where it could have had a serious effect. The advantage of the war clause, then, seems to be in controlling adverse selection.

sult of war. Under the status clause, the cause of death does not matter; under the result clause, it is all-important.

Both types of clauses have given rise to endless litigation—so endless it is impractical even to summarize here.[61] The principal type of litigation, however, seems to have been over whether the wording of the clause makes it a status clause or a result clause. These cases arise, for example, when a soldier is killed in a tavern brawl or dies as a result of a common civilian disease. Unless the wording is so clear as to make the clause unquestionably a status clause, the courts tend to bend over backward to interpret it as a result clause. Because of the confusion that has surrounded the status clause, the majority of life insurers use the result clause. Since the New York statutes require that all war clauses shall be interpreted as result clauses rather than as status clauses, it is not surprising to find that all life insurers domiciled in New York use the result clause.

Another type of litigation involves the time when a person might be said to be in military service. When the term "active service" is used, courts have excluded the period of training. In one amusing decision (amusing to us but not to the insurance company involved) a court held that the words "while on duty as a soldier" did not include a sailor who died of appendicitis while in the service. The court made a definite distinction between a soldier and a sailor, which distinction the men of the services have always insisted exists as a matter of pride in their own superior branch (whichever that might be). This decision indicates the importance of carefully spelling out to the courts just what the war clause intends to exclude. Implied intention means little to a court eager to protect the family of the serviceman.

In addition to litigation over the interpretation of the clause and the nature of the death is that over the existence of war itself. This problem arises in the time interval between enemy attack, as at Pearl Harbor, and actual declaration of war by the Congress; between the end of actual hostilities and the declaration of the end of the war; and in such situations as the Korean "police action" and the Vietnam "conflict." Judicial decisions will depend on how strictly the court wishes to interpret the term war. Although in cases such as the Korean conflict the majority of courts have interpreted the clause broadly, a few courts have held strongly to the concept that Congress must declare war before war clauses take effect.

---

[61] For such a summary and citations, cf. Krueger and Waggoner, *op. cit.*, chap. 18.

11
Policy Options

In addition to the general provisions of the life insurance contract discussed in Chapter 10, the policy contains provisions offering the policyholder several choices (1) in case of surrender of his policy, (2) in the method of applying policy dividends, and (3) in the method of payment of proceeds. The three types of options are called nonforfeiture options, dividend options, and settlement options.

1. NONFORFEITURE OPTIONS

Except for short-duration term policies and term policies which have expired, no policy which has been in force more than a minimum amount of time (generally one to two years) can be terminated without value upon surrender by the insured. From almost the beginning of level premium insurance, introduced in England by Old Equitable in 1762, at least some companies have recognized that under a level premium plan of insurance, the policyholder who surrenders his policy before maturity has contributed more than his share of premiums for the protection he has received, and deserves some type of refund.[1] Nonforfeiture values arise from three sources: (1) higher initial premiums than necessary to pay for the death protection afforded by the policy; (2) compound interest on these excess premiums at a rate guaranteed by the company; and (3) survivorship benefits for an amount determined by mortality rates guaranteed by the company.[2]

Early attempts at making refunds of premiums in event of termination often were confined merely to a statement that the company would give consideration to a refund in case of surrender or would "purchase back" the policy for an "equitable consideration." In 1851 the Scottish Widows' Fund and Equitable Assurance Company of Edinburgh added contract sur-

---

[1] This same principle was introduced in health insurance when, in 1960, Southwestern Life began offering noncancellable, guaranteed renewable disability income policies with cash values.

[2] Review Chapter 1 for a refresher on the source of nonforfeiture values.

render values to its policies. By 1861 most United States companies had established rules for granting nonforfeiture values, and some included them in the policy as a contractual right. In 1861 Elizur Wright, member of the first Board of Insurance Commissioners of Massachusetts, effected the passage of a state law requiring extended insurance as a nonforfeiture value; and most companies began to adopt definite forms of nonforfeiture values. Following the Armstrong investigation in New York (1905), states not yet having nonforfeiture laws generally adopted them.

Life insurance policies today provide for several nonforfeiture values, any one of which may be elected by the policyholder within (usually) 60 days after the due date of any premium in default; and if no such election is made, then a stated (automatic) form of paid-up benefit becomes effective. The nonforfeiture values are guaranteed in the contract and are not subject to change, once the policy is issued.

The three most common forms of nonforfeiture options found in policies are (1) cash value, (2) reduced paid-up insurance, and (3) extended term insurance. Because the cash value is the basis of the other two options, it will be discussed first.

Cash Value.   Before the passage of the Standard Nonforfeiture Law, completed in most states prior to 1948, the amount of the cash value was the legal reserve required in any given policy, subject to a surrender charge of not more than $25 for each $1,000 of insurance. The purpose of the surrender charge was to enable the company to recover that part of the cost of issuing the policy which had been charged against surplus.[3] Cash surrender value usually was offered only after the expiration of the first 3 policy years, and the surrender charge usually diminished yearly and disappeared entirely after the policy had been in force for a minimum number of years, 20 for example.

The reserve less surrender charge method of figuring surrender values was subject to criticism. In the first place, the legal reserve for any policy is based on mortality and interest assumptions developed to measure the solvency of the company rather than to measure any one policyholder's equitable share in the assets of the company. The interest and mortality assumptions used for reserve computations are not usually the assumptions used in calculating premiums. Furthermore, because the legal reserve is based on mortality and interest assumptions only, it cannot reflect the incidence of expenses. This limitation made the use of a surrender charge necessary. The surrender charge itself was misunderstood and was often interpreted as a penalty for discontinuing the contract rather than as a

---

[3] Acquisition costs (commission to the agent, medical fee, investigation fee, state premium taxes, all the clerical costs involved in underwriting and issuing a new policy) take so much of the first year premium that the net amount remaining for the company is substantially less than that needed to finance the legal reserve required for the policy without drawing on surplus. The resulting charge against surplus is restored from future renewal premiums, which are greater than the amount required to offset year by year additions to legal reserves.

charge for high first year costs that otherwise would be recovered from future premiums. These criticisms, along with the desire to substitute sound actuarial principles for heretofore crude standards for surrender values, led to the development and passage of the Standard Nonforfeiture Law.

Under the Standard Nonforfeiture Law, no relationship is fixed between the cash surrender value and the reserve, and no surrender charge is made. Instead, the minimum value required is determined according to a special formula designed for that purpose. This formula fixes the maximum first-year expenses that may be charged against each type of policy at each age for purposes of determining the nonforfeiture value. This first-year expense is amortized over the premium paying period of the policy. The formula develops an "adjusted premium" which is the net annual level premium for any given policy plus the amount sufficient to amortize the first year expenses within the policy premium paying period. The current minimum nonforfeiture value is the present value of the company's obligations under the policy less the present value of the adjusted premiums, using actuarial assumptions yielding no less than that produced by the 1958 CSO Table at $3\frac{1}{2}$ percent.[4]

The Standard Nonforfeiture Law does not require that a surrender value be given after any specified arbitrary period of time but instead requires that such value be given at whatever time and for whatever amount such value is produced by the formula. Thus, one policy at one age may produce a surrender value at the end of the first policy year, whereas another will not show any values for several years.[5] The result is less inequity now in nonforfeiture values than under the old reserve less surrender charge method of computing them, where no distinction would be made among plans, amounts of insurance, ages of issues, policy durations, and the reserve valuation methods used.[6]

Companies can—many do—provide cash values in excess of the minimum required by law. The objective is to return to each policyholder as nearly as possible his equitable share in the assets of the company, without impairing the position of the continuing policyholders. Therefore, in developing their schedules of nonforfeiture values, companies take into consideration the opportunity afforded policyholders for adverse selection (both mortality and financial), the cost involved in handling the surrender,

---

[4] If this paragraph is not clear, then try it again after reading Chapter 27. The 1958 CSO Table became mandatory in 1966. Originally the minimum values were based on the 1941 CSO Table.

[5] The Nonforfeiture Law does not require a cash value until the end of three years. Values developed prior to that time need be only some form of paid-up insurance benefit, the form of which is to be left up to the company.

[6] Life insurance companies are given the option to use a method of computing their legal reserve liability that makes an allowance for high first year expenses. Cash values based on reserves computed in this manner should not require as high a surrender charge as would be required when reserves are computed on a full level premium basis. See Chapter 27 for a discussion of methods of computing reserves.

and the obligation that surrendering policyholders have to contribute to the surplus of the company as payment for the added security they had received from that surplus.[7]

Insurers are not required to disassociate cash values from the reserve; they are required only to provide at least the minimum values. Thus, a policy provision as follows will satisfy the regulators: "In determining the cash values a deduction has been made from the reserve. During the first policy year, the deduction is $16 for each $1,000 of face amount. The deduction decreases by one eighth in each succeeding year until there is no deduction in the ninth and subsequent policy years."

Insurers are required to include a statement in their policies of the formulas used in computing nonforfeiture values. The foregoing cash value provision is an illustration of one these statements.[8] Life insurers must show in their policies the specific policy year-end values for each of the first 20 policy years. Most policies show these values also for the end of the policy years in which the insured reaches ages 55, 60, and 65.

Table 11–1 shows examples of the cash values of several policies of one company on various anniversary dates for selected issue ages.

The accumulation of cash value is often one of the selling points that agents use in their efforts to write whole life policies. The whole life policy is frequently sold to policyholders as a financial instrument designed to accomplish one of two purposes: the creation of an estate for the family of the policyholder in the event of his premature death, and the building of a fund to be liquidated as a retirement income for the policyholder in the event of his survival to retirement age. The plan is for the policyholder to surrender the policy at retirement age and have the guaranteed cash values paid to him under one of the guaranteed life income settlement options.[9]

The cash surrender clause of a policy requires the proper surrender of the policy to the company. What is a proper surrender is usually spelled out in the policy, and requires that the policy owner elect the option in writing and file such election with the home office of the company. The election must include a written surrender of all claims. The insurance

---

[7] Those insurers that see no relationship between policy surrenders and the insured's health, make no charge for adverse mortality selection in setting their nonforfeiture values. However, most insurers do make charges to compensate for the liquidity problem inherent in surrenders for cash. The cost of processing policy surrenders may be spread over all policies by including it in the expense loading charge or it may be charged against surrendering policyholders only.

[8] See Chapter 27 for an illustration of another method of stating the basis of nonforfeiture values.

[9] The question of equity has been raised regarding the use of standard mortality assumptions in computing the cash surrender value for policies covering persons in poor health. It has been suggested that mortality assumptions which reflect the poorer health of the insured be used. This would produce higher cash values for policyholders who are in "poor health" when they reach age 65 and would make it unnecessary for them to exchange unequal values with the insurer if they wish to use their cash value to fund their retirement income. See Robert I. Mehr, "New Settings for Old Stones," *Journal of Risk and Insurance*, Vol. XXXIV, no. 3 (September, 1967), pp. 477–79.

TABLE 11–1

Continuous Premium Whole Life
Cash Value per $1,000 of Face, 1958 CSO 2 ½%, Participating

End of Policy Year	Age at Issue		
	20	30	40
1	$ 0	$ 3	$ 8
2	14	21	33
3	28	40	57
5	49	69	96
10	104	146	198
20	236	315	406
At age 65	623	578	506

20-Pay Life
Cash Value per $1,000 of Face, 1958 CSO 2 ½%, Participating

End of Policy Year	Age at Issue		
	20	30	40
1	$ 8	$ 13	$ 18
2	32	41	52
3	56	70	87
5	96	121	148
10	207	257	310
20	472	577	687
At age 65	739	739	739

20-Year Endowment
Cash Value per $1,000 of Face, 1958 CSO 2 ½%, Participating

End of Policy Year	Age at Issue		
	20	30	40
1	$ 28	$ 28	$ 29
2	73	73	74
3	118	119	120
5	203	204	205
10	434	435	435
20	1,000	1,000	1,000

Term to Age 65
Cash Value per $1,000 of Face, 1958 CSO 2 ½%, Participating

End of Policy Year	Age at Issue		
	20	30	40
1	$ 0	$ 0	$ 0
2	2	5	8
3	11	15	20
5	19	26	33
10	40	54	61
20	86	97	62
At age 62	59	54	45
At age 65	0	0	0

terminates when both the statement of election and the policy are received at the home office of the insurer. The insurer can waive receipt of the policy. What happens when the insured elects to surrender his policy but dies before completing the required procedure? The beneficiary is not likely to be content with the cash surrender value so he is apt to sue for the face amount of the insurance if the insurer claims that the surrender had been legally completed. The beneficiary would stand a good chance of winning the suit, although he cannot be assured of winning because court decisions have not all gone the same way. Cases involving the question of whether a policy has been surrendered occur with sufficient frequency for insurers and beneficiaries to be concerned about the surrender procedure.

Paid Up for a Reduced Amount.   Reduced paid-up insurance is the nonforfeiture value used by a few companies as automatic if no option is elected by the insured within 60 days after the due date of the defaulted premium.[10] In these companies, if the policyholder fails to pay his premium and makes no overtures to the company about the disposal of his policy, the company automatically applies the paid-up reduced amount option.[11]

Under the reduced paid-up insurance nonforfeiture option, the company uses the net cash value of the policy to buy a paid-up policy of the same type for the amount that can be purchased at the net single premium rate for the insured's attained age. The net single premium is based on the interest and mortality assumptions used in computing the cash value. The paid-up insurance under any form of a whole life policy will be whole life. It will be paid-up endowment under that type of contract. The reduced paid-up insurance nonforfeiture option usually is not included in term insurance polices.

The net cash value is the cash value for the face amount of insurance at the date of default, increased by the cash value of any dividend additions and the amount of any dividend accumulations and decreased by the amount of any indebtedness to the company against the policy. The examples in Table 11–2 show the amounts of paid-up insurance available at the end of given policy years, based on several ages of entry on three policy plans, assuming no dividend additions, accumulations, or policy indebtedness.

The paid-up option should be elected when the policyholder's need for insurance protection has decreased but will continue to exist until the maturity date of the policy. For instance, at age 65 financial protection against death is still needed for at least final expenses. If the policyholder

---

[10] Because of the small death benefits that will usually be involved under this option, it is not common to use this as the automatic option.

[11] It is not widely understood by policyholders that even if they do nothing after failing to pay a premium, some value will continue in force for some time thereafter—provided there was a paid-up value under the nonforfeiture valuation formula at the time. Cases are not uncommon of beneficiaries who discovered long after the death of the insured that the old policy on which premiums had not been paid for years was still in force for some value at the death of the policyholder. The beneficiary should never discard a lapsed policy found among the effects of the deceased, but instead should check with the company to see if it still has value.

TABLE 11-2

Continuous Premium Whole Life
Paid-up Values per $1,000 of Face, 1958 CSO 2 ½%, Participating

End of Policy	Age at Issue		
Year	20	30	40
5	$ 143	$ 163	$ 184
10	274	310	343
15	393	437	478
20	499	547	591

20-Pay Life
Paid-up Values per $1,000 of Face, 1958 CSO 2 ½%, Participating

End of Policy	Age at Issue		
Year	20	30	40
5	$ 282	$ 284	$ 283
10	541	543	537
15	780	779	772
20	1,000	1,000	1,000

20-Year Endowment
Paid-up Values per $1,000 of Face, 1958 CSO 2 ½%, Participating

End of Policy	Age at Issue		
Year	20	30	40
5	$ 292	$ 292	$ 290
10	554	554	549
15	780	788	783
20	1,000	1,000	1,000

Term to Age 65
Paid-up Values per $1,000 of Face, 1958 CSO 2 ½%, Participating

End of Policy	Age at Issue		
Year	20	30	40
5	$ 128	$ 158	$ 182
10	253	304	338
15	371	431	468
20	480	539	575

has in force more death protection at retirement than he feels will be needed to pay the cost of dying (funeral expenses, taxes, and so on), he can convert some or all of the insurance to the reduced paid-up insurance option, making it unnecessary to continue premium payments and allowing him to spend more of his retirement income for the cost of living. If he does not need all of the reduced paid-up insurance available, he can use the cash values of some of his insurance to increase his retirement income.

Reduced paid-up insurance continues to pay dividends if the original policy was participating. Reduced paid-up insurance has cash and loan values. If reduced paid-up insurance is not the automatic option, and it usually is not, the insured must request this option within the time specified in the policy, usually three months after lapse.

Extended Term. The extended term option is commonly used as the automatic option in the event that the policyholder fails to elect one of the other nonforfeiture provisions within the required time. Under this option the company uses the net cash value of the policy to purchase term insurance for the full face amount of the policy (less any policy loans outstanding) for the length of time that can be supported using a net single premium for term insurance at the insured's age at the time of default. The net single premium used in computing the extended term benefit may be based either on the 1958 CSO Table or on a special table developed to serve as the maximum mortality basis for determining the value of the extended term benefit. The special table, known as the 1958 CET Table (Commissioners 1958 Extended Term Table) recognizes the higher mortality generally experienced under extended term insurance.

A look at the policies of several companies will show that some companies use 1958 CSO exclusively whereas others use 1958 CET exclusively. The two tables may be combined as illustrated by the following provision: "The 1958 CSO Table is used . . . except . . . for the first five years of extended term insurance for which the 1958 CET Table is used." The rationale of using the CET Table for the first five years is that these are the years in which the mortality experience under extended term is adverse.

If, in endowment insurance, the cash value will extend the term beyond the maturity date, the amount of net cash value in excess of that needed to continue the face amount to maturity will be used to purchase a pure endowment—i.e., endowment payable only if the policyholder lives to the endowment date. In other words, if a $10,000 endowment policy with 5 years to run to maturity is placed on an extended term option, it will be handled as follows: First, assume the cash value of this particular policy is $5,674 and that the amount required for a net single premium for a $10,000 term policy for 5 years at the age of surrender is only $546. The $5,128 remainder would be used to purchase a pure endowment. The amount of 5-year pure endowment that can be purchased at the policy holder's attained age with a net single premium of $5,128 is $6,165. If under this option the insured dies within five years, his beneficiary will collect $10,000 (the amount of the extended term insurance); however, if he lives for 5 years, he will collect $6,165 (the amount of the pure endowment).

Under extended term, the full amount of the policy (assuming no accumulated dividends[12] or policy indebtedness) remains in force for a limited period of time instead of (as in the reduced amount option) a reduced amount of insurance remaining in force for the full original policy period. The extended term option is, in fact, a misnomer. It should be called reduced term because it reduces rather than extends the term of the original policy.

---

[12] If, because of accumulated dividends, the term of insurance under the extended term option will extend to or beyond the insured's attained age of 100, reduced paid-up insurance will be provided.

Table 11–3 shows the length of time each of several policies will remain in force for their full amounts, assuming given ages of issue, if these policies are put on the extended term option at the end of the policy years indicated and no dividend credits or policy indebtedness are involved.

TABLE 11–3

Continuous Premium Whole Life

Extended Term Durations per $1,000 of Face, 1958 CSO 2½%, Participating

End of Policy Year	Age at Issue					
	20		30		40	
	Years	Days	Years	Days	Years	Days
5	18	181	15	102	10	243
10	24	319	19	56	13	176
15	26	97	19	313	13	330
20	25	292	19	76	13	107

20-Pay Life

Extended Term Durations per $1,000 of Face, 1958 CSO 2½%, Participating

End of Policy Year	Age at Issue					
	20		30		40	
	Years	Days	Years	Days	Years	Days
5	28	252	21	274	14	363
10	35	278	27	67	18	349
15	38	356	29	342	21	136
20	Paid up		Paid up		Paid up	

20-Year Endowment

Extended Term Durations and Pure Endowment[a] per $1,000 of Face, 1958 CSO 2½%, Participating

End of Policy Year	Age at Issue								
	20			30			40		
	Years	Days	Pure Endowment	Years	Days	Pure Endowment	Years	Days	Pure Endowment
5	15	0	$250	15	0	$215	15	0	$ 93
10	10	0	536	10	0	517	10	0	454
15	5	0	765	5	0	778	5	0	757
20	Matured			Matured			Matured		

[a] The amount of endowment to which the insured will be entitled if living on the maturity date. Under the extended term option, the amount of death protection remains the same as long as the extended term runs, but the amount of endowment payable is lower than it would be if the premiums were continued to the maturity date.

Term to Age 65

Extended Term Durations per $1,000 of Face, 1958 CSO 2½%, Participating

End of Policy Year	Age at Issue					
	20		30		40	
	Years	Days	Years	Days	Years	Days
5	7	195	7	179	4	162
10	13	27	9	175	5	44
15	14	84	9	59	4	64
20	13	122	7	236	2	126

HANDLING A POLICY LOAN.   When there is a loan outstanding against a policy that is to be continued as extended term insurance, the amount of the loan is deducted both from the face of the policy and from the cash value. This means that a smaller amount of insurance is extended for a period shorter than would be the case had there been no indebtedness. Were the loan deducted from the cash value only, the policy would be extended for even a shorter period.

Assume a $10,000 policy issued at age 21 which has been in force 20 years on the continuous premium whole life basis. Assume further that the policy has indebtedness against it for $1,000, and that the policyholder decides to discontinue premium payments, forget the loan, and put the insurance on the extended term, nonforfeiture option. A 20-year-old continuous premium whole life policy of $10,000 issued at age 21 in one company has a cash value of about $2,547. When this policy is placed on the extended term basis, the loan is subtracted from both the face amount and the cash value of the policy. Thus, this policy will extend $9,000 for as many years as $1,547 will provide at the net single premium for term insurance at the attained age of 41.

At first glance it might seem unfair to subtract the amount of the loan from both the face amount and the cash value of the policy. On closer examination, however, the logic of this procedure becomes apparent. If the amount of the indebtedness were not subtracted from the face amount of the insurance when the policy is put on an extended term basis, the result could be adverse selection, making it profitable for anyone to borrow heavily on his policy when he reaches his deathbed, and then surrender it for extended term insurance for its full amount. The effect would be to increase the insurance, contrary to all good underwriting practices.

Suppose that shortly after he borrows the $1,000, the insured in the foregoing case decides to cash in his policy. He will be entitled to collect only $1,547, since he has already received $1,000. Suppose, instead of cashing in the policy, he dies shortly after getting the loan. His beneficiaries will collect only $9,000, since the face of the policy as well as its cash value is encumbered by the loan. If he neither dies nor cashes in his policy but instead converts it to an extended term contract, his present insurance (in this case $9,000) is continued for the period purchased by the remaining cash value (in this case $1,547). Therefore, the insured gets full value— the adjustment in the amount of the term insurance extended does not impose any penalty on him. The situation is just the reverse when there are dividend accumulations. The amount of the accumulations is added to the face amount of the term extended and to the cash value used as the net single premium. This seemingly double adjustment upward does not impose any penalty on the company.

The usual policy provides that the insurance shall be nonparticipating when placed on an extended term basis, and that a loan cannot be granted if the policy is in force as extended term insurance. However, policies on an extended term basis may be surrendered for their cash value. Under some policies the right of the insured to participate in the surplus of the insurer is not withdrawn when the policy continues in force as extended term insurance. These usually are not the policies with the most favorable extended term rates for the insured.

When a policyholder no longer can continue premium payments and yet wishes to keep his insurance in force, he must choose between reduced paid-up insurance, extended term insurance, or the combination of the two that best suits his objectives. He will seek the optimum tradeoff among the amount of insurance, the duration of coverage, and the preservation of cash values. His health might also be a controlling factor. If his health is poor, he might be inclined to select the extended term option. Because the insurers recognize that adverse selection is inherent in the extended term benefit, they make that benefit automatic in the event of premium default in the hope of neutralizing the effect of conscious selection against them.

If for some reason, premiums cannot be paid out of current funds and this reason is the result of a temporary condition, premiums should be paid with a premium loan until the temporary financial embarrassment has passed. If one of the paid-up insurance nonforfeiture options is selected, the policyholder may never be able to replace his policy with one as good as the one surrendered. Another important reason for using a premium loan rather than one of the nonforfeiture options is to keep in effect disability benefits written with the policy. Double indemnity and disability riders terminate upon conversion of the policy to reduced paid-up or extended term insurance.

2. DIVIDEND OPTIONS,

Life insurance policies may be issued on either a participating or a non-participating plan. Under the participating plan, policyholders are entitled to policy dividends as declared by the company. These dividends reflect the difference between the premium charged for a given class of policies and the full cost (broadly defined) of these policies as experienced by the company. Under the nonparticipating plan, policies are written for a premium lower than the gross premium charged for participating insurance in the same company.

The Nature of Dividends.   Dividends distributed to participating policyholders are not profits in a commercial sense, but instead are a return of an overcharge of premium.[13] That portion of the company's earnings for the year not deemed necessary to strengthen surplus or contingency reserves may be distributed among individual policyholders.[14] The method of calculating dividends is rarely if ever stated in the policy contract. Instead,

---

[13] See Chapter 21 for a discussion of tax laws relating to policy dividends.
[14] See Chapter 27 for a discussion of the source of surplus and the problems involved in its apportionment.

the policy makes some such statement as "This policy shall share in the divisible surplus of the company. Its share shall be determined annually by the Company and credited as a dividend. The first dividend shall be payable in equal parts on each premium due date during the second policy year if the premium then due is paid. Each dividend thereafter shall be payable on the policy anniversary."[15]

The dividend clause often includes a provision for the payment of dividends for the fraction of the policy year in which the policyholder dies. The practice on such postmortem dividends varies from full payment of the current year's dividend to a pro rata share. No fractional dividends, however, are paid upon surrender of the policy.

Participating policies offer the policyholder several options for the use of his dividends. Aside from the option of taking his dividends in cash, the insured may elect (1) to apply the dividend toward the payment of the premium, (2) to leave the dividend to accumulate with interest credited annually at a guaranteed minimum rate of interest, (3) to use the dividend to buy paid-up additions to the policy, (4) to apply the dividends to the cash value of the policy to (a) pay up the policy in fewer years, (b) convert a whole life policy into an endowment policy, or (c) shorten the endowment period, and (5) to use the dividend to buy one-year term insurance. The automatic option varies among companies, being cash in some companies, the accumulation option in others, and the paid-up addition option in still others. The statutes of some states specify the dividend option that is to be automatic if no other is selected by the policyholder. Currently about 21 percent of all policy dividends are taken in cash, about 26 percent are used to pay premiums, 28 percent are left to accumulate at interest, and 25 percent are used to purchase additional insurance.

Payment in Cash. Cash dividends are taken most frequently when the policy is paid up. Unless there is some particular reason why the policyholder wants the dividend in cash, he should consider the advantages of one of the other options.

Application toward Payment of Premiums. Usually, the company's premium notice will show the gross premium, the amount of the dividend, and the net premium due. The policyholder has only to send his check for the net premium, which, together with the dividend, will take care of

---

[15] Annual distribution of policy dividends is required by the laws of many states, particularly New York, where the system of deferred dividends popular in the late 19th and early 20th century led to abuses castigated by the Armstrong Committee. Cf. Chapter 29. Even where not required, the practice of annual policy dividends is usually followed. However, dividends paid over longer periods, quinquennially, for example, are not unknown and have their advocates. Under the laws of New York and those of a number of other states, dividends are not restricted exclusively to regular annual payments. Extra dividends at reasonable intervals or dividends on policy terminations are allowed. Extra and terminal dividends, however, are carefully supervised by the insurance regulatory departments of the states in order to prevent a disproportionate amount of funds from being used for these types of dividends. In general, these special dividends must not be excessive in comparison with the regular annual dividends apportioned on the policies in preceding years, otherwise, they will be declared inequitable.

the premium due for that period. In order to afford a reasonably adequate life insurance program, many families must depend on policy dividends to help meet their premium obligations.

Accumulation at Interest.   At the option of the policyholder, dividends will be retained by the company and accumulated at not less than a guaranteed rate of interest specified in the policy, compounded annually. If the company earns more than the guaranteed rate, the dividend accumulations may participate in the excess earnings.

Companies may include in the contract a provision automatically applying accumulated dividends at the expiration of any grace period to the settlement of any past-due premiums, if the accumulated dividends are sufficient for that purpose. If the dividend accumulations are insufficient to meet the full annual premium, they may be used automatically to pay the corresponding quarterly, semiannual, or monthly premium but never to pay a fraction of these premiums.

Even in the absence of such a provision, the general rule of law is that the insurer cannot lapse the policy if it has accumulated dividends under the policy sufficient to pay the stipulated premium unless the insured directs otherwise.[16]

If the premium is in default and the dividend accumulations are insufficient to pay a full premium, unless withdrawn they will be applied to increase the period of time for which the policy will be continued in force under the extended term insurance, nonforfeiture provisions.

The contract also usually provides that dividend accumulations may be withdrawn at any time provided they have not been applied under a nonforfeiture option.

If dividend accumulations are neither withdrawn, used for premium payments, nor applied under a nonforfeiture option, they will be included in the cash settlement made at the time the policy matures as a death or endowment claim or upon the surrender of the policy.

Dividends left to accumulate can amount to a rather sizable sum over a period of time. For example, although present dividend and interest scales are not guaranteed for the future, in one company dividends left to accumulate under a $10,000 continuous premium whole life policy issued today at age 25 would, at age 65, add $7,472 to the $6,030 guaranteed cash value in the policy. In terms of retirement income, the dividend accumulations would increase the guaranteed monthly life income from $40.28 to $90.19 (male) 60 months certain. Dividend accumulations, therefore, can substantially increase the retirement values in an insurance program.

---

[16] Practice in the application of dividend accumulation varies from contract to contract. However, in at least one case (*Indianapolis Life* v. *Powell*, 104 S.W. (2d) 157 [Tex. Civ. App. 1937]), it has been held the obligation of the company to apply any dividends it holds to premium payment even though the policy provided that "no premiums shall be construed as paid, either wholly or in part, by reason of dividends remaining with the company under the accumulation option." Also see *Lomar* v. *Aetna Life Ins. Co.*, 85 Fed. (2d) 141, 142 (10th cir.)

Paid-Up Additions. The policy usually provides that, upon the election of the policyholder, dividends may be applied to the purchase of additional paid-up participating insurance of the same type, usually referred to as "dividend additions." This option usually is not available with term insurance. Providing insurance at net single premium rates, these options represent the least expensive way a policyholder can purchase insurance, since no charge for expenses is added to the rate. For example, the gross rate at age 25 for a $1,000 single premium whole life policy in one company is $413.67, more than 41 percent of the face of the policy.[17] In this same company, a policy dividend of $1 at age 25 will buy $2.94 of paid-up insurance. The effective rate here is only about 34 percent of the amount of insurance, since it is the *net* rather than the *gross* rate.[18] These paid-up additions are generally eligible for future dividends along with the original contract, but at a lower rate because, purchased at net rates, they do not participate in expense savings. Table 11–4 indicates the amount of paid-up insurance purchased in a representative company by a cash dividend of $1 at the ages given for whole life and for endowment at age 65.[19]

TABLE 11–4
Amount of Paid-up Insurance Purchased by a Cash Dividend
of $1 (Whole Life and Endowment) 1958 CSO 2 ½ %

Attained Age	Whole Life	Endowment at Age 65
20	$3.27	$2.72
25	2.94	2.43
30	2.65	2.18
35	2.38	1.95
40	2.14	1.74
45	1.93	1.56
50	1.75	1.40
55	1.60	1.26
60	1.47	1.13

Over a period of years, paid-up additions can produce a substantial amount of insurance. For example, if dividends on a $10,000 continuous premium whole life policy issued at age 25 were used to buy paid-up additions, by age 65, the amount of additional paid-up insurance purchased by the insured under one company's *present* dividend scale would amount to $8,614.

Companies usually provide that the paid-up additions may be surrendered at any time for a cash surrender value equal to the full reserve

---

[17] A $10,000 policy would have a premium of $3,872 and a $100,000 policy, $38,492. The rate structure calls for a reduction in premium of $5 for each $1,000 in excess of $5,000.

[18] Net rate used here means gross rate less cost of operation and should not be confused with the same term used to designate gross rate less dividend.

[19] Rates will vary from company to company. These are based on the 1958 CSO at 2½ percent interest.

value of the insurance. That amount will always equal or exceed the amount of the dividends used to purchase the additions.

The paid-up additions dividend option can be selected for current dividends at any time by the insured without furnishing evidence of insurability. If the insured wishes to convert accumulated dividends to paid-up additions, he might be asked to show evidence of insurability in order to eliminate adverse selection in the use of the option.

The Accelerative Option.   Two methods are available by which dividends may be used to pay up a policy in fewer years, to convert a whole life policy into an endowment, or to shorten an endowment period. One method is to accumulate the dividends at interest until they, plus the reserve value of the policy,[20] equal the net single premium for a paid-up policy of the same amount at the attained age of the insured. At that time, the policy will (upon request) be endorsed as fully paid up. For example, the foregoing $10,000 continuous premium whole life policy issued at age 25 could be paid up at age 49 if the paid-up option were exercised, assuming, of course, no change in the dividend scale or interest rates. If the insured dies before age 49, his estate collects the face of the policy plus the dividends. At age 49 the cash value of the policy plus dividend accumulations equals $5,597, the net single premium for a $10,000 whole life policy at that age.

Under this same method, the dividends can accumulate until they, plus the reserve value of the policy, equal the face amount of the policy, at which time the policy upon request is matured as an endowment. Under this plan, if death occurs before these values equal the face amount, both the face amount and the dividend accumulations are paid to the beneficiary. For example, the foregoing $10,000 continuous premium whole life policy issued at age 25 could mature as an endowment at age 59 if dividends were left to accumulate at interest, assuming no changes in the dividend scale and interest rates. At age 59 the reserve value of the policy plus the value of the accumulated dividends equal $10,000. If the policyholder under this plan dies before age 59, his estate collects both the face amount of the policy and the accumulated dividends.

The second method is the use of the accelerative option. Under this option, the dividends are credited directly to cash values rather than accumulated separately at interest. In this event, if the insured dies early, his estate collects only the face amount of the insurance. Under the accelerative dividend option, the $10,000 continuous premium whole life policy used in this illustration could be paid up before age 49, and it could endow at an age earlier than 59 because as each dividend is paid the reserve is increased, reducing the amount at risk.[21] With less at risk, a smaller pro-

---

[20] This is an expression of convenience. Actuarially, there is no reserve per policy but only the total reserve for all policies.

[21] The amount at risk has been defined here as the face amount of the policy less the reserve.

portion of the premiums to be collected will be needed than originally anticipated to pay the cost of insurance and, therefore, more can be used to build the reserve.[22]

The application of either of these methods of paying up the policy in fewer years—converting a whole life policy into an endowment or shortening the endowment period—saves the policyholder the expense costs allocated to the remaining premiums, which no longer have to be paid.

One-Year Term Option. Some companies include the option to purchase additional one-year term insurance with the dividends. The amount of one-year term insurance that can be purchased with dividends under this option generally is limited to the cash value of the policy. When the current dividend, plus any accumulations of dividends that were not needed for the purchase of term insurance in the past are no longer sufficient to purchase this amount of insurance, the option is terminated. For example, on a continuous premium whole life policy issued at age 40, the termination date in one company, assuming current dividend scales, will not be reached until the 25th policy year when the insured is aged 65. These estimates assume that the dividends not used to purchase one-year term insurance are taken in cash or used to buy paid-up additions. If the excess dividends were accumulated at interest, the projected period of the option would be 28 years; at the insured's age 68.

If the option is not selected at the time the policy is issued, evidence of insurability will be required if it is selected later.

The maximum rates at which one-year term insurance will be purchased must be included in the policy. Table 11–5 is illustrative of the maximum standard rates used by one insurer. However, insurers may charge lower rates and they usually do.

TABLE 11–5
Cost of Paid-Up Term Insurance for One Year
per $1,000 of One-Year Term Insurance

Age	Premium	Age	Premium	Age	Premium
25	$1.86	40	$3.40	55	$12.52
30	2.05	45	5.15	60	19.59
35	2.42	50	8.01	65	30.58

An older variation of the one-year term option allows the insured to apply the entire dividend to purchase one-year term insurance rather than limiting the amount of term insurance to the cash value of the policy. For example, a $10,000 policy issued at age 30 will have a 10th year dividend in one insurer of $67.50. The cash value of the policy would be $1,460.

---

[22] While this point could be explained in terms of the survivorship benefit concept, it is, perhaps, more easily understood in terms of the decreasing insurance increasing investment concept.

Under the newer version of the one-year term option, the insured can apply $4.96 of his dividend for the purchase of one-year term insurance for $1,460, and take the rest in cash, accumulate it at interest, or use it to buy $134 of paid-up whole life insurance. Under the older version of the one-year term option, the insured can apply the entire $67.50 to purchase $19,850 of one-year term insurance for that year.

Which Dividend Option to Select.   The solution to the problem of selecting a dividend option is by no means cut and dried, although several guideposts may be established.

If the policyholder is operating on a tight budget, perhaps the only choice he has is to use his dividends to pay premiums. If, on the other hand, he can afford to select one of the other options, he has to make a choice among paid-up additions, accumulations at interest, the accelerative option, and in some cases the one-year term option. If he believes that it is more important that he increase his death protection than his retirement protection, paid-up additions are the proper choice, assuming, of course, that the one-year term insurance option is not available. Paid-up additions will increase both death and retirement protection but will add more to death than to retirement protection.

If the greater need is for retirement protection, then the accelerative option is the proper choice. Under this option, there is no increase in death protection whatsoever, because the dividends are used to increase cash values. Only the face of the policy will be paid upon death of the insured.

The accumulations at interest option, frequently called the deposit option, seems to stand between the accelerative option and the paid-up additions option. It offers more death protection but less retirement protection than the accelerative option and more retirement protection but less death protection than the paid-up additions option.

The cash value of paid-up additions in many cases will not be much less than the value of dividend accumulations. Thus, the insured can have the benefit of increased protection through the years and then cash in his additions at age 65, if he so desires, and still have nearly the same amount of cash as if he had left the dividends to accumulate.

When federal income tax considerations are important to the decision, paid-up additions or the accelerative option might be the most attractive. For example, the cash value of the accumulations under a continuous premium whole life policy in one company, based on a 20-year projection of its current dividend scale and current interest rate, would be $2,751.10 for a $10,000 policy issued at age 45. The cash value of paid-up additions would be $2,536.77, or just about 7.8 percent less. When it is held in mind that interest on dividends left to accumulate is taxable in the year credited, whereas the increase in the cash values of the additions is not, the net value to the policy owner of the additions is nearly always in excess of that of the accumulations, in spite of the fact that paid-up additions had also provided additional insurance.

Several circumstances make the selection of the one-year term option useful where it is available. If the death protection is inadequate, the one-year term option provides a method of increasing the protection at a faster rate than under the paid-up additions option. If the cash value is used as collateral for a loan, the one-year term option can retain the face amount of the insurance as death protection. The one-year term insurance equal to the cash value of the policy offsets the indebtedness. In any situation in which the cash value is encumbered, the one-year term option offers relief.

3. OPTIONAL METHODS OF SETTLEMENT

An important purpose of life insurance is to provide an income for the beneficiaries upon the death of the insured, or for the insured himself at retirement. In keeping with this thought, life insurance companies have developed a number of income settlement options which are included in most life insurance policies. These options may be elected either by the policy owner while living or, if the policy owner does not elect one, by the beneficiary after the policy owner's death. The options apply to the proceeds of the policy and usually to the cash values if payable to the insured. Some insurers have contract restrictions on the applicability of some settlement options to cash values, requiring that the policy be in force for a given minimum number of years such as 5 or 10 or that the insured be at least 55 years old.[23] The election of a settlement option by the policy owner precludes the beneficiary from selecting an option unless the right to change is left to the beneficiary. The policy contract of one company states the matter thus:

(a) By Owner.   The owner may:

1. elect a settlement option for death proceeds during the lifetime of the insured. Any such election may be changed during the insured's lifetime.

2. revoke any existing election and elect a settlement option for death proceeds during the 60 days following the date of death of the insured if the insured immediately before his death was not the owner. Any such election shall be final.

3. elect a settlement option for surrender or maturity proceeds. Any such election shall be for the owner as direct beneficiary.

(b) By Direct Beneficiary.   A direct beneficiary may make an election of a settlement option if no election is in force when this policy becomes payable. Such election shall be subject to any remaining rights of the owner.

---

[23] Under certain conditions, a number of insurers will permit the use of cash values (and endowment proceeds) to provide income to persons other than the insured. (See *Who Writes What in Life and Health Insurance,* an annual publication of the National Underwriter Company, Cincinnati, Ohio.)

(*c*) **By Contingent Beneficiary.** A contingent beneficiary may make an election of a settlement option if the policy proceeds become payable to such contingent beneficiary and if no election is in force. Such election shall be subject to any remaining rights of the owner.

The proceeds of the policy at maturity are paid to the beneficiary or policy owner in a lump sum, unless some other plan of settlement agreement is chosen.[24] Most death payments are taken in a lump sum, although in a significant minority of cases death payments from life insurance policies are settled under one of the income options.

The most common optional modes of settlement offered by policy contracts are interest only, installments for fixed periods, installments in fixed amounts, and life income. Insurers usually place a limit on the minimum amount of funds they will hold under these options and on the minimum size of each periodic payment, these usually being $1,000 or $2,000 for the size of the fund, and $10 or $20 for the amount of the periodic payment to each beneficiary.

Interest Only. Under the interest only option, sometimes called the deposit option because it resembles money on deposit in a bank, the company holds all or a part of the proceeds or cash values and pays the payee a contractually guaranteed rate of interest or a higher rate as may be determined annually by the company in view of its earnings. The policy owner may provide, if he wishes, that no part of the principal sum shall ever be withdrawn by the primary payee, being payable to a secondary payee or to the estate of either the beneficiary or policy owner upon death of the primary beneficiary.[25]

The policy owner may, on the other hand, direct that the proceeds be held at interest with the right of the beneficiary to withdraw in whole or in part. For example, a policy owner might direct that proceeds from a $20,000 policy be held at interest only, with the interest payments payable to his widow as long as she shall live, but granting her the right to withdraw principal amounts not to exceed $500 in any one year. An important use of the interest only settlement with the privilege of partial withdrawal is to provide an emergency fund for the widow that she may use in case there are unexpected expenses beyond her income for the year. The policy might also provide for the withdrawal of the full $20,000 without any restrictions.

Another use of the interest only option with right of full withdrawal is

---

[24] Except in family income, family maintenance, or other policies where, under the insuring clause, the insurer agrees to pay an income of so much a month for a stated period or to a stated date, before the lump sum is payable.

[25] Many companies hesitate to agree to pay any remaining proceeds back to the estate of the policy owner, as contrasted to payment to the estate of the last surviving beneficiary. Payment to the estate of the insured may necessitate reopening that estate half a century or more after the policyholder's death. Moreover, such an arrangment can be a factor in disqualifying the proceeds for the federal estate tax marital deduction. State laws on perpetuities also could be involved in paying the excess to the estate.

to create an estate clearance fund which will be needed soon after but not immediately upon the death of the insured. The interest only option is more appropriate than the lump-sum settlement for this purpose, since the fund will earn interest from the date of death until a withdrawal is made. Many companies will permit the policyholder to direct that at his death the proceeds shall be held and accumulated at interest until named minor children have reached a specified age, usually college age. Because the laws of several states prohibit the accumulation of income except for a minor beneficiary, life insurers generally will not accumulate the interest under an interest only option for adult beneficiaries.

The interest only option is used also in insurance planning when there is reason to defer the payment of the policy proceeds to a later date. A common period for deferral is to the end of the widow's social security dependency income. As soon as the youngest child reaches age 18, the mother's social security income terminates until she reaches age 60. A $10,000 policy purchased to offset the loss of this social security income may be held at interest after the insured's death until it is needed. A few companies where permitted by law will agree to accumulate the interest payments at compound interest for the deferred period; but most companies require the beneficiary to take the interest payments in cash.

Another reason for deferral is to take advantage of higher guarantees (contract rates) on some policies than on others. For example, the contract rate under the interest only option of one insurer is $2.50 a month per $1,000 for contracts issued in the 1920's and 1930's, $2.47 for the first half of the 1940's, $1.88 for those contracts issued during the last half of the 1940's during the 1950's, and early 1960's, and $2.26 currently. The insured's portfolio of policies with other insurers may contain policies with contract rates for the interest only option as high as $2.87 a month per $1,000 of proceeds and as low as $1.65.

On policies involving the mortality risk, a life income option, 10 years certain, for example, the contract rates for this same insurer over the same time period, using female age 60 rates, moved from $6.43 a month per $1,000 to $6.16 to $5.69 to $5.60 and to its current rate of $4.95. Wide variations may exist among the contract rates in the policies contained in the insured's portfolio, even among contracts that have been issued recently. For example, in the early 1960's one insurer used a contract rate of $5.38 compared to the $5.60 used by the insurer cited above. In the later 1960's the $5.38 rate was reduced to $5.23 whereas the $5.60 rate was reduced to $4.95. Projections of increased life expectancies account for the continued decrease in contract rates under life income options even though higher interest assumptions are now used, 3 percent as against $2\frac{1}{2}$ percent in one company, and $2\frac{3}{4}$ percent as against $2\frac{1}{4}$ percent in the other.

The policies with the lower contract rates should be liquidated first to meet the income needs for the early years after the insured's death, and those with the higher contract rates should be placed on the interest only option until they are ready for liquidation under one of the other options.

Because the older policies assume mortality experience more favorable to the annuitant, the newer policies are better used for fixed period income needs, while the older policies would be preferable for providing lifetime income. The face amount of the policy could be kept intact under the interest only option until the newer policies are liquidated and then be liquidated on a lifetime income option. In this way, the beneficiary can obtain the greatest value from the guarantees. Unfortunately, however, many companies do not allow the beneficiary complete flexibility in the use of options. Some insurers are more liberal than others, and there is a wide variation among practices.[26]

The usual rule is that the beneficiary must elect the option within six months after the insured's death in order to get the benefit of the contract rates. If an interest only option is selected, one of the liquidating options can be taken later at contract rates if done within a limited period after the insured's death. However, the liquidating option does not have to be effective within this limited period. It must only be elected. Thus, the beneficiary can take advantage of favorable contract rates by making the election within the specified time period, to have his insurance settled under an interest only option for, say, 10 years, and then liquidated under a life income option. The danger, of course, is that the beneficiary is then stuck with a life income option that might work to his disadvantage if his health later deteriorates. Therefore, he might want to consider electing a refund option so at least the principal will be returned to his estate at the expense of a smaller income for life.

The contract rates set the minimum values that the insurer will pay under the optional modes of settlement. The rates actually paid may exceed the minimum under some options and will vary from time to time over the period of the contract. The rates used at any given time are called current rates. For example, while the contract rate for the interest only option may produce $2.26 a month per $1,000 of insurance, the current rate may produce $3.30 a month.[27]

The time limit under which an insurer will hold insurance proceeds under an interest only option is usually 30 years or the lifetime of the primary beneficiary if he should survive the insured by more than 30 years. In some estates, the insurance proceeds are large enough to provide a sufficient lifetime income to the beneficiary from interest alone. The proceeds may then be held in full for the secondary beneficiary.

The uses of the interest only option in life insurance programming and estate planning are discussed in Chapters 20 and 21.

Installment for Fixed Period.   Under the installment for fixed period option—sometimes called the installment certain, or time, option—the

---

[26] See *Who Writes What?, op. cit.*

[27] More so in the past than at the present, a few insurers paid a lower interest rate on funds subject to withdrawal than on those which were nonwithdrawable.

proceeds are retained by the company and paid in equal annual, semiannual, quarterly, or monthly installments, including both principal and interest, for a definite number of years, regardless of the lifetime of the beneficiary. Upon the death of the primary beneficiary, the payments either are continued to a designated payee or their commuted value is paid to the beneficiary's estate.

Under this fixed installment option, the length of the income period selected determines the amount of each installment. Interest on unpaid proceeds is based on a rate specified in the policy, with excess interest allowed as earned. The principal sum is gradually decreased with each installment, thus decreasing the amount subject to excess interest earnings. Therefore, the amount paid in each installment under participating options might decrease as the principal decreases, even though the rate of interest paid remains unchanged.

The fixed period option is useful when an income is wanted for a specific number of years, for example during the period between the time when the mother's social security benefits stop (when she no longer has a child under 18 in her care) and when the widow's benefits start (at age 60). The fixed period option is used to provide income over the four years of college.

TABLE 11–6
Guaranteed Installments of Principal and Interest per $1,000 of Proceeds

Number of Years Payable	Monthly 2½%	Monthly 2¾%	Monthly 3%	Monthly 3½%
5	$17.70	$17.80	$17.91	$18.11
10	9.39	9.50	9.61	9.83
15	6.64	6.75	6.87	7.10
20	5.27	5.39	5.51	5.75
25	4.46	4.59	4.71	4.96
30	3.93	4.06	4.18	4.45

Table 11–6 shows the amount of guaranteed monthly income per $1,000 of proceeds which will be paid under the fixed period option under various interest rates for the number of years indicated. Under participating options, these payments will be increased by dividends as determined by the company. The withdrawal value at any time is the commuted value of any unpaid installments, computed on the basis of the contract rate of interest. A minimum amount of monthly income payments per $1,000 of insurance proceeds is usually fixed at between $4 and $6 a year. If the insurer sets $5 as its minimum then, looking at Table 11–6, the fund will have to be liquidated in less than 25 years unless the interest paid is more than 3½ percent.

The time option is an inflexible option. No limited withdrawals are allowed because they would require the expense of establishing new (lower) periodic amounts. However full withdrawal may be allowed under the agreement.

The time option was first used by company practice in 1867. About 1889, companies began including the option by rider. Soon thereafter, companies began to include the option in the body of the policy. Today these options are nearly universally granted.

Installments in Fixed Amounts.   The installments in fixed amounts option—often called the amount option—provides for payment of an unvarying annual, semiannual, quarterly, or monthly installment of a predetermined amount until the proceeds and the interest thereon are exhausted. The desired size of each installment determines the length of the income period, in contrast to the fixed period option, where the length of the period selected determines the amount of the income.

Since the fixed amount option provides for installments in definite sums, any excess earnings apportioned on the unpaid principal will lengthen the income period rather than increase the size of the payment. Any fractional amount of the proceeds and interest remaining at the end of the income period will be paid with the last full installment.

Table 11–7 illustrates the guaranteed length of time for which a given monthly income will be provided by various amounts of proceeds at 3 percent under this option.[28]

TABLE 11–7

Length of Time Various Incomes Are Provided by Various Amounts of Proceeds—3% (Amount Option)

Monthly Income Desired	$,1000		$3,000		$5,000		$10,000	
	Years	Months	Years	Months	Years	Months	Years	Months
$ 50	1	8	5	4	9	6	22	10
75	1	1	3	3	6	0	13	5
100	0	10	2	7	4	5	9	6

One point should be kept in mind in deciding whether to select the amount option or the time option when a liquidation on an annuity certain basis is desired. Some policies mature at death with a loan outstanding against them. In such cases the time option would reduce the amount of each periodic payment, whereas the amount option would reduce the number of period payments. Also, the amount of the insurance proceeds may have been increased by dividend additions. Under the time option, these additions increase the amount of each payment, whereas under the amount option the number of periodic payments will be increased.

---

[28] Occasionally, a company will guarantee higher interest rates under fixed period and fixed amount options than it will under the interest only option.

The amount option is a more flexible option than the time option. A limited or unlimited right of withdrawal can be given the beneficiary because withdrawals will not affect the amount of each periodic payment. They affect only the duration of the payment. The beneficiary can be given the right to have the periodic amounts increased or decreased. For example, if there are excess interest earnings, the beneficiary may prefer that the periodic payments be increased rather than having the duration of the payments extended beyond the period during which the funds are needed most. Also, payments can be made, say, for 10 months a year to finance a college education, with two or three payments a year to pay tuition and fees. Unless there is some special reason to use the fixed time option, the flexibility of the fixed amount option would seem to suggest its use where a liquidating option on other than a life income basis is desired.

The fixed amount option made its first appearance in 1901. It did not become generally used until the twenties and thirties.

Life Income.   Under the life income option, the proceeds of the policy are retained by the company and paid in equal annual, semiannual, quarterly, or monthly installments for as long as the payee lives. Often the option guarantees payments for a minimum number of years, usually 5, 10, or 20, or guarantees to continue the installments until an amount equal to at least the proceeds of the policy are paid. (This latter variation will be recognized as an installment refund annuity option.) At the death of the payee, the present value[29] of any unpaid guaranteed installments will be paid in one sum to the executors or administrators of the payee, or payments will be continued to, or commuted for, any named contingent payee.

The life income options offer the payee the advantages of the annuity discussed in Chapter 6. If the insurance proceeds are sufficient to provide the level of income needed when settled under the life income option, that option is worthy of serious consideration, for it provides the insured or his beneficiary a given income for life.[30] However, in giving serious consideration to the life income option (or to any other long-term option) the danger of relying on a fixed-dollar income to sustain real purchasing power for years into the future cannot be ignored.

Table 11–8 gives the guaranteed monthly incomes payable for $1,000 of face amount under the life income option for life only and for 5, 10, and 20 years certain and for the installment refund option, using a 3 percent interest assumption. Since mortality assumptions also affect the amounts guaranteed under the contract, all companies using 3 percent interest as-

---

[29] Usually commuted on the basis of 2½ percent to 3 percent compound interest per annum.

[30] Do not be confused by the term "the insured or his beneficiary." The option is used by the insured to provide himself with a retirement income with the cash values of a whole life policy or the proceeds of an endowment. The option is used by the beneficiary (whether selected by the insured or beneficiary) to provide her with a lifetime survival income upon death of the insured.

TABLE 11–8

Monthly Income per $1,000 at Various Ages under a Life Income Option (3%)

Age		Life	Years Certain				Installment
Male	Female	Only	5	10	15	20	Refund
25	30	$3.23	$3.22	$3.21	$3.20	$3.19	$3.18
30	35	3.38	3.37	3.36	3.35	3.34	3.32
35	40	3.57	3.56	3.55	3.54	3.51	3.49
40	45	3.81	3.80	3.79	3.76	3.72	3.70
45	50	4.12	4.11	4.08	4.04	3.97	3.95
50	55	4.52	4.50	4.46	4.37	4.26	4.27
55	60	5.03	5.01	4.92	4.77	4.58	4.67
60	65	5.72	5.67	5.50	5.24	4.90	5.18
65	70	6.68	6.57	6.25	5.76	5.19	5.84

sumption will not show the same rates appearing in Table 11–8 because different insurers use different mortality assumptions. For example, $1,000 will provide a monthly lifetime income of $5.03, for a woman age 60, according to Table 11–8. The contract option offered by another insurer, using a 3 percent interest assumption, would provide the same woman $5.12 a month. No expense loadings are used in computing the option values.

A glance at Table 11–8 will reveal that a life only option is not significantly attractive for a woman, even at age 65. At age 65, the income under a life income only option is just $0.22 a month per $1,000 more than under a life income option, 10 years certain. This amounts to only about 1.6 percent increase in income. Because survivorship benefits for a woman age 65 would not be high during the next 10-year period, the increase in income granted to her for a life income only option compared to a life income, 10 years certain option would be small.

A practice of some companies is to pay dividends for excess interest earned during the guaranteed period but to dispense with participation after the guaranteed period expires. Other companies allow no participation dividends under any type of life income settlement option, whereas still others allow participation under all life income options for the full life of the option.

Some insurers use lower interest assumptions in computing the benefits for the guaranteed period than for the life income period. A period certain life income option is a combination of the fixed period option with a deferred life income option, with the deferral period equal to the duration of the fixed period. For example, one prominent insurer guarantees 2¾ percent for the fixed period portion of the option and 3 percent for the deferred life income part of the option.

Withdrawal privileges are allowed by some insurers under a life income option but only for the fixed period payments. For example, if a widow age 40 elects a life income option, 20 years certain, under a $100,000 policy and decides at age 50 to have the 120 remaining guaranteed payments of $372 commuted she can withdraw a cash sum of $39,200.[31] At the expiration of the 20-year guaranteed period (10 years hence) the beneficiary will again collect $372 a month if she is still alive. The life income portion of the option as a rule may not be withdrawn because such a privilege would lead to adverse mortality selection against the insurer. Beneficiaries who become seriously ill might be inclined to withdraw these funds whereas the healthy ones would leave them with the insurer.[32]

Since the amount payable to the beneficiary under a life income option is based partly on the age and sex of the beneficiary, satisfactory proof of the beneficiary's age and sex must be submitted at the time the policy becomes a death claim. The policies of some insurers include a clause providing for an adjustment of income after the life income payments have begun, if new evidence shows the age or sex of the payee to be different than that upon which payments are based. However, most policies do not include such a clause.

Joint and Survivorship. Some contracts include as an option the privilege of having the cash values or proceeds distributed as an income payable until the death of the last survivor of two persons. The option may or may not offer a minimum number of guaranteed payments, and most often is selected when the cash value of a policy or the maturity proceeds of an endowment are taken as a retirement income for a husband and wife. The joint and survivorship option guarantees income to a man and his wife as long as either shall live, whereas the use of the regular life income option would provide a retirement income only as long as the policyholder himself lives or for the guaranteed period, if that be longer. The joint and last survivor option also is used when it is desirable to provide a lifetime income for two beneficiaries, a mother and a father, for example. The amount of each payment under the option is based on the ages of both beneficiaries. Some options provide for a decrease in the income upon the first death to two-thirds of the joint income.

Table 11–9 shows the monthly installments per $1,000 of proceeds payable under the joint and last survivorship option in a given company.

The option was first issued in 1901 as a special agreement. Now many companies will include the option by rider and some include it in the contract.

Life Annuity Option. Some insurers in addition to, or instead of, the life income only option offer what is known as an annuity option under which the proceeds or cash value of the policy can be applied to purchase a nonparticipating straight life annuity contract at current rates.[33] The

---

[31] The amount of $39,200 is the present value of $372 a month for 120 months computed using 2½ percent interest.

[32] In those very few cases where withdrawal is permitted during the life income only period, the insurer will require evidence of good health.

[33] This option gives the beneficiary or the insured the benefit of any change in interest or mortality assumptions that may be favorable at the time of election.

TABLE 11–9

Special Joint and Survivor Settlement Monthly Installments per $1,000 of Proceeds

Age		*Life Annuity as Long as Either Lives*	*Life Annuity Reduced to ⅔ at First Death*	
		Joint and Survivor Income	*Joint Income*	*Income to Survivor*
Male	*Female*			
60	56	$4.12	$4.75	$3.17
60	57	4.17	4.81	3.21
60	58	4.23	4.87	3.25
60	59	4.29	4.94	3.29
60	60	4.34	5.00	3.33
60	61	4.40	5.07	3.38
60	62	4.46	5.14	3.43
65	61	4.60	5.38	3.59
65	62	4.67	5.46	3.64
65	63	4.75	5.54	3.69
65	64	4.82	5.63	3.75
65	65	4.90	5.72	3.81
65	66	4.97	5.80	3.87
65	67	5.05	5.89	3.93

amount of each annuity payment is increased by 3 percent (in some companies, 4 percent) over that paid under a similar annuity policy because there are no additional commissions and taxes to pay. Also offered in some contracts is the privilege of selecting a period certain life income or a period certain joint and last survivor income using current rather than contract rates.

Other Options.   Most life insurance companies will, in addition to the optional modes of settlement offered in the contract, permit the election by the policyholder in advance of his death, or by the beneficiary thereafter, of any reasonable and sound mode of settlement. Many companies, further, will write special settlement agreements which they will attach to and make a part of the policy contract.[34] For example, some companies will write a remarriage clause in the option agreement under which an income will be paid to the primary beneficiary (in this case the widow) until she remarries. Upon proof of her remarriage, the funds go to the secondary beneficiary. Notification and burden of proof of remarriage usually are the responsibility of the contingent beneficiary or guardian.

Opportunities Provided through Settlement Options.   The use of income settlement options rather than lump-sum settlements offers the insured and his beneficiary several opportunities. The options provide certain convenient and economical quasi-trust services. The fund is managed by the insurance company and not exposed to the hazards of investment by inexperienced hands. The annuity principle of liquidation can be applied to

---

[34] At the present time it is the practice of some companies to provide in special settlement agreements that the options selected under them shall be the options, not in the policy, but those in use by the company at the time the option goes into effect.

life insurance proceeds and cash values and thus provide the largest possible return commensurate with the degree of safety afforded. All but the interest only option offers exclusive income tax advantages to a widow-beneficiary.[35] By use of the option the beneficiary can be given the protection of the spendthrift trust clause as described in Chapter 9. Furthermore, use of the options helps the insured solve problems associated with common disaster as described in Chapter 10. And use of the interest only option assures that the policy proceeds will earn interest immediately upon the insured's death until the funds are needed.

Problem in Using Settlement Options. The planning of income insurance programs through the use of settlement options offers several problems. The guaranteed payments under a participating (dividend-paying) option are so conservative that it is difficult to know how much insurance is necessary to provide a given income. The question is whether to plan the program on the basis of the low guarantees or on what the companies are likely to pay. If the answer is the latter, how does one estimate what the company will be paying (*a*) when the option becomes effective and (*b*) throughout its duration.[36]

Inflation and growth impose other problems in the use of conventional settlement options. Any long-range financial plan based on a fixed-dollar income is exposed to the purchasing power risk. In this age of inflation, this can be a serious matter. The use of settlement options may foster too heavy a reliance on fixed-dollar incomes. Fixed-dollar incomes also deny the beneficiaries an opportunity to share in the growth of the economy, and higher living standards brought about through this growth. The use of a variable annuity settlement option has promise as an instrument for offsetting the purchasing power risk inherent in the fixed-dollar options and for giving the beneficiary a stake in a growing economy.

Settlement options with a life contingency factor are restricted in their usefulness to beneficiaries or policy owners who are in poor health. These options could be made more useful if mortality assumptions reflecting differences in hazards were used in computing the values under life income options.

It has been suggested that the rate of return paid to the beneficiary under a liquidating option be related to what the insurer can earn on the proceeds of the policy (new money) rather than on what the insurer earns on its total investment portfolio, and that this rate be fixed throughout the payout period.[37] For example, assume that $100,000 of life insurance proceeds become available upon the death of the insured and these funds can be

---

[35] Cf. Chapter 21.

[36] It is interesting to note that when life insurance agents plan an insurance program for a client, they use the guaranteed options only, that is, they do not consider anticipated dividend in determining the amount of insurance needed to fund the program. However, they do use anticipated, though not guaranteed, dividends in projecting the cost of the program.

[37] Mehr, "New Settings for Old Stones," *op. cit.*

invested by the insurer in an amortized loan yielding 5 percent net.[38] These funds could be liquidated under a settlement option using a fixed 5 percent for the period. If the period selected for liquidation is 15 years, the beneficiary could be paid $781.80 a month. Under this arrangement there would be no dividends (no excess interest earnings in which to participate), and if the option had withdrawal privileges the liquidation value of the asset would have to be allowed to fluctuate inversely with current interest rates. As noted, a number of insurers offer a nonparticipating life annuity option, no period certain under which the insurer's current rates are used in computing benefits. Even nonparticipating refund life annuity options are offered at current rates. But as yet, no settlement option without a life contingency is offered on a nonparticipating basis at *new* money rates.

The use of settlement options in life insurance programming is discussed in Chapter 20.

---

[38] Net rate here means after margins for expenses and profits.

12

Industrial Life and Health Insurance

Up to this point the discussion of life insurance has been concerned primarily with what is called ordinary life insurance—i.e., life insurance issued in face amounts of $1,000 or more with premiums payable on an annual, semiannual, quarterly, or monthly basis. The modifying term "ordinary" is used to distinguish this form of life insurance from other forms that were subsequently introduced to the market fully equipped with identifying handles such as, for example, industrial and group. With the advent of industrial life insurance and later group life insurance, the pristine form had to have a label. That label is "ordinary," meaning customary, normal, usual, and common. This chapter is concerned with industrial insurance. Group insurance is discussed in Chapters 15 and 16.

1. DEFINITION OF INDUSTRIAL LIFE

In a model law drafted by the National Association of Insurance Commissioners, industrial life insurance is defined as:

. . . that form of life insurance, the policies for which include the words *Industrial Policy* as a part of the descriptive matter; and (*a*) under which the premiums are payable weekly, or (*b*) under which the premiums are paid monthly or oftener, but less often than weekly, if the face amount of insurance provided in such policies is $1,000 or less.

The model law, with minor exceptions, has been incorporated in Section 201 of the Insurance Law of New York and in the insurance laws of a number of other states. For example, under Section 201 of the New York law, the amount of weekly premium life insurance that can be placed on any one life is limited to $1,000 regardless of the number of policies involved. Moreover, the size of monthly premium industrial policies is restricted by New York law to amounts *less* than $1,000. Policies written for $1,000 or more must be issued as ordinary insurance. The reason for the New York restriction is that the prices of ordinary life insurance are lower than industrial insurance prices, and the law wants to prohibit an insurer from offering a higher priced industrial policy when the amount of insurance involved is sufficient to qualify for a lower priced ordinary policy.[1]

The foregoing model definition of industrial life insurance or the New York modifications of it does not operate in every state. For this reason, industrial insurance is difficult to define since it means different things to different companies, especially with respect to monthly premium policies.

Distinctive Characteristics.   The Institute of Life Insurance defines industrial life insurance as "life insurance issued in small amounts, usually not over $500, with premiums payable on a weekly or monthly basis. The premiums are generally collected at the home by an agent of the company."[2] While the characteristics of industrial life insurance included in this definition are distinctive they are not necessarily unique. Some insurers issue monthly premium ordinary insurance in amounts less than $1,000 and collect the premiums at the door of the insured.

While there has been some tendency in recent years toward pricing and proposing industrial insurance in terms of face amounts, as is done in ordinary insurance, traditionally the quotations in rate manuals have been in terms of amount of weekly (or monthly) premiums. The sale is a 25 cents a week, or 50 cents a week policy as contrasted to the ordinary practice of selling a $2,000 or $5,000 policy. The result is odd amounts of insurance, $329, for example, for a 25 cents a week nonparticipating 20-payment whole life policy issued at age 30 in one company.

For many years, the only insurance available on the lives of young children was that obtainable through industrial policies.

Other distinctive characteristics of industrial insurance relate to policy provisions and underwriting standards. These will be discussed later.

Origin and Development.   The term "industrial" was originally used to identify weekly premium insurance because these policies were intended to be sold to workers in industry, primarily hourly wage earners who could not afford (or were incapable of budgeting for) the higher, less frequent, premium payments necessary to purchase ordinary insurance. This branch of insurance, as it has turned out, could not now be more inappropriately named. Speak of industrial life insurance to anyone other than the life insurance cognoscente and he will think you are talking about life insurance purchased by industry for the benefit of employees. But the term "industrial" remains in the insurance codes and persists in the literature.

The first industrial policy was issued by Prudential of England on November 13, 1854, and the first claim was paid on January 4, 1855. The introduction of industrial insurance in the United States was made by the

---

[1] See Joseph M. Belth and E. J. Leverett, Jr., "Industrial Life Insurance Prices," *Journal of Risk and Insurance,* Vol. XXXII, No. 3 (September, 1964), pp. 367–83 for an empirical study of industrial versus ordinary life insurance prices.

[2] Institute of Life Insurance, *Life Insurance Fact Book,* 1969, p. 114.

namesake of the Prudential of England, the Prudential Life Insurance Company of America, organized in Newark, New Jersey, in 1875, as the Prudential Friendly Society. The Metropolitan and the John Hancock followed the Prudential four years later in offering industrial life insurance.

Industrial life insurance comprises only about 3 percent of the total life insurance in force in this country. The size of the average industrial policy is about $450 and compares with an average size of more than $5,000 for ordinary insurance and an average of more than $5,500 per group life insurance certificate. The amount of industrial life insurance purchased in 1966 was $7.1 billion, representing about 9.8 million policies, the first year since the introduction of industrial policies that fewer industrial than ordinary policies were sold.[3]

During the last half of the decade of the 60's, industrial life insurance in force decreased at an annual rate of nearly 1 percent while ordinary life insurance in force increased at an annual rate of more than 8 percent, and group insurance in force increased at an annual rate in excess of 13 percent.[4]

Nearly one half of all industrial life insurance in force in the United States is in the South. Only about one fourth of the ordinary and group life insurance in force is in the southern states. During the period 1956–66, industrial life insurance in force in the United States decreased 1.1 percent, while increasing 28.7. percent in the East South Central states, 21.5 percent in the West South Central states, and 18.4 percent in the South Atlantic states.[5]

Economic gains of workers who need and can afford more life insurance protection than provided under industrial policies, the discontinuance of the sale of weekly premium industrial insurance by the giant industrial insurance writers (Metropolitan, Prudential, and John Hancock), the rapid growth of group life insurance, the gradual increase in group life insurance coverage for dependents, the wide availability of ordinary family policies covering children, the writing of monthly premium (and even weekly premium) ordinary policies, and the expanded social security program have been responsible for curbing the national growth of industrial life insurance.

---

[3] Much of what formerly would have been industrial insurance is now being sold as monthly debit ordinary insurance. In 1966, 29 percent of all ordinary life insurance policies, representing 12 percent of the face amount of all ordinary life insurance purchased in that year, were written as monthly debit ordinary policies. The average size monthly debit ordinary policy is about four times the size of the average industrial policy.

[4] See the *Life Insurance Fact Book, op. cit.,* for current figures which are likely to be even less encouraging to industrial insurers, despite the bright future predicted for industrial life insurance by economics professor Jack Blicksilver of Georgia State College in his study subsidized by the Life Insurers Conference and reported in the *National Underwriter,* Life Insurance Edition, February 3, 1968.

[5] The bright future for industrial insurance predicted by Professor Blicksilver appears to be restricted to its future in the South, a variation on the theme that the South shall rise again, if in fact increased sales of industrial insurance is a measure of progress. See *Life Insurance Fact Book, op. cit.,* for current figures.

2. INDUSTRIAL LIFE INSURANCE POLICY CONTRACTS

Types of Contracts. Many of the same types of policies written in ordinary insurance are written in industrial insurance. The range is narrower but the present tendency is toward an increase in the number of forms. Whole life paid up at 65 or 75 is more common than continuous premium whole life. Twenty-pay life is also a common form. Twenty-year endowment policies were once popular for children; however, many companies have stopped issuing short-term endowments on a weekly premium basis, offering them, instead, on the less expensive monthly premium plan.[6]

The scarcity of continuous premium whole life and especially term forms might be considered unfortunate, since, in theory at least, the purchasers of industrial insurance are those who cannot afford the premiums on policies of $1,000 or more. One principle of life insurance buying is that when dollars available for life insurance premiums are extremely scarce, they should be used to purchase as much premature death protection as possible unless extenuating circumstances rule this principle inapplicable. Obviously, the limited payment and endowment plans common in industrial insurance do not buy as much face amount per premium dollar as could be purchased under a continuous premium whole life plan or under one of the term plans.

Industrial insurers probably would argue that extenuating circumstances do rule out the foregoing principle. They would contend that for a large number of people, weekly premium life insurance is the only form of savings the policyholder has and that term insurance would eliminate this small though important savings feature. They would point out that the endowment form was introduced in 1892 and sold mainly as a savings plan. They also would insist that the industrial buyer is so governed psychologically that he would not buy any insurance which fails to offer "living benefits." Finally, they would recall that, for the most part, industrial policies first issued in the United States were continuous premium whole life. Limited payment policies were introduced later because it was found that the burden of continuous payments in late years was too heavy for the typical industrial policyholder at that time.

Policy Provisions. In general, the principles involved in, and the provisions of, the industrial policy are similar to, if not identical with, those of the ordinary contract. However, there are a number of important differences, most of them a result of the special nature of the business, the small size of policies, and the type of customers served.

Because of the small amounts of insurance involved, the industrial policy cannot economically offer some of the options found in ordinary life insurance contracts. On the other hand, these small amounts make it possi-

---

[6] Industrial endowments are prohibited in New York, although monthly premium ordinary may be written on an endowment plan for amounts less than $1,000, provided dividend options and policy loan provisions are eliminated.

ble to offer a greater degree of liberality in some provisions of industrial than can be offered in ordinary. The following are the major differences usually found:

LOAN VALUES.   Loan values generally are not provided in weekly premium industrial policies. Since the face amount is small, the loan value also would be small, and the cost of servicing policy loans would be disproportionate to the money involved. Monthly premium industrial policies, however, grant loan privileges subject to a minimum amount, customarily $10.

ASSIGNMENT.   To reduce administration costs and to discourage industrial policyholders from indiscriminately assigning their policies, general assignment of the industrial policy is usually prohibited. Assignment to a bank is usually permitted, however, thus making it possible for the industrial policy to be used as collateral. The bank assignment clause is a requirement of the New York State law.

OPTIONAL SETTLEMENTS.   Again because of the small amounts of insurance involved, industrial policies usually do not provide for settlement options. Sometimes annuity certain options are found in monthly premium industrial policies issued for a face amount of $500 or more.

DIVIDEND OPTIONS.   Participating industrial policy dividends usually do not begin before the fifth year on weekly premium policies nor before the end of three years on monthly premium contracts. It is uncommon to find dividend options. Dividends are paid annually and on one basis only, usually as paid-up additional amounts of insurance, or, less often, as a premium credit.

NONFORFEITURE PROVISIONS.   Extended term insurance is available as early as the end of the first six weeks in policies of some companies and after six months in others. After three years of premium payment (in some companies, five) the industrial policy usually gives the insured the other nonforfeiture options: a paid-up policy for a reduced amount or cash surrender values. The minimum nonforfeiture values for industrial policies issued since 1968 must be based on the Commissioners 1961 Standard Industrial Mortality Tables. Since values are so small in industrial policies, the choice of nonforfeiture provisions is withheld until the end of the third year because the expense of paying them—in contrast to granting extended term insurance—would be disproportionate to the values involved.

CONTESTABILITY.   The application usually is not made a part of the industrial policy, so there is little to contest. Nevertheless, an incontestability clause is included which makes the policy incontestable after it has been in force for one year during the insured's lifetime. The policy usually provides a basis for contest by providing that if the applicant received treatment for a serious physical condition within the two years prior to the application, failure to report such treatment is grounds for rescission.[7]

---

[7] The applicant is not expected to judge the seriousness of a condition for which he has been treated but only to report all treatment. Assume that he fails to report a visit to his physician 10 months before the application. If it turned out this treatment was for a

SUICIDE. Because the amount of insurance involved in an industrial policy is small, some insurers do not deem it necessary to include the usual suicide clause found in ordinary life insurance. However, other insurers will use the typical suicide clause exempting the insurer from liability if the suicide occurs within two years after the policy is in force.

REINSTATEMENT. The industrial reinstatement clause is more liberal than that found in ordinary life insurance policies in that, upon reinstatement, defaulted premiums may be paid without interest. It is less liberal in that the reinstatement period is shorter—two instead of three years. Companies' practices in reinstatement are usually more liberal than the terms of clause. The two-year limit on the reinstatement period is frequently disregarded, but interest is charged on past-due premiums starting with the end of the second year. In some companies industrial policies in force for more than five years may be reinstated without evidence of insurability. Other companies allow reinstatement without proof of insurability, regardless of the time the policy has been in force, if the lapse period does not exceed a maximum period, such as 16 weeks.

Some insurers allow premiums in arrears to be made a lien against the policy, thus relieving the policyholder of the burden of paying cash at the time of reinstatement. Interest is charged on the amount of the lien.

CHANGE OF PLAN. Usually, the industrial policy contains a provision allowing the insured on any policy anniversary date to change from the more expensive weekly premium industrial plan to the less expensive monthly premium industrial plan. Some companies also will allow a combination of several industrial policies into an ordinary policy. The technical procedure in such a change is to credit the ordinary policy with the total value of the reserve liability attributable to the converted industrial policies. The premium rate for the new ordinary policy will be established on the basis of an age of issue that would have produced the amount of reserve established as of the date of conversion. It follows, therefore, that the higher the reserve, the lower will be the assumed issue age and consequently the lower will be the new premium.

GRACE PERIOD. The grace period is usually four weeks on weekly premium plans and 31 days on monthly premium plans.

BENEFICIARY DESIGNATION. Originally, industrial policies did not provide for the designation of a named beneficiary. Instead, the policy, under a facility of payment clause, was payable to anyone who appeared to be entitled to the proceeds as evidenced by possession of the policy or by proof of having paid the funeral expenses. The New York law now restricts this type of beneficiary arrangement. So in most industrial policies issued today, the insured may name a beneficiary. To take care of special

---

common cold, it would hardly justify contest; however, if it turned out to be for, say, a malignancy, the failure would be grounds for contest. The burden of proof of lack of seriousness (and materiality) of an unreported treatment is on the insured or his beneficiary, since the insured is obligated to report all treatments, leaving the company to form its own conclusions about the situation.

situations that might arise, industrial policies still retain a modified facility of payment clause which provides that if the beneficiary does not survive the insured or if the beneficiary is a minor or legally incompetent, the company may pay the proceeds to any relative of the insured who appears to be equitably entitled to them. The clause avoids the cost and delay involved in the appointment of an administrator or guardian.

DEATH BY ACCIDENTAL MEANS AND DISMEMBERMENT. Multiple indemnity for death resulting from accidental means, available as a policy rider in most ordinary contracts, is included in all industrial policies and is automatically charged for in the premium.[8] Also included is a dismemberment provision. Loss of two limbs or total loss of sight carries a lump-sum benefit equal to the face of the policy, and the policy will be endorsed as paid-up insurance for the full amount of the policy. Loss of one limb or one eye entitles the insured to a benefit equal to one half of the policy face and a paid-up policy for the full amount. Unlike ordinary policies, no age limit is placed on this benefit. If an accident causing loss of a limb also causes death, the loss of limb benefit will be an offset against the multiple indemnity benefit. The multiple indemnity benefit coverage terminates when the policy is placed on a reduced paid-up or extended term nonforfeiture option.

MONEY BACK OPTION. Industrial policies contain a clause allowing the insured to surrender the policy within the first few weeks (commonly two) and receive a refund of all premiums paid—i.e., he is not charged for the cost of the insurance protection he has received during the "approval" period.

PREMIUM REDUCTION. Many industrial policies provide that if the insured pays the premiums to an authorized company office rather than to the house-to-house agent, he will be entitled to a refund of, say, 10 percent at the end of the year. Some companies allow the policyholder who pays the premium directly by means of a money order to deduct the cost of the money order.

PAYOR BENEFIT. A payor benefit, under which premiums payable until the child reaches a given age, 21 for example, is available on industrial policies written on children for an additional premium just as in ordinary juvenile policies.

Differences in Underwriting Practices. Several practices differ between the underwriting of industrial and ordinary policies.

NO MEDICAL EXAMINATION. The standards for determining whether a policy will be issued without a medical examination are more relaxed in industrial than in ordinary insurance with the result that industrial policies do not usually require a medical examination. However a medical examination sometimes is required for applicants at older ages if the application reveals a need for it. Even when required, the medical is usually

---

8 Since life insurance contracts are not contracts of indemnity (Chapter 9), the purist cringes when payments in excess of the face of the policy are called multiple indemnity.

both less intensive and less extensive than that given (or supposed to be given) in ordinary insurance. The amount of insurance involved is too small to warrant expensive underwriting costs.

RANGE OF STANDARD. Many applicants who would be accepted for ordinary policies only at extra premiums qualify for industrial policies at standard premiums. Again, the small amount at risk makes for liberal underwriting standards, especially since the premium rates allow for higher mortality costs.

3. PREMIUM PAYMENT AND COLLECTION

The industrial life insurance agent, commonly called a debit man, is charged primarily with the duty of collecting premiums on the route assigned him, even though the industrial policy contract carefully specifies that the premium is payable at the home office and that it only *may* be paid to the agent.[9] Secondarily, it is the duty of the industrial agent to sell new industrial and ordinary policies, on which he receives a commission. He must also service policyholders in his *debit* (territory) as new developments in family situations occur or as claims arise.[10]

A debit in its purest sense is the sum of the premium an agent is required to collect each week. A debit may consist of as many as 1,000 or even more policyholders. The debit book changes each week as surrenders and claims are deducted and new business and revivals are added. The collection work of the debit agent is expected to be completed by Thursday morning so that the rest of the week can be spent canvassing for new business. In most agencies, the policies written by an agent outside his own territory are transferred to the agent in whose territory they are written, in order to control collection cost. Usually an agent receives as many new policyholders by the transfer system as he loses; so there is little objection to the plan.

4. COST OF INDUSTRIAL LIFE INSURANCE

There is much misunderstanding about the cost of industrial insurance. This form of insurance has been more widely criticized and maligned than any other branch of the industry.[11] Because the price is demonstrably higher to the policyholder, critics have implied that companies make excessively large amounts of money on industrial policies at the expense of the lower income groups for which these policies are primarily written.

---

[9] If the agent fails to collect the premium, the policyholder is still held responsible for paying it to the company within the usual four week grace period.

[10] The term "debit" originally meant the amount of premium to be collected by the agent on the insurance in force in his territory. Its meaning has now expanded to include a given number of policyholders, a particular territory, and a type of marketing system.

[11] See *Investigation of Concentration of Economic Power, Temporary National Economic Committee,* Monograph 28, 1940, and Monograph 28A, 1941.

Price Comparisons. Some writers make a careful distinction between the premium for and the price of life insurance.[12] They contend that only part of the premium is used to purchase life insurance protection and the rest is used to build cash values. They recognize the possible legal and actuarial inconsistencies implied in this approach but contend that such a concept "is the only basis on which a meaningful analysis of life insurance prices can be built."[13]

Ignoring the premium versus price distinction for the moment and using nonparticipating policies to eliminate the dividend variable, the following differential in premiums between industrial and ordinary life insurance policies written in the same company may be noted. Three plans (continuous premium whole life, 20-payment whole life, and 20-year endowment), two insurers, and three issue ages (20, 30, and 40) are used to present illustrative, though not necessarily typical, differences in premiums.

TABLE 12–1

Percentages by which Nonparticipating Premiums for Industrial Policies Exceed Those for Ordinary Policies

Continuous Premium Whole Life $1,000 of Coverage

	Issue Ages		
	20	30	40
Company A	20.5%	29.0%	40.0%
Company B	0.5	21.5	39.6

20-Payment Whole Life $1,000 of Coverage

	Issue Ages		
	20	30	40
Company A	29.1%	38.4%	37.5%
Company B	20.4	32.2	45.9

20-Year Endowment $1,000 of Coverage

	Issue Ages		
	20	30	40
Company A	20.0%	21.9%	31.4%
Company B	16.7	22.9	27.2

The percentage differences shown in Table 12–1 are at best only a rough indication of the degree to which industrial insurance is more expensive than ordinary insurance in the two companies whose rates were used in the computations. These percentages would accurately measure the differ-

---

[12] Joseph M. Belth, *The Retail Price Structure in American Life Insurance* (Bloomington, Indiana: Bureau of Business Research, Graduate School of Business, Indiana University, 1966), p. 2.

[13] *Ibid.*, p. 35.

ences in premiums for ordinary and industrial policies only if the ordinary premiums were adjusted to reflect the payment of weekly rather than monthly premiums, and if the industrial premiums reflected the discount allowed for payment of premiums at an authorized office of the insurer rather than at the insured's home. Further adjustments in premiums need to be made to reflect the lack of comparability of the two policies. For example industrial premiums include dismemberment disability benefits and multiple indemnity benefits for deaths arising from accidental means; ordinary premiums quoted usually do not include these benefits. The comparison cannot be validated by the simple addition of the disability and double indemnity rates to the ordinary rate, since the disability clause attachable to the ordinary policy is much broader than that included in the industrial contract. The other differences in policy provisions are not reflected in these percentages nor is the difference in age classification procedure considered: the next birthday in the industrial policy versus the nearest birthday in the ordinary policy.

Note that the percentage differentials shown in Table 12–1 differ not only between the companies used but also among types of policies and ages of issue. If the size of the policy were increased, the differentials would be even greater. For example, if a $5,000 continuous premium whole life policy were used at issue age 30, the differential would be 95.5 percent for Company A and 77.1 percent for Company B. The quantity discounts given for the higher amounts of ordinary life insurance account for the greater percentages by which the premiums for industrial insurance exceed those for ordinary insurance.

When the level price method[14] is applied to determine the comparative mean level prices of a sample of industrial policies and a sample of ordinary policies each issued for $1,000 on a continuous premium whole life basis to males age 35, the mean level prices of industrial insurance exceed those of ordinary insurance by 33.3 percent.[15] The prices include waiver of premium and accidental death benefits and the discount in industrial insurance for premiums paid to one of the authorized offices of the company. The computations are based on the payment of monthly premiums for ordinary insur-

---

[14] This method views the price of life insurance as the payment for life insurance protection which decreases each year as the cash value of the policy increases. The level price is an average of the yearly prices for the period selected, and its calculation involves computing the price of protection (policy face less cash surrender value) for each year and combining the yearly prices into one level price for the period, using appropriate interest, mortality, and lapse rates. See Belth, *op. cit.*, p. 19 for an outline of the method of computing level prices for various periods, and pp. 33–69 for a discussion of the techniques and decisions involved in developing a level price, and pp. 281–300 for an explanation and description of a computer program developed for performing the numerous computations necessary to develop a level price.

[15] The sample included 37 industrial insurers and 28 ordinary insurers. The actuarial assumptions used are 3 percent interest, the X_{18} table of mortality with select data for the first five policy years, and lapse rates based on one half Linton's A Table (first-year lapse rate of 5 percent, leveling at 1 percent in the 15th year). See Chapter 24 for a discussion of mortality tables, and Chapter 25 for a discussion of lapse tables.

ance and weekly premiums for industrial insurance.[16] "Despite the size of the difference between the industrial and ordinary means, the industrial policies of some companies in the distribution reflect a *lower* price than the ordinary policies of some companies."[17] Thus, the "best buy" in industrial insurance could be more attractive than the "poorest buy" in ordinary insurance.

Reasons for Higher Prices for Industrial. The foregoing discussion illustrates that, in general, a policyholder can expect to pay a higher unit cost for industrial than for ordinary insurance. The higher premium rates and prices of industrial insurance result from three factors: (1) higher mortality costs, (2) higher cost of administration, and (3) higher lapse rates.

HIGHER MORTALITY COST. Although the death rates among industrial policyholders have been dropping faster than the death rates among ordinary policyholders, the differences in these rates are still significant enough for the insurers to use special mortality tables in their industrial business. These tables have been accepted by the various states.

Two reasons for the difference in industrial and ordinary mortality rates are: (1) Industrial insurance is sold to people in lower income classes a high percentage of whom are black. The mortality rate among Negroes has been higher than that among Caucasians. Industrial policyholders, on the average, have not in the past enjoyed as favorable working conditions, living standards, and health facilities as those who purchase ordinary insurance. Improvements in environmental health, living standards, and medical care are gradually being reflected by a lessening of the differential between mortality rates used in industrial and ordinary premium computations. (2) The underwriting (selection) standards for industrial insurance are less rigid than those for ordinary insurance. Medical examinations and inspection reports are the exception in industrial insurance, and the range of insurability at standard rates is wider in industrial insurance than in ordinary insurance.

HIGHER ADMINISTRATIVE COST. The cost of administering a dollar of industrial insurance is higher than the cost of administering a dollar of ordinary insurance. One reason is that the face amount of insurance written under industrial policies is so low, making for a high unit cost per policy.[18] Furthermore, the expense of door to door collection of premiums adds to the cost of servicing industrial insurance. A study undertaken a number of years ago indicated that for one insurer about 90 percent of the higher cost

---

16 The data used are those found in Belth and Leverett, *op. cit.,* pp. 367–83.

17 *Ibid.,* p. 372. Greater dispersion was found among the prices of ordinary policies than among the prices of industrial policies included in the study. The coefficients of variation were as follows: ordinary, 0.199, and industrial, 0.139.

18 Quantity discounts given in ordinary insurance recognize the lower fixed cost per unit associated with policies of high amounts of insurance. For example, in one insurer the nonpar premium per $1,000 of continuous premium whole life, issued to a male age 25, would be 7.53 percent less for a $10,000 policy than for a $5,000 policy.

of handling industrial insurance over ordinary insurance was attributed to the additional expense in collecting premiums of small amounts at frequent intervals, and at the door of the insured.[19] Little has happened in the intervening years to lead one to suspect anything drastically different today. Efforts have been made in both industrial and ordinary insurance to control costs in the face of a sharply rising trend by the efficient use of data processing equipment. However, as of this moment, the industrial insurers have not come up with an electronically operated and computer controlled robot that can successfully and efficiently collect premiums from house to house.

HIGHER LAPSE RATES. The lapse rate of industrial insurance is higher that that of ordinary insurance. The higher rate is partly the result of the greater frequency of premium payment. Each time a premium falls due, the policyholder is faced with the question, to pay or not to pay.[20] The holder of an ordinary policy faces that decision 1, 2, 4, and sometimes 12 times a year. The weekly premium policyholder faces the question 52 times a year. Obviously, the more times he is faced with the decision, the greater is the chance that he will succumb to temptation.

A factor that is probably even more important is the type of people who are sold industrial policies. Low income hourly wage earners are not likely to be able to incur extra expenses or to absorb a temporary interruption of income and continue to pay the premiums week by week when the insurance man knocks at the door (or rings the bell, buzzer, or chimes).

Two other factors account for the higher lapse ratio among industrial policyholders:

Improper Selling. If a policyholder is not properly sold in the beginning, he is always a potential lapser. Industrial insurance has undergone serious criticism for high pressure selling. A person who is pressured into buying something he cannot afford, for a need he does not understand, is a likely prospect for lapsation. Some of the high pressure selling used by agents is attributed to the pressure these agents are under from their managers to meet quotas. Spokesmen for industrial insurance argue that high pressure selling is the exception rather than the rule. Policy lapses also are the exception rather than the rule. Lapsation is expensive—especially if it occurs during the early months of the policy.

Improper Servicing. Poor service can be the result of the lack of adequate training facilities for agents and from the high rate of turnover

---

[19] Malvin Davis, *Industrial Life Insurance* (New York: McGraw-Hill Book Co., 1944), p. 138.

[20] According to one great life insurance enthusiast, this question involves a serious moral principle. Speaking at the 1914 meeting of the National Association of Life Underwriters in Cincinnati, the late Professor S. S. Huebner is reported to have said that the proper education in life insurance would lead one to believe that a person has committed a crime if he dies without life insurance. Of the poor departed one, it should be said: "He did not die, he absconded." Cf. R. Carlyle Buley, *A Study in the History of Life Insurance* (New York: Appleton-Century-Crofts, Inc., 1953), p. 442.

among agents.[21] However, a number of companies make a conscientious effort to improve the quality of their debit agency forces by applying scientific techniques to agency recruiting, training, and supervision. They also attempt to encourage their agents to concentrate on business that is not likely to lapse by using a compensation system that is weighted in favor of business which continues in force. The result has been to reduce the overall lapse rate of industrial insurance, since the agent gains by concentrating on quality business.

5. INDUSTRIAL HEALTH INSURANCE

Industrial health insurance policies are those sold on a weekly premium basis to the same types of people who purchase industrial life insurance. Underwriting standards are lax and the policies are usually issued for small benefits ($16 or $20 a week for disability income, $5 to $10 a day for hospital care, and $150 maximum surgical scheduled) and for very limited income benefit durations (usually not more than 26 weeks). Industrial health policies generally are cancellable at any time and are renewable only at the option of the insurer. Unlike industrial life insurance, industrial health insurance has never been an important factor in the market. Like industrial life insurance, and for the same reasons, industrial health insurance is more expensive than ordinary insurance (the term "ordinary health insurance," by the way, is never used): higher incidence of loss (higher morbidity rates), higher expenses, and higher lapse rates.

Companies that sell industrial health insurance usually sell industrial life insurance and their agents write both types of coverage, often for the same clients. In fact, industrial health insurance was developed in this country by industrial life insurance companies who began writing weekly premium health insurance in the early 1900's.

Industrial health insurance policies usually cover total disability resulting from accidents or sickness; and use the strict "any occupation" definition of disability. The policies generally contain more restrictions than are found in ordinary policies.

6. APPRAISAL OF INDUSTRIAL INSURANCE

Several textbook writers make apologies for industrial insurance:

Critics of industrial life insurance allege that it is subject to an excessive lapse rate, with consequent loss or added cost to policyholders. This criticism does not seem to be warranted, particularly in respect to policies issued by the larger com-

---

[21] The better industrial writers will resent this statement. They will point out—and correctly—that their selection, training, and supervision plans are more careful than those of most ordinary companies and that a high percentage of their agents hold the CLU designation, generally considered to be a mark of the professionally trained underwriter.

panies. The experience of the larger companies indicates that the weekly premium lapse rate is reasonable in relation to that on monthly premium ordinary or industrial policies taking into account the great lapse opportunity for weekly premium business.[22]

When all proper factors are considered, the difference in cost between industrial and ordinary is reasonable. It should be remembered that industrial insurance was designed for those who either could not or would not purchase and retain ordinary life or individual health insurance.[23]

It is difficult to accept that a reasonable solution to the problem of those "who either could not or would not purchase and retain ordinary life or individual health insurance" is to offer them something that is more expensive.[24]

A cynic might say that the major question about . . . industrial policies is what, if anything, they are good for. . . . This is not to imply that the contracts are a "gyp". . . . It is probable that . . . these contracts are no more profitable for the companies than other types of insurance. . . . Industrial policies provide a means for a person of low income and poor savings habits to obtain a minimum amount of short term disability protection at a cost within his weekly budget. . . . While the relative cost of industrial insurance is high in proportion to its benefits . . . it cannot be denied that the device has made it possible for millions to obtain insurance. Most of these would not have obtained coverage on any other basis. . . . Much of the market for industrial insurance is also served by group insurance, and as the group principle grows, the relative amount of industrial insurance will continue to decline. . . . But for the present, there are many persons who cannot or will not obtain coverage on any other basis.[25]

Thus, industrial insurance is admittedly expensive and has been viciously criticized in the past. Yet through industrial insurance thousands of working people have received at least some small amount of money upon the death of a member of the family to pay the cost of burial. Others have received cash from maturing endowments, and still others have drawn on cash values to help out during times of emergencies. Funds have been made available through industrial health policies to help pay medical expenses and partially offset loss of earnings during total disability. For many industrial policyholders, life insurance represents their only form of savings, even though very small.

The important question is how to achieve the benefits of industrial in-

[22] Dan M. McGill, *Life Insurance* (rev. ed.; Homewood, Illinois: Richard D. Irwin, Inc., 1967), p. 731.

[23] S. S. Huebner and Kenneth Black, Jr., *Life Insurance* (6th ed.; New York: Appleton-Century-Crofts, 1969), p. 591.

[24] There are those who point out that while the "more expensive argument" is correct, it is also unreasonable and academic. They argue that $0.25 a week is vastly different than $13 a year, and insist that this is a real argument supporting industrial insurance and not an apology for it.

[25] O. D. Dickerson, *Health Insurance* (3rd ed.; Homewood, Illinois: Richard D. Irwin, Inc., 1968), p. 479.

surance without its excessive costs. The premiums spent for industrial policies could have purchased much more life and health insurance coverage if they had been spent for ordinary policies. The average size industrial life policy purchased in 1968 was $786. Surely the average premium for these purchases would have been more than enough to purchase ordinary insurance, giving these buyers much more life insurance protection and potential cash value for their money. Certainly there is need for vigorous consumer education programs in life and health insurance.

13

Health Insurance

Life and health insurance deal with the same economic factor—expenses and loss of earning power arising from a fortuitous event. Accident and health departments of life insurance companies write over 55 percent of the health insurance premium volume in the United States.

1. THE NEED FOR HEALTH INSURANCE

Injury and sickness can bring about two kinds of financial loss: (1) loss of income resulting from inability to work and (2) expenses of medical, hospital, and nursing care, including all the incidentals such as prescription drugs.

Annual admissions to nonfederal hospitals in the United States during the late 1960's exceeded 14 percent of the civilian population. On a typical day, more than 0.3 percent of the civilian population were occupying hospital rooms, and their average length of stay amounted to about 8 days. Annually, the average American had more than 8 days of restricted activity and nearly 4 days of bed disability as a result of illness or injury. Nearly 7 percent of all personal consumption expenditures and 6 percent of personal disposable income went for medical care.[1]

The fundamental questions are how can a person finance the cost of medical care and how can he replace the loss of income arising from his inability to work. For the theoretical average person, that is one who goes to the hospital once every 7 years for an 8-day stay, spends about 7 percent of his personal consumption expenditures on medical care, and loses about 7 workdays a year, the answers to these questions might not be too difficult. That is, the answers might not be too difficult if he has the average number of dependents, the average amount of savings, and the average income. He could handle his medical expenses and his living expenses during

---

[1] Sources: American Hospital Association, Chicago, Illinois; Health Insurance Institute, New York City; United States Department of Health, Education and Welfare; Health Insurance Association of America, New York City; and United States Department of Commerce. Current statistics are probably no more encouraging than the ones cited here.

periods of disability from his current income, accumulated savings, and by drawing on his credit resource.

But there are wide variations from these averages. Some people enter the hospital more often than once every 7 years, and many stay in the hospital more than 8 days. Medical expenses can easily exceed 6 percent of any given person's disposable income, and a person's loss of time from work may be measured in terms of weeks, months, years, or even a remaining lifetime. And, of course, many people have incomes well below average, and have little or no savings. Large numbers have more than the average number of dependents. The probability of average experience for any person is infinitesimal. The number of people who can individually bear the risk of medical care expenses and disability income losses is small and is limited to the independently wealthy.

Two questions have been raised: (1) how can a family's medical care expenses be financed and (2) how can its income be maintained during periods of disability of its wage earner? Currently the answers are being found through public plans, employee benefit plans, and individual plans. This chapter is concerned with individual health insurance plans. Health insurance in employee benefit plans is discussed in Chapter 16.

2. TYPES OF COVERAGE AVAILABLE

Although health insurance[2] covers vary widely, they may be classified as to the nature of the peril involved and the type of loss covered.

Nature of the Peril.   On the basis of the nature of the peril involved, health insurance covers can be classified as to accident insurance and sickness insurance.

ACCIDENT COVERAGE.   Insurance against loss from accident is the grandfather of all health insurance coverages. Accident insurance[3] is still widely sold under separate policies and as a part of contracts covering both accident and sickness. Benefits may be limited to lump sums or may include a series of periodic payments to offset loss of earned income.[4] In general,

---

[2] Health insurance has been defined by the Committee on Health Insurance Terminology of the Commission on Insurance Terminology of the American Risk and Insurance Association as "Insurance against loss by sickness or bodily injury. The generic term for those forms of insurance that provide lump-sum or periodic payments in event of loss occasioned by bodily injury, sickness, disease, or medical expense and that include such forms as accident insurance, sickness insurance, medical expense insurance, accidental death insurance, and dismemberment insurance. The form is sometimes called 'accident and health,' 'accident and sickness,' 'accident insurance,' or 'disability income insurance.' " Also, the term *health insurance* is sometimes used to designate *sickness insurance* only (*q.v.*) or *medical expense insurance* only (*q.v.*).

[3] Accident insurance is defined by the Commission as "A form of health insurance against loss by bodily injury."

[4] Loss that is either real or presumptive. For instance, a policy may pay a weekly or monthly benefit during a period of time during which the insured is unable by reason of accidental bodily injury to perform any of the duties of his own occupation. During that time, he might be able to work at some other occupation and, in fact, might do so and earn income while still receiving the benefits from the policy. In other words, it is presumed that inability to perform the duties of his own occupation will mean loss of income; if it does not, the benefit is nevertheless paid.

accident insurance policies provide valued payments[5] for accidental death and dismemberment. When the policy does not include loss of time (income) benefits, valued benefits are usually available for certain fractures and dislocations. Where loss of time benefits are written, valued benefits for fractures and dislocations may be optional—i.e., the insured may, at the time of the injury, select these valued benefits in lieu of the loss of time benefits. Occasionally, the policy may provide for the payment of valued benefits for fracture or dislocation plus loss of time benefits.

In addition, accident policies may also offer certain expense benefits for the actual cost of hospitalization, medical, nursing, and surgical care up to a given blanket maximum[6] or for a flat amount payable without regard to the actual cost incurred. A waiver of premium benefit for total disability may be offered under accident insurance.[7]

Certain frill benefits may also be offered; for example, multiple benefits (double, triple, or even more) for certain uncommon causes of injury such as hurricanes, tornadoes, lightning, or explosions of steam boilers. Multiple benefits may extend to the insured who is injured in a common carrier or while a passenger on a passenger elevator.[8]

The various benefits under an accident policy are usually scheduled in the policy and rated separately. The insured may select only that coverage he wants.

SICKNESS COVERAGE.   Sickness insurance[9] developed more slowly than accident insurance, largely because of the lack of reliable statistics and because of the greater moral hazard involved.[10] Sickness coverage is rarely sold separately from accident coverage, except for dread disease policies.

With the exception of death, dismemberment, loss of sight, and dislocation and fracture benefits, the types of benefits available under sickness coverages are the same as those offered under accident coverages.[11] However, basic medical benefits under sickness insurance usually are written scheduled rather than blanket.

---

[5] That is, stated fixed amounts. Thus the valued benefit for loss of sight of both eyes may be $1,000.

[6] That is, lumping all covered costs together rather than setting up a schedule of maxima that will be paid for each type of expense.

[7] Under this benefit, premiums are waived after a waiting period and the insurance continues in force.

[8] Multiple benefits for uncommon accidents lend themselves to dramatic sales presentations with little or no addition to the premium. In one sense, they are difficult to justify. Why does a man need larger benefits because his disability is from the explosion of a steam boiler than he does if he is disabled by a fall down the steps? These frill benefits are now falling from the scene although they remain in large numbers of policies issued earlier.

[9] Defined by the Committee on Health Insurance Terminology as a form of insurance against loss by illness or disease. Illness and disease do not include accidental bodily injury. Sickness insurance may provide benefits for loss of time or expense incurred by pregnancy.

[10] It is easier to fake disability from sickness than it is to fake disability from accident.

[11] Sickness insurance never covers death, death by sickness being deemed "natural" death and covered only by life insurance. Also, sickness does not produce dislocations, fractures, and so forth.

Types of Losses Covered.   Based on the kinds of losses covered, health insurance covers are of three types: income covers, specific loss covers such as loss of life, sight, or limb, and expense covers.

INCOME COVERS.   Policies covering accident and sickness are written to pay the insured a weekly indemnity if he becomes disabled. The covers are written for temporary disability and for long-term disability. They may also be written to cover partial as well as total disability.

LOSS OF LIFE, DISMEMBERMENT, AND LOSS OF SIGHT.   Accident policies frequently are written to provide specific payments for the accidental loss of limb or sight. These benefits are scheduled in the policy and relate to the capital sum, the amount paid to a designated beneficiary in the event the insured dies accidentally.

EXPENSE COVERS.   Health insurance is written to cover a wide variety of medical expenses.[12] These covers include hospital insurance, surgical insurance, regular and major medical insurance, dental care, dread disease, and psychiatric care.

Hospital Coverage.   Policies are offered that cover the cost of hospital room and board and, to a varying degree, the charges incidental to hospitalization.[13] This type of coverage is the most extensive in number of persons covered and in volume of premiums written.[14] The coverage is written on an individual basis, family basis, or group insurance basis.

Hospital expense policies cover two basic items: daily charges for hospital board and room (and the floor nursing and routine services included in that charge) and the charges for miscellaneous (or ancillary) hospital expenses such as operating room, laboratory, and similar costs. Maximum limits are set for daily charges, miscellaneous hospital expenses, and for the number of days of hospital care.

Also available are hospital policies that provide a flat amount per day of hospitalization regardless of expenses incurred.[15] Thus the policy will pay,

---

[12] Medical expense insurance is defined by the Committee on Health Insurance Terminology as "A type of health insurance that provides benefits for most types of medical expenses such as for physicians, hospital, and nursing service and medication. These benefits may be related to actual expense, specified sums, or services rendered. Such insurance sometimes includes benefits for prevention and diagnosis, as well as treatment, rehabilitation, supplies, and equipment. This term should be used to include covers called *hospital surgical insurance* and *medical care insurance.*"

[13] "Miscellaneous" or "ancillary" charges such as operating room, anesthesia, drugs, dressings, and so forth.

[14] For current figures, see the *Source Book of Health Insurance* annual published by the Health Insurance Institute, New York City. Recent figures show that more than 80 percent of the population in the United States had some form of private hospital insurance coverage, more than 74 percent had surgical expense coverage, more than 59 percent had regular medical insurance, nearly 29 percent had major medical insurance, and just under 28 percent had some type of formal nongovernment protection against loss of income. About 73 percent of all health insurance premiums were for hospital and medical coverage, and 27 percent for loss of income.

[15] This type of policy is often called an indemnity policy (in an attempt to make a distinction from the reimbursement type policy). The term "indemnity" is inappropriate. A possible substitute name, but one having no standing in common usage as of now, is a "valued" hospitalization policy, or "valued benefit" policy.

say, $50 a day for a maximum of 60 days, 90 days, 6 months, or a similar period if the insured is necessarily confined to a hospital. The benefit may be stated in terms of monthly payments. The policy form may include dependents, although the per diem for dependents may be less than that for the insured. The same coverage is often offered as a rider on a disability income policy or even on a major medical policy, with the maximum benefit limited to the amount of the deductible under the major medical policy.

A third type of hospital expense coverage offered is the service incurred plan, most widely seen in the various Blue Cross contracts. In this type of coverage the basic benefit is not cash but payment of covered expenses when the insured[16] is confined in a hospital participating in the particular plan. Cash benefits are usually paid only when the insured is confined in a hospital that does not participate in the Blue Cross plan under which he is covered. Under the plan, limits are placed on the number of days of hospital care provided.

Surgical Expense Coverage. The basic form of surgical expense coverage is a schedule of specified maxima that will be paid for various listed operations, which list includes most surgical procedures known. Allowance for procedures not listed usually is made by a provision that the benefit will be that of the most nearly related procedure.

In the schedule, the most expensive types of surgical procedures carry the maximum benefit with all others scaled down proportionately. A typical schedule will list 35 or more procedures ranging from the maximum benefit for cutting into the cranial cavity or removal of a lung or portion of the vertebrae down to, perhaps, 5 percent of the maximum for suturing a wound. The coverage provides that the "regular and customary charges" will be paid for any operation up to the listed maximum. The schedule is referred to in terms of its maximum benefit. Thus, a schedule that pays up to $400 for some several procedures is called a $400 schedule.

Surgical schedules vary not only in maximum amounts for major operations but also in the proportion of this maximum that is allotted to lesser procedures.

Surgical schedules may be an integral part of a hospital expense policy, they may be attached by rider, or they may be attached to an accident policy or a loss-of-time policy by rider.

Regular Medical Expense Coverage. Medical expense coverage is written to cover physicians' bills other than surgery. It is of several types: it may be written to pay irrespective of disability; it may be restricted to expenses while a policyholder is disabled as defined in the policy; or it may be restricted to payment of such expenses only while the insured is hospitalized.

Any one of three limitations, or a combination of them, is common in

---

[16] Most Blue plan carriers will contend that they are not insurers and that the coverage they offer is not insurance. This contention is often successful in winning tax advantages for them in various jurisdictions and succeeds in keeping them out from under full insurance department regulation in nearly all jurisdictions.

medical expense coverage: (1) exclusion of the first few calls by the physician; (2) a limit on the amount of reimbursement per call or per day; (3) an aggregate amount that will be paid for medical attendance. Benefits may be added to most medical expense plans to pay the costs of scheduled diagnostic procedures, or such procedures may have blanket coverage but be limited in aggregate amount.

As mentioned, an accident policy often includes blanket expense coverage under which all medical costs (hospital, surgical, physician, and so on) will be reimbursed on a nonscheduled basis up to an aggregate amount per claim. Blanket expense coverage also is available through limited policies that cover expenses for certain diseases only, such as poliomyelitis, scarlet fever, meningitis, tetanus, dipththeria, cancer, and some others. In such policies the maximum that will be paid overall is usually high: $5,000 to $10,000 or even more in some policies.

Medical expenses may also be provided for through a medical or nurse rider on a disability income policy. Under such rider a flat amount per day is paid for a stated number of days (or months) if the insured requires regular medical care or the services of a registered nurse.

Medical expense coverage is also available through the Blue Shield plans on a semiservice incurred basis—i.e., participating physicians agree that in the case of persons covered by the plan whose incomes are below a certain level (varying from community to community), the amount paid directly to the doctor by the Blue Shield plan is full payment. However, in the case of covered persons with an income above the agreed maximum, the payment made by Blue Shield is only partial payment, the physician being free to charge as much more as he wishes.[17] Such arrangements have not proved entirely satisfactory. Often the maximum income level is unrealistically low, or the additional fee the physician charges above the maximum is so high as to lead the subscriber (insured) to wonder if the additional amount might not have been the total fee in absence of the Blue Shield plan.

Major Medical Coverage.[18]   Major medical coverage (using medical expense broadly to include not only physicians' and surgeons' bills but also hospital board and room, ancillary charges, nursing care, prosthetic de-

---

[17] Historically, the medical profession has charged according to its presumption of the ability of the patient to pay. Thus, any two patients may pay entirely different amounts for the same treatment. As a body, the profession pursues this principle down to the lowest level: the patient with no ability to pay is not charged—or at least no real effort is made to collect any bill sent him. To an extent, hospitals also charge on presumed ability to pay. For this reason, Blue Cross plans pay on a service incurred basis only for semiprivate facilities. If a Blue Cross patient wishes private facilities, the plan makes an allowance on the charges rather than paying for all services incurred. (When the statement is made that Blue Cross pays for services incurred, it should be held in mind that it pays for such services *only* if they are covered in the contract. The Blue Cross–Blue Shield plans have exclusions and limitations just as do other insurance policies.)

[18] Major medical insurance is defined by the Committee on Health Insurance Terminology as "A type of health insurance that provides benefits for most types of medical expense incurred up to a high limit, subject to a large deductible. Such contracts may contain internal limits and a percentage participation clause (sometimes called a 'co-insurance clause')."

vices, and so on), written on an individual, family, or group basis, provides virtually blanket protection for medical expenses up to a given maximum such as, for example, $10,000 or $20,000. The coverage includes a deductible—i.e., the first $250, $500, $750, or $1,000 of expenses are not paid, thus reducing the cost of the insurance, not only through eliminating the cost of the small claim and its administration, but also by reducing the moral hazard through avoiding some duplication with other coverage.

Usually the maximum benefit applies to each accident or each sickness. For a new accident or sickness, or even a recurrence of a previous one, if separated from the treatment for it by some such period as six months, the maximum is again available. Sometimes, especially in coverage extending beyond the ages of 60, 65, or 70, the maximum may be an aggregate: When covered expenses for any and all accidents or sicknesses have totaled the maximum, the policy expires.

Participation clauses are in widespread use in major medical policies (and sometimes even in basic hospitalization policies for certain coverages such as ancillary charges).[19] The clause provides that after the deductible has been accumulated, the insurer will pay a given percentage (75 or 80 percent being common) of the charges incurred up to the maximum. The underwriting theory involved is that if the insured is paying part of the cost, he will have a greater incentive to recover—and less incentive to use unnecessary services.[20]

Major medical insurance is usually written on top of existing hospital, surgical, and medical expense coverage. In such cases, what is known as a "corridor deductible" may be applied: the deductible is whatever is paid by the basic plan plus some amount such as, for example, $100 or $200. Whenever medical bills not covered by the basic plan exceed the deductible, the major medical plan becomes operative. To illustrate, assume a corridor deductible of $200 and covered medical bills of $1,200, of which the basic plan pays $900. The covered person pays the next $200, and the major medical plan, assuming an 80 percent participation, pays $80 of the final $100. In other major medical plans, the full amount paid under a basic plan may be applied toward fulfilling the deductible requirement.

Deductibles in major medical are usually on a "per case" basis. Thus,

---

[19] "Percentage participation" is defined by the Committee on Health Insurance Terminology as "A provision in a health insurance contract that the insurer will share covered losses in agreed proportions." It is still customary to call the participation clause coinsurance, an appellation that is confusing to those acquainted with coinsurance as it is used in fire insurance policies.

[20] Another way of handling the problem of overutilization or prolongation of medical services is to put internal limits in the major medical policy. A common internal limit is the amount that will be paid for hospital daily board and room. Because private duty nursing is often overutilized when expenses are covered on a blanket basis, some policies that do not include an overall participation clause will have one that applies to nursing care only. A third type of internal limit is a maximum amount per operation or series of related operations. Some major medical policies are even using a surgical schedule. Internal limits are contrary to the principle of major medical, which is to offer blanket coverage; however, overutilization of medical facilities and overcharging for services have seriously threatened the continued existence of the coverage in its pristine form.

under a $500 deductible plan, $500 of covered expenses must be incurred because of a specific accident or sickness before the insurance becomes payable. In some plans deductibles are applied on an annual basis; whenever the covered person has accumulated during a year a total of all bills for all accidents or sicknesses in excess of the deductible, the insurance starts paying. The year may be defined as any 12 consecutive months or it may be defined as a calendar year, that is January 1 through December 31. Some insurers write a monthly family deductible plan to gear the deductible to the realities of monthly budgeting so common to many family units. Under the family budget deductible, the insurer reimburses the insured for all covered medical expenses incurred by the family in a given month in excess of a specified amount such as $25 or $50.

Comprehensive Medical Expense Coverage. A modified type of major medical insurance, known as comprehensive, is usually a plan with a low deductible, $25, $50, or $100, but with the high maximums found in major medical insurance. The plan is not written on top of a basic plan. Therefore, the first dollar of expense incurred applies to the deductible. The plan is written primarily in group insurance contracts. In some cases no deductible or participation percentage is applied to hospital or surgical expense.

Dental Care Coverage. Dental care coverage is written by insurance companies through group policies and through individual and family policies. It is included in some major medical policies. It is also written under prepaid contracts with dental service plans sponsored by dental societies through nonprofit dental service corporations. Coverage varies widely among the plans as to benefits offered, participation and deductible clauses used, limitations, and exclusions.

The coverage under dental insurance usually includes oral examinations, fillings, and extractions. It may or may not include the cleaning of teeth, orthodontics, X rays, bridgework, and drugs. Preexisting conditions (a mouthful of neglected teeth) are handled in various ways: excluded until restored, excluded for a limited period, or by charging a higher first-year premium. Deductibles may be higher the first year. Maximums may be increased each year up to a predetermined limit. The participation may be 80 percent for the cost of some dental services and 60 percent for the cost of others. There may be 100 percent reimbursement of certain scheduled benefits.

Nursing Home Care Coverage. When nursing home care coverage is provided, it is usually included as an extension of hospital care policies or of major medical policies. Some Blue Cross plans offer coverage for nursing home care, and several insurance companies offer nursing care coverage outside of that which may be provided under major medical and hospital insurance. Specific nursing home care coverage is written along with other medical care coverage, especially for people over age 65, and generally is sold on a mass basis. It is anticipated that more skilled nursing home care insurance will be written by insurers as the standards for nursing home care improve. Care is less expensive in a nursing home than in a hospital and the use of nursing home care during the convalescent period would reduce the overall cost of medical care. Insurers along with nearly everyone else are searching for more efficient methods of providing and financing medical care.

Vision Care. A few contracts have been written to cover vision care but these have been group contracts. Several prepayment plans have been developed by optometrists but these plans have not had the success achieved by the dental plans. The cost of eye care is included in medical expense policies written by insurance companies, particularly for disease of, or injury to, the eyes. However, these are not the expenses for which vision care coverage is designed. Vision care coverage is for eye examinations, refraction tests, and the fitting of glasses. The expenses covered by vision care plans usually are low and hardly susceptible to insurance.

3. TYPES OF HEALTH INSURANCE POLICIES

Accident, sickness, and medical expense policies may be classified in a number of ways. One basis of classification already noted is the underwriting technique used: individual and group insurance.[21] Other bases for classifying health insurance policies are the continuation provisions used, underwriting standards applied, breadth of benefit provisions offered, and the form of contract.

Continuation Provisions. A major difference among health insurance contracts is in the provisions for the renewal of the policy from term to term. Any of the covers that have been discussed can be written on any one of the following bases:

1. Term contract.
2. Cancellable contract.
3. Optionally renewable.
4. Conditionally renewable.
5. Guaranteed renewable.
6. Noncancellable contract.

TERM CONTRACT. A term contract is one "that makes no provision for renewal or termination other than by expiration of the policy term." [22] At the end of the policy term (as defined in the policy), the coverage expires. If continued coverage is wanted, a new policy must be purchased. No renewal provision is included in the policy. A typical term contract is a trip travel accident policy such as one purchased to cover a round-trip air flight.

---

[21] The Committee on Health Insurance Terminology defines individual insurance as "A contract of health insurance made with an individual that covers him and, in certain instances, specified members of his family." It defines group insurance as "A contract of health insurance made with an employer or other entity that covers a group of persons identified as individuals by reference to their relationship to the entity."

[22] This definition is that of the Committee on Health Insurance Terminology.

CANCELLABLE CONTRACT. A cancellable contract is one "that may be terminated by the insurer or insured at any time." The premium for a cancellable contract and the contract terms and benefits may be changed at any time simply by asking the insured to accept a rider or a waiver on the policy. If insured refuses, the insurer can cancel the policy. Of course, the insurer cannot cancel his obligation under a policy for a claim that has already originated. Widespread public criticism of the cancellation of health insurance, increased competition from the major life insurance companies writing policy forms without cancellation provisions, and legislation in a few states restricting the right to cancel (and to refuse to renew) have reduced the number of contracts with a cancellation clause. The cancellation provision is now found mostly in restricted forms of coverage, especially those issued with little or no underwriting. The principal advantages of cancellable forms are that they are less expensive, and have less strict underwriting standards. Therefore, some persons who are unable to afford noncancellable policies or who could not qualify physically or by reason of hazardous occupation for noncancellable insurance can have some health coverage under the cancellable form.

OPTIONALLY RENEWABLE CONTRACT. An optionally renewable contract is one "in which the insurer reserves the right to terminate the coverage at any anniversary or, in some cases, at any premium-due date, but does not have the right to terminate coverage between such dates." At any renewal date, the premium may be changed or a restrictive rider added. In effect, the company can say one of three things: "We will not renew this policy." "We will renew this policy only for $X of additional premium." "We will renew this policy only if coverage or benefits are restricted by the following rider."

Optionally renewable coverage is the most common type of coverage in force for a variety of reasons: (1) the premium rates for optionally renewable policies are substantially lower than those for comparable noncancellable or guaranteed renewable covers, (2) benefits are often more liberal; for instance, sickness benefits may be payable for life as contrasted to benefits payable to age 65 only, as in most noncancellable or guaranteed renewable forms, and (3) underwriting is more liberal, making it possible for some persons who would not be issued a noncancellable or guaranteed renewable policy on an unrestricted basis to purchase unrestricted coverage on optionally renewable forms.

There has been much public criticism of the failure of insurers to renew optionally renewable policies. As a result, a number of states have passed laws restricting the right of renewal.[23]

---

[23] For example, New York restricts the reasons for nonrenewal of hospital, surgical, and basic medical expense plans to fraud, moral hazard, overinsurance, discontinuance of a class of policies, and other reasons approved by the Superintendent of Insurance. The right to cancel because of deterioration of health alone is specifically prohibited. These restrictions apply after the policy has been in force two years.

It is sometimes contended that there is no practical difference between a cancellable policy and an optionally renewable policy. In both, the insurer may withdraw from the exposure if it turns out that its selection has been poor or if the health or moral condition of the insured deteriorates.[24] However, there can be a significant difference. In a cancellable form, the insurer can terminate the coverage in five days (assuming the terms of the model Uniform Provisions Law apply and that they have not been superseded by special state law). In the case of an optionally renewable form, the insurer must wait until the next renewal date.

CONDITIONALLY RENEWABLE CONTRACT.   A conditionally renewable contract is one "that provides that the insured may renew the contract from period to period or continue the contract in force to a stated date or an advanced age, subject to the right of the insurer to decline renewal only under conditions defined in the contract." Such a clause may read—

Insured shall have the right to renew this Policy until the next Anniversary Date following the Insured's (usually 65 or 70th) birthday except for the following reasons only:

a) Nonpayment of premium on or before due date or during the specified grace period; or

b) If the Insured is no longer engaged in the profession, occupation or association; or

c) If renewals are declined on all like policies in force on members of the named profession, occupation or association in the State named herein. In such case, written notice shall be given to the Insured at least 30 days prior to renewal date; or

d) Renewal of the Policy after the Anniversary Date following the Insured's ———— birthday shall be at the option of the Company only.

Under a conditionally renewable contract, the insurer cannot refuse to renew solely on grounds of deterioration of health. Under an optionally renewable or cancellable provision, coverage for an insured who has suffered a heart attack may be[25] terminated—or renewed only with a waiver of liability in event of any further cardiovascular renal condition. Under a conditional termination right clause, the policy could not be terminated for this cause alone.

Conditionally renewable policies are commonly issued in franchise cases under which all members of a profession, occupation, employer, or association of some type are offered coverage on a group basis.

GUARANTEED RENEWABLE CONTRACT.   A guaranteed renewable contract is one "that the insured has the right to continue in force by the

---

[24] Implicit in cancellable and optionally renewable is a temptation to lower selection standards or even to practice little or no selection because the insurer can withdraw from an exposure that proves bad after acceptance. This practice is known as postclaim underwriting.

[25] "May be" because many companies writing optionally renewable and cancellable coverages say that they rarely if ever terminate for deterioration of health alone.

timely payment of premiums for a substantial period of time[26] during which period the insurer has no right to make unilaterally any change in any provision of the contract while the contract is in force, other than a change in the premium rate for classes of insureds. Premiums may not be changed for an individual but only for classes of insureds, objectively determined."

The guaranteed renewable form is a relatively recent innovation, and what constitutes a "class of insureds" is not clearly defined. Such definition will eventually come from commissioners' rulings and court litigation, later, perhaps, finding its way into state insurance statutes. Undoubtedly a class could be all holders of a form selected by entry age on all females. Some guaranteed renewable clauses refer not to classes but to "all holders of this policy form." In that case, rates could only be increased on all holders. Others refer to all policies in a state. In such a case, rates could only be increased for all insureds in a given state.

The guaranteed renewable contract was developed to enable insurers to experiment with broader coverage for medical expenses and still promise the insured that his coverage would not be terminated if loss estimates on which the rates were based proved inadequate. The cost of medical care has been advancing at a rapid rate with all predictions being for the advance to continue.[27] It is only natural that insurers would be reluctant to issue medical expense insurance that was guaranteed renewable at a guaranteed rate.[28] Guaranteed renewable forms make it possible to give the policy-holder assurance that his coverage will continue in force while not requiring the company to make impossible guesses as to future limits of losses.

The guaranteed renewable form was developed primarily to handle the problem of inflation in medical expense costs, but it has now been adapted to disability income coverage. The application of guaranteed renewability to a disability income form is somewhat of an anomaly. Disability income coverage is written under a valued form.[29] Inflation cannot lead to higher claims under a valued form; but deflation could be a problem, and was during the Great Depression of the 1930's, when the high value of the dollar became an inducement to malingering and faked claims.

---

26 The National Association of Insurance Commissioners has approved a definition of guaranteed renewable that specifies that for a policy to be called "guaranteed renewable," it must make the policy renewable at the insured's option to at least age 50 or for 5 years if issued after age 44. Most guaranteed renewable contracts on the market guarantee renewability to age 65, although other ages such as 62, 70, and even life are to be found.

27 The cost of medical care (all items) in the 10-year period ending in 1969 increased about 50 percent. Hospital room rates increased about 150 percent. (United States Department of Labor, Bureau of Labor Statistics.)

28 A guaranteed renewable major medical policy issued at a guaranteed rate would be priced out of the market in competition with an optionally renewable form, because the guaranteed rate would have to attempt to reflect increased medical costs and would require a loading for the risk inherent in that type of projection.

29 A valued form is defined by the Committee on Health Insurance as "relating to an agreement by the insurer to pay a specified amount of money to or on behalf of the insured upon the occurrence of a defined loss."

NONCANCELLABLE CONTRACT. A noncancellable contract is one "that the insured has the right to continue in force by the timely payment of premiums set forth in the contract for a substantial period of time[30] as also set forth in the contract, during which period the insurer has no right unilaterally to make any change in any provisions of the contract while the contract is in force.[31] These contracts are not cancellable; the right of renewal or continuance usually is guaranteed to an advanced age (for example, 65). The expression, 'noncancellable and guaranteed renewable,' is used interchangeably with the term here defined; however, *noncancellable* is to be distinguished from *guaranteed* renewable (*q.v.*)."

The difference between guaranteed renewable and noncancellable is the premium guarantee. Whereas the guaranteed renewable premium can be increased (by classes of insureds), the noncancellable premium schedule is fixed for the duration of the policy. For this reason, the insurer must be strict in selecting its insureds under a noncancellable policy. Noncancellable insurance is commonly issued only to persons in the two highest occupational classifications (AAA and AA in Conference classification coding).[32] These two classifications include persons subject to no occupational hazard to health or life and who might be loosely classified as executive, professional, and white-collar workers. Premium rates for similar benefits usually are higher under the noncancellable form than under any of the other forms, because of the risk involved in fixing premiums so far in advance.

The rate for noncancellable coverage does not have to be level (i.e., the same throughout the life of the policy as at entry age). It can be a separate premium. The renewal clause guarantees only that the premium will not be changed from that stated at the time of issue. Formerly, noncancellable policies called for an increased rate at about age 50–55. Sometimes there were two or even more changes as the insured progressed into the older ages. This is not common today; but in recent years, a number of companies are offering a noncancellable policy with a low entry rate that increases after a few years. The philosophy underlying this plan is the same as that underlying the modified life policy: Younger insureds, especially, may wish to postpone the full rate until a later age, at which time they believe they will be better able financially to pay a higher premium.

It should be noted that a noncancellable policy is noncancellable as to both insurer and insured. Once the insured has paid a premium, he cannot terminate and demand a pro rata refund. The only way he can terminate the policy is by refusing to pay the next premium. To mitigate this condition,

---

[30] Cf. footnote 29.

[31] The insurer can, however, amend the policy or the rate as a condition of reinstatement if the policy has been lapsed and reinstatement is requested.

[32] The "Conference" classification system, probably the most widely used of any one occupational classification system, was developed by the old Health and Accident Underwriters Conference, an intercompany association absorbed in the 1950's by the Health Insurance Association of America. However, many companies develop their own systems and use different letter or numeral classification codes.

two modifying clauses can be found (in optionally renewable and guaranteed renewable as well as in noncancellable).

(1) Ten days free inspection. A number of states require insurers to make a statement approximating as follows:[33]

Ten days are allowed from the date of receipt of this policy to examine its provisions, and the policy may be surrendered within said 10-day period; and upon surrender, any premiums paid will be immediately returned in full. If the policy is surrendered, the liability of the Company shall not extend to claims having their origin during the inspection period.

(2) Noncancellable as to insurer; cancellable as to insured. This clause[34] provides that although the insurer cannot cancel, the insured may cancel and demand a refund of part of the current premium.

Noncancellable covers were written as early as 1885 in Great Britain, but the form was not introduced in the United States until 1907. By 1921, at least nine companies offered the policy. Because of highly adverse claim experience during the Great Depression of the 1930's, nearly all insurers discontinued writing noncancellable policies. However, with the growth of interest in health insurance that started in the 1950's (and particularly with the entry of many large life insurance companies into the health insurance business), interest in the noncancellable form revived.

While in the past it has been common to call noncancellable forms a class of health insurance[35] such usage no longer has validity. Today some insurers issue optionally renewable, guaranteed renewable, and noncancellable policies with identical provisions except for the renewal clause and for certain uniform provisions that state law requires be different in optionally renewable and guaranteed renewable forms.[36]

Any form of coverage (medical expense or disability income) can be written with any of the renewal clauses discussed; however, it is not common to issue medical expense forms with a noncancellable provision because they are, as pointed out, reimbursement forms and claim cost under them is directly affected by inflation. It is impossible to set premiums

---

[33] This statement may be a policy provision, may be a rider (even in the form of a paste-on sticker), or even a statement made in a letter of transmittal of the policy. However, enough states are now requiring the statement that many companies put it in all policies.

[34] This clause does not appear to have much intrinsic value and may contribute to one of the problems of the health insurance business—rewriting of policies. It is a practice in health insurance to encourage an insured to drop a policy in one company to take a similar (always, of course, presented as a "better") policy in another company. That the insured cannot cancel any health policy except a policy containing the cancellable provision has a tendency to slow down rewriting. Putting in a "cancellable as to insured" clause simply makes it easier for the rewriting agent to operate. While it can be argued that since there is no cash value in health insurance policies, there is no loss when the cover is shifted. However, there is always the loss of the time that has already run under the initial contestable period of the policy superseded.

[35] The common classification was commercial, noncancellable, and industrial policies. The Committee on Health Insurance Terminology does not even recognize the term "commercial."

[36] Statutory provisions for health insurance policies are discussed in Chapter 14.

for 35 or 40 years into the future when there is no way to determine what the losses will be so many years hence. This is not to say that noncancellable medical expense forms cannot be found; but in proportion to the number of medical expense covers offered, they are rare. Guaranteed renewable forms are much more common for assuring the continuous availability of medical expense insurance.

In some policies, noncancellation provisions and guaranteed renewable provisions are combined: the policy is noncancellable to age 60 or 65 and guaranteed renewable thereafter. No one knows what the long-run effect of the possession of medicare insurance by the elderly population will be on the utilization of medical facilities—except to be sure that it will increase. Guaranteed renewability seems to be a necessary safeguard for policies owned by retired people.

GROUP RENEWABILITY. The foregoing discussion of continuation provisions (renewability) applies to individual (and family) policies. Continuation provisions under group contracts may be classified as follows:

1. Provisions affecting the continuance of the master contract (or segment thereof)

a) guaranteed renewable.

b) limited renewal right (this being applicable under a contributory plan where the policy may be terminated if less than a certain percentage of those eligible remain covered).

c) optionally renewable.

2. Additional provisions affecting continuance of coverage of the individual

a) subject to continuance of employment (or membership in an insured group).

b) cancellable as to a class within a group.

Underwriting Standards. Another classification of health insurance policies is based on underwriting standards, and in some ways overlaps with the one based on termination provisions. As mentioned, the strictest underwriting standards are applied to the noncancellable forms and the most liberal standards are applied to cancellable forms. Mass merchandised franchise, blanket, and credit health insurance covers, older age policies, special risk policies, substandard policies, and business overhead expense policies are policies that are classified according to underwriting standards used. The mass merchandised forms are discussed in Chapter 16.

OLDER AGE POLICIES. Older age policies (sometimes called senior citizen policies) are contracts which are issued beyond the normal insuring age of 60. Comprehensive hospital and medical benefits are provided under social security (medicare) for those age 65 or older. Although medicare benefits are broad in scope, they do not provide complete protection. Private insurance is available to supplement medicare benefits, sometimes written under a mass enrollment plan offered by several insurance companies.

Enrollment periods in designated states are announced periodically, and lifetime protection is written without a physical examination and without concern about the applicant's medical history. Impairments existing before the contract is issued are covered after a specified waiting period. Benefits usually are designed to complete a sound health insurance program for the insured by filling the gaps in medicare without creating any overlaps. As can be seen by reviewing the benefits under medicare, sufficient gaps are found to make supplemental private coverage desirable.

Gaps under medicare exist under both the basic plan and the supplementary plan. Under the *basic plan* medicare provides up to 60 days in a participating hospital (after the insured pays the first $40 of cost himself),[37] all but $10 a day for an additional 30 days, and all but $20 a day for an additional 60 days, this latter 60 days being subject to a lifetime reserve which the patient may use as he sees fit. These benefits are paid for each "spell of illness," that is, the period beginning with the admission to the hospital and ending after the patient is out of the hospital or nursing home for 60 consecutive days. Benefits for psychiatric hospital services are subject to a 190-day lifetime limit. The patient must absorb the cost of the first three pints of blood furnished him. Coverage is for semiprivate room, board, and necessary hospital and nursing services. A private room is covered only if medically indicated. The basic plan covers up to 20 days in a nursing home, and all but $5 a day for an additional period of 80 days for each spell of illness after a stay of at least 3 days in the hospital and within 14 days of discharge. The basic plan covers up to 100 home health visits by nurses, interns, or other health workers from qualified home health agencies (but not from doctors) in the 365 days following release from a hospital or nursing home after a stay of at least 3 days.

The coverage under the *supplementary plan* provides benefits to offset costs of home, hopsital, office calls of physicians, surgeons, radiologists, pathologists, anesthesiologists, psychiatrists, and dental suregons; rental of medical equipment; ambulance; X-ray therapy; artificial eyes, limbs, and braces; surgical dressings, casts, and splints; prescription and nonprescription drugs not self-administered; diagnostic studies during any 20-day period performed or supervised by a hospital medical staff; and up to 100 visits during a 365-day period by visiting nurses, medical social workers, aides, technicians without the requirement of prior hospitalization. All of the medical services under the suplementary plan are subject to a $50 calendar year deduction and a 20 percent participation on the part of the patient. Payment for psychiatric care is limited during any calendar year to $250 or 50 percent of the expenses, whichever is smaller.[38]

An appropriate medical expense policy for a person age 65 or older

---

[37] After 1968 the $40 deductible may be adjusted to reflect relative increases in the cost of hospital care, using a formula that produces a two-year time lag.

[38] Social Security Act, secs. 1812, 1813, 1814, 1833, and 1861. See applicable paragraphs.

and covered under medicare would be a major medical policy integrated with medicare, that is, one that would pay those expenses not provided for under either the basic or supplementary medicare plans. For example, the coverage would include such items as the initial $40 of hospital expense, the $10 daily charge after 60 days, the $20 charge after 90 days, and the full charge after 150 days; private nursing, prescribed drugs, extended psychiatric services, and extended care in a nursing home.

SPECIAL RISK POLICIES. A special risk policy (sometimes called a specialty policy) offers the customary benefits or any combination of benefits found in orthodox health insurance policies but usually features higher benefit limits and are used by insurers in underwriting hazards not acceptable under orthodox policies. Some examples are war hazards, bomb tests (coverage of personnel engaged therein), test flying, the nonappearance of an actor or performer (payable to the employer, not employee) by reason of accident or sickness; loss of license by a commercial pilot because of disability; accidents to amateur or professional athletes, or any other hazardous exposure. The list of hazards covered by special risk policies is limited only by the imagination.

Special risk underwriting and rating are subjective—i.e., they depend almost entirely on the judgment of the underwriter because experience is too limited to supply any meaningful statistics. Thus the exposure presents a special risk as well as a special hazard.

SUBSTANDARD POLICIES. Policies designed specifically to cover physically impaired persons are called substandard policies, a designation not acceptable to public relations men who would prefer such a name as special qualified impairment policy. These policies are issued to persons who cannot meet the normal health requirements of a standard health policy. Coverage is given in consideration of an increase in premium, or through a waiver of medical conditions. In some cases, when these policies are written for people who have had a serious illness, such as cancer, heart trouble, or diabetes, coverage is given for a recurrence of the impairment but for a benefit level lower than that for other illnesses.

BUSINESS OVERHEAD EXPENSE POLICIES. Business overhead expense coverage might be compared roughly to business interruption insurance. It is a reimbursement form, and, as such, is subject to the general tax rules applying to business property insurance rather than those applying to business health insurance. Premiums are a deductible business expense, and benefits are includible as gross income.[39] A special policy form enumerating the overhead expenses covered is necessary if the premiums are to be income tax deductible. Premiums for a *regular disability income policy* even if the benefits are to be used exclusively to defray overhead expenses are not deductible, but neither are proceeds reportable as income.[40]

---

[39] Rev. Rul. 55–264, 1955–1 CB 11.
[40] Rev. Rul. 54–480, CB 1958–2, 62.

Overhead expenses include such items as rent, taxes, power, insurance, clerical salaries, and similar expenses. Overhead expenses, however, do not include such items as inventory, capital retirement on mortgage loans (but do include the interest on the loan), wages or salary of the proprietor, and wages of a professional performing duties that had been performed by a disabled professional.[41]

The business overhead policy form may be issued only to natural persons who are legally liable for the debts of a business. Therefore, it cannot be issued to corporations but only to sole proprietors (which includes all self-employed professional persons) and partners. When the policy is written on partners (or in a situation involving joint occupancy,)[42] each insured is covered for only that percentage of the overhead expenses for which he is liable: one half each in a 50–50 partnership or joint tenancy.

The benefit period is usually short term—12 to 36 months—on the theory that if a partner or proprietor is disabled longer than 12 to 36 months he will probably sell or liquidate his interest. Amount limits are usually high, more than $1,000 a month not being uncommon.[43] Further, it is common to write the insurance in addition to whatever personal loss of time coverage the applicant may have, that is the underwriting rules limiting the amount of loss of time coverage on any one life are waived for this coverage.

While technically the policy may be written on anyone who is legally liable for the debts of a business, in practice most insurers will write the coverage only in cases in which the applicant's personal services play an important role in the business operation. Some insurers even confine the coverage to professional men.[44]

---

[41] For instance, the wages or salary paid by a physician to another physician who is his assistant or substitute are not reimbursable.

[42] Such as two lawyers using a common office and clerical staff but not under articles of partnership.

[43] Of course only the amount of loss is paid under the policy; thus, if an insured has $1,000 a month coverage but his overhead expenses during any month of disability were under $1,000 he receives the lesser amount—just as in fire insurance where the amount paid is limited to the amount of the loss, if this amount is less than the amount of the insurance.

[44] The problem that arises when the business is mercantile in nature is best illustrated by a story: In the early days of business overhead expense, an insurance company executive argued that the form would be made available to anyone who was legally liable for the debts of a business. He quickly revised that opinion when a restaurant owner covered under one of his company's business overhead expense policies sustained a multiple fracture of a leg and was bed-confined in traction. While so confined, he continued to do all the menu planning for the restaurant, all the buying (by phone), and kept all the books from his bed. Since these were the major functions he performed while not in bed, it was obvious that he was not disabled in the sense contemplated in rating the policy; yet it would have been impossible for the insurer to get any court to agree that a man confined to bed in traction is not disabled within the meaning of the term as understood by a layman—usually the legal test. The insurer paid the claim, but immediately changed the underwriting rules.

Breadth of Benefit Provisions Offered. Health insurance policies may be classified as to the range of benefits offered. Some policies offer broad protection whereas others offer highly restricted protection. Of course no health insurance policy is completely free of limitations, but some have more limitations than others. When a policy contains unusual exclusions, conditions, or reductions of a restrictive nature the policy is called a limited policy.

Some fraternal and ethnic organizations offer forms of health insurance benefits to members, usually on a restricted basis.[45] It is common for certificates of some fraternal coverage to exclude a long list of diseases and disabilities and to pay reduced benefits for still other diseases. Medical expense coverage is rarely found.

Limited policies are those covering only specifically named accidents or diseases. Examples are dread disease contracts covering a few relatively rare but highly expensive sicknesses such as poliomyelitis, scarlet fever, tularemia, diphtheria, and so on. Cancer is sometimes included.[46] Benefits under such policies are written on a blanket basis—$5,000, $10,000, $20,000, for example.

Other examples of limited policies are travel ticket, newspaper, and automobile accident policies. Travel ticket, once sold as a stub on a railway ticket, is now commonly sold over the ticket counter or, especially in airports, from vending machines. Air travel ticket coverage is written blanket for high amounts. Newspaper policies[47] usually limit coverage to a small list of accidents with benefits graded by type of accident, higher indemnities being payable for less frequent accidents such as common carrier accident and low benefits for the more common types of accidents. Travel ticket, newspaper, automobile accident, and similar policies nearly always include a relatively high principal sum to be paid for accidental death and a relatively high capital sum to be paid for loss of sight or dismemberment.

Limited policies are a source of public misunderstanding. In the first place, it is common in advertising and selling them to play up the relatively large capital and principal sum benefits and the maximum benefits payable for rare accidents such as those involving a common carrier. The minor benefits payable for common accidents are not usually noticed by the buyers. When they are injured, they think in terms of the maximum benefits that were stressed in the advertising copy. Further, the public, always hunt-

---

[45] Note the term "usually." Some larger fraternals offer coverages in every way comparable to that of regular insurance companies. In fact, these fraternals pioneered some of the coverage now considered standard. The text discussion refers principally to the hundreds of small fraternal societies to whom insurance coverage is only an incidental service.

[46] Often cancer is covered by rider for an additional premium and for a maximum amount less than that for other covered diseases.

[47] The form takes its name from the fact that it is often sold in conjunction with newspaper subscriptions, the premium being an addition to the regular carrier-delivery rate for the paper; however, the same form is also offered frequently by direct mail and retains its newspaper name.

ing bargains in insurance, buys these policies in lieu of adequate coverage. Many states require that a limited policy carry a surprint on the face in red, "This is a limited policy. Read the provisions carefully." It would be interesting to know what percentage of owners of limited policies have followed this admonition.

The Form of the Contract. Most health insurance is written as a separate policy covering loss of income or the expense of medical care or both, resulting from accident or illness. Some health insurance is written in connection with other benefits, such as the medical payments coverage written with automobile insurance. Still other health insurance is written as a rider to life insurance policies. Riders to life insurance policies offering accident or disability protection are not usually classified along with other health insurance coverage. Since they are written as a part of life insurance policies rather than separately, they are often bypassed in discussions of health insurance. These riders are: (1) Multiple indemnities for accidental death; (2) waiver of premium in case of disability; (3) waiver of premium and monthly income in case of disability.

MULTIPLE INDEMNITY. For an additional premium, most life insurers will attach a rider under which they agree to pay a multiple of the face amount of the policy if death results directly and independently of all other causes from external, violent, and accidental means occurring before the end of the policy year nearest the insured's 65th birthday and within 90 days of the accident.[48] The most common multiple indemnity is double indemnity, or twice the face of the policy. Triple indemnity (sometimes confined to common carrier accidents) is written by some insurers.

The extra premium for the rider is payable only during the regular premium paying period but not beyond the date at which the multiple indemnity coverage expires. The premium for double indemnity is low, less than 0.1 percent of the face amount of the policy at ages under 45. Multiple indemnity coverage does not continue when one of the nonforfeiture options such as extended term or reduced paid-up is selected. Multiple indemnity coverage also does not apply to additions purchased with policy dividends.

WAIVER OF PREMIUM. For a small extra premium,[49] it is common to

---

[48] Multiple benefits are not payable if death occurs as a result of any one of a number of conditions. It is necessary for the insured to read his policy carefully. One insurer, for example, excludes death resulting from suicide, drugs, sedatives, medicine or anesthetics, taking poison, inhaling gas or fumes, any illness or disease, bodily, physical or mental infirmities, bacterial infection other than that occurring in consequence of accidental and external bodily injury, medical or surgical treatment, participation in riot, participation in insurrection, operating, riding in, or descending from any kind of aircraft except as fare-paying passenger in a licensed plane operated by a licensed pilot, a state of warfare, military, naval, or air service of any country at war, civil commotion or hostile action, commission of an assault or felony, and homicide or intentional injuries inflicted by another.

[49] For instance, on a participating ordinary life policy with one insurer, the premium for a disability waiver at age 25 is $0.37 per $1,000; on a 20-pay life, it is $0.24.

attach to a life insurance policy a rider providing that in event the insured becomes totally disabled before a stated age such as 60 or 65,[50] the premiums will be waived for the duration of the disability after a specified waiting period, such as 6 months. It is common to provide for a refund of any premiums paid during the six months, once the waiting period has been satisfied. When premiums are waived on a participating policy, the insured continues to receive the dividends, and the nonforfeiture values continue to increase.

Some insurers define total disability in their policies as that which renders the insured incapable of engaging in *any* work for remuneration or profit. However, the courts interpret this definition to mean any work for which the insured is, or becomes, reasonably fitted by education, training, or experience. Other insurers are now defining total disability in their policies in terms of "own occupation" for a specific period—24 months, for example—and any occupation thereafter. Certain disabilities are considered total by their nature. Among these are the loss of sight in both eyes or the loss of the use of both arms or both legs, or of one arm plus one leg.[51]

DISABILITY INCOME RIDERS.   Some insurers will issue a rider providing that in the event of total disability they will not only waive premiums but also pay a monthly income for the duration of the disability[52] or until the insured reaches age 65. If the insured is still disabled at age 65, the face of the policy is payable in a lump sum or under installment options. A six-month waiting period following a disability is a common condition for eligibility for benefits. The amount of the monthly disability income is a percentage of the face amount of the life insurance—1 percent, for example.

Disability income coverage under life insurance riders generally terminates at age 55 or 60. An insured who is disabled before that time, however, continues to receive his benefits until death or age 65 when the face amount of the policy is paid. As a rule, these riders are issued only on applicants between such ages as 15 and 50. Insurers place a maximum limit on the amount of monthly income benefits they will write regardless of the face amount of the life insurance purchased. This limit is usually lower than that available through separate disability income insurance policies. The relatively recent increase in the availability of guaranteed renewable and noncancellable disability income policies has reduced the importance of disability income riders on life insurance policies.

When a disability income rider is attached to an endowment policy, the disability income ceases at the maturity date of the endowment.

---

[50] In some older policies, the expiration date was as early as 55.

[51] A person who has lost the use of both legs, for example, but can continue in his occupation will nevertheless be considered totally disabled under the terms of the policy.

[52] It may seem contradictory to say that benefits will be paid for the duration of a permanent disability since by definition "permanent" should mean lifetime. However, courts have held that there need be only a reasonable assumption that the disability is permanent, which means that recoveries from permanent disabilities are not unknown.

Disability income benefits are not payable for disability beginning after a policy has been placed on a nonforfeiture option such as extended term or paid-up for a reduced amount.

The price of the rider is low. The annual premium per $10 of monthly income per $1,000 of face amount on an ordinary life policy, participating plan, at age 25 in one insurer is $2.86. On a 20-pay life policy in the same insurer, the price is $3.44.

4. TYPE OF HEALTH INSURANCE PURVEYORS

Nearly 1,800 private insuring organizations offer a wide variety of health insurance plans. These include insurance companies, Blue Cross and Blue Shield organizations, medical society approved plans, and a number of independent health insurance plans.

Insurance Companies.   The predominant type of health insurance organization is the insurance company, currently writing over 60 percent of all health insurance premiums. About 69 percent of the insurance companies writing health insurance are life insurance companies, 28 percent are casualty insurance companies, and only about 3 percent are specialty companies writing health insurance exclusively.

Producers' Cooperatives.   Cooperative health insurance plans are set up by employees' associations, employers, unions, consumer groups, student groups, hospitals, medical associations, and medical clinics. They are frequently termed nonprofit plans because they are usually organized under laws exempting them from certain taxes imposed on regular insurance companies. It may be argued that these plans are no more nonprofit than a mutual insurance company. However, they do differ from mutual insurance companies in one major respect. Mutual insurance companies are organized as consumers' cooperatives whereas cooperative health insurance plans usually are organized as producers' cooperatives. The key to the difference is in who bears the financial risk, the consumers or producers of the covered hospital and medical services. The financial risk in a mutual insurance company rests with the insureds who not only own the company but who also are the consumers of the hospital and medical services that are underwritten by the company.[53] The financial risk in cooperative health insurance plans rests with the hospitals and physicians who furnish the services and not with the persons who "subscribe" to the insurance.

Chief among the cooperative health insurance plans in size and extent of operations are the Blue Cross and Blue Shield plans. In addition there are a number of direct service plans known as group practice prepayment plans.

BLUE CROSS PLANS.   The name Blue Cross is applied to those 76 independent nonprofit membership corporations providing protection against

---

[53] See Chapter 28.

the cost of hospital care who have been authorized by the American Hospital Association to use the name and emblem of Blue Cross. Blue Cross insurance is a system of providing hospital service and care rather than of paying direct cash reimbursement or stated amount benefits to the insured. Hospitals agree to provide Blue Cross subscribers[54] with certain services at predetermined contract prices charged to the plan. If for some reason the plan is not financially able to pay the participating hospital the contract price, the hospital agrees to accept a pro rata payment. Benefits in Blue Cross contracts are usually express in terms of a specified number of days of hospital care. Room and board benefits, including general nursing, usually are on a full-service basis in semiprivate rooms.[55] However, exceptions will be found not only among the various Blue Cross plans but also among the certificates given to subscribers of the same plan. For example, some plans place a dollar limit on the daily hospital room and board benefit and others include a deductible or a participation clause. Full coverage is usually given for hospital services such as drugs, laboratory, operating room, oxygen, basal metabolism, electrocardiogram, and other extras. Here again there are exceptions. In some plans maximum amounts are allowed for the costs of one or more of these services. In others, a particular service might not be covered at all. For example, whereas a few plans cover X-ray therapy on a full-service basis and even fewer cover it subject to a maximum dollar amount, most plans do not cover it, even in part. While the majority of plans cover anesthesia in full, a significant minority do not include this service, and a few cover its cost subject to a maximum amount.

The Blue Cross subscriber must be admitted to a cooperating hospital in order to have expenses covered up to maximum amount. However, when he must be hospitalized in a nonplan hospital, he is allowed a stated number of dollars per diem. Furthermore, if a Blue Cross subscriber has the customary full service coverage for a semiprivate room and wants or needs to be alone, his contract most likely will call for the plan to allow him a fixed number of dollars a day toward a private room.

The foregoing discussion should be sufficient to dispel a common impression that the Blue Cross plan is one plan written on a national basis. Blue Cross is composed of a host of independent plans having in common the right to use the name Blue Cross. The independent Blue Cross plans are loosely coordinated at the top by the American Hospital Association and the Blue Cross Association. The responsibilities for establishing minimum standards for plans, for providing guidance to those plans that ask for it, and for maintaining smooth operating relations between the plans and the hospitals are assumed by the American Hospital Association. The Blue

---

[54] The Blue plans seek to avoid orthodox insurance terminology and, therefore, do not speak of their insureds as policyholders or even insureds.

[55] Semiprivate originally meant two-bed rooms, but now means four- and even eight-bed rooms.

Cross Association represents the plans in national affairs through marketing services, education, research, professional relations, and public relations. It operates system-wide services such as a computerized communication system, the Interplan transfer agreement for subscribers transferring coverage from one plan to another, and the Interplan Bank for Blue Cross subscribers utilizing benefits away from their home areas. It accepts responsibility on behalf of the plans for national enrollments and serves as a prime contractor to the United States government in performing administrative intermediary functions under medicare. It aids in the administration of the Local Benefit Agreement for National Accounts, an arrangement obviously for giving local benefits to national accounts.

Blue Cross plans are established primarily on a group basis, although individual enrollments are available continuously in some plans and community enrollments are encouraged in others by having enrollment periods of one or two weeks once or twice a year. When national accounts or a group of accounts in a given industry are handled through Blue Cross plans and uniform benefits are desired nationally, an interplan syndicate is used to tailor the needs to the company or industry.[56]

BLUE SHIELD PLANS.   The name Blue Shield is applied to those 75 prepaid expense plans operated by medical societies who have been authorized by the National Association of Blue Shield plans to use the name and emblem of Blue Shield. Blue Shield plans provide medical and surgical expense insurance to subscribers usually on a semiservice incurred basis. Some plans are written on a full-service basis where the participating physicians perform the services offered under the plan without additional charge to the subscriber. The physician is paid the amount scheduled in the plan.

Most plans offer partial service benefits. Only subscribers with incomes below certain limits are given full benefits. Those with incomes above the limits will be required to pay the physician the difference between his normal fee and what he receives for his services from the Blue Shield plan. Approval standards for Blue Shield plans offering service benefits require that the income limit be set high enough to include 75 percent of the population in the area in which the plan operates.

A few plans offer a cash rather than a service benefit. Under these plans, there is a schedule of benefits covering various services but the physician can charge what he wants. The subscriber must pay the difference between the doctor's charge and the amount credited from the plan. However, by far the majority of benefits provided under Blue Shield plans are for serv-

---

[56] The Blue Cross Association also owns an insurance company, the Health Service, Inc., which offers a standard national contract, with rider, to companies operating over several plan areas. The plan is not tailored as in the syndicates. Local plans underwrite the benefits to the extent that they can meet the benefits of the uniform national agreement. The H.S.I. underwrites directly those benefits that cannot be handled by local plans.

ice rather than indemnity benefits. If the plan is financially unable to pay the contract price, participating physicians agree to accept a lower amount.

If a subscriber uses a nonparticipating physician, the plan usually will pay the amount due to the subscriber or to the physician if so directed by the subscriber.

Blue Shield plans cover a large percentage of those who are covered under Blue Cross plans. In some geographical areas the two plans are under the same board and are operated by the same staff. Even where the plans are not jointly managed they generally work together on enrollments and on coordinating benefits.

The National Association of Blue Shield plans serve the individual plans much in the same way that individual Blue Cross plans are served by the American Hospital Association and the Blue Cross Commission. The Blue Shield plans do not have a Local Benefit Agreement for National Accounts nor an Interplan Bank. Subscribers who use physicians in another area pay their own bills direct and look to their home plans for reimbursement. Syndicates, however, are used for national accounts, and many times Blue Shield plans are combined with Blue Cross plans in these syndicates.[57]

DENTAL SERVICE CORPORATIONS.   State dental societies have formed nonprofit organizations for the sale of prepaid dental care plans under which participating dentists agree to perform the services offered to subscribers to the plans. The plans, although colorless and without a cross or a shield, bear the same relationship to dentists and dental care expenses as the Blue Shield plans bear to the medical profession and the cost of medical care, and the Blue Cross plans bear to the hospitals and the cost of hospital care. The National Association of Dental Service Plans is the coordinating agency for professionally sponsored state dental service corporations.[58]

GROUP PRACTICE PREPAYMENT PLANS.   Medical group practice involves a formal organization of physicians who provide medical services to the public and share the group practice income according to some agreed-on formula. The practitioners share facilities, personnel, and equipment. A group practice prepayment plan matches medical group practice with a system for budgeting the cost of medical care. Members of a prepayment plan pay dues to the plan in return for the right to medical services as needed. The plan organizes the staff and facilities necessary to satisfy the needs of its members.

Group practice prepayment plans may be civic in nature and operated as consumers' cooperatives or they may be private in nature and operated as producers' cooperatives sponsored and owned by physicians. Some group

---

[57] The National Association of Blue Shield Plans own an insurance company, the Medical Indemnity of America, Inc. M.I.A. operates for Blue Shield plans much in the same way as H.S.I. operates on behalf of Blue Cross plans. In fact, M.I.A. and H.S.I., though seperate insurers, operate jointly in soliciting and servicing national accounts.

[58] Optometric vision service organizations have been formed in a number of states to offer vision care prepayment plans. The American Optometric Association sponsors the Vision Institute of America to coordinate the various prepayment plans.

practice prepayment plans are sponsored and operated by employers, unions, or joint management–labor boards.

Benefits under a group practice prepayment plan generally are broader than those under coverage offered by insurance companies and the Blue plans. For example, coverage is not limited to accidents and sickness but includes physical examinations and other preventive treatment.

14

The Health Insurance Policy

The prospective purchaser of health insurance is faced with a great array of policy forms. One researcher found 300 different contracts, no two of which were identical. Fortunately, enough order can be created out of chaos for a reasonable discussion of the health insurance policy.

The laws of all jurisdictions require the inclusion in every health insurance policy (with certain exceptions, to be mentioned later) of a set of uniform provisions relating to what might be called the operational conditions of the policy. In addition, the policy will include insuring agreements, benefits provisions, and exclusions, all of which vary widely among policies. In this chapter the uniform provisions will be outlined first and then the coverage provisions (insuring agreements, benefit clauses, and exclusions) will be discussed.

1. UNIFORM PROVISIONS

About 1909, state legislatures began to study the problem of unduly restrictive claim practices and other abuses in the health insurance business. In order to offset much of this criticism, the National Association of Insurance Commissioners drew up a group of standard provisions for health insurance policies. By 1911 this set of provisions, with some state by state variations, was put into law in most jurisdictions; and the requirement was made that any health insurance policy issued in the jurisdiction must contain this set of provisions exactly as worded in the law.

Over the years between 1911 and 1950, amendments by various states to their standard provision laws had decreased the degree of uniformity of requirements from state to state. The standard provisions had become less standard with the passing years. Developments in the business had made some of the old standard provisions less applicable and these changes had been reflected in variations and amendments in the laws of the various states. As a result, the National Association of Insurance Commissioners drafted a new set of laws and recommended their adoption by the various regulatory jurisdictions. The model law drafted by the NAIC was entitled, "Uniform Individual Accident and Sickness Policy Provisions," and the set of provisions itself has come to be known as the uniform provisions. All but two jurisdictions (Louisiana and Alaska) require the use of the uniform provisions in all individual policies issued in their jurisdiction.

The uniform provisions cover the same general area as the standard provisions, with changes adapting them to modern health insurance. Unlike the standard provisions, the uniform provisions need not be worded verbatim. The insurance commissioner may accept any wording that gives the insured protection in substance at least equal to what the law intends. Further, whereas the standard provisions were numbered in sequence and the numbering had to be included in the policy,[1] the uniform provisions are not numbered; however, each has a descriptive title, which must be used in the policy. Among the uniform provisions, 12 are mandatory and 11 are optional. In addition, the uniform provision law establishes certain regulations involving policy conditions not embodied in the policy provisions themselves. The law does not apply to workmen's compensation, reinsurance, blanket insurance, or group coverages. Disability riders on life policies also do not come under the uniform provisions law.

The uniform provisions usually will be found grouped together[2] in a policy under some such heading as Uniform Provisions, Statutory Provisions, Required Provisions, or the like.

The title Uniform Provisions can be misleading. The layman, and many agents, think that since the provisions are uniform, there is no need to check them in comparing policies. Uniform implies that they will be the same in every contract. This is not the case. In the first place, one policy may contain only the mandatory provisions; whereas another may include one or several of the optional provisions, almost all of which add restrictions. Further, some of the mandatory provisions even have options within them, as will be seen from the following brief summary of the provisions. Careful contract analysis must include a review of the uniform provisions in any given policy.

Mandatory Provisions. The following is a brief résumé of the content of each mandatory uniform provision. The following sideheads constitute the title of the provision as set forth in the model law and which is to be used in the policy. Note again that these provisions are not numbered.

Entire Contract—Changes. The policy and endorsements, if any, constitute the entire contract. Changes are valid only if endorsed on the

---

[1] This requirement created an awkward situation: not all of the standard provisions were mandatory; but if one of the optional provisions was omitted, the policy showed a skip in numbering, leading the insured to think that perhaps something had been left out in printing the policy form, an annoying experience indeed.

[2] The grace period provision is often found lifted out of the grouping and placed earlier in the policy format.

policy by an executive officer of the company. An agent cannot waive provisions or alter the terms of the contract as printed.

TIME LIMIT ON CERTAIN DEFENSES. After three years,[3] no misstatements in the application may be used to void the policy or deny a claim *except fraudulent misstatements.* A policy that the insured has the right to continue in force by timely payment of premium until at least age 50 or for at least 5 years if issued after age 44 may contain in lieu of this provision one entitled "Incontestable," which eliminates the "except fraudulent misstatements."[4] The incontestable provision itself has an option within it. The insurer is allowed the option of making the contestable period exclude any period of time during which the insured is disabled. Assume an extreme case in which an insured is disabled the day after his policy goes in force and remains disabled for the rest of his life. If the insurer had elected to include this latter option in the policy, the policy would never become incontestable.

Note that a guaranteed renewable or noncancellable policy is not required to use the incontestable clause. The only requirement is that the Time Limit on Certain Defenses be used. Therefore, it is necessary to examine the policy to see whether it contains the time limit or incontestable clause and if it includes the incontestable clause, whether that clause has the optional phrase that excludes periods of disability.[5]

A second paragraph under Time Limit on Certain Defenses is required. After three (in the model law) years, a claim may not be reduced or denied on the grounds of a preexisting condition. Thus, in effect, preexisting conditions are covered after the contestable period.

GRACE PERIOD. A grace period shall be granted for payment of premiums after the premium due date, during which the policy remains in force. (The grace period does not apply to the initial premium.) The model law specifies that the period must not be shorter than 7 days for weekly premium policies, 10 days for monthly premium, and 31 days for all other premiums. In many states the model law has been amended to lengthen the grace period for weekly premium and monthly premium policies. In a cancellable policy, the grace period clause may be modified

---

[3] The model bill of NAIC specifies three years; most states require not more than two years.

[4] There is an argument that omission of the reference to fraudulent misstatement does not improve the clause since a contract obtained by fraud is void from its inception. But this is general contract law which does not seem to apply when the incontestable period commences in a health insurance policy.

[5] Nothing in the law specifically prevents the insurer from using the incontestable clause in an optionally renewable policy. Because that clause is more liberal than the time limit clause, it would seem that an insurer should have no trouble in getting incontestability approved. But when one insurer included an incontestable clause in its optionally renewable policy, the insurance department of one state refused to accept the filing on the ground that "it might confuse the insured."

so as to be subject to the right of the insurer to cancel; and in an optionally renewable policy, it may be modified to state that the grace period does not apply if 5 days (in some states as much as 30 days or more) prior to the due date, the insurer has notified the insured of its intention not to renew.

REINSTATEMENT. If the insurer accepts a premium for a lapsed policy, it is reinstated without any application for reinstatement. If a reinstatement application is required and a conditional receipt is given with the application, reinstatement is automatic if the application is not refused within 45 days from date of receipt of the application. A reinstated policy will cover only injuries suffered after the date of reinstatement, and only sickness that begins 10 days after the reinstatement date. A reinstatement premium shall be applied to a period for which the premium was not paid, but, except for policies that are noncancellable or guaranteed renewable, the reinstatement premium cannot be applied retroactively for a period of more than 60 days.[6]

NOTICE OF CLAIM. Written notice of a claim must be given within 20 days of the commencement of the loss or as soon thereafter as is reasonable. Notice to the insurer or its agent with information sufficient to identify the insured is sufficient. In case of loss of time (disability income) benefits payable for at least two years, notice of continuation of the disability is required every six months unless the insured is legally incompetent.

CLAIM FORMS. Claim forms must be supplied by the insurer to the insured within 15 days of receipt of notice of claim. If the claimant does not receive such forms, he will be deemed to have complied with the proof of loss provision if he submits written proof of the occurrence, character, and extent of the loss.

PROOF OF LOSS. The insured must submit proof of loss for loss of time benefits within 90 days of the termination of any period for which the insurer is liable and within 90 days of the date of occurrence of any other loss. If it is not reasonable to file proof of loss within 90 days, it must be filed as soon as possible but in no case later than one year, unless the insured is legally incompetent.

TIME OF PAYMENT OF CLAIMS. Claims for specific losses will be paid immediately on receipt of proof.[7] Loss of time claims will be paid at the intervals specified in the policy (usually weekly in industrial policies and monthly in others) but never less frequently than monthly.

PAYMENT OF CLAIMS. Death benefits will be paid to the named beneficiary, or to the estate of the insured if no beneficiary is named or if the

---

[6] Application of a retroactive premium to the entire past period is permitted in guaranteed renewable and noncancellable policies to allow the insurer to make up the special reserve for these policies required by the laws of most states.

[7] This provision is not construed to prevent the insurer from taking time to check on the validity of the claim.

beneficiary predeceases the insured. All other benefits are payable to the insured.[8] This provision has two optional paragraphs, either, both, or neither of which may be included, at the option of the insurer.

a) Up to $1,000 of any indemnity may be paid to any relative by blood or marriage, or to anyone else the insurer deems to have a valid claim if the beneficiary is the insured's estate, a minor, or someone legally incompetent to sign a release. This clause, often found in weekly premium life insurance policies, is commonly called a "facility of payment" clause, and is another of the variations to be found in the mandatory uniform provisions that should be checked in any policy analysis. The facility of payment clause could be useful in avoiding possible delay and expense in achieving an equitable distribution of insurance proceeds.

b) Medical expense indemnities may, at the option of the insured, be paid to any vendor of medical service or care.

PHYSICAL EXAMINATION AND AUTOPSY.   The insurer shall have the right and opportunity to examine the person of the insured while the claim is pending when and as often as may be reasonably required and to perform an autopsy where it is not forbidden by law. The right to examine the person of the claimant is important to help the insurer manage the moral hazard, and the insurer is likely to find it necessary to exercise this right. However, insurers seldom ask for an autopsy.

LEGAL ACTIONS.   No legal action to collect a claim shall be started sooner than 60 days or later than 3 years from the time proof of loss is required to be furnished. The purpose of a minimum time limit is to give the insurer adequate time to process the claim. The maximum time limit requirement is to allow the insurer to terminate its liability under the policy within a reasonable time, thereby reducing the size of the reserve needed for losses reported but not yet settled.

CHANGE OF BENEFICIARY.   Consent of the beneficiary is not necessary to change the policy unless the beneficiary has been named irrevocably. The reference to an irrevocable beneficiary may be omitted, and there need be no provision in a policy for an irrevocable beneficiary.

The Optional Provisions.   Any one, all, or none of the following provisions may be included in a policy but if the policy covers any subject contained in one of the optional provisions, then it must use the substance of the provision as set forth in the law. A similar provision which, in the opinion of the state insurance commissioner, is more favorable to the policyholder than the statutory provision may be used instead. Optional provisions entitled "Change of Occupation," "Misstatement of Age," and

---

[8] The insured does not have to be the person suffering the loss. An ownership form is possible in health insurance policies as in life insurance policies. If a person other than the subject of the insurance is the owner then the benefits go to the owner and not to the person on whom the insurance is written. The most common use of the ownership form is in key man health insurance to indemnify an employer for loss of the services of a key employee.

"Conformity with State Statutes" are the ones most commonly found in policies.

CHANGE OF OCCUPATION. If the insured changes his occupation to one more hazardous than that in which he was engaged when the policy was issued, or if he is injured or contracts sickness while performing the duties of a more hazardous occupation *for compensation,* benefits will be reduced to equal the amount that the premium he has paid would have purchased at the rate for the more hazardous occupation. If he changes to a less hazardous occupation, he may apply for a rate reduction. Note that the application of this clause could lead to a situation that would be ignored by the typical insured unless the clause is specifically called to his attention: A college instructor who is assigned an AAA classification might agree to paint his student's house as a way of earning extra money during the summer when classes are not in session. A painter is a Class B risk (quite a way down the scale, the Conference classifications running AAA, AA, A, B, and so on). If he is injured or disabled while painting the house, he automatically takes a Class B rating, which produces a substantially higher premium; therefore, his benefits would be substantially reduced.[9]

MISSTATEMENT OF AGE. If age was misstated in the application, the benefits paid will be those the premium would have purchased at the correct age. Note that while an understatement of age will *decrease* benefits, an overstatement will *increase* them.

The inclusion of the misstatement of age provision is both a liberalization and a restriction. If the misstatement of age clause were not contained in the policy, then a misstatement of age may be considered a material misrepresentation, and material misrepresentations can be a basis for the insurer to avoid the contract. The misstatement of age clause liberalizes the policy in that it does not allow the insurer to avoid the policy but instead allows only an adjustment of the level of the benefits to the premium paid. On the other hand, once the policy has passed the contestable period, misrepresentation of age could not be held a cause for denying or reducing a claim (unless the policy uses the optional phrase, "except for fraudulent misstatement" and fraud in the misstatement of age somehow can be proved).

The optional provisions do not include a misstatement of sex clause. Misstatement of sex can create problems in health insurance similar to those created in life insurance because sex is also an important variable in the underwriting and rating of health insurance (p. 208).

OTHER INSURANCE IN THIS INSURER. The insurer may use one of two provisions relating to other insurance with the same insurer. (*a*) If

---

[9] For example, in one company the amount of premium it takes to buy a $100 a month benefit under a 2-year, optionally renewable disability income policy with a 30-day waiting period issued to a Class AAA risk would buy only $62 of benefit for a Class B risk.

the insured has other insurance with this insurer aggregating more than a maximum benefit specified in the provision (amount specified is at the option of insurer), the excess shall be void, and the premium for the void portion refunded. (*b*) If the insured has more than one like policy with this insurer, he or his beneficiary may elect the policy under which to be paid; the others are void; and the premium for them must be refunded.

INSURANCE WITH OTHER INSURERS. The heading "Insurance with Other Insurers" contains two uniform provisions. One relates to benefits payable on a service or expense incurred basis, and the other relates to all other benefits such as, for example, disability income benefits and dismemberment benefits. In effect, both are the same. If duplicating coverage exists of which the insurer has not been notified, the liability of the insurer will be the pro rata proportion that the insurer's limits of liability bear to the total amount of insurance in force. Thus, for example, if an insured had two policies each providing a disability income benefit at $400 a month and one of the policies contained an other insurance clause, that policy would be liable for only $200 because its pro rata proportion to the total indemnity in force is one half. Premiums for benefits not payable are to be returned. Subject to the approval of the commissioner, the insurer may specify the nature of duplicating coverage. Unless otherwise specified, the provision will not be construed to cover group insurance, medical payments under an automobile insurance policy, coverage provided by a hospital or medical service organization, union welfare plans, employee or employer benefit organizations, third party coverage, or benefits required under compulsory statutes such as workmen's compensation.[10]

RELATION OF EARNINGS TO INSURANCE. If loss of time benefits under all policies in force on the insured at the time of claim exceed his income at that time or his average income for the past two years—whichever is higher—the liability of the insurer using this clause shall be for the proportionate amount of such benefits as the amount of the monthly earnings bears to the total amount of monthly benefits; but the reduction must not make the total benefits payable under all the policies less than $200 a month. Premiums paid during the two-year period for the portion not collectable will be returned. Assume that an insured has 2 policies, each containing this provision and each agreeing to pay $500 a month in benefits, or an aggregate of $1,000. Assume further that at the time of disability, the insured is earning only $500 a month and that during the 2-year period preceding disability, he averaged only $475 a month. Since he was earning more at the time of disability than his average during the

---

[10] It should be noted that this provision would be useless in a policy guaranteeing renewability because the only penalty the insurer can assess when notified of duplicating coverage is to terminate its own coverage, and guaranteed renewable and noncancellable policies once issued cannot be terminated or altered.

2 previous years, the prorating would be based on $500 a month, which is only half of his aggregate coverage; therefore, each policy would pay only $250 a month—half of his current earnings.[11]

The provision also permits specifying the nature of "other coverages" and declares that in the absence of such specification, the provision shall not be construed as including any coverage provided pursuant to any compulsory benefit statute, including workmen's compensation or employer's liability statutes, or benefits provided by union welfare plans or by employee or employer benefit organizations. Further, it is specified that the provision can be used only in policies guaranteeing renewability to at least age 50 or for 5 years if issued after age 44.

UNPAID PREMIUMS. Premiums unpaid at the time of claim may be deducted from the claim payment.

CANCELLATION. The insurer may cancel on five days' notice[12] and refund the unearned premium pro rata. After the initial term, the insured can cancel, effective on receipt of his notice by the insurer, and the insurer will refund the unearned premiums on a short-rate basis.[13] Cancellation is without prejudice to claims arising prior to the cancellation.

CONFORMITY WITH STATE STATUTE. Any provision of the policy that, on the effective date of the policy, is in conflict with the statutes of the state in which the insured resides at the time of issue is automatically amended to meet the minimum requirements of that state. The purpose of this provision is to eliminate the expense of having to write special forms in a few states having atypical requirements.

ILLEGAL OCCUPATION. Liability is denied if the loss was incurred while the insured was committing or attempting to commit a felony or while he was engaging in an illegal occupation, if these actions were a contributing cause of the loss.

INTOXICANTS AND NARCOTICS. Liability is denied if any loss is a result of the use of intoxicants or drugs unless administered on the advice of a physician.

Other Requirements of the Uniform Provisions Act. In addition to the mandatory and optional provisions, the model uniform provisions law sets up certain other requirements for health policies.

1. The entire monetary and other considerations must be expressed in the policy.

2. Effective and termination dates must be expressed.

---

[11] How the framers of the model bill could parlay the explanation of this provision, as they did, into a 500-word statement containing only four sentences, one of which is 250 words long, is a feat that has this author baffled.

[12] Five days are specified in the model law. A number of states have passed legislation requiring a longer period of notification. The most liberal notice is required by North Carolina where the length of the period of notice increases from 30 days the first year to 2 years after the policy has been in force for 8 years.

[13] The short rate provides a refund less than that produced on a pro rata basis.

3. The policy may cover only one person, except that it may be amended to include a spouse and dependent children under 19.[14]

4. The type used in the policy must be at least 10 point (2 points larger than the type usually used in newspapers), and no undue prominence may be given to any portion of the text, except that heads may be larger.

5. Exceptions and reductions that apply to the policy in general must be grouped under a descriptive head; however, those exceptions applying only to a particular provision may be carried in the section dealing with that provision.

6. The only items that can be made a part of a policy by reference rather than by being printed in the policy are rates, classes of risks, and a short-rate table.

7. A policy in violation of the act shall be construed as though it conformed to the act.

8. No policy provision can restrict or modify the act.

9. Statements in the application shall be binding only if a copy of the application is attached to and made a part of the policy; and if the insured requests a copy of any reinstatement application and does not receive it in 15 days, no statements on the reinstatement application shall bind the insured.

10. Only the applicant can alter a statement on the application.

11. False statements on the application may bar recovery only if the statements are material to the risk.

12. Supplying claim forms, acknowledging receipt of notice of a claim, and investigation of a claim shall not constitute a waiver of defense against the claim.

13. The policy will remain in force for any part of a policy term that extends beyond the age limit, and acceptance of a new premium after that term keeps the policy in force, subject to any cancellation provisions in the policy.

14. If misstatement of age leads the insurer to accept a premium beyond the age limit, its only liability is for return of the premium.

15. The act does not apply to workmen's compensation insurance; reinsurance; blanket or group insurance; and riders covering permanent and total disability issued with life insurance or annuity contracts.

The insurer may, with the approval of the commissioner, omit or modify any provision inapplicable or inconsistent with the coverage provided in the policy.

---

[14] This provision is usually interpreted to mean that the child must be under 19 at the time of issue but that the coverage can extend to a later age. Many medical expense forms will cover a child to age 21, 22, or even 23, presumably on the theory that the child is probably still in school during those ages.

2. COVERAGE PROVISIONS: LOSS OF INCOME

Beyond the requirements of the uniform provisions law, an insurer is free to develop its own individual policy provisions and to present them in the policy in any order it chooses. Most policy draftsmen will place the statutory provisions at the end of the policy, preceding them with the insuring agreements, benefit clauses, and policy exclusions.

Discussion of coverage provisions can be handled more effectively by considering loss of income covers and health expense covers separately. Particular provisions common to both types of covers will be discussed only in connection with loss of income coverage in order to avoid repetition.

Only loss of income policies that are more or less typical of the current guaranteed renewable or noncancellable forms will be discussed.[15] Bear in mind that, as stated, the wording and sequence of clauses in policies may vary widely, but the overall effect of the provisions of any policy will be approximately the same.

Consideration, Policy Term, Date of Issue.   Consideration, policy term, and date of issue may be covered under one heading in the policy or they might be set forth in the policy schedule, under definitions or elsewhere. If they are grouped under one heading they might read as follows:

This policy is issued in consideration of the statements and agreements made in the application, a copy of which is attached hereto and made a part hereof, and of the payment of the Premium stated in the Policy Schedule.

The first Term of the Policy begins on the Date of Issue and ends on the first Renewal Date, except as it may be continued in force by reason of the Grace Period.

All such terms begin and end at 12 noon, Standard Time, at the place of residence of the Policy owner (or "Insured").

This Policy may be renewed, subject to the Renewal Provisions set forth herein, by the timely payment of premiums in advance to the Company or its authorized representative.

In the policy from which these provisions are quoted, the Date of Issue and First Renewal Date are set forth in the Policy Schedule.

Note that in this contract, as in many life insurance contracts, the stated consideration is the application and the payment of the premiums. This means that the only obligations binding on the insured to create the contract are to complete and sign the application which becomes a part of the policy and to pay the initial premium. The insured need continue to pay the premiums only as long as he wishes to keep the policy in force. Although the policy says that the application is part of the consideration, the consideration technically is the payment of the initial premium for that is

---

[15] The use of the modifying words "more or less" is in recognition of the difficulty in typifying any health insurance policy.

the value given up by the insured in exchange for the insurer's promises contained in the contract.

THE APPLICATION. The application generally asks for the usual personal information for purposes of identification; it also asks for a description of the type of plan for which the application is made and the name of the beneficiary, if any, of the insurance. Moreover, the application searches for information about other insurance, declined applications, and the health and accident history of the applicant. For use in the underwriting of loss of time benefits, the application sometimes asks about the applicant's monthly earnings.

The applicant is requested to sign the application, and it is on the basis of these questions that the policy is issued. He certifies that he has read the answers and that they are correct[16] and agrees that recovery shall be barred if misstatements material to the risk are made with intent to deceive.[17]

The application usually states that the insurance will not take effect until there has been settlement for the premium and the policy has been issued as applied for. As with life insurance contracts, the policy generally goes into force on the date of the application if the first premium is paid with the application and the insured is acceptable; otherwise, it does not go into force until the first premium is paid on delivery of the policy while the insured is in good health. If the settlement is partial, the policy will remain in force for a pro rata fraction of the original period.

Attached to the application is an authorization to any physician to give medical information concerning the applicant to the company or its representative. Whether there will be medical examinations for guaranteed renewable and noncancellable policies depends upon factors such as the type of plan, the amount of the insurance, and the age of the applicant.

Some few policies—notably those providing short-term accident and other limited coverage—do not always make the application part of the policy and, therefore, do not attach a copy. These are usually policies on which there is no underwriting in the sense of selection. As noted under the Uniform Provisions, statements in the application cannot be used in defense of a claim if the application is not attached to the policy.

Insuring Agreements. The insuring agreements will indicate broadly what the insurer promises to do for the insured. An insuring agreement might read as follows:

---

[16] In view of the importance of the statements on the application, the applicant himself should fill it out. As a practical matter, however, since the applicant is unacquainted with the form, and the form must be filled in so it can be photostated, it is universally the practice for the agent to ask the applicant for the answers and then write them on the form himself. Although some applicants do, no applicant ever should sign the application without reading the questions and the answers filled in by the agent.

[17] It is remarkable what a poor memory many applicants have when it comes to health history; and it is interesting how many applicants who obtained the policy by fraudulent concealment of details of poor health history will cry fraud at the insurer when a claim is denied.

The company will pay for disability of the Insured commencing while this policy is in force and resulting from accidental bodily injuries sustained while this policy is in force and not contributed to by any other cause (hereinafter called "such injuries") or from sickness, the cause of which is contracted while this policy is in force (hereinafter called "such sickness"), subject to all the provisions and conditions hereof.

Three specific items in this illustrative clause require elaboration: accidental bodily injury, independence of all other causes, and preexisting conditions.

ACCIDENTAL BODILY INJURY.   Under the foregoing insuring agreement, coverage is offered for accidental bodily injury. It once was the custom (and still is, in some limited policies not subjected to careful underwriting at the time of issue) to specify that injury must be caused by accidental means.

The distinction between accidental bodily injury and injury by accidental means is subject to widespread misunderstanding, so much so that there is a tendency for courts to ignore the difference between the two terms. A number of courts, however, still uphold the distinction. Injury caused by accidental means refers to injuries that result from an act that is unforeseen, unexpected, or unusual. An injury that is itself unexpected but nevertheless follows from ordinary means, voluntarily employed, in a way that is not unusual or unexpected, cannot be the result of accidental means. For example, a male student decides to carry a coed's trunk up to the fourth floor of the sorority house as a favor to her. In the process, he strains his back. While he has suffered an accidental bodily injury, he has not suffered an injury from accidental means. A strained back is a probable consequence of carrying a heavy object up four flights of stairs (or one flight, for that matter). Legally, a prudent man is capable of anticipating the possible consequences of any voluntary action he undertakes. However, if in carrying the trunk up the stairs the student trips over a stack of IBM cards left lying on the next to last step of the third flight and falls with the trunk coming down on him breaking a rib, he has suffered an injury by accidental means. Tripping over a stack of IBM cards is not a probable consequence of carrying a trunk up a flight of stairs or anywhere else except perhaps through a card-carrying IBM machine.

If it appears that the distinction is a fine one, it should be remembered that the courts have also found it so. Accidental means is being used less and less.[18] The principal reasons that accidental means is disappearing

---

[18] However, it is still commonly, though not universally, used in accidental death benefit riders written with life insurance. Formerly, some insuring clauses in health policies specified that the injury must be a result of "external and violent" means, sometimes adding, "leaving visible wounds or contusions." Although now virtually extinct in health contracts, this wording also is still common in accidental death benefit riders used with life insurance policies. Court interpretation of the term "violent," however, is liberal. It seems that the size of the force operating on the body is unimportant. The court considers all force violent, including the bite of a tiny insect. The "visible wound or contusion" clause nevertheless is

from the accident policy are competition and the problems that the insurers have with the courts in trying to enforce the provision. For an example, when the insured died as a result of a self-administered, non-suicidal overdose of narcotics, the insurer denied benefits under the accidental means provisions. The Pennsylvania Supreme Court reversed the lower court's decision in favor of the insurer, thus abandoning what it called an artificial distinction between accidental means and accidental results. The court believed it was proper for an insurer to include a contractual limitation in its policy to avoid claims such as this one but insisted that any such limitation be spelled out in precise language.[19]

In an action to collect benefits under an accident policy, the insured, driving his car at night on a mountain road in Colorado, failed to make a curve and was killed. The evidence clearly showed that the road was highly dangerous, that the insured had previously driven the road twice (though not at night) and was familiar with the dangers; that he was driving at a high and dangerous rate of speed and shortly prior to the fatal accident had been given a traffic violation ticket for speeding; and that a passenger in his car had complained about the way the insured was driving. The policy covered death by accidental means. The insurance company disclaimed liability and defended this action on the ground that the insured's death was not by accidental means, because the deceased was speeding over a relatively unknown, dangerous road at night and should have foreseen the consequences of his intentional acts—i.e., that the decedent's death was not unusual, unexpected, or beyond anticipation, and that it was the inevitable result of his own deliberate acts and therefore not by accidental means.

The trial court held for the plaintiff, and the Supreme Court said that it was cognizant of a distinct split of authority among the various appellate courts throughout the country. It recognized that many courts have supported the insurer's contention that when a policy specifies accidental means the immediate or proximate cause of the death must be accidental, and if death results as the natural and probable consequences of the voluntary acts of the insured, death does not occur by accidental means. Also it observed that this was the general view prior to 1934 and was followed by the United States Supreme Court.[20] But it pointed out that Justice Cardoza dissented from the majority opinion, and in the 30 years since that dissent, an increasing number of courts of last resort have followed Cardoza's rationale.

---

strictly interpreted by the court. For the beneficiary to collect under an accidental death benefit rider so hedged, the insured must have been in an accident sufficiently violent to have abrasions, bruises, or cuts on his corpse. An exception is made in the case of accidental drowning or of internal injury revealed by autopsy.

[19] *Beckham* v. *Travelers Insurance Co.,* 225 A (2d) 532 (Pa. 1967). "None are more hopelessly enslaved than those who falsely believe they are free" (Goethe).

[20] *Landress* v. *Phoenix Mutual Life,* 291 V.S. 491, 54 Sup. Ct. 461, 78 L.Ed. 934, 90 H.L.R. 1382.

In the present case the court held that the average man when buying an accident policy draws no distinction between accidental means and accident and gives no consideration to it. He has no comprehension of a strict and technical interpretation. Therefore, the use of the term accidental means in the policy here involved was synonymous with accident.[21]

INDEPENDENCE OF ALL OTHER CAUSES.   Note the phrase in the insuring clause, "not contributed to by any other cause." If a student, while crossing a bicycle towpath on the campus, suffers a dizzy spell and falls in front of an oncoming rider and has a rib broken in the ensuing collision, the accidental bodily injury has not been without contribution of any other cause. For another example, consider the case of an automobile driver who has a heart attack, crashes into a tree, and suffers multiple fractures and contusions. His injuries have not been independent of other causes.[22]

The purpose of the "not contributed to by any other cause" provision in accident coverage is to allow the insurer to avoid having to pay a claim under an accident policy for a loss due largely to a health condition. However, in cases where a disease following an accident causes death or disability, courts allow recovery under an accident policy if it can be shown that the injury set in motion the chain of circumstances resulting in the loss, regardless of a contributing or concurrent disease. For instance, if a young man suffers pneumonia following an automobile accident in which he was involved, the contract probably will be held to cover for the resulting disability loss if it can be shown that the disease is the direct result of the accident. The recovery would be based on the doctrine of proximate cause, which can be defined as follows:

> In the event of the concurrence of several causes, the loss will be deemed to have been caused by the dominating peril so long as there exists an unbroken chain of cause and effect between the peril and the loss, whether or not the peril is active at the consummation of the loss. Proximate cause means the immediate, efficient cause *without which* the results could not or would not have happened.

In an action to collect under an accidental death policy, the undisputed evidence reflects that the insured met death by drowning; that for several years the insured had been subject to epileptic seizures; that at the time of his death he was working near the edge of a ditch which contained about four feet of water and that he suffered an epileptic seizure which

---

[21] *Scott* v. *New Empire Insurance Co.,* 400 P. (2d) 953 (1965) N. Mex. Sup. Ct. "Happy the man who early learns the wide chasm that lies between his wishes and his powers" (Goethe).

[22] The burden of proof that there was a contributing cause is on the insurer. In one case, a trial court directed a verdict in favor of the insurer when evidence indicated that before the insured fell into the ditch, he dropped his shovel, making no attempt to break his fall. An autopsy disclosed a heart attack recent enough to have occurred at the time of the fall.

caused him to fall into the water-filled ditch and drown. The question presented is whether for such death his beneficiaries are entitled to payment, since the insurance company pleaded the exclusionary language that the death was "caused or contributed to, directly or indirectly, wholly or partially by disease, or by bodily or mental infirmity." When the plaintiffs established that the insured met his death by drowning then the burden shifted to the insurance company to establish that the death was caused proximately by "disease or by bodily or mental infirmity." The trial court held for the insurance company and the plaintiff appealed. The Arkansas Supreme Court said that it was a question of fact for the jury as to whether the infirmity was the proximate cause of the accident, and that the trial court had ample evidence to sustain the finding against the plaintiff.[23]

PREEXISTING CONDITIONS. Note that in the sample insuring clause quoted a few pages earlier, the policy does not cover preexisting conditions: the injury must occur and the sickness must commence while the policy is in force.[24]

Injury is fairly commonly defined as injury occurring after the issue date of the policy. It is possible to impose a probationary period, that is a period of time after the issue date during which no benefits will be paid. The wording would be to the effect, ". . . injury occurring after the policy has been in effect for _____ days (or weeks)." Because, as noted, the determination of injury is on a reasonably objective basis, probationary periods for injury are not common. However, probationary periods for sickness are usual in disability income policies. They may be general or they may be imposed for only specified types of sickness. Specific types of sickness on which probationary periods are sometimes posed are "female disorders," "disorders of the urogenital tract," and so forth. In evaluating policies, it is important to look for probationary periods.[25]

Several definitions of sickness are to be found: "first occurring," "first commencing," "beginning while this policy is in force," "first manifesting itself after the effective date" are examples. All except the last one preclude any sickness that can be traced to a preexisting condition. Suppose an insured applies for a disability income policy without any idea that he is suffering from what is actually a developing cancer. Later, after the policy is issued, he becomes disabled as a result of cancer. Technically, he might not have a legitimate claim for disability income benefits. However, as a matter of claim administration, many companies would honor

---

23 *Jackson* et al. v. *Southland Life Insurance Co.,* 393 S.W. (2d) 233 (1965) Sup. Ct. Ark.

24 The policy specifies that it is effective from 12:01 A.M. Standard Time on the policy date at the place of residence of the insured.

25 The probationary period might be classed as a form of postissue underwriting, designed primarily to reduce antiselection. The applicant may have contracted a sickness or disorder and may be applying for the policy because he knows the sickness or disorder is developing. Insurers that do not use a probationary period for sickness rely on careful underwriting to detect such situations.

such a claim if there is clear evidence that there had been no medical diagnosis of the condition prior to the date of the application and no symptoms recognizable to a layman. The "first manifesting" provision recognizes this type of situation, and means in effect that if there was no diagnosis of a condition prior to the date of application and no symptoms recognizable to a layman, the claim will be honored even though it can be proved beyond doubt by medical testimony that the disorder or disease had its actual origin prior to the effective date of the policy.

Definition. Various terms may be defined in the particular provisions as they appear in the policy. However, in recent years the trend has been to develop a separate section of the policy and call it Definitions. The terms usually defined in this section are disability, physician, elimination period, recurrent disabilities, and policy owner.

TOTAL DISABILITY. Various restrictive definitions of total disability may be found in disability income policies: bed confined, house confined, total loss of business time, any occupation, own occupation, and presumptive disability.

Bed Confined. For the insured to be considered totally disabled under the bed confined restriction, he must be literally confined to bed. This definition was once used in industrial health insurance policies (i.e., policies written on a weekly premium basis, with the agents collecting the premiums at the home of the insured).[26] Because of the highly restrictive nature of the bed confining definition of disability, the courts will not uphold it. Therefore it is rarely, if ever, included in policies today. It does not appear to make much sense anyway.

House Confined. Under a house confinement restriction, the insured must be "continuously confined within doors" to qualify for benefits. Usually trips to a physician's office, clinic, or hospital on orders of the physician are excepted from the restriction. Because courts have interpreted the house confined restriction liberally, it is now rarely used. It might be used in policies providing for long-term (such as lifetime) benefits following a period of disability defined in terms of occupational capability. Thus, a policy might provide that the insured will be considered totally disabled for the first 60 months if he is unable to perform the duties of any occupation and for life thereafter if house confined. The house confined definition might also be included in "female riders" attached to disability income policies (particularly noncancellable or guaranteed renewable ones) issued to women. In these riders, it may be provided that if the insured (a female) is married or not regularly employed outside her home at the time of the occurrence of disability, total disability shall be defined as house confinement.[27]

---

[26] These policies are misnamed. See Chapter 11 for discussion of industrial life insurance.

[27] Married women who work are subject to an extra moral hazard: They may not be dependent on their earnings for a living; therefore, they may decide eventually to stop working but to give disability as a reason in order to collect benefits for as long as the benefit period

Total Loss of Business Time. The total loss of business time definition means literally that the insured must be unable to perform the duties of any occupation for wages, compensation, or profit. This definition is not widely used. When it is used, it may be combined with the phrase, "Inability to perform the duties of his own occupation"—that is, "Inability to perform the duties of his own occupation and experiences total loss of business time."

Inability to Perform the Duties of Any Occupation. Literally, the inability to perform the duties of any occupation means that the insured cannot claim total disability if he can sell pencils on a street corner. However, no court will interpret this definition that literally; rather it will interpret it to mean inability to perform the duties of any occupation for which the insured is reasonably suited by education, training, or experience.[28] Therefore, most insurers word the clause in the way the court would interpret it. Variant wordings are found, some of which will include phraseology that, in effect, makes the "any occupation" one that pays within the same range as the insured's own occupation or enables him to maintain approximately the same economic status as before. This type of definition might be called an economic status definition. Also to be found, but rarely, is "any occupation for which he is reasonably suited . . . or can become suited." This wording is designed to force rehabilitation if rehabilitation is possible.

Inability to Perform Each and Every Duty of His Own Occupation. The own occupation definition is the most liberal definition in use today. Interestingly, the own occupation definition was in widespread use early in the history of disability income insurance. The more restrictive wordings developed to curb the abuses of the own occupation definition. "Any occupation" was largely a depression development; and a return to own occupation began in earnest in 1950. Insurers reinstated the own occupation definition on a limited basis, defining total disability as inability to perform the duties of one's own occupation for the first 12 months only and thereafter as inability to perform the duties of any occupation. Under competitive pressure, the length of time that own occupation runs has extended to two, three, and now five years—five years being the time limit

---

in the policy runs. Anyone, female or male, whose place of business is not outside his home is a difficult risk to underwrite. If he can conduct his business while at home, how is it possible to learn objectively whether or not he is working while claiming to be disabled?

[28] However, the insured would seem to do better to select a policy with wording that he does not have to go to court to have interpreted. Two philosophies of claim adjustment are recognizable: (1) "Inasmuch as a court would interpret (any given provision) more liberally than it is worded in the policy, we'll settle on the basis of the more liberal wording." (2) "If we are taken to court, the court will interpret the provision more liberally than it is worded; but very few claimants, proportionately, go to court; therefore, we'll try to make settlement on the basis of the restrictive wording and accede to the more liberal interpretation only if the insured starts litigation."

used in policies issued by what might be termed "better insurers."[29] Some companies are using more than five years for the own occupation period; one, at least, uses own occupation for the duration of the disability even if the benefit period runs to age 65. Whether or not there will be a general extension of the own occupation period beyond five years is dependent on the claim experience under the five-year forms. (This experience at least in part is a function of economic conditions; a period of depression might flood own occupation insurers with claims, so much so that insurers will again retreat to any occupation as the total disability definition).[30]

A qualification of the own occupation definition that was introduced about 1960 is "inability to perform own occupation and does not perform any occupation." Note that this wording does not say the insured must be unable to perform another occupation but only that he is not allowed to perform one and still be considered totally disabled. The wording was devised to take care of a situation, for example, in which a surgeon because of a skin disease is unable to perform an operation but can take a job as chief of the hospital staff. The administrative job while perhaps not netting him as much compensation as did surgery, nets an attractive income and one that no court would hold greatly lowers his economic status. He applies for disability income under an own occupation definition. The insurer denies the claim on the ground that he is performing his own occupation, that of a physician. He contends that his occupation is that of a surgeon, and that since he cannot perform surgery he is disabled under the terms of an own occupation definition. The court upholds his claim.

Although the "perform no occupation" restriction appears to be a sound underwriting safeguard, it is rarely found because it is difficult to sell in competition with an unrestricted own occupation clause.

Presumptive Disability. Policies may provide for presumptive disability, worded, for example, as follows:

Specified Disabilities—The entire and irrecoverable loss of the sight of both eyes, or the use of both hands, or both feet, or of one hand and one foot, will be considered as Total Disability for as long as such entire loss may continue.[31]

Note that in the provision quoted, the loss referred to is "loss of use." Also to be found is a presumptive disability provision that specifies "loss

---

[29] Because better is a subjective adjective, this observation about what better insurers do might be considered questionable; so it is carefully noted for the record that there are insurers who can make a strong case for being in the better classification who do not use a period as long as five years.

[30] It is difficult to determine whether such liberalizations (and the high benefit limits being allowed today) are the result of more knowledgeable underwriting or of the coming of age of a generation of underwriters who have forgotten the traumatic loss experiences of the Great Depression.

[31] The wording implies that "irrecoverable loss" can be recovered; however, the contradiction is not absurd. Claim files include cases of claimants who went on permanent disability "temporarily." Loss of use could be diagnosed as irrecoverable and yet recovery be effected.

of," with loss of defined as severance at or through the wrist or ankle joint. Obviously, this is a more stringent definition. It would not cover loss of use by reason of paralysis, severance of nerves or tendons, and so forth.

Physician. Definitions of total disability always include the qualifying provision that the insured must be under the "regular care and attendance of a physician other than the insured." However, in cases of static disabilities, the requirement is usually not enforced. The definition of physician is usually "a legally qualified physician or surgeon." Thus, the qualifications of a physician depend on the laws of the state in which he is licensed. Naturopaths, chiropractors, osteopaths, and so forth qualify if the law in the states where they were licensed class them as physicians. Some few policies define a physician as one holding the degree of doctor of medicine, a definition that is more restrictive, of course.

Elimination Period. The elimination period, also called waiting period, is defined as the number of days at the beginning of a continuous period of disability for which the monthly income is not payable.[32] Elimination periods reduce claims frequency and lower administrative costs. Therefore, the premium can be lowered if an elimination period is written into the policy. The longer the elimination period, the lower will be the premium. The savings in premiums, however, increase at a diminishing rate as the waiting period increases. The drop in premiums between a 30- and 60-day waiting period, for instance, will be less than the drop between first day coverage and a 30-day elimination period. Common elimination periods are 30, 60, and 90 days, although longer or shorter waiting periods are available.[33]

Recurrent Disability. Policies frequently make provisions for recurrent disabilities. One such provision is as follows:

If following a period of disability for which indemnity is payable under this policy, the Insured shall resume his regular occupation and perform all the important duties thereof for a continuous period of six months or more, any subsequent disability commencing while this policy is in force and resulting from or contributed to by the same cause or causes shall be considered a new period of disability and indemnified as sickness, but if said period during which the In-

---

[32] An elimination or waiting period is to be distinguished from a probationary period, the latter being a period of time from issue date of the policy during which no benefits at all are payable (or some type or types of benefits are not payable). A probationary period runs only once: from issue date. A waiting or elimination period (which corresponds to a deductible in reimbursement covers) applies at the beginning of every separate disability.

[33] Carefully selected elimination periods generally are desirable because it is not economical to purchase insurance to cover losses that can be paid out of the pocket without distress. It may be nice to receive a claim check for a few days of disability, but except in rare instances it costs more in premium money to get the benefit than the benefit is worth. Everyone knows someone who has "made money" on his insurance coverage, but such a person is an exception. If he were not, the insurance business could not survive. Insurance should not be viewed as a profit-making venture for the insured.

sured resumes his regular occupation shall be less than six months, such subsequent disability shall be deemed a continuation of the preceding disability, and the Company's liability for the entire period, including such preceding disability or disabilities, shall be subject to the applicable Maximum Indemnity Period.

Six months is the most commonly required interval in individual disability income policies; but longer and shorter periods are found. After each recurrence period, the elimination period is again imposed and the maximum benefit period is again opened. If the recurrent period has not expired, another period of disability from the same cause is considered a continuation of the old period, and the elimination period is not again imposed. Benefits begin on the first day of the recurrence, but the period for which disability benefits have been received counts toward the maximum benefit period.

Assume a two-year benefit maximum. The insured is disabled for a year, goes back to work for five months (under a six-month definition), and suffers a recurrence. Benefits for the recurrence begin with the first day, but he now has only one year of benefits left. On the other hand, if he has been disabled a year and works seven months before a recurrence, the waiting period is again imposed, but he has a new benefit period of two years. If, however, the benefit period is to age 65, a recurrence does not adversely affect the benefit period. For example, the insured is disabled for one year and recovers. If he has a recurrence he still has benefits to age 65 even though the recurrence is within the recurrence period. On the other hand, by being within the recurrence period, he escapes reimposition of the elimination period. Therefore, if the benefit period is a fixed number of years as contrasted to benefits to a stated age (usually 65), the shorter the recurrence period, the more advantageous for the insured because it makes it possible for him to establish a new benefit period sooner. If the benefits are to a stated age, establishment of a new benefit period means nothing; so the longer the recurrence period, the more advantageous because it reduces the chance of a reapplication of the elimination period.

A difference in the wording of the recurrent disability provision will be found among disability income policies. One might read as follows:

. . . unless . . . there is an interval between the two periods of disability during which the Insured engages in a gainful occupation and performs all the duties of such occupation on a full-time basis for a period of at least six consecutive months. . . .

The provision quoted above specifies return to "a gainful occupation." The provision quoted earlier refers to a return to "his own" occupation. The latter is more restrictive. A man might return to *some* occupation full time (and thus break the recurrence period, should that be desirable) without being able to return to *his own* occupation. Note that whereas own occupation is *more liberal* in defining disability, it is *more restrictive* when defining the condition that breaks the recurrence period.

Policy Owner. Some companies issue the disability income policy in an ownership form. An ownership form permits someone other than the subject of the insurance to own the policy.[34] In such forms, the subject of the insurance is referred to as the insured and the owner as the policy owner, the latter then being defined in some such terms as:

Policy owner means that person so designated in the Policy Schedule. The Policy owner may exercise every right and privilege conferred upon him by this Policy or agree with the Company to any change or amendment of this Policy unless otherwise provided by amendment hereto.

Benefit Provisions. A disability income policy will usually (but not necessarily) have a heading, "Benefit Provisions." Whether or not the heading is used, the following group of provisions will be found in the policy.

MONTHLY BENEFIT FOR TOTAL DISABILITY. If a policy covers accident (injury) only, or accident and sickness, both of them for identical benefit durations, only one monthly benefit provision will be found in the policy. If the policy covers both accident and sickness but allows the insured to select different maximum benefit durations for each cause of disability, it will use two different provisions. Wording of a provision covering both accident and sickness might be as follows:

If the Covered Person (or "Insured") shall suffer a Total Disability, the Company will pay either the Monthly Accident Benefit or the Monthly Sickness Benefit, but not both concurrently, beginning on the day of disability specified in the Policy Schedule but not exceeding the time specified for any one such disability in the schedule of Maximum Benefit Periods. One thirtieth of the Monthly Benefits for either Accident or Sickness will be paid for each day of any period of disability of less than one month's duration.

This provision may also state the age, most commonly 65, at which payment of benefits will cease and may also limit the maximum benefit duration for benefits starting at very late ages.[35]

WAIVER OF PREMIUM. A provision for waiver of premium in event of total disability is not universal in disability income policies; but when it is offered, it is nearly always a part of the policy contract, with the premium included in the premium rate for the policy rather than a rider at an extra premium.

---

[34] Third party ownership of disability insurance policies including accidental death benefits can offer an estate tax advantage. But in general, third party ownership has fewer advantages in health insurance than in life insurance where cash values are involved and taxation often turns on the matter of ownership. Cash values in disability income insurance are extremely rare at this stage of its development. However, the ownership form finds some use in the area of the business applications of health insurance. Cf. Chapters 20 and 21.

[35] Benefit durations longer than to age 65 are rare in any form of disability income coverage and nearly nonexistent in noncancellable and guaranteed renewable policies. In policies terminating benefits at 65, the duration of benefits beginning after age 64 is usually limited to one or two years as a loss control device to reduce the temptation to use a faked disability or to malinger to produce a retirement income from a disability income policy.

Three variations are common in waiver of premium provisions in disability income policies. (1) Variation in the number of days of disability that must have passed before the waiver begins. The most common waiting period is 90 days but other waiting periods from as short as 60 days to as long as 365 are to be found. (2) Variation as to retroactive status. While waiver of premiums falling due after the end of the waiting period is more common, retroactive waiting periods are to be found. A retroactive provision states that in event of disability not only will premiums falling due after the waiting period be waived but also any premiums paid during the waiting period will be refunded.[36] (3) Variation as to duration of waiver. Two provisions are found. (*a*) A provision that the premium will be waived during the benefit period. Thus if the policy has, say, a two-year benefit maximum, the premium will be waived during the first two years of disability only. If disability continues beyond two years, not only will benefits cease but also coverage will cease unless premiums are resumed even if the disability is continuing. (*b*) Waiver for the duration of the disability. Illustrating again with a two-year benefit policy, if the disability continues beyond two years, benefits cease but the policy remains in force without premium payment as to other benefits in the policy and as to new disabilities (including a recurrence of the old disability after the recurrence period).

OTHER BENEFIT PROVISIONS. A disability income policy containing only the benefit provisions discussed above is known in the business as a stripped or stripped down policy. It may be said to provide basic protection against loss of income by reason of disability. However, there are a number of other benefit provisions that can be added to a disability income policy. In the past, it has been more common to include these other benefits than it is today. Many insurers who offer stripped policies will make many of these other benefits available by rider at an additional premium charge.[37]

Accidental Death and Dismemberment. Accidental death and dismemberment is one of the most frequent other benefits included in a disability income policy; and virtually every company confining its policy to the basic benefits will offer AD & D as a rider. Two terms used in connection with AD & D need defining. (1) Capital sum, which is defined[38]

---

[36] Without the retroactive feature, a disability of as long as 364 days could occur without the waiver being of any actual benefit to the policy owner: Assume an annual premium is paid on a due date and disability occurs the next day. If the waiver of premium is only for premiums falling due after the waiting period, no premium will fall due for 364 days, and no benefits will be derived from the provision if recovery occurs within that time.

[37] It is extremely difficult to make generalizations such as these since there are nearly 1,100 insurance companies writing health insurance policies, and each has more than one policy form. Positive statements concerning "many" and "more" could be made only after a tabulation of the provisions of every policy form on the market, a task neither this author nor anyone he knows has undertaken. Such a tabulation would be futile anyway. Individual insurers issue new forms and revise old ones so frequently that a detailed tabulation would be out of date before it could be recorded, much less published.

[38] By the Committee on Health Insurance Terminology.

as "the maximum amount payable in one sum in event of accidental dismemberment. When a contract provides benefits for kinds of dismemberment, each benefit is an amount equal to, or a fraction of, the capital sum." (2) Principal sum, which is defined[39] as "the amount payable in one sum in event of accidental death and, in some cases accidental dismemberment. When a contract provides benefits for both accidental death and accidental dismemberment, each dismemberment is an amount equal to the principal sum or some fraction thereof." As it will be noticed, there is some overlap in these definitions, and in the usage within the business, capital sum and principal sum tend to be used interchangeably. In this text accidental dismemberment benefits will be referred to as the capital sum and accidental death benefits as the principal sum.

Accidental death benefits alone are sometimes offered, but dismemberment benefits alone are infrequently offered.[40] Accidental death itself is an uncomplicated benefit. A typical provision might read:

If Injury as defined in the Policy shall result directly and independently of all other causes within 90 days from the date of accident in the death of the Insured, the Company will, in addition to all other benefits payable under the Policy, pay $——.

Accidental death benefits are usually sold in units of $1,000. When they are offered by rider, the number of units purchased is left up to the insured, with the insurer setting a maximum amount that will be issued on any one insured. However, when the accidental death benefit is a policy provision as opposed to a rider, the amount for that particular benefit is not subject to choice by the individual, but is tied in with the amount of disability income benefit, say $2,500 per $100 a month of disability benefit up to a maximum of, say, $10,000.

When dismemberment coverage is combined with accidental death coverage, the clause might read:

If Injury as defined in the Policy shall result directly and independently of all other causes within 90 days from the date of accident in any of the losses set forth below, the Company will, in addition to any other benefits payable under the Policy, pay:

For loss of

Life . . . . the Principal Sum
Both hands, both feet, or the sight of both eyes
. . . . the Principal Sum[41]

---

39 *Ibid.*

40 This is another of those statements that needs to be qualified with the notation that the author has never made a tabulation of all of the myriad of policies that are offered (nor does he know of any such tabulation) to prove this statement to be true. Therefore, let the statement be qualified by "among the policies that have come to the author's attention. . . ."

41 Sic. The term "principal sum" rather than "capital sum" is used in the policy quoted here, despite the differentiation between these terms as discussed in this text.

Either hand or either foot or the sight of either eye
.... One half the Principal Sum
Except that only one amount, the largest, shall be payable for injuries as a result of any one accident.
Loss with regard to hands and feet shall mean actual severance through or above the wrist or ankle joints. Loss with regard to eyes shall mean complete and irrecoverable loss of entire sight.

If the amount of the capital and principal sum is fixed and not subject to choice by the insured, the benefits may be stated in dollar amounts rather than as a whole or a fraction of the sum.[42]

Lifetime Accident Benefit. Optionally renewable disability income policies sometimes offer accident benefits for the duration of the disability with no maximum time limit. Guaranteed renewable and noncancellable policies might offer lifetime accident benefits restricting sickness benefits to age 65. The lifetime accident benefit may be included in the policy contract itself, or—perhaps more often—is available by rider for an extra premium. The chance of loss being low, the premium is modest, varying with the benefit duration of the policy to which it is attached.[43]

Partial Disability. Coverage for partial disability may be written as a policy provision or as a separate rider for an additional premium. The definition of partial disability will vary among policies and will depend upon how total disability is defined in the policy. A policy defining total disability in terms of house confinement will usually offer a fractional benefit (commonly one half) for nonconfining disability. If the total disability definition is "total loss of business time," partial disability will usually be loss of 50 percent of business time. When total disability is defined in terms of inability to perform any occupation, the definition of partial is usually ability to perform some but not all of the duties of any occupation. If the definition of total disability is the inability to perform the duties of one's own occupation, the definition of partial disability will be the inability to perform one or more of the major duties of one's own occupation.

Partial disability benefits usually are restricted to periods following total disability. A number of insurers will write partial disability benefits for accidents without the requirement that it follow a total disability.

Partial disability represents somewhat of an anomaly in underwriting philosophy. Historically, the benefit seems to have been devised as a way to permit an insurer to shorten periods of total disability. For instance, an insured may have recovered from a total disability to the extent that he can

---

[42] Accidental death benefits are nearly universally offered as a rider on life insurance policies, often referred to as double indemnity as discussed in Chapter 13.

[43] For example, in a given insurer, the rates per $100 of monthly benefit in a noncan to age 65 policy with a 30-day elimination period for accident and sickness, AAA occupational classification, issue age 35, are: 1-year benefit duration policy, rate for lifetime accident rider, $10; 2-year benefit, $8; 3-year, $7.25; 4-year, $6.50; 5-year, $6; 10-year, $5; to 65, $3.50.

return to work half days; however, if he does, he is no longer considered totally disabled under most definitions of total disability, and his benefits cease; yet his earned income may not return to the predisability level or to the level of his total disability income. Therefore, the insured, rather than accept a reduction in income, continues to claim total disability instead of returning to work part time. In theory, if the policy offers benefits for partial disability the insured may move from the higher benefits of total disability coverage to the lower benefits of partial disability coverage, thus reducing the insurer's total loss experience.

Special Allowances. Disability income policies may include special allowances for periods of hospitalization, home nursing care, medical care for accidents, persistency, or for the payment of annual premiums. Thus, a disability income policy may provide for an extra benefit during hospitalization (in the policy or as a rider). Commonly, this benefit will be a multiple of the regular disability benefit—i.e., if the regular benefit for total disability is $100 a month, the benefit will be increased to $200 a month while the insured is hospitalized. In the case of long-term disability benefits, the extra hospital benefit will be payable for a duration shorter than that over which the disability income is paid. Another provision sometimes found (again in the policy or as a rider) is waiver of the elimination period if the disability causes hospitalization. For instance, a policy providing disability income benefits after the first 30 days may agree to pay these benefits starting with the first day of hospitalization even though the elimination period has not expired. Still another possible provision is a stated value benefit if the insured suffers a disability requiring either hospitalization or the use of a trained nurse in the home. This benefit is usually stated in dollar units—i.e., the insured may select multiples of $100 a month (regardless of the amount of monthly disability benefit) up to some maximum per month, say $500. The hospital or home nurse benefit is payable in addition to the regular monthly disability income benefit. A provision (most often by rider) may offer coverage for medical expenses incurred as a result of accident. Medical expense coverage for accidents usually is blanket coverage, paying all expenses up to some maximum such as $5,000. This benefit also is payable in addition to the regular disability income benefit.

It is common to provide that if an injury results in a need for treatment by a physician or in a need for hospital emergency room treatment and no other disability benefits are payable under the policy, the cost of the medical treatment will be reimbursed up to a maximum usually expressed as a fraction of the total monthly disability benefit offered, say 25 percent.

To encourage the insured to renew his policy, a few companies provide that the benefits will be increased each year of consecutive renewal by some percentage (usually 10 percent) up to a maximum increase of 100 percent.

The common method of defraying the cost of premium collection is to include this cost in the annual premium. If the insured chooses to pay his premium more frequently than annually, the extra collection cost (and the loss of interest involved) would be loaded into the fractional premium. Some few companies quote a base rate on a monthly or quarterly basis and increase the benefits if premiums are paid annually.

Frill Benefits. Several benefits are offered that are called frill benefits because their primary value seems to be the opportunity they give the salesmen to dazzle their prospects with the chance of collecting large sums of money in exchange for an insignificant premium. They appear to have no real place in the insurance portfolio of the buyer. One of these benefits is multiple indemnity for specified accidents. Multiple amounts of benefits may be offered in event disability occurs as a result of particular, specified accidents, usually limited to injuries arising from accidents to public conveyance or elevators or to injuries incurred as a result of being crushed by the falling walls of a burning building if the insured is inside the building at the time, or to injuries sustained as a result of a steam boiler explosion, or of some other low-frequency occurrences. The multiplication may apply to any principal sum contained in the policy.

Optionally renewable coverages at one time commonly included a table of stated value benefits for dislocations and fractures. Those insurers that still offer the benefit usually do so on any one of several bases: (1) the stated benefit is payable in lieu of the monthly benefit; (2) it is payable *at the option of the insured* in lieu of monthly benefit; (3) it is payable in addition to the monthly benefit; and (4) it will be the minimum payable regardless of how short the period of defined disability is from the dislocation or fracture, if indeed there is any disability at all.

A few insurers offer a return of premium benefit in disability income policies, usually a rider at an extra premium of about 30 percent of the base premium. The benefit provides that if the insured has no claims (or aggregate claims of not more than a stated maximum) in some period such as 20 years, all premiums paid will be returned.[44] Another possible version of the return of premium rider is to provide that at expiry date (such as age 65), the difference between premiums paid and benefits received will be refunded.

The foregoing listing of other possible benefit provisions should not be considered exhaustive. The possible benefit provisions are limited only by the imagination of the policy draftsman and his ability to convince insurance departments of their justification.[45] However, the list does represent the other provisions (and riders) that are most commonly found in older policies in force and in policies currently on the market.

---

[44] The extra premium charged is used to build a fund which, together with interest earned and benefits of survivorship, will equal the amount of the premiums at the end of 20 years. This provision also serves as a claims control device. Presumably many insureds with claims minor to their pocketbook and to their expected premium refund will not file them in order to preserve their right to a refund.

[45] Another restrictive influence is the ability to interest reinsurers in new ideas.

The student should not be expected to remember all of the provisions discussed. The purpose of the discussion is to show that infinite variations in benefit provisions are available and that no assumptions relative to the benefit structure of disability income policies can be made merely on the basis that "this is a disability income policy."

Exceptions and Limitations. As pointed out in the discussion of the uniform provisions, exceptions and limitations pertaining only to specific provisions in the policy may be stated in that provision, but those general to the policy must be grouped under a descriptive heading such as Exceptions, or Exceptions and Limitations, or Exceptions, Limitations, and Reductions, or Not Covered, or some language equally as clear. Note, however, that certain particular exceptions may be stated in the uniform provisions themselves, such as "illegal occupation," "while committing a felony," "use of intoxicants and narcotics." The current trend is toward a reduction in the number of exceptions. The most common exceptions still found are the following.

Self-inflicted Injury. This may be worded simply "intentional self-inflicted injury" or may also be more inclusive as in "intentionally self-inflicted injury including any attempt at suicide."

War or Act of War. The usual wording of this exception is "war, declared or undeclared, or any act of war."

Active Military Duty. The wording will follow the lines of ". . . injury sustained or sickness which begins while the Insured is on full-time active duty as a member of the military (land, sea, or air)[46] forces of any country whether or not such country is at war. Upon receipt of written proof, any premium or pro rata part of a premium paid for any period of such full-time active military duty shall be returned to the insured."

Another version of the exclusion used by many insurers provides exclusion of coverage while on active military duty "other than active duty for a period of training not exceeding 60 days duration." Some insurers provide:

Upon the Covered Person entering such service on a full-time, active duty basis, the Policy owner may suspend the policy and receive pro rata refund of premium. Thereafter, upon application made within 31 days of termination of said active duty basis, this policy may be reinstated without evidence of insurability by payment of the pro rata premium to the end of the then current premium interval, after which time, the regular premiums shall be resumed.

It should be noted that the reinstated policy would not cover any disability having its origin during the active duty military service period because it was not in force during that time.

GEOGRAPHICAL LIMITATIONS. Originally coverage under health (and life) insurance policies contained geographic restrictions. Coverage was void "outside the United States," "in Indian territory," "west of the Missis-

---

[46] Policies with the new look add "or space."

sippi," and so on. Gradually geographical restrictions disappeared from life insurance and, also, from health insurance policies. Subsequent to World War II and the impetus the development of aviation has given to travel, plus general international turmoil, geographical restrictions have been reappearing in health insurance policies. A common restriction is worded along the following lines:

> . . . payments shall not be made for injury sustained or sickness that begins while the Insured is outside the Home Areas if such injury is sustained or such sickness begins after the Insured has remained outside the Home Areas for six months or longer; nor shall payments for any continuous period of disability be made for more than six months under the Benefit Provisions of this policy while the Insured is outside of the Home Areas. Home Areas means the 50 states of the United States of America, the District of Columbia, Canada, the Canal Zone Puerto Rico, and the Virgin Islands.

Some policies provide that the coverage will be void outside the home areas unless permission to make the trip is obtained in advance and in writing from the insurer.[47] Some policies impose geographical restrictions for only the first six months after the effective date—a device to weed out those who take the coverage with the intention of immediately traveling or residing abroad.[48]

HERNIA AND BACTERIAL INFECTION.   The policy might state that a loss caused or contributed to by a hernia will be considered to be a loss resulting from sickness. Also any loss caused by disease, bodily infirmity, or any bacterial infection other than a bacterial infection occurring as a

---

[47] This is tantamount to a flat exclusion because few insureds would know to apply for permission. In fact, because it is well established that few insureds ever read their policies, it is probable that the vast majority of people with policies containing a geographical restriction even know of its existence. Few agents will go all out to impress the restriction on the buyer, particularly since policies without the restriction are on the market. (However court decisions are beginning to appear that hold that since everyone knows that the insured is not likely to read his policy, the unexpected restrictions in these policies are not to be applied. See *Gerhardt* v. *Continental Ins. Co.,* 225 A (2d) 328, N.J. Sup. Ct.)

This footnote is not to be taken to imply that geographical exceptions are not a valid loss control safeguard. *First,* health conditions (and the exposure to injury particularly during times of an international crisis) are not always as favorable in areas outside the North American continent as they are in it. *Second,* for an insurer not regularly transacting business abroad, the process of settling a claim originating abroad (involving communications, language, currency exchange, and so forth) can be costly. *Third,* the problem of independent inspection is nearly insurmountable, which makes it necessary to rely almost exclusively on the ethics of the insured plus those of the vendor of medical care, who may consider all alien corporations fair game. And *fourth,* the cost of living is less in certain areas outside the home areas than in the home areas. The amount of monthly disability income that would not be worth malingering for in the United States might be well worth malingering for in a less expensive (and perhaps more exotic) far-off place.

[48] While applications usually ask if travel abroad is contemplated, it is difficult to prove that a no answer was false. It is possible that a person might take a policy more than six months in advance of moving abroad while actually intending at the time of application to make the move, but more likely such a person will purchase a policy without a geographical restriction since such policies are to be found.

consequence of accidental injury on the exterior of the body will be considered to be a loss resulting from sickness. As mentioned, many disability income policies provide longer benefits and shorter elimination periods for disability resulting from injury than for disability resulting from accident. Thus the insured has an incentive to claim that a given disability has been caused by injury. While hernia may result from an act (lifting) and thus seem to be injury, the primary cause of the disability is a structural weakness in the abdominal wall, which is more in the nature of a sickness than an injury. Because an argument can be made that an infection can have an accidental origin, the policy eliminates any attempt to do so by specifically stating that, for purposes of the coverage involved, only particular causes of infection shall be deemed accidental.

PREGNANCY, CHILDBIRTH, OR MISCARRIAGE. Disability income policies usually exclude disability resulting from pregnancy, childbirth, or miscarriage—it being deemed (rightly or wrongly) that the insured has a choice in the matter; and whenever the insured may choose to incur a disability, the exposure may be difficult to underwrite.[49]

AIR FLIGHT. Some policies exclude disability resulting from an air flight except on regularly scheduled airlines operating between stated points. More frequently today the exclusion reads:

Travel or flight in, or descent from or with, any aircraft, unless the Insured is being transported solely as a passenger without any duties relating to the aircraft or flight.

Sometimes insurers issuing disability income policies with this type of "aviation participation" exclusion will amend the policy by rider for selected applicants who do private flying, usually for an additional premium. Whether or not the insurer will issue the rider is usually based on the insured's flying experience and amount of time he regularly spends flying. Other insurers are no longer using the exclusion in keeping with the trend toward reducing the stated number of exclusions. However, questions about private flying will nearly always be asked in the application, and the company may decline to issue the coverage or agree to issue it only with an exclusion rider or at an increase in premium if the insured holds a private pilot's license.

The foregoing exclusions are the most common ones found in policies currently being issued. Of course some policies contain fewer exclusions than others. In fact, in some policies the only exclusion found is war or act of war.

---

[49] At least one claims man swears that he once received an accident claim for a pregnancy. The female insured argued that because she had not intended to become pregnant, her condition was an accident. A policy covering accidental pregnancies perhaps could be written (and now probably marketed) to cover single women, or married women beyond a given age, or even below a minimum age.

3. COVERAGE PROVISIONS: HEALTH EXPENSE

The two principal types of expense covers are (1) the basic forms of hospital, surgical, and medical and (2) the catastrophe form known as major medical. Each of these two basic types of policies will be discussed to the extent that they involve principles or provisions foreign to loss of income coverages.

Insuring Clause. Health expense policies cover the perils of accidental bodily injury and sickness or disease. Both the basic and the catastrophe forms include not only the named insured as in loss of income coverage but also may include "any eligible member of insured's family named in the application." Eligible members of the family usually are restricted to the insured's spouse and the unmarried dependent children of the insured. Age limits are placed on the eligibility of the children. The maximum age usually may be 18 or 21, or even higher for children who are full-time students, and the minimum ages may be 14 days, three months, or any minimum that will exclude coverage immediately at birth. Policies usually provide that additional new members are covered upon written application of the insured and upon payment of the required premium, if any.[50] Coverage for members of the family is not common in surgical and basic medical expense insurance (nongroup) but can be obtained through a surgical rider on a family hospital expense policy.

Definitions. In addition to the definitions found in disability income contracts, terms commonly defined in expense policies include the following: (Hold in mind, of course, that each policy draftsman has his own ideas on definitions; so that policies will vary in wording to at least some degree.)

---

[50] Under the law in most states an individual policy of insurance may be issued to only one person except that a spouse and dependent children under 19 may also be covered. This law is generally interpreted as meaning that no child over 19 can be covered for the first time under a family policy but may be continued beyond that age if the entry age was prior to age 19. In some policies an eligible child is covered automatically until the next premium due date, by which time the insurer must be notified of the new child and be remitted any additional premium required. Divorce, annulment, or legal separation terminates the coverage of a spouse. Some policies provide that in the event of the death of the insured, the spouse becomes the insured, and still fewer provide that in the event of the death of the parents, the coverage on the children becomes paid up until the children reach a specified maximum age or are married.

Many medical policies provide that upon termination of coverage on a child by reason of marriage or age, the child may convert the coverage to an individual policy without evidence of insurability. The application for conversion must be made within a specified time (often within 31 days of termination). Many insurers add the provision that they may reject the application if the applicant already has in force duplicating coverage. The new policy will be on a form then being issued by the company and shall not contain any limiting rider or endorsement that was not applicable to the family policy. In some policies, this conversion privilege is extended to a spouse whose relationship with the insured has been terminated by reason of divorce, annulment, or legal separation.

Hospital is usually defined as a "lawfully operated" institution for care and treatment of sick and injured persons with 24-hour nursing service, facilities for diagnosis and major surgery, and which is not, except incidentally, a "place of rest, place for the aged, place for drug addicts, a place for alchololics, or a nursing or convalescent home."

Convalescent Home. Convalescent home care is increasingly being added to the coverage offered under major medical policies. A convalescent home is defined as an institution with organized facilities for medical supervision and 24-hour nursing service for the care and treatment of post-hospital patients and with a bed capacity of six or more persons. Some definitions will add that there must be a registered nurse on duty 24 hours a day and that the services of a physician must be readily available. The definition usually states that a convalescent home shall not include a place of rest, place for the aged, place for drug addicts, or a place for alcoholics.

Nurse. A nurse is defined as a graduate or registered nurse othen than one who ordinarily resides in the insured's home or who is a member of the insured's immediate family.

Benefit Period. The benefit period is related to any one sickness or injury of a covered person and is defined as the period of time from the date the first expenses applicable to the deductible are incurred during which benefits will be paid. The length of the benefit period varies among policies, one-, two-, and three-year benefit periods being common. Five-year benefit periods can be found. Some policies dispense with the benefit period and are content to rely on the maximum amount payable to control liability. Other policies provide that if the covered person is still hospitalized when the benefit period expires, the benefits will be continued until he is discharged, subject to the policy maximum. It is also possible to find policies that provide that benefits will be continued after the expiration of the benefit period if the covered person is totally disabled at that time. It is neither common nor infrequent for the policy to contain a provision that if, at end of the benefit period, the covered person has not used up the maximum benefit, he may establish a new benefit period by again satisfying the deductible.

An example may clarify this provision. Assume a policy written for a maximum benefit of $10,000, a deductible of $1,000, and a benefit period of 3 years. During the 3 years, the covered person incurs $5,000 in expenses above the deductible for a single injury or single sickness. If a new benefit period can be established by reintroducing the deductible amount he would pay the next $1,000 (the deductible again) and begin drawing benefits for expenses in a new benefit period. However, the benefit for the new period would be only the difference between the expenses incurred in the first benefit period and the policy maximum. Once his expenses pass the $10,000 maximum, all benefits cease whether in the first or in any subsequent benefit period.

Benefit Provisions. The benefit provisions under the basic coverages and those under major medical are sufficiently different to merit separate treatment.

HOSPITAL SURGICAL EXPENSE COVERAGE.   Basic hospital surgical insurance coverage provides for hospital confinement expenses, usually actual charges for room and board up to a maximum amount per day and for a maximum number of days per hospital confinement.[51] A hospital confinement is defined as all periods of hospital confinement separated by less than six months unless due entirely to unrelated causes. Some policies fix the limit as a contract year rather than as a hospital confinement. The limit applies separately for each member of the family. Some few plans pay a fixed dollar benefit irrespective of actual charges, whereas others provide full coverage for room and board without a per diem limit, but restrict the service to a given class such as semiprivate rooms.

Hospital surgical insurance policies usually cover necessary hospital services (ancillary charges) up to a maximum measured in terms of a given multiple of the room and board daily maximum, such as 15 or 20 times the daily rate for room and board when the patient is confined to the hospital for a minimum period such as 18 to 24 hours.[52] The purpose of the minimum confinement period is to eliminate coverage for diagnoses. Surgical fees are covered usually on a scheduled basis. A $500 surgical schedule might, for example, list maximums of $500 for the removal of a portion of the lung, $250 for the amputation of a foot, $125 for removal of a benign tumor, $62.50 for removal of a cyst requiring hospital confinement, and $25 for a cyst removal not requiring hospital confinement.

Some hospital surgical policies offer coverage for accident emergency treatment where an insured receives emergency treatment in a duly constituted hospital but is not confined as a registered bed patient. The limit is usually a given multiple (commonly 3) of the daily room and board benefit, and the treatment must be received within 24 hours from the time of the accident.

The hospital forms generally exclude pregnancy, childbirth, miscarriage, or complication from these causes, but usually offer separate maternity benefits. The maternity benefit usually does not become effective until the policy has been in force for 10 months and is generally limited to a benefit equal to a given multiple (such as 10) of the daily room and board benefit, payable as a lump sum.

A few hospital surgical forms offer benefits for nursing expenses, some only while the insured is in the hospital, and others extending to nursing care at home.

A provision for waiver of premium in the event of disability is rarely

---

[51] In addition to the primary benefit period, a few plans offer a reduced benefit for a secondary period.

[52] In some policies the hospital services benefit is subject to a special deductible; in others the insurer pays 100 percent of the first $200 of hospital extras and 80 percent of the expenses in excess of $200. Other variations will be found.

found in health expense policies either as a part of the contract or as a rider at an extra premium.

MAJOR MEDICAL COVERAGE.   The benefits provided under major medical insurance may be discussed under five headings: (1) the deductible, (2) maximums, (3) participation, (4) covered charges, and (5) specified diseases.

The Deductible.   The deductible in major medical insurance often is $250 but sometimes $500 or more. In most major medical policies, but not all, the deductible must be accumulated in a stated period of time. The period is set forth in the benefit clause, and its length varies among policies, running generally from 90 days to 6 months. If within this period the insured or a covered family member accumulates covered medical expenses equal to the deductible, the insurer will pay those expenses in excess of the deductible (subject to maximums set by internal limits and to the overall policy maximum and to any percentage participation clause). Should the required deductible not be accumulated within the period set, the insured must start over. For example, assume a policy with a 6-month accumulation period for a $500 deductible. In 6 months, the insured (or a covered member of the family) has covered expenses from 1 injury or 1 sickness totaling $400. He has not qualified for benefits. His expenses continue and amount to another $100 in the 7th month. He still does not qualify for benefits. He must accumulate this $500 medical expense during 1 consecutive 6-month period.[53]

The deductible clause may also provide that in the event the insured suffers a second disability within the same 12-month period, the deductible for the second disability may be waived or reduced.

A number of major medical policies provide that if more than one family member incurs medical expenses by reason of a common accident, the deductible shall apply only once—to the aggregate expenses of all injured family members. Some policies provide that if two or more members of the family suffer the same communicable disease within a period of time (say six months), the deductible, if completely exhausted by the first illness, shall not apply to the second (or other) cases. These provisions are called common accident and common sickness clauses.

Maxima.   Major medical policies are written with a maximum benefit of some such amount as $10,000 or $20,000. The maximum may apply to each disability[54] or to a calendar year or benefit period. Other plans have

---

[53] The type of deductible just described is commonly called an each disability deductible. A calendar year deductible applies the deductible to aggregate expenses during a calendar year. When aggregate expenses exceed the deductible, the insured qualifies for benefits. A calendar year deductible may apply to the aggregate expenses of an individual or to the aggregate expenses of the family. Another form of deductible, called a benefit year deductible, aggregates expenses during *any* period of 12 consecutive months (not merely a calendar year). Another form is a monthly deductible called the family budget deductible: all covered expense incurred in the family each month in excess of the deductible amount qualifies for benefits.

[54] Except where an insured suffers concurrent sickness.

a lifetime maximum known as an aggregate. Such plans commonly allow the insured, if he can prove insurability, to reinstate the aggregate limit after a given amount of benefits has been received. Aggregate limits are more common than annual limits or benefit period limits but less common than a maximum benefit for each disability. In some policies a per case maximum will be used for physical injury and illness with a lifetime aggregate maximum applying to mental illness. Further, some policies written on a per case maximum basis will provide for continuation after age 65 on an aggregate benefit basis. Provision for continuation beyond age 65 was more common prior to medicare than it is now. Most of the current guaranteed renewable major medical policies now written can be renewed only to age 65, some providing "age 65 or eligibility for medicare, whichever is earlier."

Participation. Participation is widely used in major medical insurance to require the insured to share in each loss as a device to control over-utilization of medical services. Although it is possible to find policies that do not include a percentage participation, the vast majority of major medical policies provide that some percentage less than 100 percent of the incurred expense will be paid. Common percentages in individual major medical are 75 and 80 percent.

The participation percentage may be applied to all covered expenses including those that are subject to an internal limit. For instance, if the maximum covered amount for hospital daily board and room is $35, then assuming an 80 percent participation the maximum that will be paid is $28. If a surgical schedule is used, and a given procedure is listed at $500, the maximum that will be paid is $400. While it is now common practice in major medical contracts to apply the participation percentages to all covered expenses, there appears to be a trend toward setting up two classes of expenses, often labeled Class A expenses and Class B expenses. Those expenses already subject to an internal maximum (such as daily room and board, convalescent home care, and surgery) are classified "A" and all others are classified "B." The participation percentage applies only to Class B expenses. Thus, in the foregoing example, under a class-type participation clause, the insured would be paid $35 for his day in the hospital and the full amount listed in the surgical schedule.

Covered Expenses. Covered expenses in major medical policies are limited to those expenses recommended by a legally qualified physician and then only for an amount not in excess of the usual and customary charges for necessary treatment.[55] Expenses usually covered in a major medical policy are the following:

---

[55] Traditionally the pricing of medical care and services has been based on the ability of the buyer to pay. The practice of adding to regular charges when the patient is insured has been widespread enough to cause the American Medical Association to issue a statement to its members that insurance is not to be considered added ability to pay.

Hospital room and board (up to a per diem maximum in most policies, although some few policies have no per diem maximum).

Convalescent home care (not always covered in every major medical policy) immediately following a period of hospitalization, usually limited to some such period as 60 days and by a daily maximum amount, often half the daily hospital board and room allowed.

Professional services of a legally qualified physician in connection with surgery, including preoperative and postoperative examination, care, and treatment. In its original concept, major medical insurance offered blanket coverage, and no internal limit (such as hospital per diem or surgical maximum) was put in the contract. Experience later demonstrated the need for certain internal limits for purposes of loss control. Today, nearly all policies set some kind of limit on surgical charges, either a maximum amount per procedure or series of related procedures (such as $1,000, $1,500, or the like) or else use a schedule of amounts that will be paid for various procedures listed in detail.

Professional services of a legally qualified physician for medical services.

Hospital services and supplies.

Drugs and medicines.

Artificial limbs or eyes.

Casts, splints, trusses, braces, or crutches.

Oxygen, its administration and the rental of equipment for rendering the service.

X-ray service and laboratory examinations.

Use of radium or radioactive isotopes.

Rental of wheel chair, hospital-type bed, iron lung, or other mechanical equipment.

Professional services of a private duty graduate nurse (and, in some policies, a licensed practical nurse) other than a member of the insured's family.

Dental surgery not excluded under "not covered."

Physiotherapy.

Local ambulance service (and sometimes other than local service).

Specified Diseases. Some major medical policies provide that if a family member contracts poliomyelitis, spinal meningitis, encephalitis, leukemia, tetanus, multiple neuritis, diphtheria, scarlet fever, smallpox, rabies, elephantiasis, or tularemia after the date of issue of the policy but while the policy is in force, the company will pay 100 percent of all covered charges incurred over an extended benefit period beginning with the date of the first treatment but not in excess of the maximum benefit. In other words, the benefit period is extended say from one year to three years, and the deductible and participation provisions are waived. Transportation of the patient by regular commercial airline or railroad to a hospital or sanitarium qualified to provide the necessary initial treatment is paid. This coverage is simply the dread disease coverage which was first written as polio coverage. In some contracts the list is smaller, leaving out rabies and tularemia. In others, the list may be longer including cerebral meningitis and typhoid. Some policies may not include this coverage but it may be available as a rider.

Exceptions and Limitations. A few policies contain no list of exclusions or of items not covered. The draftsmen of these policies reason that it is sufficient to list only what is covered. These policies will nevertheless by their definitions exclude various exposures; for instance, the definition of hospital will exclude rest homes. However, the usual procedure is to include a schedule of exclusions in the policy. The expense covers contain many of the same exclusions as found in income covers. In addition, the following exclusions commonly are found:

Costs in a Veterans' Administration hospital or any hospital operated by a government or instrumentality of government.[56]

Costs in hospitals in which there would be no charges except for the existence of insurance.

Mental disorder (although most policies provide coverage for expenses while the patient is in a hospital not devoted exclusively to the care and treatment of mental disorder; sometimes an aggregate maximum is applied to these in-hospital expenses; rarely, if ever, are benefits provided for outpatient care).

Injuries and sickness covered by workmen's compensation laws.

Costs covered by any federal, state, or other governmental law or plan. This would exclude duplication with medicare and medicaid (benefits under Title XIX of the social security law).

Dental care and treatment except that necessitated by accidental damage to natural teeth.

Cosmetic or plastic surgery except that caused by accidental injury while the policy is in force or a congenital defect of a child born while the policy is in force and if the child is a covered member.

---

[56] According to the United States General Accounting Office, about 21 percent of the veterans who received care in VA hospitals in 1969 had some form of private health insurance. Were private insurers required to reimburse the VA for hospital care provided for non-service-connected disabilities incurred by these insureds, these reimbursements would amount to $40 million during fiscal 1971 based on government estimates. Legislation has been proposed by President Nixon to "require insurance companies to reimburse the Veterans Administration for general hospital care of veterans with non-service-connected medical problems who have purchased private health insurance but who elected to receive that care in VA hospitals. . . ." President Nixon believes that "insurers should not be relieved of payments because their policyholders choose to be treated in VA hospitals." Aside from the policy exclusion, it has been held that private insurers are not liable for payment to the VA because no medical or hospital expenses are incurred by the insured veteran when treated in a VA hospital. Thus, the need for legislation is clear if the VA is to obtain reimbursement from the insurers, unless the insurers would voluntarily agree to pay for medical care furnished by the VA.

Examinations for eyeglasses or hearing aids or the cost of eyeglasses or of hearing aids.

Transportation except local ambulance service to and from the hospital.

This list of additional exclusions may be abbreviated or extended, according to the underwriting practices of the insurer.

15

Insurance in Employee Benefit Plans: Group Life Insurance

Insurance performs an important function in the funding of employee benefit plans. Although individual life and health insurance policies are used in some cases to provide benefits for key employees (cf. Chapter 22) and to fund a number of pension trusts (cf. Chapter 19,) the more significant role is played by group insurance. It is only natural that insurance would have a major part in the development of employee benefit plans because most of these plans are designed to give employees a measure of economic security in dealing with the risk they and their families face in a wage-oriented society.

1. EMPLOYEE BENEFIT PLANS

Employee benefit plans may be defined broadly enough to include the whole gamut of nonpaycheck benefits running all the way from those required under Title II of the Social Security Act to such fringe benefits as paid vacations and to beyond the fringe benefits as company provided recreational facilities. Applying the broad concept of employee benefit plans, the costs of these plans in the aggregate now amount to 30 percent of the payroll and that percentage is expected to double in less than a decade, as the social revolution taking place in this country continues to achieve benefits through social security legislation and collective bargaining. An all-inclusive definition, however, would have little conceptual value for the purposes of this discussion.

Definition of Employee Benefit Plans. The annual review of employee benefit plans in the *Social Security Bulletin* adopts a narrow concept of employee benefit plans but one that has analytical values for the treatment of the subject in the context of this chapter. In the *Bulletin* employee benefit plans are defined as:

any type of plan sponsored or initiated unilaterally or jointly by employers and employees and providing benefits that stem from the employment relationship and that are not underwritten or paid directly by government. . . . The intent is to include plans that provide in an orderly, predetermined fashion for (1) income maintenance during periods when regular earnings are cut off because of death, accident, sickness, retirement, or unemployment and (2) benefits to meet expenses associated with illness or injury.[1]

Not included in the definition are "such fringe benefits as paid vacations, holidays, and rest periods; leave with pay (except formal sick leave); savings and stock-purchase plans; discount privileges; and free meals."[2] Also not included are federal old age, survivors, and disability insurance benefits, benefits under medicare, and benefits under workmen's compensation and unemployment compensation statutes.

The definition of employee benefit plans adopted for this text is restricted to *private* plans on a formalized basis offering income replacement benefits in the event of the death, disability, unemployment, or retirement of the worker, and hospital, surgical, and medical expense benefits for the worker and his family in the event of accident or illness.

The Magnitude of Employee Benefit Plans.   Statistics on the size and growth of employee benefit plans show the increasing importance of these plans in the American economy.[3]

In a recent year the amount contributed by employers and employees to finance private employee benefit plans as defined here equaled more than 46 percent of the after-tax profits earned by American corporations, and 100 percent of the amount paid by these corporations as dividends to their stockholders. Employer and employee contributions to employee benefit plans amount to nearly 7 percent of wages and salaries paid to employees of private industry.[4]

Current Trends in Employee Benefit Plans.   Employee benefit plans continue to be involved in an evolution that produces changes not only in the breadth but also in the depth of coverage. New types of coverage making strong gains are comprehensive dental care plans and prescription drug plans. In evidence, also, is an increasing use of long-term disability income coverage in employee benefit plans. Potential widows are being offered protection against loss of their "interest" in their husband's accumulated retirement credits by the inclusion of benefits for widows surviving husbands who die before reaching retirement age; and some plans include pension credit benefits that keep up a man's status in a retirement plan while he is disabled and unable to work.

---

[1] Alfred M. Skolnik, "Ten Years of Employee Benefit Plans," *Social Security Bulletin,* Vol. 29, No. 4 (April, 1966), p. 19. Mr. Skolnik is with the Office of Research and Statistics, Social Security Administration, U.S. Department of Health, Education, and Welfare.

[2] *Ibid.*

[3] Current statistics on employee benefit plans should be available in the *Social Security Bulletin,* usually in the March or April issue. Expect a two-year time lag.

[4] *Ibid.*

A trend toward plan liberalization is found in most types of coverage. Hospital coverage is being offered for longer stays; the duration of benefits for short-term disability is being extended; early retirement provisions are being liberalized; and benefit structures are being adjusted upward to reflect increases in both the cost and standard of living. Employers also are assuming a larger part of the cost of employee benefit plans.

Philosophical Overtones.   An important philosophical change appears to be evolving in how employee benefit plans are viewed. Originally, employee benefits were considered by employers and the general public to be *gratuities* that could be withdrawn at any time. (Many employers still regard these benefits as voluntary employer plans granted to employees to increase employee productivity and to be clothed with the restrictions necessary to assure employers, rather than employees, their benefits.) Employees also considered these benefits to be gratuities and were appreciative of them.

Later, the view developed that employee benefit plans were an obligation of the employer to his employees, the same as the employer's obligation to pay wages in cash. This view is based on the theory that employees earn these benefits just as they do their wages and that, consequently, the funds committed to finance these plans belong to the employees and are therefore not gratuities. Of course this wage concept of employee benefit plans ignores the contention that the employer might believe he is buying something in employee attitude and loyalty with the dollar he spends for employee benefits that he does not expect to get with the dollar he spends for direct wage payments.

A new concept of employee benefit plans is emerging, one that relates neither to the specific productivity value of these benefits to the employer nor to the employee's concept that employee benefit plans are payments for employment. This concept, similar to that of workmen's compensation, is one of a *nonwage social obligation* of industry, a form of social benefit, the cost of which is a proper cost of industry. The public, workers, and even some employers are beginning to accept the view that the social costs of operating a free enterprise system should not have to be borne by the individual workers in that system but by the enterprises that operate under the system.

While this later view has its merits, it also has some social implications that are both disturbing and challenging. The *disturbing* features are that not all workers are covered under employee benefit plans and that the public is apathetic about the consequences. If the public is to rely on industry to solve certain social problems through collectively bargained or voluntarily provided employee benefit plans, how are the problems of unemployment, illness, survivorship, and old age to be solved for those who have no employee benefit plan coverage? Some of the people who most need help with these problems are without these social benefits. Among those who want to see a broadly gauged program of social benefits, some fear has been expressed that successes with private employee benefit plans will dull efforts at expansion of public plans. Their fear is based on what they believe to be organized labor's lack of concern for providing publicly what it has been able to get privately for its members, and on management's traditional opposition to an expanding role of government in planned individual economic security. If private employee benefit plans could be expanded to cover those now without benefits, these fears would be abated. The *challenge,* therefore, is to interest the general public in the private employee benefit plan movement so that third parties become concerned with the shape and direction of the movement and, hopefully, help to chart its course in the public interest.[5]

The Employee Benefit Plan Discipline. Many professional and technical skills are involved in the planning and administration of employee benefit plans. The discipline of employee benefit plans cuts across many areas of the arts and sciences, attracting the interest of students of law, medicine, economics, actuarial science, finance, accountancy, and labor relations. Aside from the employers and employees themselves, many third-party institutions are actively engaged in the business of developing, servicing, and supervising employee benefit plans. These include banks, trust companies, hospital and medical care associations, firms of employee benefit plan consultants, and insurance companies. This chapter is concerned primarily with the role of insurance companies in providing life insurance coverage in employee benefit plans. The next four chapters are concerned with health insurance and retirement plans. In order to eliminate repetition or overlap, subject matter relating to all three types of employee benefit plans (life, health, and retirement) are discussed either in this chapter or in one of the next four.

2. HISTORY AND DEVELOPMENT OF GROUP INSURANCE

The meteoric rise of group insurance in this country is one of the phenomena of the insurance business. The first group life insurance policy was written in 1911 by the Equitable Life Assurance Society of New York on the lives of about 125 employees of the Pantasote Leather Company. At the beginning of the next year, the Equitable formed a group department, and in July, 1912, it wrote $5,946,564 on the lives of 2,912 employees of Montgomery Ward and Co., a case so large that it brought group insurance immediately to the attention of the American public.

From the start, nearly 60 years ago, group life insurance has grown and prospered so that today about $500 billion is in force in the United States covering the lives of more than 75 million people under nearly 300,000

---

[5] For an interesting philosophical study of fringe benefits, see Donna Allen, *Fringe Benefits: Wages or Social Obligations?* Cornell Studies in Industrial and Labor Relations, Vol. XIII (Ithaca, New York: New York State School of Industrial and Labor Relations, 1964).

group policies. About 86 percent of the group life insurance in force covers employer-employee groups.[6] The average coverage per employee in employer-employee groups is more than $7,000. Plans administered by unions, or jointly by unions and employers, make up about 5 percent of the group life insurance in force. The average coverage per employee in these groups is about $2,500.

Group life insurance represents more than 36 percent of all life insurance in force in the United States. This compares with about 20 percent at midcentury.

Phenomenal as has been the growth of group life insurance, its current growth is not so marked as that of group health insurance.

Several types of group health coverage are available. The oldest is loss of income protection, first introduced in 1910. Today, more than 35 million people have disability income protection under insured group plans. The next form to be introduced was group hospital expense, first written in December, 1929, on 1,500 schoolteachers by the Baylor University Hospital, Dallas. Today over 80 million persons are insured against the expense of hospital care under group policies issued by insurance companies. In 1938 the first group surgical expense plan was written. This coverage has proved as popular as group hospital coverage, so that the numbers insured are about the same under both types of plans. Group medical expense insurance was introduced in the 1940's; today more than 60 million are covered under regular medical expense group insurance policies. Group major medical was introduced in 1949. The popularity of this form is growing rapidly. Today, over 70 million people are covered by insurance companies under group major medical policies.[7] The first group vision care expense insurance was written in 1957, but this coverage has not met with much interest. The first group dental expense insurance coverage was written by the Continental Casualty Insurance Company on August 1, 1959, to cover approximately 1,200 employees of the Dentist Supply Company and their families. Today more than 2 million persons are covered under either group dental expense insurance policies or dental service contracts.

At the close of World War II, the total annual group health premium in the United States was about $200 million. At the present time, it is about $6.2 billion. Group health insurance premiums represent about 67 percent of all health insurance premiums written in the United States. This compares to about 50 percent at midcentury.

---

[6] Other groups include professional societies, employee associations, union and joint employer-union, fraternal societies, depositors in banks, shareholders of credit unions, and participants in mutual fund contractual plans. For current statistics on group life insurance, see the *Life Insurance Fact Book, op. cit.*

[7] To the foregoing numbers, additions must be made for coverage under Blue Cross, Blue Shield, and medical society plans (about 60 million) and under a number of independent plans (about 9 million).

The first modern group annuity contract was issued on Christmas Day, 1921. Termed a group pension plan at that time,[8] it called for the employer to purchase *annually* for each employee a single premium deferred annuity of $10 a year to commence at age 65. An employee who retired after 30 years of service would receive an annuity of $300 a year (30 × $10). By 1929, the deposit administration group annuity was introduced. Instead of the employer's purchasing annually a single premium deferred annuity for each employee, he contributes to an unallocated fund held by the insurance company. When the employee reaches retirement age, these accumulations are used to purchase for him a single premium immediate annuity in the amount called for under the pension formula. A variation of the deposit administration plan was introduced in 1950 under the name of immediate participation guarantee plan. Instead of purchasing a single premium immediate annuity for each employee when he reaches retirement age, the retired employees are paid their pension benefits direct from the unallocated fund. Another variation of the deposit administration plan was introduced in 1961. It took the name separate or segregated accounts, and is designed to accommodate employers who want a part of their contributions invested in common stocks.[9]

In terms of annuity income provided, group annuities make up more than 80 percent of all annuities in force with life insurance companies. This compares with about 50 percent at midcentury.

3. NATURE OF GROUP LIFE INSURANCE

In group insurance, the underwriting is done for the group and not for individuals in the group. Selection and rating is based on the group as a whole, and the policy is issued to the group. The insureds themselves are not contracting parties. Members of the group are issued certificates of participation and booklets describing the coverage in the master policy.

Definition of Group Life Insurance. Not long after the first group insurance policies were written, studies were made to determine to what extent, if any, this new form of insurance should be regulated by the states. The National Association of Insurance Commissioners in 1917 de-

---

[8] The name was changed to annuity because of the disrepute into which the term pension later fell as a result of unfavorable experience with nonactuarial pensions. One of the worst such experiences from a public relations standpoint was that of Morgan & Company, a packing firm which merged with Armour & Company in 1923. Morgan had established a pension plan in 1909, limiting its maximum liability to $500,000. At the time of merger, 600 employees had already retired under the plan, and actuaries calculated that over $7 million would be necessary to pay the promised benefits. A member of the Morgan family voluntarily contributed $500,000 to the fund, but that succeeded in postponing the debacle by only 14 months, at the end of which time all benefits ceased leaving 600 old people high and dry. The disaster received nationwide newspaper attention.

[9] The types of group annuities and their variations will be explained in detail in Chapter 19.

veloped the first standard definition of group life insurance. The original definition was as follows:

Group life insurance is hereby declared to be that form of life insurance covering not less than 50 employees with or without medical examination, written under a policy issued to the employer, the premium on which is to be paid by the employer or by the employer and employees jointly and insuring only all of his employees, or all of any class or classes thereof determined by conditions pertaining to the employment, for amounts of insurance based upon some plan which will preclude individual selection, for the benefit of persons other than the employer; provided, however, that when the premium is to be paid by the employer and employee jointly and the benefits of the policy are offered to all eligible employees, not less than 75 percent of such employees shall be so insured.

Although this original definition has since been drastically amended in a number of ways to be described later, it is still a good description of the basic and distinguishing features of group life insurance. Under this definition group life insurance (1) requires a minimum number of participants, (2) may be written with or without a medical examination, (3) is written under a master policy, (4) requires someone other than the insured to pay part of the premium, (5) must have eligibility standards for participation and a benefit formula which precludes selection against the insurance company, (6) requires at least 75 percent participation of those eligible if the plan is contributory and 100 percent participation if the plan is noncontributory, and (7) must not be written for the benefit of the employer.

The current definition of group life insurance is contained in the model group life insurance bill adopted by the National Association of Insurance Commissioners in December, 1956. This bill with its amendments either has been adopted in whole by the states or used as a model for the group insurance law in force. Some states have no group insurance law, and thus the restrictions discussed below will not apply as a matter of statute (although insurers might adhere to them because they are based on sound underwriting principles).

The current definition, except for placing a limit on the amount of insurance that can be written on one life, is more liberal than the original one, as will be seen as the discussion develops.

The statutory definition lays out the rules for issuing group life insurance. Since in some states variations from the model bill will exist, statutes must be checked for the exact definition in any given state. These variations, however, will not be extreme. The basic characteristics of the latest model bill are as follows:

ELIGIBLE GROUPS. Eligible groups have been broadened from employees of one employer to include the following. (1) Multiple employer groups—i.e., employees of more than one employer when grouped under a trustee. The grouping can be arranged either by a combination of employers in the same industry, as through a trade association, or by one or more labor unions whose members are employed by more than one employer. The policy is issued to the trustee. (2) Members of a labor union are also eligible for group insurance under the model law. A trustee is not needed because the policy may be issued directly to the union. (3) Debtors of a common creditor may be covered by group insurance. The debt may arise out of a loan or out of a purchase. Thus, the creditor may be a finance company or a vendor. The policy in these cases is issued to the creditor.

The above groups, including the single employer group, are the only ones provided for under the model bill. One or more additional groups are made eligible under the laws of a number of states. Among these are association groups such as teachers, lawyers, and other professional groups; units of state troopers, the state police, the national guard, and the naval militia; depositors or investors in financial institutions such as credit unions, savings banks, and mutual funds; members of fraternal societies, veterans' organizations, or trade associations; members of agricultural cooperatives; and dependents of employees covered under group life insurance policies. The enabling laws for insurance on these groups specify that the group shall have been formed prior to seeking the coverage and shall have a legitimate purpose other than that of obtaining insurance.

That more types of groups are eligible for coverage in some states than in others reflects, to some extent, the varying degrees of strength of state life underwriters' (agents) associations. Organized life insurance agents seek to contain group insurance. They see in its expansion a serious threat to their markets and charge that it deprives the insured of needed consultation services only a professional agent writing individual insurance can provide. The absence or presence of legislative pressure groups on behalf of potential group buyers also accounts for the variations in eligibility requirements. On the basis of sound underwriting theory, the only restriction that seems necessary is that the group shall have been formed prior to seeking the coverage and shall have a legitimate purpose other than that of obtaining insurance. If a medical examination were required, even this restriction would seem unnecessary.

ELIGIBLE GROUP MEMBERS. In an employee group, all employees of the employer may be eligible, including retired employees. Directors of a corporation, partners in a partnership, or a proprietor in a sole proprietorship are eligible for coverage only if they are bona fide employees actively engaged in the conduct of the business. In a creditor group, all debtors are eligible who have a binding obligation to repay at and from the date the insurance becomes effective for the specific debt. All members of the union are eligible for coverage under a policy issued to a labor union.

Although all employees are eligible under the model bill, the employer may establish eligibility standards that will cover only a certain class of employees.[10] However, any class he decides to cover must be determined

---

[10] The statutes of some states prohibit establishing classes for group insurance purposes based on race, sex, or age.

by conditions of employment.[11] For instance, an employer might cover only hourly wage workers, or only salaried workers. A college might cover only the teaching and not the clerical and maintenance staffs. It might further restrict the coverage only to those members of the teaching staff who hold the rank of assistant professor or higher.

It is customary in most plans to require a probationary period of service, say 60 days or 3 months, as a condition of eligibility. The waiting period avoids the clerical work involved in handling temporary or transient employees. Also, part-time employees or seasonal workers usually are excluded.

In creditor groups the creditor may choose to cover only certain debtors, but in setting up an excluded class he must do so on conditions relating to the debt. For example, he may exclude all secured loans but cover unsecured loans.

The insurer might also set up standards for eligibility. One is the actively at work requirement, which specifies that the employee must be on the job at the time he becomes eligible for insurance or for increases in his coverage. (This requirement is designed to give some measure of health selection, of course.) Also, companies usually require, under a contributory plan, that an employee must make application for insurance within 31 days after becoming eligible, or he will be required to submit evidence of insurability upon application for membership. Other cases in which evidences of insurability will be required are the in-and-outers. Once out, evidence of insurability is required to get back in if there has been no termination of employment. If there has been a termination of employment, evidence of insurability is required to reenter the plan only if the terminating employee had converted his policy to ordinary insurance under the conversion privilege to be discussed later. (These requirements are to reduce antiselection; that is, to protect against the high possibility that those in ill health will choose to come in.)

PAYMENT OF THE PREMIUM. Under the model bill, only in creditor groups may the person whose life is insured pay the entire premium. The creditor, of course, may, if he wishes, pay all of the premium himself or share it with the debtors. Only in multiple employer groups is the person whose life is insured not allowed to contribute specifically to the cost of his insurance; the premium must be paid by the trustee from funds contributed by the employers, by the unions, or by employer and union together. In employer and union groups, the employer or union must pay either all or part of the premium. If the employer or union pays all of the premium, the plan is known as noncontributory; if they pay only part of the premium, the plan is known as contributory (because the insured employee or union member must contribute to the premium funds). A few

---

[11] A class based on desire for the coverage rather than on conditions of employment obviously would lead to adverse selection.

states restrict employee contributions to a maximum of $0.60 per month per $1,000 of insurance on standard rated groups.[12]

In contributory plans, each employee is usually required to contribute a flat amount per $1,000 regardless of his age or sex.[13] The effect is that a young man will be paying a higher percentage of the cost of his insurance than will an older man. Actually, at ages under about 42 or 44, the customary employee's contribution of $0.50 or $0.60 a month per $1,000 of insurance will more than take care of the group tabular gross premium for his coverage.[14] Beyond these ages, the tabular cost of the insurance is greater than the employee's contribution.

If the employer or union were not required to pay part of the premiums the plan might not work. The rates necessary for older employees might make the average rate, when spread among the participants on the basis of each $1,000 of insurance, unattractive for the younger members of the group. These younger members, if insurable, might refuse to join the plan, leaving only the older members and the impaired risks. The rate per $1,000 would then have to be increased, making it too high for the younger members of the older group so they, too, would drop out. A further increase in the rate would be necessary with similar results. But if the employer or union pays part of the premium, then the contribution rate can be kept attractive for nearly all employees.

However, debtors can be required to pay the full premium in creditors' groups without affecting the stability of the plan even though a flat premium is charged everyone regardless of his age and health. Although the younger and healthier debtors are victims of unfair discrimination, they do not reject the insurance either because they are unaware of the high cost or because of high-pressure salesmanship on the part of the creditor. The borrower also might feel that he must take the insurance or he will be denied the loan. Because the payment of the insurance premium will be included in the loan repayment schedule, the borrower frequently looks at the insurance premium as part of the cost of the loan.[15]

---

[12] In addition to the $0.60 maximum, New York has an alternate restriction limiting aggregate employee contributions to 75 percent of the premium paid for the coverage. The alternate basis is seldom used. For extra risk groups the maximum monthly employee contributions are $0.70, $0.75, and $0.80 per $1,000 of insurance. Many contributory plans fix the employee contributions at $0.50 a month per $1,000 of insurance.

[13] In some contributory plans, lower contributory rates are fixed for women than for men, or for employees below a given age than for those above that age.

[14] Yearly renewable term insurance in amounts of $10,000 can be purchased on an individual basis for under $6 a year ($0.50 per month) per $1,000 until age 35, and for under $7.20 a year ($0.60 per month) per $1,000 until age 41. Even when comparable coverage is available at a lower premium initially, that premium will increase as the employee becomes older, and soon will exceed the $6 or $7.20 annual contribution per $1,000 of insurance. At that time, the group policy will become more economical for the employee, but in order to get the coverage he must prove insurability, something he cannot be certain of doing.

[15] Under some plans, the older as well as the younger debtor may be overcharged. See discussion of creditor group life insurance later in this chapter.

Because there is no underwriting reason why employees should not be allowed to contribute under multiple employer group plans, recent amendments to state group insurance laws have permitted such contributions.

SIZE OF THE GROUP.   The original definition of group insurance fixed the minimum size of employee groups at 50, but this number has been reduced to 10 in the current definition. Labor union groups must cover at least 25 at date of issue; multiemployer or trusteed groups must cover at least 100, and not less than an average of 5 per employer unit. If the plan is established by an employers' association, at least 600 persons must be covered at date of issue unless 60 percent of the employers whose employees do not already have group life insurance participate. In creditor groups at least 100 new entrants must be expected yearly.[16]

The underwriting rules of some insurers will not permit them to accept groups as small as the law allows without special safeguards.[17] At one time companies wrote small groups at rates in excess of standard, but as competition for baby groups developed, rates gravitated back to standard levels. In creditor groups, companies may insist on a volume of insurance standard as well as the 100 new insured every year requirement. In multiemployer cases, in addition to the 100 lives the insurer may require that the case produce an annual premium of not less than a given amount a year. These are just a few examples to show that company underwriting rules sometimes are more stringent than the law requires.

Two factors account for the requirement of a minimum number of lives: selection and cost. The group should be large enough to reduce the likelihood of adverse selection against the insurer and, of lesser importance, to achieve the economies of administration upon which the differential between group and individual rates is based.

Selection.   The larger the group, the less the likelihood that the insurance will be taken solely to cover some eligible employee who otherwise would be uninsurable. Group insurers reason also that a large group is less apt to have a disproportionate number of impaired lives. While a

---

[16] Remember that these are the provisions of the model law. In some states the requirements may be stricter; in others they are not so strict. For a single employer, three states have a minimum of five employees. For labor union groups, a minimum of 10 members are required in nine states plus the District of Columbia, and a minimum of only 2 is required in one state. Illinois, which has a group insurance law, requires no minimum for labor union groups but requires 10 for a single employer group. Two states require only 50 new entrants yearly for creditor group life insurance, and one state requires only 25 (New York). Three states with group insurance laws set no minimum for creditor group. For multiemployer groups, one state requires 250 lives; one, 75 lives; two, 50 lives; three, 25 lives; and two, 10 lives.

[17] Typical of the safeguards required for the baby groups are evidence of insurability for all employees or for those scheduled for higher amounts; limit on the amount that can be written on any one life; a higher percentage of participation than normal on contributory plans; the requirement that either the plan be noncontributory or the employee's contribution be less than 50 percent; and more information about the group members, weighed more carefully before approving the case.

minimum of 50 or even 25 can be useful in reducing adverse selection, it is doubtful that a minimum of 10 is truly effective. The fact that the minimum number of persons needed to form a group has been decreasing over the years indicates that the insurers are giving less and less attention to group size as a means of guarding against adverse selection. The desire to expand their group business has led the insurers to find other methods to deal with the problem of antiselection.

Cost. An advantage of group over individual insurance is its lower cost. The principal reason for its lower cost is lower expenses; for instance, the employer assumes certain clerical functions. Also, the insurer is able to spread certain fixed costs over a large volume of insurance. Unless the group is large enough to yield a high enough premium volume, this cost advantage would be negligible. The principal cost saving in writing groups as small as 10 employees would be in sales commissions. The first-year commission on group life insurance involving an annual premium of $1,200 in one company would be $240 the first year, and $36 for each year thereafter. The commission on a similar type of insurance (yearly renewable term) written on an individual basis in this same company and involving an annual premium of $1,200 would amount to $360 the first year, $120 a year the next two years, $72 a year the next three years, and $24 a year thereafter. The amount of group insurance purchased the initial year with the $1,200 would be about $227,000 assuming all employees to be age 40. The amount of individual insurance purchased with this amount, assuming the same age, would be about $169,000.[18]

PERCENTAGE OF GROUP. The model bill requires that in noncontributory plans 100 percent of those eligible must be covered, whereas in a contributory plan at least 75 percent of the then eligible employees must subscribe to the plan.[19] These rules apply in all but the multiemployer trusteed groups where all eligible persons must be covered, but this actually is no exception since covered employees are not allowed to contribute under these plans.

The participation provision is the one provision of the model law that all states with group insurance statutes have adopted. Even in those states which have no group law, insurers insist on the 100 percent and 75 percent rules to reduce adverse selection and to hold down expenses. Of course, 100 percent participation is desirable even in contributory groups to eliminate adverse selection and control unit cost, but the lawmakers and the insurance underwriters recognize the near impossibility of enrolling 100 percent of those eligible. Some will refuse to join on religious grounds; and others just procrastinate because of lack of sufficient motiva-

---

[18] Commission scales and premium rates vary among companies both for group insurance and for ordinary insurance.

[19] Where evidence of insurability is required, the rules allow for the exclusion of those who fail to meet the standard before the percentages are applied.

tion. The 75 percent participation rule allows a practical margin to take care of the nonbelievers.[20]

AMOUNT OF INSURANCE. The model bills have two provisions dealing with amounts of insurance: benefit formulas and benefit maximums.

Benefit Formulas. The model bill for the regulation of group creditor insurance limits the amount of life and health insurance on the debtor to the amount of the debt.

In employer, union, and trusteed groups, the law requires that the amounts of insurance under the policy must be based upon some plan precluding individual selection either by the employee, employer, union member, or union. Therefore, the amount of coverage for each person insured must be established by a predetermined rule called a formula or schedule and not by the individual choice of the one whose life is covered. The purpose of this rule, of course, is to eliminate selection against the insurer or the group which could occur if members of the group who are in poor health were allowed on their own initiative to take disproportionately large amounts of insurance. Because large groups are to a degree self-rated (the degree of self-rating depending on the size of the group), any encouragement of adverse selection could result in selection against the group as well as the insurer.

Five methods of determining the amount of insurance on the lives of individual participants are in use:

1. A flat amount for everyone, such as $5,000 for each covered employee.

2. The employee's salary or salary bracket, either an amount equal to, say, 1 year's salary or $5,000 for employees earning under $5,000 a year, $7,500 for those earning $5,000 to $10,000, and so on. The wage brackets and amount of coverage for each are, of course, established by the employer or union.

3. Based on the employee's job classification; for instance, $5,000 for employees in no supervisory capacity, $10,000 for department heads, $20,000 for officers, and so on—again the classifications used and amounts for each being the choice of the employer.

4. Length of service; for example, $4,000 for employees with less than 5 years' service, $8,000 for those with from 5 to 10, and so on. This method is seldom used today.

5. A combination of any of the above methods; for instance, $2,000 for nonsupervisory employees with less than 5 years of service, increasing to $5,000 at the end of 5 years; $5,000 for department heads with less than 5 years of service, increasing to $10,000 after 5 years; and so on.

---

[20] One group plan recently was bogged down because of the refusal of several employees to sign up for the coverage. The employer, so the story goes, called in the spokesman for the "uncooperative" employees and told him bluntly that those employees who do not sign up for the plan will be fired. "In that case," said the leader of the holdouts, "you can count us in. Up until now, no one had explained to us in such clear terms the benefits of signing up."

A sixth plan, no longer in use, but one that seems to have merit, was the plan used by Montgomery Ward in its prototype program in 1912 but abandoned in 1921 for one of the standard plans because the cost was too high in face of declining business. The plan provided $100 as a burial benefit and then one year's salary up to a maximum of $3,000 to the estate or beneficiaries of employees who had no dependents. For employees with dependents, the dependent wife or husband was given a lifetime annuity, 4 years certain, for an amount equal to 25 percent of the employee's salary. The income ceased when the widow or widower remarried. This type of benefit formula is in keeping with the philosophy that employee benefit plans are a nonwage obligation of industry.

Use of the employee's salary or salary brackets to determine the amount of insurance is the most common method, although in a number of trusteed plans or plans established through collective bargaining, a flat amount per employee is used.

Benefit Maximums. The maximum placed on the amount of insurance in creditor groups is set in the model bill at $10,000 on any one life. In some states the limit is fixed at $5,000. Insurers, however, set their own limit based on the total outstanding indebtedness of the group to be insured. The larger the total amount of outstanding indebtedness, the higher will be the maximum the insurer will place on any one life. For example, if the amount of outstanding indebtedness is between $250,000 and $400,000, the maximum might be fixed at $3,000. If the outstanding obligations are between $700,000 and $850,000, the maximum on any one debtor might be set at $7,500. Each insurer will develop its own schedule. The reason for requiring that the maximum bear some relationship to the total outstanding debt is to assure a practical spread of risks in order to achieve a uniform claim experience.

The maximum limit on any one life in all other groups is fixed in the amended model bill at 150 percent of compensation but in no event less than $20,000 nor more than $40,000. These restrictions apply only to group term insurance. Twenty-two states and the District of Columbia have enacted the $20,000/$40,000 limits. Twenty states, including the large industrial states of New York, California, Michigan, and Massachusetts, have no limits on the maximum amount of group life insurance that may be issued on any one life. In two states a fixed benefit maximum has been set without regard to the employee's salary, one by statute, the other by department ruling. The remaining six states have limits which are more liberal than that of the model bill. The limitations on maximums apply to the state in which the master policy is issued. For example, although Illinois has $20,000/$40,000 limits, the Illinois employee of a New York based company could have any amount on his life despite the Illinois limit.

One point of controversy within the life insurance business is the question of whether there should be a limit on the amount of group coverage that can be written on one life. The interests of insurers and their agents have some areas of conflict.

Life insurance agents' associations fight attempts to increase the maximum coverage allowed under group life insurance. They offer public interest arguments in defense of their stand, arguments that the two major company associations (The Life Insurance Association of America and the American Life Convention) no longer support. The agents contend that group life insurance ceases to serve a social purpose when it is used by highly paid executives to build a large potential estate. Furthermore, they argue, the extension of group life insurance threatens to crowd out the commissioned agents who provide a useful social function in building a strong life insurance industry in America and in providing for the people a life insurance service not available elsewhere. They maintain that the writing of group life insurance in amounts that attempt to make group term a substitute for an individually prescribed and tailored permanent life insurance program is not in the public interest.

Those who oppose restrictions on group insurance profess to see no evidence to support the agents' fears. They believe that group insurance might even encourage people to purchase more individual coverage to complete a satisfactory life insurance program. Furthermore, they do not accept the contention that the use of large amounts of term insurance is against the public interest, especially since they can point to the growing practice of continuing the coverage on retired employees through pension plans, deferred profit sharing plans, and salary savings plans.

A Joint Committee on Reexamination of Group Policy, appointed by the Life Insurance Association of America and the American Life Convention in 1960, proposed that a nondiscrimination rule be substituted for a specific limit on the amount of group life insurance. Under this rule, higher salaried employees are not to receive a higher amount of insurance in relation to salary than that offered to lower salaried employees in the group. The associations adopted the report in the fall of 1960, but no state has yet incorporated the rule into its law.[21]

Just as in creditors' groups, insurer underwriting rules limit the amount of insurance that can be written on one life in employer, union, and trusteed groups. The maximum that can be written on one life usually bears a relationship to the total amount of insurance in force on the group. For example, the single life limit might be $5,000 if the total insurance on the group is less than $500,000; if more than $500,000, but less than $750,000, the limit on a single life might be $10,000; and so on, increasing as the total insurance in force increases. Each insurer has its own schedule of maximums, and many insurers consider other factors in addi-

---

[21] A major Illinois insurance company attempted to get the Illinois $20,000/$40,000 restriction removed in the 1965 Assembly, but could not get the bill out of committee. Similar efforts will be made again in Illinois and in other states.

tion to insurance in force. Among these are whether the plan is contributory or noncontributory, the extent of the employers' contribution in contributory plans, number of employees covered, and the benefit schedule down the line. The insurer usually requires that there be a reasonable relationship between the amount of insurance on an employee and his annual earnings, something like a maximum of three times earnings.

One purpose of restricting maximums is to guard against adverse selection. Therefore, if an employer develops a benefit schedule under which amounts of insurance for certain employees exceed the insurer's single life limit for the case, the amounts in excess of the limit will be granted only if the employees involved can provide evidence of insurability.

Another purpose of the limit may be to reduce the chance of wide fluctuations in claims experience. When this is the case, the employer usually can retain his benefit schedule by allowing the group to be charged either for the cost of reinsuring the excess amounts or the costs of building a special fund to average out fluctuations in mortality experience.

4. THE GROUP LIFE POLICY

For convenience of discussion, the holder of the master contract in the group case is referred to here as the employer and the participating individuals as employees. The insurer is referred to as the company. However, wherever the term employer is used, the terms trustee, creditor, or association could be substituted; and wherever the term employee is used, the terms union member, debtor, or association member could be substituted.

Only one policy contract is issued in the group case: the master contract issued to the employer. The individuals whose lives are insured are not policyholders; they are participants in the plan. The evidence of insurance given them is not an insurance policy but a certificate of participation, or, as most group men prefer to call it, certificate of insurance.

Standard Provisions in Group Life Insurance. The model group bill sets up a number of provisions which must be included in substance in the group life insurance master policy. Provisions more liberal to the insured or policyholder will be allowed. State laws vary as to the standard provisions required, although most states having a group insurance code have accepted the standard provisions prescribed by the model bill. Where a group policy covers insured persons in several states, the statutes of the state in which the policy is issued usually govern. The model group law of the National Association of Insurance Commissioners makes mandatory the following provisions in group policies:

1. A grace period of 31 days during which the death benefit coverage shall continue in force, unless the policyholder shall have given the insurer prior written notice of discontinuance. The policyholder may be

held liable for the payment of a pro rata premium for the time the policy was in force during the grace period.

2. Incontestability after two years, both as to the policyholder and the person whose life is insured. As for the latter, this provision is important only when evidence of insurability is required.

3. Applications, if any, shall be attached to the policy and statements made by the policyholder and participants shall be representations.

4. A provision stating the conditions, if any, under which the company may require evidence of insurability of any person eligible for coverage.

5. A statement of how misstatement of age is to be adjusted. Unlike individual insurance, the premium usually will be adjusted so that it will provide the full protection to which the employee is entitled under the benefit formula in use, neither more nor less than this amount. This is a more equitable arrangement than adjusting the insurance to the premium as in the case of individual insurance, because employees are entitled to the full amount of insurance arranged for them under the group formula. The cost of insurance to the employee under a contributory group plan does not vary with his age. However, when the benefit schedule is related to age, the policy usually provides for an adjustment of the benefit.

6. A facility of payment clause that allows the insurance company to pay the proceeds of the policy to any one or more surviving close relatives of the deceased employee, or to the executor of his estate in the event that there is no living named beneficiary. This clause also allows the company to pay up to $100 a month to any person or institution who appears to the company to have assumed responsibility for the care, custody, or support of a minor beneficiary or one that is incapable of giving a valid release for payment.

7. Certificates of participation shall be issued to each employee covered, stating insurance benefits, the beneficiary, and the rights and conditions of the insured in case of termination of employment or of the group contract. These rights are as follows:

a) If employment is terminated, the insured may without providing evidence of insurability elect within 31 days to take an individual policy on any plan but term for the same amount for which he was covered under the group contract at the premium applying at his attained age. This provision does not apply to disability benefits.

b) If the master policy is terminated, an employee who has been covered for at least 5 years may take an individual policy on any plan except term for an amount not exceeding the smaller of *either* the amount terminated less the amount of any new or reinstated group coverage effected within 31 days *or* $2,000.

c) In case the insured dies after termination of employment or of the master contract but within the period during which he had the right to take an individual policy, he shall be covered under the group policy even though no application for the individual policy had yet been made.

8. A final standard provision requires that if the plan is written on a basis other than term, it must contain equitable nonforfeiture provisions. Naturally, the provisions discussed in (6) and (7) above do not apply to creditor groups. A standard provision designed specifically for creditor groups is the requirement that the insured debtor be furnished a statement that his life is insured and that any death benefit paid will be applied to reduce or retire the debt.

Other Group Life Policy Provisions. The following provisions, in addition to the standard provisions, usually are found in group life contracts. It will be noted that group life insurance contracts do not contain the suicide exclusion found in individual insurance.

TEMPORARY SUSPENSION OF EMPLOYMENT. The policy usually provides that in the case of sickness or temporary layoff, the insurance may be continued on the life of the employee for a period of several months under an arrangement that eliminates adverse selection. A request for an extension of this period usually will be granted to the employer if he continues to pay the premium for the employee on leave.

CLERICAL ERRORS OF EMPLOYER. A clerical error on the part of the employer, such as failing to notify the company that an employee has become eligible for coverage, shall not deprive the employee of such coverage.

DISABILITY. Some group life policies provide that if an employee becomes totally disabled for a duration of, say, at least nine months prior to age 60 (age 65 in a few contracts) and remains disabled to the time of his death, the amount of insurance on his life at the time of disability will remain in force. This is, in effect, a *waiver of premium* clause. Annual notice of the continuation of the disability is required. A *maturity value disability* benefit provision is written in other group life insurance contracts under which, if total and permanent disability occurs before age 60 (age 65 in some contracts), the proceeds of policy become payable, usually on a 5-year installment basis, as a disability claim rather than a death claim. A third type of disability provision found in some group life policies is the *extended death benefit.* Under this clause, if the insured employee dies within one year after termination of his employment, the group life insurance benefit is paid provided the employee had been continuously and permanently disabled since leaving his employment and was under age 65 at death. The lifetime waiver of premium clause is the most popular type of disability benefit in group life insurance contracts currently in force, with the maturity value benefit running a close second and the extended death benefit a poor third. The maturity value benefit was the most common until 1932. From 1932 to 1938, if a policy had a disability benefit, it was the extended death benefit. The waiver of premium benefit was introduced after 1938 and grew in popularity. Currently, the maturity value benefit has regained its popularity.

INSTALLMENT SETTLEMENT OF PROCEEDS. Although most group

insurance benefits are paid in a lump sum, the group policy usually permits the employee or his beneficiary to elect an installment settlement of policy proceeds. Nearly all companies provide for the fixed amount or fixed installment options. Some companies will make available the other options customarily offered in individual policies. The life annuity rates payable under the options when available generally are not guaranteed in the policy but are the rates payable by the company at the time the option is selected.

RETIRED EMPLOYEES.   Group policies may provide for the continuation of coverage on retired employees. In such cases the amount of insurance may be reduced. It is customary for the employer to pay the entire cost of postretirement protection even if the plan is contributory for active employees.

EMPLOYEES COVERED.   Employees who become eligible for coverage under a noncontributory plan are covered automatically without any action on their part. Those who become eligible under a contributory plan must make a written request to the employer (in form of an enrollment card) within a stated time after becoming eligible—31 days, for instance. If they wish to enroll in the plan after the enrollment period expires, they may be required to furnish evidence of insurability at their own expense.

ALTERATIONS OF POLICY.   As is typical of all life insurance policies, the group contract declares that no agent shall have the right to alter or amend the policy, to accept premiums in arrears or extend the due date, to waive any required proof of claim or extend the date when such proof is due. No change in the policy is valid unless approved by an officer of the company (and the specific officers authorized to make changes may be specified) and evidenced by an endorsement or amendment signed by the officer and attached to or written in (usually rubber-stamped) the policy.

BENEFICIARIES. The employee shall have the right to name a beneficiary and to change his beneficiary at any time by filing written notice of the change with the company and having it endorsed on his certificate. Should the employee die before the actual endorsement is made, the change is effective as of the date of notice. The company, however, shall not be held liable if the proceeds have already been paid before the notice was received. The group insurance statutes prohibit the naming of the employer as beneficiary.

ASSIGNMENT.   Traditionally, the policy has prohibited employees from assigning rights under a group life insurance policy. This provision denies the employee the right to have the proceeds paid on the group policies sheltered from federal estate taxes (cf. Chapter 21). Until 1968, it was not clear whether an employee could remove the insurance proceeds from his gross estate by assigning all incidents of ownership in the coverage even though the assignment prohibition was either not included in the policy or eliminated from it by endorsement. The problem was whether the employee could legally assign his right to convert his group insurance policy upon termination of his employment and whether the right of the employee to cancel his insurance by terminating his employment was an incident of ownership that could not be assigned. The Internal Revenue Service ruled in 1968 (Rev. Rul. 68–334 restated as Rev. Rul. 69–54) that an employee who irrevocably assigns all incidents of ownership in his group insurance certificate, including the conversion privilege, has effectively removed the value of the proceeds of the group insurance from his gross estate. However, if the policy does not give the employee the right to convert the group coverage to individual coverage upon termination of employment, then an irrevocable assignment does not remove the proceeds of the insurance from the employee's estate since he retains the right to cancel the insurance by termination of employment, a right considered to be an incident of ownership.

Both the state law and the provisions of the policy must permit assignment for the employee to exclude the proceeds from his gross estate. Many states have passed laws authorizing the assignment of group life insurance, and it was held by a federal district court in *Landorf* v. *U.S.* (Ct. Clms., 3–14–69) and by the Tax Court in *Gorby's Estate* (53 T.C. 12, 10–27–69) that unless a statute specifically prohibits such an assignment, it is permitted. Furthermore, the nonassignable restriction is being eliminated in a growing number of group life insurance policies.

The policy does not prohibit the assignment of the master policy, which assignment might be desirable in case of a merger, for example.

REGISTER OF PARTICIPANTS. The policy requires the employer to keep a record or register that retains up to date the names of participating employees, the amount for which each is covered, the date of entry into the plan, and the time and amounts of any increases or decreases in coverage.

DUE DATE, COMPUTATION, AND PAYMENT OF PREMIUM. (1) Premiums usually may be paid monthly, quarterly, or semiannually, and the time and frequency of payment may be changed upon the written request of the employer. (2) Premiums are payable in advance. (3) The company will compute an average rate based on ages of the members of the group (not based on the average age of the members), using the initial schedule of benefits and the employee data supplied by the employer. (4) At any renewal date, or whenever the terms of the policy are changed, the employer or the company may request a recomputation of the rate to reflect any new schedule of benefits or any major change in the age distribution of employees. (5) The initial premium and the premium on any renewal date shall be the average rate per $1,000 applied to the total amount of insurance in force on all employees, regardless of the age of each participant. (6) Any premium adjustments involving the return of unearned premiums to the employer shall be limited to the 12-month period immediately preceding the date when evidence is received by the company that such adjustments should be made. Since premiums are paid in advance, a refund is due when the number of employees is reduced.

POLICY DIVIDENDS AND NONPAR ADJUSTMENTS. If the policy is participating, dividends will be paid in cash to the employer or, on his written request, used toward payment of the next premium. If the plan is nonparticipating, provision usually is made for a retroactive adjustment of the premium if experience indicates that adjustment is merited. An employer usually is entitled to an adjustment if the total of claims paid plus a retention percentage is less than the premiums collected. The retention percentage, to be discussed later, is based on the amount the company estimates is necessary for administration costs, contingency reserves, insurance costs,[22] and a margin for profit. Should dividends or adjustments exceed the amounts contributed by the employer in a contributory plan, the excess must be used for the benefit of the employees—refunded to them, used to enable them to skip contributions for a period, or applied to buy additional insurance or benefits.

RENEWAL. When the plan of insurance is 1-year term, the policy contains a provision permitting the employer to renew the contract at the end of the policy year and at the end of each subsequent year, contingent upon (1) payment of premiums, (2) 75 percent participation in contributory cases and 100 percent in noncontributory cases, and (3) the minimum number required by the policy (or statute) for a group.

THE CERTIFICATE OF PARTICIPATION. The master policy requires the company to issue to the employer for delivery to each employee an individual certificate stating the insurance to which the employee is entitled and to whom benefits are payable, and summarizing the provisions of the policy affecting the employee.[23]

Surrender of the certificate is a condition precedent to the payment of a death claim or to the exercise of any rights under the policy.

The certificate itself certifies that under a group policy, identified by policy number, the employee is entitled to named benefits subject to the provisions of the master policy; and it identifies the beneficiary. It then gives a summary of the policy provisions affecting the employee, such as:

1. Authority of agents.
2. Cessation of insurance.
3. Conversion privileges.
4. Disability benefits.
5. Change of beneficiary and facility of payment.
6. The benefit formula or schedule.
7. Settlement options.
8. Prohibition of assignment.

---

[22] The insurance cost is to pay for bad experience in other groups—i.e., to pay some of the claims in other groups when these claims exceed the premiums collected from those groups. There is always the possibility that the claims in any group will exceed premiums collected. Rates must include an insurance charge to offset this contingency. The larger the group, the smaller is the percentage added in the retention limit for the insurance charge. The insurance charges are discussed later in this chapter.

[23] The certificate is neither a contract between the employee and the insurance company nor between the employee and his employer.

It also usually contains space for endorsement of any change of beneficiary or amendment of the coverage.

5. UNDERWRITING AND RATING GROUP LIFE INSURANCE

The underwriting and rating of group insurance go hand in hand.

Underwriting. In group insurance the basis of underwriting is the group covered, in contrast to individual insurance where the basis of underwriting is each individual insured. The group underwriter is not interested in any one individual who is participating in the plan, but in whether or not the composition of the group is such that it can be insured.

Group underwriting differs from individual policy underwriting also in that less emphasis is placed on accepting or rejecting the risk outright and more emphasis on designing a sound plan for the group. In other words, it is necessary to underwrite the details of the plan of insurance itself, especially in order to obtain an adequate spread of risk and to gain the economies of group operation. The lack of antiselection is not automatic with group insurance but must be consciously provided for in arranging schedules of benefits, fixing eligibility requirements for coverage, determining the maxium scale of employee contributions, and supervising the administration of the plan. Neither are the economies of a group operation automatic. They also must be provided for in the design and administration of the plan.

Since the underwriting unit is the group, the health of any one given individual is of no consequence except as it may affect the average. Thus group insurance requires no medical examination of individuals to be covered.[24] Even individuals with impairments or conditions that would require an extra premium in an individual plan, or who would be uninsurable under an individual plan, can be included. The theory is that they will be offset by the extra healthy individuals who are included under the plan. Group operates on the theory that if the group is selected, there will be no need to select the individuals, and the average of the group experience will approximate that of a similar number of individually selected lives. If the group itself contains a large number of employees engaged in extra hazardous occupations, or if the employees' working conditions, living conditions, or moral environment are substandard, the underwriter may load the premiums to reflect these adverse underwriting factors.

The group covered under the master contract is, as far as the individuals in it are concerned, a random group, since under a noncontributory plan all eligible members are covered; and under a contributory plan, 75 percent must be covered. This eliminates much of the choice on the part of the individual participant and is the essential feature in group underwriting.

---

[24] As the commissioners' definition states, group insurance *may* require a medical examination. In practice it rarely does except where the amount of insurance scheduled for a given life is in excess of some limit fixed by the insurer.

Where persons to be insured are allowed to decide whether or not to take the coverage, as in individual policies, there will be, on the average, a tendency for a higher proportion of the poor risks to seek the insurance. This, as has been explained, is called antiselection or adverse selection. Given an opportunity, the public will select against the company, giving it proportionately more poor risks than good risks.

Two additional factors make it possible in a group plan to write insurance without underwriting the individual members.

1. A group of employees is to a certain extent preselected. Employers hesitate to hire people in poor health. Some even require a medical examination as a condition of employment. The percentage of impaired risks, therefore, is held down.

2. There is some tendency for employees whose health deteriorates to drop out of employment and thus out of the group. In the case of group life, although an individual is entitled to take an individual policy without examination, the overall rate of such conversions is small, running at about 10 percent.

In employer associations and, to a large extent, unions, the same factors indicated above, which tend to reduce the number of impaired lives, also are applicable. They do not apply, however, to creditor and association groups.[25] In creditor group there may be no element of preselection. However, since creditor group usually covers persons buying on installments for the period over which they are in debt, individual participants are insured for relatively short periods of time so that the lack of preselection apparently is unimportant. In a few states the maximum duration of installment loans for which group credit life insurance may be written is 60 months, except for mortgage loans where the maximum duration may be 35 years. As an additional underwriting precaution, persons who will be over age 65 at the scheduled maturity date of the indebtedness or, in some plans, persons who are 65 years of age or older at the time the debt is incurred are excluded from coverage.

The lack of preselection in group insurance seems to be no problem if sound underwriting controls (effective central administration office, proper design of plan and rates to control antiselection by age, and an adequate participation requirement to control antiselection by health) are established.[26]

Rating. Group insurance rating involves two types of rating systems: manual rating and experience rating. The first year premium for a new group policy is determined according to manual rates. Premiums for sub-

---

[25] In some creditors' groups, however, there may be a form of underwriting of the debtor by the creditor similar to the underwriting of employees by the employer. Few creditors will lend to unemployed workers.

[26] Perhaps the real question is whether use of individual evidence of insurability is ever proper for group insurance.

sequent years are determined by a prospective experience rating formula. After the completion of each policy year, dividends or retroactive rate credits may be available to group policyholders on the basis of their experience for that year. In prospective experience rating, renewal premiums are set on the basis of expectations for the next year. In retrospective experience rating, refunds are given on the basis of performance for the year completed.

MANUAL RATING. The term "manual" has several meanings, the most common of which pertain to the use of hands (manual labor) or the use of a handy book (a student's or teacher's manual). It is in this latter sense that the word manual is used here. Manual premiums for group insurance frequently are computed by modern electronic equipment using employee population data supplied by the employer, tabular gross premium rates, policy constants, advance expense adjustment factors, and, where applicable, extra loadings for special hazards.

The insurer usually will require the following employee data to compute the gross premium for a group insurance policy: year of birth, sex, date of employment, occupation, and earnings. From these data the amount of insurance allocated to each employee and the average rate for the group can be determined.

Suppose the benefit schedule is based on a combination of years of service, earnings, and occupation. For example, assume that all employees except those in managerial positions are given death benefits equal to 1 year's salary if they have had less than 10 years of service and $1\frac{1}{2}$ times their annual salary for service of 10 years or more, and that managerial employees are given $1\frac{1}{2}$ times their annual salary for service of less than 10 years and 2 times their annual salary for 10 or more years of service. If the data supplied by the employer show that employee A has 15 years of service and is earning $10,000 a year in a nonmanagerial position and that employee B has 8 years of service and is earning $16,000 in a managerial position, the amounts of benefits allocated to them are $15,000 for A and $24,000 for B. The computer can be programmed to allocate the amounts of insurance to each employee based on the benefit formula.

Tabular Gross Premium Rates. Tabular gross premium rates per $1,000 of group life insurance are a function of age and are computed using the 1960 Commissioners Standard Group Mortality Table, 3 percent interest, and a loading of $33\frac{1}{3}$ percent.

The 1960 CSG Table (reproduced as Table 15–1 on page 363) is based on the intercompany studies of the Group Mortality Committee of the Society of Actuaries and represents the 1950–58 mortality and disability experience under group policies written by most of the important writers of group life insurance. The studies are restricted to employer-employee groups of 25 or more employees and exclude the few industries classed as extra hazardous. By using a semiscientific method, the experience under the three types of disability provisions discussed earlier was translated into death claims and combined with the mortality rate.[27] The actual experience was enriched to allow the companies a margin (1) to handle expected adverse variations in experience from year to year, (2) to permit the companies to write most groups at standard rates, (3) to adjust for a higher expected mortality rate where large amounts of insurance are involved (the basic experience was reported on the basis of number of lives and not on amounts of insurance), (4) to give greater weight to accidents as a cause of death at the younger ages, and (5) to provide for the cost of the privilege given certificate holders to convert into individual policies without evidence of insurability. The result was a loading of about 20 percent of the mortality rates reported plus a constant of about one death per thousand persons at each age. Over the range of ages from 16 to 60, the margin is equal to nearly 46 percent of the basic rate. For the range of ages 61 to 100, the margin is about 33 percent of the basic rate.[28]

The tabular gross premium per $1,000 of group term insurance at age 25 is shown in Table 15–2 on page 365 to be $2.97. It was figured as follows:

1. The expected cost of the benefit based on the 1960 CSG Table is $2.26 (Table 15–1).

2. Premiums are paid at the beginning of the year, but it is assumed that claims are paid evenly throughout the year. Premiums therefore can be expected to earn interest for an average of six months. The assumed rate of interest is 3 percent. A compound discount table will show that $0.98529 invested at 3 percent will accumulate to $1 in 6 months. Therefore, only $2.26 × 0.98529 or $2.23 is needed at the beginning of the year to accumulate to $2.26 in 6 months. This amount ($2.23) is called the net premium.

3. To arrive at the tabular gross premium, the net premium is increased by a loading of 33⅓ percent. The 33⅓ percent loading on $2.23 amounts to $0.74. The tabular gross premium then is equal to $2.23 plus $0.74 or $2.97 (Table 15–2).

Computing the Manual Rate. The manual rate charged an initial group is a weighted average reflecting the composition of the group. The premium is the gross rate times the amount of insurance written. The gross rate is computed from the tabular gross premiums plus a policy constant of $2.40 per thousand for the first $40,000 of insurance to offset the high cost of

---

[27] Seventy-five percent of the waiver of premium claims, 50 percent of the maturity value claims, and 100 percent of the extended death benefit claims were counted as death claims. The 75 percent rule is supported by statistics, the 50 percent rule is based on judgment, and the 100 percent rule was adopted for its simplicity.

[28] At ages 0 to 15, where there was no group mortality experience, the 1960 CSG Table show mortality rates equal to 117.5 percent of that shown for these ages in the 1958 CSO Table. This percentage extends the relationship existing between these two tables at age 18. At advanced ages where the amount of group mortality data was considered insufficient for credibility, the group mortality rates with margins were arbitrarily set at 105 percent of that produced for those ages under the 1958 CSO Table.

TABLE 15-1
Commissioners 1960 Standard Group Mortality Table

Age	Deaths per 1,000	Number Living	Number Dying	Expectation of Life— Years
0	8.32	10,000,000	83,200	66.86
1	2.07	9,916,800	20,528	66.41
3	1.79	9,896,272	17,714	65.55
3	1.72	9,878,558	16,991	64.67
4	1.65	9,861,567	16,272	63.78
5	1.59	9,845,295	15,654	62.88
6	1.53	9,829,641	15,039	61.98
7	1.48	9,814,602	14,526	61.08
8	1.45	9,800,076	14,210	60.17
9	1.42	9,785,866	13,896	59.25
10	1.42	9,771,970	13,876	58.34
11	1.45	9,758,094	14,149	57.42
12	1.48	9,743,945	14,421	56.50
13	1.55	9,729,524	15,081	55.58
14	1.63	9,714,443	15,835	54.67
15	1.72	9,698,608	16,682	53.76
16	1.81	9,681,926	17,524	52.85
17	1.90	9,664,402	18,362	51.95
18	1.99	9,646,040	19,196	51.04
19	2.03	9,626,844	19,542	50.14
20	2.09	9,607,302	20,079	49.25
21	2.14	9,587,223	20,517	48.35
22	2.18	9,566,706	20,855	47.45
23	2.21	9,545,851	21,096	46.55
24	2.24	9,524,755	21,335	45.65
25	2.26	9,503,420	21,478	44.76
26	2.28	9,481,942	21,619	43.86
27	2.30	9,460,323	21,759	42.96
28	2.33	9,438,564	21,992	42.05
29	2.36	9,416,572	22,223	41.15
30	2.40	9,394,349	22,546	40.25
31	2.45	9,371,803	22,961	39.34
32	2.51	9,348,842	23,466	38.44
33	2.60	9,325,376	24,246	37.53
34	2.71	9,301,130	25,206	36.63
35	2.85	9,275,924	26,436	35.73
36	3.02	9,249,488	27,933	34.83
37	3.21	9,221,555	29,601	33.93
38	3.45	9,191,954	31,712	33.04
39	3.72	9,160,242	34,076	32.15
40	4.02	9,126,166	36,687	31.27
41	4.37	9,089,479	39,721	30.39
42	4.75	9,049,758	42,986	29.53
43	5.18	9,006,772	46,655	28.66
44	5.64	8,960,117	50,535	27.81
45	6.15	8,909,582	54,794	26.97
46	6.70	8,854,788	59,327	26.13
47	7.31	8,795,461	64,295	25.30
48	7.98	8,731,166	69,675	24.49
49	8.72	8,661,491	75,528	23.68

TABLE 15–1 (Continued)

Age	Deaths per 1,000	Number Living	Number Dying	Expectation of Life— Years
50	9.52	8,585,963	81,738	22.88
51	10.40	8,504,225	88,444	22.10
52	11.37	8,415,781	95,687	21.32
53	12.44	8,320,094	103,502	20.56
54	13.61	8,216,592	111,828	19.82
55	14.88	8,104,764	120,499	19.08
56	16.24	7,984,165	129,663	18.36
57	17.70	7,854,502	139,025	17.66
58	19.24	7,715,477	148,446	16.97
59	20.87	7,567,031	147,924	16.29
60	22.62	7,409,107	167,594	15.63
61	24.51	7,241,513	177,489	14.98
62	26.60	7,064,024	187,903	14.34
63	28.86	6,876,121	198,445	13.72
64	31.31	6,677,676	209,078	13.11
65	34.00	6,468,598	219,932	12.52
66	37.00	6,248,666	231,201	11.94
67	40.32	6,017,465	242,624	11.38
68	44.01	5,774,841	254,151	10.84
69	48.03	5,520,790	265,159	10.32
70	52.33	5,255,531	275,022	9.81
71	56.86	4,980,509	283,192	9.33
72	61.58	4,697,317	289,261	8.86
73	66.42	4,408,056	292,783	8.41
74	71.53	4,115,273	294,365	7.97
75	77.04	3,820,908	294,363	7.54
76	83.14	3,526,545	293,197	7.13
77	89.98	3,233,348	290,987	6.73
78	97.71	2,942,411	287,503	6.35
79	106.25	2,654,908	282,084	5.98
80	115.48	2,372,824	274,014	5.63
81	125.32	2,098,810	263,023	5.30
82	135.63	1,835,787	248,988	4.99
83	146.35	1,586,799	232,228	4.70
84	157.51	1,354,571	213,358	4.42
85	169.20	1,141,213	193,093	4.15
86	181.46	948,120	172,046	3.89
87	194.39	776,074	150,861	3.65
88	208.16	625,218	130,144	3.41
89	223.08	495,069	110,440	3.17
90	239.55	384,629	92,138	2.94
91	258.06	292,491	75,480	2.70
92	279.23	217,011	60,596	2.47
93	303.76	156,415	47,513	2.23
94	332.49	108,902	36,209	1.99
95	368.80	72,693	26,809	1.73
96	420.59	45,884	19,298	1.45
97	512.84	26,586	13,634	1.13
98	701.56	12,952	9,087	.80
99	1,000.00	3,865	3,865	.50

TABLE 15–2

Tabular Gross Premium Rates per $1,000 of Group Term Insurance
1960 CSG Table at 3% Loaded by the Basic Loading Percentage
(Ages 15–95)

Age Nearest Birthday	Annual	Semiannual	Quarterly	Monthly
15	$ 2.26	$ 1.14	$ 0.57	$ 0.19
16	2.38	1.20	0.60	0.20
17	2.50	1.26	0.63	0.21
18	2.61	1.31	0.66	0.22
19	2.67	1.35	0.67	0.23
20	2.75	1.39	0.69	0.23
21	2.81	1.42	0.71	0.24
22	2.86	1.44	0.72	0.24
23	2.90	1.46	0.73	0.25
24	2.94	1.48	0.74	0.25
25	2.97	1.50	0.75	0.25
26	3.00	1.51	0.76	0.25
27	3.02	1.52	0.76	0.26
28	3.06	1.54	0.77	0.26
29	3.10	1.56	0.78	0.26
30	3.15	1.59	0.80	0.27
31	3.22	1.62	0.81	0.27
32	3.30	1.66	0.83	0.28
33	3.42	1.72	0.86	0.29
34	3.56	1.79	0.90	0.30
35	3.74	1.88	0.94	0.32
36	3.97	2.00	1.00	0.34
37	4.22	2.13	1.07	0.36
38	4.53	2.28	1.14	0.38
39	4.89	2.46	1.23	0.41
40	5.28	2.66	1.33	0.45
41	5.74	2.89	1.45	0.49
42	6.24	3.14	1.58	0.53
43	6.81	3.43	1.72	0.58
44	7.41	3.73	1.87	0.63
45	8.08	4.07	2.04	0.68
46	8.80	4.43	2.22	0.74
47	9.60	4.84	2.42	0.81
48	10.48	5.28	2.65	0.89
49	11.45	5.77	2.89	0.97
50	12.51	6.30	3.16	1.06
51	13.66	6.88	3.45	1.16
52	14.94	7.53	3.77	1.26
53	16.34	8.23	4.13	1.38
54	17.88	9.01	4.51	1.51
55	19.55	9.85	4.94	1.65
56	21.34	10.75	5.39	1.80
57	23.25	11.71	5.87	1.97
58	25.28	12.73	6.38	2.14
59	27.42	13.81	6.92	2.32
60	29.72	14.97	7.50	2.51
61	32.20	16.22	8.13	2.72
62	34.95	17.61	8.82	2.96

TABLE 15-2 (Continued)

Age Nearest Birthday	Annual	Semiannual	Quarterly	Monthly
63	$ 37.92	$ 19.10	$ 9.57	$ 3.21
64	41.13	20.72	10.39	3.48
65	44.67	22.50	11.28	3.78
66	48.61	24.49	12.27	4.11
67	52.97	26.68	13.37	4.48
68	54.82	29.13	14.60	4.89
69	63.10	31.79	15.93	5.34
70	68.75	34.63	17.36	5.81
71	74.70	37.63	18.86	6.32
72	80.90	40.75	20.43	6.84
73	87.26	43.96	22.03	7.38
74	93.97	47.34	23.73	7.95
75	101.21	50.98	25.56	8.56
76	109.23	55.02	27.58	9.24
77	118.21	59.55	29.85	10.00
78	128.37	64.67	32.41	10.86
79	139.59	70.32	35.25	11.81
80	151.71	76.42	38.31	12.83
81	164.64	82.94	41.57	13.93
82	178.19	89.76	44.99	15.07
83	192.27	96.86	48.55	16.26
84	206.93	104.24	52.25	17.50
85	222.29	111.98	56.13	18.80
86	238.40	120.09	60.20	20.16
87	255.38	128.65	64.48	21.60
88	273.47	137.76	69.05	23.13
89	293.08	147.64	74.00	24.79
90	314.71	158.54	79.46	26.62
91	339.03	170.79	85.61	28.68
92	336.84	184.80	92.63	31.03
93	399.07	201.03	100.77	33.75
94	436.82	220.05	110.30	36.95
95	484.52	244.08	122.34	40.98

small groups less an advance expense adjustment factor to allow for the cost reduction that accompanies the increase in the size of the group. The expense adjustment factor applies only to groups producing annual premiums (tabular plus policy constant) of $2,400 or more.[29] If the policy is written for an extra hazardous industry or includes the maturity value disability benefit, an extra premium is added.

Assume a group with an employee population of 50 employees and that each employee is given $10,000 of life insurance. Assume further that the industry is not one of the few rated extra hazardous, and that the disability benefit is the waiver of premium type and therefore does not require an additional premium. Assume the following age distribution of employees:

29 The amount of the advance expense adjustment factor depends upon the size of the tabular gross premium plus policy constant.

Age	Number	Age	Number
20	10	50	10
30	10	60	10
40	10		

TABLE 15–3

Advance Expense Adjustment Factors for Use with Commissioners 1961 Standard Group Life Insurance Premium Rates

Net Premium Plus Basic Loading Percentage Plus Policy Constant (Annual Basis)		Net Premium Plus Basic Loading Percentage Plus Policy Constant (Monthly Basis)		Advance Expense Adjustment Factor
Under $ 2,400		Under $ 200		0%
2,400 – $	2,999	200 – $	249	1
3,000 –	3,599	250 –	299	2
3,600 –	4,199	300 –	349	3
4,200 –	4,799	350 –	399	4
4,800 –	5,399	400 –	449	5
5,400 –	5,999	450 –	499	6
6,000 –	7,199	500 –	599	7
7,200 –	8,399	600 –	699	8
8,400 –	9,599	700 –	799	9
9,600 –	11,999	800 –	999	10
12,000 –	17,999	1,000 –	1,499	11
18,000 –	35,999	1,500 –	2,999	12
36,000 –	59,999	3,000 –	4,999	13
60,000 –	119,999	5,000 –	9,999	14
120,000 –	179,999	10,000 –	14,999	15
180,000 –	239,999	15,000 –	19,999	16
240,000 –	359,999	20,000 –	29,999	17
360,000 –	419,999	30,000 –	39,999	18
480,000 –	719,000	40,000 –	59,000	19
720,000 –	and over	60,000 – and over		20

The gross premium charged for an initial group term policy would be figured as follows:

(1) Age	(2) Number of Employees	(3) Amount of Insurance per Employee in $1,000 Units	(4) Total Amount of Insurance in $1,000 Units	(5) Tabular Premium for Age Class	(6) Total Premium for Age Class
20	10	10	100	$ 2.75	$ 275.00
30	10	10	100	3.15	315.00
40	10	10	100	5.28	528.00
50	10	10	100	12.51	1,251.00
60	10	10	100	29.72	2,972.00
	50		500		$5,341.00

Policy constant ($2.40 × 40) 96.00

Tabular premium plus policy constant $5,437.00
Less advance expense adjustment factor ($5,437 × 0.06) 326.22

Total gross premium $5,110.78
Average rate per $1,000 ($5,110.78 ÷ 500) $ 10.22

In the above illustrative computation, the total amount of insurance in units of $1,000 (column 4) is multiplied by the tabular premium for each age class (column 5) to produce the total premium for the age class (column 6). The $96 policy constant ($2.40 $\times$ 40) is added to the total premium for all age classes (total of column 6) bringing the amount to $5,437. Since this amount lies between $5,400 and $5,999 it is discounted by an advance expense adjustment factor of 6 percent, reducing the total to $5,110.78 (see Table 15–3 on page 367). The total gross premium, $5,110.78, is then divided by 500, the number of $1,000 units of insurance written for the group (the total of column 4) to give the average rate. The average rate, $10.22 per $1,000, is the rate that will be used for adjustments in amounts of insurance involving new entrants and terminations regardless of the ages of such entering or terminating employees. It will continue to be used until a new rate is calculated upon renewal of the policy. The premium rate computed in the foregoing illustration is the minimum initial premium that can be charged for new groups written in Maine, Michigan, New York, Ohio, and Pennsylvania. When no minimum premium law governs, insurers frequently charge premiums lower than those produced by these rates. Most of the group life insurance written is subject to these minimum premiums because of the extraterritorial application of the New York law: Insurers writing business in New York must adhere substantially to the New York law on business written elsewhere.

Premiums on group insurance generally are paid monthly, and, using the 1961 scale, are equal to 8.458 percent of the annual premium. In the foregoing illustration, the monthly premium would be $10.22 $\times$ 0.08458 or $0.86 a month per $1,000. Under a contributory plan, the employees might be asked to pay as much as $0.60 of this premium. Manual rating in group life insurance makes no distinction between the rates charged males and females, but in some contributory plans, employers ask for lower contributions from female employees than from male employees.

If the group requires an extra rating (i.e., if it is substandard), an amount is added to the total premium which represents the estimated difference between standard and expected mortality for the year (in the case of group term). If only part of the group is subject to the extra hazard (as, for instance, an organization with two plants, only one of which is engaged in extra hazardous work), the cost of the extra premium is, nevertheless, distributed over the entire group. The average rate is always the same for each member of the group regardless of his age, sex, or the job he performs.

EXPERIENCE RATING. The initial premium charged for a group life insurance policy is the manual premium. Renewal premiums are adjusted to reflect (1) the experience of the "average" group in the class or (2) the experience of the particular individual group to be rated, one, the other, or both, depending on the size of the group and the number of years of experience available for the group. Renewal premiums for small groups are determined by class experience; for large groups they are determined by the group's own experience; and for in-between groups they are weighted, determined partly by class experience and partly by the group's own experience.

Group insurance is a highly competitive business. In order to retain their clients (and attract new ones), insurers are forced to use experience rating plans that appeal to buyers. The basic elements in an experience rating formula are (1) claims, (2) expenses, (3) risk charge, and (4) reserve for claims fluctuations.

Claims. One factor in the renewal premium to be charged the group is the probable future claims experience for the group. The probable claims experience for a group of, say, 100 employees will be that of the average of the entire class of which the particular group is a part, because 100 employees is an insufficient number for the experience of the particular individual group to be statistically significant.[30] However, the experience with a group of 2,000 employees might have full statistical significance. Its own experience would be used to measure its expected claims. The statistical significance of the experience with a group of 500 employees might be assigned a value of 25 percent so that the expected claims for that group would be a weighted average composed of 25 percent of its own experience and 75 percent of the experience for the entire class. If the group of 500 has accumulated experience for 5 years, the statistical significance of this experience might be assigned a value of 60 percent. In that event the expected claims for the group would be a weighted average composed of 60 percent of its own experience and 40 percent of the experience for the entire class.

Suppose that the previously described case involving 50 lives and an initial manual premium of $5,110.78 is up for renewal. Because the group is small, its expected claims will be based on the insurer's claim experience for all groups in the same class. If the insurer's manual loss ratio (incurred claims ÷ manual premium) for the class after adjustments for trends is 70 percent, then the expected claims experience for the group is $3,577.55 ($5,110.78 × 0.70). And that is the claims charge projected for the group.

Suppose the group had $6 million of insurance spread over 2,000 lives. If the initial manual premium for the group is $57,678.48 and the adjusted manual loss ratio is 50 percent, the expected claims projected for the group would be $28,839.20 ($57,678.40 × 0.50). The credibility given to the experience of this group is 100 percent because the group is large enough for its experience to have full statistical significance.

If the group had only 500 lives, then its own experience would have

[30] For a group of 100 lives that has been insured for 5 years, there will be enough experience for it to have some statistical significance, perhaps about 25 percent.

some, but not full statistical significance in projecting future claims. Suppose that the group had $2 million of insurance on these 500 lives with an initial manual premium of $19,729.60 and an adjusted manual loss ratio of 60 percent producing $11,837.76 in claims ($19,729.60 × 0.60). The average experience for the class would produce expected claims of $13,810.72 ($19,729.60 × 0.70). Using the aforementioned 25–75 weighted average, the expected claims for the group would be projected at $13,317.48 [($11,837 × 0.25) + ($13,810.72 × 0.75)].

In measuring the probable loss ratio for a group, the insurer considers all death claims paid, all disability claims approved (75 percent of the face amount of the insurance for waiver of premium claims and the present value of proceeds to be paid under maturity value claims), any changes in the reserve for claims incurred but not reported, claims reported but not paid, and assessments for the additional mortality expected from the adverse selection when the privilege of converting group coverage to individual coverage is exercised by members of the group ($65 to $85 per $1,000 of converted insurance, or in the small groups, 1 or 2 percent of the total premium).[31]

A ceiling may be put on the total claims to be charged against a particular group for the policy period. This limit will vary by the size of the group and is expressed in terms of loss ratios. It might be 200 percent for a group of 500 lives and as low as 110 percent for a very large group. The loss limit excludes from the individual group experience that has no statistical significance. The abnormal claims are charged to all groups and are spread among individual groups as a contingency or excess claims charge. A group large enough to produce a stable year to year claim experience is, in effect, self-rated for normal losses (100 percent credibility is given to its normal experience) and is insured only against catastrophic losses, that is, claims in excess of the annual loss limit.

Expenses. The premium charge must be large enough to cover not only expected claims but also expenses incurred by the insurer in soliciting, servicing, and administering the group insurance plan. These costs include sales (commissions and salaries), printing (policy, certificates, booklets, and forms), servicing (claims, consultations, additions, and deletions), and administration (billing, records, and general overhead). In addition, premiums must be sufficient to pay taxes associated with the case and to yield a profit. Where economically feasible, these expenses are charged directly to

---

[31] Those in bad health are thought to be more inclined to convert their policies, while those in good health may not take advantage of the conversion privilege. Often, however, even employees who are uninsurable fail to convert their coverage. Sometimes the reason is ignorance, lack of interest, or coverage under another group; at other times, it is the inability to pay the premium for permanent insurance. Were it possible to convert the term forms, the chances are that a larger percentage of group coverage would be converted. Currently, only about 1.25 percent of employees leaving a group convert their group coverage to individual insurance, and it is suspected that most of these are otherwise uninsurable.

the particular group involved, otherwise they are spread among the groups by formula designed to charge each group as closely as possible for the expenses incurred on its behalf. For example, commissions and premium taxes can be charged directly to each group without expensive record keeping, but a system that allocates certain administrative expenses (each postage stamp, each guest luncheon check, each phone call, and so on) on an exact basis would not be worth the cost involved.

The systems used to allocate expenses to particular groups vary among insurers. Certain administrative and servicing expenses usually are assessed on the basis of a fixed amount for the contract, a given amount for each group member, and a specific amount for each claim. These flat charges may be arranged so that they bear a lower ratio to the total premium charged for large groups than for small groups. Premium taxes vary widely among the states.[32] Some insurers charge each group the exact premium tax paid for that group, whereas others charge an average tax rate for all groups. Commissions paid usually are charged directly to the group, although where the commission scale used provides for a higher first-year commission and scaled down renewal commissions, the insurer may amortize the extra first-year commission over several years rather than charge it all to the group immediately.

Risk Charge. In addition to the charge for probable future claims experience and for those expenses of the insurer not associated with claims, a risk charge (sometimes called an insurance charge) is added to cover claims not charged against the group. A risk charge is added also to cover additional claims in years when actual claims exceed predicted claims. This charge enables the insurer to return cash refunds to groups that earn experience credits and to build a general surplus and contingency reserve as a buffer against catastrophes (epidemics and earthquakes, for example) that might adversely affect the insurer's financial position. The size of the risk charge varies inversely with both the number of lives covered and the amount of the loss limit.

Claims Fluctuation Reserve. In addition to the charge for a contribution to the general surplus of the insurer to build a contingency fund, the group may be required to build a special claims fluctuation reserve to be held by the insurer. The purpose of the reserve is to allow the insurer to improve the predictive qualities of the exposure by extending the time over which claims can be forecast. With the accumulation of the claims fluctuation reserve, the risk charge can be reduced.

RETROSPECTIVE RATING. Retrospective rating is an extension of experience rating, using much the same formula but some different figures.

---

[32] The premium tax ranges from a high of 4 percent to a low of 1.7 percent. The most common rate is 2 percent. The rates are not applied uniformly to the same base in all states, and tax offsets vary widely among states, so it is necessary to look beyond the rate itself for an adequate comparison of premium taxes among the states. In 10 states, domestic insurers are exempt from premium taxes.

The purpose of experience rating (renewal rating) is to establish an adequate and equitable ex ante (from before) premium for the coming year based on *projected* claims experience, *estimated* expenses, risk charges, and profit charges. The purpose of retrospective rating is to establish a reasonable and equitable ex post (from after) premium for the policy year just completed based on *actual* claims incurred, *actual* expenses charged to the group, risk charges, and profit charges.

The sum of the risk charge, profit charge, and expense charge is technically known as the retention. If the retention plus the incurred claims and additions to the claims fluctuation reserve is less than the premium earned, the excess is refunded to the policyholder. If the retention plus incurred claims exceed the premium, the deficit is charged against the claim fluctuation reserve, carried forward against the experience of the group in subsequent years, or absorbed by the insurer.[33] In the retrospective rating formula, the claims experience of the particular group may be given a higher credibility factor than that used in the renewal rating formula. For example, the credibility factor used in the renewal rating formula for a group of 500 lives might be 25 percent whereas a 60 percent credibility factor might be used in the retrospective rating formula. Furthermore, the expense allocations used in a retrospective rating formula are more likely to reflect the costs attributable to the group than the formula allocations used in experience rating.

Retrospective experience rating is treated in greater detail in Chapter 16, where both the asset share and tabular methods are discussed.

6. GROUP PERMANENT LIFE INSURANCE

While the vast majority of group life insurance policies are written as one-year renewable term, an increasing number of group contracts are written as group permanent. Group permanent plans are used where group life insurance is designed to protect against both premature death and old age, or, even more commonly, where the employer wishes to give the employee a paid-up policy at retirement. Two major types of group permanent are written: unit purchase and level premium.

The Unit Purchase Plan. The more popular group permanent plan is the unit purchase plan, known generally as the group paid-up plan. The plan involves a combination of single premium whole life insurance with decreasing term insurance. Usually the amount of group term purchased on each employee will decrease as the amount of permanent insurance increases, so that the total amount of insurance in force on his life remains

---

[33] Because of the highly competitive nature of the group insurance market, insurers are not likely to carry forward large experience deficits against a group for fear that the group will shift its business to another insurer in order to start off with a clean slate. Indeed, the sophisticated insurance buyer may be able to get his insurer to absorb all of any experience deficit.

constant.[34] Customarily, the employer's contributions are used to buy group term insurance, whereas those of the employee are used to purchase units of paid-up group permanent. Since the employees' contributions remain constant, the additional amount of paid-up permanent purchased decreases each year because the rate goes up as the employee's age advances.

For example, assume that the employee under the benefit formula is entitled to group insurance equal to his annual salary of $8,000. He is 25 years old when he becomes eligible for coverage. If the employee contribution rate is the customary $1.30 a month per thousand (it could be more or less), his premium the first year will buy $453.04 of paid-up whole life insurance and his employer will pay for $7,546.96 of 1-year term insurance. Next year his contribution will buy $430.56 of paid-up whole life giving him a total of $883.60 of paid-up insurance, leaving his employer to purchase $7,116.40 of 1-year term insurance. Assuming no changes either in his contribution rate or the rates for paid-up group permanent, by the time the employee reaches age 65 he will have accumulated $11,448 of paid-up life insurance.[35] Of course, the older the employee is when he enters the plan, the less will be his paid-up life insurance at retirement. For example, if he had started at age 40, assuming the same $8,000 benefit, his paid-up life insurance at age 65 would be only $5,858.32. For this reason, instead of a flat rate for each employee, some plans call for a contribution rate which varies with the age of the employee at the outset but remains level throughout the period of coverage. The monthly contributions per $1,000 of insurance might be set at $1 for those under age 30, $1.30 for those 30 to 39, $1.95 for those 40 to 49, and $2.60 for those over age 50. Special arrangements involving a continuation of term insurance after retirement sometimes are made for employees who are within 20 years of retirement when the plan is installed, because they will not have had time to build an adequate amount of paid-up group permanent life insurance coverage.

In the usual case, group term is terminated when the employee resigns, is fired, or retires, but it may be converted by the insured at attained age. The group permanent remains in force because it is paid-up insurance. Instead of retaining the permanent insurance, however, the ex-employee, if he so desires, may exercise the option of taking the cash surrender value of the policy. Cash surrender values, however, are not allowed while the employee remains under the group plan.

---

[34] That is, assuming that the employee does not shift from one benefit class to another.

[35] A case such as this might lead the employer, at first blush, to consider a lower rate of contribution for employees entering at such young ages, since this employee will have paid-up insurance of $8,000, the amount of his scheduled benefits, by the time he passes age 49. This means that the employer will not be participating in the plan during the last 16 years. But since normal progress and cost-of-living increases will likely raise the salary of this young man to a figure well over $8,000 a year long before he passes age 49, chances are that his paid-up insurance will never equal his formula benefits, and his employer will continue to participate in the plan.

The Level Premium Plan. Under the level premium plan of group permanent, any policy other than term can be used. Life paid up at age 65, endowment at age 65, retirement income, whole life, and life paid up at 85 are common. In level premium group permanent, the employees' rights upon termination of employment depend upon the nature of the vesting. If the plan is noncontributory and no rights are vested in the employee, then all he has is the right to convert to an individual policy. The employer is refunded the cash value. If the plan is contributory or is a vested non-contributory one, the employee may take the cash value or the paid-up value, or he may continue the entire amount of the coverage in force by paying the full premium direct to the company. If the group permanent is used to fund a qualified pension plan, the employee will be entitled to receive at least his contributions and, in some instances, interest on them, which may exceed the cash value.[36]

Whereas the usual purpose of the unit benefit group permanent is to fund a paid-up life insurance policy for employees at retirement, the usual purpose of level premium group permanent is to fund income benefits for employees at retirement under a qualified pension plan. The difference in the way in which the two plans are taxed accounts for the difference in the circumstances under which they are used. Where reasonable in amount, employers' contributions to group permanent are a deductible business expense if the plan is qualified as a pension plan under Treasury Department regulations. (If the plan is not qualified but the rights of the employees are currently nonforfeitable, the contributions of the employer still will be deductible as a business expense.)

The income tax consequences to the employees depend on whether or not the plan is qualified as a pension plan. In nonqualified plans where the rights of the individual employee are nonforfeitable, the employee must report as taxable income in the year paid the full amount of the group permanent premium paid on his behalf by his employer. In qualified plans, the employee reports as taxable income only that part of the group permanent premium paid by the employer that is used to provide life insurance. The taxable income reported is the cost of one-year term insurance for the amount of life insurance provided. The remainder of the premium paid by the employer is treated as deferred income, to the employee.

Since premiums paid by employers on nonmedical group term life insurance in amounts not in excess of $50,000 need not be reported as income by the employee, the usual procedure in nonqualified plans is to use the unit purchase (group paid-up) plan under which the employer's contributions are used to buy the group decreasing term insurance, and the employee's contributions are used to buy the group permanent paid-up cover-

---

[36] A qualified pension plan is one that is approved by the Internal Revenue Service for favorable tax treatment. Pension plans are discussed in Chapter 17.

age. In this way, the employee gets the greatest tax advantage from the plan.

In qualified plans, the procedure used is reversed. The level premium plan of group permanent insurance is used. Under it, the employee's contributions are allocated, first to pay for the insurance protection at one-year term rates, and the employer's contributions are used, first to build the cash values. By this method of allocating premiums, the employee is given the most favorable income tax treatment.

A simpler solution for qualified plans (and the logical one under a noncontributory plan) would seem to be to provide for death benefits through group term life insurance and to fund the pension benefits through a group annuity contract.

7. WHOLESALE (FRANCHISE) LIFE INSURANCE

Wholesale life insurance is an adaptation of some of the principles of group insurance to groups that are too small to qualify for group coverage. Wholesale insurance is used also in some large groups where the required percentage of participation cannot be obtained under a contributory plan, or where the employer pays none of the premium. When separate life insurance contracts of the same form are issued to members of an association on a mass marketing basis, the plan is called franchise life insurance, or sometimes, simply, association group.

Under wholesale life insurance plans individual policies are issued to each person in the group, and individual underwriting is done. Physical examinations may be required, although in practice they are usually waived in favor of a statement about the health of the applicant. The employer, while not applying for the insurance, signs an agreement with the company to pay the premiums. The plan may be contributory or noncontributory, but in either case the employer is responsible for the payment of the premium, and (if the plan is contributory or wholly financed by employees) for its collection from employees.

Wholesale life insurance is also available under certain conditions on a guaranteed issue basis, especially where a high percentage (75–100 percent) of eligible employees are covered. A guaranteed issue basis means that individual underwriting is eliminated. The availability of guaranteed issue contracts usually is determined by the amount of insurance involved, the nature of the group, and the number of persons covered.

Wholesale or franchise life insurance is written under conditions designed to eliminate as much adverse selection as possible. The amount for which the employee is insured is not left up to him but is set by a predetermined schedule.

As in group life insurance, the usual plan of insurance is one-year term. The insured names his own beneficiary and has possession and control of the policy (instead of having only a certificate of participation). The contract usually includes the conversion privilege. Because of the small size of the group covered and consequently a higher administration cost, the premium for wholesale (franchise) life insurance is higher than for group life insurance.

Since the number of participants required under group life insurance has been reduced, wholesale life insurance has found less application than formerly, except as franchise coverage written on members of professional societies, employee associations, and other types of groups indirectly related to employment or occupation.

8. GROUP CREDIT LIFE INSURANCE

Credit life insurance is issued through a lender or lending agency to cover payment of a loan, installment purchase, or other obligation in the event of death of the debtor. About 90 percent of the credit life insurance in force in the United States is written under group contracts. The contract is between the insurer and the lender. The borrower is given a certificate by the creditor indicating the coverage afforded under the master contract.

Credit life insurance is term insurance usually written for the amount of the loan and decreasing as the loan is repaid. If the amount of the indebtedness exceeds the maximum limit per life, the debt is not fully insured until the unpaid balance of the loan is reduced to the maximum limit.[37] The policy usually provides for the termination of insurance on debtors who become delinquent and remain so for a specified period.

Group credit insurance is a simple operation. The creditor issues the certificate of insurance to the debtor, computes and remits the premium on each payment date, and forwards a transcript of the death certificate to the insurer for claim payments. Claims may be paid to the creditor by the insurer direct or the creditor may be authorized to draw a draft on the insurer for the amount of the claim. A claim form showing the amount of the outstanding indebtedness is completed by the creditor and sent to the insurer.

Premiums are usually paid monthly and are computed under one of two simple formulas, both of which use a flat rate unrelated to the age of the borrowers. Under one formula the premium is based on the amount of insured indebtedness outstanding at the time the monthly premium is due. Under the other formula the premium is computed on a single premium basis. The rate is applied to the total amount of insured loans originating

---

[37] Under some policies when the indebtedness exceeds the maximum amount of insurance permitted on a single life, the amount of insurance is restricted to the percentage of the unpaid debt that the individual life limit bears to the initial indebtedness. Thus, if the single life limit is $4,000 and the initial indebtedness is $5,000, then the amount of insurance is equal to 80 percent of the amount of the outstanding balance. The debt is never fully insured under this arrangement.

during the month. Under the outstanding balance formula the rate base is $1,000 of outstanding balance, for example, $0.84 per $1,000 of outstanding balance. Under the single premium formula the rate base is $100 of initial indebtedness, for example $0.55 per $100 of initial indebtedness repayable in 12 monthly installments. When the debtor is charged specifically for the insurance as is customary, he is required by the lender to pay the full cost of the insurance in advance, regardless of whether the monthly outstanding balance or single premium formula is used by the lender in computing the remittances due the insurer. The total cost of the insurance is added to the loan and the debtor pays the full financing charges even though under the monthly outstanding balance formula the lender does not have to remit the full premium in advance.

Premium rates vary widely among insurers and among insureds of the same insurer. For example, borrowers of one finance company pay single premiums from a low of $0.44 to a high of $0.75 per $100 of initial balance, to be repaid in 12 equal installments. The coverage is underwritten by 5 insurers: 1 in 23 states, another in 15 states, 1 in 7 states, and 2 insurers each writing in 1 state. In one state, for example, group credit life insurance underwritten by one insurer is offered through the Automobile Dealers Association of that state at 4 rates per $100: $0.50, $0.60, $0.75, and $1. The rate charged by all except 2 dealers using the plan is $1. The other 2 charge $0.75. Nationwide specialty automobile finance companies make group credit life insurance available to car purchasers in this state at much lower rates. One automobile finance company using a group contract underwritten by one insurer charges $0.375 per $100 whereas another using a different insurer charges $0.386. These two finance companies pay no commissions to the automobile dealers whereas the dealers get a 40 percent commission on the $0.75 rate and a 55 percent commission on the $1 rate for insurance written through the facilities provided by the Association.

The lender cannot charge the borrower more than the premium to be paid to the insurer. But the lender can receive an experience dividend on his group insurance contract just as an employer may receive dividends under his group insurance contract. For example, dividends on group credit life insurance policies have become an important source of revenue to a number of finance companies.[38]

Group Credit Life Insurance and Public Policy. Elected and appointed public officials at both state and federal levels have expressed concern about the type of competitive system under which group credit life insurance is marketed. Insurers also have shown some concern. A system that produces such wide variety in the premiums charged similar borrowers suggests a type of competition that is not in the public interest. Normal

---

[38] *Consumer Credit Industry* (Hearings before the Subcommittee on Antitrust and Monopoly of the Committee of the Judiciary, U.S. Senate, 90th Cong., Part 3 [Washington, D.C.: U.S. Government Printing Office, 1968]), pp. 2093–99.

competitive forces in the distribution of group credit insurance tend to raise the cost of the insurance to the borrower. In many cases the rate is negotiated between the insurer and the lender and is set at that level which will provide the highest profit to the lender. The borrower is usually a pawn in the process because his primary interest in obtaining the loan is likely to make him a captive insured.

STATE REGULATION. The National Association of Insurance Commissioners in 1957 drafted a model bill for the regulation of credit life and health insurance. The model bill, revised in 1960, was designed to correct the abuses that the 1954 United States Senate Subcommittee on Antitrust found to exist in the sale of credit life insurance, such abuses as requiring the borrower to pay more for the insurance than the benefits warranted and failure to disclose to the debtor the nature and cost of the coverage. Thirty-one states and the District of Columbia have enacted the model bill in substantially the form recommended by the NAIC. Three additional states have enacted statutes which give the insurance commissioner broad authority to regulate credit life and health insurance. Of these 35 jurisdictions, 27 have promulgated supplemental regulations. The insurance commissioners in six states where no special statutes relating to credit insurance were enacted use their general regulatory authority to issue regulations substantially similar to the 1954 model rules and regulations prepared by a subcommittee of the National Association of Insurance Commissioners.

Under the legislation or regulation concerning the sale of credit life insurance, the lender is required to furnish the insured debtor evidence of his insurance, the borrower cannot be charged more for his coverage than the premium paid by the creditor to the insurer, the debtor must be given a refund of the premium on the declining balance of credit life insurance as of the time the insurance is cancelled, and the insurance must provide benefits that are reasonable in relation to the premium charge.

There is general agreement that with a few exceptions the states have dealt with the abuses of lack of disclosure, charging borrowers premiums higher than those charged by the insurers, and failure to refund unearned premiums. But the abuse of overcharging still exists in all but a few states. An insurance company executive explained the problem clearly before a United States Senate subcommittee:[39]

In the sale of other forms of insurance, competition produces reasonable rates because the purchaser is seeking the best possible benefits at the lowest possible rates. . . . In the case of Credit Insurance, however, while the debtor usually pays for the insurance, he is not the real purchaser. . . . Because the costs are passed on to the debtor, there is no incentive on the part of the creditor to hold down the cost. In fact, the situation is often just the reverse. When the creditor pays a higher premium for credit insurance and passes it on to the debtor, he stands to gain more in the form of either a commission or a dividend or retrospec-

---

[39] See statement of Kenneth C. Nichols, *ibid.,* pp. 2348–52.

tive rate credit, based on the experience of his case. . . . In December of 1959, the NAIC recommended that at least 50 percent of the premium dollar should be returned to the debtor public in the form of claim payments. Thereafter, a number of States which enacted the model bill adopted the 50 percent minimum loss ratio principle but many of them permitted insurers to change rates which produce loss ratios substantially below 50 percent. Many did not establish maximum rates and others permitted insurers to charge as much as 75 cents or more (per $100). . . . [An NAIC] study of credit life insurance experience for the years 1960 through 1962 . . . showed that the claim rate for $100 indebtedness repayable in 12 monthly installments was approximately 30 cents. . . . The . . . study also documented the extent to which the 50 percent minimum loss ratio benchmark was not being achieved. It showed, for example, that 45 percent of companies writing group credit life insurance included in this study . . . had loss ratios of less than 50 percent. The average loss ratio of this business was approximately 40 percent. . . .

Types of Rate Regulation. Twenty states and Puerto Rico have established prima facie acceptable credit life insurance rates. Three of these states use a decremental sliding scale. For example, in New Jersey for cases averaging less than $250,000 of insurance the maximum rate is $0.64 per $100 of initial indebtedness repayable in 12 monthly installments. The rate decreases until it reaches $0.44 for cases averaging $5 million or more of insurance in force. The decremental scale in New York also ranges from $0.64 to $0.44. In Vermont, the scale is from $0.70 to $0.40. In the 18 other jurisdictions, the maximum prima facie rate is a flat amount running from $0.50 in Connecticut to $0.90 in certain circumstances in Texas. (The Texas rate is $0.70 to $0.90 depending upon the amount of indebtedness and the basis used to remit premiums to the insurer.)

The 50 percent loss ratio bench mark adopted by the NAIC was an attempt to give meaning to the model bill provision that a policy be disapproved by the commissioner if the benefits provided are not reasonable in relation to the premium charge. Under this bench mark the commissioner is directed to disapprove a rate producing a loss ratio of under 50 percent. The 50 percent loss ratio bench mark has been specifically adopted in 17 states including 15 that have established rates which prima facie meet the 50 percent loss ratio standard.

In 13 states consumer credit laws establish a maximum permissible credit life insurance rate (4 states) or grant authority to either a creditor regulatory agency (5 states) or the insurance commissioner (4 states) to set a maximum rate. These rates run from a low of $0.60 in Oregon and Pennsylvania to a high of $1 in Georgia, Louisiana, and Mississippi.

The president of a life insurance company having 20 percent of its business in credit life insurance and writing this form of insurance for credit unions told the United States Senate subcommittee investigating credit insurance:[40]

---

[40] See Statement of Robert E. Vanderbeck, *ibid.,* pp. 2620–23.

I do not believe that the American public should be satisfied with any insurance program that takes nearly half of the premium for expenses. . . . (I)t would be my observation that the 50 percent should be increased to 65 percent with a decremental sliding scale upward from that level based upon type of coverage and size of case.

Statements supporting the 50 percent bench mark and opposing a decremental scale also can be found in the published hearings of the subcommittee.[41]

Federal Concern. At the conclusion of the credit insurance hearings before the United States Senate Subcommittee on Antitrust and Monopoly, the committee chairman, Senator Hart, said:[42]

One fact is crystal clear from these subcommittee hearings—some lenders and sellers on credit are making windfall profits at the expense of the borrowers. . . . So long as . . . distortion of normal competition continues, the inequities will persist. The usual answer has been—leave it to the States. . . . The truth is that state regulation simply has not done the job. Does this mean that Federal rate regulation is the only answer? Not necessarily. There is another solution. . . . Remove the impediments to the free flow of competition. . . . This could be done effectively by simply forbidding lenders or sellers from making a profit, either directly or indirectly, on the sale of credit insurance in connection with a business transaction. . . . Such a law would make true competition possible.

---

[41] See, for example, the statements of Paul Boyer, *ibid.,* pp. 2138–41, and of R. Donald Quackenbush, *ibid.,* pp. 2290–95.

[42] *Ibid.,* pp. 2626–28.

16

Insurance in Employee Benefit Plans: Group Health Insurance

Most of what has been said in the previous chapter of the theory of group life insurance also applies to group health insurance. The number of similarities between group health and group life is greater than the number of differences. The differences result principally from the nature of the perils covered and the greater liberality in defining (or not defining) eligible groups.

1. THE NATURE OF GROUP HEALTH INSURANCE

Group health insurance, unlike group life insurance, was allowed to develop without any special legislation or control designed specifically for it. Companies writing it had only to comply with the general statutes relating to insurance until 1937, when Illinois enacted the first state group health insurance law.

Model Group Health Definitions. Two model group health insurance definitions have been prepared: one in 1940 by the National Association of Insurance Commissioners, and the other in 1948 (with later amendments) by the old Health and Accident Underwriters Conference, drafted for the National Association of Insurance Commissioners.

Neither model bill has been adopted in its entirety by the states, but both have had at least some influence on the 35 states that have group health insurance laws. The current edition (1957) of the conference (now Health Insurance Association) bill is less strict than the NAIC bill in that it requires no minimum number of lives in a group and fixes no specification for minimum participation. The NAIC bill requires a minimum of 25 lives and a minimum participation requirement of 75 percent of the eligible group if the plan is contributory and 100 percent if it is noncontributory.

Among states having group health insurance laws, 1 state requires the group to have at least 15 members; 16 states require at least 10; 7 states require a minimum of 5; and 4 states require a minimum of 2. (Apparently, the lawmakers in these last four states reason that it takes at least two to form a group.) In the remaining states, the minimum is left to the discretion of the underwriting departments of the companies. The elimination of the participation percentage requirement has not been so readily accepted. Seventeen of the states with laws require a minimum participation, but not all of them fix the requirement at the 75–100 percent level.

In general, group health insurance is more liberally defined in the statutes than group life insurance. More types of groups are eligible. The conference bill states that group health insurance may be issued to any group that is eligible for group life insurance. Furthermore, the bill states that group health insurance may be written for any other substantially similar group which, in the discretion of the commissioner, may qualify for such coverage. The only restriction seems to be that the group must have been organized and maintained in good faith for purposes other than that of obtaining insurance. The definition is broad enough to include coverage of dependents of the primary insured employee or association member. In group health insurance, covered group members may pay the entire premium, there being no requirement as in group life insurance that the premium be paid in part by the employer or union.[1] Finally, no statutory maxima of the amounts of insurance that may be written on each member of the group are established, leaving this underwriting decision entirely to the companies.

The greater freedom given to the writing of group health insurance than to the writing of group life insurance can be explained partly by the lack of effort on the part of insurance agents to push for restrictions on group health insurance. When group health insurance was developing, there was little interest in individual health insurance, either on the part of the agents or the public. Competition from Blue Cross- and Blue Shield-type organizations, operating on the group principle, led the insurance companies to develop competitive group contracts. The trend toward group insurance in health insurance did not produce the emotional reactions that this trend did (and still does) in life insurance.

---

[1] Group health insurance may be written without employer contribution because rates do not vary so widely among ages. If this statement is not clear, refer to the discussion in Chapter 15 of the reason for requiring employer contributions for group life insurance. Further, since group plans currently return in claims about 90 percent of premium and individual plans return only about 55 percent, it is possible to write "member pay all" plans at premiums lower than those charged for individual policies. Again, it must be held in mind that part of the lower cost is illusionary: The employer is assuming certain rather heavy clerical costs in handling collections, policy issue, and even claim settlement.

However, while there is no statutory requirement that the employer pay part of the premium, the need for the cooperation of the employer in the area of claims control is considered so important that some insurers might decline to issue policies in which the employer does not participate in the premiums.

Insurance companies are free to establish their own underwriting rules as long as these rules are not in conflict with state law. In states having no minimum group requirement or no minimum participation requirement, the insurer might set as the minimum number of insureds acceptable as 5, 10, or even more. It might require 75 percent participation if the plan is financed in whole or in part by the employees, and 100 percent participation if financed in whole by the employer. The insurer may not wish to accept certain types of groups even though these groups are eligible under the law. Although the law sets no maximum on benefit levels, the insurer will do so to avoid malingering.

Eligibility Standards. Group health insurance plans generally include eligibility standards similar to those found in group life plans. These standards are designed to protect the insurer against adverse selection and to control administrative costs. The standards relate to periods of probation, actively at work requirements, handling of temporary and part-time employees, grace periods for enrollment in contributory plans, the requirement that employees be bona fide, and the requirement in contributory plans that there be evidence of insurability in the case of in-and-outers—that is those employees who pick up the coverage, drop it, and pick it up again.

2. THE GROUP HEALTH INSURANCE CONTRACT

Just as the group life contract differs in some ways from the individual life policy, so does the group health contract differ in some ways from the individual health policy.

Differences in Group and Individual Contracts. Most group health policies provide benefits arising from nonoccupational accidents and illnesses only. Occupational disabilities are left to the coverage required under workmen's compensation laws. Because the disability income payable under workmen's compensation laws usually is low, some employers ask that their group policies covering short-term disability income include benefits for loss time resulting from occupational injuries, especially in those industries where the added cost for this coverage is nominal. Sometimes a supplementary contract providing only for occupational loss of time is written in lower amounts to integrate with workmen's compensation benefits so that a disabled employee is paid the same disability income benefits whether his disability is occupational or nonoccupational. Under group long-term disability income plans, coverage is usually included for loss of income arising out of industrial accidents and diseases. Because workmen's compensation medical benefits generally are adequate and therefore do not need to be supplemented, occupational coverage for medical care is not necessary in group policies. The exclusion of occupational disabilities is not usual in individual policies, except in policies written for people engaged in hazardous occupations. (An exception is with policies written under a franchise plan, which are often written on a nonoccupational basis.) Duplication of reimbursement benefits with workmen's compensation is virtually uniform in individual medical and hospital expense policies.

The uniform provisions, required by law to be contained in individual health insurance contracts (see Chapter 14), are not required in group health insurance contracts. These provisions for the most part relate to the obligations of the insurer and the insured at claim time. Provisions in group policies on claim handling usually are more liberal than those under the uniform provisions, so that the use of these provisions would be restrictive.

Other examples of restrictions sometimes found in individual policies that are commonly omitted in group contracts are those clauses relating to prorating benefits for other insurance (although a "coordination of benefits" clause is now commonly used in group insurance), change of occupation, misstatement of age, and the time limit for legal action. Provisions similar to those set forth in the uniform provisions which are protective to the policyholder, however, are required in group policies.[2]

Some Important Similarities.   Several important provisions appear in both group and individual contracts. These include beneficiary provisions in accidental death coverages, notice of loss, proof of loss, and time period for filing suits. In addition, the insurer may reserve the right to refuse renewal of the group policy on any renewal date. The right to refuse a renewal applies only to the master contract. No individual participant may be cancelled or denied renewal except by termination of the entire group.

Termination of the master contract or of an individual certificate is without effect on prior disability, just as with terminations of individual policies. Moreover, in most regular insurer plans (but not all Blue Cross–Blue Shield group plans), a period is allowed after termination during which claims developing out of conditions existing at the time of termination are covered. For example, group hospital and surgical benefits usually are payable for three months after termination if the claims are the result of a condition existing when the contract was terminated but which did not require hospitalization or an operation at that time. This extended benefit generally applies only to illnesses causing the insured to be totally disabled at the time his coverage terminates. Pregnancies in progress at termination are covered; and any maternity benefits applicable are paid if incurred within nine months after termination, even if pregnancy was not known to be in progress at the time the contract or certificate expired.[3]

---

[2] In the Health and Accident Underwriters Conference bill, only three standard provisions were proposed: (1) Only statements made in writing should be used to avoid or reduce the insurance and, in the absence of fraud, all statements should be deemed representations and not warranties; (2) a certificate of insurance should be delivered to each covered employee setting forth the essential features of the coverage; and (3) new employees and dependents might be added to the group from time to time in accordance with the terms of the policy.

[3] This is true in substantially all group health insurance plans covering maternity, but not always in group practice prepayment plans and Blue Cross–Blue Shield group plans.

Similar Provisions in Group Health and Group Life. Some important provisions are common to all group insurance. Since these provisions were explained in Chapter 15, they need only be mentioned here. They include the clauses dealing with dividend or retroactive rate reductions, payment and adjustment of premiums, employer reports, assignment, the grace period, employer omissions, and now, more frequently, the conversion privilege.

3. TYPES OF HEALTH INSURANCE COVERAGE

Group insurance can cover virtually all insurable health losses in any combination.

Disability Income Coverage. Disability income coverage is of two types—short term and long term. Short-term disability coverage is the older of the two and the more prevalent. It is designed to replace some of the loss of earnings resulting from the inability to work because of illness or accidental injury. Weekly or monthly indemnities are paid in event of disability as defined in the policy.

Customarily, disability under short-term coverage is defined as the inability of the insured to perform any and every duty of his own occupation. Some contracts define disability simply as the inability of the insured to perform his regular work. Benefits for partial disability are not available under short-term disability income coverage. Income benefits resulting from accidents may begin with the first day of disability, whereas a short waiting period, three or seven days being common, is required for sickness benefits. Benefits usually are payable for 13 or 26 weeks, except that benefits for disability from pregnancy, if covered at all, will be limited to 6 weeks, for example. The amount of the benefit is scheduled in the policy and usually bears some relationship to salary, generally not more than $66\frac{2}{3}$ percent nor less than 50 percent. Sometimes benefits are related to occupation or are set at a fixed amount for all employees, especially under negotiated plans.

The eligibility requirements for long-term disability coverage generally are more restrictive than those for short-term coverage. They usually require employees to have reached a given minimum salary, to have had a minimum number of years of service, or to have a supervisory or managerial position. Lower income workers have relatively attractive long-term disability benefits under social security. Nevertheless, restrictive eligibility requirements under long-term disability income coverage may soon be relaxed as these benefits are integrated with social security and become full-fledged members of the employee benefit plan family.

Disability in long-term disability income coverage usually has two definitions: the inability of the insured to engage in *his* own occupation for an initial period of one or two years, and the inability of the insured to perform *any* occupation for which he is reasonably fitted by education, training, or experience, at the expiration of the initial period. Benefits for partial disability frequently are available under long-term disability income coverage, but usually on a restricted basis.

Under long-term disability coverage, waiting periods of six months are common if the plan is integrated with short-term disability coverage, and 60- or 90-day waiting periods are common if there is no short-term disability income coverage. The duration of the benefit period may be as long as to age 65 or even for life in some plans or for 2 years, 5 years, or 10 years in others. Benefit amounts usually are higher than those for short-term plans, and generally are related to earnings with some maximum such as $1,000 or in large groups even $2,000 a month. Long-term disability income benefits usually are integrated with other forms of disability income coverage so that benefits will not be duplicated. Offsets are taken against such benefits as social security and disability benefits payable under pension plans. Offsets, however, are not usually taken against benefits payable under individual disability income insurance policies owned by the insured.

Group disability income coverage usually has few restrictions. Disabilities not covered under the usual individual policy frequently are covered under group policies: disabilities such as those caused by alcoholism, drug addiction, and mental illness. Self-inflicted injuries or injuries or illnesses suffered outside the United States or Canada usually are excluded.

Accidental Death and Dismemberment.   Group coverage is usually written to pay benefits for accidental loss of life or of body members. Accidental death and dismemberment coverage sometimes is written without loss-of-time benefits, and frequently pays for occupational as well as nonoccupational injuries. In hazardous industries, however, it is usually written for nonoccupational accidents only. When written without loss-of-time benefits, it is usually written as a supplement to group life insurance. It is sometimes written separately for large amounts, for example, for $100,000 or more. The amount of coverage is written in terms of a principal (or capital) sum with a schedule of benefits expressed in multiples or fractions of the principal sum. The principal sum, for example, is paid for accidental death or the loss of two or more body members (eye, hand, or foot), and one half the principal sum for the loss of one member. A loss of a member is precisely defined. For example, loss of the use of the hand is not sufficient; it must be severed at or above the wrist. For there to be a loss of an eye, the entire sight from that eye must be lost and irrecoverable. Under some plans, twice or even three times the principal sum is paid for death or dismemberment arising from various travel accidents (usually common carrier), or if the accident results in total and permanent disability.

Accidental death and dismemberment coverage contains the usual self-inflicted injury exclusion and also excludes losses resulting directly or indirectly, wholly or partially, from wars, insurrections, riots, commission of assaults or felonies, diseases of the mind or body, and, sometimes, occupational injuries. Death must occur within 90 days of the accident.

Accidental death and dismemberment coverage is attractive chiefly because it is inexpensive and not because it fills any separate need. The amount of the principal sum, when written with group life insurance, usually equals the amount of group life insurance except when the amount of life insurance is in excess of $10,000 or $20,000. Then a maximum of $10,000 or $20,000 might be set.

Hospital Expense. Hospital expense benefits usually are expressed in terms of two sets of charges: hospital room and board, and miscellaneous hospital expenses. Hospital room and board may be covered for actual costs up to a given maximum amount per day, $25, for example, and for a given maximum number of days, 70, for example, while miscellaneous or special hospital expenses are covered, usually on an unallocated basis, up to a maximum of some multiple of the allowance for daily room and board, 20, for example. It is common to allow a substantial amount in excess of the fixed multiple of the room allowance, but under an arrangement whereby the insurer pays three fourths and the insured pays one fourth of the amount over the given multiple. Maternity benefits up to a maximum of about 10 or 15 times the daily room benefit or up to a flat amount may be allowed. To control the cost, some group hospital insurance plans pay no benefits for the first few days of hospital stays.

Hospital expense insurance usually covers dependents of the employees. Dependents include the employee's wife or husband and his unmarried children. For coverage, dependent children are variously defined but more commonly are restricted to those under age 19 and over 2 weeks old. A few plans define dependents broadly, and include those who would be considered dependents by the Internal Revenue Service.

Surgical Expense. Indemnities for surgical procedures are written, usually as set forth in a schedule of maxima for each procedure, as in individual health insurance policies. For unscheduled surgical procedures, the insurer agrees to pay an amount in keeping with the amounts paid for scheduled procedures. Schedules are not standardized so that all $300 schedules will not pay the same for each surgical procedure. For example, under one $300 surgical schedule, the maximum benefit for a tonsillectomy with adenoidectomy is $40; in another it is $45. Specific additional amounts may be payable for the services of an anesthesiologist and for administration of anesthetics. Specific benefits may also be payable for obstetrical procedures. Fractions or multiples of the basic schedule may be written to accommodate the needs of the group.

Nursing Home Care. An increasing number of group contracts offer coverage for nursing home care as a part of the coverage made available under major medical and hospital expense insurance. Nursing home care coverage can be expected to increase particularly as group plans for retired employees are developed and purchased to supplement benefits offered under medicare, and as continuing efforts are made to control the cost of hospital care coverage by providing alternative care in skilled nursing homes for the non-aged as well as for the aged. The growth of nursing home coverage can be expected to follow the growth of qualified nursing homes.

Psychiatric Expense Coverage.   Currently, nearly all group health insurance policies issued cover in-hospital treatment for nervous and mental disorders, and about 85 percent cover out-of-hospital treatment for mental illness. As the demand for psychiatric expense cover increases, coverage over and beyond (or in lieu of) that offered under policies written to cover hospital and medical expenses will become an important part of an employee benefit health insurance package.

Major Medical Expense.   The purpose of major medical is to pay the large medical expenses. It is blanket coverage for nearly all hospital, surgical, and medical care expenses between a deductible and an aggregate maximum, usually written with a participation clause under which the insured pays 20 percent or 25 percent of the covered expenses. Group forms of major medical offer the same ranges of covered expenses, kinds of maximum limits, types of deductibles, participation provisions, and exclusions offered by the individual major medical policies, described in Chapter 13. When major medical is written without hospital, surgical, and regular medical expense coverage, the deductible is an initial deductible; that is, the employee bears the cost of his medical expenses up to the deductible limits. In some group health insurance programs where there are no basic health plans, the deductible is small, perhaps only $50, and the plan is called comprehensive medical expense insurance rather than major medical insurance. Aside from having a small deductible and sometimes a low or no participation arrangement, comprehensive medical is the same coverage as major medical. When major medical is written in combination with a basic plan, as is the usual case, the deductible will be either a corridor deductible or an integrated deductible. A corridor deductible requires the insured to assume expenses equal to the deductible after the basic plan is exhausted, before any liability is assumed under the major medical plan. An integrated deductible allows the amount of benefits paid under the basic plan to be applied to the deductible. If the benefits paid under the basic plan are less than the amount of the deductible, the effect is to have a small corridor deductible. If the benefits paid under the basic plan are larger than the amount of the deductible, then the amount of the deductible is assumed to be equal to the basic plan.

Dental Care Coverage.   One of the most recent covers to be included in group health insurance plans is dental care, under which 50 to 80 percent of the expenses of oral examinations (including X-rays and cleanings), fillings, extractions, inlays, bridgework, dentures, oral surgery, anesthesia, treatment of gum diseases, root canal therapy, and orthodontics are paid after the insured absorbs the first $25 or $50.

Vision Care Coverage.   Major medical insurance ordinarily does not cover the cost of eye examinations, refractions, correctional vision care, and eyeglasses. (In many major medical plans, however, eye injury or disease and certain ophthalmic materials are covered). Group vision care insurance has been introduced to pay the cost of vision care although very little demand seems to exist for this coverage. The coverage, when written, usually includes a deductible of $5 or $10, a maximum limit of $10 to $20 for each covered expense, a percentage participation requirement, restrictions on benefits (such as 1 set of lenses a year), and exclusions of certain types of vision care (such as contact lenses and sunglasses). Usually 100 percent participation of the group is required and dependents are not covered. Because the expenses involved in vision care usually are neither high nor unexpected, both the need for and suitability of vision care coverage is questionable.

Out-of-Hospital Drugs. The expanded use of prescription drugs to control illness has led to the inclusion of coverage for out-of-hospital legend drugs (those which by law require a written prescription) in a growing number of group medical care plans. A calendar type deductible usually is used.

4. SPECIAL FORMS OF MASS HEALTH INSURANCE COVERS

Three special forms of mass health insurance covers are written: franchise, blanket, and credit.

Franchise Health Insurance. Franchise insurance is the health equivalent of wholesale insurance in life insurance. It is designed to fill the need of a group of employees too few in number to qualify for group health insurance or to cover members of associations or holders of a given credit card with individual contracts sold under a mass marketing system in which administrative techniques usually associated with group insurance are often utilized. As in wholesale life insurance individual policies are issued to insureds, and unless a high percentage of those eligible enroll in the plan individual selection standards may be practiced.

Blanket Health Policies. A blanket insurance policy (often called "blanket group") is a contract that protects all members of a certain group against the insured perils. While this sounds like a definition of group insurance, blanket differs from group in that no individual insured is specifically named and no certificates are issued. Examples of types of groups usually written under blanket policies include passengers of a common carrier, students at a college, spectators at a sports attraction, members of a volunteer fire department, members of the football squad, campers at a camp. In general, the membership of a blanket group changes frequently, and the policy covers this changing membership. It is a sort of for whom it may concern type of coverage which usually is limited to blanket accident medical expenses and accidental death and dismemberment benefits.

Group Credit Health Insurance. Group credit life insurance may be written to include benefits in the event of the total and permanent disability of the debtor-insured. But purchasers of group credit insurance are interested in indemnity in the event of the temporary disability of the debtor-insured, usually for a period exceeding two weeks or a month. Group credit health insurance can be purchased to pay the disabled debtor's monthly payments until he recovers or until his debt is discharged, whichever comes first. In some plans, the benefits are payable retroactively to the first day of the debtor's disability if this disability remains continuous for a qualification period of, say, 14 days. In other plans, benefits are paid only for the period following the qualification period. The retroactive payment provision can lead to malingering; and for this reason, there is a tendency to avoid writing it.

5. UNDERWRITING GROUP HEALTH INSURANCE

The purpose of underwriting in group health insurance is the same as in any form of insurance, group or individual: to produce a profitable combination of exposures at premium rates that have a practical degree of equity among these exposures. Each insured must be required to pay as nearly as possible the expected value of his loss exposure plus his fair share of the insurer's cost of doing business. Underwriting, therefore, is closely related to rating and policy design.

While the objective of underwriting is the same in all forms of insurance, special problems may be present in group underwriting that are not found in individual underwriting (and vice versa, of course). Particular problems may be found in group health underwriting not found in group life underwriting, and the problems are likely to differ among the various kinds of group health covers.

Specific problems found in group underwriting not found in individual underwriting are (1) to determine whether the proposed group and plan are legal under the group insurance laws of the state and (2) to determine whether the plan design can be administered efficiently and rated properly.

Problems found in group health insurance underwriting not found in group life insurance underwriting are principally those associated with controlling the moral hazard. The underwriters of group health insurance are much more concerned with loss control devices than are the underwriters of group life insurance. For example, as among the various types of health insurance covers, more concern is given to the problem of underwriting benefits for married women under long-term disability than under short-term disability income plans. Also because dependents are covered under medical care plans, more concern is given to the problem of duplication of benefits in the underwriting of medical care benefits than in the underwriting of short-term disability income benefits.

Disability Income Benefits.   A number of factors are considered in underwriting disability income coverage (and other group health insurance coverage). These include the type of group, the size of the group, the environment of group members, the level of benefits, the duration of benefits, eligibility standards for coverage under the plan, eligibility standards for benefits under the plan, the participation percentage in contributing plans, and persistency experience in remaining with past insurers. The underwriting standards to be applied generally are more strict for small than for large groups, for long-term disability income benefits than for short-term disability income benefits, for association groups than for employer groups, for groups whose members are exposed to substandard environmental conditions than for groups whose members live and work in a healthful and wholesome economic and moral climate, and for groups that change insurers frequently than for those that tend to stay with one insurer.

SHORT-TERM DISABILITY.   Both the loss exposure and the risk under group short-term disability insurance are low. The benefit period is usually under one year, most commonly 13 or 26 weeks. The scale of benefits usually is low, generally less than $100 a week. The insurers have a vast amount of loss experience to enable them to forecast loss rates within reasonable ranges, and any errors can be quickly corrected because premiums may be adjusted annually.

The eligibility standards for coverage generally required in group life insurance are required in group disability income coverage: actively at work, full-time regular employee, and a reasonable probationary period (which, in some covered positions, may be none at all). Unlike the practice in group life insurance, disability income coverage usually is not continued during periods of layoffs because of the moral hazard involved in writing disability income coverage for unemployed persons. In writing disability income coverage, underwriters are vitally interested in the relationship between benefit levels and employee earnings as a means of controlling the moral hazard. They usually prefer to restrict the benefits to not more than two thirds of normal earnings. The absenteeism rate of the employer is of interest to the underwriter as a clue to possible malingering among employees, as is the attitude of the employer toward absenteeism. Lax employment practices and lack of follow-up on employees reporting "sick" can have an adverse effect on loss ratios.

LONG-TERM DISABILITY.   Because both the loss exposure and the risk under group long-term disability income insurance are higher than under group short-term disability income insurance, underwriters apply a more restrictive range of standards to eligibility requirements and plan design in underwriting group long-term than group short-term disability income coverage.

In long-term disability income coverage the benefit period is expressed in years (5, 10, or to age 65) rather than in weeks. Furthermore, since long-term plans generally are restricted to high-paid employees, benefit schedules offering more than $1,000 a month are not uncommon.

Group long-term disability income coverage is newer, and less widely purchased, than is short-term coverage; so the experience accumulated by insurers under long-term plans is not extensive. In addition, because of the low frequency rate of long-term disability claims, it takes more experience and a larger number of exposures to develop the same degree of claims predictability for long-term disability income insurance as for short-term disability income insurance.

The combination of a large loss exposure and a statistically inadequate basis for predicting claims requires the underwriter to give special attention to underwriting factors in long-term disability income coverage that would be of less concern to him in the underwriting of short-term disability income coverage.

Preferred groups for long-term disability income coverage are those composed of employees not exposed to a significant unemployment hazard. Underwriters do not want to be subjected to claim problems arising out of attempts of insureds to use disability income insurance benefits as supplementary unemployment compensation benefits. Employers who have experienced low rates of turnover among the classes of employees to be included in the group generally present no underwriting problems. Groups thought to be exposed to a significant unemployment hazard are (1) those in unstable industries, (2) those in new companies, and (3) those with a high percentage of married women.

Groups composed of a highly restricted eligibility class yielding only a few employees also are considered to be problem groups. Higher benefit levels and longer duration periods usually may be written for large groups than for small groups without requiring individual members of the group to give evidence of insurability. Eligibility standards that exclude large numbers of married women from the group and that impose long periods of employment before allowing an employee to be included in the group sometimes are necessary as underwriting control devices.

A further underwriting control found in some plans is the requirement that income from sources such as social security benefits, disability income benefits provided under pension plans, and personal disability income insurance benefits be applied as offsets against group long-term disability income benefits in order to keep disability benefits under two thirds of the employee's after-tax, predisability earnings.

Medical Care Benefits.   The underwriters of medical care benefits are concerned with most of the problems that face the underwriters of disability income and life insurance coverage. They are confronted also with additional problems, mainly those associated with the underwriting of small, frequent losses that are, in some cases, within the control of the insured employees and their physicians. Medical care underwriters have a major interest in the probability of (and opportunity for) benefit abuses, and, therefore, encourage plan designs that eliminate both duplication of benefits and overutilization of medical facilities. Cost control devices are written into the plan, and these are discussed later.

Medical care insurers working through the industry-supported Health Insurance Council are committed to a program of loss control. The association works with hospital and physician review committees to study whether the level of medical charges is reasonable, whether the surgery was, in fact, necessary, whether the patient was given unneeded medical services, and whether the frequency of the service was excessive. In other words, those who finance the cost of medical care services are working with those who who provide it to make the providers more cost conscious. No effort is made through cost control to reduce the effectiveness of medical care services, only to increase their efficiency.

Medical care problem groups are (1) those composed of a large percentage of female employees; (2) those composed of a high percentage of older employees; (3) those composed of a high percentage of workers exposed to seasonal unemployment; (4) those composed of a high percentage of single employees living alone or married couples, both of whom work outside the home; (5) those groups that change frequently from one insurer to another; and (6) those groups in which the employee pays all or in which the employer pays only a small amount of the cost.

The frequency and severity of medical care expenses are higher for women and for older people than for men and for younger people. Workers exposed to seasonal employment understandably tend to put off medical attention, that needed surgery, for example, until just before layoffs, and they are in no hurry to leave the hospital. Furthermore, they tend to postpone medical attention for their dependents until their jobs are again available. Single workers living alone find the hospital an ideal place to be when they are too sick to stay home alone. Hospital care is also the solution to home care for couples both of whom work outside the home. Groups that move from insurer to insurer are suspect of dodging necessary rate increases. Employee pay all groups are quick to respond negatively to premium increases by looking for another insurer, and they lack the claim control of an employer who has a financial stake in the plan.

Underwriters try to build cost controls into the plan provisions. For example, medical care benefits extended to retired employees usually are for amounts less than that given active workers, and these benefits also are made excess over medicare benefits payable under social security. Benefits usually are also restricted in some manner for employees who are no longer actively at work because of disability leave, layoff, strike, resignation, or discharge. For example, medical care coverage may be continued for, say, one year for those on disability leave and for two weeks for those on layoff or strike. For those who have resigned or who have been discharged, coverage ceases immediately, except for employees and their dependents who are ill at the time of termination. For them, coverage will be continued for a specific period, say, three months for hospital and surgical benefits and one year for major medical benefits.

An antiduplication (coordination of benefits) clause may be used to restrict benefits payable to employees who are covered under other group policies. For example, if husband and wife are working, both may be covered under two group plans, under one as the employee and under the other as a dependent. An antiduplication clause restricts the maximum benefits payable under the combined coverage to total expenses incurred.

As a cost control device, the insured is usually expected to bear part of his loss. This is accomplished by the use of participation and deductible clauses and by setting specific benefit maximum at levels below those that could be expected to reimburse the insured fully for his expenses.

One underwriting problem in group medical care insurance, not found in group disability income coverage, is that of handling dependents. If a dependent is, or just had been, hospitalized when the insurance goes into effect, his coverage usually does not begin until 31 days after termination of his hospital confinement.

6. RATING GROUP HEALTH INSURANCE

Group health insurance rates are computed separately for each type of coverage. In general, the principles applied in the rating of group life insurance are applied in the rating of group health insurance.

The Society of Actuaries has a Committee on Experience under Group Health Insurance, which collects, processes, and publishes morbidity statistics supplied to it by major group health insurers. Various actuaries have taken these statistics, supplemented them with other data, and prepared special studies that have been useful in developing tabular premium rates for the various types of group health coverage.[4] However, no commissioners standard group tables or industry tabular gross premium tables have been prepared for group health covers. Group health insurers are not subject to minimum initial premiums. Theoretically, group health insurers must satisfy only the broad rule that premiums be sufficient to cover reasonable assumptions for claims and expense experience.

Each group health insurer prepares its own manual rates from its own experience and from the tabular rates developed from the basic data in the special morbidity studies published by the Society of Actuaries. In preparing its manual rates, the insurer adjusts its basic data for general morbidity trends and for its estimate of how its own claims experience is likely to differ from these data because of variations in company underwriting philosophy, market areas, claims administration, and types of groups written. An allowance for expenses, a margin for contingencies, and a risk charge are added to the expected value of the claims, to arrive at the final gross manual premium.

The gross manual rate is adjusted for a number of variables, such as the personal characteristics of the group (age, sex, and income levels), the geographical location of the group, the industry in which the group is employed, the size of the group, the administrative procedure to be used,

---

[4] These studies have been published in the *Transactions of the Society of Actuaries.*

and the trends in the cost of medical care services. These adjustments are made either through a schedule of surcharges or discounts, or by a classification system built into the manual. The method varies among insurers and among covers. As in group life insurance, the initial premium charged a new group is the manual premium except where this group has been insured with another insurer and has accumulated sufficient experience to warrant a modification of the manual premium, either up or down.

Experience rating is used retrospectively and prospectively in group health insurance, just as in group life insurance: (1) to give premium refunds to those groups whose actual experience has been better than projected[5]; and (2) to raise or lower the premium charged on each renewal for those groups with poorer or better than expected experience.

Manual Rates. The importance of the factors to be considered in manual rating varies among the different group health insurance covers.

DISABILITY INCOME COVERAGE. The 1947–49 Basic Morbidity Table for Males, Group Accident and Sickness Insurance, an excerpt from which is shown in Table 16–1, is frequently used as basic data for computing manual rates for group short-term disability income coverage.[6]

TABLE 16–1

Excerpts from the 1947–49 Basic Morbidity Table for Males,
Group Accident and Sickness

Duration t (days)	Tabular Cost of $1 of Weekly Benefits for Duration of Disability t or Less		Duration t (weeks)	Tabular Cost of $1 of Weekly Benefits for Duration of Disability t or Less	
	Annual	Monthly		Annual	Monthly
3	0.0820	0.0068	13	0.6440	0.0537
4	0.1078	0.0090	14	0.6598	0.0550
6	0.1564	0.0130	26	0.8011	0.0668
7	0.1790	0.0149	27	0.8099	0.0675
13	0.2788	0.0232	52	0.9645	0.0804
14	0.2908	0.0242	53	0.9691	0.0808

Using this table, the basic monthly premium for a disability income plan under which benefits are paid for 26 weeks after a seven-day waiting period would be as follows:

Tabular cost, 27 weeks	$ 0.0675
Tabular cost, 7 days	−0.0149
Monthly claim cost per $1 of weekly benefit	$ 0.0526

---

[5] In a few groups, a retrospective charge is provided for in the event that the experience is worse than anticipated.

[6] The source of this table is Morton D. Miller, "Group Weekly Indemnity Continuation Table Study," *Transactions of the Society of Actuaries*, Vol. III (1951), p. 55.

An insurer using this table will adjust the figures to reflect current trends and to take cognizance of its own experience. Assume that after studying available data, the insurer concludes that the monthly claim cost per dollar of weekly benefit under the foregoing plan (26 weeks after a 7-day waiting period) should be adjusted upward by 2 percent. The tabular monthly claim cost for the plan then would be set at $0.0526 × 1.02, or $0.0537 per dollar of benefit.

The next step is to add margins to handle expenses and contingencies. The insurer determines these margins with one eye on the amount of premium it figures it needs to handle the business profitably and with adequate safety margins, and the other eye on the constraints imposed by competition. These margins usually include a constant of so much per dollar of weekly benefits plus a percentage of the tabular net or gross premium. For example, assume that the insurer determines that it needs (or can get) $0.004 per dollar of weekly benefits plus 25 percent of the gross premium, then the monthly gross premium for $1 of benefits, 26 weeks maximum after a 7-day waiting period, would be $0.0537 plus 0.004 divided by 0.75, or $0.0769.

Assume that the group to be covered has 100 employees and the benefit level is $50 a week, maximum 26 weeks after a waiting period of 7 days. If the group is an all-male group in a standard industry with no significant percentage of the coverage on overage or underage people or on unskilled labor, and the group is not transfer business from another insurer, the initial premium for the group will be $0.0769 × 50 × 100 or $384.50 monthly, subject to a volume discount or loading, if any, to be discussed later.

If the group is not a standard male group, then additional margins would have to be added for those claims costs not reflected in the tabular cost. Claims costs usually are higher for women than for men; so a margin is added to offset this additional cost when the group includes females. Assume that the insurer determines that under a 26 week maximum benefit period with a 7-day waiting period, the female cost is 50 percent higher than the male cost, then the premium will be loaded 50 percent for females, usually according to brackets based on the percentage of females in the group. The brackets are usually of intervals of 10 percentage points, such as less than 11 percent, 11 percent through 20 percent, and so on. The loading is based on the midpoints in the brackets, such as 5 percent, 15 percent, and so forth.

If 18 women are in the foregoing group of 100 employees, then the female loading for the group would be as follows: 0.85 × (0.15 × 1.50) or 107.5 percent, since 18 is in the 11 through 20 percent bracket and the midpoint in this bracket is 15 percent. So 15 percent of the premium will be loaded by 50 percent. This loading increases the monthly manual premium for the group to $384.50 × 107.5, or $413.34. Some insurers, rather than loading the male rate for female coverage, determine the premiums separately for males and for females. Separate rating of the sexes is standard in group long-term disability insurance coverage.

In many companies premiums for short-term disability income insurance for the usual group ordinarily do not reflect the ages of the group members even though studies show that short-term disability income claim costs increase with the age of the members. However, if a significant percentage of the coverage written for the group is on persons over a given age, the insurer will add an extra charge to offset the expected higher claims rate. Conversely, if a significant percentage of the coverage is written on persons under a specific age, the premium will be reduced to give credit for the expected lower claims rate. What percentage is significant, what ages are specified as the breaking points, and what size debit or credit to be used are individual matters for the insurer to decide.

Suppose that the insurer writing the foregoing group of 100 employees has determined that if 10 percent or more of the coverage is written on persons over age 65, the premium for that coverage will be loaded 300 percent and that if more than 25 percent of the coverage is written for persons under age 30, the premium for that coverage will be reduced 50 percent. If this group has 15 people over age 65 and 28 people under age 30, then the monthly premium will be adjusted further as follows:

$$(0.57 \times \$413.34) + 3 (0.15 \times \$413.34) + 0.5 (0.28 \times \$413.34),$$
producing a premium of $595.21.

Some insurers classify their group short-term disability income manual rates according to age (usually in five-year intervals), rather than adjust premiums for significant deviations from "normal" patterns of age distributions.

If the group is employed in an industry that presents an unusual health hazard, the premium will be loaded to cover additional expected claims. Only a few industries today require special loadings, because improved production techniques have reduced the health hazard in many industries. If the foregoing group is employed in the manufacturing of rock-wool, and the insurer's loading for this industry is 15 percent, then the premium would be increased to $595.21 $\times 1.15$ or $684.41. The extra premium is charged for coverage written on a nonoccupational basis because it reflects the extra health hazard associated with employment in that industry.

If the percentage of total coverage on unskilled employees exceeds a specified percentage, a special loading may be required. Assume that the insurer underwriting the above group requires a loading if the percentage of coverage on unskilled workers exceeds 50 percent. Because the percentage of total coverage on unskilled employees in this group is only 15 percent, no loading is required.

The group is a new group, that is, not transferred from another insurer; therefore, no adjustments need be made for previously poor experience.

Because expenses do not increase in direct proportion to the amount of premium, a volume discount (or charge) is applied to manual premiums. The volume discount table used by the insurer of this group shows a discount of 5 percent for a monthly premium volume of between $500 and $699. After applying the 5 percent discount to the $684.49 premium, the manual premium becomes $684.49 × 0.95 or $650.27 monthly. The volume discount, however, is not applied until the manual premium for all health covers has been computed. If the total monthly manual premium for all health covers written by this insurer for this group amounted to $2,000, the discount would be 16 percent. (If the total monthly premiums were only $250, this insurer would add an additional charge of 5 percent.)

The principles used in rating long-term disability are the same as those used in rating short-term disability except it is customary in long-term disability to use separate manual rates for each age or age classification and for males and females.

ACCIDENTAL DEATH AND DISMEMBERMENT.   The manual rates for accidental death and dismemberment coverage are computed in a manner similar to that used for computing rates for short-term disability income coverage, except fewer variables are used. Except for 24-hour coverage, that is coverage that includes both the occupational and nonoccupational hazard, the only variable used is one for extra hazardous exposures such as noncommercial flying. No adjustments are made for the age distribution of the group or for the number of females in the group. For nonoccupational coverage, the usual flat manual rate is $0.06 per month for each $1,000 of principal sum. This rate is computed from intercompany data supplied by the Society of Actuaries. Expense loadings are light because a good part of the expenses are absorbed in the loadings for the other group covers with which accidental death and dismemberment are written. Of course, in the unusual case where accidental death and dismemberment is written as separate cover, the expense loading is increased.

For occupational coverage, four industry classes are used. For example, in one company clerical and professional workers in banks, insurance companies, and other offices are rated A and are charged $0.07. Actors and actresses are rated B and charged $0.105. Workers in breweries are rated C and charged $0.14. Policemen and firemen are rated D, which means that they are individually rated rather than class rated. The rate that the insurance company will charge to write accidental death and dismemberment occupational coverage for policemen and firemen depends upon the insurer's appraisal of the extra hazard involved in the particular case being rated.

MEDICAL CARE COVERAGE.   The procedure involved in developing manual rates for medical care coverage is essentially the same as in disability income insurance. Data compiled by the Society of Actuaries, hospital, medical, and dental associations, intracompany experience, and the federal government are studied to produce tables of claim frequencies and average claim values. Manual rating for medical care coverage, however, is more complicated than rating for disability income coverage because of the large number of variables involved. Medical care manual rates must reflect the increasing cost of medical care, the relationship between the cost of medical care and the income of the patient, the variation in the cost of medical care in various parts of the country, and the wide variety of benefit plans written.

Group Hospital Insurance. The manual premium for group hospital insurance is a composite of the cost of the room and board benefit and the cost of the hospital extras. For example, one insurer's manual premium for a group hospital expense plan providing maximums of $25 a day for room and board for 70 days and 20 times the daily benefit amount for hospital extras, written on an all-male group in Cleveland, Ohio, would be $5.07 monthly per employee. This premium is a composite of $3.02 for hospital room and board charges and $2.05 for hospital extras. For dependents' coverage the monthly premium per employee is $5.66 to cover 1 dependent and $10.56 to cover 2 or more dependents, or, instead, a composite dependents' premium of $8.97 may be charged to cover all dependents. The $8.97 is made up of $5 for hospital room and board and $3.97 for hospital extras.

As in group short-term disability income coverage, the percentage of coverage written on females affects the manual premium for group hospital expense coverage. If, under the foregoing plan, 20 percent of the coverage is written on females, the manual premium for this insurer would be $5.29 monthly per employee. If 70 percent of the coverage is on females, the monthly premium per employee would be $5.61

Unlike group short-term disability income coverage, manual premiums for group hospital expense coverage are adjusted according to geographic area. The ancillary service benefit written with group hospital expense insurance is written blanket and is subject to wide geographical variations in costs.

One insurer shows the following variations in its per employee monthly manual premium for the above plan of group hospital expense insurance written on a group where 60 percent of the coverage is on females.

New York, New York	$5.09	Dallas, Texas	$5.81
Indianapolis, Indiana	5.31	Denver, Colorado	6.03
Cleveland, Ohio	5.56	Detroit, Michigan	6.26

All insurers do not use the same classification system.

In general, for any given case, the applicable geographical area is the one in which at least some given percentage of employees work. If a group has a significant number of employees in more than one area, a composite average will be computed for the group. For example, suppose that the group includes 500 workers—20 in New York, 300 in Indianapolis, and

180 in Dallas. This insurer's rule is that if less than 5 percent of the employees are in any given area, these employees are assumed to be in the area with the highest premium. The 20 employees in New York, therefore, are grouped with the 180 Dallas employees. The manual premium for the group, assuming 60 percent of the coverage is on females and the benefits are a maximum of $25 a day for 70 days and 20 times daily benefits for hospital extras, will be computed as follows:

$$300 \times \$5.31 = \$1,593$$
$$200 \times \$5.81 = 1,162$$
$$\text{Total} \qquad = \$2,755$$

$2,755 ÷ 500 = $5.51, the average monthly rate per employee for the group.

As in group disability income coverage, a margin will be added to the manual premium for group hospital expense coverage if a disproportionate amount of the coverage is on older or retired employees. Extra premiums also are charged for groups employed in specified industries and for groups in which there is a large percentage of unskilled workers.

In the discussion of group disability income coverage, mention was made of premium volume loadings or discounts. The premium for group hospital expense coverage is subject to these loadings and discounts. In the foregoing case, the discount would be 17 percent if only hospital expense coverage were written, but if other group health covers are written, the premiums are combined before the loading or discount is applied.

Group Surgical Insurance. Manual premiums for group surgical insurance, of course, depend upon the amounts in the surgical schedule and on whether obstetrical benefits are included. As in hospital expense coverage, the premiums vary directly with the percentage of coverage on females. Geographical adjustments might be made in the manual premiums for group surgical expense coverage, but usually industry loadings do not apply to the premium for group surgical expense benefits.

For a group of workers in Cleveland, Ohio, composed of 40 percent females, one insurer has a manual premium of $1.07 per month per employee for a $300 surgical schedule excluding obstetrical benefits. If obstetrical benefits are included, the premium is $1.25 per month per employee. The composite premium for dependents is $2.40 per employee excluding obstetrical benefits, and $3.54 per employee including obstetrical benefits. Premium volume loadings and discounts apply to group surgical expense benefits.

Group Medical Expense. The manual rating of group medical (physician) expense coverage presents no new variables. The manual rates reflect rather broadly the experience variations expected as to industry, percentage of female coverage, "unusually high" proportion of coverage on older or retired employees, territory, premium size, and plan variation.

Group Major Medical. The development of manual rates for group major medical insurance is more complicated than the development of manual rates for other group health covers. More variables must be considered in major medical insurance, and some of the same variables that are recognized in other group health covers have greater significance in major medical insurance.

While the claims rate under basic medical care coverage is affected by the age of the employee (the older the employee, the higher the expected value of the claim), the variance between the average expected claims for all ages combined and the average expected claims for each 5-year age class (under 30, 30 to 35, 35 to 40, . . . 65 and over) is not large enough to warrant special consideration for age in manual rating unless a large percentage of the coverage is written on employees past age 55 or 60 or under age 30. The average claim rates in major medical insurance, however, vary significantly among the 5-year age classification, more than 450 percent between the under age 35 and the over age 65 group, more than 250 percent between the age 35 to 40 and the age 60 to 65 groups, more than 100 percent between the age 40 to 45 and the age 55 to 60 groups, and more than 25 percent between the age 45 to 50 and the age 50 to 55 groups.[7] One reason for the greater increase in claim costs with age is that the deductibles used with major medical eliminate the frequent small claims found at young ages, leaving the relatively more severe claims that occur at older ages.

Claims vary more widely among geographical areas under major medical coverage than under basic medical coverage. For example, data compiled by the Society of Actuaries and by individual companies show that the expected claim cost in the highest cost area is about 70 percent more than it is in the lowest cost area under major medical expense coverage, but only about 20 percent more under basic medical coverage. The claim costs among locations differ more widely under major medical coverage than under basic medical coverage because major medical benefits are blanket, whereas a large part of the benefits under basic coverage are scheduled and, therefore, subject to more underwriting and claim control.

The area classifications are not the same for basic medical coverage and for major medical coverage. For example, in the rate manual of one insurer, six area codes are used for basic medical coverage and nine area codes are used for major medical coverage. Area three for basic coverage and area four for major medical are standard, that is they require no adjustment in the tabular rates for territorial variations. For basic medical coverage, area one calls for a discount of 8.5 percent and area six requires a loading of

---

[7] These figures are based on a study by Alan M. Thaler, "Group Major Medical Expense Insurance," *Transactions of the Society of Actuaries,* Vol. 3. (1951), p. 429 ff.

12.5 percent. For major medical coverage, area one is given a discount of 24 percent and area nine is increased by a loading of 40 percent.

The highest priced area for major medical may not be the highest priced area for basic medical.

A variable used in rating group major medical coverage that is not considered in the rating of other group health insurance covers is the income of the persons insured. Studies have shown that the participation clauses used in group major medical policies do not deter persons in high-income groups from asking for expensive medical care services, because these people generally want them, expect them, and can afford to pay for them. The expected value of claims at the various ages is about 150 percent more for those earning in excess of $25,000 than for those earning less than $5,000, and about 65 percent higher for those earning between $10,000 and $15,000 than for those earning between $5,000 and $10,000.

The inflation in the cost of medical care requires that a trend factor be included in projected medical care claims costs so that these increased costs will be reflected in the manual rate. The cost of medical care increased more than 50 percent during the sixties. Because major medical coverage is written blanket, rather than scheduled, the increase in the cost of medical care services is quickly reflected in mounting claim costs. The deductibles are consumed faster and the bills for covered expenses accumulate at a more rapid rate. The American consumer not only is paying more per unit of medical service, he is buying more units.

Students of the subject of the cost of medical care point out that since the price index does not adjust adequately for changes in the quality of medical care, the inflation in the cost of medical care has not been as great as that suggested. Notwithstanding, the cost of group major medical coverage is closely related to the dollar cost of medical care and to the amount that private consumers spend on medical care services.

The number of females in the group, the plan provisions, the industry, and the type of employees affect the manual rate for group major medical coverage, just as they do for basic coverage. The rate manual of one insurer (Table 16–2) shows the following standard monthly rates for a group of 10 to 24 lives for major medical coverage with a $100 corridor deductible, 80 percent–20 percent participation, $10,000 maximum, and written on a per disability basis.

The basic coverage required with this plan depends upon the area in which the group is located. If the plan is written in area three, Champaign, Illinois, for example, the basic plan must provide at least $21 a day hospital room and board benefit for a maximum of 31 days, 20 times daily benefits for hospital extras, and a $300 surgical schedule. If the plan is written in area nine, Los Angeles, for example, the basic plan must provide at least $28 a day hospital extras, and a $400 surgical schedule. If the base hospital plan daily benefits are at least $5 higher than the minimum required for the area, the base rate is decreased by 25 percent.

TABLE 16–2
Dollar Rates for Employees and Dependents

Number of Employee over 65 Yrs.

Employees earning $10,000 yr. or more	Less than 10%		10% but under 20%		20% but under 30%		30% but under 40%		40% but under 50%	
	Emp.	Dep.	Emp.	Dep.	Emp.	Dep.	Emp.	Dep.	Emp.	Dep.
Less than 10%	1.53	2.50	1.85	2.81	2.15	3.12	2.45	3.45	2.75	3.76
10% but less than 20%	1.88	3.06	2.25	5.33	2.62	3.81	2.99	4.21	3.35	4.54
20% but less than 30%	2.21	3.61	2.65	4.06	3.08	4.50	3.54	4.95	3.97	5.42
30% but less than 40%	2.56	4.17	3.08	4.70	3.58	5.22	4.08	5.74	4.60	6.27
40% but less than 50%	2.90	4.73	3.48	5.33	4.05	5.91	4.63	6.50	5.20	7.10

The foregoing manual rates are adjusted for female exposure as follows:

Less than 25%	No adjustment
25% to 45%	Increase 4%
45% to 65%	Increase 8%
65% to 85%	Increase 12%
85% to 100%	Increase 15%

The rates also are adjusted for the area in which the group is located. For example, a 30 percent decrease is given for area one, no adjustment is made for area four, and an increase of 40 percent is charged for area nine. As in the other forms of group health coverage, the final premium is subjected to volume loadings or discounts.

Experience Rating. Experience rating in group health insurance is basically the same as in group life insurance. It is used prospectively to determine the renewal premium for the group and retrospectively to determine dividends or retroactive rate adjustments for a completed policy period.

PROSPECTIVE EXPERIENCE RATING. In the discussion in Chapter 15 of experience rating of group life insurance, the concept of credibility was introduced. Credibility refers to the statistical significance that can be accorded to the loss experience of a given group in establishing the premium for that group. Credibility is expressed as a factor that varies directly with (1) the size of the group, (2) the number of years of experience available for the group, (3) the loss frequency rate produced by the group, and (4) the number of covers written for the group. The credibility factor varies inversely with the maximum amount of losses that may be chargeable to the group in a policy year. This maximum, called the loss limit, is expressed as a percentage of the premium and generally varies with the size of the group. It might be 250 percent for one group size and 125 percent for another. Claims in excess of the limit are not included in the group's experience, but are pooled with those of other groups.

In the experience rating formula, the credibility factor can be any number from zero to one. For example, in medical care and short-term disability covers, for groups consisting of 100 persons, the credibility factor might be 0.20 if experience for only 1 year is available and 0.65 if five years of experience have been accumulated. For groups of 500 persons, the credibility factor might be 0.75 if 1 year of experience is available, but 0.80 if 5 years of experience have been accumulated. For groups of 25 persons and only 1 year of experience, the credibility factor might be 0.00, whereas for groups of 1,500 persons the credibility factor might be 1.00.

Because of the low loss frequency rate and the high loss severity rate produced under long-term disability coverage, a far larger group is required to experience rate this coverage than is required to experience rate short-term disability income and medical expense coverage. Claims experience under long-term disability coverage is generally pooled with that of other groups, with little or no credibility given to the experience of the particular group.

When several types of group covers are written for a particular insured by one insurer, the practice is to combine the coverage for experience rating. Because random fluctuations in claims under each coverage can be offsetting, the total loss experience under the combined covers is likely to be more stable. Therefore, a higher credibility factor is assigned to the combined experience than could be assigned to the experience under each separate coverage.

In prospective experience rating (renewal rating), the experience of several years will be taken into consideration, but the most recent experience is usually given the greatest weight.[8] In medical care coverage, claims experience is adjusted to reflect the trend toward higher cost of medical services. This adjustment usually produces a higher renewal premium even for those insurers with experience better than that anticipated in the current premium. Because there is no clear-cut secular claims trend in disability income coverage, no adjustment of the claims experience under this coverage is necessary. Disability income claims, however, do tend to fluctuate inversely with business conditions: more business, less claims; less business, more claims, but no allowance is generally made in the experience rating formulas for this type of fluctuation. Experience rating for disability income coverage produces higher renewal premiums for those insureds with experience worse than that anticipated in the current premium and lower renewal premiums for those insureds with experience better than that anticipated in the current premium.

The renewal premium for a group policy is fixed at a level high enough to cover expected claims, expected expenses, and a risk charge.

Claims Charge. The claims charge is developed from the average experience of the particular group, or on a weighted average of the class experience and the experience of the particular group. The claims charge, when expressed as a percentage of the premium, is called the loss ratio charge. The loss ratio charge may be expressed as follows:

$$\frac{C}{P} = \frac{z A + (1 - z)E}{P}, \text{ where}$$

$C =$ Claims charge.

$P =$ Premiums earned for past years adjusted to present rate levels.

---

[8] If the group coverage has been in force only one year and the experience under it is poor, the insurer may consider that experience to be an aberration and not penalize the insured for it. Insurers have noted that a larger than normal number of claims occur during the first policy year when past-due surgery and other medical treatment are sought soon after the policy becomes effective and these services consequently become less of a financial burden to the patient.

$$\frac{C}{P} = \text{Loss ratio charge.}$$

$z = $ Credibility factor.

$A = $ Actual claims incurred by the particular group over the past years adjusted to give higher weight to the recent year and, in medical care coverage, to reflect trends in claims cost.

$E = $ Expected claims over the past years based on the average experience of the class of groups adjusted to reflect trends.

Assume that a disability income group insurance policy with a benefit level of $50 a week, maximum 26 weeks after a waiting period of 7 days, was written 5 years ago covering a group of 100 employees. During this 5-year period, the earned premiums, adjusted to present rate levels, were $20,000; the actual claims incurred, after adjustments, were $13,000; and the expected claims, after adjustments, on the class of groups were $17,600. The credibility factor is 0.65 because of the size of the group and its 5 years of experience.

Applying the foregoing formula, the loss ratio charge for the group can be computed as follows:

$$\frac{C}{\$20,000} = \frac{0.65\,(\$13,000) + (1 - 0.65)\,\$17,600}{\$20,000}$$

$$C = \$15,610$$

The loss ratio charge is $\dfrac{\$15,600}{\$20,000}$ or about 78 percent.

If the renewal premium for this group, based on the average experience on the class of groups, would be $4,000, then the claims charge for this group would be 78 percent of $4,000 or $3,120.

Assume that the group had only 10 employees and that all of the other figures were also one tenth of their former size, that is earned premiums were $2,000; actual claims incurred were $1,300; and expected claims on the class of groups were $1,760. The credibility factor would now be zero because the group is too small for its own experience to have any statistical validity.

Applying the formula, the loss ratio charge for the group can be calculated as follows:

$$\frac{C}{\$2,000} = \frac{0\,(\$1,300) + (1 - 0)\,\$1,760}{\$2,000}$$

$$C = \$1,760$$

The loss ratio charge is $\dfrac{\$1,760}{\$2,000}$ or about 88 percent.

If the renewal premium for this group, based on the average experience on the class of groups, would be $400, then the claims charge for this group would be 88 percent of $400 or $352.

Assume that the group had 1,000 employees and that all of the other figures were also 10 times their original size, that is, earned premiums were $200,000; actual claims incurred were $130,000; and expected claims on the class groups were $176,000. The credibility factor would now be one because the group is large enough for its own experience to have full statistical significance.

Applying the formula, the loss ratio charge for the group can be figured as follows:

$$\frac{C}{\$200,000} = \frac{1\,(\$130,000) + (1-1)\,\$176,000}{\$200,000}$$

$$C = \$130,000$$

The loss ratio charge is $\dfrac{\$130,000}{\$200,000}$ or 65 percent.

If the renewal premium for this group, based on the average experience on the class of groups, would be $40,000, then the claims charge for this group would be 65 percent of $40,000 or $26,000.

The figure for *claims incurred* is not the same as that for *claims paid*. At the end of the policy year, there will be claims approved but not yet paid, claims reported but not yet processed, and claims incurred but not yet reported. Some claims incurred in a previous year will be paid in the current year, and some claims incurred in the current year will not be paid until a subsequent year.

The claims charge used in computing renewal rating is based on incurred claims and not on claims paid. The relationship between incurred claims and paid claims may be expressed as follows:

$$IC = CP + CR - \ddot{CR} \text{ where}$$

IC = Incurred claims.

CP = Chargeable claims paid.

CR = Allocated claim reserve liability at the end of policy year.

$\ddot{CR}$ = Allocated claim reserve liability at the beginning of the policy year.

Claim reserves for a case are estimates of the amount needed to pay all losses incurred during the policy year. For known claims (those reported but not yet settled) the reserve is computed by multiplying the number of outstanding claims by an average value per claim. The average value per claim is determined by the insurer from its experiences with the group (and with the class of groups) and is, of course, adjusted to reflect trends.

Claims incurred but not yet reported are estimated on the basis of experience, using some such statistically reliable ratio as the ratio between incurred but unreported claims to paid claims during the final quarter of previous policy years for the group and for the class of groups.

For example, assume a disability income group insurance policy with a benefit level of $50 a week, maximum 26 weeks after a waiting period of 7 days, covering a group of 100 employees at an annual premium of $3,-500. If, at the end of the policy year, the number of known claims outstanding is 3 and the average value per claim is $100, the reserve liability for claims reported but not yet settled would be estimated at $300. Furthermore, if over a 3-year period the ratio of incurred but unreported claims to paid claims during the final quarter of the policy year averaged 40 percent after necessary adjustments and the amount of cash claims paid during the final quarter of the current year was $800, the claim reserve liability for unreported claims would be estimated at $320 ($800 $\times$ .40). The total claim reserve liability would be estimated at $620 ($300 + $320), or 17.7 percent of the annual premium, a realistic percentage for short-term disability income coverage.

Assume that the claim reserve liability at the beginning of the policy year was estimated at $500 and that chargeable claims paid during the year was $3,000. Using the foregoing formula $IC = CP + CR - \overset{..}{CR}$ to figure incurred claims for the year, incurred claims are found to be $3,120 which is $3,000 + $620 − $500.

Expense Charges. Expenses as well as claims are experience rated for renewal premiums. Cost accounting techniques are employed to allocate expenses among group cases. More precise methods are used in computing dividends or retrospective rate credits than in establishing renewal premium rates. Since greater refinement in retrospective experience rating, insofar as practicable, gives the policyholder the benefits of savings in expenses to which he contributes and charges the policyholder for those extra expenses that are incurred on his behalf, the lack of precision in renewal experience rating creates no problem of rate equity. Expense charges are usually based on a percentage of premiums, a charge per group member, a charge per contract, and a charge per transaction. The charges are set to reflect the savings to the insurer involved when the insured does much of the administration work associated with the group, such as accounting and claims administration. Variations in commission scales and premium tax rates are considered. Much of the discussion on the experience rating of expenses for group life insurance discussed in Chapter 15 applies to the experience rating of group health insurance. The two types of covers are frequently combined and experience rated as a unit.

Risk Charge. In Chapter 2 of this text, Harold Cremér was quoted as follows: "The object of the theory of risk is to give a mathematical analysis of the random fluctuation in an insurance business, and to discuss the various means of protection against their inconvenient effect."[9]

The purpose of the risk charge in the experience rating formula is to compensate the insurer for handling the risk associated with the exposure. The insurer takes the risk that the claims incurred by a given group or class of groups will be greater than the amount specifically charged for claims. The claims charge is an estimate based on probable future claims. As a result of random fluctuations, incurred claims could well exceed projected claims. For example, actual claims might exceed probable claims when there is an epidemic or a business recession or when there is an abrupt increase in the cost of medical care or in the use of medical services. The risk charge provides the insurer funds with which to protect itself against the "inconvenient effect" of random fluctuations.

Although insurers use different methods of computing the risk charge, generally the amount of the charge is related to the degree of risk involved. The degree of risk is measured by the probabilities of deviation from expected claims.

For example, suppose that the short-term disability income claims for each year over the past 10 years in 2 groups have been as follows:

Group A (500 Employees)				Group B (50 Employees)			
1	$10,000	6	$11,000	1	$1,500	6	$ 600
2	15,000	7	16,000	2	1,300	7	1,600
3	16,000	8	14,000	3	2,000	8	400
4	8,000	9	16,000	4	300	9	900
5	9,000	10	15,000	5	2,200	10	2,200

The total claims for the 10-year period would be $130,000 for Group A and $13,000 for Group B. The arithmetic mean or expectancy for each year is $130,000 ÷ 10 or $13,000 for Group A, and $13,000 ÷ 10 or $1,300 for Group B.

What is the probability that results next year will be quite different from these long-run averages? With what degree of confidence can a prediction be accepted that claims will not exceed $13,000 next year in Group A or $1,300 in Group B? (Out of the past 10 years, claims in Group A exceeded $13,000 6 times, and claims in Group B exceeded $1,300 5 times.) Useful statistical tools to deal with questions of this type are those that measure dispersion. A commonly used measure of dispersion is the standard deviation.

The standard deviation is the square root of the variance of a distribution. The variance can be computed by squaring the mean of the distribution and subtracting it from the average of the squares of all values in the distribution.

[9] Footnote 11, Chapter 2.

The square of the mean in Group A is $13,000^2$ or $169 million. The average of the squares of all values in Group A is computed as follows:

$10,000^2 =$	$100,000,000	$11,000^2 = $	121,000,000
15,000^2 =	225,000,000	16,000^2 =	256,000,000
16,000^2 =	256,000,000	14,000^2 =	196,000,000
8,000^2 =	64,000,000	16,000^2 =	256,000,000
9,000^2 =	81,000,000	15,000^2 =	225,000,000
		Total	$1,780,000,000

$1.78 billion ÷ 10 = $178 million, the average of all values in distribution A. The variance in Group A is equal to $178 million — $169 million or $9 million. The standard deviation is the square root of $9 million or $3,000, and is about 23 percent of the mean.

The square of the mean in Group B is $1,300^2$ or $1.69 million. The average of the squares of all values in Group B is computed as follows:

$1,500^2 =$	$2,250,000	600^2 = $	360,000
1,300^2 =	1,690,000	1,600^2 =	2,560,000
2,000^2 =	4,000,000	400^2 =	160,000
300^2 =	90,000	900^2 =	810,000
2,200^2 =	4,840,000	2,200^2 =	4,840,000
		Total	$21,600,000

$21,600,000 ÷ 10 = $2,160,000, the average of all values in distribution B. The variance in Group B is equal to $2,160,000 — $1,690,000 or $470,-000. The standard deviation is the square root of $470,000 or $685.60, and is about 53 percent of the mean.

Although in absolute dollars the standard deviation in Group A ($3,-000) is larger than in Group B ($685.60), the standard deviation relative to the mean of the distribution is higher in Group B (53 percent) than in Group A (23 percent). The total risk charge will be higher for Group A but the risk charge percentage will be higher in Group B because the risk is greater in Group B. The total risk charge can be expected to vary directly with the standard deviation of the expected claim. The percentage risk charge can be expected to vary directly with the ratio of the standard deviation of expected claims to the mean of the distribution.

The more stable the experience of the group, the lower will be the per unit risk charge. In small groups, where the applicable credibility factor is low, the experience of the group is, to a large extent, pooled with that of other groups. The risk charge is then based principally on the experience of the pool rather than on the experience of the individual group.

A number of insurers reduce the risk charge for each year that the group remains with the insurer because of the contributions the group has made over the years to the surplus or contingency reserve of the insurer. Other insurers assume a constant year to year risk for the group and make no adjustment in the risk charge unless a newfound change develops in year to year loss experience.

The risk charge is less for groups that achieve stability of loss experience by combining several covers under one policy.

RETROSPECTIVE EXPERIENCE RATING.   Prospective experience rating looks to the coming year and has as its function the setting of renewal premiums. Retrospective experience rating looks to the year just completed and has as its function the determination of dividends or retroactive rate credits. The formulas used to determine dividend or rate credits are of two types: asset share and tabular. The asset share method is used for large groups with a high credibility factor, whereas the tabular method is used for small groups with low credibility.

Asset Share.   The factors and concepts used in asset share retrospective experience rating are essentially the same as those used in prospective experience rating. The figures used in retrospective experience rating formulas, however, may differ from those used in prospective experience rating formulas. For example, the credibility factor used by some insurers in computing incurred claims may be larger in retrospective than in prospective experience rating, that is more weight is given to the insured's own experience than to class experience in determining dividend or retroactive rate adjustments than is given to the insured's own experience in determining renewal rate adjustments. In any event, the credibility factors applied to renewal rating are more likely to comply closely to statistical theory than are the credibility factors used with retrospective experience rating. Practical considerations, such as competition from other insurers and the possibility of self-insurance, frequently require a compromise with results produced by mathematical formulas, and these compromises are found more often in the retrospective experience rating calculations than in the prospective experience rating considerations.

Expenses are experience rated and are more carefully allocated among particular groups in retrospective experience rating formulas than in prospective experience rating formulas. Cost accounting techniques are used to develop formulas that produce just distributions of administrative costs, commission expenses, taxes, risk charges, and profit charges in order to achieve equity among insureds.

The retroactive rate adjustment formulas used by insurers not only vary among insurers but also vary from time to time within a given insurer. The principles applied, however, are common; only the importance assigned to the different components in the formula varies.

The retroactive rate credit or dividend formula may be expressed as follows:

$D = P - [(zA) + (1 - z)E + e]$, where

$D =$ Dividends or retroactive rate credit.

$P =$ Earned premium (sometimes includes interest earnings on advance premiums and special contingency funds).

$z =$ Credibility factor.

$A =$ Actual claims incurred by the group over the past year.

$E =$ Expected claims over the past year based on the average experience of the class of groups.

$e =$ Expenses chargeable to the group as determined by applicable formula.

Assume that a disability income group insurance policy with a benefit level of $50 a week, maximum 26 weeks after a waiting period of 7 days, was written on a group of 200 employees at an annual earned premium of $8,000. Assume that the losses incurred were $5,200, that the credibility factor was 0.40, that the expected claims over the past year, based on the average experience of the class of groups, were $7,040, and that the expenses charged to the group were $800. The dividend or retroactive rate credit payable to the group would be figured as follows:

$D = \$8,000 - [(0.40 \times \$5,200) + (1 - 0.40) \$7,040 + \$800]$

$D = \$8,000 - [\$2,080 + \$4,224 + \$800]$

$D = \$8,000 - 4,104$

$D = \$896$

Suppose the actual losses were $7,300, exceeding the expected losses by $260. A dividend or retroactive rate credit nevertheless would still be payable to the group. The dividend or rate credit would be figured as follows:

$D = \$8,000 - [(0.40 \times \$7,300) + (1 - 0.40) \$7,040 + \$800]$

$D = \$8,000 - [\$2,920 + \$4,224 + \$800]$

$D = \$8,000 - \$7,944$

$D = \$56$

Thus a dividend of $56 would be paid to this group, even though it was carried at a loss. The predividend loss is $100 figured as follows: $8,000 − ($7,300 + $800) = −$100.

If, in the foregoing illustration, the credibility were 0.70 rather than 0.40 and the actual losses incurred were $7,300, no dividend would be paid. Applying the formula, a negative dividend would result:

$D = \$8,000 - [(0.70 \times \$7,300) + (1 - 0.70) \, \$7,040 + \$800]$

$D = \$8,000 - [\$5,110 + \$2,112 + \$800]$

$D = \$8,000 - \$8,022$

$D = -\$22$

Retrospective experience rating as applied in group health insurance is usually designed to provide a policy dividend or a retroactive rate credit. Only rarely are group policies written to provide for retroactive rate charges or assessments where claims and expenses are in excess of that allowed in the rate structure. In some group plans, however, deficiencies in premiums may be charged (in whole or in part) against favorable experience in future years.

If the insurer wants to retain the insured as a customer, the insurer will not allow the deficit to become so large that the insured will be encouraged to look elsewhere for his coverage in order to make a fresh start. Market constraints affect what the insurer can do in carrying forward deficits. Some insurers handle the problem of deficiencies by requiring the insured to build a claim stabilization reserve to which deficits are charged. The insured usually is given credit for the interest earned on the stabilization fund.

Tabular Approach. The tabular approach to retrospective experience rating is applied to small groups. For small groups the premiums are based nearly completely on class experience and the expense ratios are relatively high. The dividend or retroactive rate credit is based on a simple formula that relates refunds to percentages of the premium charged. The refund percentages vary by such factors as the claim rate, the amount of the premium, and the number of years the policy has been in force. The objective is to achieve an equitable distribution of the divisible surplus that is allocated to these plans.

Retrospective experience rating formulas, both tabular and asset share, vary widely among insurers and are not published. Only the general principles of the formulas used have been discussed here.

7. REASONS FOR USING GROUP LIFE AND HEALTH INSURANCE

Three reasons for establishing a group insurance plan in any given business are to improve industrial relations, to meet the demands of unions, and the desire of the employer or key men to obtain their own personal insurance at low rates.

Industrial Relations. Much is made of the industrial relations aspects of group insurance by writers and salesmen. Group insurance plans are said to attract better employees, reduce employee turnover, and improve morale and efficiency; but it would appear that the value of group insurance in attracting and holding employees is at least open to question.

The value of any condition of employment depends on contrast. If two jobs offer the same conditions, those conditions are no factor in influencing a person in the choice of or encouraging a person to remain on a job. Today, group insurance is so widespread in business and industry that it offers no contrast. Whichever job he chooses, the employee will usually be covered under a group life and health insurance plan; and nearly any other job to which he might shift will be covered also. It is possible that the lack of an attractive group plan might prove a disadvantage in obtaining employees and holding them; but under today's conditions it would appear that the existence of a good plan has little effect in obtaining or holding employees.

Group insurance improves employee morale and hence efficiency by reducing the financial worries of employees. The effect of group insurance in this respect is probably less important in life insurance than in health insurance. Few healthy people worry much about dying or the effect of their death on their dependents—except when forced to do so by the life insurance agent. However, people are conscious of the costs of medical and hospital care, and are kept reminded of these costs by constant publicity given to them. Group health insurance will lessen their worry about possible loss.

Demands of Unions.   Group insurance is a fundamental part of the scope of collective bargaining. Employee financial security is of vital concern to unions. Unions recognize that group insurance is an effective way of providing this security. The direct demand of unions for group insurance has been one of the principal reasons for establishing group insurance plans. Either the union makes a direct demand on the employer to establish a plan, or the employer establishes it in anticipation of union demands. Employers may feel that they have better control over plans established independently of unions and that they enjoy a greater advantage in employee relations by initiating the plans themselves. However, the employer cannot establish a plan independently of the union if the union chooses to bargain for it.

"Get It Wholesale."   Some group plans are established because the employer in a smaller business or the executives in a larger one look at group insurance as a way to get insurance at less than the individual policy rates. Because premiums paid by the employer for group insurance are deductible as a business expense, the effective cost of group insurance is further reduced. In a large business, where ownership and management are divorced, executives find it easy to sell themselves on life and health insurance when the premiums are to be paid out of corporate funds. Stockholders rarely object. The owner-manager in the small business may be just as much intrigued with the tax savings involved and the low cost of group coverage on his own life and health as he is with the needs of his employees. The appeal of group insurance to executives is especially strong if these executives are otherwise uninsurable.

8. AN APPRAISAL OF GROUP INSURANCE

Although the amount of group insurance in force is influenced by economic conditions, group insurance has become so much a part of the employment picture that even the severest economic depression could have no more than a temporary effect upon it.

Group life insurance has already begun to replace industrial insurance as the form of protection most often owned by lower income groups. Group also is having an effect on the ordinary life insurance business by taking care of the demand for the smaller policy.

Both industrial and ordinary life insurance were well developed before group appeared on the scene. In health insurance, strides in the effort to write individual coverage were not made until the 1950's, when the group plan of writing insurance already was well established and booming. It is possible that, because of the greater efficiency of group insurance, individual health insurance will never develop to the ranking position that individual contracts have achieved and still hold in the life insurance business. People generally need more than their group insurance to complete their life insurance programs; but group health insurance, especially for medical care, is often sufficient. While group life insurance usually supplements individual life insurance, group health insurance frequently supplants individual health insurance. Only in the area of long-term disability income protection has group insurance not become a major limiting factor to the growth of individual contracts, and even here the trend is toward the writing of more long-term disability income insurance on a group basis.

Group Insurance and the Agency System. While group insurance technically is sold under the agency system, it probably would be more realistic to describe the marketing of group insurance as a channel which utilizes services of the agency system merely because that system is there and traditional. Agents may initiate group cases, but details more often are handled by salaried group representatives. Ususally there is little agent-client relationship between either employer and agent or employees and agent. In the small or medium-size group case, an enterprising agent might take advantage of the opportunity to serve individual employees as a means of developing sales of additional insurance if the need exists; but, by and large, the individual agent plays a minor role.

Occasionally, some companies will write group insurance around the agent—i.e., they will write it direct and pay no commissions. This trend was given much impetus in 1954 by the federal employees' case in which $6.7 billion of group life was placed in force on 1.7 million federal workers with payment of only a token commission. Unions bargain for group coverage written direct without commissions. The New York law, however, requires that a commission be charged against every group case regardless of whether the commission is paid.

Some individual agents and the life agents' association are active in fostering or protecting legislation which keeps group life insurance from expanding. For the most part, companies have no fears at all about the expansion of group insurance into any area that can be underwritten, although they are sometimes restrained in their pronouncements on the subject as a matter of maintaining good relations with their agency forces.

Group and Society.   Group insurance offers a number of advantages over ordinary insurance. These advantages must not be overlooked in any appraisal of group insurance. One of the principal advantages is its ability to provide low-cost insurance protection by using efficient marketing and administrative techniques. It also spreads insurance to a number of people who would otherwise be without it. Among this group are those who are not sufficiently motivated to buy insurance, those who feel that they cannot afford insurance, and (most important) those who are uninsurable under individual contracts. The social importance of group insurance is recognized in the tax laws, which (in general) allow the cost of group insurance as a deductible expense to the employer and do not consider the premium the employer pays as taxable compensation to the employee.

9. BASIC DECISIONS IN ESTABLISHING GROUP INSURANCE PLANS

In the formation of a group insurance plan, several decisions will have to be made.

Contributory versus Noncontributory Plans.   Should the plan be contributory or noncontributory? The noncontributory plan is simpler to administer. All employees of an eligible class are automatically covered, thus eliminating the task of selling the plan to 75 percent of those qualifying. The possibility of troublesome clerical errors is reduced.

The contributory plan makes it possible for the employer to offer higher limits of coverage without a correspondingly higher premium outlay on the part of the employer. On the other hand, income tax considerations favor the noncontributory plan. The entire cost of a noncontributory plan is a deductible business expense. Under the contributory plan, employees are not allowed to deduct their contributions in reporting income for tax purposes. The opportunity to pay 100 percent of the premium with tax-free dollars gives the noncontributory plan a decisive cost advantage to the participating employee. Premiums paid by employers for group insurance need not be reported as income by the participating employees except for amounts of life insurance in excess of $50,000. Thus, the employee receives, in effect, a tax-free increase in income in the amount of the premium.

Some argue that the contributory plan makes the employee more conscious of his insurance and consequently the employee relations value of the plan is more effective. Others argue that the noncontributory plan is more acceptable to the employee because he looks upon it as a gift. Under the contributory plan, the employee tends to think that he is paying for what he gets. He may overlook or discount his employer's contribution. In fact, some employees under a contributory plan do not even understand that the employer is paying any part of the cost.[10]

Eligibility. A decision must be made whether to insure all employees or to set up standards of eligibility. It is common to exclude all employees with less than a specified minimum period of service in order to exclude temporary and transient employees. It is permissible to limit coverage by restricting the plan to certain departments, to the wage roll only, salary roll only, or any other group as long as it does not result in adverse selection. Also, it must be determined whether retired employees, employees temporarily laid off, or employees on leaves of absence are to be covered. Cost is an important factor in these decisions.

Types of Coverage. Under a group life plan, there is little decision involved in type of coverage. The employer needs to decide only whether the plan is to be group term exclusively or whether some group permanent is to be included. In a group health plan there are many decisions to be made: Should the plan include only hospitalization and surgical benefits (the most widespread coverages in group health)? Should it include loss of time coverage (perhaps the most important, since bills can be paid if income continues)? Should it provide for long-term disability income? Should it contain provisions for medical reimbursement, diagnostic expense, drugs, psychiatric care, nursing home care, dental care, and vision care, and so on? Should there be a catastrophe coverage in the form of major medical? If so, should it be integrated with a basic plan or stand alone as the only medical coverage?[11] Should the plan include coverage that integrates with medicare?

The Formula or Schedule. To some extent, the types of coverage purchased will depend on how much the employer feels he can budget for premiums. The budget is also important in determining the schedule of benefits. Employers usually like to provide life insurance benefits equal to at least one year's income, although there are many cases where much less than this amount is provided. In health insurance a decision often will have

---

[10] This is largely the fault of those employers who fail to merchandise their group plans. Group plans should be given publicity on a continuing basis. One way to keep employees reminded of their group insurance is to give each employee an annual statement of how much money the employer has paid in premiums for insurance benefits for that employee.

[11] Good insurance-buying principles would suggest that there be no coverage for the small, frequent loss which can be budgeted. Insurance should be purchased only for the large, infrequent loss which can not be budgeted. This would suggest that first-dollar coverage be eliminated. Whereas this conclusion would be logical in individual coverage, it is not necessarily so in group coverage. Income tax considerations account for the difference. In employer financed plans, the cost of the insurance is deductible by the employer and not reportable as income to the employee. The effect is to be able to pay first-dollar losses with tax-free dollars. Also, the cost of trading dollars (which is the case in first-dollar coverage) is not so expensive in group as in individual coverage because insurers pay out about 90 percent of the premiums collected. The tax savings more than offset the 10 percent loading paid to the insurance companies.

to be made whether to offer a wide range of coverages with low limits or to offer only a few coverages with more adequate limits.

The Company to Buy from.   If the employer already has some coverage and is adding more, he usually will want to make further purchases from the same company. Placing all group coverage in one company reduces administrative detail. Moreover, the more insurance an employer has with a given company, the better is his bargaining position on rates, service, and claims. The higher combined premium is likely to result in a lower retention limit.

The reputation of the company for promptness in handling claims and other details of service also will have a bearing—probably more bearing after the plan is installed than before. Most employers assume, unless they have convincing evidence to the contrary—perhaps from another employer —that service from any well-known company will be about the same as that from another. However, after the plan is installed they may become dissatisfied with the service and decide to switch the plan to a different company. The ability of the company to meet the desired specifications of the plan can often be an important factor in selection of the company.

A major factor in choice of company in many cases is cost. Costs of identical plans tend to vary among companies. One of the factors in the rate is the retention limit—the amount of the premium retained by the company for contingencies, expenses, and profit. In the larger group case, bargaining over the size of the retention assumes a role in the choice of the insurer. Competition is keen, often even sharp. The size of the retention a company feels it must have is a matter of variables which a company can interpret in a number of ways. The buyer tries to drive down the retention rate[12] and will sometimes consider only the company which offers the lowest one. Differences in retention rates, however, often are small, so that the "price" buyer will usually have several companies from which to make a choice.

One device sometimes used in competitive bidding in group insurance is the level commission plan. The agent might request that his commission be loaded in the quoted rate as a level commission rather than as a high first-year commission in order to produce a lower first-year rate and give him a competitive advantage with the strictly price buyer. Some buyers request and obtain quotes that include only the minimum commission allowable under the law.

Basically, the cost of a group life and health insurance program equals the benefits paid plus the money required to deliver these benefits to the covered employees. The employer has the choice of providing the benefits through the insurance mechanism by using commercial insurance contracts, nonprofit associations offering prepaid hospital, surgical, and medical care

---

[12] In fact, he occasionally succeeds in driving it down to a level that makes many observers of the group business raise their eyebrows.

protection (Blue Cross, Blue Shield, and independent plans), or group practice prepayment plans; or the benefits can be paid directly by the employer from his own assets (self-insurance in some cases; noninsurance in others).[13]

The amount to be paid in benefits to covered employees is fixed in the benefit schedule. The variables are the costs of delivering the benefits and the cost of the risk associated with the program. If the plan is insured, the risk cost variables are the contingency funds required by the insurer and the profit expected by the insurer. The net cost of an insured program is the amount of funds retained by the insurer after claims have been paid to employees and dividends have been paid to employers.

If the benefits are to be paid by the employer from his own resources, the risk cost variable is the amount which equals "the difference between the net profit that would be received if future loss incidence could be perfectly forecast and the profit received when the same loss incidence is experienced without the ability to forecast."[14] Part of this cost is anxiety. Another part is the cost of maintaining sufficient liquid assets and credit lines to meet claims, the frequency and severity of which are abnormally high. The net cost of an uninsured or self-insured program is the cost of administering the plan and the cost of the risk.

Initial rates quoted on a particular plan for a given employer are likely to vary among insurers because potential loss rates, expenses, and risk costs are not estimated alike by all insurers. Also, some insurers attempt to "buy the business" by quoting a low initial rate with the hope of raising the rate significantly at the end of the first policy year. However, rates among insurers in subsequent years are likely to be closer together, the difference being the amount retained by the insurer for premium taxes, general administrative costs, claims administrative expenses, sales expenses, contingency reserves, risk charge, and profit.

Retention rates vary among insurers. Some operate more efficiently than others. Some may seek higher contingency reserves and profits from new groups to offset poor companywide underwriting experience in the past.

The claim charge includes the charge for the claims reserves held to pay unreported claims, claims in process of settlement, and claims which have not yet been paid. Insurers are not alike in their practices with respect to claims reserves. The insurer's practice in claims reserving is of importance to the buyer. Some insurers are overly conservative and overstate the amount that they are likely to need to pay claims, thus increasing the charge to the buyer. Some insurers might not return unused claims reserves to the policyholder after a reasonable time following the termination of the policy.

---

[13] Cf. Chapters 13 and 28.
[14] Robert I. Mehr and Bob A. Hedges, *Risk Management in the Business Enterprise* (Homewood, Illinois: Richard D. Irwin, Inc., 1963), p. 85. See also pp. 66–67.

In group health insurance, a decision has to be made whether to use the facilities of commercial insurance companies entirely or insure the hospital and surgical exposures with service plans like Blue Cross and Blue Shield. Competition has all but eliminated the many points of difference which formerly existed between the "Blues" and the insurance companies. If the hazard is less than the average, experience rating might give insurance companies a cost advantage over those Blues that do not experience rate their policies. If the hazard is greater than average, the community rate usually employed by the Blues might give the service plan the advantage. Economies of combining all group coverages with one insurer could give insurance companies the cost advantage.

17

Insurance in Employee Benefit Plans: Retirement —An Overview and Tax Aspects

In a basically agricultural economy of small independent farmers with large families who earn their living off the land, the aged can be retained in the family group without too great a financial burden on the family. In a business economy of small proprietors, owners of family operated enterprises can pass their interests to their families upon reaching retirement, in return for which the families will provide the income necessary for support of those retired. Both the retired farmer and retired businessman may wish to render limited services to the farm or business.

In an economy such as exists in the United States today, where industrialization, urbanization, big business, big agriculture, and small families are predominant, economic care of the aged often is beyond the financial capacity of the family. In addition, not only is the tradition of the family caring for its own breaking down but also the will to do so.

1. PROVIDING ECONOMIC CARE FOR THE AGED

How to provide economic care for the aged is a significant question. Since efficient and competitive enterprise generally has no place for the superannuated employee, it is often impossible for the retired worker to provide a sufficient income in his old age on a pay as you go basis. Some persons who are retired from their regular jobs do take work elsewhere but most commonly this work is part time or is in low-pay self-employment. The income from postretirement jobs frequently is insufficient to provide the purchasing power needed by retired workers. Therefore, the job of taking care of the retired worker and his dependents today seems to fall on

(1) the worker's ability and effort to accumulate a retirement fund during his working years, (2) the government, (3) the employer, (4) personal gifts, and (5) private charity. Usually the retired worker depends upon more than one of these sources of income—preferably some combination of earned income from postretirement employment, income from (and liquidation of) personal savings, social security retirement income, and company pension plans.

Self-Reliance for Old Age Income. For a considerable period throughout the social and economic development of the United States, the problem of providing for an old age income was predominantly thought to be one that should be solved by the individual himself. In today's economy, however, the problem of amassing a competence out of one's earnings is a difficult one—difficult not only in absolute terms but difficult also in terms of the things that must be foregone during productive years. It is not human nature to give up present things for future benefits. Furthermore, mass marketing methods now in vogue do not encourage thrift. The American economy is geared to mass production. To maintain full employment, goods have to be sold so that they will not pile up in the warehouses and lead to curtailment of production.

To sell these goods, distributors resort to powerful advertising and other sales promotion methods. One of the most effective methods has been the development of installment selling with "nothing or little down" and "easy" monthly payments. With effective advertising and sales presentations making man dissatisfied with what he has and with installment selling under easy payment plans, making it possible for him to buy the things that are supposed to make him happy, there is no wonder that he finds it difficult to save. Actually instead of saving a part of present income for future use, the tendency for many people is to spend part of expected future income for present use.

Even if one had a burning desire to save and were not susceptible to high-pressure selling and advertising, he must still face three other obstacles: inflation, increasingly high standards of living, and the progressive income tax.

INFLATION. The problem created by inflation is an important consideration in planning for retirement. The government is committed to a policy of maximum employment consistent with private enterprise. A high level of investment is essential to the maintenance of full employment.[1] A number of distinguished economists argue that a gently rising price level is necessary to stimulate business activity to motivate growth in

---

[1] Any major decrease in private investment spending will have to be offset by government spending if the level of employment is to be maintained. Although government economic policy is directed toward the maintenance of private investment spending, it does not preclude heavy increases in deficit-financed government spending, should such a program become necessary for the continuation of economic prosperity.

productive capacity, and to maintain maximum employment. Professor Alvin H. Hansen argues:

A high degree of stability in the value of money must be an important consideration of public policy. Yet we are . . . in considerable danger of making a fetish of rigid price stability. This fetish could easily become a serious obstacle to optimum growth and expansion. . . . If, fearful of short-run instability, we fail to place the economy under the pressure of an aggregate demand adequate to produce full employment, we shall not ever discover what our potentialities for growth are.[2]

Professor Hansen does not consider the evils of moderate price increases to be serious. In discussing the evil that accumulated savings are eaten into by inflation, Professor Hansen says "It is well to remember that nothing eats so dangerously into family savings as deflation and unemployment."[3]

However, voices are still heard from distinguished economists in defense of a policy of price stability. Professor Henry C. Wallich writes:

Unemployment hurts a limited number of people seriously, but for the most part temporarily. Inflation hurts large numbers, usually less severely, but the damage done to savings and relative income positions tends to be permanent. If inflation should ultimately lead to a severe depression we shall end up with the worst of both worlds. . . . In the short run all sorts of good things can be promised and performed by the high pressure economy—fuller employment, more output, more growth. . . . It has been argued that permanent inflation must inevitably accelerate from a creep to a run. As its victims learn to defend themselves, by obtaining quicker wage and salary adjustment or through escalation, the beneficiaries must move their own demands ahead faster and faster to preserve their gains. . . .

But even if it does not accelerate, continuing inflation will . . . do increasing harm. The distortion of investment decisions, the discouragement of saving, the compulsion to speculate, the misallocation of resources, the strengthening of the monopoly position of firms owning old and low-cost equipment . . . the inherent instability of an economy in which everything is worth what it is only because it is expected to be worth more next year; the fluctuation in the value of "inflation hedges" produced by uncertain speed of the inflation; the need to concentrate all efforts on staying ahead of the game—all this does not add up to a satisfactory picture of a stable and rapid growing economy. And, as the moralistically inclined may feel tempted to add, a society in which all contracts and financial promises are made with the afterthought that they will be partly cancelled by inflation does not offer a morally elevated picture either. . . . Few of the critics of inflation would claim that they can see its ultimate consequences. It may lead to a collapse into deep depression, or simply to more inflation with stagnating growth. Or more likely, it will lead to price controls imposed under

---

[2] Alvin H. Hansen, "The Case for High Pressure Economics," in E. S. Phelps, B. Balassa et al. (eds.), *Problems of the Modern Economy* (New York: W. W. Norton and Company, Inc., 1966), pp. 305 and 309. The article was selected from Professor Hansen's book *The American Economy*, published in 1957.

[3] *Ibid.*, p. 308.

the pressure of impatient citizens or politicians. The immediate sacrifices that a policy of stable prices demands seem preferable to any of these.[4]

Regardless of the "fetish" for price stability, it seems likely, based on recent historical observations, that it is not unrealistic to expect prices to rise significantly over the working lifetime of an employee and throughout his retirement period. Thus, the young man who plans his retirement income on the basis of current price levels may find his planned income grossly inadequate when he reaches retirement age.

GROWTH.   Even were it realistic to expect no long-run deterioration in the value of the dollar (stable price levels), the young man who plans his retirement income on the basis of current income patterns may not be satisfied with his planned income when he reaches retirement age. Based on recent historical observations, it is not unrealistic to expect standards of living to rise significantly over the working lifetime of an employee and throughout the period of his retirement. It seems unreasonable to expect the typical worker to be able to plan a retirement income program for himself that will give him an income that reflects improved living standards throughout the period of his retirement. It does seem reasonable, however, for retirement income programs to be arranged so that retired employees can share in benefits accruing from economic growth even though this growth occurs after the employee has retired. Self-reliance for growth-oriented retirement programs can be at best only a partial solution to the problem.

THE PROGRESSIVE INCOME TAX.   The progressive income tax adds another difficulty for the individual who seeks to plan his own retirement income program. Increases in wages and salaries often accompany rises in the general price level. However, with the progressive income tax rate the worker retains only a decreasing proportion of each wage increase. Higher wages, therefore, in themselves might not be a solution to the problem of old age financing. Even the higher paid executive might not be able to plan for his own retirement and still maintain the standard of living expected of him.

Government Plans.   A second approach to the problem of financing old age security is for the government to arrange retirement programs. Because of the difficulty the individual faces in accumulating a competence by direct savings, the government has found it both economically desirable and politically expedient to enter the pension financing business. This was accomplished through the Social Security Act of 1935 (effective 1937) and its many subsequent amendments.

The purpose of social security is to provide a floor upon which a comfortable retirement income can be built by the individual. There are, of

[4] Henry C. Wallich, "The Case Against High-Pressure Economics," in Phelps, Balassa et al., op. cit., pp. 310, 311, and 312. This article was written for the American Assembly in 1958.

course, wide differences of opinion as to how high the floor should be. Some want it at a level that will provide a minimum decent standard of living. Others want it low enough so that additional income will be necessary to provide a minimum decent standard of living. Still others want it high enough to provide a comfortable standard of living.

The government also plays a role in the retirement picture by granting certain important tax advantages to private industrial pension plans approved by the Internal Revenue Service. The nature of and the requisites for these tax advantages will be discussed later.

Employer Plans. The third method of handling the problem of old age financing is for the employer to assume some of the burden. Some will argue that the burden is never assumed by the employer because funds used by him to finance retirement benefits are a part of labor cost which otherwise would have been available for wages.[5]

Spurred by the rise in the social philosophy of employer responsibility for the welfare of employees, by inducements offered under federal income tax legislation, and by the demands of organized labor, employers have been entering the field of old age financing in increasing numbers. Today about 34 million people are covered under formal private pension plans, an increase of about 47 percent during the Sixties. Assets of private pension plans are in excess of $125 billion, an increase of nearly 140 percent during the Sixties. The number of persons covered by private pension and the assets of the private pension industry are expected to continue their growth, but at a slower rate.[6]

The rate of growth in the numbers covered is expected to decrease because the number covered is already quite high in relation to what could be expected if all workers *reasonably* considered eligible for private pensions were covered.[7] The rate of growth in private pension fund assets is expected to be slower because with the maturing of a pension fund a significant change occurs in the relationship between the payments into and out of the fund. During the early stages in the life of a pension fund, benefit payments usually are small and can be handled from earnings on assets. The fund, therefore, grows each year by the amount contributed by employers or employers and employees jointly. As the pension plan approaches maturity, benefit payments increase and much of the amount contributed is needed to pay these benefits. The fund will grow only by the

---

[5] This reasoning does not recognize that the employer expects to gain certain additional advantages through granting his employees a pension—advantages that he might not gain by paying out the funds in the form of direct wages. Cf. Chapter 15.

[6] The President's Committee on Corporate Pension Funds and Other Private Retirement and Welfare Programs estimates that by 1980 42 million people will be covered by private retirement plans with assets of about $225 billion. (*Public Policy and Private Pension Programs* [Washington, D.C.: U.S. Government Printing Office, 1965], p. 10.)

[7] Daniel M. Holland, *Private Pension Funds: Projected Growth* (New York: National Bureau of Economic Research, 1966), chap. 2.

amount earned on accumulated assets coupled with whatever slight excess remains from contributions over benefits.[8]

When the fund fully matures, its level will remain stationary. The sum of contributions plus earnings on accumulated assets will be sufficient to pay benefits, with no surplus for growth nor deficiency for decline. This latter conclusion will hold true only if the following wholly unlikely conditions prevail: (1) the employee population remains stable, (2) the mean age, the median age, and the modal age of the employees remain the same, and (3) the actual experience with respect to mortality, withdrawals, expenses, investment performance, and other actuarial assumptions conforms to that projected in establishing the rate of contributions to and withdrawals from the fund.

2. PENSION PLANS CLASSIFIED

Private pension plans may be informal or formal. If formal, they may be funded or unfunded. If they are funded, they may be classified as to whether they are uninsured or insured and as to whether they are qualified under the Internal Revenue Code or are nonqualified plans. If they are insured, they may be classified as to whether the funds paid by the employer (and employees) to the insurer are used to purchase or pay for either cash value life insurance or deferred annuities for the individual participants at the time that these funds are paid in, or whether these funds are held in an unallocated account and used to purchase annuities for employees as they retire (or, if they are entitled to them, as they leave their jobs before retirement).

Informal versus Formal. The informal pension plan is hardly any plan at all. The employer decides whom he will pension and for how much at the time the pension payment commences. The plan is purely discretionary in nature. In practice, of course, retirement ages and incomes by classes of employees do tend to become established under a discretionary plan, but the employee has no formal promise that he will receive anything. Thus he has no sound basis for personal financial planning. By and large, such plans have not proved to be a solution to the retirement problem. A *formal* pension plan will define the rights and benefits of the employee in advance, setting forth eligibility standards both for participation in the plan and for the receipt of benefits. It also establishes a formula for the amount of the pension and for any other payments such as death, disability, or severance benefits. The number of informal plans in existence today is insignificant.

Unfunded versus Funded. Informal plans usually are not funded. A formal plan, however, may be unfunded or funded. When the employer pays the retirement benefits out of current earnings directly to the em-

---

[8] *Ibid.,* chaps. 3 and 4.

ployees as their benefits mature, the plan is unfunded. The *unfunded* plan is called pay as you go, although the designation is not particularly apt. Owe as you go is more fitting because in any formal plan obligations accrue during the employees' working lifetime. If funds to finance them are not set aside in the years the benefits accrue, it is inconsistent to say that the employer is paying as he goes when he is actually owing as he goes.

The problem of providing employees security with respect to promised benefits has become an important social issue, one that is discussed in Chapter 18 *infra*. Among the basic formal private pension plans covering more than 25 workers, about 700 are unfunded. Nearly one half of these 700 plans cover fewer than 100 persons but 12 of them cover more than 5,000 employees. All unfunded plans combined cover about 500,000 employees for basic benefits.[9]

When the employer puts aside money in excess of that required to pay pension benefits currently payable to retired employees and transfers this money to a trustee (usually a bank) or to an insurance company, he is advance funding. When he puts away enough each year to offset his accruing liability for the current service of covered employees and in addition has accumulated sufficient assets to offset the initial past service liability (pension credits earned before the plan is installed) the plan is fully funded. Whether the plan has to be *fully* funded to be actuarially sound is a moot question.[10]

Various methods of funding and their relationship to the question of the actuarial soundness in pension financing are discussed in Chapter 19 *infra*. At that point, it will be shown that actuarial soundness in a pension plan relates not only to the *method of funding* but also to the actuarial assumptions used.

In late 1966, the American Institute of Certified Public Accountants issued an opinion prepared by its Accounting Principles Board under which corporate earnings statements now are to recognize pension expenses in unfunded plans on the same basis as in funded plans; that is, these expenses must be charged off in the year in which pension rights are earned. At the time the report was issued, many corporations with unfunded plans charged off pension costs only when the money was paid out to retired employees. The purpose of the 1966 pension cost opinion was what the institute called another major step in its "accelerated campaign to make financial reports more useful to investors" by reducing the number of acceptable accounting principles so as to make it easier for stockholders to compare earnings of one corporation with that of another.[11]

---

[9] *Public Policy and Private Pension Programs, op. cit.*, p. 6.

[10] See Dorrance C. Bronson, *Concepts of Actuarial Soundness in Pension Plans* (Homewood, Illinois; Richard D. Irwin, Inc., 1957).

[11] Other important aspects of the opinion included the requirements (1) that pension costs be charged against income each year on a consistent basis and that the benefits of overfunding (previous overpayments into the fund or capital gains through appreciation

The principles used in accounting for the cost of pension plans for the purpose of reporting earnings to stockholders and those used in reporting earnings to the Internal Revenue Service, of course, are not necessarily the same. The tax considerations in pension plan financing are discussed later in this chapter.

Once considered a funding device (and still in use) is the balance sheet method of funding. Under this plan, accrued pension obligations are carried as a liability or as a restriction against surplus on the balance sheet. It is a crude method of funding, for it does not earmark *specific* assets for pension financing. It is only slightly removed from the unfunded plans which pay benefits from current earnings. The only difference in the two plans is in the cost accounting. Under the unfunded plan the pension cost is charged as an expense in the year paid, whereas in the so-called balance sheet funded plan the cost of pensions is charged as a reserve to the year in which the liability is incurred. The balance sheet plan gives the illusion of sufficient funds to pay benefits without the necessity of drawing on current income. Also, the tax deduction will have to be taken in the year the benefit is paid rather than in the year in which the accrual of pension benefits is charged.

Two prerequisites of sound pension funding are (1) conservative estimates of the cost of benefits based on sound actuarial data and (2) the deposit of funds into a separate account to be used to pay pension benefits. The balance sheet method does not satisfy the second of these requisites.

Uninsured versus Insured. Two funding agencies are available: trust companies and insurance companies. When a trust is used as a funding agency, the plan is called an uninsured or self-insured plan; when an insurance company is used, the plan is called an insured plan; and when both funding agencies are used in connection with the same plan, the plan is said to be split funded.

THE UNINSURED PLAN. Under the uninsured plan, a trust fund is established for the benefit of employees. The employer (and in some plans the employee also) makes periodic contributions to the fund in amounts actuarially calculated to fund the pension on the basis of the funding method selected. The employer uses whatever actuarial assumptions (mortality, interest, turnover, salary, retirement, and disability rates) he deems reasonable. Some employers will use more conservative assumptions than

---

in the value of securities) be spread over a period of not less than 10 years; (2) that the amount charged against income in reports to stockholders be within the minimum and maximum limits established in the statement of the opinion for pension costs and not necessarily the sum actually transferred to a pension fund in a given year; and (3) that there be more extensive disclosure in annual reports to stockholders, including a statement of the company's pension accounting and funding policies, the amount of the provision for pension cost for the year, and the nature and effect of significant matters affecting comparability with past financial reports. See *Opinion of the Accounting Principles Board Number 8,* American Institute of Certified Public Accountants, Inc., New York City, November, 1966.

others. The amount of the contributions under a given plan will be a function of both the actuarial assumptions and the actuarial cost method chosen.[12] The trustee invests the money, accumulates the earnings, and distributes the benefits to eligible employees.[13]

INSURED PLANS.   In a trusteed plan, the pension fund stands on its own feet—i.e., there is no averaging of experience with other pension funds.[14] In an insured plan, investment experience generally is averaged among all plans. Mortality experience and administration expenses are partly allocated on an average basis and partly on the performance of the individual plan, with the size of the group controlling the division. In trust fund plans no guarantees are available, whereas the insured plans offer guarantees, the nature and extent of which vary with the type of plan. In the insured plan, the insurance company will assume the responsibility for administering the plan, investing the funds, and providing actuarial services. In a trust fund plan, these responsibilities are divided among the employer, the trustees, and the consulting actuary.

Insured plans account for about 28 percent of all persons covered under private pension plans and they control about 30 percent of the assets held to fund private pensions.

Allocated versus Unallocated Funding Instruments.   Funding instruments may be classified as to whether the funds are immediately allocated to each participant under the plan or whether the allocation is deferred until the participant reaches retirement age. Trust fund plans usually are unallocated unless the trust agreement requires the immediate purchase of life insurance or annuities for each participant as funds are received.

Insured plans are unallocated when the insurer accumulates the funds under a deposit administration group annuity and then allocates them to each participant when he reaches retirement age. They are allocated when individual life insurance or annuity contracts, group permanent life insurance, or paid-up deferred annuity certificates under conventional group deferred annuity contracts are purchased for each employee in the year his pension credits are funded. Insurance companies developed unallocated funding instruments in an effort to become more competitive with banks as funding agencies for pension plans. Types of funding instruments are discussed in Chapter 19.

Nonqualified versus Qualified.   A private pension plan may be nonqualified or qualified. A nonqualified plan is one that does not meet the requisites of the Internal Revenue Service. The employer using a nonqualified plan is willing to sacrifice the federal tax advantages accorded qualified plans in exchange for the freedom to establish whatever cover-

---

[12] Actuarial assumptions and actuarial cost methods are discussed in Chapter 19.

[13] For a brief but comprehensive discussion of the trust fund plan and an explanation of its claimed advantages, cf. Hamilton and Bronson, *Pensions* (New York: McGraw-Hill Book Company, Inc., 1958), chap. 7.

[14] An exception is in the use of common trusts where investment experience is averaged.

age requirements, benefit structures, and financing methods he deems best for his company.

A qualified pension plan is one that is approved by the Internal Revenue Service and, as a consequence, is given favorable tax treatment. Most pension planners are not willing to put other considerations ahead of tax consequences. Therefore, they design and finance pension plans with the objective of qualifying under the Internal Revenue Code and its interpretive regulations.

3. TAX LAWS AND RETIREMENT PLANNING

Favorable tax treatment has contributed significantly to the design and growth of private pension plans in the United States. Private pension plans were first favored by legislation in 1926 when Congress granted an income tax exception to investment income earned on funds held by pension trusts. Because some employers established pension trusts during periods of high earnings only to revoke them during periods of low earnings to recapture these funds, Congress incorporated nondiversionary standards in the Revenue Act of 1938. Under that act, funds held by pension trusts were required to be used for the exclusive benefit of employees, so pension trusts had to be made irrevocable.

The current standards applicable to qualified pension plans are those enacted in the Revenue Act of 1942 as amended in 1954.

Requirements for Qualification. For a private pension to become qualified for favorable tax treatment, it must satisfy the requirements set forth under Section 401a of the 1954 Internal Revenue Code and under Section 1.401 of the regulations implementing the code. These requirements are designed to grant favorable tax treatment only to those plans that serve a useful purpose.[15]

Some members of the public who have concerned themselves with the private pension plan movement believe that the requirements for qualification need to be expanded to include safeguards necessary to assure workers for whom contributions are made that benefits will in fact be paid to them upon their retirement.[16]

The basic requirements for qualification of a private pension plan by the Internal Revenue Service are as follows:

1. The plan must be for the exclusive benefit of the employees or their beneficiaries.
2. Fund assets or income may not be diverted to the employer's use until all liabilities to employees covered under the plan are met.

---

[15] *Private Pension Plans* (Hearings before the Subcommittee on Fiscal Policy of the Joint Economic Committee, 89th Cong., 2d sess., April 26, 27; May 2, 1966, Part 1 [Washington, D.C.: U.S. Government Printing Office, 1966]), p. 1.

[16] *Ibid.* Also *Public Policy and Private Pension Programs, op. cit.*

3. The plan must be nondiscriminatory with respect to employees covered.

4. The plan must be nondiscriminatory with respect to contributions and benefits.

5. Where a trust is required, the trust must be valid and bona fide, and created in the United States by a written instrument under Section 501a of the Internal Revenue Code. A trust is not required, for example, when pension plans are funded through insurance companies under a group plan.

6. Either the contribution required of the employer or the benefits promised to the employees must be fixed.[17]

7. Forfeitures may not be applied to increase the benefits otherwise payable under the plan.

8. The plan must be in writing, permanent, and communicated to the employees.

9. The plan must provide primarily retirement income benefits.

An explanation of each of these requirements follows.

EXCLUSIVE BENEFIT OF EMPLOYEES. To be qualified, a pension plan created by an employer must be exclusively for his employees and their beneficiaries.[18] The employer, therefore, is not allowed to participate in a qualified plan. This requirement creates no problem under the corporate form of business organization because the corporation is the employer. Its stockholders, if employees of the corporation, are eligible to be covered under qualified plans on the same basis as any other employee of the corporation. Under the sole proprietorship or partnership form of business organization, a problem does arise. Before 1963, sole proprietors and partners were not permitted to be covered under a qualified pension plan set up for their employees.

Some relief was given to sole proprietors and partners under the Self-Employed Individuals Tax Retirement Act (commonly called the Keogh Act) which became effective January 1, 1963. Under this act, sole proprietors and partners are allowed to participate in qualified pension plans as self-employed persons but not as employees. The attractions offered to self-employed under the Keogh Act are less enticing than those offered to owner employees of corporations. The relatively more restrictive provisions under the Self-Employed Individuals Tax Retirement Act will be explained at the appropriate point in this chapter.

---

[17] Benefits expressed in terms of units as in the variable annuity plan qualify under this provision.

[18] Former employees and employees on leave may be included in this plan. The regulations define beneficiaries as "the estate of the employee, dependents of the employee, persons who are the natural objects of the employee's bounty, and any person designated by the employee to share in the benefits of the plan after the death of the employee."

No Diversion of Fund Assets or Income. No part of the fund assets or its income may be recaptured by the employer until all liabilities to employees under the plan are satisfied. Thus, under insured plans, policy dividends or experience rating credits must be used to pay the next premium before further contributions are made by the employer. Of course, if excess premiums are paid because of misstatement of ages or because of some clerical error, the employer may recover the amount of his overpayment upon correction of the mistake.

Furthermore, in the event the plan is terminated and funds remain after all liabilities have been discharged, these funds can revert to the employer as overpayments arising from what is called an "actuarial error." Under a fully funded plan, when investment earnings and mortality rates, for example, are greater than those projected by the actuaries, the assets of the fund will exceed its liabilities. Upon discharge of these liabilities and termination of the plan, the remaining assets can revert to the employer.

Nondiscriminatory Coverage. Alternate standards are set up under the Internal Revenue Code to measure whether coverage under a private pension plan is nondiscriminatory. One is a percentage standard and the other is a classification standard.

Percentage Standard. To meet the percentage requirement, at least 70 percent of all employees must be eligible and at least 80 percent of the eligible group must be covered. Before applying the percentage, certain employees may be excluded: part-time workers (those employed for not more than 20 hours a week), seasonal workers (those employed for not more than five months in any calendar year), and employees who have been with the company less than 5 years.

Assume that a corporation has 500 employees. Fifty employees are part time, 60 are seasonal workers, 190 have been employed less than 5 years, and 50 under age 30 have had five or more years of service. The company has designed a pension plan under which all full-time employees at least 30 years old with 5 or more years of service are covered. To determine whether this plan will qualify under the percentage standard, the following steps are necessary:

1. Determine the number of employees with respect to whom the percentage requirement is inapplicable:

    50   part-time workers
    60   seasonal workers
    190   employed less than 5 years
    ———
    300

2. Determine the number of employees with respect to whom the percentage requirement is applicable:

500 total employees
—300 employees to whom the percentage
       requirement is inapplicable
_____
200 full-time employees with 5 or more
       years of service

3. Employees ineligible to participate because of age requirement:

50 employees with 5 or more years of
   service have not reached age 30.

4. Total eligible employees:

200 full-time employees with 5 or more
       years of service
—50 under age 30
_____
150 total employees eligible to participate

5. Percentage of full-time employees with 5 or more years of service eligible to participate:

$$150 \div 200 = 75 \text{ percent}$$

Because more than 70 percent of the full-time employees with five or more years of service are eligible to participate in the plan, the plan would qualify if 80 percent of the eligible employees ($0.80 \times 150 = 120$) participate. If less than 120 employees participate, the plan would not qualify under the percentage standard. The purpose of the 80 percent requirement is to prevent a plan from qualifying when participation in the plan favors highly paid employees even though eligibility standard for coverage does not discriminate against low-paid employees. Were it not for the 80 percent rule, an employer could qualify his plan by meeting the 70 percent requirement and then requiring such high contributions from employees that only highly paid employees could afford to participate in the plan.

The percentage standard is generally called the arbitrary rule.

Classification Standard. Plans not meeting the percentage requirement can qualify if they cover employees under a classification system found by the Commissioner of Internal Revenue not to be discriminatory in favor of employees who are officers, shareholders, supervisory employees, or high salaried employees. Under this standard the commissioner has wide discretionary powers. The code and the regulations make it clear that the use of specific classifications to establish coverage eligibility standards are not to be considered discriminatory per se. Their use will be considered discriminatory only if they, in the opinion of the commissioner, yield discriminatory results.

The codes states:

[a] Classification shall not be considered discriminatory . . . merely because it excludes employees . . . whose entire annual wages do not exceed the maximum

taxable under Social Security . . . or merely because it is limited to salaried or clerical employees.

The regulations explain that the foregoing classifications are not the only ones that in themselves are discriminatory. Under the regulations, any eligibility requirement for coverage such as, for example, workers in a given department, employees with a minimum number of years or service, or employees who meet a minimum age requirement will qualify under the classification standard as long as it does not violate the nondiscrimination requirement.[19]

A contributory plan covering all employees but with contributions required of participating employees so burdensome as to make the plan acceptable only to higher paid employees would be considered discriminatory in favor of such highly paid employees.[20]

Under the classification standard (generally called the discretionary rule) each case will be tested by the Internal Revenue Service to determine whether it discriminates in favor of officers, stockholders, supervisory employees, and other highly paid employees.

NONDISCRIMINATORY CONTRIBUTIONS AND BENEFITS. The benefit must not discriminate in favor of officers, stockholders, supervisors, or highly salaried executives. Again the commissioner has wide latitude in interpreting this requirement, but the code makes it clear that a plan will not be discriminatory simply because (1) the contributions or benefits bear a uniform relationship to the total compensation, or to the basic rate of compensation of such employees, or (2) because the rate of contributions or benefits applied to earnings subject to the social security tax differs from the rate applied to those earnings in excess of the maximum subject to this tax. Any plan, however, that promises higher benefits based on wages in excess of that covered by social security (or one that promises benefits based only on the amount in excess of the social security maximum wage base) must meet the nondiscriminatory rules set up by the Interal Revenue Service for integration of benefits with social security.

TAX-EXEMPT TRUST, CUSTODIAL ACCOUNTS, OR DIRECT METHOD. The plan must be funded through a qualified trust, a bank custodial account, or one of a limited number of direct methods. The use of one of these funding agencies as a part of a plan does not preclude the use of another type as a part of the same plan.

Trusts. When a trust is used as the funding agency, the trust must be a valid tax-exempt domestic trust created in writing.[21] In order to have tax-exempt status, a pension trust must not engage in prohibited transactions

---

[19] A pension plan may not discriminate on the basis of membership in a union, for to do so would be in violation of Section 8a of the National Labor Relations Act.

[20] Revenue Ruling 65–178 states that employee contributions not in excess of 6 percent of the compensation are not ordinarily considered to be burdensome.

[21] The Revenue Code, however, states that if the trust would qualify for exemption except for the fact that it is a trust created or organized outside the United States, contributions may be deductible by the employer.

with the employer. Prohibited transactions include such activities as lending the employer money at less than reasonable rates of interest and without adequate security, buying substantial amounts of securities or other property from the employer for more than adequate consideration, and selling to the employer any substantial part of its securities or other property for less than adequate consideration. The trust can buy debentures of the employer if these debentures are not bought at greater than market price, the amount owned after the purchase will not exceed 25 percent of the issue, not more than 50 percent of the issue belongs to dependents of the employer at time of purchase, and the amount invested in securities issued by the employer or related persons will not be more than 25 percent of trust assets.

Custodial Accounts. A bank custodial account is treated as a qualified trust if the funds are invested in regulated investment companies (mutual funds) issuing only redeemable stock or in annuity, endowment, or life insurance contracts issued by an insurance company. The investment company stock must be registered in the name of the custodian or its nominee, and the employee covered under the plan must be the beneficial owner. However, just as under a trust, the particular employee need not have a nonforfeitable interest in the stock. In the event of a forfeiture of an employee's beneficial ownership in the stock, the beneficial ownership of the stock must pass to another employee covered by the plan. Annuity, endowment, and life insurance contracts must be held by the custodian until distributed under the terms of the pension plan.

Direct Method. Under some funding arrangements, neither a trust nor a custodian is needed. A contract between the employer and an insurance company under a group plan is the most common direct method in use. A master contract issued by the insurer spells out the terms of the plan. The employer pays the premium directly to the insurer, and the insurer agrees to pay benefits according to the provisions of the plan. The insurance company, in effect, serves as the trustee or custodian.

Other media available under the direct method are nontransferable individual annuity or retirement income contracts issued by an insurance company with the title held by the employee or by the employer for the benefit of the employee, a *nontransferable* face amount certificate treated as an annuity under the code but issued by an investment company, and a special nontransferable United States Rertirement Plan Bond registered in the name of the employee.

When one of the direct methods other than a group plan is used, the employee must be given full and immediate vesting of benefits, a feature not usually found in corporate pension plans but one that is required in plans for the self-employed (Keogh plans).[22] When an individual life

---

[22] A benefit is vested if its payment is not contingent upon the employee's continuation in employment. The vesting is immediate if it commences when the employee enters the plan and it is full if all accrued benefits are vested.

insurance or annuity contract is used to fund a qualified pension plan, the policy must be either nontransferable or owned by a qualified employee trust.

DEFINITE BENEFITS OR FIXED CONTRIBUTIONS. A plan designed to provide retirement benefits for employees will be considered a pension plan if the employer contribution under the plan can be determined actuarially on the basis of definitely determinable benefits or if such contributions are fixed without being geared to profits. The purpose of this requirement is to differentiate between a qualified pension plan and a qualified deferred profit sharing plan. These plans must be distinguished because the amount allowed the employer as a tax deduction under a qualified pension plan may be different from that allowed him under a qualified deferred profit sharing plan. The difference in the tax status of employers under qualified pension plans and under qualified profit sharing plans is discussed later in this chapter.

Deferred Profit Sharing Plans. Deferred profit sharing plans may be used to provide retirement benefits for employees. For qualification, the plan must meet the same exclusive benefit, nondiversion, and nondiscriminatory rules that apply to qualified pensions. The definite benefit or fixed contribution rules do not apply. Only a definite predetermined formula for allocating the contributions made to the plan among the participants and for distributing the funds accumulated under the plan is required. (Until mid-1956 the regulations required a qualified profit sharing plan to include a definite predetermined formula for fixing the amount of the employer's contribution to the plan. This requirement was discontinued when the Court of Appeals for the Sixth, Seventh, and Ninth Circuits held that a predetermined formula for employer's contribution was not necessary.)

The plan may allocate contributions to employees on the basis of service, earnings, or a combination of service and earnings. More weight may be given to each year of service beyond a given minimum, such as 1 unit for each year of service up to 6, 2 units for each year of service in excess of 6 but less than 12, and 3 units for each year of service in excess of 12. The age of the employee, however, cannot be a factor in the allocation formula.

The allocation formula determines how much of the employer's contribution is to be credited to each participant. The distribution formula determines when and how much a participant may withdraw before retirement and is related to a fixed number of years, the attainment of a stated age, or to the occurrence of an event such as layoff, illness, disability, death, or severance of employment. In all plans, the participant is entitled to his full interest at retirement, in most plans the full interest of the participant is paid at his death, and in a number of plans the participant is entitled to his full interest in the event of his disability. In most plans, the participant is entitled to a share of his interest upon severance of employement.

Deferred profit sharing plans appeal to employers who do not want to make a commitment to fund predetermined benefits or to assume predetermined fixed contributions but still wish to grant some sort of retirement income to their employees.

FORFEITURES NOT ALLOWED TO INCREASE BENEFITS. Pension plans must expressly provide that forfeitures arising from severance of employment, death, or for any other reason will not be used to increase employee benefits otherwise payable. Forfeitures, if any, must be used at least once during each taxable year to reduce the amount of the employer's contribution under the plan. Forfeitures, however, can be anticipated in figuring the plan's projected cost. Forfeitures arising after the plan is terminated or after the employer makes his final contribution to the plan can be used to increase benefits.

The code and regulations prohibiting forfeitures from increasing benefits apply to qualified pension plans. They do not apply to qualified deferred profit sharing plans. Qualified deferred profit sharing plans may include a provision under which forfeitures are used to increase employee benefits, but the forfeitures must not result in prohibited discrimination.

WRITTEN, PERMANENT, AND COMMUNICATED. A qualified pension or profit sharing plan must be a definite written program which is communicated to the employees.

Permanency. The term "plan" is considered to imply permanency. A pension plan set up during years of high tax rates and abandoned within a few years *without a valid business reason* when profits fall does not satisfy the requirement of permanency. Also a pension plan that is abandoned soon after pension benefits have been fully funded for employees in whose favor discrimination is prohibited will not meet the permanency requirement.

The commissioner in deciding upon the permanency of the plan will consider the circumstances and facts of each case including the probability (based on the company's financial history) that the employer will be able to continue the contributions required under the plan. Valid business reasons for terminating a plan include the demand of employees for a substitution of a salary increase for employer pension contributions, business mergers, financial difficulties, and the liquidation of the business.

For profit sharing plans contributions are not required every year but as viewed by the Internal Revenue Service a single or occasional contribution from profit does not meet the requirement of permanency. Recurring and substantial contributions are necessary.[23]

---

[23] The Internal Revenue Services refuses to apply in other circuits decisions of a particular United States Court of Appeals. In one case the court held to be qualified a profit sharing plan calling for a single contribution. In another case the court declared qualified a profit sharing plan under which contributions were made by the employer for only two years after the plan had been determined to have tax-exempt status. The plan included an agreement by the company to contribute to the fund a part of its annual profits over a minimum level. Contributions were discontinued because of insufficient earnings. The United States Court of Appeals for the Ninth District, backing the tax court, ruled

Communication. The most effective way of communicating the salient features of a plan is to furnish each employee with a copy of the plan. If this is not feasible, various substitutes may be used such as a booklet or a conspicuous notice on the company bulletin board stating the nature of the plan, the eligibility requirements, the benefit structure, the provisions for vesting, the contribution rate if employees are to contribute, and where on the company's premises and at what reasonable times the complete plan may be inspected by employees. In the case of a profit sharing plan, the employer contribution formula, if any, must also be included in the announcement.

BENEFITS PRIMARILY RETIREMENT INCOME. A pension plan must be primarily for retirement benefits. However, incidental death benefits, disability benefits prior to retirement, and medical benefits for retired employees may be included in a qualified pension plan. But layoff, sickness, and accident benefits or benefits for hospitalization or medical expense *prior* to retirement cannot be provided under a qualified pension plan.

A qualified profit sharing plan must be primarily for deferred compensation. Accordingly, as mentioned, the plan must provide for distribution of the funds after a fixed number of years or upon the participant's reaching a given age. Prior distributions, however, are allowed for such events as layoffs, illness, death, retirement, or severance of employment. Since the principal purpose of a profit sharing plan is to accumulate funds for its participants, a qualified plan cannot allow participants before retirement to elect irrevocably death benefits only, to the exclusion of retirement benefits. A constructive distribution, however, can be made of funds allocated to the account of a participating employee through the purchase of *incidental* life and health insurance benefits for the employee and his family.

Death Benefits. In a definite benefit pension plan, life insurance benefits are considered incidental if they are not more than 100 times the scheduled monthly retirement income benefit. This rule reflects the 100 to 1 ratio found in the typical retirement income policy that pays $10 monthly retirement income for each $1,000 of life insurance. Because a whole life policy or an endowment policy will provide death protection in excess of 100 times the annuity income available from their cash value, these policies cannot be used as the *sole* funding instrument in a qualified pension plan of the definite benefit types.[24] Whole life or endowment insurance, however, can be used to fund a qualified pension plan when combined with a side fund large enough to raise the monthly retirement income benefit to 1 percent of the face amount of the policy.

---

that the plan, nevertheless, continued to qualify for tax benefits because the employer never abrogated the agreement. However, because of the adamant stand of the Internal Revenue Service, a deferred profit sharing plan will lose its qualified status if contributions are not recurring and substantial unless a court battle can be won to retain this status.

[24] The age 65 cash value of a $10,000 continuous premium whole life policy issued at age 20 will provide a retirement income of only about $50 a month. A $10,000 endowment at age 65 will provide a retirement income of only about $70 monthly.

On the other hand, a whole life policy can be used as the sole funding instrument when the plan is of the fixed contribution type rather than the definite benefit type if two conditions are met: (1) the aggregate premiums paid for the policy are less than 50 percent of the aggregate of the contributions allocated to the employees at any particular time and (2) the trustee is required to surrender the policy for its cash value before or at maturity or to distribute the policy to the participant at retirement.

In plans not funded with life insurance, the 100 to 1 rule is used to set the maximum self-insured death benefits allowable.

Post-retirement death benefits under qualified pension plans can equal 50 percent of the employee's base salary in the year preceding retirement if the cost of the providing that benefit adds less than 10 percent to the cost of the plan.

None of the foregoing rules prohibit the payment of the credited pre-death accumulations to the deceased participant's beneficiaries.

Under qualified profit sharing plans, the life insurance benefits associated with retirement income and single premium endowment policies are considered incidental regardless of the face amount of these policies. For all other life insurance policies, the rules for determining whether the insurance is incidental are the same as those applied to fixed contribution pension plans with one exception: The rules apply only to those funds which have not been accumulated for at least two years. Profit sharing funds that have accumulated for two or more years can be used for the purchase of life insurance without restriction because then the distribution is considered to have been deferred. Contributions made to the profit sharing fund in the current year will not be available for the purchase of whole life insurance without the restriction until two years later.

Health Benefits. A qualified pension plan can include benefits in the event that the covered employee becomes permanently and totally disabled before he reaches retirement age. These benefits may be insured or paid directly from the pension fund.

Incidental health insurance including hospital and medical care benefits may be purchased with profit sharing funds for participants. Any part of the funds that have accumulated two or more years can be used to purchase health insurance. Health insurance purchased with funds that have accumulated less than 2 years is considered incidental if the aggregate of premiums paid for the coverage does not exceed 25 percent of the funds allocated to the employee's account. If both health insurance and whole life insurance are purchased, one half of the premiums paid for the life insurance is included in the 25 percent limitations.

Health insurance is rarely purchased with profit sharing funds because federal income tax laws favor other methods of providing this coverage.[25]

A qualified pension plan may provide hospital and medical expense

---

[25] See pp. 452–53.

benefits for retired employees and their dependents.[26] Medical benefits, however, must be subordinate to retirement benefits. Such benefits are considered subordinate if, starting with the time medical benefits are added, the aggregate of contributions for these benefits and for life insurance benefits does not exceed 25 percent of the aggregate of contributions made during the same period for retirement benefits, exclusive of those used to fund the initial past service liability (the amount required to fund benefits earned before the plan is installed).

Postretirement medical benefits included with qualified pension plans can be funded by employer contributions only or through joint contributions by the employer and employees.[27] A separate bookkeeping account is required for medical care funds, but assets can be commingled with retirement funds for investment. The employer's contribution must be reasonable and ascertainable and the nature and amount of the medical benefits must be specified in the plan. The usual rules relating to nondiversion, forfeitures, and prohibited discrimination apply to postretirement medical care plans.

4. SPECIAL RETIREMENT PLANS

The discussion to this point has been concerned with rules for qualifying regular pension plans and deferred profit sharing plans. Two types of retirement plans require separate treatment: plans for the self-employed and plans for employees of certain nonprofit corporations and of public school systems.

Self-Employed (Keogh) Plans. Before January 1, 1963, sole proprietorships and partnerships could qualify pension and deferred profit sharing plans covering their employees, but the owners of these businesses could not be included in the plans. This was true even though the sole proprietor or partner was actively engaged in the operation of the business. The only business owners who could be covered under qualified pension and deferred profit sharing plans were employee stockholders.

The Self-Employment Individual Tax Retirement Act of 1962 (the Keogh Act) and its subsequent amendments made it possible for owner employees of unincorporated businesses and for other self-employed persons to be covered under qualified retirement plans.

The act makes a distinction between self-employed individuals and owner employees. A self-employed person is one who owns not more than a 10 percent interest in the capital or profits of a partnership. An owner employee is one who owns the entire interest in an unincorporated trade or business or more than a 10 percent interest in the capital or profits of a partnership.

---

[26] The term "retired employees" includes those who have been retired early by reason of permanent disability. A separation from employment is a requirement for retirement.

[27] If retirement benefits are financed by employer contributions only, the medical benefits still can be financed through joint contributions or vice versa.

"Keogh plans" are subject to a special set of restrictions that are not applicable to plans that exclude owner employees and self-employed individuals. Therefore, employee stockholders still retain some advantage over employee owners of unincorporated businesses.

SPECIAL REQUIREMENTS TO QUALIFY KEOGH PLANS. To qualify, a retirement plan covering self-employed individuals must meet several special requirements. Some of these requirements apply only to plans that include owner employees (as defined) whereas others apply to all self-employed persons including owner employees.

Restrictions Applying Only to Owner Employee Plans. It will be recalled that in order to qualify a pension or deferred profit sharing plan (those covering employees of corporations and nonowner employees of unincorporated businesses) the coverage requirements must not discriminate in favor of supervisory and highly paid personnel. Keogh plans covering owner employees, however, must cover *all full-time* employees having *three years* of continuous service except for those plans established before the owner employee himself has had three years of continuous service. In those plans, the same waiting period applied to the owner employee must also be applied to other full-time employees. Thus, if the plan is initiated after the business completes its second year, the continuous service requirement for full-time employees must be fixed at two years.

Under the usual qualified plan the employer may require the employee to contribute as a condition of coverage if the contribution rate is not burdensome, but under a Keogh plan covering owner employees, an employee must be allowed to participate under a contributory plan even though he does not choose to contribute.

The usual qualified plans are allowed to have provisions that defer the vesting of benefits in the employees but a Keogh plan covering owner employees must grant all covered employees full and immediate vesting. Immediate nonforfeitable rights in the plan must be given to the participants. No conditions can be set forth that would cause a participant to lose his accumulated benefits.

Distributions under a qualified pension plan can be made to any participating employee upon severance of his employment or for early retirement in accordance with the provisions of the plan. Funds accumulated under a qualified deferred profit sharing plan can be distributed to a participant upon the attainment of a stated age or upon the happening of some event such as illness. Except in the case of permanent and total disability or death, a Keogh plan cannot allow distributions for *owner employees* until they reach age 59½. Distributions to be made to *nonowner employees* are not restricted by this rule.

Retirement distributions to owner employees must be fixed at an age not later than 70½. The owner employee need not retire at this age. He can continue to work and have contributions made to the plan on his behalf, but he must draw his retirement annuity at that age. Other employees need not draw their retirement annuity until they retire regardless of whether or not they have passed age 70½.

If the owner employee dies before receiving full distribution of his interest, the remaining interest must be paid to the beneficiary within five years or it must be used within five years to provide the beneficiary an immediate life annuity or an annuity certain for a period not to exceed the life expectancy of the beneficiary. These rules apply regardless of the owner employee's age at the time of his death. They do not apply to nonowner employees.

A maximum is placed on the amount of contributions that can be made on behalf of owner employees. This maximum is the lesser of $2,500 or 10 percent of the income earned from the business. These limitations apply only to owner employees and do not include within them the amounts used to purchase health insurance nor the amounts allocated to the purchase of incidental life insurance.

An exception to the 10 percent limitation allows a level premium retirement annuity or insurance policy to be purchased and maintained for the owner employee if the annual premiums contracted for do not exceed 10 percent of the owner employee's average annual earnings for the preceding three-year period. Only annual earnings not in excess of $25,000 may be included in the averaging process. Therefore, total premiums paid for owner employees under the averaging rule are limited to $2,500 including the cost of life and health insurance. Owner employees who take advantage of the three-year averaging rule must apply the rule to other covered employees if by doing so the contributions made for them would be increased.

As noted earlier only *voluntary* employee contributions are permitted under Keogh plans covering owner employees. Under contributory plans, owner employees are allowed to contribute the lesser of 10 percent of their earned income or $25,000 provided other employees are allowed to make voluntary contributions at the same rate. Thus, an owner employee who has an earned income of $25,000 can contribute a deductible $2,500 to the plan as an employer and a nondeductible $2,500 as an employee. Owner employees having no employees are not permitted to establish contributory plans.

Keogh plans may be profit sharing or pension plans. If the contributions to the plan are based on a percentage of the participants' compensation, the plan is a pension plan. If the contributions are based on the earned income of the self-employed individual, the plan is a profit sharing plan.

The usual qualified deferred profit sharing plan does not require a definite formula for determining the contributions to be made on behalf of the participants, but in profit sharing Keogh plans covering owner employees a definite formula is required. The formula must define profits for purposes of the plan and specify the percentage (or schedule of percentages) of profits to be contributed for the benefit of participants other than owner employees. If a variable factor is used in the formula, its value must not be subject to the discretion of the owner employee.

A qualified pension or profit sharing trust must not engage in transactions defined as prohibited. These prohibitions generally do not forbid transactions with the creator of the trust if such transactions are reasonable and do not impair the security of the employees. Trusts used with Keogh plans covering owner employees, however, may not engage in any transactions with the creator.

Restriction Applying to All Keogh Plans. Aside from the tax treatment of contributions to and distributions from Keogh plans (a subject to be discussed later), there is only one special rule that applies both to plans that include owner employees and to plans that do not include owner employees. This rule relates to the period over which distributions may be made to participants. It sets the following as the maximum periods.

1. The life of the participant.
2. The lives of the participant and his spouse.
3. A period certain not longer than the life expectancy of the participant.
4. A period certain not longer than the joint life and last survivor expectancy of the participant and his spouse.

501c (3) Organizations and Public School Systems. Section 403b of the Internal Revenue Code provides for special treatment of nonqualified annuity plans for employees of Section 501c (3) organizations. These organizations include particular nonprofit corporations and any community chest, funds, or foundations organized and operated exclusively for religious, charitable, scientific, testing for public safety, literary, and educational purposes or for the prevention of cruelty to children or animals. Special tax treatment of nonqualified annuity plans is not accorded employees of all nonprofit organizations but just those that come under 501c (3).

In addition to 501c (3) organizations special treatment of nonqualified annuities also are accorded employees of public schools operated directly by governmental units even though these schools might not be considered 501c (3) organizations.[28]

For an employee to be eligible for the benefits granted under 403b, his employer must purchase an annuity contract for him, and that contract must be both nontransferable and owned by the employee. His rights in the contract must be nonforfeitable. Life insurance benefits in combination with the annuity are allowed only to the extent that they do not exceed 100 times the scheduled monthly retirement benefit. This means that $1,000 of life insurance per $10 a month retirement benefit is allowed.

---

[28] Some schools operated by separate educational instrumentalities can qualify as 501c (3) organizations, and, as such, their employees can receive special tax benefits not given employees of public schools not also 501c (3) organizations. These special tax benefits are discussed later in this text.

Annuities written under 403b are in effect nonqualified deferred compensation plans with a special advantage to the annuitants in that their rights in the contract are nonforfeitable without the annuitants incurring a current income tax liability. In this respect, the plan has the same advantage to the employees as a qualified pension plan. Unlike qualified plans, 403b annuities can be written for one or more employees without regard to any rules against discrimination. The annual amount that can be paid by the employer in annuity premiums on behalf of an employee without that employee incurring a current tax liability is limited. The limitation depends upon whether the annuity is purchased with or without a salary reduction.

If the annuity is purchased with a salary reduction, the amount that an employee can ask his employer to put into the tax sheltered annuity is limited by an exclusion allowance for any one year, calculated as follows:

$$X = (A + B) \cdot \frac{n}{5 + n} - B$$

where

X is the maximum exclusion allowance for the year.

A is the total appointment salary during the current calendar year.

B is the total employer contributions to annuity or pension plans prior to the start of the year.

n is years of service including the current calendar year.

Assume an employee with 12 years of service to the end of the current year has a current salary of $10,000. He has not yet participated in the tax sheltered annuity plan but on his behalf his employer had contributed $3,000 to a qualified pension plan over the past 12 years.

Applying the foregoing formula, the employee can authorize a contribution of $6,176 (minus his employer's current contribution to the pension fund on his behalf) for the purchase of an annuity for the current year ($10,000 + 3,000) $\times$ $12/17$ − $3,000 = $6,176. The amount that he can authorize for purchase of an annuity will decrease in successive years unless he receives unusually large salary increases.

The employee usually will not want to authorize the maximum especially where he has large accumulated past service increments. He might like to spread the past service increments uniformly over the remaining years of anticipated service. In this event he would use the following formula:

$$X = \frac{A \cdot Y - 5B}{5F - Y}$$

where

X is the exclusion amount to be applied during the current calendar year.

A is the total appointment salary during the current calendar year.

Y is the total years of service (past and future).

B is the total employer contribution to annuity or pension plans prior to the start of the year.

F is the number of future years of service anticipated, including the current year.

Assume that the employee is 37 years old and anticipates retirement at age 65. The foregoing formula will limit his annuity contribution for the current year to $3,850 (less the employer's current contribution on his behalf to the pension plan).

If the annuity is purchased without a salary reduction, the amount that the employer can put into an annuity for an employee without that employee incurring a current income tax liability is calculated using the following formula:

$$X = \frac{AN}{5} - B$$

where

X is the amount to be excluded from current income.

A is the total appointment salary during the current calendar year.

N is the years of service including the current calendar year.

B is the total employer contributions to annuity or pension plans prior to the start of the year.

In the foregoing illustration, the limitation would work out as follows:

$$X = \frac{(\$10,000)\ (12)}{5} - \$3,000 = \$21,000$$

5. TAX STATUS OF THE EMPLOYER UNDER QUALIFIED PLANS

Subject to certain limitations set forth in the Internal Revenue Code, contributions made by an employer to qualified pension and deferred profit sharing plans can be deducted by him as business expense in the year the contribution is made.

If the pension or deferred profit sharing plan does not qualify (i.e., does not get the approval of the Internal Revenue Service), contributions made by the employer are deductible by him and taxable as income to the employee either in the year when a contribution is paid or in the year when a benefit is made available. If the employee's right in the plan is non-forfeitable, the year in which a contribution is paid governs the tax status of the transaction; if the employee's right in the plan is forfeitable, the year in which a benefit is made available governs. By qualifying a plan, the employer may deduct his contributions in the years in which they are paid, and the employee is taxed in the years in which he receives benefits, regardless of the nature of the employee's rights. The advantage of qualifying a plan, therefore, is to give the employer a current deduction without having his contributions taxed immediately as income to the employee.

Pension Plans.   The code places certain limitations on the amount of pension contributions that the employer can deduct as a business expense in any one year. The purposes of these limitations are twofold: (1) to prevent the employer from charging off excessive compensation and (2) to prevent the employer from overfunding the pension to gain tax deductions in what he might consider to be the most favorable years. The restrictions are as follows:

1. The contribution must qualify as an ordinary and necessary business expense. Furthermore, both the contribution (when added to all other employee compensation) and the amount of the pension must be reasonable in relation to the services rendered by the employee. This limitation is subjective and general but it does prohibit a corporation from deducting contributions for employees whose activities on behalf of the business are negligible.

2. More specifically, the employer may deduct up to 5 percent of the total compensation of covered employees. This maximum may be reduced later if an actuarial analysis reveals that 5 percent is more than necessary to fund the benefits under the plan. Data supporting the 5 percent deduction must be submitted to the commissioner in the second year and at least every fifth year thereafter. If, as is likely to be the case, the cost of funding the plan exceeds 5 percent, the excess can be deducted in the year contributed if it does not exceed the aggregate level amounts necessary to fund the pensions for all employees during their remaining service.[29]

3. As an alternate to the 5 percent rule, the employer may elect the 10 percent rule, or what is called the normal cost method of funding. The normal cost is the level amount needed to fund a given pension, assuming contributions are spread over the entire working period of each employee. For those employees who had service prior to the establishment of the plan, a past service liability is created. This liability will equal the sum of the contributions that were missed during the years between the employee's employment date and the installation of the plan, augmented by interest and survivorship benefits based on the actuarial assumptions used in the plan.

The 10 percent or normal cost rule limits the employer's annual deduction to the normal cost of the plan plus 10 percent of the initial past serv-

---

[29] This provision is subject to the limitation that if the remaining unfunded cost with respect to any three persons is more than 50 percent of the entire remaining unfunded cost, it must be spread over at least five years.

ice liability. The amount that can be deducted each year to fund initial past service liability is called the "standard 10 percent base." Normally, under the 10 percent rule it will take between 11 and 12 years to fully fund past service liability because the annual decrease in the unfunded liability will equal the standard 10 percent base *less* accrued interest and survivorships. The standard 10 percent base remains level unless it is changed to correct an actuarial error, to adjust for a revaluation of assets, or to allow for a retroactive increase in benefits.

If an employer's contribution in any year exceeds the maximum amount allowable, the excess may be carried forward to the first year in which the maximum allowable exceeds the amount contributed.

Deferred Profit Sharing Plans. Employer contributions to profit sharing plans usually are predetermined by formula and are based on a percentage of profits. Employer contributions, therefore, fluctuate year to year along with profits. The basic limitation on the amount of employer contributions to a qualified deferred profit sharing plan that can be deducted in a taxable year is 15 percent of the compensation paid to employees who share in the employer's contribution. Because the amount of contributions fluctuates from year to year, the amount contributed in some years might exceed the 15 percent deductible limit, whereas in other years the amount contributed might be under the maximum deductible limit. When the contributions are less than the maximum deductible limit, the employer is given a *credit carry-over;* when they are more, he is given a *contribution carry-over.*

A credit carry-over is good until used. The amount of credit carry-over that can be used in any one year is limited to 15 percent of the then current compensation paid to employees who share in the employer's contribution. Thus, where there is sufficient carry-over, an amount equal to 30 percent of payroll may be deducted, 15 percent for current contribution and 15 percent for credit carry-over.

A contribution carry-over can be used in any year in which aggregate contributions are less than 15 percent of aggregate covered payroll. Contribution carry-overs can be used to bring the aggregate deductions to the 15 percent. The aggregate (cumulative) deduction cannot exceed 15 percent of the aggregate (cumulative) payroll. (See illustration on page 449.)

Combination Pension and Profit Sharing Plans. When an employer has both a qualified pension plan and a qualified deferred profit sharing plan covering the same employees, he is subject to the specified individual plan limitations on the annual amounts that can be deducted for contributions to each plan plus a combined limitation of 25 percent of the compensation of the employees covered by the plans. If the annual combined contributions exceed the 25 percent limit, the excess can be carried over and deducted in future years subject to the limitation that in no year can the combined deduction exceed 30 percent of the then current compensation of participating employees.

Illustration: Qualified Pension Plan. Assume that in 1966 an employer with 500 employees established a qualified pension plan. In that year his annual payroll was $3 million for employees participating in the plan. For purposes of this illustration the assumptions are made that (1) the payroll remains constant from 1966 through 1970, (2) the benefit structure is not changed, (3) the normal cost of the plan remains constant, and (4) there are no changes that require a reevaluation of the initial past service liability. The pension plan provides for $5 a month times the years of full-time service from entry age for each employee until his retirement at age 65. The actuarial assumptions used in computing the cost of funding the plan are (1) the 1951 Group Annuity Table set back one year, (2) a 4 percent interest rate, (3) a low turnover table (T–1), and (4) an average retirement age of 65.[30]

Assume that the 10 percent rule (normal cost plus 10 percent of past service liability) is used to establish the maximum limit for deductions of employer contributions. Based on the actuarial assumptions used, the normal cost of the plan in 1966 was computed to be $118,932 annually. The initial past service liability was computed to be $2,461,100.[31] The maximum annual limit for deduction of employer contributions to the pension fund would be the sum of $118,932 (the normal cost) and $246,110 (10 percent of the initial past service liability) or a total of $365,042. After the initial past service liability is fully funded, the maximum annual deduction will be the normal cost.

Assume that the employer's contributions to the plan from 1966 through 1970 were as follows: $500,000; $250,000; $365,042; $250,000; and $300,000. The amounts deductible each year will be computed as follows:[32]

Taxable Calendar Years	1966	1967	1968	1969	1970
Amount of contributions paid in year	$500,000	$250,000	$365,042	$250,000	$300,000
Amount carried over from previous year	0	134,958	19,916	19,916	0
Total deductible subject to limitation	500,000	384,958	384,958	269,916	300,000
Limitation applicable to year	365,042	365,042	365,042	365,042	365,042
Amount deductible for year	365,042	365,042	365,042	269,916	300,000
Excess carried over to succeeding years	134,958	19,916	19,916	0	0

[30] Actuarial assumptions are discussed in some detail in Chapter 19. Do not worry about them now.

[31] The methods used to compute the normal cost and the initial past service liability are discussed in some detail in Chapter 19.

[32] This format is published by the IRS to illustrate the application of the Code.

Illustration: Deferred Profit Sharing. Assume that instead of a qualified pension plan the employer had set up a qualified deferred profit sharing plan with a contribution formula of 15 percent of net profits before federal income taxes. Retain the assumptions of a $3 million steady annual covered payroll and assume further that net profits before federal income taxes for the period from 1966 through 1970 were as follows: $3.5 million; 0; $6.5 million; $666,667; and $4,333,333. The amounts deductible each year would be computed as follows:[33]

Taxable Calendar Years	1966	1967	1968	1969	1970
1. Amount of contributions:					
a) In taxable year	$525,000	0	$ 975,000	$100,000	$ 650,000
b) Carried over from prior taxable years	0	$ 75,000	0	75,000	0
2. Primary limitations applicable to year: 15 percent of covered compensation	450,000	450,000	450,000	450,000	450,000
3. Secondary limitation applicable to year:					
a) Twice primary limitation	—	—	900,000	—	900,000
b) (1) Aggregate primary limitation (cf. item 2)	—	—	1,350,000	—	2,250,000
(2) Aggregate prior deductions (cf. item 4 (c))	—	—	525,000	—	1,600,000
(3) Excess of (1) over (2)	—	—	925,000	—	650,000
c) Lesser of (a) or (b) ..	—	—	900,000	—	650,000
4. Amount deductible for year on account of					
a) Contributions in year ..	450,000	0	900,000	100,000	650,000
b) Contributions carried over	0	75,000	0	75,000	0
c) Total	$450,000	$ 75,000	$ 900,000	$175,000	$ 650,000
5. Excess contributions carried over to succeeding years	$ 75,000	0	$ 75,000	0	0

Illustration: Combination Pension and Profit Sharing Plans. Assume that the employer established both the retirement and the deferred profit sharing plans just described and that all of the assumptions made concerning these plans and the employer's contributions to them still hold. The amounts deductible each year would be computed as follows:

[33] This format is published by the IRS to illustrate the application of the Code.

Taxable Calendar Years	1966	1967	1968	1969	1970
1. Amount deductible for					
a) Contributions to pension	$365,042	$365,042	$ 365,042	$269,916	$ 300,000
b) Contribution to profit sharing	450,000	75,000	900,000	175,000	650,000
c) Total	815,042	440,042	1,265,042	444,916	950,000
2. Amount carried over from previous year	0	65,000	0	515,042	59,958
3. Total subject to limitations (item 1 plus item 2) ...	815,042	505,042	1,265,042	959,958	1,009,958
4. Primary limitation applicable to year: 25 percent of covered compensation	750,000	750,000	750,000	750,000	750,000
5. Secondary limitation applicable to year: 30 percent of covered compensation	—	900,000	—	900,000	900,000
6. Amount deductible for year on account of					
a) Contributions in year ..	750,000	440,042	750,000	444,916	900,000
b) Contributions carried over	—	65,000	0	455,084	0
c) Total	750,000	505,042	750,000	900,000	900,000
7. Excess contributions carried over to succeeding years	65,000	0	515,042	59,958	109,958

Keogh Plans. The deductibility of contributions made on behalf of self-employed individuals covered under Keogh plans is the full amount of the annual contribution, subject to a maximum of 10 percent of the earned income of the self-employed person or $2,500, whichever is lower. Where the self-employed individual is covered under more than one Keogh plan, the deduction is allocated among the plans. No contribution or credit carry-overs are permitted for the self-employed. Each year stands on its own. In the event that a portion of the amount contributed is used to purchase life or health insurance on the self-employed individual the amount so allocated is not deductible.

Contributions made to Keogh plans on behalf of participants other than the self-employed are subject to the rules applicable to regular qualified plans.

501c (3) Organizations and Public Schools. Because 501c (3) organizations and public schools generally pay no income taxes, little question arises with respect to the deductibility of contributions to 403b annuity plans. For purposes of social security taxes and benefits, payments of 403b annuity premiums are considered wages if they are paid in lieu of wages, that is if the premiums are a result of a salary reduction plan. If the annuity payments are in addition to the employee's regular salary, they are not considered wages for social security purposes.

6. TAX STATUS OF THE FUND UNDER QUALIFIED PLANS

Pension and deferred profit sharing funds are deposited with trustees or insurance companies. When a trust fund plan is used, the trustee usually is a bank but sometimes natural persons serve as trustees of pension and deferred profit sharing plans. The trustees and insurance companies invest the funds and accumulate the earnings on them. What is the income tax status of these earnings?

Trust Fund Accumulations.   Earnings of qualified pension or profit sharing trusts are exempt from income tax as long as these earnings are not unrelated business income. Unrelated business income includes income from any trade or business regularly carried on by the trust or by a partnership of which the trust is a member. If there is a rental income from a business lease of property purchased with borrowed funds and the lease is for a term in excess of five years, unrelated business income includes that proportion of the rental income that the amount of the year-end indebtedness on the property bears to the year-end. *adjusted basis* of the property.[34] Also included as unrelated business income is the rent from the lease of personal property unless that personal property is leased with real property. Personal income tax rates are applied to unrelated business income in excess of an allowable $1,000 specific deduction.

Specifically excluded from the category of unrelated business income are dividends, interest, royalties, and capital gains. Also excluded are rents except for the limitations already mentioned. Therefore, earnings from the usual investment portfolio of a qualified pension or profit sharing trust is income tax–free.

Insurance Company Accumulations.   Since 1961, life insurance companies have not been taxed on income earned on assets allocated to qualified pension and deferred profit sharing plans. The amount of life insurance company investment earnings exempt technically does not include all earnings on qualified pension and profit sharing assets held by the insurer. The exemption applies to the earnings on those funds that are attributable to the book reserve for life insurance and annuity contracts written to fund these plans. Earnings on assets attributable to contingency reserves (voluntary reserves set aside to provide a safety margin to offset possible adverse fluctuations in mortality and investment experience from that guaranteed by the insurer to the fund) are not exempt from life insurance company income taxation since these funds are attributable to the insurer's surplus rather than to employee benefit plans.

---

[34] Adjusted basis means the cost that would be used in computing the capital gain or loss that would arise from the sale of the property.

Under the laws of most states, insurers may accept pension and profit sharing fund contributions from employers and invest them in a portfolio held as a separate account, that is, an account segregated from the insurer's general investment portfolio. Unlike the insurer's general investment portfolio, the segregated account portfolio may be heavily invested in equities. Investment yields earned and capital gains realized in a segregated account accrue directly to the pension fund and therefore are not subject to the income tax levied on life insurance companies.

The exemption of interest earned on assets attributable to the book reserve on insured qualified pension and profit sharing plans applies to insured qualified Keogh plans and to plans written for 501c (3) organizations and public school systems.

7. TAX STATUS OF EMPLOYEE PARTICIPANTS UNDER QUALIFIED PLANS

Employee participants in qualified pension and deferred profit sharing plans can be affected by three types of taxation: the income tax, the estate tax, and the gift tax.

The Federal Income Tax. A favorable income tax consideration is that the participating employee does not have to report as current income contributions made on his behalf to qualified pension and profit sharing plans except where there is life insurance written in connection with the plan. In this case, the employee must report only the cost of the term insurance for the amount at risk. The cost of the amount at risk is determined by multiplying the difference between the face amount of the insurance and its cash value at the end of the year either by the one-year term rate charged by the insurer, or that set forth by the Internal Revenue Service. The IRS term rate is low. For example, at age 25, it is $1.93 per $1,000; at age 35, $3.21; at age 45, $6.30; and at age 55, $13.74. Thus in a year in which the face amount of the policy exceeds its cash value by $14,000 a 45 year old insured would have to report as income 14 $\times$ $6.30 or $88.20. If the plan is a contributory plan and it provides that employee contributions will be used first to pay the insurance cost, there will be no reportable current income if the employee's contribution for the year exceeds $88.20.

The foregoing rules also apply to qualified Keogh plans and to tax sheltered plans written for 501c (3) organizations and public school systems.

Under qualified pension plans, funds cannot be used to purchase health insurance for participating employees. Health insurance may be purchased with qualified deferred profit sharing funds, and when this is done the cost of the insurance is taxed as a current income to the employee. Because premiums paid by the employer for *individual* health insurance policies for his employees are deductible by the employer as a business expense and are not reportable as income to the employer it is better for health insurance to be purchased direct by the employer rather than through the profit sharing trust. (For life insurance coverage, only the premiums for group insurance are both deductible by the employer and not reportable as income by the employee, and, even then, the employee must report as income employer-paid premiums for coverage in excess of $50,000).[35]

INCOME TAXATION UPON DISTRIBUTION.   When pension or deferred profit sharing funds are distributed (or made available) to a participating employee (or his beneficiary) an income tax liability will arise. The nature of this liability will depend upon (1) whether the plan is contributory or noncontributory, (2) the reason for the distribution, and (3) the time period over which the distribution is made.

Pension and profit sharing plans can be contributory or noncontributory, that is, employees may or may not be required to make contributions to the fund (or, as in some plans, employees may be allowed to make voluntary contributions to the fund). Under contributory plans, the employee's payments to the fund are made with after-tax dollars, therefore the employee incurs no additional income tax liability when these funds are returned to him. The employee's total contribution includes not only what he has paid into the fund by means of deductions from his salary but also amounts contributed by his employer that were, nevertheless, treated as taxable income to him, such as, for example, the cost of any incidental life insurance included with the plan. (Employees covered under noncontributory plans also incur no additional income tax liability upon the return of employer-paid funds that were treated as employee taxable income.) The employee's contribution to the fund is called the *consideration paid*. As will be seen later, the consideration paid is important in ascertaining not only the income tax liability but also any estate or gift tax liability that might be involved.

Distributions from pension and profit sharing funds may be made to participating employees at normal retirement, at early retirement because of permanent and total disability, upon severance of employment, or upon termination of the plan. Distributions may also be made to pay the medical expenses of retired employees. In addition, distributions can be made from deferred profit sharing funds to participating employees during periods of illness, layoffs, and for medical expenses prior to retirement. Distributions from pension and profit sharing funds also can be made to the beneficiary of a participating employee following his death. As will be seen later, an important consideration can be whether the distribution is made in conjunction with the termination of the participating employee's service with his employer.

When the full amount credited to the employee participant's account is paid to the recipient within one taxable year, the distribution is called a lump-sum distribution; when the distribution is made as periodic pay-

---

[35] If the group term life insurance is purchased by the trustee rather than by the employer, the cost of the insurance is taxable income to the employee.

ments over several years, the distribution is called an annuity distribution. Whether the distribution is made as a lump sum or as an annuity is an important consideration in measuring the resulting income tax liability.

The distribution may be made by the trustee in the forms of cash or he may distribute life insurance contracts, annuity contracts, or securities of the employer corporation. When the distribution is in the form of insurance or annuity contracts the disposition that the recipient makes of these contracts determines the income tax consequences of the distribution.

Lump-Sum Distributions. Before the Tax Reform Act of 1969 a lump-sum distribution made to the employee participant was taxed as a capital gain if the employee severed his employment. If employment was not severed, the lump-sum distribution was taxed as ordinary income. The measure of the capital gain or ordinary income then as now is the excess of the payment received over the consideration paid by the employee participant.

The Tax Reform Act of 1969 modified the application of the long-term capital gains tax treatment. It precluded from such treatment that portion of the distribution which represents benefits accrued for plan years beginning after December 31, 1969. That part of the distribution representing (1) employer contributions for prior years, and (2), all appreciation of, and earnings on, investment, whenever accrued, will still be considered a long term capital gain. However, new rules apply to the computation of the capital gains tax. The tax on long term capital gains will continue to be computed by adding $\frac{1}{2}$ of the gain to the individual's adjusted gross income. But the former maximum tax rate of 25 percent, applicable to the long term capital gain will now apply only to the first $50,000 of that amount. On amounts in excess of $50,000 the maximum rate will be increased to $29\frac{1}{2}$ percent for 1970, $32\frac{1}{2}$ percent for 1971, and 35 percent for 1972. Note that this maximum rate applies only to the amount in excess of $50,000.

Employer contributions, the distribution of which will henceforth produce ordinary income, include both the actual contributions and plan forfeitures reallocated to the employee. In some cases, it may be difficult to establish the precise amount of post-1969 employer contributions. Presumably the IRS will establish regulations which will provide rules of presumption. If, however, the employee cannot establish the amount, the entire distribution will seemingly be considered ordinary income.

The effects of excluding these employer contributions from long term capital gains tax treatment is greatly mitigated by a special averaging rule which may be applied to the portion now taxed as ordinary income. The application of this averaging rule is as follows:

1. If the employee-participant has participated in the plan for at least 5 years, then upon death, disability, or distribution for any reason, *after* his attaining age $59\frac{1}{2}$, his tax liability is computed by calculating the

additional tax which would be incurred by adding ⅐th (14²⁄₇ percent) of the ordinary income portion of the distribution to his basic income in the taxable year and multiplying that amount by 7. In computing his basic income, compensation (other than deferred compensation) received from the employer during the applicable tax year is to be excluded, as well as the portion of the distribution taxed as a long term capital gain.

2. If the distributee has participated in the plan for at least 5 years, but the distribution is made *prior* to his attaining 59½ for any reason *other* than death or disability the 7 year "forward averaging" rule described in 1. above will apply, *except* that in computing the basic income, compensation received from the employer for the applicable tax year *cannot be excluded.*

3. If the individual has participated in the plan for *less* than 5 years the averaging rule will not apply regardless of his age or the reason for the distribution.

An alternative lump-sum distribution averaging rule applies if it yields a tax higher than that produced under item 1 above. Under this rule the tax on that portion of the gain producing ordinary income is equal to 7 times the tax resulting from treating as taxable income ⅐th of the gain in excess of personal exemptions.

The following example illustrates the application of the two rules: Assume that an employee retires at age 60 after participating 30 years in a noncontributory pension plan. His wife is 58 years old. He elects a lump-sum distribution of $66,000. The amount contributed by his employer was $11,000 before January 1, 1970. After January 1, 1970, his employer had contributed $19,000 including that amount representing the employee's pro rata share of forfeitures arising from terminating employees whose benefits were not vested. His salary during the year of retirement was $20,000. He had $5,000 of other taxable income.

Under method 1, his tax would amount to:

⅐th of employer's contribution after 1969 (⅐ × $19,000)	$2,714	
Other taxable income	5,000	
Total taxable income	$7,714	
Tax		$1,326
Other taxable income	5,000	
Tax		810
Increase in tax		$ 516
Tax on ordinary income portion of lump-sum distribution (7 × $516)		$3,612

Under method 2, his tax would amount to:

Employer's contribution after 1969	$19,000
Personal exemptions (2 at $750)	1,500
Taxable income	$17,500
$\frac{1}{7}$th of income	2,357
Tax on $\frac{1}{7}$th of employer's contributions after 1969	358
Tax on employer's contribution (7 × $358)	$ 2,506

Since $3,612 is greater than $2,506, method 1 will be applied in this case.

The lump-sum distribution rule applies regardless of the purpose of the distribution: normal retirement, disability retirement, termination of the plan, or death. When the plan is terminated and the funds are distributed to the participants all in one year, the taxable amount received by the participants is not treated as a lump-sum distribution unless at the same time the business is also terminated by sale or liquidation. The employee must be separated from the service of his employer for the lump-sum distribution rule to be applied. Severance of employment is strictly interpreted and is independent of salary continuation. Where lump-sum distributions are to be made from pension and profit sharing funds in connection with a corporate merger and reorganization, particular attention needs to be given to the arrangements affecting employment if the lump-sum distribution tax treatment is sought.

Because death of an employee automatically severs his employment, the lump-sum distribution rule applies to such distribution made to a sole beneficiary.

The beneficiary will take the same cost basis held by the employee participant, reduced by any tax-free payments made to the employee participant prior to his death. The beneficiary is accorded a special employee death benefit exclusion under which the first $5,000 of taxable benefits are exempt. Of course, if the employee's beneficiary receives payments from the employer that otherwise would be taxed as ordinary income, the beneficiary will use the $5,000 exclusion against this income.

In order for a distribution to be taxed as a lump-sum distribution, the full amount credited to the employee participant's account must be distributed within one taxable year. Thus, if there is more than one beneficiary and any one of them elects to receive annuity payments from the trust, payments to the other beneficiaries are taxed as ordinary income even though these beneficiaries elect to receive all of their allocated benefits within one year. However, if a trust distributes an annuity contract to one beneficiary and makes lump-sum distributions to the others, the lump-sum treatment is accorded the distributions because then the full amount credited to the employee participant's account will have been distributed within one year.

The income tax treatment of the distributed annuity contract involves the question of constructive receipt.[36] Constructive receipt is at issue when a lump-sum distribution is made available to a participant unconditionally without penalty such as the forfeiture of his right to continue in the plan or the forfeiture of some of the credits he has accumulated under the plan. If the distribution is payable in a lump sum but the recipient is given the option to elect an annuity payment, no constructive receipt will be held if the recipient elects a nontransferable annuity within 60 days after the lump sum becomes available. When the distribution is made in the form of an annuity contract, the cash value of the annuity is not held to be constructively received if, within 60 days of its receipt, the annuity is made nontransferable. No income tax liability is incurred unless the policy is surrendered for its cash value or until payments from the annuity contract are received.[37]

If the distribution is in the form of a life insurance policy, the cash value of that policy will not be considered as constructively received if, within 60 days after the distribution, the recipient converts the policy into a nontransferable annuity containing no life insurance coverage.

If the annuity or life insurance policy is distributed to an employee who has severed his employment and that policy is surrendered in the year distributed, the taxable amount is treated as a lump-sum distribution. If it is surrendered in a later year, the taxable amount is treated as ordinary income.

In general, death benefits payable under life insurance policies are excludable from taxable income. However, where life insurance policies are used to fund qualified pension and profit sharing plans, only that amount by which the value of the policy is increased by the employee's death is excludable. The beneficiary must report as income an amount equal to the policy's cash value immediately before the insured's death.

Capital gains treatment is not accorded lump-sum distributions under Keogh plans nor under 403 (b) plans. These distributions, whether they are made before or after the death of the participant, are taxed as ordinary income. However, for those taking lump-sum distributions under Keogh plans under which contributions have been made for at least five years, a special averaging rule offers some relief. Under this rule, the tax on the gain is the greater of (1) five times the amount by which the tax bill would be increased by adding one fifth of the gain to other adjusted gross income or (2) five times the tax that would result on only one fifth of the gain after deducting the amount allowed for personal exemptions.

Annuity Distributions. Benefits payable to an employee participant or his beneficiary as periodic payments are subject to rules governing the taxation of annuities with special modifications applicable to employee

---

[36] For income tax purposes, if funds are made available to a person and he does not elect to receive them, these funds are generally treated as though they have in fact been received, thus the term constructive receipt.

[37] Annuity contracts issued before 1963 need not be made nontransferable upon their distribution to avoid taxation of their cash value as constructive receipt.

benefit plans. In determining the income tax liability for annuity payments received from a qualified pension or profit sharing plan, one of two rules will be applied.

Under one rule, the annuitant determines the ratio of his investment in the plan to his expected return from the plan and excludes a similar portion of each annuity payment from his gross income. For example, a male employee receiving a retirement income of $3,000 a year for life only starting at age 65, has an expected return of $45,000, using the expected return multiple 15 prescribed in the annuity regulations interpreting the code.[38] If the employee had contributed $10,000 to the pension fund and none of the employer's contributions had been taxed as current income to the employee, the ratio of his investment in the plan to his expected return is 10 to 45, or two ninths (22.2 percent). Therefore, the employee will exclude two ninths of each annuity payment from gross income and report as ordinary income only seven ninths of the $3,000 or $2,333 a year. The exclusion ratio will continue even though the employee lives beyond his expected 15 years.

If the retirement income is guaranteed for a fixed number of years, the value of this guarantee is charged against the employee participant's investment in the plan. For example, if in the foregoing illustration the $3,000 a year is guaranteed for a minimum of 10 years, the employee participant's investment would be reduced 15 percent.[39] The exclusion rate, consequently, would be reduced from 22.2 percent to 18.9 percent. The amount of income to be reported will increase from $2,333 to $2,433.

In noncontributory plans, the employee's investment is usually zero. The exclusion ratio, therefore, will also be zero; so the employee will have to report as gross income all of his annuity payments.

If, during the three year period beginning on the date the annuity payments begin, the employee receives an aggregate amount equal to or greater than his investment in the plan, an alternate rule applies. Under this rule, the employee excludes from gross income all annuity payments received until he has excluded an amount equal to his investment in the plan. Thereafter, all annuity payments received are included in gross income. If, in the foregoing illustration, the employee's contribution to the plan had been $9,000 (or less) rather than $10,000, the employee would have excluded from gross income the full $3,000 of annuity payments received each year until he had recovered his investment, after which he would report the full $3,000 as ordinary income each year.

These rules apply also to annuity benefits payable to the beneficiary of an employee participant following his death. If, upon termination of em-

---

[38] Reg. 1.72–9, Table I—Ordinary Life Annuities—One Life-Expected Return Multiples. For males age 65, the multiple is 15. For males age 60, the multiple is 18.2. For females age 65, the multiple is 18.2, the same as for males age 60.

[39] Reg. 1.72–9, Table III—Percent Value of Refund Feature. The percentage is a function of age, sex, and duration of guarantee.

ployment, the amount that an employee can withdraw is limited to his own contributions (if any), his rights in the plan are considered to be forfeitable. When the employee's rights in a pension plan are forfeitable, the beneficiary can treat the previously mentioned $5,000 employee's death benefit as additional investment in the plan, and consequently increase the applicable exclusion ratio. Thus, if following the death of an active employee participant who had contributed $5,000 to the plan the surviving beneficiary is entitled to $2,400 a year for 10 years, the amount excludable from gross income each year could be $1,000, figured as follows:

Investment in the plan		
Employee participant's contributions	$5,000	
Employee death benefit	5,000	$10,000
Expected return		
$2,400 × 10		$24,000
Ratio of investment to expected return		10 to 24
Excludable amount		
10/24 × $2,400		$ 1,000

The amount to be reported by the beneficiary as ordinary income each year would be $1,400.

When a retirement income is paid to an employee participant under a joint and survivorship annuity, the survivor continues to use the same exclusion ratio. However, the $5,000 employee's death benefit exclusion does not apply. Upon the death of an employee participant who has been receiving his retirement income under a refund or period certain life annuity, the payments to his beneficiary are excludable from gross income until these payments plus those received tax free by the employee equal the employee's investment in the plan. After that, the full amount of each payment is ordinary income. The $5,000 employee's death benefit exclusion is available if the employee participant's rights in the plan in excess of his own contributions were forfeited.

If the death benefit payable to the beneficiary of an employee participant are paid from life insurance proceeds settled under one of the annuity options, only that part of the life insurance proceeds equal to the predeath cash values are taxable under the annuity rules. The rest is excluded as life insurance proceeds. If the plan is noncontributory, the employee participant's investment is equal to the aggregate cost of the insurance that was taxed to him currently plus the $5,000 employee's death benefit, if applicable. If the beneficiary is the surviving spouse of the employee, an annual interest exclusion of up to $1,000 is allowed.

Under Keogh plans, distributions to beneficiaries of self-employed persons do not qualify for the $5,000 income tax free employee death benefit. Also not qualified are distributions made to death beneficiaries under a 403b plan unless the plan was established by a 501c (3) organization that also falls within the definitions of 503b (1), (2), or (3). Not included among these organizations are public schools. Most other organizations that have tax sheltered annuity plans are included.

If the retirement plan specifically provides for early retirement in event of disability, the income paid to the employee prior to normal retirement age will be treated as income received under a wage continuation plan. If the plan is contributory, that part of the benefit attributed to the employee's contribution is excludable from gross income as a personal health insurance benefit. However, no part of the employee's contribution will be considered as attributable to disability income benefits unless otherwise specified in the plan. Some or all of the benefit attributable to the employer's contribution will be excluded as a wage continuation payment made because of personal injury or sickness. The excludable amount is up to $100 a week after a 30-day waiting period. If the amount of the payment under the wage continuation plan is not more than 75 percent of the employee's regular weekly pay he can exclude up to $75 a week during the last 23 days of the 30-day waiting period unless he is hospitalized in which event he can exclude up to $75 a week for the entire 30-day waiting period. In any case, the $100 a week maximum applies after the 30-day waiting period. After the employee reaches normal retirement age, he loses the disability pension exclusion, and the annuity rules apply. This sick pay exclusion is not available to self-employed individuals under a Keogh plan.

An income averaging rule gives relief to taxpayers who receive a large taxable income in a single taxable year. It should be noted that taxable income received under employee benefit plans is considered eligible income under this rule with but two exceptions: (1) lump-sum benefits that are taxed as capital gains and (2) premature distributions received by an owner employee under a Keogh plan.

The Estate Tax. A lump-sum payment or the value of an annuity distribution paid to a beneficiary of a deceased employee under a noncontributory qualified pension plan is exempt from federal estate taxes. The exemption does not apply to amounts payable to the estate of the deceased employee. In a contributory plan only that portion of the death benefit attributable to the employee's contributions is taxable.

In some states death benefits under employee benefit plans are subject to state inheritance and estate tax laws; in other states these benefits are exempt. Exemptions, where they exist, are the result of statutes, court decisions, and opinions of attorney generals. Wide variations exist among the states. For example, in Illinois, although there is no statutory provision, the practice is to tax death benefits fully if they are paid subsequent to the decedent's retirement, and only to the extent of the employee's contribution if they are paid prior to his retirement.[40] Employee benefits are treated under New York law in the same manner as under the federal law. In

---

[40] In re *Daniels Estate*, 112 N.E. (2d) 56, it was held that in profit sharing plans, the amount of the decedent's vested interest at the time of his death is taxable.

Maine, proceeds of qualified employee benefit plans are exempt if they are paid to the decedent's spouse or children. Death benefits under pension plans are not excluded under Massachusetts law.

Death benefits paid under a qualified profit sharing plan and under 403b annuity plans for employees of favored employers [those who are 501c (3) organizations falling within the definitions of 503b (1), (2), and (3)] are treated for federal estate tax purposes in the same way as are payments under qualified pension plans. Death payments made to beneficiaries of a self-employed person under a Keogh plan and to beneficiaries of participants in 403(b) plans written for nonfavored employers such as public schools are not exempt from federal estate taxes.

The Gift Tax. When an employee designates his beneficiary irrevocably under a qualified pension plan, he makes a taxable gift equal to the value attributable to his contributions. It follows, therefore, that under a noncontributory plan no gift tax liability can be incurred. These same gift tax rules apply to employees under a qualified profit sharing plan and to employees of favored employers under 403(b) plans. They do not apply to self-employed individuals under a Keogh plan nor to employees of nonfavored employees under 403 (b) plans. Under these plans, an irrevocable beneficiary designation or the election of a survivorship annuity is considered a gift and the value of the interest transferred is treated as a taxable gift.

18

Insurance in Employee Benefit Plans: Retirement Plan Design

A study of employee benefit plans for retirement income involves a great deal more than tax considerations—principally considerations of finance and employee relations. The requirements for qualifying private pension plans do not specify the *exact* plan design. Pension planners have some leeway regarding such basic features as (1) the qualifications necessary for an employee to be eligible to participate; (2) the conditions under which benefits are payable; (3) the types of benefits payable; (4) the level of benefits; and (5) the extent, if any, to which the employees are asked to participate in the financing. Neither do the requirements for qualifying the plan specify the *precise* funding policy to be used. The code establishes certain minimum and maximum standards relating to plan design and funding policy, but the pension planners are free to operate within these limits, leaving them a number of determinations to make from many possible combinations.[1] Plan design is discussed in this chapter and funding policy is discussed in the next chapter.

The constraining factors fashioning the terms of the plan are cost, competitive conditions in the labor market, and the desire for an effective policy of personnel and employee relations. A ruling of the National Labor Relations Board, upheld by the Court of Appeals, Seventh Circuit, added an additional constraint. These two bodies held that the Labor Management Relations Act of 1947 made the terms of pension plans subject to collective bargaining.[2]

---

[1] Code restrictions are discussed in Chapter 17.

[2] *Inland Steel Company* v. *United Steelworkers of America*, 77 NLRB 4 (1948); *Inland Steel Company* v. *National Labor Relations Board*, 170 Fed. (2d) 247, 251 (1949); and 336 U.S. 960 (1949).

1. ELIGIBILITY FOR PARTICIPATION

The percentage standard (arbitrary rule) and the classification standard (discretionary rule) for determining whether a plan satisfies the non-discriminating coverage requirement were discussed in Chapter 17.[3] Although some plans, primarily negotiated plans providing uniform or service related benefits and some noncontributory plans with flexible funding arrangements, will cover all employees, these rules make it clear that all employees need not be covered for the plan to be qualified. Therefore, it is necessary for the terms of the plan to specify who is covered. Under these terms, coverage for some classes of employees may be excluded whereas coverage for other classes may be deferred. Excluded classes might be part-time employees, seasonal workers, employees whose earnings do not exceed the social security wage base, workers who are overage when the plan is installed, employees outside the bargaining unit for which the plan is written, and hourly employees. Deferred classes might include employees under a given age and employees who have not met a minimum service requirement. The purpose of restrictive participation requirements is to control cost, principally administrative cost for the deferred classes and benefit cost for the excluded classes.[4]

Pension Plans. Coverage for any class of employees which produces a high turnover rate often is deferred. A time period study of employee data might reveal a high turnover, for example, among employees with less than three years of service, or for females under age 27 or for males under age 25. Further analysis might indicate that the highest turnover occurs among females under age 23 with less than 5 years of service and among males under age 25 with less than 3 years of service. To save administrative costs (record keeping and the costs involved in some funding arrangements that would require the purchase of and then the early surrender of life insurance or annuity contracts) the plan design might specify participation requirements as follows: for females, at least age 23 and at least 5 years of service; for males, at least age 25 and at least 3 years of service.

It will be recalled that, under the arbitrary rule, workers employed for not more than 20 hours a week and those employed for not more than 5 months in any calendar year may be excluded in applying the percentage test. Employers usually prefer to confine participation rights in a pension plan to full-time regular employees so as to provide the maximum benefits for these employees per dollar of cost. They feel no moral obligation or social pressure to provide retirement benefits to part-time or seasonal

---

[3] See p. 432 ff.

[4] If the plan provides for immediate vesting, deferred participation requirements also are used to control benefit costs. See p. 471 ff. for discussion of the concept of vesting.

workers. Whether they will continue to feel no social responsibility for these employees is another question and one not to be taken lightly.[5]

Employees whose earnings do not exceed the maximum amount subject to the social security tax may be excluded without violating the classification standard of the code. But the exclusion of these employees will restrict the level of benefits that can be scheduled for the employees who are covered. The nature of these restrictions is explained later in this chapter when benefit formulas are discussed. Employers who exclude workers whose gross earnings fall within the social security tax base are trying to keep the cost of their plan low while giving something more than social security retirement benefits to those earning in excess of the social security tax base. Furthermore, some authorities expect that adequate retirement income benefits eventually will be assumed by the social security system, and that a private pension system no longer will be essential.[6]

The historical notion that public benefits should be limited to a basic floor of protection that needs supplementing by private pension plans in order to afford retired employees a "reasonably adequate" income is being reexamined. The question of whether social security should be extended to provide the major part of retirement income is being strongly debated.[7] There is a great deal of support for the contention that a public program is vastly superior to a private program in attaining the goal of universal coverage and that "the private program should supplement the public program by providing optional nonuniversal benefits."[8]

Employees who have reached some maximum age, say 50 or 60, when hired or when the plan becomes effective, are denied participation rights in some plans because of the high cost of funding reasonable retirement benefits for these employees. The maximum age limitation might be ap-

---

[5] That there is no social obligation to grant other than regular full-time employees the right to participate in pension plans is by no means a settled issue especially in a changing political, economic, and social environment. Professor Merten C. Bernstein asserts: ". . . many part-time workers are second wage earners in a family, usually wives, upon whom a family's standard of living depends. . . . It is far from 'clear' that part-time workers should be excluded from what is considered the proper area of pension coverage. . . . Income substitutes for their earnings will become steadily more urgent." Merten C. Bernstein, "The Future of Private Pension Plans," *Journal of Risk and Insurance,* Vol. XXXIV (1967), p. 20.

[6] Howard Young, Actuarial Consultant, Social Security Department, International Union, United Automobile, Aerospace and Agricultural Implement Workers of America—UAW, in supporting suggestions for improvements in private pension plans argues: "My view is that any benefits which we have agreed—by our legislative procedures—are desirable for all should be provided through the public program. . . . It must . . . be emphasized that . . . improvements (in private plans) are not alternatives to the needed revamping of the public program." (Howard Young, "Discussions of Papers on the Future of Private Pensions," *Journal of Risk and Insurance,* Vol. XXXIV [1967], p. 35.)

[7] See Robert M. Ball, "Policy Issues in Social Security," *Social Security Bulletin,* June, 1966; the Report of the Advisory Council on Social Security—1965; and Ray M. Peterson, "The Future of Private Pension Plans," *Journal of Risk and Insurance,* Vol. XXXIII (1966), pp. 604–6.

[8] Young, *op. cit.,* p. 35.

plied to new employees only, with all present employees otherwise eligible included in spite of a maximum age limitation. Or, the maximum age limitation might be set at age 60 for present employees and age 50 for new ones.[9] How the employer intends to fund the plan might affect his decision on whether he will use a maximum age limitation and what that limitation will be. The questions of concern in establishing a funding policy are discussed in Chapter 19.

When current employees are excluded under a maximum age limitation, they frequently are given some retirement benefits on an informal unfunded basis to achieve some degree of equity and to improve productive efficiency by retiring older, less productive workers.

Other classifications may be used to exclude employees covered under an alternative pension plan. The plan may cover workers in one collective bargaining unit or in one plant, or the plan may cover salaried employees only. Unless hourly workers are earning the same as salaried workers, plans covering only salaried employees might not qualify under the Internal Revenue Code.[10]

With respect to requirements for eligibility for participation in qualified pension plans, a special cabinet committee appointed by President Kennedy to reappraise legislation and administrative practices relating to private pension programs concluded that "it is inequitable and undesirable for . . . plans . . . to be limited to clerical or salaried employees unless there is a showing of special circumstances or to require an inordinately long waiting period before an employee is covered."[11] With respect to the showing of special circumstances, the committee recognized that in some cases it would be impractical "to avoid differential treatment among groups of employees" and ". . . that the need for flexibility in developing retirement programs for different groups of employees should be respected where adequate reasons are shown and unjustified discrimination does not result."[12] With respect to a waiting period for coverage, the Committee recommended that it "be set at not more than three years, which . . . is ample to exclude transient employees."[13] The committee recognized "that reasons of administrative convenience and cost . . . may justify the exclusion of temporary and part-time employees. . . ."[14]

---

[9] If all present employees who are officers, stockholders, supervisors, or highly paid can qualify under the rules set for new employees, the establishment of different eligibility requirements for present employees than for future employees will not be considered discriminatory.

[10] Commissioner v. Pepsi-Cola Niagara Bottling Corp., Fed. (2d) C.A. 2, 6-28-68.

[11] President's Committee on Corporate Pension Funds and Other Private Retirement and Welfare Programs, Public Policy and Private Pension Programs (Washington, D.C.: U.S. Government Printing Office, January, 1965), p. 59.

[12] Ibid., pp. 60–61.

[13] Ibid., p. 61.

[14] Ibid., p. 60. It should be pointed out that no sweeping legislation has yet resulted from the Cabinet committee's report.

Profit Sharing Plans. Eligibility requirements for participation in deferred profit sharing plans usually are less restrictive than those for pension plans principally because the objectives of a profit sharing plan are to raise output and lower costs "through the direct participation of the employees . . . in the total results of the enterprise as measured by profits."[15] With these objectives, it would make sense to keep restrictions at a minimum. Coverage of employee groups with a high turnover rate will not necessarily work to the disadvantage of the employer in a deferred profit sharing plan because accumulations not available to employees upon termination of employment are credited to the continuing employees. Owner employees of corporations will thereby share in these forfeited benefits.[16] Maximum age restrictions generally are not used because allocations to older workers create no cost problem. Participants are entitled only to the accumulations credited to their accounts and age is not used as a factor in the formula for allocating profit sharing funds among participants. As a rule there is no minimum age requirement, but a service requirement is common, usually one, two, or three years, with a few requiring as many as five years.[17] Rarely are there salary requirements for participation in profit sharing plans because only a few of these plans integrate benefits with social security.[18]

Commonly, a requirement for participation is that the employee be a full-time employee, which by definition normally means that he works at least 20 hours a week and at least 5 months a year.[19] Although some plans restrict coverage to certain classes of employees under an arrangement that does not produce prohibited discrimination, most deferred profit sharing plans are broad coverage ones rather than limited coverage plans.[20] If the

---

[15] J. J. Jehring, *Increased Incentives through Profit Sharing* (Evanston, Illinois: Profit Sharing Research Foundation, 1960), p. 2.

[16] The plan must not discriminate in favor of stockholders, officers, supervisory employees, and other highly paid employees, however. The Regulations state: "Funds in a . . . profit sharing plan arising from forfeitures on termination of service . . . must not be allocated to the remaining participants in such a manner as will effect the prohibited discrimination."

[17] B. L. Metzger, *Profit Sharing in Prospective* (2d ed.; Evanston, Illinois: Profit-Sharing Research Foundation, 1966), pp. 53–54. Shorter waiting periods usually are required for cash profit sharing plans.

[18] *Ibid.*, p. 54.

[19] *Ibid.*, p. 53. B. L. Metzger in observing that the practice of restricting coverage to full-time employees is not universal (in 11.7 percent of the sample of 94 deferred profit sharing plans studied, full-time employment was not a requirement for eligibility for participation) noted: "Some managements feel that regular, permanent, part-time employees are members of the stable work force and, as such, make their own particular contributions to corporate excellence. In accordance with this reasoning, these part-time people should be eligible for profit sharing participation. . . ."

[20] *Ibid.*, p. 43. The only employee group not eligible for participation in a majority of deferred profit sharing plans is the union production/operating group. Of the firms studied with plans, only about 39 percent (45 firms) employed union production/operating workers. Among these 45 plans, only 46.7 percent (21 plans) covered union production/operating workers. In commenting on this latter statistic, Metzger wrote: "Union employees are often excluded from profit sharing programs either because the companies are already contributing

highest paid third of the eligible employees make up less than one half of the plan's participants, the plan will be judged to be nondiscriminatory by the Internal Revenue Service. Conversely, if the highest paid third of the eligible employees make up one half or more of the plan's participants, the plan will be considered to be discriminatory.

2. CONDITIONS UNDER WHICH BENEFITS ARE PAYABLE

Plan designers must not only stipulate the conditions under which employees are eligible for coverage but also the conditions under which they are eligible for benefits.

Because the primary purpose of a qualified pension plan is to provide retirement incomes for participating employees, the usual requirement that must be met to qualify for benefits is the attainment of a specified age. The plan will specify a normal retirement age. It might also provide for early retirement and for late retirement.

Normal Retirement Age. The normal retirement age is the earliest age at which the employee is entitled to full benefits under the plan's formula. In some plans a minimum service requirement is superimposed on the age requirement, common service periods being 10 and 15 years. The use of a minimum service requirement grows out of the concept that pension benefits should in some way be a function of the service rendered by the employee and that benefits payable to employees with only a few years of service would not only be costly to the employer but the amount of the benefit would be insignificant.

Age 65 has become the magic age for normal retirement primarily because this is the age at which the worker can retire and collect full social security benefits. The normal retirement age need not be the same for all employees. It might be 65 for some occupations and lower for other occupations, the classical example being in the airline industry where the normal retirement age is lower for flight than for nonflight personnel. It might be age 65 for all employees except for those age 55 or more at the time the plan is established. For this group the normal retirement age might be set at age 70 to permit high age, low service employees to accumulate a more reasonable pension benefit and to reduce the employer's cost by giving him more time to fund past service credits and to reduce the amount needed to fund the benefits. The cost of a given monthly pension benefit obviously is less for a person age 70 than for a person age 65 because of the additional interest and survivorship benefits accruing from age 65 to age 70, and the lower expected payout period at age 70 than at age 65.

Obviously not everyone (if anyone) becomes useless or disenchanted with work exactly at age 65 or some other arbitrary retirement age. Some

---

to some other health, welfare, pension, or other insurance program on behalf of their union employees or . . . unions have already bargained special benefits and/or disproportionate wages for their members."

employees continue to be productive beyond the normal retirement age whereas the productivity of others will be on the wane long before the normal retirement age is reached. So why should there be a normal retirement age when retirement is an individual rather than a class matter? From the standpoint of the employer, the principal reasons appear to be financial and administrative. A normal retirement age reduces the problem of making reasonable actuarial estimates of costs under a definite benefit formula and does not force the employer to determine in each case when an individual employee should be retired. From the standpoint of the employee, a normal retirement age offers him security. He knows that he will not be retired before the normal retirement age, even though a normal retirement age may force him to retire before he is ready. The knowledge that he could be forced to retire before he is ready might give the employee the incentive to make the necessary financial and emotional preparation for retirement.

In selecting the normal retirement age, aside from the very real consideration of the minimum age for full benefits under social security, an important consideration is the objective of the retirement program. Is its objective to remove unproductive old workers who seriously hamper business efficiency? Or, is its objective to provide old employees an opportunity to quit work and live the life of leisure that young men yearn for but old men fear. If it is the latter, the retirement age can be highly flexible with the minimum age a function of what the employer believes he can afford to finance.

If the objective is to retire employees when their efficiency is seriously impaired, the normal retirement age should be fixed at that age where, on the average, it would be less expensive to pay employees a reasonable retirement income than to keep them on the payroll. Obviously, since the expense of retiring an employee with a reasonable pension varies inversely with the age of retirement, and the cost of retaining an employee beyond his most productive years varies directly with the employee's age, an age eventually will be reached where the cost of retaining the employee will exceed the expense of retiring him at a reasonable pension. While this observation has conceptual simplicity, it may not offer the employer much help in selecting a normal retirement age for his plan. While he has the data necessary to make estimates of the cost of various levels of retirement benefits at various ages he probably does not have the data required to project the cost of retaining employees beyond various age limits. So the magic age of 65 is usually selected as the normal retirement age.

Early Retirement.   Under many plans employees who meet certain conditions, such as reaching at least age 55 and completing at least 10 years of service, may, at their option, retire early at a reduced benefit. The benefit is scaled down from the normal retirement amount to reflect the difference in the actuarial cost of early retirement. For example, assume that the normal retirement age is 65 and that the pension formula produces a retirement income of $400 a month at that age. The pension plan allows participation in retirement benefits at age 55 at the option of the employee. At that age the pension formula produces a retirement income of $250 a month (fewer years of services, lower average earnings). But because of actuarial adjustments to reflect higher pension costs at age 55, the pension benefits using one set of actuarial assumptions would be reduced to $105 monthly. If early retirement were deferred to age 60, the formula would produce $300 a month but that amount would be scaled back to $195 a month following the actuarial adjustment.[21]

Early retirement may be conditioned not only on the employee's age and service but also on the employer's consent or on the physical condition of the employee.[22] Some plans require that the employee be a victim of permanent and total disability to qualify for early retirement.

The provision for early retirement helps to overcome the limitations of a normal retirement age where everyone is treated as a homogeneous part of a class rather than as an individual. Obviously, the value to an employee of an early retirement privilege depends upon the amount of income that must be sacrificed to take advantage of the privilege. Inclusion of early retirement privileges can be expensive to the employer, and the reduction of benefits for early retirement is a means of controlling cost.

Because "it is obvious that instinctively the worker has deep inner resistance to withdrawal from work,"[23] it seems logical to expect that the employer can grant employees earlier retirement privilege without full actuarial reduction of benefits and not incur a significant increase in cost. In estimating the cost of early retirement, the actuary will make assumptions as to the number of employees that will retire early and the ages at which they will retire. He can then prepare estimates of the costs of various benefit adjustments for early retirement. The employer can select the adjustment scale that is priced reasonably in terms of what he is willing to pay for flexibility in his employee retirement plan.

Late Retirement. A number of plans make a distinction between normal and mandatory retirement age. For example, early retirement at reduced benefits may be permitted at age 55 at the employee's election, normal retirement at full benefits may be fixed at age 65, and late retire-

---

[21] These are adjustments for males. For females, the adjusted monthly pensions would be $120 and $202, respectively. Because females have a longer life expectancy at age 65 than do males, the percentage reduction in retirement benefits assessed for early retirement for females is lower than that for males.

[22] It is not customary to require employer consent for early retirement. When it is required, the benefit level must not exceed the amount vested at the time of early retirement, if the plan is qualified under the Internal Revenue Service.

[23] Julius Hochman in *The Social and Biological Challenge of Our Aging Population* (New York: Columbia University Press, 1950), reprinted in William Haber and Wilbur J. Cohen, *Social Security Programs, Problems, and Policies* (Homewood, Illinois: Richard D. Irwin, Inc., 1960), p. 103. Mr. Hochman says, "The evidence accumulated by geriatricians and psychiatrists amply indicates that retirement is frequently followed by crisis and severe emotional disturbance. . . ."

ment at normal benefits may be permitted at age 68 at the employee's election. Note that even though the benefits of employees who elect early retirement are reduced, the benefits of employees who elect late retirement are usually not increased because of the incentive it would give employees to retire late. Cost savings on late retirements can be anticipated in developing the scale of adjustments for early retirement benefits. In those plans where employers want to encourage late retirements, higher benefits are paid for late than for normal retirement. The higher late retirement benefit may be the result of (1) an actuarial adjustment designed to equate the benefit with that provided at normal retirement age, (2) the accumulation of additional benefits because of additional years of service, or (3) an increase in the average compensation upon which the pension is based. Whether items (2) and (3) will affect the level of the pension will depend upon the pension benefit formula, a subject to be discussed later in this chapter.

Many plans contain provisions under which a willing employee at his employer's request can be retained beyond the mandatory retirement age. Usually each case must be acted upon individually, sometimes at the board of directors level.

The conditions under which benefits other than retirement are paid are examined in the following section.

3. TYPES OF BENEFITS PAYABLE

Under pension plans several types of benefits may be available to participating employees: (1) lifetime income benefits at retirement, (2) benefits in event employment is terminated prior to reaching minimum retirement age, (3) death benefits (4) widow's pension, and (5) disability benefits.

Retirement Income Benefits. The normal form of retirement benefit usually is a life income payable to the retired employee only, with payments ceasing upon his death.[24] However, the employee generally has the option before or at retirement to select a joint and last survivorship annuity or a refund annuity in lieu of the pure life annuity.[25] As a cost control measure, the plan might require that the option be selected several years prior to retirement, otherwise virtually all employees in poor health at retirement will select a refund option. Under some plans, a retiring employee might be required to show evidence of good health before being allowed to elect one of the annuity options. Some plans give employees the option to have their pension benefits commuted into a lump sum at retirement because lump-sum distributions offer some employees an income tax advantage.[26]

---

[24] If the plan is a contributory plan and the retired employee dies before he has recovered an amount equal to his accumulated contributions, his beneficiary is paid the deficiency in a lump sum.

[25] See Chapter 6 for a discussion of types of annuities.

[26] See Chapter 17 for discussion of the income taxation of pension benefits.

The amount payable under the lump-sum option should be a function of the employee's life expectancy and the level of interest rates at the time the employee retires.

In reaching decisions about options to be offered and conditions to be imposed on their selection, pension designers must consider what arrangements give the best balance between the benefits of providing flexibility and the cost of achieving this flexibility.

Benefits upon Termination of Employment. Under a contributory pension plan, the employee always is entitled to a refund of his contributions upon voluntary or involuntary termination of his employment. The usual practice is to return these contributions augmented by a modest rate of interest, although under some plans no interest is included in the refund. The failure to include provisions for payment of interest on the employee's contributions would be unfair and therefore unwise. The same logic that supports refunding the employee's contributions when he terminates his employment also supports including interest with that refund. Funds contributed by an employee are his own savings and should be returned to him with interest. Under some plans, the terminating employee is given the right to leave his accumulated contributions with the pension fund for distribution as an annuity at retirement age. Because the cost of administering this option is expensive for the individual employer, it is rarely used except in those plans administered by an insurance company. Furthermore, since so few employees take advantage of the deferred annuity option when offered, there seems to be little reason to give terminating employees other than cash withdrawals of their contributions.

VESTED BENEFITS. With respect to benefits upon termination of employment, the principal variation among pension plans revolves around the disposition of benefit rights not attributable to employee contributions. The disposition of these rights is a function of the vesting provisions of the plan. Vesting is defined as the "attainment by a participant of a benefit right, attributable to employer contributions, that is not contingent upon a participant's continuation in specified employment." "A benefit the payment of which is not contingent upon a participant's continuation in specified employment" is known as a vested benefit.[27]

Types of Vesting Provisions. The two extremes of vesting are (1) vesting of pension benefits at retirement only and (2) immediate and full vesting of pension benefits as they are earned. Vesting at retirement offers no benefits upon termination of employment unless the employee at the time of his termination qualifies for immediate retirement benefits by having met the plan's age and service requirements. Under immediate and full vesting the employee's "rights to vested benefits are acquired . . . commencing immediately upon his entry into the plan" and "all accrued

---

[27] *Bulletin of the Commission on Insurance Terminology of the American Risk and Insurance Association,* Vol. 1, No. 4, p. 2.

benefits of a participant become vested benefits."[28] Most vesting provisions currently found in pension plans are at neither of the extremes, offering something more than vesting at retirement only and something less than full and immediate vesting.[29]

The intermediate types of vesting may be classified as to (1) the time of vesting, (2) the amount of vesting, and (3) the conditions of vesting.

If vesting is not immediate, then obviously it is deferred. Deferred vesting is "that form of vesting under which rights to vested benefits are acquired by a participant commencing upon the fulfillment of specified requirements (usually in terms of attained age, years of service and/or plan membership)."[30]

If vesting is not full then obviously it is partial. Partial vesting is "that form of immediate or deferred vesting under which a specified portion of the accrued benefits of a participant becomes a vested benefit."[31] Partial vesting may be graduated or progressive; for example, no vesting for the first five years and then 10 percent vesting for each year of service thereafter, to reach full vesting in 15 years. This vesting arrangement is known as graded vesting, "that form of immediate or deferred vesting under which an increasing proportion of the accrued benefits of a participant becomes a vested benefit in accordance with a specified formula and requirements (usually in terms of attained age, years of service, and/or plan membership)."[32]

The most common type of intermediate vesting is deferred and full vesting with a service requirement of 10 or 15 years and an age requirement of 40 or 55.[33]

Vesting may be unconditional or conditional. Conditional vesting is "that form of vesting in a contributory plan under which entitlement to a vested benefit is conditional upon the nonwithdrawal of the participant's contribution."[34] Conditional vesting is common, especially in those plans not funded with individual life insurance and annuity contracts. Vesting may also be contingent, a "form of vesting under which entitlement to a vested benefit is conditioned upon the circumstances surrounding the employee's termination of service or his conduct at the time of and after separation of employment."[35] For example, a plan may provide for a forfeiture of vested rights if the employee voluntarily terminates his employment, or if his employment is terminated by his employer because of an act of em-

---

[28] *Ibid.*, Vol. 2, No. 1, pp. 1–2.

[29] See *1965 Study of Industrial Retirement Plans* (New York: Bankers Trust Company, 1965) and *Labor Mobility and Private Pension Plans,* BLS Bulletin No. 1407 (Washington, D.C.: U.S. Department of Labor, 1964).

[30] *Bulletin of the Commission on Insurance Terminology, op. cit,.* Vol. 2, No. 1, p. 2–3.

[31] *Ibid.*

[32] *Ibid.*

[33] BLS Bulletin No. 1407, *op. cit.* About 68 percent of the 15,818 plans studied had deferred and full vesting provisions.

[34] *Bulletin of the Commission on Insurance Terminology, op. cit.,* Vol. 2, No. 1, p. 2.

[35] *Ibid.*

ployee infidelity. The vesting provisions under most pension plans are not contingent. Vested benefits are given regardless of the reason for the termination of employment.

A final type of vesting is locked-in vesting, a "form of vesting in a contributory plan under which the participant has no right to withdraw his contributions after benefits attributable to employer contributions have vested. . . ."[36] Locked-in vesting is not at all common but the concept has merit, particularly for employees beyond, say, age 50 or 55 who have accumulated valuable pension rights financed by their employers. To prevent these employees from throwing away these rights when their employment is terminated, under a few plans employee contributions are not refunded if the termination occurs after the employee reaches a given age, 50 or 55, for example. Instead, his contributions are locked in to provide him a paid-up pension when he reaches the minimum retirement age.

THE VESTING ISSUE. The question of vesting of benefits in pension plans has become a public policy issue, and various vesting standards have been proposed by federal administrative and legislative committees. Under the provisions of the Internal Revenue Code, a pension plan need not offer vesting to meet the standards for qualification as long as the plan is active and continuing. However, to the extent that benefits are funded or are credited to the employees' account, the plan must contain provisions for the vesting of all accrued employee benefits if the plan is terminated. Although the Internal Revenue Code does not specifically require vesting for operative plans, the Internal Revenue Service has required vesting where the lack of vesting might result in discrimination in favor of higher paid employees.

Those who argue the case for vesting would add a minimum vesting requirement to the conditions that must be met to qualify a pension plan for favorable tax treatment. One proposal calls for alternative standards: full vesting upon the attainment of age 45 and the completion of 15 years of continuous service; or graded vesting starting at 50 percent of earned credits upon completion of 10 years of continuous service and the attainment of age 45, with an additional 5 percent for each year of continuous service thereafter reaching full vesting after 20 years of continuous service.[37] Another recommendation is for a graded deferred vesting system based on service only without any provision for a minimum age. The formula recommended would vest 50 percent of accrued pension credits after 15 years of service, with full vesting at the end of 20 years.[38] Still

---

[36] Ibid., p. 3.

[37] A proposed "Pension and Employee Benefit Act," introduced by Senator Jacob K. Javits, who for several years now has been seeking tighter pension laws.

[38] Public Policy and Private Pension Programs, op. cit., p. 42. The recommendation of the Cabinet committee did not specify that the vesting from the 15th to the 20th year would be 10 percent additional for each of these years but that probably is what was implied. Also, the recommendation did not specify that the years of service must be continuous as in the case of the Javits proposal.

another proposal calls for vesting of normal retirement benefits after 10 years of service with no minimum age requirement. Service before age 25 would be disregarded if such service is not credited under the provisions of the plan.[39]

The arguments for 10-year vesting and no age requirement was put as follows:

. . . 10 years is a sufficiently extended period of time for the value of an employee's service to be explicitly recognized for pension purposes. It represents about one fourth of the typical working life of an employee. Loss of benefits for such a period of service, were an employee to move elsewhere, would, therefore, represent a substantial reduction in his retirement security. . . . The staff carefully considered but rejected allowing vesting to be deferred until a certain age. With an age requirement set at 45 years or above—which seem to be the levels suggested by some—too large a segment of an employee's working life could be excluded from pension coverage if he were to change employment before he reached age 45.[40]

The Case for Compulsory Vesting.   Proponents of federal vesting standards base their argument on two important considerations: the desire for fair treatment of employees and the need for an efficient system of private pension plans. The argument requires that the concepts of equity and efficiency as they relate to private pension plans be clearly defined. Obviously, those who oppose compulsory vesting standards would not concede that they are arguing against equity and efficiency.

The crux of the "fairness" argument for compulsory vesting is stated as follows:

Without vesting of benefits, employees can find themselves devoting large portions of their working lives to an employer only to find when a move is necessary, that those years have bought nothing toward their security on retirement.[41]

As a matter of equity and fair treatment, an employee covered by a pension plan is entitled, after a reasonable period of service, to protection of his future retirement benefit against any termination of his employment. Vesting validates the accepted concept that employer contributions to pension plans represent 'deferred compensation' which the individual worker earns through service with his employer.[42]

A man who has devoted 15 years of his life to working under a plan in the expectation of pension has earned something . . . and he ought not to be told in his later years . . . that his rights have been forfeited. . . .[43]

---

[39] This is the proposal of the Inter-Agency Staff Committee as outlined by Assistant Secretary of the Treasury Stanley S. Surrey in an Address to the American Pension Conference, New York City, May, 1967.

[40] *Ibid.*

[41] *Ibid.*

[42] *Public Policy and Private Pension Programs, op. cit.,* p. 39.

[43] Senator Javits in the *Congressional Record,* Feb. 28, 1967, p. S2689.

The premise upon which the fairness argument for compulsory vesting is based has not gone unquestioned. Typical of one counterargument is the statement that

Equity and fairness do not require that an employee get back everything that he or his employer contribute when he terminates his employment after several years, but merely that he get what he bargained for under informal, noncoercive and fair bargaining procedures.[44]

Typical of another counterargument is the observation that

at any given level of contributions to a pension program, vesting provisions result in some reduction in benefits for workers who remain covered by the plan until retirement age. Proposals for required vesting, therefore, rest on the assumption that pensions must, for reasons of equity, allocate more funds to those who leave and less to those who retire.[45]

The gist of the argument that compulsory vesting is necessary for an efficient system of private pension plans is found in the following observations made by the President's Committee on Corporate Pension Funds:

By bringing pension benefits to additional workers . . . vesting strengthens the private pension system and the security function it is expected to perform.[46]
    . . . If a choice must be made between a system that provides a higher level of benefits but only for those who remain with their employer until retirement age against one that assures a slightly lower level of benefits to all workers after a reasonable period of service, public policy clearly must choose the latter.[47]
    The effective functioning of the Nation's labor market system rests on the individual worker's freedom to change jobs to parts of the economy where his services can be better utilized. . . . The lack of vesting in private pension plans . . . clearly is a deterrent to mobility for important segments of the labor force. . . .[48]

The President's Committee recognized that compulsory vesting would increase the cost of pension plans but concluded that the additional cost would be modest. The Committee concluded:

In summary, the most complete available information indicates that the added cost of adopting the basic features of the Committee's recommendations (50 percent of accrued pension credits after 15 years of service, with full vesting at the end of 20 years) would be . . . under 5 percent for a large majority of pension plans. Rarely would the added cost exceed 10 percent of present expenditures. . . .[49]

---

[44] Representative Thomas B. Curtis in the *Congressional Record*, April 24, 1967, p. H4541.

[45] *Public Policy for Private Pensions*, Hewitt Associates (Libertyville, Illinois, August, 1966).

[46] *Public Policy and Private Pension Programs, op. cit.*, p. 40.

[47] *Ibid.*, p. 41.

[48] *Ibid.*, p. 40.

[49] *Ibid.*, p. 46.

The "efficiency" argument for compulsory vesting also has been challenged, just as the fairness argument. The President's Advisory Committee on Labor-Management Policy made these observations about the recommendations of the President's Committee on Corporate Pension Funds:

> Private . . . pension plans are voluntarily instituted frequently by collective bargaining, and their terms vary . . . in consideration of . . . factors fashioned by economic circumstances of particular companies and industries. A vesting requirement may unduly burden the maintenance of existing plans or hamper the establishment of new plans. . . . These considerations are particularly compelling with respect to the numerous private pension plans (covering about one fifth of all employees in private pension plans) in which the funds available for pension purposes and limited to a fixed contribution by employers, e.g., so many cents per employee hour worked or per unit of production. Under these circumstances, the limited funds available have been used as the parties deemed best, entirely for the needs of long-service employees. In some cases the amounts available under such plans for benefits at retirement would be significantly reduced if vested rights were established. In addition, to require such fixed contribution programs to provide vested rights may deprive large numbers of employees in certain industries of the opportunity to secure any private pension benefits at all.[50]

In essence the argument is that compulsory vesting would reduce efficiency because it would discourage the establishment of new plans and weaken existing plans. A further line of counterargument holds that lack of vesting is not the culprit that interferes with labor mobility and the effective functioning of the nation's labor market system.

> The presumption that pension plans inhibit worker mobility is widely accepted. . . . Almost without exception, however, it is agreed that other practices —seniority, for example—are intermeshed with the accumulation of pension rights and may, on balance, be more significant deterrents to worker mobility.[51]

Nothing short of immediate vesting would eliminate the holding power of pension plans and give the flexibility needed for transitions in a fast-changing technologically oriented society. Vesting provisions short of immediate full vesting "create short-term barriers to voluntary movement; that is a worker may feel 'locked-in' a plan during the period immediately before he qualifies for vesting because he is so close to assuring himself of a right to a valuable asset."[52] Compulsory vesting deferred for a period of 15 years may have little influence on labor mobility. The Bureau of Labor Statistics noted that "since the propensity of workers to change jobs undoubtedly declines as they grow older and as they accumulate more service (hence security in their employments), high age and long service require-

---

[50] *Ibid.*, Appendix D., pp. 4–5.
[51] *Labor Mobility and Private Pension Plans*, BLS Bulletin No. 1407 (Washington, D.C.: U.S. Department of Labor, 1964), p. 1.
[52] *Ibid.*, p. 22.

ments in vesting provisions counteract the theoretical mobility potential of vesting."[53]

One interesting counterargument against compulsory vesting and all the other recommendations contained in the *Report to the President on Private Employee Retirement Plans* is expressed by the President of the United Mine Workers of America who believes that "private pension plans do not operate by public grant of privilege like franchised public utilities and thus protected from hazards of competition." He suggested that the proposals "be set aside and that recommendations be prepared for necessary improvements in the Federal Old Age, Survivors and Disability Insurance system, so that it will better serve as the nation's basic instrument for assuring the payment of a more meaningful minimum retirement income for most people."[54] On the other hand, Walter P. Reuther, President of the UAW, told the Joint Economic Committee of the Congress in December, 1967, that a minimum vesting requirement is long overdue. He said that Congress should require vesting of all accrued pension benefits for employees with 10 or more years of service, but that plans which provide benefits less than some specified minimum level should be exempt from the vesting requirement.

The Vesting Decision.   The trend is not only toward providing some form of vesting but also toward more liberal vesting provisions. Studies show that of the conventional plans as distinguished from the negotiated pattern-type plans, 97 percent provided some form of vesting as of 1965 compared with 90 percent as of 1960 and 75 percent as of 1955.[55] The studies revealed that 26 percent of the plans vested if the service requirement was met by age 45, whereas 5 and 10 years earlier these percentages were 18 percent and 10 percent. Of the pattern plans, 94 percent provided some form of vesting. These percentages were 82 percent and 41 percent 5 and 10 years earlier. Among the pattern plans, 80 percent vested if the service requirement was met by age 45; these percentages for 5 and 10 years earlier were 50 percent and 20 percent.

The trend toward more vested plans and more liberal vesting rights reflects the acceptance by employers that in most cases the benefits of vesting outweigh its costs. The pension designer's task is to develop the vesting arrangement that maximizes the efficiency of the plan and this means the arrangement that produces the most efficient relationship between the value of and the cost of vesting. The dollar costs of various vesting arrangements can be estimated using appropriate actuarial assumptions relative to withdrawal rates, mortality rates, and interest rates. The dollar values of various

---

[53] *Ibid.*, p. 23.

[54] *Public Policy and Private Pension Programs, op. cit.*, Appendix D, p. 13. Remarks by W. Anthony Boyle.

[55] *1965 Study of Industrial Retirement Plans* (New York: Bankers Trust Company, 1965), pp. 19–20; *1960 Study of Industrial Retirement Plans* (New York: Bankers Trust Company, 1960), pp. 17–18.

vesting arrangements are not so easily estimated. For example, what values should be assigned to the following advantages of vesting: (1) better employee relations (disgruntled employees can leave without losing accumulated pension credits), (2) greater interest in the plan by younger employees (a plan under which employees must work for years before they own anything in it has little present reality), (3) flexibility in the labor market by increasing the mobility of workers to accommodate change in technology, (4) the strength that vesting gives to the nation's program for retirement protection, (5) greater ease in qualifying the plan for tax deduction under the Internal Revenue Code, (6) the desire to treat terminating employees as having earned pension rights with the minimum of restrictions, and (7) the urge to honor what might be considered to be a social obligation to vest pension benefits. These values must be subjective unless they show up in greater efficiency on the job, and even then their measurement is by no means clear and precise.

Death Benefits.   In keeping with the philosophy that an employee's contributions to the plan must be recovered by the participant or his beneficiary, contributory plans provide for a refund of the employee's contributions (with interest in some plans; without interest in others) in the event of his death prior to retirement. In the event that death follows retirement, contributory plans customarily refund to the participant's beneficiary the difference, if any, between the total amount of contributions paid by the participant to the plan and the total amount of retirement benefits paid by the plan to the participant. Refunds of employee contributions are not death benefits because these refunds would be made upon any termination from the plan regardless of cause.

When an employee elects to receive his retirement income in the form of a joint and last survivorship annuity or a refund annuity, benefits may become payable upon his death. These benefits also are not death benefits; they result from a tradeoff of lower periodic lifetime income payments in exchange for the survivorship or refund benefit.

But some pension plans include a true death benefit, particularly those funded through individual life insurance policies and through group permanent life insurance contracts. Group annuity plans or trust fund plans usually do not provide for a death benefit. Anticipated mortality experience is discounted in measuring the cost of the plan.[56] When death benefits are provided under group annuity or trust fund plans they are usually restricted to a flat amount or related to the salary of the participant.

In most cases, group life insurance plans rather than pension plans are considered to be the better vehicle for providing death benefits. Lump-sum death benefits in excess of $5,000 paid under a pension plan are subject to federal income taxes whereas death benefits paid under a life insurance policy are not taxable as income. For federal estate tax purposes, however,

---

[56] See Chapter 19 for a discussion of actuarial cost assumptions.

the law favors death benefits under pension plans because these benefits, if paid to a named beneficiary, are not includable in the participant's estate. Proceeds paid under a life insurance policy are includable in the participant's estate if the participant retains incidents of ownership in the insurance. Where the potential estate tax liability imposes a significant problem to the participant it might be possible for him to arrange his group coverage so as to eliminate the insurance proceeds from his estate.[57]

Widow's Pension. Under some pension plans a retiring employee without advance notice may elect to take his retirement income as a joint and survivorship annuity rather than as a life annuity. Most joint and survivorship annuity options designed for pension plans provide that the participant receive a level periodic income as long as he lives but that his survivor receive a lifetime income of a reduced amount. The customary reduction in the amount payable to the widow is 50 percent or $33\frac{1}{3}$ percent. This type of option is a form of widow's pension because it allows the selection at the time of retirement rather than requiring advance notice of several years. The retiring employee, of course, receives a lower periodic pension but the plan must absorb the cost of adverse selection. For example, if the plan allows the participant to retire at age 60, he can decide to retire anytime after that age when his health deteriorates, and saddle the plan with the obligation to pay his widow a pension for life if he predeceases her. The cost to the plan "is a particularly difficult cost to evaluate; nevertheless, the cost of such a provision is significant."[58]

Typically, the participant must elect the joint and survivorship annuity in advance of retirement. This type of arrangement creates no additional cost to the plan and provides no additional benefit. The widow of a participant who dies after electing the option but before reaching retirement age would not be entitled to a pension because the joint and survivorship annuity does not become effective until the participant retires. To overcome the discontinuity in this type of arrangement some plans include a rollback provision under which the survivorship annuity becomes effective upon the death of the participant even though that death occurs before the annuitant reaches retirement age. If the employee is asked to accept a further reduction of his annuity income as payment for exercising the rollback option then, of course, the arrangement is not a true widow's benefit. But if the costs of the rollback privilege are absorbed by the plan, then the plan offers a true widow's pension. To qualify for the widow's benefit on death before retirement, the employee would have had to elect the joint and survivorship annuity in lieu of the normal straight life annuity. If his wife predeceases him before he retires, he would still receive only that amount payable under the joint and survivorship option and not the higher amount that would have been payable under the straight life annuity.

---

[57] See Chapter 21 for discussion of life insurance in estate planning.

[58] Meyer Melnikoff, *Proceedings of the October 1962 Meeting of the American Pension Conference,* New York City, p. 14.

Widows' benefits are not common in pension plans in the United States although they are used extensively in Europe.[59] However, they are now receiving more attention.

The number of variations possible among the specifications for widows' benefits are limited only by one's imagination. Eligibility may be a function of the age of the participant when he was hired, his age when he was married, his age when he died, and his years of service. The commencement date of the widow's benefit may be a function of her age and the termination date may be a function of her marital status. The widow's benefit may be conditioned upon the participant's selection of a joint and survivor annuity option for his pension. The amount of the widow's pension may be a function of (1) the amount of the normal pension accrued by the participant at the time of his death, (2) the amount of benefit that would have been payable to the participant if he had retired early on the day of his death, or (3) the amount of benefit that would have been payable to the participant if he had retired on the day of his death and had elected an immediate joint and survivorship option.

In deciding whether to include a true widow's pension benefit, the plan designer must consider its probable cost based on actuarial assumptions relating to the variables governing the probability that the widow's pension will have to be paid and the probable duration of the payments. He must then consider whether the funds needed to pay for the widow's benefit can be used better to finance higher pension benefits for all employees or to enrich the group life insurance benefits for all employees.

Disability Benefits. Workers are on occasion required to retire from a job because of permanent disability. Disability retirement can create an even greater financial strain on the employee and his family than does normal retirement. A number of pension plans recognize the problem of permanent and total disability and make some arrangement for permanent disability protection.

In some plans a form of permanent disability protection is offered by allowing the disabled worker to retire early at an actuarially reduced benefit level. If the age and benefit level for early retirement is the same regardless of whether the participant is disabled, the plan then offers no special disability protection. However, if the requirements for disability retirement are less strict than those for early retirement (fewer years of service, lower age level), the plan does provide a disability benefit distinct from early retirement. A further distinction may be made between disability retirement and early retirement. Under some plans, pension credits continue to accumulate for the disabled participant who is then given full retirement benefits when and if he reaches normal retirement age.

---

[59] Clark T. Foster, *ibid.*, p. 3. "The principal reason for the lack of concern is that, unlike the situation in Europe, most employers in the United States provide survivors' benefits in the form of group life insurance."

Some plans provide for a disability benefit unrelated to retirement benefits, and express this benefit as a percentage of earnings at the time of disability or as so much a month for each year of service. Eligibility requirements usually restrict disability benefits to employees who have accumulated some such service period as 10 years and have reached some such age as 50. Therefore, young employees as a rule are given no permanent disability income protection through pension plans. An exception may be found in some pension plans that are funded through individual life insurance policies that provide a monthly disability income benefit of some such amount as $10 per $1,000 of face amount of life insurance.

When the disability benefit is funded through individual life policies, the definition of disability included in the pension plan must conform to that used in the life insurance policy (for example, a total disability existing continuously for at least six months that prevents the participant from engaging for remuneration or profit in an occupation, his own for the first 24 months and in any occupation thereafter for which he is reasonably fitted by education, training, or experience). If disability benefits are paid directly from the pension fund, the plan may include any definition of disability that its designers consider proper (for example, a period of incapacity lasting for six months after which the participant, in the judgment of a physician, is totally incapable of further performance of substantially gainful employment with a reasonable probability that such incapacity will be permanent). Note that in this latter example a disability is not presumed to be permanent simply because it lasts six months, and, therefore, does not result in temporary disabilities automatically being treated as permanent disabilities.

The better way to provide total and permanent disability benefits for employees is to arrange for these benefits through long-term group disability income insurance with benefits payable to the normal retirement age. The retirement plan can assume the responsibility for paying benefits beyond the normal retirement age. The employer can continue to fund his liability for disabled employees under the pension plan just as he does for active employees or he may add a benefit to his group health insurance policy under which the pension fund will receive periodic payments sufficient to offset the annual cost of accumulating retirement benefits for disabled employees. The advantages of using long-term group disability insurance rather than provisions written into a pension plan to cover permanent and total disability are that employees under age 50 are more likely to be covered and the administrative problems associated with disability income protection are better handled by insurers experienced in the handling of this type of protection.

MEDICAL EXPENSE BENEFITS. Assets accumulated in pension funds may be segregated into a special account (although the funds may be commingled with all retirement funds) to provide specified medical expense benefits for *retired* employees, their spouses, and dependents. The right to accumulate qualified pension funds for medical care expenses of retired employees, their spouses, and dependents has been effective only since 1962. Some pension plans have incorporated provisions for accumulating funds for medical benefits and use the funds to pay medical expenses up to the amounts specified in the plan or to pay premiums on behalf of retired employees for group health insurance or for the voluntary supplementary medical insurance available under medicare.[60]

Plan designers should consider the income tax advantage of providing medical expense benefits (particularly the payment of premiums for the voluntary supplementary medical insurance under medicare) for retired employees through the pension plan even if this means reducing the amount available for payment of retirement income benefits. If the retired employee pays his own medical expenses, he can deduct only that amount in excess of 3 percent of his adjusted gross income. If he pays his own health insurance premiums, he can deduct only 50 percent of the amount paid subject to a maximum annual deduction of $150. In noncontributory plans all of his retirement income is included as gross income and in contributory plans most of his retirement income is treated as gross income.[61] But medical expenses paid for the retired employee, his spouse, or dependents under a qualified pension plan either direct or as premiums to purchase medical expense insurance are not includable in the gross income of the employee.

Benefits under Profit Sharing Plans.   While the principal function of a qualified deferred profit sharing plan is the same as that of a qualified pension plan, the mechanics of a deferred profit sharing plan require more liberal vesting arrangements. If an employee under a pension plan terminates his employment before his benefits are vested the effect must be to reduce the cost of the plan to the employer.[62] However, in a profit sharing plan, if an employee terminates his employment before the accumulated employer's contributions made on his behalf are vested, these accumulations may be, and usually are, allocated among the remaining participants in the plan. Such an arrangement could lead to discrimination in favor of highly compensated employees, supervisors, officers, and stockholder-employees who, over the long run, are likely to be the remaining participants. Therefore, more liberal vesting provisions are required in profit sharing plans than in pension plans to gain approval of the Internal Revenue Service.[63]

Benefits under a deferred profit sharing plan usually become fully vested

---

60 Part B, Title XVIII, Social Security Act.

61 See page 453.

62 The regulations permit the employer, in estimating the future cost of a pension plan (technically known as valuation of liabilities of a pension plan), to anticipate the effect of forfeitures. Normally assumptions are made as to withdrawals in making actuarial cost projections. Forfeitures may not be used to increase the benefits employees would otherwise receive.

63 If prohibited discrimination does not result, provision *may* be made in profit sharing plans to use forfeitures to reduce employer contributions which otherwise would be required under the contribution formula contained in the plan.

upon the death, permanent disability, or retirement of the participant. Most plans provide some form of vesting in the event of severance of the participant's employment before death, disability, or retirement, the most common being graded vesting with full vesting after 10 or 20 years of service or after 10 years of participation in the plan. A very small percentage offer immediate full vesting. Usually the terminating employee has the same vested benefits whether he resigns or is fired.[64]

It is argued that liberal vesting offers a temptation to an employee to quit his job in order to get his hands on the money that has been credited to him under the plan. However, a study by the National Industrial Conference Board reveals that vesting does not strongly influence resignations.[65]

The primary objective of deferred profit sharing plans is to help build financial security for participants and their families in the event of the employees' permanent disability, retirement, or death. However, severance benefits are an important by-product of deferred profit sharing plans and should be given serious consideration in formulating vesting provisions. Adequate severance benefits appear to be a desirable feature of deferred profit sharing plans.

Preseverance benefits are made available under some deferred profit sharing plans in order to make these plans more flexible and also more appealing to younger employees without losing sight of primary long-term objectives.[66] When preseverance benefits are made available, certain restrictions on the participants' access to these benefits are necessary so that all funds to the credit of the participants will not be treated as current income for tax purposes when employer contributions are made and as interest is earned.[67]

Withdrawal and loan privileges are the principal preserverance benefits provided under deferred profit sharing plans although most noncontributory plans offer neither type of benefit. Most contributory plans offer either loan or withdrawal privileges or some sort of combination of the two.[68]

Distributions are permitted under profit sharing plans after at least two years. Thus if the plan permits withdrawals, the maximum that can be allowed is the total amount in the fund less the contributions made and the interest earned during the previous two years. However, the plan may

[64] Metzger, op. cit., pp. 67–69.

[65] F. B. Brower, Sharing Profits with Employees ("Studies in Personnel Policy"), No. 162 (New York: National Industrial Conference Board, Inc., 1957), p. 36. Brower concludes, "If the company is prosperous, and the profit sharing benefits are substantial and continuing, this is the best inducement for the employee to continue with the company. This argument has been found very effective in several companies faced with employees wanting to leave and obtain their vesting rights."

[66] J. J. Jehring, Pre-Severence Benefits in Deferred Profit Sharing (Evanston, Illinois: Profit Sharing Research Foundation, 1956).

[67] Under the doctrine of constructive receipt, a person is considered to have received funds that are made available to him regardless of whether or not these funds have actually been distributed if they are made available without penalty.

[68] Metzger, op. cit., pp. 70–71.

not permit withdrawal up to the legal maximum. A number of contributory plans restrict withdrawals to employee contributions. Others restrict them to a given percentage of the amount vested. Furthermore, withdrawals usually are allowed only for hardship cases. However, where employee contributions are voluntary, employees usually are allowed to withdraw their own contributions without restriction. The amount withdrawn less the participant's own contributions is taxable as income in the year received. In formulating withdrawal provisions, plan designers want to make them liberal enough to be of value to the participants but not so liberal as to permit participants to lose sight of the basic long-term financial security intent of deferred profit sharing plans.

Access to profit sharing funds may also be provided through a loan provision. The loan has an advantage over withdrawal in that the borrowed funds are not treated as taxable income to the participants. Furthermore, the participant may deduct the interest he pays for the loan. Equally important is that the loan must be repaid thereby preserving the long-term objective of the plan.

The plan must include the terms under which loans will be made. If the specified interest rate is too low and the specified repayment schedule is too lenient, the Internal Revenue Service may refuse to qualify the plan. Generally the amount that can be borrowed is limited to 75 percent of the participant's equity in the employer's contributions and 100 percent of his equity in his own contributions. The loans may be restricted to specific purposes such as home construction or repair, home mortgage payments, expenses of illness or death in the family, education of the children, or for any sound purpose in keeping with the long-term objectives of the plan. A waiting period may be required in order to protect the liquidity position of the fund.

4. LEVEL OF BENEFITS

The size of the benefits to be paid employees upon retirement is an important consideration in designing a pension plan. The employer must be concerned not only with the adequacy of the pension benefits but also with his ability to finance it. In fixing the benefit formula, management will have to reach a compromise between its desire to give employees an attractive pension and the even stronger urge to return reasonable profits to the owners of the business.

Pension benefits usually are of the conventional type in which periodic benefits are expressed in terms of a fixed amount of dollars. An increasing number of plans are expressing benefits in terms of an investment unit with a variable dollar value. Some plans combine the fixed dollar and variable features.

Benefit Formulas. Benefit formulas either establish a definite benefit or a definite contribution. Definite benefit formulas are the flat amount, the flat percentage of earnings, the flat amount unit benefit, and the percentage unit benefit. Definite contribution formulas are known as money purchase formulas.

DEFINITE BENEFIT FORMULAS. Under the *flat amount* formula, all participants upon retirement are given the same benefit regardless of their earnings, age, and to some extent their years of service. For example, all employees meeting some minimum credited service requirement such as 25 years will be given a monthly retirement benefit of, say, $100 a month. Employees who reach retirement age with less than 25 years of credited service will be given a reduced benefit, for example, $80 a month for 20 years, or $60 a month for 15 years.

The flat amount formula has been used in a number of negotiated plans but upon renegotiation many of these plans have been modified so that the flat amount became the minimum benefit if the formula to be used in its place produces a lower benefit.

A formula that relates pension benefits to earnings but not to years of service is the *flat percentage formula*. Under the flat percentage formula, a pension equal to a given percentage of the employee's average annual compensation is paid to all employees completing a minimum number of years of credited service. The flat percentage formula gives no reward to years of credited service beyond the minimum. Employees who fail to meet the minimum service requirement are given a proportionately reduced pension. The percentage used varies widely among plans being as low as 15 percent in some plans and as high as 70 percent in others with the common range being 20 percent to 50 percent. The average compensation to which the percentage applies may be the average earnings of the employee over the full period of his participation in the plan or, more commonly, the average of his earnings over the final few years of his participation. Earnings to be counted usually exclude overtime pay and bonuses.

A formula that relates benefits to years of service but not to earnings is the flat amount unit benefit formula. Under the *unit benefit formula* the employee is given one unit of benefit per month for each year of credit service. Credited service may be less than actual service because the years of service rendered by the employee before he becomes eligible to participate in the plan might not be counted. Also, there might be a maximum set for the number of years to be credited. Furthermore, years of service beyond the normal retirement age also might not be counted. In addition, credit might not be given for service rendered before the plan is installed. A full year of credited service usually will require a minimum number of hours worked such as, for example, 1,600. A participant who has worked fewer hours than the minimum usually will be given partial credit for the year.

Under the flat amount unit benefit formula, the employee will be given, say, $4 for each year of service. Under this formula an employee with 30 years of service would receive a monthly pension of $120. The flat amount unit benefit formula is used in a number of negotiated plans and the amounts range widely, some providing $2 or less and others $5 or more.

The unit benefit formula may be used to relate benefits not only to years of service but also to earnings by using a percentage formula. Under the percentage formula, the employee will be given, say, $1\frac{1}{2}$ percent of earnings for each year of service. Using this formula an employee with 30 years of service would receive a monthly pension of 45 percent of earnings. The earnings to which the percentage is to be applied in determining the amount of the pension may be the compensation earned during the year in which the unit benefit is accumulated (career average) or upon earnings during the last 5 or 10 years before retirement (final average). Many variations of the final average compensation plan are in use such as compensation for the year immediately before retirement or average compensation for the five consecutive years of highest pay. Because inflation has made benefits computed on the basis of the career average inadequate, a final average earnings formula is becoming popular.

The percentage of earnings used in the percentage formula plans vary widely, being 1 percent or less in some plans and 2 percent or more in other plans.

When an established company puts in a pension plan, a number of employees will be on the payroll who have already accumulated many years of service. If the percentage is to be applied to the career average earnings, the years of past service usually are rewarded at a lower rate than are years of service rendered after the plan has become effective.[69] For example, the employee may be given a monthly pension equal to 2 percent of earnings for each year of future service and 1 percent for each year of past service. The differential is justified by the higher cost of providing past service benefits.[70]

The discrimination against past service credits may be only illusory. The 1 percent used in the foregoing illustration to determine the amount of the past service benefit is applied to the employee's current earnings at the time the plan is installed rather than to the amount he actually earned while rendering the past service. Because of normal increases in earnings over the years of employment, the higher base will compensate to some extent for the lower rate.

Plans under which the percentage applies to final earnings usually apply

---

[69] The Commission on Insurance Terminology has defined past service benefit as "that portion of a participant's retirement benefit that relates to his period of credited service before the effective date of the plan." Future service benefit is defined as "that portion of a participant's retirement benefit that relates to his period of credited service after the effective date of the plan." (*Bulletin of the Commission, op. cit.*, Vol. 1, No. 2, May, 1965.)

[70] The cost of providing past service benefits is greater than the cost of providing current service benefits because of the role that interest earnings play in pension financing. No interest will be earned on unfunded past service benefits. In contributory plans, a differential between past service and current service is further justified because past service benefits must be financed entirely by the employer.

the same percentage for each year of service allowed. However, limitations may be placed on the amount of past service credits allowed either by ignoring past service credits in excess of a given number, counting only those past services credits earned beyond a specific age, or eliminating the first 5 or 10 years of past service.

The percentage unit benefit formula is widely used because of the prevailing opinion that it is equitable to reflect both earnings and service in determining the size of the pension.

Under the flat amount, flat percentage, and unit benefit formulas, the benefits are determined in advance by a fixed formula. The projected cost will fluctuate according to interest, mortality, expense, and employee turnover assumptions; funding methods used; employee population data; and in many plans also according to trends in salary and wage scales, and the ages at which employees choose to retire.[71] Obviously the cost will be a variable factor, although the benefit is based on a fixed formula.

MONEY PURCHASE FORMULAS. Some business firms are willing to install a pension plan only if the costs can be budgeted in advance and related to unit cost of production. These firms use the money purchase formula. Under this plan a percentage of the worker's pay (normally from 5 to 10 percent) is set aside by the employer and sometimes matched by the employee. The contributions may be based only on the earnings in excess of or below a given amount. The amount of the retirement benefit will be determined by how much the contributions can buy. The amount of retirement annuity that can be purchased with the contribution each year will decrease as the employee grows older. (A deferred annuity costs more when purchased at age 40 than when purchased at 35.) Higher contributions produced by increased earnings may to some degree offset the normal increase in cost from advancing age. (Employees are expected to earn more as they advance through the ranks and as inflation pushes up wage levels.) The employee, however, bears the risk of an increase in the annuity rate scale of the insurer.

While the definite cost associated with the money purchase plan appeals to the employer, the indefinite amount of the benefit it produces is not attractive to the employee.

The plan is particularly unattractive to employees with a relatively long past service record (contributions made for past service will not purchase comparable benefits at the employee's current age) and to the employees who join the plan at advanced ages (contributions for them will be made for fewer years and each contribution purchases a comparatively small benefit). To make the money purchase plan more palatable to these employees, some employers apply the formula only to future service, handling past service by a unit benefit formula or a minimum benefit. For employees

---

[71] Cost of pension benefits is discussed in Chapter 19.

who enter the program at older ages, a higher percentage of earnings may be contributed than for those who enter the plan at younger ages.

Profit Sharing Plans.   Some employers prefer to relate the amount of their contributions for employee retirement to profits rather than to payroll especially if their profits fluctuate widely from year to year.[72] How much of the company's profit will be turned over to finance retirement benefits will vary widely among companies. Some companies will have no formula leaving the amount of the contribution to be determined by management on a year to year basis.[73] The Internal Revenue Service, however, requires that there be frequent and recurring contributions. Other companies will use a formula: a percentage of gross profits; a percentage of net profits; a percentage of the profits available after the payment of a minimum dividend on common stock; a percentage of the net profits available after deducting a fixed percentage of invested capital; or a graded percentage of net profits, i.e., 5 percent of the first $25,000, 8 percent of the next $25,000, and so on. Obviously if the employee has to accept a deferred profit sharing plan rather than a bona fide pension plan, the least he should be asked to take is a formula plan and not a discretionary plan.

The plan must provide a definite predetermined formula for allocating among the employees the profits apportioned to the fund. Allocation formulas usually consider earnings and service. A system of points can be developed for each year of service and each $100 of annual earnings.

In some deferred profit sharing plans, employees are required to contribute a percentage of their salaries in order to participate in the employer's contributions.

The retirement benefit available to the employee is determined in the same why as in the money purchase pension plan.

Integration with Social Security.   Pension formulas frequently take into consideration benefits payable under social security. These plans either reduce the benefits otherwise provided under the formula by a percentage of the employee's social security benefit or exclude employees who earn less than a given level of compensation, usually the maximum earnings subject to social security taxes when the plan is installed or revised. As long as the combined pension and social security benefit does not result in discrimination in favor of higher paid employees, these types of benefit formulas will meet the qualification rules of the Internal Revenue Service.

Plans with formulas that consider social security payments in fixing the

---

[72] Because the qualification requirements for deferred profit sharing plans will not allow contributed profits to be allocated to employees on the basis of the ages of the participants, a retirement plan based on profit sharing is not likely to handle adequately the retirement needs of employees who are near retirement when the plan is installed.

[73] The President's Committee on Corporate Pension Funds and other Private Retirement and Welfare Programs recommended in its report "that, in order to qualify for special tax treatment, a profit sharing plan be required to provide for employers' contributions in accordance with a predetermined formula . . . which could only be changed for valid business reasons." (*Public Policy and Private Pension Programs, op. cit.,* p. 68.)

level of private pension benefits are called integrated plans. The Internal Revenue Service has developed regulations for integrating qualified retirement plans with two types of integrated plans—the offset plan and the excess plan.

THE OFFSET PLAN.   An offset pension plan is one under which the retirement benefit payable to a participant is reduced by a percentage of his social security benefit.

An offset plan meets the integration rules if the total benefits of the plan are offset by no more than a maximum of 83⅓ percent of the employee's primary insurance amount (dependent's benefits do not count) set by the social security amendments of 1967, or a maximum of 75 percent of the employee's primary amount set by the Social Security Act in effect on the day the employee retires. These maximum percentages apply only to those plans that fit the following conditions:

1. No preretirement death benefits are provided.
2. The normal form of retirement benefit is a straght life annuity (no postretirement death benefit).
3. A minimum of 15 years of service is required to qualify for full benefits.
4. Normal retirement age is at least 65 for males and 60 for females.

If the plan does not conform to all of the foregoing conditions, the maximum percentage integration rate is reduced. For example, if the plan offers preretirement benefits found in the typical retirement annuity or retirement income policy, the basic maximum integration rate is reduced by one ninth. If the normal retirement benefit is a life annuity, 10 years certain, the basic maximum integration rate is reduced by 10 percent. If the plan provides for early retirement (before age 60 for women, age 65 for men), it can be integrated by deferring the applicable offset until age 60, female, and age 65, male, and then reducing the applicable offset by the percentage obtained by dividing the years of actual service by the years of potential service to age 60, female, and age 65, male. If the plan provides for normal benefits with less than 15 years of service, the maximum offset rate is reduced by one fifteenth for each year of service under 15 accumulated by the employee at the time he retires.

The offset plan is rarely used because of its lack of appeal to employees. Employees pay social security taxes and fail to understand why any part of their social security retirement benefits should be used as an offset against benefits payable under their employer's retirement plan. Furthermore, they object to increases in social security retirement benefits being used to reduce their employer's cost rather than to improve their own retirement programs. The concept of the offset plan is at best questionable. Private programs should be designed to add to public programs rather than to take away from them.

THE EXCESS PLAN. An excess plan is one under which employees are covered only if their annual earnings exceed a given amount, usually the maximum wage base for social security at the time the plan is established or revised. A modified excess plan is one that does not exclude earnings under a given level but provides higher benefits for earnings above a given level, again usually the maximum wage base. The modified excess plan is viewed as a uniform plan for the lower benefits and an excess plan for the stepped-up benefits.

An excess plan providing straight percentage retirement benefits meets the integration rules if the benefits based on an employee's annual earnings in excess of those covered by social security do not exceed a maximum rate of 30 percent. The 30 percent figure is computed as follows: the employee's retirement benefit under social security is assumed to equal 36 percent of the average monthly wage base increased to 54 percent (1½ times) to reflect survivorship benefits. It is assumed that the employee pays 50 percent of the cost thus producing a maximum integration rate of 27 percent (one half of 54 percent). The Internal Revenue Service raised the percentage arbitrarily from 27 percent to 30 percent in recognition of an expectation of future amendments to the Social Security Act.

An employee's covered compensation is the average of his maximum wages covered by social security during his career. If an employee were always covered by the maximum wage base, his average covered compensation may be determined in accordance with the following age brackets:

Employees Reaching Age 65	Covered Compensation
Before 1972	$5,400
1972 through 1978	6,000
1979 through 1993	6,600
1994 through 2,000	7,200
2,001 ------	7,800

Thus, for an employee reaching age 65 in 1977, normal retirement benefits under an excess plan would be limited to 30 percent of $6,000. For an employee reaching age 65 in 1990, benefits would be limited to 30 percent of $6,600. For employees reaching age 65 in 1999, the limit would be 30 percent of $7,200, and it would be 30 percent of $7,800 for employees reaching age 65 in the year 2006. The employee's average compensation must be based on a period of not less than five consecutive years.

The 30 percent rule applies only to those plans that meet the same four conditions established for the offset plan relating to preretirement death benefits, the normal retirement annuity, years of service, and normal retirement ages, plus one additional condition: the plan must be noncontributory. The adjustment factors for the maximum integration rate are the same for the excess plan as for the offset plan regarding preretirement death benefits, normal retirement annuities expressed in terms of period certain guarantees, and for plans under which employees with less than 15 years of service can qualify for normal retirement benefits. However, for plans allowing early retirement benefits, the adjustment factor requires a reduction of the maximum integration rate by one fifteenth for each year that benefits begin for females before age 60 and for males prior to age 65. If the plan is contributory, the maximum integration rate may be increased by one eighth or one twelfth of the employee's contribution depending upon the nature of the plan.[74]

A unit benefit plan meeting the foregoing five conditions is properly integrated if the benefit for each year of credited service is no more than 1 percent of the employee's excess compensation for that year; no more than three fourths of 1 percent of the employee's average annual excess compensation; no more than 1 percent of actual annual compensation in excess of (a) $4,800 prior to 1968 and (b) maximum wages covered by social security after 1967; or no more than three fourths of 1 percent of the employee's average annual compensation in excess of (a) $4,800 prior to 1968 and (b) maximum wages covered by social security after 1967.

A money purchase plan is properly integrated if the employer does not contribute more than 6 times the maximum allowable rate under an integrated unit benefit plan when the rate of employer contributions is based on actual compensation.

The excess plan is the popular method of integrating private pension plans with social security.

Desirable Level of Retirement Income. Pension experts generally agree that the minimum pension when combined with social security should equal at least 50 percent of preretirement income to be considered adequate.[75] But if the benefit is fixed at this level throughout retirement, the retired employee is exposed to the purchasing power risk and is denied the opportunity to share in an increasing standard of living arising out of a growing economy. To protect the annuitant against the adverse effects of rising prices and to give him a stake in a growing economy, some plans provide for variable benefits. The benefits may be related to a cost-of-living index adjusted for improved living standards, or the benefit may be expressed in terms of a fixed number of units which vary in terms of their dollar values. This latter arrangement is the variable annuity. Under the

---

[74] If the plan's benefits and employee contributions are based on current compensation, and the plan is a unit benefit plan without life insurance benefits, the maximum benefit rate may be increased by one eighth of the employee's contribution rate. If the plan's benefits are based on average annual compensation and the employee contribution rate is based on actual compensation, the allowable increase is one twelfth of the employee's contribution rate.

[75] The 50 percent reduction is based on the assumption that one half of preretirement income would enable the retired employee to maintain his general preretirement standard of living because of lower living costs: entertainment is at a slower pace, maintenance expenses for clothing, transportation, and food are lower, homes are paid for, and the children are no longer dependent.

variable annuity plan the size of the retirement annuity payment fluctuates according to the market value of the investment portfolio supporting the annuity. When the variable annuity plan is used the employee's dollar benefits are converted into units at the unit value when the conversion is made.

Another form of variable pension benefit is the escalated benefit under which the retired employee's benefit is increased by a given percentage each year.

Variable pensions of one type or another are gaining in popularity as both labor and management accept the thesis that the economy has built-in inflationary biases, and respond to the need for giving full consideration to solving the difficulties that inflation and growth create for the worker living on pension income.

5. EMPLOYEE PARTICIPATION IN FINANCING

An important question in pension planning is whether the employee should be asked to contribute a portion of the cost. Should the plan be contributory or noncontributory?

In answering this question, the problems of administration, cost, control, and employee relations need to be considered.

The Issues.   The noncontributory plan has the advantage of ease of administration. A noncontributory plan automatically covers everyone in the group without having to use pressure to get employee participation. In addition to eliminating the selling job, the noncontributory plan cuts out the paper work involved in withholding funds from participating employees, and reduces the possibility of clerical errors.

Some cost considerations favor the contributory plan both from the employer's and the employee's point of view. More attractive benefits can be offered employees for each dollar spent by the employer. The additional benefits purchased through employee contributions usually are better dollar for dollar than the employee could purchase individually for the same amount of money.

But income tax considerations favor the noncontributory plan. The employer may deduct as necessary business expenses the contributions he makes to qualified pension plans and the employee does not have to report these contributions as current income, except those contributions used to purchase life insurance for him in conjunction with the pension plan. The employee reports the pension income only when he receives it at which time he is likely to have a lower marginal tax rate. Furthermore, if the employee's accumulated pension benefits under noncontributory plans are paid within one taxable year to the employee upon termination of employment or to his beneficiary upon his death, these payments are accorded favorable income tax treatment as discussed in Chapter 17. Also, death benefits paid from employer's contributions to qualified pension plans are not subject to the federal estate tax in the deceased employee's estate.[76]

As for control, the employer expects to have full freedom in administering the plan when he is financing its entire cost. On the other hand, when the cost is shared, employees may expect to be given some degree of responsibility in planning and administering the program. In negotiated plans, however, the method of financing may have little to do with administration and control. Unions tend to favor noncontributory plans as well as retention of some measure of control. They reason that since money spent for pensions is money which might otherwise be spent for wages, workers should have some say as to how this money is spent.

Some argue that contributory plans have greater employee relations value because only the employee who appreciates the plan will enroll in it. When he pays part of the cost, the employee is more conscious of plan benefits, and consequently the coverage does not go unnoticed. Others argue that noncontributory plans are better for employee relations. Employees are likely to look upon noncontributory plans as free, whereas they might assume that under contributory plans they are paying the full cost. The employer's contribution might be ignored completely.

Realistically, it seems that the employee relations value of a pension program is not dependent on any one particular method of financing it. Employees rarely object when the employer picks up the check. However, if an adequate pension program is possible only under a contributory plan, employees usually will prefer to pay part of the cost rather than accept a cheap plan.

Practical Considerations.   Employee contributions under a contributory plan may be related to benefits or to employer contributions. For example, under a defined benefits plan, the employee may be given a retirement benefit equal to 2 percent of his compensation for each year of credited service. The employee's contributions might then be fixed at one and one-half or two times that amount, making the employee contribute 3 or 4 percent of his compensation per year. How much of his own retirement benefit an employee's contribution will purchase will be a function of the age of the employee, the compensation (career average or final pay) upon which benefits are based, and the actual (as distinguished from the projected) cost of each dollar of benefits.

Under a defined contributions plan, the employee may be asked to contribute a percentage of earnings related to the contribution made by the employer. For example, the employer and the employee may each con-

---

[76] The estate and gift tax exemption of employer financed benefits from qualified retirement plans were judged to be inequitable by the President's Committee on Corporate Pension Funds and Other Private Retirement and Welfare Programs (*Public Policy and Private Pension Programs, op. cit.,* pp. 66–67). The Committee recommended the elimination of the special gift and estate tax exemptions afforded qualified pension plans.

tribute 6 percent, or the employee may be asked to contribute 5 percent and the employer 10 percent.

There is no definitive answer to the question of how much an employee should be asked to contribute. A decision on this matter involves a mix of financial and labor considerations centering around industry-wide and company wage levels and structure, current and long-term profit outlook, size of pension desired, and the nature and level of other employee benefit plans.

If contributions are to be asked from employees to support a system of employee benefits, it would seem that because of income tax considerations it would be better for the employees if these contributions were made toward the financing of retirement and disability income benefits rather than used to help finance survivorship or medical care benefits. All benefits paid under life insurance and medical care insurance plans are income tax-free. Disability income benefits payable under a noncontributory plan are reportable as income to the employee when he receives them subject to a deduction of $100 a week after a 30 day waiting period.[77] Under a contributory plan, disability income benefits attributable to the employee's contributions are excludable from gross income.[78] Thus a contributory disability income plan will provide some nontaxable income during the first 30 days, and some additional nontaxable income beyond the 30 day period if the benefits are in excess of $100 a week. Under a noncontributory retirement plan, all benefits are reportable as income when received but under a contributory retirement plan the employee may exclude from his taxable income an amount equal to his contribution to the plan.

The following observations can be made about the mix between noncontributory and contributory plans in the United States. (1) About 75 percent of the plans are noncontributory; (2) about 75 percent of the covered employees are participating in noncontributory plans; (3) most multiemployer plans are noncontributory; (4) about 30 percent of the single employer plans are contributory; and (5) a higher portion of nonbargained plans than bargained plans are contributory.[79] In some plans, contributory and noncontributory employees are given the right to make contributions to increase their pension. The earnings on these contributions are not taxed until they are distributed to the employee.[80]

---

[77] If the sick pay received is not more than 75 percent of the employee's regular weekly wage, the employee can exclude up to $75 a week sick pay during the first 30 days provided he is hospitalized for 1 day during the 30-day period. If he is not hospitalized, and his sick pay is not more than 75 percent of his regular pay, he can exclude up to $75 a week during the 23 days following a 7-day waiting period.

[78] The proportion of benefits received which are attributable to employee contributions is an amount which bears the same ratio to the total amount of benefits received as the total amount of employee contributions over the last three years bears to the total amount of contributions (employee and employer) paid over these same years.

[79] *Labor Mobility and Private Pension Plans, op. cit.,* p. 7.

[80] The Internal Revenue Service will not object to voluntary contribution provisions in a pension plan if these contributions are restricted to a reasonable amount. The Internal

6. PRIORITIES OF ALLOCATING PLAN ASSETS

Provision must be made in the pension agreement for allocating the fund assets among the participants whose benefits are vested in the event that the plan is terminated or contributions are discontinued. If the funding instrument (see Chapter 19) is allocated, the participant usually receives the paid up benefits already purchased for him. If the funding instrument is unallocated as in a trust fund plan or certain types of insurance company plans, a system of priorities usually is established. The plan may provide that after employees are returned their own contributions, the fund assets will be distributed in the following order, usually as paid up annuities: (1) retired employees (2) employees not yet retired but past normal retirement age (3) disabled employees (4) employees not yet retired but past early retirement age and (5) employees with vested interests. Any remaining funds are distributed to the other employees not included in the foregoing classes.

Another system sometimes used provides for the allocation of assets to purchase benefits for accumulated current service credits for all employees, with any remaining assets used to honor past service credits on a pro rata basis.

It is important that the resulting allocation plan not discriminate in favor of the prohibited group of employees if the plan is to be qualified (see Chapter 17).

Revenue Service considers that a maximum of 10 percent of earnings is reasonable. If employee optional contributions are matched by the employer, then a maximum of 6 percent is reasonable, otherwise discrimination ordinarily results. An Internal Revenue Service ruling specifies that if an employee is allowed to withdraw voluntary contributions before severing his employment, he must forfeit the accumulated interest on these contributions.

19

Insurance in Employee Benefit Plans: Retirement Funding Policy*

If the employer pays his retired employees their pension benefits each year from current cash flow,[1] he has no further decisions to make regarding funding policy. He has simply decided upon a policy of no funding.[2] But if the decision is made to set aside funds in excess of that amount needed to pay current benefits to employees who have already retired, then a number of issues relating to this policy of funding need to be resolved.[3] These include the questions of (1) the degree to which the plan will be funded, (2) the actuarial cost method to be used, (3) the actuarial cost assumptions to be made, (4) the funding agency to be chosen, (5) the funding instrument to be selected, and (6) the funding medium to be designated.

---

* The funding illustrations used in this chapter assume (1) no change in the benefit formula between the entry age of the employee and his retirement at age 65; (2) no disability benefits; (3) no vesting; (4) a $4\frac{1}{2}$ percent interest assumption; and (5) a termination rate based on the 1960 Standard Group Annuity Table combined with low turnover rates. The formulas for developing the illustrations and the computations used in arriving at the results are described in the appendix to this chapter.

[1] Cash flow is the difference between cash inflow and cash outflow over a particular period. If the net cash inflow is positive, the firm's stock of cash increases. If it is negative, the stock decreases. A sound, profitable business should have no trouble meeting its pension obligations even in periods of negative cash flow and a temporarily low cash position. Credit resources generally will be available.

[2] The fact that he has decided not to fund the plan, however, does not mean that he has no interest in the valuation of his obligations under the plan. Measurement of pension obligations is discussed later in this chapter.

[3] It is assumed that the funding policy will be so designed that the plan will be approved as qualified by the Internal Revenue Service. Therefore the funds will be set aside irrevocably and will be turned over to a trustee or an insurance company.

496

1. THE DEGREE OF FUNDING

The degrees of funding can range all the way from no funding at all to perpetuity funding. A no-funding system, sometimes curiously called funding by current disbursements,[4] requires all pension payments to be made directly by the employer. No payments are made from a special irrevocable pension fund because no fund will have been accumulated. And, because there is no accumulated fund to earn investment income, no part of the pension benefits will be paid from income tax-free investment income.

A perpetuity funding system requires that the employer set aside in one lump sum a fund sufficient to honor all pension obligations as they mature without the employer ever having to make additional contributions. Under perpetuity funding, all pension benefits will be paid from income tax-free investment income.[5] Perpetuity funding is at best only a theoretical concept. In the first place, no business would be willing to use its assets to fund its pension obligations in perpetuity even were it able to do so. In the second place, perpetuity funding is likely to be actuarially impossible. A condition precedent for perpetuity funding is a stable employee population. In addition the actuary must not underestimate the value of the variables that go into determining the ultimate cost of the plan;[6] otherwise the fund would not be adequate to support the plan's benefit structure on a perpetual basis.

The process of making a decision on the degree of funding to be achieved involves a tradeoff of the costs and benefits of using the current disbursements approach with those of using a funded approach. A funded approach may be one of terminal funding or of advance funding. Advance funding may be partial or full. A plan is partially funded and meets the funding requirements of the Internal Revenue Service when there is full funding of benefits accumulating for employees after the plan has been established (current service credits) and the unfunded "liability" for the benefits granted to employees under the terms of the plan when the plan is established (past service credits) is frozen by funding the current interest on this "liability." A plan is fully funded when (1) the annual contributions to the fund are sufficient to cover the accumulating "liability" for current service credits for that year and (2) the fund has

---

[4] Rather than use the contradictory term current disbursements funding to describe a plan that is not funded, the terminologists have chosen to substitute the expression current disbursements approach to meeting pension obligations as a means of distinguishing this approach from funded approaches. Current pension financing seems a more appropriate term.

[5] The entire one-time contribution will not be deductible by the employer in the year made. The employer's annual deduction is limited by Section 404 of the Internal Revenue Code. The amount of contribution in excess of the maximum allowable deduction can be carried forward from year to year until the full deduction is taken. See Chapter 17.

[6] These variables are discussed later in this chapter.

received contributions sufficient to cover the accumulated "liability" for past service credits.[7]

Current Disbursements Approach. The current disbursements approach has some attractions and some limitations.

BENEFITS.   An important benefit of the current disbursements approach is that little money is needed initially to operate the plan. The employer does not have to accumulate funds with a trustee or insurance company over long periods of time in advance of their disbursement to retired employees. Instead these funds can be invested in the employer's business, and in many cases, produce earnings which even after taxes will exceed the tax-free earnings produced by insurers or trustees managing qualified funds. Furthermore, since there is no need to qualify a current disbursements pension plan, the employer has greater freedom in designing the plan. He can discriminate in favor of key employees. In fact, the current disbursements approach is used by a number of employers to provide selected employees with benefits in addition to those provided under qualified plans.

Under the current disbursements approach, the financial burden of providing the pensions is not spread over all or even part of the working lives of covered employees. Instead it is spread over the period during which employees are retired. Because more and more employees will be in the retired class as the plan ages, the incidence of the burden is shifted from the initial years of the plan to the later years of the plan. For example, assume that the plan is written for a work force with a stationary population, which means that the number of people of each sex reaching the qualifying age for retirement benefits will be replaced by an equal number of people of each sex reaching the qualifying age for coverage.[8] Under the current disbursements approach, the financial burden of the plan will be low initially but will rise steeply until it reaches a plateau. If the age for coverage is 25 and the age for retirement is 65, the plateau will be reached in 40 years when the size of the retired group will be stabilized. At the plateau level, the burden of financing the plan will be higher than it would be under funded plans regardless of the degree of funding. The reason, of course, is that a part of the pension payments under funded plans is paid from interest earned on the accumulated funds.

COSTS.   The unevenness over time of the burden of pension obligations

---

[7] Quotation marks are used to enclose liability to indicate that accrued credits usually are not liabilities in the legal sense of the word because the employer generally is not legally obligated to pay benefits under the plan. (See Benjamin Aaron, *Legal Status of Employee Benefit Rights Under Private Pension Plans* [Homewood, Illinois: Richard D. Irwin, Inc., 1966], and Edwin W. Patterson, *Legal Protection of Private Pension Expectations* [Homewood, Illinois: Richard D. Irwin, Inc., 1960].)

[8] If the plan's qualifying age for retirement is 65 and its qualifying age for coverage is 25, then a stationary population means that the number of men and women reaching age 65 will be replaced by an equal number of men and women age 25. The concept of a stationary population is useful for measuring the incidence of the burden of financing pension plans under various degrees of funding. Obviously pension planners do not deal with stationary populations.

and the lack of tax-free investment income to offset the higher ultimate financial burden of the plan are among the costs to be considered in evaluating the current disbursements approach in comparison with the funded approach to pension finance.

Other costs of the current disbursements approach are financing inflexibility and employee dissatisfaction. Under the current disbursements approach, the plan has to be financed entirely by the employer. Unless the employer funds the plan, he is in no position to ask the employees to contribute to the cost of providing the benefits. Furthermore, financing flexibility is restricted in that the employer has to make the payments to the retired employees as the payments fall due. His contributions will vary from year to year according to the pension payments to be made, a variable over which the employer has no control if he is to meet the obligations he has assumed under the plan. Under a funded plan, the employer is in a position to vary his annual contributions independently of the pension payments to be made, a flexibility that could be helpful during periods of financial strain. During periods of reduced cash flows (or great cash needs) payments to a qualified pension fund usually can be reduced or postponed with little or no repercussions, but reduction or postponement of pension benefits payable to retired employees would create serious problems both in employee relations and in public relations.

Employees are not satisfied with current disbursement plans because they believe that these plans do not provide the security that should be accorded their pension benefits. Payment of benefits are dependent upon (1) the ability of the employer to pay these benefits as promised and (2) the willingness of the employer to pay the promised benefits. If for financial or other reasons the employer decides to terminate the plan, retired employees will no longer receive their monthly check and active employees will not get the pensions that they were led to believe would be provided for them during their retirement. Employees look to funded plans to give some sort of security to their retirement benefits although there is some awareness that funding in and of itself does not provide the maximum security for employees. The security of employee pension benefits is a function both of the reasonableness of the actuarial assumptions made in estimating the cost of the benefits and the degree to which the benefits are funded.

Types of Funding. Two types of funding are possible: terminal funding and advance funding.

TERMINAL FUNDING. Under terminal funding, benefits are not funded during the active life of an employee. However, when the employee retires, his benefits are funded in full by the employer who transfers to a trustee or insurance company the full amount of money necessary to provide the benefits as scheduled.[9] For example, if an employee is to be

---

[9] Under some plans, a system of postretirement funding is used where the employer does not fund benefits immediately in full. Instead he spreads the burden over a period of several

retired on a $200 monthly pension at age 65, no part of the pension is funded until the employee reaches age 65. Then the entire pension is funded by a deposit of about $27,000 with the trustee or insurer.[10] Terminally funded plans will be approved as qualified plans if they otherwise satisfy the qualification requirements of the Internal Revenue Service.[11]

Benefits. The benefits of terminal funding when compared with the current disbursements approach are that the financial burden of providing pensions is spread less unevenly over time, the burden at the plateau level will be lower, and employees will be less dissatisfied. Assuming a stationary population, the financial burden of the plan would be level at a contribution amount that would be initially higher and ultimately lower than under a current disbursements approach. The burden at the plateau level would be lower because investment earnings would be used to cover part of the pension payments. Employees will be less dissatisfied because at least the benefits for the retired workers would be secured.

When compared with advance funding, terminal funding offers the employer the benefit of a lower initial financial burden since only the benefits of retired employees need be funded. However, since the employee population is not stationary, terminal funding produces an uneven financial burden over the years. Annual outlays are likely to fluctuate widely especially during the early years of the plan, perhaps requiring contribution of such size in some years as to be inconvenient if not damaging. A study of the age distribution of employees will reveal if this is likely to be the case. If it is, then a system of postretirement funding under which the obligations to retired employees are funded over several years rather than at one time might provide the necessary relief.

Costs. One cost of terminal funding when compared with the current disbursements approach is the heavier financial burden that it produces in the earlier years. Funds need to be made available to cover the present value of the entire pension for each employee when he retires rather than just the month by month payments as under the current disbursements approach. Furthermore, in order to deduct the contributions in the year made the employer must qualify the plan. Therefore, another cost is the freedom that he must give up in order to meet the requirements for qualification, plus the expenses involved in qualifying the plan.

Terminal funding has most of the same costs as the current disbursements approach when compared with advance funding: financial inflexi-

---

years. These systems of funding also are called terminal funding to distinguish them from advance funding.

[10] The exact amount to be deposited is a function of the interest, mortality, and expense assumptions used in its computation.

[11] Terminal funding may be used to fund those negotiated plans under which the employer agrees to pay retirement benefits to employees who reach retirement age during the term of the collective bargaining contract. These plans will qualify if "the expected contributions will not be less than the full cost of prospective pensions for employees expected to retire under the plan" while the labor contract is in force.

bility and employee dissatisfaction. The opportunity to use several years over which to spread the burden of postretirement funding allows for at least some, though not much, flexibility of financing and the funding of benefits for the retired employee cuts down some of the employee dissatisfaction. Yet employers must finance the full cost of the pension, and active employees are given no benefit security.

ADVANCE FUNDING. Under advance funding, accumulations are made on a systematic basis during the active working lives of the employees to offset the cost of the pensions when they become payable. Given the actuarial assumptions, the degree of funding achieved is a function of the actuarial cost method used.

Benefits. A number of benefits arise from the advance funding of pension plans. Again the central question is whether these benefits outweigh their costs. Among the retirement plans covering 26 or more participants, only about 2 percent are unfunded plans.[12] Therefore, it would appear that the benefits of advance funding are so overwhelming for most pension planners that only in a few cases do these benefits fall short of costs.

Specifically, the benefits of advance funding are the opportunity for gaining some flexibility in spreading the financial burden of the plan, the chance to offset the cost of the plan with the maximum amount of tax-free investment income, and the possibility of gaining the maximum employee relations value from the plan. The extent to which these benefits are achieved is in some measure a function of the degree of advance funding.

Costs. Advance funding has the same costs as terminal funding when compared with the current disbursements approach. When compared with terminal funding, advance funding has the cost of a heavier financial burden in the early years of the plan. The employer may find it more profitable to invest the funds in his own business rather than place them with an insurance company or trustee for investment.

2. ACTUARIAL COST METHODS

Several methods are available for determining the amount of the employer's periodic contributions to the fund. These methods, known as actuarial cost methods, are defined as "a particular technique for establishing the amount and incidence of the normal costs, supplemental costs, and actuarial liabilities pertaining to the benefits of a pension plan."[13]

The normal cost referred to in the definition is the annual cost accrual for current service. The supplemental cost is the cost for service rendered

---

[12] President's Committee on Corporate Pension Funds and Other Private Retirement and Welfare Programs, *Public Policy and Private Pension Programs* (Washington, D.C.: U.S. Government Printing Office, January, 1965), p. 5–6.

[13] This definition is the one approved by the Commission on Insurance Terminology of the American Risk and Insurance Association.

before the plan was established and for increases in the benefits provided under the plan for service rendered before the benefit structure was amended. The actuarial liability is the amount by which the present value of the total benefits under the plan exceeds the sum of the present value of the total normal cost of the plan and the plan's assets. It is a measure of the supplemental liability under the plan.

Two actuarial cost methods broadly classified are the accrued benefit cost method and the projected benefit cost method. Under the accrued benefit cost method, normal cost and supplemental liability are handled separately. Under the projected benefit cost method, normal cost and supplemental liability may be separated or they may be handled together. The projected benefit cost method may be computed on an individual basis or on an aggregate basis.

The Accrued Benefit Cost Method. The accrued benefit is defined as:

one under which the actuarial costs are based directly upon benefits accrued to the date of cost determination, such benefits being determined either by the terms of the plan, or by some assumed allocation of total prospective benefits to years of service. With respect to the determination of the annual cost of the plan, the method assumes that a precisely determinable unit of benefit is associated with each year of a participant's credited service.[14]

The accrued benefit cost method is easily applied to pension plans using a unit benefit formula. For example, if under the benefit formula, the employee is provided a pension of $5 monthly at age 65 for each year of continuous service, the employer may contribute enough each year to fund in full the cost of a $5 monthly pension commencing at age 65. By the time a new employee now age 35 reaches age 65, the employer will have fully funded 30 separate pension units of $5 each, giving the employee a retirement income of $150 a month.[15] The amount of contribution needed to fund the accruing $5 pension benefit will increase each year. Understandably, the amount necessary to fund a $5 monthly pension varies inversely with the time period over which the fund can earn interest and reap the benefits of survivorship. At age 35, it would take $108.77 to fund a life income of $5 monthly starting at age 65. At age 40, it would take $149.98; at age 60, $433.40; and at age 64, $555.14.[16]

SUPPLEMENTAL LIABILITY. The foregoing computation assumes a new employee age 35. Suppose the plan is new and the 35-year-old employee has 10 years of credited service before the effective date of the plan? Here a supplemental liability is created.

A supplemental liability is a separate element of actuarial cost which appears when the actuarial cost method establishes future regular cost accruals whose actuarial present value is less than the actuarial present value of total projected

---

14 *Ibid.*

15 This assumes, of course, that the plan is insured or that the actuarial assumptions used prove to be adequate.

16 Cf. Appendix to this chapter, Section B1 (16) for the computations.

benefits of the plan. Such supplemental liabilities are generally (but not always) the result of applying the actuarial cost method on the assumption (explicit or implicit) that the actuarial cost accruals began before (a) the establishment of the plan, (b) the commencement of funding (or other recognition of cost accruals), or (c) a plan amendment increasing benefits.[17]

This supplemental liability frequently is called initial past service liability, or simply past service liability.

In the foregoing plan of $5 monthly at age 65 for each year of continuous service, the initial past service liability for the 35-year-old employee with 10 years of service would be the cost of a $50 monthly pension (10 × $5) commencing at age 65 funded at age 35. This would amount to $1,087.70, which is 10 times the $108.77 cost of funding the $5 monthly pension.

FUNDING THE SUPPLEMENTAL LIABILITY. Under the accrued benefit cost method, the normal cost of the pension for the 35-year-old employee with 10 years of past service would be funded on the $108.77 to $555.14 step-rate basis as illustrated, but the past service liability of $1,087.70 would be handled separately.

For qualified plans, the minimum contribution required by the Internal Revenue Service is an amount sufficient to fund current service cost each year and to cover the interest on the initial past service liability. Beyond that, the employer is free to adjust his contributions to whatever levels best fit his financial plans as long as he does not overfund. He may vary his contributions from year to year according to his cash position. Thus, with respect to the foregoing 35-year-old employee, the employer must contribute $108.77 this year to fund the current service cost and $48.95 to pay the interest on the unfunded past service liability, making a total of $157.72.[18] It will have increased to $198.96 when the employee reaches age 40, and to $600.10 when he reaches 64. The past service liability will remain unfunded. The minimum total contributions of the employer would be the sum of similar computations made for all covered employees. The illustrations here are based on one employee for the sake of simplifying the explanation.

If the employer wishes, he can fund the entire past service liability with a single contribution of $1,087.70. However, the maximum annual deduction that he can take for income tax purposes is 10 percent of the initial past service liability. This would amount to $108.77 a year for 10 years.

If the employer chooses to contribute only the maximum amount that can be deducted for income tax purposes each year, he can fund the $1,087.70 past service liability for this employee by contributing $108.77 a year for 12 years and $58.73 in the 13th year. More than 10 years of contributions are needed to fund the past service liability at the rate of

---

[17] See footnote 13.
[18] The interest of $48.95 is 4½ percent of $1,087.70.

10 percent a year in order to pay off the accumulating interest on the unpaid balance.

A common practice is to fund the past service liability over a 25-year period. In this event, the $1,087.70 of past service liability could be funded at the rate of $73.35 annually for 25 years, using a 4½ percent interest assumption. This level amount would be added to increasing normal cost during each of the first 25 years. Then the past service liability will have been retired.

Projected Benefit Cost Methods.   Instead of funding each benefit in full as it accrues, the employer may prefer to project the total benefit for the employee and fund its cost with equal annual contributions over the working life of the employee. A projected pension of $150 a month at age 65 for a new employee age 35 can be funded with level contributions of $221.58 a year.[19] This annual level amount of $221.58 compares with the step rates under a unit benefit system that starts at $108.77 for the first year and increases each year, reaching $555.14, the cost of funding the final $5 monthly benefit earned for the 30th year of service. How these two systems will affect the aggregate annual burden on the employer is a function of the age distribution of the employees. If the plan is written for a work force with a stationary population, the aggregate annual burden on the employer will be the same regardless of whether the plan is funded on the unit system or on a level basis.

FUNDING THE SUPPLEMENTAL LIABILITY.   How the employer funds the past service liability incurred when the plan is first installed also affects the amount of his periodic contributions. If it is assumed that the past service liability incurred when the plan was installed, has already been funded, then the employer has to concern himself only with how he would fund the normal cost of the plan, assuming also that there have been no amendments increasing benefits for services already performed and that the actuarial assumptions used in the computations have been realistic.[20]

Suppose, however, that the plan is just now being installed and that the 35-year employee had already accumulated 10 years of recognized service under the plan. This would mean that he already would have accumulated a monthly pension of $50 commencing at age 65. The employer has the problem of deciding how to fund his liability for the pensions already earned by this employee, and others like him, before the plan became effective.

The Attained Age Basis.   Under the level contribution projected benefit cost method, the employer may choose to fund his pension obligations on an attained age basis, lumping past service benefits with current service benefits and spreading the cost over the remaining working life of

---

[19] Cf. Appendix to this chapter, B2 (19) for the computation.

[20] The normal cost is defined as the cost of benefits earned for service rendered after the pension plan is installed, and after any amendments increasing the level of benefits for service already rendered.

the employee. Thus, for example, assuming a benefit formula of $5 monthly for each year of credited service, the 35-year-old employee with 10 years of past service will have accumulated a pension of $200 a month at age 65. This pension may be funded by an annual contribution from the employer of $295.44, of which $73.86 is used to fund past service liability and $221.58 is used to fund current service cost although there is no such specific allocation.[21] Thus, under this system the contributions are level and the past service liability is fully funded by the time the employee retires.

Under the more common funding system, past service liability and normal costs are handled separately rather than lumped together.

Entry Age Normal. When past service liability is handled separately under a level contribution projected benefit cost method, a system known as entry age normal is used. Under this system, the assumption is made that the normal cost of the plan has been funded each year from the age at which the employee entered employment or would have become eligible to participate in the plan. For example, assume that an employee with 10 years of covered service is age 35 when the plan is established. Under the benefit formula he is to receive a monthly pension at age 65 equal to $5 for each year of service. Thus, after 40 years of service his pension will be $200 monthly.

Under a level contribution system, the normal cost figured from the entry age 25 would be $141.61. The past service liability equals $2,266.05, the accumulated value of $141.61 a year for 10 years augmented by $402.31 in interest earnings, and $447.74 in survivorship benefits.[22]

The employer can meet the minimum funding requirements of the Internal Revenue Service by an annual contribution of $141.61 to fund the normal cost plus $101.97 to offset the interest on the unfunded past service liability—a total of $243.58 annually. The contribution will remain level and the past service liability will remain unfunded. If the employer chooses to fund the past service liability at the maximum rate allowable as a deduction under the income tax law, he can contribute $226.60 a year for 12 years and $122.36 in the 13th year. At this time the past service liability will have been funded and his total annual contributions $368.20 (which is $141.61 plus $226.60) will be reduced to $141.61, the normal cost. A common practice is to fund the past service liability over 25 years. In this event, his contributions would be $152.82 to fund past service liability and $141.61 to fund normal cost, making a total contribution of $294.43 a year for 25 years and $141.61 a year thereafter for the remaining 5 years.

Note that under entry age normal method of funding, the past service

---

[21] The pension earned by service performed after the plan is established equals $150 or three fourths of the total pension. Therefore, under the attained age level-contribution system of funding three fourths of the contributions ($221.58) is used to fund current service costs and one fourth ($73.86) is used for funding past service liability. Cf. Appendix to this chapter, B3 (20) for the computations.

[22] Cf. Appendix to this chapter, B4 (22) for the computations.

liability is higher than under the accrued benefit cost method. In this particular illustration, it is $2,266.05 compared to $1,087.70, assuming an employee age 35 with 10 years of credited service and a pension at age 65 of $5 monthly for each year of credited service. The reason is that total contributions from age 25 to age 35 would have been much higher under the projected benefit cost method than under the accrued benefit cost method. Furthermore, since the size of both the interest earnings and survivorship benefits is a function of total contributions, these elements also would have been higher.

AGGREGATE LEVEL COST METHOD.   An aggregate as distinguished from the individual level cost basis just discussed can be used in determining the amount of the employer's periodic contribution. Under the aggregate method, the contributions are computed on a collective basis without identifying particular individuals. Thus, rather than computing the level contribution for the employee age 35 and for each of the other employees separately, the contributions are computed for all employees as a group.

For example, assume the employee population data in Table 19–1. The

TABLE 19–1
Employee Population Data

Age Bracket	Midpoint in Bracket	Number of Employees	Total Annual Earnings	Average Annual Earnings	Average Years of Past Service
20–24	22	8	$ 36,000	$ 4,500	3
25–29	27	10	55,000	5,500	3
30–34	32	20	120,000	6,000	7
35–39	37	18	108,000	6,000	10
40–44	42	19	123,500	6,500	12
45–49	47	15	105,000	7,000	19
50–54	52	12	96,000	8,000	20
55–59	57	10	83,000	8,300	30
60–64	62	8	80,000	10,000	32
Totals			$796,500		136

pension formula provides for an annual retirement benefit at age 65 equal to 1½ percent of average annual earnings for each year of credit service. Assume that all employees are male and that earnings will remain the same.[23] The annual contribution under the aggregate level cost method is computed by multiplying the total annual earnings for each age bracket by the quotient of the present value of total projected benefits divided by the present value of total future earnings projected for each age bracket. Table 19–2 shows the necessary computations.

---

[23] These assumptions are unrealistic but they do help to simplify the illustration, because otherwise separate computations would have to be made for female employees and projections of salary scales would have to be made to determine benefit amounts.

TABLE 19–2

Illustration of Computation under Projected Benefit Cost Method—Aggregate Level Cost*

Midpoint Age Bracket (1)	Total Annual Earnings (2)	Total Years of Covered Service (Age 65 − Col.1 + Col.9) (3)	Total Projected Benefits (1½% of Col.2 × Col.3) (4)	Present Value of a Deferred Life Annuity Due of One Payable at Age 65 (t-1; 4½%) (5)	Present Value of Total Projected Benefits (Col.4 × Col.5) (6)	Present Value of Life Annuity of One Payable to Age 65 (t-1; 4½%) (7)	Present Value of Future Earnings (Col.2 × Col.7) (8)	Average Years of Past Service (9)
22	$ 36,000	46	$ 24,840	0.611	$ 15,277	12.617	$ 452,212	3
27	55,000	41	32,828	0.990	32,500	13.723	754,765	3
32	120,000	40	72,000	1.516	109,152	14.457	1,745,640	7
37	108,000	38	61,560	2.173	133,770	14.650	1,582,200	10
42	123,500	35	64,838	2.928	189,845	13.765	1,699,978	12
47	105,000	37	58,275	3.787	220,687	11.965	1,256,325	19
52	96,000	33	47,520	4.865	231,185	9.541	915,936	20
57	83,000	38	47,310	6.362	300,986	6.576	545,808	30
62	80,000	35	42,000	8.528	358,176	2.820	225,600	32
Total	$806,500	343	$451,171		$1,621,578		$9,068,464	136

* Cf. Appendix to this chapter, Section B5, for the computations in column 5, and Section B6 for the computations in column 7.

Based on the computations in Table 19–2, the annual contributions by the employer, assuming a noncontributory plan, needed to fund the plan under the aggregate level cost method would be the quotient of $1,621,578 (the total for Column [6]) divided by $9,068,464 (the total for Column [8]) multiplied by $806,500 (the total for Column [2]), or 0.1788 × $806,500, giving a product of $144,402. The annual contribution rate of 17.88 percent of total annual covered payroll will continue to be the employer's contribution under the following set of assumptions: (1) the benefit formula remains unchanged; (2) the earnings of the employees remain unchanged; (3) the termination experience conforms to the assumptions in the t-1 table; (4) the interest earned equals exactly $4\frac{1}{2}$ percent; and (5) no new employees are added.[24] These assumptions, of course, are unrealistic. Fund assets might accumulate more rapidly (or less rapidly) than anticipated; more (or fewer) employees will terminate than anticipated; inflation (or deflation) and increased (or decreased) productivity will not only alter the pay scales but will also cause a revision in the benefit structure; and business expansion (or contraction) will affect the numbers employed. Therefore, the contribution percentage will have to be computed periodically to keep it realistic.

The foregoing illustration of the aggregate level cost method of computing the employer's annual contributions under a noncontributory plan is based on the combined funding of past and current service costs. However, past service liability may be segregated and handled separately under the aggregate method just as under the individual method. Where the past service liability is treated separately, the present value of total projected benefits in Column (6) would be reduced by the present value of the benefits attributable to past service. For example, in the age 20–24 bracket, the past service benefits would be 3 (Column [9]) times $1\frac{1}{2}$ percent of $36,000 (Column [2]), or $1,620. The present value of these benefits is the product of $1,620 times 0.611 (Column [5]), or $960. The present value of total projected current service benefits would be $15,277 (Column [6] minus $990, or $14,317. Similar computations would have to be made for each of the other age brackets. The annual employer contribution rate would then be the quotient of the present value of total projected current service benefits divided by the present value of future earnings (Column [8]). This rate would amount to much less than 17.88 percent since the average years of past service (Column [9]) represent nearly 40 percent of the total years of covered service (Column [3]). The annual contribution of the employer would be the product of the contribution rate applied to total annual earnings plus the amount set aside to reduce (or at the minimum freeze by paying the interest on) the past serv-

---

[24] Another important assumption is that no arithmetical errors have been made in the foregoing computations, an assumption that makes the author a bit uneasy. This assumption also applies in all the other computations in this text, and the author has the same timidity about them.

ice liability. The amount contributed, if any, for funding past service liability is a function of the period over which the funding is to be spread. Common periods are 20 to 30 years or the time elapsing until the youngest participating employee is retired.

Funded Ratio. Throughout the foregoing discussion mention has been made of initial past service liability. However, additional liability for past service can develop even though initial past service has been funded if the benefits are later enriched.

The value of the fund assets plus the present value of contributions to meet current costs divided by the present value of projected benefits is called the funded ratio and is a measure of benefit security. The higher the ratio, of course, the greater the degree of employee benefit security. A number of factors can reduce (or increase) the funded ratio. Examples of these are a change in actuarial assumptions, a change in the value of accumulated assets, and a change in the benefit structure.

Defined Contribution Plans. Under the traditional defined contribution plan, the annuity received by the employee is a function of the amount of contribution paid by the employer rather than the other way around. Contributions are usually expressed as a fixed percentage of the earnings of the employees covered. Actuarial cost methods can be used to determine what these benefit levels are likely to be. However, in negotiated plans both benefits and contributions are likely to be fixed, with contributions usually expressed in terms of so many cents an hour. Actuarial cost methods are used to determine the benefit levels that can be provided, taking into consideration expected changes in the level of the payroll. Usually, past service liability is funded on an irregular basis, depending on the amount of the fixed contribution available after paying the normal cost of the plan.

3. ACTUARIAL COST ASSUMPTION

Given the benefit formula, the employee population data, and the actuarial cost method to be used, the size of the employer's scheduled periodic contributions to noncontributory pension plans is a function of the actuarial cost assumptions used.

The principal actuarial assumptions of concern in developing pension cost estimates are (1) mortality rates, (2) turnover rates, (3) disability rates, (4) retirement rates, (5) salary rates, (6) interest rates, and (7) expense rates. These assumptions are estimates, of course, and no one expects the experience to be just as projected. The most that can be asked of the actuary is that he give systematic attention to the selection of his assumptions and that he review them periodically to test their appropriateness in view of the changes likely to take place in the underlying conditions affecting these assumptions. Only the projected cost is a function of the actuarial assumptions used. The ultimate cost of the plan is a function of the actual benefits paid, actual expenses incurred, and actual investment income earned. The challenge to the actuary is to keep projected cost in line with the cost that ultimately will be experienced.[25]

The actuary's job is to make the necessary valuation of the plan's assets and liabilities so that the employer is informed of the plan's funded ratio and knows what changes he needs to make in his contributions if he wants to maintain a given funded ratio. The liabilities of the plan are the present values of the pension payments to be made to active employees when they retire and to employees already retired. The assets of the plan are the value of the funds already accumulated and the present value of the periodic contributions budgeted by the employer. While the services of an actuary might not be needed in the valuation of assets accumulated from previous contributions, his services are essential in computing the present value of employer contributions.[26] The principal factors that concern the actuary in making his valuations are whether the employee will become eligible to collect benefits, what the size of benefits will be if he is eligible, how long will he collect them, and the interest rate to be used in discounting the value of these expected benefits to the date of the valuation.

Mortality Rates.   Mortality rates are used to measure (1) the probability that an employee will survive to retirement age and thus qualify for pension benefits and (2) the probable length of time that a pensioned employee will live to receive benefits. Mortality rates also are used in computing the present value of employer contributions under the various actuarial cost methods. Where death benefits are provided under the plan, mortality assumptions are necessary for projecting the cost of these benefits.

The projected cost of retirement benefits under pension plans varies inversely with the rate of mortality assumed in the computations because deaths cancel the necessity for paying retirement benefits. In funded plans, deaths among participating employees enhance the relative value of employer contributions already made. The projected cost of any death benefits varies directly with the assumed mortality rate.[27] Several mortality tables have been developed for use in computing annuity values.[28] The most popular one used for pension cost projections is the 1951 Group Annuity

---

[25] Sometimes an employer fails to understand that the ultimate cost of a pension plan is independent of its projected cost. As a result, he might be misled into making his funding arrangements on the basis of the lowest cost projection provided him by some actuary in private practice who hopes to become the plan's actuary.

[26] The question of the valuation of investments held in a pension fund is one that does concern actuaries who are not content with valuations based on acquisition costs or market prices, but who seek what they believe could be a more realistic approach to the valuation of investment portfolios to be held over the long term.

[27] See Chapter 24 for a detailed discussion of the nature, construction, and development of mortality tables.

[28] The same mortality tables cannot be used in projecting the cost of annuity benefits as are used in projecting the cost of life insurance benefits. (See Chapter 24.) For example, a man age 35 would have a 78.7 percent chance of surviving to age 65 using the 1951 Group Annuity Table, but he would have only a 69.7 percent chance of surviving to age 65 using the Commissioners 1960 Standard Group mortality table, a table used in group life insurance rate making.

Table with various projection scales designed to reflect mortality improvement. A projection scale records the effects of assumptions made about the rate of mortality improvement to some particular date or as of some particular date. For example, under the 1951 Group Annuity Table, a male age 35 or female age 30 has a 78.7 percent chance of surviving to age 65. If the GA 1951 mortality rates are projected to 1965, a man age 35 has an 81.8 percent chance of surviving to age 65. And if the GA 1951 rates are projected as of 1965 into the indefinite future, a 35-year-old male or 30-year-old female would have an 85.6 percent chance of surviving to age 65. Note that for females the table is set back 5 years.

A common practice is to project the mortality rates to a recent date based on what is known as "projection scale C," and to set the ages back one year.[29] An age set back one year means simply that the figures given in the table for age 36, for example, are the ones used for dealing with participants age 35.

If the actuary has some reason to believe that the group with which he is dealing will experience mortality higher or lower than that shown in the 1951 Group Annuity Table, he will make the necessary adjustments by applying whatever projection he believes is suitable and by adjusting the ages to whatever levels he believes is appropriate. As the group develops mortality gains or losses, the actuary can modify his assumptions to conform with observed experience.

Of all the actuarial assumptions used in projecting the cost of a pension plan, actuaries have the most confidence in their mortality assumptions because of the proven reliability of mortality statistics.

Turnover Rates. Turnover rates are used to measure the probable number of employees who will leave the service of their employer prior to reaching normal retirement age. The projected cost of retirement benefits under a pension plan varies inversely with the rate of employee turnover assumed in the computations because employee terminations prior to full vesting relieve the employer from paying part, or all, of the retirement benefits. In funded plans, turnover among participating employees enhances the relative value of employer contributions. "Savings" from employee turnover are discounted in estimating the total benefits to be paid under the plan and in computing the present value of employer contributions under the various actuarial cost methods. Turnover rates are used

---

[29] "Projection scale A" assumes that mortality rates will continue to decrease at the same rate as during the relatively recent past. "Projection scale B" assumes that there will be a smaller rate of decrease at the younger ages and a higher rate of decrease at the older ages because those at the older ages are more likely to benefit from scientific discoveries applicable to the art of medicine. Projection scale C assumes that since mortality rates among group annuitants are higher than those among individual annuitants, a higher rate of improvement can be anticipated in the mortality rates among group annuitants. Therefore, under projection C the assumption is made that the mortality rate reduction will be one and one half times that of projection B but in no event more than an annual reduction of $1\frac{1}{4}$ percent.

appropriately in cost projections only for periods where there is no vesting or where the vesting is less than full.

The rate of employee turnover in any company is a function of a number of variables: the distribution of employees as to age, sex, length of service, and pay period; the strength of the economy; the industry in which the company operates; and the company's personnel policy. A higher rate of turnover is expected among female than among male employees, among younger employees than among older employees, among employees with a short period of service than among employees with a long period of service, and among hourly employees than among salaried employees. Established companies in stable or growing industries are expected to have lower turnover rates than are new companies in new industries or old companies in declining industries. Companies with attractive wage scales, working conditions, and benefit programs are likely to experience lower turnover rates than are companies with marginal wage scales, working conditions, and benefit programs. Economic conditions also affect the turnover rate. During periods of recession, some employees hold on to jobs which in the normal course of events they would have left and others are discharged from jobs which ordinarily they would have kept. In periods of booming prosperity, timid employees lose some of their timidity and change jobs in search for greater success.

Several turnover tables have been developed for use by actuaries in pension cost projections.[30] Tables are available for low, moderate, and high turnover. Turnover tables are similar to mortality tables except they reflect the probable rate at which employees at each age will withdraw from their employer's service. For example, under one table, 5 percent of male employees age 35 will resign or be discharged before they reach age 36, and 4.6 percent of male employees age 36 will no longer be employed at age 37. In most tables the withdrawal rate reaches 0 at age 50 or 55.

Actuaries do not have the same comfortable feeling in working with turnover tables as they have in working with mortality tables. Because of their lack of confidence in predicting withdrawal rates, actuaries tend to use low withdrawal rates in their initial projections and then later make adjustments in these rates as experience develops. They might even prepare two sets of cost projections, one based on low turnover and the other on moderate turnover, and leave it up to the employer to select the one he believes to be the most appropriate.

Disability Rates.   Under some plans, a disability pension is granted to those who become totally disabled before reaching normal retirement age. When such a benefit is included in the plan, the actuary has to consider the morbidity contingency in projecting the cost of the plan. He must work

---

[30] See T. F. Crocker, H. M. Sarason, and B. W. Straight, *Actuaries Handbook* (Los Angeles: Pension Publications, 1955).

with morbidity statistics that reflect both the rate of disability and the duration of disability. A disability rate measures the probability of the occurrence of disability at each of a series of ages. The duration of disability measures the average severity of a disability commencing at each of a series of ages. The disability rate is expressed as the occurrence of X disabilities per 1,000 of exposures. The duration of disability is expressed as $X per $1 of annual disability benefit.

The rate and duration of disability among a given group of employees are a function of the distribution of employees as to age, sex, and occupation; how disability is to be defined; the personnel practices of the employer; and the strength of the economy. Disability rates are higher among females than among males, among older employees than among younger employees, among some types of occupations than among other types of occupations, in plans where disability is defined loosely than in plans where disability is defined strictly, in those plans where disability benefits are generous than in those plans where the benefits are meager, in those companies that use the disability provision to retire employees whose efficiency is impaired by increasing inactivity resulting from relatively minor causes than in those companies where disability retirement is permitted only when a genuine disability occurs, and in those companies that are the most adversely affected by downswings in the economy.

Because so many variables affect the rate and duration of disability among participants in a particular pension plan, actuaries often find general statistics inadequate for projecting the cost of a disability benefit in a pension plan. Statistics developed by insurance companies are of some use, but they are limited to the extent that the plan's definition of disability and the plan's administration of the disability provision differ from that reflected by the insurer's statistics. Therefore, the selection of appropriate disability incidence and duration rates presents the actuary a problem that requires not only careful analysis but also a great deal of speculation in reaching a solution which at best can only be tentative. Frequent periodic reviews of the disability experience developed under the plan can be helpful in making necessary adjustments in the assumed rates.

Mortality rates, turnover rates, and disability rates often are combined into termination rates which are used to project the rate of employees at each age who can be expected to receive retirement benefits.

Retirement Rates. The pension system under which the University of Illinois faculty and staff are covered fixes age 60 as the normal retirement age and age 68 as the mandatory retirement age. An employee who defers his retirement beyond age 60 accumulates additional benefit units and the value of each unit is likely to be higher because it is based on an average of the employee's five highest years of earnings. Even so, each year that an employee postpones his retirement, the cost of the benefits is reduced because when the higher benefits are discounted for interest and mortality for a shorter duration the product is less than when lower benefits are discounted for a longer duration. The gains from interest and mortality are more than sufficient to offset the higher benefits

Therefore, in projecting the cost of pension plans that have a flexible retirement age, the actuary will want to reflect the rate of retirement in his estimates. Retirement rates indicate the probable percentage of eligible participants at each age between the normal retirement age and the mandatory retirement age that will retire at that age. Assume the following retirement rates:

Age	Retirement Rate
60	0.02
61	0.04
62	0.06
63	0.08
64	0.10
65	0.40
66	0.20
67	0.20
68	1.00

These rates mean that 2 out of every 100 reaching age 60 will retire; 4 out of every 100 participants not yet retired will retire at age 61; 40 percent of the participants not yet retired will retire at age 65; and all of the participants not yet retired will retire at the mandatory age of 68.

Rather than use a table of retirement rates, the actuary may find it simpler to use an average age of retirement for projecting the cost of a plan. For example, he may assume that the average age of retirement is 66 and base his cost estimates on that figure.

If early retirement is permitted without reducing the benefit to its actuarial equivalent, the retirement rates for ages at which retirement is permitted also must be considered by the actuary in his cost projections.

Salary Rates. Where the retirement benefit is related to the employee's compensation, the rate at which the employee's compensation increases affects the cost of the plan and, therefore, should be considered by the actuary in making his cost projections. Changes in the rates of compensation are not easily anticipated; nevertheless, actuaries do make attempts at doing so. Salary rates usually are expressed as a ratio of the anticipated earnings upon which the pension benefits are to be based to current earnings at the attained age of the employee. A schedule of salary rates at five-year intervals may appear as follows:

Age	Salary Scale	Age	Salary Scale
22	2.50	47	1.20
27	2.00	52	1.10
32	1.50	57	1.05
37	1.40	62	1.02
42	1.30	67	1.00

These rates mean the pension for an employee now age 27 and earning $8,000 a year would probably be based on average earnings of $16,000 a year ($8,000 $\times$ 2), and that the pension for an employee now age 37 earning $8,000 a year would probably be based on average earnings of $11,200 a year.

Salary rate progressions are likely to be higher for males than for females and for executives than for the general employee. Salary rate progressions also will differ among industries and among companies within the industry. In developing salary rate progressions the actuary will study historical data for the particular group involved.

The use of salary rates in projecting pension costs has the effect of increasing these cost projections. The use of withdrawal rates has the effect of reducing pension costs. Since salary rates and withdrawal rates would counteract one another to some extent and since both rates are at best rough estimates, some actuaries choose to ignore them both hoping that the results obtained would be no worse than if they used them both.[31]

Salary rates usually are limited to measuring normal salary increases based on years of service and job promotions. They generally do not attempt to project the across-the-board types of salary increases that are associated with inflation and improvements in the general level of productive efficiency. Projections of this latter type would produce current service costs that would be high relative to current payroll. For example, assume a conservative 2½ percent increase in productivity and an equally conservative 1½ percent increase in the cost of living.[32]

Under these modest assumptions a 35-year-old man employed at $9,000 annually will be earning $29,191 when he reaches retirement age without considering his probable normal salary progressions. Using the previously illustrative table of salary rates, this progression would be at the rate of 1.44. Applying this rate (1.44) to the $29,191, the final projected salary would be $42,035. A benefit formula providing 1½ percent of final pay for each year of service would produce an annual pension at age 65 of $18,916. The current service charge for this pension using the projected benefit cost method, the 1951 Group Annuity Mortality Table, 5 percent interest, and a low turnover rate (t-1) would be $2,148. If the normal salary rate were applied without allowance for inflation and growth, the

---

[31] If salary rates are used, the Internal Revenue Service requires the use of turnover rates. However, turnover rates may be used without the use of salary rates.

[32] Herman Kahn and Anthony Weiner in their book *Toward the Year 2,000: A Framework for Speculation* (New York: Macmillan Company, 1967) assume a 2½ percent annual increase in productivity in their low projection and a 4 percent increase in their high projection. Lawrence A. Mayer in his article "The Diverse $10,000-and-Over Masses," *Fortune,* December, 1967, assumes a 3 percent annual gain in productivity. There appears to be a consensus among economists that the economy has built-in inflationary biases that are not likely to falter. The "result is a gradual upward drift of prices over the long run." (Lloyd G. Reynolds, *Economics* [Homewood, Illinois: Richard D. Irwin, Inc., 1966], p. 600.)

final salary would be $12,960, producing a pension of $5,832. The current service charge for this pension would be only $666. And if no salary rate were used in the cost projection, a pension of $4,050 would be produced with a current service charge of $453. Because the use of salary rates substantially increases the current service cost of the plan, some employers prefer that their actuaries ignore salary rates in making cost projections and adjust for these increases as they arise.

Interest Rates. Cost projections made for pension plans involve discounting to the present the estimated future payments under the plan. For example, if the estimated total value of payments to be made at age 65 for 20 employees now age 35 is $50,000, the present value of these obligations is a great deal less than $50,000; the amount being an inverse function of the interest rate used in the discounting process. If a 5 percent rate is used, the present value of obligation would be $11,569. A 4 percent rate would produce a higher present value of $15,416, and a 6 percent interest rate would produce a lower present value of $8,705. Note two observations from these illustrative figures: (1) the importance of the interest rate in pension cost projections and (2) the sensitivity of the projected cost of pension plans to changes in the interest assumption.[33] At 5 percent, a $50,000 obligation due in 30 years is valued at 23.14 percent of its face amount. At 4 percent, it is valued at 30.83 percent of its face amount and at 6 percent it is valued at 17.41 percent of the face amount of the obligation. An increase from 5 to 6 percent decreases the obligation by nearly 25 percent. A decrease from 5 to 4 percent increases the obligation by about 33 percent.

The interest assumption also has a significant impact in computing the employer's annual contributions needed to fund the plan. For example, the employer's contribution over a 30-year period to fund a pension obligation for an employee age 35, assuming a 5 percent interest rate, would be only about 51 percent of that required were no interest rate used in the computation. At 6 percent, the employer's contribution would be only about 46 percent and at 4 percent about 57 percent of that required without the use of interest assumptions.

Selection of the interest rate to be used by the actuaries usually is the job of investment specialists employed by the funding agency selected to manage the plan's investments. However, actuaries, being aware of the sensitivity of cost to small changes in interest rates, urge prudence in selection of these rates in order to keep the assumptions realistic.[34] The

---

[33] The effect of interest assumptions on the projected cost of pension plans is a function of the age distribution of those covered under the plan and the termination and retirement rates used in making the projections. The importance of the interest rate varies inversely with the average age of the population covered and the termination rates and directly with the retirement rates.

[34] Exceptions will be found. Sometimes an actuary will work knowingly with unrealistic assumptions. His objective may be to show low projected costs by using interest assumptions that appear to be unrealistic. (The word *appear* is used here because what might appear to be an excessive interest assumption to one actuary might not appear to be

funding agency's investment experience with funds of various sizes and with investment policy restrictions designed for various degrees of conservatism can be useful in the selection of an interest assumption particularly if this experience is adjusted to reflect projected changes in the investment climate.

Expenses. It costs money to create and maintain a pension plan, money in excess of that paid to participants in benefits. Expenses associated with the establishment and administration of a pension plan are of several types: developmental, legal, actuarial, financial, and administrative. Regardless of who makes the payment directly to those who perform the promotional, legal, actuarial, financial, and administrative services in connection with the plan, the cost is ultimately borne by the employer.

Where insurance companies are used as the funding agency, most of the expenses will be paid by the insurer out of premiums collected from the employer and from investment income generated by the fund's assets. Insurers have their own legal, actuarial, financial, and administrative service staffs. The employer will incur some direct legal expense not included in the premiums paid. To the degree that the employer becomes involved in the plan's administration he will incur administrative expenses beyond those covered in the premium. And in some plans funded through insurance companies, the employer might use a consulting actuary of his own rather than rely on the insurer's actuarial services.[35] The expense allowance added to the premium by insurers varies among the type of funding instrument used and the amount of premium dollars generated. The percentage of the gross premium allocated for expenses is higher for individual insurance and annuity contracts than for group annuity contracts, and lower for group annuity contracts that produce a substantial amount of premiums than those that produce a moderate amount of premiums.[36] If the expense allowance added to the premium turns out to be more than enough to cover expenses associated with the plan, the insurer will take this into consideration in developing the dividends (or rate adjustment credits) allowed the employer.

Where trust companies are used as funding agencies, many of the expenses associated with the plan are paid directly by the employer (some-

---

excessive to another. For example, to most actuaries a 9 percent assumption would appear to be excessive but to a few less conservative actuaries a 9 percent assumption would appear to be a realistic expectation from an aggressive equity investment policy.) In some cases the actuary might knowingly work with excessively low interest assumptions to overstate the cost in order to hoodwink union negotiators or to cover up a policy of overfunding.

[35] In conventional group annuity plans and individual policy pension trust plans where the funds are allocated to specific employees, the employer must rely exclusively on the insurer's actuarial service. But in deposit administration plans where the funds are unallocated to particular employees, the employer is free to seek less conservative actuarial advice than he would probably receive from his insurer's actuarial staff. Allocated and unallocated funding instruments are discussed later in this chapter.

[36] Expense allowance for the various types of insured funding instruments are discussed later in this chapter.

times by the trust fund itself). The employer deals with his own attorney, consulting actuary, and trustee. He also performs much of the administrative work for the plan and allocates these costs to the plan.[37] The investment expenses of a trust fund plan usually are charged against the earnings of the fund and are expressed as a percentage of assets. The percentage reduces as the size of the fund increases. (In some insurance plans, investment expense charges are also related to the size of the fund.)

In drawing any conclusion about projected cost estimates of a pension plan, it is important to know what allowances, if any, have been made for future expenses associated with the management of the plan.

4. FUNDING AGENCIES

A funding agency is "an organization or individual that provides facilities for the accumulation of assets to be used for the payment of benefits under a pension plan, or an organization that provides facilities for the purchase of such benefits."[38] The funding agency usually is a life insurance company, a bank, or a group of individuals acting as trustees.[39] When the funding agency is a trustee (usually the trust department of a bank), the plan is called a trust fund plan.[40] All plans funded through insurance companies are called insured plans, but the amount of insurance involved in the plan is a function of the type of funding instrument used. Funding instruments are discussed later in this chapter.

Trust Fund Plans. Slightly more than 70 percent of the persons cov-

---

[37] The future expenses of a pension plan when loaded into an annuity premium are taken into consideration in evaluating the plan's liability. However, although the Treasury Department will allow the future expenses of a trust fund plan to be considered in the valuation of the plan's liabilities, actuaries usually ignore expenses in their valuation formulas. The reason is that the employers usually charge the current operating expenses of the plan to general administrative expenses rather than to the plan.

[38] See footnote 13.

[39] Individual trustees are commonly used in multiemployer plans. (U.S. Department of Labor, *Multiemployer Pension Plans under Collective Bargaining*, Bulletin No. 1326, Spring, 1960 [Washington, D.C.: U.S. Government Printing Office, 1962].) A multiemployer pension plan is one covering the employees of more than one employer under which contributions are paid into and benefits are paid from a pooled fund. Usually contribution rates and benefit provisions are uniform. Multiemployer pension plans nearly all result from collective bargaining and account for about one third of all employees covered under negotiated plans and about one sixth of all participants under private pension plans. (Joseph J. Malone, *Collectively Bargained Multi-Employer Pension Plans* [Homewood, Illinois: Richard D. Irwin, Inc. 1963].)

[40] Sometimes trust fund plans are loosely called self-administered plans. Truly self-administered plans are handled entirely by the employer without the use of either a trustee or an insurer and without the benefits of qualification under the Internal Revenue Code. Trust fund plans are frequently called "uninsured" or "noninsured" plans. This designation also is a misnomer because the trustee may be purchasing individual life insurance and annuity policies with the trust fund assets.

ered under private pension plans are participants in trust fund plans, and these plans hold slightly more than 70 percent of private pension fund assets.[41] Trust funds not only are the leading but also the oldest type of pension funding agency. Under trust fund plans, the employer turns over his contributions (and those of his employees also, if the plan is contributory) to the trustee who invests the money, and as the participants become eligible for benefits pays out these benefits according to the terms of the plan.

The trust fund plan is primarily used either by employers with a large enough number of employees to be able to predict, with an acceptable degree of accuracy, the mortality rate among his employees or by employers with sufficient financial strength and with risk aversion at a degree low enough to permit them to retain the risk of adverse mortality fluctuation. While some trusteed plans provide that the funds shall be invested in immediate annuities at the time an employee retires, trust fund plans, by and large, do not use insurance.

The traditional arguments for trust fund pension plans have been: (1) greater economy of operation, (2) greater flexibility in establishing and administering the benefit formula, (3) the possibility of more profitable investment experience since there is more investment freedom, and (4) greater flexibility in the selection of actuarial cost methods and actuarial assumptions. Nearly all the advantages claimed for the trust fund plan can be matched by the latest forms of insured plans. As will become apparent as the discussion develops, insurers have been successful in their efforts to develop departures from the conventionally insured plans to improve their competitive position as pension funding agencies.

Insured Plans. Service as a funding agency for pension plans is an important part of the business of life insurance companies. Nearly 25 percent of the assets set aside by life insurance companies as policy reserves to meet their obligations to policyholders and their beneficiaries as they fall due are for obligations incurred under insured pension plans.

The traditional arguments for insured pension plans have been: (1) guaranteed benefits; (2) pooling of investments; (3) pooling of mortality; and (4) the providing of actuarial, legal, financial, and administrative services at low cost. As the discussion develops, it will become evident that all types of insured plans do not offer the traditional advantages claimed for insured plans. The efforts of insurers to offer funding instruments that are competitive with trust fund plans has resulted in the development of insured plans that have assumed more of the characteristics of trust fund plans and less of the characteristics of the traditional insured plans.

---

[41] See the following publications for current statistics: *Life Insurance Fact Book* (New York: Institute of Life Insurance Annual), and *Corporate Pension Funds* (Washington, D.C.: Securities and Exchange Commission, Annual Statistical Release).

5. FUNDING INSTRUMENTS

A funding instrument is defined as "an agreement or contract governing the conditions under which a funding agency performs its function."[42] In the trust fund plan, the funding instrument is the trust agreement. In an insurance company plan, the funding instrument is the insurance or annuity policy. Both the trust agreement and the contract with the insurer include the terms under which the funding agency accumulates, administers, and disburses the plan's assets.

Funding instruments may be classified as allocated or unallocated. The distinction is based on whether the funds as collected are allocated to purchase benefits for individual employees or are accumulated on an unallocated basis for the benefit of all covered employees. The funding instrument in a trust fund plan generally is unallocated except in those plans under which the trust agreement requires (or authorizes) the purchase of individual life insurance policies for each participant.

Because the primary concern of this book is life insurance, the principal interest here is in the funding instruments used by life insurance companies in funding pension plans. These instruments may be classified broadly into those involving group policies and those involving individual policies.

Group Deferred Annuity.   The group deferred annuity consists basically of a contract between the employer and the insurance company for the purchase of deferred retirement annuities for each of the employees participating in the plan. As in group life and health insurance, a master contract is issued to the employer, with certificates of participation given to the individuals under the plan. The plan may be either contributory or noncontributory. If the plan is contributory, usually a specified percentage of the number of employees, customarily 75 percent, will be required to participate. Companies usually set a minimum on the number of lives, 10 for example. As a rule, companies also have a minimum annual premium requirement, making a special administrative charge on plans falling below either a minimum aggregate annual premium or a minimum premium per participant. The purpose of these minimum requirements is to effect the administrative economies responsible for the rate advantage that group annuities offer over individual annuities.

An employee's rights in the annuities in event of termination of employment depend on whether or not the annuities purchased for him are vested. If the plan is noncontributory and not yet vested, he receives nothing. If it is vested, the employee keeps the paid-up annuities already purchased for him. If the plan is contributory but not vested, his contributions—but not those of his employer—are returned to him with or without interest. If the plan is contributory and vested at the time of termination, the employee

---

[42] See footnote 13.

may withdraw his own contributions in cash and retain the paid-up annuities purchased by the vested portion of the employer's contributions. Or, if
he wishes, he can leave his own contributions in the plan to provide paid-up
annuities on them as well as on the vested portion of the employer's contributions. If he elects to keep the paid-up annuities, he still retains the
right to withdraw his own contributions in cash at any time prior to his
normal (65) retirement age. Some contracts offer the employee a vested
interest only if he takes his own contributions in the form of a paid-up
annuity; if he subsequently cashes out his annuity, he forfeits his interest
in the employer's contribution.

Usually the plan forbids the employee to withdraw his contributions
prior to termination of employment. In case of death before retirement,
contributory premiums are returned to the estate or designated beneficiary
of the employee; however, it is not common to grant death benefits from
the employer's contributions. In case of death after retirement, the annuity
may or may not pay a refund. The basic annuity purchased with the employer's contributions usually is the pure life annuity. Refund annuities
would materially increase the cost. Employee contributions customarily
are used to purchase a modified refund annuity calling for a refund to the
deceased's beneficiary or his estate of any amount by which his contributions exceed the total benefits he has received.

While group annuities at one time contained provision for income in
event of disability, today it is rare to find such provisions in the conventional group annuity. Provision may be made to allow early retirement for
disability within 10 years of the normal retirement date at a reduced amount
determined actuarially.

When employment is terminated by other than retirement, nonvested
annuities purchased with the employer's contributions are cancelled and
their values credited to the account of the employer to be applied toward
future premiums. A charge of 5 percent is made when the cancelled annuities are newly purchased ones. Unless the amount of the cancelled annuities
is large, no tangible evidence of good health will be required. If the amount
is large, the company may require a medical examination of the terminating
employee or may hold up the credit (paying interest on it meanwhile), for,
say, five years.[43]

The company usually reserves the right to modify the terms of the group
annuity contract. Any modification or change in the contract is without
prejudice to annuities already purchased. Four conditions under which the
insurer may discontinue the plan are: (1) nonpayment of premiums, (2) a

---

[43] Costs under the plan are based on the assumption that premiums paid for those who
die before retirement will be used to help pay the benefits of those who live beyond their
life expectancy—just as in the case of any annuity benefits. Therefore, to give credits to
the employer on account of the termination of an employee before retirement who is in
ill health would be in effect adverse selection and would upset cost calculations. Some
companies, however, ignore the health question, granting full credit on termination and
adjusting for adverse selection in the dividend or rate reduction formula.

drop in the number of eligible employees below the minimum required, (3) a drop in the participation percentage in a contributory plan below the required percentage, and (4) refusal of the employer to consent to new conditions imposed under the terms permitting contract modifications. As far as the insured is concerned, the plan may be discontinued at any time.[44] Annuities already purchased, however, remain in force.

RATES.   Rates for the conventional group annuity usually are based on a modification of the 1951 Group Annuity Mortality Table and from $3\frac{1}{2}$ to $4\frac{1}{2}$ percent interest.[45] An expense loading of 5 percent of the gross premium typically is charged although the expenses actually incurred will be higher for the small groups and lower for the large groups. Adjustments for equity among groups is accomplished by adding a separate annual administrative charge for small groups and by the dividend formula for large groups.

It was once the practice to guarantee group annuity rates for the life of the contract. The contract usually provided, however, that rates could be changed on or after the fifth anniversary of the contract but such rate changes would not apply to future annuities purchased for employees who were enrolled in the plan prior to the date of change. Since 1935 the general practice has been to guarantee the initial rates for premiums received during the first five contract years only, with changes thereafter applying to everyone under the plan. After the first five years, rates may be changed annually.

Rate guarantees and conditions for purchase of annuities for past service credits are the same as those applying to the purchase of annuities for future service credits. Only past credit annuities purchased during the initial guarantee period take the initial rates.

DIVIDENDS OR RETROACTIVE RATE CREDITS.   If the experience of the group is better than that projected in the premium structure, a dividend or rate credit is given to the employer. How large a role the mortality experience of a particular group plays in determining its own dividend depends upon the credibility assigned to that group. The credibility given to a particular group is a function of its size and the number of years that the policy has been in force. For its own mortality experience to be a significant factor in the dividend formula, the group must be large and the plan must have been in effect a number of years. The dividend to be paid is a function not only of mortality experience but also of the level of operating expenses

---

44 The Internal Revenue Service places restrictions or penalties on discontinuance of such plans. These restrictions are designed to prevent employee benefit plans from being used as tax avoidance schemes. Also, if the plan is a part of a union collective bargaining agreement, discontinuance will be restricted by that agreement.

45 The GA 1951 Table is based on intercompany mortality experience from 1946 to 1950 with a projection scale to reflect trends in mortality improvement and a safety margin for the benefit of below-average groups. Companies modify this table by setting the age back one or two years and varying the projection scale.

(sales and administrative) of the insurer, its investment performance, and the level of contingency reserve required by the insurer for the particular plan.

In computing the dividend or retroactive rate credit, the insurer reviews the experience of each group policyholder for the year. The following formula is used to determine whether a particular group produces a gain or loss:

$$E = p\,(1 + i) - (b + e + c + r)$$

where

E is the gain or loss for the year.
p is the total earned premiums attributable to the particular group.
i is the net rate of investment income earned.
b is the benefit disbursements made under the plan.
e is the expenses chargeable to the plan.
c is the contingency reserve under the plan.
r is the annuity reserve liability under the plan.

The total earned premium attributable to the particular group (p) is made up of all annuity premiums paid during the current year plus the accumulated balance of premiums earned in prior years. A measure of premiums earned in prior years is the sum of the annuity reserve liability and the contingency reserve. These reserves will be discussed later in this section.

The net rate of investment income (i) is handled in one of two ways. The traditional method is to use the rate of return on the insurer's total investment portfolio without regard to when the money was paid in by the employer. Thus, if the net rate of return on the insurer's total investments averaged 4.8 percent, then 4.8 percent would be the net rate of investment income used in the dividend formula even though the insurer earned a net rate of 6 percent on funds invested during the current year.

Because employers by using trust fund plans could earn more investment income on their funds than the average portfolio rate earned by insurance companies, insurers found themselves at a competitive disadvantage in the business of serving as funding agencies for pension plans. To improve their competitive position, a number of insurers use the investment year (or new money) approach in computing the net rate of investment income earned. They use a series of interest rates in their dividend formulas designed to reflect the net investment earnings on the funds in accordance with when they were invested and reinvested.

Benefit disbursements (b) include annuity payments, the return of employee contributions, and the payment of cash to terminating employees whose benefits are vested. The amount of annuity payments charged to the plan will be the group's own experience modified by the average experience of the insurer with all groups. The degree of modification of the group's own experience is an inverse function of the size of the credibility factor assigned to the group.

The expenses chargeable to the plan (e) include a reasonable share of the insurer's general overhead figured on the basis of acceptable cost accounting principles, sales expenses, direct cost of services performed, taxes, administrative expenses directly associated with the plan, and a reasonable profit for stockholders in a capital stock company.

The contingency reserve (c) is the amount that the insurer expects the plan to accumulate over a period of years to fund any additional annuity claims arising from successful efforts of the medical arts to prolong life, to offset adverse mortality fluctuations from year to year, and to fund the expenses associated with the payment of claims and the servicing of annuitants long after the master policy is terminated. The relative size of the contingency reserve ultimately required by the insurer is an inverse function of the number of participants in the group, and the scale varies widely among insurers. The Life Insurance Company Income Tax Act of 1959 makes it more efficient for the insurer to develop a buffer against adverse experience by using conservative assumptions in evaluating the annuity reserve liability rather than creating high contingency reserves.[46]

The annuity reserve liability is the present value of the insurer's obligations arising from annuities issued and outstanding under the master policy. These obligations include those under deferred annuities purchased for active employees and those past the deferred period that are currently being liquidated to provide benefits to retired employees. The amount of the annuity reserve liability under a given plan is a function of the mortality and interest assumptions used as a basis for valuation.[47]

If the equation $E = p\,(1 + i) - (b + e + c + r)$ produces a plus amount, that amount is a gain for the year and may be refunded to the employer as a dividend or retroactive rate credit. However, the insurer has no legal obligation under the policy to pay this amount or any part of it as a dividend or retroactive rate credit. What the insurer promises under the policy is that it "will determine annually the dividend, if any, to which this contract may be entitled" and pay that amount in cash to the employer.

Although only about 8 percent of the insured pension plans in the United States are group deferred annuities, they cover about 25 percent of all persons covered by insured plans.

Group Deposit Administration Annuity.   One objection of the employer to the conventional group annuity is the lack of flexibility in the handling of its costs. The employer's contributions are used annually to buy deferred single premium annuities. Employers have been inclined to look with favor on the trusteed plan, where the financing is more flexible and the funds are not actually committed on behalf of any one employee

---

[46] See Chapter 29.
[47] See Chapter 27.

until he reaches retirement age. The deposit administration variation of the group annuity plan was developed by the insurance companies to offer the employer some of the advantages of the trust fund plan while still offering him an insured plan. The flexibility gained by the deposit administration plan, however, is at the expense of some of the guarantees of the conventional plan.

The group deposit administration annuity retains many of the underwriting requirements and benefit features discussed in connection with the conventional group annuity. Only the basic differences between the two plans are discussed.

THE CONVENTIONAL DEPOSIT ADMINISTRATION PLAN. Under the conventional deposit administration plan, or DA plan, as it is commonly called, instead of immediately allocating the periodic contributions of the employer to the purchase of a deferred annuity for a particular employee the purchase is delayed until the employee is ready to retire. Contributions in the meantime are accumulated as a deposit with the insurance company. As each employee becomes eligible for retirement, funds are taken from the account to purchase a single premium immediate annuity to provide the benefits scheduled under the retirement plan. The annual deposit required of the employer will be the amount the actuary estimates will be needed to fund the plan adequately. The insurance company does not guarantee the adequacy of the fund. The insurance company will require, however, that the DA fund be large enough each year to purchase the annuities for employees scheduled to retire during that year. The retirement benefit is guaranteed on all annuities purchased from the deposit administration fund.

The DA plan gives greater flexibility than the conventional group annuity in the selection of the retirement age and in the establishment of a relationship of benefits to final average salary. No "normal" retirement age is necessary in the deposit administration plan. Instead, an assumed distribution of retirements may be used, based on experience. That is, the employer surveying past retirement ages determines how many employees may be expected to retire at different ages—or in different age brackets. This distribution may then be used as the assumption for future rates of retirement, thus reflecting costs more accurately than the assumption of a normal retirement age of 65, as is common under the group deferred annuity plan.[48]

Further, the deposit administration plan, by postponing purchase of any annuities to actual retirement age instead of purchasing them annually, permits benefits to be based on the final average salary, a figure not determinable until actual retirement is effected.

Since annuities are not purchased until the employee retires, the em-

---

[48] While the normal retirement age may be flexible under the DA plan and an assumed distribution of retirement ages may be used in the funding assumptions, the insurance company must insist on a maximum retirement age to prevent the policyholder from selecting against the insurance company by not retiring employees in ill health.

ployer receives no specific credits from the insurer for terminations. This does not mean that the employer receives no cost savings resulting from a termination. He receives immediate credit for terminations under the DA plan, since the terminated employee is eliminated from the cost calculation next following his date of termination. Also, allowance may be made for anticipated terminations in measuring the size of the deposit the employer is required to make into the fund each year to meet the established schedule of benefits.

The insurance company usually guarantees a minimum rate of interest and the maximum percentage charged for administration on all funds deposited during the first five years. Annuities enter the picture only at the time of retirement of an employee, and their purchase rates are usually guaranteed with respect to all money deposited under the contract in the first five years, regardless of when this money is usually applied to buy benefits.[49]

Under the DA plan, actuarial calculations must be made for terminations, salary increases, early and late retirements, and so forth. The employer is free to hire independent actuarial consultation, or the insurance company will furnish the service. This freedom to use independent actuarial services[50] is one of the attractions of the plan. Employers often feel insurance company standards are too rigid and require higher deposits than are actually necessary.[51]

IMMEDIATE PARTICIPATION GUARANTEE PLAN. A variation of the group deposit administration annuity developed to meet the competition of the trust fund plan is the immediate participation guarantee plan, first written in 1950. Sometimes called the "pension administration plan" or "direct-rated deposit administration plan," it seeks to combine the flexibility of trust fund plans with the guarantees of insured plans.

Group deferred annuities and conventional deposit administration plans remove from the control of the employer the deposits made to fund benefits. Further, the employer's participation in any cost savings is deferred through the operation of the dividend formula. Finally, these plans involve the creation of contingency reserves. In competition, advocates of trust fund

---

[49] Interest guarantees might be graded, providing, for example, a guarantee of 4.75 percent for the first five years, 4.25 percent for the next five years, and 3.75 percent thereafter. These guarantees apply only to money deposited during the first five years. An annual contract charge of several hundred dollars is usually assessed against plans producing premiums under a given amount. The annuity purchase rate guarantees are based on interest, mortality, and loading assumptions similar to those used in the group deferred annuity.

[50] Also, the independent pension consultant, who often originates a pension case, might suggest deposit administration since it could mean the continuation of his services on a retainer's fee for as long as the plan is in effect, or for as long as he is available, whichever is shorter.

[51] Usually any standard that can be justified on the basis of the employer's experience will be acceptable to the insurance company.

plans point out that these plans enable the employer to keep more of the funds in his business, reflect immediately any gains in cost factors, and make a contingency fund unnecessary. Instead of having a contingency reserve for losses, such losses are made up by additional contributions to the plan if and as needed. The immediate participation guarantee plan (IPG) seeks to achieve for the employer these "advantages" of the trust fund plan.

As in the conventional deposit administration plan, a fund is established into which contributions for the cost of benefits are deposited. This fund is credited annually with the actual net rate of interest earned by the insurance company, including capital gains and losses. A minimum rate of interest usually is guaranteed as in the conventional deposit administration plan. The fund is charged annually with actual administration expenses and credited or charged with mortality gains or losses. Under the IPG plan, no annuities are purchased from the fund when an employee retires as in the conventional DA plan. Instead, all benefit payments are charged directly to the fund. For accounting (valuation) purposes upon the retirement of an employee, the fund is, in effect, debited with the gross single premium for an annuity equal to the amount necessary to pay the scheduled benefits. At the end of the year, any excess of the single premium over the amount paid in benefits is returned to the fund. The fund is then debited for the cost of a new annuity for the next year, the rate being at the attained age of the retired employee but on the schedule of rates prevailing at the time of his retirement.

In other words, everything is handled on an immediate basis, thus giving the employer immediate participation in all cost factors.[52] This is one of the characteristics that gives the plan its name. In exchange for this immediate participation, the employer sacrifices many of the guarantees of the group deferred annuity plan, and some of those of the conventional deposit administration plan.

In effect, the IPG plan resembles the trust fund plan with the insurance company performing the functions of the trustee. One important difference, however, is that once an employee has retired, the insurance company guarantees his future benefits. This is one of the guarantee features of the plan that gives it its name. It is in this connection that the combination of the flexibility of the uninsured plan plus some of the guarantees of the insured plan is achieved through IPG.

In IPG, the employer is relatively free to make any contribution rate assumptions he considers reasonable. The insurance company merely sets a minimum and maximum rate of annual contributions. The employer alone

---

[52] Such as mortality improvement, interest earned on funds left with the company, administration expense, turnover. In the self-administered and IPG plans (and, to some extent, in conventional deposit administration plans), the employer always thinks of participation in terms of potential gain. Advocates of "immediate participation" will usually illustrate these potential gains in contrast to the conventionally insured plans. Rarely, however, is equal stress given to the potential losses (or increased expenses, to put it another way). Immediate participation applies not only to gains but also to losses.

is responsible for any deficits which develop in the plan. The one requirement the insurance company has is that the fund be large enough at all
times to pay the benefits promised for employees already retired. Should
the level of the fund fall to that minimum, the contract provides that annuities will be purchased for those already retired. What happens to those
under the plan but not yet retired is up to the employer.

In general, the IPG plan guarantees that all money deposited in the plan
during an initial period of, say, five years, plus all interest earned on that
money, can be applied to the purchase of annuities at a scale of guaranteed
rates. After the expiration of the initial rate guarantee, the company is free
to alter the rates at which future contributions may purchase annuities.

An IPG plan may be discontinued either by the insurance company or
by the employer. If the plan is discontinued, the following alternatives for
handling money already deposited are available:

1. The fund could continue to operate until such time as the amount in
it drops to the minimum required, whereupon it would come under the
provisions for automatic discontinuance and revert to a closed annuity contract.

2. The difference between the amount required to buy annuities on
those already retired and the total amount in the fund could be used at the
time of discontinuance to buy deferred, paid-up annuities on those not yet
retired to the extent of the funds available.

IPG contracts sometimes provide that the employer may transfer the
IPG funds to another funding agency upon payment of a surrender charge.

Under a modified version of the IPG plan, the accumulating deposits
are handled on an immediate participation basis but the liquidation is
handled under the conventional deposit administration arrangement
whereby single premium lifetime annuities are purchased for retiring employees.

The IPG plan is a modification of the DA plan, and together they represent about one tenth of all insured plans and protect about three fifths of
all persons covered under insured pension plans.

Group Permanent. As explained in Chapter 15, group life insurance
can be written wholly or partially in the form of permanent policies as
contrasted to the customary one-year term contract. Group permanent may
be used to fund a retirement plan as well as to provide a life insurance
plan. The general characteristics of group permanent were discussed in
Chapter 15 and need not be repeated here.

The policy form most commonly used in group permanent plans (sometimes called group insurance annuity plans) is the retirement income contract. Also popular are endowment at age 65, whole life paid up at age 65,
and continuous premium whole life. These forms build endowment or
cash values which, under an automatic annuity option, convert to retirement income at retirement age.

The group permanent plan can use a benefit schedule which provides a retirement income based on a flat percentage of salary. Salary usually is considered in terms of brackets with so many units (commonly, $10 a month[53]) of retirement benefits purchased on a level premium basis for each salary bracket. Insurance adjustments resulting from changes in salary sufficient to change brackets are made usually on contract anniversaries. Years of service may be given weight in the benefit schedule by use of a unit of benefit for each year of service rather than a flat percentage of earnings.[54]

The group permanent plan will have a normal retirement date as in the group annuity. The selected date is the earliest date for retirement with "full" benefits. If the plan permits early retirement, the available cash value can be used to purchase an immediate annuity of whatever size it will buy at the attained age of the employee. In the case of late retirement, the usual plan is to start retirement benefits at the normal age even if the employee remains at work. The employee might be allowed to defer his retirement by taking the interest only option, to be converted later to a life income for a higher amount upon retirement. While the procedure of delaying retirement and crediting the employer with the benefits not paid can be worked out in a group permanent plan as in the group annuity, the former plan is not so well adapted to the arrangement because of the large death benefits payable upon death before retirement.

In death before retirement, the employee's beneficiary receives the face amount of the insurance on his life. If the plan is based on a retirement income contract, the cash value may be more than the face amount. In that case, the cash value is paid just as under an individual retirement income insurance policy. Usually the standard forms of settlement options are available to the beneficiary.[55]

In case of death after retirement, the benefit payable to a beneficiary varies according to the type of annuity income selected. Usually, the employee may elect any one of the standard annuity settlement options available from life insurance companies in lieu of the customary life income option, if the election is made before retirement date.

In event of termination of employment prior to vesting, under noncontributory plans the cash value is credited to the employer to be used for future premiums. If the plan is contributory, the employee's withdrawal value is equal to the cash value on the amount of insurance purchased by his contributions. In more liberal plans the employee's withdrawal value prior to vesting may be his contributions plus interest. If the plan is fully

---

[53] Some companies offer plans that provide other than $10 units, the amounts written in any particular case being largely a matter of the relative emphasis in the plan on death and retirement benefits.

[54] Death benefits under this plan would increase each year.

[55] Cash settlement is common.

vested, the withdrawing employee is entitled to the cash value on the entire amount of insurance on his life.

The employee may elect to take his withdrawal value in the form of reduced paid-up life insurance. In that event the amount by which the original insurance exceeds the paid-up benefit may be converted without evidence of insurability to an individual policy of any type except term.

The group permanent contract, like group annuities, may be discontinued by the employer at any time by nonpayment of premium. It may be discontinued by the insurance company if the number of participants or the percentage of participation drops below the required minimums.

Premiums in group permanent plans are level for each unit of purchase. Usually, the initial rate structure is guaranteed for a period of from three to five years. Thereafter, rates may be adjusted, but only as to new entrants into the plan or additional units for those already covered. Dividends are payable under participating contracts and experience credits are granted under nonpar contracts.

Group permanent life insurance plans are used to fund about 5 percent of the insured pension plans and cover about 3 percent of the participants under insured plans.

Individual Contract Pension Trust.   In addition to the various group life insurance and group annuity plans as funding instruments for retirement plans, individual life insurance or annuity policies are used. Under these plans, a corporate or individual trustee is set up[56] who applies for the policies, holds possession and title to the individual policies, collects the money to pay the premiums, and sometimes receives benefits for payment to the employee or his beneficiary. It is more common, however, for the benefits to be paid directly to the individual.

The individual contract pension trust is most widely used by small groups, the average plan covering about 13 participants. Insurance companies engaged in the group business usually will not write an individual contract plan for large groups. They prefer to write such groups on a group basis because it is less expensive, easier to administer, and more flexible.

Several types of policies may be written in the individual contract plan as under the group permanent plan; however, again as under the group permanent plan, the most common contract traditionally was the retirement income policy, and the most common annuity contract, the retirement annuity. Since retirement income insurance costs only slightly more than the retirement annuity, the insurance form was generally used. Currently, the use of a split funded plan with either whole life insurance paid up at age 65 or continuous premium whole life combined with a separate equity investment fund is popular in individual contract pension trusts. One

---

[56] The trustee is set up in order to qualify the plan, and also for administrative convenience.

problem with the insurance form is that evidence of insurability is required. Retirement annuity contracts, however, may be purchased for the uninsurable employees.

The problem of the uninsurable employee has been minimized by the guaranteed issue contract. Under this contract the insurance company agrees to write a maximum amount of insurance on each participating employee without evidence of insurability. The maximum may be a given figure such as $30,000 or it may be related either to the number of lives covered or to the average amount of insurance written under the plan: 10 to 14 lives, $15,000, and so forth; or three times the average but in no case more than $30,000.

The individual contract pension trust is adaptable to the customary range of eligibility standards and benefit formulas found in other plans. Some benefit formulas may be awkward to administer, however, requiring the issuing of several policies for each employee throughout his working life to reflect changes in salary brackets. Since some companies will write disability income coverage as riders to individual policies, total and permanent disability income protection can be made available with the individual contract pension trust.

Death benefits before retirement under the plan depend upon the type of policy used. If a retirement income policy is used, the death benefit will be the face amount of the insurance or the cash value, whichever is the larger. For any other type of life insurance policy, the death benefit is the face of the policy. If the retirement annuity contract is used, the death benefit is the premiums paid or the cash value, whichever is the larger. These death benefits, except for the portion purchased with employee contributions, do not have to be made available to the employee's beneficiary. They can be used by the trustee to pay future premiums on behalf of the employer. The vesting provisions of the plan determine the disposition of the death benefit.

Withdrawal benefits before retirement, in the retirement annuity and the retirement income policy, are the cash values computed according to the terms of the individual contracts. The terminating employee is always entitled to a return of his own contributions, sometimes without but usually with nominal interest. If the plan is not vested, the balance of the cash value of the terminated contract goes to the trustee to be used to finance future employer contributions. If the plan is fully vested, the employee is entitled to the entire cash value of the policy and he may exercise one of the several options. He may continue the contract in force by paying the premiums; he may exercise one of the paid-up options in the policy; or he may elect to collect the cash value either in a lump sum or in periodic payments.

Death benefits after retirement depend, of course, upon the type of annuity settlement used. In the individual contract pension trust, the basic annuity frequently is life income with a period certain guaranteed. The annuitant, however, may choose the actuarial equivalent under any other of the common forms.

If the individual policy pension trust is discontinued:

1. Cash values can be used to purchase paid-up deferred annuities.

2. The employee can take over full premium payments or the policy can be reduced in size if he wishes to pay a smaller premium.

3. The cash value of the policies can be made available to employees.

Individual contract pension trust plans account for about two thirds of all insured pension plans, but cover less than one ninth of all persons protected under insured plans.

6. FUNDING MEDIA

Funding agencies may invest the fund's assets in fixed dollar obligations, equities, or in some combination of the two. Traditionally life insurance companies have invested primarily in government bonds, corporate bonds, and real estate mortgages. Corporate stocks and real estate account for less than 10 percent of general investment portfolios of life insurance companies. The regulatory laws under which life insurance companies operate limit the investments of the general account to small amounts of equities.[57]

In a trust fund plan the investment powers of the trustees are spelled out in the trust agreement. The trustees may be given broad powers to invest the funds in whatever investment media appears appropriate for achieving the objectives of the fund subject, of course, to any limitations imposed by local law. If the trust agreement is silent on the investment authority of the trustees, then these trustees are limited to those investments that are legal for trust funds in the state where the trust was created.

Separate Accounts.   Life insurance companies in their efforts to compete successfully with trust fund plans were able to get authorization to establish separate accounts for use in handling pension funds. These separate accounts are not subject to the restrictive investment regulations applicable to the insurer's general assets. The separate account is designed to accommodate employers who want to use equities as a funding medium.

The separate accounts are maintained by the insurer in much the same way as common trusts are maintained by banks.[58] In both instances, the funding agency selects the investments for each pooled account. The insurer and bank may create pooled accounts for common stocks, real estate mortgages, and corporate bonds and the employer is allowed to select how

---

[57] See Chapter 29.

[58] Some insurers will maintain individual separate (segregated) accounts for plans involving sums large enough for diversified investment portfolios. Trust fund plans commonly maintain segregation of assets for each trust except where the trust agreement permits the plan to participate in common trusts by purchasing units or shares of a commingled fund.

he wishes his contributions spread among these accounts. The insurer or bank retains the responsibility of picking the particular investments to be purchased.

Under separate account funding of insured pension plans, the Securities and Exchange Commission requires that employee contributions be included as a part of the general investment funds of the insurer where they will be accumulated by the insurer at a guaranteed minimum rate of interest. No investment guarantees are made on the separate accounts. Annuity purchase rates, however, have the same types of guarantees found in other deposit administration plans.

7. CHOICE OF AGENCY, INSTRUMENT, AND MEDIA

In making decisions as to funding agencies, funding instruments, and funding media to use, several considerations seem to be important, not the least of which are the types of benefits to be provided under the plan and the types of benefit formulas to be used.

For example, if true death benefits are to be provided under the plan, then an insurer might be the appropriate funding agency with group permanent life insurance as the appropriate funding instrument. If the number of participants is insufficient to qualify for a group policy or if the amount of death benefits provided for under the plan exceeds the underwriting limits for the particular group, then the appropriate funding agency might be a trust with individual life insurance policies as the appropriate funding instrument. This latter arrangement is known as an individual policy pension trust and is defined as a plan administered by trustees who are authorized to purchase individual level premium policies or annuity contracts for each participant in the plan. A trustee is necessary as a legal entity to administer the plan and to own the policies purchased to fund the plan.

The principal advantage of providing death protection through a qualified pension plan is that benefits not attributable to employee contributions are not included in the participant's taxable estate.[59] However, they are subject to income taxes. The controlling question here is whether it would be more advantageous on the average for the death benefits to be subject to the federal estate tax or subject to the federal income tax.[60]

If the benefit formula is based on the final earnings of the participants or if the formula provides for annuities that are not fixed in amounts but are variable, responding to an index reflecting changes in the cost of living and changes in the standard of living, a trust fund plan or one of the un-

---

[59] The amount of death benefits that can be provided under a qualified plan is limited. See Chapter 17.

[60] Benefits payable under a group life insurance plan are included in the taxable estate but are not included as taxable income.

allocated funding instruments in an insured plan would seem appropriate. The appropriate funding medium might well be an equity separate account under the deposit administration insured plan or an equity common trust under a trust fund plan.

For plans including a small number of employees but seeking a degree of flexibility beyond that offered under the individual policy pension trust, a combination plan (known also as split funding) might be appropriate. A combination plan is one under which an individual policy pension trust is combined with a side fund accumulated in equity investments through either a trust fund plan or a deposit administration separate account. The auxiliary fund, known also as a conversion fund, may be invested in fixed dollar obligations rather than equity investments if that is what the employer wants.

Specific Factors Involved. Decisions as to funding agencies, funding instruments, and funding media involve tradeoffs among objectives. The principal objectives are flexibility, security, favorable financial cost, and service.

Flexibility may be desired in the range of benefits that can be offered, the type of benefit structure that can be used, in the pattern of funding, and in the investment policy of the fund.

Benefit security involves the nature of the guarantees made by the insurance company for each dollar of contribution received. Allocated funding instruments offer more guarantees than are available under unallocated funding instruments. Variations exist among the types of unallocated funding instruments as to the nature of the guarantees made by the insurer. Trust fund plans offer no guarantees. How important guarantees are in a pension plan is a function of the financial strength of the employer whose fund is guaranteed.

The financial cost of any plan depends upon the nature and level of benefits, the investment earnings on the fund, and the expenses associated with establishing and administering the plan. A number of factors discussed earlier in this chapter affect the cost of the plan benefits, given the nature and level of these benefits. None of them are a function of the type of funding agency, funding instrument, or funding media. They are functions of such actuarial factors as mortality rates, employee turnover, retirement rates, and salary scales.

Investment earnings and plan expenses are a function of the funding agency, funding instrument, and funding media. Because of the interrelationship between the funding agency, funding instrument, and funding medium when allocated funding instruments are used, it is impossible to discuss one without the other when comparing investment earnings and plan expenses. Thus, the basic question is whether group deferred annuities and individual policy pension trusts offer a rate of return on investments and a schedule of expenses competitive with that offered through unallocated funding instruments, particularly deposit administration separate accounts and trust fund plans.

If the past is any key to the future, the investment return on allocated funding instruments will be less than that earned on unallocated funding instruments when the funding media used with unallocated funding instruments include a significant proportion of common stocks. The funding media used with allocated funding primarily are fixed dollar obligations. As between insurer separate account funding and trust fund plans, there is no reason to believe that as a group one will do better than another with the investments it manages. Some banks will turn in better investment performances than some insurers and some insurers will turn in better investment performances than some banks. When investment results is the key to selection of a funding agency, the question is not one of which type of funding agency but one of which funding agency regardless of the type. Banks and insurers become substitutional for one another.

Expense items vary between funding agencies and among funding instruments. Insured plans incur two types of expenses not found among trust fund plans: commissions to agents and brokers and state premium taxes. Both types of plans are subject to administrative and investment expenses. Commissions are the highest for individual policy pension trusts and lowest for group annuity policies. The commission scale for group permanent life insurance, while a great deal less than that for individual policy pension trusts, still is higher than that for group annuities.

The administrative expenses associated with an insured plan are likely to be the same, on the average, as those associated with a trust fund plan, unless the employer retains his own actuary in which case the administrative expenses of an insured plan are likely to be higher. In group plans, the commissions paid are not a particularly significant item but the state premium tax in those 25 jurisdictions where such taxes are levied can be a considerable item, ranging from 1 to 3 percent of annuity premiums. On the average, all expenses excluding investment expenses amount to about 3 percent of the annuity considerations paid to insurers in the aggregate, that is including those states in which no premium taxes are assessed against annuity considerations.

The quantity and quality of services rendered to the plan in general is not a function of the type of funding agency used, but of the particular funding agency and actuarial firm employed to service trust fund plans. The typical insurer might perform better than some actuarial consulting firms, and other actuarial consulting firms might perform better than the typical insurer. However, the insurance company is better equipped than the banks to perform the service of paying benefits to widely scattered payees. They have developed a system for claim payments and usually operate nationwide. Banks must depend on their correspondents in dealing with pensioners (and those with vested benefits).

8. PENSION FUNDING AND PUBLIC POLICY

The minimum funding currently required for plans qualified by the Internal Revenue Service is that annual contributions to the plan be sufficient (1) to offset the liability accruing for the current service of participating employees and (2) to cover the interest on the accumulated unfunded past service liability as of the time the plan is established and as of the time the plan is amended. Proposed changes in legislation are directed toward requiring that the unfunded liability be liquidated over a specified period of time.

Proposed Minimum Funding Standards. The various proposals from governmental committees concerned with pension plans would require the eventual full funding of all accrued liabilities. The Cabinet committee concludes that

liabilities accruing from credits for past service should be funded fully over a period that roughly approximates the average work life of employees but not more than 30 years from the inception of a new plan or (with reference to existing plans) from enactment of the requirement. Other accrued liabilities that may arise (such as those attributable to retroactive benefit increases, recognition of an individual's service prior to coverage under the plans, actuarial adjustment, etc.) should be funded fully on the same basis as past service liabilities but within 30 years after the event giving rise to the liability.[61]

The Interagency Staff Committee would give pension plans 25 years to bring their assets up to a level equal to their vested liabilities. "More specifically, a plan would each year have a funding target—in terms of a percentage of assets measured at market value to vested liabilities—which it must meet, and this target would be increased at an annual rate equal to four percent of vested liabilities."[62]

The Javits bill would require existing plans to liquidate their unfunded past service liability within 40 years, and new plans to liquidate their unfunded past service liability within 30 years. Furthermore, experience deficiences (actual experience is less favorable than projected experience thus creating an unplanned deficit) that develop would have to be liquidated within five years of their certification. A report by a certified actuary would be required when the plan is initiated and triennially thereafter.[63]

THE CASE FOR FUNDING STANDARDS. The case for funding standards centers about the need to give employees greater security.

Pension plans without adequate funding may turn out to be empty or only partially fulfilled promises. . . . Inadequate funding puts the risk of financial

---

[61] *Cabinet Committee Report,* p. 52.

[62] *Survey Remarks, op. cit.*

[63] Exemption would be given to multiemployer pension plans enrolling at least 25 percent of the employees of its industry, if employment appears stable, and no one employer has more than 20 percent of the plan's participants.

loss on the employee, since the employee can usually expect benefits only from the funds in the plan that are in the hands of the trustee or the insurance company. . . . Funding is necessary to assure that workers with vested rights will have their expectations fulfilled.[64]

According to the Interagency Staff Committee, "it is . . . inescapable that the employers and the Government have a common goal, to provide the security of the employee by assuring the resources from which benefit commitments can be met."[65]

THE CASE AGAINST FUNDING STANDARDS. The case against minimum funding standards seems to be based on the undesirable effects that the restraining influence can have on the development and liberalization of private pension plans and the belief that the government should concentrate its efforts on "assuring the payment of a more meaningful minimum retirement income for most people" through "necessary improvements in the Federal Old Age, Survivors and Disability Insurance System," rather than through reforming the private pension system.[66]

Various members of the Advisory Committee on Labor Management have made these observations:[67]

If we were to apply the recommended minimum funding requirements suggested . . . to many plans . . . the reserve for accrued benefits would need to be increased by several times or, in the alternative, benefit levels would need to be slashed correspondingly, although no imperative need is shown for either; . . . pension plans which are not fully funded can nonetheless be actuarially sound; . . . stipulating funding beyond (the present minimum requirements) involves the danger of slowing down pension plan improvements and discouraging new plans from coming into existence, or driving old plans out of business.

It has been argued that persons with accumulated past service are likely to be the ones to be neglected when new plans are established if the proposed funding standards are adopted.

The problem of determining standards for measuring compliance with proposed funding regulations has been raised:

Since different methods and different assumptions produce different net liabilities, just what is meant . . . by "all current service liabilities" and . . . "all accrued liabilities." The calculation of these amounts depend upon the actuarial funding method used and upon the (actuarial) assumptions . . . (used). Literally hundreds of different estimates could be used without using methods or assumptions which were unreasonable.[68]

---

[64] *Cabinet Committee Report, op. cit.,* pp. 50, 51, and Appendix P, p. 7.

[65] *Survey Remarks, op. cit.*

[66] *Cabinet Report, op. cit.,* Addendum, p. 13.

[67] *Ibid.,* Addendum, pp. 13–14.

[68] Carl H. Fischer, "Is Governmental Regulation Inevitable?" Address before the Conference of Actuaries in Public Practice, New York, October, 1966.

The effect likely would be for many plans to use the methods and assumptions that would produce the lowest measure of liability or for the government to prescribe the standards and place pension plans "in an actuarial straitjacket."[69] "There are no universal methods or assumptions properly applicable in the valuation of all pension plans. Further, any officially selected set of requirements would become obsolete."[70]

In addition to pension funding proposals, there have been proposals to guarantee full payment of all vested pension rights through a reinsurance plan funded by mandatory contributions from tax qualified pension plans. There are many areas of controversy on the reinsurance issue. Some are technical and others are philosophical, and all are beyond the scope of this chapter.

Appendix to Chapter 19
A Mathematical Note on Pension Funding

This appendix is for the mathematically orientated student who is interested in developing a technical understanding of the funding methodology used in Chapter 19.

The appendix is divided into four sections. The sections are lettered A through D, with a subscript following each letter to denote the order within the section.

The first section explains and defines certain actuarial notations $(l'_x, \ddot{a}'_x, {}_n|\ddot{a}'_x, {}_n|\ddot{a}_x^{(12)'})$ and certain commutation symbols (D'_x, N'_x). These symbols used in pension funding formulas are simply abbreviations for basic pension funding concepts, such as "the number of persons living and employed at age 35," noted by l'_{35}, or "the present value of a retirement income of \$100 per month, commencing when a person now age 45 reaches age 65, contingent upon his continuous employment with the company," noted by $20|\ddot{a}_{45}^{(12)'}$.

The second section consists of the computations for the funding illustrations in Chapter 19. These computations are based on a 4½ percent interest assumption, low turnover assumptions, mortality assumptions consistent with those in a standard group annuity table, and no vesting. Each part of Section B is related to a footnote in Chapter 19. The footnote num-

---

[69] *Ibid.*
[70] *Ibid.*

ber will be in parenthesis following the section subdivision. For example, $B_3^{(20)}$ means that the third part of Section B is in reference to footnote 20 of Chapter 19.

The third section illustrates how changes in interest and termination assumptions affect the valuation of pension obligations and their expected costs. (Note that with higher interest assumptions and higher termination rates, the relative amount by which annual contributions increase each year is higher because interest earnings and survivorship benefits will play a larger role in the funding results).

The fourth section demonstrates how various vesting arrangements affect the valuation and cost of pension obligations.

SECTION A: ACTUARIAL NOTATIONS AND SYMBOLS

A_1. **Termination Tables.** In pension planning the actuary is concerned with the contingencies of terminations which includes death, disability, and turnover. He acquires this information from the termination table which best approximates the experience of a particular group within a particular industry.

The termination tables range from a low termination rate to a high termination rate. These rates are based on data obtained from studies of mortality, disability, and turnover experience. Two sets of termination data are presented below in tabular form. Both sets reflect the mortality experience contained in the 1960 Standard Group Annuity Table. The differences in the termination rates are confined to different projections of employee turnover. One industry, or company within that industry, may consider low turnover assumptions appropriate, whereas another may consider moderate turnover assumptions appropriate. The termination table which best approximates the company's experience will be selected.

Excerpts from two such tables are presented in Table 19–A–1.

Table 19–A–1

Moderate Termination		_Low Termination_	
Age (x)	l'_x	Age (x)	l'_x
35 . . . . 3313.4525		35 . . . . 3841.5665	
36 . . . . 3160.6491		36 . . . . 3746.0415	
37 . . . . 3018.1887		37 . . . . 3662.3008	
50 . . . . 1856.4732		50 . . . . 3209.4303	
51 . . . . 1816.1499		51 . . . . 3188.6486	
52 . . . . 1781.6438		52 . . . . 3165.7344	

In the foregoing tabulation, $1'_x$ is the actuarial notation for the number of people age x who are living and employed for a particular company within a particular industry.

A₂. Funding a Retirement Income through Various Forms of Annuities

Pure Endowments. The concept of expectation can be used to explain the present value at age x of a t-year pure endowment of 1, and noted by $_tE_x$. If p is the probability that a person will receive a payment of R, the product $\$R \cdot p$ is called his expectation. Further, suppose the payment of R is deferred for t-years, then the present value of his expectation is $\$R \cdot v^t \cdot p$, where $v^t = (1 + i)^{-t}$ and i is the assumed rate of interest.

If the payment of R in t-years is contingent upon the employee's survival and continued employment with the company, then the probability (p) becomes $_tp_x' = \dfrac{l'_{x+t}}{l'_x}$, where l'_{x+t} is the number of people alive and working for the company at age $x + t$ and who started work for the company at age x. The present value of R is the product $\$R \cdot v^t \cdot {}_tp_x'$, referred to as a t-year pure endowment of R and noted by $\$R \cdot {}_tE_x'$.

Annual Payment Life Annuities Due. A life annuity due is composed of a series of payments made at the beginning of the payment period. It is denoted by $\ddot{a}_x$ where x represents the annuitant's age. For retirement income, x is usually 65. Figure 19–A–1 illustrates a retirement income of $1 per year.

FIGURE 19-A-1

Payment Amounts $1	$1	$1	$1
Payment Periods 1	2	3	β

Where $\beta = w - x - 1$ (w is the age at which the annuitant dies; in this table $w = 110$). Therefore β is the number of years of payments.

The present value of a series of payments contingent upon an employee's termination, $\ddot{a}_x'$ can be expressed as the sum of a series of pure endowments as illustrated in the following equations:

$$\ddot{a}_x' = 1 + \frac{vl'_{x+1}}{l'_x} + \frac{v^2 l'_{x+2}}{l'_x} + \cdots + \frac{v^{w-x-1}l'_{w-1}}{l'_x} \quad \text{(equation 1)}$$

$$= 1 + {}_1E_x' + {}_2E_x' + {}_3E_x' + \cdots + {}_{w-x-1}E_x' \quad \text{(equation 2)}$$

$$= \sum_{t=0}^{t=\beta} {}_tE_x' \quad \text{(equation 3)}$$

Commutation Symbols—D_x' and N_x'. In order to simplify the number of computations involved in calculating an annuity as shown in equation 2, the following commutation symbols were developed: $D_x' = v^x l_x'$, and $N'_x = \sum\limits_{t=0}^{t=\beta} D'_{x+t}$ where $\beta = w - x - 1$.

Thus, $\ddot{a}'_x = \sum\limits_{t=0}^{t=\beta} v^t \dfrac{l'_{x+t}}{l'_x}$, where $\beta = w - x - 1$ (equation 4)

$$= \sum\limits_{t=0}^{t=\beta} \dfrac{D'_{x+t}}{D'_x}, \text{ where } \beta = w - x - 1 \quad \text{(equation 5)}$$

$$= \dfrac{N'_x}{D'_x} \qquad\qquad\qquad\qquad \text{(equation 6)}$$

By multiplying both the numerator and the denominator of equation 4 by v^x

$$\left(\dfrac{v^{x+t} l'_{x+t}}{v^x l'_x} = \dfrac{D'_{x+t}}{D'_x} \right) \quad \text{equation 5 was developed. Since } N'_x \text{ was defined as}$$

$\sum\limits_{t=0}^{t=\beta} D'_{x+t}$ equation 6 is substituted, reducing the number of operations

from as many as 1,295,029 (that is, $109 \times 109 \times 109$, if $x - 1 - w = 110$) to 2, that is a simple division, N'_x divided by D'_x.

The following is an example of a possible commutation table.

TABLE 19–A–2

Age	D'_x	N'_x
15	5167.2044	55563.4049
16	4672.7351	50396.2005
17	4225.5834	45723.4654
106	17	26
107	7	9
108	2	2
109	0	0
110	0	0

After the D'_x column is calculated ($D'_x = v^x l'_x$) for ages 15 through

110 the N'_x column is calculated ($N'_x = \sum\limits_{t=0}^{t=\beta} D'_{x+t}$, where $\beta = w - x - 1$)

by working backwards along the D'_x column. That is $N'_x = N'_{x+1} + D'_x$, with reference to the foregoing commutation table: $N'_{109} = N'_{110} + D'_{109} = 0, N'_{108} = N'_{109} + D'_{108} = 2, N'_{107} = N'_{108} + D'_{107} = 9, \cdots, N'_{15} = N'_{16} + D'_{15} = 55563.4049$.

Annual Payment n-year Deferred Life Annuity Due. The deferred life annuity due is similar to a life annuity due except that the first n-payments are omitted. The annuitant receives payments starting at age $x + n$ rather than at age x; the annuity, however, is purchased by the employer on the annuitant's x^{th} birthday. The present value of the annuity is denoted by $_n|\ddot{a}'_x$ and is expressed as follows:

$$_n|\ddot{a}'_x = \sum_{t=n}^{t=\beta} {}_tE'_x, \text{where } \beta = w - x - 1 \qquad \text{(equation 7)}$$

$$= \sum_{t=n}^{t=\beta} \frac{D'_{x+t}}{D'_x}, \text{ where } \beta = w - x - 1 \quad \text{(equation 8)}$$

$$= \frac{N'_{x+n}}{D'_x} \qquad \text{(equation 9)}$$

Life Annuities Due Payable m times Per Year. The present value of a life annuity due payable m times per year is denoted by $\ddot{a}_x^{(m)'}$. Figure 19–A–2 illustrates a retirement income of $\$1/m$ payable at m equal intervals. The total amount paid to the annuitant amounts to $\$1$ per year.

FIGURE 19–A–2

$-Payment Amounts	1/m	1/m	1/m	1/m	1/m	1/m	1/m
Payment Periods	1/m	2/m	3/m	m-1/m	1 year	2 years	β

Note: $\beta = w - x - 1$ (w is the age at which the annuitant dies, $w \le 110$), that is, β is the number of years of payments.

$$\ddot{a}_x^{(m)'} = \frac{1}{m} \sum_{t=0}^{\infty} {}_{t/m}E'_x \qquad \text{(equation 10)}$$

$$\doteqdot \frac{N'_x - \dfrac{m-1}{2m} D'_x}{D'_x} \qquad \text{(equation 11)}*$$

The n-year Deferred Life Annuity Due Payable m times Per Year. The present value of this annuity is denoted by $_n|\ddot{a}_x^{(m)'}$. The notation $_n|\ddot{a}_x^{(m)'}$ is similar to $\ddot{a}_x^{(m)'}$ except that the first n times m payments are deferred.

---

* Woolhouse's Formula corrected through the second term. That is, if

$$\sum_{i=0}^{m} f(x_0) + f(x_{1/m}) + f(x_{2/m}) + \ldots + f(x_m), \text{ where } m = \frac{m \cdot n}{n}$$

then $\displaystyle\sum_{i=0}^{m} f(x_i)f = m[f(x_0) + f(x_1) + \ldots f(x_m)] - \frac{m-1}{2}(f(x_m) -$

$$\frac{n^2 - 1}{12n} [f(x_m) - f(x_0)] + \frac{n^4 - 1}{720m^3} [f'''(x_m) - f'''(x_0)] + \ldots$$

and $\displaystyle\sum_{i=0}^{m} f(x_i) \doteqdot n[f(x_0) + f(x_1) + \ldots + f(x_m)] - \frac{n-1}{2} f(x_0)$

$$_n|\ddot{a}_x^{(m)\prime} = \frac{1}{m} \sum_{t=n}^{\infty} {}_{t/m}E_x' \qquad \text{(equation 12)}$$

$$\doteqdot \frac{N_{x+n}' - \dfrac{m-1}{2m} D_{x+n}'}{D_x'} \qquad \text{(equation 13)}\dagger$$

In retirement income plans the payments are made monthly ($m = 12$).

SECTION B: ILLUSTRATIONS OF FUNDING COMPUTATIONS

All computations in this section are based on $4\frac{1}{2}$ percent interest assumptions and low termination assumptions.

$B_1{}^{(16)}$. **Single Payment Necessary to Fund Monthly Pension of \$5 at Age 65, at Various Attained Ages.**

TABLE 19–B–1

$$12\,(\$5)\,_n|\ddot{a}_x^{(12)\prime} \doteqdot 12(\$5)\,\frac{N_{x+n}' - 11\!/\!24\,D_{x+n}'}{D_x'}, \text{ where } n = 65 - x$$

(1)	(2)	(3)	(4)	(5)	(6)
Age (x)	N_{65}'	$11\!/\!24\,D_{65}'$	D_x'	$_n|\ddot{a}_x^{(12)\prime}$	$12(\$5)_n|\ddot{a}_x^{(12)\prime}$
35	1561.2908	69.17143	823.0723	1.81286	108.77
40	1561.2908	69.17143	596.9418	2.49960	149.98
60	1561.2908	69.17143	206.5676	7.22339	433.40
64	1561.2908	69.17143	161.2696	9.25232	555.14

$B_2{}^{(19)}$. **Annual Level Contributions Necessary to Fund a \$150 Monthly Pension at Age 65 for New Employees, Aged 35.**

$$\frac{12(\$150)\ddot{a}_{65}^{(12)\prime} \cdot _{30}E_{35}'}{\ddot{a}_{35:\overline{30}|}'} \doteqdot \$1800\,\frac{N_{65}' - 11\!/\!24 D_{65}'}{D_{35}'} \cdot \frac{D_{35}'}{N_{35}' - N_{65}'}$$

$$\doteqdot \$1800\,\frac{N_{65}' - 11\!/\!24 D_{65}'}{N_{35}' - N_{65}'} \text{ where } \begin{aligned} N_{35}' &= 13679.2578 \\ N_{65}' &= 1561.2908 \\ D_{65}' &= 150.9195 \end{aligned}$$

$$\doteqdot \$1800 \times (0.1231)$$

$$\doteqdot \$221.58$$

---

† Once again, Woolhouse's Approximation Formula was applied.

$B_3^{(20)}$. **Annual Level Contributions Necessary to Fund a \$200 Monthly Pension at Age 65, Attained Age 35, Entry Age 25, Showing Allocation between Contributions for Past Service Liability and Current Service Cost.**

$$\frac{12 \cdot (\$200) \cdot \ddot{a}_{65}^{(12)\prime} \cdot {}_{30}E_{35}^{\prime}}{\ddot{a}_{35:\overline{30}|}^{\prime}} = \frac{12(150 + 50) \cdot \ddot{a}_{65}^{(12)\prime} \cdot {}_{30}E_{35}^{\prime}}{\ddot{a}_{35:\overline{30}|}^{\prime}}$$

Using $B_2^{(19)}$

$$\doteq \$221.58 + 600\,(0.1231)$$

$$\doteq \$221.58 + \$73.86$$

$$\doteq \$295.44$$

Contributions for Past Service Liability = \$ 73.86

Current Service Cost   = \$221.58

$B_4^{(22)}$. **The Annual Level Contribution Necessary to Fund a \$200 Monthly Pension at Age 65, Using Entry Age Normal Method, and Showing Amount of Accumulated Past Service Liability, Attained Age 35, Entry Age 25.**

Note: ${}_{40|}\ddot{a}_{25}^{(12)\prime} = \ddot{a}_{65}^{(12)\prime} \cdot {}_{40}E_{25}^{\prime}$ (applicable to B_2 (19) and B_3 (20))

$$\frac{12\,(\$200)\,{}_{40|}\ddot{a}_{25}^{(12)\prime}}{\ddot{a}_{25:\overline{40}|}^{\prime}} \doteq \$2400\,\frac{N_{65}^{\prime} - {}^{11}\!/_{24}D_{65}^{\prime}}{D_{25}^{\prime}} \cdot \frac{D_{25}^{\prime}}{N_{25}^{\prime} - N_{65}^{\prime}}$$

$$\doteq \$2400\,\frac{N_{65}^{\prime} - {}^{11}\!/_{24}D_{65}^{\prime}}{N_{25}^{\prime} - N_{65}^{\prime}}$$

$$\doteq \$141.60 \text{ (4 place accuracy)}$$

$$N_{25}^{\prime} = 26844.9810$$

$$N_{65}^{\prime} = 1561.2908$$

$$D_{65}^{\prime} = 150.9195$$

The annual level payment commencing at age 25 and ending at age 65 necessary to fund an age 65 retirement income of \$200 per month is \$141.60.

The Past Service Liability for an employee now age 35 with 10 years of past service is \$2266.05, computed as follows:

(1) Annual Payments 10 × \$141.60 $\doteq$ \$1416.00

(2) Interest Earnings \$141.60 $\ddot{s}_{\overline{10}|.045} - 10(141.60)$ $\doteq$ 402.31

(3) Survivorship Benefits (4) − [(1) + (2)] $\doteq$ 447.74

(4) 12 (\$200) ${}_{30|}\ddot{a}_{35}^{(12)\prime} - \$141.60\,\ddot{a}_{35:\overline{30}|}^{\prime}$ $\doteq$ \$2266.05

Note: ${}_{30|}\ddot{a}_{35}^{(12)\prime} = 1.81286;\ \ddot{a}_{35:\overline{30}|}^{\prime} \doteq 14.7228;\ \ddot{s}_{\overline{10}|.045} \doteq 12.8412$

B_5 (Column 5, Table 19-2 in Text of Chapter 19). **The Computation of the Present Value of a Deferred Life Annuity Due of One Payable at Age 65.**

TABLE 19-B-2

$$_n|\ddot{a}'_x = \frac{N'_{x+n}}{D'_x} \text{, where } n = 65 - x$$

Age (x)	N'_{65}	D'_x	$_n|\ddot{a}'_x$
22	1561.2908	2556.1807	0.611
27	1561.2908	1577.5350	0.990
32	1561.2908	1029.3744	1.516
37	1561.2908	718.5406	2.173
42	1561.2908	533.2395	2.928
47	1561.2908	412.3096	3.787
52	1561.2908	320.9424	4.865
57	1561.2908	245.4093	6.362
62	1561.2908	183.0770	8.528

B_6 (Column 7, Table 19-2 in Text of Chapter 19.) **The Computation of the Present Value of an n-Year ($n = 65\text{-}x$) Temporary Life Annuity Due of One Issued at Age x.**

TABLE 19-B-3

$$\ddot{a}'_{x:\overline{n}|} = \frac{N'_x - N'_{x+n}}{D'_x} \text{, where } n = 65 - x$$

(1)	(2)	(3)	(4)	(5)
Age (x)	N'_x	N'_{65}	D'_x	$\ddot{a}'_{x:\overline{n}|}$
22	33812.3475	1561.2908	2556.1807	12.617
27	23210.2656	1561.2908	1577.5350	13.723
32	16545.8324	1561.2908	1029.3744	14.547
37	12088.1417	1561.2908	718.5406	14.650
42	8901.5707	1561.2908	533.2395	13.765
47	6494.4640	1561.2908	412.3096	11.965
52	4623.1232	1561.2908	320.9424	9.541
57	3175.1557	1561.2908	245.4093	6.576
62	2077.6154	1561.2908	183.0770	2.820

SECTION C: THE EFFECT OF INTEREST AND TERMINATION ASSUMPTIONS ON PROJECTED COST OF PENSION OBLIGATIONS.

The actuarial assumptions are used not only in determining the projection of the expected cost of the pension obligation but also in deriving the employer's annual contributions.

Tables 19–C–1 through 19–C–4 illustrate how different interest and termination assumptions affect the projected cost of pension obligations.

Table 19–C–5 summarizes the effect of interest and termination assumptions on the projected cost of a $100 a month pension payable at age 65 for employees age 27 and 57.

C_1. **Amount Needed to Fund a Retirement Income of $100 Monthly at Age 65, $4\frac{1}{2}$ Percent Interest and Low Termination Assumptions, at Various Attained Ages.**

TABLE 19–C–1

$$_n|\ddot{a}_x^{(12)\prime} = \frac{N_{x+n}^{\prime} - \frac{11}{24} D_{x+n}^{\prime}}{D_x^{\prime}} , \text{ where } n = 65 - x$$

Age (x)	$N_{65}^{\prime}$	$D_{65}^{\prime}$	$D_x^{\prime}$	$\$100 \; _n|\ddot{a}_x^{(12)\prime}$
22	1561.2908	69.17143	2556.1807	$ 58.373
27	1561.2908	69.17143	1577.5350	94.585
32	1561.2908	69.17143	1029.3744	144.954
37	1561.2908	69.17143	718.5406	207.657
42	1561.2908	69.17143	533.2395	279.821
47	1561.2908	69.17143	412.3096	361.892
52	1561.2908	69.17143	320.9424	464.918
57	1561.2908	69.17143	245.4093	608.012
62	1561.2908	69.17143	183.0770	815.022

C_2. **Amount Needed to Fund Retirement Income of $100 Monthly at Age 65, 5 Percent Interest and Low Termination Assumptions, at Various Attained Ages.**

TABLE 19–C–2

$$_{n|}\ddot{a}^{(12)\prime}_{x} = \frac{N'_{x+n} - \tfrac{11}{24} D'_{x+n}}{D'_{x}} \text{, where } n = 65 - x$$

Age (x)	N'_{65}	$\tfrac{11}{24} D'_{65}$	D'_{x}	$\$100 \, _{n|}\ddot{a}^{(12)\prime}_{x}$
22	1107.0065	50.7202	2301.3643	$ 45.898
27	1107.0065	50.7202	1386.7806	76.168
32	1107.0065	50.7202	883.5621	119.540
37	1107.0065	50.7202	602.2128	175.400
42	1107.0065	50.7202	436.3711	242.061
47	1107.0065	50.7202	329.4519	320.619
52	1107.0065	50.7202	250.3979	421.843
57	1107.0065	50.7202	186.9517	565.004
62	1107.0065	50.7202	136.1781	775.665

(Compare Table 19–C–2 with 19–C–1 to determine effect of interest assumptions on projected costs.)

C₃. **Amount Needed to Fund Retirement Income of $100 Monthly at Age 65, 4½ Percent Interest and Moderate Termination Assumptions, at Various Attained Ages.**

TABLE 19–C–3

$$\$100 \, _{n|}\ddot{a}^{(12)\prime}_{x} = \$100 \frac{N'_{x+n} - \tfrac{11}{24} D'_{x+n}}{D'_{x}} \text{, where } n = 65 - x$$

Age (x)	N'_{65}	$\tfrac{11}{24} D'_{65}$	D'_{x}	$\$100 \, _{n|}\ddot{a}^{(12)\prime}_{x}$
22	853.9141	37.8318	2503.7396	$ 32.594
27	853.9141	37.8318	1509.8387	54.050
32	853.9141	37.8318	937.9195	87.009
37	853.9141	37.8318	592.1506	137.816
42	853.9141	37.8318	384.1886	212.417
47	853.9141	37.8318	255.8299	318.994
52	853.9141	37.8318	180.6233	451.814
57	853.9141	37.8318	134.4760	606.860
62	853.9141	37.8318	100.1300	815.022

(Compare Table 19–C–3 with 19–C–1 to determine the effect of termination assumptions on projected costs.)

C₄. Amount Needed to Fund Retirement Income of $100 Monthly at Age 65, 5 Percent Interest and Moderate Termination Assumptions, at Various Attained Ages.

TABLE 19-C-4

$$_n|\ddot{a}_x^{(12)\prime} = \frac{N_{x+n}^{\,\prime} - {}^{11}\!/_{24} D_{x+n}^{\,\prime}}{D_x^{\prime}}, \text{ where } n = 65 - x$$

Age (x)	$N_{65}^{\prime}$	${}^{11}\!/_{24} D_{65}^{\prime}$	$D_x^{\prime}$	$\$100 \; _n|\ddot{a}_x^{(12)\prime}$
22	605.4537	27.7404	2254.1508	$ 25.628
27	605.4537	27.7404	1327.2701	43.526
32	605.4537	27.7404	805.0620	71.760
37	605.4537	27.7404	496.2846	116.407
42	605.4537	27.7404	314.3968	183.752
47	605.4537	27.7404	204.4183	282.613
52	605.4537	27.7404	140.9215	409.954
57	605.4537	27.7404	102.4432	563.935
62	605.4537	27.7404	74.4797	775.665

(Compare Tables 19-C-1, 19-C-2, 19-C-3, and 19-C-4 to determine the effect changes in both interest and termination assumptions have on projected costs.)

C₅. Summary of the Results of Tables 19-C-1 Through 19-C-4 for Two Ages: 27 and 57.

TABLE 19-C-5

Age (x)	Interest Assumption (%)	Termination Assumption	$\$100 \; _n|\ddot{a}_x^{(12)\prime}$ $n = 65 - x$
27	4½	Low	$ 94.585
57	4½	Low	608.012
27	5	Low	$ 76.168
57	5	Low	565.004
27	4½	Moderate	$ 54.050
57	4½	Moderate	606.860
27	5	Moderate	$ 43.526
57	5	Moderate	563.935

Note that the termination rate has an insignificant effect at higher ages upon the projected cost of the pension obligation.

SECTION D: THE EFFECT OF VESTING ON THE PROJECTED COSTS OF PENSION OBLIGATIONS

Throughout Chapter 19, the valuation of the various pension obligations was computed under the assumption of no vesting. This is an unrealistic assumption, particularly for qualified plans, as is noted in Chapters 17 and 18.

The valuation of a vested pension obligation is based upon the cost of a nonvested pension obligation plus an additional charge for vesting, expressed as a percentage of the nonvested pension cost. The vesting charge is a function of: (1) the mortality, disability, and turnover of the group; (2) the age and sex distribution of the group; (3) the degree of vesting; and (4) the vesting eligibility requirements.

D_1. Vesting Charges for 100 Percent Vesting for Age 22 Male, and Age 22 Female: Low Termination Assumptions.

TABLE 19–D–1
Charges for 100 Percent Vesting as Specified:
Low Termination Assumption

Age (x)	Sex	Vesting Eligibility Requirements		Additional Charge for Vesting
		Age Requirement	Years of Service Required	
22	Male	None	0	0.189
22	Female	None	0	0.384
22	Male	None	10	0.109
22	Female	None	10	0.223
22	Male	35	10	0.079
22	Female	35	10	0.173
22	Male	40	10	0.038
22	Female	40	10	0.101

D_2. Vesting Charges for 100 Percent Vesting for Age 22 Male, and Age 22 Female: Moderate Termination Assumptions.

TABLE 19–D–2

**Charges for 100 Percent Vesting as Specified:
Moderate Termination Assumptions**

Age (x)	Sex	Vesting Eligibility Requirements		Additional Charge for Vesting
		Age Requirement	Years of Service Required	
22	Male	None	0	.5625
22	Female	None	0	1.4008
22	Male	None	10	.2862
22	Female	None	10	.6254
22	Male	35	10	.2072
22	Female	35	10	.4635
22	Male	40	10	.1058
22	Female	40	10	.2630

Table 19–D–1 is based upon a low termination assumption, whereas Table 19–D–2 is based upon a moderate termination assumption. Observe how the various independent variables within each table affect the vesting charge, and how the vesting charges are affected by the termination assumptions used.

20

Programming Income Insurance

One of the most frequently asked questions is, "How much insurance should I own?" The best answer is an adaptation of Abraham Lincoln's reputed reply to the query, "How long should a man's legs be?" Lincoln's response was, "Long enough to reach the ground."

Just so, the answer to the question, "How much insurance should I own?" is, "Enough to cover your needs," subject, of course, to the ability to pay premiums. Since most people can use more insurance than they are willing to budget for premiums, an intelligent job of insurance buying requires efficiency in use of dollars available for premiums. A useful technique for achieving efficiency in the use of premium dollars is programming.

1. PROGRAMMING DEFINED

Programming is the process through which an efficient preloss plan for an effective postloss balance between resources needed and resources available is developed to handle the perils of premature death, disability, and retirement. Through the process of programming the resources presently available and those to be purchased through insurance are coordinated into an integrated financial plan.

Steps in Programming. Six steps are involved in the programming process:

1. Determine the purposes for which postloss resources are needed.
2. Determine the amount of resources needed to satisfy each purpose based on individual objectives.
3. Determine the extent to which present resources will satisfy these objectives.
4. Determine the kinds and amounts of additional resources required.
5. Coordinate the post loss resources into an integrated financial plan.
6. Arrange the necessary safeguards to protect the financial plan.

It should be noted that the title of this chapter is *not* "Programming Life Insurance" but "Programming Income Insurance." It has been demonstrated previously that three perils can interrupt the flow of income: death, old age, and disability. An income insurance program is therefore, a three-legged stool. To try to base it on two legs—death and old age, as is the case when programming is confined to postdeath and postretirement resources alone—is to leave the program in precarious balance.

2. PURPOSES FOR WHICH POSTLOSS RESOURCES ARE NEEDED

Since no one set of postloss resource needs is universally applicable to everyone, programming must be done on an individual basis. A number of basic purposes for which resources may be needed should be reviewed in the light of their appropriateness for individual objectives. These basic purposes are as follows:

1. Executor fund.
2. Mortgage retirement fund.
3. Emergency fund.
4. Education fund.
5. Family period income.
6. Lifetime income for the widow.
7. Retirement income.

Executor Fund.   After death, a last expense or clearance fund is needed to dispose of the body and provide a place to store it. However, these are by no means the only possible costs involved. Following death, usually there are unpaid bills for medical services, hospital services, nursing care, and other such items, which can amount to large sums. In cases of serious illness, no one thinks about economizing or cutting corners on anything that might help: specialists, treatments, transfusions, operations, transplants, oxygen tents, special foods, medicines—anything to keep the patient alive.

Included in the total clearance bill will be outstanding current bills. Nearly everyone operates at least partly on credit: charges accumulated under credit cards; separate charge accounts at various stores; a club account; the utility company services; accrued federal, state, and local taxes; and other obligations outstanding.

Mortgage Retirement Fund.   Mortgage retirement is the second common cash need. In most family budgets, mortgage payments (or the monthly rent for housing) are the largest single items, running 25 percent and sometimes even more of monthly income. Thus, if mortgage payments can be eliminated or even reduced, a much smaller income will satisfy basic family needs. Therefore, sufficient resources should be made available in a lump sum to pay off the mortgage debt, if prepayment is acceptable under the terms of the morgage contract.

Emergency Fund. The best the typical man can do with his financial plan is to provide a minimum livable income for his family in the event of his premature death. Such minima offer no leeway in case of emergencies which require extra cash.

Emergency needs include such items as extraordinary repairs of household equipment, special tax assessments, and the occurrence of major uninsurable losses or expenses.

Education Fund. While the importance of the college education fund depends on the circumstances, attitude, and overall philosophy of each individual family, it is becoming increasingly important for young men and women to obtain a college degree to compete effectively in the labor market. Of course, the value of a college education cannot be measured solely in terms of economic values. As more and more families enjoy the cultural benefits of higher education, its importance will not be questioned but taken as a necessity just as is a high school education today. Therefore, funds to finance four or more years of higher education for sons and daughters might be a needed resource.

Income Needs. A successful financial plan should provide for a family period income during the dependency of the children and a lifetime income in the event of the disability or death of the breadwinner. It should also provide for a retirement income. The lifetime income should be sufficient to provide for the breadwinner and his spouse following his disability and for his widow following his death. The retirement income should be sufficient to provide for both the husband and wife as long as either is alive.

Family Period Income. The family period is that period during which there are dependent children. It usually ends when the youngest child reaches age 18. At age 18 most children have completed high school and are capable of full-time work. The child may elect alternatively to attend college. If he makes this election, resources needed for his support usually are considered as a part of the education fund discussed above. The amount of resources made available in the program for higher education would determine if part-time work will be necessary for the student.

Lifetime Income. After the child rearing period the objective is to provide an income for the life of the widow or disability of the breadwinner. If children can go to work, they can always support a widowed mother or help her support herself. They can also help support a disabled father. However, most people find repugnant the idea of full dependency on their children at anytime in life. The responsibility of supporting parents creates a hardship on the children that can be crippling to their economic and even emotional lives. Receipt of such support places the parent or parents in an uncomfortable role. Even if it is not possible to arrange for complete economic sufficiency, provision for at least some income will lighten the burden on the children and give the parents a feeling of some independence.

Also, where there are several children, the obligation to support the widowed mother or disabled father may not fall equitably upon all the children, thereby creating disunity in the family, a development that neither parent wants to encourage.

RETIREMENT INCOME. Loss of income can result from outliving one's productive capacity as well as from disability or death.

To anyone under, perhaps, 50, retirement seems distant. Just as it is hard to visualize the horror of a train wreck killing 500 people in China, so it is difficult for the individual of 30 or even 40 to visualize the horror of the inability to earn a living at far-off 65. When the train wreck comes to one's own locality, however, his attitude toward it is much different. Unfortunately, when old age comes to one's own backyard, it is too late to do anything about it. The cure for dependency at 65 is best started at an earlier age.

3. AMOUNT OF RESOURCES NEEDED

Far more difficult than determining the nature of the needs is determining the amount of cash or income necessary to fill these needs. It stands to reason that, given no constraints, most people would like to arrange an income sufficient to provide a standard of living to which they and their families are accustomed. However, there are constraints.

First of all, a man's resources are limited. His decision problem is one of a trade off between the use of resources for current living expenses and the use of resources for providing for postloss expenses.

In the second place, even if a man is both able and willing to budget the necessary resources to purchase sufficient disability or postdeath income, he might face another limitation: the underwriting standards of insurers. For example, insurance companies restrict the amount of disability income insurance they will write on any one person. Also, the insurer requires the proposed insured to qualify for the insurance in accordance with the rules set forth by the underwriting department.

4. RESOURCES AVAILABLE

The next step after determining resources needed is to subtract from them resources currently available. An important resource to consider in financial planning is social security benefits. These include retirement benefits to workers and their families, death benefits to the survivors of deceased workers, disability benefits to eligible persons and their dependents, and medical expenses for the aged.[1]

---

[1] The amount of social security benefits, being a matter of legislation rather than contract, is changed so frequently that there is little point (and some danger) in quoting exact figures in a book. The reader has no way of knowing from the book itself whether or not the figures quoted are current. Up-to-date figures are available free in pamphlet form from any social security office.

Other assets in the typical financial plan are those found in employee benefits plans: group life insurance, disability income, medical care, and retirement income benefits. Employee security plans are widespread and are continuing to grow in importance. Even self-employed professional men, through an association group or a professional corporation, often own large amounts of group insurance and even pension benefits.

In addition to employee benefits, one or more life insurance policies are usually already in force. Also, there might be an individual disability income insurance policy and a medical care insurance policy in force to supplement benefits payable under employee benefit plans.

In the process of programming, it is essential to identify the postloss resources currently available. In addition to social security benefits, life and health insurance proceeds, and payments under employee benefit plans, postloss resources include all real and personal property currently owned that will be available, real and personal property that will be inherited, and the potential earning capacity of the survivors.

5. RESOURCES REQUIRED

Obviously the difference between the amount of postloss resources needed and those currently available will be the amount of postloss resources required to complete the program.

Postloss resources can be acquired gradually by accumulating them through savings and investment or by purchasing them through an insurance contract. The problem with the accumulation method for all income loss exposures except retirement is that the loss may occur before there is sufficient time to accumulate the necessary resources. Thus, there might well be insufficient postloss resources in event of death or disability if one relies solely on what he can accumulate during his productive years. Therefore, he must purchase these resources through insurance policies.

Just as the amount of income provided in the typical plan is a compromise between wants and ability to pay, so also is the choice of methods to be used to fill the gaps in needed resources. When the resources are to be provided through life insurance, the choice often is between what appears to be the best policy for the purpose and the policy for which the insured is willing to make the financial sacrifices necessary to pay the premium.

Determining which is the best policy is dependent upon the nature of the need to be covered. For example, whole life insurance might well be the most efficient method to provide for the last expense fund because that need will exist until death. Of course, the clearance fund need does not have to be met by life insurance; but since no man knows when he will die, unless he uses life insurance, he will have to maintain liquid assets equal to whatever cash amount he estimates will be needed at death. Thus, if it is assumed that $5,000 will be necessary to take care of clearance expenses, then without life insurance the individual will have to have $5,000 in liquid assets on hand today, and keep them on hand throughout his future lifetime— a rather large order for the typical family man. Moreover, the clean-up bill will be paid with 100 cent dollars that is, a $5,000 clearance bill will cost $5,000. On the other hand, if life insurance is used the $5,000 clearance bill likely will be paid with less than $5,000.

Life insurance is the most efficient way to provide the money to pay clean-up expenses. The act of dying creates the need for the money; and life insurance proceeds, maturing because of death, furnish the cash to offset death expenses. An asset which has its highest value at liquidation (in this case, death) is especially valuable for clean-up expenses.

One difficulty involved in programming life insurance for final expenses is that death often comes after a protracted illness leading to the accumulation of medical and hospital bills. While reasonably accurate estimates can be made of the size of other final expenses, possible medical and hospital bills are a matter of guesswork. If they cause the need for cash to exceed the amount of life insurance assigned for clean-up expenses, the rest of the program may be upset. The family will have to dip into resources intended for other uses. The result is that often, in an attempt to play it safe, more life insurance is assigned to the clean-up fund than is needed. While it is true that money left after final bills are paid is not lost, it is also true that if these resources had not been assigned to the clean-up fund, their use might have been more efficiently arranged in the program.

The solution to this problem is medical expense insurance, using the term in the broadest sense to include all insurable expenses of illness: physician, surgeon, hospital, nurse, drugs, and so on. Since such insurance, subject to its maximum, automatically adjusts itself in size of benefits to the size of the bills incurred, the guesswork regarding how much should be allotted for medical expenses in the clean-up fund is reduced.

Since medical insurance should be part of the insurance program of every family, no special medical policy for clean-up purposes is necessary. The same policy that handles medical expenses in case of recovery will pay these expenses in case of death.

The mortgage retirement fund is an example of a need which exists only for a specific period of time. Note also, that the amount of resources needed to satisfy the mortgage retirement need decreases from month to month as the principal of the mortgage debt is reduced. Life and health insurance policies can be purchased to provide the resources needed for this purpose.

While a lump-sum payment can be arranged under a life insurance policy to provide the postdeath resources needed to retire a mortgage debt,[2]

---

[2] Too often neither the agent recommending and placing the mortgage insurance nor the mortgagor takes the trouble to check prepayment provisions. As a result, families sometimes find themselves with cash on hand to pay off the mortgage but with a mortgage contract which prohibits early prepayment. Also, some mortgages will penalize prepayment, especially in the early years of the contract. If there is a penalty provision, then the amount of mortgage insurance should be increased to cover it, if, in spite of the penalty, prepayment is financially advantageous.

no lump-sum payment can be arranged under a disability income insurance policy for this purpose, or for that matter to meet the need for any purpose requiring a lump-sum settlement. Resources to be provided through insurance to meet postloss needs following disability have to be arranged on an income basis regardless of the nature of the need. Perhaps one day insurers will develop a disability income insurance policy that is more responsive to the needs of the buyer.

One of the postdeath emergency needs is for funds to pay the expenses arising out of the illness of a surviving family member. As in the case of the final medical expenses, it is impossible to estimate how much might be needed in the emergency fund for medical bills. Rather than tie up money in an emergency fund to meet the unbudgetable expenses of medical care, it is simpler and more economical to provide for these costs by arranging for enough family income to pay premiums on medical care insurance. So, as long as insurance is available, laying aside cash in an emergency fund to meet possible medical bills is inefficient. Income programming usually requires close budgeting, and medical care insurance facilitates close budgeting. Only the deductible amounts and the amounts required to offset any coinsurance obligations should be provided for in the emergency fund.

The foregoing are just a few examples of how life and health insurance can be programmed to obtain an efficient preloss arrangement for an effective postless balance between resources needed and resources available.

With respect to death or disability, the amount of new insurance to be purchased is a function of the amount of each unfilled need, while the kind of new insurance is a function of the nature of each unfilled need. But, as explained in Chapter 8, when one considers life insurance as a possible resource for retirement income the amount of cash value generated at age 65 to fill that need also is a function of both the kind and amount of new insurance purchased.

6. COORDINATING POSTLOSS RESOURCES

The process of programming income insurance is a technique used to coordinate postloss resources into an integrated financial plan. Disability income insurance is written in terms of an income of so many dollars a week or so much a month. Life insurance, however, is written in terms of a given one-sum face amount. The face amount of a life insurance policy can be translated into an income through the use of one of the settlement options.

An important consideration in a financial plan involving life insurance is the efficient use of settlement options. Which settlement option to select, as will soon become apparent, depends upon the nature of the need to be filled with the life insurance proceeds. For example, in some cases the proceeds are best held at interest and later paid in a lump sum, whereas in other cases the proceeds are best paid out as an annuity, either as a life annuity or as an annuity certain. The settlement options provided in nearly all life insurance policies, briefly reviewed, are as follows.[3]

Interest Only.   The proceeds of the policy may be left with the company at interest. Under this settlement the company pays not less than the guaranteed rate as a monthly, quarterly, semiannual, or annual income, as desired, except that most companies have some limitation on the minimum amount they will pay in any one installment, such as $10. Usually, the beneficiary may be given the right to withdraw "in whole or in part," or the insured may have elected to restrict the withdrawals to a maximum in any one year.

In using the interest only option, at least two rules should be followed: (1) Life insurance proceeds should not be tied up so tightly that in event of an emergency need they cannot be drawn upon. (2) The beneficiary should not be left an inadequate income from interest in an attempt to preserve principal.

Fixed Period Option.   The fixed period option provides for equal payments over a specified period of time. When selected for the beneficiary by the insured, it should be chosen with extreme caution. Although election of, say, the 10-year time option may be justified at the time the election is made, it may be wholly unrealistic by the time the policy matures. Suppose the option is selected for the readjustment income (p. 569). This may be a useful income arrangement when there are dependent children, but if the children are grown by the time the policy matures, the widow might be far better off if the proceeds were paid to her as a life income. Again, educational policies often are arranged to pay proceeds over a fixed period of four years, starting on a given date. Suppose, however, that on that date the son is in the armed forces or the daughter is already married. If the fixed period option has been elected, the proceeds will have to be paid over the four designated years, regardless of how ridiculous the arrangement might be at the time the policy matures.[4]

If unusual situations peculiar to a nontypical program should present special reasons for using fixed period options, they should always be analyzed carefully to determine whether some other option would serve the purpose better.

---

[3] Group life insurance policies and weekly premium industrial life insurance policies often prove to be the exception. Monthly premium industrial policies sometimes provide for limited options. Group insurance policies usually offer a fixed period or fixed amount option at rates guaranteed in the master contract. A number of group policies offer some form of life income option but usually at rates in effect at the time of the death of the insured.

[4] The argument that the insured can change the election if his situation changes at any time prior to his death is insufficient. What an insured can do and what he will do often are not the same thing. (1) He may die before he realizes that the fixed period option is incorrect for the new situation. (2) Insureds simply do not review their programs often enough to keep them always up to date.

Specified Amount Option.   Under the amount option, policy proceeds are paid out in installments of a fixed amount until the principal (and interest credited to it) are exhausted. The option, also called "principal and interest to exhaustion," is probably the most widely used option in programming.

If, in using the amount option, several policies are involved in making up a given amount of income, the policies should be arranged to pay *concurrently* and not *consecutively*. If two policies are arranged to pay consecutively and one is lapsed or impaired by a loan, there could be a gap between the cessation of payments from one and the beginning of the payments from the other.

The amount option, like the interest-only option, has the advantage of flexibility. Restricted or full withdrawal privileges may be granted. The beneficiary may also be given the right to increase or decrease the amount of each installment within or without limits. The beneficiary may be given the right even to have installments eliminated for certain months during the year—summer, for example, when the children can work or when there are no school expenses.

Life Income Option.   As the name indicates, the life-income option provides income for the life of the payee. In fact, it is often called "the annuity option," since in effect—if not purely technically—the proceeds of the policy are used by the company to buy a single premium annuity on the life of the policyholder or beneficiary.

The use of the life income option is practical only when (1) the amount of the insurance proceeds is sufficient to provide the level of income needed and (2) the age of the beneficiary is high enough to produce an attractive differential between the payments made under the interest only option and those made under the life income option. Table 20–1 compares the amounts of income available to a female beneficiary under three settlement options, all based on 3 percent interest: life income with payments guaranteed for 10 years, interest only, and 10-year installment amount.

TABLE 20–1

Comparison of Monthly Income per $1,000 of Proceeds to a Female from
Life-Income Option, Interest Only Option, and 10-year Installment Option

(interest assumption 3%)

Age	Life Income Option 10 Years Certain	Interest Only Option	10-Year Installment Amount Option
20	$2.96	$2.47	$9.61
25	3.07	2.47	9.61
30	3.20	2.47	9.61
35	3.35	2.47	9.61
40	3.53	2.47	9.61
50	4.05	2.47	9.61
60	4.90	2.47	9.61
65	5.50	2.47	9.61
70	6.22	2.47	9.61
75	7.03	2.47	9.61

The most important use of the life annuity option in programming is to provide a lifetime income for an elderly widow and to arrange the insured's own retirement benefits.

7. THE PROCESS OF PROGRAMMING—AN ILLUSTRATION

The process of programming is best illustrated by use of an example. The following example has been developed to illustrate the basic principles of programming and has been kept simple without being unrealistic. The recommendations suggested for solutions to the programming problems are not to be taken as the only possible solutions but as an illustration of the programming process.

The Facts.   Briefly outlined, the essential facts are assumed to be as follows:

Family Data
    Father   Age 33.
                    Occupation: Accountant
    Mother   Age 30.
                    Occupation: Housewife
    Son   Age 5.
    Daughter   Age 3.
Income Data
    After-tax income: $1,000 monthly.
Resources Available
    Social security: Fully and currently insured.
    Employee benefit plans:
        Group term life insurance on life of father: $5,000.
        Group disability income insurance on father: 50 percent of gross
            monthly salary, 1 week elimination period, 26 weeks maximum
            duration.
        Group hospital, surgical, and medical expense coverage (dependents
            included): $30 daily maximum for hospital room and board
            plus full coverage for necessary hospital services and supplies
            for a maximum period of 70 days, benefits for surgical proce-
            dures subject to a $300 maximum surgical schedule, and bene-
            fits for nonsurgical medical fees of $5 times the number of days
            of covered hospital confinement.
        Group major medical (dependents) included: $10,000 aggregate
            lifetime benefit with an automatic reinstatement of $1,000 per
            year, a 20 percent participation clause, and a $100 corridor de-
            ductible.
        Retirement benefit: $400 a month at age 65 if settled under a joint
            and ¾ survivorship annuity.

Accumulated Savings:
$1,000 in a savings and loan association.

100 shares of common stock in American Telephone and Telegraph Corporation. For total worth see today's Wall Street Journal for the price per share.[5]

Life Insurance In Force (in addition to that provided under employee benefits)

Father   Continuous Premiums Whole Life: $10,000
(Waiver of premium benefit)
Group credit life insurance to handle the outstanding balance on loan to finance the purchase of the family automobile.

The Objectives.   The objectives and how they can be met may be discussed in terms of the three basic perils: death, disability, and retirement.

DEATH.   In the event of his death the father wants resources to be available to meet the following needs: $4,255 as a last expense or executor's fund, $20,000 to cover the outstanding balance of his 30-year mortgage, $5,000 for an emergency fund, some income to offset part of the cost of the college education of his children, a minimum monthly income of $570 during the first 13 years when both children are under age 18, $500 monthly during the next two years while only one child is under age 18, $300 a month for 15 years until his widow is age 60, and $250 a month as a lifetime income to the widow from age 60.

Social security provides no mother's or widow's benefit between the time the youngest child is age 18 and the widow is age 60, a time known as the blackout period. The maximum family benefit from social security is $388 per month. For the family period, these benefits may be programmed as follows: $388 per month until the son is age 18 and then $249 until the daughter is age 18.[6] After the blackout period, when the widow reaches age 60, social security will provide her a lifetime monthly benefit of $132.[7]

Social security provides a lump-sum benefit of three times the insured's retirement benefit (Primary Insurance Amount), not to exceed $255. Social security also provides a monthly income of about $139 for each child after

---

[5] If the author knew what that price would be at the time this is read he would have either bought it long or sold it short. While this sounds logical, it isn't really, because if he were that clairvoyant he might know about some budding IBM's instead in which to buy long and some crumbling buggy whip company to sell short.

[6] The social security amounts used in this program are those in effect in 1969, and it is assumed that the father dies in 1969. Benefits are based on the average covered monthly wage which in 1969 was $532. Since his earnings are above the average covered monthly wage base, and this base rose sharply in 1966 and again in 1968, his average monthly covered wage will increase with each year that he works at his current salary. If he dies in 1974, his average monthly wage would be $562, based on the schedule of covered wages as of 1969.

[7] The social security amounts used in this program do not reflect the amendments passed in December, 1969. One of these amendments increased benefits across the board by 15 percent, effective January, 1970. That current social security benefits are different from those programmed in this text is of no concern because the purpose here is to illustrate the programming process.

age 18 while he is a full-time college student, unmarried and under age 22. There is a four-year limit per child and no more than two children per family may receive benefits. The father believes that the social security benefit is sufficient to satisfy the education need since the children can work part time even while full-time students and still have some time left to participate in a few selected demonstrations.

The $5,000 of group term insurance provided by the father's employer will satisfy the emergency fund need while his $10,000 continuous premium whole life policy is best used to provide income. Under the life income option, his $10,000 policy will provide $49 per month for a 60-year-old widow. By placing the proceeds under the interest option (with full withdrawal rights in order to provide the necessary flexibility), the family will receive an additional $21 monthly income until the widow reaches age 60.

Present resources available when matched against resources needed produce a deficit representing resources required. These required resources are those needed for the mortgage retirement fund, the executor's fund, the family period income, and the widow's lifetime income.

Because the last expense or executor's fund will be needed regardless of when death occurs, $4,000 of permanent insurance should be used to provide this resource, preferably life paid up at age 65. However, budget constraints might require the use of a modified premium whole life policy with its low premiums during the early years of the policy.

The amount of resources necessary to satisfy the need for the mortgage fund decreases month to month as mortgage payments are made. Therefore, a decreasing term policy or supplemental term rider (or whatever brand name the insurer chooses to use—for example, a mortgage redemption policy) can be used to cover this need.

The remaining $69 a month of the widow's lifetime income can be completed with $14,000 of continuous premium whole life insurance. The policy will provide $29 a month under the interest only option until the proceeds are liquidated under the life income option. A $37,000 policy made up of $19,000 of term and $18,000 of whole life insurance can be used as a resource for the $250 a month needed to complete the social security suspension period income. This insurance will provide $76 a month during the family income period under the interest only option until it is needed for the social security suspension period. For the 2-year period after the son reaches age 18 until the daughter reaches age 18, $125 monthly is needed. This amount can be provided with a $2,800, 5-year renewable and convertible term policy held at interest only, for 13 years and then settled under the amount option. To complete the program, only $6,000 of decreasing term insurance is needed to furnish the $50 monthly for the 13 years until the son reaches age 18.

Table 20–2 summarizes the program for postdeath resources. Note that the 100 shares of A.T.&T. stock and the $1,000 in savings and loan shares are not programmed. These resources can be used as a cushion to enrich

TABLE 20-2. Programming Postdeath Resources

	Special Funds				Monthly Income Needed			
					Family Period		Widow's Lifetime	
	Executor's Fund	Mortgage Fund 30 Years	Emergency Fund	Education Fund	For 13 Years until Son Is Age 18	For 2 Years until Daughter Is Age 18	For 15 Years until Widow Is 60	For as Long as Widow Lives
Amount of postdeath resources needed	$4,255	$20,000	$5,000	$139 a month for each child*	$570	$500	$300	$250
Postdeath resources available — Social security { Group term 5,000 ; Whole life, 10,000 }	255		5,000	139 a month for each child	388	249		132
					21	21	21	49
Total postdeath resources available	255		5,000	139 a month for each child	409	270	21	181
Gaps in postdeath resources required	4,000	20,000	0	0	161	230	279	69
New resources to be acquired: Whole life, 4,000	4,000							
Decreasing term, 20,000		20,000						
Whole life, 14,000					29	29	29	69
Whole life, 18,000; Term, 19,000					76	76	250	
Term, 2,800					6	125		
Decreasing term, 6,000					50			

* $139 a month for each child is the amount of social security benefits payable using the 1969 benefit scale.

the program, particularly during the children's college education period to supplement their social security income.

DISABILITY.   In the event of his disability, the father wants resources to be available to meet the following needs: a minimum monthly income of $750 during the first 13 years when both children are under age 18, $700 monthly during the next 2 years while only 1 child is under age 18, and then $600 a month for life. He also wants some income to offset part of the cost of the college education of his children.

Resources available include funds from employee benefit plans, social security, life insurance, and savings. Disability income under the company's employee benefit plan will provide the father a maximum of 6 months income equal to 50 percent of his pretax earnings which, at his current salary, would amount to $500 a month. His savings could be drawn upon to provide the needed resources for the 1-week elimination period and to provide the $250 a month needed to bring the total to $750 during these 6 months.

Social security disability income benefits begin with the seventh month of disability. These benefits can be programmed as follows: $388 a month during the first 13 years when both children are under age 18, $296 a month for the next 2 years while only 1 child is under age 18, and then $185 a month for the next 17 years until the father reaches age 65. A social security benefit of $93 a month will be paid to each child beyond the age of 18 up to age 22 if he is unmarried and is in school.[8]

A disability freeze provision of the social security law preserves the survivorship and retirement benefits of persons who qualify by meeting certain coverage requirements. It is assumed in this illustration that these coverage requirements have been met. Thus, his social security retirement pension will be $254 a month while both he and his wife are alive, $185 a month if his wife predeceases him, and $139 a month for his widow if she survives him.

Under the company pension plan, accumulated credits are vested in the event of disability. These credits amount to a pension of $100 a month starting at age 65.

The values of his group life insurance policy and his continuous premium whole life policy are protected by a waiver of premium benefit. If the $10-000 continuous premium whole life policy is surrendered for its cash value and settled under a life income option at age 65, it would provide the insured a $30 monthly income.[9] The new permanent insurance to be pur-

---

[8] The disability benefits programmed here, like the survivor benefits programmed earlier, assume that the father becomes disabled in 1969 and that the children continue in school until age 22 and are unmarried. If the father escapes disability until 1974, benefits will be higher for reasons explained in footnote 6 supra. The father's income will be $200 a month for the 17 years preceding age 65, and the childrens' education income will be $100 a month, based on the 1969 schedule of course.

[9] Since the premium will continue to be waived beyond age 65, the insured would use the loan value of the policy to provide the $30 monthly income rather than surrender the policy for its cash value. Also, because of his poor health the life income option would not be his cup of tea.

chased to complete the death protection needs will provide $45 a month at age 65.

Assuming that the father becomes disabled immediately, the gaps in post-disability resources are as follows: after a 6-month elimination period, $362 a month for 13 years; $404 a month for the next 2 years; $415 a month for the following 17 years; and then $171 a month for life if he and his wife are alive. If he survives his wife, the gap is $115. If his wife survives him, the gap will be a maximum of $109, the actual amount depending upon the widow's age at the death of her husband. The older she is when her husband dies, the higher will be the income provided her under her husband's life insurance which has been kept in force under the waiver of premium provision. (A higher life income per $1,000 of insurance proceeds is paid to a widow starting at age 70 rather than at 65.)

The gaps are filled as follows: a $500 monthly disability income policy, with a 6-month elimination period and benefits to age 65; retention of the life insurance to protect the widow and family; and accumulation of savings from the excess disability income provided before age 65 to be used after age 65. Table 20–3 summarizes the postdisability resource program.

RETIREMENT. The father wants to plan for retirement at age 65, at which time his wife will be age 62. His income objective is $775 monthly while both he and his wife are alive, reducing to $580 monthly upon his or her death. Present resources available are his company pension plan, which may be programmed to provide $400 a month while both he and his wife are alive, reducing to $300 a month to the survivor; the cash value of his permanent life insurance policy of $10,000, which may be programmed to provide $30 a month to the husband; and his social security which will provide $293 a month while both he and his wife are alive, $213 monthly if he survives his wife, and $160 monthly if she survives him.

The gaps in the program are $52 monthly while both husband and wife are alive, $37 monthly if the husband survives the wife, and $120 monthly if the wife survives the husband. These gaps are filled by purchasing permanent life insurance to cover much of the additional resources needed for the death protection program. A $22,500 life paid up at age 65 on the husband will fill the $120 monthly income needed if the wife survives the husband after his retirement. The cash value of $9,500 of continuous premium whole life insurance will fill the $52 gap in the combined retirement income needed and the $37 gap in the income needed if the husband survives the wife after his retirement. Table 20–4 summarizes the postretirement resource program. The completed income program is illustrated by Chart 20–1.

Additional Issues. The foregoing program considers the income needs in the event of disability but does not reflect the need for medical care expenses associated with accidents and illnesses. Neither does it consider the question of resources needed in the event of the disability or death of the mother or children.

TABLE 20–3. Programming Postdisability Resources

		Monthly Income Needed							
		Family Period Income					Lifetime Income		
							For Life after Age 65		
		For First 6 Months of Disability	For 13 Years until Son Is Age 18	For 2 Years until Daughter Is Age 18	For College Education Period	For 17 Years until Father Is Aged 65	Husband and Wife Alive	Husband Survives Wife	Wife Survives Husband
Amount of postdisability resources needed		$750	$750	$700	$93 a month for each child*	$600	$600	$450	$450
Postdisability resources available	Employee benefit plan, short-term disability income	500							
	Social security		388	296	93	185	254	185	139
	Company Pension plan						$100	75	75
	Old and new life insurance cash values and proceeds						75	75	Not less than 127
	Savings	250							
Total postdisability resources available		750	388	296	93 a month for each child	185	429	335	341
Gaps in postdisability resources required		0	362	404	0	415	171	115	109
New resources to be acquired	Disability income insurance policy 6-Month elimination period benefits payable to age 65		500	500	500	500			
	Retention of the life insurance program								Not less than $109
	Savings accumulated from excess programmed income		163	115				115	

TABLE 20–4
Programming Postretirement Resources

		Monthly Income Needed		
		If Husband and Wife Both Survive	If Husband Survives Wife	If Wife Survives Husband
Amount of postretirement resources needed		$775	$580	$580
Postretirement resources available	Social security	293	213	160
	Company pension plan	400	300	300
	Cash value of $10,000 whole life policy	30	30	
Total retirement resources available		723	543	460
Gaps in postretirement resources available		52	37	120
New resources to be acquired	$22,500 of paid-up whole life insurance at age 65, purchased to complete death resource plan			120
	Cash value of $9,500 of continuous premium whole life policy, purchased to complete death resources plan	52	37	

MEDICAL CARE RESOURCES. As is becoming increasingly common, the medical care expenses of the family are handled to a large extent through group health insurance on the breadwinner with coverage extended to the dependent family members. Because of the nature of the group coverage, the father needs to provide for resources to handle only the 20 percent participation and the maximum annual deduction of $100. It is assumed that credit resources can be drawn upon to handle these expenses if current and accumulated resources are insufficient. Medicare benefits are available under social security to covered persons when they reach age 65. These benefits and the types of health insurance that can be purchased to integrate with them are discussed in Chapter 13. The basic and major medical coverage provided by the employer continues after retirement and integrates with medicare.

Medical care resources for the surviving spouse and for the dependent children in the event of the death of the husband can be provided through the conversion of the group major medical insurance coverage to an individual policy. The foregoing program has made no specific allocation of resources to pay the necessary premiums for the converted coverage. Perhaps additional postdeath resources should be made available through life insurance to fund these premiums.

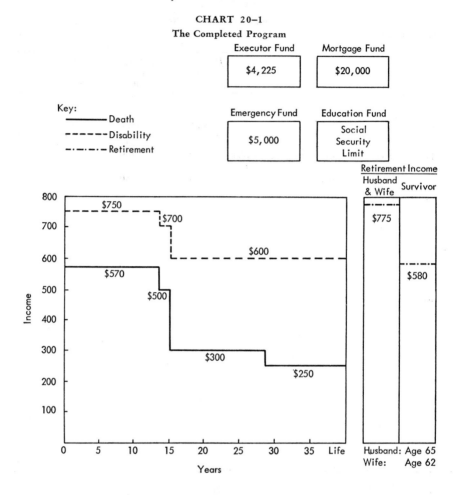

CHART 20-1

The Completed Program

INSURANCE ON THE LIFE OF THE WIFE. The death of the wife causes a need for resources to pay the expenses associated with her death and to fund the cost of replacing the services she provides during the family period.

Insurance on wives is widely neglected because the need for it is so little recognized. Income insurance is thought of in terms of replacement of earned income, and the male usually considers himself the only or the major member of the family contributing to earned income. While the wife in a family may not be bringing in a check each pay period, she is providing services that, in the event of her death or disability, can be replaced only by a substantial addition to the family budget. Moreover, the income value of the wife's services is both income and social security tax free, whereas the cost of domestic servants is not only subject to social security taxes, but also is not a fully tax-deductible expense. Therefore, the economic contribution made by the wife to her family is more valuable financially than it appears on the surface.

In addition to the need for resources to pay for her last expenses and for funds to finance the cost of replacement of her services, two other resource needs may arise from the death of the wife:

1. Resources to replace the loss of income tax savings afforded by filing a joint return.
2. Resources to replace the loss of social security benefits during the family income period and retirement.

If his wife should die, the father believes he should program $3,000 for last expenses and $200 per month until both children are in high school. A $3,000 continuous premium whole life policy on the life of the wife would provide the resources needed for the last expense or executor's fund. By purchasing a 10-year $20,000 decreasing term policy on the life of his wife, the father can provide $200 a month income upon the death of his wife until the children are in high school, assuming there are no more children.

In the event that the wife becomes disabled, there will be a need for resources to hire household help. With the wife, as well as the children to take care of, the need might be for more than $200 a month. Unfortunately disability income insurance on women who do not have a job outside the home generally is unavailable, although a few insurers will write disability income insurance on housewives for an amount up to $100 a month for a benefit period of up to 2 years.

INSURANCE ON THE LIVES OF THE CHILDREN. Insurance on the lives of children often absorbs premium dollars which should be used for protection on the life of a parent. For this reason, it normally would seem practical to withstand the pressures to buy life insurance on the lives of children unless the premium budget is sufficient to include coverage on children along with adequate coverage on the parents. However, if the father is committed to the idea that the lives of his children should be insured, he might wish to give consideration to the purchase of the family policy under which term insurance is provided for the children, term insurance that is convertible to whole life insurance at the end of the coverage period for amounts up to five times the basic coverage. Insurance on the life of the wife also is included in the family policy.[10]

READJUSTMENT INCOME. Many programmers consider a readjustment income essential because few breadwinners can afford an income replacement program that will permit a family to continue the same standard of living. They hold that it is nearly impossible for the family to reduce expenditures to a sharply lower level the very instant earned income is interrupted and that it takes time to cut living expenses. They base their beliefs

---

[10] See Chapter 7 for a discussion of the family policy.

TABLE 20–6

**Amount of Life Insurance Required to Provide
a Monthly Readjustment Income (3%)**

Years	$100 a month	$200 a month	$300 a month
1	$1,184	$2,368	$ 3,552
2	2,333	4,666	6,999
3	3,449	6,898	10,347

on two ideas. First, if after-the-loss income can be dropped by stages—say to $675 a month the first year, $625 the second, and reach a level of $570 the third year, the family will have time to make an orderly readjustment both in their expenditures and in their style of life. Second, it takes little additional life insurance to provide a readjustment period income. Table 20–6 shows the amount of life insurance required to provide $100, $200, and $300 a month for one, two, and three years.

The programming illustration in this chapter does not provide for a readjustment income. Because dollars for premiums are limited it seems better to provide an effective livable income for as long as possible even though it requires a sacrifice of a higher income during the first few post-loss years. Furthermore, planning readjustment disability income through insurance could well be an impossible task. Company underwriting rules are likely to prohibit the writing of as much disability income insurance as is required to provide a reasonable readjustment income in most cases. The maximum amount of disability income insurance allowable may be necessary for the basic income. So, too, the additional cost of arranging for the disability income to be paid to age 65 (when it can be replaced by retirement income) rather than for just one or two years is attractive. For example, a monthly disability income of $100 for one year would cost about $30 annually. The same $100 income payable to age 65 would cost about $55, less than twice as much for many more years of protection.

Tradeoffs. The objective of programming income insurance is to do the most efficient job possible of covering loss exposures with the amount of money that can be budgeted for insurance premiums. The process of determining the amount of resources needed usually becomes a problem of deciding upon the minimum amount of income on which a family can operate effectively. In practice, the life insurance agent finds that his job is to persuade clients to lower their estimates of the amount of cash and income resources needed following disability, death, or retirement. Many life insurance agents will approach the problem of determining how much income to assign to each need by first getting a commitment from the client on how much he is both willing and able to budget for insurance and then covering as many needs as possible in order of their importance. A procedure such as this naturally produces tradeoffs situations. What is the order of importance of the need for postloss resources? Whose set of values are predominant?

For example, the cost of the program just developed might well prove to be more than the budget can stand. In this event, the insured might be convinced that the cost of purchasing the resources needed to provide his widow the programmed lifetime income is prohibitive. Consequently, he will exclude that need at this time and purchase only enough resources for the family income period. He is satisfied with this decision because he can rely on the potential earning capacity of his widow to provide the resources necessary for her own care after the children are assumed to be self-supporting, and for her own retirement needs.

RULES IN TRADEOFFS. When considerating tradeoffs among needs, two general rules should prove helpful:

1. *Keep First Needs First.* Some needs have more appeal than others. An example is the college education fund. It is not at all uncommon for parents to buy high-premium educational endowment policies while leaving the need for grade or high school income inadequately covered.

Furthermore, it would seem to be inefficient to insure the lives of children for more than death expenses, particularly if the amount of insurance on the life of father is inadequate. Clear thinking on the subject would suggest that the best way to protect the children is to increase the insurance on the life of the father. After all, what has a dead parent done for his child if he has bought a $5,000 endowment at age 18 on the life of his child at the expense of $15,000 of continuous premium whole life insurance on his own life.

Also, the so-called living needs, such as income for retirement and the lure of increasing cash values as a "savings account" nearly always seem to have great market appeal. Often, people are quicker to purchase high premium policies to build up cash values than they are to buy low premium policies offering more adequate premature death protection.

2. *Look to the Future.* A young unmarried man will have no need for resources to provide income for a widow and, hopefully, children, but what are the possibilities for the future? To the young unmarried man, retirement income has far more appeal than income for a family that does not yet exist. The result is that he might load up with high-premium retirement insurance before he is married, only to find that in a few years his need to provide for postdeath resources is vastly greater—or at least more pressing —than is his need to provide for postretirement resources. At this time, however, he might find that many of his available premium dollars are going into the retirement fund. To change his policies to lower premium forms and buy added insurance with the premium savings he will have to be insurable—something he cannot be sure of. A sound program must cover not only today's needs but also provide flexibility for future needs.

8. PROGRAMMING SAFEGUARDS

The foregoing discussion has dealt with three principal issues: (1) the amount of resources that will be needed in the event of (a) the death, disability, or retirement of the breadwinner and (b) the death or disability of dependent family members other than the breadwinner; (2) the deficiencies in the amounts of resources currently available to meet these needs; and (3) the kinds and amounts of resources to be purchased to offset those deficiencies that are to be handled through insurance.

Programming income insurance involves more than determining needs and how to meet them. It requires the use of proper safeguards to assure that the needed resources are paid to the appropriate people, that they are not dissipated before they satisfy their planned objectives, that efficient use is made of the dividend options associated with participating life insurance, that these resources are provided on an efficient basis, that an effort is made to protect these resources from being eroded through inflation, and that the program is reviewed periodically in an attempt to keep it up-to-date.

Paying Resources to the Appropriate People.   Paying the resources to the appropriate people involves three issues: (1) the designation of the beneficiaries, (2) the problem of creditors' rights and (3) the question of common disaster. These issues are discussed at length in Chapter 9 and 10.

If the purpose of the life insurance is to provide an executor fund, it would seem logical that the insured's estate be named the beneficiary of the policy because the obligation to pay the estate clearance expenses (debts, funeral expenses, estate administration, and taxes) falls upon the estate and the estate executor or administrator should be provided with the funds necessary to pay these expenses. Tax considerations, however, could affect the advisability of naming the estate as beneficiary. These considerations are discussed in Chapter 21 of this text. To pay the proceeds to his estate, the insured designates his beneficiary as himself, his estate, his legal representatives, or his executors, administrators, or assigns.[11]

If the purpose of the life insurance is to create resources to provide income to the widow and children, then the insured should name his wife as primary beneficiary, specifically giving her first name, her maiden last name, and his own last name—i.e., Mary Smith Jones.[12] The children should be named as secondary beneficiaries.[13]

In naming the children as beneficiaries, their full name and relationship

---

[11] In six states (Florida, Iowa, Maine, North Dakota, South Dakota, and Tennessee), some or all of the policy proceeds payable to the estate of the insured under certain conditions may be held to be paid to the insured's heirs as statutory beneficiaries.

[12] Of course, if he divorces Mary Smith and marries another Mary Smith, there could be confusion unless he carefully identifies which Mary Smith Jones he intends to be the beneficiary under the policy.

[13] Cf. Chapter 10 for a discussion of minors as beneficiaries of life insurance policies.

should be carefully spelled out. Care must be taken to avoid the problem of excluding children who now are only a gleam in father's or mother's eye. The solution appears to be to name the current children, using a class designation such as children of the insured, including Tom, Dick, and Harry. Where there are illegitimate children, to avoid problems of litigation they should be specifically named. Also any illegitimate child not yet conceived should be provided for, although to bring up that possibility in family discussions of beneficiary designations might lead to a marital crisis. Stepchildren also should be specifically named.

The advantages of an individually named beneficiary are discussed in Chapter 21 of this text.

Since it is possible that neither the primary nor secondary beneficiary may survive the insured, a final beneficiary should be named. It is customary to name the estate of the insured as the final beneficiary in the event that all the beneficiaries predecease the insured. If the insured does not own the policy, the owner should be named the final beneficiary.

A secondary payee should be named to receive payments being made under one of the installment settlement options should the initial beneficiary die before the full amount of the policy proceeds are liquidated. Since it is possible that the secondary payee may not survive the initial payee, a final payee should be named. It is customary to name the estate of the last surviving payee as the final payee to avoid the expense of reopening the insured's estate.

If the insured does not want the funds to go to someone for whom he feels no responsibility, he can name as final beneficiary, or payee, some worthy institution such as the University of Illinois that, hopefully, will outlive all other beneficiaries or payees.

To assure that beneficiary designations are kept up to date, they should be reviewed periodically, and changes made when necessary. Divorces, death of a beneficiary, the marriage of children, alterations in the specific needs for resources, and various new interests may require a change in the beneficiary designation to assure continued efficiency in the program.

CREDITORS' RIGHTS.   The primary purpose of most life insurance in force is to provide resources to take care of the income needs of widows and their children. It is possible for the insured to arrange his insurance so that these resources will be available for this purpose rather than for the purpose of retiring the insured's or beneficiaries' obligations to creditors. Chapter 9 describes ways to accomplish this objective.

COMMON DISASTER.   The possibility always exists that the insured and his beneficiary will die simultaneously, perhaps as a result of a common accident. In planning his financial program, the insured must take this possibility into consideration in arranging his insurance. The various problems and their suggested solutions are discussed in Chapter 10.

Protection against Dissipation.   Proceeds of life insurance may be dissipated not only by creditors' claims, assuming the insurance is incorrectly written, but also by indiscriminate or careless use of the policy loan provision. If the insured borrows against the cash value of his policy, the amount of available postdeath resources is reduced by the amount of the loan. Arrangements should be made to hedge the loan by the purchase of an amount of term insurance to replace the postdeath resources dissipated by the loan.

Postdeath resources may be dissipated by failure to pay the premium. The inclusion of an automatic premium loan provision in the policy will protect the insured against loss arising out of his carelessness in overlooking a premium payment.

If his failure to pay the premiums arises because of his inability to continue premium payments into the future, then he must carefully consider the tradeoffs involved in taking the extended term nonforfeiture value, the paid-up reduced amount nonforfeiture value, and the cash surrender value. The factors to consider in this tradeoff problem were discussed in Chapter 11 of this text.

Efficient Use of Dividend Options.   The policyholder has a choice of four methods of receiving annual dividends declared under participating life insurance plans. The common options, as discussed in Chapter 11 of this text, are: (1) to take the dividends in cash or use them to reduce the next annual premium payment, (2) to leave them with the insurer who will accumulate them with interest credited annually at a guaranteed minimum rate of interest, (3) to use them to buy paid-up additions to the policy, and (4) to use them to buy one-year term insurance.

The paid-up additions option frequently is preferable for several reasons. Paid-up additions will increase both potential postdeath and postretirement resources. The cash values of paid-up additions in many cases will not be much less than the value of dividend accumulations. The paid-up additions option offers an advantage because interest credited under the dividend accumulation option is taxable in the year the interest is credited, if the funds are subject to withdrawal. However, the annual increases in the cash values of the paid-up additions are not subject to income taxes in the year credited. These values will never be taxed as income if the policy matures as a death claim. How these increments in value are taxed if the policy is surrendered for its cash value is discussed in Chapter 21 of this text.

The factors to consider in the tradeoff among the various dividend options are discussed in detail in Chapter 11.

Providing the Resources in an Efficient Manner.   All life and health insurance policies do not offer the same values per premium dollar. Therefore, when a resource is to be provided through insurance, it does not mean that it should be provided through any insurance policy that happens to be offered by any insurance company through any agent or broker.

Professor Belth found "A large amount of price variation in life insurance, not only on similar plans of insurance in different companies but also, in some cases, on different plans in the same company."[14] This suggests that the buyer should do some comparison shopping. However, few people have the knowledge and skill required to make cost comparisons among life insurance policies. To aid those who are concerned with the problem of cost comparison, a compendium of life insurance prices has been pre-pared by a publishing house which combines the required knowledge of policies, rates, values and practices.[15]

Price is not the only consideration in making an efficient purchase of life and health insurance. Other considerations are noted in Chapter 28.

Efficiency requires that there be a limit to the number of policies and insurers that are analyzed prior to a purchase decision. The costs involved in making these analyses present an important constraint. The ideal approach would be to deal with an insurance brokerage firm that has made a business of finding those insurers that offer the buyer reasonable values for his premium dollars.[16]

Efficiency in providing resources through insurance means also that the proper mix of policies be purchased, that is, that decreasing term life insurance be used where appropriate and that limited payment whole life or endowment policies not be used where inappropriate. It also means that elimination periods in disability income policies and deductibles in medical care policies be chosen wisely.

Efficient provision of resources through life insurance requires the judicious selection of settlement options among the policies. Some policies provide more attractive settlement option values than others. Once the settlement arrangements have been determined, the mix of options selected among policies should be the one that provides the most income for the periods chosen.

Another matter relating to efficiency is to arrange premium payments to

---

[14] Joseph M. Belth, *The Retail Price Structure in American Life Insurance, op. cit.,* p. 238.

[15] *Cost Facts On Life Insurance* (Cincinnati: National Underwriter Company, 1969). This publication shows cost figures of 141 insurers for various issue ages, policy durations, amounts of insurance, and plans of insurance. Three cost methods are used: the traditional net cost method, where interest is ignored; the equalized cost method, which considers interest foregone; and the benefits cost bases, which takes into account not only interest rates but also mortality and lapse rates. For example, the publication will show the following average annual cost per $1,000 of insurance for a $25,000 continuous premium whole life issued at age 35 figured for a 20-year duration under the three methods for four different insurers.

Insurer	Traditional Method	Equalized Cost Method	Benefits Cost Method
1	$−6.81	$2.08	$ .47
2	−4.63	5.35	3.77
3	−2.14	4.36	1.83
4	+1.58	8.98	6.67

For further discussion see Chapter 28 of this text.

[16] Note the term "reasonable values." This does not mean necessarily the "best" values but coverage at prices which are not excessive. The costs of finding the best values may exceed the benefits to be derived from these values.

avoid extra charge for greater than annual frequency of payment. The advantage of several annual premium due dates spread throughout the year has to be weighed against the advantage of the quantity discounts that might be lost if several small policies rather than one large policy are purchased.

Protecting Resources against Inflation.   Inflation presents a serious problem in financial planning. For the 4-year period ending in 1964, the average annual increase in the consumer price index was 1.18 percent. For the 3-year period ending in 1967 the average annual rate of increase was 2.88 percent. The increase was 4.65 percent for the year 1968, and 5.5 percent for 1969. From June, 1965, to December, 1969, consumer prices increased 19 percent.

Some economists argue that there is a tradeoff in the economy between inflation and unemployment. They believe that an annual rate of inflation of about 3 percent is necessary to avoid an unemployment rate in excess of 4 percent. Those economists that do not accept this view nevertheless believe that the best that can be hoped for in terms of price stability is an annual rate of price inflation of not less than 1.5 percent. The question appears to be the magnitude of expected inflation rather than whether inflation is expected.

An income insurance program must consider the adverse effects of erosion of resources through inflation. Because of inflation, more after-the-loss resources will be needed and these resources will have to provide an increasing stream of income to the beneficiaries. Note that the program developed in this chapter is static. It assumes no inflation. Neither does it provide for an increasing standard of living. Also, it calls for level annual premiums.

When life insurance is purchased to provide resources for the support of dependents, logically the insurance should provide these dependents an income that escalates at a rate sufficient to offset anticipated increases in prices and perhaps in living standards. The concept of the level premium and that of the level payout is not in step with the real world. Escalated benefits should be programmed and the premium payments should be distributed over the working lifetime of the insured under an arrangement whereby the premium is increased periodically to adjust to projected upward movements in the income of the premium payer.[17]

In order to offset the effects of inflation which may require additional resources at death, a few insurers write life insurance coverage that adjusts to changes in the cost of living as measured by the consumer price index. The cost-of-living policy is discussed in Chapter 7. As a means of protecting the proceeds of the policy from inflation after the death of the insured, these proceeds can be placed in a variable annuity for orderly liquidation.

---

[17] See Joseph M. Belth, "Dynamic Life Insurance Programming," *Journal of Risk and Insurance*, Vol. XXXI, No. 4 (December, 1964), and Robert I. Mehr, "Some Thoughts on Life Insurance Product Development," *Journal of Risk and Insurance*, Vol. XXXV, No. 4 (December, 1968).

Disability income also should be written with escalated benefits, but these benefits seem to be available only under group insurance contracts.

For retirement income, accumulation through an annual premium variable annuity or through a mutual fund with the option, where available, to use a variable annuity for liquidation at guaranteed mortality rates seems to offer a good solution to the planning problem.[18]

One source of inflation protection available for the program developed in this chapter is that provided through probable increases in social security benefit levels. The government appears to consider it a moral commitment to offer some purchasing power protection to those relying on social security benefits. Another source of inflation protection is the participating settlement options. The figures used in the program illustrated in this chapter are based on the guaranteed interest rates offered by companies under their settlement options. For example, most companies guarantee 3 percent for their installment options but are currently paying nearly 5 percent. When a financial program is based on the guaranteed rates of interest, the resources needed will show a larger amount than would be necessary were the program to be based on current interest rates. Benefits paid on the basis of interest rates higher than those assumed in the program will produce a margin of protection against inflation.

Keeping Program Up-to-Date.   The program should be reviewed periodically and an effort made to modify the program to reflect changes in the objectives of the insured. Family situations change, resources accumulate that have not been considered in the program, and sights are usually raised as income increases.

9. DYNAMIC PROGRAMMING

As mentioned, the foregoing discussion has centered on static programming. The status quo has been assumed insofar as resources are concerned, both those available before the loss and those needed and available after the loss. In the program developed to illustrate the process, no consideration was given to the forces that are likely to change the balance between postloss resources needed and those available.

------

[18] A new life insurance policy may be available in the future that will permit policyholders to accumulate equity-based cash values through level premium whole life or endowment policies. Under these policies, cash values and reserves would be expressed in terms of units of a separate account to be invested primarily in common stocks. The value of the units would reflect the investment performance of the separate account. Death benefits also would be variable, adjusted for changes in the value of the policy reserve, but a minimum death benefit could be provided through a flexible term insurance rider. To permit the writing of this policy, changes will be necessary in state insurance laws. Various industry and regulatory groups are working on the necessary enabling legislation. Questions also will have to be resolved with the Securities and Exchange Commission. The chairman of a prominent life insurer estimates that it will take at least until 1973, maybe longer, to clear the path for the issuance of this policy.

Factors Likely to Alter the Balance.   The dynamic forces that affect the equilibrium between needed and available postloss resources are of two basic origins: endogenous and exogenous.

ENDOGENOUS FACTORS.   The endogenous factors are those that will affect the insured's financial state even in a society void of economic and social change. In assessing endogenous influences, the external environment is considered to be fixed. Such factors as the purchasing power of the dollar, the real per capita consumption expenditure, the real per capita income, social security programs and benefits, and tax burdens are assumed to be the same tomorrow as they are today.

Examples of endogenous factors that can be expected to upset a static life insurance program are increasing earnings arising out of normal progression in employment, a progressively rising standard of living made possible by additional earnings, an increasing rate of savings as higher shares of earnings are allocated to investment programs, and changing family financial responsibilities as children are bred and eventually reach financial independence.

EXOGENOUS FACTORS.   The exogenous factors affecting the financial status of the insured are those arising from the operation of the total economy, from the policy of the government toward the economic welfare of its people through modifications in the social security system, and the tax policy of federal, state, and local governmental units. Two basic characteristics of the economic systems, that operate to throw static programs out of balance are (1) the increasing standards of living made available per man-hour worked as a result of technological improvements, and (2) the increasing cost of living brought about by the inflationary biases in the system.

Suggested Methods of Helping to Preserve the Balance.   A system known as dynamic programming offers one method of approaching the problem of preserving the balance between needed and available postdeath and postretirement resources.[19] The data given for the family programmed in this chapter include the ages of the family members, the current income of the father, social security benefits payable under the then-current law (1969), current level of benefits under employee benefit plans, accumulated savings and investments at that time, and the life insurance in force. Dynamic programming would require that assumptions be made about the character of the endogenous and exogenous factors that are likely to affect the balance between postloss resources needed and those available. These assumptions would relate to the probable future pattern of earnings, probable changes in living standards, probable changes in family financial

---

[19] See Joseph M. Belth, "Dynamic Life Insurance Programming," *Life Insurance Selling,* Vol. XLIV, No. 2 (February, 1969) for an abridged and updated version of an earlier paper of the same title, *op. cit.*

responsibility, probable changes in the level of employee benefits, probable changes in the value of the dollar, probable changes in social security benefit plans, and probable changes in the tax burden.

Table 20–2 summarizes the static program for postdeath resources and Table 20–4 summarizes the static program for postretirement resources. These resources are expressed in terms of 1969 dollars. It cannot be assumed that these dollar resources when converted into goods and services will provide the same amount years into the future as they will provide today. Neither can it be assumed that these resources will permit the same relative difference between the preloss and postloss standards of living in the future as they do today.[20] Yet these assumptions appear to be implicit in a static program. A dynamic program for postdeath and for postretirement resources would be expressed in terms of varying amounts of dollars into the future. Each component of the postloss equation—resources required less resources available equals resources needed—would be expressed in terms of projected values for each year, considering anticipated changes in price levels, living standards, savings accumulations, and family financial responsibilities. A computer can be programmed to determine the amount of life insurance face amount needed each year to provide the resources necessary to retain the postdeath balance between resources needed and resources available. The computer also can be programmed to determine the amount of life insurance cash values needed at retirement age to balance postretirement resources needed with those available from other sources. It can then indicate the amount and kinds of permanent life insurance and the amount and kinds of term life insurance necessary to complete the program.

A number of insurers are using their computers to help their agents program their clients' life insurance. But, by and large, the programming that is done even with the use of computers is static. Life insurance agents have not been trained in the skills needed for an effective job of dynamic programming.

Another approach to the problem of preserving the balance between needed and available postloss resources is through the development of new life insurance policies. One such policy could be an increasing benefits survivorship annuity with various modifications to mesh premium inputs with the ability to pay cycle and to gear income outputs to the income needs cycle.[21] A variable life policy modeled after the variable annuity is another type of dynamic life insurance policy that could be helpful.[22] Still another

---

[20] Even were the father to die today (the assumption made in static programming for postdeath resources), it cannot be assumed that the level of resources provided will enable his family to retain its initial per capita shares of the gross national product—that is, the family will not be given the opportunity to share in the fruits of a growing economy.

[21] See Robert I. Mehr, "Some Thoughts on Product Development in Life Insurance," *op. cit.* Under a survivorship annuity, the beneficiary is paid a periodic income upon the death of the insured. Flexibility to handle changes in family responsibilities can be accomplished through guaranteed insurability riders.

[22] *Ibid.* Cf. footnote 18, this chapter. Also see Robert I. Mehr, "Has the Life Insurance Company Product Become Obsolete," *Journal of Insurance*, Vol. XXIX, No. 1 (March,

type of policy is one that will automatically adjust to the needs of the insured as he proceeds through his life cycle.[23]

In discussing dynamic life insurance programming, Professor Belth wrote:

> . . . even if dynamic programming is found to be impractical in the daily work of life insurance agents, it could possibly be put to use in the development of new types of life insurance policy contracts. In short, the concepts underlying dynamic life insurance programming may have potential in helping the life insurance industry to meet more effectively the life insurance needs of the buying public.[24]

Life insurance companies generally have not been alert to the need for new policies as distinguished from old policy forms with new twists. When Old Equitable issued four policies at its first meeting at White Lion Inn in Cornhill, England in 1762, every basic form available now more than 200 years later had been offered.[25] "New" policies offered have been only some slightly different combinations of term, endowment, and whole life insurance rather than reflecting a change in basic concepts. There is some hope that the last third of the 20th century will bring not only revolutionary thinking but also revolutionary results in life insurance product design.

1962), in which it is suggested that the basic policy be an annual premium deferred variable annuity and that term insurance riders expressed in fixed purchasing power units be used to provide death benefits.

23 Cf. Robert I. Mehr, "A Life Adjustment Policy," *Journal of Insurance,* Vol. XXVIII, No. 2 (June, 1961). Here the need for a new policy form designed specifically for the young unmarried male is discussed, and a suggested policy form is developed.

24 Joseph M. Belth, *op. cit.,* p. 70.

25 Robert I. Mehr and Robert W. Osler, *Modern Life Insurance* (New York: Macmillan Co., 1949), p. 682.

21

Insurance in Estate Planning

As the term is commonly used, estate planning includes not only estate conservation but also estate creation. Thus, the matters discussed in Chapter 20 actually are a part of estate planning in the broad sense. The term may be used also in a restricted sense to mean the protection of an existing estate by developing plans for the disposition of the estate that give the maximum benefit to the recipient. Included in the role of estate planning is the prudent use of estate assets during the lifetime of the estate owner by utilizing arrangements which are not in conflict with his aims and philosophy. Thus, estate planning includes the creation, administration, and distribution of an estate.

Estate planning in the narrow sense has three fundamental objectives: (1) reduction of the cost of transfer, (2) arrangement for the most economical method of paying transfer costs which cannot be eliminated, and (3) development of changes in the character of estate property so as to make wise use of assets. Many techniques have been developed to achieve these objectives. Life insurance plays a vital role in a number of these techniques. The life underwriter, together with the lawyer, who coordinates all activities and prepares the necessary legal documents; the accountant, who gathers much of the needed information; and the trust officer, who is prepared to provide expert fiduciary services where needed—all these make up the estate planning team. Each expert provides the service of his field.

It is the purpose of this chapter to describe the role of the life underwriter as a member of the estate planning team and to show how life insurance may be used to protect estates. The tax aspects of life insurance policies also are a subject of this chapter.

1. THE ROLE OF THE AGENT IN ESTATE PLANNING

Why has the life insurance agent become a member of the estate planning team? Why has he joined the field of the experts such as accountants, lawyers, tax consultants, and trust officers? A number of reasons justify the presence of the life underwriter.

Life Underwriters as Advisors in Personal Finance. For years, life insurance men have undertaken the responsibility of motivating men to save. They have helped and encouraged men to create estates. It is only logical that they should help men conserve and protect their estates once they have been accumulated.

The canons of ethics of the American Bar Association prevent an attorney from actively soliciting business. Instead, he must wait for the clients to approach him. Accountants also abide by a similar code of ethics prescribed by the American Institute of Accountants.

On the other hand, life underwriters can and are expected to be aggressive. It is proper for them to bring up the subject of estates and to urge that action be taken to put them in order. The life insurance agent fills a gap between counsel and client. He is often the moving force behind the creation of the plan.

A working knowledge of estate planning can, and does, lead the underwriter to the ideal type of client. He calls on and talks with men of substantial means. He is able to help them distribute their assets in the most advisable way. He helps them arrange their estates to eliminate the probability that assets will have to be sacrificed at forced sale to raise the cash necessary to pay the costs of estate transfer.

All Life Insurance Men Are Not Qualified to Assist in Estate Planning. Estate planning has many facets. It requires knowledge of the law of wills, trusts, and taxation—to name a few. Taxation problems are further divided into estate tax, inheritance tax, gift tax, and income tax problems. The insurance man who attempts to join the estate planning team must be familiar with these concepts in addition to being an expert in life insurance.

2. THE COST OF ESTATE TRANSFER

Estates shrink as they pass from one individual to another. Several factors are responsible.

Administration Cost. All property does not pass directly from a decedent to his heirs or devisees. While title to real property passes directly, title to personal property becomes vested in the personal representative of the decedent's estate, who is appointed by the probate court to collect the personal assets of the decedents, pay all debts, taxes, and costs of administration, and to distribute the remainder to the next of kin or legatees under the will. The appointed representative is called either an executor or an administrator.[1]

---

[1] When a person dies testate (with a will) and has nominated someone to be the personal representative of the estate, the court usually appoints that nominee if he is qualified and is willing to serve. That person is called an executor. If a person dies intestate (without a will) the court appoints a representative to administer the estate. That person is called an administrator.

Estimates have been made on the cost of estate administration. On the average they run between 4 and 5 percent of the size of the estate. For an estate of $50,000, the estimated cost would be approximately $2,300, whereas the estimated cost would be $6,900 for an estate of $150,000.

On estates of $500,000, the estimated administration cost is about $22,500, and for a $1 million estate it is $43,000. These are, at best, rough estimates. Obviously, they will vary widely from case to case depending upon the character of the estate property, the complexity of the estate distribution plan, the number of states in which property is located, and whether or not the will is contested. At any rate, administration cost is an important item in estate shrinkage.

Debts.   Before estates may be passed to heirs, all debts must be paid. Since most people use credit facilities, there are usually debts to be paid out of the estate. The size of the debt will vary with the size of the estate, the length of the last illness, and the habits of the deceased.

Studies have been made to approximate the average total debts in estates. The average amount of debt ranges between 4 and 6 percent. The percent of total debts to gross estate declines as the size of the gross estate increases. For example, the average debt on a $100,000 gross estate is $5,600 or 5.6 percent. On a $1 million gross estate the average debt is $45,000 or 4.5 percent. Like estimates of administrative costs, these too can fluctuate widely depending on characteristics peculiar to each individual estate.

Taxes.   One of the major causes of shrinkage in the transfer of estates is taxes, which cut deeper than most people realize. Death taxes are levied by both the federal and state governments and are of two types: (1) an estate tax, which is a tax on the right to transfer property at death and is measured by and collected from the estate and (2) an inheritance tax, which is a tax on the right of the beneficiaries to receive property and is collected from them. The federal death tax is an estate tax. Commonly, the owner of a modest estate thinks of the federal estate tax, at least, as being the problem of the millionaire. Yet if a man owns a home, a car, a reasonable amount of life insurance, and has a few investments here and there, estate taxes begin to be a problem. Anyone who will leave more than $60,000 after deductions for administration expenses, funeral costs, and debts faces an estate tax problem; and while it may be possible to arrange the $60,000 estate so that the problem is eliminated, the owner needs to go into the matter thoroughly.

In addition to the federal estate tax, state death taxes must be taken into consideration in estate plans. States impose one, two, or three of the following types of taxes: (1) an inheritance tax, (2) an estate tax, and (3) a credit estate tax that can be used as an offset to the federal tax. The first is imposed on and measured by the shares received by the individual beneficiaries. The second, like the federal tax, is imposed on and measured by the estate before it is broken down into shares. The third is a type of tax levied when the amount of death taxes produced under the regular state death tax laws is less than the amount of credit allowed under the federal tax law for state death taxes actually paid. Its purpose is to bring the state levy up to the maximum credit.[2] Only the state of Nevada imposes no death taxes whatsoever; and while rates in most of the states are low in comparison to federal estate tax rates, the exemptions even to Class A[3] beneficiaries are as low as $5,000 in some jurisdictions.[4]

Still other taxes can cause estate shrinkage: (1) accrued federal and state income taxes not wholly covered by payroll withholdings; and (2) accrued personal and real property taxes.

Other Factors Causing Shrinkage. Two other factors can cause shrinkage in an estate:

1. When an estate passes from the owner through the executor administrator to heirs or legatees, it loses the benefit of the management of the original owner, whose knowledge of the peculiarities of the estate and whose management skill, particularly in the case of the estate containing business interests, may have been the major factor in making it profitable.

2. The beneficiary of an estate is interested primarily in income, not capital appreciation, as the estate owner may have been; consequently, estate property that is ideal for an active businessman may not be ideal for a widow. Few businessmen, if possessed of foresight enabling them to know they would die within a year, would leave the character of their estate unaltered. Such changes, made by the executor or the beneficiaries, often involve loss which must be offset with life insurance if the estate value is to be preserved. Actually, the executor may be limited by law as to the types of investments he can retain, unless the will gives him discretion.

3. THE PROBLEM OF ESTATE LIQUIDITY

The major problem of estate protection is that of offsetting the shrinkage factors in estate transfer.

The Necessity of Planning for Shrinkage. The costs of estate transfer must be paid in cash in relatively short order. Usually, debts, administration expenses, and state death taxes have to be paid within a year. Federal estate

---

[2] Five states (Alabama, Arizona, Arkansas, Florida, and Georgia) have only the credit estate tax. Only Nevada, Mississippi, North Dakota, Oregon, Utah, South Dakota, and West Virginia do not have this tax. Thus, in most states, the maximum credit for state death taxes is taken. Credit is allowed only on taxable estates exceeding $40,000. For a taxable estate of $40,000 to $90,000, the maximum credit is 0.8 percent of the amount in excess of $40,000. For taxable estates from $90,000 to $140,000 the maximum credit is $400 plus 1.6 percent of the amount in excess of $90,000. A table of maximum credits is published in the Internal Revenue Code, and these credits progress upward to $1,082,800 plus 16 percent on the amount in excess of $10,040,000.

[3] Class A beneficiaries are usually the surviving spouse, children and grandchildren, parents, and grandparents. However, the definition varies from state to state, in some few instances including only the surviving spouse.

[4] District of Columbia, Hawaii, Louisiana, New Jersey, Ohio, and Virginia, for example. For a good digest of state death taxes see the *Advanced Underwriting and Estate Planning Service,* Vol. 1, sec. 3 (Indianapolis: Research and Review Service).

taxes must be paid within 15 months after death or they incur interest costs and, in some cases, special penalties. Estates, therefore, should contain sufficient liquidity to meet these costs, or a forced sale of preferred estate assets, which will raise cash more readily, might be necessary.[5]

THE NATURE OF THE ESTATE. A liquid asset is one which can be converted into cash on a moment's notice and without loss of value. Accordingly, cash is the most liquid of all assets. Aside from life insurance, government bonds and widely circulated listed stocks[6] are perhaps the most liquid of earning assets. If estates were made up in large part of highly liquid assets, the problem of forced liquidation would not be serious. Liquidity, however, costs money. As a general rule, liquid assets produce a lower rate of return than nonliquid assets. Many estate owners are reluctant to sacrifice yield for liquidity.

ADVANCE PLANNING. To avoid forced liquidation, advance estate planning is necessary. It is strange how few people plan their estates to avoid forced liquidation; too few people really understand what forced liquidation means. Forced liquidation does not mean that the less desirable assets of the estate will be liquidated, leaving the more desirable ones for the heirs. It means that the best part of the estate will be sold—the safest and most liquid investments are usually used to meet the costs of estate transfer.[7]

The Small Estate. The necessity for advance planning is not confined to the large estate. Estate planning may also be important in the relatively small estate, even though death taxes are not a significant consideration. Cash will be needed to meet estate administration costs, to retire debts, and to pay accumulated income and property taxes. The relatively small estate is just as apt to be without sufficient cash as is the large estate. Liquidation losses are likely to be felt more acutely by the beneficiaries of a small estate because the amount to begin with is small and the losses could reduce the standard of living of the survivors to the subsistence level.

4. HANDLING ESTATE TRANSFER COSTS

If an estate owner wants to prevent the forced liquidation of estate assets to meet estate transfer costs, he must arrange in advance for the necessary estate liquidity.

---

[5] Usually the income produced by the estate is insufficient to pay the estate transfer costs and provide an adequate income for the dependent survivors. A loan is not generally a feasible solution to the problem since the executor usually does not have the authority to borrow money for the estate. Therefore, should he borrow on behalf of the estate, he would be personally liable. Even where the executor has authority by will to borrow money, a loan is not an adequate solution; the loan may not be easy to arrange, and the interest cost may be as expensive as liquidation losses.

[6] Where one individual owns a large block of stock in one company, the entire block may not be as liquid as a few shares, since an effort to sell a large block of stock may depress the market for that stock.

[7] Cases are on record in which families have lost control of a business because of the necessity for forced liquidation of a portion of stock to pay estate transfer costs.

One method would be to keep on hand a large cash fund. Obviously, this method is uneconomical. There is no reason to hold idle cash to pay expenses which have an uncertain due date if insurance can be arranged for the uncertainty.

The Use of Life Insurance.   The most logical method of meeting estate obligations is through life insurance. Under a life insurance plan, the same contingency (death) which creates the estate liability will create an offsetting estate asset. Furthermore, the value of the life insurance at death, when the cash is needed, is greater than it will ever be during the life of the insured. An earning asset which has a higher "death liquidated value" than living "going concern value" is especially useful in estate planning. The use of life insurance to pay estate settlement costs allows the current estate to be passed intact to the heirs and legatees.

Not only does the use of life insurance to pay estate obligations avoid liquidation losses in estate settlement but it also reduces the cost of estate transfer. It makes it practical for the insured to maintain a less liquid but higher income-producing estate. It lessens the problems of estate settlement, thus reducing the cost of administration. The immediate cash provided by the insurance enables the executors to take advantage of all cash discounts for prompt payment.

In the small estate the death tax problem is not an important consideration. In the large estate, however, the tax problem is one which must be given serious attention. Life insurance purchased to pay death taxes can be arranged so as to keep the insurance out of the estate of the deceased. Under present tax laws, in order to prevent the insurance proceeds from becoming subject to estate tax liabilities in the estate of the insured, the insured must not have any incidents of ownership in the policy and his estate must not be the beneficiary. Incidents of ownership include the right to the cash values and proceeds, the right to change the beneficiary, and the right of assignment. If the insured has any such right, either alone or acting with someone else, the proceeds will be taxable in his estate. It does not matter who pays the premium on the policy. The insured may pay it himself, and the proceeds still will not be taxable in his estate if the estate is not named beneficiary and if the beneficiary has ownership of the policy with no more than 5 percent chance of reversion to the insured. Unless specifically prohibited by state law and the provisions of the group policy, an employee by assigning all incidents of ownership in the coverage, including the right to convert the coverage into permanent insurance in the event of termination of employment, may remove group insurance proceeds from his taxable estate.

Arranging Insurance for Estate Liabilities.   The type of life insurance policy which should be used for estate protection purposes depends upon the nature of the estate. In large estates where income is taxed in high brackets, there may be a tax advantage in buying single premium life insurance to meet estate obligations. The annual interest and survivorship increments to the cash value under the single premium (as well as annual premium) policy accrue tax free.

Where the estate is invested in the controlling shares of a business, it may not be desirable to liquidate any of these shares to buy single premium life insurance. The best plan may be to use part of the income from these assets to pay premiums for annual premium life insurance. The same may be true of other assets which the estate owner may wish to hold.

The amount of life insurance needed would depend upon an estimate of (1) the costs of estate transfer and (2) the loss of income, if any, resulting from the change in estate management.

Other things being equal, the executor of the estate should be the beneficiary of the policy, since he will have to pay all estate transfer costs. However, other things usually are not equal, as the following discussion will show.

THE SMALLER ESTATES.   In the relatively small estates there may be some advantages in naming the wife as a revocable beneficiary. Life insurance proceeds paid to a named beneficiary are not subject to state death taxes in a number of states.[8] Moreover, proceeds paid to a named beneficiary do not go through the general estate for probate; so certain probate expenses will be saved. The disadvantage of naming the widow as revocable beneficiary is the lack of assurance that she will use the funds to pay the estate liabilities. This, of course, might be an advantage if it were to prove more attractive to retain the insurance proceeds than to preserve the general estate.

If the insured wants to make sure that the policy proceeds will be used on behalf of the estate and, for the reasons given, does not want to name his estate as beneficiary, he may use a revocable life insurance trust. The trustee is named beneficiary of the policy and is authorized to purchase assets from the general estate (or to make loans to it) in amounts necessary to pay off the estate liabilities. The executor is given the authority to sell to or borrow from the trustee by the insured in his will. The disadvantage of this arrangement is the added cost involved.

THE LARGER ESTATES.   In the larger estates none of the above beneficiary arrangements may be satisfactory. Life insurance payable to the estate or to revocable beneficiaries (individuals or trustees) is taxable under the federal estate tax laws. A beneficiary arrangement which will exclude the life insurance proceeds from the estate of the insured may be desirable. One such arrangement is for the proceeds to be payable to an owner bene-

---

[8] In all but 19 states, life insurance paid to a named beneficiary is exempt from state death taxes even if the insured retained an incident of ownership. In 14 of these 19 states, special exemptions varying from $10,000 to $75,000 are granted for proceeds paid to named beneficiaries. Four of the five states not providing exemptions impose only a credit estate tax, so no state death taxes need to be paid unless there is a federal tax. The fifth state, Arizona, has an estate tax with tax brackets equal to the maximum state death tax credit allowed under Section 2011(b) of the Internal Revenue Code. It has no inheritance tax.

ficiary with someone other than the insured being designated as successor owner in the event of prior death of the beneficiary owner. As mentioned earlier, although the insured may pay the premiums, he must have no incidents of ownership in the policy. The disadvantages of this arrangement are the same as the revocable beneficiary designation plus the fact that the owner beneficiary can cash in the policy before the insured dies. Also, if she predeceases the insured, the value of the policy will be includable in her taxable estate.

If the insured has adult children, a better plan might be to have one or more of them owner beneficiaries of the policy. This will also ease the tax problem in the wife's estate, since the policy will not be taxable in her estate if she predeceases her husband. Furthermore, if she outlives her husband, the insurance proceeds will not increase her estate and thus raise her potential estate tax liability. The children can use the proceeds to buy estate property and thereby give the necessary liquidity to the estate.

In order to guarantee that the policy proceeds will be used to provide estate liquidity, the insured can create an irrevocable trust to own and be the beneficiary of the insurance. The trust agreement can authorize the trustee to purchase estate assets from the executor or to lend the executor cash to provide the necessary estate liquidity. The insured's will can give to the executor the authority to sell to or borrow from the trustee. If the trust beneficiary has only a life interest in the trust income (i.e., no right to terminate the trust and take over the property), the trust property will not be taxable in the beneficiary's estate.

If the plan is designed to free the insured's estate of the insurance proceeds, the owner beneficiaries must not be under any *legal* obligation to use the policy proceeds on behalf of the estate. Otherwise they will be taxable in the insured's estate. Also, if the insured pays the premiums on the insurance, these premiums will constitute a gift on which a gift tax may be payable.

The policy proceeds should be placed on the interest only option with full right of withdrawal. In this way the proceeds can earn interest until the funds are needed.

5. REDUCING ESTATE TRANSFER COSTS

Estate planning involves not only providing estate liquidity to pay the cost of estate transfer but also arranging the estate to reduce these costs. In the small estate the principal objective is to save administration costs, whereas in the large estate the major concern is to reduce the tax liability.

The principal method of effecting savings in estate administration costs is to arrange for the property to be transferred to the beneficiary without its having to be probated.[9] The purpose is to bypass probate and other ad-

---

[9] To probate means to establish the authenticity or validity of a will. This is done in a probate court, a special court limited to the administration of decedent estates.

ministration costs, and to eliminate the risk of having the estate owner's distribution plan contested by disappointed actual or would-be heirs. The costs and delays involved in defending against a contested will can be expensive.

To save federal estate taxes, a properly drawn will and the use of other transfer devices can be effective. These estate transfer devices—life insurance paid to a named beneficiary, wills, gifts, trusts, and joint ownership —need examination.

Life Insurance Payable to a Named Beneficiary.   Life insurance should usually be made payable to a named beneficiary rather than to the insured's estate. A named beneficiary, it will be recalled, saves probate costs because the proceeds will be paid directly to the beneficiary rather than first passing through the estate. Furthermore, as previously mentioned, the use of a named beneficiary will exempt the insurance proceeds in whole or in part from death taxes in virtually every state. Federal estate taxes, of course, are unaffected by the naming of the beneficiary unless the insured has given up all incidents of ownership.[10] Another advantage of paying policies to a named beneficiary rather than to the estate is the speed of settlement. Estates take time to settle, but life insurance proceeds are paid without delay.

The advantages of life insurance as estate property make it a candidate for consideration in lieu of other estate property currently held by the estate owner. It might prove beneficial to convert certain estate property into single premium life insurance or to use the income from the estate to buy annual premium insurance to utilize the investment advantages of life insurance.[11]

Wills.   Upon a person's death, his property may be distributed either under the laws of descent and distribution[12] or by will. The laws of descent and distribution are state laws prescribing how property is to be allocated in the absence of a will.[13] Unless a person wants his property distributed in accordance with the "public will" made by his state legislature, he had bet-

---

[10] IRC, Section 2042, includes as an incident of ownership any reversionary interest in the policy (either by law or contract) that exceeds 5 percent of the value of the policy immediately before the death of the insured. The reverter interest is valued actuarially and is based upon the probability of the insured surviving the beneficiaries.

[11] Cf. Chapter 8 for a discussion of the investment attributes of life insurance.

[12] Laws of descent specify how real estate passes to heirs, whereas laws of distribution indicate the method of disposing of personal property.

[13] The Illinois law, for example, provides that one third of each parcel of real estate and of personal property goes to the surviving spouse, and two thirds to the children equally, or their issue *per stirpes* (one from whom a family is descended). If there is no surviving spouse, real and personal property goes to all the children equally, or their issues *per stirpes*. If there are no children, one half of the real estate and all of the personal property goes to the surviving spouse, and the other one half of the real estate is shared by the parents, brothers, and sisters equally. If there is only one parent, he or she receives two shares, and if there are deceased brothers and sisters, their issues share *per stirpes*. If there are no children or spouse, the parents, brothers, and sisters share equally. Where the decedent leaves no heirs, his property passes to the state under the escheat statutes. *The statutes vary among the states.*

ter make his own will. Although he does not have complete freedom in making his will,[14] he can design one more in keeping with his objectives than the one written for him by the state.

Through a will, the testator[15] can discriminate among his children, leaving the largest shares to the ones that deserve (or need) them the most. If the estate is small, the testator may not wish to divide the estate but to leave it entirely to his wife to provide her with a livable income. The testator may wish to include persons not covered by the laws of descent and distribution, or to leave specific property to certain designated individuals rather than to leave them shares in the net estate. Another advantage of a will is that it allows the testator to select his own executor.

THE MARITAL DEDUCTION.   In the case of an estate passing between husband and wife by reason of death, a marital deduction is allowed in the federal estate tax by Section 2056 of the code. The marital deduction has important applications in estate planning. In some situations it will be impossible for the estate owner to take full advantage of the marital deduction without executing a will. In estate planning, it is highly important that this deduction be clearly understood. The marital deduction is whatever the deceased leaves the surviving spouse outright or under a nonterminable interest,[16] up to 50 percent of the adjusted gross estate.[17] Inasmuch as the portion of the estate qualifying for the marital deduction is not subject to estate tax, use of it can effect material savings.

Assume a married man owns assets worth $220,000, including securities, cash, business interests, real estate, life insurance, and all other assets. When he dies and his estate tax is computed, the first step is to deduct all obligations he owes, funeral expenses, estate administration costs, uninsured casualty losses, and state death taxes paid on charitable bequests. Suppose these amount to $20,000, leaving an adjusted gross estate of $200,000. As stated, the marital deduction is whatever the deceased leaves his wife outright or under an arrangement involving a nonterminable interest, up to one half of his adjusted gross estate. Thus, if he leaves his wife $50,000, then that amount is the marital deduction. If he leaves her $100,000 outright, then $100,000 is the marital deduction. If he leaves her the entire $200,000 outright, then the marital deduction is still only $100,000 because

---

[14] The rights of the surviving spouse usually are protected by state law, and some states restrict the amount of charitable contributions. Rules against perpetuities and accumulation of income also restrict the testator.

[15] The person who makes a will.

[16] A terminable interest is one in which the spouse's interest in the proceeds is for life only, or one that will terminate or fail upon the lapse of time or the occurrence or non-occurrence of an event or contingency; provided an interest passes or has passed to someone other than the surviving spouse or his or her estate, and such other person may possess or enjoy the proceeds after the interest of the surviving spouse fails. IRC, Section 2056(b)(6).

[17] The adjusted gross estate is the gross estate minus funeral expenses, administration expenses, debts, state death taxes paid on charitable bequests, and uninsured property and casualty losses suffered during the estate settlement period. (IRC, Sections 2053 and 2054.)

of the 50 percent ceiling. Thus, the marital deduction in this estate can be any amount up to $100,000.

Here is what the absence of a will in Illinois, for example, can mean with respect to the marital deduction. Under Illinois law, when a husband dies without a will and leaves children, the wife automatically is entitled to an undivided one third and the children to an undivided two thirds of the estate.

Therefore, where a husband dies intestate (without a will) and the estate is, say, $200,000, the wife would get $66,666 outright from the husband, and the children would receive the balance. This means that the marital deduction would be $66,666, with a resulting tax liability of about $13,000. By the simple expedient of a will leaving half the estate to the wife, the estate tax would be $4,800, a tax reduction of over $8,000.

THE LIFE UNDERWRITER AND WILLS.   Typical of the genuine importance of the position of the life underwriter is the substantial service he can render to his policyholders by discussing wills.[18] Rarely will an attorney ask a client about his will. To do so is considered unethical. He must wait for the person to come to him—even if he waits so long that the individual dies intestate with all the trouble and loss to dependents an intestacy can produce. But a life insurance agent, who understands what the absence of a will can mean with respect to the marital deduction, for instance, will invariably find out if there is a will.

Living Gifts.   One method of reducing estate administration costs and death taxes is to reduce the value of the estate by making living transfers (gifts) of assets to someone else. The motive for the transfer, however, must be strictly a living motive—i.e., the transfer must not be made in contemplation of death, or the gift may be set aside and the property taxed in the decedent's estate.

The Revenue Act provides that transfers of property made more than three years prior to the death of a decedent shall not be taxed as a transfer in contemplation of death. However, if the death occurs during the three-year period from the date of the gift, the presumption is that it was made in contemplation of death. The burden of proof that it was otherwise is on the estate. It is desirable, therefore, to establish clearly that a living motive exists when a transfer of property is consummated. Typical living motives

---

[18] Bar associations are extremely jealous of any action on the part of laymen which they interpret as encroaching on the practice of law. For example, in one instance, a member of the Illegal Practices Committee of a bar association informed a life insurance agency specializing in the sale of insurance for estate planning purposes that he considered it an illegal practice of law for a life underwriter to discuss with a client what provisions should be contained in his will even if the life insurance agent recommended that he consult his lawyer about the changes. The extent to which an agent can enter into a discussion of a will, according to the committee member, is to recommend that the client see his lawyer. Any recommendations as to provisions should be made only to the lawyer, who will then pass them on to the client if the client comes to see him. While this opinion is extreme, it does illustrate the care that agents must exercise in talking to prospects and policyholders about wills.

include providing an independent income for relatives, the giver's withdrawal from business, lower income (but not estate!) taxes for the donor, and the like.

When a gift is made, a gift tax liability may be incurred. Every individual has a lifetime gift tax exemption of $30,000. In addition, he has an annual exclusion of $3,000 per donee. If he gives away more than $3,-000 in any one year to any person, his annual exclusion will be exceeded and he must then turn to his $30,000 lifetime gift tax exemption. For example, if in one year he gives away $5,000 to each of two persons, the difference between that figure and his $3,000 annual exclusion per donee must be taken out of his $30,000 lifetime gift tax exemption, leaving an unused total of $26,000. If he gives away, say, $29,000 during the following year to any one individual, he will have entirely used up his $30,000 lifetime exemption, and from then on he will have left only the $3,000 annual exclusion per donee. Therefore, in subsequent years if he makes a gift of more than $3,000 to any one person, the excess over $3,000 will be a taxable gift.

The foregoing rules apply to single men or women. In the case of married men and women, the rules are more favorable.

A married person may give away, with the consent of the spouse, $6,000 annually per donee without gift tax liability, and he and his spouse jointly have a lifetime gift tax exemption of $60,000 over and above the annual exclusion. This is accomplished by taking advantage of the marital deduction applicable to gift taxes which considers a gift of property owned by either spouse as being made 50 percent by the wife and 50 percent by the husband. It is important to note, in connection with gifts made by a spouse, that the law requires the consent of the other spouse before the combined exemptions and exclusions will apply; i.e., if the husband gives away, say, $6,000, he can claim only a $3,000 annual exclusion unless his wife consents to the gift. If she consents, the other $3,000 is considered as a gift from her. If the gift is one of $8,000, then $4,000 is considered as a gift from each spouse so that $1,000 is deducted from the $30,000 lifetime exemption available to each party.

Even when gifts are subject to a gift tax liability, they are quite likely to be taxed at a rate far lower than the same amount of property would have been taxed under the estate tax rate. For one thing, the gift tax rate is about 25 percent less than the estate tax rate. The actual differential, however, is likely to be greater, since both tax structures are progressive. For example, a taxable living gift of, say, $10,000 might be taxed in 10.5 percent gift tax brackets,[19] whereas if the property had remained in the estate to be transferred at death, it might be taxed in, say, 30 percent estate tax brackets.[20] By taking assets out of high estate tax brackets and placing them in tax-free or low gift tax brackets via living transfers, more of the estate can be conserved for the beneficiaries.

---

[19] This assumes that taxable gifts of $20,000 have already been made.
[20] This assumes a taxable estate of $150,000.

Estate plans often include gifts of life insurance and annuities on the lives of the donee. It is especially popular to make these gifts to children and grandchildren.

However, if the gift of life insurance as with any gift is made within three years before death, the decedent's estate must establish living motives for the gift. Otherwise, the proceeds would be includable in his gross estate.

If a donor makes a gift of a life insurance policy on his life more than three years before his death, retains no incidents of ownership in the policy, and pays no further premiums, the policy proceeds normally will not be included in his gross estate. However, if the donor continues to pay premiums on the policy after relinquishing all incidents of ownership, part of the proceeds will be taxed at his death. The Internal Revenue Service has held in Revenue Ruling 67–463 that premiums paid by the donor within three years of his death constitute a transfer of an interest in the death proceeds. The value of this interest is measured by the proportion the amount of premiums paid in the three-year period bears to the total premiums. For example, assume the donor made a gift of a $100,000 policy with an annual premium of $2,000. Assume that he had paid 12 annual premiums, 3 of them falling within 3 years of his death. Under the IRS ruling, the amount of proceeds to be included in the donor's estate is $25,-000, which is $3/12$ of the total proceeds of $100,000.

However, the IRS ruling has been challenged by those who hold that only the sum of the premiums paid in the three years prior to death is included in the donor's estate—in this example, only $6,000. The issue has come up in four cases—two in federal district courts and two in the Tax Court. A U.S. District Court in Michigan in July, 1968, ruled against the IRS, holding that only the amount of the premium paid in contemplation of death is included in the deceased's estate. In December, 1968 a U.S. District Court in Texas ruled in favor of the IRS, holding that an interest in the policy was kept alive by premium payments in contemplation of death, and that the value of this interest is measured by the value of the life insurance policy proceeds in accordance with the IRS formula. However, this decision was overruled in April, 1970 by the Fifth U.S. Circuit Court of Appeals. In September, 1969, and again in January, 1970, the IRS had adverse rulings by the Tax Court, which held that payment of the premiums did not constitute a constructive transfer of interest in the policy, so that only the dollar amount of premiums paid in contemplation of death are in the deceased's estate. In the September, 1969 case four dissenting judges believed that the deceased had transferred more than just money used to pay premiums; he had transferred a property right in the insurance, which was kept in force by such premium payments. Thus, the value of the transferred property should be measured in terms of the life insurance policy proceeds purchased with these premiums. Only one of these cases has been ruled on by a Circuit Court as of May 1, 1970. So, until the issue is finally settled, the donor of a life insurance policy on his own life should play it safe by shifting to the donee the obligation to pay the future premiums, if any, on this policy.

Insurance is a valuable asset for the donee and is a good gift medium. It is likely to be held by the insured until needed for a given and necessary purpose rather than haphazardly dissipated in careless spending and investing. Also, a life insurance policy can be paid for on an annual basis so that the donor can take advantage of the annual $3,000 exclusion available for each donee.

Trusts.   Another instrument used effectively in estate planning is the trust, testamentary or living. Under a trust, the donor (settlor) transfers property to a second person (trustee) for the benefit of a third party (beneficiary).[21]

TESTAMENTARY TRUSTS.   A testamentary trust is a trust created under a will: Bob provides under his will that certain assets go to Irwin in trust for Margaret. The trust, therefore, does not become operative until the death of the settlor.

A number of reasons may impel a man to create a testamentary trust. He may wish to arrange for professional management of the estate; he may want to control the use of the estate income; he may have minor children for whom otherwise a guardian of the property would have to be appointed; he may wish to protect the estate from the creditors of the beneficiaries through a spendthrift trust clause; or he may wish to reduce estate taxes and estate settlement costs. Only the last of these reasons needs elaboration.

A testamentary trust will not reduce estate taxes upon the death of the testator nor will it reduce estate settlement costs. The potential trust property remains in the estate of the testator until distributed to the trust after the will is probated. It is handled and taxed like all other property. The trust, however, can be set up to reduce taxes and administration cost upon the death of the trust beneficiary. If the trust beneficiary is given a life interest only in the trust income and does not hold a general power of appointment over the trust property at her death, the property is not taxable in her estate.[22] In this way successive death taxes are eliminated.[23] Since the

---

[21] The settlor may not be the sole beneficiary under a trust, although he may be a co-beneficiary. He also may be the trustee or a co-trustee.

[22] A general power of appointment is one which may be exercised in favor of the trust beneficiary, her estate, or her creditors. The trust beneficiary, however, may be given the right to invade the principal if this power is limited to amounts needed for necessary support, education, or medical care.

[23] The federal estate tax allows an estate tax credit, however, on prior transfers to decedents as follows:

Within 2 years	100% credit
Within 3 or 4 years	80% credit
Within 5 or 6 years	60% credit
Within 7 or 8 years	40% credit
Within 9 or 10 years	20% credit
Over 10 years	0% credit

property does not enter her estate, it need not go through probate; so these costs also are not incurred.

LIVING TRUSTS.   A living trust is one that becomes operative during the lifetime of the creator. Living trusts may be either revocable or irrevocable.

Revocable Trusts.   A revocable trust is one in which the creator reserves the right to terminate the trust and reacquire the property. Aside from the advantages offered to the creator by the testamentary trust, the revocable living trust offers additional uses. The creator can reduce estate administration cost if the trust remains in force after his death. Furthermore, the beneficiaries will continue to receive their allocated income (and principal) after the death of the creator without having to wait until a will is probated. Finally, a revocable trust, by meeting certain standards, can offer income tax advantages.[24] Investment income can be transferred from the higher tax brackets of the creator to the lower tax brackets of the trust or its beneficiaries by placing the investment property in trust.[25] Furthermore, if the

---

[24] Income from a trust will not be taxable to the grantor unless the corpus will revert to him within 10 years after the trust is created; he can terminate the trust within 10 years after its creation; he can control the use of trust property or income; he can use the trust income for his own benefit; or he may exercise administrative powers for his own benefit. The concept that husband and wife are one economic unit was adopted by the 1969 Tax Reform Act. Therefore, the income of a trust will be taxable to the grantor if that income can be controlled by or used for the benefit of the grantor's spouse. IRC, Section 673(c), dealing with short-term reversionary trusts, makes an exception to the first rule above if the reversionary interest is not to take effect until the death of the beneficiary. The short-term reversionary trust is discussed later in this chapter.

[25] Subject to the exceptions noted in footnote 24, a trust is a separate tax entity. For income tax treatment, trusts may be classified either as simple or complex. A simple trust is one that must distribute all of its income currently and has no provisions for charitable or capital distributions. The trust income is taxable to the beneficiary in the year earned. The trust itself will be taxed only on capital gains allocated to the corpus. It is allowed a personal exemption of $300 but no standard deduction. All other trusts are called complex trusts. Income held and accumulated for beneficiaries is taxable to the trust, generally under the same rules applying to individuals. The trust has a personal exemption of $100 but no standard deduction. For the most part, an unlimited deduction is given for amounts allocated to charity. Beneficiaries of a complex trust to whom income is required to be distributed currently and to whom other amounts are distributed or are distributable must report as income such amounts that do not exceed the distributable net income of the trust. Before the 1954 Revenue Code, when a trustee accumulated the income from the trust and later distributed it to the beneficiary (usually during periods of low income) the beneficiary would be taxed on the income received at the tax rates applicable to his income in that year. The taxes paid by the trust over the years would be credited against his tax. The 1954 Code introduced the 5-year throwback rule under which the accumulated income of the trust for up to the previous 5 years was treated for income tax purposes as though it had been received during these years. The 1969 Tax Reform Act extended the throwback to an unlimited period for accumulations beginning in 1969 in order to further restrict the tax advantages of accumulation trusts. A short-cut method is available for use by beneficiaries in computing their income tax on accumulation distributions. The accumulation distribution (not counting the current year) is divided by the number of years accumulated and added to the gross income for each of the previous 3 years to determine the additional tax for these years. The total additional tax so computed is divided by 3 and multiplied by the number of accumulated years. This amount less the taxes paid by the trust is the tax on the accumulation distribution excluding the distribution for the current year.

property is not sold before the death of the creator, the value at the creator's death becomes the acquisition cost for computing capital gains in the event of a sale thereafter.[26] This latter tax advantage gives the revocable trust an edge over *inter vivos* gifts if no estate tax problem is involved.

In a revocable trust, the transfer of property from the grantor to the trustee does not constitute a taxable gift, but payments of income from the trust to the beneficiary do result in a taxable gift by the creator.

Irrevocable Trust. An irrevocable trust is one in which the creator has not retained the right to terminate the trust and reacquire its property. The principal advantage of the irrevocable trust over the revocable trust in estate planning is the reduction of death taxes. An absolute and irrevocable transfer of property to a trust takes the property out of the grantor's estate and eliminates the estate tax on it. The transfer, however, becomes a taxable gift.[27] The same income tax advantages are available under the irrevocable trust as under the revocable trust with one exception: the grantor's cost basis plus any gift taxes paid on the transfer will govern acquisition costs for establishing capital gains, even though the sale takes place after the death of the insured. If the fair market value of the property at the time of the transfer is less than the grantor's cost basis plus gift taxes, the basis for determining capital losses will be the fair market value at the time of the transfer.

A useful estate planning tool is the sprinkler trust under which the trustee has discretionary powers to distribute trust income or principal among a given class of beneficiaries in whatever portions and at whatever times he chooses, usually in accordance with the needs of these beneficiaries and at times which will produce the greatest income tax savings to these beneficiaries. If one of the trust beneficiaries is the trustee, all of the trust income will be treated as income to him unless he is limited in his power to sprinkle the income by clearly understood standards relating to such factors as the beneficiaries' health, support, and education. As a precautionary measure, a corporate trustee or some independent party should be named as co-trustee.

SHORT TERM REVERSIONARY TRUSTS. Short term reversionary trusts —i.e., trusts under which the corpus (body) of the trust or the income therefrom reverts to the grantor after a specified period or event—were long the subject of litigation and confusing Internal Revenue Service reg-

---

[26] The standards indicated in footnote 24, of course, do not have to be met to enjoy this latter advantage since the trust property is taxable in the grantor's estate.

[27] Whether the $3,000 annual gift tax exclusion allowed for each donee applies to gifts in trust depends upon whether the gift is of a present rather than future interest. The exclusion applies only to present interests. A present interest is an unrestricted right to immediate use of such property or the income from it. For example, if a trust is created under which the income is to be paid to the wife as long as she lives, with the trust property passing to the son upon the wife's death, two gifts are considered to have been made. The wife receives a present interest in the form of a life estate, whereas the son receives a future interest in the form of a remainder interest. The $3,000 exclusion applies only to the gift to the wife.

ulations until the Revenue Act of 1954, which clearly defined their taxable status. The 1954 law opened the way to effecting legal tax savings through such trusts, which savings can be combined advantageously with life insurance in a number of ways, some few of which will be mentioned by way of illustration.

Generally speaking, the 1954 Revenue Act provides that the grantor will not be subject to tax on the income of a noncharitable trust if the term of the trust is for at least 10 years or until the death of the income beneficiary, whichever occurs first, if the income is not paid to or accumulated for the benefit of the grantor or used to discharge one of his legal obligations. (The term for a charitable trust is two years if the income is payable to a specified church, church organization, tax-exempt school, or tax-exempt hospital.)

The short-term trust, therefore, offers persons in higher income tax brackets a chance to transfer income from property or securities from their own higher tax brackets to the lower tax brackets of the trust or trust beneficiary, or both, without the necessity of giving away the corpus of the trust permanently. Thus, for instance, a parent in a 59 percent tax bracket can save on his tax bill by placing some of his income-producing property in a short-term, reversionary trust. Under this arrangement, instead of 59 percent of the income from the property going for taxes, as it would if received by him, the income is paid to the trust and is taxed at the lower rate applied to the lower income of the trust or trust beneficiaries.[28]

Such a trust can be set up with the trustee directed to use the income to purchase various types of life insurance, such as educational insurance on a child, insurance on the life of a grandchild, insurance on a partner or co-stockholder, and insurance on a son during the first few years of his marriage when his need for protection is high but his ability to pay is low. The short-term trust may also be used to provide an income to help support relatives where there is no legal obligation to do so; or to help a son get started in his business or profession.

It is even possible to set up such a trust to pay for life insurance on the life of the grantor if (1) the income is payable directly to a trust beneficiary

---

[28] The trust can be directed to pay the trust income to the grantor's young children in annual amounts equal to the sum of their personal income tax exemption and low-income allowance. The Tax Reform Act of 1969 increased the personal exemption from $600 to the following schedule: 1970, $625; 1971, $650; 1972, $700; and 1973 and after, $750. The Act replaced the minimum standard deduction of $300 with the following schedule of low-income allowances: 1970, $1100; 1971, $1050; and 1972 and after, $1,000. Thus each child can be paid the following scheduled amounts free of income taxes: 1970, $1,725; 1971, $1,700; 1972, $1,700; and 1973 and after, $1,750. If at least $100 of the income paid to each trust beneficiary is attributable to dividends on corporate stocks, the amount of tax-free payments can be increased by $100, making a total of $1,850 by 1973. The funds paid by the trust to the children will escape income tax because they are distributions and as such are deductible by the trust in arriving at its taxable income. The creator can continue to take personal exemptions for each child as dependents, assuming they meet the dependency requirements. The trust can be directed to use the remaining income, if any, to purchase 10-pay life insurance on the lives of the children.

who has (2) the full authority to use the money in any way he or she sees fit. If there is no trust requirement or other binding agreement that the income is to be used to buy insurance on the grantor, but the trust beneficiary so uses it of his or her own free will, then the insurance so purchased will be considered to be owned by the beneficiary and not includable in the grantor's estate at the time of his death. Thus a temporary trust could be set up for 10 years and the income used by the trust beneficiary (voluntarily and entirely at the beneficiary's option) to purchase 10-pay whole life. At the end of the 10 years, the insurance will be fully paid up and will be the property of the beneficiary. The corpus of the trust could then revert to the grantor. The insurance would have been paid for from favorably taxed income (compared to the tax that would have been paid had the income been taxed to the grantor), and yet the corpus of the trust will not be permanently lost to the grantor.

Short-term reversionary trusts constitute taxable gifts, the amount of which is the value of the transferred property minus the value of the grantor's retained interest. The Internal Revenue Service provides tables for calculating these values. The factor for a 10-year reversionary trust is 0.291081. Thus, a taxable gift of $29,108.10 would be involved in the transfer of $100,000 into a 10-year reversionary trust. Should the grantor die during the effective period of the trust, only the discounted or reversionary value of the trust will be included in the grantor's estate for estate tax purposes. In the above case this value will range from $70,891.90 if death occurs in the 1st year to $96,618.40 if death occurs in the 10th year. Small savings, therefore, in estate taxes are possible under the short-term reversionary trust.

LIFE INSURANCE TRUST.   A life insurance trust is a type of living trust under which the property involved consists wholly or partly of life insurance policies held by and/or payable to the trust. The policies can be made payable to the trust either by beneficiary designation or by assignment. The procedure to use depends upon the purpose of the trust. If the sole purpose of the trust is to collect, invest, and distribute the proceeds of the policies, this purpose can be accomplished by naming the trustee as beneficiary under the policies. If the trust is irrevocable, the trustee should be named as an irrevocable beneficiary. Where the trustee is to perform certain duties with respect to the policies during the lifetime of the insured or where the policies are to constitute living gifts to the trust, a transfer of the policy to the trustee by assignment is the appropriate procedure. In the latter case, the trustee also should be named the beneficiary.

A life insurance trust may be funded or unfunded. Under the funded insurance trust, the trustee has the obligation to pay the premiums on the insurance from property transferred to him by the grantor. The premiums are paid either from the trust income or from trust property if the trust income is insufficient. The trust may be partially funded with the grantor paying that part of the premiums which cannot be met out of trust income. In an unfunded trust, the premiums are paid directly by the insured. No property is turned over to the trust to fund the premiums.

One of the uses of a life insurance trust has already been discussed: to provide estate liquidity. Other uses are to integrate the insurance estate with the other estate in order to achieve a single plan of estate administration; to gain more discretion in insurance settlements than is available through life insurance settlement options; to make the appointment of a guardian of the property unnecessary in cases where the insurance proceeds are for the benefit of minors; and to arrange for the investment of life insurance proceeds in types of securities likely to offer some hedge against inflation.

Tax Aspects of Life Insurance Trusts. The tax consequences of a life insurance trust depend upon whether the trust is revocable or irrevocable, the same as in other living trusts. If revocable, there are no tax consequences, whether funded or unfunded; i.e., no gift tax liability is incurred, and there are no special income or estate tax savings. In an irrevocable funded life insurance trust, there are no income tax consequences if the income from trust property is earmarked to pay premiums on the life of the grantor. Such payments are considered taxable income to the grantor.[29]

The values of the policies turned over to an irrevocable trust and the future premiums paid on them by the insured are taxable gifts. Whether the $3,000 annual gift tax exclusion applies to these gifts depends upon whether the trust beneficiary is given a present or future interest in the policies. To establish a present interest and thus allow the donor the $3,000 annual exclusion, the trust beneficiary must be given an immediate right to the policy and to all its benefits.

The insurance policies are treated at death in the same way they would have been treated had there been no trust: the proceeds are not part of the insured's taxable estate if he has retained no incidents of ownership in the policy.[30] As for property transferred to a funded life insurance trust, the same principles of estate taxation apply as are applied to any other living trust.

Joint Ownership with Right of Survivorship. A useful device for estate transfer is joint ownership. Real estate may be held in joint tenancy, which means that upon the death of a co-owner the property automatically passes to the surviving owners and not to the heirs of the deceased.[31] Two or more people may also own personal property as joint owners. For the property to pass automatically to the surviving co-owners, they must clearly specify that they hold the property as joint owners with right of survivorship and not as owners in common.

---

[29] IRC, Section 677(a)(3). If, however, the income is used to pay premiums on the lives of persons other than the grantor, the income is taxable to the trust and not to the grantor.

[30] If, however, the trustee is under *legal* obligation to use the proceeds on behalf of the insured's estate, they become taxable in the insured's estate.

[31] When co-owners wish to leave their interests to their heirs rather than to the surviving owner, they must hold the property as tenants in common rather than joint tenants.

The advantage of joint tenancy and joint ownership with the right of survivorship is that the property automatically passes to the survivor without passing through the deceased's estate for administrative purposes. This arrangement has no federal estate tax advantages, however, because if the deceased paid for the property from his own funds, the full value of the property is taxable in his estate. There might be some state death tax advantages because a few states exempt jointly held property entirely, and some others tax only the fractional interest held by the deceased as though the property were held in equal shares as tenants in common. A number of states treat jointly held property in the same manner as it is treated by the federal government: the share paid for by the decedent is taxable.[32]

There may be some federal tax disadvantages to the creation of joint tenancy or joint ownership with right of survivorship. As between husband and wife, the creation of joint ownership in personal property will be treated as a taxable gift made by the tenant whose proportional interest in the property is less than his proportional contribution to the purchase price.[33] As between others than husband and wife, the creation of a joint tenancy in real estate as well as in personal property can result in a taxable gift.[34] Thus, gifts of joint ownership have the disadvantage of incurring possible gift tax liability without any offsetting decrease in estate tax liability.

In small estates where potential gift and estate tax liability create no problem, a gift in joint ownership with right of survivorship has an advantage over a full ownership gift or a gift as tenants in common. It will accomplish the purpose of reducing estate administration cost while at the same time giving the wife, as surviving owner, a new cost basis for figuring capital gains in event the property is sold after the husband's death. The new cost basis will be the value at the husband's death rather than the original cost to the husband.[35] In the event of inflation, this is an advantage since the value at death is likely to be greater than the original cost.

In the larger estate the use of joint ownership with right of survivorship might not be desirable. Factors to consider in making the decision are: the gift tax problem; the problem of successive taxation in the estate of the survivor; the problem of proving the amount contributed by the survivor to

---

[32] By way of example, Missouri law provides that property held jointly with right of survivorship passes to the surviving co-owner tax free, except where the joint ownership was created in contemplation of death; Illinois law provides that jointly held property is taxable as if the property had been held in equal shares in tenancy in common; Wisconsin law provides that jointly held property is taxable to the extent of the decedent's fractional interest in it; Iowa provides that property held jointly with the right of survivorship is taxable to the survivor, except such part as can be shown to have originally belonged to the survivor and never belonged to the decedent; and Indiana law is the same as Iowa law except that real estate held as tenants by the entirety (a joint estate with right of survivorship between husband and wife) is not taxed.

[33] Joint bank accounts and government savings bonds are excluded.

[34] IRC, Section 2515, provides that a joint tenancy in real estate between spouses shall not be treated as a gift even though all or most of the purchase price is contributed by one spouse.

[35] IRC, Section 1014(b)(9).

the purchase price; and the problem of assuring that the property will be distributed according to the desires of the estate owner. In this latter connection, he will have no assurance that a second husband of his widow may not gain more from his estate than will his children.

Business Interests. When the estate includes a business interest, life insurance can play a major role in estate plans. As discussed in Chapter 22, death of the owner can cause severe shrinkage in the value of the business interest. When the owner of a business dies, the business is either liquidated or reorganized.

If the decision is to liquidate the business, life insurance might be necessary to facilitate this liquidation and to protect the general estate from business debts. Estate planning for business liquidation is usually confined to sole proprietorship. In partnerships and close corporations, the plan is nearly always one of reorganization. Life insurance is used to finance a buy and sell agreement.[36] Each partner or stockholder will insure the lives of the others so that upon a death, life insurance will be available to the survivors to purchase the interests of the deceased at the agreed upon price. The plan assures that the business interest will be liquidated promptly and fairly and will thereby reduce the cost of estate administration.

6. EXAMPLES OF ESTATE TAX PLANNING

The difference that estate planning can make in the conservation of an estate may be illustrated by the following examples. These examples are confined to estate tax planning only, but similar illustrations could be developed to demonstrate the advantages of planning for other estate shrinkage factors.

Assumptions. The following plans assume that the husband predeceases his wife by at least 10 years and that the wife's share received after the husband's death is fully intact at her death. Also, it is assumed that the husband has not previously utilized his lifetime gift tax exemption. An adjusted gross estate of $200,000 is assumed for a married man with two children.

The Plans. Six estate plans are outlined.

Plan 1

Leave $200,000 life estate[37] to wife by will giving her no power of appointment of the remainder at her death

Tax when husband dies	$31,500[38]	
Tax when widow dies	None	
Net retained by wife		$168,500
Net acquired by children		168,500

---

[36] See Chapter 22.

[37] A life estate is an arrangement whereby the beneficiary has the right to enjoy the income as long as he or she lives. Upon death of the beneficiary, the property goes to a secondary beneficiary who has already been named.

[38] Tax rates used throughout this chapter are those in effect at the time of this writing.

There is no second tax when the wife dies because the property was neither given to the wife outright nor did she have a general power of appointment of the remainder at her death. For these same reasons, the estate did not qualify for the marital deduction.

Plan 2

Leave $200,000 outright by will to wife		
Tax when husband dies	$ 4,800	
Tax when widow dies	30,136	
Net retained by wife		$195,200
Net acquired by children		165,064

The reason for higher taxes upon the death of the widow is that her estate will not have the benefit of the marital deduction.

Plan 3

Leave $100,000 outright to wife by will		
Leave $100,000 life estate to wife by will without power of appointment		
Tax when husband dies	$4,800	
Tax when widow dies	4,044	
Net retained by wife		$195,200
Net acquired by children		191,156

In this plan the husband leaves his wife half the estate outright and the other half in a life estate. When the husband dies, the half he leaves his wife outright ($100,000) qualifies for the marital deduction. To the marital deduction is added the $60,000 estate tax exemption, leaving a final net taxable estate of $40,000 on which the estate tax is $4,800. When the widow dies, only the amount left to her outright is taxable. Since she retained $95,200 after taxes, her taxable estate, after the $60,000 exemption, will be $35,200 which will yield a tax of $4,044.[39]

Plan 4

Leave $100,000 life estate to wife by will without power of appointment		
Liquidate one half of his holdings ($100,000), which will buy $150,000 **single** premium life insurance on husband (payable to wife)		
Tax when husband dies	$10,900	
Tax when widow dies	15,128	
Net retained by wife		$239,100
Net acquired by children		223,972

In this plan it is assumed that the husband is using one half of his holdings ($100,000) to buy single premium life insurance on his life, and

---

[39] For simplicity these illustrations ignore the deductions for funeral expenses, administration costs, debts, and so on in the widow's estate.

that he retains incidents of ownership in the policy. The life insurance proceeds qualify for the marital deduction of up to $125,000 (one half of the estate) leaving a taxable estate of $65,000 after the $60,000 exemption.

If the insured gives up all incidents of ownership in the policy, his estate tax liability will be reduced to $4,800 since his taxable estate would be only $40,000.[40] However, he would incur a gift tax liability of $953,[41] so his net tax savings would be $5,147.[42] The tax liability in the widow's estate will be increased, but only to the extent of the tax on the additional estate made possible by the tax savings in the husband's estate. The widow's taxable estate will be $84,419,[43] which will yield a tax of $16,337. The net acquired by the children would be $228,082, an increase of $4,110 as a result of the insured's giving up the incidents of ownership in his life insurance.

Plan 5

Leave $100,000 life estate to wife by will without power of appointment
Leave $50,000 outright to wife by will
Buy and give now a $25,000 single premium annuity to son on his life
Buy and give now a $25,000 single premium annuity to daughter on her life

Tax when husband dies	$4,800	
Tax when widow dies	None	
Net retained by wife		$145,200
Net acquired by children		195,200

In this plan the $50,000 left outright to the wife qualifies for the marital deduction, since it is less than one half of the adjusted gross estate, which is now $150,000. The $50,000 in annuity gifts to the children will not incur a gift tax liability if the wife consents because of the privilege of splitting gifts. The husband and wife have a joint $6,000 annual exclusion per donee, and a joint lifetime exemption of $60,000.

Plan 6

Leave $75,000 life estate to wife by will without power of appointment
Leave $75,000 outright to wife by will
Buy and give now a $25,000 single premium annuity to son on his life
Buy and give now a $25,000 single premium annuity to daughter on her life

Tax when husband dies	$1,050	
Tax when widow dies	935	
Net retained by wife		$148,950
Net acquired by children		198,015

---

[40] $100,000 − $60,000.

[41] The value of the gift would be $100,000, the cost of the policy. A marital deduction of $50,000, a lifetime exemption of $30,000, and an annual exclusion of $3,000 reduces the taxable gift to $17,000 which, according to the gift tax rates, yields a tax of $953.

[42] $10,900 − ($4,800 + $953). Actually, the tax savings will be a little more, since payment of the $953 in gift taxes reduces the estate by that amount, thus reducing estate taxes another $172.

[43] $150,000 − ($953 + $4,628 + $60,000).

This plan takes full advantage of the marital deduction leaving the widow one half of the adjusted gross estate. The husband's taxable estate will be only $15,000.[44] The widow's taxable estate will be only $13,950,[45] since the life estate does not incur a second tax.

THE WIFE DIES FIRST.   In the above illustrations, it was assumed that the husband dies first. But what happens if the wife dies before the husband? What is the amount of the estate tax due when the husband subsequently dies? Take Plan 3, for example. If the wife is not alive when the husband dies, there can be no marital deduction. In that case the tax is $31,500 instead of $4,800.

Since there is usually no way of predicting accurately who will die first, life insurance on the wife could be used to offset the loss of the marital deduction. The husband can insure his wife (naming the children as absolute and irrevocable beneficiaries) for the amount of the excess tax liability payable, ($22,656),[46] or the children can insure their mother's life for that amount. Then the children will have $22,656 of life insurance proceeds if the mother dies first. Subsequently, at the death of the father, the net estate received by the children will amount to $168,500 after taxes. Accordingly, the children's inheritance will finally total $191,156, of which $22,656 came to them at their mother's death and $168,500 at their father's death.

Which Plan Is Best?   The answer to this is a personal one. Decide first on objectives, and then develop the plan which best meets these objectives.

These examples of estate tax planning are given as indications of the many combinations that can be made in estate planning with and without the utilization of life insurance to accomplish desired, specific objectives.

Life underwriters frequently hear: "I am much more interested in the welfare of my children than I am in the future of my wife. She may get married again; she is extravagant; and the plan I want is one where my wife will have enough income during her lifetime but in which she cannot touch the principal."

Such an arrangement can be made and in a way which will still save estate taxes. Two life estates or trusts may be arranged. In one of them his wife will get the income for her lifetime, and at her death the remainder will go to the children. In the second life estate or trust, his wife will get all the income during her lifetime and will have the power to leave the property to any one she chooses at her death.

These two different types of life estates contain different powers of appointment. In one, his wife is limited to leaving the corpus of the estate to persons designated by her husband. In the other, she may leave it to anyone.

When his wife has the power to leave the corpus to anyone she chooses,

---

[44] $150,000 — ($75,000 + $60,000).
[45] $75,000 — ($60,000 + $1,050).
[46] $31,500 — ($4,800 + $4,044).

it will qualify for the marital deduction at her husband's death but will be fully taxable in her estate at her death. When she is restricted in appointing the persons to receive the corpus at her death (the children, in this case), the corpus will be taxed in her husband's estate, but it will not be subject to tax again in her estate when she dies.

7. INCOME TAXATION OF LIFE INSURANCE POLICIES

It is impractical in a text such as this to discuss all the income tax aspects of life insurance policies. Only the commonly asked questions are treated here.[47]

Taxation of Proceeds.   Proceeds of a life insurance policy may be payable in a lump sum, in fixed installments, or as a life income to the beneficiary. They may also be held at interest. Proceeds paid as a lump sum by reason of death are not taxable as income. The one exception to this rule involves policies transferred for value. If A purchases from B an existing policy for $10,000 on B's life, paying B $3,000 for it, and then pays another $1,000 in premiums before B's death, he is taxed on the $6,000 gain. The rule is that if a policy is transferred for value, the difference between the proceeds and the sum of the purchase price plus premiums paid by the transferee is taxable income. Exceptions to this rule are: (1) If the transferee is the person whose life is insured, no income tax liability is incurred on the gain and (2) no income tax liability is incurred where the policy is transferred to a partner of the insured, to a partnership in which the insured is a partner, or to a corporation in which the insured is a shareholder or officer. Note, however, that a transfer between stockholders does not fall within this exception.

Proceeds payable under a fixed installment option involve taxable income. Only that portion of each installment settlement representing a return of principal is excluded. The law seeks to tax only the interest, and even here a surviving spouse is allowed an annual exclusion of $1,000 in otherwise reportable income. For example, if the widow receives 10 annual installments of $11,380 instead of a lump sum of $100,000 she will report only $380 annually as taxable income. Ten thousand dollars is excluded as return of principal and $1,000 is tax free under the widow's exclusion, leaving only $380 as taxable income. If the beneficiary were someone other than a surviving spouse, taxable income would amount to $1,320 annually.

Proceeds payable as a life income also involve reportable income. In this case the net policy proceeds are divided by the life expectancy of the beneficiary at the insured's death, using the same mortality table used by the insurance company in computing the benefits. The amount obtained is the annual deduction. The excess is reportable as income subject to the $1,000

---

[47] For up-to-date information on federal income, estate, and gift taxes as they relate to life insurance, see the *R & R Tax Handbook,* published by the Research and Review Service, 1720 East 38th Street, Indianapolis, Indiana.

annual surviving spouse exclusion. If the life income option guarantees a minimum number of payments then before prorating proceeds over the primary beneficiary's life expectancy, the actuarial value of the guaranteed payments is subtracted from the proceeds. The actuarial value of the guaranteed payments is found by computing the present value of the contingent beneficiaries' interest using the mortality and interest assumptions applied by the company in figuring the option. Period certain benefits paid to a contingent beneficiary are taxed only to the extent of any excess interest paid.

If the proceeds are left at interest, the entire amount of the interest payable is subject to the income tax in the year paid. There is no $1,000 exclusion for the surviving spouse. If the proceeds are later paid out under one of the policy's liquidating options, the $1,000 interest exclusion will become available to the spouse.

Any "excess interest" paid under any of the above options is treated the same as guaranteed interest, and will be taxable subject, of course, to the $1,000 surviving spouse exclusion where applicable.

In general, the $1,000 surviving spouse exclusion applies only if the settlement option selected is a contractual right, either contained in the policy or made a part of it by endorsement prior to the insured's death. Only one surviving spouse exclusion can be taken regardless of the number of policies the deceased held. However, a widow may have two exclusions if she has survived two husbands and if both husbands left her insurance.

Taxation of Endowment Policies.   The difference between the net proceeds paid by the insurance company and the total premiums paid by the policyholder for the insurance represents taxable income to the insured when an endowment policy matures as a living claim.

For instance, assume a person buys a $100,000, 20-year endowment and his total premiums less dividends and charges for double indemnity, waiver of premium, and disability income over the 20 years amount to $85,000. The policy matures, and he receives a $100,000 check from the insurance company. The $15,000 gain is subject to the income tax as ordinary income, not as a capital gain. However, the $15,000 gain is eligible for income averaging. The insured can take advantage of income averaging if he has eligible income in a single taxable year that exceeds by at least one fifth his average taxable income for the preceding four years, and such excess is more than $3,000.[48]

If the policyholder is in high income tax brackets or if he is not eligible to take advantage of income averaging, he may prefer to spread the gain over an extended period by taking the proceeds in installments. In this case

---

[48] The income tax averaging provision is found in Section 1301 of the Internal Revenue Code. It was liberalized by the Tax Reform Act of 1969 by reducing the amount by which income must exceed the four year average from one third to one fifth and by including capital gains, gambling gains, and taxable income from gifts and inheritances formerly excluded.

income taxes will be payable on that part of each annual installment which exceeds the quotient obtained by dividing the insured's policy cost by the number of years over which the proceeds are to be liquidated. If the life income option is selected, the amount of each payment subject to tax is computed in accordance with the tax rules for annuities discussed later in this chapter. The basis for the cost of the contract is the sum of the net premiums paid.

If the policy does not include an installment option, or if the option is exercised after the expiry of 60 days beyond the maturity date of the policy, the full gain will be taxed as ordinary income under the doctrine of con- structive receipt. If the policy proceeds are then paid in installments, the cost basis of the contract for income tax purposes becomes the face of the contract rather than premiums paid.

Taxation of Cash Values. Two questions are important in discussing the taxation of cash values of life insurance policies: (1) the growing cash values of policies while they are in force and (2) the cash values of policies upon surrender.

Annual increments in cash values are not subject to income taxes. There can be no income tax on cash value accumulations until the policy is sur- rendered, and then the excess of surrender value over net premiums paid is taxable as ordinary income. Thus, if an insured surrenders a policy for $25,000 on which he has paid $16,000 net in premiums, he will be taxed on $9,000. However, the $9,000 is eligible for income averaging.

It is not necessary to subtract the cost of insurance from the premiums paid in computing the gain. Therefore, all the gain is not taxable. That part which was used to pay premiums, in effect, is excluded. In the above illustration, if the actual cost of insurance protection received over the life of the policy was $8,000, then the insured actually gained $17,000[49] rather than $9,000, although only $9,000 is taxable.

If the cash values are taken under an installment or annuity option, and a tax liability is involved, the rules governing the tax are the same as those applicable to endowment proceeds settled under income options.

Taxation of Dividends. Dividends on life insurance policies are not taxable income because they constitute a premium refund. If dividends are left with the company to accumulate at interest, the amount of interest cred- ited is taxable in the year credited. If the policyholder does not have the privilege of withdrawing the interest without withdrawing his accumula- tions in full, the interest is not currently taxable.[50]

Dividends applied to buy paid-up additions or one-year term insurance create no tax liability. They are viewed as dividends received in cash and then used to buy single premium insurance.

---

[49] $25,000 − ($16,000 − $8,000) = $17,000. The actual amount invested was only $8,000, since the other $8,000 was used to purchase the protection which the insured enjoyed over the life of the policy.

[50] *Massachusetts Mutual Life Insurance Company* v. *U.S.*, 288 U.S. 269.

Taxation of Conventional Annuities. The amount subject to the income tax is the annual annuity income less the amount which, according to the Internal Revenue Service, represents a proportionate return of principal or what the Service calls the expected return. The return of principal (called annual exclusion) in an annuity certain is found by dividing the purchase price by the number of years over which installments are paid. The amount excluded each year under a life annuity is found by dividing the purchase price by the expected total return and then multiplying the guaranteed annual return by the resulting fraction. The figure obtained is excluded and the remainder is taxable as ordinary income. The total expected return is found by multiplying the guaranteed annual income by the life expectancy of the annuitant determined from tables furnished by the Internal Revenue Service. An illustration of the application of the formula is developed in Chapter 6.[51] If payments are for a period certain and life thereafter, the cost is reduced by the actuarial value of the guaranteed payments for the period certain. The values of payments certain and of refund features are calculated by use of special tables provided by the Internal Revenue Service. The annual exclusion continues throughout the life of the contract even though the annuitant has already received a full return of his principal tax free. The amount of the exclusions at that time represent insurance gains rather than a return of principal and as such are not taxable.

Taxation of Variable Annuities. Payments received under a variable annuity contract are taxed in much the same manner as payments under the fixed dollar annuity. The annuitant divides the amount of his net investment in the contract by his tabular life expectancy and deducts the resulting figure each year from his annuity income as a return of principal. The remainder is taxable income. As in the fixed dollar annuity, he deducts the actuarial value of any refund feature in figuring the amount of his net investment. If the total payments received in any one year are less than the annual excludable amount, the annuitant may elect to take a new start for the next year. In this event, he recalculates both his net investment in the contract and his life expectancy as of the new starting date.[52]

Taxation of Health Insurance. In general, benefits paid under individually owned health insurance policies are not includable as gross income for the federal income tax.[53]

Subject to a maximum of $150, one half of the premiums paid on policies providing reimbursement for medical care expenses (including amounts

---

[51] See p. 131.

[52] Reg. 1.72–2(b)(3), 1.72–4(d)(3), 1.72–5(f), and 1.72–7(d).

[53] IRC, Sections 101 and 104(a)(3); Reg. § 1.101–1(a). However, benefits received in one year from a policy or policies covering medical-hospital and similar reimbursement costs must be reported up to the amount of any deduction as medical expense that has been taken for them in a previous year. Reg. § 1.104–1(d) and 1.213–1(g).)

paid for the diagnosis, cure, mitigation, treatment, or prevention of disease or for the purpose of affecting any structure or function of the body, and for transportation essential to medical care) is deductible if the insurance is for the benefit of the taxpayer, his spouse, or dependents. Premiums in excess of the allowable special deduction may be treated as medical expenses and deducted if the taxpayer itemizes his deductions and his medical expenses exceed 3 percent of his adjusted gross income.

Premiums paid for insurance against physical impairments or loss of earnings are not deductible, and only the pro rata share of premiums used to fund medical care benefits is deductible when the policy provides both medical care benefits and loss of time benefits.

In a type of policy known as "business overhead expense," which names certain items of overhead expense for which the insured will be reimbursed in case of disability, premiums are fully deductible as a business expense. However, the proceeds from the policy will be includable as gross income for income tax purposes. Note, however, that premiums paid on a regular disability income policy are not deductible even though the intent is to use proceeds to pay business overhead.

Death benefits from a health insurance policy paid to the insured's estate or other beneficiary are treated as life insurance policy benefits.

Premiums on Life Insurance.   Premiums paid for personal life insurance are not a deductible expense. Interest paid on loans made to finance the purchase of annual premium life insurance, endowments, or annuities is not deductible if paid in accordance with a purchase plan anticipating systematic direct or indirect borrowing against the increases in the policy's cash value. However, a deduction for interest will be allowed if no part of 4 of the annual premiums due during the first 7 years is paid by indebtedness. Interest on a loan to purchase single premium policies is not deductible; and the law treats as a single premium any policy on which substantially all of the premiums are paid in less than five years or on which a substantial number of premiums is either prepaid or deposited under a premium deposit plan.

8. REPLANNING A CONTINUING NECESSITY

Tax and estate planning for any given estate is not a one-time matter. Reexamination must be a frequent occurrence. In the first place, the situation of the estate owner changes continually. Dependent children grow up. An heir dies. A new heir is born. The nature and character of assets change.

In the second place, tax laws, regulations, and rulings habitually change. For instance, at one time life insurance up to $40,000 was exempt from the federal estate tax. That law was changed, requiring replanning of every estate which had taken it into account. Also, the test of whether a policy was to be included in the estate of the insured once depended on who had the incidents of ownership; the law was changed to add to the test of ownership the question of who paid the premiums; now it has been changed back to the ownership test only; tomorrow it may be changed to some other basis. Before 1948 there was no such thing as a marital deduction.[54] Once the interest element in limited installment payment of proceeds was nontaxable if the insured elected the option for the beneficiary prior to death; then for a few years it was nontaxable no matter who elected the option; currently it is taxable in any case except for the $1,000 exclusion to a surviving spouse. Before 1954 jointly owned property took a cost basis equal to the cost paid by the donor decedent in computing taxable gains on subsequent sale. Now jointly owned property included in the decedent's taxable estate takes a new cost basis—the value at the time of the decedent's death. Also, before 1954, the creation of a joint tenancy in real estate between husband and wife involved a taxable gift. Since 1954 the creation of a joint tenancy between husband and wife in real estate no longer is considered a taxable gift.

As pointed out in several places throughout this chapter, the Tax Reform Act of 1969 with its income tax changes has affected estate planning. Now, reform of the federal estate and gift tax laws appears to be in the offing. These laws have been under attack for some time. For example, in 1967 Secretary of the Treasury Fowler stated that these laws place "a high premium on the form and timing of the transfer of property," and in 1969 the House Ways and Means Committee was told that the "existing estate and gift tax system could well be characterized as a governmental levy on poor advice." In 1970, the U.S. Congress had before it recommendations of the Treasury Department for reform to eliminate the inequality between intervivos and testamentary transfers of property by combining the gift and estate tax into a unified tax system with one exemption and one rate schedule applying to all transfers of property. The Treasury Department has also recommended that any value at the time of the transfer in excess of the transferor's acquisition cost be subject to the capital gains tax. A further recommendation has been that property transferred between spouses be free of tax. If any of these recommendations are enacted into law, their effect on estate planning will be significant.

Unless frequent reexaminations of any estate plans are made, unnecessary taxes are almost inevitable, to say nothing of delays in estate settlement, losses on estate values, and increased administration costs.

---

[54] Except as such a deduction was obtained in effect in states operating under the law of community property, which is of Spanish heritage, as contrasted to common law, which is of English heritage.

22

Business Uses of Life and Health Insurance

Life and health insurance are used in a number of ways to protect a business. Since the field of business life and health insurance is highly technical, the insurance agent operating in it usually must work with lawyers and accountants. The lawyer helps with the legal complexities, such as the buy and sell agreements, stock repurchase agreements, and special tax issues. The accountant helps with the problems of valuation, premium budgets, and types of purchase plans. The insurance agent's principal contribution is to uncover the needs for life and health insurance in the business and to motivate the owners to satisfy these needs. In addition to the lawyer, accountant, and insurance agent, a fourth party may be involved: a trust officer. A trust company frequently participates in business insurance as a depository in escrow; when this is true, the trust officer will want to have the agreements checked by his own counsel.

Four basic uses of business insurance are:

1. To protect the business against financial loss in the event of the death or extended disability of a key man, and to help attract and retain the key man in the business.

2. To salvage the value of a sole proprietorship upon the death or extended disability of the owner.

3. In a partnership, to prevent the liquidation of the business in the event of the death of a partner, and to preserve the value of his share. In the event of the disability of a partner, to prevent heavy financial drains on the partnership, and to preserve the value of his interest.

4. In a close corporation, to enable surviving shareholders to retain management control and to assure an equitable price for the shares in the estate of the deceased stockholder. In event of disability, to prevent the same type of losses mentioned in the case of partnership insurance.

In addition to these basic uses, business life and health insurance offers collateral advantages in the form of business stability and improved credit. Business life insurance, under certain circumstances, also offers a source of capital, confidential borrowing, and tax-free additions to surplus.

1. KEY MAN INSURANCE

Plants, equipment, and material do not make a business unless they are turned into a product that is merchandised by men of technical and executive ability. Wipe out the personnel, and the business is destroyed. An important function of key man insurance is to protect a business against financial loss resulting from the death or disability of a key employee. "What corporate purpose could be considered more essential than key man insurance?" asked the Federal Court of Appeals for the Third Circuit in a case involving key man insurance.[1] "The business that insures its buildings and machinery and automobiles from every possible hazard can hardly be expected to exercise less care in protecting itself against the loss of two of its most vital assets—managerial skill and experience."

Who Are "Key Men"?   The key men in any business are those employees whose loss by reason of disability or death would cause the business a serious financial loss. They are also those employees who are important enough to the business to merit a continuation of their salaries during periods of disability, to an amount beyond that provided under the usual group disability plan or sick leave arrangements established as the personnel policy of the company, and for whom special deferred compensation arrangements may be important to wed them to their jobs. Such people are not always those with titles. They are those whose roles and interest in the business are more than mere drawing of salary. Conversely, the man with a title is not always a key man. He may be a functionary, replaceable with comparative ease. Discovering who are key men in a business requires a careful study of the nature and operation of the particular business at hand.

Key men fall into many categories. Top executives are obvious examples. Less obvious, but often equally important, are research workers, sales managers and top salesmen, department heads, the company treasurer or accountant—any employee who will be costly to replace because (1) training a new man will take time and money and/or (2) efficiency in his department will fall sharply while a replacement is being trained.

Protection against Death or Disability of Key Man.   The business protects itself by buying life and health insurance on the key man and naming itself as beneficiary. After determining who the key man is, the problem is to determine how much and what kind of insurance to buy.

DETERMINING INSURABLE VALUE.   Determining the insurable value of a key man is rarely subject to precise formulas. Usually, the value is arrived at arbitrarily by giving consideration to several factors:

1. *What would it cost to replace the key man if he were to die or become disabled?* It is infrequent, except in a small business such as the typi-

---

[1] *Emeloid Co.* v. *Commissioner,* 189 Fed. (2d) 230, p. 233.

cal sole-proprietorship, that any employee, however valuable, eventually cannot be adequately replaced; but such replacement will nearly always involve costs. If replacement comes from the "ranks below," it is rarely that the new man can step into the job with no loss of efficiency in the department. The probable cost of the reduced efficiency, in terms of profit, needs to be estimated. If the replacement must come from outside the company, a replacement of equal ability will often require a higher salary. In all probability, the desired man is secure in his present position. A new job is a gamble. If nothing else, there may be conflicts of personality even though his work is eminently satisfactory. Therefore, to be attracted, he must be offered a large enough differential to compensate him for the risks of moving. A study of the personnel market might help in estimating the value of a key man in this connection.

2. *What portion of company profit is traceable to the key man?* In most cases this will probably be difficult to answer precisely; in others, such as that of a salesman, it may be relatively easy to estimate.

3. *How much investment would be lost if the key man were to die or become disabled?* Large sums might be invested in a research or developmental project that would be a total loss in event of the death or disability of a key man. One man might be solely responsible for the development and operation of a specialized department, or he might be the guiding genius or even the sole worker on an expensive advertising or merchandising campaign that would have to be scrapped entirely if he were lost.

4. *How much of the loss is the company willing to insure?* The amount of key man insurance will depend, not so much on a rough estimate of the key man's value as on the amount of money the company is willing to spend for indemnity in case of death or disability.

5. *How much salary will the company want to pay the disabled key employee, and for how long?*

TYPE OF POLICY. The type of life insurance policy to buy for key man indemnification depends upon the purpose for which it is bought. If the policy is bought for indemnification only in the event of the death of the key man and there is no interest in collateral cash value benefits, then some form of term insurance will be sufficient. If the purpose is to provide the company with indemnity in the event of the death of the key man while at the same time funding a special retirement benefit for the key employee, then the policy should be the one that gives the balance needed between the face amount of the insurance and the cash value at the retirement age of the key man.[2]

For total disability, some insurers still offer a disability income rider which can be attached to the key man life insurance policy if it is a perma-

---

[2] It would seem that corporations concerned about tax liability under the accumulated earnings tax might want to confine their key man life insurance purchases to policies carrying premiums no higher than the lowest premium form of permanent insurance.

nent form. However, a separate disability insurance policy may be used effectively to provide for the loss occasioned by long-term disability. For temporary disability (disability lasting less than six months) the business may choose simply not to insure the loss at all unless the exposure can produce exceptionally high losses. In that event, a special temporary disability insurance plan providing high limits for short periods can be purchased, although the market for such coverage is limited. A few insurers write special disability policies with maximum monthly payments of, for example, $25,000 for a maximum benefit duration of 6 months after a 1-month waiting period, to cover special key man disability insurance needs only, particularly to protect lenders of funds and suppliers of venture capital to firms whose principal attraction is the talent, skill, and character of its chief executive. The policy is not written to provide disability income benefits to the executive himself.

THE TAX ASPECTS.   The customary arrangement in key man insurance is for the business to purchase the policy, retain all incidents of ownership, pay the premium, and name itself as beneficiary. The key man himself has only to give his permission for the insurance. Aside from that, he is completely outside the transaction.

When the business is the beneficiary, it cannot deduct the premium for life insurance.[3] The same rule applies with respect to health insurance with one exception. Where professional or business overhead expense health insurance provides *specifically* for reimbursement for the business overhead expenses of a sole proprietor, professional man, or partner in the event of his absence due to injury or sickness, the premiums are deductible.[4] Such a policy is treated for tax purposes as business interruption insurance. Even though the proceeds are taxable, as soon as they are received they are used to pay business expenses which are deductible.

The proceeds of a key man life insurance policy paid to the business are specifically exempt from income tax.[5] By analogy, it would appear that the proceeds paid under key man health insurance would also be exempt. While logic does not always produce the right answer in tax situations, there is reason to believe that it does in this case since the provisions of Section 1.104–1, paragraph (d) of the regulations do not specifically rule out the exclusion of disability insurance benefits.[6]

The tax rules with respect to gains or losses on surrender values of key

---

[3] This, of course, seems inconsistent with the decision in the Emeloid case, quoted earlier, which upheld the purchase of business insurance as being for an essential business purpose, and likened its purchase to the purchase of property insurance. Yet premiums paid by a business for property insurance are deductible, whereas those paid for life insurance are not.

[4] Rev. Rul. 55–264, CB 1955–1, p. 11. This must be a specific overhead expense policy form. An ordinary loss of time policy will not qualify. (Rev. Rul. 59–480, CB 1958–2, 21.)

[5] Cf. Section 104(a), Internal Revenue Code of 1954.

[6] Cf. *Castner Garage, Ltd.*, 43 B.T.A.1.

man life insurance are no different from the rules discussed in Chapter 21 in connection with personal insurance.

Retaining the Key Man. Life insurance may be used to fund plans designed to attract and retain key employees. Several devices have been used for this purpose.

DEFERRED COMPENSATION PLANS.   One method of compensating stockholder employees, officers, and other key employees has received considerable attention: deferred compensation. In qualified pension plans, employer's contributions to pension funds are deductible in the year made, whereas the employee does not have to report these contributions as income until the year payments are received, as explained in Chapter 17. It is sometimes desirable to grant to certain employees deferred compensation benefits beyond those included in the qualified plan. To try to include these benefits in the basic pension plan might disqualify it on the grounds that it discriminates against the lower paid employees. Therefore, they must be handled on a supplementary basis. The problem is how to set up the supplementary plan.

Assume a key man with a salary of $60,000 a year. At that time his tax bracket is high. After payment of taxes, his net take home pay is much less. So he might get together with his company (or like to) and say:

How about paying me $50,000 a year instead of $60,000 a year for the next 20 years? At the end of that time, I'll retire, and you can pay me $20,000 a year for 10 years. Right now, I'm 45 years old. If you pay me $60,000 a year for 20 years, that will total $1.2 million. On the other hand, if you pay me $50,000 a year for 20 years, then that total will be $1,000,000, leaving a differential of $200,000. I'll draw that $200,000 by taking $20,000 a year for 10 years.[7] In that way I'll reduce my income tax liability for the next 20 years, and when I retire at age 65, I'll be in the lower $20,000 tax bracket and have more exemption. This will reduce the cost of financing my retirement to the extent of the tax savings effected.

The corporation could underwrite the future $10,000 a year liability by buying a deferred annuity for the employee.

However, such a plan will not save the employee any taxes, because if he were entitled to draw $60,000 instead of $50,000, he would nevertheless pay income tax on the entire $60,000 because of the "theory of constructive receipt," under which amounts that could be drawn at will are considered as actually paid.

Suppose, however, the employer says to the key man:

We should like to pay you a bonus, but we cannot afford to pay it now. We want you to be happy and satisfied with your earnings from this company, and we want you to stay with us. So here's what we'll do: We will continue to pay you your present salary, which is all we can afford right now, and we will

---

[7] For the sake of simplicity, this illustration disregards the fact that the respective present values would not be equal.

promise you that when you retire 20 years from now, we will give you $20,000 a year even though you are not actually working for us in an active capacity at that time.

In a case like this, since the employee was not entitled to receive the money immediately, the theory of constructive receipt apparently would not apply. This, then, would seem to be an opportunity to use life insurance to underwrite the future bonus: to assure the employee he would get it, and to provide the employer with the funds when the promise became due. However, the widespread interest in such plans came to the attention of the Treasury Department. The Department indicated that if an employee's right to future compensation is "nonforfeitable," the commuted value of the employer's promise to pay would be construed as taxable income in the year the promise is made. By nonforfeitable the Internal Revenue Service appeared to mean no ifs, ands or buts attached to the employee's right to get the money in the future.

If, on the other hand, the corporation says to the employee: "If you continue to work for us until you reach age 65, we will pay you $20,000 a year until your death *as long as you are not working for a competitor,*" then vesting is *conditional* and not *absolute.* In that case a constructive receipt interpretation seems unlikely.

However, the Internal Revenue Service now considers a mere unsecured promise to pay income in the future not to constitute taxable income to the employee currently, and that the employee's right to future compensation need not be forfeitable.

Setting up the Insurance. Life insurance can be used to fund a deferred compensation plan. The policy should be bought by the employer on the life of the employee, with the employer as the beneficiary. The type of policy to be used depends upon whether the deferred compensation plan is to be tied in with a key man indemnification plan and whether the widow is to receive any benefits in the event of the death of the key man while he is still employed.[8] If the plan creates a contingent liability for the employee only and ignores employer key man indemnification, an annual premium deferred annuity will be sufficient. If the plan calls for a contingent obligation to the widow in the event the employee dies, an endowment at age 65 may be used. Usually a whole life policy is preferable to an endowment policy, since at age 65, for example, the employer may want to continue the plan. If the plan does not include the widow but is to double as key man indemnification, then the policy should be a whole life of the type

---

[8] Generally, it is better to eliminate the widow from the deferred compensation plan and cover her instead with the split dollar plan to be discussed later. Income tax laws give preferential treatment to insurance proceeds payable by reason of death. Funds paid by employers to the widow of a deceased employee are subject to income tax after a one-time $5,000 exemption. However, under practically every circumstance, no income tax is due on life insurance proceeds to the beneficiary, or, in this case, to the corporation.

which provides the desired balance between the face amount needed at death for indemnification and the cash value needed to fund the employee's benefit at age 65.

In no case should the employee hold any incidents of ownership in the policy. The deferred compensation agreement and the insurance must be kept separate. The obligation of the employer to pay the deferred compensation benefits must be independent of the insurance. In fact, no reference should be made to the insurance in the employment agreement. The purpose of the insurance is to give the business added financial resources which will help it maintain a sound financial position in face of its potential liabilities. The reason for keeping the employment agreement and the insurance separate is income tax consequences. Without the separation there is a chance that the premiums paid by the employer will be considered current taxable income to the employee.

The Tax Aspects. Premiums paid by the employer for life insurance policies are not deductible expenses. The cash values or endowment proceeds paid to the employer are taxed in the same way as they are in personal insurance. Proceeds received by the employer (beneficiary) at the death of the employee are not taxable. Deferred compensation paid to the employee or his widow is deductible as a business expense in the year paid. As for the employee, if the employment agreement is properly drawn, the employee incurs no tax liability prior to retirement and then only for the amounts actually received.[9] If the plan guarantees payments to the widow upon the employee's death, the present value of these payments at the time of the employee's death must be included in his estate for estate tax purposes. The widow must report as income, for tax purposes, all amounts in excess of the first $5,000. The widow, however, can deduct from these payments the amount of the estate tax paid on them.

$5,000 EXEMPTION. An employer may pay the widow (or estate) of a deceased employee up to $5,000 after his death, and the widow (or estate) does not have to report the money as income for tax purposes. However, if the deceased employee had more than one employer, the exemption applies only to a total of $5,000. His beneficiary can not claim an exemption for each $5,000 paid by each employer. The employer, of course, can deduct the $5,000 payment as a business expense.

Life insurance may be used to fund these payments. The employer insures the life of the employee and names himself as beneficiary. Premiums are not deductible nor are proceeds reportable for income tax purposes. The

---

[9] The employee must have no vested rights in the plan before reaching retirement age and all benefits must be paid periodically and directly by the employer. If, as a condition for the deferred compensation, the employee agrees to serve as a consultant after retirement, he should have the contract drawn so as to make him an independent contractor rather than an employee in order not to subject his deferred compensation to social security taxes when he receives it nor to expose himself to loss of social security benefits.

employer gains a tax advantage when he collects the proceeds tax free and deducts as an expense the amount paid over to the widow of the deceased employee.

SPLIT DOLLAR PLANS.   The split dollar plan uses a policy with a cash value (whole life or endowment) as a vehicle to tie key executives to the company. The annual premium is shared by the employer and the employee. The employer's portion each year is that amount which equals the increase in cash value. The employee pays the remainder. When the increase in the cash value is equal to or greater than the annual net premium (when a participating policy is used, the net premium is the initial annual premium minus the annual dividend) the employer pays the full premium and the employee pays nothing. One drawback of this premium arrangement is that the employee has to pay the full first-year premium, since customarily the policy contains no cash value in the first year. However, more and more companies are developing minimum-size policies (i.e., $50,000) which contain a first-year cash value.

Basic Split Dollar Plan.   Under the basic split dollar plan the employer owns the policy, but the employee is given certain rights in it through an employment agreement. For example, the employee is given the right to name a beneficiary who will receive all the proceeds which exceed the cash value of the policy at the time of death. If, for some reason, the plan is terminated prior to the death of the key employee, the employee generally is given the option to purchase the policy from the employer for its cash value.

Collateral Assignment Plan.   A modified version of the split dollar plan is the collateral assignment arrangement under which the policy is owned by the employee rather than the employer but is assigned to the employer as collateral for a series of annual loans (generally non-interest-bearing) equal to the annual increases in the cash value of the policy. The employee names the beneficiary, but under the collateral assignment the employer's claim for the amount of the indebtedness is discharged before the remaining proceeds are distributed to the beneficiary.

An advantage of the collateral assignment plan is its simplicity. Existing policies can be used, and should a decision be made to terminate the plan, all that needs to be done is for the employee to pay off the indebtedness and recover the policy.[10] The funds to retire the indebtedness can be obtained from the insurer under a policy loan. A disadvantage of the collateral assignment plan is that the employer cannot utilize the cash value of the policy as an asset in the business, since his rights in the policy are limited by the terms of the assignment, as discussed in Chapter 10. If ownership of the policy's cash value is important to the financial position of the firm, it will have to use the basic split dollar plan.

---

[10] The advantage of using an old existing policy owned by the key employee is that annual increases in the policy's cash values will be greater than the net premiums due, thus eliminating any further premium outlays by the key employee.

Basic Difficulties. **Two** basic problems with the split dollar plan are: (1) the employee's protection decreases each year as the employer's total premium contributions increase; (2) since most policies have low cash values in the early years, the employee's portion of the premium may be too high for him to handle.

The problem of decreasing protection can be overcome by using the "fifth dividend option" available with many participating policies. The annual dividends purchase one year term insurance not to exceed the cash value in the policy. Table 22–1 illustrates the operation of the split dollar plan when used in conjunction with the one-year term dividend option. The illustration is based on one company's dividend and premium scales in use at the present time. Except for the guaranteed values, actual results will depend on future experience.

Other dividend options can be used to provide a higher death benefit than normally provided for under the basic plan. Also term riders may be attached to the base policy to offset this declining protection problem. For example, an increasing term rider can be used with some nonparticipating policies to solve the problem of decreasing protection.

The problem of initial high premium contributions required by the employee can be handled in several ways.

One way is to level the employer's premium contributions by dividing the cash value at 65 by the number of years remaining until the employee reaches age 65. For example, the guaranteed cash value at age 65 for the split dollar plan illustrated in Table 22–1 is $55,700 (Column 1). Under the level contribution plan, the employer would pay this $55,700 in 30 equal annual installments—the period elapsing from employee age 35 to his age 65—resulting in an annual payment of $1,853. Since the annual premium for the policy is $2,438, the employee will pay only $585 the first year compared to $2,238 without the level premium modification. For the second year the employee would pay $328 computed as follows: gross premium ($2,438) less dividends after purchase of 1-year term insurance ($257 as shown in Column 4) less employer's contribution ($1,853).

Another way is for the employer to lend the employee sufficient funds to pay a large part of the first premium and for the employee to repay the loan over a specified period of years. Still another way is for the employer or employee to use a policy already in existence on the employee's life. Patently, this avoids the problem of initial high premium contributions required by the employee.

Tax Considerations. The "measurable economic benefit" received by the employee from his employer in connection with life insurance policies used in split dollar plans initiated after November 13, 1964, is taxable to the employee as current income. This economic benefit is the sum of the cost of the life insurance protection received by the employee under the plan plus the value of the dividends used for his benefit, minus the premium paid by the employee. The cost of the life insurance protection is figured by applying the one-year term rate published by the Internal Revenue Service (called the P.S. 58 Table) or by the insurer to the amount of proceeds payable to the employee's beneficiary. For example, the employee's taxable income for the fifth year of the split dollar plan illustrated in Table 22–1 would be $794, figured as follows: The value of the death benefit of $100,000 (Column 11) payable to the employee's beneficiary is $414 using the P.S. 58 rate of $4.14 per $1,000 at age 39. The value of the dividend accruing to the employee is $408 (Column 2), and the premium paid by the employee is $28 (Column 9). The sum of $414 plus $408 minus $28 is $794.[11]

Under the split dollar plan, the employer cannot deduct any premiums he pays, and the proceeds received by reason of death are not taxable.

HEALTH INSURANCE FOR KEY MEN. In a company where little or no health insurance is given the employees on a group basis, the employer can use individual health insurance plans to attract or retain key men. These plans offer favorable tax treatment. Payments made by an employer to a disabled employee are deductible by the employer if these payments are made under a documented plan which has been communicated to the covered employee and if the benefits are reasonable in relation to the employee's salary for services rendered.[12] The benefits are not taxable to the employee if they satisfy one of the following conditions: (1) reimbursement for medical care, (2) payments for permanent injury or loss of bodily function, or (3) payments in lieu of wages during absence from work as a result of bodily injury or sickness. This latter condition has the following qualifications: Payments are excluded up to a rate of $100 a week after a waiting period of 30 days. If the payments do not exceed 75 percent of the employee's regular weekly wage, payments may be excluded up to $75 a week during the first 30 days after a 7-day waiting period. However, if the employee is hospitalized for at least 1 day, the 7-day waiting period does not apply.

The medical care and disability income benefits offered key employees need not be insured to qualify for the tax advantages. The benefits are deductible when paid. However, to regularize the cost of these benefits and to avoid exposure to catastrophic losses, the employer may choose to insure the exposure. In this case, he will purchase disability income and medical care insurance on the selected employees and have these benefits paid directly by the insurer to the employees. The premiums paid by the employer are deductible as a business expense under Section 162 of the

---

[11] Policies used to fund split dollar plans initiated prior to November 14, 1964, are governed by Revenue Ruling 55-713. Under this ruling, the employee incurs no income tax liability. The employer is considered to have made the employee an interest-free loan.

[12] In a sole proprietorship and partnership, tax deduction cannot be taken for benefits paid to owners, even though they are actively engaged in the business. However, in a corporation deductions can be taken for shareholder-employees, although it would appear that to safeguard the deduction it might be well to include in the plan a few selected key nonshareholder-employees.

TABLE 22–1

Split Dollar Plan Using One-Year Term Dividend Option

Age: 35 | Plan: Ordinary Life | Amount: $100,000 | Annual Premium: $2,438

Year	Guaranteed Cash Value End of Year (1)	Dividend at End of Previous Year (2)	Cost of One-Year Term Additions (3)	Acc. Divs. Beg. of Year after Purchase of Term (4)	Term Additions Purchased Beg. of Year (5)	Combined Death Benefit* (6)	Increase in Combined Cash Value for Year† (7)	Premium Paid by Employer (8)	Premium Paid by Employee (9)	Total Paid to Date by Employer‡ (10)	Death Benefit for Employee (6)−(10) (11)
1	$ 200	$ 0	$ 0	$ 0	$ 0	$100,000	$ 200	$ 200	$2,238	$ 200	$ 99,800
2	2,100	263	6	257	2,100	102,357	2,157	2,157	281	2,357	100,000
3	4,100	311	13	563	4,100	104,663	2,306	2,306	132	4,663	100,000
4	6,000	360	20	921	6,000	106,921	2,258	2,258	180	6,921	100,000
5	8,000	408	28	1,331	8,000	109,331	2,410	2,410	28	9,331	100,000
6	9,900	457	38	1,793	9,900	111,693	2,362	2,362	76	11,693	100,000
7	11,900	499	50	2,300	11,900	114,200	2,507	2,438	0	14,131	100,069
8	14,000	542	63	2,854	14,000	116,854	2,654	2,438	0	16,569	100,285
9	16,000	584	78	3,453	16,000	119,453	2,599	2,438	0	19,007	100,446
10	18,100	627	95	4,097	18,100	122,197	2,744	2,438	0	21,445	100,752
15	27,600	825	219	7,930	27,600	135,530	2,737	2,438	0	33,635	101,895
20	37,200	1,011	453	12,451	37,200	149,651	2,832	2,438	0	45,825	103,826
25	46,600	1,184	877	16,912	46,600	163,512	2,630	2,438	0	58,015	105,497
30	55,700	1,341	1,617	19,822	55,700	175,522	2,157	2,157	0	69,740	105,782

* Includes accumulated dividends. The death benefit will be increased by any post mortem dividend payable and by interest on accumulated dividends from the preceding policy anniversary to the date of death.

† Increase in guaranteed cash value for the year plus increase in accumulated dividends at the beginning of the year.

‡ Death benefit for employer is equal to total paid to date by employer.

Note: The 42nd policy year is the last year for which the accumulated dividend fund is sufficient to purchase one-year term additions equal to the full guaranteed cash value under this policy.

Internal Revenue Code, provided they are in consideration of personal services actually rendered by the employee, and do not constitute unreasonable compensation for services performed. Under Section 106 of the Code, the premiums paid by the employer are not taxable income to the employee. Unlike the rules restricting coverage under qualified pension plans, the employer may discriminate in favor of officers, executives, supervisors, and other highly paid employees, covering them only.[13]

2. SOLE PROPRIETORSHIP INSURANCE

The predominant type of business structure in the United States and Canada is the sole proprietorship, under which one man owns the business alone, without partners or shareholders. From the standpoint of estate planning, it is one of the most dangerous of all types of business structures. Rarely, however, does the sole proprietor realize this fact.

Ask the gift shop owner, druggist, or garage owner where the family support would come from if he were to die or become disabled. His answer nearly always will be, "The business will provide an income." In many cases the business not only will fail to provide an income but it may also be an expense to the family and cut deeply into other available estate assets.

The Problem in Sole Proprietorships.   The estate problem in the sole proprietorship organization arises from the fact that the law recognizes no difference between the business and the personal estate. The sole proprietor, however, usually thinks of his business as something apart from his personal estate.

Actually, his business and personal estate—the home, the car, the savings account—are one and the same thing. His business assets can be attached to pay his personal debts, and his personal assets can be attached to pay his business debts. They are interchangeable. Many are the cases in which errors in business judgment have caused losses of personal fortunes as well as instances in which extravagances in personal living have caused losses to business estates.

When a Sole Proprietor Is Disabled.   In most cases the sole proprietor is not only the owner and manager of the business, he is also a full-time employee. Therefore, when he becomes disabled the business is without the services of a key employee. If the disability is of lengthy duration, his services will need to be replaced.

One of two solutions is usual:

1. Someone from the family steps in and does his work: his wife, perhaps. This, however, might not be satisfactory. If his disability is such that

---

[13] Tax courts have found that amounts paid for medical care expenses were in excess of a reasonable amount in relation to salaries for personal services actually performed. For this reason, the use of insurance to level the payments from year to year might be useful in preventing unusually high payments to an employee in any one year—payments that might be considered in excess of a reasonable relationship to salary for work performed.

he cannot work, he might need full-time care at home. If his wife has to run the business, then she must hire someone to take care of the house. This will create an added drain on the family budget. It also is likely that his wife will not be capable of performing his job as efficiently as he did. The probable result is that the income will drop, while at the same time expenses will increase.

2. A manager is hired. He will have to be paid, thus reducing the income to the family. Further, unless the manager is as efficient as the proprietor, the income from the business will drop. If he is as efficient, he will be entitled to, and probably will demand, a high salary. In the case of many sole proprietorships, the business provides only one good income: that of the owner manager. If a nonowner manager also must be paid a good income, what is left for the owner?

Disability income insurance on the sole proprietor can be used to help offset the financial problems involved in each of the above courses of action.

If the proprietor's wife is capable of running the business, then there will be additional income to pay for the cost of her replacement in the home. If she is not capable of maintaining the level of business profits, the disability income insurance will help to offset the drop in family income.

If a manager must be hired (or an existing employee promoted to the position of manager), the disability income insurance will provide a fund that can be used to pay the additional costs of business management and to cushion a possible decline in profits resulting from the change in management. Inasmuch as disability insurance purchased on the proprietor is personal insurance,[14] proceeds from it will be income tax free. Therefore, the amount of insured income needed will be less than the amount of gross income to be offset.

Short-term disability of the owner which produces inconvenience in the business but no serious financial loss to the business is not a subject for business insurance. The discussion above refers to disabilities of durations long enough to create a major financial problem.[15]

If the disability is permanent, there should be sufficient coverage to

---

[14] Since the business and personal estate of a sole proprietor are one and the same, any sole proprietorship insurance is, in the final analysis, personal insurance. However, the existence of the business creates new insurance needs, a different viewpoint on the part of the insurance buyer, and a different basis for the evaluation of insurable needs. Hence, it seems valid to classify sole proprietorship as business insurance even though there is no business ownership as encountered in some forms of business insurance.

[15] What constitutes a short-term disability in such a case depends on how long the business could get along without the services of the proprietor without either (1) incurring additional expense for someone to perform his duties or (2) causing a serious drop in profits. In a one-man business, cost or loss might start almost immediately. When the total of that cost or loss mounts to a point that will be a financial hardship (as contrasted to inconvenience), then insurance should be available. In a larger proprietorship with a number of employees, it might be several months before the absence of the proprietor would have serious financial effects. The elimination period in the coverage is, then, a matter of the individual case involved.

enable the sole proprietor to dispose of the business. He might wish to sell the business to an outsider or, if he has a son, he might wish to continue the business until his son is ready to take over. Sole proprietorship disability insurance will enable him to (1) take his time in making a sale so that he can gain the most advantageous price, in contrast to a distress sale, (2) enable him to keep the business until his son is old enough and experienced enough to manage it. If he has a logical buyer, he might wish to consider a disability buyout agreement, to be discussed later in this chapter.

When a Sole Proprietor Dies.   When a sole proprietor dies, the business does not pass immediately to his heirs or devisees. It becomes a part of his estate, to be disposed of by the executor or administrator. Actually, one of two things will happen: the executor[16] will sell or liquidate the business, or he will make an effort to operate it.

1. The executor will dispose of the business. Unless (a) the last will and testament of the sole proprietor contains express instructions "in direct, explicit, and unequivocal language" for continuing the business,[17] or (b) all the heirs are adults and agree to assume the responsibilities for the continuation of the business, the legal duty of the executor is to dispose of the business as rapidly as possible. He has no choice in the matter, because he has no right to leave the estate assets invested "in trade"[18] any longer than absolutely necessary. If he continues to operate the business beyond the time necessary for its sale or liquidation, he may be held personally responsible to the heirs for any loss as well as for all debts he incurred for the business.

Exactly how long an executor may leave estate assets in the business is a matter to be determined by the court in any given case. The executor, however, because of his exposure to liability, will tend to dispose of the business as quickly as possible. The sale, being a forced sale, will not be conducive to a favorable price. However, in any event, the amount realized from the disposal of the business asset is apt to be much less than the sole proprietor had expected. It is entirely possible that the liquidation losses will be so severe that the business estate will be inadequate to pay its own settlement costs. If this proves to be the case, then other estate assets will have to be used for this purpose: the bank account, the home, and, in some cases, family life insurance.[19]

The first need of the sole proprietor, then, is to protect his general estate against the debts of the business. He should provide enough cash through

---

16 Although there is a distinction between an *administrator* and an *executor* (cf. Chapter 21), the term *executor* will be used herein to mean either one.

17 Thompson on "Wills," Section 142–43.

18 Cf. *24 Corpus Juris 55,* Section 474–75.

19 If the family's personal life insurance is made payable to named beneficiaries, it usually will not be subject to the claims of the insured's creditors. If it is made payable to the insured's estate, then it becomes a part of the estate and can be used to pay estate debts. Cf. Chapter 9.

life insurance payable to his estate to meet all the business debts and estate administration costs without forcing liquidation of his so-called personal assets.

2. The executor will make an effort to operate the business. If there is an express provision[20] in the will permitting the executor to operate the business, the executor may attempt to run it. However, before he can do this there must be enough cash available in the estate to pay estate debts, administration costs, and estate taxes, or the business might have to be liquidated for that purpose. It should be held in mind, also, that the existence of an authorization to continue the business is not a mandate to the executor. If he undertakes to operate the business, the courts will take the position that the decision was voluntary on his part and hold him personally liable for all debts incurred by him in the operation of the business.[21] But if continuation of the business has been authorized, he is entitled to indemnification for any of these debts out of the general estate or out of any assets specifically earmarked in the will for the conduct of the business. However, should the newly created business debts exceed available estate assets, the executor would have to pay the excess without indemnification. A cautious executor will be hesitant, therefore, to operate the business, even when specifically authorized to do so.

How successful the executor's operation of the business will be also is problematical. The nature of the sole proprietorship is such that much of its value as a going business is traceable to the proprietor himself. The business is successful because the proprietor himself made it that way. (Had there been others in the business equally responsible for its success, the business undoubtedly would have been organized as a partnership or a corporation.) The executor, however, rarely will be as effective in the management of the business as was the owner. Not only will he be less experienced in that particular business operation, but he probably will also have his own work to look after so that he will be able to devote only part time to his duties as executor. People who traded with the business because of the good will created by the proprietor are likely to drift away, and suppliers may be hesitant to extend additional credit. Creditors may demand immediate payment of all debts, a right they have upon the death of the sole proprietor, irrespective of the maturity date of the obligations.

---

[20] A typical provision might read: "I authorize my executors for the time being to carry on, during such period as they shall think fit, the trade or business of ————, now carried on by me, and for that purpose to retain and employ therein the capital which shall at my death be employed therein, and such additional capital as they shall think fit to advance from time to time out of my residuary estate, with power to employ at such salary as they shall think fit, any manager of the said business, and generally to act in all matters relating to the said business as if they were beneficially entitled thereto; and my executors shall be free from all responsibility for losses arising in the prosecution of the said business." Quoted from *R & R Advanced Underwriting & Estate Planning Service*, Vol. II (Indianapolis: Research and Review Service).

[21] Cf. *11 Ruling Case Law*, Section 147.

Too often the continuation of the business by the executor results in a nightmare for the executor himself, accompanied by a steady reduction of business so that in the end he is forced to liquidate it anyway—and in view of the decline of the business, perhaps for even less than if the business had been liquidated immediately.

The need for sole proprietorship life insurance for business continuation (as distinguished from business liquidation) is to provide enough cash (*a*) to guarantee that the business will not have to be liquidated to raise cash for administration costs, debts, and taxes; (*b*) to provide the executor with working capital to carry on the business;[22] and (*c*) to guarantee sufficient assets to indemnify the executor for debts contracted in running the business.[23]

IF THE BUSINESS PASSES TO THE HEIRS. If, as a result of successful planning and a fortunate selection of an executor, the business does survive to pass to the heirs, sole proprietorship insurance can be helpful.

When the heir does take over active management, he or she may not be able to earn as much from the business for the first few years, at least, as was earned by the deceased proprietor. Sole proprietorship life insurance can make up the loss. Also, the insurance proceeds will be useful in helping the heirs maintain the credit rating of the business and retain its employees.

However, the advisability of turning over a sole proprietorship to the heirs to be held as income property is open to serious question. If the heirs are unsuccessful in operating the business, they may dissipate their inheritance from the general estate in an attempt to save the business. In this event, the business becomes a liability rather than an income-producing asset. Therefore, many sole proprietors recognize from the start that the most desirable plan of handling their business in event of death is to dispose of it.

IF THE BUSINESS IS TO BE SOLD. If the proprietor makes up his mind that disposal of the business is the best method of handling the estate problem relating to it, he may either (1) leave the disposal problem to the executor or (2) arrange for his own buyer in advance. In either case, sole proprietorship insurance is needed.

If the buyer is to be located after death occurs, the proprietor should recognize two facts:

a) It will take time to arrange a favorable sale. In the meantime, cash will be needed to keep the business going and retain customers and good will until a buyer is located. Customers and good will usually make up a good part of the value of a sole proprietorship. A going business is worth more than the liquidation value of its inventory, equipment, and other assets. Life insurance can provide the needed cash to continue the business in operation and to preserve its values until it is sold.

---

22 To offset the possibility of more stringent credit conditions.
23 So as to reduce or eliminate the possibility of personal loss to the executor

b) No matter how competent the effort to maintain the value of the business after the loss of the owner, that value is almost certain to decline. As has been said, the sole proprietor himself is one of the most important sources of value in the business. When he is no longer associated with the business its value is almost certain to decline. In estimating the value of his estate, the sole proprietor, therefore, must take this probable shrinkage into consideration and, if necessary, offset it with additional insurance protection so that his estate can continue to provide the income necessary for the maintenance of his family.

If the proprietor decides to arrange for a buyer in advance, the problem of finding the buyer after death will be eliminated, but two new ones will be introduced: first, assurance that the buyer will go through with the purchase, and second, guaranteeing that the buyer will have the money to pay the agreed-upon price.

The first problem is a matter of contract. A contractual agreement can be drawn up under which the proprietor agrees to sell and the buyer agrees to purchase the business at a price to be determined by the agreement.

The second problem is a matter of sole proprietorship insurance.

In its simplest form, the sole proprietorship buy and sell arrangement contemplates that insurance on the proprietor will be bought and paid for by the prospective purchaser of the business. If the buyer is not able to finance the premiums necessary to purchase all the insurance needed, provision may be made in the agreement for the insurance proceeds to be used as a down payment, with the remainder of the purchase price, as fixed by the agreement, to be paid over a period of years out of the income from the business. If the proprietor wants his family to have a fixed sum in cash immediately upon his death and that sum involves more insurance than the buyer can afford, the proprietor may arrange to advance part of the necessary premiums, to be paid back by the buyer in addition to the purchase price.[24]

When sole proprietorship life insurance involves postmortem purchase of the business under a buy and sell agreement, a trust may prove advantageous. Proceeds of the policies are paid into the trust, and the trustee handles all details of the transfer. The trust arrangement is more flexible and less complicated than paying the proceeds to the buyer who, in turn, must deal with the executor in effecting the transfer. For one thing, the executor will have a prejudicial interest in the transaction (the interest of the estate), whereas the trustee is likely to be impartial, interested in

---

[24] It is sometimes contended that if the proprietor must advance part of the premiums to the prospective buyer, he might be better off to use the money to buy personal insurance and have, at his death, the insurance *and* the business. Actually, each estate problem must be studied individually to determine the best solution for the objectives involved. Often the principal problem is to get the business out of the estate. Otherwise, its debts or deficit operation may drain the general estate, since the two are legally one and the same. Personal insurance does not assure that this will be done.

neither the buyer nor the seller, but only in carrying out the terms of the agreement.

A disability income rider plus waiver of premium on the sole proprietorship life insurance can be used to help fund a disability buyout agreement. For instance, assume a $50,000 sole proprietor life insurance policy taken at age 45 on a continuous premium whole life basis with a disability income and waiver of premium rider. The nonpar or net after dividend premium for such a policy in one company would be about $1,800 a year. In case of the disability of the sole proprietor as defined in the rider,[25] and the agreement to sell the business in such event, the potential buyer will receive $10 per month per $1,000 of face amount—or $500 a month income—and he has $1,800 a year waived in premiums that can be applied on the purchase price. If disability income coverage is not available as a rider to the sole proprietorship life insurance, or if income before the end of the waiting period specified in the rider is advisable, a specific disability income policy may be purchased.

If the disability income payments plus the waived premiums are inadequate to pay the purchase price over a reasonable length of time, the payments can be supplemented out of business income. Since disability income insurance does not pay off in lump sums,[26] the terms of payment in the buy and sell agreement should not require a large down payment. The buyer might be able to raise a small down payment out of his own resources or through a loan.[27]

The continuous premium whole life form with waiver of premium and monthly income disability is ideal to fund a buy and sell agreement. In case of death the proceeds of the life insurance will provide the buyer with the cash to complete the purchase. In case of disability the monthly income will provide funds for the periodic payments, and the waiver of premium will continue the values of the policy, which will be available at death to complete the payments, or at an earlier date should the cash values of the policy equal the balance outstanding on the purchase price. The loan value could be borrowed at that time and turned over to the seller. Since the waiver of premium will keep the policy in force, the policy loan will not have to be repaid until the death of the insured, when the policy proceeds are reduced by the amount of the outstanding indebtedness. Interest paid on the loan in most cases will be deductible as an expense for income tax purposes. The disability income will continue to be paid, and the owner

---

[25] Usually defined as "total and permanent"; however, case law has so altered the definition commonly used in such riders that, despite the rider language, it amounts to total disability with a waiting period. Usually, also, disability must occur before some such age as 55 or 60—55 in the policy quoted.

[26] Except for disability from dismemberment or loss of sight, for which capital sum coverage is available.

[27] The loan can be made against the business assets or against the cash values of the life insurance written to fund the agreement in case of death.

of the policy will collect the death or endowment benefits, less the policy loan, when they mature.

Such buy and sell arrangements in sole proprietorships most often are made between the proprietor and a key employee or employees. When so made, they tie the employees closer to the business and help to eliminate turnover among key employees.

Occasionally, the best solution to the problem of the disposition of the business is incorporation. Such a plan might be wise where there is a minor child and the proprietor wishes to hold the business for him. If there is a key employee in the business capable of running it, an answer could be to incorporate the business upon the death or disability of the proprietor, selling the key employee a portion of the stock and placing control of the business in a trust until the child reaches an age at which he is capable of handling it himself. If disability rather than death causes the sale, and the proprietor can comprehend what is going on, he might retain the stock and vote it himself.

3. PARTNERSHIP INSURANCE

Corpus Juris defines a business partnership as *"a contract of two or more competent persons, to place their money, effects, labor and skill, or some or all of them, in lawful commerce or business, and to divide the profit and bear the loss, in certain proportions."*[28]

Two principles should be held in mind with respect to the partnership: (1) Each partner in a general partnership (the most common type) is fully liable for all debts and obligations of the firm to the extent of his personal estate and (2) at the death of a partner, the firm, in the absence of an agreement to the contrary, is legally terminated as to future business irrespective of the desires of the surviving partners.[29] Business problems can arise out of the disability or death of a partner, and life and health insurance can be of help in solving these problems.

When a Partner Is Disabled. Except in the case of a "silent" partner, disability of a partner deprives the firm of a key employee. If he is disabled for a long period of time, it will be necessary to hire someone to do his work. In the case of a personal service partnership, the income of the firm may be reduced by the amount of business lost because of the inability of the disabled partner to handle it.[30] At the same time, the disabled man is

---

[28] 47, 640, Section 1.

[29] It is sometimes stated that the death of a partner *terminates* the partnership. In the legal sense of the term terminate, it does not. After dissolution, a partnership remains as a firm as long as is necessary to wind up preexisting obligations. However, dissolution—which is effected whenever a partner withdraws as well as when one dies—operates with respect to all future business transactions. A dissolved partnership may not take on new business commitments.

[30] Some of the business attracted to the firm because of any given partner, of course, will continue and can be handled by one of the other partners.

entitled to his division of the partnership profits and, perhaps, a continuation of his so-called salary or drawing account. It is possible to draw the partnership agreement so that any partner's share of the firm income is in proportion to his active contribution to it. However, the partnership arrangement usually grows out of and cultivates a close personal relationship among the members of the firm. The chances are that even if partners are not contractually bound to continue income to a disabled partner, they will feel morally obligated to do so. As a result, the income of all partners will be reduced.

Such loss of income can be avoided by the use of partnership disability insurance under which each partner carries disability income insurance and agrees to eliminate or reduce his drawing account in case of disability.

When a Partner Dies.   The partnership relation is a personal one. It subjects each partner to responsibility for the acts of the other or others. Because it is such a close relationship, the law protects the right of a person to select his partners. No one can choose a partner for another, nor can anyone elect to be the partner of another unless the other is willing. The entire act of effecting a partnership is *voluntary*. Therefore, unless there is an agreement or a statute to the contrary, the death of a partner dissolves (except as noted in footnote 29) the partnership and leaves each surviving partner free to choose new associates.

The business must be either *liquidated* or *reorganized*, and the choice is not entirely up to the surviving partners. The law provides only for liquidation, except where the heirs of the deceased partner may agree to permit their inherited share of the business to remain in the partnership,[31] in which case they become partners. However, if the heirs are minors they cannot give consent to reorganization, so unless there is a partnership buy and sell agreement, liquidation of the business is the only choice. Also, if the heirs are not minors and are unwilling to join the firm, or if the surviving partners do not want them as new partners, again liquidation usually is the only choice in absence of a partnership buy-and-sell agreement.

If liquidation is necessary, the surviving partners become trustees in liquidation, saddled with the responsibility of trusteeship, bound to act promptly and honestly and to render an accounting of their acts to the personal representatives (executors or administrators) of the deceased.[32]

Forced liquidation is an unfortunate solution, for rarely will the full value of the assets of the business be realized. The surviving partners may find themselves without a business or jobs. Business debts that cannot be paid from funds realized from the sale of the business assets can cut into the personal funds of the surviving partners and the estate of the deceased. Since the estate can be held liable for the entire debt of the partnership, the

---

[31] *20 Ruling Case Law 990,* Section 226.

[32] For a description of the role of the survivors as trustees, cf *40 American Jurisprudence,* Section 306.

heirs of the deceased may not only fail to realize anything from the business but may also find other estate assets depleted because of the business.

So, if for some reason it is decided that upon the death of a partner the business shall be liquidated instead of reorganized, sufficient life insurance on each partner will be needed to offset liquidation losses and to protect the other assets of the surviving partners and those of the deceased partner's estate against the debts of the business.

If the firm is to be reorganized,[33] four courses are open:

1. The surviving partner or partners may be named heir or heirs of the deceased.

2. The surviving partners may take in the heirs of the deceased as partners.

3. The survivors may agree to take in as a partner, purchasers of the heir's interest.

4. The survivors may purchase the interest of the heirs.[34]

INHERITING THE SHARE OF THE DECEASED. Obviously, partners will name each other as heirs only where the survivor is a person to whom the deceased partner normally would make a bequest, as in father and son partnership where the father leaves his interest to his son. However, since fathers sometimes do bury sons, a problem could arise unless the son also leaves his interest to his father. But in the usual case, the son will leave his interest to his wife, and unless his wife is active and knowledgeable in the business, and has a good relationship with her father-in-law, it would be better to arrange for the disposition of the son's interest through a buy and sell agreement with his father in the event that the son dies first.

TAKING IN THE HEIRS OF THE DECEASED AS PARTNERS. As previously mentioned, the nature of the partnership relationship is close and personal. The surviving partners wish to select their own partners. It would be unusual if the heirs had the same qualities that made the deceased partner attractive to the survivors. Further, the heirs rarely will want to go into the firm as active partners. Usually they have no experience in the business and no interest in working in it. They might be a little more willing to be silent partners (i.e., nonworking partners), but the surviving partners may not be able or willing to support nonworking partners. Usually, the survivors do not want new partners and the heirs do not want an interest in a partnership. They want money.

TAKING IN THE PURCHASER OF THE HEIRS' INTEREST AS A PARTNER. The survivors are under no obligation to take in as a partner a prospective purchaser of the heirs' interest. Although occasionally the surviving partners and heirs may be able to agree on a purchaser, it is poor estate and

---

[33] Reorganization will nearly always be the desire of the surviving partners, whose jobs as well as money are tied up in the firm.

[34] There is a fifth method of reorganization: the heirs may buy out the partners. Usually, however, the survivors will not be interested in this method of reorganization since it leaves them without a business; and rarely will the heirs want the business.

business planning to leave the disposition of the interest of the deceased partner to a chance sale agreement.

PURCHASING THE INTEREST OF THE HEIRS. In most cases the only satisfactory method of reorganization is for the surviving partner or partners to purchase the interests of the heirs. The problems involved here are (a) reaching an agreement with the heirs as to the terms of the purchase and (b) financing the purchase.

Reaching an agreement as to terms will prove no simple matter in the majority of cases. In the first place, the survivors will have to deal with an executor who is under obligation to obtain the best "deal" possible for the heirs. Usually, therefore, he will set a high price. If his asking price is refused, he has evidence that the interest of the heirs is not worth as much as they expected. If he compromises, the heirs may feel he made unnecessary concessions.

In the second place, it is difficult for the heirs to realize that the business without the services of the deceased is worth less than it was while he was still alive. If they think that a reasonable capitalization rate for the business is 10 percent, they would assign a value of $400,000 (given an anticipated $40,000 in annual earnings) for his share of the business, whereas the entire assets of the firm, and even its value as a going business, may be worth far less than that figure.

Often the attempt to buy out the heirs after the death of a partner results in a stalemate over price that can be resolved only by liquidation; and liquidation is rarely to the gain of either the survivors or the heirs.

The solution is an advance agreement that in the event of the death of one partner, the survivors shall have a right to acquire the deceased's interest and are obligated to purchase it at a price set in the agreement or determined by a formula established in the agreement. This is the partnership buy and sell agreement.

Disability of a partner can also be covered with a buy and sell agreement.[35] One method is to agree that each partner will carry disability income insurance on his own life and that during an initial period of disability as defined in the policy (say two or three years), he will receive a gradually decreasing income from the partnership itself. If the disability continues beyond the initial period, the other partner or partners will then buy out his interest in installments, the transfer of interest to be effected by making out to him a series of notes, payable, say, over a 72-month period. Alternatively, the arrangement might be to convert a permanently disabled partner into a silent partner. Assuming there is also partnership life insur-

---

[35] There is at least one dissenting opinion. R. W. Hilgedag, in "Should Disability Be Covered in the Buy-Out Agreement," *The Insurance Salesman,* July, 1957, p. 55, argues that the treatment of the disability of a partner should be covered in the articles of partnership, not a buy and sell agreement: "Disability insurance—vital to the partnership or close corporation—should be in the form of what is loosely called key man rather than buy-out." This position has been directly attacked by William Harmelin and Morris Friedman, *Disability Insurance in the Business Buy-Out Agreement* (Indianapolis: Rough Notes Company, 1958).

ance, each partner may be given the option of purchasing the policy on his life held by the disabled partner—but until such purchase is made and paid for, the disabled partner must maintain the life insurance in force (although a time limit for the exercise of purchase option may be set). A partnership entity plan and cross-purchase (both to be discussed shortly) are also possible.[36]

In the case of death buyout agreements, two types are possible: the *survivorship* agreement and the *purchase* agreement.

The *survivorship* agreement provides that upon the death of a partner, his interest shall vest in and become the property of the surviving partners, either at his death or upon the payment of a stated amount. Since this type of agreement makes a direct transfer, it might be challenged as an attempt to make a testamentary distribution of property outside of a will.[37]

The *purchase* buy and sell agreement uses the language of purchase and sale. Each partner agrees that if he dies, his estate will sell his partnership interest at the price and terms set in the agreement. He also agrees that if he is predeceased by any other partner, he will purchase his pro rata share of the interest of the deceased. The agreement provides that the deceased's personal representative (executor or administrator) will make the necessary transfers. The legality of this type of agreement has seldom been successfully challenged.[38]

The funded buy and sell agreement offers a planned solution to the problem of disposal of a partnership interest. The price is established in advance by a formula which is likely to be equitable, since it was determined by the partners under the most favorable conditions for achieving equity. The parties, in making the agreement, do not know on which side of the transaction they will find themselves when it is carried out. If they survive, they are the buyers; if they die, they are the sellers.

The agreement guarantees that the heirs will sell and that the surviving partners will buy the interest of the deceased partner. The only problem that remains is whether the buyers will have the money to carry out the agreement. The certainty of a buy and sell agreement loses its effectiveness

---

[36] For a discussion of the tax considerations involved in various types of disability buy-out agreements for partnerships, cf. Harmelin and Friedman, *op. cit.*, and Hugh M. MacKay, "Disability, Retirement or Death of a Partner," *Journal of the American Society of Chartered Life Underwriters*, Vol. XII, No. 1 (Winter, 1958), pp. 53ff.

[37] Most of the litigation concerning the legality of buy and sell agreements has been over the survivorship type. The preponderance of opinion has upheld its legality, starting with *McKinnon* v. *McKinnon*, 56 Fed. 409 (1893). There has been some contrary opinion; for example, cf. *Ferrara* v. *Russo*, 40 R.I. 533, 102 A. 86 (1917) or *Gomez* v. *Higgins*, 130 Ala. 493, 30 S. 417 (1900).

[38] An instrument that is testamentary in character operates only by reason of the death of the maker. The instrument of a purchase-type buy and sell agreement is operative the day it is signed. The element of present existing contractual rights distinguishes this type of agreement from the survivorship type. Cf. *Ireland* v. *Lester*, 298 Mich. 154, 298 N.W. 488 (1941).

if it is not funded, i.e., if no funds are arranged in advance to meet the obligation.

While there may be other methods of funding a buy and sell agreement, insurance will almost always prove the best solution. The situation which creates the need for funds—death or disability—also creates the funds needed: the insurance proceeds. If insurance is used to fund the agreement, the partners will not have to drain their personal resources, nor will they have to borrow to carry out the terms of the agreement. Partnership insurance provides the amount of money needed,[39] at exactly the time it is needed and on the most efficient basis.

How the Insurance Is Arranged. The insurance to fund the buy and sell agreement can be arranged in several ways. The most popular plans are the *cross-purchase* and the *partnership entity*.

THE CROSS-PURCHASE PLAN. Under the cross-purchase plan, each partner individually buys and maintains enough insurance on the lives of the other partners to fund the purchase for which he is obligated.

The cross-purchase plan has a number of advantages; among them:

1. Since each partner owns and pays the premiums on the policies on the lives of the others, he pays exactly in proportion to his benefits.

2. The proceeds of the policies are not subject to estate taxes, since the deceased holds none of the incidents of ownership in the policy on his life.

3. The purchase price sets the cost basis for the income tax of the share purchased in case of its later sale.

4. The plan is flexible since, in the case of more than two partners, the survivor may purchase any amount of the deceased's share agreed upon rather than an amount which is in direct proportion to his share in the partnership. For instance, among three equal partners, one might wish to purchase only 25 percent of the interest of a deceased partner, leaving the other 75 percent to the other surviving partner. Under a cross-purchase plan in which each partner is acting as an individual buyer, this arrangement can be made.

The fact that one of the partners may be much older than another sometimes is considered a disadvantage of the cross-purchase plan, under which each pays the premiums on the life of the others.[40] The older man in such

---

[39] It is not necessary for the insurance to equal the full amount of the value of the deceased's share. In fact, where the price is to be set by a formula taking into account current financial factors, it is impossible to have the life insurance equal the exact amount, for that amount is unknown until after the death of a partner. If the full amount cannot be insured, the life insurance can be considered a down payment, with the balance to be paid under arrangements set forth in the agreement.

[40] Where there is a wide difference in age and proportionate ownership shares, it may sometimes prove impossible for younger members of the firm to pay the premiums on policies on older members directly, as under the cross-purchase plan. In that case premiums may be pooled: either each partner contributes to the pool in proportion to his ownership interest or the total premiums are divided by the number of partners, each paying an equal amount. The buy and sell agreement should arrange, when necessary, for the reimbursement

a case is paying a lower premium than the younger man. This arrangement, however, is not inequitable, since, according to the laws of probability, the younger men are more likely to collect on the policies they have purchased.

The one serious disadvantage of the cross-purchase plan arises when there are a number of partners. Only two policies are necessary when there are only two partners. If there are three partners, six policies are necessary. A four-man partnership requires 12 policies. If there are 10 partners, 90 individual policies will be necessary. For this reason and others,[41] where a partnership is composed of a large number of partners, the entity purchase plan is most common.[42]

THE ENTITY PLAN. Under the entity plan the buy and sell agreement specifies that upon the death of a partner, the partnership itself will purchase the share of the deceased partner for the account of the surviving partners. The insurance on the life of each partner is owned by and made payable to the partnership. The partnership pays the premiums out of partnership income.[43] The cash values are carried as assets of the firm.[44]

The following points regarding the entity plan will be useful as a basis for comparing it with the cross-purchase plan:

1. The indirect but real premium burden of the plan will rest more heavily on the larger interest partners in contrast to those with smaller interests. An inequity is also created against the older partners in favor of the younger partners. While these features often make the plan more acceptable to those with smaller interests and to younger firm members, who usually are less able to pay the higher premiums required under the cross-purchase plan, they do require an adjustment in setting the purchase price for the shares of the larger interest and of the older firm members.

2. The policies and proceeds are company assets and, as such, are subject to the claims of creditors of the firm. Thus, payment of the funds intended for the purchase of the share of a deceased partner could be delayed

---

to the estate of the deceased for his premium contributions. Except under peculiar circumstances, the entity plan, to be discussed later, usually will prove a better way of meeting the problem of excessive premiums for some partners.

[41] One of the "others" being that the sale of the cross-purchase plan calls for convincing each partner that he should spend money out of his pocket for premiums on insurance on the other partners. It is easier to sell a man on spending "company money," even when company money in the case of a partnership is actually the individual partner's money.

[42] A variation of the individual ownership cross-purchase plan is the joint ownership plan under which the policies on the lives of the individual partners are jointly owned by the other partners who pay the premiums jointly and are the joint beneficiaries.

[43] The premiums, of course, are not deductible as a necessary business expense for income tax purposes.

[44] Under the 1954 Revenue Act, for some purposes, at least, a partnership can be dealt with as an entity apart from individual owners; thus the entity plan referred to previously. The tax code says, "If a partner engages in a transaction with a partnership other than in his capacity as a member of such partnership, the transaction shall be considered as occurring between the partnership and one who is not a partner." I.R.C., Section 707 (A).

or the amount depleted entirely.[45] Of course, in the other plan, the proceeds are subject to the claims of the creditors of the individual partners.

3. The result of the payment of the premiums by the firm is the same as though each partner had paid them in direct ratio to his interest in the partnership. Under the cross-purchase plan, each partner owns the cash values in the policies he has purchased on the lives of the other partners; under the entity plan, the cash values are owned by the partnership. Therefore, in setting the purchase price for a deceased partner's share, the formula must take into account both the cash values of the insurance owned on the lives of the surviving partners and the proceeds of the policy on the life of the deceased partner.

4. The deceased's interest in the firm will be divided among survivors in exact proportion to their present interests, which may be an advantage or disadvantage.

Who Shall Be the Beneficiary?   In the cross-purchase plan, the *surviving partners* usually are the beneficiaries, since they are the ones obligated by the agreement to buy the interest of the deceased. Under the entity plan, *the partnership itself* usually is the beneficiary, since it is the party obligated by the agreement to purchase the deceased's interest.

In either type of plan, *a trustee as beneficiary* will usually prove the most advantageous arrangement. The trustee receives the proceeds, turns the money over to the personal representative of the deceased, and secures the necessary transfers and releases. Not only does the trusteed plan provide for impartiality and relieve the survivors of the details of direct negotiations, but it also permits clear segregation of the partnership insurance proceeds from the proceeds of the personal life insurance carried by the deceased. As another function, the trustee can also serve during the life of the agreement by handling details such as collection and payment of premiums and acting as a depository for the policies.

It is possible to make the policy payable to the *widow or other named beneficiary* of the insured. This plan is often considered desirable by partners who wish to give their beneficiaries the advantage of the installment options in the policy or to avoid the expense and delays of having the proceeds go through their estate, as they will have to do if paid to other than the insured's beneficiary. This plan also is fraught with dangers. The beneficiary might claim both the proceeds and the partnership share. In fact, in one such case[46] the agreement was held to be unclear, and the widow was allowed to keep both the proceeds of the policy and the partnership share.[47]

---

[45] If the financial condition of the firm is such that its assets are insufficient without the insurance, the insurance proceeds can be helpful in preventing the partners from being saddled with a personal liability for firm debts. (It must be remembered that a general partner has unlimited liability for the debts of the partnership.)

[46] *Price* v. *McFee,* 196 Md. 443, 77 A. (2d) 11.

[47] There is also a tax danger for the survivor or survivors. In *Legallet* v. *Commissioner,* 41 B.T.A. 294, the amount of the insurance proceeds paid direct to the widow of the deceased partner by the policy was not allowed as part of the cost basis of the partnership share

When the insured's beneficiary is named, the partnership interest is in the estate, but the purchase price for it goes directly to that beneficiary. Creditors with claims against the estate may object to the transfer of estate assets (the partnership interest) without any direct compensation to the estate. A number of companies make it possible for the heirs of the deceased to use the settlement options under the policy, even though the policy is made payable to the surviving partner or to the partnership. Various plans are available, for example, the "additional direct beneficiary" arrangement. Under this plan, after the terms of the buy and sell agreement have been executed, the direct beneficiary releases the policy proceeds for the additional direct beneficiary (the insured's beneficiary) who can take them under the settlement options.

Personal Service Partnerships. The personal service partnership (such as a firm of lawyers, investment bankers, a medical partnership, and the like) often will use an income continuation agreement instead of a lump-sum payment. Under this plan it is provided that for a specified number of years after the death of a partner, the firm will share a percentage of its profits with the heirs of the deceased. Sometimes there will be two agreements: one a regular buy and sell agreement covering tangible assets including receivables, and the other an income continuation agreement covering the deceased's share in future earnings. Life insurance can be used to fund both agreements.

4. CLOSE CORPORATION INSURANCE

In many corporations, the stock is owned by a limited number of people, most if not all of whom also are active in the business, usually as officers or executives. This type of organization is called a close corporation.

The close corporation has an existence apart from the individual stockholders. However, the relationship among the stockholders is nearly exactly as among partners. In fact, the relationship is so intimate and personal that the close corporation is often called an incorporated partnership. Unlike the partnership, however, the withdrawal or death of a stockholder has no legal effect on the continuation of the business, although it will necessitate a realignment of ownership which can create problems—unless proper plans are made to take care of the contingency.

The relationship among stockholders in the close corporation is so close that it breeds the same feeling of moral responsibility for one another as is often found in partnerships.[48] Further, the close corporation is closed

---

of the survivor when he subsequently sold the firm assets. As a result, he was forced to pay a higher capital gains tax than would have been necessary had he or the firm received the proceeds and paid them over to the widow.

[48] This is not to say that all partners and close corporation stockholders feel a moral responsibility for the welfare of one another. Examples of partners and close corporation stockholders who live in absolute hatred of one another could be found. The point is that

because the existing stockholders do not want to admit new stockholders—at least stockholders they cannot select for themselves.

Out of the close relationship of close corporation stockholders grows the need for close corporation insurance.

If a Stockholder Becomes Disabled. The effect of the disability of a close corporation stockholder who is also an employee of the firm is nearly identical with that resulting from the disability of a partner. He will continue to share in the profits of the company although contributing nothing to them. A replacement for him will have to be hired, costing additional money. Probably the company will feel an obligation to continue his salary over a long period of time. If the stockholder is a key man, as is often the case, the corporation may suffer a loss of income as well as incur additional expenses. Disability income insurance can be used in the close corporation to offset these extra expenses and the loss of profits.

Furthermore, it might be desirable for the close corporation and its employee-stockholders to enter into a disability stock redemption agreement under which the stock of a disabled employee must be sold by the employee and purchased by the corporation at a price to be set by a predetermined formula if the employee becomes totally disabled as defined for a period of, say, two years. The agreement should provide that the purchase price should be paid over a period of years and that disability insurance be purchased to fund the agreement. Disability as defined in the agreement should correspond to disability as defined in the policy. If a buyout agreement is not acceptable to the employee-stockholder because of the possible adverse capital gains tax consequences, an agreement to exchange his voting common shares to nonvoting cumulative preferred shares might be an acceptable alternative for providing him with an income and eliminating a possible source of disruption in the growth plans of the corporation.

When a Stockholder Dies. When a close corporation stockholder dies, there is no legal effect on the company. His shares become a part of his estate, eventually passing on to the heirs. However, here is where trouble lies.

While a partner cannot be forced to take in a partner against his will, a close corporation can be forced to take in as a stockholder the heir of a deceased stockholder or the person to whom the heir has sold his inherited stock. Anyone who holds legal title to stock becomes a part of the company regardless of what may be the wishes of the surviving stockholders. The new member might even be a competitor. The surviving stockholders could do nothing to keep him out or to bar him from full information about the operations of the firm.

Such is the major problem created for the surviving stockholders at the death of a close corporation stockholder.

---

partners or close corporation stockholders usually become associated because they know and have an interest in one another. This close relationship usually is conducive to the development of a feeling of obligation for one another's welfare.

The heirs of the deceased minority stockholder are faced with problems, too. Stock in a close corporation in which one is not actively engaged might be a speculative investment. Since close corporations are normally highly dependent on the skills and abilities of a limited number of stockholder-executives, the degree of safety of principal might be low unless the close corporation is a prime candidate for acquisition by some company seeking expansion by the merger route. Earnings on such stock might be unpredictable for the same reason. Further, dividend earnings may be low because employee-stockholders are frequently more interested in plowing profits back into the business than in declaring dividends on the stock; and they may vote themselves salary increases and bonuses which take up a large part of what might have been profits available for dividend distribution. The old stockholders with the controlling interests could freeze the new, unwanted stockholder out of the business. It is true that minority stockholders have enforceable rights and can sue to force the distribution of surplus or profits as dividends and to stop unreasonable salary and bonus payments, but any investment under which the owner must argue with others about return and must resort to costly law suits is hardly the kind of investment to leave to an heir.

Another problem faced by the estate or heir might be the lack of liquidity of the stock. If the estate or heir wishes to sell stock in a close corporation, he has difficulty in finding a buyer, and if lucky enough to find a buyer, has even more trouble establishing a price. The very factors that keep close corporation stock from being a good investment for heirs also prevent it from being a good investment for anyone who does not intend to work actively for the company or whom the firm would not accept as an employee even if he were willing. Since future earnings on the stock are unpredictable, and since there is no market established for the stock, its value is not clear. The seller is prone to value it high. The buyer is prone to value it low because of its inherent drawbacks. The gap between the two valuations is often too great for successful negotiation.

The heirs of a majority stockholder are also faced with problems. While it is true that by their control they can set whatever business or financial policies they wish and, in effect, say to the minority stockholders, "Do as we say or get out," the nature of the close corporation is such that often heirs of a majority interest cannot get along without the co-operation of the minority. As has been brought out, many if not all of the minority stockholders in the usual close corporation are also key employees in the firm. The heirs are often not acquainted with the business or not enough interested in it to risk losing the key men. Also, since the minority stockholders are active employees, they are in a position to sabotage the heirs, should they wish.

If the minority stockholders are left to run the business while the majority heirs are inactive in the company, the minority can conduct the business so that dividends to the heirs become negligible. For instance, they can put profits back into the business, living on their salaries. Further, as minority stockholders, the survivors could exercise rights that could cause the majority heirs embarrassment and trouble.

Finally, if heirs inheriting a majority interest wish to sell, the minority interests may not have the money to buy at a price that will give the heirs anything like their proportionate share of the going business. The problems of finding an outside buyer have been discussed.

One more problem faces the heirs of a deceased stockholder: valuation of the stock for tax purposes. Since there is no yardstick in the form of an established market price (and rarely a value established by a prior sale close enough in time to have any bearing), there can be a wide discrepancy between the value set on the stock for federal estate tax purposes by the executor and the value set by the government. Trust officers report that the valuation problem of stock in close corporations, for estate tax purposes, represents one of the greatest difficulties in estate administration and often results in excessive administration costs. On the other hand, if the buy and sell agreement and the method of valuation used in it have been negotiated at arm's length and in good faith, the government will consider the valuation of the stock under the agreement as acceptable for tax purposes.[49]

Thus, for both the surviving stockholders and the heirs, the best arrangement in the vast majority of cases will be for the survivors to buy, and the heirs to sell, the stock of a deceased stockholder. Again, in view of the problems encountered when an attempt is made to negotiate the sale after the death of the stockholder, such problems being the same as those in the partnership, the best way to handle the sale is through a buy and sell agreement among the stockholders, put into effect while they are all alive. Such agreement is, of course, of little value unless there is also money to pay for the stock. The agreement can be funded in various ways but, as in the partnership buy and sell agreement, life insurance offers the best method in the vast majority of cases.[50]

How the Insurance Is Arranged.   The two most common types of purchase agreements are the *individual* and the *stock retirement* plans.

Under the *individual plan,* each stockholder agrees to buy a portion of the stock of the deceased stockholder. Each purchases, owns, and maintains the insurance necessary to fund his purchase. The cross-purchases arrangement to fund a buy and sell agreement in a close corporation is the same as in a partnership, and has the same advantages with respect to equity in results, estate tax implications, the setting of a cost basis for tax purposes in the event of later sale of the stock, and flexibility. It has the additional advantage of freeing the proceeds of the policy from the claims of the creditors of the corporation.

---

[49] *May* v. *McGowan,* 194 Fed. (2d) 396. (Numerous other cases could be cited.)

[50] If one of the partners or stockholders is uninsurable, other funding methods will have to be used with him. Life insurance can continue to be used with the insurable partners or stockholders.

Under the *stock retirement plan,* the corporation agrees to purchase the stock of the deceased shareholder, and purchases, maintains, and owns the insurance necessary to fund the agreement.[51] This plan is the counterpart of the partnership entity plan. The advantages and disadvantages of the stock retirement plan are to a large extent the same as those of the entity purchase plan. However, there are issues that need to be considered in choosing between a cross-purchase plan and a stock retirement plan that are not present in choosing between a cross-purchase plan and a partnership entity plan. These issues include the questions of (1) the income tax burden and (2) the validity of the stock retirement plan.

In the partnership plans, it makes no difference who pays the premium —the partners or the partnership—insofar as the income tax burden is concerned. Since the partnership is not a separate tax entity, whatever the partnership earns is taxable as income to the partners. Premiums paid by the partnership are not deductible as an expense, and therefore are considered as part of the partnership income taxable to the partners. In the corporation plans, it makes a tax difference who pays the premium. Premiums paid by the corporation are not deductible by the corporation; but since a corporation is a separate tax entity, they are not reportable as income to the stockholder. Earnings of a corporation are taxable to the stockholder only when they are paid out as dividends. Therefore, the choice of plans can affect the tax burden. For example, the corporation can pay the premium directly or increase the salaries of the employee-stockholders to allow them to pay the premiums. The tax question can be important in the decision because the premiums on the insurance are a nondeductible expense for the corporation, whereas salaries are deductible for the corporation but reportable as income to the stockholder. Thus, which plan will cost less in income taxes depends on a comparison between the marginal tax rate being paid by the corporation and the marginal tax rates being paid by the individuals. If the corporation is paying more than the individual shareholders, the individual stock purchase plan will cost less in taxes. If the stockholder is paying more than the corporation, then the stock retirement plan will cost less.

Another issue in choosing between the cross-purchase plan and the stock retirement agreement is whether the corporation is authorized by law to buy its own stock. An Illinois corporation may purchase its own stock except where such purchase will reduce net assets below a value equal to

---

[51] Where the stockholder is also an employee, the agreement often calls for him to sell and the corporation to buy his stock in the event he severs employment. The price for his stock is set in the agreement, either at an actual figure or through the establishment of a formula. Cash values in the insurance carried on his life can be used to fund the purchase. However, since cash values may be insufficient at the time the stockholder leaves employment, and since it might be financially impossible for the corporation to meet the agreed price, provision may be made for the corporation to pay the balance in installments or to allow the stockholder to dispose of the stock himself if the corporation is unable to meet the established price or make a satisfactory settlement.

stated capital and certain designated surplus items. The Illinois law is typical. However, while the laws of most states permit the corporation to purchase its own shares out of capital surplus, subject to certain conditions such as authorization in its articles of incorporation or approval of its stockholders, in a few states a corporation may purchase its own shares out of earned surplus only.

Who Shall Be the Beneficiary?   Problems of beneficiary designation under close corporation insurance are the same as those under partnership insurance. If the cross-purchase plan is used, the stockholders themselves can be made beneficiaries of the insurance they carry on each other. If the stock retirement plan is used, the corporation can be the beneficiary. The value of a trustee as beneficiary in the close corporation case is the same as in the partnership case. The problems and disadvantages of naming the heirs direct beneficiaries or naming the estate of the insured are also the same.

The Buy and Sell Agreement.   When the solution to the problem of the disposition of the interest of the deceased stockholder (or partner) involves the use of a buy and sell agreement funded by life insurance, a number of vital points need to be covered in the agreement. These include a clear-cut statement of the purpose of the agreement and the mechanics of how the purpose is to be accomplished—that is, whether there is to be a cross-purchase agreement, an entity or stock retirement plan, and whether a trustee is to be used. If a trustee is to be used, his duties should be spelled out.

Details of the life insurance to be purchased to fund the agreement should be included. These details relate to such matters as the amounts of life insurance to be purchased on each stockholder or partner; the type of policies to be bought; who is to pay the premium; who is to be the beneficiary; the restrictions on the exercise of such policy rights as loan privileges, surrender, and change of beneficiary; and, in cross-purchase plans, the disposition of the policies held on the lives of the survivors by the estate of the deceased.

The price at which the interest of the deceased is to change hands needs to be specified. This may be done either by establishing a stipulated price subject to periodic review and adjustment according to a defined procedure, or by setting forth the method to be used for valuation at the time of death.

Valuation methods used are the current book value of the interest or the average book value over a given period of time, the capitalized average earnings of the interest using a specified multiple, the use of an appraisal board of arbitrators to be selected according to procedures spelled out in the agreement, the value set by the tax authorities for state and federal death taxes, or some combination of the foregoing factors with the weights clearly delineated. A minimum value may be set equal to the amount of insurance purchased to fund the agreement.

The agreement needs to cover the question of how to pay the balance of the purchase price if the value of the interest exceeds the amount of insurance. Usually this is handled through a series of interest-bearing notes arranged for convenient maturities. Both the interest rates and the maturity rates need to be scheduled in the agreement.

The agreement usually will provide that if a stockholder or partner wants to sell his interest during his lifetime he must offer it to the other stockholders or partners at the price specified in the buy and sell agreement.

Finally the agreement should spell out the conditions under which it can be revoked or altered. Aside from the mutual agreement to terminate, termination usually is automatic in the event of bankruptcy, receivership, the simultaneous death of a specified number of stockholders or partners, and the inability of a stockholder or partner to carry out its terms relating to the insurance to be carried.

For disability buy and sell agreements, aside from those of the foregoing provisions that are applicable, the agreement needs to clearly define disability.

5. MISCELLANEOUS USES OF BUSINESS INSURANCE

In addition to the business uses of life and disability insurance that have been discussed, several others may be important.

Collateral Uses. Many of these miscellaneous uses are actually collateral advantages of the uses of disability and, especially, life insurance for key man protection, business interest liquidation, and business continuation. They serve as predeath or predisability advantages of the insurance which is purchased for postdeath and disability uses. These uses are:

1. Key man insurance aids in establishing credit for a business. Creditors and lenders are aware of the importance of key personnel to the financial standing of the business. Many a bank loan has been made or line of credit extended, not so much because of the financial aspects and physical characteristics of the business, but because John Doe is president, or general manager, or in some other key position. Creditors recognize the added strength that key man life insurance gives to a firm.

The value of key man disability insurance is far less understood by creditors and lenders, largely because so little key man disability insurance is in force. Yet the effects are the same whether a man's services are lost to the business because of death or because of disability. Inevitably, as the use of business disability insurance spreads,[52] its value in strengthening credit will increase.

2. Life insurance policies other than term are good collateral for loans. The life insurance company is contractually bound to make such loans up

---

[52] One of the problems here is finding an insurer that will write an amount of disability income insurance on an employee sufficient to cover not only the employee's need for disability income but also the employer's need for key man disability protection.

to the cash value of the policy at a contractually set rate of interest regardless of the money market at any given time. Therefore, during periods of tight money the loan values of life insurance policies are an attractive source of funds.[53] Banks and other lending agencies always will accept life insurance policies as collateral for loans.

Policy loans made by the insurance company have another value: They can be made confidentially. Occasions arise when a business firm may not want it known in banking or credit circles that a loan was needed.

3. Business insurance also can be used as an aid to corporate financing. Where the success of a business enterprise is recognized to be largely dependent on one man, or where a stock is being issued to finance a program of development the success of which will be largely in the hands of one man, it is possible to use key man insurance to back the issue and thus add a margin of safety that will make the issue more attractive to investors. In event of the key man's early death, proceeds from the policy can be used to retire the stock.[54]

4. Key man life insurance permits accumulations that are less liable to criticism from stockholders. This is especially important where there are minority stockholders not actively engaged in the business. To them, the accumulations may seem to be a means of avoiding payment of dividends. Minority stockholders have distinct legal rights. They have been known to cause the business embarrassment and expense by threatening or bringing suit against officers for alleged attempt to accumulate surplus to avoid payment of dividends.[55] Such stockholders are less likely, however, to look upon the cash values in key man insurance as an unreasonable accumulation of earnings.

Other Primary Uses. A number of other uses of business insurance are available that are primary rather than collateral uses. These are:

Credit Insurance. Life insurance is widely used as security for credit or

---

[53] During the money crunches of 1966 and 1969–70, the loan values of life insurance policies were particularly attractive—attractive to the insured but not to the insurer!

[54] It appears from a study of court decisions in such cases (cf. *Ellsworth* v. *Lyons,* U.S. Circuit Court of Appeals, 6th dist., 181 Fed. 55, and *Tweedie Footwear Corp.* v. *Fonville,* Texas Court of Civil Appeals, 115 S.W. [2d] 421) that the proceeds would have to be payable to a trustee for the specific benefit of the holders of the block of stock rather than to the corporation.

[55] There is also the possibility that accumulation of cash funds to redeem stock of shareholders will be subject to the imposition of an accumulated earnings tax. Edwin M. Jones, counsel for New York Life, speaking before the insurance section meeting of the New York State Bar Association, was quoted by the *National Underwriter* (Chicago, March 12, 1960) as stating, "In two cases where substantial sums were accumulated and used to redeem stock of shareholders, the penalty tax was imposed. In neither case was insurance purchased. It may be that these cases indicate that the way to avoid the accumulated earnings tax is to buy life insurance since the use of insurance requires less cash to be accumulated. In any event, there are cases supporting the view that the purchase of insurance has a reasonable business purpose when such insurance is designed to provide for continuity of management. My personal view is that this proposition will one day be firmly established in the law."

loans. The creditor or lender may require the borrower to assign existing life insurance as collateral; or the lender may himself purchase and maintain life and disability insurance on the borrower. Credit insurance is widely used to guarantee installment purchases, usually in the form of group insurance, as discussed in Chapter 15.

Group Insurance. As noted in Chapters 15 and 16, group life and health insurance is important in funding employee benefit plans.

Insurance in Pension Plans. The use of life insurance and annuities in pension and profit sharing plans is discussed in Chapter 19.

6. TAXES AND BUSINESS LIFE INSURANCE PLANNING— A SUMMARY

Life insurance tax planning, while a major consideration in any type of life underwriting, is especially important in the field of business insurance. It is here that many pitfalls, unknown to the uninformed, can be avoided and that substantial reduction of income and estate tax liability can be accomplished.

Life insurance may be purchased to fund agreements among partners or stockholders. Jones and Smith are partners. They come to an agreement that when one of the partners dies, the survivor will buy the partnership interest from the estate of the deceased. The deceased's wife agrees to sell at a price determined in advance.

To assure that the funds required are available and to obtain those funds at the lowest possible cost, life insurance is purchased. Jones buys a $30,000 policy on Smith's life, and Smith buys the same amount on Jones's life. When Jones dies, Smith has enough money from the proceeds of his insurance on Jones's life to provide him with the means of buying Jones's partnership interest from Jones's estate.

In the absence of a trust agreement, most insurance authorities consider that the best arrangement is for Jones to be the beneficiary on Smith's policy and for Smith to be the beneficiary on Jones's policy. Frequently, however, the partners will name as beneficiary the wife of the person whose life is insured. This can be expensive in taxes.

For example: Jones and Smith each have a $30,000 original interest in the firm, so each buys a $30,000 policy on the other's life. Jones's wife is beneficiary of the policy on his life, and Smith's wife is the beneficiary of the policy on Smith's life. Jones dies, and his wife gets the $30,000 proceeds from the insurance company. Jones' interest in the partnership is delivered to Smith.

Smith now owns a $60,000 business in which he originally invested $30,000. If he had been the beneficiary on Jones's policy, he would have received the proceeds from the insurance company and turned over the $30,000 to Jones's wife in exchange for the partnership interest.

However, since Jones's wife received the $30,000 direct from the insurance company, Smith still has only his original $30,000 invested in a business now worth $60,000 to him. If he later sells the business he will have to pay income tax on the difference between his original $30,000 investment and whatever price he receives for the business. On the other hand, if he had been Jones's beneficiary, he would then have had a $60,000 investment in the business, and his cost basis for tax purposes would be $60,000, not $30,000.

The same principle would apply on an agreement to buy out costockholders in a corporation.

Circumstances alter cases, and in many instances it is advisable for the corporation to be the beneficiary under a stock purchase plan; but it is important to consider whether the surviving stockholders would not fare better under a cross-purchase plan with each stockholder paying the premiums on the lives of the others and with the surviving stockholders named as beneficiaries.

Brown, Jones, and Smith are the sole stockholders of a small corporation. Each owns 100 shares. They enter into a cross-purchase agreement under which each insures the others. Brown dies, and as beneficiaries on Brown's life, Jones and Smith each receive $10,000 in insurance proceeds, which they use to buy Brown's stock from his estate.

Jones and Smith now own 150 shares each. Their cost basis for those 150 shares owned by each is the original cost of their 100 shares plus the $10,000 each received from the life insurance company and which each used to buy Brown's stock. When, as, and if Jones or Smith sells his stock, his income for tax purposes will be the amount by which the selling price of his stock exceeds the sum of his original investment plus the $10,000 of life insurance proceeds.

On the other hand, if the corporation were the beneficiary and used the insurance proceeds to buy the stock from Brown's widow, subsequently retiring the stock from the corporate treasury, Jones and Smith would then own all the stock in a corporation whose book value had increased because of the retirement of Brown's stock, but both Jones and Smith would still have as their cost basis only their original investment in their respective stock interests.

It will be recalled, however, that there might be an income tax advantage for the corporation to pay the premiums under the entity plan. The corporation can pay the premiums without such premiums being taxable as dividends to the stockholders or as salaries to employee stockholders. If the money were paid out first to the stockholders and used by them to buy the insurance under a cross-purchase plan, the money would be taxable income to the stockholders and unless considered salaries would not be deductible by the corporation.

Deductibility of Premiums.   Life insurance premiums are not deductible when paid on the lives of partners or sole proprietors. Premiums are deductible as a business expense when paid by corporations only when the corporation is not the beneficiary and holds no incidents of ownership. If, for instance, the Consolidated Corporation pays the premiums on the life of an officer or other employee and that employee's wife is the beneficiary, the premiums are deductible by the corporation provided, of course, that the corporation has no incidents of ownership. The amount of the premiums, however, constitutes additional taxable income to the employee whether he be an officer or a general employee. Group insurance is an exception to this rule.

It is important to bear in mind that the life insurance premiums, when added to other compensation such as salaries and bonuses, must be reasonable. The total must not be so out of line that the Internal Revenue Service will consider it excessive compensation for the amount and type of services rendered by the stockholder or officer.

The premiums, moreover, must be clearly shown to constitute compensation to the employee. In one case a stockholder employee who was a corporate officer was paid a salary and, in addition, under an agreement among the stockholders, the corporation paid the premiums on his insurance. The court held that the premium payments were not additional compensation but were dividends and therefore not deductible as business expense.

The income tax treatment of health insurance premiums is slightly different. The reasonableness of health insurance premiums is determined independently of the total compensation paid to the insured. The employer can deduct reasonable premiums paid to maintain health insurance on the employee for the employee's benefit.[56] In a 1960 case[57] the Tax Court held that premiums on health insurance for the benefit of certain corporate executives were deductible, even though a substantial part of their salaries was disallowed as exceeding reasonable compensation. On this matter the court said: "It is not unusual for a corporation to provide such insurance. The amounts paid were neither unreasonable nor excessive . . . the payments cannot, therefore, be regarded as dividends."

Section 303 of the Internal Revenue Code. If a corporation buys a part of its stock from a stockholder, the price paid to the stockholder usually will be treated as a taxable distribution. This is the rule under Sections 301 and 302 of the IRC. But under Section 303, where stock is included in the gross estate of the decedent, a redemption of such stock by the corporation for an amount equal to the sum of death taxes, funeral, and administrative expense will not be considered a taxable distribution if the value of the stock owned in the corporation is more than 35 percent of the value of the decedent's gross estate or 50 percent of the value of his taxable

---

[56] Remember that, unlike life insurance premiums, these premiums do not constitute taxable income to the employee (IRC, Section 106).

[57] *Ernest, Holdeman, and Collet, Inc.,* 19 T.C.M. 40 (1960).

estate.[58] Life insurance on the principal stockholder, purchased and owned by the corporation, can provide the funds necessary to purchase the stock from his estate. The use of this plan enables the surviving stockholders to retain the business interest and thus help perpetuate the control of a family corporation.

Before a 1969 amendment to the Internal Revenue Code, there was a question whether an accumulation to be used to purchase stock under a Section 303 redemption would be considered in appraising accumulated earnings for the application of the accumulated earnings tax. Two circuit courts and the Tax Court had held such accumulations to be for the personal benefit of the stockholder and not for a reasonable business purpose. However, the 1969 amendment provides that amounts needed for a Section 303 redemption in the year in which a stockholder dies or a later year are for reasonable business needs. But the amendment made no reference to earnings accumulated in the years prior to the stockholder's death. Since the accumulated earnings tax applies only for the year in which the earnings are retained and assessed, annual premium life insurance appears to be an appropriate instrument for funding Section 303 redemptions. The premiums paid in any one year obviously would be less than the full amount needed to fund the redemption were the entire amount set aside in any one year as a lump sum. Retained earnings only in excess of $100,000 are subject to review by the Internal Revenue Service.

Income Taxation of Group Insurance.   Payments of premiums by an employer for group life insurance are a deductible business expense and, except for the cost of coverage in excess of $50,000, do not constitute taxable income to employees. There are, however, certain restrictions and rules that must be applied. The employee must not name the employer as beneficiary, and there must be no blanket or individual assignment of the policies to the employer. Group insurance premiums on the lives of employees are deductible business expenses not only for corporations but also for partnership employers or employers who are sole proprietors.

The Technical Amendments Act of 1958.   A new subchapter to Chapter 1 of the Internal Revenue Code was added in 1958. This addition, known as Subchapter S, makes it possible for an unincorporated business to incorporate while retaining the tax status of a partnership if the corporation meets certain conditions.[59] These corporations, sometimes referred to

---

58 If stock of two or more corporations is included in the gross estate, the combined stock may be treated as the stock of a single corporation for the purposes of applying the 35 percent or 50 percent tests provided that his gross estate includes more than 75 percent of the outstanding stock of each corporation.

59 The conditions are that there must not be more than 10 stockholders; all stockholders must consent to the election to be taxed as a partnership; there can be only one class of stock; the stockholders must be individuals or estates; the corporation must not be an alien corporation; the corporation must not own 80 percent or more of a subsidiary corporation; more than 80 percent of the corporation's gross receipts must not be derived from foreign sources; and more than 20 percent of the corporation's gross receipts must not be derived from certain sources of personal holding company income: rents, royalties, dividends, interest, annuities, and security transactions.

as Subchapter S corporations, are treated as regular corporations for all except tax purposes.

The significance of this act to the field of business insurance is that fringe benefits unavailable to business owners under the partnership or proprietorship form of business organization can be made available to the stockholders of Subchapter S corporations. Since partners and proprietors are employers rather than employees, they are not eligible to participate in qualified pension and deferred profit sharing plans. But in a Subchapter S corporation the stockholders who work for the corporation are employees along with the other working force and are therefore entitled to be included in a qualified pension or deferred profit sharing plan and enjoy its tax advantages.

Prior to the Tax Reform Act of 1969, Subchapter S corporations were treated just like any other corporation with regard to qualified pension plans. However, the Tax Reform Act established a maximum level of contribution which may be made on behalf of a "shareholder-employee" for taxable years beginning after December 31, 1970, without creating a current tax liability for him. This maximum is 10 percent of compensation or $2,500, whichever is less. A shareholder employee is defined as any individual owning more than 5 percent of the corporation's outstanding stock. Although the corporation may make any contribution on behalf of a shareholder employee called for by the plan, the amount by which the contribution on his behalf exceeds the foregoing limit will be taxable to him as current income. In the event that the amounts contributed are forfeited for any reason, he will be entitled to a deduction in the year of forfeiture.

Available to a Subchapter S corporation but unavailable to owners in a partnership or sole proprietorship is the $5,000 tax-free death benefit which can be paid to the stockholder-employee's widow upon his death. Also, the corporation can purchase health insurance on the stockholder-executive without the premiums being taxable income to the employee. A partnership or proprietorship cannot purchase health insurance on its owners with tax-free dollars.

The Technical Amendments Act of 1958 included among its 103 sections other provisions affecting business life insurance. An important one deals with the income tax treatment of nonforfeitable annuity retirement income contracts purchased by tax-exempt educational, charitable, or religious organizations. The law was amended to provide that premiums paid by such organizations for employee nonforfeitable annuities that are not a part of a qualified pension plan are to be taxed to these employees only to the extent that they exceed a given exclusion determined by applying a formula set up in the act. This formula is discussed in Chapter 17.

23

Underwriting the Insurance

Mortality and morbidity tables are employed in the calculation of life and health insurance premiums. The tables used are a compilation of mortality and morbidity experience among insured lives. Therefore, when new persons are added to the insured group, they must be comparable to those upon whose lives the tables are based if the loss rate for the group is to approximate the experience shown in the tables.

The process by which an insurer determines whether or not and on what basis it will accept an applicant for insurance is know as "underwriting the insurance" or "selecting and classifying the insured." The former is probably the better term. The latter might imply that the process is one of choosing only the best insureds, which is not the case. Instead, the process is one of determining whether the expected loss of the applicant is equal to, more than, or less than that anticipated by the insurer in its standard premium schedule. The insurer will have a range above the average expected loss at which it will accept applicants at standard premiums. Beyond that range, the applicant will be charged a higher premium, or in some cases be denied the insurance. Thus, underwriting involves techniques not only for reaching decisions whether applicants should be accepted for insurance but also for assigning them to appropriate rate classes.

Industry figures show that out of every 100 regular ordinary life insurance policies applied for, 3 are rejected.[1] About 60 percent of the rejections are for serious health impairments; the rest are primarily for hazardous occupations. About 53 of every 1,000 ordinary policies currently issued and paid for, representing about 6.4 percent of the amount of ordinary insurance purchased, require an extra premium.[2]

---

[1] This is not a picture of the insurability of the American public at large, but only of people who apply for ordinary life policies. Among those who don't apply, and therefore do not appear in this summary, are (1) those who know they would not be accepted, and hence never apply in the first place, and (2) those whom the agents know would not be accepted and whom they therefore never solicit.

[2] Heart conditions account for 33 percent of the extra rate policies; weight problems account for 16 percent; other medical reasons, 29 percent; hazardous occupations account for 12 percent; and all other causes account for the remaining 10 percent.

Ideally, companies would like to be able to offer some type of coverage to everyone who applies, because rejections cause adverse public relations and often are both irritating and discouraging to agents.

Sometimes the applicant has just been examined by his own physician and told he has "absolutely nothing to worry about." Too often the medical examiner, despite instructions, reminders, and cajolery from the company, pats the applicant on the back, and remarks, "You passed with flying colors."

The family physician who is treating an individual patient does not have statistical evidence to support his prognosis. He may feel it is better not to frighten the patient about a condition, or he may consider whatever condition exists to be compensated. However, the home office medical director and underwriting department are dealing with a mass of exposures. They know that a given impairment about which the family physician is not concerned in the individual case will produce greater mortality in the mass.

In the case of the physician making the examination, his function is not to "pass" any applicant. His function is only to report his findings to the company. Rarely is he even qualified to form a judgment. Insurance medicine is a technical branch of the profession in which few practicing physicians are qualified.

The situation can be aggravated when a company upon rejecting an applicant is unable to tell the applicant or the agent the reason, since it may be confidential. The result can be an ex-applicant who publicly criticizes the company and an irritated agent engaged in protracted correspondence with the company about the case.

This chapter is concerned with the various classifications of acceptable applicants and with the information used by the insurer in making underwriting decisions. It also deals with the nature and expense of nonmedical life insurance and with the importance of reinsurance.

1. THE NECESSITY FOR UNDERWRITING

Because applicants for insurance are not random and do not have the same loss expectancy at a given age, underwriting is necessary to avoid adverse selection and to achieve equity among policyholders.

If one knew he were going to die or become disabled tomorrow, he would beg or borrow the largest sum of money he could get to buy insurance tonight. But as long as death or disability is not imminent, the typical person thinks next week, next month, next year will be soon enough for him to insure. When the public is left to its own initiative to buy insurance, among those who apply for it will be those in bad health or engaged in hazardous occupations. As a result, mortality or morbidity among a group that includes unsolicited and unselected applicants will be greater than that anticipated among solicited and selected applicants.

Therefore, the company must either rate up or reject all applicants whom it can recognize as not measuring up to its standards. Were a company not to apply rigid underwriting standards and, instead, insure all applicants at standard rates, applicants who might be rated up or rejected by other insurers would gravitate to that company. This phenomenon is known as adverse selection or antiselection. An insurer involved in antiselection eventually would be out of business because (1) to remain solvent it soon would have to charge a premium that would reflect the average loss expectancy of its insureds, (2) that loss expectancy will be higher than the average loss expectancy of insurers using generally accepted underwriting standards to rate up or reject applicants with high loss expectancy, and (3) the difference in the premium that the antiselected insurer would have to charge would be too high for it to be able to attract sufficient numbers of insureds to be able to continue in business.

Equity Among Policyholders. A second objective of underwriting is to achieve equity among policyholders. This means that within broad classification limits a policyholder should be charged a premium in accordance with the burden that his exposure places on the insurer. The objective is one of achieving a practical degree of equity, not perfect equity. Even under the most sophisticated rating system, any premium rate is theoretically inequitable for every applicant except the average one. Since the average is a statistic rather than a human being, it becomes technically correct to state that any premium rate is inequitable for all applicants. However, the operation of the insurance principle depends upon large numbers. If there are too many classifications, there will not be a large enough group of people in any one of them for the law of large numbers to operate. Companies must therefore use classifications sufficiently broad to produce stability of experience. Thus, there is a limit to the extent to which inequities can be eliminated.[3]

The purpose of selection and classification of insureds is to reduce the degree of rate inequity among policyholders. How this is done will become apparent as the discussion progresses.

---

[3] The degree of rate inequity for a given policyholder increases with the extent that his expected mortality or morbidity is above or below that of the average of the classification in which the insurer's underwriting standards place him. Those with loss expectancies below the average pay more than is necessary to uphold their share of the burden whereas those with loss expectancies above the average pay less than is necessary to uphold their share of the burden. It is anticipated that within any classification, a number of policyholders with loss expectations lower than the average will be available to offset to a large extent those policyholders with loss expectations higher than the average. The insurer determines how far above or below the average expected mortality or morbidity for a given classification it will go within that classification before assigning the applicant to a different classification. The difference in the expected mortality or morbidity between policyholders at the top and the bottom of the range within a class would be higher than the difference in the expected mortality or morbidity between policyholders at the top of the range of one class and those at the bottom of the range of the next highest class. Such is the inequity inherent in class rating.

2. UNDERWRITING FACTORS

Several different underwriting factors are used by underwriting departments of life and health companies. Among them are (1) age, (2) sex, (3) plan of insurance, (4) occupation, (5) residence, (6) race and nationality, (7) family and personal history, (8) physical condition and physique, and (9) financial condition. Some discussion of the nature and importance of each of these factors will be helpful in understanding both the questions asked on a life insurance policy application and the reasons why some applicants are rated up or are rejected.

Age. Insurers establish maximum ages above which they will not issue policies. The maximum age for new life insurance varies among companies and is commonly 70 or 75. An exception usually is made for term insurance where the maximum age is commonly set at 60.[4]

Several explanations may be given for establishing maximum age limits. As a practical matter, the number of applications for life insurance which could be obtained above age 70 or 75 would be insufficient to constitute a group large enough for the safe operation of the law of large numbers. At these ages the need for new life insurance is frequently small or nonexistent, the cost is nearly prohibitive, the possibility of meeting the medical requirements is remote, the medical examination generally is ineffective in revealing degenerative conditions, and the probability of adverse selection is high. Patently, adverse selection is suspect when people apply for high-cost insurance when they have little need for postdeath resources.

However, some companies recognize that at times there may be a need for new life insurance beyond the published maximum age limit. To meet this demand, they have developed a special set of rates for applicants up to, perhaps, 10 years above the regular limit. These rates are confined to one or two plans of insurance and are adjusted to take care of the problem of antiselection.

A few companies set the minimum age limits at which they will write insurance. These limits are one day, one week, one month, three months, six months, or even a year. The purpose of eliminating coverage during these early months is to avoid the high expected losses associated with infant mortality experience. Because of the small need for insurance at these younger ages, insurers frequently limit the amount of insurance they will write on children, and require that the amount be reasonable in relation to the amount of insurance on the person who is supporting the child. Insurers

---

[4] Insurers may have different maximum age limits at which they will issue different types of policies. One insurer, for example, sets age 70 as the maximum age at which it will write new continuous premium whole life policies, but will issue at age 80 new endowments at age 90, and whole life paid up at age 95. This insurer sets age 60 as the maximum age at which it will issue 5-year, nonrenewable convertible term policies, age 55 as the maximum age at which it will issue 5-year renewable term insurance, and age 54 as the maximum age at which it will issue nonrenewable convertible term to age 65.

have found that the financial condition of the parents is an important consideration in assessing the expected survival rate of infant children.

In writing insurance nonmedically, that is without requiring the applicant to submit to a medical examination, age is an important factor. Companies usually will not write nonmedical insurance beyond ages 40 or 45, and the maximum amount of nonmedical insurance that will be written generally is an inverse function of the age of the applicant. Age limits also are established for the writing of disability benefits.

Age affects the underwriting of disability income and health expense insurance because the incidence and duration of disability increase with age. The rate of loss under long-term disability policies increases with age about as rapidly as does the rate of death. But under health expense policies and short-term disability income policies, the loss rate remains fairly constant until about age 55, when it increases sharply with age.

Sex.   In general, women are accepted for life insurance on the same basis as men, although this has not always been true. It was commonly considered, even well into the 1920's, that the loss potential among women was greater than among men, and that women should either pay a higher premium or not be accepted at all. The childbirth hazard is now considered to be so minor as to have no practical effect upon mortality experience, being offset by the more sheltered lives of women.[5] Moreover, it is statistically observable that women, on the average, live more than five years longer than men. Insurers are now making life insurance available to women at lower premiums than are charged men, recognizing that women have become important buyers of life insurance and no longer represent a greater physical and moral hazard. About 70 percent of all women in the United States are insured under some form of life insurance. About 30 percent of all ordinary life insurance policies are purchased on the lives of women, and these policies represent about 12 percent of all ordinary life insurance purchased in the United States.

While many insurers will write any plan of life insurance on the lives of women, some few insurers have restrictive rules regarding the writing of term insurance. These rules limit term insurance to one or more of the following: single women, self-supporting women, self-supporting single women, business and professional women, women who can show that a satisfactory need exists, and women who have substantial means in their own right.

These varying rules relating to the writing of term insurance on women

---

[5] To avoid sarcastic annotation in the margin by the feminist contingent, we explain that by "more sheltered lives" we mean, for instance, that fewer women than men work outside the home; hence the statistically average woman is exposed to a smaller number of chances of traffic accident and contagion, to name just two hazards. Moreover, women show a smaller incidence of coronary breakdown, stomach ulcer, nervous breakdowns, and other disturbances generally considered to be aggravated if not created by the vicissitudes of business life. However, the number of women working outside the home is increasing as the trend toward two-income families continue. About 1 family out of every 3 has a working wife compared to 1 out of every 20 at the turn of the century.

present an interesting example of how differently life insurers view underwriting factors. Obviously some insurers believe that term insurance on dependent women presents a problem of adverse selection that can be avoided by such rules.

A number of companies will not write disability income insurance for women, and most of those that do will write only short-term benefits on self-supporting females engaged in an occupation requiring them to leave home. Some companies make disability benefit provisions for single women cancellable upon marriage. However, in a few companies housewives may be able to purchase disability income insurance for small amounts ($100 a month, for example) and for benefits of short durations (1 or 2 years, for example). The dollar limit of monthly income disability benefits written for women in some companies may be lower than that written for men. Also, the maximum age to which the coverage is issued and the maximum age at which disability may occur (in some companies) are lower for women than for men. For example, a company may pay a maximum of $750 a month for a male and issue the policy up to age 55, requiring that disability occur before age 60. For a female the maximum amount may be only $400 and the corresponding age limitations may be 50 and 55. Underwriting rules for the waiver of premium disability benefit for women usually are not so strict. It is generally available for self-supporting females, and a growing number of companies will write the coverage for dependent housewives. The age limits at which the rider will be issued are lower in some, but not many, companies for women than for men.

Plan of Insurance.   Before the development of substandard underwriting, it was common practice for companies to be considerably more liberal in underwriting higher premium plans of life insurance. Higher premium plans require higher reserves per $1,000 of insurance, and consequently the company has progressively less at risk under these plans. Hence, applicants who would have been considered uninsurable for a continuous premium whole life plan may have been insured at standard rates under a short-term endowment plan.

The practice of dealing with impairments by restricting the plan of life insurance is in use today but on a more limited scale. For example, an applicant with a slight health or physical condition, the effects of which are usually postponed until later years, might be insurable at standard rates under an endowment plan which expires prior to the years in which the impairment is likely to affect mortality. Thus, to illustrate, an overweight person at age 25 might be insurable at standard rates under a 20-year endowment plan because the effects of overweight do not begin to be seriously felt until the middle years. However, this same applicant might be rated substandard for a continuous premium whole life policy.

Finally, the plan of insurance is important in underwriting because the amount at risk is different under different policies; hence, companies often have stricter underwriting rules for certain types of policies. Some plans themselves tend to invite adverse selection. Whereas a given applicant might be eligible for continuous premium whole life insurance, he might not be eligible for a family income policy, term policy, or a preferred risk contract. The trend in underwriting now, however, is to give less attention to type of policy. Many companies apply the same selection standards to term insurance as a whole life insurance but allow for expected adverse selection in their rate structure.

The plan applied for in health insurance is important since some types of plans can be issued to certain impaired applicants, whereas others cannot. For instance, in some cases it is considered proper to issue an accident-only policy where coverage for both accident and sickness could not be issued.

Occupation. Certain occupations are considered extra hazardous and not to be written at standard rates. In the rate book of one company, approximately 750 occupational duties requiring other than standard rates are listed.[6] Some samples are reproduced below.

| | | Ratings for | |
	Life Only	Disability Income Rider and Waiver of Premium	Accidental Death Benefit
Abrasive Manufacture			
Clay, crushing furnace, grinding and sizing depts.			
Foremen (supervising only), inspectors	$2.00	WP only, 150%	200%
Other workers	3.50	Unacceptable	Unacceptable
Other departments			
Foremen and inspectors	Std.	WP only	Std.
Graders, wheel testers, packers, shippers, and so on.	Std.	WP only, 150%	200%
Other workers	$2.00	Unacceptable	Unacceptable
Acetylene Gas Manufacture			
Foreman (supervising only), compressor engineers, generator tenders, skilled workers	Std.	WP only	200%
Other workers	$2.00	WP only, 150%	Unacceptable
Amusements and Sports			
Baseball, basketball, golf, tennis, squash players	Std.	Yes	Std.
Circus employees	Unacceptable		
Football and hockey players	Std.	WP only, 150%	200%
Horse racing			
Starters	Std.	WP only, 150%	200%
Trainers (best grade), trotting horse drivers, and stablemen	$2.00	Unacceptable	Unacceptable
Jockeys	Unacceptable		
Others	Inquire		
Prize fighters	Unacceptable		
Racers, auto and motorcycle	Unacceptable		
Wrestlers	Unacceptable		

[6] Occupational mortality has been improving over the past years, with the resulting tendency among life insurance companies to reduce or eliminate ratings on a number of occupations.

Note that, in this listing, some of the jobs may be standard for life insurance alone but substandard or uninsurable for waiver of premium, disability income or accidental death benefit riders.

The insurability of various occupations or duties and the ratings they take vary from company to company; however, there is almost always agreement that certain obviously hazardous occupations—of steeplejacks, to give an extreme example, or bartenders, race car drivers, workers in plants manufacturing explosives, and sand blasters—are to be rated at least substandard. Even here there may be no general agreement among companies as to the extent of ratings, i.e., how much of an extra premium should be charged.

The hazardous nature of any particular occupation arises from a greater incidence of accident in that occupation, from duties or working conditions of a nature which adversely affect health, or from environmental conditions which either attract people of low economic or mental status or place the individuals in contact with people of questionable character.

For underwriting purposes, the company is interested in how long the applicant has been in his present job, and, if less than two years, the nature of his previous occupation. This information is necessary since a previous occupation might affect the present state of health of the applicant as well as have a bearing on the moral hazard. A question of concern, too, is whether or not the applicant has an occupational history which suggests a return to a former hazardous occupation. Once a life insurance policy is issued it cannot be rated up should there be a subsequent change in occupation. However, many insurers will remove occupational ratings after the insured has changed to a less hazardous occupation, subject to evidence of insurability, and in some cases subject to a waiting period of one full year of service in the new occupation.

Avocations also are important in underwriting because professors may engage in motorcycle racing as a hobby and students may engage in ski acrobatics.

Occupation has a direct bearing on the hazard in health insurance. While the introduction of plant safety devices has reduced the direct occupational hazard in many lines of work, there are still differences in claim experience among occupations.

Each company uses a manual or system of occupational classifications. The health insurance rate book lists occupations in alphabetical order and assigns a code to each. Here is an excerpt from a typical occupational classification for an optionally renewable disability income policy:

AAA	Abstractor, office duties only
AAA	Accountant
B	Acetylene, gas plant employee
B	Acid plant employee
B	Actor, actress, acrobatic, or gymnastic work
AAA	Advertising, office or sales duties only

Some companies develop their own classification systems and manuals. Probably most companies use one of the systems developed by either the

Bureau of Accident & Health Underwriters or the Health & Accident Underwriters' Conference, intercompany associations that were subsequently merged into the present Health Insurance Association of America. The Bureau manual contains 14 classifications, coded A through M. The Conference has 2 manuals, 1 with 11 classifications and 6,200 listings, coded AA to J, and the other a simplified classification with 1,380 listings, coded AAA, AA, A, and B.

Noncan occupational classification systems are usually simpler, partly because the higher rate of noncan is in itself selective, limiting the great bulk of applications to the professional, executive, and white-collar classes, and partly because there has never been any real statistical basis for such classifications. An illustrative noncancellable and guaranteed renewable classification system is as follows:

(1) Office or clerical work in a stable business
(2) White collar groups not meeting the requirements for Class 1
(3) One-man occupations
(4) Skilled manual workers
(5) Insurable risks with some occupational hazard.

The agent fills out the application on the basis of the classification applying to the applicant. The home office checks his classification.

Residence. Although health and, hence, mortality may be adversely affected by various climates and sanitary conditions in different areas, these variations usually are not considered, at least as among locations in North America. Among companies writing business abroad, however, permanent or long-term residence in unhealthful climates or in areas where sanitary conditions are bad may call for either higher premiums or rejection.

If the applicant has changed his residence within the past two years, the company wants to know the place of previous residence. This information is important since it can have a bearing on the present state of health of the applicant and may indicate whether or not he may be expected to settle permanently in a location which is undesirable from an underwriting point of view. Also, it has its value for purposes of identification and for the investigation of other underwriting factors.

Race and Nationality. Certain races can be shown statistically to have a mortality rate higher than that expected among "Caucasians." Certain nationalities have environment and living standards such that they may produce impairments that continue through one or more generations even after these people migrate to a different country. Since the mortality experience among the non-Caucasian races has been improving at such a rapid rate, and because of the fear of being suspected of unfair discrimination, race is becoming less important as an underwriting factor. In fact, insurers to a large extent have officially, if not practically, eliminated the special discriminatory treatment of races.[7] A reasonable period of residence in this country, however, is usually required before life insurance may be written

---

[7] Some states have laws forbidding any differences in rates based solely on race.

on new immigrants. This requirement is to allow time for the new immigrant to adjust to new living conditions and to establish a reliable medical and personal history.

Family and Personal History. The health records of both the insured and his family are considered important to underwriting decisions.

In general, family history is important only if it reveals something which might adversely affect the longevity of the applicant, such as cardiovascular renal diseases. Rarely will favorable family history offset the adverse effect of personal history.

Age and the state of health of parents, brothers, and sisters are requested on the application blank, since this information is considered as having at least some bearing on the longevity of the offspring. If the applicant's father or mother is no longer living, the insurer wants to know the age and cause of death. The same information is required for deceased brothers and sisters. Even though there is reason to question both the accuracy of the family history reporting and the exact effect of heredity on life expectancy, insurers usually will give some weight to unusually good or bad history in making its underwriting judgment because statistical studies have shown that *ceteris paribus* those applicants reporting good family histories show a mortality rate of about 26 percent lower than those reporting poor family histories.

Early deaths of family members are not in themselves justification for rejection; they control the underwriting decision only if early death resulted from something which could be transmitted to children by inheritance or childhood contact.

The personal history of the applicant himself is more directly important in appraising the exposure—health record, habits, environment. All these are important in measuring not only the physical hazard involved but also the moral hazard. In fact, the habits, environment, and reputation of the applicant are considered so important that there is an investigation of these history factors by professional and disinterested investigators, commonly employees of organizations conducting a credit investigation business. The nature and significance of the inspection report is discussed later.

The character of the applicant is one of the most important yet most intangible underwriting factors. What is his marital history? What are his business ethics? What is his general reputation? Does he show evidence of sufficient moral stamina to stand up in adversity? If not, physical adversity or economic adversity may make him an expensive policyholder.

The application blank itself, by including a series of questions, also attempts to determine the information relating to the personal history, habits, and environment of the applicant. Heavy drinking, excessive use of drugs, and dangerous living are grounds for rejection. Habits relating to air travel also are important. If there appears to be an unusual aviation hazard,[8] the

---

[8] Travel in company owned planes, on commercial airlines, whether scheduled or not, and on military aircraft is not considered to be an unusual aviation hazard. Commercial airline pilots, who in former years had to pay higher premiums for insurance if they could

company may charge an extra premium to cover the additional hazard or may limit the amount of insurance that will be issued. Life insurance policies do not exclude deaths resulting from aircraft accidents, although where there is a severe aviation hazard, a partial exclusion rider may be used in policies issued in those states which permit their use.[9]

Physique and Physical Condition.   Physical condition, of course, has a direct effect upon longevity. The insurance companies want to know about an applicant's sight, hearing, heart, arteries, nervous system, lungs, tonsils, teeth, kidneys, and so forth. They judge the applicant in the light of their knowledge of the effect of any discovered impairment or disorder on longevity in general, and not as it may affect any one individual's life span. Consequently, while a practicing physician might not consider a given impairment as serious in the light of an individual's health, habits, and environment, the life insurance medical department may consider it cause for increasing the premium or rejection in view of statistics which show that out of a large group of persons with the impairment, more will die than standard insurance mortality tables would indicate.

For example, the practicing physician, with a chance to observe an individual over a period of time and with full knowledge of all his affairs, might consider an elevation of blood pressure a temporary functional disturbance brought about by a passing condition. On the other hand, the life insurance physician, having no chance to observe the individual over a continuing period of time or lacking positive evidence as to his past history, but having before him only the report of an elevated blood pressure on one or a series of examinations, will give the matter serious consideration. He has statistical evidence that high blood pressure has an adverse effect on mortality in the mass. Even if he knows that the condition is functional rather than organic, he also has evidence that a certain percentage of functional cases will eventually become organic. He cannot judge by the individual case; he must judge by mass experience.

In general, impairments can be grouped into three classes: temporary, static, and progressive.

An example of a temporary impairment is a peptic ulcer. An example of a static impairment is an amputation (assuming that it was the result of a localized condition such as an injury and not of a general, progressive disease or disturbance which amputation cannot arrest). Amputation of one limb is usually not cause for rejection or for an extra premium, although it

---

get any at all, now usually can purchase coverage at standard rates. Even private pilots within some particular age range who do not fly more than a given number of hours a year, and who are experienced, are covered at standard rates. The unusual aviation hazard includes the private pilot who is either too old, too young, inexperienced, or flies more than a given number of hours annually. Crew members of aircraft also present an unusual aviation hazard. Some insurers consider travel in a privately owned plane to represent an unusual aviation hazard.

[9] Disability and accidental death benefit provisions of these same policies commonly carry some aviation restrictions of their own.

may have an effect upon the underwriting of waiver of premium accidental death benefits.

An example of a progressive impairment is cancer. Progressive impairments, however, may eventually become static impairments. For instance, cancer, at least in the early stages, often can be completely arrested by X ray or operation. A history showing a successful cancer operation 10 years ago with no evidence of recurrence can be considered in an entirely different light from existing cancer or cancer operated upon recently. Diabetes is an impairment which some companies will consider as changing eventually from a progressive to a static stage. Within the past few years, a number of companies have begun to accept diabetics whose condition has proved to be completely controllable by the use of insulin.[10] At one time diabetics were universally rejected.

The general physique of the applicant is important. Marked variations from the average height and weight, for instance, are considered adverse factors, since such deviations affect mortality in the mass. The distribution of weight is a factor for consideration. A rule of some companies is that if the waist measurement exceeds the expanded chest measurement, an overweight condition is present. Overweight is much more serious than underweight. The effect of underweight and overweight on mortality must be evaluated in the light of personal and family history. Generally speaking, underweight is not seriously regarded as an impairment;[11] however, when coupled with a family history of tuberculosis, or when malnutrition is suspected, it will cause careful scrutiny.

Physical condition of the applicant obviously is important in writing insurance that covers sickness. It is sometimes not understood why it is also important in underwriting accident insurance. Poor health increases the chance of a person's becoming a victim of an accident, and also can intensify or prolong the disability resulting from an accident.

Financial Status. Obviously, an application for a policy calling for a total premium outlay (adding any existing insurance on the life) completely out of line with the size, source, and stability of the applicant's income is cause for underwriting suspicion. Either the policy is not going to be accepted by the applicant if issued, or there is a good chance that the policy will result in early lapse. A life insurance company is not eager to pay either for medical examinations or for the cost of issuing policies only to have them rejected when issued or lapsed before enough premiums are col-

---

[10] The common practice is to charge a higher premium.

[11] Recent studies indicate that persons between the ages of 15 and 45 that are as much as 20 percent underweight show better mortality experience than do people in those ages who are of average weight. People over 45 who are as much as 10 percent underweight show better mortality experience than do those over 45 who are of average weight. As for overweight, studies show a lesser improvement in mortality over the past years than has been experienced by those of average weight. Overweight, therefore, is becoming more seriously regarded by underwriters. See *Build and Blood Pressure Study,* a two-volume study published in 1959 by the Society of Actuaries, Chicago, Illinois.

lected to permit the company to recover the acquisition costs in connection with them.[12]

What constitutes overinsurance at any income level is difficult to define. Any two men at the same salary level and with the same family responsibilities are apt to have different ideas as to what constitutes a reasonable percentage of income to budget for life insurance premiums. Five percent may seem to be too much for one of them whereas 20 percent may seem to another man to be no burden at all. Underwriters review each application to determine whether in their opinion the amount of insurance proposed bears a reasonable relationship to the income of the applicant. The underwriters may use an arbitrary rule as a guide. One such rule is the 20 percent rule which permits that amount of life insurance to be written that could be purchased under the continuous premium whole life plan with 20 percent of the applicant's income. In applying the rule, the total amount of insurance in force on the life of the applicant is considered. If the application calls for an amount in excess of the arbitrary limit, it may signal a cause for underwriting concern.

The arbitrary nature of the rule and its general uselessness is seen in its application. Given the same income young people can purchase more insurance than can older people. Also, at extremely low and extremely high levels of income, the 20 percent rule could produce overinsurance. For example, if 20 percent of a $400 monthly income were used for insurance only $320 would be left for other expenses. Twenty percent of a monthly income of $5,000 would produce $1,000 which might purchase an amount of insurance so large as to seem undesirable from an underwriting standpoint. In the latter case, an unusual set of circumstances may be cause for altering the underwriting attitude toward what constitutes overinsurance. For example, people with large estates might purchase insurance for tax purposes in amounts which otherwise would seem excessive.

Underwriting rules restricting the amount of insurance allowable on any one insured often are influenced by the ability of the company to get reinsurance. Most companies do not retain the entire face amount of a large policy themselves but reinsure part with other companies.

The amount of insurance applied for together with other insurance owned is particularly important in underwriting disability income coverage. There is a point where the level of disability income benefits payable in relation to after-tax earned income has a bearing on the insurer's claim experience. Underwriters do not want their insureds to have disability income insurance benefits in amounts sufficient to dull their incentive to return to work. Many insurers hold that the maximum safe amount of monthly disability income benefit is about 80 percent of the insured's after-tax income at monthly income levels of less than $2,000.

---

[12] See Chapter 24 for discussion of acquisition costs.

Special Considerations. In reviewing an application for life or health insurance, underwriters attempt to sort out uncommon hazards that affect the mortality or morbidity rate of the applicant. They are not interested in the hazards that affect the normal members of the group. Thus, moderate consumption of alcohol is ignored. Also ignored is the use of tobacco, except where a special nonsmoker's policy is written at a reduced premium. Not ignored are the use of drugs, promiscuity, adultery, excessive gambling, and unethical business dealings. Which, if any, of these items will eventually be ignored depends upon whether society will view them as being common to the normal members of the group. Air travel, once seriously considered in underwriting, is now ignored. Perhaps space travel will proceed through the same cycle as it is introduced and develops.

Because intangibles such as habits, environment, financial responsibility, and character have much more bearing on the incidence, size, and duration of health insurance claims than on life insurance claims, greater scrutiny is required in health insurance underwriting.

3. SOURCES OF UNDERWRITING INFORMATION

Five principal sources of underwriting information are: (1) the application, (2) the medical examination or statement of health,[13] (3) the agent's report, (4) the inspection report, and (5) the Medical Information Bureau.

The Application. A reproduction of the application is found in every ordinary life insurance policy.

Part I. This part of the application is filled out by the agent in the presence of the prospect.

One of the first questions asked is *date of birth*. The importance of this question is obvious, since the premium rate for life insurance is based on age. In the case of ordinary insurance, age of applicant for rate purposes is usually considered to be that of his nearer birthday.[14] Hence, for ordinary insurance, age changes midway between calendar birthdays.[15] The applicant is considered aged 25 from the time he is 24 years and 6 months until he is 25 years and 6 months. In the case of industrial insurance, the age for the next birthday is used. The applicant is rated as age 25 as soon as he passes his 24th birthday. "Age change" is the term used to designate the date on which an individual becomes the next higher age for rate purposes.

---

[13] In nonmedical life insurance, the statement of health is the substitute for the medical examination.

[14] A mortality table can be constructed on a basis of last birthday, next birthday, or nearest birthday. For the purposes of determining the applicable rate, the age count rule must match that of the mortality table; i.e., if the table is based on nearest birthday, then age must be counted to nearest birthday.

[15] The purchase price for a single premium life annuity generally is based upon the number of full years plus full months of age that may be completed at the date of issue. The annual premium for a retirement annuity is based upon the nearest age at issue, as in the case of regular life insurance. Cf. Chapter 6.

Former as well as present address is asked in all applications in order to facilitate the inspection investigation if the applicant is too new in his present location for the inspector to find people who know much about him.

Occupation is asked in order to determine whether the applicant is engaged in a hazardous occupation, and, for the same reason, specific duties must be given in addition to "kind of business." If the applicant has been in his present occupation less than two years, he must give his former occupation. Applications also inquire about aviation activities.

The application form asks whether or not there are *negotiations for other policies* now pending or contemplated. The overinsurance picture might change when all policies pending are added to those already in force. Whether the applicant has ever had an *application for life insurance declined or postponed,* or was offered a policy with a rated-up premium or on a plan other than applied for, is asked. If the answer is yes, space is provided for an explanation. Companies are especially careful of applicants who have a history of rejection.

Applications often ask if the applicant is a *member of the reserve forces* of any branch of the U.S. Army, Navy, Marine Corps, or the National Guard. By itself, an answer in the affirmative is not considered cause for rejection, rating, or change of plan by most underwriting departments, but it may, together with other unfavorable factors, have bearing on acceptance, rejection, or rating.

Any contemplation of *change of occupation* or *change of residence* to a foreign or tropical country must be noted since such a change might materially affect the hazard.

The final set of questions in Part I of the application is concerned with who is to own the policy, the type of policy applied for, the amount, special benefits, methods of paying premiums, whether a conditional receipt has been issued, how dividends are to be applied (if a participating policy), and the beneficiary designation or designations.

Part I of the application closes (except for the agent's certification, to be discussed separately) with the details of total insurance already in force: year of issue, name of company, amount, and annual disability income, if any. The importance of this information has already been discussed.

Part II. The second part of the application consists of the applicant's statements to the medical examiner as to personal history and is to be completed by an authorized medical examiner for the company in the presence of the prospect. Consider the questions in Part II, medical. The application goes into considerable detail regarding the prospect's past history and present health condition. There is a request for a statement of every illness, disease, injury, and operation since childhood and every physician or practitioner consulted in the last five years. A long series of questions to be answered yes or no includes inquiries about such things as X rays, electrocardiograms, blood tests, other laboratory tests; whether or not the applicant has ever had albumin, sugar, and so on; whether he has been in a hospital, clinic, or the like for observation or treatment; whether he has ever changed occupations or residence because of health and whether he has been on a restricted diet within a year; whether he has made a claim for disability or compensation based on sickness or accident; whether his health is impaired, or whether he is in any way deformed or crippled; and whether he has ever had any one of a number of specific diseases or disturbances. Questions regarding his use of alcohol or narcotics are considered highly important in underwriting the application.

The family record asks the age, health details, and cause of death (if death has occurred) regarding the applicant's spouse, father, mother, brothers, and sisters.

If the applicant is an adult female, there is a futher series of questions regarding pregnancy, maternity, and disturbances indicative of trouble with the female generative organs.

The foregoing questions are those which are asked of the applicant by the medical examiner, and the signature of the insured certifies that the answers have been correctly recorded by the medical examiner. The signature also waives all provision of law forbidding a physician from disclosing any knowledge or information which he has acquired in examining or attending the applicant. This waiver permits the company to make inquiry of any physicians who have attended or treated the applicant in the past. As a practical matter, such inquiries are not made unless it appears that they would have a bearing on the hazard.

NONMEDICAL INSURANCE. Part II of an application for a policy issued nonmedically consists of statements in lieu of medical examination and covers many of the same questions as those asked by a medical examiner, except that they are asked by the soliciting agent: height, weight, all diseases, illnesses, and so on; physicians or practitioners consulted; X rays, electrocardiograms, blood tests, albumin, and various specific diseases and disturbances; the use of alcohol and drugs; family records; and the additional questions if the applicant is an adult female. Omitted, of course, are the questions to be answered by the physician as the result of a physical examination. That the physical condition of the applicant is not disregarded when a policy is issued nonmedically is apparent.

Both the number of companies issuing nonmedical policies and the limits in amount of insurance that will be taken on the plan from any one applicant have increased considerably in the past few years. A principal reason for this trend is the accumulation of favorable experience with nonmedical insurance. Other factors are the lack of availability of medical examiners and the increasing cost of medical examinations. An advantage of nonmedical insurance to the agent is the elimination of one more obstacle to the sale of insurance. Some people object to the time and trouble involved in submitting to a physical examination. Some even are afraid of physical examinations.

Nonmedical insurance as written today was first tried in Canada, where the experiment was made because of the difficulty and cost of getting the medical examiner and the applicant together in rural provinces. Also, it was felt that in the small communities, agents usually knew their prospects well and could do a competent job of preselection. The use of nonmedical in the United States was originally limited to rural districts for the same reasons. However, it expanded steadily from the rural areas into the small towns and later into the large cities. With the cursory examination that some physicians give a life insurance applicant today—and the proof of the cursory nature may be found in the taking of an examination—it would seem unlikely that nonmedical applicants are any more poorly selected than a number of those who have submitted to medical examinations. This is especially true when the agent himself does a conscientious job of selection. However, studies show that the mortality rate is higher among nonmedically issued policies than among those policies issued following a medical examination.[16] For the lifetime of the policy, the present value of the extra mortality expected under nonmedical insurance varies with the age of the insured and runs from $0.75 per $1,000 under age 30 to $18 per $1,000 from ages 45 to 49. At ages 35–39, it is $3.50 per $1,000 and at ages 40–44 it is $9 per $1,000.

Limitations customarily found in the writing of nonmedical insurance are the ages at which it will be issued, the maximum amount that will be written, the plans that will be written, and the degree of insurability of the applicant that is acceptable. The practice is to write nonmedical insurance up to age 40 or 45 for maximum limits of amounts varying according to the age of the applicant. For example, one insurer has the following nonmedical limits:

Limit Written in One Year

Ages	Amount
0–4	$10,000
5–30	25,000
31–35	15,000
36–40	5,000

Aggregate Limit Written until Examined

Ages	Amount
0–40	$25,000

Thus, in this company, an applicant age 31 can purchase $15,000 nonmedically during the current year and another $10,000 during the next year. If he is examined and found insurable, say at age 35, he can then purchase $5,000 a year nonmedically from age 36 through age 40. The aggregate limit would no longer apply.

---

[16] Society of Actuaries, *1964 Reports of Mortality and Morbidity Experience,* Chicago, Illinois.

With another insurer the limits written until examined are the same as the limits written in one year and are as follows:

Ages	Amount
0–35	$40,000
36–40	20,000
41–45	7,500

Each insurer sets its own limits on the amounts it will write nonmedically based on how it interprets its own statistics. Its goal is to balance the lower expenses of nonmedical insurance against its higher mortality cost. Some companies will write up to $60,000 at young ages. Other companies restrict the amounts to $20,000.

Nonmedical usually will not be written on a term plan. When it is written on plans requiring premiums lower than those charged for continuous premium whole life, the maximum limits may be reduced. Nonmedical will not be written for substandard applicants unless the cause of the substandard exposure grows from an accident hazard arising from an occupation. Currently, about two of every three ordinary policies are issued nonmedically.

The Medical Examination.   Part III in the application for a medical policy (technically not part of the application) consists of the physician's answers to questions based on his examination of the applicant: marks of identification (to be sure that a healthy person is not being substituted for an unhealthy one), general appearance, race, height, weight, body measurements, the findings of a urinalysis, heart action, condition of nervous system, lungs, stomach, kidneys, muscles, joints, glands, eyes, ears, and all such matters. Finaly, the examiner is asked if he knows anything in connection with the insured's physical condition, family history, or past health not already recorded which would affect the insurability, and if he does, whether he is sending confidential information on it to the home office. The physician also is asked about the applicant's habits with regard to the use of stimulants and narcotics.

In addition to the medical examination, the applicant's own physician may be contacted for information to help clarify a particular situation.

The Agent's Certification.   One of the sources of underwriting information is the agent's report or certification, which appears at the end of Part I of the typical application.

The certification requires the agent to tell how long and how well he has known the applicant; if he has any unfavorable information regarding the applicant's health, character, habits, and so on; the approximate amount of money the applicant is now putting into life insurance; and his estimate of the applicant's net worth and annual income. An additional report is requested on women concerning the source of income and who will be responsible for the premium; whether the husband carries insurance on his own life and in what amount, and if he carries less than his wife, why he does so; the maiden name of the married applicant and, if she is a widow, the cause of her husband's death. This certification usually requires, also, that the general agent or manager name the soliciting agent and give the names of several references who have known the applicant for several years. The company wants to know, too, whether the applicant sought the insurance or was solicited by the agent. Companies are fearful of possible adverse selection when the applicant is unsolicited.

The help of the agent in the selection of insureds can be of great value to the underwriting department. If the agent is personally acquainted with the applicant, lives in the same area, and is acquainted with other people who know him, he may be able to provide useful information. In any event, as one company states in its rate book, the following is true:

The final responsibility of selecting risks necessarily rests upon the proper officials at the Home Office. The agent may, however, practice a preliminary selection which will be greatly to his advantage. One measure of an agent's worth to the company is the amount of gilt-edged business which is placed and paid for. In the long run, the agent will earn more money by spending his best efforts in finding prospects who are good risks than in spending this amount of effort in trying to argue the company into taking risks which should not be accepted or by trying to induce the company to reduce a rating.

Careful "field underwriting" is even more important in health insurance than in life insurance because of the greater importance of moral hazard, which is hard to determine from a written application only. Note the use of the word "risk" in the quotation. A good risk as used here means that the expected loss will be no greater than that allowed for in the premium charged.

The Inspection Report.   An important source of underwriting information on an applicant is the inspection report. The use of inspection reports for supplemental and confirming information on the applicant arises from an original practice of making inquiries among his friends regarding his reputation and habits in order to discover anything of a fraudulent or "off-color" nature about the application. However, both because the territorial activities of companies widened, and because friends often gave prejudiced information, companies began to check applicants through disinterested local correspondents who either knew the applicant or were able to collect information about him from his neighbors and business associates. Some companies eventually established their own inspection departments, and among the larger companies a few of these departments are still in existence.

Today the usual practice is to use a commercial credit investigation agency, or a bureau especially established for the purpose, to make inspection reports on applicants for life and health insurance policies or applicants for agents' contracts. There are several of these commercial investigation agencies. They provide a means of gathering unbiased information, since inspection agencies have no interest, one way or the other, whether the information reported is favorable or unfavorable.

Inspection reports on smaller policies where they are no contradictions or complications in the application are simple and relatively brief. The making of credit investigations is so common a practice in everyday business transactions that an inspection agency may have data on the applicant even before the insurance company makes inquiry. It needs to do only a little checking to bring the data up to date or to find requested information that it does not already have. There is a tendency to eliminate inspection reports on small policies as a move toward economy. Not only do inspection reports themselves cost money, but also there are costs involved in handling and using them.

In the case of larger policies or of questionable applications, a more detailed investigation may be requested. The ability of the large commercial credit investigation organizations to find obscure facts is sometimes almost incredible, so much so that the question of the invasion of privacy has been raised and legislation proposed to protect the public from activities of credit investigating agencies.

Questions answered on the usual inspection report concern the identity of the applicant, his occupational duties, his participation in aviation, his finances, health, habits, and reputation.

The inspection report is also considered the primary source of information relating to moral hazard. In a typical inspection form, this information appears as follows under the classification, "reputation":

Do any of the following apply to this applicant:
Heavy debts?
Domestic trouble?
Drinking habits?
Connection with illegal liquor?
Irregular beneficiary?
Is his general reputation as to character and morals good?
If not, give details.
Do you recommend him for life insurance?

Specific comments are asked concerning the exact duties of the applicant's occupation and any part-time occupation; line of business in which he is engaged and how long he has been so employed together with his previous employment record and present financial standing; his marital status, number of children, home surroundings, and standing in the community; his driving habits; sports activity; and details of his environment (living quarters).

The inspection report is considered an invaluable source of underwriting data. It serves as a good check on information gained from other sources. Sometimes the services of inspection companies also are used to clarify circumstances surrounding questionable death claims.

The Medical Information Bureau. A final source of underwriting data is the Medical Information Bureau, known throughout the industry as the MIB. The Medical Information Bureau, an association of life and health insurance companies,[17] is a clearinghouse for information relating to applicants for life insurance. Its purpose is to enable life and health insurance companies to detect misrepresentations of facts and thus to guard the interests of existing policyholders against imposition and fraud.

The bureau obtains its information from member companies, who submit reports on all applicants showing any one of a given number of impairments. These impairments may be those affecting the health, any family health history, or habits of the prospective insured. The information which a company reports is limited to its finding of a medical impairment and does not indicate the action taken. The bureau is never told whether the insurance was issued as applied for, declined, or rated. Moreover, it does not reveal the name of the reporting company.

The fact that a report has been made on the individual simply alerts another company to some impairment which might not otherwise be revealed to that company. Since the underwriting practices of life and health insurance companies are not the same, it is a common occurrence for one company to accept an applicant who has been rated or declined by a previous company.

The information on individuals is reported in code by the MIB and is available only to a restricted group of people in a subscribing company and chiefly for the purpose of processing an application for life insurance. The Recording and Statistical Corporation, a subsidiary, records on a card the information provided for each person and makes a duplicate available for the member companies. When a company receives an application, it checks it against its MIB files and uses the data as added underwriting information.

4. CLASSIFICATION OF INSUREDS

The evaluation and classification of applicants are functions of the underwriting department. For the most part, the process of evaluation is a matter of correlating information reported about the applicant with its statistically observable effect, if any, on longevity and morbidity. Armed with the information about the applicant and an understanding of how the information relates to the applicant's insurability, the underwriters must determine whether the applicant is acceptable at standard rates, acceptable only at rates higher than standard, or not acceptable at all.

Formerly, trained clerks used to pass on applications based on their own interpretation of the data submitted. Difficult cases were referred to

---

[17] The MIB was originally organized in 1902 by the Medical Directors' Association. This connection was terminated in 1946 when the MIB was reorganized as an unincorporated association of member life insurance companies. There is no longer any legal connection between the MIB and the Medical Directors' Association.

the supervisors. A few of the small companies still operate in this way. Others use objective rating systems.

Numerical Rating. Wherever human judgment enters in, there is always a residual margin of error despite the amount of training the human mind has been given. Consequently, there has been an effort in the science of underwriting to standardize its operations. Perhaps the most common method of standardization is the numerical rating system.[18]

Although there are many variations in use, the basis of the numerical system is the calculation and assignment of debits and credits for the various factors involved in the underwriting of an applicant. The average applicant is assumed to have a rating of 100. Points are subtracted (credited) to his rate for underwriting factors that are known or suspected to result in loss experience better than average, and are added (debited) to this rate for factors that are known or suspected to result in loss experience which is poorer than average. The extent of the debit or credit of specific items varies from company to company according to that company's own experience and according to its interpretation of published experience. An illustrative example which bears no particular relation to any one company's system follows.

Assume that the applicant is a 30-year-old college professor, 5 feet 10 inches tall, weighing 220 pounds, and has a good personal health record and family history. The application and inspection report reveal that he went into his profession as a result of a reformation from habits somewhat tipsy. All sources of underwriting information report that he has suffered no relapses in a considerable time. Although, as a given individual, he probably never will, the company has statistics which show that a certain percentage of chronic tipplers will go back and sign the pledge again, "for life, same as the last time." It has further been determined statistically that in any large group of former alcoholics, the mortality will be at least 25 percent above standard. Consequently, the numerical rating system debits the application 25 or more points.[19] There is a debit of another 25 points because of the extent to which the applicant is overweight. His good family history creates a credit of 10 points.

And so the process goes on down the list of underwriting factors, debiting some and crediting others. In the end, the total of the debits is added to 100, and from that total is subtracted the sum of the credits. The resulting figure, assuming that the schedule of value of debits and credits is accurate to begin with, will indicate the degree to which mortality can be expected to vary from standard. If the final figure is 95, for instance, then the mortality to be expected on this applicant is 5 percent below standard mortality; i.e., 5 percent better experience is expected than for standard exposures;

---

[18] Developed early this century by Dr. O. H. Rogers, Medical Director, and A. H. Hunter, actuary of the New York Life Insurance Company.

[19] A debit of 25 points is usually given where the insured has been a total abstainer for a number of years; much higher debits are given where the reform has been recent.

if the total is above 100, say 125, then 25 percent greater mortality is to be expected. Companies generally will accept, at standard rates, applications scoring not more than 125. Some companies, particularly those not writing "extra risk" insurance, may be more liberal.[20]

The values and inaccuracies in the numerical system have long been a subject of discussion and treatises. Old-school medical directors and actuaries were extremely reluctant to agree that applicants could be satisfactorily evaluated without individual scrutiny by those trained in medical and actuarial sciences. A particular criticism was that interrelationships among factors will not be evaluated properly, being in combination a greater hazard than the sum of them separately indicates, for example, underweight and tuberculosis. Another criticism was that since underwriting is an art and not a science, it is not subject to the exactness of numerical rating. Nevertheless, the numerical rating system has been accepted as the most practical method available and one that can be successfully applied if used intelligently. Various modifications of the numerical system handle cases of interrelated factors more satisfactorily. In borderline cases the application can be submitted to the medical director or the actuary, whereas the normal run of applications can be processed smoothly by trained and experienced clerks with a minimum of expense and loss of time, and with a more uniform evaluation than by any other known method, considering the pressure of time on the medical experts and the element of human judgment involved.

Classes of Applicants.   Broadly speaking, applicants may be classed either as insurable or uninsurable.

A rate can be figured for any age and any physical condition. Obviously, however, as the mortality and morbidity hazard increases, the rate for insurance will eventually become too high for the applicant, and, at this point insurance becomes economically impractical. Under these conditions the applicant is, for all practical purposes, uninsurable. Insurable applicants are divided into two broad classes—standard and substandard. Rarely will term insurance be issued for substandard exposures, and the amount of insurance written under other plans may be restricted by those insurers who are not confident of their ability to rate the extra hazard appropriately.

Extra-Hazard Life Insurance.   Extra premium charges as a result of specific disease or impairments are nearly as old as modern life insurance, which may be said to have begun with the establishment of the Equitable Society of England. In 1762 Old Equitable was charging an additional premium to insure applicants who had suffered from gout, for applicants with hernia, for applicants who had not had smallpox, for applicants with the "female hazard" (women under 50), and for beer retailers.

It was 134 years later, however, before the insurance of substandard lives made its appearance in the United States. In 1896 the New York Life

---

[20] Note the term "extra risk insurance." It should be called extra hazard insurance in keeping with the definitions developed in Chapter 2.

Insurance Company entered the field on an extensive scale following a study of the mortality experience among applicants rejected over the previous 15 years. As a result of this investigation, a measure was devised of the effect of certain impairments on the mortality of a representative group. The company then issued policies written for an extra premium designed to cover the expense of the additional mortality.

New York Life was alone in the substandard field for a considerable period of time, and it was not until the publication in 1910 of the Medico-Actuarial investigation, a joint project of the Actuarial Society of America and the Association of Life Insurance Medical Directors, that very many companies were willing to issue such policies. Subsequent studies have convinced an increasing number of companies that substandard insurance can be issued on a scientific basis.

METHODS OF RATING EXTRA HAZARD INSURANCE. Several methods of rating substandard applicants have been designed to reflect the nature of the extra hazard since some hazards increase with the age of the insured, others decrease with the age of the insured and still others remain constant.

Lien Plan. Under the lien plan the standard premium is paid, but less than the full face amount of the policy is payable if death occurs within a specified number of years. Frequently the size of the lien decreases yearly to reflect the decreasing nature of the hazard. Because the lien plan is simple and policyholders have a certain optimism about the possibility of surviving the lien period, the plan would be useful where the extra hazard decreases with age were it not for its serious limitations. What appears to be a disproportionately large lien is necessary to offset the extra hazard because a given increase in the percentage of expected mortality will induce a much smaller increase in the premium necessary to offset it. Total premiums reflect not only mortality but also expenses and reserve financing, and neither of these items increases in proportion to the extra mortality expected.[21] Another limitation is that the lien is placed on the policy during the years when the insurance is needed most. The lien plan is rarely, if ever, used in the United States today. In some states the lien plan is prohibited under laws which do not permit insurers to settle death claims for amounts less than the face of the policy. However, lien plans are used in Canada and Great Britain.

Rated-up Age. The rated-up age plan assumes that, for insurance purposes, the age of the applicant is a given number of years higher than his chronological age. For example, a man 35 years old may be charged the rate for a man 40 years old. This plan is suitable when the extra mortality increases in amount with age, i.e., when the difference between the standard rate of mortality and the rate of mortality for the substandard group increases with age. Reference to the death rate per 1,000 in the CSO mortality table reproduced in Chapter 24 will illustrate that the differences in the

---

[21] If you do not understand the foregoing point, maybe you will after you have studied Chapters 25 and 27.

mortality rates between any given age and the rated-up age increase as the ages involved increase. For example, consider the mortality rates per 1,000 at the following ages.

Age	Mortality Rate per 1,000
30	2.13
35	2.51
40	3.53
45	5.35
50	8.32

The difference in mortality rate at age 30 and at age 35 is 0.38 per 1,000. Between ages 35 and 40, it is 1.02; between 40 and 45, the difference is 1.82; and it jumps to 2.97 between ages 45 and 50. Thus, although a rated-up age policy carries a level premium, the insured would be, in effect, paying an increasingly higher extra mortality cost each year the policy is in force.

Few impairments increase the mortality rate to the extent of that assumed by the rated-up age plan. Simplicity both for the insurer and the insured is the principal advantage of the rated-up age plan. For the insurer it is easy to administer, and for the insured it is easy to understand. The rated-up age plan, once widely used, is still popular today with a number of insurers.

Flat Additional Premium. Under the flat additional premium plan, a constant additional premium (an extra premium which does not vary by age) is added to the standard premium rate. For example, one company charges a flat additional premium of $5 per $1,000 of insurance for window cleaners. This means that although the standard premium for $10,000 continuous premium whole life insurance at age 30 is $201.80, a window cleaner at this age would be required to pay a premium of $251.80. On all policies except short term, the flat additional premium, like the rated-up age method, provides for an increasing mortality hazard. Since the amount at risk decreases each year, the constant additional premium results in heavier mortality loadings each year. Therefore, when the extra hazard is constant it is necessary to calculate the average extra hazard and load the premium accordingly.[22] Since the mortality exposure decreases faster under an endowment policy, these policies generally call for a lower extra premuim for the same impairment than would be charged for a term or whole life policy.

For the policyholder, the rated-up age plan is more favorable than the flat additional premium plan when identical premiums are required. Part of the extra premium collected under the rated-up age plan is used to build higher cash values and, if participating, to pay higher dividends. Cash

---

[22] It is felt that a decreasing extra-premium charge would create too many problems of administration.

values and dividends, however, are unaffected by the flat additional premium plan or the lien plan.

Extra Percentage Tables.   A convenient and common device for use in substandard rating is the extra percentage table. Under these tables, a set of premiums is computed using mortality rates consistent with the percentage of expected mortality over standard mortality. For example, insurance will be written at standard rates if the expected mortality is less than 125 percent of standard mortality. However, if expected mortality exceeds standard mortality by 125 percent or more, special tables are used that produce premiums higher than would be produced at standard rates. Extra percentage tables are designated either by letters or numbers such as Tables A, B, C, or 1, 2, 3, up to Tables P or 16. Each table reflects a mortality range: Table A shows a range of 125 percent to 145 percent of standard mortality; Table B, a range of 146 percent to 165 percent; Table C, a range of 166 percent to 190 percent; and Table P, a range of 451 percent to 500 percent above standard. An intermediate classification (AB) is frequently found to reflect a range of 125 percent to 137.5 percent of standard mortality. One insurer may write extra hazard insurance only through Table C, whereas others will write it through Table P. A few insurers will write extra hazard insurance up to 1,000 percent of standard mortality.

Illustrative rates as used by one insurer for three different policy forms are shown in Table 23–1.

Note that the extra premium at age 25 in Table A is less than 10 percent of the standard premium and that in Table P it is about 108 percent of the standard premium, even though the extra premium in Table A is based on 125 percent of standard mortality and the extra premium in Table P is based on 500 percent of standard mortality. This is because the standard premium is based on a tabular mortality scale enriched to allow a margin for safety and includes a loading for expenses. The extra premium, however, reflects the difference between expected extra mortality measured against actual standard mortality rather than against tabular standard mortality, and it does not include an expense loading except for those expense items such as sales commissions and premium taxes which are a function of the level of premiums.[23]

Mortality rates increase with age. Since the percentage of expected mortality over standard mortality remains the same throughout the duration of the policy, higher margins for extra mortality are provided with increasing age. (A constant percentage of an increasing amount yields an increasing amount.) Therefore, the extra percentage plan serves best where the extra hazard is expected to increase with age.

The extra percentage tables may be used for substandard rating in several ways. They may be used to determine the additional premium to be added to standard premiums under the flat additional premium method. Extra

---

[23] Cf. Chapters 24 and 25 for further clarification.

TABLE 23-1

Extra Premiums Per $10,000 of Insurance At Illustrative Ages (Participating)

	Continuous Premium Whole Life			20 Payment Whole Life			20-Year Endowment		
	Standard Premium	Extra Premium Table		Standard Premium	Extra Premium Table		Standard Premium	Extra Premium Table	
Age		A (125 Percent)	P (500 Percent)		A	P		A	P
25	$173.50	$ 17.10	$ 186.40	$299.50	$ 23.10	$ 308.70	$495.30	$ 8.00	$ 176.20
35	237.25	24.20	282.50	366.30	26.90	332.40	510.70	10.90	223.20
45	340.50	38.30	470.10	460.00	36.80	467.90	551.20	23.20	403.20
55	515.00	65.50	858.60	605.00	63.40	933.50	649.40	50.20	910.40
65	826.00	120.10	1,692.60	870.30	129.10	1,360.40	883.50	125.50	1,326.47

percentage tables also are used to determine the age to assign the applicant under the rated-up age plan. Here the age assigned to the applicant is one that will correspond in mortality experience as nearly as possible to that indicated by the percentage table. Finally, the extra percentage table may be used as the basis for rating without any particular reference to the other two plans. In this event, reserves and cash values are based on the higher than standard mortality assumptions used in developing the premium rate. These mortality assumptions also are used in the dividend formula.

In plans with extra premium ratings, the extended term nonforfeiture option usually is not provided, and the automatic option is the paid-up insurance at a reduced amount. Where the extended term option is available, the values are computed using the higher than standard mortality assumptions.

Standard Premiums with Limitations Imposed. Several plans for handling substandard exposures involve no additional premium charge. One such plan is to offset the extra hazard by using special dividend classes for these exposures. The actual experience among this class of exposures in relation to standard tabular mortality is used in the dividend formula to reflect any additional hazard. This plan is used only when the extra hazard is not expected to produce losses in excess of tabular mortality, and sufficient exposures can be insured in the class to make it workable.

Another method for treating substandard exposures is to issue the policy at a standard premium but to restrict the plan under which it will be issued to high premium forms, such as endowment insurance. This approach may be used effectively when the extra hazard is not likely to be important until the later years in the duration of the policy when the amount at risk is substantially reduced.

Removal of Ratings. It is common practice for a company to reconsider an extra premium rating for physical impairment in the light of a new medical examination, most frequently paid for by the insured. If the physical impairment is shown to have disappeared, the extra rating will be removed from the premium.

It could be contended that removal of a rating for an improvement in physical condition is not valid, for it constitutes selection against the company. In the operation of the insurance principle, the individual is a member of a group. The mortality for the group is based on the average of all entrants and assumes as many in the group who will prove to be better than the average as there are those who fall below it. If those whose condition improves are taken out of the group, then the average mortality of the group will become higher.

As a practical matter, however, most companies will reconsider ratings and, if extra premiums are clearly no longer justified, will remove them. If insurers were not willing to remove the extra premium, the now standard insureds most likely would surrender their policies and purchase insurance elsewhere at standard rates—a logical and understandable action on their part. The technical error brought about is adjusted in advance by allowing a margin of safety in the calculation of the extra charge.

Removal of the extra premium based on a hazardous occupation is theoretically sound if the insured has changed his occupation to one less hazardous. However, it is customary to impose a waiting period before eliminating the extra charge in order to make sure that the change is not temporary. A medical examination may be required to determine whether or not the insured's health was affected by his former work. Extra premiums based on occupation usually are refunded for the periods during which the insured was no longer in a hazardous occupation.

Since extra premiums once removed cannot be reassessed, companies must give careful consideration before eliminating them.

Extra Hazard Health Insurance.   If the applicant for health insurance does not fall into what is termed "standard ranges," one of several actions may be taken by the insurer.

1. The applicant may be rejected and no insurance issued to him.

2. He can be issued coverage at reduced limits. As a simple illustration, assume the applicant has applied for $800 a month disability income benefits but already has $300. Instead of the $800 applied for, he could be offered $200.

3. He can be issued a modified plan. As mentioned previously, the company might offer an accident-only policy where it would not offer accident and sickness, or the insurer might offer a 2-year loss-of-time benefit period where the applicant has applied for benefits to age 65.

4. He can be offered a longer waiting period. An applicant with a history of severe hay fever who applies for first-day benefits might be acceptable only if the policy contained a waiting period of 30 days before benefits begin for any claim.

5. He can be offered a waiver. The waiver is a provision attached to the policy excluding the company's liability for a stated condition or conditions. For instance, a prospect with a history of phlebitis might be acceptable at standard rates with a waiver of liability for phlebitis and varicose veins.

6. He can be offered coverage at an increased premium rate, a common type of substandard underwriting in life insurance but not usual in health insurance except for hazards relating to occupations. Under the extra premium plan, the pure premium (i.e., the premium before the addition of administration expenses and acquisition costs) is increased by a given percentage determined, to some extent, by subjective probabilities and then later modified by the insurer's and reinsurer's experience. Patently, because of its relatively recent development extra premium rating in health insurance requires experimentation. But despite the lack of credible experience upon which to develop a premium that insurers could accept with a high degree of confidence, a large number of insurers are now using extra premium rating for physical impairments as well as for occupational hazards. Substandard underwriting on an increased premium basis is com-

plicated by intangible factors. While it is possible to compile statistics on the added hazard of certain conditions, it is more difficult to determine what effect any given disability will have on the moral fiber of differing policyholders.

7. He may be covered by what is known as a qualified impairment plan, under which he is issued a regular policy except that benefits payable for a recurrence of a stated condition are restricted either by requiring a longer waiting period before disability benefits begin for a claim involving that impairment or by writing a reduced maximum benefit period for such claims. Restrictions for claims under major medical insurance involving the stated impairment may be a higher deductible, a lower maximum benefit, and a higher participation percentage by the insured. An extra premium may be charged for the qualified impairment policy, and the insurer's underwriting requirements usually prohibit the writing of the policy until after the applicant has enjoyed a period free of the stated condition.

ADVANTAGES OF EXTRA HAZARD INSURANCE. Extra hazard insurance is socially desirable, since it makes life and health insurance available to more people than could otherwise obtain it if only standard applicants were accepted by the company. Over 5.5 million extra hazard life insurance policies are in force for more than $30 billion of insurance. About 15 percent of the health insurance is written on an extra hazard basis.

5. THE EFFECT OF SELECTION ON COST

The foregoing discussion of risk selection reveals clearly its direct effect upon cost. The cost of life and health insurance is a function of the mortality or morbidity of those insured. The higher the mortality, the higher is the cost of insurance. Consistently poor selection of applicants will mean that policyholders will pay more for their insurance.

The purpose of selection is integral to rate making, and upon good selection depends not only adequacy of funds to meet contractual obligations but also the degree of equity among policyholders.

6. LIMITS OF RETENTION

All companies set maximum limits on the amount of life insurance they will retain on an individual life. This amount varies from company to company and, in general, is in some proportion to the size of the company as measured by its surplus. Usually, the smaller the company, the lower the limit of retention, since large claims affect small companies much more adversely than they affect large companies. The retention limit of small and new companies might be $5,000 or even less, whereas for the large company the retention limit will be hundreds of thousands of dollars. (The giant companies may have retention limits in excess of $1 million.) Not only does the retention limit vary among companies, but also it may vary within a given company according to age of issue, type of policy, and class of applicant. For example, for all types of policies issued at standard rates except term and modified life, a company might retain $200,000 for applicants between the ages of 21 and 55, but only $130,000 for those 56 to 60, and $100,000 for those between 10 and 20. These retention limits might be cut in half on term and modified life policies. For substandard applicants, a lower schedule of retention limits might be in effect.

Regardless of its retention limits, as a practical matter a company does not like to reject an application from a desirable policyholder simply because the amount for which he may wish to insure legitimately is more than the company can handle. If the company refuses to accept the total application, it might end in losing the amount it is willing and eager to insure.

The Nature of Reinsurance.   To solve the problem of low retention limits on the one hand and large applications on the other, life insurance companies resort to a process known as reinsurance.[24]

Under the reinsurance system, a company accepts an application, if it is acceptable, for whatever the amount may be, regardless of whether or not it exceeds the company's retention limit, and issues to the applicant a policy for that amount. There are, of course, gross limits on how much a company will write even with reinsurance.[25] Some insurers set the limit in terms of dollars whereas others have no announced set limit, handling each application as a special case. It would, therefore, be more accurate to say a company accepts an application for any amount within reason in view of its underwriting philosophy and the reinsurance facilities it has available. It then takes the amount of the policy in excess of its retention limit to a reinsurance company, which agrees to pay that amount when the policy becomes a claim.[26]

For a simple illustration of reinsurance, suppose the retention limit of a company receiving an application for $25,000 is $15,000. The company which has received the application (called the "direct-writing" company) issues a policy in its name for the full $25,000 and then reinsures (cedes) $10,000, which is the amount in excess of its retention limit. If the policy becomes a claim during its first year, the direct-writing company will contribute $15,000 out of its own funds, while the reinsurer will make up the other $10,000.[27] The payment by the reinsurer, however, is to the company which issued the policy rather than to the policyholder's beneficiary. The

---

[24] Not all companies engage in reinsurance transactions. A few large companies and some fraternals prefer to limit their writings to those amounts which they feel they can handle themselves.

[25] For example, one company has a gross limit of $1 million, but a retention limit of $400,000.

[26] Many companies accept reinsurance, and a number actively solicit it. There are a few companies that do not sell directly to the public at all but deal only in reinsurance.

[27] The distribution of the claim burden, should the loss occur in a subsequent year, will depend on how the reinsurance contract is written.

full claim check is written and signed by the company which issued the policy to the insured.

As far as the policyholder is concerned, there is no difference between a claim paid wholly by the company issuing the policy and a claim paid jointly by that company and its reinsurer. If the reinsurer fails to pay its share of the claim, the direct-writing company still is responsible to its policyholder. The policyholder himself is not a party to the reinsurance agreement, nor does he usually know anything about it.

DISASTER REINSURANCE.   The concentration of population in urban areas and the concentration of employees in larger and larger plants, coupled with the writing of group insurance, has increased interest in a type of blanket reinsurance called disaster reinsurance. This coverage provides a method of stopping losses to the insurer under individual as well as group policies in case of a multiple-person accident. It supplements the basic, underlying reinsurance plan.

Under the disaster reinsurance plan, the ceding company purchases an amount of reinsurance per accident retention limit. For instance, assume the ceding company wishes a retention limit of $100,000 per accident. It might then purchase disaster reinsurance for a limit of $3 million per accident. Should a disaster occur in an area or plant in which the ceding company has a number of policyholders and death claims totaling $2 million result, the entire loss in excess of the $100,000 per accident retention would be paid by the disaster reinsurance.

The limit of coverage under disaster reinsurance is automatically reinstated following a claim so that the full limit immediately becomes available for a subsequent disaster.

Types of Life Reinsurance.   Two types of life reinsurance are (1) year renewable term and (2) coinsurance.

THE YEARLY RENEWABLE TERM PLAN.   Under the yearly renewable term plan (sometimes called risk premium reinsurance) the company reinsures only the net amount at risk in excess of its retention limit. The net amount at risk on any policy is the difference between its face amount and the amount of its terminal reserve. As the terminal reserve increases year by year, the net amount at risk in excess of the retention limit decreases and so does the amount of reinsurance. For example, when the terminal reserve on a $25,000 policy is $5,000, then only $20,000 is at risk. Thus, a company with a net retention limit of $15,000 in this case would have to reinsure only $5,000 for that year under the yearly renewable term plan. The reinsurer simply multiplies the net amount at risk under the reinsurance agreement at the beginning of any year by the reinsurer's yearly renewable term rate for the attained age in order to arrive at the reinsurance premium. Reinsurance rates are highly competitive and provide for only a small expense loading since the reinsured absorbs the acquisition and underwriting expenses. (Note the use of the term "reinsured." This term is used here because of its simplicity. The technical term is "ceding company," and means the company originating the insurance and surrendering some or all of it to another insurer.) In the foregoing illustration if the insured were now aged 37, then the reinsurance company would charge the yearly renewable term rate for age 37, say $4.59 per $1,000, and apply it to $5,000 of insurance for a premium of $22.95 for a male in the standard underwriting class. Next year the amount at risk will be less and so will be the amount of reinsurance. The rate, per $1,000 will be higher, of course, say $4.85.

The yearly renewable term plan of reinsurance is preferred by the smaller companies since it enables them to keep a larger amount at risk on each reinsured contract, and to retain more of the premium for investment.

The plan is simple to administer, there being no commissions, nonforfeiture values, and dividends, and because the insurance is term insurance experience refunds are easily computed. Where the reinsurer is not licensed to do business in the reinsured's state, one-year renewable term reinsurance is attractive because the reinsured company cannot offset required reserves with reserves on reinsured business.

THE COINSURANCE PLAN.   Under the coinsurance plan the company reinsures the amount of the original contract that exceeds its retention limit and continues this amount of reinsurance in force throughout the life of the contract. For example, if a company with a net retention limit of $50,-000 writes a policy for $75,000, it will reinsure $25,000 and continue this amount of reinsurance in force until the policy becomes a claim. The reinsurer will be entitled to one third of the premium less acquisition and certain other expense allowances, and will be liable for a corresponding proportion of claims, nonforfeiture values, and dividends.[28]

The attractions of the coinsurance plan are that the reinsurer guarantees to adjust its dividend scale on the reinsurance to that of the reinsured, thus assuring that the net cost of the reinsurance will follow that of the reinsured. Also the reinsurer accepts part of the responsibility of setting up first-year reserves, which reserves, as mentioned, are a drain on surplus.

If a company wishes to reinsure on a coinsurance basis with an insurer not licensed in its state, it may use a modified plan whereby the ceding company in effect retains the entire reserve under the contract. As stated, reserves held on reinsurance ceded to a company not licensed in the state usually are not allowable as a deduction from the reserve liability of the ceding insurer. Another reason for using the modified coinsurance plan is the desire of the ceding company to hold and invest the money it collects. The modified coinsurance plan differs from the yearly renewable term plan

---

[28] In the past, mortality experience under large policies generally was not so favorable as experience under smaller policies. Since dividends usually are based on average mortality experience, reinsurers often found themselves forced to pay dividends in excess of those earned by the larger policies that they were reinsuring on a coinsurance basis. Thus, there was a tendency for the reinsurers to prefer the decreasing term basis of reinsurance under which no dividends were paid by the reinsurer. A number of yearly renewable term plans, however, do include what are called participating agreements under which mortality gains on reinsurance of amounts less than a given figure are shared.

in that the amount at risk decreases each year for both the ceding company and the reinsurer, rather than initially for the reinsurer only. One reason for using the modified coinsurance plan rather than the yearly renewable term plan is that the reinsurance premium is not negotiated but, instead, is based on premium charged to the policyholder. Another reason is that the net cost of reinsurance will be less during the early years because the reinsurer will absorb some of the initial expenses, thus reducing the problem of surplus drain arising from the writing of new business.[29]

Types of Health Reinsurance.   The two most commonly used forms of health reinsurance are quota share and surplus share. Quota share is also sometimes referred to as coinsurance; however, strictly speaking, it is not exactly comparable to the term coinsurance as used in life reinsurance.

THE QUOTA SHARE PLAN.   Under the quota share plan, a stated percentage of all benefits of a certain type are reinsured. For instance, a health insurer may reinsure 50 percent of every loss of time benefit or 50 percent of every medical care benefit. This plan is most often used by new companies. The plan is particularly appropriate for an insurer willing to trade off premium volume for the help of its reinsurer in reviewing the underwriting of each applicant and for the rendering of other technical assistance.

THE SURPLUS SHARE PLAN.   Under the surplus share plan, the ceding company reinsures all policies written in excess of its retention limits. The amount of such share is usually determined by the proportion that the amount beyond the retention limit bears to the total amount of such indemnity in force on a particular exposure. Assume a policy with a $25,000 accidental death benefit and a monthly loss of time benefit of $600. Assume further that the company's retention on the accidental death benefits is $10,000, and on the loss of time, $400. In that case it would reinsure a three-fifth share of the accidental death and a one-third share of the monthly income benefit. (The amount of the accidental death benefit in excess of the retention limit is $15,000, or three fifths of the $25,000 written. The amount of the monthly indemnity in excess of the retention limit is $200, or one-third of the $600 written.)

One variation of the surplus share type of reinsurance is an arrangement under which a policy written for more than a given amount of coverage is reinsured for some stated share of the policy amount, say 60 percent, so all policies written in excess of a company's retention are reinsured on a uniform basis. Thus, in the foregoing illustration both the accidental death benefit and the monthly income benefit would be reinsured for a three-fifth share (60 percent), since both are written for amounts in excess of the retention limit.

Under surplus share, the ceding company is relieved of shock loss exposures but does not, as in the case of quota share, reinsure a portion of every policy issued. It retains the full premium on all the smaller policies.

---

[29] See Chapter 27.

EXCESS OF LOSS PLANS.   Several types of excess of loss reinsurance plans may be written. The excess of loss plans differ from the share plans in that the reinsurer agrees to pay only losses that are in excess of a given amount. The amount may be related to losses per person, losses per accident or epidemic, or total losses per class of business written. One method is excess of loss per person reinsurance used—for example, with major medical insurance under which claims in excess of a given amount per person are reinsured. For instance, the ceding company may pay the first $5,000 of loss per person on $20,000 maximum indemnity major medical policies and reinsure 80 percent of the excess over $5,000.

Another excess of loss plan is disaster reinsurance applying to losses in excess of a stipulated amount arising from accidents or epidemics of catastrophic proportions. The operation of disaster reinsurance for health coverage is the same as that described earlier in this chapter for disaster life reinsurance.

Still another type of excess of loss plan is nonproportional reinsurance, also called excess loss ratio reinsurance, and is written to guarantee that the reinsured's incurred losses for the year will not exceed a given percentage of its earned premium on a particular class of business. This type of reinsurance is not extensively written in health insurance because it presents serious problems. In theory, nonproportional reinsurance protects the ceding company against unpredictable fluctuations in loss experience such as those produced, for example, by an epidemic. However, excessive loss ratios also can be a result of poor underwriting and other forms of mismanagement. Unless there is a large spread of exposures with a long history, the reinsurer would have to take over, almost literally, the operation of the ceding company in order to guarantee its loss ratio.

Reinsurance Agreements.   A company may handle each policy on which it needs reinsurance on an individual basis; i.e., the company may wait until it has a need for reinsurance, then "shop" for a reinsurer. This method has the disadvantage of delay in issuing the policy to the applicant. The company may not wish to accept the application until it determines whether reinsurance will be available. Meanwhile, of course, the applicant may withdraw and purchase his insurance elsewhere. This method still finds some use in the life insurance business, particularly in locating reinsurance for that portion of the excess for which the insurer does not have regular reinsurance contracts.

Because of the disadvantages of case by case shopping, or street reinsurance, as it is sometimes called, it is customary to provide for reinsurance facilities in advance of need with contracts or "treaties." The treaties may be either facultative or automatic.

FACULTATIVE.   The facultative treaty is only a little more than a step away from individual shopping, for the reinsurer has the right to accept or reject any reinsurance submitted after a survey of each individual case. Also the ceding company is under no obligation to submit any business it prefers to retain. The facultative plan has the advantage of agreement in advance regarding the form of reinsurance effected, the terms and amount of the premium, the commission, if any, to be paid by the reinsurer to the reinsured, and other details relating to the reinsurance, eliminating the expense of separate policies for each case since the memoranda data coupled with the terms of the contract serve the same purpose.

The disadvantage of the facultative treaty is that the ceding company does not know, in advance, whether it will be able to obtain the reinsurance sought, although by constant dealings with one reinsurer it comes to know within reasonable limits what that reinsurer will and will not accept.

AUTOMATIC. Treaties may also be automatic—i.e., the reinsurer agrees that it will assume liability automatically for the excess over the ceding company's retention limits (up to a certain maximum) on any application acceptable to the ceding company, and the writer agrees to cede all amounts in excess of its retention limit. Thus the policy may be written at once, and the insurer knows in advance exactly how much reinsurance it will be possible to obtain. More than one reinsurer may be involved in a given reinsurance treaty in which case the basis for sharing the loss among them will be set forth in the treaty.[30]

The maximum reinsurance acceptable to the reinsurer usually bears a scheduled proportion to the retention limit of the ceding company.[31] The proportion decreases as the size of the net retention limit of the ceding company increases. To illustrate: with a $10,000 net retention maximum, it may be able to obtain automatic reinsurance for four times its own limit. It is then able to issue a $50,000 policy without any shopping for reinsurance. If, however, it were to raise its net retention limit to $25,000, the automatic treaty might not provide reinsurance for more than twice the amount of the retention limit, making it possible to issue a policy for $75,000 without additional reinsurance facilities.

When an application is submitted for an amount which exceeds the maximum available through automatic treaties, the treaty may provide that the excess be submitted on a facultative basis, or it may be necessary for the insurer to shop for it. Reinsurance treaties also are written in combination, being automatic for standard business and facultative for substandard business.

Also, modified versions of automatic treaties are written. Under one version, for example, the reinsurer agrees to accept the reinsurance ceded at the reinsured's discretion. Another version gives the reinsurer the op-

---

[30] Reinsurance arrangements involving reciprocal agreements among several companies to exchange reinsurance are known as reinsurance pools. Under such arrangements each company is given an opportunity to take as much reinsurance as it cedes.

[31] In some situations involving special hazards, a reinsurance company might accept the entire risk if the ceding company does not want any of it. This procedure has made possible the development of adequate exposure units and underwriting experience to handle effectively business which otherwise might have gone uninsured.

portunity to deny reinsurance on specific applicants when it has underwriting information that would dictate this action.

The advantage of the automatic treaty is that it avoids delay in binding the insurance.

The Reinsurance Contract.   The contract between the reinsurer and the reinsured includes a number of matters of importance to the transaction. It stipulates: (1) whether the reinsurance is to be written under a yearly renewable term plan, a coinsurance plan, or a modified coinsurance plan; (2) the schedule of reinsurance premiums, and a statement of how the premiums are to be settled; (3) the ceding commission scale, if any; (4) the reinsured's authority to settle claims; (5) the reinsurer's obligation to pay claims in a lump sum; (6) the reinsurer's obligation to pay its share of the full claim to insolvent reinsureds, even though their obligations are scaled down; (7) the duration of the agreement after cancellation by either party; (8) the basis for experience dividends to be paid to the reinsured; (9) the nature of the reinsured's obligation to cede, and the reinsurer's obligation to accept reinsurance.

Other Reinsurance Services.   The use of reinsurance to write amounts in excess of the company's retention limit is not its only use: companies commonly reinsure a large part of their substandard business; double indemnity and disability riders often are reinsured. An important reinsurance service to many companies is the underwriting advice and assistance given by the reinsurer. In other than unusual circumstances, the underwriting services of reinsurance are far more valuable to small than to large companies, which have their own expert underwriting departments.

Reinsurance has fostered the growth of new companies, which, of necessity, must have very low retention limits until their growth allows them to make better use of the law of large numbers in predicting their losses. When an insurer wishes to eliminate a given coverage or to withdraw from a given territory, reinsurance offers a convenient method of transferring the business to another insurer.

Reinsurance itself may also be reinsured. The process of reinsuring reinsurance is called *retrocession.*

24

The Tools of Rate Making

Throughout this book, reference has been made to premium rates, policy reserves, and cash values. It is only logical to expect that curiosity might have been aroused as to how they are computed.

As was stated in Chapter 2, the basis of insurance is found in that branch of mathematics known as the theory of probability. Fortunately for most readers, this is not a text in mathematics. It does not seek to instruct potential actuaries. Instead, it seeks only to explain basic rate making principles so that the general student of life insurance will have at least a fundamental knowledge of the "why's" of rate calculation. This chapter is concerned principally with the tools of life insurance rate making. Chapter 25 will give some attention to health insurance rate making.

Three factors are involved in computing a life insurance rate: mortality, interest, and operating expenses. Lapse rates, discussed in the appendix to this chapter, also may be considered in premium computations. These factors may be said to be the tools of rate making.

1. MORTALITY TABLES

The mortality table is a convenient method of expressing probabilities of living and dying, and is used along with interest and expense assumptions to calculate a rate necessary to produce premiums sufficient to pay claims based on these assumed probabilities.

The mortality table is not, as its form might suggest, the mortality history of a group recorded until there are no longer any survivors. It is, rather, the assembly of a series of relationships between the probable number dying and the number living at any given age. For example, the Commissioners 1958 Standard Ordinary Mortality Table (1950–54), commonly called the 1958 CSO Mortality Table (see Table 24–1), shows the relationships between the probable number dying and the number living at each age from 0 to 100.[1] To illustrate: of 9,575,636 people assumed

---

[1] The 1958 CSO Table is used in this chapter and in Chapter 25 for illustrative purposes only. Its use here should not be taken to mean that this is the mortality table actually used by insurers in computing their rates.

TABLE 24–1. Table of Mortality (1950–54) Commissioners 1958 Standard Ordinary

Age	Number Living (l_x)	Deaths Each Year (d_x)	Deaths per 1,000 ($1,000_{q_x}$)	Expectation of Life ($\overset{\circ}{e}_x$)
0	10,000,000	70,800	7.08	68.30
1	9,929,200	17,475	1.76	67.78
2	9,911,725	15,066	1.52	66.90
3	9,896,659	14,449	1.46	66.00
4	9,882,210	13,835	1.40	65.10
5	9,868,375	13,322	1.35	64.19
6	9,855,053	12,812	1.30	63.27
7	9,842,241	12,401	1.26	62.35
8	9,829,840	12,091	1.23	61.43
9	9,817,749	11,879	1.21	60.51
10	9,805,870	11,865	1.21	59.58
11	9,794,005	12,047	1.23	58.65
12	9,781,958	12,325	1.26	57.72
13	9,769,633	12,896	1.32	56.80
14	9,756,737	13,562	1.39	55.87
15	9,743,175	14,225	1.46	54.95
16	9,728,950	14,983	1.54	54.03
17	9,713,967	15,737	1.62	53.11
18	9,698,230	16,390	1.69	52.19
19	9,681,840	16,846	1.74	51.28
20	9,664,994	17,300	1.79	50.37
21	9,647,694	17,655	1.83	49.46
22	9,630,039	17,912	1.86	48.55
23	9,612,127	18,167	1.89	47.64
24	9,593,960	18,324	1.91	46.73
25	9,575,636	18,481	1.93	45.82
26	9,557,155	18,732	1.96	44.90
27	9,538,423	18,981	1.99	43.99
28	9,519,442	19,324	2.03	43.08
29	9,500,118	19,760	2.08	42.16
30	9,480,358	20,193	2.13	41.25
31	9,460,165	20,718	2.19	40.34
32	9,439,447	21,239	2.25	39.43
33	9,418,208	21,850	2.32	38.51
34	9,396,358	22,551	2.40	37.60
35	9,373,807	23,528	2.51	36.69
36	9,350,279	24,685	2.64	35.78
37	9,325,594	26,112	2.80	34.88
38	9,299,482	27,991	3.01	33.97
39	9,271,491	30,132	3.25	33.07
40	9,241,359	32,622	3.53	32.18
41	9,208,737	35,362	3.84	31.29
42	9,173,375	38,253	4.17	30.41
43	9,135,122	41,382	4.53	29.54

TABLE 24–1 (Continued)

Age	Number Living (l_x)	Deaths Each Year (d_x)	Deaths per 1,000 ($1,000q_x$)	Expectation of Life ($\overset{\circ}{e}_x$)
44	9,093,740	44,741	4.92	28.67
45	9,048,999	48,412	5.35	27.81
46	9,000,587	52,473	5.83	26.95
47	8,948,114	56,910	6.36	26.11
48	8,891,204	61,794	6.95	25.27
49	8,829,410	67,104	7.60	24.45
50	8,762,306	72,902	8.32	23.63
51	8,689,404	79,160	9.11	22.82
52	8,610,244	85,758	9.96	22.03
53	8,524,486	92,832	10.89	21.25
54	8,431,654	100,337	11.90	20.47
55	8,331,317	108,307	13.00	19.71
56	8,223,010	116,849	14.21	18.97
57	8,106,161	125,970	15.54	18.23
58	7,980,191	135,663	17.00	17.51
59	7,844,528	145,830	18.59	16.81
60	7,698,698	156,592	20.34	16.12
61	7,542,106	167,736	22.24	15.44
62	7,374,370	179,271	24.31	14.78
63	7,195,099	191,174	26.57	14.14
64	7,003,925	203,394	29.04	13.51
65	6,800,531	215,917	31.75	12.90
66	6,584,614	228,749	34.74	12.31
67	6,355,865	241,777	38.04	11.73
68	6,114,088	254,835	41.68	11.17
69	5,859,253	267,241	45.61	10.64
70	5,592,012	278,426	49.79	10.12
71	5,313,586	287,731	54.15	9.63
72	5,025,855	294,766	58.65	9.15
73	4,731,089	299,289	63.26	8.69
74	4,431,800	301,894	68.12	8.24
75	4,129,906	303,011	73.37	7.81
76	3,826,895	303,014	79.18	7.39
77	3,523,881	301,997	85.70	6.98
78	3,221,884	299,829	93.06	6.59
79	2,922,055	295,683	101.19	6.21
80	2,626,372	288,848	109.98	5.85
81	2,337,524	278,983	119.35	5.51
82	2,058,541	265,902	129.17	5.19
83	1,792,639	249,858	139.38	4.89
84	1,542,781	231,433	150.01	4.60
85	1,311,348	211,311	161.14	4.32
86	1,100,037	190,108	172.82	4.06
87	909,929	168,455	185.13	3.80
88	741,474	146,997	198.25	3.55

TABLE 24-1 *(Concluded)*

Age	Number Living (l_x)	Deaths Each Year (d_x)	Deaths per 1,000 $(1{,}000q_x)$	Expectation of Life $(\overset{\circ}{e}_x)$
89	594,477	126,303	212.46	3.31
90	468,174	106,809	228.14	3.06
91	361,365	88,813	245.77	2.82
92	272,552	72,480	265.93	2.58
93	200,072	57,881	289.30	2.33
94	142,191	45,026	316.66	2.07
95	97,165	34,128	351.24	1.80
96	63,037	25,250	400.56	1.51
97	37,787	18,456	488.42	1.18
98	19,331	12,916	668.15	0.83
99	6,415	6,415	1,000.00	0.50

to be living at age 25 the probability is that 18,481 will die before they become 26; of 9,373,807 living at age 35, probably 23,528 will die before 36; and of 6,415 living at age 99, probably all of them will die before 100.

What's in a Mortality Table?   Table 24-1 is the Commissioners 1958 Standard Ordinary Mortality Table. It is made up of five columns: "Age," "Number Living," "Deaths Each Year," "Deaths per 1,000," and "Expectation of Life."

The "Age" column runs from 0 through 99. Why does it stop at age 99? Why not include ages 100 and beyond? According to the table, out of 6,415 people alive on their 99th birthday, 6,415 will probably die before they reach 100 years of age. In other words, the table states that probably all the people reaching age 99 will die before they reach 100. Since it is presumed that no one will live to be 100, there is no point in extending the table beyond age 99. There are some authenticated cases of people living past age 100, but statistically they are so few that they can be ignored for purposes of rate making.[2] The age at which all are dead is called the "limiting age."

The "Number Living" column starts with a group of 10 million individuals at age zero. Any number, however, could have been used as a starting figure and any age as a starting age. (For instance, the American Experience Mortality Table, published in 1868 and based on mortality experience covering the years 1843–58, started with 100,000 individuals at age 10, and was extended in 1900 to age 0.) The number used at the starting age chosen is called the "radix."

The figures in the "Deaths Each Year" column are the probable number of people out of the given group at that age who will die before reaching

---

[2] Annuity tables, which are based on the experience of annuitants, run to higher ages— to age 109 in one table.

their next birthday. This figure is the other half of the relationship between the number living and the number dying. It is the difference between the figures for two successive ages in the "Number Living" column, since the figures in the "Number Living" column are reduced each year by the probable number dying during the previous year.

By reducing the "number living" by the "deaths each year," the table makes it easy to determine the probable number of deaths over a period of years out of any starting group. For example, using the 1958 CSO Table to determine the probable number dying over a five-year period out of 9,575,636 living at age 25, all that is necessary is to subtract the number living at age 30 (9,480,358) from the number living at 25. The remainder is 95,278, the probable number dying in the five years.

In theory, the "Deaths per 1,000" column is similar to the "Deaths Each Year" column. The figures in both of these columns are the "death part" of the living-dying relationship. However, in the "Deaths Each Year" column, the "living part" of the relationship is the *number assumed to be living* at the beginning of the year, whereas in the "Deaths per 1,000" column, the living part of the living-dying relationship is always *1,000*.

The final column, "Expectation of Life," is the average number of additional years which those at any given age can be expected to live. For example, based on the 1958 CSO Table of Mortality, life expectancy at age 97 is 1.18 years. The table shows that there are 37,787 living at the beginning of age 97. Out of this group, 18,456 will probably die between ages 97 and 98; 12,916 between 98 and 99; and 6,415 between 99 and 100. The average age of death of the group is computed as follows:

Number Dying		Age of Death		Aggregate Age
18,456	×	97.5	=	1,799,460.0
12,916	×	98.5	=	1,272,226.0
6,415	×	99.5	=	638,292.5
37,787				3,709,978.5

The total aggregate age (3,709,978.5) divided by 37,787 (the number of individuals in the group) equals 98.18, which is the average age of death for the group. Life expectancy of the group, therefore, is 1.18 years.

It should be noted that, contrary to the general impression of a large part of the public, the life expectancy of any one individual does not enter into the computation of his life insurance premium in any manner. For example, the life expectancy at age 25 is 45.82, 1958 CSO; but the probability of death in the next year is 1.93 per 1,000. The rate for a five-year term policy issued at age 25, if based on life expectancy, would be zero because the life expectancy at that age exceeds the five-year term by more than 40 years. Yet during this five-year period, 95,278 out of 9,575,636 will die, and the premium must allow for these deaths.

Life expectancy figures, however, have some uses. They are used in figuring taxable income under annuities, as explained in Chapters 6 and 21; they are used in comparing mortality tables and in studying improvements in longevity or in comparing longevity among countries, sexes, and races; they are used to measure the duration of "life expectancy" term policies as discussed in Chapter 4; and they are used as an aid in measuring damages in liability claims involving death or disability.

Relationships in a Mortality Table. Possession of any one of the following sets of figures will make it possible to determine the remaining three columns in a mortality table: (1) the number of people surviving at each age from an original group of individuals; (2) the number of people dying during each age from an original group of individuals; (3) the number of people dying at each age out of the number living at the beginning of the age. The following examples will illustrate the relationship in a mortality table.

Assume that from an original group of individuals, the number living at the ages tabulated below is:

Age	Number Living		Age	Number Living
27	3,179,474		32	3,146,482
28	3,173,147		33	3,139,403
29	3,166,706		34	3,132,129
30	3,160,119		35	3,124,602
31	3,153,388			

The first four columns of a mortality table (ages 27 through 34) may be developed from these data as follows:

First, compute the "Deaths Each Year" column: Since 3,179,474 individuals were living at the beginning of age 27 and only 3,173,147 were living at the beginning of age 28 (the end of age 27), then 6,327 must have died during the year. The process is repeated for each of the other years as indicated below:

Age	Living Beginning of Year		Living End of Year		Deaths During Year
27	3,179,474	—	3,173,147	=	6,327
28	3,173,147	—	3,166,706	=	6,441
29	3,166,706	—	3,160,119	=	6,587
30	3,160,119	—	3,153,388	=	6,731
31	3,153,388	—	3,146,482	=	6,906
32	3,146,482	—	3,139,403	=	7,079
33	3,139,403	—	3,132,129	=	7,274
34	3,132,129	—	3,124,602	=	7,527

Then compute the "Deaths per 1,000" column by dividing the number dying during the year by the number living at the beginning of the year, and multiplying the answer by 1,000. At age 27, 6,327, the number dying, is divided by 3,179,474, the number living. This gives 0.00198995, which represents the chance of death for 1 member of the group. When this figure is multiplied by 1,000 it gives 1.99, which is the expected number of deaths from each 1,000 members of the group. This process is repeated for each age group as shown below:

Age	Deaths Each Year		Number Living			Deaths per 1,000
27	6,327	÷	3,179,474	× 1,000 =		1.99
28	6,441	÷	3,173,147	× 1,000 =		2.03
29	6,587	÷	3,166,706	× 1,000 =		2.08
30	6,731	÷	3,160,119	× 1,000 =		2.13
31	6,906	÷	3,153,388	× 1,000 =		2.19
32	7,079	÷	3,146,482	× 1,000 =		2.25
33	7,274	÷	3,139,403	× 1,000 =		2.32
34	7,527	÷	3,132,129	× 1,000 =		2.40

The following are the completed first four columns of the table:

Age	Number Living	Deaths Each Year	Deaths per 1,000
27	3,179,474	6,327	1.99
28	3,173,147	6,441	2.03
29	3,166,706	6,587	2.08
30	3,160,119	6,731	2.13
31	3,153,388	6,906	2.19
32	3,146,482	7,079	2.25
33	3,139,403	7,274	2.32
34	3,132,129	7,527	2.40

The "Expectation of Life" column is omitted because it cannot be computed unless the table is completed to the age at which all members of the group are dead ("limiting age"). In the case of the 1958 CSO Table, the limiting age would be 100.

Constructing a Mortality Table. Raw data used in the construction of a mortality table usually are collected by age classes. From the following raw data, several steps are necessary to complete a section of a mortality table (from ages 35 through 40).

Age	Number Living	Number Dying
35	300,000	753
36	250,000	660
37	750,000	2,100
38	630,000	1,896
39	540,000	1,755
40	630,000	2,224

First, list the ages. Next, figure the "deaths per 1,000." The process is identical with that used in the foregoing example.

Age	Deaths Each Year		Number Living			Deaths per 1,000
35	 753	÷	300,000	× 1,000 =		2.51
36	 660	÷	250,000	× 1,000 =		2.64
37	 2,100	÷	750,000	× 1,000 =		2.80
38	 1,896	÷	630,000	× 1,000 =		3.01
39	 1,755	÷	540,000	× 1,000 =		3.25
40	 2,224	÷	630,000	× 1,000 =		3.53

In constructing the table it is possible to assume any number as the number living at age 35; consequently 100,000 will be used as the radix. If 100,000 were living on their 35th birthday and 2.51 per 1,000 died before reaching 36, then 251 would be the probable number of deaths during the year. The probable number surviving to age 36 would be 99,749. The probable number dying during age 36 would be 99,749 × 2.64 or 263. The process would be continued until the calculation of the number dying for age 40. The completed table is below.

Age	Number Living	Deaths Each Year	Deaths per 1,000
35	 100,000	251	2.51
36	 99,749	263	2.64
37	 99,486	279	2.80
38	 99,207	299	3.01
39	 98,908	321	3.25
40	 98,587	348	3.53

Use of Mortality Tables. The following examples will illustrate how the mortality table is used in computing projected claims under life insurance contracts:

Example 1: What would be the charge (excluding interest and expenses)[3] for a one-year term policy issued at age 35 assuming 1958 CSO mortality? This table shows that if 9,373,807 individuals were insured at age 35, 23,528 would probably die before they reached age 36. Furthermore, if these individuals were insured for $1,000 each the projected claims would amount to $23,528,000. The proportionate share of these claims per policyholder would be $2.51.[4]

Example 2: What would be the charge (excluding interest and expenses) for a $1,000 single premium pure endowment at 65 issued at age 30?[5] If 9,480,358 pure endowments were sold, the probable number of claims would be 6,800,531. Since each claim would amount to $1,000, total claims would be $6,800,531,000. The cost per policyholder would then be $6,800,531,000 ÷ 9,480,358 or $717.33.

---

[3] The role of interest and expenses in premium computations is deferred until later in the chapter.

[4] $23,528,000 ÷ 9,373,807.

[5] A pure endowment is a policy which pays nothing if the insured dies before reaching endowment age but pays the face amount upon reaching that age.

The first step in computing the premium for any life insurance or annuity contract is to tabulate the amount of projected claims. A mortality table is essential for this task.

Mortality tables also are important in the valuation of reserve liabilities and for the calculation of nonforfeiture values. Companies might, for example, use the 1958 CSO Table for the valuation of reserves, but a less conservative one for computing premiums and nonforfeiture values. Especially is this true in figuring premiums for a nonparticipating policy where a dividend cannot be used to refund excess premiums resulting from the use of tables with ultraconservative safety cushions.

Safety Margins. Not only must a mortality table be based on adequate statistical data, but it should also provide a safety margin to allow for unpredicted increases in the death rate and for temporarily adverse mortality fluctuations.[6] When the table is to be used to establish minimum standards for legal reserves, appropriate margins must be allowed to make the table safe for all companies, for example those with liberal underwriting as well as those with strict underwriting and those national in scope as well as those regional in scope.

In some of the older mortality tables, a safety margin was assured by using data gathered from a period which had higher mortality rates than the present or than was anticipated in the future.

The newer tables, however, are first computed from relatively recent mortality data, to which is added a safety margin computed mathematically. (This is sometimes called "enriching" the table.) For example, the following are the death rates per 1,000 from the 1958 CSO Mortality Table, first without and then with safety margins.

Age	Without Safety Margin	With Safety Margins	Age	Without Safety Margins	With Safety Margins
20	0.84	1.79	50	6.71	8.32
25	0.93	1.93	55	10.93	13.00
30	1.08	2.13	60	17.56	20.34
35	1.41	2.51	65	27.61	31.75
40	2.36	3.53	75	63.80	73.37
45	4.03	5.35	85	140.12	161.14

Annuities. On first thought, one might assume that a given mortality table would work as well for annuities as it does for life insurance. An analysis of the question, however, reveals four reasons why this is not true.

First, the safety factors that are built into a life insurance mortality table would have the opposite effect if the table were to be used for annuity rates. They would result in the establishment of an unsafe rate

---

[6] Insurance companies, for example, witnessed a temporary but drastic mortality fluctuation during the influenza epidemic of 1918–19.

rather than in a margin of safety, by projecting a lower survival rate than indicated by the basic data.

Second, while a decreasing trend in mortality rates is a factor of safety for life insurance rate computation, it tends to make the table unsafe for annuities. If a life insurance policyholder lives longer than projected in the table, the company has a gain from mortality; however, for every year that annuitants live longer than the table predicts, the company has a loss from survival.

Mortality rates have been decreasing. For example, based on mortality statistics for the general population, the life expectancy at birth in 1939–41 was 63.6 years. By 1949–51 it had risen to 68.1 years, and by 1959–61 to 69.9 years. Although some of this increase was brought about by an improvement in infant mortality, analysis shows that more than one half of it was a result of a decline in the death rate beyond age 25. Life expectancy at age 65 also has increased during this period from 12.8 in 1939–41, to 13.8 in 1949–51, and to 14.4 in 1959–61.

Third, in an annuity table, companies find it necessary to distinguish between the sexes. Mortality rates for females are much lower than for males.[7] Since women are heavy buyers of annuities, companies take this mortality differential into consideration. This difference usually is handled by rating women down four or five years, thus avoiding the necessity of using two tables.[8]

Until the 1950's, life insurance companies made no differential in life insurance rates based on sex.[9] Currently, many companies offer policies to women at rates lower than those charged men.[10]

Fourth, because people who are not in good physical condition are not likely to buy annuities, mortality among people who purchase annuities is apt to be lower than among those who purchase life insurance.

Annuity mortality tables will, therefore, show fewer deaths and a greater expectation of life at any given age than will mortality tables used to compute rates and values for life insurance. For example, the Annuity Table for 1949—Male (1939–49) projects a life expectancy at age 65 of 15.01

---

[7] According to the Industry Actuarial Advisory Committee to the NAIC, Subcommittee on Deficiency Reserves and Mortality Tables Review, the average level of ultimate mortality on males is about 5 percent higher than the corresponding level for the mixture of males and females included in standard ordinary mortality experience.

[8] For example, a woman aged 65 would be assumed to have the same death rate as a man aged 60 or 61.

[9] One reason companies for so long did not differentiate between life insurance rates for men and women of the same age is that policies on women usually are for a lower average amount. The added expense of issuing small policies, it was thought, offset the lower mortality cost.

[10] Companies may require a minimum amount of insurance for the woman to be eligible for the lower premium; the lower premium may not be given for some policies; the lower premium may be established by an age set back or by a separate schedule of rates based on the 1958 Female CSO Table; the insurer may offer a lower rate on one special policy only such as, for example, a Ladies Economy Exclusive, whatever that is.

years, whereas the 1958 CSO Table projects only 12.90 years. Two factors make this difference even greater than it appears: (1) the 1958 CSO is based on more recent data and (2) the 1958 CSO data include female as well as male mortality experience. Since mortality experience is improving, and since women live longer than men, the tables would show an even greater difference if the basic data were comparable.

Types of Mortality Tables. A two-way system of classifying mortality tables may be used. (1) They may be classified on the basis of the type of population used in the sampling procedure. Mortality tables may be divided into those based on general population statistics and those based on insured population statistics. (2) They may be classified according to the weight they give to recently medically selected lives. Mortality tables may be divided into select, ultimate, and aggregate.

TYPE OF POPULATION. A number of different mortality tables have been published. Some are based on U.S. population statistics, and others are based on insurance company statistics. The National Office of Vital Statistics periodically prepares a group of mortality tables showing mortality rates in the country among males and females, among white and non-white, among rural and city dwellers, and among native and foreign born in various sections of the country. The data from which these tables are prepared are not entirely accurate because of errors made by the census takers and processors, and because of inaccurate and inadequate information given by the people. These tables are not used in insurance rate making or in computing reserves, not only because they contain errors but also because life insurance companies select insureds rather than insure all applicants. Consequently, mortality experienced by the companies should be less than that stated in the general population tables. If applicants were not occasionally rejected, adverse selection probably would produce mortality experience higher than the general table.

Table 24–2 shows the variation between general population statistics and those based on insured lives.

TABLE 24–2

Deaths per 1,000

Age	1958 CSO Basic* (without Safety Margin)	1949–51 Census
20	0.84	1.35
30	1.08	1.79
40	2.36	3.68
50	6.71	8.76

* These mortality figures are based on mortality statistics for the period 1950–54. Were they based on the 1949–51 period used in the census figures, there would be even greater disparity, since mortality experience is improving.

A number of tables have been developed from statistics on insured lives and on the lives of annuitants. The data upon which these tables are based are usually accurate because they come from the records of the companies. Insurance companies, by the nature of their business, must maintain accurate records of birthdates and dates of death. Where necessary, insurance companies, by pooling experience, can develop sufficient data to produce credible mortality tables.

WEIGHT GIVEN TO RECENTLY SELECTED LIVES. Mortality tables developed from statistics on insured lives may be select, ultimate, or aggregate.

A *select* mortality table is one that gives full weight to the effect of recently selected lives on mortality rates. Therefore, it must show for each age a series of mortality rates based on the duration of the policy.

Two groups of insured individuals, both aged 35, would not be expected to experience the same rate of mortality if one group was insured five years ago and the other last year. The second group will still show the effect of selection based on physical, occupational, and moral standards. However, when these same two groups reach age 40, five years hence, their mortality rates would probably not differ greatly. Thus, from a practical standpoint, there would seem to be no need to continue the select character of the table any further.

Table 24–3 is an excerpt from a select table. Notice that the table shows six mortality rates for each age, one for each of six years of insurance. When the 5-year select period expires, the insured will be age 40 and will be assumed to have the same mortality expectation as every other insured age 40 with a policy duration in excess of 5 years.

TABLE 24–3
Select Mortality Table—Rates per 1,000

Age at Issue	Years of Insurance						Attained Age
	1	2	3	4	5	6 and over	
35	.91	1.09	1.32	1.60	1.96	2.36	40
36	.95	1.18	1.45	1.78	2.20	2.64	41
37	1.03	1.29	1.61	1.99	2.45	2.95	42
38	1.12	1.43	1.79	2.21	2.73	3.28	43
39	1.23	1.58	1.98	2.46	3.02	3.63	44
40	1.35	1.73	2.19	2.71	3.33	4.02	45

Select tables have wide use in the life insurance business. Many insurers use them in computing premium rates for participating and nonparticipating policies. They also are used for analysis of internal operations, such as underwriting, dividend apportionment, surrender value schedules, and projecting the profitability of new business.

An *ultimate* mortality table shows the rate of mortality at various ages for lives beyond the select period—i.e., it shows the rate of mortality after the effect of selection has worn off. The mortality rate for a group age 35 on an ultimate table will show the expected mortality under policies which have been in force for more than 5 years. The 1958 CSO Table, as well as some tables used in making participating (and nonparticipating) rates and in establishing minimum reserve standards, are ultimate tables.

Aggregate tables are developed from data on all insured lives with no distinction made as to how long the lives have been insured. Recently selected lives are combined with lives which have been insured for many years. Aggregate tables are not used in developing life insurance premium rates because the ultimate tables give the companies an extra margin to help with the high first-year expenses involved in selling and issuing the policy. Companies not seeking this additional margin use select tables; otherwise they use ultimate tables.

Basic Tables.   Basic mortality tables are those developed from insurance company experience without the inclusion of a safety margin. Since 1934 a group of major companies has maintained a continuous mortality investigation on the basis of their combined experience. The statistics so obtained are used periodically by the mortality committee of the Society of Actuaries to construct basic tables. They are used also by company actuaries to construct tables to serve as standards with which they can compare their own company's experience. In addition, the basic data when modified by the insurers are used to prepare mortality tables to serve as a basis for computing premium rates for insurance.

Both select and ultimate tables are prepared. Select mortality rates are provided each year for the preceding year. Ultimate mortality statistics are provided in five-year age groups.[11] In addition to select and ultimate mortality data for ordinary insurance, mortality investigations are made of the experience on juvenile ordinary policies, policies of large face amounts, group life insurance, and, when applicable, war. The main purpose of these investigations is to study mortality trends.

These investigations serve as a basis for change in mortality tables but since frequent changes in the mortality tables used for premium calculations, reserve computations, and nonforfeiture values are neither practical nor necessary, such changes are made only at long intervals.[12]

Development of Mortality Tables.   "Traditionally, the actuary has interested himself primarily in the measurement of the span of human life and the determination of the probabilities of death and survival over specific periods. From the first crude table of mortality constructed by Halley, of comet fame, through the speculations on the possibilities of a mathematical

---

[11] For policies in force 6 to 15 years, only standard, medically examined issues are used. The experience during the 16th and subsequent policy years covers all standard issues, those medically examined and those issued nonmedically.

[12] Not necessary because gains from mortality are (1) anticipated in calculating the rate, (2) returned as dividends, or (3) both; not practical because of the high cost of computing new rates and issuing new policy forms and rate manuals based on them. The importance of a new table has far more significance in the regulation of reserves than in the computation of a premium rate, as discussed later in this chapter.

law resulting in the empirical formulas of Gompertz and Makeham, to the modern actuarial techniques, we have seen a constant and continuing search for information which would reduce the risk of error in the making of estimates as to future mortality experience. Accuracy in these estimates is necessary in our business to reduce the risk of financial loss to the insurer and to increase the degree of fairness with which the losses insured against are apportioned among those insured."[13]

LIFE INSURANCE TABLES. Until 1900 the actuaries' table, more precisely known as the English Seventeen Offices Table of 1843, was commonly used in the United States. This table was based on the experience of British companies. After 1900 and until 1948 the American Experience Table of Mortality, based on the mortality statistics of a period from 1843 to 1858 taken from the experience of the Mutual Life Insurance Company of New York was generally used. A number of policies are still in force today that were issued on the basis of the American Experience Table of Mortality.

Two mortality tables upon which a great many policies in force today were issued are the Commissioners 1941 Standard Ordinary and the 1941 Standard Industrial Tables, adopted by most states as the basis for reserves and nonforfeiture values on all policies issued in the mid-1940's until January 1, 1966.[14] The Commissioners 1941 Standard Ordinary Table is based on mortality experience of a large group of companies between 1930 and 1940, and is weighted to give an adequate safety margin.

The 1941 Standard Industrial Table is based on the industrial mortality statistics of the Metropolitan Life Insurance Company from 1930 to 1940, and is weighted to give an added margin for safety. It soon replaced the Standard Industrial Table of 1907, which was based on the mortality

---

[13] Alfred N. Guertin, "Actuarial Trends in the Life Insurance Field," University of Connecticut, *Insurance Lecture Series,* Spring, 1952.

[14] Many efforts were made to encourage the development and adoption of a new mortality table long before the development of the 1941 CSO Tables. However, the opponents had always been successful in blocking the moves. The chief arguments for a new table were: (1) the American Experience Table was out of date; (2) it did not represent the average of all companies; (3) a new table would show the fallacy of the contention that companies were overcharging by using the old tables; (4) the public demanded a new table; (5) professional critics of life insurance—meaning people who made money out of yellow journalism attacks on the business—often made a point of the use of out-of-date mortality tables without explaining how the premium is adjusted through the dividend formula (and in other ways) to reflect more recent experience. The principle objections to a new table were: (1) the present table served the purpose well enough because the companies knew how to allow for its error, so there was no need in going to the expense of developing a new one; (2) a newer table might create serious problems for new companies since it might result in higher reserves; (3) a new mortality table might give less margin for expenses under New York and Wisconsin laws since it will give lower net premiums; (4) a new table might cause some companies to be more selective in their underwriting, which some people argued would not be in the public interest; (5) lower net premiums resulting from new mortality tables might cause the public to demand lower gross premiums. For a good discussion of arguments over the desirability of a new mortality table and other matters relating to the history of mortality tables, see R. Carlyle Buley, *A Study in the History of Life Insurance* (New York: Appleton-Century-Crofts, Inc., 1953).

statistics of the Metropolitan from 1896 to 1905, as the basis for computing reserves and surrender values for industrial policies.

The newest mortality table for ordinary life insurance is the 1958 Commissioners Standard Ordinary Table developed by the National Association of Insurance Commissioners and the Society of Actuaries. While the impetus for the work on this table grew from the deficiency reserve problem,[15] the Industry Advisory Committee to the NAIC's Subcommittee on Deficiency Reserves and Mortality Tables Review concluded that an important need for a new mortality table existed regardless of the deficiency reserve problem. Its June, 1958 report pointed out that the 1941 CSO Table was less representative of current experience than the American Experience Table was at the time the 1941 CSO Table was developed.

The 1958 CSO Table was developed from a mortality table called X_{17}, which was devised by the Society of Actuaries. The basic data underlying the table are the combined ultimate mortality experience on $170 billion of standard ordinary insurance of 15 large companies during the period between 1950 and 1954 policy anniversaries and involved death claims of nearly $2 billion. The basic table is a graduated[16] mortality table constructed from these data. The unadjusted death rates at the young adult ages were less than half of those of the 1930–40 study used for the 1941 CSO Table, and in no case were they more than 81 percent of the earlier rates.

The basic unadjusted mortality table was compared with individual company experience to study deviations, using both the 15 large companies whose figures made up the table and also the experience of 33 smaller companies. This comparison showed a range of actual to projected deaths of from 65.3 percent in the company with the most favorable experience to 115.7 percent in the company with the least favorable experience. Because

---

[15] Improvements in mortality experience have made it possible for companies to reduce their premiums. Minimum reserves, however, had to be maintained on the basis of the 1941 CSO Table at 3½ percent. In New York, the maximum interest assumption for reserve calculation was 3 percent. The formula for computing reserves (Chapter 27) is the present value of projected claims less the present value of projected net premiums. In New York, the amount of each premium used in the projection at that time must not have been less than that yielded by using the 1941 CSO mortality assumptions at 3 percent. If the company charged a gross premium less than this amount, it was required to set up a reserve to offset the deficiency in future premiums. For example, at age 35 one company charged $18.92 per $1,000, nonpar for its continuous premium whole life policy. The net level premium for this policy figured on the basis of 1941 CSO at 3 percent would have been $19.13. This policy, therefore, would have required a deficiency reserve equal to the present value of a life annuity due of $0.21 a year figured at 3 percent interest and 1941 CSO mortality. This would have amounted to $4.34 initially. If the reserve were based on the 1958 CSO Table at 3 percent, no deficiency reserve would have been necessary since the net level premium figured on this basis would be only $16.29. (If you do not completely understand this note but get the general idea, this should be sufficient for now.)

[16] Raw mortality data do not reveal a continuous and regular rise in the death rate from low to high ages. Especially are there likely to be irregularities at the very young and very old ages. To iron out these irregularities and to produce a graduating mortality curve, actuaries must adjust the raw data by applying one of the formulas developed for this purpose. The procedure is known as graduation, and the table that results is called a graduated table.

mortality rates representing average company experience, without margins, would not be appropriate for a mortality table used by all companies as a basis for determining policy reserves, a safety margin was adopted ranging from a low of 15 percent (ages 64–93) to a high of 236.1 percent (age 10).[17] Comparison of the 15 companies' combined experience showed actual deaths to be about 83.6 percent of those projected in the adjusted table.[18] The lowest percentage for any of the 15 companies was 79 percent and the highest was 88 percent.[19]

The newest mortality table for industrial insurance, the 1961 Commissioners Standard Industrial Mortality Table, was developed using the mortality experience of 18 companies during 1954–58 for policies on the lives of white males and females. For ages under 10, 17,004,693 policy years producing 18,689 death claims were used. For ages 10 and higher, $86,356,443,374 of insurance years (amount of insurance times the number of years) producing $674,043,039 in death claims was used. The number of policies for ages under 10 rather than the amounts of insurance was used as the basis for computation because of the problem of adjusting graded benefits under juvenile policies.

Safety margins in the 1961 CSI Table range from a low of 25 percent at the higher ages to a high of 195.5 percent at the lower ages. These margins are designed to reflect the variations in underwriting standards among insurers and variations in the composition of the group insured.[20]

The use of the 1961 CSI Table became mandatory as the basis for computing minimum reserves and nonforfeiture values for all industrial policies issued beginning January 1, 1968.

The newest mortality table for group insurance is the 1960 Commissioners Standard Group Mortality Table explained and reproduced in Chapter 15 of this text.

ANNUITY TABLES.   Although several other annuity tables have been developed (the McClintock Table for 1896, the American Annuitants'

---

[17] The percentage margins vary widely among ages. For example, at 10-year intervals the margins are: age 0—11.8 percent; 10—236.1 percent; 20—113.1 percent; 30—97.2 percent; 40—49.6 percent; 50—24.0 percent; 60—15.8 percent.

[18] Thus, from an aggregate point of view, the average percentage margin for all ages combined is: 19.6 percent, computed as follows: $\dfrac{100 - 83.6}{83.6}$. This compares with a 16.4 percent average margin on the 1941 CSO Table.

[19] A separate table, 1958 CSO-A, was prepared by adding a loading of 0.75 deaths per 1,000 to 130 percent of the 1958 CSO Table mortality rates. This table is specifically designed to provide for both the higher mortality experienced by some companies under the extended term nonforfeiture benefit and the expense of maintaining this benefit in force. In computing reserve liabilities under ordinary policies insurers are allowed to use an age down to three years younger for female lives. (This is called a rate-down, or, specifically in this case, a three-year rate-down for women.)

[20] A CSI Extended Term Table with the same additional mortality rates as used in the CSO Extended Term Mortality Table has been constructed for use in computing values under this nonforfeiture provision.

Table for 1920, and the Combined Annuity Table for 1928), the most important ones are the 1937 Standard Annuity Table, the Annuity Table for 1949, the Group Annuity Table for 1951, and the 1955 American Annuity Table.

The 1937 Standard Annuity Table is the one most extensively used on older annuities but on newly issued annuities more recent tables are used. The basic data from which this table was constructed were the experience of clerical employees covered under group life insurance during 1932–36 for those ages below 60. For ages 60 and above, the experience of individual annuitants was used.

The Annuity Table for 1949 is significant because it introduced for the first time projection factors to reflect continued improvements in mortality rates.[21] The experience with male employees not more than 55 years old and females 50 years or less, covered under group annuities in the major companies was used, and the experience of annuitants covered under individual immediate straight life annuities was used for ages over 55 male and 50 female. The basic data were based on the early and middle 1940's but were adjusted to 1949. Two sets of projections were developed: Scale A is based upon the continued improvement of mortality at the same annual rates as in the past; Scale B projects a lower rate of improvement at younger ages and a higher rate of improvement at older ages than has taken place in the past.[22] The table with various modifications in the projection factors is used in determining rates for annuity contracts and in determining the amounts of periodic income guaranteed per $1,000 of life insurance when settled under a lifetime income option.

The Group Annuity Table for 1951 (GA 1951) for ages under 56 was developed by applying Projection Scale B, adjusted for one year's decrease, to the Annuity Table for 1949. For ages over 65 the 1946–50 intercompany experience on retired group annuitants adjusted for three years' decrease under Projection Scale B was used. Extrapolation was applied to arrive at ages 56–65.[23] The projection factors were used to adjust the mortality to the 1951 level. For example, the data for the intercompany experience (1946–50) tended to represent that of 1948, thereby requiring a three-year adjustment to bring the data to 1951.

---

[21] Life insurance mortality tables are static in that they are based on mortality experience for a given period, making no adjustment for anticipated mortality improvement. Until 1949, annuity tables also were static. Insurers using the 1937 Standard Annuity Table had to adjust to reflect mortality improvement by rating ages down as the table became obsolete. For example, a person age 65 had to be rated as though he were age 63 or age 62.

[22] The theory of Projection Scale B is that improvements in mortality in the early years has already brought the rate so low that further decreases should not be expected at the same rate. The rate of improvement at the higher ages, however, should be expected to increase because this is the group that is most likely to benefit from advances in medical science.

[23] Extrapolation is a statistical process for estimating a quantity which depends on one or more variables by extending the variables beyond their established ranges.

A safety margin was added to the table by reducing male mortality rates by 10 percent and female rates by 12.5 percent, thus providing an absolute margin that increases with age. Because the credibility of the data at the advance ages was considered lower than those at the lower ages, the increasing margins seemed to be appropriate. The 10 and 12.5 percent safety margins were arbitrarily selected.

The GA 1951 Table was the first mortality table to be based on the experience of group annuitants. Projection Scale C was developed to keep the table current. This scale projected greater improvement than Scale B because mortality rates among group annuitants are higher than those among individual annuitants, and therefore can be expected to improve at a faster pace. (Projection Scale C is based on an assumed mortality rate reduction equal to $1\frac{1}{2}$ times that projected in Scale B, but in no event more than a 1.25 percent annual reduction in mortality from the basic table.

The GA 1951 Table with full or modified Projection C is widely used in computing rates and reserves for group annuities. A common modification is to project the mortality rates to the current year and then set back the ages one year to allow for further improvements.

The 1955 American Annuity Table was developed to provide reasonable rates for annual premium deferred annuities and life income settlement options involving intervals of many years between the time the contract is written and rated and when the annuity payments are to begin. The table is based on data submitted to the Society of Actuaries by the major life insurance companies and reflects the 1948–53 experience under individual annuity contracts. In order to produce a table of combined experience, female data were treated as male data set back five years. The effect is to understate mortality at lower ages and to overstate it at higher ages. Future decreases in the mortality rate is projected at an average annual rate of approximately 0.9 percent at age 40 and beyond. The effect is to set the age back 1 year every 10 years. Thus the premium for an annual premium deferred annuity commencing at age 65 issued to a man 45 would be based on the current mortality rate for a man aged 63.

The 1955 American Annuity Table is used by a number of companies in computing rates on individual annuities and in computing values on life income settlement options.

2. INTEREST

Because premiums are paid in advance of claim payments, insurance companies have money to invest. Investment earnings are considered in computing the cost of insurance.

In the actuarial illustrations in this chapter, Chapter 25, and Chapter 27, an assumption of $2\frac{1}{2}$ percent interest is used. Even though the net rate of interest earned by life insurance companies on their invested assets has been in an upward trend since 1947, a number of leading insurance companies still use 2½ percent in computing their rates and reserves. Other companies use 2¾ percent, 3 percent, and a few even use 3½ percent.

Life insurance companies, on the average, have increased the return on invested assets, after investment expenses but before federal income taxes, from the low point of 2.88 percent in 1947 to in excess of 5 percent at the close of the decade of the 1960's. Because the premiums and values are guaranteed over a long period of time, participating life insurance companies generally are ultraconservative in the interest assumptions they use, relying on their dividend formulas under participating policies to pass on to their policyholders the interest earnings in excess of the assumed rate.

Types of Interest. The two types of interest are simple and compound.

SIMPLE INTEREST. Under simple interest, the interest is paid to the investor each year as it is earned, and the investor has the problem of reinvesting it if he so desires.

For example, if $100 is invested at 2½ percent *simple* interest, the earning is $2.50 a year and is actually paid to the investor. The amount of interest also is $2.50 in each of the following years. As a result, the amount of simple interest earned in 4 years, for example, is 4 times $2.50 or $10.

COMPOUND INTEREST. Under compound interest, the interest earned each year is added to the principal and reinvested for the next year. In this way the principal constantly increases each year by the amount of the interest earned during the preceding year. Consequently, since the size of the principal increases each year, so does the amount of interest earned.

For example, if $100 is invested at 2½ percent *compound* interest, the return is $2.50 the first year. During the second year, interest is earned not only on the original principal of $100 but also on the previous interest earning of $2.50, which has been reinvested. Thus, in the second year, the interest earned would be $2.56. For the third and fourth years, the interest would be $2.63 and $2.69. For the 4 years the total interest earned would be $10.38. This compares with $10 earned at *simple* interest.

Since it is assumed that life insurance companies keep their interest earnings reinvested until funds are needed to pay claims, compound interest is assumed in the calculation of life insurance rates and reserves.

Table 24–4 shows the value of $1 invested at 2½ percent compound interest for the years indicated.[24]

Present Value. Compound interest amount tables show how much $1 at a given rate of interest will accumulate to at some specified future date. Present value tables show the reverse; i.e., they show how much (assuming a given rate of compound interest) must be on hand now in order to accumulate to $1 at a specified date in the future. For example, at 2½ percent compound interest, in order to have $100 at the end of one year, $97.56

---

[24] The formula for these values is $S = P (1 + i)^n$ where S is the amount; P, the principal; i, the rate at which interest is to be compounded; and n, the number of years involved.

TABLE 24–4

Amount of 1 at $2\frac{1}{2}\%$ Compound Interest $(1 + i)^n$

Year	$2\frac{1}{2}\%$	Year	$2\frac{1}{2}\%$	Year	$2\frac{1}{2}\%$
1	1.02500	16	1.48451	31	2.15001
2	1.05063	17	1.52162	32	2.20376
3	1.07689	18	1.55966	33	2.25885
4	1.10381	19	1.59865	34	2.31532
5	1.13141	20	1.63862	35	2.37321
6	1.15969	21	1.67958	36	2.43254
7	1.18869	22	1.72157	37	2.49335
8	1.21840	23	1.76461	38	2.55568
9	1.24886	24	1.80873	39	2.61957
10	1.28008	25	1.85394	40	2.68506
11	1.31209	26	1.90029	41	2.75219
12	1.34489	27	1.94780	42	2.82100
13	1.37851	28	1.99650	43	2.89151
14	1.41297	29	2.04641	44	2.96380
15	1.44830	30	2.09757	45	3.03790

must be invested. If \$100 is needed at the end of 10 years, then at $2\frac{1}{2}$ percent compound interest, \$78.12 must be invested now.[25] Table 24–5 shows the present value of 1 due in the number of years indicated at $2\frac{1}{2}$ percent. The present value concept is an important concept in life insurance mathematics because the present value of future obligations and the present value of future premiums to be collected must be equated.

Use of Interest in Rate Computation. The method of figuring the cost of two different types of insurance contracts, if interest and expenses are excluded, has already been explained. Interest can now be introduced into the computation. Under the assumption that claims are paid at the end of the year and premiums are paid at the beginning of the year,[26] it becomes necessary to determine how much would be charged at the beginning of the period, assuming a given rate of compound interest, in order to have enough to pay claims projected under the mortality assumptions used.

---

[25] The present value of \$1 due one or more years from now is found by the following formula:

$$P = \frac{S}{(1 + i)^n}$$

P is present value, S is the sum (in this case \$1), i is the rate at which interest is to be compounded, and n is the number of years. Thus the present value of 1 due five years from now at $2\frac{1}{2}$ percent is:

$$P = \frac{1}{(1 + 0.025)^5} \text{ or } 0.88385.$$

Just as in the practical use of algebra, no one ever stops to calculate a logarithm (or a square root), even though he might have been taught how to go about it, so no one in the practical use of present values ever stops to calculate them as has been done here. Instead, tables of present values are available. The actuarial symbol for the present value of 1 is v^n. v^n equals $1/(1 + i)^n$.

[26] These assumptions are examined in Chapter 25.

TABLE 24–5

Present Value of 1 at 2 ½ % Compound Interest (v^n)

Year	2½%	Year	2½%	Year	2½%
1	0.97561	16	0.67363	31	0.46512
2	.95181	17	.65720	32	.45377
3	.92860	18	.64117	33	.44270
4	.90595	19	.62553	34	.43191
5	.88385	20	.61027	35	.42137
6	.86230	21	.59539	36	.41109
7	.84127	22	.58087	37	.40107
8	.82075	23	.56670	38	.39129
9	.80073	24	.55288	39	.38174
10	.78120	25	.53939	40	.37243
11	.76215	26	.52624	41	.36335
12	.74356	27	.51340	42	.35448
13	.72542	28	.50088	43	.34584
14	.70773	29	.48866	44	.33740
15	.69047	30	.47674	45	.32917

Example 1. Assuming 1958 CSO at 2½ percent, how much (excluding expenses) would be charged for a $1,000 one-year term policy issued at age 35?

Reference to the mortality table on page 688 shows that if 9,373,807 individuals age 35 are insured, probably 23,528 will die before they reach age 36. In other words, if each of these individuals has a $1,000 policy, the projected claims for the group would be $23,528,000. The process thus far is identical with that used in the mortality examples; however, to take interest into consideration, it is necessary to find the present value of these claims; i.e., to find out how much money is needed now to have $23,528,000 at the end of the year. To find this figure, multiply the amount of claims by the present value of 1 for one year at 2½ percent compound interest. This computation ($23,528,000 × 0.97561) gives $22,954,-152.08. To obtain the cost per policyholder, divide the present value of projected claims by the number insured (9,373,807). The answer ($2.45) is the net premium for a $1,000 one-year term policy at age 35, 1958 CSO, 2½ percent.

The computation is shown below in tabular form.

Age	Projected Claims	Amount of Insurance	Amount of Projected Claims	Years of Interest	Present Value Factor	Present Value of Projected Claims
35	23,528	$1,000	$23,528,000	1	0.97561	$22,954,152.08

	Present Value of Projected Claims	Number Insured	Premium
	$22,954,152.08 ÷	9,373,807 =	$2.45

Example 2. How much would be charged (excluding expenses) for a $1,000 *pure* endowment at age 65 issued at age 30, assuming 2½ percent

compound interest and 1958 CSO? If 9,480,358 pure endowments are sold to people age 30, the projected number of claims will be 6,800,531. (The mortality table shows this number alive at age 65.) Since each of these policies is for $1,000, the total amount of projected claims would be $6,800,531,000. Next, find the present value of these claims by multiplying this figure by the present value of 1 at 2½ percent compound interest for 35 years (0.42137). The reason for the 35-year discount period is that the premiums are to be collected at age 30 but benefits will not be paid until age 65 (end of age 64). As a result, premiums will earn interest for 35 years. This computation ($6,800,531,000 × 0.42137) gives $2,865,539,-747 as the present value of projected claims. Next, divide this figure by the number insured (9,480,358) to get the single premium charged with each policyholder. The result is $302.26.

The above computation is shown below in tabular form.

Age	Projected Claims	Amount of Insurance	Amount of Projected Claims	Years of Interest	Present Value Factor	Present Value of Projected Claims
30	6,800,531	$1,000	$6,800,531,000	35	0.42137	$2,865,539,747

Present Value of Projected Claims		Number Insured		Premium
$2,865,539,747	÷	9,480,358	=	$302.26

Effect of Interest and Mortality Assumptions on the Premium. Either a change in interest assumptions or a change in mortality assumptions will affect the size of the premium. A change from a 2½ percent to a 3 percent assumption, for example, would decrease the net annual premium on a continuous premium whole life policy from $12.55 to $11.28, using the 1958 CSO Table. The higher the rate of interest, the greater will be the contribution by investment earnings and the lower will be the direct cost to the policyholder. A change from higher to lower mortality assumptions also will decrease the premium. The net annual premium at age 25 for a continuous premium whole life policy would be $20.50, using CSO 1941 assumptions at 2½ percent compared with $17.67 using the CSO 1958 assumptions at 2½ percent. The lower the mortality rate, the longer will be the average period over which the company will hold the money and earn interest on it. Also, the lower the mortality rate, the higher will be the survival rate among premium payers, and consequently the greater will be the average number of premiums the company will collect from each policyholder. Thus, each premium can be lower than it would be under higher mortality assumptions. Premiums, therefore, vary inversely with changes in interest assumptions and directly with changes in mortality assumptions.

3. EXPENSES

The premium computations illustrated in earlier paragraphs provided for enough money to pay projected claims based on given interest assumptions. They allowed nothing for the cost of doing business nor for profits in a stock company.[27] They are net premiums[28] and were computed by taking only two factors into consideration: mortality and interest. The $2.45 computed in Example 1 is the net premium for a one-year term policy issued at age 35, and the $302.26 computed in Example 2 is the net premium for a pure endowment at 65 issued at age 30.

Only a subsidized insurance plan can operate on the basis of net premiums. A mutual insurer would have to add a charge for handling the insurance, paying the taxes, and for building various contingency funds to meet adverse fluctuations in interest earnings and mortality experience. A stock insurer would need, in addition to all the above, a margin for profits. Providing an allowance in the premium for these charges is called loading; and just to add confusion, the allowance itself is called the loading.

The premiums quoted by the insurers in their rate books are called gross premiums and include an allowance for expenses. They are computed either by adding the expense loadings to the net premiums or by a direct computation which is independent of the valuation net premiums.[29] Premiums for participating policies customarily are computed by addition of an expense allowance to the net premium whereas premiums for nonparticipating policies typically are calculated directly by considering mortality, interest, and allowances for expenses, contingencies, and profit all in the same computation.

The technique of loading involves three objectives: (1) to cover all expenses and contingencies, (2) to have the funds for expenses when needed,[30] and (3) to spread the cost equitably among the policyholders.[31] Loading is primarily a problem in cost accounting rather than one of actuarial science.

---

[27] The use of conservative mortality and interest assumptions gives a margin for expenses or for profits upon which some companies rely to a degree in fixing their final premium rates.

[28] The terms gross and net as used here must be distinguished from the same terms as applied to (1) participating premiums before and after dividends or (2) premiums including and excluding commissions.

[29] Valuation net premiums are discussed in Chapter 27. The valuation net premium may or may not be the same as the net premium to which the loading is added. It is the same only if identical mortality and interest assumptions are used in both computations. See Appendix B to Chapter 25 for a simple illustration of a direct computation of a gross premium.

[30] As will become clear later (Chapter 27), practical difficulties are involved in achieving this objective under level premium plans.

[31] As will be seen later, in participating insurance some of these objectives are shifted in part to the dividend scale and handled only in a rough way in the loading formula.

ACQUISITION COSTS. By far the largest of all expenses to be considered are those in connection with putting new business on the books. For example, on a $1,000 policy issued at age 25, total costs of acquisition might be $20 while costs in connection with the administration of the policy after the first year may drop to $2.50 a year. Acquisition costs could be loaded onto the premium in the year incurred. However, this approach would involve a premium differential, making the premium for the first year substantially higher than subsequent premiums. While such a plan is used occasionally, particularly in mutual assessment and some health insurance policies, it is usually not considered good practice. Companies do not want to emphasize the high acquisition cost nor does the public like to pay heavier first year premiums. Hence costs of acquisition are amortized over the total premium paying period, and a level amount is added to the net premium each year. The amount by which the first-year reserve exceeds the amount of premium left after acquisition costs and death claims are paid is charged against surplus. The surplus account is replenished from subsequent premiums.

GENERAL OVERHEAD LOADING. All expenses designated as general overhead in any type of business—clerical salaries, furniture and fixtures, rent, management salaries, and so on—must be considered. The allocation of these costs is unaffected by the size of the premium, probably little affected by the face amount of the policy, but is most likely affected by the number of policies.

LOADING FOR CONTINGENCY FUNDS. Once a level premium legal reserve policy has been issued, the premium cannot be changed, even should unforeseen contingencies make the premium rate in the policy inadequate. Assessment insurance plans can take care of such contingencies, theoretically, by levying an extra charge against the policyholders. Legal reserve companies, however, allow for the possibility of increased expense or decreased earnings by establishing various contingency funds.

The amount of loading for contingency funds will vary in relation to the type of policy and the amount at risk—i.e., the excess of the face amount of the policy over the policy reserve.

IMMEDIATE PAYMENT OF DEATH CLAIMS. One of the items which might be considered in arriving at the gross premium is a charge to offset the loss resulting from the payment of death claims throughout the year rather than at the end of the year as assumed in the net premium computation.

Relying on large numbers, it is safe to assume that death payments will be reasonably uniform during the year, and therefore that on the average all death claims will be paid six months before the end of the year, or about six months earlier than is assumed in calculating net premiums. This means that in any year there will be a loss to the company of approximately one half of one year's interest on the funds used to pay mortality costs for that year. Allowance may be made for this loss through an expense loading or by using continuous functions in the computation of the net premium which recognize conditions closer to reality.

Methods of Loading. In discussing acquisition costs, contingency funds, and general overhead loading, three classifications into which expenses of operation may fall have been considered. These are: (1) Expenses which vary with the size of the premium. These include, for example, agents' commissions, agency expenses, and premium taxes. (2) Expenses which to some degree vary with the face amount of the policy. Examples here can be found in underwriting cost. Insurers spend more money obtaining information to underwrite large policies than they do to underwrite small ones. Also, it frequently costs more to service holders of large policies because they may require special settlement agreements, beneficiary arrangements, and other estate planning services. (3) Expenses which are constant regardless of the size of the premium or the face amount of the policy. Examples are record keeping, premium administration, claims administration, and general overhead. The more policies the insurer has in force, the less will be the constant expense per policy.

The first step in loading is to determine into which of the three categories each type of expense falls.[32]

Obviously, it would be inequitable to lump all operating expenses and divide by the number of policies in force, because each policy does not contribute equally to company expenses. Just so, it would be inequitable to assess all loading in proportion to the size of the premium or the face amount of the policy. Hence, the system of loading used by any one company is a combination of a percentage of premium, percentage of face amount, and a fixed amount per policy. Therefore, gross premium rates per $1,000 usually will vary with the size of the policy.

Companies, for example, may achieve a graded premium scale by charging a higher premium per $1,000 for policies $5,000 and below; a lower premium per $1,000 for policies between $5,000 and $10,000; and still lower premiums per $1,000 for policies between $10,000 and $20,000, $20,000 and $25,000, $25,000 and $50,000, and over $50,000. Other companies issue special policies at lower premium rates but require a high minimum amount of insurance. Still other companies have a rate structure which charges less and less for each additional $1,000 of insurance up to a given maximum. The most common method of grading premiums by amounts of insurance is to charge a flat policy fee. For example, the insurer may charge a flat fee of $10 per policy regardless of its size, or it might charge a flat fee of $2 per $1,000 of insurance but in no event more than $10 a policy. The policy fee usually is set below that amount necessary to

---

[32] Policies of large amounts may be separated and allocated a reduced loading percentage.

cover the fixed expense per policy so as not to overburden the purchasers of policies of small amounts.

Because graded premiums do not adequately reflect the constant expense per policy, it is necessaary to determine the average amount written per policy and to load the premium accordingly. For example, if a given fixed cost per policy is $6.30 and the average amount of insurance per policy is $9,000, then a loading of $0.70 per $1,000 would be sufficient to meet this cost assuming that the premiums are in no way graded by the size of the policy. Purchasers of smaller policies will be paying less than their share, whereas purchasers of larger policies will be paying more than their share. To the extent that premiums are graded by the size of the policy, these inequities are reduced.

In loading systems, the same percentage of premium or the same percentage of the policy amount cannot be used for all ages and still achieve the degree of equity desired without making suitable adjustments through the dividend formulas.[33] For example, based on 1958 CSO at $2\frac{1}{2}$ percent, the net level premium for $1,000 continuous premium whole life insurance issued at age 20 is $10.75. At age 50 it is $32.38. A 25 percent loading based on premiums would produce about $2.69 at issue age 20, and about $8.09 at issue age 50. Since some of the expenses do not vary with the size of the premium, if $2.69 is adequate for the policy issued at age 20, then $8.09 must be excessive for the policy issued at age 50. A loading of $5 per $1,000 of insurance would produce an excessive amount at age 20 if it is adequate for age 60.

The same percentages also cannot be used for all plans and achieve the desired degree of equity. At age 20 the net level premium for a 20-payment whole life policy figured on the basis of 1958 CSO at $2\frac{1}{2}$ percent is $19.48 per $1,000. A loading of 24 percent of this amount would produce $4.87 compared to $2.69 for the continuous premium whole life policy. If the $2.69 is adequate, then the $4.87 would be excessive because the expenses of these two policies do not bear the same relationship to their premiums. A "modified percentage" plan of loading has been developed to help achieve equity. A common plan is to load the continuous premium whole life with 25 percent of its net premium but to load the limited payment whole life policy with $12\frac{1}{2}$ percent of its net premium plus $12\frac{1}{2}$ percent of the net premium for a continuous premium whole life policy issued at the same age.[34]

A flat amount per $1,000 of insurance may be used along with the modified percentage loading plan to help achieve some semblance of equity

---

[33] Generally, comparatively simple formulas are used in setting the loading on participating policies since the dividend scale is relied upon to produce the necessary equity. Dividend formulas are discussed in Chapter 27.

[34] The endowment may be loaded with $6\frac{1}{4}$ percent of its net premium, $6\frac{1}{4}$ percent of the net premium for a limited payment life issued at the same age for the same premium payment period, and $12\frac{1}{2}$ percent of the premium for the continuous premium whole life issued at the same age.

between the loading at different ages of issue. A combination of both a fixed percentage of the premium and a flat amount per $1,000 would to some extent counteract the bias inherent in each method.[35] Thus, the foregoing percentages could be reduced and a flat amount of several dollars per $1,000 of insurance could be added.

Term insurance presents a special loading problem. An additional loading is usually charged to take care of the initial adverse selection, and to cover the adverse selection resulting from renewal and conversion privileges.

As may be expected, the system of loading used by any one company will usually vary from that of other companies,[36] and even the system of loading used by any given company for the calculation of present rates may not be the same as was used to calculate rates in the past, nor the same as may be used to calculate rates in the future.

Nonparticipating Policies. That there is a difference between the problems involved in determining the loading for participating policies and those involved in calculating the loading for nonparticipating policies is apparent. The company must attempt to figure the expenses more accurately and equitably for nonparticipating policies because there is no way to make adjustments later. However, in participating policies, unless inequities and inadequacies in loading are far more serious than even mediocre actuarial ability might produce, these inequities and inadequacies can be adjusted by varying the dividend scale.

The gross premium for nonparticipating policies must be sufficient to pay claims and expenses, to build contingency reserves, and to provide a profit; but it must be low enough to allow the company to compete successfully in the marketplace. This means that the actuary must attempt to achieve preciseness in his projections of mortality, interest, and expense rates. For nonparticipating insurance, more realistic assumptions are necessary for premium computations than are prescribed for minimum reserves.[37] In fixing these assumptions the actuary either can use what he considers the most likely experience and then add a profit factor or he can use slightly more conservative assumptions (but less conservative than those used in participating insurance) and let the profit arise from achieving better than projected results.

---

[35] If the aggregate loading is to be adequate, then one based on a given percentage of premium would yield an excessive amount at the high issue ages and an inadequate amount of the low issue ages. Conversely, one based on a flat amount per $1,000 would yield an excessive amount at the low issue ages and an inadequate amount at the high ages of issue. These observations already have been demonstrated.

[36] Some companies may load their premiums excessively to produce a surplus for high policy dividends, whereas others will prefer to keep their premiums low even if this means their dividends will not appear competitive. These latter companies prefer to make their premiums more attractive than their dividends.

[37] It is because of this fact that the problem of deficiency reserves (discussed in footnote 15) arose.

The actuary, in selecting his mortality assumptions, may use the data compiled by the Society of Actuaries or that of his own company (if his company is large enough to produce credible experience). Of course, he can use some combination of the two. Select, rather than ultimate, tables are used by some actuaries, since they more nearly reflect actual experiences. With death rates declining, mortality tables based on current experience will become obsolete before the expiration of many of the policies that were priced on the basis of these tables. This suggests that a projection scale to adjust for expected mortality improvements would be necessary to achieve rate equity between new and old policies. However, projection scales are not used in life insurance rating.

What is a realistic interest assumption for the future? This is, in fact, an impossible question. One would have to be psychic to predict accurately the course of future interest rates over the duration of a life insurance policy. But since aggregate results are significantly affected by small changes in the interest rate,[38] the actuary is forced to answer the above question. In doing so, he tends to be conservative, but not as conservative for nonparticipating as for participating insurance.

Estimating future expenses connected with a policy is not an easy problem, either. Premium tax rates can be changed by state legislatures; alterations can be made in the federal income tax provisions and rates;[39] and changes in the general price level can affect the cost of general overhead expenses.

After the actuary has decided on his mortality, interest, and expense assumptions, the task of computing the gross premium becomes one of applying a formula.[40] Under the formula the nonparticipating gross single premium[41] is the sum of the present value of projected future claims and the present value of expenses to be incurred, both figured at the policy issue date. How to compute these values and how to translate them into level premiums are the subject of Chapter 25.

Expense Ratios.   Often an attempt is made, especially in competitive

---

[38] Long-run results are more sensitive to a miscalculation of interest rates than to an equal miscalculation of mortality rates because, as a policy continues in force, its investment factor becomes increasingly more important and its mortality factor increasingly less important.

[39] Allowance for federal income taxes usually is made in the interest assumptions rather than in the expense loading, the interest assumptions being net after taxes.

[40] Some formulas allow for an additional factor: lapse rates (see the appendix to this chapter). Expenses are higher in the first year than in any other year. However, the expense loading is spread on a level basis over the entire premium paying period. If a policyholder terminates his policy, the expenses incurred by that policy may have exceeded the amount of expense money collected to offset them. Only through the continuation of the policy and the payment of its premium will the company recover its high first-year expenses. The withdrawal rate is an allowance to offset the loss occasioned by early withdrawal. Many companies handle the withdrawal problem through their nonforfeiture valuation formula. Nonforfeiture valuation is discussed in Chapter 27.

[41] The full premium including the loading.

selling, to use comparisons between the expense ratios of different companies to indicate economy of operation. The expense ratio is essentially a relationship between operating expenses and premiums. Comparisons imply that if the ratio of expenses to total premiums is low, economy of operation is indicated.

Such comparisons are invalid because they may contain figures arrived at on such differing bases as to render them useless for the purpose of comparing operating economy. Moreover, since acquisition costs are such a large part of loading, the company writing a large amount of new business—generally a desirable development, since the operation of the insurance principle depends upon the constant addition of new exposure units—will tend to show a higher percentage of incurred expenses to total premiums than will the company writing a small volume of new business.

Expense ratios indicate the degree of accuracy with which the company has estimated its expenses, not the economy of operation. For example, if two companies had the same expenses and one used a higher estimate for loading, that company would have a lower expense ratio, assuming all other elements in the rate calculation were the same.

Appendix to Chapter 24
Lapse Rates

In Chapter 23, nine selection factors for underwriting the insurance were discussed: (1) age, (2) sex, (3) plan of insurance, (4) occupation, (5) residence, (6) race and nationality, (7) family and personal history, (8) physical condition and physique, and (9) financial condition. All of these factors except the financial condition of the insured are discussed solely in terms of their effect on the mortality rate to which the insured is subject. The financial condition of the insured is discussed also in terms of exposure to high lapse rates.

Lapse Rates as a Tool in Rate Making. When gross premiums are computed independently of net premiums, separate attention is likely to be given to lapse rates. Lapse rates and mortality rates taken together produce a termination rate which is used to project the number of premiums the insurer is likely to collect at each premium payment period. (Policyholders who die or who lapse their policies pay no more premiums.) Taken separately, mortality rates project the obligations the insurer is likely to incur because of death claims and lapse rates project the obligations the insurer is likely to incur because of surrender payments to lapsed policyholders.

Lapse rates are considered to be important to the pricing of life insurance.[1]

In Chapter 24, three conventional tools of rate making are discussed—mortality, interest, and expense. Mortality and interest assumptions are necessary in calculating the net premium, while the expense factors are added to the net premium to determine the gross premium.

A simplified method of computing gross premiums is discussed in Appendix B of Chapter 25. Under the conventional method, expenses are segregated into broad classifications, one of which is acquisition costs. In the simplified method, expenses are further segregated into an item called lapse expenses.

Lapse Rates Defined.   A lapse is any termination of a policy prior to the death of the insured or the maturity of the policy. When a lapse takes place within the early policy years, before the cost of issuing the policy can be recovered from the premium payments, this unfunded cost must be apportioned to the remaining or to future policyholders.

Lapse rates vary considerably among life insurance companies. "Each company's rate is influenced by many factors, including the types of policies written and the ratio of new policies to older ones in force with the company."[2] Since there is no standardized formula for defining lapse rates, these rates may differ not only among insurers as to experience but also as to how the lapse rate is formulated. Nevertheless, some generalizations can be made about lapse rates. They may be expressed in terms of premium volume, number of policies in force, or the face amount of insurance in force. They can be expressed in terms of the probability of withdrawal during successive policy years in tabular form similar to mortality tables. Linton's A Table reproduced below is an example of one such table.[3]

The four parts of the Linton Lapse Table are: policy year, death rate, withdrawal rate, and total termination rate. The policy year is the number of years that the policy has been in force. The death rates are those of the American Men Select Mortality Table, using age 40 as the entry age. The withdrawal rates are calculated by dividing the total number of policies per block of business (policies of a given type issued in the same year to insureds of the same age and insurability classification) that are voluntarily terminated during each policy year by the number of policies that persist throughout that particular policy year.

Some generalizations can be observed from Linton's A Table, particularly about the differences in mortality and lapse rates. While mortality is

[1] Charles F. B. Richardson and John M. Hartwell, "Lapse Rates," *Transactions of the Society of Actuaries,* Vol. III (Chicago: University of Chicago Press, 1951), pp. 338–74, and Joseph M. Belth, "The Impact of Lapse Rates on Life Insurance Prices," *Journal of Risk and Insurance,* Vol. XXXV, No. 1 (March, 1968), pp. 17–34.

[2] Institute of Life Insurance, *Life Insurance Fact Book, 1968,* p. 50.

[3] M. A. Linton, "Return under Agency Contracts," *Record of the American Institute of Actuaries,* Vol. XIII (1924), p. 287.

Linton's A Table

Policy Year (1)	Death Rate (issued at age 40) (2)	Withdrawal Rate (3)	Total Termination Rate (4)
1	0.004	0.100	0.104
2	.005	.060	.065
3	.006	.050	.056
4	.006	.044	.050
5	.007	.040	.047
6	.008	.036	.044
7	.009	.032	.041
8	.009	.029	.038
9	.010	.027	.037
10	.011	.025	.036
11	.012	.024	.036
12	.013	.023	.036
13	.014	.022	.036
14	.015	.021	.036
15	.016	.020	.036
16	.017	.020	.037
17	.019	.020	.039
18	.021	.020	.041
19	.023	.020	.043
20	...	...	...

a function of age and generally increases as the age of the insured increases, the lapse rate is a function of the policy year and generally decreases as the number of policy years increase.

Both mortality and lapse rates could be tabulated in terms of factors other than age or policy years. They can be related to income, occupation, or demographic region of the insured; amount or frequency of premium payment; plan of insurance; whether policy loans are outstanding; and how long the agent who wrote the policies has been in the life insurance business.[4]

History of Lapse Studies. Lapse rates have been of major concern to life insurance companies for many years. High lapse rates, especially during the early years of the life insurance business in the United States, resulted in heavy losses to the insurers.

At the eighth annual meeting of the American Life Convention in August of 1913, an actuary, I. Smith Homans, delivered a paper on "Waste From Lapsation" in which he reported his findings from one of the first statistical studies on lapsation in the United States.[5] This paper

---

[4] Richardson and Hartwell, *op. cit.*

[5] Carlyle Buley, *The American Life Convention 1906–1952,* Vol. I (New York: Appleton-Century-Crofts, Inc., 1953), p. 412.

had the effect of generating greater interest in the problem of lapsation. The following year, the American Institute of Actuaries had a discussion on methods of improving persistency and sought to develop an equitable policy on reinstatement.[6]

By the 1920's the focus on the problem of lapsation was transferred to the agent. The interest turned to the events which precede and accompany the sale. One of the most extensive lapsation studies during this era was undertaken by M. A. Linton.[7] He attempted to associate lapsation with the type of agent and the experience of the agent.

By 1929, the insurance industry knew that economic conditions had an effect on voluntary terminations. This conclusion became more apparent throughout the thirties. By the end of the depression a large number of lapsation studies had been carried out. These studies attempted to link lapse rates with such determinants as: income, occupation, age, sex, premium payment, and amounts of insurance.[8]

Not until 1949 was there any analysis measuring the interaction of the various factors affecting voluntary termination.[9]

The most thorough lapsation study conducted in the fifties was Charles F. B. Richardson and John M. Hartwell's study of "Lapse Rates" reported in Vol. III of the *Transactions of the Society of Actuaries*, 1951. They reviewed the complete history of lapse studies and arrived at the conclusion that "the efforts to prevent early lapsation have produced little gain, even though much more is known about the characteristics of good quality business."[10]

In the era of the sixties persistency studies have continued but not until 1967 did anyone publish an illustration of a method of gross premium calculation that incorporates lapsation into the tools of rate making.[11] A discussion of this method appears in Appendix B of Chapter 25.

---

[6] American Institute of Actuaries, "Methods for Conserving Business," *Record of the American Institute of Actuaries,* Vol. III, p. 284.

[7] Linton, *op. cit.,* pp. 283–319.

[8] Life Insurance Sales Research Bureau (now Life Insurance Agency Management Association), *Reports,* Committee on Persistent Business; Conservation Rewards, Conservation Records, Terminations, Persistency, and Agents' Compensation.

[9] Life Insurance Agency Management Association, *Reports:* "Persistency, 1942–1947," and "The Persistency Rates, 1949."

[10] Richardson and Hartwell, *op. cit.,* p. 340.

[11] Joseph M. Belth, "Calculation of Life Insurance Gross Premiums: A Suggested Modification of the Traditional Textbook Approach," *Journal of Risk and Insurance,* Vol. XXXIV, No. 3 (September, 1967), pp. 385–96.

25

Computation of Premiums

Although the vast majority of life insurance policies are purchased on a level premium basis, computation of a premuim rate begins with the calculation of the net single premium. The net annual level premium is then computed from the net single premium. The two must be mathematically equivalent.

This chapter first summarizes the steps involved in calculating the net single premium. Then these steps are applied to the computation of single premiums for three basic forms of life insurance policies and for three basic forms of annuities. Next the procedure for converting single premiums into level premiums is explained. Finally, the computation of premiums for health insurance is discussed.

The chapter includes two appendixes, one to explain the use of commutation symbols and algebraic formulas for computing net premiums and the other to explain the computation of a gross premium by use of a linear algebraic equation.

1. TWO ASSUMPTIONS

In this chapter, two assumptions are made in the computation of premium rates for life insurance: (1) premiums are paid at the beginning of the year; (2) claims are paid at the end of the year.

The first assumption is realistic because the first premium must be paid before the policy goes into force; and unless each of the following premiums is paid when due (or within the grace period), the policy will not continue as originally written, but instead will lapse without value or be placed on one of the nonforfeiture options. Premiums paid more frequently than annually require special treatment.[1]

---

[1] A third assumption must be made for premiums paid more frequently than annually, if, as is the usual case, the balance of the annual premium is not required should death occur after the payment of one monthly or quarterly premium. This assumption is that the monthly deaths will be one twelfth of the projected annual deaths. This assumption is not realistic because projected death rates rise with age on a continuous basis. They increase monthly as well as yearly.

The assumption that claims will be paid at the end of the year, however, does not reflect the true state of affairs. Insurance companies pay their claims promptly upon completion of the necessary forms. They realize that death creates costs that must be paid before the end of the policy year, and that widows and orphans are not interested in fasting for the sake of simplifying actuarial computations. Nevertheless, the assumption is used to simplify calculations. How the actuary compensates for this assumption was discussed in Chapter 24.

2. NET SINGLE PREMIUM

The net single premium for any life insurance policy is the equivalent of the present value of the projected future claims under the policy based on given interest and mortality assumptions. For example, if 1,000 people of a given age are insured for $1,000 each for a period of five years and the projected deaths are 10 in the first year, 11 in the second, 12 in the third, 13 in the fourth, and 14 in the fifth year, a fund of $55,520 at the beginning of the period (assuming a 2½ percent interest return) will be just enough to meet all claims projected during the term of the agreement. The cost for each of the 1,000 participants will be $55.52 per policy ($55,520 ÷ 1,000).

It works out as follows: The $55,520 collected in advance will earn $1,388 during the first year. At the end of the year a total of $10,000 will be paid in death claims, leaving $46,908 to be invested throughout the second year.[2] This amount earns $1,173. After paying $11,000 in claims, $37,081 is available for investment the third year, and earns $927. Claim payments of $12,000 at the end of that year leave $26,008 to earn $650 interest during the fourth year. After subtracting $13,000 for claims, $13,658 is available to earn interest during the fifth year. This fund, invested at 2½ percent, will amount to $14,000 at the end of the year, which is the exact amount needed to pay projected claims at that time.

The question now is how this figure of $55.52 per policy was computed? In Chapter 24 the use of mortality tables and interest assumptions in rate making was described. The application of these mortality tables and interest assumptions to specific problems can now be reviewed. The mortality assumptions to be used in the following pages are those contained in the 1958 CSO Table reproduced on page 688. Remember that in practice, however, companies may use mortality assumptions that are more in line with their own experience. Nevertheless, the use of the 1958 CSO assumption here does serve to illustrate the principle involved. The interest assumption used in this chapter is 2½ percent. Here again, companies vary

---

[2] Remember the assumption that premiums are paid in advance and claims are paid at the end of the year.

as to their interest assumptions, but the assumption used here is sufficient to illustrate the principle involved.

Steps in Calculating the Net Single Premium.   To calculate a net single premium, the actuary needs to know (1) the plan of insurance, (2) the mortality table to be used, and (3) the rate of interest to be used.[3] With this information, eight steps are involved in computing a net single premium.

Step 1. Determine what constitutes a claim. Two types of contingencies can be covered: the contingency of survival and the contingency of death. The annuity is an example of coverage for the contingency of survival, for under annuity contracts the insurer is obligated to pay only as long as the insured lives.[4] Term insurance is an example of coverage for the contingency of death, for under a term insurance contract the insurer is obligated to pay only if the insured dies during the term of years for which the policy is written. The endowment policy is an example of a combination of both survival and death claims.

Step 2. Determine when claims are assumed to be paid. Claims may be paid at the beginning of the year, at the end of the year, or at any time during the year. Under life insurance policies, claims are paid as incurred, but the assumption is made that they are paid at the end of the year.[5] Under an annuity contract, claims are paid at the end of each income period if the annuity is an ordinary annuity, and at the beginning of each income period if it is an annuity due.

Step 3. Find (from "number living" column of the mortality table) the number living at the issue age. In computing the premium, it is assumed that the number issued is the number living as shown on the mortality table for the age at which the policy is issued.

Step 4. Determine the probable number of claims per year, and multiply the figure for each year by $1,000. If the number insured is assumed to be the number living at the age of entry, then the number of death claims each year must be found in the deaths per year column for that year in the mortality table and for each succeeding year within the policy period. The number of living claims (if the policy covers that contingency) will be the figure in the number living column of the mortality table for the year or years involved.

Step 5. Determine the years of interest involved, and find the present value factor applicable for each of these years. The calculation here de-

---

[3] He would also need to know if death benefits are assumed to be payable at the end of the year of death or at the date of death. As previously mentioned, this discussion assumes that the benefits are payable at the end of the year of death.

[4] The fact that some annuities have a cash or installment value after death does not alter this statement, as will become apparent in the calculation of an annuity rate.

[5] Some actuaries compute premiums on the basis that claims are paid as incurred. This calls for the assumption that deaths, on the average, occur in the middle of the year, and that claims, therefore, are paid six months before the end of the year.

pends on the time at which claims are to be paid. If they are to be paid at the end of the year, then the funds for the first-year claims will earn one year's interest; those for the second year will earn two years' interest, and so forth. If claims are to be paid at the beginning of the year, funds for first-year claims will earn no interest; for the second year's claims, one year's interest; and so on. The present value factors can be found in a present value table for the interest rate assumed.

Step 6. Calculate the present value of total claim payments for each year during the period of coverage. Multiply the amount of the claims for each year by the present value factor for that year. For instance, the value of the claims at the end of the first year will be multiplied by the present value factor for one year; the amount of the second-year claims will be multiplied by the present value factor for two years, and so forth.

Step 7. Calculate the present value of all future claims. The computation here is merely the sum of the present values of claims for each of the years insured, as computed in Step 6.

Step 8. Calculate the net single premium. The net single premium is the present value of all future claims divided by the number living at the age of entry.

How each of these eight steps is used in calculating the net single premium for term, whole life and endowment insurance policies and for several types of annuity policies can now be illustrated.

The Net Single Premium for Term Insurance. The net single premium for a $1,000 five-year term policy issued at age 25 is calculated as follows:

1. What constitutes a claim? Death.

2. When are claims assumed to be paid? Although they are paid during the year, they are assumed to be paid at the end of the year.

3. How many are living at issue age? 9,575,636 (Number living at age 25).

4. What is the probable amount of claims per year?

Age (a)	Number of Claims (b)	Amount of Insurance (c)	Amount of Claims (b × c)
25	18,481	$1,000	$18,481,000
26	18,732	1,000	18,732,000
27	18,981	1,000	18,981,000
28	19,324	1,000	19,324,000
29	19,760	1,000	19,760,000

5. How many years of interest are involved? Since the assumption is that claims are paid at the end of the year, the following are the number of years of interest: age 25, 1 year; age 26, 2 years; age 27, 3 years; age 28, 4 years; age 29, 5 years.

The present value factors for each of the number of years involved are: 1 year, 0.97561; 2 years, 0.95181; 3 years, 0.92860; 4 years, 0.90595, 5 years, 0.88385.

6. What is the present value of the claims for each year?

Age (a)	Amount of Claims (b)	Years of Interest (c)	Present Value of 1 (d)	Present Value of Claims (b × d)
25	$18,481,000	1	0.97561	$18,030,248
26	18,732,000	2	.95181	17,829,305
27	18,981,000	3	.92860	17,625,757
28	19,324,000	4	.90595	17,506,578
29	19,760,000	5	.88385	17,464,876
				$88,456,764

7. What is the present value of all future claims? $88,456,764.

8. What is the net single premium of a five-year term issued at age 25? The total probable claims of $88,456,765 are divided by 9,575,636—the number living at age 25.

$$\$88,456,764 \div 9,575,636 = \$9.24.$$

Whole Life Policies. A whole life policy is essentially a term policy which covers for the life of the insured rather than for a limited period. To abbreviate the illustration, the net single premium for a $1,000 whole life policy issued at age 92 will be calculated.

1. What constitutes a claim? Death.

2. When are claims assumed to be paid? They are assumed to be paid at the end of the year.

3. How many are living at issue age? 272,552 (Number living at age 92).

4. What is the amount of claims per year?

Age (a)	Number of Claims (b)	Amount of Insurance (c)	Amount of Claims (b × c)
92	72,480	$1,000	$72,480,000
93	57,881	1,000	57,881,000
94	45,026	1,000	45,026,000
95	34,128	1,000	34,128,000
96	25,250	1,000	25,250,000
97	18,456	1,000	18,456,000
98	12,916	1,000	12,916,000
99	6,415	1,000	6,415,000

5. How many years of interest are involved? The years of interest are shown in Step 6 for ages 92 through 99, the year when all members of the group are assumed to be dead.

6. What is the present value of claims per year?

Age (a)	Amount of Claims (b)	Years of Interest (c)	Present Value of 1 (d)	Present Value of Claims (b × d)
92	$72,480,000	1	0.97561	$ 70,712,213
93	57,881,000	2	.95181	55,091,715
94	45,026,000	3	.92860	41,811,144
95	34,128,000	4	.90595	30,918,262
96	25,250,000	5	.88385	22,317,213
97	18,456,000	6	.86230	15,914,609
98	12,916,000	7	.84127	10,865,843
99	6,415,000	8	.82075	5,265,111
				$252,896,110

7. What is the present value of all future claims? $252,896,110.

8. What is the net single premium for a whole life policy issued at age 92? The total probable claims of $252,896,110 are divided by 272,552—the number living at age 92.

$$\$252,896,110 \div 272,552 = \$927.88.$$

A more realistic whole life policy would be one issued at age 25 rather than at age 92. So that this figure will be available for use in computing a net level premium, the following is an abbreviated table showing the calculations of a net single premium for a whole life issued at age 25.

Age	Amount of Claims	Years of Interest	Present Value of 1	Present Value of Claims
25	$18,481,000	1	0.97561	$18,030,248
26	18,732,000	2	.95181	17,829,305
27	18,981,000	3	.92860	17,625,757
28	19,324,000	4	.90595	17,506,578
29	19,760,000	5	.88385	17,464,876
95	$34,128,000	71	0.17322	5,911,652
96	25,250,000	72	.16900	4,267,250
97	18,456,000	73	.16487	3,042,841
98	12,916,000	74	.16085	2,077,539
99	6,415,000	75	.15693	1,006,706
				$325,236,476,740

Here the present value of future claims would be $325,236,476,740, which, divided by 9,575,636, equals $339.65, the net single premium for a whole life issued at age 25.

Endowment Policies. The net single premium for a $1,000 endowment at 65 issued at age 55 is computed as follows:

1. What constitutes a claim? Claims are paid to those dying before age 65 and to those living at age 65.

2. When are claims assumed to be paid? They are assumed to be paid at the end of the year. The living claims are paid at the end of the endowment period.[6]

3. How many are living at issue age? 754,191 (Number living at age 55).

4. What is the amount of claims per year?

Age	Number of Claims	Amount of Insurance	Amount of Claims
55	108,307	$1,000	$ 108,307,000
56	116,849	1,000	116,849,000
57	125,970	1,000	125,970,000
58	135,663	1,000	135,663,000
59	145,830	1,000	145,830,000
60	156,592	1,000	156,592,000
61	167,736	1,000	167,736,000
62	179,271	1,000	179,271,000
63	191,174	1,000	191,174,000
64	203,394	1,000	203,394,000
65	6,800,531	1,000	6,800,531,000

5. How many years of interest are involved? The years of interest are as shown in Step 6; since the living claims at age 65 are paid at the beginning of the year, there will be no interest earned during that year. Therefore, the same present value factor is used for the death claims paid at the end of age 64 and the living claims paid at the beginning of age 65.

6. What is the present value of the claims for each year?

Age (a)	Amount of Claims (b)	Years of Interest (c)	Present Value of 1 (d)	Present Value of Claims (b × d)
55	$ 108,307,000	1	0.97561	$ 105,665,392
56	116,849,000	2	.95181	111,218,047
57	125,970,000	3	.92860	116,975,742
58	135,663,000	4	.90595	122,903,895
59	145,830,000	5	.88385	128,891,846
60	156,592,000	6	.86230	135,029,282
61	167,736,000	7	.84127	141,111,265
62	179,271,000	8	.82075	147,136,673
63	191,174,000	9	.80073	153,078,757
64	203,394,000	10	.78120	158,891,393
65	6,800,531,000	10	.78120	5,312,574,817
				$6,633,477,109

[6] Under endowment at age 65 policies, the endowment benefit generally is payable to those who are living on the anniversary of the policy on which the insured's age, at nearest birthday, is 65. If the policy is a 20-year endowment, for example, the living claims are paid to those living at the end of 20 years (the beginning of the 21st year).

7. What is the present value of all future claims? $6,633,477,109.

8. What is the net single premium for an endowment at age 65, issued at age 55? The total probable claims of $6,633,477,109 are divided by 8,331,317—the number living at age 55.

$$\$6,633,477,109 \div 8,331,317 = \$796.21.$$

Life Annuity Five Years Certain. The net single premium for a $1,000 life annuity, five years certain, issued at age 90,[7] is computed as follows:[8]

1. What constitutes a claim? Claims are paid annually for five years dead or alive and thereafter for each year as long as the annuitant is alive at the end of the year.

2. When are claims paid? At the end of the year.

3. How many are living at issue age? 468,174.

4. What is the amount of claims per year?[9]

Age	Number of Claims	Amount of Annuity	Amount of Claims
90	468,174	$1,000	$468,174,000
91	468,174	1,000	468,174,000
92	468,174	1,000	468,174,000
93	468,174	1,000	468,174,000
94	468,174	1,000	468,174,000
95	63,037	1,000	63,037,000
96	37,787	1,000	37,787,000
97	19,331	1,000	19,331,000
98	6,415	1,000	6,415,000

5. How many years of interest are involved? Since claims are paid at the end of the year, the years of interest involved are those shown in tabular matter for Step 6.

6. What is the present value of claims for each year?

Age	Amount of Claims	Years of Interest	Present Value of 1	Present Value of Claims
90	$468,174,000	1	0.97561	$ 456,755,236
91	468,174,000	2	.95181	445,612,695
92	468,174,000	3	.92860	434,746,376
93	468,174,000	4	.90595	424,142,235
94	468,174,000	5	.88385	413,795,590
95	63,037,000	6	.86230	54,356,805
96	37,787,000	7	.84127	31,789,069
97	19,331,000	8	.82075	15,865,918
98	6,415,000	9	.80073	5,136,683
				$2,282,200,607

7. What is the present value of all future claims? $2,282,200,607.

8. What is the net single premium for a life annuity, five years certain,

---

[7] This unrealistic age of issue is assumed for purposes of simplicity, i.e., to reduce the number of calculations involved.

[8] The 1958 CSO Table will be used in this and other annuity illustrations, although more realistic results would be obtained by using an annuity mortality table. Nevertheless, the principle is the same regardless of the table used.

[9] The full number buying the policy (468,174) will be paid claims during the first five years; only those living thereafter will continue to be paid claims.

issued at age 90? The total probable claims of $2,282,200,607 are divided by 468,174—the number living at age 90.

$$\$2,282,200,607 \div 468,174 = \$4,874.68.$$

3. NET LEVEL PREMIUMS

Few people are able to purchase life insurance on a single premium basis, and even fewer are willing to do so. They want to budget their insurance into a series of annual payments, either for life or for a limited number of years. Broadly speaking, two plans are available for the purchase of life insurance on an annual premium basis: (1) yearly renewable term insurance and (2) the level premium plan.

Yearly Renewable Term Plan. Under the yearly renewable term plan, the insured pays a single premium for one year of insurance and has the right to renew the policy without proving insurability for additional one-year periods at the premium applicable for the age of renewal. The premium increases each year with the increase in the rate of mortality. The net premium for this policy (sometimes called the net natural premium) is the mortality cost in accordance with the mortality table used for each year, discounted for one year. Accordingly, the net premiums each year for a yearly renewable term policy of $1,000 issued at age 25 and renewable for five years, would be:

First year	$1.93 × 0.97561 =	$1.88
Second year	1.96 × 0.97561 =	1.91
Third year	1.99 × 0.97561 =	1.94
Fourth year	2.03 × 0.97561 =	1.98
Fifth year	2.08 × 0.97561 =	2.03

If this were renewed for 30 years, the rate would rise to $11.90 × 0.97561, or $11.61 per $1,000, in the 30th year. The one-year discount factor is used in each computation because, under the yearly renewable term plan, only the cost of one-year term insurance is paid each year. Because the premium is paid at the beginning of the year and claims are assumed to be paid at the end of the year, one year's discount is involved each year.

The vast majority of the insuring public not only does not like to pay for its insurance with a large single premium, it also does not like premiums that increase each year. Thus, a man age 25 seeking coverage for the whole of life probably would prefer a net annual level premium rather than a net single premium of $339.65 or a net premium starting at $1.88 and progressing to, perhaps, a prohibitive level. For example, the net yearly renewable term premium at age 70 is nearly 26 times that at age 25.

Level Annual Premium Plan. The level annual premium plan is a method by which premiums are spread evenly on an annual basis over the duration of the policy or over a limited number of years.

A division of the net single premium by the number of years over which the premium is to be paid will not produce a sufficient net level annual premium. A simple division of this type ignores the two important factors in rate making: interest and mortality.

In computing the net single premium, it is assumed that the company collects the entire premium in advance and earns interest on it until the funds are used to pay claims, one, two, three, four, and more years hence. Under the level annual premium plan, only part of the full net single premium is collected in advance. Consequently, there will be a substantial loss in interest on the unpaid portion. Allowance must be made in level annual premium computations to offset this loss.

The net single premium computation also assumes that the full net single premium is paid by everyone. However, the level annual premium is collected only from those who are alive on each succeeding premium due date. Under this plan, death cancels the obligation to pay further premiums. Therefore, the level annual premium must compensate for the possible cancellation of premium obligations.

How can an allowance for the loss of interest and premiums be computed? A level premium can be looked on as being an annuity payable to the company by the policyholder. The premium payments for a 20-year term or for a 20-pay life is a temporary life annuity for 20 years, whereas the net level premium for a continuous premium whole life policy is a whole life annuity, both payable by the policyholder to the company.

Use of the Annuity Due in Computing the Net Level Annual Premium. Since premiums are paid at the beginning of the year[10] the net level premium is an annuity due. An annuity due, it will be recalled is one under which "benefits" are paid at the beginning of the income period rather than at the end of the period, as in an ordinary annuity. And, since the payments are contingent on the continued life of the annuitant, the annuity due is a life annuity due.

TEMPORARY LIFE ANNUITY DUE. The net single premium for a five-year annual temporary life annuity due of one issued at age 25 is computed as follows:

1. What constitutes a claim? Claims are paid annually to those alive.
2. When are claims paid? At the beginning of the year.
3. How many are living at issue age? 9,575,636.
4. What is the amount of claims per year?

---

[10] Level premiums are nearly universally computed on an annual basis; i.e., the premium is the amount due at the beginning of each policy year. Premiums payable at more frequent intervals are called fractional premiums and are installments of the annual premium. Any unpaid installments at the time of the death of an insured were once deducted from the claim. For instance, if an insured who paid his premiums quarterly died in the first quarter, the three unpaid installments were due and were deducted from the policy proceeds. The current practice among many companies, however, is to collect premiums only until the end of the month in which death occurs, refunding any part of the premium paid beyond that time. The loss of the fractional premiums is absorbed in the rate margins.

Age	Number of Claims	Amount of Annuity	Amount of Claims
25	9,575,636	1	9,575,636
26	9,557,155	1	9,557,155
27	9,538,423	1	9,538,423
28	9,519,442	1	9,519,442
29	9,500,118	1	9,500,118

5. How many years of interest are involved? Since claims are paid at the beginning of the year, the following are the years of interest: age 25, none; age 26, one year; age 27, two years; age 28, three years; age 29, four years.

6. What is the present value of claims for each year?

Age	Amount of Claims	Years of Interest	Present Value of 1	Present Value of Payments
25	9,575,636	0	1.00000	9,575,636
26	9,557,155	1	.97561	9,324,056
27	9,538,423	2	.95181	9,076,766
28	9,519,442	3	.92860	8,839,754
29	9,500,118	4	.90595	8,606,632
				45,422,844

7. What is the present value of all future claims? 45,422,844.

8. What is the net single premium for a five-year temporary life annuity due issued at age 25? The total probable claims of 45,422,844 are divided by 9,575,636—the number living at age 25.

$$45,422,844 \div 9,575,636 = 4.74.$$

WHOLE LIFE ANNUITY DUE. The net single premium for a whole life annuity due is computed in the same manner as a temporary life annuity due, except that it is computed from issue age through age 99.

For example, the net single premium for a whole life annuity due of one issued at age 25 is computed as follows:

Age	Amount of Claims	Years of Interest	Present Value of 1 at 2½%	Present Value of Payments
25	9,575,636	0	1.00000	9,575,636
26	9,557,155	1	.97561	9,324,056
27	9,538,423	2	.95181	9,076,766
28	9,519,442	3	.92860	8,839,754
29	9,500,118	4	.90595	8,606,632
95	97,165	70	.17755	17,252
96	63,037	71	.17322	10,919
97	37,787	72	.16900	6,386
98	19,331	73	.16487	3,187
99	6,415	74	.16085	1,032
				259,212,467

Here 259,212,467 ÷ 9,575,636 = 27.07, present value of a whole life annuity due of one.

The net single premium for a temporary life annuity due of 1 for 5 years at age 25 was found to be 4.74. Thus, a single payment of $4.74 at the age of 25 is the mathematical equivalent of a series of annual payments of $1 made at the beginning of each of the 5 years from ages 25 to 29 inclusive, on behalf of those who survive each year.[11] Consequently, if the net single premium for a 5-year term policy issued at age 25 (1958 CSO, 2½ percent) is $4.74, it follows that the net level annual premium would be $1. If the net single premium were $500, the annual premium would be $500 ÷ 4.74 or $105.49.[12]

To find the net level annual premium for any policy, the net single premium is divided by the present value of an annual annuity due of one for the premium paying period. It should be stressed that the annuity due is for the term of years over which premiums are to be paid. This may or may not be the same as the term of the policy. For instance, a whole life policy may call for continuous premiums or the premium period may be limited. If it is a continuous premium policy, then the present value of a whole life annuity due is used. If it is a 20-pay policy, the present value of a temporary life annuity due for 20 years is used.

Steps in Calculating the Net Level Annual Premium.   The following are the steps in calculating a net level premium:

1. Determine the net single premium for the policy.
2. Determine the present value of an annual life annuity due of one for the premium paying period.
3. Determine the net level annual premium by dividing the results obtained in Step 1 by the results obtained in Step 2.

To illustrate the steps, the net level premiums for a limited payment and for a continuous payment policy are computed as follows:

Limited-Payment Life Policies.   What would be the net level premium for a $1,000 5-pay whole life policy issued at age 25?

1. What is the net single premium for the policy? This was calculated previously and found to be $339.65.
2. What is the present value of a five-year temporary life annuity due of 1 per annum? This was calculated previously and found to be 4.74.
3. Determine the net level annual premium: $339.65 ÷ 4.74 = $71.66.

---

[11] If no allowance were made for interest and mortality, the present value would be the sum of the annual payments—in the foregoing illustration $5 instead of $4.74. The $0.26 margin in this illustration is the allowance for interest and projected premium loss per $1,000 of level annual premium.

[12] The equation is 500:x = 4.74:1.00. The formula for solving this equation is the means times the extremes. Thus, 4.74x = 500, or x = 500 ÷ 4.74.

Continuous Premium Whole Life. What would be the net level annual premium for a continuous premium whole life policy issued at age 25?

1. What is the net single premium for the policy? This was computed previously and found to be $339.65.

2. What is the present value of a whole life annuity due of one premium? This was calculated previously and found to be 27.07.

3. Determine the net level annual premium: $339.65 ÷ 27.07 = $12.55.

Endowment, Term, and Annuities. The procedure for calculating the net level annual premium for other than whole life policies presents no new problems. To find the net level annual premium, the net single premium for any policy is divided by the present value of an annual life annuity due for the premium paying period. For a 10-year term policy, the life annuity due would be for 10 years; for a 20-year endowment, the life annuity due would be for 20 years. In the case of a pure deferred annuity at age 65 paid for on an annual premium basis from an issue age of, say, 35, the life annuity due would be for 30 years.

Special Policy Combinations. Rate calculation for the many special policy combinations that will be found, such as family income, family maintenance, double protection, and retirement income, are based on the same principles used in computing rates for term, whole life, and endowment. To compute the net level annual premium for any of them, all that is necessary is to find the present value of all projected future claims per policy (net single premium) and divide this amount by the present value of a life annuity due of 1 per annum for the premium paying period.

The net single premium on a double protection policy, for instance, is the sum of the present value of the projected claims under the term and under the whole life portions of the policy. The net level annual premium can then be computed by using the appropriate life annuity due for the premium paying period. In some cases the premium paying period for the entire policy will be for the whole of life, whereas in other cases the premium paying period might be divided, one part for the whole of life and another part for the period during which the term protection is offered.

4. HEALTH INSURANCE PREMIUMS

Basically, the calculation of a premium rate for health insurance coverage is the same as that for life insurance. A "pure" or net rate is determined, to which is added a margin for expenses, contingencies, taxes and profits.

The specialized underwriting problems and unique characteristics of health insurance introduce actuarial problems in rate making for health insurance that are not found in life insurance. For instance, it is considerably more difficult to define disability on a basis that will lead to objective treatment of claims than it is to define death. Also, claim frequencies and average claim values under health insurance do not have the same stability as do mortality rates, but tend to vary from time to time, partly as a result of variations in economic conditions.[13] Health insurance rates are based more on judgment and less on statistics than are life insurance rates.

Pure or Net Rate. The pure insurance premium is obtained by multiplying the claim rate by the average value of the claims. The claim rate[14] is the percentage of claims occurring during the year out of a given number of exposures. The average value of the claims[15] may be a fixed dollar amount as in accidental death and dismemberment coverage; or it may be a function of the duration of disability, as in disability income insurance, or of the level of expenses as in medical care coverage.

Claim frequency and severity rates are determined by statistical analysis. Available statistics for health insurance are limited. The Actuarial Society of America in 1926 and the Society of Actuaries in 1952 published statistics based on life insurance disability riders.[16] The Society of Actuaries also prepares statistics on double indemnity benefits and provides statistics on a regular basis for group and individual health insurance.[17] The Bureau of Accident and Health Underwriters (now merged into the Health Insurance Association of America) published statistics on individual health insurance. It published accident insurance experience for 1931–40 and 1948–51; and medical care insurance statistics for 1939–41, and sickness insurance experience for 1952 and 1953. Also, most companies have accumulated statistics from their own experience which they use in developing rates. A 1964 Commissioners Disability Table also is available for use in computing minimum reserves, checking the adequacy of premiums, and for premium computations. This table is based on data collected from 17 companies reflecting the first year of total disability claims incurred in 1958–61. As health insurance matures, better statistics undoubtedly will become available and rate making will take on more of a scientific flavor than has been true in the past.

Term Rates. Most rate making starts with the calculation of the pure premium rate for a term of one year. If the peril is accidental death, the pure insurance rate is the probability of accidental death multiplied by the amount of insurance. For example, if the claim rate is 1 in 2,000 and the amount of insurance is $1,000, then the pure insurance rate for a term of one year is $0.50. While accidental death rates vary with the age of the

---

[13] A period of economic depression will greatly increase claim frequencies and claim values. The man who is unemployed has less incentive to get well.

[14] Also called "claim frequency rate" and "probability of occurrence."

[15] Also called "average severity of the claim" and "claim severity rate."

[16] Actuarial Society of America, *Report of Committee on Disability Experience* (New York, 1926), and Society of Actuaries, "Report of Committee on Disability and Double Indemnity," *Transactions of the Society of Actuaries,* 1952 Reports.

[17] Reports on experience under various types of health coverage are found in the *Transactions of the Society of Actuaries* Report numbers. See, for example, the reports for 1958, 1959, 1961, 1963 and 1965.

insured, the variation is not considered significant enough to vary premiums by ages, particularly at the ages at which the coverage is commonly purchased. A Society of Actuary study based on data from 1951–58 shows accidental death rates per 1,000 to be 0.424 at age 1, falling to 0.198 at age 9, rising to 0.583 at age 19, falling to 0.286 at ages 33–35, and rising again after age 35 but remaining under 0.583 until age 64.[18]

Under a disability income policy, a specified amount is paid after a given waiting period for each period of disability, subject to a maximum duration. The average value of a claim under a disability income policy is a function of both the claim frequency (the probability that a covered disability will occur) and the claim severity (the probable duration of a covered disability). The claim severity is a function of the waiting period and the maximum benefit period in the policy.

Continuance tables have been prepared for use in computing the average value of disability income claims. These tables combine claim frequency rates and claim severity rates. Table 25–1 is an excerpt from a continuance table based on data provided by the Conference Modification of Class 3 Disability rates.[19]

TABLE 25–1

Continuance Table, Age 40, Excerpts

(per 100,000 lives exposed)

(1) Days X	(2) Number Disabled for Exactly X Days	(3) Number Disabled for X or More Days	(4) Total Number of Disability Days Accumulated through Day X
1	1,410	32,810	32,810
2	1,810	31,400	64,210
3	2,010	29,590	93,800
8	1,480	20,100	211,990
9	1,210	18,620	230,610
10	1,090	17,410	248,020
70	38	1,800	572,667
71	36	1,762	574,429
72	34	1,726	576,155
73	32	1,692	577,847

The relationships among the columns in Table 25–1 are as follows: The values in Column 3 decrease each year by the previous value in

---

[18] Society of Actuaries, "Report of Committee on Disability and Double Indemnity," *Transactions of the Society of Actuaries,* 1958 Reports.

[19] The Conference Modification of Class 3 Disability rates is based on the 1926 study cited in footnote 16 of this chapter. Class 3 is that class which has the highest claim rates. The modifications were developed by the Health and Accident Underwriters Conference, now a part of the Health Insurance Association of America.

Column 2, and the values in Column 4 increase each year by the previous values in Column 3. Thus, the total number disabled for 3 or more days (Column 3) is the number disabled for 2 or more days less the number disabled exactly 2 days (Column 2), and the total number of disability days accumulated through the third day (Column 4) is the total number of disability days accumulated through the second day plus the number disabled for 2 or more days (Column 3).

The values in Column 4 may be used to compute the net premium rate for a disability income policy as follows: assume a disability income policy issued at age 40 paying $1 a day after a 10-day waiting period for a 60-day benefit period. Column 4 shows that out of 100,000 lives exposed at age 40, 248,020 days of disability will be accumulated through the 10th day. Since there is a 10-day waiting period, no disability income payments will be made for these days. The total number of disability days accumulated through the 70th day is 572,677. The disability days for which income payments will have to be paid, assuming 100,000 active lives insured, would be those accumulated after the 10th day through the 70th day.[20] This is computed by subtracting 248,020 from 572,667, making a total of 324,647 disability days for which $1 will have to be paid. The net premium per policyholder would then be $324,647 divided by 100,000, or $3.246 per $1 of daily disability income benefit.

Note that in the foregoing example, the aggregate premium of $324,647 is the sum of anticipated daily benefit payments without adjustment for interest. The same value per dollar of claims is assigned to the benefits paid on the 11th day of disability as on the 70th day of disability, ignoring that funds to be used to pay benefits for the 70th day can earn interest 60 more days. However, insurers generally do not consider interest when computing disability income premiums unless the benefit duration is more than a year.

Claims originate throughout the year, but for the purpose of premium computation it is assumed that, on the average, claims originate at midyear. So, when premiums are paid in advance they are discounted for six months' interest. Also, since only those alive at midyear can possibly become disabled, the premiums are further discounted for six months of mortality.

Continuance tables also are used in computing premium rates for hospital insurance. They are similar to disability continuance tables. Column 1 in both is the same. In the hospital continuance table, Columns 2, 3, and 4 are headed: Number of Hospital Cases Confined Exactly X Days; Number of Hospital Cases Confined X or More Days; and Total Number of Hospital Confinement Days Accumulated through Day X. Continuance tables are used in computing premiums for hospital expense insurance in the same manner as they are used in computing premiums for disability income insurance. Hospital continuance tables are prepared for children,

---

[20] The 70th day is used because the maximum duration of benefits is 60 days *after* a 10-day waiting period.

adults under age 65, adults over age 65, males, females, and for various types of admissions—surgical, for example. For hospital extras, statistics are available as an aid in computing the average benefit per insured. Claim frequency rates also are available for aid in developing premiums for surgical benefits. Various statistical studies have been published for use in developing premiums for major medical insurance.[21] Various factors affecting the premium for major medical insurance are the participation percentage, geographical area, the nature of the deductible, the types of internal limits in the policy, and the maximum amount of coverage. Premium computation for major medical insurance is expected to become more complex as the nature of the variables that affect the cost of the coverage becomes more apparent.[22]

Level Premium. If claim rates and average claim values do not vary greatly over the years covered by the benefit offered, a level premium can be achieved simply by using the pure premium at all ages. If the claim rate and average claim value do vary significantly, benefits can be reduced at older ages, rates can be jumped by age groupings, or a level premium can be calculated much in the same way as one is calculated for life insurance: a single premium is developed equal to the present value of the one-year premiums for all ages covered and then divided by the present value of an annuity due of 1 per annum payable to the age at which the coverage expires.

The level premium method generally is used in calculating rates for non-cancellable, guaranteed renewable policies. It is not customary to offer cash values with these policies. However, the probability of lapses may be discounted in computing the premium rate.

Loading. The pure insurance rate must be loaded for acquisition costs, expenses, regular and contingency reserves, and profit in a stock insurer or policy dividend in a mutual insurer.

The largest item of acquisition cost is agents' commissions. Two types of commission plans are used in health insurance: (1) Level plan: a relatively low (compared to life insurance) first-year commission of, say, 25 percent, followed by the same commission rate on each subsequent annual renewal. (2) Unlevel: a relatively high first-year commission as in life insurance, followed by relatively low renewal commissions—say, 40 percent, plus 10 percent renewals. The level plan will produce a greater loading factor if the business persists less than two years, whereas the unlevel plan will produce a higher loading factor if the average persistency of the busi-

21 Morton D. Miller, "Gross Premiums for Individual and Family Major Medical Expense Insurance," *Transactions of the Society of Actuaries*, Vol. VII; Lowell M. Dorn, "New York Life Morbidity Experience under Individual and Family Major Medical Policies," *Transactions of the Society of Actuaries*, Vol. XV.

22 Charles A. Siegfried, "Some Considerations Involved in the Analysis of Major Medical Expense Insurance Experience," *Transactions of the Society of Actuaries*, Vol. X.

ness is more than two years. For instance, the 25 percent level plan will cost 75 percent of one year's premium for a persistency of three years, whereas the 40 percent first year 10 percent renewal unlevel plan over the same period will cost only 60 percent of one year's premium. On the other hand, if the policy persists only one year, the level plan will cost 25 percent of one year's premium, whereas the unlevel plan will cost 40 percent.

The problems of determining appropriate loadings for the various expense items, contingencies, profits, and taxes are the same in health insurance as in life insurance, and these problems were discussed in Chapter 24.

Making Up the Premium.   Rates are usually calculated on a unit basis, say $1,000 as the unit for accidental death and dismemberment benefits and $100 per month as the unit for loss of time benefits. A unit for hospital expense is usually $1 per day of benefit, whereas unit cost for surgical is based on the maximum benefit in the surgical schedule. The premium for any policy is the total of the unit rates involved.

Rating Factors.   The rate for a health insurance policy is based on three factors: age, occupation, and sex. The occupational factor is more important for accident insurance than for sickness insurance, but premium rates and other underwriting practices in connection with sickness insurance as well as accident insurance generally depend upon the type of occupation of the insured.

The rate for optionally renewable disability income insurance usually does not vary with age until age 55. Because of the increase in the morbidity rate at later ages, the rate after age 55 usually is higher. Hospital, surgical, and basic medical care plans have one rate for adults and another for children. Again at later ages, a differential may be charged because of the higher morbidity rate. Guaranteed renewable disability income policies and major medical insurance are usually rated on a level premium plan and graded by age. Children, however, take a flat rate under major medical insurance.

Studies have shown that women experience a higher rate of disability than men. The cost of health insurance, therefore, is usually higher for women than for men. (Commonly, of course, disability income insurance is written on employed women only.)

Elimination Periods.   It is common in disability income policies to provide for an elimination or waiting period for each disability—particularly for sickness coverage. Under such clauses, benefits do not begin until the end of the first few days or weeks of each period of disability. Thus, the company pays and charges only for the larger, more uncertain part of losses. As a result (1) the pure premium can be reduced because a smaller amount is paid out in claims and (2) loading can be reduced because the expenses of handling numerous small losses is eliminated.

Appendix A to Chapter 25
A Mathematical Note

In Chapter 25, premiums were computed arithmetically. However, in practice premiums are computed algebraically. In order to understand the formulas used by the actuary in his work, the student must first learn a new language—the language of symbols or notation.

Mortality Symbols. The symbol for the number of persons living is (l). The age involved is represented by a subscript placed beside the l. Thus, the number living at age 25 would be represented by l_{25}. The mortality table column indicating the number of people living at each age in the table is labeled l_x, x representing the age involved.

The number dying is indicated by the symbol (d). The age is shown by a subscript opposite the symbol. Therefore, the number dying at age 21 is d_{21}. The death column in the mortality table is headed by d_x.

The rate of mortality is reflected by the symbol q_x, which indicates the proportion of lives aged x dying during the year. The rate of mortality per 1,000 column in the mortality table is labeled $1,000q_x$.

Thus, the following equations may be established:

1. $d_x = l_x - l_{x+1}$ [1]

2. $q_x = \dfrac{d_x}{l_x}$ [2]

One additional column usually found in the mortality table is expectation of life, the average number of years to be lived in the future by lives now aged x. The symbol $(\overset{\circ}{e}_x)$ is used to express this figure and it is the label used for that column.[3] Another symbol used with mortality tables is (w), the last year in the table at which l_x is larger than zero. On the 1958 CSO Table, this is age 99 since age 100 is the limiting age of the table.

Interest Symbols. In life insurance, actuaries are interested in present values, at compound interest, of sums due both to be paid and to be received

---

[1] Assume age 25. The number dying at age 25 is 18,481 (1958 CSO). The number living at age 25 is 9,575,636. The number living at age 26 is 9,557,155. 18,481 = 9,575,636 − 9,557,155.

[2] The rate of mortality at age 25 is 18,481 ÷ 9,575,636 or 0.193 percent or 1.93 per 1,000.

[3] Two expectations of life figures are computed: curtate and complete. Curtate (reduced) includes only the full years involved, leaving out any fraction of a year, whereas complete expectation of life includes the fraction. The symbol for curtate expectation is (e_x); for complete $(\overset{\circ}{e}_x)$.

in the future. The symbol for the present value of 1 due in n years is (v^n).[4] At 2½ percent, v^n equals 0.9756098 [5] where n is one year. Where n is two years, v^n is 0.9518144.[6] Actuaries work with tables of v^n values.

Symbols for the Expression of Premiums. The following symbols are used to indicate premiums:

$A^1_{x:n\rceil}$ = The net single premium for n-year term.

A_x = The net single premium for whole life.

$A_{x:n\rceil}$ = The net single premium for n-year endowment.

a_x = The net single premium for an immediate whole life annuity.

$\ddot{a}_{x:n\rceil}$ = The net single premium (present value) for temporary life annuity due.

$\ddot{a}_x$ = The net single premium (present value) for whole life annuity due.

$_nE_x$ = The net single premium for n-year pure endowment.

P_x = Net annual level premium for continuous premium whole life.

$_nP_x$ = Net annual level premium for limited-payment whole life.

$P^1_{x:n\rceil}$ = Net annual level premium for n-year term.

$P_{x:n\rceil}$ = Net annual level premium for n-year endowment.

Formulas for Net Single Premiums. For an n-year term policy, the formula for the net single premium is:

$$A^1_{x:n\rceil} = \frac{vd_x + v^2 d_{x+1} + v^3 d_{x+2} + v^4 d_{x+3} + \cdots + v^n d_{x+n-1}}{l_x}. \tag{1}$$

For a whole life policy, the net single premium formula is:

$$A_x = \frac{vd_x + v^2 d_{x+1} + v^3 d_{x+2} + v^4 d_{x+3} + \cdots + v^{w-x+1} d_w}{l_x}. \tag{2}$$

For an n-year endowment, the net single premium is:

$$A_{x:n\rceil} = {}_nE_x + A^1_{x:n\rceil} =$$

---

[4] The formula for computing present value is $P = A(1+i)^{-n}$ where P is the present value, A the amount, i the compound rate of interest, and n the number of years involved. The symbol (v) is $(1+i)^{-1}$. Thus $P = Av^n$. Where A is 1, P becomes v^n.

[5] $P = 1(1+0.025)^{-1}$ or $\dfrac{1}{1.025}$ or 0.9756098.

[6] $P = 1(1+0.025)^{-2}$ or $\dfrac{1}{(1.025)^2}$ or 0.9518144.

$$\frac{vd_x + v^2 d_{x+1} + v^3 d_{x+2} + v^4 d_{x+3} + \cdots + v^n d_{x+n-1} + v^n l_{x+n}}{l_x}. \quad (3)$$

For an immediate whole life annuity, the net single premium is:

$$a_x = \frac{v l_{x+1} + v^2 l_{x+2} + v^3 l_{x+3} + v^4 l_{x+4} + \cdots + v^{w-x} l_w}{l_x} \quad (4)$$

Commutation Symbols. Numerous computations would be necessary to work out the above formulas. To reduce the amount of arithmetic required, a set of commutation symbols have been created. The values of these symbols are presented in tabular form in what are called commutation columns. The columns are based on a given mortality table and a given interest assumption. Table 25–A–1 shows the commutation columns for the 1958 CSO at 2½ percent. The symbols shown in these columns are (D_x), (N_x), (C_x), and (M_x). Their meanings are as follows:

$$D_x = v^x l_x.$$
$$N_x = D_x + D_{x+1} + D_{x+2} + D_{x+3} + \cdots + D_w.$$
$$C_x = v^{x+1} d_x.$$
$$M_x = C_x + C_{x+1} + C_{x+2} + C_{x+3} + \cdots + C_w.$$

Here is how the commutation symbols are used to simplify the arithmetic of premium computations. Note that the denominator in formulas (1) through (4) is l_x. If the denominator and numerator in these formulas are multiplied by v^x, the denominator becomes $v^x l_x$, which, as indicated above, is represented by symbol (D_x). The numerator in formulas (1) through (3) becomes $v^{x+1} d_x + v^{x+2} d_{x+1} + v^{x+3} d_{x+2}$ etc. Since the symbol (C_x) is used to indicate $v^{x+1} d_x$, the formula for the net single premium for an n-year term policy can be written as follows:

$$A^1_{x:\overline{n}|} = \frac{C_x + C_{x+1} + C_{x+2} + C_{x+3} + \cdots + C_{x+n-1}}{D_x}. \quad (5)$$

The formulas for whole life and n-year endowments are written:

$$A_x = \frac{C_x + C_{x+1} + C_{x+2} + C_{x+3} + \cdots + C_w}{D_x}. \quad (6)$$

$$A_{x:\overline{n}|} = \frac{C_x + C_{x+1} + C_{x+2} + C_{x+3} + \cdots + C_{x+n-1} + D_{x+n}}{D_x}. \quad (7)$$

Since the symbol (M_x) is used to express $C_x + C_{x+1} + C_{x+2} + C_{x+3} + \cdots + C_w$, the formula for the net single premium for an n-year term policy can be further reduced to:

$$A^1_{x:\overline{n}|} = \frac{M_x - M_{x+n}}{D_x}. \quad (8)$$

TABLE 25–A–1

1958 CSO Table
Commutation Columns—Interest at 2½%

Age	D_x	N_x	C_x	M_x
0	10000000.0000	324850104.9680	69073.1710	2076826.7172
1	9687024.4290	314850104.9680	16632.9566	2007753.5462
2	9434122.5838	305163080.5390	13990.2787	1991120.5896
3	9190031.7084	295728957.9552	13090.0808	1977130.3109
4	8952794.4741	286538926.2468	12228.1241	1964040.2301
5	8722205.5791	277586131.7727	11487.5189	1951812.1060
6	8497981.3556	268863926.1936	10778.2903	1940324.5871
7	8279935.2370	260365944.8380	10178.0782	1929546.2968
8	8067807.4636	252086009.6010	9681.6066	1919368.2186
9	7861350.0557	244018202.1374	9279.8558	1909686.6120
10	7660329.9546	236156852.0817	9042.8478	1900406.7562
11	7464449.7860	228496522.1271	8957.6178	1891363.9084
12	7273432.4866	221032072.3411	8940.8062	1882406.2906
13	7087090.8833	213758639.8545	9126.8500	1873465.4844
14	6905108.1581	206671548.9712	9364.0939	1864338.6344
15	6727326.7826	199766440.8131	9582.3146	1854974.5405
16	6553663.2627	193039114.0305	9846.7536	1845392.2259
17	6383971.1254	186485450.7678	10090.0279	1835545.4723
18	6218174.4633	180101479.6424	10252.3993	1825455.4444
19	6056259.3006	173883305.1791	10280.6243	1815203.0451
20	5898264.9735	167827045.8785	10300.1828	1804922.4208
21	5744104.7377	161928780.9050	10255.1657	1794622.2380
22	5593749.4258	156184676.1673	10150.6810	1784367.0723
23	5447165.8414	150590926.7415	10044.0865	1774216.3913
24	5304263.9929	145143760.9001	9883.7932	1764172.3048
25	5165007.9517	139839496.9072	9725.3439	1754288.5116
26	5029306.7854	134674488.9555	9617.0037	1744563.1677
27	4897023.7928	129645182.1701	9507.1611	1734946.1640
28	4768076.9758	124748158.3773	9442.8900	1725439.0029
29	4642339.5370	119980081.4015	9420.4356	1715996.1129
30	4519691.3751	115337741.8645	9392.0634	1706575.6773
31	4400062.8465	110818050.4894	9401.2183	1697183.6139
32	4283343.0569	106417987.6429	9402.5686	1687782.3956
33	4169468.7479	102134644.5860	9437.1317	1678379.8270
34	4058337.1968	97965175.8381	9502.3390	1668942.6953
35	3949851.0856	93906838.6413	9672.2130	1659440.3563
36	3843840.9771	89956987.5557	9900.3401	1649768.1433
37	3740188.4751	86113146.5786	10217.2318	1639867.8032
38	3638747.0704	82372958.1035	10685.3232	1629650.5714
39	3539311.8617	78734211.0331	11222.0794	1618965.2482
40	3441765.0620	75194899.1714	11853.1042	1607743.1688
41	3345966.5023	71753134.1094	12535.2926	1595890.0646
42	3251822.2774	68407167.6071	13229.3739	1583354.7720
43	3159280.1784	65155345.3297	13962.4424	1570125.3981
44	3068262.0685	61996065.1513	14727.5918	1556162.9557

Age	D_x	N_x	C_x	M_x
45	2978698.8164	58927803.0828	15547.3085	1541435.3639
46	2890500.3526	55949104.2664	16440.4699	1525888.0554
47	2803559.9048	53058603.9138	17395.7457	1509447.5855
48	2717784.6405	50255044.0090	18427.9447	1492051.8398
49	2633069.2135	47537259.3685	19523.3861	1473623.8951
50	2549324.6723	44904190.1550	20692.9455	1454100.5090
51	2466453.0891	42354865.4827	21921.2231	1433407.5635
52	2384374.4270	39888412.3936	23169.1325	1411486.3404
53	2303049.8123	37504037.9666	24468.5917	1388317.2079
54	2222409.2905	35200988.1543	25801.7117	1363848.6162
55	2142402.4988	32978578.8638	27171.9031	1338046.9045
56	2062976.8254	30836176.3650	28599.9098	1310875.0014
57	1984060.3996	28773199.5396	30080.3536	1282275.0916
58	1905588.3725	26789139.1400	31604.8230	1252194.7380
59	1827505.7998	24883550.7675	33144.7659	1220589.9150
60	1749787.7198	23056044.9677	34722.7242	1187445.1491
61	1672387.2632	21306757.2479	36286.6291	1152722.4249
62	1595310.6622	19633869.9847	37836.1144	1116435.7958
63	1518564.5694	18038559.3225	39364.2006	1078599.6814
64	1442162.1578	16519994.7531	40858.9196	1039235.4808
65	1366128.5462	15077832.5953	42316.6940	998376.5612
66	1290491.6985	13711704.0491	43738.1310	956059.8672
67	1215278.1249	12421212.3506	45101.6207	912321.7362
68	1140535.6099	11205934.2257	46378.0358	867220.1155
69	1066339.5743	10065398.6158	47449.5963	820842.0797
70	992881.7500	8999059.0415	48229.7870	773392.4834
71	920435.3077	8006177.2915	48625.9779	725162.6964
72	849359.6946	7085741.9838	48599.9832	676536.7185
73	780043.7396	6236382.2892	48142.0663	627936.8353
74	712876.2140	5456338.5496	47376.6752	579794.7690
75	648112.3021	4743462.3356	46392.1628	532418.0938
76	585912.5111	4095350.0335	45261.0951	486025.9310
77	526360.8716	3509437.5224	44008.9628	440764.8359
78	469513.8465	2983076.6508	42627.3426	396755.8731
79	415434.9294	2513562.8043	41012.5834	354128.5305
80	364289.7989	2098127.8749	39087.3533	313115.9471
81	316317.3241	1733838.0760	36831.6174	274028.5938
82	271770.6619	1417520.7519	34248.4382	237196.9764
83	230893.6600	1145750.0900	31397.0289	202948.5382
84	193865.0736	914856.4300	28372.4430	171551.5093
85	160764.2229	720991.3564	25273.7507	143179.0663
86	131569.3974	560227.1335	22183.1949	117905.3156
87	106177.1855	428657.7361	19177.1362	95722.1207
88	84410.3641	322480.5506	16326.1748	76544.9845
89	66025.3978	238070.1865	13685.6613	60218.8097
90	50729.3636	172044.7887	11291.0955	46533.1484
91	38200.9638	121315.4251	9159.6932	35242.0529
92	28109.5415	83114.4613	7292.8738	26082.3597

TABLE 25–A–1 (concluded)
1958 CSO Table
Commutation Columns—Interest at 2½%

Age	D_x	N_x	C_x	M_x
93	20131.0686	55004.9198	5681.8884	18789.4859
94	13958.1795	34873.8512	4312.1729	13107.5975
95	9305.5630	20915.6717	3188.7449	8795.4246
96	5889.8533	11610.1087	2301.6880	5606.6797
97	3444.5103	5720.2554	1641.3408	3304.9917
98	1719.1569	2275.7451	1120.6380	1663.6509
99	556.5882	556.5882	543.0129	543.0129

For whole life and n-year endowments, the formulas are:

$$A_x = \frac{M_x}{D_x}. \tag{9}$$

$$A_{x:\overline{n}|} = \frac{M_x - M_{x+n} + D_{x+n}}{D_x}. \tag{10}$$

For the net single premium for a whole life annuity, the numerator in formula (4) after multiplying by v^x becomes:

$$a_x = \frac{v^{x+1}l_{x+1} + v^{x+2}l_{x+2} + v^{x+3}l_{x+3} + \cdots + v^w l_w}{v^x l_x}. \tag{11}$$

Symbol (D_x) represents $v^x l_x$, so substituting D_x in the above formula it reads:

$$a_x = \frac{D_{x+1} + D_{x+2} + D_{x+3} + D_{x+4} + \cdots + D_w}{D_x}. \tag{12}$$

Commutation symbol N_x is used to indicate $D_x + D_{x+1} + D_{x+2} + D_{x+3} + \cdots + D_w$. The above formula, therefore, can be written:

$$a_x = \frac{N_{x+1}}{D_x}. \tag{13}$$

Application of the Formulas. The net single premium for a $1,000, 20-year term policy issued at age 25 can be computed as follows, using the commutation columns (1958 CSO, at 2½ percent) and formula (8), and multiplying by $1,000, the amount of the insurance.

$$1,000A^1_{25:\overline{20}|} =$$
$$1,000 \left(\frac{1754288.5116 - 1541435.3639}{5165007.9517} \right) = \$42.21. \tag{14}$$

The net single premium for a $1,000 whole life policy issued at age 25 using formula (9) would be:

$$\$1,000A_{25} = \$1,000 \left(\frac{1754288.5116}{5165007.9517} \right) = \$339.65. \qquad (15)$$

For a 20-year endowment issued at age 25, the net single premium for a $1,000 policy using formula (10) would be:

$$\$1,000A_{25:\overline{20}|} =$$
$$\$1,000 \left(\frac{1754288.5116 - 1541435.3639 + 2978698.8164}{5165007.9517} \right). \qquad (16)$$
$$\$1,000A_{25:\overline{20}|} = \$617.92$$

The net single premium for an immediate whole life annuity of $1,000 a year issued at age 65 using formula (13) would be:

$$\$1,000a_{65} = \$1,000 \left(\frac{13711704.0491}{1366128.5462} \right) = \$10,036.91. \qquad (17)$$

Note how much simpler the arithmetic is in working out formulas (8), (9), (10), and (13) than would be the case in solving formulas (1), (2), (3), and (4). The use of the commutation columns greatly facilitates premium computations.

Formulas for Net Annual Level Premiums. The net annual level premium is computed by dividing the net single premium by the present value of an annuity due of 1 per annum for the premium paying period. For a 20-year term policy, a 20-year endowment, or a 20-pay whole life policy, the net single premium is divided by the present value of a 20-year temporary life annuity due. For a continuous premium whole life policy, the net single premium is divided by the present value of a whole life annuity due. The formula for the present value of an n-year temporary life annuity due is developed as follows:

$$\ddot{a}_{x:\overline{n}|} = \frac{l_x + vl_{x+1} + v^2l_{x+2} + v^3l_{x+3} + \cdots + v^nl_{x+n}}{l_x}. \qquad (18)$$

If both the numerator and denominator of this formula are multiplied by v^x, the results are:

$$\ddot{a}_{x:\overline{n}|} = \frac{v^xl_x + v^{x+1}l_{x+1} + v^{x+2}l_{x+2} + v^{x+3}l_{x+3} + \cdots + v^{x+n}l_{x+n}}{v^xl_x}. \qquad (19)$$

Substituting the commutation symbol (D_x) in the above formula, it becomes:

$$\ddot{a}_{x:\overline{n}|} = \frac{D_x + D_{x+1} + D_{x+2} + D_{x+3} + \cdots + D_{x+n-1}}{D_x}. \qquad (20)$$

Since commutation symbol (N_x) is used to express $D_x + D_{x+1} + D_{x+2} + D_{x+3} + \cdots + D_w$, formula (20) can be written:

$$\ddot{a}_{x:\overline{n}|} = \frac{N_x - N_{x+n}}{D_x}. \tag{21}$$

For the whole life annuity due, the formula is:

$$\ddot{a}_x = \frac{D_x + D_{x+1} + D_{x+2} + D_{x+3} + \cdots + D_w}{D_x}. \tag{22}$$

Since the numerator in the above formula is the commutation symbol (N_x), the formula can be written simply:

$$\ddot{a}_x = \frac{N_x}{D_x}. \tag{23}$$

The formula for the net annual level premium for an n-year term policy (formula [8] divided by formula [21]) becomes:

$$\frac{M_x - M_{x+n}}{D_x} \div \frac{N_x - N_{x+n}}{D_x} \text{ or } P^1_{x:\overline{n}|} = \frac{M_x - M_{x+n}}{N_x - N_{x+n}} \tag{24}$$

For an n-payment whole life policy, the formula is:

$$\frac{M_x}{D_x} \div \frac{N_x - N_{x+n}}{D_x} \text{ or } {}_nP_x = \frac{M_x}{N_x - N_{x+n}}. \tag{25}$$

For an n-year endowment, the formula is:

$$\frac{M_x - M_{x+n} + D_{x+n}}{D_x} \div \frac{N_x - N_{x+n}}{D_x} \text{ or } P_{x:\overline{n}|} =$$
$$\frac{M_x - M_{x+n} + D_{x+n}}{N_x - N_{x+n}}. \tag{26}$$

For a continuous premium whole life policy, the formula is:

$$\frac{M_x}{D_x} \div \frac{N_x}{D_x} \text{ or } P_x = \frac{M_x}{N_x} \tag{27}$$

Application of the Formulas.   The net annual level premium for $1,000, 20-year term issued at age 25 would be:

$1,000 \, P^1_{25:\overline{20}|} =$

$$1,000 \left(\frac{1754288.5116 - 1541435.3639}{139839496.9072 - 58927803.0828} \right) \text{ or } \$2.63.^* \tag{28}$$

For a 20-payment whole life policy, the premium would be:

$1,000 \, {}_{20}P_{25} =$

$$1,000 \left(\frac{1754288.5116}{139839496.9072 - 58927803.0828} \right) \text{ or } \$21.68.^* \tag{29}$$

For a 20-year endowment:

$$\$1{,}000\ P_{25:\overline{20}|} =$$

$$\$1{,}000 \left(\frac{1754288.5116 - 1541435.3639 + 2978698.8164}{139839496.9072 - 58927803.0828} \right)$$

$$\text{or } \$39.44.^* \qquad (30)$$

For a continuous premium whole life:

$$\$1{,}000\ P_{25} = \$1{,}000 \left(\frac{1754288.5116}{139839496.9072} \right) \text{ or } \$12.55.^* \qquad (31)$$

Appendix B to Chapter 25
Direct Method of Gross Premium Computation

In Chapter 24 the traditional method of calculating the net level premiums was discussed. To obtain the gross premium it was necessary to add a margin for expenses, contingencies, profits, and taxes. However, the gross level premium may be computed directly—that is, independently of the net premium. The approach used in this appendix is that developed by Professor Joseph M. Belth, "to provide students with a clearer understanding of the nature of the process."[1] Professor Belth says that his "system is designed primarily as a teaching device rather than as a description of the way in which life insurance companies actually calculate gross premiums."[2] Its function is to show how the factors that affect gross premiums are related. However, the system does have operational utility because, given a set of relevant assumptions, it provides the insurer with a technique for testing the adequacy of its price structure in terms of its financial objectives.

The Price Structure. The components of the price structure for nonparticipating life insurance are gross premiums and cash surrender values. For participating policies, a third component is dividends. The adequacy of the insurer's price structure can be modified by changing any one or more of these components. Thus, if under a given set of relevant assumptions a proposed price structure would produce an income more than, or less than, an amount sufficient to meet the insurer's financial objectives, that structure

---

* Rounded off.

1 Joseph M. Belth, "Calculation of Life Insurance Gross Premiums: A Suggested Modification of the Traditional Textbook Approach," *Journal of Risk and Insurance,* Vol. XXXIV, No. 3 (September, 1967), p. 385.

2 *Ibid.*

can be made to produce the desired income by altering the components, using a trial and error system to reach the appropriate results. Such alterations would include changing the proposed schedule of gross premiums, the proposed schedule of cash surrender values, and the proposed dividend scale, one or all, and in varying degrees until the suitable price structure is developed.

However, to simplify the illustration here the trial and error method will not be used. Instead, a schedule of cash surrender values (shown in Table 25–B–1, Column 6) and a scale of dividends (shown in Table 25–B–1, Column 7) will be given as constants. A linear algebraic equation (to be developed) will be used to arrive at the gross level premium (GP). As a further simplification, the illustration is confined to one group of policies—a $10,000 participating continuous premium whole life policy issued to men 50 years old.

Relevant Assumptions. Just as assumptions must be made in the traditional method of computing the net premium, so must assumptions be made in the direct computation of gross premiums. The relevant assumptions deal with interest rates, mortality rates, lapse rates, expense rates, and profit rates. For purposes of this discussion, the realism of these assumptions is not at issue because the focus is entirely on the methodology rather than on the results.

THE INTEREST RATE. The interest rate assumed is 5 percent. The present value of 1 payable in t years appears on Table 25–B–1, Column 5. The formula for the present value of 1 due in t years is $P = (1 + i)^{-t}$, and the notation for $(1 + i)^{-t}$ is v^t.

MORTALITY RATES. The mortality rates assumed are those of Nelson and Warren's III Select and Ultimate Tables.[3] The rates from the select table are those for males at issue age 50 with the select mortality running for 15 years. The rates for attained ages 65 through 79 are taken from the ultimate table. These mortality rates are shown in Table 25–B–1, Column 3.

LAPSE RATES. The lapse rates assumed are indicated in Table 25–B–1, Column 4. The first 10 policy years correspond to Linton's A Table.[4] The rates for the remaining 20 years are extended arbitrarily to correspond with Belth's lapse assumptions.[5]

EXPENSE RATES. The assumed expenses are (a) those expressed as a percentage of the gross premium, (b) those expressed as a flat amount per policy, (c) those arising out of death claims, and (d) those associated with surrender claims.

Expenses that are expressed as a percentage of the gross premium are

---

[3] Nelson and Warren. *Principal Mortality Tables* (Kansas City), pp. 66–69.

[4] M. A. Linton, "Return under Agency Contracts," *Record of the American Institute of Actuaries,* Vol. XIII (1924), p. 287.

[5] Joseph M. Belth, "Calculation of Life Insurance Gross Premiums: A Suggested Modification of the Traditional Textbook Approach," *Journal of Risk and Insurance,* Vol. XXXIV, No. 3 (September, 1967), p. 385.

TABLE 25–B–1

Assumed Mortality, Lapse, and Interest Rates
Scheduled Cash Surrender Values and Dividends

($10,000 participating continuous premiums whole life policy, issue age, 50)

Policy Year — t (1)	Attained Age (2)	Mortality Rate — x (x) (3)	Lapse Rate (4)	P.V. of 1 Payable in t years (v^t) $i = 5\%$ (5)	Cash Surrender Value ($) (6)	Dividends ($) (7)
1	50	0.00279	0.1000	0.95238	40	32.40
2	51	.00382	.0600	.90703	230	37.40
3	52	.00481	.0500	.86384	430	42.20
4	53	.00560	.0440	.82270	620	47.30
5	54	.00634	.0400	.78353	820	52.20
6	55	.00714	.0360	.74621	1,020	56.70
7	56	.00807	.0320	.71068	1,220	61.40
8	57	.00910	.0290	.67684	1,430	65.90
9	58	.01027	.0270	.64461	1,620	70.50
10	59	.01159	.0250	.61391	1,830	75.00
11	60	.01318	.0260	.58468	2,000	79.10
12	61	.01520	.0280	.55684	2,210	83.10
13	62	.01739	.0320	.53032	2,400	87.30
14	63	.01969	.0380	.50507	2,600	91.40
15	64	.02324	.0440	.48102	2,790	95.60
16	65	.02727	.0480	.45811	2,970	99.70
17	66	.02977	.0520	.43630	3,160	103.70
18	67	.03255	.0560	.41552	3,370	107.70
19	68	.03558	.0580	.39573	3,560	111.50
20	69	.03891	.0600	.37689	3,740	115.50
21	70	.04251	.0680	.35894	3,930	119.40
22	71	.04634	.0770	.34185	4,100	123.30
23	72	.05034	.0870	.32557	4,320	127.20
24	73	.05446	.0980	.31007	4,510	131.40
25	74	.05875	.1100	.29530	4,690	134.20
26	75	.06337	.1230	.28124	4,880	138.10
27	76	.06855	.1510	.26785	5,050	143.10
28	77	.07451	.1810	.25509	5,230	146.90
29	78	.08134	.2300	.24295	5,410	149.60
30	79	.08895	.91105	.23138	5,590	154.40

assumed to be 70 percent of the GP in the first policy year, 10 percent of the GP for the second through ninth years, and 5 percent of the GP thereafter. The 70 percent for the first year is made up of 55 percent for agent's commission, plus 13 percent for agency management expenses, plus 2 percent for state premium taxes. The 10 percent for the second through the ninth years is composed of 5 percent for agent's commission, 3 percent for agency management expenses, and 2 percent for state premium taxes; the 5 percent thereafter includes 2 percent for agent's commission, 1 percent for agency management expenses, and 2 percent for state premium taxes.

The other expenses assumed are as follows. (1) Expenses per policy are $90 for the first year and $6 thereafter. (2) Death claim expenses are $40 per claim. (3) Surrender value claim expenses are $10 per claim.

PROFIT RATES.   The profit per block of business is equal to the income (premium and investment income) derived from the block of policies, minus the expenses and claim payments attributed to these policies. A block is defined as the number of policies of the same type, the same face amount, issued to a homogeneous group of the same age. In this illustration, a block of 100,000 policies is assumed. The policies are $10,000 continuous premium whole life, participating, issued to men at age 50, at standard rates.

The profit assumed is expressed as a combination of a flat amount per policy and a percentage of the gross premium. The present value of the profit per policy in the original block is assumed to be $20 plus 30 percent of one level GP. The term "profit" as used in this discussion is broad, and includes allowances for contingency margins and additions to surplus.

Operational Assumptions.   Four additional assumptions are made to simplify the mathematics of the illustration. They involve the time of payment of premiums, expenses, and claims; the independence of mortality and lapse rates; the setting of a fixed termination date for all policies; and the restriction of the source of income to premiums only.

TIME OF PAYMENT ASSUMPTIONS.   Premiums, expenses expressed as a percentage of the gross premium, and expenses expressed as a flat amount per policy are assumed to be paid at the beginning of the year. Assumed to be paid at the end of the year are death claims, death claim expenses, cash surrender value claims, surrender value claim expenses, and dividends.

INDEPENDENCE OF MORTALITY AND LAPSE RATES.   Table 25–B–2 shows that the mortality and lapse rates are both mutually exclusive and independent of one another. That is, in Table 25–B–2 the number living and persisting in policy year t is derived by subtracting both the number dying and the number lapsing in policy year t–1 from the number living and persisting in policy year t–1. Note that the number living and persisting as shown in Table 25–B–2, Column 5 for policy year 2 (89,721) is derived from the number living and persisting as shown in Column 5 for policy year 1 (100,000) less the sum of the number dying in policy year 1 (279 as shown in Column 6) and the number lapsing in policy year 1 (10,000 as shown in Column 7). Thus,

$$100,000 - [279 + 10,000] = 89,721.$$

The mortality rates and the lapse rates are applied separately to the number living and persisting at the beginning of the year. The 10,000 lapses for the first year were computed by applying the 0.10 lapse rate (Table 25–B–1, Column 4) to the 100,000 living and persisting in policy year 1.

The 279 deaths for the first year were computed by applying the 0.00279 mortality rate (Table 25–B–1, Column 3) to the 100,000 living and persisting in year 1. The result is a double decrement, and Table 25–B–2 is a double decrement table.

TABLE 25–B–2

Double Decrement Table

Policy Year — t (1)	Attained Age (2)	Mortality Rate — x (3)	Lapse Rate (4)	Number Living and Persisting (5)	Number Dying* (6)	Number Lapsing* (7)
1 50	50	0.00279	0.1000	100,000	279	10,000
2 51	51	.00382	.0600	89,721	343	5,383
3 52	52	.00481	.0500	3,995	404	4,200
4 53	53	.00560	.0440	79,391	445	3,493
5 54	54	.00634	.0400	75,453	478	3,018
6 55	55	.00714	.0360	71,957	514	2,590
7 56	56	.00807	.0320	68,853	556	2,203
8 57	57	.00910	.0290	66,094	601	1,917
9 58	58	.01027	.0270	63,576	653	1,717
10 59	59	.01159	.0250	61,206	709	1,530
11 60	60	.01318	.0260	58,967	777	1,533
12 61	61	.01520	.0280	56,657	861	1,586
13 62	62	.01739	.0320	54,210	943	1,735
14 63	63	.01969	.0380	51,532	1,015	1,958
15 64	64	.02324	.0440	48,559	1,129	2,137

* Rounded to the nearest whole number for illustrative purposes.

FIXED TERMINATION DATE FOR ALL POLICIES. It is assumed that all policies remaining in the 30th year are terminated in that year. Note for attained age 79 (Table 25–B–1, Column 2) that the sum of the mortality rate of 0.08895 (Table 25–B–1, Column 3) and the lapse rate (Table 25–B–1, Column 4) equal 1. Therefore, the assumption is that no one will continue his policy beyond attained age 79, and that by attained age 80 all policies in the original block of 100,000 will have been terminated either through payment of a death claim or a cash surrender value claim.[6]

SOURCE OF INCOME. A final operational assumption is that gross premiums will be treated as the sole source of income, even though investment earnings are an important source of income to life insurers. However, this assumption does not mean that investment income is ignored. The reduction of all items in the formula to their present values, by discounting them at the assumed rate of interest (5 percent) for the appropriate number of years, eliminates the need for a separate investment income item in the

---

[6] The computations could have been carried on through the limiting age of the mortality table, but the benefit of doing so for this illustration would not be worth the effort.

formula. The effect of this discounting process is to reduce the amount needed for expenses and for the payment of claims by the amount of the assumed investment income, thus retaining the equivalence of the items in the equation.

Calculation of the Gross Premium. The profit equation offers a useful method of gross premium calculation—

$$PV \text{ (profit)} = PV \text{ (GP)} - PV \text{ (expenses plus claim payments)}.$$

This equation says that the present value of profits per block of business is equal to the present value of the gross premium per block of business minus the present value of both the expenses and the claim payments associated with that block of business.

In order to derive the gross premium per policy, it is necessary to analyze the components of the equation.

THE PRESENT VALUE OF PROFITS. The present value of the profits per block of business is defined as the number of policies per block times the profit objective per policy. The profit objective per policy has been defined as $20 plus 30 percent of one level GP. The size of the block has been assumed to be 100,000 policies. Thus,

$$PV \text{ (profit)} = 100,000 \text{ ($20 + 30\% GP)}, \text{ or } \$2,000,000 + 30,000 \text{ GP}.$$

THE PRESENT VALUE OF GROSS PREMIUMS. The derivation of the present value of gross premiums requires an understanding of the concept of the time value of money, explained in Chapter 24. A sum of $1 payable a year from now is worth less than $1 now if the interest rate is greater than zero $(i > 0)$. If interest is 5 percent, a sum of $1 payable a year from now is worth $0.9538 now [1 $(1 + i)^{-1}$ or v^1, see Table 25–B–1, Column 4].

The present value of the gross premium payments is equal to the sum of the present values of these payments times the number of people who make the payments. That is,

$$PV \text{ (GP)} = \sum_{t=1}^{30} (N)_t \text{ (GP)} v^{t-1}$$

where N_t is the number of people living and persisting in policy year t (Table 25–B–2, Column 5) and v^t is the present value of 1 payable t years from now (Table 25–B–1, Column 5).

Table 25–B–3 illustrates the computation of the present value of gross premiums for the first three years. If this procedure is continued through attained age 79, the present value of GP will be the total of Column 4 in Table 25–B–3, or $916,790 (GP).[7] Note that since premiums are assumed to be paid at the beginning of the year, no discount factor is applied to the premiums to be paid the first year. Therefore, the present value factor is 1.000 for that year.

---

[7] In the foregoing illustrations and in those to follow, the numbers have been rounded to the nearest whole real number.

TABLE 25–B–3

Present Value of Gross Premiums for Attained
Ages 50 through 52: An Illustration

(1) Attained Age (Table 25–B–1, Column 2)	(2) Number Living and Persisting (Table 25–B–2, Column 5)	(3) Present Value of 1 (v^t) (Table 25–B–1, Column 5)		(4) Present Value of Gross Premium (GP)
50	100,000	1.00000	=	100,000 (GP)
51	89,721	0.95238	≅	85,449 (GP)
52	83,995	0.90703	≅	76,186 (GP)
Total	$\sum\limits_{t=1}^{30} (N)_t (GP) v^{t-1}$		=	$916,790 (GP)

THE PRESENT VALUE OF EXPENSES AND CLAIMS PAYMENTS. The
present value of the expenses and claims payments associated with the block
of business is the summation of the following seven present value series:
(1) death claim payments, (2) death claim expenses, (3) cash surrender
value payments, (4) surrender value claim expenses, (5) dividend payments, (6) expenses per policy, and (7) expenses that are a percentage of
the gross premium. The computation of the present value of the foregoing
items is similar to the method of calculating the present value of gross
premiums as previously illustrated.

Present Value of Death Claims. The present value of death claims is
equal to the sum of the present values of the death claims for each year. The
death claims for each year is the product of the number dying in that year
times $10,000. That is,

$$PV \text{ (death claims)} = \sum_{t=1}^{30} (d)_t \, \$10,000v^t,$$

where $(d)_t$ is the number dying in policy year t (Table 25–B–2, Column 6).

Table 25–B–4 illustrates the computation of the present value of death
claims for the first two years.

If this procedure is continued through attained age 79, the present value
of death claim payments will be the total of Column 5 in Table 25–B–4, or
$114,271,799. Note that since death claims are assumed to be paid at the
end of the year, a discount is applied for the first year.

Present Value of Death Claim Expenses. The present value of all the
death claim expenses is the sum of the number dying each year (Column 6,
Table 25–B–2) times the present value (Column 5, Table 25–B–1) of
$40, the death claim expense per policy. The total present value

$$\sum_{t=1}^{30} (d)_t \, \$40v^t$$

is $457,087.

TABLE 25–B–4

Present Value of Death Claim Payments for Attained Ages 50 and 51:
An Illustration

(1) Attained Age (Table 25–B–1, 25–B–2, Column 2)	(2) Number Dying (Table 25–B–2, Column 6)	(3) Amount of Claims ($10,000 × Column 2)	(4) Present Value of 1 (v^t) (Table 25–B–1, Column 5)	(5) Present Value of Death Claims (Column 3 × Column 4)
50	279	$2,790,000	0.95238	$ 2,656,130
51	343	3,430,000	0.90703	3,111,112
Total		$\sum_{t=1}^{30} (d)_t \, \$10,000 \, V^t$	=	$114,271,799

Present Value of Cash Surrender Payments. The present value of the cash surrender value payments is the summation of the number lapsing in each policy year (Table 25–B–2, Column 7), times the present value of the cash surrender values (Table 25–B–1, Column 6). That is

$$PV \text{ (cash surrender value payments)} = \sum_{t=1}^{30} (L)_t \, (C)_t \, v^t,$$

where $(L)_t$ is the number lapsing in year t, and $(C)_t$ is the cash surrender value payable to those lapsing in year t. For the 30 policy years, the total present value of cash surrender payments amounts to $69,076,738. Because surrender value payments are assumed to be paid at the end of the year, each payment is discounted for t years.

Present Value of Surrender Value Claim Expenses. The present value of the surrender value claim expenses for the 30 policy years is the summation of the number lapsing each year times the present value of $10, the assumed surrender claim expense per policy. That is,

$$PV \text{ (surrender value claims expenses)} = \sum_{t=1}^{30} (L)_t \, (\$10) v^t.$$

For the 30 policy years, the present value of surrender value claim expenses amounts to $449,162.

Present Value of Dividend Payments. The procedure for computing the present value of dividend payments is similar to the foregoing procedure except that no first year dividends are paid to the 10,279 whose policies terminate the first year either because of death (279, Table 25–B–2, Column 6) or lapse (10,000, Table 25–B–2, Column 7). The only ones who will receive a first-year policy dividend are the 89,721 (Table 25–B–2, Column 5) who are living and persisting after the first policy year. Thus, the amount of the first year's dividend payment is 89,721 times the first year's dividend payment (Table 25–B–1, Column 7) or 89,721 times $32.40. However, dividend payments for each year after the first one are not contingent on the policyholder's living and persisting to the end of the year. These payments are the product of the dividends times the number living and persisting at the beginning of the year. Thus, the second year's dividend payment per block of business is $37.40 (Table 25–B–1, Column 7) times 89,721 (Table 25–B–2, Column 5).

The present value of dividend payments is the number of persons living and persisting at the end of the first policy year, times the present value of dividend payments at the end of the first policy year, plus the summation of the product of the number living and persisting each year after the first, times the present value of the dividend payments in those years. That is,

$$PV \text{ (dividend payments)} = N_2 P_1 v + \sum_{t=2}^{30} N_t P_t v^t$$

where N is the number of people living and persisting and P_t is the amount of the dividend payment per policy in policy year t. For the 30 policy years, the total present value of dividend payments amounts to $57,159,437. Because dividend payments are assumed to be paid at the end of the year, each payment is discounted for t years.

Present Value of Flat Expenses per Policy. Expenses of flat amounts are assumed to be apportioned to each policy, in this case $90 per policy in the first policy year and $6 per year per policy thereafter. The amount of these expenses for any year is the number living and persisting at the beginning of that year (Table 25–B–2, Column 5) times the flat charge per policy for that year. The present value of the total of flat expenses per policy is the number of policies initially in the block (100,000) times $90, plus the summation of the product of the number living and persisting each year thereafter, times the present value of $6. That is,

$$PV \text{ (flat expenses per policy)} = \$90 \, (N)_1 + \sum_{t=2}^{30} (N)_t \, \$6 \, v^{t-1}.$$

For the 30 policy years, the total present value of flat expenses per policy amounts to $13,900,738. Because these expenses are assumed to be paid at the beginning of each year, the present value in period t is lagged 1 year $(t-1)$. Thus, the present value of the first year's flat expenses is $(100,000) \times \$90 v^0$ where $v^0 = 1$ (a number raised to the 0 power is 1).

Present Value of Expenses Expressed as a Percentage of GP. Expenses based on a percentage of *GP* are assumed to be apportioned to each policy, in this case 70 percent for the first year, 10 percent for the second through the ninth year, and 5 percent thereafter. The amount of these expenses for any year is the number living and persisting at the beginning of that year (Table 25–B–2, Column 5) times the percentage of *GP* appropriate for that year. The present value of the total of expenses based on a percentage of *GP* is the number of policies initially in the block (100,000), times .70*GP*, plus the summation of the product of the number living and persisting each year from the second year to the ninth year, times the present value of $.10GP$, plus the summation of the product of the number living and persisting for the 10th year and each year thereafter, times the present value of $.05GP$. That is,

PV (expenses as a percentage of GP) =

$$(N)_1 (.70GP) \text{ plus } \sum_{t=2}^{9} (N)_t (.10GP) v^{t-1} \text{ plus}$$

$$\sum_{t=10}^{30} (N)_t (.05GP) v^{t-1}.$$

For the 30 policy years, the total present value of expenses that are expressed as a percentage of GP amounts to $137,315GP$. Because these expenses are assumed to be paid at the beginning of each year, the expenses for each year are discounted $t - 1$ years.

Solving the Equation. The sum of the present values of the 6 expense and claim payment items associated with the block of 100,000 continuous premium whole life policies is $255,314,941 plus $137,315GP$. Earlier, the present value of gross premiums was found to equal $916,790GP$, and the present value of profits was found to be $2,000,000 + 30,000GP$.

By recalling the profit equation, PV (profit) = PV (GP) − PV (expenses plus claim payments) and inserting the correct values for the variables,

$$\$2,000,000 + (30,000) \, GP =$$
$$(916,790) \, GP - [\$255,314,941 + (137,315) \, GP]$$

a linear equation in terms of the gross premium can be solved:

$$916,790GP - 30,000GP - 137,315GP = 2,000,000 + 255,314,941; \text{ so}$$
$$749,475GP = 257,314,941,$$
$$GP = 257,314,941 \div 749,475$$
$$\therefore GP \cong 343.33$$

Table 25–B–5 gives a summary of the values of the items in the equation and illustrates the solution to the profit equation. The mathematical notation for the calculation is given in Table 25–B–6.

TABLE 25–B–5

Summary of Gross Premium Calculations

Present Values:

(1) Profit	$ 2,000,000 + 30,000 *GP*
(2) Gross premiums	(916,790) *GP*
(3) Face amount payments	114,271,779
(4) Death claim expenses	457,087
(5) Cash surrender value payments	69,076,738
(6) Cash surrender claim expenses	449,162
(7) Dividend payments	57,159,437
(8) Flat expenses per policy	13,900,738
(9) Expenses expressed as a percentage of gross premiums	(137,315) *GP*

Solution to Profit Equation:

$$PV \text{ (profit)} = PV \text{ (GP)} - PV \text{ (expenses + claim payments)}$$
$$(1) = (2) - [(3) + (4) + (5) + (6) + (7) + (8) + (9)]$$
$$\$2,000,000 + 30,000 \, GP \cong (916,790) \, GP - \$114,271,779 - \$457,087 - \$69,076,738$$
$$- \$449,162 - \$57,159,437 - \$13,900,738 - (137,315) \, GP$$
$$\cong 779,475 \, GP - \$255,314,941$$
$$(749,475) \, GP \cong \$257,314,941$$
$$\therefore GP \cong \$343.33$$

TABLE 25–B–6

Mathematical Notation for the Gross Premium Calculations

$$PV \text{ (profit)} = PV \text{ (gross premiums)} - PV \text{ (expenses plus claim payments)}$$

PV (profit):

PV (objective per policy $\times$ No. in block) $= (\$20 + 0.30 \, GP) \times (100,000)$
$$= \$2,000,000 + 30,000 \, GP$$

PV (GP):

$$\sum_{t=1}^{30} [(\text{no. living and persisting})_t GP \, v^{t-1}] = (916,790) \, GP$$

PV (expenses plus claim payments):

PV (face amount payments) $= \sum_{t=1}^{30} (\text{no. dying})_t (\$10,000) v^t$
$$= \$114,271,779$$

PV (death claim expenses) $= \sum_{t=1}^{30} (\text{no. dying})_t (\$40) v^t = \$457,087$

PV (cash surrender value payments) $= \sum_{t=1}^{30} (\text{no. lapsing})_t (\text{cash surrender value})_t v^t$
$$= \$69,076,738$$

PV (cash surrender value claim expense) $= \sum_{t=1}^{30} (\text{no. lapsing})_t (\$10) v^t$
$$= \$449,162$$

PV (dividend payments) $=$ (no. living and persisting at end of 1st policy year) (dividend for that year) v PLUS
$$\sum_{t=2}^{30} (\text{no. living and persisting})_t (\text{dividend})_t v^t$$
$$= \$57,159,437$$

PV (flat expenses per policy) $= \sum_{t=1}^{30} (\text{no. living and persisting})_t (\text{expenses per policy})_t v^{t-1}$
$$= \$13,900,738$$

PV (expenses expressed as a percentage of GP) $= \sum_{t=1}^{30} (\text{no. living and persisting})_t (\text{percentage of } GP)_t v^{t-1}$

$$PV \text{ (profit)} = PV \text{ (GP)} - PV \text{ (expenses plus claim payments)}$$
$$\$2,000,000 + 30,000 \, GP \cong (916,790) \, GP - 255,314,941 + (137,315) \, GP$$
$$GP \cong \$343.33.$$

26

Financial Management: Statements and Assets

The financial management and condition of an insurance company are a concern of the law, which not only sets rigid standards for the company's investments and disbursements but also makes its transactions subject to constant review by state regulatory authorities. In order for these insurance departments to obtain information that will enable them to judge whether a company is fulfilling the requirements of the law in its financial transactions and whether it is in sound condition as defined by the law, each company is required to submit a highly detailed annual statement. In the United States these statements are filed with the insurance department in each state and territory in which the company is licensed to do business. In Canada they are filed with the Dominion department, which assumes the primary responsibility for the solvency of companies licensed by it.

While the annual statements of companies licensed in a given state are on file with the department in that state and are public records, open to inspection by anyone on demand, the annual statement required by a state is designed primarily to provide information for the use of the department rather than to present the information in a form readily understandable by the layman. These statements are highly complex and do not follow the form customary in ordinary corporate annual statements.

The insurance company annual statement is further complicated to the extent that state laws require different information or a different presentation of the same information. At one time in the history of regulation of the insurance business, every state had its own annual statement form, or "blank." Thus a company licensed in several states had to develop information for and fill out several different blanks. Since developing the information for and filling out an annual statement blank is an expensive and complicated procedure, the use of different blanks requiring different information by different states was highly unsatisfactory. To remedy the problem, the National Association of Insurance Commissioners developed a uniform report known as the "convention blank," because the NAIC was then called the National *Convention* of Insurance Commissioners. This blank was developed in 1872 as one of the first projects of the newly organized association. With the exception of the gain and loss exhibit, the 1872 convention blank was used without revision until 1951. The gain and loss blank was revised in 1939. In its present form, the convention blank is accepted by all states as providing the information needed or wanted.

While the convention blank is uniform for all states, the financial statement for any given company may vary from state to state. Certain assets may be admitted in one state but not admitted in another.[1] At times in the past, different states have required different methods of valuing certain types of securities.[2] Other differences could be cited; but the point here is that there can be a variation in the financial statement of a company from one state to another even though the annual statement form used is the same for all states.

Insurance companies have been criticized from time to time for the complicated nature of their annual statements. Critics charge that the statements cannot be understood by either the insuring or investing public. Two points with respect to this confusion need to be stressed: (1) The form of the annual statement is prescribed by state insurance departments, not by insurance companies. (2) Insurance departments are interested in developing information that will enable them to judge the condition and transactions of companies in relation to the law. The information desired by the departments and the form in which they wish it presented may or may not be of interest or significance to the general public.

For policyholders and the public, all companies prepare and publish condensed annual statements in a form understandable to anyone who has a rudimentary acquaintanceship with corporate annual statements. Many companies develop attractive reports which have sound advertising and public relations values while at the same time presenting general financial and operational information of interest to the policyholder. The information given in these reports includes the surplus position of the companies, mortality and expense rates, net interest earned, the company's investment policy, and figures which show the nature and extent of the company's growth.

In addition to the convention reports developed for the regulatory authorities and the annual reports developed for policyholders, companies prepare interim financial reports for the use of management. This chapter is concerned only with the reports required by state officials.

---

[1] Admitted assets are those which the law of the state allows to be used to determine the excess of assets over liabilities.

[2] For example, in the years 1917–21 and 1931–33 when, because market prices were abnormally low, many states permitted valuation of nonamortizable securities at higher than market value.

1. THE CONVENTION BLANK

The convention blank as revised in 1951 calls for several different groups of statements. Three of them are financial statements: the balance sheet, summary of operations, and surplus account. These are followed by a gain and loss exhibit. There are 15 other exhibits and 20 schedules relating to the summary figures used in the financial statements. In addition, there are 50 general interrogations, 30 of which are grouped on one page. These questions pertain to the entire business of the company.

The nature of these statements, exhibits, schedules, and interrogatories will be discussed briefly.[3]

As in any business, the three most important statements are the balance sheet, profit and loss statement, and allocation of surplus.

The balance sheet for a life and health insurance company is given on pages two and three of the convention blank. In the form required, it is similar to the balance sheet of any type of business. Assets are given on the left-hand page and liabilities and net worth on the right-hand page. Different sections of the balance sheet will be discussed later.[4]

The profit and loss statement (on an accrual basis) is presented on page four of the blank in the form of a summary of operations. Income applicable to the period is stated whether or not it has been received. Expenses applicable to the period are deducted whether or not they have been paid.

Income items consist of life and health insurance premiums, considerations for annuities and supplementary contracts, dividend accumulations, and investment income. Charged against this income are policy benefits paid or payable, interest on policy or contract funds, increases in reserves, commissions, general operation expense, taxes, licenses and other fees, and dividends.

Allocation of surplus is shown on the bottom of page four of the blank as a double column form. The left-hand column is a statement of the source of the surplus funds; for example, surplus carried over from the previous year, gains during the current year, and net capital gains. On the right is a statement of the distribution of surplus funds; for example, dividends to stockholders (if any), increases in contingency reserves and in

---

[3] A detailed discussion of each of the items of an annual statement requires a development of a background of technical knowledge of both actuarial and accounting theory beyond the scope of this book, or of the course for which it is intended as a text. The purpose of this discussion is to acquaint the student with the general nature of the blank in order to facilitate understanding of company assets, liabilities, and surplus, and the problems of financial management. For a comprehensive discussion of the Convention blank see Joseph C. Noback, *Life Insurance Accounting: A Study of the Financial Statements of Life Insurance Companies in the United States and Canada* (Homewood, Illinois: Richard D. Irwin, Inc., 1969).

[4] Assets are discussed later in this chapter. Liabilities, capital, and surplus are discussed in the following chapter.

unassigned surplus, and net capital losses. A gain and loss exhibit appears on pages five and six of the convention blank. This exhibit is divided into two sections: operations by classes of insurance issued, and increases in reserves.

Operations by classes or "lines" is a breakdown of the items in the summary of operations. The purpose of the exhibit is to show the contributions of each of the following classes of business to the surplus of the company for the year:[5]

Industrial
Ordinary
    Life insurance
    Total and permanent disability insurance
    Accidental death insurance (double indemnity)
    Annuities
    Supplementary contracts
Group
    Life insurance
    Annuities
Health
    Group
    Individual

The section on reserves begins with a statement of the previous year's reserves for each line or subdivision included above, with the exception of health insurance. To the previous year's reserves are added assumed net premiums,[6] assumed interest, and other increases. From the total are deducted assumed mortality, other costs, and payments on terminations.[7] The remainder is the reserve as of the end of the year.[8]

Another required statement is the policy exhibit. This exhibit, found on pages 15 and 16, is divided into three parts:

Ordinary Business
    Whole life and endowment
    Term
    Group
    Dividend additions
Industrial Business
    Whole life and endowment

---

[5] Remember these figures are after the payment of policy dividends and therefore represent net gains or losses.

[6] Net premiums refer to valuation premiums without the expense loading.

[7] Note the use of the terms "assumed interest" and "assumed mortality." These mean that if the reserve basis of the policy is 1958 CSO at $2\frac{1}{2}$ percent, then $2\frac{1}{2}$ percent and the 1958 CSO tabular mortality are used regardless of the actual interest earned or mortality experienced.

[8] This is known as the retrospective method of calculating a terminal reserve, which will be explained in detail in Chapter 27.

Term
Dividend additions
Annuities
Individual annuities
Group annuities
Supplementary contracts involving life contingencies

The exhibit starts with a statement of the number of policies in force at the end of the previous year and the amounts involved. To this is added the number and amount of policies issued, revived,[9] and increased during the year covered by the statement.

From the total arrived at are deducted policies which have become claims, matured as endowments, expired, surrendered, lapsed, decreased in amount,[10] withdrawn, and terminated by disability.[11] The remainder is the number of policies and amount of insurance in force as of the end of the year for which the statement is made.[12]

Under each of the divisions of the annuity section, the number of such annuities is listed. Also listed are the amounts of the annual income now payable, income deferred but fully paid, and income deferred but not fully paid.

A note at the end of the exhibit gives the number of policies and the amount of insurance which has been reinsured.

The general interrogatories sections found on pages 11, 17, 21, and 43 request the answers to a series of questions about the company and its operations. Often these questions are designed for the purpose of gathering statistics on trends in the business and have little or no bearing on the financial position of the company. They might even be asked in connection with a study by the NAIC Blanks Committee for use in deciding whether more schedules should be added or others dropped. Examples of questions in the interrogatory section are the number, kind, and amount of the company's stock outstanding; whether or not the company has a retirement plan for agents and employees; in what states, territories, and countries the company operates.

Deposit schedules found on page 18 are of two types: special and general. In the special schedule are included deposits not available for the protection of all policyholders, such as a deposit required of a U.S. company for the exclusive protection of Canadian policyholders. The general deposit schedule includes a schedule of all other deposits.

---

[9] Lapsed policies reinstated.

[10] Most of the decreases result from policies being put on the paid-up nonforfeiture option.

[11] Such termination arises under a type of policy that provides for payment of the face amount in installments commencing at the time of disability or maturing at age 65 in event the policyholder is continuously disabled prior to that age.

[12] The statement also will show transfers from one form to another, the most common of which are conversion of term to whole life and the conversion of whole life to extended term.

In addition to the gain and loss exhibit and the policy exhibit, there are 14 other exhibits from pages 7 through 14. Briefly these exhibits are as follows:

1. Breakdown of premium receipts, dividends applied as premiums, premiums on reinsurance ceded, and commissions into the following categories:

> Industrial life
> Ordinary life insurance
> Total and permanent disability insurance
> Accidental death insurance (double indemnity)
> Annuities
> Group
> > Life insurance
> > Annuities
> Health
> > Individual policies
> > Group policies

Figures in each category are divided into first year, renewal, and single premiums.

2. An analysis of investment income, derived by subtracting taxes, licenses, fees (computed in Exhibit 6), and investment expenses (computed in Exhibit 5) from the total interest, dividends, and real estate income (computed in Exhibit 3).

3. A detailed report of total interest, dividends, and real estate income shown in Exhibit 2.

4. Breakdown of capital gain and loss on investments by showing the increase or decrease in book value and the profit and loss on the sale or maturity of all investments of the company.

5. Expenses incurred in life and health insurance operations.

6. Taxes, licenses, and fee for life and health insurance operations.

7. Analysis of dividends of policyholders.

8. A detailed explanation of the reserves shown for the different types of life insurance policies outstanding.

9. A detailed explanation of health insurance reserves.

10. Funds held by the company not involving life contingencies, such as funds held under fixed amount and fixed period settlement options and dividend accumulations.

11. A report of life insurance claims in process and as yet unpaid.

12. Determination of the amount of the company's ledger assets.

13. Breakdown of all assets into ledger, nonledger, nonadmitted, and admitted.

14. An analysis of nonadmitted assets.

The 18 schedules other than deposits appear on pages 19 through 45. They are, briefly, as follows:[13]

A. A list of real estate owned and of real estate sold during the year. Real estate owned is divided into that owned at the beginning of the year and that acquired during the year. Information concerning description, cost, market value, income produced, and expenses in connection with the property is required.

B. A report of mortgages owned and changes made during the year. These mortgages are classified according to the states and foreign countries in which they are held. Also farm and other mortgages are handled separately. A distinction is made, too, between purchase money mortgages and all other mortgages. Loans more than three months overdue but not yet in process of foreclosure, mortgages over $250,000 or representing more than one half of 1 percent of admitted assets, loans on which interest or taxes are delinquent for more than a year, and several similar items are listed separately. A detailed list of foreclosures during the year also is required.

C. A schedule of loans secured by collateral.[14]

D. A schedule describing the type, cost, book values, and market values (and for bonds, amortized values) of stocks and bonds owned; purchased (or otherwise acquired); sold, redeemed, or otherwise disposed of during the year. Also included is the amount of income from stocks and bonds and the rate of earnings on stocks for the previous three years; a summary of bonds purchased during the year with their descriptions, name of seller, cost, and par value; a similar type of summary of securities sold during the year, including profit or loss.

E. Balance in each bank account as of the date of the statement plus the highest balance in each such account during each month of the year and interest received on such accounts. Amounts on deposit in any suspended banks or trust companies are listed separately.

F. A list of the amounts of all claims resisted or compromised during the year divided into (1) those disposed of and (2) those still in process at the end of the year. Claims are divided into death, disability, double indemnity, and other.

G. Payments over $1,000 made to trade associations, rating bureaus, service organizations; all salaries, compensation and emoluments, excepting bona fide commissions paid to or retained by agents, received in the current year by: (1) each director or trustee regardless of the amount, (2) each of the 10 officers or employees receiving the largest amounts, and (3) any other person, firm, or corporation if the amount received was in excess of $20,000, except for amounts included in Schedules I, J, and K.

---

[13] For purposes of simplicity, these schedules are discussed in the order appearing on the blank. Notice, however, their illogical arrangement. For example, Schedules H, N, and O deal with health insurance. Schedules A through E deal with assets and so does Schedule X.

[14] Few companies have any such loans outstanding.

In the case of employees who are not directors or officers and who were paid less than $20,000, it is necessary to show only the total number of such employees and the total amount paid them.

H. An analysis of health insurance experience with respect to premiums, claims, and expenses. The analysis segregates group from individual policies and further divides these classes into types of coverage.

I. Commissions on loans and purchase or sale of property which exceed $5,000, including name and address of the person receiving the commission and the amount involved in the transaction.

J. Names and addresses of persons paid legal fees of $500 or more and the nature of the service for which the fee was paid. Amounts under $500 are reported in total.

K. Itemization of all expenditures made in connection with matters before legislatures and other government departments.

L. A report of the last annual meeting: names of candidates for director and votes cast for each, and a copy of the minutes of the meeting.

M. Examples of dividend rates paid during the year on the different classes of policies and a statement of the method by which the dividends were calculated.

N. Premium and loss experience on various types of health policies.

O. Analysis of health insurance claims arranged by types of coverages and broken down into amounts paid, unpaid, and estimated.[15]

S. A list of amounts recoverable from reinsurance companies.

T. Premium collections for life insurance and annuities classified by states.

X. Unlisted assets, consisting of assets of doubtful or no value, with particulars about any property acquired, sold, or transferred to or from this schedule during the year.

New York sets a limit on the amount which may be used for expenses.[16]

In order to administer the law, the New York department requires companies doing business in that state to complete Schedule Q. This schedule calls for the following types of information: a comparison of first-year field expenses incurred with the limit allowed, comparison of total field expenses incurred with the limit allowed, and for mutual insurers, also a comparison of total expenses incurred with total expenses allowed.

As stated, many of the schedules are detailed breakdowns or listings of figures required in the statements. Some of the schedules require the information only as part of the general policy of giving publicity to all insurance company transactions, whereas others require information necessary to permit the regulators to measure whether insurers are complying with the restrictions in the code.

---

[15] Estimated health claims are those incurred but not yet reported.

[16] N.Y. Insurance Law, Sections 212 and 213 (McKinney, 1969). Cf. Chapter 29 for a brief discussion of these limitations.

2. ASSETS

Although the policy reserve of a life insurance company often is referred to as a "fund," it is simply a bookkeeping figure, actuarially determined, to measure the liability of the company under policy contracts outstanding. Thus the reserve is a liability; and it is necessary for the company to hold assets to offset that liability if the company is to remain solvent. Assets represent the values owned by the company which are available to offset liabilities and the ownership interest in the company.

Types of Assets. The instructions for filling out the annual statement blank state that "each class of assets should be entered . . . at its final value." To determine this final value, five terms relating to life insurance company assets must be defined: *ledger, nonledger, gross, nonadmitted,* and *admitted*.

Ledger assets arise from an excess of income over disbursements. In addition, they reflect any write-up of the value of an asset (which shows as income) and the value of any write-down (which shows as a disbursement). They reach the financial statement through normal double-entry book-keeping procedure, that is from vouchers through journal to ledger. Examples of items included in ledger assets are cash on hand, real estate, mortgage loans, stocks and bonds, policy loans, and furniture and fixtures.

Nonledger assets are those to which a value is attached but which arise out of transactions not yet completed. They do not go through the ledger but are inventoried at the end of the accounting period and entered directly on the financial statement. Examples are interest due and accrued but not yet collected, and uncollected premiums due. A nonledger asset could be made a ledger asset if the insurer chooses to handle the item through the ledger. For example, accrued interest receivable could be converted into a ledger asset by setting up and debiting a ledger asset account for interest due and accrued but not yet collected, and crediting interest income. An asset may have a ledger value and a nonledger value. These are combined in the balance sheet. For example, if common stocks are carried in the ledger at cost, there will be a nonledger value equal to the difference, if any, between the cost and market value of these stocks.

Gross assets are the total of ledger and nonledger assets.

Nonadmitted assets are assets which cannot be included in determining the solvency of the company, i.e., they cannot be counted in measuring the amount by which assets exceed liabilities. Examples of typical nonadmitted assets are any of the company's own stock which it may own or loans secured by the company's own stock; supplies on hand; furniture and equipment (except in many states the depreciated value of large electronic data processing equipment); advances to agents; the amount by which the book value of any asset exceeds the valuation as determined by the state insurance department; uncollectible premiums; uncollectible deposits in failed banks; and uncollectible past-due interest on investments. Non-admitted assets usually are those that cannot be counted upon to produce funds in the event the insurer is liquidated.

Admitted assets are the net after nonadmitted assets have been deducted from gross assets. Expressed as a formula, *ledger assets + nonledger assets — nonadmitted assets = admitted assets.*

The final value of assets asked for on the annual statement blank is that of admitted assets.

Valuation of Assets. The admitted assets of a life insurance company consist mainly of stocks, bonds, mortgage loans, other types of loans, real estate, and cash. For the purpose of the annual statement, each of these assets must be assigned a value. If they are overvalued (or undervalued, for that matter) the statement will not be a fair measure of the company's financial condition. Therefore, a fair value must be assigned to admitted assets.[17] Since the surplus of mutual life insurance companies rarely exceeds 10 percent of legal reserves,[18] it also is important that valuation standards for assets be flexible enough to prevent unnecessary insolvencies during adverse market reactions.[19] In many cases the state insurance department prescribes the method of valuation. Valuation problems in the past have been and still are being studied by both the industry and the regulatory authorities. The common methods of valuing assets today are:

Cash. Obviously, the value of cash, on hand or in banks, is the dollar amount itself.

Loans. Loans are valued at the amount lent plus accrued interest minus the amount repaid.

Real Estate. Real estate held by a life insurance company may be classified

---

[17] Liabilities must also be fairly valued. This is a subject for Chapter 27.

[18] In some states the law restricts the amount of surplus, including those reserves not classified as statutory liabilities (i.e., voluntary reserves), which a mutual life insurer can accumulate. The typical limitation is 10 percent of the legal reserve as computed by the insurer. Any surplus in excess of this amount must be paid in dividends. The maximum size of the statutory surplus is a function of the size of the legal reserve. The size of the legal reserve is a function of the interest and mortality assumption used and the method applied by the insurer in computing its reserve. The more conservative the assumptions and the method adopted by the insurer the higher will be its legal reserve and consequently the higher will be the maximum surplus it can accumulate. Because many insurers believe that the statutory surplus maximum is too low, they are inclined to compute their reserves conservatively. Furthermore, when reserves are computed conservatively liabilities are overvalued, producing a hidden surplus. By understating asset values insurers also are able to build an additional hidden surplus.

[19] A mandatory securities valuation reserve (MSVR) was instituted by the National Association of Insurance Commissioners in 1951 to protect against adverse fluctuations in the values of bonds and stocks. The reserve is designed as a stabilizer to reduce the impact of rising and falling markets on the insurer's surplus. The reserve is accumulated by annual increments until it reaches a specified maximum. The size of each annual increment is a function of the admitted asset value of bonds and stocks and of the amount of net realized and unrealized capital gains on securities during the year. Net capital losses are allowable as a deduction. The maximum limitation on the MSVR is about $1\frac{1}{2}$ percent to $2\frac{1}{2}$ percent of assets in the large companies.

into three types: (1) property necessary to the operation of the business; (2) property acquired in satisfaction of a debt (such as property obtained through the foreclosure of a mortgage); and (3) property purchased for investment income. Property necessary to the operation of the business is usually valued at cost, including the cost of improvements, less depreciation. Property acquired in satisfaction of a debt normally is valued at the amount of the debt. Property purchased for investment income is valued on the basis of its cost. However, in no event may real estate be valued at more than its market value.

Nonamortizable Securities. Regulations of most states establish two classes of securities, nonamortizable and amortizable. A typical classification of nonamortizable securities includes all stocks because they do not have a maturity date, bonds in default as to principal or interest, bonds not amply secured and bonds yielding in excess of a given percentage on the current market. Nonamortizable securities, with the exception of preferred stocks which meet certain earnings and dividend requirements, must be valued at their fair market price. The problem is that of determining just what is the fair market price. Since the stock exchanges best reflect the market price of listed securities these are generally used as the valuation basis. However, valuation of listed securities is left to the Committee on Valuation of Securities of the National Association of Insurance Commissioners, which promulgates annual valuation rules based largely on ratings in security manuals and current market prices. Customarily, the Committee recommends the market quotations as of December 31. Unlisted stocks usually are valued at their last public sale price, or at the bid or asked price. If there have been no recent sales, common stock may be valued at book value.[20] Insurance company stocks in some states must be valued at book; in others at market.

In 1957 the National Association of Insurance Commissioners adopted the "one-fifth rule" for the stabilization of the value of those preferred stocks which meet certain dividend and earnings requirements. This rule allowed life insurance companies to value qualified perferred stocks at a figure between the price quoted in the market on the last day of the year of the report and the amount shown in the statement for the previous year. One fifth of the difference between these two figures was added to or subtracted from, as the case may be, the previous year's value. Thus, if a qualified preferred stock had a market value of $80 a share on the last day of the statement year and was valued in the previous statement at $90 a share, the value admitted in the new statement would have been $88 a share. If the situation were reversed, i.e., if $80 in the previous year's statement had been related to a current market value of $90, the new statement value would have been $82 a share. Thus, fluctuations up and

---

[20] Book value of common stock is found by dividing capital plus surplus minus preferred stock by the number of common shares outstanding. In applying this formula, the surplus should not include reserves required by statute.

down in the preferred stock market were minimized in the valuation of qualified issues.

The one-fifth rule was discontinued after 1964 by the National Association of Insurance Commissioners. The NAIC accepted the argument that preferred stocks meeting certain earnings and dividend requirements should be treated as a fixed income security, and valued at cost. Consequently, all preferred stocks purchased after 1964 and meeting the tests are valued at cost. Preferred stocks purchased before 1965 may be valued at their December 31, 1964, one-fifth rule value or at their original cost.

Amortizable Securities. In general, to be eligible for valuation on an amortized basis, a bond must not be in default as to principal or interest, must have a maturity date, must be amply secured,[21] and must fall into one of the following classes: (1) issued, assumed, or guaranteed by the U.S. or Canadian government; (2) special revenue bonds of a political subdivision or corporation bonds in the four highest grades of a recognized rating agency; (3) corporate bonds on which the yields to maturities do not exceed a given figure;[22] (4) approved by the National Association of Insurance Commissioners' Committee on Valuation of Securities; and (5) foreign bonds approved by the committee.

Amortizable securities[23] are valued according to a procedure under which their original cost is written up or down by gradual stages until the book value equals par at maturity date. The purpose of valuation on an amortized basis is to eliminate the fluctuation in asset values that would result if market values were used. The effect is to place a higher than market value on the bond when the market interest rate moves up, and a lower than market value on the bond when the market rate of interest moves down. Why this is true is explained in the following paragraphs. For those bonds acquired through direct placement, the amortized basis provides a convenient method for valuation because no public market value quotations are available.[24]

---

[21] The term "amply secured" does not necessarily mean secured by the pledge of specific assets but secured in the sense of being safe as indicated by a favorable working capital position and earnings record. The commissioners set up certain tests for measuring the adequacy of the security.

[22] This is called the yield test. The theory behind this rule is that unusually high-yielding bonds often are not considered to be of good quality and for that reason their valuation on an amortized basis is denied. The effect of this ruling is to require the use of market value. The yield on a bond is a function of the relationship between the interest payments and the market price. Since the interest payments are fixed, the yield increases as the market price goes down. For extraordinarily high yielding bonds, these low market values are the ones admitted on the annual statement.

[23] Amortized value in its strict or narrow sense refers only to bonds bought above par. The excess value is written down over the life of the bond so that the valuation at maturity date is par. However, the term is used (though technically incorrectly) to cover the reverse process, i.e., writing up, the technical name for which is "accrual of discount."

[24] Direct placements are broadly defined as securities not offered for public sale and include securities acquired directly from the issuers, securities acquired from investors who had acquired them from the issuers, and securities acquired from investment bankers or at

A bond is a document certifying a debt of a specific amount of money payable at the end of a designated period. For example, a $1,000 20-year bond certifies that a debt of $1,000 is due 20 years from its date of issue. The debt carries an interest rate known as the bond or coupon rate. If the bond has a 5 percent rate, it promises in addition to pay $50 a year during each of the 20 years of its life. The $50 is a fixed contractual obligation and will not vary during this 20-year period. Perhaps interest rates in the market might rise to 7 percent at one time and drop to 4 percent at another, depending upon conditions in the money market. If the market rate rises above the bond rate, the bond will sell at a discount; i.e., the bondholder in a sale will have to accept less than $1,000 for his $1,000 bond. The reason is simple. If the purchaser paid $1,000 for the bond, he would get only a 5 percent return on money which is worth more than 5 percent. Therefore, he would be willing to pay for the bond no more than that amount which would make the entire transaction yield him the market rate of interest.

For purposes of illustration, assume that the market rate of interest for this type of investment risk is 7 percent. What will be the price of the bond in question? The price is the function of three factors: (1) the bond rate (5 percent), (2) the market rate (7 percent), and (3) the length of time until the bond matures (assume this to be 10 years). Bond tables are published from which the price of the bond can be ascertained. A quick reference to one of these tables will give a price of approximately $857.90. If an investor purchases a $1,000 5 percent bond due in 10 years and pays $857.90 for it, the investment will yield him 7 percent. The effective annual return will be $50 plus an annual write-up. On the straight line method which gives approximate yields only, the annual write-up would be $14.21. The $14.21 annual accumulation (or write-up) is computed by dividing the bond discount, $142.10,[25] by the number of years until the bond matures (10). The $64.21 ($50 plus $14.21) gives an effective yield of approximately 7 percent on a mean or average investment of $928.95.[26] For valuation purposes, the bond will be entered at cost ($857.90) when it is purchased, but will be increased in value by the write-up each year so that by maturity it will have reached a value of $1,000. If the market rate is

competitive bidding when there was no public distribution. The first category represents the most important source of direct placements for life insurance companies. Direct placements account for more than 80 percent of the corporate bonds held by U.S. life insurance companies at the present time. One advantage to the issuing corporation of direct placement is that the securities are exempt from registration with the Securities and Exchange Commission. Another advantage is lower distribution costs. The insurance companies (chiefly the large ones) find direct placement advantageous because it enables them to get a larger portion of the issue than they could obtain at a public sale.

[25] The bond discount ($142.10) is the face amount of the bond ($1,000) minus the price of the bond ($857.90).

[26] The average investment ($928.95) is the average of the initial investment of $857.90 and the terminal investment of $1000. The annual interest received, $50, plus the annual increase in the write-up of the investment value, $14.21 equal the annual return of $64.21.

4 percent instead of 7 percent, the bond would sell at a premium. Assuming the other facts are the same as above, the bond would sell for about $1,081.80. The annual amortization cost (write-down) would amount to $8.18 on the straight line method. This means that the effective earning each year is $50 minus $8.18 or $41.82, which on a mean investment of $1,040.90 yields an effective return of approximately 4 percent. The bond will be valued at $1,081.80 when purchased, but will be written down each year so that on its maturity date its valuation will be equal to its maturity value.

The Actuarial Method. The simple procedure just described does not produce the exactness often desired in the valuation of bonds for purposes of the annual statement. Instead of the same amount of write-up or write-down every year as in the straight line method, an actuarial method is available under which the actual amount of effective interest earned each year on the book value for that year is computed. For discounted bonds, the effective interest amount less the bond interest payment is equal to the write-up for any period, whereas for premium bonds, the bond interest payment less the effective interest amount is equal to the write-down. Tables 26–1 and 26–2 may help clarify the point.

TABLE 26–1

Discount Bond Illustration

Bond $1,000—Bond Rate 5%
Purchase Price $857.90—Effective Rate 7%
(10 years to maturity)

Years to Run	Initial Book Value	Bond Interest	Effective Interest	Write-up	Terminal Book Value
10	$857.90	$50	$60.05	$10.05	$867.95
9	867.95	50	60.75	10.75	878.70
8	878.70	50	61.51	11.51	880.21

TABLE 26–2

Premium Bond Illustration

Bond $1,000—Bond Rate 5%
Purchase Price $1,081.80—Effective Rate 4%
(10 years to maturity)

Years to Run	Initial Book Value	Bond Interest	Effective Interest	Write-down	Terminal Book Value
10	$1,081.80	$50	$43.27	$6.73	$1,074.07
9	1,079.07	50	43.16	6.84	1,072.23
8	1,072.23	50	42.89	7.11	1,065.12

In tables 26–1 and 26–2 the value in the last column is the valuation used for the year in question. If the tables in these illustrations were to be carried to completion, the book value at the end of the 10th year would equal $1,000, the maturity value of the bond payable at that time.

Efforts currently are being made to devise new and more realistic methods of valuation. Much progress has been made with respect to bond valuation, but a great deal of study needs to be given to stock valuation. More realistic valuation methods to many authorities mean methods that give less weight to liquidation values and more consideration to what might be considered stable, long-run values. After all, as will soon become apparent, life insurance company investment portfolios do not require the liquidity assumed in the valuation formulas.

3. INVESTMENTS

Life and health insurance companies are more than risk bearing institutions. They are major financial institutions investing large sums of money every business day of the year.

The sources of new funds available for investment by life insurance companies consist chiefly of:

1. Premiums collected in early policy years under the level premium plan that are in excess of those needed to pay claims and expenses for those years.

2. The accumulation of funds under the pure endowment portion of endowment and retirement income policies.

3. Funds left with the company under policy settlement options.

4. Funds left with the company under dividend options.

5. Funds made available (a) when expenses are less than the amount built into the premium, (b) when the mortality and morbidity experience is better than the mortality and morbidity assumed in computing the premium, and (c) when investment earnings are higher than the interest rate assumed in computing premiums.

6. Funds obtained from the sale of capital stock[27] and from paid-in surplus.

These funds could be held in cash to be paid out as required under policy contracts. However, because the interest that can be earned on these funds significantly reduces the amount of premiums policyholders will have to pay, these funds are invested to yield a return.[28] In anticipation of this return, the company guarantees a minimum rate of interest in computing premiums, cash values, and values under settlement options, and in retaining dividends for accumulation under the dividend accumulation option.

The types of assets permissible for the general investment account of life insurance companies are set by state law. In the main, they are confined to

---

[27] Applies only to capital stock companies. See Chapter 28.
[28] The investment return includes interest, dividends, and capital gain.

what may be called "first lien" securities: bonds and mortgages, although limited investment in equity securities and rental real estate are authorized.[29]

Investment Qualities Required. The fundamental quality sought in life insurance company investment policy is safety of the dollar value of the principal. Within the constraints necessary to maintain a safe investment portfolio, life insurers seek to maximize the yield obtained on their investments. To some extent they also make an effort to channel funds into projects that have favorable social implications.

Because the obligations of life insurance companies are expressed in terms of fixed amounts of dollars, it is considered essential in life insurance company investment policy and in the laws that regulate this policy that insurers invest principally in senior securities.[30] Any substantial investment in equity securities generally is prohibited not only by law but also by the investment committees of insurance companies.[31]

The laws of most states recognize that diversification of investments is essential to a safe investment portfolio, and consequently limit the proportion of assets which an insurer may invest in any single type of investment. Insurers generally have diversified their investments far beyond the legal requirement, not only by classes of investments and within these classes, but also by geographical distribution and by maturity dates. In addition, investments of life insurance companies are diversified among industries, companies, types of security, and the times at which the funds are committed.

Liquidity, the ability of an asset to be converted into cash immediately and without loss of value, is of little importance to a life insurance company investment portfolio. In the first place, the commitments of life insurance companies are long term, and consequently, their assets can be invested in long-term debt. Life insurance company investments generally are purchased to be held to maturity for the income they provide. They are not usually purchased to be liquidated before maturity. In the second place, life insurance companies have investments maturing at frequent intervals, providing a source of liquidity for the portfolio. In the third place, cash receipts arising from premium income and investment earnings continue to grow so that, except in an extreme emergency not yet witnessed,[32] life insurance companies as a group always will have cash income sufficient to

---

[29] State regulation of the investments of life insurance companies is discussed in Chapter 29.

[30] Where insurers issue contracts under which no fixed dollar amounts are guaranteed, it is considered safe for the insurer to invest funds supporting these contracts in equity securities. The investment risk is shifted to the contract holder.

[31] Exceptions are made for the investment of funds accumulated in segregated accounts for deposit administration pension plans and for the investment of funds in separate accounts used for funding variable annuities.

[32] Such an emergency would have to be more extreme than that of the depression of the 1930's. During the depression years, total revenue of the business always exceeded total disbursements. Premium income alone exceeded total disbursements in all but three years, 1932, 1933, and 1934. Cf. Chapter 8.

meet cash needs. Total income of life insurance companies (premiums and investment income) is running at a rate nearly three times that of disbursements (death payments, endowment payments, annuity payments, surrender payments, policy dividends, and disability payments). This is not to say that no life insurer finds itself short of cash. However, these shortages usually arise from commitments made to borrowers. When the insurer experiences a level of policy loans in excess of that anticipated in its financial planning, as can happen during periods of tight money, the insurer might have to rely on bank credit to obtain the funds necessary to honor its loan commitments. Finally, every policy written today contains, as a result of state law, a "deferment clause" permitting the company to postpone payment of any cash or loan value (except a loan to pay premiums) for a period of time, usually up to six months. The use of the deferment privilege could help to prevent a serious loss resulting from a forced liquidation of assets if cash calls suddenly exceeded the amount of cash readily available.

The investment policy of life insurance companies is geared toward seeking the highest rate of interest compatible with the required degree of safety not only because life insurance companies are business institutions attempting to maximize productive efficiency but also because life insurers must operate in the marketplace and can minimize the cost of insurance to policyholders by increasing the rate of return on their investments. The maximization of productive efficiency may become of increasing importance to life insurers as buyers become more price conscious and attempt to utilize available techniques for making price comparisons before making their purchases.

At one time the yield problem was acute. In 1923 the net rate of interest earned on life insurance company investments was 5.18 percent. At that time it was common to guarantee $3\frac{1}{2}$ percent or even 4 percent in computing premiums. From the high point of 1923 the net rate of interest earned declined steadily to a low of 2.88 percent in 1947. This rate was below the average rate guaranteed on all policies outstanding in some companies. As a result, dividends on some participating policies were reduced and higher premiums were charged for new policies.[33] Holders of nonparticipating policies were not affected of course, except in those very few cases where insurers became insolvent and had to be rehabilitated. Although life insurers' net investment income before taxes has moved up substantially since 1947 and is currently in excess of 5 percent, who can say whether the margin between the interest guaranteed on all outstanding policies and the interest earned could not again fall to a dangerous level. Policies being written today include interest guarantees ranging from $2\frac{1}{2}$ percent to $3\frac{3}{4}$ percent. That life insurance companies base their rates and values in part on

---

[33] The process of reserve strengthening was used also under which lower interest assumptions were used in computing the reserve liability of the insurer. The effect was to increase the reserve and decrease the surplus by a corresponding amount.

guaranteed interest assumptions makes adequacy of yield an important investment consideration aside from competitive factors.

Life insurance companies offer one of the largest pools of capital in the country, and there is a feeling in some quarters that a part of these funds should be invested in ways that would help solve some of the social problems facing the nation, particularly those associated with improving the working and living conditions in the inner cities. At a White House meeting on September 13, 1967, the life insurance industry acting through the joint committee on urban problems of the American Life Convention and the Life Insurance Association of America made a pledge to divert $1 billion into investments designed to improve conditions in the central cities. Eighteen months later $900 million of this amount had been committed or disbursed for projects not ordinarily considered because of the low financial return relative to the risk involved. The types of projects undertaken under the program were designed to improve housing and to finance job-creating enterprises in the core city areas in 227 cities in 42 states. Specifically, $681 million was used to provide 63,000 housing units, ranging from rent supplement housing projects to single family homes for low- and moderate-income families. Another $219 million was invested in job-creating enterprises and community services providing 30,000 permanent jobs for core city residents. Projects calling for $100 million were under review, virtually completing the initial $1 billion pledge.

The $1 billion pledge was an amount equal to about 10 percent of the net increase in life insurance company assets for 1967. A second $1 billion pledge was made by the life insurance industry in the spring of 1969, and the hope was expressed that a larger proportion of the second billion-dollar program can be devoted to the creation of new jobs for core area residents and to the development of minority business enterprises, two of the most vital needs of the inner cities. Life insurance company executives were hopeful that their effort would help to improve the quality of the cities and that significant gains for the people of the cities would be achieved through the life insurance urban program. However, they believe that a massive cooperative effort by other elements of the private sector, by government at all levels, and by the active participation of concerned individuals is needed if the life insurance urban program is to produce a major impact on the condition of the cities.

Types of Investments.   Life insurance investments are distributed among government securities, corporate bonds, mortgages, real estate, stocks, policy loans, and a few miscellaneous investments. Although the law restricts investments to certain particular types and, for some types, only for certain given maximums, life insurance companies have wide discretion as to their choice of investments among these classes. Wide variation among company investment portfolios will be found. The following tabulation shows the percentage distribution among the types of assets held in the composite investment portfolio of United States life insurance companies in a recent year.[34]

U.S. government securities ...	2.4 percent	Mortgage loans	37.2 percent
Foreign bonds	0.4 "	Real estate	3.0 "
State, provincial, and			
local bonds	2.7 "	Policy loans	6.0 "
Corporate bonds	36.5 "	Cash	0.9 "
Corporate stocks	6.9 "	Miscellaneous assets	4.0 "
		Total	100.0 percent

GOVERNMENT SECURITIES.   Traditionally, aside from fluctuations in the bond market, U.S. government bonds offer the highest degree of dollar safety of any investment; but they also offer the lowest investment yields. Prior to World War I, few U.S. government bonds were owned by life insurance companies. However, during both World War I and World War II, companies invested heavily in U.S. Governments.[35] At one point during World War II, U.S. bonds represented about half of the total investments of the companies. Holdings of these bonds have decreased significantly since the war, as safe and higher yielding private investments have become available. Today about 2.4 percent of the assets of U.S. life insurance companies are invested in U.S. government securities. This compares with nearly 46 percent in 1945. Shortly after World War II life insurers began to liquidate their low-yielding U.S. government securities taking advantage of the prices pegged by the government.

Specified Canadian government bonds are eligible for life insurance company investments. Some states, however, limit the amount of assets that can be placed in such obligations. For instance, New York restricts the amount to 10 percent of admitted assets unless the company has Canadian policyholders, in which case up to one and one half times the assets necessary to offset the reserve liability on those policies may be invested in Canadian government bonds. At present, less than 0.2 percent of U.S. life insurance company assets are invested in Canadian government bonds.

State, county, and municipal bonds vary in suitability. Many issues are acceptable, but they usually produce yields lower than that which can be obtained from other securities. Less than 3 percent of the assets of U.S. life insurance companies currently are invested in state and local bonds.

CORPORATE BONDS.   Corporate bonds have long been an important medium for the investment of life insurance company funds. There are few restrictions on bond investments.[36] The only questionable class of cor-

---

[34] See the Institute of Life Insurance, *Life Insurance Fact Book,* current edition, for the most recent percentages.

[35] Aside from patriotic motives, life insurance companies purchased large amounts of government bonds during the war because these bonds were available as an investment outlet. If more profitable, safe investments had been available, life insurance companies probably would have purchased fewer government bonds.

[36] The Armstrong Committee recommended no restrictions on investments in bonds. The overall recommendations of the committee were for vast restrictions in every phase of life

porate bond is the collateral trust bond, which is secured by shares of stock. It is a suitable life insurance company investment, according to some experts, only if the corporate shares used as collateral would themselves be suitable for investment.

The only legal restrictions on bonds relate to those which are not fully secured or are in default as to the payment of interest.[37]

Corporate bonds (railroad, public utility, and industrial) constitute about 37 percent of the assets of life insurance companies in the United States.

MORTGAGES.   In general, the mortgage loan is well qualified as an investment for life insurance companies. If an adequate margin has been maintained between the amount lent and the appraisal value of the property, the loan is well secured. Mortgage lending offers an opportunity for both geographical diversification and diversification of credit risks. Furthermore, it offers a relatively high rate of return for the degree of security involved. On the other hand, mortgage loans are relatively expensive to initiate and to service, and foreclosure in case of defualt is costly and sometimes harmful to public relations. Moreover, since most mortgages can be paid off in advance, there is a tendency in times of falling interest rates for mortgage borrowers to "refinance" by paying off the old mortgage and making a new one at a lower rate of interest.

Prior to the depression of the 1930's, mortgages customarily were payable in a lump sum at maturity date. The depression popularized the monthly payment mortgage, which greatly increases the safety of the loan, since the margin between appraisal value and the debt constantly increases. The security of certain mortgage loans has also been enhanced since the depression by FHA insurance and the guaranteed GI mortgage of the Veterans Administration. However, only about 25 percent of the dollar amount of mortgage loans held by life insurers is in mortgages insured by the FHA or guaranteed by the Veterans Administration.

The total of life insurance assets invested in both farm and nonfarm mortgage loans amount to about 37 percent of the admitted assets of U.S. life insurance companies. About 40 percent of all mortgage loans are for one- to four-family residential properties; about 20 percent are for apartment developments, about 30 percent are for commercial properties, and the remainder is for farm properties.

REAL ESTATE.   At the present time, direct investment in real estate amounts to about 3 percent of admitted assets, commercial properties ac-

---

insurance company operations. See Chapter 29 for a discussion of the Armstrong Committee and its recommendations. The New York law places no limit on the amount of corporate bonds that can be held in an insurer's portfolio provided these bonds meet the qualifying "earnings over interest" test and the total amount of bonds of one insurer does not exceed 5 percent of the insurer's admitted assets. Insurers may invest up to one half of 1 percent of admitted assets in bonds of corporations that do not meet the test.

[37] The New York law states that, to be eligible, bonds must be adequately secured and not predominantly speculative.

count for 64 percent of the real estate investments, home and branch offices represent about 27 percent of life insurance company real estate holdings, residential properties make up 6 percent of the real estate held by life insurers, and all other types equal the remaining 3 percent.

Considered highly speculative, real estate was barred by law in nearly every state as an investment for life insurance companies until the mid-1940's.[38] An insurance company was allowed to own only whatever real estate properties—such as home office and branch offices—it needed for the convenient transaction of its business plus any real estate it might have acquired by mortgage foreclosure. Foreclosed real estate had to be disposed of in a specified period of time—within five years, for example, under the New York law.[39]

Today, all but a few states have laws permitting investment in real estate. The percentage of assets which can be invested in real estate, however, is limited, and many states prohibit investment in certain types of real estate, the exclusion list varying from state to state but including such prohibitions as hotels, agricultural property, mines, quarries, amusement enterprises, and clubs. New York permits a life insurance company to invest up to 10 percent of its admitted assets in housing developments, but restricts the investment in commercial real estate to 5 percent of admitted assets. Taking advantage of these laws, life insurance companies were pioneers in the construction of large-scale housing developments. They have also played a role in the construction of shopping centers by purchasing them from developers and leasing them back for management. Because the percentage of assets a company can invest in these types of projects is limited, only the largest companies have shown interest in them.

Other types of real estate in which life insurance companies have invested include retail stores, industrial sites, supermarkets, office buildings, and the like. A popular type of investment transaction has been the purchase of industrial or business property from the industry or business, followed by a leaseback to the former owner. The transaction releases working capital for the business,[40] as well as offering it certain tax advantages.[41] Another type of real estate investment is the purchase of the land upon which a building stands and then a leaseback to the building owner.

---

[38] Virginia was one of the first states to pass legislation permitting life insurance companies to hold investment real estate. The law became effective in 1943.

[39] An extension of time usually is allowed if market conditions are such that a sale within the five-year period would be unwise.

[40] The sale and leaseback of property enable the corporation to realize in working capital the full market value of the building, whereas a mortgage loan would release only a given percentage of its value. Under New York law, life insurers may lend only up to 66½ percent of the value of commercial properties.

[41] The tax advantage arises out of the right of the tenant to deduct rents paid as a regular business expense. The profit on the sale of the building, if any, is taxed as a capital gain. The insurance company can deduct depreciation anew on the building based on the cost of the building to the company regardless of how completely the building had been depreciated by its former owner.

For example, an insurance company purchased from the building owners the land on which the Empire State Building stands.

STOCKS. Stocks once formed a considerable part of life insurance company assets. The Armstrong investigation and the recommendations arising from it led to legislation that all but eliminated stock investment for many years. The investigating committee recommended that the state insurance law be amended virtually to prohibit investment of assets in any class of stock, common or preferred. That amendment was passed in 1906. Since most of the other states amended their insurance laws in light of the findings of the New York investigation, investment in stocks by life insurance companies was at a virtual standstill everywhere in the United States until 1928. In that year New York amended its law to allow limited and restricted investment in preferred and guaranteed issues. During the 1940's a number of states changed their laws to allow some investment in common stocks, and, in 1951, the law was liberalized in New York. The current New York law restricts investments in common stocks to 5 percent of admitted assets or one half of its policyholders' surplus, whichever is lower. Not more than 2 percent of the outstanding common stock of any corporation may be held.[42] There are no restrictions on the amount of preferred stock that may be purchased so long as the issues meet the standards prescribed for them.

One practical objection to investment in common stocks to fund contractual guarantees for specified dollar amounts is the problem of fluctuating values. Common stocks must be valued at the official market price as determined by the NAIC. Thus, a severe drop in market prices of common stocks could eliminate the surplus of an insurer if it had a high percentage of its assets invested in common stocks, making the company legally insolvent, unless the Valuation Committee of the NAIC established arbitrary value for these securities. Currently, about 7 percent of all U.S. life insurance company assets are invested in stocks. Common stocks are responsible for more than three fourths of the total of stock investments. The percentage of life insurance company assets invested in common stock can be expected to increase with the growing interest in equity-based contracts (variable annuities and segregated accounts for funding pension plans).

POLICY LOANS. Policy loans are 100 percent secured. Default on the loan results in cancellation of a like amount of liability under the contract. However, policy loans are not encouraged by life insurance companies. In the first place, many of them are in the category of small loans, which are expensive to handle. In the second place a policy loan may be a prelude to a lapse. Moreover, the loan provision is a source of adverse selection against the insurer. If interest rates are historically low, policyowners usually can borrow money from banks on the security of assigned policies at rates

---

[42] However, most states place no restrictions on the amount of common stocks of a particular corporation that can be owned by a life insurer, and those that do usually allow more than the 2 percent New York limitation, usually 10 percent.

lower than the loan rate set in the policy if the size of the loan is adequate.[43] If interest rates are historically high, policyowners find the loan values on their policies particularly attractive. For example, if they can borrow on their policies at 5 percent rather than elsewhere for 7 percent, it would require no high powered financial wizard to determine the best source of borrowed funds. Currently, policy loans exceed 6 percent of the assets of U.S. life insurance companies.

The adverse investment selection against insurers brought about by guaranteed interest rates on policy loans come in for a great deal of attention and study as the decade of the 1960's drew to a close with interest rates perched at their all time highs.[44]

MISCELLANEOUS INVESTMENT. Various minor investments may be held by life insurance companies. One example is collateral loans, of which few are made. Another is investment in transportation equipment—for example, railroad rolling stock leased back to the railroad, jet aircraft leased to airlines, and leased fleets of automobiles and trucks. Life insurance funds have also been used in pipeline and toll road financing and various other projects. Since the legislation of several states allows companies to invest a small percentage of assets without restriction, any type of investment or speculation might be found in the portfolios of companies controlled by these laws. For example, an Illinois company[45] once invested funds in a large quantity of cheese, hoping to make a profit from the increase in its value resulting from the aging process.

---

[43] The life insurance company, with a contract interest rate for policy loans, is bound to that rate no matter what the conditions of the loan market are at the time the loan is made. Also, the same interest rate is charged on small loans as on large ones. Therefore, the contractual rate must be large enough to handle the high cost of making small loans.

[44] Cf. Chapter 10 for a discussion of the kind of change now being made by some insurers in the interest guarantees written into the loan provisions of new policies.

[45] Illinois companies may invest 5 percent of their admitted assets in anything they wish. New York law permits an insurer to invest up to 2 percent of its admitted assets without restriction.

27

Financial Management: Liabilities and Net Worth

In the preceding chapter, the nature and problems associated with accounting for and management of assets were discussed. The other side of the accounting equation, *assets = liabilities and net worth,* is the subject of this chapter.

1. THE NATURE OF LIABILITIES AND NET WORTH

The concept of a liability at first seems tricky, for it is not something that can be touched or seen. It is a figure on paper which serves as a yardstick for measuring the adequacy of assets. If assets are not sufficient to offset liabilities, the company is technically insolvent.[1] A liability exists wherever a company is "liable" (bound or obligated) to pay out assets now or in the future. Policy reserves are the principal liability of a life insurance company. They measure the net accrued liability of a company with respect to future benefits.

The concept of net worth is not difficult. It represents the ownership interest in the business. It follows that this figure is the difference between what the business owns (its assets) and what it owes (its liabilities). It is composed of two items: surplus and capital.

Life Insurance Company Liabilities. The nature of the liabilities of a life insurance company can be clarified by a brief look at the items that appear on the right-hand (or liability and net worth) side of a condensed annual statement for a typical company.

POLICY RESERVES. The life insurance policy reserve represents the amount which, together with assumed future net valuation premiums and interest, will be exactly sufficient to enable the company to pay all benefits (death and survivorship) as they become payable, if the company's experi-

---

[1] It is true that a company could be solvent although its assets were less than its liabilities, since the valuation of both assets and liabilities contain some element of uncertainty.

ence is precisely in accordance with its valuation assumptions relating to interest and mortality.[2]

The statutes of 34 states require the insurer to create a deficiency reserve when the gross premium charged for a given class of policies is less than the valuation net annual premium. The valuation net annual premium is the net premium actually used in computing an insurer's policy reserves.[3] The required deficiency reserve in any given year is equal to the net valuation premium less the gross premium multiplied by the present value of a life annuity due of one for the remaining premium paying period.[4]

Reserves under health insurance policies are discussed later in this chapter.

Policy reserves for life insurance, health insurance, and annuities make up roughly 87 percent of the liabilities of all U.S. life insurance companies.

POLICY PROCEEDS AND OTHER FUNDS LEFT WITH INSURER.   Liabilities of insurers under life insurance policies include the value of policy proceeds left with the company under settlement options,[5] dividends left to accumulate at interest, funds deposited to pay future premiums as they become due, and cash values payable on policies cancelled because of premium default where the payment of the cash surrender value is the automatic option. These items are liabilities because they measure the value of obligations of the insurer to its policyholders.

POLICY CLAIMS.   At the time the financial statement is prepared, there will be claims reported but not yet paid. The value of these claims must be shown as a liability. Also, there will be claims incurred but not yet reported. The value of these claims must be estimated and reported as a liability.

DIVIDENDS.   Since policy dividends are declared on December 31 for payment on policy anniversaries in the following year, and since policy anniversaries are distributed throughout the calendar year, the company must show on its annual statement a liability for dividends declared to policyholders. Dividends payable to stockholders also must be shown as a liability if they have been declared but not yet paid.

---

[2] Another way of explaining the concept of the reserve is to view it as the excess of the present value of future claims (a liability) over the present value of future net valuation premiums (an asset), both figured on the basis of the interest and mortality assumptions used. Note the use of the term valuation premiums. The valuation premium is something less than the gross annual premium paid by the policyholder and often is something different from the net annual premium (gross premium minus expense addition) charged the policyholder.

[3] The concept of the valuation net annual premium is discussed later in this chapter.

[4] For the benefit of those readers who have studied Appendix A, Chapter 25, the formula for the deficiency reserve is

$$(VP\text{-}GP)\ddot{a}_{x+t:\overline{n}|} = \frac{N_{x+t} - N_{x+n}}{D_{x+t}}$$

[5] Settlement options involving life contingencies are shown under policy reserves as a part of annuity reserves.

COMMISSIONS, TAXES, AND EXPENSES. At the time of the statement, various expenses incurred but not yet paid will have to be shown as a liability. Two important items here are commissions and taxes. Agents will have earned commissions which have not yet been paid. Also, many taxes, particularly federal income taxes, are payable after the end of a fiscal year; thus, the company will be liable in the current year for taxes which have accrued in the preceding year.

SECURITY VALUATION RESERVE. A mandatory security valuation reserve is maintained to offset possible adverse fluctuations in the value of security holdings. Although the law requires that this reserve be shown as a liability, it is more in the nature of a net worth item. It reduces unassigned surplus by earmarking part of it as a contingency reserve.

OTHER LIABILITIES. Other liabilities include unearned investment income and dividends, funds deposited by mortgagors to pay taxes and insurance on mortgaged property, amounts due to reinsurers for premiums, amounts due to the reinsured for claims, provisions for experience rating refunds, borrowed money, interest payable on policy and contract funds due or accrued and liability for employee benefits.

Net Worth Items. The principal items in the net worth section of a life insurance company balance sheet are surplus and capital.[6] The capital account, of course, appears only in statements of capital stock companies. The surplus is divided into special surplus funds and unassigned surplus.[7] Surplus funds arise from the creation of contingency reserves. These reserves are voluntary as distinguished from the required policy reserve and the mandatory security valuation reserve.

SPECIAL SURPLUS FUNDS. Voluntary reserves are set up for contingencies to provide a margin for safety. Sometimes the reserve is simply called a special contingency reserve and is created to offset adverse fluctuations in mortality experience or investment earnings. At other times it may be separated into several reserve accounts such as a mortgage valuation reserve, asset fluctuation reserve, investment reserve, mortality fluctuation reserve, special group life insurance reserves for epidemics, and voluntary reserves to strengthen the reserves for those policies written at higher interest and mortality assumptions than the company now believes are realistic.

How much of its surplus an insurer shows as assigned is a matter of management philosophy. Some insurers will earmark its entire surplus as a general contingency reserve, and therefore show no surplus. Management

---

[6] The Convention Blank (Chapter 26) does not provide a special column for net worth. Net worth items are called below-the-line items since they appear at the bottom of the liability page. Liability items are called above-the-line items.

[7] The term "special surplus fund" is used in the Convention Blank. However, use of the term "fund" is misleading. Surplus is not a fund. The American College Dictionary (Random House, New York) defines "fund" as a stock of money or pecuniary resource. Accordingly, a fund would be an asset. Perhaps a better term would be "appropriated" or "assigned" surplus—that is, that portion of the excess of assets over liabilities segregated for specific purposes.

may prefer to avoid use of the concept of surplus in its annual report so as not to give its policyholders the impression that earnings are being retained that otherwise would be paid to policyholders as dividends.

How the insurer segregates its surplus seems to make no difference to the regulatory authorities. In those states where mutual insurers and participating stock insurers are subject to a maximum limitation on the accumulation of surplus, except for paid-in surplus, the entire surplus, regardless of what it is called, appears to be subject to that limitation.[8]

UNASSIGNED SURPLUS. Put in nontechnical terms, unassigned surplus, sometimes called free surplus is the margin by which the admitted assets of the company exceed the sum of liabilities, special surplus funds, and paid-in capital and surplus, if any.

CAPITAL STOCK. The capital stock account represents the dollar value nominally assigned to shares issued to stockholders. This account, of course, is found only in stock companies and will not appear on the books of mutual companies.

2. THE POLICY RESERVE

Policy reserves are the obligation of the company to its policyholders and must be set up as a liability and valued according to the laws of the state.

State statutes specify the minimum basis for valuation of policy reserves. On currently issued policies, all states require that policy reserves must not be less than those calculated on the Commissioners Reserve Valuation Method using the 1958 Commissioners Standard Ordinary Mortality Table and $3\frac{1}{2}$ percent interest, or a method, mortality table, and interest rate producing, in the aggregate, larger reserves.[9]

In understanding policy reserves, it is helpful to think in terms of individual policy reserves with the aggregate liability of the company being the sum of these individual reserves. Although this concept is not realistic, as will soon be explained, it is, if carefully used, a helpful tool in explaining the nature of reserves.

It is common to refer to the reserve as a fund as though it were an asset. For the purpose of a nontechnical discussion, the misnomer is of little consequence; in fact, it is often difficult and awkward to avoid. However, it should be made clear that the reserve is not a fund. As a liability, it is an accounting measure of obligations.

Definition of Reserve. The reserve is a liability representing that amount which, together with future net valuation premiums and interest will be exactly sufficient to enable the company to meet all policy obligations as they fall due, assuming that the company's experience is precisely in

---

[8] Paid-in surplus is the excess over the par or assigned value of capital stock received from the issuance and sale of the insurer's own stock.

[9] The Commissioners Reserve Valuation Method (CRVM) is described later in this chapter.

accordance with its assumptions relating to mortality and interest. The insurer in computing its valuation premiums may use the same interest and mortality assumptions used in computing the premiums charged the policyholder or it may use assumptions that are more conservative. A commonly used set of valuation premium assumptions is 1958 CSO at $2\frac{1}{2}$ percent which produces reserves higher than those either required by law or by conservative financial management.[10]

Even when the interest and mortality assumptions used in premium computations are identical to those used in reserve computations, the valuation premium differs from the premium charged the policyholder. The premium charged the policyholder includes an expense loading. The valuation premium is a net premium based solely on mortality and interest assumptions. The use of net premiums rather than the actual premiums to be collected adds further conservatism to the method of calculating reserves, an element of conservatism required by law. If identical interest and mortality assumptions are used in computing both the valuation premium and the net premium charged the policyholder (gross premium less loading), the two net premiums even then might not be the same. The law provides for more than one method of reserve valuation. Only under the full reserve valuation method will the valuation premium and the net premium be equal when identical interest and mortality assumptions are used. Types of reserve valuation methods are discussed later in this chapter.

Time of Valuation. The reserve at the beginning of any policy year is called an *initial* reserve whereas the reserve at the end of any policy year is called the *terminal* reserve. These reserves can easily be expressed in terms of one another: The initial reserve for any year (n) is a combination of the valuation premium payable at the beginning of that year (n) plus the terminal reserve at the end of the previous year ($n-1$). The terminal reserve for any year (n) is the initial reserve for that year plus the assumed interest earnings on that beginning reserve minus the assumed mortality costs for the year. For example, the reserve at the beginning of the 20th policy year on continuous premium whole life insurance issued at age 35 would be $351.46 per $1,000, based on 1958 CSO at $2\frac{1}{2}$ percent. This is computed by adding the valuation premium ($17.67) to the terminal reserve for the 19th policy year ($333.79). The terminal reserve for the 20th policy year is the initial reserve ($351.46), increased by interest at $2\frac{1}{2}$ percent ($8.79), and decreased by assumed mortality costs ($7.71) for a total of $352.54.[11]

---

[10] Those states that limit the surplus accumulation by mutual and participating stock life insurers relate the limitation to size of the reserve. In New York, and in several other states, that limitation, except for small companies, is 10 percent. The more conservative the insurer is in valuing its reserves, the higher is the surplus it is permitted to accumulate. This seems a bit ridiculous, does it not! What it says is that the less the insurer is likely to need a contingency surplus, the more surplus it can have.

[11] How the mortality cost is computed will be explained later.

When a life insurance company prepares its annual statement, it will have on its books policies issued on every business day throughout the year. Some policies will be just starting a new policy year whereas others will be reaching the end of their current policy year. It may be assumed that on the average, all policies are midway through their policy years, since an equal number should be scattered evenly on each side of the midpoint. The reserve at the halfway mark in a policy year is called the *mean* reserve, and is computed by arithmetically averaging the initial and the terminal reserves. The mean reserve for the 20th policy year for continuous premium whole life insurance issued at age 35 is $352.00 per $1,000, 1958 CSO at 2½ percent, and is computed by averaging the initial reserve of $351.46 and the terminal reserve of $352.54. Life insurance companies use the mean reserve for purposes of computing the aggregate liability on all policies in force as of the date of the financial statement.

Approaches to Valuing Reserves. The reserve liability of a company on its outstanding policies may be calculated in two ways—prospectively or retrospectively. Also, reserves may be computed on a full net level premium basis or on a modified basis.

PROSPECTIVE AND RETROSPECTIVE METHODS. The prospective method looks at the reserve on the basis of what is assumed will happen in the future, whereas the retrospective method considers what is assumed to have happened in the past. Either approach, of course, will give the same result because the assumptions used are the same. Both methods will be illustrated presently.

The prospective approach is the one most commonly used. The state statutes under which reserves are regulated generally are couched in terms of the prospective approach.

Under contracts where the dollar amount of assumed future claims is geared to the market value of the insurer's investment portfolio (variable annuities, for example), it is not possible to compute in dollars the present value of assumed future claims. No one knows what the dollar amounts of these claims will be. For these contracts the retrospective approach might have greater conceptual simplicity because it arrives at the reserve by reviewing the insurer's past operations. Measured retrospectively, the reserve is that amount by which the accumulated value of assumed net valuation premiums collected on behalf of the policies in force exceed the accumulated value of assumed claims paid.

RESERVE SYSTEMS. The full net premium basis makes no allowance for the high first year expenses associated with selling and underwriting a policy, completely ignoring the disequilibrium between the incidence of expenses incurred and premiums collected. This disequilibrium is taken into consideration in the modified systems. At this point, only the full reserve system will be discussed. Modified systems will be explained later in the chapter.

Illustration of Reserve Computation. Computation of the reserve under the full net level premium may be illustrated using both the prospective and retrospective approach.

PROSPECTIVE VALUATION. The formula for computing reserves under the prospective method is as follows: the terminal reserve equals the present value of *assumed* future claims minus the present value of *assumed* future net level valuation premiums, both values computed on the basis of assumed rates of interest and mortality.[12]

Steps in Calculating Reserves. The steps in calculating the reserve under the prospective method are as follows.

Step 1. Based on $1,000 of insurance, determine the present value of assumed future claims for the age at which the reserve is computed. (This step involves the same procedure as the computation of a net single premium for $1,000 of insurance issued at the age at which the policy reserve is being computed, see p. 721.)

Step 2. Based on $1,000 of insurance, determine the present value of assumed future net level valuation premiums to be collected from the age at which the reserve is computed. (This is computed by multiplying the assumed net level valuation premium by a life annuity due of 1 at this age for the remaining premium paying period.)[13]

Step 3. Determine the reserve for $1,000 of insurance by subtracting the results of Step 2 from the results of Step 1.

Step 4. Determine the reserve for all insurance of a given class by multiplying the results of Step 3 by the number of thousands of dollars of insurance in force in that class. (A class includes the age of the insured and the age and type of policy—for instance, a continuous premium whole life policy issued at 25, in force 10 years.)

Application of Steps. The following is an illustration of the application of the steps involved in computing the reserve at the end of the second year on $5 million of continuous premium whole life insurance issued at age 96. The net level valuation premium per $1,000 using 1958 CSO mortality at $2\frac{1}{2}$ percent is $482.91.

Step 1. Determine the present value of assumed future claims for the age at which the reserve is computed. At the end of the second policy year, the insured is age 98. So it is necessary to find the net single valuation premium for $1,000 of continuous premium whole life insurance at age 98. This amounts to $967.[14]

Step 2. Determine the present value of assumed future level valuation premiums for the age at which the reserve is computed. To find this figure

---

[12] Assumed mortality and assumed interest are used rather than actual mortality experienced and actual interest earned for reasons to be explained later.

[13] This computation is explained on page 729.

[14] Explained on page 721.

it is necessary to multiply the assumed net level valuation premium $482.91 by the present value of a whole life annuity due of 1 a year issued at age 98.[15]

Net level valuation premium $482.91
Value of a life annuity due of 1 per
    annum for remaining period issued at age 98 .....   1.32
Present value of assumed future net level
    valuation premiums (482.91 × 1.3237) 639.00

Step 3. Determine the reserve per $1,000. This is found by subtracting the present value of future premiums ($639) from the present value of future claims ($967). It is equal to $328.[16]

Step 4. Determine the aggregate reserve. This is determined by multiplying the reserve per $1,000 by the number of thousands outstanding (5,000), giving an aggregate terminal reserve of $1,640,000.

RETROSPECTIVE VALUATION. The formula for computing reserves under the retrospective method is as follows: the terminal reserve equals the accumulated value of the net level valuation premium collected minus the accumulated value of assumed claims, both values computed on the basis of assumed rates of interest and mortality.

Steps in Calculating Reserves. The steps in calculating the reserve under the retrospective method are as follows.

Step 1. Assume that $1,000 of insurance is written for the number living at age of issue as shown in the mortality table used for computing reserves.

Step 2. Tabulate the assumed number living at the beginning of each year from age of issue to the age at which the reserve is computed and multiply these figures by the net level valuation premium for $1,000 of insurance under the type of policy involved.

Step 3. Determine the accumulated value of the net level valuation premiums by multiplying these premiums by the amount of 1 at the assumed rate of interest for the years involved and then computing their total. (If the reserve is to be computed at the end of the 10th year, the first premium will involve 10 years of interest; the second, 9; the third, 8; and so on.)

Step 4. Tabulate the assumed number dying during each year from age of issue to the age at which the reserve is computed and multiply these figures by $1,000 to find the amount of assumed claims.

Step 5. Determine the accumulated value of assumed claims by multiplying these claims by the amount of 1 at the assumed rate of interest for the years involved and then computing their total. (If the reserve is to be computed at the end of the 10th year, the first-year claims will involve only

---

[15] Explained on page 729.
[16] Rounded to the nearest dollar.

9 years of interest, since claims are assumed to be paid at the end of the year.)

Step 6. Subtract the results obtained in Step 5 from the results obtained in Step 3 and divide by the number living at the end of the year for which the reserve is computed. This gives the reserve per $1,000 of insurance.

Step 7. Multiply the results of Step 6 by the number of thousands of insurance in force in that class to obtain the aggregate reserve.

Application of Steps. The following is an example of reserve computation under the retrospective method, using for illustration $5 million of continuous premium whole life insurance issued at age 96. The reserve is calculated for the end of the second year. (The net level valuation premium was computed earlier and found to be $482.91.)

Step 1. It is assumed that $1,000 of insurance is written for 63,037 people.

Step 2. Net level valuation premium:

Age	Number Living	Net Level Valuation Premium	Aggregate Premium
96	63,037	$482.91	$30,441,198
97	37,787	482.91	18,247,720

Step 3. Accumulated value of net level valuation premiums:

Aggregate Premium	Years Accumulated	Amount of 1 at 2½%[17]	Accumulated Value
$30,441,198	2	1.0506	$31,981,523
18,247,720	1	1.0250	18,703,913
Total accumulated value of net level valuation premiums			$50,685,436

Step 4. Assumed claims:

Age	Number Dying	Amount per Claim	Aggregate Claims
96	25,250	$1,000	$25,250,000
97	18,456	1,000	18,456,000

Step 5. Accumulated value of assumed claims:

Aggregate Claims	Years Accumulated	Amount of 1 at 2½%	Accumulated Value
$25,250,000	1	1.0250	$25,881,250
18,456,000	0	1.0000	18,456,000
Total accumulated value of assumed claims			$44,337,250

---

[17] See table of amount of 1 values reproduced in Chapter 24.

Step 6. The reserve per $1,000 of insurance:

$$\frac{\$50,685,430 - 44,337,250}{19,331} = \$328.^*$$

Step 7. The aggregate reserve:

$$\$328 \times 5,000 = \$1,640,000$$

Note that the reserve is $1,640,000, whether computed prospectively or retrospectively. The excess of the accumulated value of assumed net level valuation premiums over the accumulated value of assumed claims always will be equal to the excess of the present value of assumed future claims over the present value of assumed future net level valuation premiums. Either procedure measures the reserve liability of the company.

Modified Reserve Systems. A problem in the practical operation of a life insurance company is the high first-year expense of a policy as distinguished from expenses in subsequent years. These high first-year expenses exceed the expense loading in the first year's premium. First-year commissions to the agent, medical examination fee, cost of inspection reports, policy issue—all these one-time expenses concentrated in the first year add up to an amount of money far in excess of the cost of maintaining the policy in any subsequent year. High first-year expenses could create a real problem for life insurance companies without sufficient surpluses to finance new business if some relief were not available through modified reserve systems as the following illustration points out.

Assume that the premium for a $10,000 nonparticipating continuous premium whole life policy issued at age 35 is $190, and that the total of the first-year commissions (for the writing agent and the general agent), the cost of the medical examination, the inspection report, other acquisition expenses, the state premium tax and home office administrative expense for the first year amount to $187. On the 1958 CSO Table the mortality expense at age 35 is $25.10. Without the safety factor added the tabular mortality expense would be only $14.10. But considering that mortality costs on newly selected lives are lower than those reflected on an ultimate table, assume that the first-year mortality cost is $11. Total expenses ($187) and mortality costs ($11) the first year would amount to $198. Since the premium collected is only $190 there would be a deficit of $8 even before a charge is made for the amount necessary to establish the required first-year terminal reserve for the policy. If the company valued its reserves on the full net level premium system, the required reserve liability at the end of the first year under the policy would be $156.40, thus increasing the deficit from $8 to $164.40. This $164.40 deficit would represent a drain on the insurer's surplus.

---

* Rounded to the nearest dollar. 19,331 is the number living at age 98.

Thus, the more new business a company writes, the greater is the drain on its surplus. In a strong, well-established company with a large surplus, the drain is of no consequence; but in a newer company with a small surplus and a high proportion of new business to business in force, the surplus drain may be serious. Required use of the full net level premium valuation system could force some companies to limit the amount of new business written.

The problem of disproportionate first-year expense could be solved by charging a higher premium the first year, but it is argued that this solution would not be practical because the sales forces and the buying public would object to it. Furthermore, there is no actuarial or accounting reason why a reserve valuation system that takes into account the unlevel incidence of expense cannot be used.

In recognition of the practical problems involved in the incidence of cost, modifications of the net level premium reserve valuation system have been developed, authorized, and successfully used by companies throughout the years. The various modified reserve systems differ in two respects (1) the length of the modification period and (2) the size of the adjustment allowed in the required reserve to absorb extra first-year expenses.

A summary history of the minimum reserve valuation bases for ordinary life insurance in force in New York provides a useful picture of the development of modified reserve systems.

The first modification came in 1907 when insurers were permitted to use the Select and Ultimate Valuation system. Up to that time, the full net level premium method was established as the minimum valuation basis.[18]

The Select and Ultimate Valuation system may be used in New York on all policies issued between 1907 and 1947. Also permitted to be used in New York as a minimum valuation base for policies issued during this 40-year period is the Illinois Standard valuation method.[19]

The Select and Ultimate Valuation method allowed the insurer to reduce the reserve during the first five policy years by the amount that select mortality experience was expected to reduce mortality costs that had been projected on an ultimate table. The reserve could be computed on the basis of mortality equal to 50 percent of tabular in the first policy year increasing to 95 percent in the fifth policy year. The full net premium reserve had to be charged after the fifth policy year. Because the reduction allowed under

---

[18] For policies issued until 1900, the rate of interest to be used for the minimum valuation of reserves was 4 percent and the mortality table specified was the Actuaries Table, more precisely known as the English Seventeen Offices Table of 1843. For policies issued between 1901 to 1906, the interest rate specified was 3½ percent and the mortality rate was the American Experience Mortality Table.

[19] The interest specified for policies issued between 1907 and 1947 is 3½ percent. The mortality table specified is the American Experience table, except that the American Men Ultimate Table may be used in conjunction with the Illinois Standard Valuation method for policies issued between 1930 and 1947.

this system was small compared to the high first-year expense and because the period of modification was so short (five years) the system never was popular.

The popular system during the 40-year period (1907–1947) was the Illinois Standard Valuation system. The Illinois system is identical with the Commissioners Reserve Valuation Method (to be discussed later in this section) except for the length of the modification period. Under the Illinois standard the reserve must be at least equal to the full net level premium reserve by the end of 20 years if the premium paying period is more than 20 years. Under the Commissioners Reserve Valuation Method, the modification period is the premium paying period—that is, the reserve need not be equal to the full net level premium reserve until the end of the premium paying period. The Commissioners Reserve Valuation Method became the basis for the minimum valuation of all ordinary life insurance issued from 1948 to the present.[20]

Two valuation systems used at one time were the full gross premium valuation method and the full preliminary term valuation method. The full gross premium valuation method was generally used until the latter half of the 19th century. The full gross level premium valuation system is the same as the full net level premium valuation system except that the full gross premium rather than the net valuation premium is used in computing the present value of future premiums to be collected. The gross premium system, therefore, produces a lower reserve than is produced by the net premium system.

The full preliminary term valuation method, to be discussed in the next section, was specifically prohibited in 1906 by New York and later by other states. However, a very few states did permit its use. An understanding of the full preliminary term valuation method is necessary to the understanding of the Commissioners Reserve Valuation Method now used in all states as the minimum valuation method.

FULL PRELIMINARY TERM. Under the full preliminary term system of valuation, no reserve is required at the end of the first policy year. For purposes of calculating reserves, the policy is looked upon as a one-year term policy for the first year. Thereafter it is regarded as the original policy, issued one year later, for a period one year shorter. For example, a 20-payment life policy issued at age 35 is looked upon as a one-year term policy at age 35 plus a 19-pay life policy issued at age 36. A continuous premium whole life policy issued at age 35 would be looked upon as a

---

[20] For policies issued from 1948 to an insurer selected optional date between April 13, 1959, and January 1, 1966, the mortality table specified for the minimum required reserve was the 1941 CSO. For policies issued from 1948 to 1966, the interest rate specified for the minimum required reserve was 3 percent. However, effective May 10, 1966, for policies issued between January 1, 1961, and December 31, 1970, the interest rate was increased to $3\frac{1}{2}$ percent. (Remember this discussion is still illustrating developments under the New York law.)

one-year term policy issued at age 35 plus a continuous premium whole life policy issued at age 36.[21]

Since there is no terminal reserve as of the end of the first year, the entire amount of the first-year premium is released for expenses and mortality costs.

For continuous premium whole life policies or other whole life plans which have relatively low premiums and relatively higher acquisition costs the full preliminary term valuation method may be justifiable.[22] However, for endowment policies or other forms of insurance that carry relatively high premiums and relatively low acquisition costs, excessive amounts for expenses may be released under the full preliminary term valuation method. Because the full net level premium reserve method of valuation makes no allowance for nonlevel expenses and the full preliminary term makes an excessive allowance under some policy forms, various modifications of these valuation methods have developed. The Commissioners Reserve Valuation Method is an outgrowth of these earlier modifications.[23]

THE COMMISSIONERS RESERVE VALUATION METHOD.   The Commissioners Reserve Valuation Method (CRVM) was developed by a committee of the National Association of Insurance Commissioners appointed in 1936 to study the need for a new mortality table and related topics. One of the related topics was the valuation of reserves. The basis for reserve valuation that came from the committee was a part of the Standard Valuation Law adopted by all states and applicable to all ordinary life insurance policies written beginning January 1, 1948. The law prescribed the 1941 CSO Mortality Table and $3\frac{1}{2}$ percent interest for the minimum standard using a modification of the preliminary term system (CRVM) as the minimum valuation method. The law was amended in 1965 so that policies issued after January 1, 1966, had to be valued using as the minimum basis the 1958 CSO Table of Mortality.[24]

Under the CRVM policies are divided into two classes: (1) those for which the modified net level valuation premium charged is equal to or

---

[21] It should be stressed that it is erroneous to say that the policy itself is a one-year term policy for the first year; it is only the reserve that is affected. The nature of the policy is that stated in the contract and is not determined by the method of valuing the reserve.

[22] The agent's commission is a large part of the first-year acquisition cost for any policy. Because the continuous premium whole life policy and certain other long-premium payment whole life policies have relatively low premiums, the standard practice is to pay the top commission scale on them and to pay smaller commission rates on higher premium policies.

[23] See C. W. Jordon, Jr., *Life Contingencies*, Society of Actuaries, Chicago, 1953, for a discussion of earlier modifications in the various states and in Canada.

[24] Note that this is a minimum valuation formula. A company may value its reserves more conservatively if it wishes, using any standard up to the full level premium system and using lower interest rates and less favorable mortality assumptions.

less than that charged for a 20-pay life policy issued at the same age for a like amount; and (2) those for which the modified net level valuation premium charged is in excess of that for a 20-pay life plan issued at the same age and for a like amount. Note the use of the term "modified net level valuation premium." The modified net level valuation premium is the net level valuation premium increased by the level amount necessary for the full net level reserve to be reached by the end of the premium paying period.

For policies falling in Class 1, the modified net level valuation premium would be the same as the full preliminary term valuation premium. Thus, the reserve on all policies falling in Class 1 may be valued on a full preliminary term basis if the company chooses. Therefore, there need be no first-year policy reserve.

For policies falling in Class 2, the modified net level valuation premium would be the full preliminary term valuation premium plus a level amount added each year, including the first, sufficient to bring the policy reserve up to its full net level premium reserve by the end of the premium paying period. That addition can be computed by calculating the full net level premium reserve for a pure endowment for the amount by which the Class 2 policy's full net level premium reserve at the end of the premium-paying period exceeds its reserve computed on a full preliminary term basis. The term of the endowment is the premium-paying period for the Class 2 policy. The amount so computed is the first-year reserve for a Class 2 policy as well as the amount by which the full preliminary term reserve is increased each year.

The following examples of reserve computations for policies falling under Class 2 should help clarify this elusive concept.

Example 1: A 30-year endowment insurance policy issued at age 25 would have a first-year reserve equal to the full net level premium first-year reserve for a 30-year pure endowment purchased at age 25, for an amount equal to $1,000 (the full net level premium reserve at the end of the 30-year period) minus the full net level premium reserve at the end of 30 years for a 20-pay whole life policy issued at age 25.

Example 2: The first-year reserve for a 15-pay whole life policy issued at age 25 would be equal to the full net level premium first-year reserve for a 15-year pure endowment, purchased at age 25, in an amount equal to the full net level premium reserve for a 15-pay whole life policy at the end of 15 years minus the full net level premium reserve at the end of 15 years for a 20-pay whole life policy issued at age 25.

Example 3: The Commissioners Reserve Valuation Method can be further illustrated with a 20-year endowment, the modified reserve valuation premium on which will exceed that of a 20-pay whole life policy and therefore must be valued in Class 2. Assume a 20-year endowment for $1,000 issued at age 35, 1958 CSO $2\frac{1}{2}$ percent. The method of arriving at the reserve for the policy is as follows:

Step 1. Determine the reserve for the 20-year endowment at the end of the 20th year: $1,000.

Step 2. Calculate the 20th year reserve on the full net level premium basis for a 20-pay life policy issued at age 35, 1958 CSO $2\frac{1}{2}$ percent: $624.55.

Step 3. Subtract the results of Step 2 from the results of Step 1: $1,000 — $624.55 = $375.45.

Step 4. View the results of Step 3 as the face amount of a 20-year pure endowment. The full net level valuation premium for a 20-year pure endowment of $375.45 is found by dividing this amount by the present value of a life annuity due of 1 for 20 years issued at age 35 1958 CSO, $2\frac{1}{2}$ percent: $375.45 ÷ 15.4254 = $24.34.

Step 5. The first-year reserve for the endowment policy will then be the equivalent of the full net level premium terminal reserve for the pure endowment. This is computed by accumulating the pure endowment net level annual premium for one year with interest and survivorship as follows:

a) Pure endowment net level annual premium	$24.3400
b) Interest at $2\frac{1}{2}\%$ (24.34 × 1.025)	0.6085
c) Survivorship 1958 CSO[25] $\left(\dfrac{23,528}{9,350,279} \times 24.9485\right)$	0.0615
d) Terminal reserve for first year	25.0100

Reserves for each succeeding year will be the reserve required for that year for a 20-payment life policy valued on the full preliminary term basis, plus the accumulated full net level premium reserve for the pure endowment. At the end of the premium paying period, the reserve will equal the full net level premium reserve.

Effect of Actuarial Assumptions on Reserves. The level of and pattern of growth of reserves are directly related to the interest and mortality rates assumed as well as to the reserve system used. The relationship between the interest assumptions and the reserve is more easily seen than is the relationship between the mortality assumptions and the reserve.

EFFECT OF INTEREST ASSUMPTIONS ON RESERVES. The size of the reserve varies inversely with the rate of interest assumed in its calculation.[26]

---

[25] The survivorship benefit is computed as follows: the number dying at age 35 divided by the number living at age 36 multiplied by the initial reserve plus interest. No mortality expense is charged here since this is a pure endowment.

[26] This observation is a corollary of Lidstone's Theorem that "an increase in the rate of interest produces a decrease in reserves, and a decrease in the rate of interest produces an increase in reserves, provided that the reserves increase with duration (Jordan, *op. cit.,* p. 115).

This is true because interest rates have an inverse effect on present values, and present values are used in computing reserves. Table 27–1 shows the

TABLE 27–1

Present Value at the Assumed Rates of Interest (i) of One
Due at the End of the Designated Number of Years (n)

$n \backslash i$	2%	2½%	3%	3½%
5	0.9057	0.8839	0.8626	0.8420
10	.8203	.7812	.7441	.7089
20	.6730	.6103	.5537	.5026
30	.5521	.4767	.4120	.3562
40	.4529	.3724	.3066	.2526
50	.3715	.2909	.2281	.1791

effect that the rate of interest has on the present value of one due n years hence. Note that for any year (n), as the rate of interest (i), increases (decreases), the amount of money needed to equal a given sum in n years will decrease (increase). Thus, the higher (lower) the interest rate, the lower (higher) will be present value of future claims.

Table 27–2 shows the difference in reserves made necessary by a change in

TABLE 27–2

Terminal Reserve at the End of (n) Years for $1,000 of
Continuous Premium Whole Life Insurance Issued at Age 35 and
Based on the 1958 CSO Mortality Table at (i) %

$n \backslash i$	2½%	3%
5	$ 81.05	$ 74.72
10	167.90	156.29
20	352.54	334.23
30	535.77	516.21
40	692.16	675.36
65	1,000.00	1,000.00

interest rates. Note that the reserve valuation is higher for each year under the 2½ percent interest assumption than under the 3 percent assumption. This would be true regardless of the type of policy, age of issue, and date of valuation. If the insured reaches age 100 (35 + 65), the full face amount becomes payable as a death claim.[27]

EFFECT OF MORTALITY ASSUMPTIONS ON RESERVES. At age 35, life expectancy under three different mortality tables is as follows:

American Experience (1843–58) .... 31.78 years
1941 CSO (1930–40) .... 33.44 years
1958 CSO (1950–54) .... 36.39 years

---

[27] Cf. Chapter 1.

Each table reflects an improvement in mortality. Premiums based upon them would, of course, also reflect this mortality improvement. For example, the net level annual premium for $1,000 of life insurance issued under various plans at age 35 using 2½ percent interest assumptions is shown below.

Mortality Assumption \ Policy Type	Continuous Premium Whole Life	20-Payment Whole Life	20-Year Endowment
American Experience	$22.37	$32.68	$43.91
1941 CSO	20.50	30.30	41.98
1958 CSO	17.67	27.24	40.44

What about the reserve? How does a change in mortality assumptions affect the size of the reserve? According to Lidstone's Theorem, "a constant increase in the rate of mortality produces a decrease in reserves, and a constant decrease in the rate of mortality produces an increase in reserves, provided that the reserves increase with duration."[28] Note that this theorem refers to a *constant* increase or a *constant* decrease in the rate of mortality. The word constant is an important one, as will soon become apparent.

Tables 27–3 to 27–6 show the reserve at various intervals for $1,000

TABLE 27–3

Terminal Reserve per $1,000 of Continuous Premium Whole Life Insurance, Issued at Age 35, 2½%

Year	American Experience	1941 CSO	1958 CSO
5	$ 74.07	$ 84.70	$ 81.05
10	157.02	174.39	167.90
20	345.26	362.44	352.54

TABLE 27–4

Terminal Reserve per $1,000 of Continuous Premium Whole Life Insurance, Issued at Age 50, 2½%

Year	American Experience	1941 CSO	1958 CSO
5	$128.99	$129.46	$126.09
10	260.85	257.76	251.94
20	511.15	495.96	485.44

TABLE 27–5

Terminal Reserve per $1,000 of 20-Payment Whole Life Insurance, Issued at Age 35, 2½%

Year	American Experience	1941 CSO	1958 CSO
5	$131.19	$138.43	$133.05
10	282.40	291.43	280.22
20	658.52	653.56	624.55

[28] Jordan, *op. cit.*, p. 117.

TABLE 27–6

Terminal Reserve per $1,000 of 20-Year Endowment
Insurance, Issued at Age 35, 2½%

Year	American Experience	1941 CSO	1958 CSO
5	$ 193.47	$ 202.37	$ 204.83
10	419.08	430.71	435.25
20	1,000.00	1,000.00	1,000.00

of insurance issued under various plans and different ages using 2½ percent interest assumptions. Note that the reserve is higher in six instances using the 1941 CSO mortality assumptions, higher in three instances using the American Experience mortality assumptions, and higher in two instances using the 1958 CSO mortality assumptions. If, as shown in Table 27–7, the mortality rates are lower under the 1958 CSO assumptions than under the 1941 CSO assumptions, and the mortality rates under the 1941 CSO assumptions are lower than under the American Experience assumptions, then why are the reserves not higher in every instance where the 1958 CSO mortality assumptions are used?

The answer lies in the rate of decrease in mortality rates from one table to the next. There has not been a constant decrease in the rate of mortality. For example, from the American Experience Table to the 1941 CSO Table the decrease in mortality at the early ages was very much greater than at the higher ages as shown in Table 27–7. The 1941 CSO mortality rates as a

TABLE 27–7

Mortality Tables
Deaths Per 1,000 at Various Ages

Age	American Experience Table of Mortality	1941 CSO Table	1958 CSO Table
20	7.80	2.43	1.74
25	8.06	2.88	1.93
30	8.43	3.56	2.13
35	8.95	4.59	2.51
40	9.79	6.18	3.53
45	11.16	8.61	5.35
50	13.78	12.32	8.32
55	18.57	17.98	13.00
60	26.64	26.59	20.34
65	40.13	39.64	31.75
70	61.99	59.30	49.79
75	94.37	88.61	73.37
80	144.47	131.85	109.98

percentage of the American Experience mortality rates are shown for selected ages in Table 27–8. Note the lower percentages at ages 70 and 80 than at age 60, where the two tables converge. This is because the American

TABLE 27–8

**Percentage Changes in Mortality Rates at Various Ages
from One Table to the Next**

Age	1941 CSO Mortality Rates As a Percentage of American Experience Mortality Rates	1958 CSO Mortality Rates As a Percentage of 1941 CSO Mortality Rates
20	31%	73%
30	42	60
40	63	57
50	90	67
60	99	76
70	96	82
80	91	83

Experience mortality rates rise more rapidly after about age 60 than do the 1941 CSO mortality rates, reaching 1.00 at age 96, the limiting age of the American Experience Table compared with age 100 in the 1941 CSO Mortality Table.

Comparison of the 1958 CSO mortality rates with those of the 1941 CSO mortality rates shows an even different pattern. The 1958 CSO mortality rate as a percentage of the 1941 CSO mortality rates is higher at age 20 than at age 30, and higher at age 30 than at age 40. But it is lower at age 40 than at age 50, lower at age 50 than at age 60, lower at age 60 than at age 70, and also lower at age 70 than at age 80.[29]

What have these observations to do with the effect of mortality assumptions on the size of reserves? The response is that the size of the reserve is a function not of the level of mortality but of the steepness of the slope of the curve of mortality rates from the age of valuation to the scheduled termination date of the policy. For example, if the assumed rate of mortality remained constant from age to age, there would be no terminal reserve regardless of the level of mortality. But the assumed rate of mortality increases with age; so there will be a terminal reserve, the relative size of which will depend upon how quickly the rate of mortality rises. The more rapid the rise in the mortality rate, the higher will be the reserve. Therefore, since, as can be deduced from Tables 27–7 and 27–8, in most instances the slope of the mortality curve based on the 1941 CSO assumptions will be higher than the slopes of the mortality curves based on the American Experience mortality assumptions and the 1958 CSO mortality assumptions, it is not surprising that in 6 out of 12 possible instances illustrated in Tables 27–3 to Tables 27–6 the reserve is highest when based on the 1941 CSO mortality assumptions.[30]

---

[29] The mortality rates under the 1958 mortality assumptions actually began increasing constantly as a percentage of the 1941 CSO mortality rates at age 35.

[30] For a mathematical explanation of why the foregoing conclusion holds, see Jordan, *op. cit.,* pp. 114–20, or in the second edition (1967), pp. 118–23.

3. NONFORFEITURE VALUES

From the time of Elizur Wright until the passage of the Guertin Laws[31] effective in all jurisdictions in 1948, it was common to tie nonforfeiture values to reserves. Roughly, the method of computing nonforfeiture values on policies issued before January 1, 1948, was to return the terminal reserve minus, in the early years, a surrender charge. The purpose of the surrender charge was to enable the insurer to regain part or all of the higher first-year expenses, which were to be recovered out of the premiums to be paid over a period of years.

The validity of tying nonforfeiture values to reserves was challenged on the ground that nonforfeiture values and reserves are not logically related. Reserves are concerned with measuring the insurer's net liabilities under policies outstanding, whereas nonforfeiture values are concerned with the insurer's obligation to provide an equitable settlement to policyholders who elect one of the nonforfeiture options.

What Is An Equitable Settlement?   It is generally accepted that an equitable settlement to a withdrawing policyholder is one that (1) does not allow the position of the continuing policyholders to deteriorate in any manner and (2) returns to the policyholder the *net* contributions made by his policy to the insurer subject to the foregoing constraint. The *net* contribution is the sum of the premiums paid and interest earned, less the sum of the mortality costs assessed against the policy, the allocated expenses charged against the policy, and the policy's contribution to the insurer's surplus.[32]

Therefore, a policy's nonforfeiture values should be the insurer's projection on a cumulative basis of the amount of the policy's anticipated net annual contributions to the insurer each year during the life of the policy. Because the insurer is contractually bound by these projections, they are usually made conservatively.

Breaking The Tie.   What happens when nonforfeiture values are coupled with reserve values? Conservatism in projecting nonforfeiture values means achieving a safety margin by holding down the values projected. Conservatism in projecting reserve liabilities means achieving a safety margin by holding up the values projected. Thus, one happening is that an insurer is not permitted to project both nonforfeiture values and reserve values conservatively.

---

[31] Cf. Chapter 29.

[32] Various other expenses may be specifically deducted, such as the costs associated with processing the surrender application. Furthermore, in order to preserve the equity between withdrawing and continuing policyholders, some insurers consider it necessary to include an assessment to offset what might be a degree of adverse mortality selection against the insurer. Policyholders in poor health who are in need of funds are properly advised to borrow on their policies rather than to surrender them for their cash value. For policies issued by stock insurers, contributions to profits also are deducted.

A second happening is the inequity created by such a linkage. The unreasonableness of having nonforfeiture values controlled by the actuarial assumptions and by the valuation method the insurer uses in computing its reserve is patent. What realistic relationship could there possibly be here?

The Standard Nonforfeiture and Valuation Laws (Guertin Laws) recognize that nonforfeiture values and reserve values should be independent of each other. The Standard Nonforfeiture Law defines minimum nonforfeiture values without reference to the reserve. Since the minimum nonforfeiture values on policies issued after January 1, 1948, are separate from the reserve, the reserve can be changed on these policies without affecting nonforfeiture values.

The Standard Nonforfeiture Law. Under the Standard Nonforfeiture Law, the *minimum* nonforfeiture value is based on an adjusted premium rather than on either the net level valuation premium or the net premium forming a part of the gross premium charged to the policyholder. The purpose of adjusting the premium is to amortize the assumed excess initial expenses (acquisition costs) of the policy over the premium paying period. The adjusted premium is based on the three factors generally used in rate making: mortality, interest, and expense, in contrast to the net premium, which is based on only two of these factors, mortality and interest.

In order to determine the adjusted premium, the assumed excess initial expense must be calculated. For the purpose of computing *minimum* nonforfeiture values, the maximum amount of these assumed expenses is restricted by law. The excess of first-year expense assumptions (for purposes of this calculation) may not exceed: (1) $20 per $1,000 of insurance, plus (2) 40 percent of the adjusted premium for the policy using the interest and mortality assumption employed in computing nonforfeiture values plus (3) 25 percent of the adjusted premium for a continuous premium whole life policy issued at the same age and under the same conditions, or 25 percent of the adjusted premium for the policy under consideration, whichever is less.[33] If the adjusted premium exceeds $40, then the percentages in the foregoing formula are applied to $40. The effect is to set the maximum assumed excess first-year expense allowance at $46 per $1,000 on those policies having an adjusted premium of $40 or more per $1,000.[34] In addition, the law requires that the 1958 CSO Table with a $3\frac{1}{2}$ percent interest assumption be used in determining the legal minimum values on newly issued policies.

The adjusted premium is determined by adding the net single premium (computed under nonforfeiture interest and mortality assumptions)[35] to

---

[33] Since the expense allowance is needed to compute the adjusted premium and the maximum expense allowance depends upon the adjusted premium, an algebraic equation must be developed to find the adjusted premium. These have been worked out for the usual line of policies, and tables of adjusted premiums have been published for them.

[34] $20 + [40 percent of $40] + [25 percent of $40] or $20 + $16 + $10 = $46.

[35] As distinguished from assumptions used in either gross premium or reserve computations.

the amount of the assumed excess initial expenses and then dividing by the present value of an annuity due of 1 for the premium paying period. The adjusted premium lies between the *net* premium and the *gross* premium. It is more than the *net* premium, since it provides for the amortized assumed excess initial expenses. It is less than the *gross* premium since it provides for only the assumed excess initial expenses and not for all expenses.

Minimum values may be computed by the prospective method, i.e., the present value of assumed adjusted premiums is subtracted from the present value of assumed future claims. The result is a nonforfeiture value that makes allowances for high initial expenses, and returns to the policyholder what is considered to be his just actuarial interest in the policy. If a required surrender value is derived by the adjusted premium formula method before the end of the third year, companies are not required to pay cash values but, instead, may grant their equivalent in paid-up insurance at a reduced amount.

In computing the extended term nonforfeiture value, the insurer is permitted to use mortality assumptions higher than those used for computing cash surrender values or paid-up insurance at a reduced amount.[36]

Computing Nonforfeiture Values—an Illustration.   To demonstrate the application of the foregoing concepts to a specific problem, the minimum nonforfeiture value at the end of the fifth year for $1 of 20-payment whole life insurance issued at age 40 is calculated as follows based on 1958 CSO at $2\frac{1}{2}$ percent.

Step 1. Compute the adjusted premium for $1 of continuous premium whole life insurance issued at age 40. This has to be done algebraically because factors are used in computing the adjusted premium that depend upon the adjusted premium itself. The formula is as follows:

$$x = \frac{A + \$20/1{,}000 + 0.40x + 0.25x}{\ddot{a}_{40}}$$

where

x = Adjusted premium for continuous premium whole life at age 40.
A = Net single premium for whole life policy at age 40.
$\ddot{a}_{40}$ = Present value of a life annuity due of 1 per annum at age 40.

Thus, solving the equation:

$$x\ddot{a}_{40} = A + 0.020 + 0.65x$$

---

[36] The Guertin Laws allow the company in figuring extended-term values to use mortality rates up to 130 percent of those used in computing other nonforfeiture values. The allowance is made to enable a company to offset possible adverse selection under the extended term option. The additional mortality assumption is widely used by small companies. In connection with the 1958 CSO Table, a special table, 1958 CSO A Table, was constructed to be used as a basis for extended term values.

or

$$x = \frac{A + 0.020}{\ddot{a}_{40} - 0.65}.$$

The net single premium for $1 of whole life insurance issued at age 40 is $0.46713 and the present value of an annuity due of 1 per annum at age 40 ($\ddot{a}_{40}$) is 21.84778.

Substituting these values in the equation, the adjusted premium for $1 of continuous premium whole life insurance is found to be:

$$x = \frac{\$0.46713 + 0.02}{21.84778 - 0.65}$$

or

$$x = \frac{0.48713}{21.19778} = \$0.02298.$$

Step 2. Compute the adjusted premium for $1 of 20-payment whole life insurance issued at age 40 by the following formula:

$$y = \frac{A + \$20/1,000 + 0.40y + 0.25x}{\ddot{a}_{40:\overline{20}|}}$$

where

y = the adjusted premium for the 20-payment whole life policy issued at age 40.

$\ddot{a}_{40:\overline{20}|}$ = the present value of an annuity due of 1 per annum for 20 years. (A and x are the same as in Step 1.)

Thus, working out the equation:

$$y = \frac{A + 0.020 + 0.25x}{\ddot{a}_{40:\overline{20}|} - 0.40}.$$

The present value of a 20-year life annuity due of 1 issued at age 40 is 15.14887.

Substituting the values in the equation, the adjusted premium for $1 of 20-payment whole life insurance becomes:

$$y = \frac{\$0.46713 + 0.020 + 0.005745}{15.14887 - 0.40}$$

or

$$y = \frac{0.492875}{14.748875} = \$0.0334178.$$

Step 3. Compute the present value of future adjusted premiums to be collected by multiplying the adjusted premium ($0.0334178) by the present value of a 15-year life annuity due of 1 at age 45 (12.04). This gives $0.40226. (Since the value is being computed for the end of the fifth year, 15 premium payments remain starting at age 45.)

Step 4. Subtract the present value of future adjusted premiums to be collected (Step 3) from the present value of assumed future claims at age 45 ($0.51749) to arrive at $0.11523, the nonforfeiture value per dollar of insurance at the end of the fifth year. (The present value of assumed future claims is taken at age 45 since that is the valuation age.)

Thus, for a $10,000 20-payment whole life policy issued at age 40, the nonforfeiture value at the end of the fifth year would be $1,152.30, based on 1958 CSO at 2½ percent.

In Excess of Minimum Value. The foregoing illustration produces the *minimum* nonforfeiture value based on the mortality (1958 CSO) and interest assumptions (2½ percent) used. Lower nonforfeiture values would be produced by using the maximum interest assumption of 3½ percent. The standard nonforfeiture value method used to produce the legal minimum surrender value is called *the adjusted premium method.* Other standard nonforfeiture methods are available to produce surrender values in excess of the legal minimum, and many insurers choose to use them. The methods for granting more liberal surrender benefits call for using excess initial expense assumptions lower than the maximum allowed by law or by amortizing these expenses over fewer years than the premium payment period. It is not uncommon for insurers to provide higher surrender values by combining both methods.

When the adjusted premium is reduced to provide for higher surrender values, the modified adjusted premium is called a *nonforfeiture factor.* Nonforfeiture factors may be referred to in a life insurance policy by letter designations, such as Nonforfeiture Factor A and Nonforfeiture Factor B. Nonforfeiture Factor B is lower and, therefore, produces a higher surrender value.[37] More than one nonforfeiture factor may be used in the same policy. For example, one policy states:

Nonforfeiture Factor—A shall be used in the calculation of values for the first two policy years. The value for any subsequent policy year shall be calculated by use of a factor reduced from Factor A by equal yearly decrements of an amount which will produce Nonforfeiture Factor B at the end of the fifteenth policy year or at the end of the premium paying period if earlier, after which all cash values shall be the full reserve on the basis of the 1958 CSO Table at 3 percent valued on the Commissioners Reserve Valuation Method.

---

[37] Remember the minimum legal surrender value is computed by subtracting the present value of assumed future adjusted premiums from the present value of assumed future claims. Consequently, the higher the adjusted premium, the lower is the surrender value. In the foregoing formula, when nonforfeiture factors are substituted for the adjusted premium, higher than the legal minimum surrender values will be provided, because nonforfeiture factors modify the adjusted premiums downward.

Nonforfeiture values also can be provided by using a formula different from that provided in the standard nonforfeiture law if the method used provides values equal to or in excess of those produced on the basis of the 1958 CSO Table at $3\frac{1}{2}$ percent using the standard adjusted premium method. This means that as long as the nonforfeiture values do not fall below the legal minimum, they may be computed by any formula the company wishes to adopt. A number of companies still base nonforfeiture values on the reserve less a surrender charge as was common before 1948.

The law does require, however, that the formula for computing surrender values be included in the policy.[38] For example, cash values shown in Table 11–1[39] were computed by the insurer on the basis of the 1958 CSO $2\frac{1}{2}$ percent net level premium reserve (including reserve for immediate payment of death claims and return of one half of the net annual premium whenever death occurs) less $10 per $1,000 during the first year, $5 at the end of the second year, and none at the end of the third and subsequent years. This method, of course, yields a higher cash value in the earlier years than that produced by another insurer that computes its cash values on the basis of the 1958 CSO $2\frac{1}{2}$ percent continuous functions reserve less a deduction for the first 10 years for policies under $25,000 and for the first 7 years for policies of $25,000 and over.[40] It is common to vary cash values according to policy size with typical breaks being at $10,000, $15,000, or $25,000. Other ways in which cash values differ among insurers are that some insurers vary the basis for computing their cash values according to the plan of insurance.[41] Other insurers specify more than one interest assumption in their nonforfeiture value formulas.[42]

Surrender Dividends. A discussion of surrender dividends requires an understanding of the concept of a policy's asset share. The fund accumulated by the insurer on a given policy is that policy's asset share. More specifically, it is the policy's pro rata share of the funds accumulated on behalf of the class of policies (called block of business) of which it is a

---

[38] In some states the law has been modified to require the formula only for those durations for which the specific values are not shown in the policy.

[39] See Chapter 11, page 235.

[40] Continuous functions means that the computations recognize that premiums paid for the period beyond the month of death are refunded and that death claims are payable immediately upon the receipt of due proof of death.

[41] To illustrate, in one company nonforfeiture values are computed by the Standard Nonforfeiture Value Method, equaling the full 1958 CSO $2\frac{1}{2}$ percent reserve after the 12th year in the Estate Series policies, after the 20th year in the Protector Series policies (or at end of premium payment period if earlier), at the end of the 3rd year in the Professional Equity policy, and the 6th year in the Executive Equity Limited policy, except in the Provider 3 Year Modified Life policy, where initial expenses are amortized over the life of the policy, and in the single premium plans, where the cash value always equals the reserve. (The author leaves it to the reader to speculate on the descriptive nature of the Estate Series policies, the Protector Series policies, and the Professional Equity policy.)

[42] To illustrate, one insurer specifies that the cash value shall equal the full net level premium reserve at the end of the 12th year, or premium payment period if shorter, based on 1958 CSO at 3 percent for the first 20 years, and $2\frac{1}{2}$ percent thereafter.

part. It is a function of actual mortality experienced, actual interest earned, and actual expenses incurred, as opposed to assumed mortality, assumed interest, and assumed expenses. For the initial year of the policy, its asset share, for reasons already explained, normally will be less than its reserve. However, as the policy persists it is likely that its asset share will exceed its reserve to the extent of its contribution to the earned surplus retained by the insurer. If the insured surrenders his policy at this stage, some insurers will pay as a surrender dividend a part of the amount by which the policy's asset share exceeds its reserve. The remainder of the asset share stays with the insurer as that policy's permanent contribution to the insurer's surplus.

The Standard Valuation Law provides that for participating insurance the interest rate used in reserve valuation cannot be lower than the interest rate used in nonforfeiture valuation by more than $\frac{1}{2}$ percent unless there is a plan for surrender dividends approved by the Commissioner of Insurance. Under New York law, provision must be made for a surrender dividend if any differential exists between the two valuation interest rates unless the Commissioner is satisfied that the differential is justified.

4. HEALTH INSURANCE RESERVES

In addition to life insurance reserves, companies writing health insurance report reserves in their annual statements for that class of business. The minimum health insurance reserve requirements under the New York law are typical of those applicable in other states. Under the New York statute, insurers are required to maintain reserves for all individual health insurance policies, and these reserves must equal an amount that places a sound value on liabilities under these policies. These reserves may not be less than those based on the standards set forth by regulations issued by the superintendent of insurance and in no event less than the pro rata unearned gross premium reserve for such policies.

The New York superintendent of insurance applies the standards set forth by the *1964 Report of the Industry Advisory Committee on Reserves for Individual Health Insurance Policies* submitted to the National Association of Insurance Commissioners in November of that year. These standards are generally accepted as reasonable minimum valuation standards in all states.

Reserves for health insurance may be classified in two broad categories: (1) active life reserves and (2) claim reserves.

Active Life Reserve. For health insurance policies that can be cancelled or nonrenewed by the insurer, the companies are required to maintain a reserve equal to the pro rata gross premium applicable to the period from the date of valuation to the next following premium due date. One method of computing the gross unearned premium reserve is to calculate one half of the aggregate gross premiums on policies in force at the date of valuation, on the assumption that policy anniversaries are evenly distributed throughout the year. Another method is to array the distribution of the gross premiums by months and assume that premiums are distributed evenly over the month. The gross unearned premium reserve is then computed on a monthly pro rata system. Thus, all policies issued in August are assumed to have been issued on August 15 and have an unearned premium reserve of seven and one-half months on December 31. Some insurers prorate each premium on a daily basis, particularly for group policies involving large premiums. Insurers will choose the method appropriate to their needs.

For noncancellable policies, guaranteed renewable policies, and certain other types of policies under which the insurer's right to discontinue the insurance is restricted, insurers are required to maintain minimum reserves based on specified morbidity or experience tables, a maximum interest rate, and a given reserve valuation method if the minimum reserve so produced exceeds the pro rata unearned premium reserve. For some types of coverage, for example, partial disability income benefits, specified disease benefits, and major medical expense benefits, no morbidity tables are specified in the *1964 Report of the Industry Advisory Committee on Reserves.* Instead, the committee states that the "insurer should adopt a standard which will produce reserves that place a sound value on the liabilities under such benefits."

The specifications for minimum reserves for other types of coverage are as follows: (1) disability income benefits, the 1964 Commissioners Disability Table; (2) hospital expense benefits, the 1956 Intercompany Hospital Table; (3) surgical expense benefits, the 1956 Intercompany Surgical Table; and (4) accidental death benefits, the 1959 Accidental Death Benefit Table. The interest rate specified is the maximum rate allowed in the valuation of currently issued life insurance policies. A two-year preliminary term valuation method (no reserve at the end of the first and second year) is permitted to eliminate pressure on the insurer's surplus arising out of high first-year expenses and out of disproportionately high claim costs in the early years of the policy.

The techniques used in computing reserves for health policies with premiums that are level and claim costs that increase with the age of the insured are similar to those used in developing reserves for life insurance policies.

Claim Reserves. The active life reserve measures the amount that, with premiums to be received in the future, will be sufficient to pay all claims that will be incurred if these claims develop according to the assumptions on which the active life reserve is based. However, liability for claims already incurred but not yet paid are not provided for by the active life reserve. Consequently, it is necessary to establish the insurer's liability for such claims separately from the active life reserve. This liability has, basically, two elements: (1) *the claim reserve* and (2) *the policy claim liability.*

The *claim reserve* provides for the future contingent benefits under claims existing at the valuation date. The amount of liability for future unaccrued benefits is a function of the continuance of the conditions which give rise to loss of income and to expenses for hospital and medical care. It is measured by the present value of the expected amounts payable under the policy. The insurer's own experience and assumptions usually are acceptable as a minimum reserve standard for claims under all coverages except disability income coverage for claims with a duration of at least two years.[43] In the latter event the minimum standard in many states is that produced by the 1964 Commissioners Disability Table at $3\frac{1}{2}$ percent.

The *policy claim liability* represents the insurer's liability for accrued benefits which would be due and payable except for completion of notice of claim and proof of loss. It differs from the claim reserve in that the liability is not contingent on the claimant's survival, his continued disability, or some other future condition. The liability has already been incurred and the policy claim is payable as soon as the formalities are completed.

Claim reserves and policy claim liabilities arise under claims for which the insurer has not received notice on the valuation date (i.e., the so-called unreported claims), as well as claims reported to the insurer prior to the valuation date but not yet settled. The reserves and claim liabilities for unreported claims are estimated from the insurer's experience with the class of policies under which the claims are incurred.

Experience under health insurance is difficult to predict with any great degree of accuracy. Claim rates and average benefits per claim exhibit considerable fluctuations and have been observed to vary with the economic cycle and as the result of epidemics. It is common, therefore, for companies to build contingency reserves as a part of surplus in order to provide for adverse fluctuations in claim experience.

5. NET WORTH

The final section of a life insurance company balance sheet deals with net worth. The net worth section also ties in with the other two financial statements, *summary of operations* and *surplus account.*

Net worth is made up of capital and surplus. Over one half of the life insurance in force in United States companies are underwritten by insurers in which there is no capital stock. These insurers, called mutual companies, are owned by the policyholders and their net worth is represented solely by surplus.

While it is common to speak of surplus as a "fund," and while it often

---

[43] Various methods have been developed by insurers for use in determining sound values for claim reserves. For a discussion of these methods see I. M. Bragg, "Health Insurance Claim Reserves and Liabilities," *Transactions of the Society of Actuaries,* Vol. XVI, pp. 17–54, 155–73.

requires circumlocution to refrain from doing so, it will be helpful in understanding the following discussion of surplus to hold in mind that it, like the reserve, is not a fund. When combined with capital, surplus is an accounting figure showing the net ownership interest in the assets of the company.[44]

Sources of Surplus.   In the computation of its gross premiums, a life insurance company assumes lower interest, higher mortality, and higher expense rates than it anticipates experiencing. As a result, the company is likely to earn excess interest and realize savings on mortality and expenses all of which go to increase surplus. Also, certain assets are revalued periodically according to market prices.[45] When the statement value is increased (decreased) surplus is increased (decreased) correspondingly. Moreover, surplus may be increased (decreased) by a sale of assets for more (less) than book value.

Furthermore, surrender of a policy may add to surplus. As previously noted when a policyholder surrenders his policy, he may not receive the full terminal reserve. If the full reserve is not paid upon surrender, surplus is increased by the difference between the reserve released and the cash surrender value paid.[46]

In addition to mortality coverage, many life insurance companies also offer certain types of health insurance coverages—waiver of premium, monthly income disability, and medical expense. Gains and losses resulting from deviations between actual and assumed morbidity will increase or decrease surplus.

Gain and Loss in Insurance.   The balance sheet indicates only how large the surplus is as of the date of the statement. It does not show the nature and causes of any changes in the surplus account. The summary of operations statement and the surplus account serve this purpose. In the computation of a gross level premium, the following items are taken into consideration: mortality, interest, and expenses. Thus, if a company experiences mortality and expenses as assumed, earns interest at the assumed rate, and increases or decreases its reserve according to the mortality and interest assumptions made, there would be no gain or loss from operations. This relationship can be shown as follows:

---

[44] In a mutual company the concept of surplus as an ownership interest seems cloudy, since a policyholder, upon withdrawal, is not entitled to a pro rata interest in the surplus. In some companies he may be given a surrender dividend, but this dividend represents only a part of his contribution to surplus and is in no event a full return of his "theoretical" interest in the company. The surplus, therefore, represents the ownership interest only of those who remain. Actually, it is difficult to say what the surplus is in terms of ownership, since if the company is dissolved, the surplus may revert to the state under the laws of escheat.

[45] Cf. Chapter 26.

[46] This should not be interpreted to mean that lapses or surrenders necessarily make a profit for the company. They may simply restore surplus which had been previously depleted when the policy was issued.

Gross premiums plus assumed interest minus assumed expenses minus increase in reserves[47] minus assumed mortality equal no gain or loss.

Since life insurers use conservative actuarial assumptions, there are likely to be operational gains. For clarification, however, the term "gain" should be defined to eliminate misconceptions.

The immediate result of a gain is to increase surplus. For nonparticipating policies, these gains represent earnings and are profit in the commercial sense as in any business firm. Therefore, in pricing nonparticipating policies, assumed and actual experience must be related as closely as possible to produce the profit rate desired by the insurer.[48] Although reserves on nonparticipating policies just as on participating policies must be valued according to the conservative standards of the law, premiums must be calculated on assumptions that are realistic in terms of the insurer's goals.

However, for participating policies, gains are not all profits in the usual sense of the word, because a portion of them is expected to be returned to the policyholder as a dividend. A margin for dividends is customarily loaded into the gross premium for participating policies.

A large gain from operations is no standard in itself of operational efficiency. Because gains arise largely from the difference between assumptions and experience, a large gain can be developed simply by using highly conservative assumptions.[49] Since the gains of a life insurance company are the result of the difference between assumed income and disbursements and actual income and disbursements, the relationship can be rewritten as follows:

Gross premiums plus actual interest[50] minus actual mortality minus actual expenses minus increase in reserves[51] equal gain or loss.

THE SUMMARY OF OPERATIONS STATEMENT.   The foregoing relationship is what is effected in the summary of operations statement.

First, the gross premiums accrued are determined by adding the premiums on annuities, life insurance, health insurance, supplementary contracts with life contingencies, and supplementary contracts without life contingencies (period certain in settlement options, and so on).

Next, the interest earned is added to the gross premiums. This interest is determined by adding the net investment income (interest less taxes, investment management expenses, and other such expenses) and the net capital gains.

Then costs of claims are deducted. These include payments made for

---

[47] Or plus decreases in reserves.

[48] Because no dividends are paid to policyholders, the premium need not contain the "fat" added to participating premiums to provide a margin for these dividends.

[49] This is not to say that operational efficiency of a company cannot result in gains. The greater the efficiency, the more favorable will be the experience when compared to given assumptions.

[50] Including capital gains and losses.

[51] Or plus decreases in reserves.

death benefits, matured endowments, annuity benefits, disability benefits, sickness benefits, and disbursements under supplementary contracts (with and without life contingencies).

Deductions are then made for general insurance expenses; taxes, licenses, and fees; commissions; and expenses of investigating claims.

Finally, allowance for increases and decreases in the reserve is made by subtracting the decrease in reserve resulting from policy terminations and adding the increase in reserves from the advancing duration of old policies and the issuance of new insurance.

The result is the net gain from operations. The summary of operations section of the annual statement continues with a deduction for policy dividends.

THE SURPLUS ACCOUNT. It is the function of the surplus account to tie together the results of the balance sheet and the summary of operations to show both the gain or loss and the size of the surplus as of the time of the statement. The surplus account tells, first, the source of funds and, second, their application.

The account is a double columned statement. The left-hand side shows the source of surplus. It starts with the surplus at the end of the previous year, listing the unassigned surplus and the special surplus funds for that year. To the sum of these two figures is added the gain determined in the summary of operations after the deduction of the policyholders' dividends. Next is added any capital gain not included in the summary of operations. Last is added the amount, if any, of surplus paid in[52] during the year. The total of these items shows the source of surplus during the year.

The right-hand half of the surplus account shows the application of surplus during the year, i.e., how the surplus was used. The first item is the amount of dividends to stockholders. Next is added any increase in reserves resulting from any change in the basis of valuation. After this, the amount of special surplus funds at the end of the year is added. The remainder necessary to balance the account is the amount of unassigned surplus at the end of the year.

Distribution of Surplus. Two decisions must be made in the management of unassigned surplus: (1) how much should be allocated to divisible surplus and (2) how the divisible surplus should be apportioned among the individual policyholders.

THE DIVISIBLE SURPLUS. Dividend scales are a matter of company philosophy. For competitive reasons, companies seek to maintain a liberal dividend policy but not at the expense of sound financial management. As policy reserves increase over the years, so must contingency reserves if the companies are to achieve their goal of a given relationship between the two. Therefore, the divisible surplus each year *on the average* must be less than

---

[52] Only in rare instances will there be any surplus paid in during the year. Surplus paid in is to be distinguished from earned surplus. It is much like capital in that it is paid in by its owners to strengthen the company.

the annual gains from mortality experience, investment results, and operational efficiency. Once a dividend scale is established, however, it is usually continued unchanged for as long as it is practical to do so. Thus the divisible surplus for any one year does not have any fixed relationship to the year to year increases in surplus. The dividend scale may be maintained by drawing on past accumulations when the current gain in surplus is insufficient to support it.[53] When gains in surplus are more than sufficient to maintain the dividend scale, the excess is retained in the surplus account. Companies prefer not to alter their dividend scales from year to year to reflect annual experience, because of the expense and inconvenience involved. Only when a clear lasting trend in annual surplus gains is discernible will a company change its dividend scale to reflect it. The new dividend scale, like the old, becomes the product of the wisdom and knowledge of company management.

A number of states limit the amount of surplus that can be accumulated by the insurer to 10 percent of its policy reserve. The restriction is designed to prevent insurers from building surpluses large enough to encourage inefficiency and waste at the expense of their policyholders. The surplus restriction does not apply to companies writing only nonparticipating policies. However, in some states a limitation is imposed on the amount of surplus that a stock company writing participating policies can transfer from participating surplus to stockholders' surplus.

In most states dividends must be apportioned and paid annually. Insurers are not allowed to use the tontine system under which dividends are deferred for a given number of years and then distributed to the survivors as was once the case.[54]

APPORTIONMENT OF DIVIDENDS. The apportionment of dividends to stockholders is simply a matter of dividing funds available for dividends by the number of shares outstanding. The process is the same as in any corporation. Dividends on stock are equitably distributed when paid to stockholders in proportion to their shareholdings.

The problem of an equitable distribution of policy dividends is not so simple. First of all, policy dividends are not profits, but a return of an overcharge of premiums.[55] To distribute them among policyholders in the same manner as profits are distributed among stockholders would be inequitable, since policyholders contribute in different proportions to expense loadings, mortality costs, and investment funds. The problem becomes one of constructing a formula for the apportionment of dividends

---

[53] New York law prohibits dividend payments during the first year of insurance unless the dividend was actually earned for the policy based on reasonable interest, mortality, and expense assumptions. (The problem here is determining what are "reasonable" expense assumptions.)

[54] Cf. Chapter 29.

[55] Thus, in the annual statement the amount of policyholder dividends never actually enters surplus but is handled in the summary of operations.

among policyholders in accordance with the contribution of each to the divisible surplus.

In apportioning the divisible surplus, it would be unfair to base the distribution on any one factor such as face amount of the policy, size of the premium, or level of the reserve. For example, it would be unfair to distribute savings in expense loading on the basis of the face amount of the policy when the amount any policy contributes toward savings in expenses of operation depends only in part on the size of its premium per $1,000.[56] Again, it would not be equitable to distribute excess interest earnings and investment gains among policies on a basis of either the face amount of the insurance or the size of premium when the contribution of each policy to the total of these gains is in proportion to its investment values as measured by the policy reserve. A policy with a high reserve, for instance, certainly has contributed more to any excess interest earnings and investment gains than one requiring a low reserve or no reserve at all.

It would be inequitable to distribute gains from mortality on a basis of total premiums, the face amount of the policy, or the reserve. It might appear at first glance that distributions of mortality gains according to the face amount of the policy would be equitable. However, the contribution of each policyholder to mortality savings depends upon the amount at risk in his policy for that year; i.e., the difference between the face amount of the policy and the amount of the reserve.

Inequities will exist if an attempt is made to divide funds available for dividends on the basis of any single factor, a reality that has not always been recognized. In the early days of life insurance in America, dividend funds were divided among policyholders either arbitrarily or on the basis of premium payments. One of the earliest methods of dividend apportionment was to credit each policy with an additional amount of insurance equal to a given percentage of the gross premium paid.

It should be understood that it is impossible to achieve complete equity in dividend allocation and retain the objectives of simplicity and economy of operation.[57] Mortality gains, excess interest earnings, and expense savings vary among policies on the basis of factors other than amount at risk, policy reserves, and size of premium. For example, the residence of the insured, his occupation, and the duration of the policy, to name a few, can affect the contribution of each policy to mortality savings. The interest rate in effect at the time premiums are paid (new money rates) would affect the contributions of each policy to interest earnings. And the degree of underwriting investigation necessary, the differences in state premium

---

[56] Policies of high face amounts usually contribute more to surplus than do policies of low face amounts since quantity discounts do not fully reflect the savings associated with writing policies of higher amounts.

[57] Simplicity is important so that the formula can be explained, if need be, by the agent to the policyholder in terms that both can understand.

tax rates, and the amount of service required will affect the contribution of the policy to operational savings.

The Contribution Plan.   The objective, therefore, should be to obtain a practical degree of equity. The search for a more equitable method of distribution than a single factor or arbitrary method of distribution resulted in 1863 in the introduction of the *contribution plan,* worked out originally by David Parks Fackler, founder of the Actuarial Society of America, then assistant to Sheppard Homans, of the Mutual Life of New York, and later actuary for the Equitable Life Assurance Society of New York. The plan was based on the theory that a contribution of a given group of policies to the earnings of a company can be found within reasonable limits by the following process:

Credit the group of policies with
1. The initial reserve.
2. The excess of the loading for gross premiums over actual expense.
3. Interest for the year on Items 1 and 2 at the *actual* rate earned by the company.

Debit the group of policies with
1. The terminal reserve.
2. The cost of insurance at the *actual* (experienced) rate of mortality.

The credit balance resulting from this process is the basis upon which that particular policy is to share in the dividend. The full credit, of course, is not returned as a dividend. Each policy is expected to make a permanent contribution to surplus. The dividend is the percentage of divisible surplus that the credit bears to the total of all credits developed.

The process involved in the Fackler plan (which originally had provided directly only for excess interest earnings and savings in mortality payments, being later modified to provide for savings in expenses) succeeded in giving the policyholder credit for excess interest earnings, savings in mortality payments, and expense savings in proportion to the contributions to the insurer's surplus attributable to these items. The Fackler plan is known as the three factor contribution system. Under this system, dividends for policies other than term that have been in force for fairly long periods and for high premium plans even in their early years will be more affected by excess interest earnings than by mortality savings because they will have accumulated large reserves. Consequently, less will be at risk per $1,000 of face amount of insurance. Conversely, dividends for term insurance and low premium whole life plans in their early years will be more affected by mortality savings than by excess interest earnings because the reserve per $1,000 on these policies is low. Therefore, more will be at risk per $1,000 of face amount of insurance. The combined effect has been that for all policies except term, dividends have increased with policy duration because excess interest has been the dominant factor in producing dividends.

The contribution plan continues to be the basis of nearly every company's formula for the apportionment of policyholder dividends. In practice, a myriad of variations has arisen; but the basic Fackler principle carries through all of them. Most companies issuing participating plans make an attempt to distribute the dividends as equitably as is practical, so that dividends are apportioned largely according to the contribution of each homogenous group of policies to the funds available for dividends. Variations among dividend formulas, company by company, mainly are differences in actuarial philosophy rather than in actuarial principle.

The Experience Premium Method. If excess interest earnings decline heavily, policy dividends will decrease with duration, a condition not considered desirable for good policyholder relations. The experience premium was introduced as a modification of the contribution system to spread the gains from mortality more evenly over the duration of the policy rather than have them weigh so heavily in the early years of the policy. The object is to reduce the extent of the reliance on excess interest earnings for dividends on policies that have been in force for relatively long durations. Under this plan, an experience premium is developed from realistic mortality and expense assumptions but with the conservative interest assumptions used in computing the actual premium payable. The annual dividend consists of the difference between the actual premium and the experience premium, plus the excess interest earned for the year. As the "realistic assumptions" prove unrealistic, they will have to be adjusted just as dividend formulas are adjusted under the unmodified plan from time to time.

Appendix to Chapter 27
A Mathematical Note on Reserve Computation

In the appendix of Chapter 25, certain symbols were explained and then algebraic formulas were developed for and applied in the computation of net premiums. Algebraic formulas also can be used in the computation of reserves.

Symbols.   The standard symbols used to express reserves are as follows:

$_tV_x$ = the terminal reserve at the end of t years for a \$1 continuous premium whole life policy issued at age x.

$_t^nV_x$ = the terminal reserve at the end of t years for a \$1 n-payment whole life policy issued at age x.

$_tV_{x:\overline{n}|} =$ the terminal reserve at the end of t years for a $1 n-year endowment policy issued at age x.

$_tV^1_{x:\overline{n}|} =$ the tth year terminal reserve for a $1 n-year term policy issued at age x.

$A_{x+t} =$ the present value of projected future claims at age $x + t$ for a whole life policy of $1 of insurance issued at age x.

$A_{x+t:\overline{n-t}|} =$ the present value of projected future claims at age $x + t$ for an n-year endowment policy of $1 issued at age x, $t \leqq n$.

$A^1_{x+t:\overline{n-t}|} =$ the present value of projected future claims at age $x + t$ for an n-year term policy of $1 issued at age x, $t \leqq n$.

$P_x \cdot \ddot{a}_{x+t} =$ the present value of future net level annual premiums at age $x + t$ for a continuous premium whole life policy of $1 issued at age x.

$_nP_x \cdot \ddot{a}_{x+t:\overline{n-t}|} =$ the present value of future net level annual premiums at age $x + t$ for an n-payment whole life policy of $1 issued at age x.

$P_{x:n} \cdot \ddot{a}_{x+t:\overline{n-t}|} =$ the present value of future net level annual premiums at age $x + t$ for an n-year endowment policy of $1 issued at age x.

$P^1_{x:n} \ddot{a}_{x+t:\overline{n-t}|} =$ the present value of future net level annual premiums at age $x + t$ for an n-year term policy of $1 issued at age x.

$_tV =$ the terminal reserve at the end of t years for any type of policy. (This symbol may be used in lieu of any one of the first four symbols above, that is, for any one of those that include the notation V.)

$P_x =$ the net level annual premium for $1 of insurance issued at age x under any type of plan.

$_tU_x =$ the accumulated value of net level annual premiums of $1 paid for t years from age x.[1]

$_tk_x =$ the accumulated value of claims paid per $1 of insurance for t years from age x.

The last 4 symbols are used in connection with computing reserves on a retrospective basis, whereas the first 11 are used in calculating the reserve on a prospective basis.

---

[1] This is called a foreborne life annuity due. It is the value of an annuity due of 1 per annum accumulated by interest and survivorship benefits. For example, if 9,575,636 people aged 25 each contributed $1 to a fund now and the 9,557,155 people who are alive at the beginning of the next year contribute another dollar, the fund will have grown to $19,856,486.45 at the end of the second year. If the fund is then divided among the 9,538,423 people alive at the end of the second year, each survivor's share will be $2.08. This would be the value of the symbol $_tU_x$ where t is 2 and x is 25.

Prospective Reserve Formulas. The prospective reserve is computed by subtracting the present value of future net level annual premiums from the present value of future claims, as of the valuation date using given mortality and interest assumptions. The following are the formulas for computing the reserve for various types of policies.

The formula for the full net level premium terminal reserve at the end of t years on a continuous premium whole life policy for $1 is:

$$_tV_x = A_{x+t} - P_x \cdot \ddot{a}_{x+t}. \tag{32}[2]$$

For an n-payment whole life policy the formula is:

$$_t^nV_x = A_{x+t} - {_nP_x} \cdot \ddot{a}_{x+t:\overline{n-t}|} \quad t < n. \tag{33}$$

If the policy is paid up, then the quantity ${_nP_x} \cdot \ddot{a}_{x+t:\overline{n-t}|}$ will be a zero and the reserve will be simply A_{x+t}, $t \geq n$.

For an n-year endowment policy the reserve is:

$$_tV_{x:\overline{n}|} = A_{x+t:\overline{n-t}|} - P_{x:n} \cdot \ddot{a}_{x+t:\overline{n-t}|} \tag{34}$$

For an n-year term policy, the reserve is:

$$_tV^1_{x:\overline{n}|} = A^1_{x+t:\overline{n-t}|} - P^1_{x:n} \cdot \ddot{a}_{x+t:\overline{n-t}|}. \tag{35}$$

The commutation columns reproduced in Appendix A to Chapter 25 can be used to work out each of the above formulas.

Example 1. Calculate the 10th-year terminal reserve per $1 of continuous premium whole life insurance issued at age 25, 1958 CSO at 2½ percent. Substituting the values of t and x in equation (32), the formula becomes:

$$_{10}V_{25} = (A_{35} - P_{25} \cdot \ddot{a}_{35}). \tag{36}$$

Substituting from equations (9), (31), and (23) (found in Appendix A to Chapter 25), the equation can be written:

$$_{10}V_{25} = \left(\frac{M_{35}}{D_{35}} - 0.01255\frac{N_{35}}{D_{35}}\right). \tag{37}$$

Using the commutation tables, the equation becomes:

$$_{10}V_{25} = \left(\frac{1659440.3563}{3949851.0856} - 0.01255\frac{93906838.6413}{3949851.0856}\right) = \$0.12175. \tag{38}$$

Example 2. Calculate the 10th-year terminal reserve for $1 of 20-payment whole life insurance issued at age 25, 1958 CSO at 2½ percent. Substituting from equation (33), the formula becomes:

$$_{10}^{20}V_{25} = (A_{35} - {_{20}P_{25}} \cdot \ddot{a}_{35:\overline{10}|}). \tag{39}$$

Substituting from equations (9), (29), and (21), the equation can be written:

---

2 The numbering is a continuation of the numbers used in Appendix A Chapter 25.

$$_{10}^{20}V_{25} = \left(\frac{M_{35}}{D_{35}} - 0.02168 \frac{N_{35} - N_{45}}{D_{35}}\right). \tag{40}$$

Using the commutation tables, the equation becomes:

$$_{10}^{20}V_{25} = \left(\frac{1659440.3563}{3949851.0856} - 0.02168 \frac{93906838.6413 - 58927803.0828}{3949851.0856}\right)$$
$$= \$0.22813. \tag{41}$$

Example 3. Calculate the 10th-year terminal reserve for $1 of 20-year endowment insurance issued at age 25, 1958 CSO at 2½ percent from equation (34), the formula becomes:

$$_{10}V_{25:\overline{20}|} = (A_{35:\overline{10}|} - P_{25:\overline{20}|} \cdot \ddot{a}_{35:\overline{10}|}). \tag{42}$$

Substituting from equations (10), (30), and (21), the equation can be written:

$$_{10}V_{25:\overline{20}|} = \left(\frac{M_{35} - M_{45} + D_{45}}{D_{35}} - 0.03944 \frac{N_{35} - N_{45}}{D_{35}}\right). \tag{43}$$

Using the commutation tables, the equation becomes:

$$_{10}V_{25:\overline{20}|} = \left(\frac{1659440.3563 - 1541435.3639 + 2978698.8164}{3949851.0856}\right) \text{ less}$$
$$.03944 \left(\frac{93906838.6413 - 58927803.0828}{3949851.0856}\right) = \$0.43473. \tag{44}$$

Example 4. Calculate the 10th-year terminal reserve for $1 of 20-year term insurance issued at age 25, 1958 CSO at 2½ percent. From equation (35), the formula is:

$$_{10}V^1_{25:\overline{20}|} = (A^1_{35:\overline{10}|} - P^1_{25:\overline{20}|} \cdot \ddot{a}_{35:\overline{10}|}). \tag{45}$$

Substituting from equations (8), (28), and (21), the equation can be written:

$$_{10}V^1_{25:\overline{20}|} = \left(\frac{M_{35} - M_{45}}{D_{35}} - 0.00263 \frac{N_{35} - N_{45}}{D_{35}}\right). \tag{46}$$

Using the commutation tables, the equation becomes:

$$_{10}V^1_{25:\overline{20}|} = \left(\frac{1659440.3563 - 1541435.3639}{3949851.0856}\right) \text{ less}$$
$$.00263 \left(\frac{93906838.6413 - 58927803.0828}{3949851.0856}\right) = \$0.00659. \tag{47}$$

Retrospective Reserve Formula.   The retrospective reserve is computed by subtracting the accumulated value of claims paid from the accumulated value of net level annual premiums collected, as of the valuation date using given mortality and interest assumptions. The formula per \$1 of insurance can be stated as follows:

$$_tV = P \cdot {}_tU_x - {}_tk_x . \quad{}^3 \tag{48}$$

The formula for $_tU_x$ (the accumulated value of net level annual premiums of 1 paid for t years from age x can be developed as follows:

$$_tU_x =$$
$$\frac{l_x(1+i)^t + l_{x+1}(1+i)^{t-1} + l_{x+2}(1+i)^{t-2} + \cdots + \cdots l_{x+t-1}(1+i)^{t-1}}{l_{x+t}} \cdot$$

$$\tag{49}$$

In order to be able to use the commutation columns to find the value of $_tU_x$, it is necessary to multiply the numerator and the denominator in the above equation by v^{x+t}. Since v is $(1+i)^{-1}$, the equation may be written as follows:

$$_tU_x = \frac{v^x l_x + v^{x+1} l_{x+1} + \cdots + v^{x+t-1} l_{x+t-1}}{v^{x+t} l_{x+t}} \cdot \tag{50}$$

And since the commutation symbol $D_x = v^x l_x$, the above formula becomes:

$$_tU_x = \frac{D_x + D_{x+1} + \cdots + D_{x+t-1}}{D_{x+t}} \cdot \tag{51}$$

Substituting the symbol N_x in the numerator of the above equation, the final formula is written:

$$_tU_x = \frac{N_x - N_{x+t}}{D_{x+t}} \cdot \tag{52}$$

The formula for $_tk_x$ (the accumulated value of assumed death claims per \$1 of insurance for t years from age x) is developed as follows:

$$_tk_x = \frac{d_x(1+i)^{t-1} + d_{x+1}(1+i)^{t-2} + \cdots + d_{x+t-1}}{l_{x+t}} \cdot \tag{53}$$

Again, in order to be able to use the commutation columns to find the value of $_tk_x$, the numerator and the denominator in the above equation must be multiplied by v^{x+t} with the following results:

$$_tk_x = \frac{v^{x+1} d_x + v^{x+2} d_{x+1} + \cdots + v^{x+t} d_{x+t-1}}{v^{x+t} l_{x+t}} \cdot \tag{54}$$

---

3 Refer back to the beginning of this section for the translation of these symbols.

And since the commutation symbol $C_x = v^{x+1}d_x$, and the commutation symbol $D = v^x l_x$, the above formula becomes:

$$_t k_x = \frac{C_x + C_{x+1} + \cdots + C_{x+t-1}}{D_{x+t}}. \tag{55}$$

Substituting the symbol M_x in the numerator of the above equation, the final formula is written:

$$_t k_x = \frac{M_x - M_{x+t}}{D_{x+t}}. \tag{56}$$

Substituting equations (52) and (56) in equation (48), the formula for computing retrospective reserves per $1 of insurance can be written as follows:

$$_t V = \frac{P(N_x - N_{x+t}) - (M_x - M_{x+t})}{D_{x+t}}. \tag{57}$$

The commutation columns can be used in computing the reserve from this formula. In calculating the 10th-year terminal reserve on insurance issued at age 25, the only variable as among types of policies will be P.

Example 1. Calculate the 10th-year terminal reserve for $1 of continuous premium whole life insurance issued at age 25, 1958 CSO at 2½ percent. Substituting in formula (57) from formula (31) and the commutation tables, the equation can be written as follows:

$$_{10}V_{25} = \frac{0.01255\,(139839496.9072 - 93906838.6413)}{3949851.0856}\ \text{less}$$
$$\frac{(1754288.5116 - 1659440.3563)}{3949851.0856} = \$0.12193. \, {}^{4} \tag{58}$$

Example 2. Calculate the 10th-year terminal reserve for $1 of 20-payment whole life insurance issued at age 25, 1958, 1958 CSO at 2½ percent. Substituting from formula (29):

$$_{10}^{20}V_{25} = \frac{.02168\,(139839496.9072 - 93906838.6413)}{3949851.0856}\ \text{less}$$
$$\frac{(1754288.5116 - 1659440.3563)}{3949851.0856} = \$0.22810. \tag{59}$$

Example 3. Calculate the 10th-year terminal reserve for $1 of 20-year endowment insurance issued at age 25, 1958 CSO at 2½ percent. Substituting for formula (30):

---

[4] The slight difference between this figure and the amount arrived at in equation (38) by the prospective method arises from the rounding off process. The small differences in examples 2, 3, and 4 exist for the same reason.

$$_{10}V_{25:\overline{20}|} = \frac{.03944\ (139839496.9072 - 93906838.6413)}{3949851.0856}\ \text{less}$$

$$\frac{(1754288.5116 - 1659440.3563)}{3949851.0856} = \$0.43463. \tag{60}$$

Example 4. Calculate the 10th-year terminal reserve for $1 of 20-year term insurance issued at age 25, 1958 CSO at 2½ percent. Substituting for formula (28):

$$_{10}V^1_{25:\overline{20}|} = \frac{0.00263\ (139839496.9072 - 93906838.6413)}{3949851.0856}\ \text{less}$$

$$\frac{(1754288.5116 - 1659440.3563)}{3949851.0856} = \$0.00657. \tag{61}$$

28

Types and Analysis of Life Insurers

Life insurance is written by three types of insurers, broadly classified as *proprietary, mutual,* and *state.* The chief difference among these types is in the nature of ownership. Proprietary insurers are corporations owned by investors. Mutual companies are in the nature of cooperatives, being corporations owned by the policyholders themselves. State insurers are owned by the government, federal or state, as the case may be, which is, theoretically, ownership by all citizens of the state.[1]

It is the purpose of this chapter to examine each type of insurer and, further, to discuss the variations among insurers of the same organizational classes.

1. STOCK AND MUTUAL COMPANIES

About 95 percent of all life insurance owned in the United States is written by stock and mutual companies. As between stock and mutual companies, stock companies are the more numerous, composing more than 90 percent of the 1,812 old line legal reserve companies.[2] However,

---

[1] In other fields of insurance, notably fire and marine, proprietary insurers include unincorporated, individual underwriters, each taking a portion of the risk. The best known group of such underwriters is that operating through the facilities of Lloyd's of London. The system of individual underwriters is not adaptable to life insurance contracts because the insured must not be able to outlive the insurer. In fire and automobile insurance, there are unincorporated cooperatives organized as reciprocal exchanges. The unincorporated cooperative form is not adaptable to life insurance for the same reason that the unincorporated, proprietary form is unsuitable.

[2] The term "old line" has no real significance. The designation was adopted during the latter half of the 19th century when competition between commercial companies and fraternal insurers was bitter. At that time fraternal organizations began to offer insurance, usually on an assessment basis and at premium rates much lower than those charged by the commercial insurers. The term "old line" was coined by the older commercial companies to emphasize the old and thus tested, and to indicate that the insurer is not an assessment insurer but a legal reserve company writing business for the general public. An old line company may be either a mutual or a stock insurer. It also may be a new company. More

mutual companies are predominant in the amount of insurance in force and in the amount of assets owned, accounting for about 53 percent of the amount of life insurance outstanding in stock and mutual companies and for about 70 percent of the assets of these insurers.[3]

Nature of Stock Companies. Proprietary insurance is issued by individuals operating through the structure of a corporation. Such corporations are called stock companies. The individual shareholders of the stock company advance the money to organize an insurer, and, in return, they share in the profits and losses. The stock life insurance company functions in the same way as any other incorporated business organization. Management control rests with the shareholders who elect the board of directors, which, in turn, elects the executive officers.

Although in a stock company the individual stockholders technically control the company, in practice stock ownership may be so widely scattered that the corporation is controlled by those who, either by ownership or by proxies, hold an amount of stock sufficient to provide the majority of votes ordinarily cast at any meeting of stockholders.

The Use of Holding Companies. A recent development in stock life insurer ownership is the increasing use of holding companies. For the most part, the holding companies are financial corporations owning or controlling one or more life insurers, property and liability insurance companies, mutual fund broker-dealer organizations, mutual fund management and investment research companies, consumer finance companies, home builders, and other financial service related corporations including only one bank. Some stock life insurers are owned or controlled by nonfinancial holding companies and conglomerates that group together companies in unrelated fields.

The control of insurers by conglomerates and noninsurance-related holding companies was viewed with alarm by the Special Committee on Insurance Holding Companies appointed by the New York State insurance department. In its 1968 report, the committee observed:[4]

[T]he dominant motives for their formation may be changing from a desire to facilitate the conduct of the insurance business to a desire to shift away from the insurance business and to subordinate insurance to other business objectives. . . .

---

than 1,300 new "old line" insurers have been formed during the past decade. Some playful "historians" claim that the fraternals coined the word and that it was originally "old lying" companies, lying about the need for higher premiums. Some professional critics of life insurance say the term refers to companies which persist in giving the public "the same old line."

[3] Mutual life insurance companies generally are older and larger than stock insurance companies. Because of the large number of new stock life insurers, stock insurers are writing an increasing percentage of the life insurance in force. Just a decade ago stock insurers had only 38 percent of the life insurance in force compared with 46 percent today. At mid-1969, 16 percent of the mutual life insurers and 52 percent of the stock life insurers were less than 10 years old. About 14 percent of the mutual life insurers and 0.4 percent of the stock life insurers were 100 or more years old.

[4] *Report of the Committee on Insurance Holding Companies,* Insurance Department of New York, 1968.

When a noninsurance holding company system includes an insurance company within it, its potential for specific harm becomes greater since tempting reservoirs of liquid assets become accessible to persons without an appreciation of security needs of the insurance enterprise, and the interests of the policyholders thus become vulnerable.

The potential costs of conflict between social purposes served by insurance and self interest of those who may control an insurer is substantial. But the inclination to profit at the expense of the policyholder, and the means by which to do it, are far more likely in a control situation than where ownership is widely distributed. . . .

[W]e urge upon those who now control or hereafter may seek to control insurance companies, that, in analyzing the courses of action open to them, they weigh most carefully the possibility that total divestment of insurers from noninsurance control may ultimately be found, by state or federal legislators, to be, not only the most feasible and effective method, but the necessary method, for protecting all of the diverse interests involved.

With respect to insurance related holding companies, Superintendent of Insurance Richard E. Stewart of New York told the joint legislative committee on insurance rates and regulation at a 1969 public hearing on insurance holding companies that "within the inherent limits of state jurisdiction, there is every reason to expect that New York with its tradition of progressive insurance laws and competent administration of those laws can meet and turn to the public benefit the present challenge of the insurance holding company."[5]

Regulatory authority over the insurance operations of holding companies and conglomerates is discussed in Chapter 29.

MUTUALIZATION OF STOCK INSURERS. Stock life insurers have been converted into mutual insurers under statutes providing the procedure for such conversion.[6] The plan of conversion must have the approval of the stockholders, the policyholders, and the insurance commissioner of the insurer's state of domicile. A dissenting stockholder who believes the conversion terms to be unfair (too low a price for his shares) may go to court in an effort to set aside the attempted conversion.[7]

The fear of eventual takeover by a holding company or a conglomerate might stimulate some stock insurer managements to seek to preserve their positions of control by attempts at mutualization of their companies.

The first stock insurer in the United States to write life insurance was the

---

[5] "Stewart Sees N.Y. Laws Meeting Challenge of Holding Companies," *National Underwriter,* Life Ed., March 22, 1969, p. 1.

[6] *New York Insurance Law,* Section 199(2) provides an example of the procedure in one jurisdiction.

[7] *Ibid.,* Section 199(4), establishes a procedure for retiring stock outstanding after an approved plan for mutualization has been in effect for more than 10 years if the company has acquired and transferred to the trustees at least 90 percent of its capital stock. This section was enacted to expedite the mutualization of a particular company, the Farmers and Traders Life Insurance Company of Syracuse, New York. A group of dissident stockholders controlling some 7 percent of the company's stock had succeeded in dragging out the mutualization of this insurer for a period well over 10 years.

Insurance Company of North America, 1794. It wrote six life insurance policies in five years, all of them short-term shipmaster policies covering mariners against the cost of ransom in the event of capture by pirates or against death while in pirate captivity. The premiums charged for these policies were from 8 to 10 percent of the amount of insurance. The charm of the INA policy kept the pirates away, so none of these policies produced a claim. The life insurance department of The Insurance Company of North America was discontinued in 1804; however, through a subsidiary, The Life Insurance Company of North America, it resumed writing life insurance in 1957, and this company showed its first profit in 1965.

Nature of Mutual Companies. A mutual insurance company is distinguished from a stock company in that voting control is technically in the hands of the policyholders, who elect the board of directors, which, in turn, elects the officers of the company who supervise its operations. Although in a mutual company control is technically in the hands of the policyholders, few policyholders ever attend policyholders' meetings or bother to send a proxy.[8] Therefore, the control of the organization usually is in the hands of a few officers who have a working majority of votes by virtue of holding proxies from policyholders.

The problem of control of mutual insurance companies by holding companies cannot arise because mutual insurers have no stock outstanding to exchange for stock in a holding company or for a holding company or conglomerate to acquire. But mutual life companies have been converted into stock insurers. With the growing interest in financial service related holding companies, more mutual life insurers can be expected to attempt conversion to stock insurers to achieve an organizational structure conducive to participation in a full-scale financial service enterprise. The word "attempt" is used here because the process is made difficult by the absence in key states of laws providing for conversion of mutual insurers to stock insurers. When a mutual insurer is converted into a stock insurer, policyholders are given stock in an amount which on some basis reflects their relative contribution to the insurer's surplus—not an easy actuarial determination.

A simpler solution for mutual insurers seeking to become a part of a holding company complex is for them either to acquire other financial service-related companies directly or through a wholly owned holding company. Organizationally, a mutual insurer could own the stock of another company quite simply if the law permitted. But restrictive insurance laws in the 50 states place a stumbling block in the path of mutuals seeking wide diversification through the ownership of other companies or of a wholly owned holding company. Insurance laws in some states are beginning to change (although gradually) to enable mutual insurers to release themselves from the regulation tangle in which they find themselves.

---

[8] Some mutual companies make a proxy to an officer of the company a part of the application for insurance.

For example, Massachusetts permitted New England Life to purchase Loomis, Sayles, a mutual fund management company.

The New England Mutual, chartered in 1835, was the first of the commercial mutual companies still writing life insurance to be chartered. However, New England Mutual did not issue its first policy until February, 1844. In the meantime, the Mutual Life of New York had been incorporated in March, 1842, and issued its first policy in February of the next year. Of the commercial mutuals still in existence it was the first to write a policy. The first life insurance corporation in the United States was the Presbyterian Ministers' Fund, Philadelphia, founded in 1759, using a charter granted by William Penn. It continues to operate today as a mutual insurer writing policies only for a limited market. It was organized as "The Corporation for Relief of Poor and Distressed Presbyterian Ministers and of the Poor and Distressed Widows and Children of Presbyterian Ministers."

Mixed Companies?   The concept of mixed companies has been used to identify insurers that have characteristics of both stock insurers and mutual insurers. The term has been adopted to describe those stock insurers in which directors are elected by some combination of stockholders and policyholders. It has also been used to distinguish those stock insurers in which profits to stockholders from participating policies are limited. A further use of the term has been to characterize those insurers in the process of a change from that of a stock insurer to that of a mutual insurer where the stock, or a large percentage of it, has been placed in the hands of a trustee. The concept of mixed companies has even been used to identify those insurers issuing both participating and nonparticipating policies.

There appears to be neither need nor justification for use of the term "mixed companies." If the insurance corporation has stockholders, it is a stock company. If it has no stockholders, it is a mutual company.

Stock Companies and Mutual Companies Compared.   Stock and mutual insurers may be compared and evaluated on the basis of management, financial strength, and price of insurance.

MANAGEMENT.   Mutual companies and stock companies both are subject to good, mediocre, or bad management. Which they have at any time bears little relation to the fundamental nature of their organization. The caliber of management depends upon executives and not upon the type of company. A stock company may be and sometimes is run for the benefit of stockholders alone. On the other hand, stock company management which puts the interest of policyholders above the interest of the controlling bloc is not unique.

FINANCIAL STRENGTH.   In judging the financial strength of a life insurance company, three factors must be considered: (1) investments, (2) reserves, and (3) surplus.

Investments.   Since all legal reserve companies operate under the same investment laws, there seems to be no reason to assume that one type of legal reserve insurer makes safer investments than another. Any variations that exist among the investment portfolios of companies are based on differences in the investment philosophy and judgment of company management and not on type of organization.

Reserves. Minimum reserve requirements for all legal reserve companies are the same in any given state. Therefore, there is no inherent advantage or disadvantage in any one type of insurer as long as it is a legal reserve company.

Surplus. Surplus, to be compared among companies, must be reduced to a percentage of obligations. A company with reserve obligations of $20 million and a surplus to policyholders (i.e., capital and surplus) of $1 million would not appear in as favorable position as a company with reserve obligations of $10 million and a surplus of $750,000. In the first case, surplus is 5 percent of obligations; in the second, it is $7\frac{1}{2}$ percent. Note the use of the word "appear." Appearances can be deceiving. Suppose that the former insurer had computed its reserve on the full net level premium basis at $2\frac{1}{2}$ percent, and the latter insurer had computed its reserve on the CRVM basis at $3\frac{1}{2}$ percent. In this event, the insurer with the surplus equal to 5 percent of reserve obligations might have more real surplus than the one with a surplus to reserve percentage of $7\frac{1}{2}$ percent.

The size of the insurer in terms of the number of insureds is important in appraising the adequacy of its surplus. A small company to be equally safe would need a higher percentage of surplus than is needed by a large one because in a small company wider deviations of actual from expected mortality are likely to occur. The greater the number of exposures, the less the uncertainty, and the less the need for relatively large surpluses.[9] Thus, the insurer with a surplus equal to 5 percent of reserves may have a more favorable surplus position than the insurer with a surplus equal to $7\frac{1}{2}$ percent of reserves if it has many more independent exposure units.

The amount the insurer has at risk in relation to its surplus is another important consideration in evaluating the adequacy of that surplus. For a given degree of financial strength, the higher the amount at risk in relation to reserve, the higher will be the required percentage of surplus to reserve necessary as a buffer against adverse mortality experience. Thus, the insurer with a surplus equal to 5 percent of reserves may have a more favorable surplus position than the insurer with a surplus equal to $7\frac{1}{2}$ percent of reserves if it has a lower ratio of reserves to insurance in force.[10]

Nothing is inherent in either type of organization that automatically assures it a larger surplus. This statement might be questioned by those who argue that the capital stock of a stock company offers an added margin of safety to policyholders. Except in the new and very small companies, the

---

[9] Cf. Chapter 2.

[10] The ratio of reserves to the amount of insurance in force is a function of a number of variables, such as volume of term insurance written, age of policies in force, age of insureds, degree of conservatism in computing reserves, and the amount of limited payment and endowment insurance plans in force.

capital stock is usually not a relatively large surplus factor. The important factor in appraising the surplus position of a company is not the ratio of capital stock to surplus but the ratio of surplus and capital to policy reserves and other liabilities. For example, take two very large insurance companies, one a stock company, the other a mutual. The mutual has a ratio of 8.36 percent of surplus to reserve liabilities, whereas the stock company has a ratio of only 6.97 percent.[11] On the other hand, another larger mutual company has a ratio of only 4.67 percent of surplus reserve liabilities. In the stock company, the capital stock represents only slightly more than 10 percent of the total surplus. A quick glance at any compendium of life insurance reports will reveal both stock and mutual companies with high and low ratios of surplus to reserve obligations. No pattern indicating a stronger surplus position for either type of insurer can be found.

PRICES.   Rate structures are a matter of the plan of insurance rather than type of company. Two rating plans are available: *participating* and *nonparticipating*. The annual premium under a participating policy generally is higher than under an otherwise comparable nonparticipating plan, but it is adjusted periodically by the payment of annual (and occasionally extra) policy dividends.[12] The annual premiums under a nonparticipating policy contain no provision for dividends. Stock companies can, and often do, issue participating policies. As a group stock insurers write about 20 percent of their insurance on a participating basis.[13] Mutual companies can, but rarely do, issue nonparticipating policies.[14]

Since participating premiums are loaded so that funds are quite likely to be available to pay dividends, the first-year premium for a given amount of insurance on a nonparticipating plan generally is lower than that on an otherwise comparable participating plan. For instance, in the rate book of one stock company issuing both participating and nonparticipating plans, the premiums for $10,000 of continuous premium whole life issued to males aged 25 are $134.50 nonparticipating and $175.90 participating. Thus a premium budget of $250 a year would buy initially about $18,400

---

[11] This ratio includes capital stock and surplus to reserve liabilities.

[12] The policy dividend is not income in a mercantile sense, but a return of the unused portion of the premium; hence it does not have to be reported for income tax purposes. The word dividend in the context of participating life insurance, unfortunately, is a bad misnomer.

[13] Many of the major stock life insurers have much more than 20 percent of their business in participating policies. Cf. Joseph M. Belth, *Participating Life Insurance Sold by Stock Companies* (Homewood, Illinois: Richard D. Irwin, Inc. 1965), p. 145. Many stock insurers issue only nonparticipating policies. Usually stock companies that issue participating plans also issue a line of nonparticipating policies.

[14] In some states mutual insurers are not allowed to issue nonparticipating policies except under certain conditions. For example, mutual insurers are permitted under Section 216(5) of the New York law to issue nonparticipating life insurance under nonforfeiture options, dividend additions, group contracts providing deferred annuities for a class of participants in a qualified pension or profit sharing plan who have terminated their participation, and contracts of reinsurance only.

of nonparticipating insurance but only about $14,200 of participating insurance in this particular company.

The nonpar rate remains less than the net participating rate (gross premium minus dividend) for a number of years. For example, the difference between the gross participating premium and the nonparticipating premium in the foregoing company for the above plan is $41.40. The present, but not guaranteed, dividend schedule for the participating continuous premium whole life contract is as follows:

Year	Dividend	Year	Dividend
1	$10.00	8	$41.11
2	20.80	9	44.80
3	23.60	10	50.00
4	26.90	12	58.10
5	29.80	15	70.70
6	33.30	18	84.00
7	37.50	20	93.40

Not until the ninth year will the dividend under this scale be large enough to bring the net participating premium below the nonparticipating premium for that year. By that time the total excess paid on the participating contract will have been $108.20, so that it will take seven more years until there is a net savings on this particular participating contract with this particular dividend scale, 15 years in all.

Two observations must be made about the foregoing comparisons and about those in the following paragraph. First, the comparisons are designed to show no more than the difference in the incidence of the burden of premium payments to the policyholder over the lives of the nonparticipating and participating policies compared, assuming the particular contracts involved and the particular dividend scales used. They are not designed to show a price comparison on either of the bases discussed in Chapter 8. The present values of expected premiums are not discounted for interest and mortality, and no effort has been made to determine the expected rate of return on the savings elements of the two policies for various durations using the Linton technique.[15] If the latter were to be done, it would be found that the imputed rate of return on the savings element of the participating policy in the foregoing illustration would exceed that on the savings element of the above particular nonparticipating policy at a duration of much less than 15 years, because the cash values of the participating policy are much higher than those of the nonparticipating policy. For example, if the two policies were surrendered at the end of 10 years for their cash values, the surrender values returned under the particular participating policy would be $281 less than premiums paid after sub-

[15] Cf. Chapter 8, pages 164 ff.

tracting dividends, whereas under the particular nonparticipating policy the surrender values returned would be $365 less than premiums paid.

The second observation to be made is that it must be *strongly emphasized* that comparison will certainly vary from insurer to insurer, plan to plan, and time to time.

The participating premium of a prominent mutual company for a $10,000 continuous premium whole life at age 25 is $173.70. This is $39.20 more than the nonparticipating premium of the foregoing stock company. Under the present dividend scale of this company the net premium on its policy will become less than that of the nonpar policy by the seventh year. The total of excess net premiums paid on the participating policy by that time equals only $93.90 which will be recaptured by the 12th year. Another prominent mutual charges $170.30 for its contract. Its present dividends will exceed the $35.80 difference by the sixth year. By that time its contract has cost a total of $66.20 more than the nonpar contract, but by the 10th year this excess will have been more than wiped out. (Remember, these illustrations are based on present dividend scales, which are subject to change. Also interest is ignored in the computations.)

An advantage claimed for nonparticipating insurance is the smaller amount of loading necessary for those expenses which vary directly with the premium. Since agents' commissions are based on gross premiums and the participating plan usually has the higher initial premium, the same rate of commission on the participating plan will produce a higher commission than it will on a nonparticipating plan. Another cost advantage of nonparticipating insurance is the absence of dividend payments. It costs money to calculate dividends, notify policyholders of the dividend amount, make out checks for those policyholders who take their dividends in cash, and maintain the accounts for those policyholders that elect one of the dividend options. Since premium taxes are based on the gross rate minus the dividend, nonparticipating policies have no advantage in this respect.

Dividend history on participating plans, as illustrated, indicates that as a general rule the total premiums paid less total dividends received for participating plans have been lower than for nonparticipating plans for those participating policyholders who live long enough to recover the higher initial premiums through increasing dividends.[16]

Advocates of a participating insurance point out that a safety margin is available in participating premiums. Insurers issuing participating policies charge a gross premium higher than they anticipate will be necessary, returning the excess as a policy dividend. If mortality or investment experience is adverse, the premium overcharge is automatically available to offset the loss in surplus. Unfavorable interest yields, increased costs of administration, or adverse mortality experience may make it necessary for participating companies to cut the dividend rate on existing policies. In this way

---

[16] Note that this statement is given as a general rule and not one that applies company by company.

increased costs in connection with insurance already in force can be charged against that business instead of being charged only against new business, as is necessary with nonparticipating policies. The participating feature, therefore, has the double-barreled advantage of (1) giving an added safety cushion and (2) permitting some degree of equity among all policyholders (new and old).

This latter observation suggests that while price projections made on the basis of current dividend structures showing participating insurance to be less expensive over minimum periods of 10 to 15 years, a downward trend in interest rates, increased mortality, and higher expenses could cause the dividends to be reduced significantly. In this event, nonparticipating insurance could be cheaper over a much longer period, even throughout the entire life of every policy in a given block.[17]

Another price advantage argued for participating policies is the privilege of using the dividends to buy paid-up additions "at *net* single premium rates, a rare bargain." While paid-up additions offer a price advantage in some companies, this advantage is not offered in every company issuing participating policies.[18] However, an important nonprice advantage of paidup additions in every case is the opportunity it offers the insured to continue to add to his insurance coverage even though he later becomes uninsurable. The use of the one-year term insurance option, referred to as the fifth dividend option, also offers this advantage.[19] It also seems to offer the insured the opportunity to purchase term insurance at unusually attractive prices.[20]

One disadvantage inherent in participating insurance is that it too often leads to selling on a basis of illustrated net cost[21]—i.e., the agent leads the buyer to believe that the net cost of the proposed insurance over the policy period will be comparable to, if not identical with, the net cost computed

---

[17] Professor Belth in his book, *The Retail Price Structure in American Life Insurance, op. cit.,* p. 165, notes that the mean of the prices for participating policies issued in 1962 based on the then-current dividend illustrations was lower than that for nonparticipating policies. Based on dividend histories, he found that for policies issued in 1930 the mean of prices for participating policies was slightly higher than that for nonparticipating policies, while the reverse was true for policies issued in 1940. (See footnote 14, Chapter 12, p. 269 of this text for a brief definition of the level price method used by Belth in making his computations.)

[18] Belth, *The Retail Price Structure in American Life Insurance, op. cit.,* pp. 124–27 and 233, Professor Belth notes that the "data suggested that paid-up additions in some companies are lower in price than the protection in their regular policies, but that the reverse is true in other companies" (p. 233). He writes, "It seems that the use of very conservative net rates will not produce low-priced protection for the insurable policyholder unless the company . . . provides that paid-up additions will participate substantially" (p. 124).

[19] Cf. Chapter 11.

[20] Belth, *The Retail Price Structure in American Life Insurance, op. cit.,* cf. Table 24, p. 103, and Table 37, p. 127.

[21] Net cost is defined as total premiums paid, minus dividends if any, minus cash value at the end of the period over which the estimate is being made.

either (1) over a past period (usually 10 to 20 years) or (2) with the current dividend scale.

Few companies writing participating insurance can honestly deny that many of their agents sell on the basis of illustrated net cost. Of course, agents are asked to tell policyholders that dividend illustrations are not to be taken as either a guarantee or an estimate that future price experience will compare with the past. In fact, accompanying all dividend illustrations is the statement that "dividend figures are illustrations only and neither imply nor guarantee future experience." Even so, no matter how carefully the policyholder has been told that dividend illustrations do not imply future experience—and this is not too often carefully explained—the policyholder may be resentful if he finds his premium after dividends greater over a period of years than was suggested as part of the inducement to buy.

Participating Insurance: Stock and Mutual Insurers Compared. A study of the prices charged for participating insurance by mutual insurance companies and by stock insurance companies offers a realistic basis for comparing stock and mutual insurers. One such study shows that the *mean* of the prices charged for participating continuous premium whole life insurance issued at age 35, male, standard rates, is lower for a sample group of mutual life insurers than for a sample group of stock life insurers.[22] The study showed substantial price variation among both mutual and stock insurers with the prices offered by some stock insurers below those of some mutual insurers. The mutual insurers in the sample were generally older and larger than the stock insurers and these variables may explain the lower mean of the prices charged by the mutuals.[23]

2. FRATERNAL INSURERS

The Uniform Fraternal Code of 1955 (revised in 1962) adopted in full or in part by many states, defines a fraternal insurer as:

Any incorporated society, order or supreme lodge, without capital stock, conducted solely for the benefit of its members and their beneficiaries and not for profit, operated on a lodge system with ritualistic form of work, having a representative form of government, and which makes provision for payment of benefits.

With the exception of the requirements for a lodge system with ritualistic form of work and for a representative form of government, a fraternal insurer appears to be similar to a mutual life insurance company: a corporation without capital stock, formed, organized, and carried on for the bene-

---

22 Belth, *Participating Life Insurance Sold by Stock Companies, op. cit.,* pp. 40–42.

23 Because the sample was not chosen randomly but on the basis of the availability of data, Professor Belth rightly refuses to make inferences from it about the life insurance business in general.

fit of its members and of their beneficiaries and not for profit. However, other differences do exist as will soon become apparent.

Distinguishing Features of Fraternal Insurance. Several features distinguish fraternal insurers from old line insurers. The distinguishing features of the fraternal insurer are the lodge system, representative form of government, the "open" contract, less stringent regulation, and a tax-free status.

While the statutes require all members of fraternal benefit societies to belong to a local lodge of the society, often the lodge system of a fraternal is merely a token. This is particularly true of the fraternal which has reached a stage of development just short of old line. At this stage, although only lodge members may be granted policies, anyone who wants to buy a policy can become a member automatically simply by purchasing the insurance.[24] Currently, educational and charitable activities are more important to many fraternals than the rituals of yesteryear.

In requiring that fraternals have a representative form of government, the statutes prohibit voting by proxy.

Fraternals issue an open policy (called "certificate") in which the by-laws and rules of the organization are a part of the contract and any amendment to them is automatically an amendment to the policy as to rates and provisions. Also, upon impairment of the society's reserves, members may be required to make an additional payment.[25]

State regulation of fraternals generally is less strict than that applying to old line companies. Reserves, for example, may be computed on a less conservative basis than the Guertin legislation requires of old line insurers; i.e., fraternals may use a combination of interest and mortality assumptions which yield lower reserves than the 1958 CSO Table at $3\frac{1}{2}$ percent. Also, fraternal sales representatives in many states need not be licensed and in others are subject to less stringent licensing requirements. Regulation pertaining to investment, however, is the same for fraternals as for other insurers.

Since fraternals are considered to be nonprofit institutions active in charitable and benevolent work, they are exempt from federal income tax and state premium taxes. They do pay filing fees whenever they file required documents with the state. Those fraternals which actually do charitable and benevolent work are entitled to their tax-exempt status, but it is feared that a number of fraternals are reaping the benefits of tax immunity

---

[24] Restrictions on membership, however, still prevail among typical fraternals. Common restrictions are those limited to members of certain national, church, and/or labor groups. A few limit membership to men only and even fewer limit membership to women.

[25] However, the Uniform Fraternal Code developed by the National Fraternal Congress and adopted by the National Association of Insurance Commissioners provides that "no change, addition or amendment shall destroy or diminish benefits which the society contracted to give the members as of the date of issuance." This Code has been enacted in nearly one half of the states.

without seriously performing any charitable or benevolent operations sufficient to justify their favored treatment.

Fraternal insurance plans originally were organized on the full assessment principle.[26] As the average age of membership increased and assessments mounted, difficulties were encountered. Fraternals soon recognized the importance of actuarially sound rate-making principles and began shifting to a legal reserve basis. When a fraternal has moved to a legal reserve basis, it may still continue to be a fraternal by virtue of holding on to its lodge system and its "social purpose." It is then known as a "legal reserve fraternal." When it has not only moved to a legal reserve basis but also has dropped its lodge system, as a few have done, it becomes an old line company. A fraternal always is a mutual. It may or may not be a pure assessment mutual. The usual metamorphosis of a successful fraternal is from an original assessment basis to a legal reserve basis (and in some cases, eventually, to an old line basis).

Advantages and Limitations.   Although fraternals are not required to maintain legal reserves as rigid as those required of old line insurers, many of them maintain their reserves on a basis as conservative as the leading old line companies.

Fraternals have an additional, theoretical safety advantage in the open contracts under which they reserve the right to levy an assessment whenever such is essential to maintain solvency. Fraternals never make a point of emphasizing this feature of their contract because buyers, as a rule, do not favor open contracts. Actually, the open contract in effect is not much different from the closed contract, since the closed contract can also be opened if reserves become deficient and company solvency is threatened. The courts can place a lien on policies of companies forced into receivership. The open contract of the fraternals simply allows the society to do what the courts can force an old line legal reserve company to do.

When fraternals are legal reserve companies, their surplus account may be similar to that of stocks and mutuals. However, many fraternals not on a legal reserve basis report "surpluses" which in reality are not surpluses at all in the true meaning of the word. Instead, they represent future ob-

---

[26] The first fraternal society was established in the United States in 1868 when John Jordan Upchurch, a railroad master mechanic, organized the Ancient Order of United Workmen. His motivating idea was to offer working men greater privileges than they found in the usual trade unions of that time. Included in the Upchurch program was a plan to provide members with protection for dependents cheaper than commercial companies were offering it. Upchurch fell victim to the lures of the assessment principle. His method of accumulating benefit funds was unsound, for there was no attempt at scientific rate making. The plan called for the payment of $1 by each member into the insurance fund. When a member died, his dependents were paid up to a limit of $2,000 in death benefit out of this fund, and another dollar was collected from each member to prepare for the next death. This was a simple, pass the hat assessment plan. No assets were accumulated to offset expected claims. However, the idea of fraternalism appealed to the notoriously gregarious nature of Americans, especially since it seemed like cheap insurance.

ligations to policyholders much as do the legal reserves in legal reserve companies, definitely a misleading use of the word surplus.[27]

Fraternals are at neither an advantage nor a disadvantage in price comparisons with ordinary insurance. Just as among old line insurers, there is a clear variation in prices charged by the different fraternals. It would be possible to find some old line insurers that charge more and some that charge less than does any given fraternal selected at random. Fraternals appear to offer insurance in low amounts (less than $500) at more attractive rates than do the industrial departments of old line insurers.

About $21 billion of fraternal life insurance is in force in the United States and Canada. Assets behind this insurance amount to over $4.5 billion. Fraternals account for just slightly less than 2 percent of all life insurance in force in the United States.

3. ASSESSMENT COMPANIES

The assessment company may or may not be a fraternal; i.e., it may write insurance only upon members of some type of lodge or social system, or it may write policies for the general public. Many states now prohibit the incorporation of any new assessment associations and require that statutory reserves be maintained on coverage issued to new members of established associations.

The assessment life insurance company operates on the principle of practical as well as theoretical mutuality. In old line mutuals, the policyholder is paid a dividend that theoretically represents operating savings of the company. However, the policyholder does not share directly in an operating loss of an old line mutual. Policy dividends can be reduced or even eliminated if the company has made no savings to share; but there can never be an increase in the initial gross premium charge. In the assessment company, the policyholder not only shares in the operating profit, through policy dividends, but also, in the event of loss, shares in that loss through an assessment—usually an additional premium.

The assessment mutual issues what is known as an "open-end contract." In effect, the insurer estimates the amount necessary for the operation of the business and the payment of claims during any premium paying period and then establishes a premium rate in accordance with this estimate. It contracts with the policyholder to return any portion of that premium that is not required for operation. It also obligates the policyholder to pay additional premiums if they should become necessary.

A "legal reserve assessment company," sometimes called a "stipulated

---

[27] This is not to imply that legal reserve insurers do not also report surpluses that are misleading by their practice of computing reserves on a conservative basis without identifying as surplus the amount by which the reported reserve exceeds the minimum statutory reserve.

premium company," is one which maintains the reserve required by law but retains a contingency clause in its policies in lieu of the required free surplus. Under this clause the company can call for additional premiums through assessment. In addition to the assessment feature, minimum premiums and reserves are required by state law. These organizations, therefore, are hybrids because they have characteristics both of assessment associations and legal reserve companies. In some states, Illinois for example, the new company is required to have an assessment clause in all contracts until the surplus reaches a given minimum amount.

Currently, only about $830 million of assessment insurance is in force in the United States—about 0.07 percent of all insurance in force in this country. These companies own about $70 million in assets.

4. SAVINGS BANK LIFE INSURANCE.

In recognition of the social and economic importance of insurance for the individual of modest income, it was suggested as early as 1874 that low-cost life insurance be written by savings banks. It was not, however, until after the Armstrong investigation[28] that such a proposal was seriously considered.

Two of the findings of the Armstrong committee disturbed Louis D. Brandeis, the father of savings bank life insurance: (1) Many companies at that time seemed to put the interests of the policyholders last on the list of considerations in the operation of the company. (2) The cost of weekly premium industrial insurance was comparatively high. So Brandeis, later Associate Justice of the U.S. Supreme Court, worked out a plan for the issuance of life insurance by the nonprofit mutual savings banks of Massachusetts. He convinced the legislature of that state that the banks would be a proper medium for the issuance of low-cost life insurance for the benefit of low-income groups. Originally, policies were to be limited in any one bank to $500 upon the life of an individual. This limit subsequently was raised to $5,000, although the insured can buy as many policies in different banks as he can qualify for up to the statutory limit of $43,000.[29] All the insurance, however, can be purchased through one bank. The originating bank serves as agent for the other banks. The $5,000 limitation does not apply to group insurance. Annuities are limited to $200

---

[28] An investigation by the state of New York, 1905, into many phases of life insurance company operations. Cf. Chapter 29.

[29] Before July 24, 1951, the maximum limit available at any one bank was $1,000. The maximum total amount available, therefore, was $1,000 multiplied by the number of authorized savings banks writing life insurance. When the maximum allowable in each bank was raised from $1,000 to $5,000 the total limit of $1,000 times the number of authorized banks was left unaltered. Since there are now 43 authorized savings banks in operation writing Massachusetts Savings Bank Life Insurance, the maximum statutory limit on any one life is $43,000.

annual income per bank.[30] Insurance may be written only for residents or people who have regular employment in Massachusetts.

In 1907 Massachusetts passed the laws necessary to permit the banks to establish insurance departments and required that the funds of the insurance department be kept separate from the banking funds. The insurance funds are not available to pay any obligations that might arise in the banking departments, nor are the banking funds liable for any obligations of the insurance departments.

Originally, in order to establish an insurance department, it was necessary for a Massachusetts savings bank to obtain, by subscription, a guaranty fund. A later provision in the law required each bank operating an insurance department to pay into a central fund 4 percent of the total premium it collected. The banks were required to continue to pay into this fund until the fund reached $100,000; that amount was reached in 1921. The purpose of the arrangement was to provide the guaranty funds for additional banks wishing to establish insurance departments. The effect was to eliminate the burden on each bank of raising its own guaranty funds.[31]

In order to minimize the cost of savings bank insurance, the use of agents is forbidden. Further, in the beginning, the expenses of the office of actuary and medical director were borne by the state.[32] The savings bank system in Massachusetts is supervised by the state insurance commission. A Division of Savings Bank Life Insurance of the commonwealth's Department of Banking and Insurance employs "instructors" to present the insurance plan before employees and similar groups.

While the savings bank system does not use solicitors or agents, it does utilize, through the medium of a cooperatively supported Savings Bank Life Insurance Council, an extensive and continuous advertising and publicity program, employing all the usual advertising media such as pamphlets, leaflets, radio, match folders, and newspapers.

---

[30] Although the statutory limitation on annual income from deferred or single premium annuities is $200 per bank, or $8,600 from all banks, the banks are free to set whatever maximum they wish as long as it is under the statutory maximum.

[31] At the present time a Massachusetts bank voting to organize an insurance department must have as a cash advance to that department (1) a special expense guaranty fund of not less than $5,000 to be applied in payment of expenses and (2) a special insurance guaranty fund of not less than $20,000 to assure the payment of claims. Under certain circumstances, in lieu of the special insurance guaranty fund, the General Insurance Guaranty Fund, with approval of the commissioner of insurance and the commissioner of banks, may contract to guarantee the risks of the insurance department of a savings bank until the bank's insurance department shall have accumulated a surplus of $20,000.

[32] Through the years 1907–1926 all expenses of the Massachusetts Savings Bank Life Insurance Division were borne by the state. During 1927–33 an increasing portion was reimbursed to the state. Since 1934 there have been no out-of-pocket expense subsidies. From 1934 to 1938 the banks have reimbursed the state at the end of each year for the actual amount spent. From 1939 to the present banks have been paying into the state one twelfth of the annual appropriation each month in advance. The Massachusetts Savings Bank Life Insurance Division is still housed, rent free, in the Statehouse.

Applications may be taken by nonissuing banks, employers, credit unions, and other types of authorized outlets, which may retain a small collection fee. Employers authorized to receive applications are not entitled to the collection fee.

The Division of Savings Bank Life Insurance assumes such functions as rate making, underwriting, and medical examinations. The individual banks have nothing to do with these operations. Through the medium of the General Insurance Guaranty Fund, mortality experience is pooled and distributed equally among the banks, thus creating a wider spread of exposures than would be possible for an individual bank to achieve.

All savings bank life insurance is issued on a participating basis. Types of policies and policy provisions are those customarily found in the commercial companies. A popular plan for premium payment is to authorize the bank to deduct premiums regularly from savings accounts.

The growth of business in force among the savings banks in Massachusetts was slow in the early years. Originally, banks were not enthusiastic about the plan. Up to 1922 only four banks had established insurance departments. However, since that time many new departments have been added, and the volume of business in force has grown substantially.

Legislation to permit the establishment of savings bank life insurance in the state of New York was passed in 1938 and in the state of Connecticut in 1941.

The requirements for the establishment of a separate insurance department by New York mutual savings banks are much the same as those for Massachusetts banks with some technical exceptions.[33] In New York, as in Massachusetts, savings banks have the same rights in general and are subject to the same limitations in their insurance operations that apply to other domestic legal reserve life insurance companies. The amount of life insurance that may be written on any one life is limited to $30,000. The entire amount may be written by a single bank under a single policy. Insurance may be written only for residents or people regularly working in New York.

Like the Massachusetts banks, New York savings banks write all the regular forms of life insurance. Individual annuities are not written. Currently 58 banks have insurance departments.[34]

Similar regulations exist for the formation and operation of an insurance

---

[33] To establish an insurance department, a New York mutual savings bank must establish a surplus fund of not less than $20,000 to meet operating expenses and losses occasioned by other causes.

[34] The New York Savings Bank Life Insurance Fund, which is outside of the New York insurance department, administers the pooling of mortality experience (called unification of mortality) among the banks, determines premiums and policy forms, and prescribes underwriting rules and regulations. In general, the fund provides the services of the actuary and medical director. The fund is financed entirely by the issuing banks which may be required to pay into the fund a given percentage of premiums received. The percentage has fluctuated between 4 percent and one half of 1 percent (now one half of 1 percent). The approval of the superintendent of banks is required for any change of this percentage.

department in a Connecticut mutual savings bank.[35] Eleven banks in Connecticut are qualified to issue insurance. The banks issue the usual line of policies. The maximum amount of insurance that may be purchased on the life of one individual is $5,000—whether purchased all in one bank or divided among several banks. This very low limit is the result of the successful efforts of the organized life insurance agents in Connecticut to block repeated proposals by the Connecticut savings banks for moderate increases in the limit since the limit was increased from $3,000 to $5,000 in 1957.[36]

The extension of the system of savings bank insurance into other states having mutual savings banks has been advocated from time to time, and bills authorizing savings bank insurance have been introduced in several state legislatures without success.[37]

Life insurance agents and their companies have charged savings bank life insurance with unfair competition. Savings banks dismiss these objections as attempts of the companies and their agents to protect their market.

Advantages and Disadvantages. The savings banks offer financially sound life insurance. Savings banks operating insurance departments must invest insurance funds in the same way they invest banking funds, except that they may make policy loans. Savings bank life insurance investments are more restricted than the investments of other legal reserve life insurance companies.

Legal reserves required of savings bank insurance are the same as those required of other legal reserve insurers.

As for surplus, the laws of the various states differ for savings bank life insurance. In Massachusetts, for example, each bank must accumulate a minimum surplus of $20,000 out of its profits. After the minimum is obtained, the bank must pay out in dividends 85 percent of profits. Unless the state actuary approves a higher figure, the maximum surplus which a bank may hold is 10 percent of its reserve. Additional protection is provided in the bank's pro rata share of the assets held by the General In-

---

[35] Here again there are technical exceptions. In Connecticut a mutual savings bank establishing a life insurance department must invest in the Savings Bank Life Insurance Company (a stock legal reserve life insurance company wholly owned by Connecticut mutual savings banks). The amount of investment required is up to 10 shares of capital stock, $100 par value, one share for each $1 million or fraction thereof of the book value of the bank's assets. The Connecticut Savings Bank Life Insurance Company deals only with Connecticut mutual savings banks, reinsuring their life insurance business, providing actuarial and underwriting technical assistance, educating and training personnel, and promoting the sale of savings bank life insurance.

[36] For a statement of the case of the Connecticut savings banks in the controversy, see Walter E. Rapp, "The Case for Increasing the Savings Bank Life Insurance Policy Limit in Connecticut," *Journal of Risk and Insurance*, Vol. XXXIV, No. 4 (December, 1967), pp. 621–27. Mr. Rapp is Executive Vice President of the Savings Bank Life Insurance Company, Hartford, Connecticut. For a statement of the case of the Connecticut insurance agents in the controversy, see Ralph M. Shulansky, "The Case Against Increasing The Savings Bank Life Insurance Policy Limit in Connecticut," *ibid.*, pp. 628–33. Mr. Shulansky is General Counsel of the Connecticut State Association of Life Underwriters.

[37] Bills to establish savings bank life insurance systems have been defeated in Delaware, Maine, Maryland, Missouri, New Hampshire, New Jersey, and Pennsylvania.

surance Guaranty Fund. Without taking into consideration the General Insurance Guaranty Fund, the average surplus today for all banks is more than 9 percent of total liabilities. This is in excess of that of many mutual and stock companies.

As to underwriting, under the "unification of mortality" system, banks showing lower than the average mortality experience for all banks pay into the General Insurance Guaranty Fund an amount determined by the actuary of the state. The banks experiencing higher than average mortality receive such contributions. However, since the underwriting is done centrally for all the individual banks, mortality experience is as uniform as the underwriting can make it. The pooling of mortality experience is not a matter of underwriting safety but is designed to iron out the expected fluctuations in mortality experience of the banks with a small volume of insurance.

Savings bank life insurance usually is offered at lower premiums, and its prices generally have been lower than those of other legal reserve companies. One factor contributing to lower prices is lower overhead charges. The banks provide the housing and clerical staff to the insurance fund. For accounting purposes, a proportionate amount of the total overhead of the bank is chargeable to the life insurance department; nevertheless, the cost of two families living under one roof usually is not double the cost of one family living alone under that roof. Also, actuarial and medical service is centralized in a cooperative bureau.

Savings banks claim they can offer life insurance at lower prices also because they pay no salesmen's commissions. Consequently, loading for the servicing of savings bank life insurance policies is less than that for the servicing of other life insurance policies. Finally, prices are lower because of a low lapse rate. The lapse rate for savings bank life insurance is currently about 2 percent a year, whereas the lapse rate for the industry generally is now running over 5 percent. Since most of the savings banks' policyholders are those with sufficient sense of responsibility to buy on their own initiative, they are less likely to lapse their policies than are those who are given the hard sell.

Savings bank life insurance accounts for more than $3 billion of insurance in force, but in Massachusetts it represents more than 6.2 percent of the total ordinary life insurance in force in that state. In New York and Connecticut, savings bank life insurance represents about 2 percent, and 0.5 percent, respectively, of the ordinary life insurance written in those states. The amounts of savings bank life insurance in force is growing markedly.

5. GOVERNMENT INSURERS

Both the state and federal governments act as life and health insurers. It is argued in some quarters that the government should not compete with private enterprise so long as private business is interested and able to provide the service at a reasonable price. Those who defend government insurers point out that, for the most part, these insurers provide insurance that is required by law as a part of a broad system of social reform, and that they have been established by democratic procedure. Insurance they claim, is a proper state service.

State Insurers.   For life insurance, only one state fund exists—the State (Life) Fund of Wisconsin. In health insurance, 4 state funds are operated under the Temporary Disability Insurance laws and 18 under the workmen's compensation insurance laws.

THE WISCONSIN STATE (LIFE) FUND.   The Wisconsin State (Life) Fund is a life insurer controlled and operated by the state of Wisconsin.

The legislature of the state of Wisconsin in 1911 authorized the Commissioner of Insurance to create a fund to issue life insurance and annuity contracts at cost. The first policy was issued in October, 1913.

The maximum amount of insurance which may be issued by the fund on one life is $10,000 and the minimum is $1,000. The fund does business only in Wisconsin. Annuities, group insurance, health insurance, and double indemnity are not issued. Waiver of premium has been issued since 1967.

The state assumes no liability other than through the fund itself. Administration of the fund is by the state treasurer. The conduct of the business is left to the state insurance commissioner. The state board of health assists in medical selection, and the treasurer of the state is the treasurer of the fund. The secretary of state audits the accounts submitted to him by the audit board, members of which also are state officials.[38] Applications are taken by designated state, county, and city officials, and state banks, and through them are forwarded to the commissioner.

The fund invests conservatively, with about 80 percent of its assets in bonds. Reserves are computed on a conservative basis, 1958 CSO at 3 percent, net level premium valuation. Its surplus position is strong.[39]

Prices are remarkably low because the fund pays no rent and no part of the salaries of the state officers who administer the fund is charged against the fund. No agents are employed, no advertising is used, the only settlement option is the interest option, and the lapse ratio generally is less than 1 percent. The life fund pays the full medical examination fee only if the applicant is accepted. If the applicant is rejected, he pays one half of the fee. Aside from the free services of state officials involved, the fund is self-supporting in that it pays all recognizable expenses.

The Wisconsin life fund has about $50 million of life insurance in force, which represents only about 0.3 percent of all ordinary life insurance in force in that state. However, the amount of life insurance in force in

---

[38] The attorney general, state treasurer, and commissioner of insurance.

[39] Not less than 10 percent of the net profits for each year shall be contributed to surplus. Such contributions shall be sufficient to maintain a ratio of surplus to admitted assets of not less than 7 percent, and may be discontinued in event such ratio exceeds 10 percent. The balance of net profits shall be distributed annually among policyholders.

the Wisconsin life fund in recent years has been growing at a rate higher than that of all other life insurance in force in Wisconsin.

STATE DISABILITY AND WORKMEN'S COMPENSATION INSURANCE FUNDS. California, New Jersey, New York, and Rhode Island operate funds to insure employer obligations under the Temporary Disability Insurance laws of those states. In Rhode Island the fund is monopolistic, whereas in the other three states the fund is competitive; i.e., employers have the option of insuring with regular insurers upon meeting certain conditions. Eleven states[40] operate competitive funds to insure employer obligations under workmen's compensation laws, and seven states[41] plus Puerto Rico operate monopolistic funds.

The Temporary Disability Insurance laws are designed to offer the employee partial protection against loss of income in event of nonoccupational accidents and illnesses. The workmen's compensation laws offer partial protection against occupational disabilities. These laws vary among the states.

Federal Insurers. The federal government offers life and health insurance through several agencies.

THE VETERANS' ADMINISTRATION. About $38 billion of life insurance is in force on the lives of veterans of the armed services. The vast majority of this amount is participating National Service Life Insurance (NSLI) issued during and after World War II; about $7.5 billion is nonparticipating National Service Life Insurance issued since 1951 under the Servicemen's Indemnity Act; and about $0.9 billion is U.S. Government Life Insurance (USGLI) on the lives of veterans of World War I.

USGLI. War Risk Life Insurance was established as a war measure in World War I to cover disability or loss of life among members of the armed forces engaged in warfare, because the military hazard during wartime on new applicants was not insured by private companies. Policies originally issued were on a one-year term basis (renewable for only five years) with the rate increasing each year. Subsequent extensions of time, however, were granted. In 1919 the term policies were made convertible to cash value forms; in 1924 the coverage was made available to all members of the armed forces; and in 1928 the insurance was made available to veterans of World War I who met certain eligibility standards.[42] The policies issued under these amendments make up what is known as USGLI.

U.S. government life insurance is legal reserve life insurance issued on a participating basis and is backed by a trust fund set up from premiums

---

[40] Arizona, California, Colorado, Idaho, Maryland, Michigan, Montana, New York, Oklahoma, Pennsylvania, and Utah.

[41] Nevada, North Dakota, Ohio, Oregon, Washington, West Virginia, Wyoming.

[42] Sale of new USGLI to veterans was discontinued in 1951. Its sale to members of the armed forces was discontinued in 1940.

collected and held in the Treasury Department, administered by the government as trustee. All costs of administration as well as claims resulting from the extra hazard of military or naval service are paid out of the general tax fund and not funds created by premiums paid in. The provisions of the policies are generally similar to those written by insurance companies, with but few exceptions.[43]

Disability income benefits are also available with USGLI.

NSLI. National Service Life Insurance was created by act of Congress in 1940. The NSLI system provided policies for persons on active duty with the military and naval forces, including the Coast Guard. It was voluntary and available to those in active service. No evidence of insurability was required if application for the insurance was made within 120 days after entrance into the service. Policies were issued on a five-year renewable term plan on a participating basis, convertible on any premium date to continuous premium whole life, 20-pay life, 30-pay life, 20-year endowment, endowment at age 60, or endowment at 65.

As in USGLI, the policy provisions are similar to those of regular company contracts with the same exceptions.

In addition to the waiver of premium disability provision that is automatically included, National Service Life Insurance policies may include a total disability income provision of $10 a month per $1,000 of insurance for an additional premium.

In National Service Life Insurance, all costs of administration, the cost of excess mortality as a result of the extra hazard of military service, and the cost of waiver of premium on account of total disability traceable to the extra hazards of military service are borne by the general tax funds. The maximum amount of NSLI any one individual may own (including any U.S. Government Life Insurance he may have) is $10,000. The insurance is backed by a trust fund held by the Treasury, similar to the fund back of U.S. Government Life Insurance.

NSLI settlement options are particularly advantageous to the beneficiary in comparison to typical settlement options of commercial insurers. Under NSLI, women are paid the same lifetime income per $1,000 of insurance proceeds as are men the same age, and the actuarial assumptions are more favorable than those used by commercial insurers. So if National Service Life Insurance is used to provide installment payments rather than a lump sum, it has an additional price advantage.

Paralleling the history of World War I insurance, National Service Life Insurance has been dropped by policyholders at a startling rate.

Servicemen's Indemnity. Issuance of new NLSI policies to servicemen

---

[43] The policy is nonassignable within certain limits; irrevocable beneficiary designations are not allowed; cash values may not be applied under settlement options; the policy is incontestable from date of issue; and if death is inflicted as a lawful punishment for a crime, the payment of death benefits is excluded.

was terminated[44] by creation of the servicemen's gratuity system in 1951. Gratuitous death benefits for all members of the armed forces were established partly as a result of public pressure against what critics termed the "government in the life insurance business," and partly as a result of studies showing that it is actually cheaper for the government to provide free indemnity than to finance the administrative machinery necessary to collect premiums, account for them, and then return a large part of them in dividends. The costs of administration of NSLI were greater than the net premiums retained.

Under the indemnity system each serviceman was automatically covered for $10,000 without any payment of premiums. Benefits were payable in 120 monthly installments of $92.90. Eligible beneficiaries were restricted. If there were no eligible beneficiaries, no benefits were payable. The money could not be paid to the estate of the deceased.

The Servicemen's and Veterans' Survivor Benefits Act. With the passage of the Servicemen's and Veterans' Survivor Benefits Act the issuance of NSLI to veterans was terminated on December 31, 1956, for all except veterans with service-connected disabilities. The Servicemen's and Veterans' Survivorship Benefits Act brought members of the armed forces under the social security system on the same basis as any other covered employee with one exception: a service member who dies without having earned a fully and currently insured status will be deemed to have that status for purposes of survivorship benefits.

Servicemen's Group Life Insurance. Beginning September 29, 1965, all active servicemen became eligible for $10,000 of group term life insurance underwritten under a blanket policy by a reinsurance pool of more than 500 commercial life insurance companies with the federal government bearing the burden of the extra hazard for military service. The Prudential Life Insurance Company of America was selected as the primary insurer and administers the plan. The insurance is allocated to the eligible insurers annually according to a predetermined formula.

The initial premium rate was set at $2 a month for the full $10,000 and is automatically deducted from the serviceman's pay, unless the coverage is specifically declined or coverage for only $5,000 is elected. In the latter case, the initial payroll deduction was $1 a month. The federal gov-

---

44 Except that within 120 days following separation from service, a veteran could apply for a five-year renewable term policy, nonparticipating, at his attained age. Effective January, 1959, these five-year renewable term plans were made convertible to a nonparticipating cash value plan or to a nonparticipating convertible term plan renewable to age 50. The disability income rider ($10 a month per $1,000) was also made available in 1959 for this new nonparticipating NSLI. A veteran who had a service-connected disability could apply for nonparticipating NSLI on one of the regular whole life or endowment plans available, if the application was filed within one year after the disability was determined by the VA to be service connected. Premiums are waived if the disability is or becomes total. For one year beginning May 1, 1965, veterans who had served after October 1, 1941, and before January 1, 1957, were given the opportunity to purchase a special form of NSLI insurance if they were ineligible for commercial insurance coverage.

ernment issues each serviceman a group life certificate giving the details of his coverage. The serviceman has the right to designate the beneficiary and to elect to have the proceeds paid to his beneficiary in 36 equal monthly installments or in a lump sum.

The group insurance coverage on the serviceman terminates 120 days after he is separated from active duty. During this period, he has the right to convert his term coverage, without evidence of insurability, into one of the standard cash value plans then being written by one of the converter companies. He pays the standard premium then being charged at his attained age by the converter company.[45] He does not get the benefit of any low priced subsidized government insurance.[46]

THE DEPARTMENT OF HEALTH, EDUCATION AND WELFARE. The only compulsory insurance in the field of life insurance is social security. It might be contended that social security is not insurance. Rates and values are not a matter of contract between the insured and the insurer but are set by legislation, which has been and will be changed frequently. Social security benefits are not mathematically based on premiums collected.[47] However, for all practical purposes, at least certain benefits under social security bear a close enough resemblance to insurance to justify their classification as social insurance.

Five types of life and health insurance benefits are available under social security: (1) retirement income benefits, (2) lump-sum death benefits, (3) income benefits for certain classes of survivors, (4) disability income benefits, and (5) medical care benefits for the aged. These benefits are important enough in the financial plans of the typical policyholder to be given special consideration by life and health underwriters in the

---

[45] If he has a service-connected disability when he is separated from the service, he may purchase NSLI insurance from the federal government as well as convert his Servicemen's Group Life Insurance coverage.

[46] Because nondisabled veterans of the Vietnam war are not given the opportunity to buy low priced life insurance from the government as were veterans of World War I, World War II, and the Korean war, U.S. Senator Philip A. Hart, Chairman of the Subcommittee on Antitrust and Monopoly of the Senate Judiciary Committee, asked the Administrator of Veterans' Affairs in a letter of June 7, 1968, to assemble from the converter companies price information to be disseminated to the Vietnam veterans to assist them in selecting converter companies in view of the wide variation in prices charged for life insurance by commercial insurers. The administrator of Veterans' Affairs rejected the request because he believed that it presented difficult communication problems, that it isolated only *one* of the factors to be considered in an insurance purchase decision, that a mass of data from 568 companies on many plans would not only be prohibitively complex but would probably confuse most veterans, and that considerable injustice could be done to many of the companies by a price disclosure system which involves the making of assumptions. For a short recital and evaluation of this exchange, see Joseph M. Belth, *"SGLI, the VA, and Life Insurance Price Disclosure," Probe*, Vol. XVI, No. 1 (January 6, 1969), pp. 1–3.

[47] Some economists feel that it would be sounder economically to pay all benefits from general taxation. They argue that nothing is to be gained by funding the benefits, either partially, as is now done, or fully, as is sometimes proposed. A funded social security system can hamstring the government in its efforts to promote economic stability through its fiscal policy. These economists, however, do recognize the psychological problems involved in eliminating the contributory feature from social security.

programming of income insurance. However, because benefit structures and eligibility requirements change so frequently, it is better to obtain details from sources that can be kept up to date more readily and efficiently than a textbook.[48]

OTHER FEDERAL INSURERS. The federal government has become an insurer under the Railroad Retirement Act and the Civil Service Retirement Act. Under these programs benefits somewhat like those provided under social security are made available to highly restricted classes of employees. For work-connected injuries of federal employees, the federal government serves as an insurer under the Federal Employees' Compensation Act.

6. DIFFERENCES AMONG INSURERS OF THE SAME TYPE

From the buyer's standpoint, more important differences result from company philosophy and practices than from type of organization. Significant variations exist among the various mutual insurers themselves as well as among the many stock and fraternal insurers.

Variations in Acceptability of Applicants. Not all companies accept the same classes of business. Some companies, regardless of whether stock or mutual, will accept juvenile applicants.[49] Others do not. Some companies, in order to restrict themselves to more favorable mortality groups and hence offer lower rates, will write only a particular type of applicant; for example, teachers, in the case of the Teachers Insurance and Annuity Association; or ministers, certain church officials, and their families only, as in the case of the Presbyterian Ministers' Fund.

Some variation in type of acceptable applicant also is found, particularly among fraternal insurers. For instance, fraternals, because of their basic structure, write members only. They further may vary by imposing membership qualifications along religious, national, or occupational lines.

Differences in Policies Issued. Companies also vary as to types of policies offered. In the main, every life insurer offers a continuous premium whole life policy or instead a paid-up at some such age as 90. They also offer several limited payment policies, endowments, and term insurance plans. A growing number of insurers offer variable annuities whereas others write only the conventional fixed-dollar annuity.

Variations of the standard policy forms differ widely. Some of these differences are a result of differences in underwriting philosophy. Policy

---

[48] Current information on social security eligibility requirements, benefits available, tax rates, and benefit formulas can be obtained from any local social security office. It also can be found in any of a number of standard reference works on life insurance, for example, National Underwriter's *Diamond Life Bulletins, Unique Manual, Little Gem;* Best's *Flitcraft's;* or Research and Review Service's *Advanced Underwriting Service.*

[49] Ages 0 to approximately 10. The age at which applicants will be considered for policies varies from company to company.

forms that one company considers sound may not be so considered by another. Another reason for the differences is the degree of emphasis insurers place on selling policies with high cash values; one company may be more aggressive than another in bringing in investable funds; consequently, one company will stress policies with a high cash value, whereas another will not deemphasize term insurance.

A significant reason for the variation among types of policies offered is competition. Small and less widely known companies (and sometimes even the large and prominent companies) design special policy forms to offer in competition with the policies of other companies. From the viewpoint of some companies the special policy form also has the advantage of not being readily comparable to the policies of other companies, thus further complicating the already difficult task of price comparison.

Because of these variations in types of policies offered, it often becomes necessary for the buyer to look beyond one company to find a policy form best suited to his needs. The competitive special policies sometimes fit a particular life insurance need better than one of the usual policies.[50]

Variations in Contract Provisions. In life insurance there are no standard policy forms. This statement is true despite the use of the term standard to designate a certain group of policies which generally bear the same name among all companies and are alike in their major provisions. Rarely, however, are two life insurance policy contracts identical. A clause here or a clause there, even a phrase here or a phrase there, could make a difference in the value of the coverage at some future time.

Nevertheless, it is possible for the buyer in general to decide what clauses, phrases, and provisions of a policy are most needed in view of the major purpose for which he purchases the policy, i.e., for instance, whether he purchases it for an estate clearance fund or for an income to his family in case of his death.

Perhaps the greatest variation among policies, even among those by the same name, is in optional modes of settlement. Options vary not only as to guaranteed amounts per installment but also as to types available.[51] For example, not all companies include the joint and survivor options.

The options printed in a life insurance contract usually are not the only ones that the companies will write. Nearly all companies will write special settlement options upon the request of the policyholder and will attach the agreement to the policy as part of the contract. Many also will make special settlement agreements with the beneficiary. However, it should be remembered that the only options the company is obligated to grant are those that

---

[50] *Who Writes What,* an annual publication of the National Underwriter Co., 420 E. 4th Street, Cincinnati, Ohio 45202, is an excellent guide to companies by type of policy issued. It attempts no ratings or recommendations, confining itself to a listing of companies by policies.

[51] Guaranteed amounts per installment vary among companies as a result of differing mortality and interest assumptions.

are either written in the policy or attached to it as a part of the policy. Other options are issued according to "company practice," and company practice may vary from time to time. Moreover, there is a difference among companies in liberality in drawing up settlement agreements. Some companies will write virtually any type of legal settlement agreement requested. Others adhere to the standard forms.[52]

The differences mentioned in company practice in writing special settlement options carry over into variations in other matters as well. For instance, there is a variation among companies regarding the automatic premium loan. Some companies include it as a regular provision in the policy, others include it only on request, and others will not write it at all. There is also a variation among the practices of companies in writing a "spendthrift" trust agreement.[53]

Special settlement agreements and spendthrift clauses represent trustee functions. The differences noted in company practices relating to them stem largely from differences in management philosophy among companies as to the extent that they should engage in operations that are more suitable for a trust. Management thinking is not agreed on the line of demarcation between the life insurance business and the trust business.

Other contract provisions which might vary among companies are those relating to disability income benefits, waiver of premium benefits, loan and surrender values, change of plan, dividend options, reinstatement, incontestability, double indemnity, guaranteed insurability, and inflation riders.[54]

Variations in Price. Variations among companies as to the prices they charge for insurance always arouse the most interest among buyers and some agents. It is impossible to determine what the differences in the prices charged by the companies will be without the use of an electronic computer and a set of data to feed into it. The set of data needed will have to be based on subjective probability assumptions about the duration of the policy; the use of the face amount of the policy to provide death benefits or the use of the nonforfeiture values to provide reduced paid-up insurance, extended term insurance, or cash values; and an assumed dividend scale. No two policies ever are exactly alike.

Companies not using agents offer insurance at lower prices. The difference in prices is to some extent the agent's commission. The agent's service to the policyholder, and especially to the beneficiary, can have a monetary value. Whether the service is worth the difference in premiums depends upon the kind and extent of service needed and rendered both to the in-

---

[52] For a good compendium of variations among settlement options and company practices relating to them, see Best's annual publication, *Settlement Options.*

[53] Under a spendthrift trust agreement the beneficiary is prohibited from invading the principal either at all or for more than a set amount in addition to the installments elected, and the creditors of the beneficiary are prohibited from attaching the principal while it is in the hands of the insurance company.

[54] Cf. Chapter 7 for a discussion of inflation riders.

sured and his beneficiary—something which cannot be determined absolutely when the policy is purchased.[55]

The price of a policy depends on its use. A company issuing a policy with a higher premium may have in that policy more favorable settlement options than a company issuing a policy at a lower premium. Which is the more expensive policy, *ceteris paribus,* may thus depend upon whether the policyholder eventually uses it to provide a lump-sum benefit (in which case the policy with the lower premium has cost him less) or for a periodic income (in which case the policy with the higher premium may cost him less).

Prices of life insurance policies often are compared on a net cost basis, i.e., total premiums paid, minus dividends if any, minus the amount collected upon surrender of the contract at the end of a given number of years.[56] Unfortunately, the practice of selling life insurance on an illustrative (current or historical) net cost basis has developed. Net cost selling is misleading because net cost illustrations are not valid in determining the price of a life insurance policy. These illustrations assume that the policy is discontinued at some given point, the ultimate period of years used in the exhibit. Unless the policy is cashed in at that time, the net cost will be other than what is shown in the illustration. For this reason, net cost illustrations are sometimes called surrendered net cost. For the policyholder who continues his insurance in force until death, net payments (premiums minus dividends) are a more suitable measure of price.

Net cost illustrations are fallacious. For instance, if enough years are included in the illustrations they often show that life insurance can be purchased free. These net cost illustrations eliminate the question of the time value of money (interest) and the value of survivorship benefits. If interest on premium deposits and survival benefits were considered in net cost illustrations, the picture would be entirely different.[57]

Finally, although price is an important consideration in the purchase of life insurance, just as it is in the purchase of other services, it is not the only consideration. The practice of net cost selling often induces policyholders to purchase insurance on a price basis alone, possibly at the expense of tradeoffs that would have been worth their additional price. It also helps to pave the way for borderline companies to write a startlingly low priced policy by restricting benefits. This is not to say that price disclosure in

---

[55] It should be pointed out that cost is not always related to service. That there is loading in the premium rate to take care of service to the policyholder does not always mean that the policyholder will receive that service. While this difference depends largely on the capability and sincerity of the agent with whom the policyholder deals, it is also related to some extent to the philosophy of the company. Once again, a good agent may render service of value over and beyond the expense loading in the premium—and so may his company. Another agent or company may not render service of value equivalent to the expense loading.

[56] Net cost illustrations published in life insurance compendiums usually are based on 10- and 20-year periods. A 20-year illustration is presented later in this chapter.

[57] Interest and survivorship benefits are explained in Chapter 1.

itself is harmful but that the usual life insurance buyer needs guidance in its use.

Professor Belth has developed what he calls a refined system for making price calculations for life insurance policies, a procedure which he named the level price method.[58] Under this system, a set of yearly prices is determined for each of the years included in the time period studied. Then by using "appropriate" mortality, interest, and lapse assumptions, these variable yearly prices are equated to a level price per $1,000 of protection for the period studied.

The refinements in the level price method over the traditional net cost method are that it considers such items as the time value of money, the decreasing amount of protection associated with increasing cash values, the probability of surviving the period studied, and the probability that the insurance will be kept in force during the period studied. However, these refinements require that "appropriate" assumptions be made, that the necessary premium data, cash value data, and dividend data be available, and that there be access to an electronic computer to handle the many computations involved in the system.[59]

Under the level price method of measuring prices, life insurance is viewed as a dual product, combining decreasing protection and increasing savings.[60] The yearly prices determined are for the difference each year between the face amount of the insurance and the cash value of the policy for that year. This approach requires that a distinction be made between life insurance prices and life insurance premiums, or to put it another way, it requires the use of the concept of annual divisible premiums. The annual premiums must be viewed as constituting two parts, the division of which varies from year to year. Only one part is used to buy life insurance protection. The other part is used to buy life insurance cash values.[61] The parts used to buy life insurance protection are considered the yearly prices of life insurance as distinguished from the life insurance premiums, and the level price of life insurance for any given period is an average of these yearly prices for that period.[62] Regardless of what one may think of the

---

[58] Belth, *The Retail Price Structure in American Life Insurance, op. cit.,* pp. 19, 33–69.

[59] Professor Belth discusses the problems of making "appropriate" assumptions (pp. 55–62) and the problems of obtaining the necessary data (pp. 62–69). Also, he describes a computer program developed for performing the numerous computations (pp. 281–300).

[60] Cf. Chapter 1, pp. 18–20 for a discussion of the decreasing protection, increasing savings concept versus the survivorship concept.

[61] It is as though the actuary in developing the premium had decided to build into it $X of varying amounts from year to year for life insurance and the residual $Y for savings, and as though when the policyholder bought the policy he had decided to pay $X of varying amounts from year to year for life insurance and to put the residual $Y in a savings account.

[62] Unlike the traditional net cost method, the level price method does not assume discontinuance of the policy at some given point. When a 20-year period of analysis is used, it means that only 20 years of data are analyzed. The usual lack of availability of data beyond 20 years is the reason that the period used by Professor Belth in his level price studies is limited to 20 years.

actuarial or legal logic inherent in the notion of a divisible premium, it must be accepted that the concept is valuable in recognizing the effect of different cash surrender value patterns on the price of a life insurance policy that fails to run its course.[63]

The price versus premium distinction could be thought of as being analogous to a distinction between the gross price and net price of an automobile, with the net price being a function of the resale price pattern of the automobile in the used-car market. For those who trade in their automobiles each year for a new one, an automobile that sells for $5,500, and has a low amount of short term depreciation, would be priced under an automobile selling at $5,300, with a high amount of short-term depreciation. For those who intend to keep their automobiles long enough for the respective depreciation amounts to converge, the higher early resale value of their cars would have no effective bearing on the relative price of these cars. And if the cars are to be held until they have only nominal junk value, there is little distinction between their gross and net prices. Just so, if a life insurance policy is held until it matures as a death claim, there would be no effective difference between its premium and its price.

Using his level-price method, Professor Belth found a wide variation in the prices charged by those insurers included in his study.[64] Wider variation was found in the prices of participating insurance than in the prices of nonparticipating policies. The 20-year level prices per $1,000 of protection charged by a sample of 88 companies for $10,000 continuous premium whole life policies (or one substantially similar) issued in 1962 to standard males aged 35 varied between $4 and $14 per $1,000.[65] The mean of the level prices was $7.55, the standard deviation was $1.52, and the coefficient of variation was 20.1 percent.[66] The prices charged by a sample of 60 companies for otherwise comparable nonparticipating insurance varied between

---

[63] There is additional value in viewing a cash value life insurance policy as decreasing protection and increasing savings in that the predeath value of a life insurance policy logically can be considered an asset of the policyholder. The postdeath value of that asset is increased only by the difference between the policy's face amount and its predeath cash value. (It should be noted that if the insurer's health has become impaired or he has otherwise become uninsured, the policy would have an intrinsic value in excess of its predeath cash value—a value that would not be reflected by the insurer in the amounts payable to him were he to surrender his policy. (Cf. Robert I. Mehr, "New Settings for Old Stones," *Journal of Risk and Insurance*, Vol. XXXIV, No. 3 [September, 1967], pp. 477 ff.)

[64] Although Professor Belth found some correlation between prices and premiums, he found greater variations in prices than in premiums. See Belth, *The Retail Price Structure in American Life Insurance, op. cit.*, pp. 73–77.

[65] *Ibid.*, Table 10, p. 73.

[66] These, of course, are statistical concepts. The mean is the arithmetic average of the distribution of the level prices of the companies in the sample; the standard deviation is a measure of dispersion (spread of the distribution) of the values about the mean and is equal to the square root of the variances. The variance is the average of the squares of the difference between the values in the distribution and the mean of the distribution. The coefficient of variation is the standard deviation of the distribution divided by the mean of the distribution. The lower the coefficient of variation, the closer together are the level prices in the distribution.

$7 and $11, the standard deviation was $0.71, and the coefficient of variation was 8.1 percent.[67]

That large differences exist among the prices charged by insurers and that insurance buyers are unaware of these differences have generated some public interest in attempting to find ways of encouraging effective price competition in the life insurance business.[68] Mr. John S. Pillsbury, Jr., 1968 Chairman of the Institute of Life Insurance remarked: "There is a growing demand that something be done by somebody to clarify the question of cost of life insurance. Adherents of the consumer movement contend that there should be some formula by which the buyer can make precise comparisons between policies and make an informed purchase decision on the basis of price. . . . I am persuaded that if the realities of the life insurance process preclude a formula answer, then we must learn to communicate clearly why this is so in a manner that will be understood and accepted. If, on the other hand, there is an answer—at least a better one than we have produced thus far—and I for one believe that there must be—then we had better put the most capable minds in our business to work promptly and creatively on this problem." (*Annual Meeting and Staff Reports,* Institute of Life Insurance, New York, 1968, p. 11.) At least two committees have been organized to study the question raised by Pillsbury—one a special joint committee formed by two major life insurance company trade associations (The Life Insurance Association of America and the American Life Convention) and the other a special subcommittee of the National Association of Insurance Commissioners.

In response to demands for credible cost comparisons of life insurance policies, the National Underwriter Company, an insurance trade publisher, released in late 1969 a new publication called *Cost Facts On Life Insurance.*[69] The volume explains and utilizes three price measurement techniques: the traditional cost method, the equalized cost method, and the benefits cost method. Using these price measurement techniques, a computer printout of cost comparisons among 141 insurers is offered for various types of policies, ages of issue, sizes of policies, and various duration periods.

The traditional cost method ignores interest, mortality, and lapse rates

---

[67] Belth, *The Retail Price Structure in American Life Insurance, op. cit.* Premium rates per $1,000 of face amount charged by the same 88 companies for the same participating policies ranged from $21 to $29. The mean of the premium rates was $24.11; the standard deviation, $1.22; and the coefficient of variation, 5.1 percent. For the same 60 companies on the same nonparticipating insurance, the premium rates ranged from $17 to $22. The mean of the premium rates was $19.32; the standard deviation, $0.63; and the coefficient of variation, 3.3 percent. (*Ibid.,* Table 12, p. 76.)

[68] Professor Belth suggests "a rigorous system of price disclosure that would make it possible for careful buyers of life insurance to obtain enough price information to permit them to make reasonably informed purchase decisions." *Ibid.,* p. 239.

[69] *Op. cit.* This publication was referred to in Chapter 20. For an explanation of the book, see Robert B. Mitchell, "How New Net-Cost Yardsticks Operate Explained in Detail," *National Underwriter* Life ed., January 10, 1970, p. 1.

in computing price illustrations. It involves a simple computation and presents a distorted picture. For example, if a $25,000 continuous premium whole life policy is issued to a 35-year old man for an annual premium of $22.75 per $1,000, the 20-year net cost per $1,000 computed under the traditional cost method would be as follows, assuming that total dividends will equal $151.88 and that the 20-year cash value is $352.54:

(1) 20 premiums ($22.75 × 20)	=	$455.00	
(2) Total dividends for 20 years	=	151.88	
(3) Net payments (1) minus (2)	=	303.12	
(4) 20-year cash value	=	352.54	
(5) Total net cost (4) minus (3)	= −	49.42	
(6) 20-year average annual cost	= −	2.47	

The 20-year average annual cost computed under the traditional cost method would be the same regardless of the insurer's dividend payout pattern so long as it pays the $151.88 over the 20-year period. It makes no difference whether the dividend payments are very low for the first 15 years and very high for the last 5 years with a substantial surrender dividend or whether they are moderate throughout the 20-year period with no surrender dividend because interest rates are not considered in the computations.

To overcome this distortion, *Cost Facts On Life Insurance* includes computations using the equalized cost method of price measurement. This method requires the use of an interest assumption to equalize the effects of differences in dividend payout patterns and in gross premium amounts.[70] Using a 4 percent interest rate, the equalized cost for the foregoing policy would be computed as follows:

(1) 20-year cash value	=	$352.54
(2) Dividends accumulated at 4 percent interest	=	210.40
(3) Total 20th year value (1) plus (2)	=	562.94
(4) Amount of 1 per annum for 20 years at 4 percent	=	30.9692
(5) Average value per year (3) divided by (4)	=	18.17
(6) Annual premium per $1,000	=	22.75
(7) Average annual cost (6) minus (5)	=	4.58

Note that item 2 here is different from item 2 in the traditional cost illustration. Here each annual dividend is accumulated at 4 percent for the remainder of the initial 20-year period. The pattern of dividends is an important consideration. Assuming total dividend payments of $151.88 during the 20-year period, item 2 will be higher if dividend payments are

---

[70] *Cost Facts* presents figures using both 2½ percent interest and 4 percent interest. The 2½ percent is considered a reasonable after-tax earnings rate for corporations, and 4 percent is considered a good average after-tax earnings rate for individuals.

moderate throughout the period than if dividend payments are very low during the early years and very high during the later years. Item 5 is the average annual amount expected to be returned to the policyholder at the end of the assumed 20 years. Item 7 is the average annual amount that will not be returned and, therefore, is the average annual cost of the policy using the equalized cost technique of price measurement.

The equalized cost method does not take mortality or lapse rates into account. To add further dimensions to cost comparisons, *Cost Facts* includes computations based on the benefits cost method of price measurement.[71]

The benefits cost method considers not only interest but also mortality and lapses, and is a measure of benefits cost, that is, the cost of providing the living and death benefits but not the benefits themselves. It is computed by utilizing techniques similar to those used in the level price method. A series of annual prices is developed to measure the prices of protection applicable to each particular year falling within the period selected. An amount assumed to be each particular year's share of the premium necessary to pay death claims is subtracted, giving the benefits cost for that particular year. For example, the benefits cost for the 10th year in the illustrative policy would be computed as follows:

(1)	Cash value end of 9th year	=	$144.80
(2)	10th year gross premium	=	22.75
(3)	Total of (1) and (2)	=	167.55
(4)	Amount of 1 at 4 percent for 1 year	=	1.04
(5)	Product of (3) times (4)	=	174.25
(6)	Cash value end of 10th year	=	164.20
(7)	(5) less (6)	=	10.05
(8)	10th year dividend	=	6.20
(9)	Price of Protection for 10th year	=	3.85
(10)	Assumed cost of death claims for year	=	1.22
(11)	Benefits cost for 10th year (9–10)	=	2.63

Similar computations are made for each year and the resulting yearly costs discounted for interest, mortality, and lapses to determine the average amount of each annual premium retained by the insurer for the period selected, 20 years in this illustration. Under the benefits cost method, the average annual 20-year price of the illustrative policy would be $3.13 if discounted for mortality and lapses, and $2.73 if discounted for mortality only. The chance that the policyholder will die or lapse the policy and thus not participate fully in the dividend increases throughout the period is reflected by the use of mortality and lapse assumptions.

Note that only the cash value at the end of the selected period is considered in the traditional cost and the equalized cost methods but that the

---

[71] The computations are made in four different ways: 2½ percent interest with and without lapse, and 4 percent interest with and without lapse. The mortality rates used are those based on the Ultimate Basic Tables Graduated Mortality Rates Per 1,000 Male Lives 1957–1960 Experience. The lapse rates used are those based on the Moorhead Table R with a first-year adjustment to reflect absence of lapses in year 1.

rate of growth of the cash value over the period will affect the results under the benefits cost method.

The $3.13 and $2.73 costs under the benefits cost method compare with minus $2.47 under the traditional cost method and $4.58 under the equalized cost method.

The traditional cost method produces the lowest prices because it ignores the earnings opportunity cost of the money paid in as premiums. The equalized cost method produces the highest prices because it takes these earnings opportunities into account. The benefits cost method shows lower prices than the equalized cost method because it includes as costs only those funds assumed to be unavailable as living benefits to policyholders or as death benefits to their beneficiaries. It includes as cost only that portion of each annual premium retained by the insurer for expenses, contingency surpluses, and profits.

Cost Facts On Life Insurance shows a wide array of prices among policies computed using any one of the price measuring techniques, and the ones that show the highest prices using the traditional method are likely to show high prices using the other methods. However, while those showing the lowest prices under the traditional method might show low prices under the other methods, there is no reason to expect them to do so.[72]

Variations in Underwriting Practices. So many variations exist among companies in underwriting practices that it is difficult to cite representative examples. One company may accept a health condition that another would not accept. Again, some companies write insurance only on standard lives, while others accept substandard business. Even among those who write substandard business, there is a variation as to how far away from standard a company will go in this direction. Some companies will write disability income protection in connection with life insurance; some will attach riders agreeing to waive future premiums in case of total disability; some will attach double indemnity riders under which the face amount of the policy will be doubled in case of accidental death; some will write one or another of these riders; and some will write none at all. Some companies will write pension trust and group insurance, and some will not. Differences exist among companies as to what are considered hazardous occupations and subject to an extra rate or not acceptable at all. The well-informed life insurance agent knows which company is most likely to accept an application for a given type of coverage from a particular type of applicant at premium rates that are competitive. However, some companies prohibit their agents, either by contract or intimidation, from dealing with other insurers on behalf of clients.[73] Fortunately, however, there are many agents

---

[72] Cf. Robert B. Mitchell, "What Sophisticated Formulas Do To Policy Cost Rankings," *National Underwriter,* Life ed., November 15, 1969. See Table 1, p. 27.

[73] Cf. Joseph M. Belth, *A Report On Life Insurance* (Bloomington, Ind.: Bureau of Business Research, Indiana University, 1967) Table 27, p. 152. For an editorial comment on this restrictive practice, see "The Right To Place Business 'Outside,'" Probe, Vol. 16, No. 24 (November 24, 1969).

who are free to place business with other insurers (free because their insurers do not enforce such restrictions, their insurers are unsuccessful in their attempts at intimidation, or their insurers subscribe to the concept that their agents are expected to act professionally, that is provide their clients the same treatment they would want for themselves).

Variations in Investment Practice. Variations in underwriting practice are equaled by variations in investment practice. The insurance laws of each state limit the types of investments that a life insurance company may make; but within the limitations of the law it is possible for investment portfolios to vary widely. For instance, some companies will invest more heavily in real estate mortgages than will others. Even among those that invest heavily in mortgages, there may be variation as to type of mortgage, some leaning more to the monthly repayment residential mortgage, while others prefer lump sum repayment commercial property mortgages. Some insurers involve themselves in construction of large-scale apartment buildings and shopping centers, whereas others do not concern themselves with major real estate investments. Those insurers interested in direct investment in real estate are governed not only by their own investment philosophy but also by the limitations imposed by the law. Some insurers are more interested in common stock investments than are others, although the total of assets that can be put into common stocks is limited by the laws of the various states. Some insurers participate in the $2 billion commitment of the life insurance industry to invest in ways that may help alleviate blighted urban conditions. Some purchase transportation equipment for leaseback to other businesses.

Variations in investment philosophy and practices arise out of differences of opinion among competent investment men as to future earnings and trends in the investment field. Investments are a specialized study, requiring a high degree of knowledge and skill. Investment practice, unlike mortality, is not subject to mathematical formulas. It is impossible to say today which investment will turn out to be best in the future. Investment men can only apply their knowledge and understanding to deciding individually which types of investments have the best outlook at the moment.

Wide differences are found not only in the composition of the investment portfolios of life insurers but also in the net rate of return on these portfolios. *Best's Life Insurance Reports* is a source of information both on how individual life insurers distribute their assets among the various classes of investments and on the yields earned by these individual life insurers.[74] These net rates of return are given for five years. They reflect the ratios that investment income, after deduction for investment expenses but before deduction for federal income taxes, bears to the mean of the assets held at the beginning of the year and those held at the end of the

---

[74] *Best's Life Insurance Reports* (Morristown, N.J.: Alfred M. Best Company, Inc., Annual).

year. By thumbing the pages of *Best's Reports,* one can observe wide differences in net investment yields, some much above and others much below the average yield earned by all U.S. life insurance companies.

With life insurers writing equity based contracts at an increasing pace, variations among insurers in the performance of their common stock portfolios will attract more attention. The common stock performance record of insurers varies even more widely among life insurers than does their performance record on their total portfolio. Professors Gentry and Pike studied the common stock investment performance of 33 life insurers for the 12-year period 1956–1967. They found that the average annual rate of return on these portfolios as a group was 8.89 percent. This compared with an average annual rate of return of 7.78 percent provided by the Standard and Poor's average of 500 stocks. The average annual rates of return among the individual insurers studied varied from a low of 5 percent for one insurer to a high of 18.1 percent for another insurer.[75]

Variations in Size, Surplus, and Reserves.   Perhaps the most noticeable variation among life insurance companies is that of size. They run the gamut from companies with a few *millions* in force to companies with many *billions* in force. Not only do companies vary in size according to the amount of insurance in force but also according to assets.

Contingency reserves and surpluses also vary among companies, for the most part as a result of different actuarial philosophies. The actuaries of one company may be able to marshal irrefutable arguments and mathematical formulas to prove the adequacy of the size of their contingency reserves and surpluses, whereas those of another company of nearly the same size will be able to marshal equally irrefutable arguments and formulas to prove that a contingency reserve of a different size is correct. Mathematics go so far; human judgment must then enter.

Differences in reserves depend upon the system adopted for their calculation. State laws set up minimum reserve standards. Companies may use higher standards than the minimum, and many do. The old and established companies usually use formulas yielding larger reserves than those used by the new companies that may lack the necessary surplus to establish larger reserves.

Variations in Sales Organizations.   Sales organizations vary among insurers (1) according to the degree of control exercised over them by the home office, (2) the skill with which they recruit, select, train, motivate, and supervise their agents and provide them with sales aids, and (3) how they compensate their agency forces.

The insurer may use a system under which a general agent is given exclusive rights to represent the company for soliciting and servicing business in a specified territory and for which he is paid a commission and a

---

[75] James A. Gentry and John R. Pike, "Rates of Return On Common Stock Portfolios of Life Insurance Companies," *Journal of Risk and Insurance,* Vol. XXXVI, No. 4 (December, 1969), pp. 545–52.

collection fee.[76] The general agent appoints, trains, supervises, and motivates agents to solicit and service the business in that territory and pays them a part of the commission he receives from the insurer. The difference between what the general agent receives from his company and the amount he pays his agents is known as his "override" or "overriding commission." The general agent is an independent operator. He pays his own expenses, finances agents, and pays for the operation of the office. The only control the insurer has over him is its right to void his contract.

A modified general agency system or a branch office system is the more common form today. Under the branch office system a salaried employee of the company is hired to manage a particular territory. He may receive commissions in addition to his salary; but this does not alter his status as an employee. He appoints and supervises the agency force on behalf of the company. Sometimes he supervises the clerical personnel of the agency; although in larger branch offices it is the practice for the company to employ a cashier as the manager of routine business and collections. The cashier may or may not be subject to the authority of the branch manager. The company pays all expenses of operation, trains the agents or supplies the branch manager with the facilities for training them, issues contracts for agents, and passes upon the qualifications of new agents whom the branch manager may propose.

Pure general agency systems and pure branch office systems are difficult to find. There is a growing tendency for the company to assume more responsibility for the financing and operation of the general agency, thus bringing the general agency system closer to the branch office system, even though the basic relationship between the general agent and his company is unchanged.

Several insurers write insurance without the use of agents. Included in the group are a few legal reserve insurers such as the Teachers Insurance and Annuity Association, the Presbyterian Ministers' Fund, and a number of life and health insurers that write insurance by mail.

Practically every life insurance company field office is on the alert for new sales personnel. To some extent, this continual search is a result of the turnover in agents, i.e., of agents leaving the business. The failure to use valid criteria for judging the potential of a prospective agent, poor training, and poor supervision contribute heavily to the turnover of agents. Those insurers that take a firm stand on agents' qualifications are likely to have lower turnover if they also do an effective job of agent training, supervising, motivating, and providing sales aids. While rule-of-thumb judgment of the fitness of men for the job of life insurance selling is still practiced,

---

[76] Earlier general agency contracts went even further in their grant of authority. One between the Northwestern Mutual Life Insurance Company and Dr. Henry Martin, dated August 22, 1861, not only authorized the doctor to solicit business, appoint agents, receive premiums, and service policyholders but also to make mortgage loans and *examine his own applicants!*

valid and reliable aptitude and interest tests have been worked out and are widely used for preliminary screening of applicants for jobs as life insurance salesmen. However, tests will not measure a man's willingness to apply himself or his ability to build a market. Furthermore, the nature of the job of selling life insurance is one that seems to produce a high agent turnover rate regardless of the practical precautions available for use in recruiting personnel. The unpopular duties of a life insurance agent are to talk about death, to persuade people to forego current consumption for dollars to be delivered at some future time, to sell an intangible product that is difficult for most buyers to understand, and to intrude on the privacy of the prospect. The job of life insurance selling requires a high degree of sales competency, dedication, and sophistication in financial matters. Relatively few people combine these traits.

In contrast to an earlier day in the business when training consisted of giving the new man a rate book, a prayer book and a pat on the back, there is today a plethora of training plans and programs. These programs are of several kinds: agency or company, commercial, campus, and institutional. The extent to which these available training tools are emphasized varies among insurers and agencies.

The basic method of compensating life insurance salesmen is the commission contract. This type of contract usually calls for high commission on the first year's premium with a much smaller commission on future premiums. For example, one insurer licensed in New York pays the following scale of commissions for continuous premium whole life policies of $5,000 or more written up to and including age 60:

> First-year commission   — 55 percent of gross premium.[77]
> Second, 3rd, and 4th year — 10 percent of gross premium.
> Fifth through 10th year   — 3 percent of gross premium.

For one-year renewable term insurance the commission scale is much lower:

> First-year commission   — 20 percent of gross premium.
> Second through 10th year — 3 percent of gross premium.

For 20-year endowment policies this insurer pays a first-year commission of 35 percent. Renewal commission rates are the same as for continuous premium whole life insurance. For a single premium policy the commission is 3 percent of the premium.

Some insurers base their commission rates not only on the type of policy written but also on the age class (sometimes at 10-year intervals) of the person whose life is insured and on whether the insurance is written on a participating or nonparticipating plan.

Insurers not licensed in New York have more freedom in developing

---

[77] For policies issued at ages 61 through 70 or for amounts written for less than $5,000, the first-year commission is 50 percent.

their commission scales because they are not subject to the New York law limiting commissions that can be paid (cf. Chapter 29). One insurer not licensed in New York pays the following scale of commission rates:

	Issue Age			
	20–24		30–39	
	1st year	2d—5th year	1st year	2d—5th year
Nonparticipating				
Continuous premium whole life	80%	10%	75%	10%
20-year endowment	50	7½	50	7½
Participating				
Continuous premium whole life	75	10	75	10
20-year endowment	45	7½	45	7½

For continuous premium whole life policies the first year commission rates of this insurer begin at 90 percent when issued at ages 0–9 and move down five percentage points for each succeeding 10-year age class so that policies issued to applicants aged 60–69 is 60 percent. These commission rates are for nonparticipating plans. For participating continuous premium whole life policies the commission rates begin five percentage points lower (85 percent for ages 0–9) and maintain this differential (55 percent for ages 60–69). If the first-year commission is 55 percent or more, renewal commission is 10 percent, otherwise it is 7½ percent. Renewal commissions are paid by this insurer for four years.

Note that the total commissions paid by the illustrative New York-admitted insurer on a $5,000 continuous premium whole life policy issued at age 25 would have been 55 percent + (3 × 10 percent) + (6 × 3 percent) or 103 percent of one year's premium whereas the illustrative company not licensed in New York would have paid 80 percent + (4 × 10 percent) or 120 percent of one year's premium, and over a much shorter period of time.

Renewal commission usually become vested (i.e., the agent's renewals will continue to be paid to him if he leaves the company) if the agent achieves certain levels of production within time periods stated in the compensation contract or completes a requisite period of service or his services are terminated by death.

Recognizing that agents are often called upon to give service to policyholders long after the renewal commissions have expired, many companies augment the system of first-year and renewal commissions with annual service fees to be paid as continuing compensation after renewals stop. These fees, commonly 2 to 3 percent of the premiums on the policies that the agent has in force, are not vested. They are paid to the agent only as long as he remains with the company. Payment of a service fee after the expiration of the renewal commission period is permitted under the New York law limiting commissions paid to agents.

Many companies pay additional commissions or bonuses per $1,000 of new business placed, basing the bonus on a satisfactory average size policy or rate of persistency, or a combination of both. There also may be additional compensation, usually in the form of a bonus, for cash with the application or for policies written on an annual rather than a quarterly premium plan. Some companies pay a bonus for larger policies by the reverse process of reducing the commission on smaller policies. The presence and nature of additional compensation in the form of various bonuses differs widely among compensation contracts and depends on the operating philosophy of the company involved.

In addition to straight compensation are various fringe benefits in the form of retirement plans and group life and disability insurance.

Companies frequently use other than the commission plan of compensation, especially for new agents. These contracts provide salary in lieu of or in addition to commission. The salary is weighted by and must be validated by production. Therefore, it is equivalent to commuting the commissions of a basic commission contract.

Under the commission contract the ordinary agent earns nothing until he starts making sales. As a result, building a satisfactory volume of production, and hence income, comes slowly for the typical new agent; hence, it has become common for companies or general agents to finance a new agent's first years in the business until his sales rise and especially until he begins to enjoy the benefit of renewals.

Financing plans vary widely. For example, under one plan, the agent's earned commissions are credited to his account to offset stipulated payments. Usually the arrangement is to continue for a period of two to three years, with the agent having the right to full commissions whenever these commissions exceed the salary. The amount of the salary usually is a function of the agent's prospective living expenses. In order to continue to qualify for salary during the specified period, the agent must satisfy requirements with respect to work habits and a minimum amount of sales. Under another plan, the agent is guaranteed a weekly or monthly income. In addition, he is guaranteed part of his commissions. In some plans he has this guarantee regardless of the amount of the commissions and in others only if the commissions exceed a specified amount. These plans provide level income to the agent during his initial period plus an incentive for increased production. Under both plans, in case of termination of employment, the agent may be liable for any deficit over commissions earned, but the usual arrangement is to "forgive" the deficit. Anyway, unsuccessful agents are not likely to return the advances.

It should be emphasized that whatever the compensation arrangement established for the new agent, he must show signs of impending success or he will not last. It is axiomatic that one has to sell life insurance in order to make a living selling life insurance.

HEALTH INSURANCE COMPENSATION.   The basic method of compensating agents for the sale of health insurance is also the commission contract; however, two different types of commission arrangements are in use.

While the predominant practice in life insurance is to "bunch" the bulk of the total commission payable into the first year, in casualty insurance the predominant arrangement is level first-year and renewal commissions, with renewal commissions being payable as long as the policy is on a premium-paying basis. Because both life and casualty insurers write health insurance, both types of commission arrangements will be found in the health insurance business.

Life insurers usually use the "unlevel" commission plan to which their agents are accustomed, although a different distribution of the renewal commissions is made. For instance, for optionally renewable policies, one life insurer pays 40 percent first-year commission, 20 percent for the second year, and 10 percent for the remaining life of the policy. For guaranteed renewable policies the scale is 50 percent for the first year, 10 percent for the next four years, and then 5 percent for the remaining life of the policy. Other nonlevel scales provide for termination of the renewal commission at the end of the 10th year and its replacement with a service fee to those agents still with the insurer. Just as with life insurance commission plans, health insurance commission plans vary among insurers not only as to scale but also as to the nature of the vesting granted to the agents.

In contrast is the level commission plan under which some insurers offer a flat 20 or 25 percent commission each year.

The graded commission plan tends to emphasize new business, whereas the level plan emphasizes business that remains in force. Although the level commission plan emphasizes persistent business, it does postpone compensation and this might make it more difficult financially for the new man in his first year or two. On the other hand, the level plan permits the building of a larger renewal income, thus giving an agent more interest in conserving and servicing his business.

7. FACTORS TO CONSIDER IN THE SELECTION OF A COMPANY

Most of the factors that should be considered in selecting a company from which to purchase insurance already have been implied. This section, therefore, is to some extent a summation.

It is patent that a buyer of life and health insurance would like to purchase his insurance from those insurers willing to give him the combination of utilities that he seeks at prices that are favorable. Utilities frequently sought from insurers are the particular coverage desired, the degree of insurer financial strength necessary for the insured to have confidence in the ability of his insurer to pay claims promptly when they occur, and the particular kinds and amounts of services needed.

Coverage Desired.   Too often the need is fitted to the policy rather than the policy to the need. If the insurer does not offer the coverage the buyer wants, other questions about the insurer are a waste of time. The buyer need not settle for a substitute plan of life or health insurance simply because the company whose agent is attempting to make the sale does not offer the particular type of cover and coverage desired. There are many types of life insurance plans, and many more types of health insurance plans, the latter with wide variations. Usually, there is no reason to compromise a want simply because a given company does not write the policy that exactly fits. The chances are that another equally good company will write the desired policy.

Financial Strength Desired.   If the insurer does offer the coverage but the buyer has some doubt about the ability of the insurer to remain solvent, then any further consideration of the insurer is a waste of time. Only dreamers believe that life insurers never die or fade away. The excellent overall record of the life insurance industry should not be allowed to lull the buyer into believing that all insurers are properly financed and are expertly managed by technically qualified personnel. Life insurers do get into financial trouble, and face formal delinquency proceedings. The buyer will do well to avoid those insurers that are underfinanced, undermanaged, and promoter-oriented.

In the matter of safety, it is hard to lay down general rules as to what makes a safe company—and this despite the fact that company safety is a basal factor to consider in buying insurance.

The amount of insurance a company has in force has little to do with safety. Insurance in force is a liability; it represents the amount of money the company has contracted to pay at the maturity of all existing policies. At first glance, it might seem that the amount of insurance in force in a given company could be so small as to render the law of large numbers inoperative. However, the small company usually retains a small percentage of the insurance it has in force. Through reinsurance it gains the necessary spread of risk.

The size of admitted assets taken alone has little to do with safety. The assets must be viewed in terms of their quality and the extent to which they are in excess of realistic reserves.

The real factors are underwriting standards, quality of investments, and the relative amount of surplus.[78] The law sets the minimum standard for investments. The extra margin of safety is in the skill of the investment

---

[78] The exact nomenclature for items making up surplus varies from company to company. The most common names are surplus funds, general contingency reserve, mortality fluctuation reserve, unassigned surplus, capital stock (if any), and special surpluses. The ratio of surplus to reserves is one objective measure of safety.

men employed by the company. The most accurate factual information available about an insurer may be obtained from the state insurance department and from reports of financial services such as *Best's Life Insurance Reports*. However, the difficulty of complete accuracy in judging safety is illustrated by two observations.

1. Were accurate, objective measurement possible, a life insurance company would never get into serious financial trouble because the state department would know exactly when to step in and order a change in practice, assuming, of course, that the insurance department were adequately staffed with trained personnel.

2. The specialized insurance reporting services such as Best's, Spectator, and Dunne's would be in agreement in their ratings (or recommendations) of life insurers.[79] Also, the mistake of giving an insurer a high rating or a recommendation in the year just before it receives a liquidation order would not be made.

Professor Denenberg notes that these "three services are not always in agreement." He observed that "when the 1965 *Life Reports* of Best's and Dunne's were compared, it was discovered that Dunne's recommends 430 companies that Best's does not, while Best's recommends only one not also recommended by Dunne's."[80] Professor Denenberg also reports:

Best's has been recommending life companies since 1935 and has graded them from 1927 to 1935. . . . [D]uring the period in which Best's either recommended or failed to recommend a life insurer . . . only three recommended insurers have been involved in delinquency proceedings . . . In the earlier period during which companies were graded . . . , only six of the delinquent companies had the highest rating. Of these six, only two had the highest rating for more than two of the years prior to the year of the delinquency proceedings, and only one for the entire period. And, the policyholders of the only company with a complete history of highest ratings finally emerged with no financial loss.[81]

Denenberg concluded:

The Financial ratings of *Best's Insurance Reports,* on the basis of historical performance, have been shown to be effective tools for avoiding delinquent insurance companies. By requiring recommended life companies . . . , and by requiring this status over a reasonable period of years, such as six, a selector can be reasonably sure of avoiding delinquent companies if Best's continues to be as efficient in rating companies as it has been in the past.[82]

Universal application of this rule by insurance buyers obviously would mean that no new insurers would be able to succeed. There are good new com-

---

[79] Best's has already been identified. Spectator is *The Spectator Desk Directory Of Insurance* (Philadelphia: Chilton Publishing Co., Annual) and Dunne's is *Dunne's International Insurance Reports* (Louisville, Kentucky: The Insurance Index, Annual).

[80] Herbert S. Denenberg, "Is 'A-PLUS' Really a Passing Grade?" *Journal of Risk and Insurance,* Vol. XXXIV, No. 3 (September, 1967), p. 373 and in footnote 11.

[81] *Ibid.,* pp. 377–78. The foregoing insurers are identified in footnotes 37, 39, and 40, p. 378.

[82] *Ibid.,* p. 384.

panies, of course, but the chances of picking a loser among them are higher than the chances of picking a loser among the well-established insurers. Therefore, if the policyholder selects a new company he had better be convinced that he is doing so with good reason.[83]

Company Prominence.   The prominence of a company is often given attention when choosing a company from which to buy. Prominence indicates that the company is well advertised and well represented, but it should not necessarily be a consideration. It is well for the buyer to remember that there are more than 1,800 legal reserve life insurance companies in the United States alone, and that the typical layman does well to name more than half a dozen. It certainly would be fallacious to say that all those he cannot name are not sound.

Service Desired.   Given that the insurer offers the product wanted and that it has the degree of financial security demanded, then the choice of insurers rests with the questions of service and price. In some cases, the decision involves a tradeoff—that is, the lower the price, the less the kinds and amounts of service. For example, savings bank life insurance and the Wisconsin Life Fund offer attractive price advantages which may, or may not, be offset by the inability of these insurers to render the kinds and amounts of service available through agency companies. Some buyers of life insurance do not want the services of an agent, whereas others do want these services and believe that they are worth the price.

However, more generally there is no tradeoff between service and price. Usually the two questions are completely divorced. In fact, one study concludes "that the absence of an agent is no guarantee of lower prices" because "some directly-purchased life insurance is actually higher in price than offered by many agency companies."[84] And in agency companies there is a wide variation in the kinds and amounts of service given, not only among insurers but also among the agents of a particular insurer.

Some insurers place more emphasis on agent training than do others, and among those that stress agent training there is a variation in the training objectives and in the effectiveness with which these objectives are accomplished. Many insurers concentrate principally on sales techniques, such as teaching their agents how to locate prospects and how to motivate these prospects to buy. Insufficient attention may be given to the educational and professional aspects of agent training. Other insurers will supplement sales training with an effort to educate their agents in life insurance product knowledge and in life insurance counseling—that is, how to use life insurance and health insurance efficiently in helping clients to solve financial problems.

Some insurers encourage their agents to prepare for and take the pro-

---

[83] Cf. Chapter 29 for a discussion of the high birth rate and high death rate of new life insurers. See, also, Jon S. Hanson and Duncan R. Farney, "New Life Insurance Companies: Their Promotion and Regulation," *Marquette Law Review,* Vol. XLIX, No. 2 (Fall, 1965).

[84] Belth, *A Report On Life Insurance, op. cit.,* p. 78.

fessional examinations offered by the American College of Life Underwriters.[85] They also encourage their agents to participate in continuing education activities by attending conferences and advanced courses to prepare themselves to do the best job possible for their clients. However, in the final analysis the amount and adequacy of the service a client can expect to get from an agent depend not only on the agent's ability but also on his desire to give this service. This leads squarely into the question of how to pick an agent.

SELECTING AN AGENT. "Too many writers on the subject of 'how to buy insurance' have made selection of the insurance company the core or major part of their work. Frequently, these same authors have had little or nothing to say about that job which often is even more important— the selection of the . . . agent. . . ."[86]

What is a good agent? The concept of a good agent in the eyes of the buyer may be different from the concept of a good agent as viewed by the company. The question here is directed to the buyer. Briefly, a good life insurance agent is one who does not allow his self-interest to interfere with the soundness of his advice; he is one who not only has up-to-date knowledge of the business but also will take the time necessary to put this knowledge to work on behalf of his client; he is one who knows the life and health insurance market sufficiently so that he can and will use only those insurers that offer his clients attractive terms, and he is one who will give his clients continuing service—that is he will periodically review his clients' needs and make the recommendations necessary to bring his client's life and health insurance program up-to-date.

For the vast majority, the most judicious method of buying life insurance is to use the services of a *good* agent. How does one find a good agent—meaning how does he go about looking for one? "What readily visible earmarks are there which will enable . . . the . . . buyer to select his agent. . . . The answer is: practically none. Practically none, that is, that are readily visible."[87] However, this does not mean that there are no sources of information for the buyer to tap. These sources may be classified into three groups: (1) local business and professional people, (2) clients of the agents, and (3) the agents themselves.[88]

---

[85] The American College of Life Underwriters offers a study course and a series of examinations leading to the award of the professional designation Chartered Life Underwriter, usually abbreviated as CLU.

[86] Robert I. Mehr and Emerson Cammack, *Principles of Insurance* (4th ed.; Homewood, Illinois: Richard D. Irwin, Inc., 1966), p. 679.

[87] *Ibid.*

[88] If the buyer has a close relative (or very dear friend) who is in the life insurance business but is not a good agent, then what? If the desire for peace in the family (or personal) relationship takes precedence over the desire to have a competent agent, the sagacious solution, perhaps, is to develop personal competence in insurance and use that close relative or dear friend as an errand boy and insurance order taker. (For those who are studying this text, presumably much of the necessary competence has been acquired to give the security that everyone ought to have against purely self-seeking life insurance agents or against life insurance agents who are incompetent.

The validity of the opinions of business and professional people (lawyers, bankers, accountants) depends upon the knowledge of these people about life insurance and their experience with the particular agents being discussed. The judgment of clients of agents may be limited by their lack of experience with other agents. It is entirely likely that many of them will not know what services to expect from a good agent. Agents themselves often are good judges of the competency of other agents.

Here two points must be noted: certain agents' comments about their competitors will tell you more about the commenting agent than about the "commentee." It is the practice of all good businessmen, in whatever line of business, to be wary of making critical remarks about their competitors. Therefore, the man who is heavily or freely critical may only be telling his listener that he himself is not a good businessman. Still, the ethical and honest agent cannot bring himself to condone clearly unethical or dishonest practices.[89]

In seeking information about agents from these various sources, it is necessary to develop a composite opinion. Those agents scoring high in the composite can be further screened, preferably by personal interview.

The prospective buyer would like to know the number of years of experience the agent has in the business. Agents who have been in the business only a few years have a lower probability of staying in the business and thus may not be around to give the client the service he has the right to expect. Is the agent free and willing to place the business with whatever insurer is best for the client? Is the agent familiar with what companies are best for what types of coverage? Does the agent attend schools, forums, and other professional educational activities on a regular basis? Does the agent provide a programming and estate planning service for his clients and keep it up-to-date? Does the agent appear to be someone with whom the client can feel comfortable in discussing confidential financial matters?

If the buyer is well informed about insurance subjects, the quickest and probably the best way for him to judge the competency of a given agent is to discuss insurance matters directly with him. The usefulness of this method, however, is strongly conditioned by the extent of the buyer's own knowledge of the subject. The buyer's knowledge must necessarily tend to be his basic measure of the knowledge of others.[90]

Price.   By definition, if the buyer chooses a *good* agent, he will not be in a position of having to purchase his insurance at unfavorable prices. One of the attributes of a *good* agent as defined here, is that he will place his client's business only in insurers that charge favorable prices. He uses what information is available to avoid high priced companies. To the extent that more meaningful price information becomes available, he will make use of it to protect the interests of his clients.

It is possible to take the many variations among companies and with

---

[89] Robert I. Mehr and Emerson Cammack, *Principles of Insurance, op. cit.,* p. 680.
[90] *Ibid.,* p. 681.

them prove that any one company is better than any other company. The task of choosing a "best company" is so shot full of if's, and's, but's, and other qualifications that even for the expert the task is impossible. Equally impossible, then, is the task for the layman. No man will get lost quicker than the man who sets out to find the best company. A practical objective is to find a good company.

Finding the best life insurance company is like trying to solve a puzzle. It looks easy in the beginning. But an hour later you throw the puzzle out the window and, in exasperation, declare, *"I give up!"* The answer is that unless you find a life insurance agent in whom there is specific and clear-cut reason for you to have confidence, you will pursue your phantom search for the best company until it is too late for protection to do your family any good. The strength of the strongest company, the lowest price of the lowest price company, mean nothing to the widow and family of the man who was so intent on buying insurance in the *best* company that he failed to buy it in *any* company. Most assuredly the costs involved in an attempt to find the best company among those that qualify in products offered, financial strength, services rendered, and prices charged are likely to outweigh the benefits to be derived.

29

The Regulation and
Taxation of Companies

Life insurance is one of the few American business institutions engaged every day in operations that may extend over three centuries. At any given time, life insurance companies may be paying off contracts made in the last century while making contracts that may not be paid off until the next century.

Such long-range operations invite public regulation. Even if the majority of policyholders had confidence in their ability to keep constant watch on developments that affect the business, they might not have that same confidence in the ability of their beneficiaries to do so. Therefore, they seek public regulation.

Furthermore, insurance is a technical business, based on mathematics and statistics. Also, legal phraseology which is incomprehensible to most laymen, and even to some lawyers who are not specialists in the field is used in insurance contracts. Since the buyer of insurance cannot hope to understand the technicalities involved, the judgment of technicians is necessary to watch the business to prevent companies from ill-advised attempts to take advantage of technical language to limit severely the coverage offered in a policy. Technicians also are needed to verify that the companies maintain standards conducive to long-range solvency so that they will be in a position to deliver on their contracts when they mature.

For the usual individual policyholder to hire experts to provide these necessary technical services would be financially impossible even if insurance companies were willing to give the same cooperation to private examiners as they are required to give to state authorities. The natural solution was public supervision in the interest of the individual policyholder. As a result, the institution of insurance in both the United States and Canada is today under the surveillance of a complicated network of governmental—and occasionally political—supervision and control. This regulation is complicated by the dual system of state and federal government authority.

1 THE HISTORY OF REGULATION

While the history of modern insurance begins in England, the history of insurance regulation begins in the United States. Modern supervision of life insurance had its beginnings in the establishment of the insurance department of Massachusetts in 1858. The Massachusetts department, an outgrowth of the lobbying activities of Elizur Wright, was but the first step in his dream of a national insurance bureau or interstate valuation commission.[1]

Elizur Wright.   Elizur Wright, an abolitionist who turned his crusading drive toward life insurance after a visit to England where he attended an auction of existing life insurance policies, was one of the outstanding personalities in the history of life insurance in America.[2]

Since surrender values in a life insurance policy were rare, it was a common practice in England for old people who could no longer pay their premiums to offer their policies for sale.[3] The buyer made himself the beneficiary of the policy and took over the premium obligations in the hope of eventually collecting more from the policy than he had put into it. At auctions where old policies were sold, the insured would "mount the block" to be inspected by prospective buyers who were interested in speculating on how much longer the policyholder would live, and hence how much they should pay for the policy. Usually, the price paid for the policy was only a very small fraction of its actuarial value.

This practice smacked so much of American slave auctions that it aroused the evangelical wrath of Wright. He returned from England later to become a lobbyist in the Massachusetts legislature for laws requiring nonforfeiture values in life insurance policies. Furthermore, Wright was convinced that reserves on whole life policies often were so inadequate that the solvency of the companies was endangered. He wanted a law establishing a state insurance commission that would not only calculate proper policy reserves but also would have the power to enforce these reserve liabilities upon the companies.

Wright calculated a monumental set of net reserve valuation tables which were adopted by Massachusetts in 1850 as a basis for judging the

---

[1] So convinced was Wright of the superiority of federal as contrasted to state supervision that he characterized the court decision in *Paul* v. *Virginia,* holding that insurance was not commerce and hence not subject to interstate regulation, as "a blow to the sound regulation of the business."

[2] Wright was graduated from Yale University in 1826 and soon thereafter became a teacher of mathematics at Western Reserve College. His interest in the antislavery movement led him to abandon teaching in 1833 to go to New York to write for and edit abolitionist journals.

[3] The Institute of Actuaries of Great Britian and Ireland later fostered a law that brought about the end of this practice.

solvency of companies. In 1858 Wright was appointed as one of a two-man board of insurance commissioners.[4] By 1861 he witnessed the passage of his nonforfeiture law by the Massachusetts legislature. While in office as insurance commissioner, Wright started and maintained a registry book in which he listed every single policy issued in the state together with yearly calculations showing what the reserve should be at any point. He kept this registry open to any policyholder. He published financial statements of companies and kept the public informed generally on the state of the insurance business. In his eight years in office, Wright forced 14 companies out of the state on the grounds of dishonest practices. Wright's capacity for irritating legislators, his candor, his constant barrage of questions about profits, expenditures, dividends, salaries, and his life insurance registry—all these and more kept the companies frantic, and irritated all who did not want sound practice and many who did. As a result, he was finally forced from office in 1867; but his labors had for all time made their impression on the course of life insurance in America. His annual reports as commissioner had been carefully studied by insurance men in England as well as in America; and those reports, together with his mathematical computations, laid the foundation for the sound development of life insurance.

Subsequently to the establishment of the Massachusetts department and the adoption of an insurance code in that state, the question of legislative regulation of life insurance came before the British parliament.[5] Investigation revealed to the satisfaction of parliament that, while there were evils in the business,[6] the degree of self-regulation being practiced by the companies was already more strict than anything the parliament of that time would consider imposing by law. It pronounced as demagogic and dangerous any legislative interference with the business. However, in acquiescence to criticism, a law was passed making it mandatory for companies to engage the services of an actuary to investigate their financial condition not less than once every 10 years. The results of such investigations were to be set forth in a report published by the Board of Trade for the information of the public.

Currently, life insurance in the United States is regulated by the individual states. Each state has a department of insurance presided over by either an elected or appointed official.[7] The department has jurisdiction

---

[4] The other member was G. W. Sargent, who was greatly overshadowed by Wright.

[5] As late as 1851, Old Equitable, with 89 years of sound operation behind it, approached parliament for a long-denied charter. It was informed that as an organization it was too ephemeral in nature to be granted the dignity of a charter.

[6] Evils bitingly satirized by Dickens in the "Anglo-Bengalee Disinterested Loan & Life Insurance Co." of *Martin Chuzzlewit*.

[7] Behind the mask of state authority are many faces. In 42 jurisdictions, the head of the insurance department is called commissioner; in 5, he is known as superintendent; in 4, director. One of these is a civil servant; 10 are elected to office; 40 are appointed. Thirty of the appointees serve at the pleasure of the governor; 10 are appointed for a definite term.

over and regulates not only domestic companies but also all foreign and alien companies licensed to do business in that state.[8]

State Regulation.   The pattern of state regulation of the business in the United States had its origin in the evolution of the country's political structure. Originally, the regulatory activities of states in all areas exceeded those of the federal government. However, as early as 1866 a bill was introduced into the U.S. House of Representatives to create a national bureau of insurance in the Treasury Department. The Senate had a similar bill before it in 1868. One year later, the U.S. Supreme Court temporarily put an end to moves designed to bring about federal regulation of insurance. In *Paul* v. *Virginia*[9] it held that "issuing a policy of insurance is not a transaction of commerce" and therefore not subject to the interstate commerce clause of the federal Constitution even when insurance is written across state lines.

The case of *Paul* v. *Virginia* was, interestingly enough, not an attempt of the federal government to regulate insurance but of a fire insurance agent to escape state regulation.[10] The Virginia law required that out-of-state companies be licensed by the state and, as a condition precedent to receiving a license, to deposit a given amount of securities with the state treasurer. Samuel Paul, a native Virginian, was appointed an agent in Virginia for a group of New York companies. He refused to comply with the deposit requirements and was, therefore, refused a license. Upon his continuing to transact business without a license, he was arrested, brought to court, convicted, and fined $50. After the highest court of Virginia upheld the decision, the case was taken to the U.S. Supreme Court on the grounds that the Virginia law violated the constitutional requirement imposed on states to grant the privileges and immunities of state law to citizens of all states, and that since insurance was commerce, state regulation of a foreign insurer was interference with interstate commerce.

On the question of granting citizens of each state the privileges and immunities of citizens in the several states, the court said that this constitutional provision was for the protection of human citizens and not corporate citizens which are creatures of state law only. On the question of the commerce clause, the court decided that issuing a policy of insurance is not a transaction of commerce within the meaning of the Interstate Commerce clause. The court said:

> Issuing a policy of insurance is not a transaction of commerce. The policies are simple contracts of indemnity against loss by fire, entered into between the

---

[8] A domestic company is one organized under the laws of the state in which it is being classified. A foreign company is one organized under the laws of a state other than the one in which it is being classified. An alien company is one organized in a country other than the country of reference. Thus, to a citizen of Illinois, an Indiana company is a foreign company and a Canadian company, an alien company.

[9] 8 Wall, 168 (1869).

[10] Nevertheless, some of those interested in bringing about federal regulation of the insurance business supported Paul in his suit.

corporations and the insured, for consideration paid by the latter. These contracts are not articles of commerce in any proper meaning of the word. They are not subjects of trade or barter offered in the market as something having an existence and value independent of the parties to them. They are not commodities to be shipped or forwarded from one State to another and then put up for sale. They are like other personal contracts between parties which are completed by their signature and the transfer of consideration. Such contracts are not interstate transactions, though the parties may be domiciled in different States. The policies do not take effect—are not executed contracts—until delivered by the agent in Virginia. They are, then, local transactions, and are governed by the local law. They do not constitute a part of the commerce between the States any more than a contract for the purchase and sale of goods in Virginia by a citizen of New York whilst in Virginia would constitute a portion of such commerce.

Hence, the *Paul* v. *Virginia* decision upheld the right of the states to regulate insurance and closed the door on federal regulation for the next 75 years.[11]

Regulation of the business prior to the establishment of the Massachusetts insurance department in 1858 and before the establishment of an insurance department in any given state was through corporate charters containing regulatory provisions. Usually, these provisions related to capital required, investments, and financial reports. Insurance companies were subject to the same type of regulation imposed on all monied corporations.

The incorporation of insurance companies by special act of the legislature was discontinued by a number of states by the middle of the 19th century in view of the formulation of incorporation statutes covering the various classes of insurers. Such legislation usually provided for reports of various kinds, but no special state official was designated to inspect such reports.

The step of selecting a special person or commission to examine insurance company reports, the next development in the history of insurance regulation, was taken by New Hampshire when it established in 1851 an ex officio commission for that purpose. Massachusetts in 1852 became the first state to provide specifically for the supervision of insurance and to appoint officials charged with that supervision. One of the earliest acts of the commissioners of Massachusetts was to establish standards of solvency for life insurance companies.

The Era of Frenzied Finance.   Starting about 1870, the line of cleavage that had always been apparent between companies operated exclusively for the benefit of the operators and those operated with a sense of trusteeship became increasingly wide. Elizur Wright, now 64, began a 15-year battle to get legislation to drive the brigands out of the business.

---

[11] There were several feeble attempts to introduce federal regulation. For example, in 1892 HR 9629 (52d Cong., 1st sess.), a bill for the creation of a federal office of commissioner of insurance was prepared, but failed to reach the floor of the House. There were also a series of additional Supreme Court cases that followed the line of *Paul* v. *Virginia,* cf. footnote 21, this chapter.

A variety of strange new practices came into the life insurance business. Tontine, which had swept France, Holland, England, Ireland, and certain German states a century before, was revived in a modified but, as Wright saw it, equally vicious form. The pristine version of the tontine system, named after Lorenzo Tonti, a neopolitan banker-physician, was introduced first in France to raise funds for the government of Louis XIV in 1689. The plan called for the payment of a single sum of money into a fund by the participating members. A payment equal to 10 percent of the initial fund was distributed each year to the surviving members, the amount going to each participant determined by the age classification to which he had been originally assigned. As the number of survivors became fewer, the value of each survivor's share increased. The last participant died 37 years later, drawing an annual predeath income equal to 245 times the original single contribution. Under this tontine system, the principal did not have to be repaid. The government's obligation ceased upon the death of the final participant.

"Tonti's idea, later carried over into the field of life insurance by the Equitable, was not only to make life insurance popular but to cause a great controversy in the world."[12] Equitable introduced its tontine policies in 1869, calling these plans a method of insuring lives "which has never before been practiced by any life insurance company and which . . . will render life assurance popular to a degree hitherto unknown."[13]

These plans called for substituting deferred dividend payments for annual dividend payments. Policyholders who survived the deferred period and had maintained their policy in force would share the dividends at the end of that period, usually designated as a stipulated period of 10, 15, or 20 years or as a period the length of which was geared to the time it would take for the premiums paid under the policy to equal the face amount of the policy when compounded at an annual interest rate of 10 percent. Under the latter arrangement, the older the policyholder was when he purchased the insurance, the shorter would be the deferred period because the policy would have a higher premium rate per $1,000 insurance. For the same reason, the deferred period would be shorter for endowment policies than for whole life policies issued at the same age. The plans permitted policyholders to select in advance the type of deferred period from the available options.

Also permitted was the advance choice of giving up surrender values in the event of lapse in exchange for the right to share in the forfeitures of

---

[12] R. Carlyle Buley, *The Equitable Life Assurance Society of the United States* (New York: Appleton-Century-Crofts, 1967), p. 18.

[13] *Ibid.*, p. 95, quoted from a sales pamphlet, *Life Insurance As Investment—Tontine— Dividend Life Assurance Policies,* issued by the Equitable in April 1869. The New York Superintendent of Insurance is quoted as follows on the inside cover: "The scheme seems to be so natural and applicable to certain classes of policyholders that like so many important discoveries in science and art, the wonder is how it could have remained so long dormant. . . ."

lapsed policies if good fortune enabled the policyholder to stay alive and keep his policy in force during the deferred period. If the policyholder chose to retain the nonforfeiture value, he was permitted to elect in advance a plan under which his policy was continued for a reduced amount of insurance in event of lapse.

Those policyholders who had lapsed their policies during the deferred period, or the beneficiaries of those who died before the expiration of the deferred period, did not share in the dividend kitty. Hence, the fewer remaining to the end of the tontine period, the bigger the share of each survivor.

The public policy arguments against the tontine system were (1) tontine kitties build up huge sums of money which might tempt companies with a weak sense of ethics to participate in long-shot investment speculations and to engage in extravagances; (2) tontine systems are contrary to insurance in that they make the rich richer and the poor poorer; (3) they promote a seeming rather than true prosperity, are not in the interest of the insured, and do not make for confidence; (4) they promote speculation which produces no socioeconomic gains; (5) they create an inequity of benefits; and (6) they are immoral because they lure policyholders into a lottery.

Tontine was but one of the evils of the business in this period. There was trickery in company management. Other transactions among those companies on the misty side of the cleavage line related to questionable high finance. Loans were made to banks in which insurance company trustees were interested; concealed loans were made to state insurance commissioners; a state commissioner was paid $3,000 to foster a bill to crush the smaller rivals of one large company; lobbying reached such proportions that in one instance $60,000 was paid to a lawyer for "work" at the state capitol in New York—and there being few regulations regarding the accounting practices of companies, the expenditure was carried on the books as taxes. Newspapers were offered (and many accepted) a dollar a line to publish attacks on Elizur Wright, who was constantly goading the companies with prophecies of disaster. Nepotism of the worst order was rampant, and in the 1870's and early 1880's financial buccaneers repeated in America all the most unsavory details of the English bonanza days. Among agents there was widespread rebating, misrepresentation, and twisting. Those companies that stuck to conservative ways and ideals of trusteeship were sneered at, abused, and assailed when they dared speak out, and were forced into setbacks from which they did not recover for years.[14]

In 1880 the trouble that was to result in the Armstrong investigation 25 years later began. The tontine bubble broke. Over 100,000 policyholders had dropped their policies, and thousands bombarded the companies in

---

[14] For a landmark study of life insurance history, see Terence O'Donnell, *History of Life Insurance in Its Formative Years* (Chicago, American Conservation Company, 1936).

person and by mail. Treated to the high-handed dismissal of their complaints, many instituted suits against the companies. They found no redress in law, for in the absence of insurance regulations to the contrary, the courts were forced to hold to the terms of the tontine contracts. Public ill will, a feeling that something ought to be done, faced the companies.

Overextension abroad, questionable financial transactions, and heavy lapsation[15] weakened the position of the companies to the place where what had been easy morality in the annual statements of many companies became serious prestidigitation. Perjury in reports became a "smart trick," a sign of dexterity. A variety of subsidiary financing brought companies into the field of investment banking. In the end, the whole sorry mess in the life insurance business was forced on the reluctant New York legislature by an internal battle for control of one of the major New York companies.

The Armstrong Investigation. On July 20, 1905, the New York legislature, in accordance with a resolution adopted by the respective bodies, established a joint Senate and Assembly committee to investigate the life insurance companies in the state.[16] According to the resolution, the appointment of the committee stemmed from the conclusions in the preliminary reports on a major New York company. These reports indicated that policyholders and their beneficiaries were not being properly safeguarded by existing laws and that a review of the insurance laws of the state was necessary because of the limited power of the superintendent of insurance. The superintendent's powers were limited to examination for solvency, whereas the reports indicated the necessity of investigating the companies more fully. The committee was organized on August 1, 1905, and began public hearings the following September 6. It continued in session consecutively for 57 meetings, closing on December 30, 1905. The committee became known as the Armstrong committee, and hearings were conducted by a brilliant counsel, Charles Evans Hughes, later to be Chief Justice of the United States Supreme Court.

The committee found even more than it had expected. Chicanery, manipulation, unholy alliances, squandering of funds stalk like nightmares through the seven aging volumes of testimony and exhibits known as the *Armstrong Report.*

---

[15] In 1895 the net gain in insurance in force for the year was one eighth of the new business written.

[16] "The committee shall . . . proceed to investigate and examine into the business and affairs of the Life Insurance companies doing business in the State of New York, with reference to the investments of said companies, the relations of the officers thereof to such investments, the relation of such companies to subsidiary corporations, the government and control of such companies, and any other phases of the Life Insurance business deemed by the committee to be proper, for the purpose of drafting and reporting to the next session of the legislature such a revision of the laws relating to Life Insurance in this state as said committee may deem proper." *Concurrent resolution adopted by the Senate and the Assembly of the State of New York, July 20, 1905.*

COMMITTEE FINDINGS.   The Armstrong investigation centered around four phases of the business: regulation, investments, expenses, and dividends, and its findings are summarized as follows:

(1) Regulation.   Directors and trustees were failing to serve as a check on management, their committees acting as "yes men" to officers. Policyholders, who are the theoretical control of mutual companies, actually had no voice in management. The committee recommended that these conditions be corrected.

(2) Investments.   Some companies were doing a banking business through ownership of bank stocks and were guilty of carrying unnecessarily large balances with such banks. Still other companies were selling securities as investment bankers for industrial corporations. Many life insurance companies were holding real estate illegally and constructing extravagant home office buildings. The committee recommended that investment in stock be prohibited and investment banking operations by life insurance companies be discontinued.

(3) Expenses.   The committee found widespread extravagances. They felt that commissions to agents and salaries to officers were too high and that too much money was being spent on lobbying. The committee recommended a limit on acquisition expenses (the amount spent to put new business on the books) and on total expenses, and that lobby expenditures be reported in detail.

(4) Dividends.   The committee opposed deferred dividends (an adaptation of tontine), holding that the system built up huge surpluses that contributed to waste and extravagance. It recommended that annual dividends be required.

RESULT OF THE REPORT.   A committee on Uniform Legislation (the Committee of Fifteen) was appointed by a conference of governors and insurance commissioners in Chicago in 1906 to study methods of strengthening insurance regulations. The New York Insurance Code of 1906, a result of the work of this committee, included about all the recommendations of the Armstrong committee and set the pattern for all state regulation throughout the country.[17] This code, and subsequent amendments— still considered the most exacting among state insurance codes—continues to influence all state codes. It covered the whole gamut of management, officers, directorate, publicity and kindred activities, administration, and investments. For instance, it required an annual statement from each company on elaborate forms; the meeting of specific regulations concerning policy forms and valuations; the adherence to expense limitations; the

---

[17] Not only does the New York code set a regulatory pattern for the country, but also it has an extraterritorial effect, for it requires that any company licensed to do business in the state, whether New York domiciled or not, "substantially comply" with the New York code, especially in matters of acqusition costs and agents' commissions, in its operations in all other states in which it does business.

observance of limits on the amount of new business;[18] the regulation of dividends; the prohibition of stock holdings;[19] limitations on the powers of officers; the insertion of nonforfeiture values and incontestability clauses; and avoidance of practices resulting in nepotism. Every phase of the business, those mentioned and others, was covered by the code resulting from the Armstrong investigation.

Other states amended and strengthened their own codes to take advantage of the lessons taught by the New York investigation and by a number of investigations conducted in other states, resulting in an improved body of state insurance law throughout the country.

The National Association of Insurance Commissioners. Some uniformity in insurance laws has been achieved through the work of the National Association of Insurance Commissioners, to which each insurance commissioner in the United States belongs. This voluntary organization came about through the efforts of the second superintendent of insurance of New York, Hon. George W. Miller. In 1871 he saw the need for uniformity in annual statement reporting, examination practices, and laws, and invited the insurance commissioners of all the states to meet in New York. Out of this meeting came the present National Association of Insurance Commissioners, generally referred to as the NAIC.

Over the years, the NAIC has been welded into a highly constructive force. Although the full organization meets only twice a year, members in the various zones into which it is divided also meet at other times, and its various committees are at work holding hearings and conferences with representatives of industry and the supervisory authorities as often as need requires or circumstances permit. A subject for legislation is given thorough study, with industry representatives encouraged to state their positions either individually or through industry committees. The result is a so-called model bill, which the commissioners are encouraged to present to their respective legislatures for enactment. State legislatures often adopt these bills.

The first broad-scale investigation of the health insurance business was conducted in 1911 by the National Association of Insurance Commissioners. It resulted in the 1912 Standard Provisions law.[20] Significantly, the Standard Provisions law, subsequently enacted in nearly all states, did

---

[18] As explained in Chapter 27, acquisition costs usually exceed the first-year premium plus the establishment of the required first-year reserve. The extra money required is a drain on surplus. The more new business that is written, the greater the drain on surplus. However, on those occasions in the past when any New York company has reached its "quota" of new business prior to the end of the year, its surplus usually has been sufficient for the department to waive the limitation.

[19] Amended in 1928 to allow investment in certain preferred and guaranteed stocks, and in 1951 to allow investment in common stocks to a restricted degree. Amendments in subsequent years have further liberalized the law.

[20] In 1950 the National Association of Insurance Commissioners developed a new model set of required provisions known as the Uniform Individual Accident and Sickness Policy Provisions. All states now either require or permit their use. Cf. Chapter 14.

not restrict the companies from experimenting with new policy forms and coverages. It simply set up the ground rules under which the business should be conducted.

The SEUA Case. *Paul* v. *Virginia* stood for 75 years. It was tested time and time again, most often by insurance companies seeking to escape state regulation.[21] The power of the federal government specifically to regulate insurance was not tested in any of these cases. Then, on November 20, 1942, the South-Eastern Underwriters Association, an organization controlling the rates for fire and allied lines in its territory, was indicted for violation of the Sherman Antitrust Act.

The charge against the SEUA[22] was that it restrained interstate commerce by fixing and enforcing arbitrary and noncompetitive premium rates, controlling agents' commissions, and using coercion, boycott, and intimidation to force nonmember companies into the conspiracy by preventing them from obtaining reinsurance facilities.

Agents who represented nonmember companies were denied the right to represent member companies, and buyers of insurance from nonmember insurers were threatened with boycotts and withdrawal of patronage. The association maintained a staff to police the agencies and companies.

The SEUA relied on the defense that since the Supreme Court had held that insurance was not commerce, the Sherman act did not apply. The district court of Georgia upheld this view, pointing out that if the finding that insurance was not commerce were to be reversed, then the reversal would have to be by the Supreme Court which itself had established the ruling in 1869. The federal government appealed the case to the U.S. Supreme Court.[23]

In a 4–3 decision, two justices excusing themselves from the case, the Court held on June 5, 1944, that when the transaction of insurance business crosses state lines, it is interstate commerce.[24] It explained that the business of insurance included many more operations than the issuing of policies, for it included "transmission of great quantities of money, documents, and communications across dozens of state lines," and these activities had been held in other decisions by the Court to be a part of interstate commerce. Even the three dissenting justices agreed that Congress has the power to regulate insurance. Their dissent was based on the contention that Congress did not intend the Sherman act to apply to insurance companies.

---

[21] See, for example, *Hooper* v. *California,* 155 U.S. 658 (1895); *Noble* v. *Mitchell,* 164 U.S. 367 (1896); *Hopkins* v. *United States,* 171 U.S. 578 (1898); *New York Life* v. *Cravens,* 178 U.S. 389 (1900); *New York Life* v. *Deer Lodge County,* 231 U.S. 495 (1913); *Northwestern Mutual Life Insurance Co.* v. *Wisconsin,* 247 U.S. 132 (1918); *Bothwell* v. *Buckbee Mears Co.,* 275 U.S. 274, 276–77 (1927); *Colgate* v. *Harvey,* 296 U.S. 404, 432 (1935).

[22] Made against about 200 of its member companies and 27 individuals.

[23] Fearing the impact of a reversal on state regulation, 36 states joined in opposing the appeal.

[24] 322 U.S. 533 (1944).

On the same day it handed down the South-Eastern Underwriters decision, the Court held unanimously that a fraternal benefit society is subject to the National Labor Relations Act because it is an insurance company and its operations affect commerce.[25] Had the U.S. Supreme Court in 1869 upheld the right of the state of Virginia to regulate the insurance business on the grounds "that states may regulate interstate affairs so long as they do not improperly burden interstate commerce, and so long as Congress has been silent,"[26] it would have been spared the embarrassment of a reversal after having held steadfastly to an awkward decision for three quarters of a century.

Thus, in two cases decided about the same time, the court changed the ground rules established in *Paul* v. *Virginia* and opened the door to federal regulation. However, it should be pointed out that these decisions did not affect the power of the states to regulate the insurance business but simply nullified those state laws which were contrary to federal regulation.

The McCarran Act.   Because the laws of many states required the use of cooperative rate making organizations in some forms of fire insurance, the immediate regulatory situation was confusing since the SEUA decision made cooperative fixing of rates a combination in restraint of trade. In order for a company to comply with the state law, it had to violate the federal law, and vice versa. The resulting confusion as well as the sweeping implications of the SEUA decision made it obvious that many readjustments would be required. As a result, the McCarran Act[27] was passed by Congress and approved on March 9, 1945.[28] The McCarran Act accomplished three purposes:

1. In order to give the states time to enact the legislation necessary to bring state law into conformity with federal law, a moratorium period was established (originally until January 1, 1948, later extended to June 30, 1948) during which the federal antitrust laws would not apply to the business of insurance except as to boycott, coercion, and intimidation.

2. It established that even after the expiration of the moratorium period, the federal antitrust acts should apply to the insurance business only "to the extent that the business is not regulated by state law."

3. It contained a declaration that the continued regulation and taxation of insurance by the states is in the public interest and that silence on the part of Congress should not be construed as a barrier to state regulation or taxation.

While Congress in the McCarran Act expressly recognized that the continued regulation by the states of the business of insurance was in the public interest, it also took steps to make insurance subject to fair trade laws. This was done by expressly making the federal antitrust laws appli-

---

[25] 322 U.S. 643 (1944).

[26] Cf. annotations to U.S.C.A. Constitution, Art. 1, No. 8, Clause 3, Note 1157.

[27] Public Law 15, 79th Cong., known as the McCarran-Ferguson Act.

[28] The insurance industry had previously sought to have Congress pass a law specifically exempting insurance companies from the federal antitrust acts.

cable to any acts of boycott, coercion, and intimidation. The McCarran Act, however, also made these laws contingently applicable to insurance in all other areas by providing that the Sherman Act, the Clayton Act, and the Federal Trade Commission Act shall be applicable to the business of insurance to the extent that such business is not regulated by state law.

Congressional deference to state regulation in any areas of interstate commerce can be justified only as long as regulation by the states continues to be in the public interest. If it should ever become apparent that this regulation is deficient or otherwise does not best serve the public, Congress stands ready to assume the primary regulatory role. Thus, it is to be expected that Congress, through one of its appropriate committees, will periodically review and assess the quality and overall effectiveness of state regulation of interstate insurance.

During the first decade after the passage of the McCarran Act, the states, under the leadership of the National Association of Insurance Commissioners, enacted laws to strengthen the regulatory role of the various state insurance departments. Since 1945 all states have enacted the Model Unfair Trade Practices Bill for Insurance, or one substantially similar. The Model Bill is the state counterpart of the Federal Trade Commission Act. In general, these laws empower the insurance commissioner to regulate, within the area of his jurisdiction, unfair competition and unfair trade practices in the insurance field, much in the same manner as the Federal Trade Commission regulates these practices in other fields.[29] The states, generally, have also enacted antitrust laws applicable to insurance, including prohibitions against interlocking insurance directorates that would substantially lessen competition. The development of state trade regulatory laws, to parallel closely the Sherman Antitrust Act, the Clayton Act, and the Federal Trade Commission Act, was thought to be necessary under the express provisions of the McCarran Act to eliminate the contingent applicability of these federal statutes.

The Federal Trade Commission's Challenge.   The generally accepted interpretation of the McCarran Act was directly challenged by the Federal Trade Commission in 1954. In that year and during the following year, the Commission issued complaints against 41 insurers, including many life companies, on the ground that the health insurance advertising of these

---

[29] The National Association of Insurance Commissioners has long recommended implementation of these laws, wherever required, by administrative regulation. This self-surveillance of the effectiveness and adequacy of state regulation, through the offices of the NAIC, has resulted in adoption by 31 states of the NAIC Rules Governing Advertising of Accident and Sickness Insurance. This NAIC code serves as a guide for regulation in other states and also served as the pattern for the Trade Practice Rules for Insurance Advertising adopted by the FTC in 1956 and rescinded in 1962.

During this period, 46 states, the District of Columbia, and Puerto Rico enacted the NAIC recommended Unauthorized Insurers Service of Process Law. These statutes permit a policyholder to sue an insurer in the state of the policyholder's residence, even though the insurer has sold the policy through the mails and is not licensed to do business in that state. The law makes the insurance commissioner of the state the agent for the out-of-state insurer.

companies was false or deceptive and, therefore, in violation of the Federal Trade Commission Act.[30] The Commission thus sought to assume general jurisdiction over interstate advertising, despite the existence of state regulatory laws covering this same subject. As expected, the insurers, their trade associations, and the NAIC entered briefs in the litigation to follow, denying the jurisdiction of the FTC.

The Commission's theory was twofold: The first argument was that the state laws could not by reason of the constitutional limitations against extraterritorial regulation effectively regulate advertising beyond its borders, thus leaving a vacuum in the regulation of interstate advertising that could be filled only by the Commission; the second argument was that the states and the Federal Trade Commission have concurrent jurisdiction in this area and that the one which first undertook to regulate, by entry of a cease and desist order, was the one which had ultimate authority.[31]

In 1958 the Supreme Court unanimously rejected these arguments and dismissed the complaints against two companies involved, both of which were agency companies, licensed by each of the states in which they did business.[32] Neither insurer did any mail-order business, and both confined their advertising largely to point of sale literature or brochures shown to the prospect by the local agent at the point of sale. The Court, in denying Commission jurisdiction, reasoned that "there is no question but that the states possess ample means to regulate this advertising within their respective boundaries." The Supreme Court laid down the following criteria for determining the area of Commission jurisdiction over insurance advertising generally:

1. The Commission's jurisdiction is limited to the advertising disseminated within those states (other than an insurer's domiciliary state) which have not enacted a regulatory law of the type contemplated by the McCarran Act. The Model Unfair Trade Practices Act or its equivalent was

<hr/>

[30] The FTC complaint was based on copy used in 1953. The insurers claimed that the criticized copy was no longer being used; that there was no evidence that anyone has been misled or deceived; that only if quoted out of context would the copy have been misleading; that there was no intention to mislead; and that states regulated advertising and, in some cases, had approved specific copy. The FTC alleged that the advertising had misrepresented the coverage offered, the benefits provided, the price charged, the insurability standards required, and the termination provisions of the policy.

[31] The Commission itself was split 3–2 on the matter of its jurisdiction. Two of the commissioners took the position that, pursuant to the mandate of the McCarran Act, the enactment of state legislation in this area denied the Commission jurisdiction insofar as nonmail-order insurance was concerned. The Commission was unanimous, however, in its position that it had jurisdiction over the advertising practices of mail-order companies on the theory that companies doing business by mail did not subject themselves to the jurisdiction of the states in which they solicited business and that the laws of those states could not by reason of due process and other limitations protect their citizens against misrepresentations reaching them through the United States mail (Commission decision of December 20, 1956, in *Matter of Travelers Health Assn.* v. *FTC*, Docket 6252; subsequently approved by the Supreme Court, 362 U.S. 293 [1960]).

[32] *FTC* v. *National Casualty Co.* and *FTC* v. *American Life Ins. Co.*, 357 U.S. 560, (1958).

specifically found to be such a law. The Court also found that each of the then 48 states had enacted the requisite laws so, that in the cases before it, no jurisdictional gaps remained and the Commission had no jurisdiction.

2. Even though a state may have enacted such a law, the Commission has jurisdiction over the advertising disseminated within the borders of such state if there are any constitutional (due process) limitations on the state's authority to regulate such advertising.

Although the Commission immediately conceded that this decision ended its jurisdiction over companies that advertised locally in states in which they were licensed, or advertised only in the form of point of sale material used by its agents, it continued to assert jurisdiction over mail-order companies and, for a while, over nonmail-order companies which advertised in the so-called mass media, such as radio, television, and national magazines. The theory was that in these instances there were due process limitations on the states' authority which rendered the state laws ineffective, thus making applicable the standby authority of the Commission.

REGULATION OF MAIL-ORDER INSURERS. The Commission's assertion of jurisdiction over the mail-order companies was challenged by Travelers Health Association. The Eighth Circuit Court ruled that the FTC had no jurisdiction, but the U.S. Supreme Court reversed the Eighth Circuit and remanded the case for further proceedings.[33]

The basis of the circuit court's holding was that the statutes of the insurer's home state (Nebraska) provided adequate regulation over the insurer's advertising practice to relieve the FTC of jurisdiction. A Nebraska statute expressly prohibits a domestic insurer from engaging "there or elsewhere" in any unfair or deceptive act or practice in the conduct of the business of insurance. The U.S. Supreme Court, rendering a six to three decision, reasoned as follows:

We are asked to hold that the McCarran-Ferguson Act operates to oust the Commission of jurisdiction by reason of a single state's attempted regulation of its domiciliary's extraterritorial activities. But we cannot believe that this kind of law of a single State takes from the residents of every other state the protection of the Federal Trade Commission Act. In our opinion the State regulation which Congress provided should operate to displace this federal law means regulation by the State in which the deception is practiced and has its impact.[34]

The U.S. Supreme Court did not consider the effect of regulation by states other than Nebraska because the circuit court had not considered

---

[33] *Travelers Health Assn.* v. *FTC,* 362 U.S. 293 (1960), reversing 262 Fed. (2d) 241 (1959). The Travelers, a Nebraska mail-order health insurance company, solicits in all states. It is licensed only in its home state of Nebraska and in Virginia.

[34] *Ibid.,* pp. 298–99. The slightly awkward wording in the last sentence of the quoted passage means that the U.S. Supreme Court believed that Congress did not intend for the McCarran Act to deny the protection available under the Federal Trade Commission Act to citizens in other states simply because the statute of an insurer's domiciliary state is worded to apply to domestic insurers' operations everywhere.

this question. However, the question was considered by the circuit court when it received the case on remand. Its unanimous opinion was that "the ultimate compulsiveness which would be necessary to enable the state to achieve control" would be absent even though the commissioner in such a state could issue a cease and desist order or an injunction on his own motion.

To the extent . . . that a state . . . must depend on any provisions, instrumentalities or processes of another state, we believe that its situation cannot, within the McCarran-Ferguson Act, be held to be 'regulated by state law.' The state must itself be legally able to do, through its own provisions, instrumentalities and processes, everything that is necessary to the effecting of control as to its situation.[35]

Thus, the FTC has jurisdiction over unauthorized mail-order insurers with respect to unfair trade practices by virtue of its power to initiate cease and desist proceedings or investigatory action.

Procedure for Handling Complaints. The FTC, working with the NAIC, developed a procedure for handling complaints involving unfair trade practices. When the FTC assumes that it has jurisdiction over a complaint, it will initiate proceedings and notify both the NAIC and the insurance commissioner in the home state of the alleged aggrieving insurer. If the FTC has no jurisdiction, it will send the complaint to the insurance commissioner of the state where the aggrieved party resides, with copies to the insurance commissioner of the state where the insurer is domiciled as well as to the NAIC. When an insurance commissioner receives a complaint he refers it to the insurance commissioner of the insurer's domiciliary state. The FTC and the NAIC are notified if that commissioner fails to take action, so that these bodies can take whatever action the complaint merits. However, the NAIC through a survey conducted in 1966 found this procedure to be ineffective.[36]

After losing the *National Casualty* and *American Hospital* cases, the FTC in 1962 withdrew its 1956 trade practice rules on health insurance advertising and in 1964 issued its "Guides for the Mail-Order Insurance Industry" to apply to companies selling insurance through the mail in states in which they are not licensed or, if licensed, do not sell through local agents.[37]

---

[35] *Travelers Health Association* v. *FTC*, 298 Fed. (2d) 820 (8th Cir. 1962).

[36] The survey revealed that complaints about deceptive advertising by unauthorized mail-order insurers had been received in 46 states, but in only 36 of them were the complaints forwarded, and in only 19 of these was the level of cooperation good. In only one state had any complaint been sent to the FTC. The procedure for handling complaints involving unauthorized mail-order insurers was found by only 4 states to be effective; 18 states found the procedure ineffective; and 15 states found the procedure to have only limited effectiveness. No opinion was expressed in 14 states.

[37] Fourteen guides designed to curb deception of health insurance buyers were issued. These guides deal with advertisements of types of losses covered; benefits payable, premium charged, and underwriting requirements; disclosure of policy provisions relating to renewability, cancellability, and termination; the use of testimonials, statistics, and statements

Mass Media Theory. The other theory—namely, that Commission jurisdiction over an insurance company depends upon the media of its advertising rather than the absence of a state's in personam jurisdiction over the company—was quickly rejected by the Commission itself.[38] The mass media theory had been advanced by Commission counsel on appeals taken by them to the Commission from recommended dismissals for lack of jurisdiction by the Commission's own hearing examiners. This rejection by a unanimous Commission of the so-called mass media theory means that the Commission's jurisdiction in this area is confined to the case of the nonadmitted mail-order insurer.

The Securities and Exchange Commission's Challenge. The FTC was not the only federal agency during this period to seek a measure of jurisdiction over insurance. In 1956 the Securities and Exchange Commission brought an action against the Variable Annuity Life Insurance Company of America (VALIC) and the Equitable Annuity Life Insurance Company (EALIC) to compel those companies to register their variable annuities with the SEC pursuant to the Securities Act of 1933. These companies had been organized in 1955 and 1956 in the District of Columbia as stock life insurance companies and were licensed there and in several other states under the insurance laws pertaining to life insurance companies. Their principal function is a special one: to sell variable life annuities.[39]

Since annuities and other insurance contracts are specifically exempt from SEC jurisdiction by the federal Securities Act of 1933 and the Investment Company Act of 1940, the principal question involved in this litigation was whether the variable annuity in the form offered by these companies is an insurance function within the meaning of these federal statutes, or whether it is a security transaction similar to that offered by a mutual fund.

The Supreme Court, in a 5–4 decision, reversed the federal district court and the Court of Appeals and held that the variable annuity as of-

---

about the insurer; statements about competitors; clarification of the identity of the insurer; misleading statements about special offers, special group rates and underwriting, and endorsements by third parties; statements about the insurer's service facilities; and advertisements in general. "Advertisements shall be truthful and not misleading in fact or in implication. Words or phrases the meaning of which is clear only by implication or by familiarity with insurance terminology shall not be used."

38 In the *Matter of Mutual Life Insurance Co. of New York,* Docket 6450 (Final Order of March 4, 1959). This rejection was foreshadowed by the Supreme Court decision in *National Casualty,* above, since the state where the advertising is read, whether that advertising be in a newspaper, magazine, or agent's brochure, would clearly appear to have constitutional authority to enforce its laws against a company over which it has in personam jurisdiction. See *Wilburn Boat Co.* v. *Fireman's Fund Ins. Co.,* 348 U.S. 310 (1954); *Prudential Ins. Co.* v. *Benjamin,* 328 U.S. 408 (1946); *Robertson* v. *California,* 328 U.S. 440 (1946); *Osborn* v. *Ozlin,* 310 U.S. 53 (1940); *International Shoe Co.* v. *Washington,* 326 U.S. 310 (1945).

39 Variable annuities are discussed in Chapter 6. Both insurers also offered, as ancillary and secondary features to the variable annuity, decreasing term life insurance on a short-term basis. This decreasing term life insurance was not involved in the SEC litigation.

fered by VALIC and EALIC was a security and not insurance within the meaning of the insurance exemptions of the Securities Act of 1933 and the Investment Company Act of 1940.[40] This decision made it clear that insurers writing variable annuity contracts would be subject to dual regulation by the SEC and the state insurance departments.

Although the Supreme Court recognized that the variable annuity clearly involves life contingencies, namely, the liquidation of the annuity consideration and the income thereon exactly over the span of life, the majority of the bench felt that, in the case before it, the absence of any guarantee that at least some fraction of the benefits will be payable in fixed dollar amounts rendered the insurance element largely superficial.[41]

A belief prevailed among interested (and optimistic) insurers that a variation of the contract involved in the VALIC case, namely, one in which the company underwrites a substantial part of the investment risk, may lead to a different result. This view was encouraged by the Court's recognition of life insurance as "an evolving institution," as well as the Court's assurance that it "would not undertake to freeze the concepts of 'insurance' or 'annuity' into the mold they fitted when the Federal Acts[42] were passed."

But when the United Benefit Life Insurance Company of Omaha introduced its flexible fund annuity in 1962 it found that this view was no more than wishful thinking. Under the flexible fund annuity, the periodic premiums paid would be placed in a separate account to be invested principally in equities. The annuity income would be paid out as a fixed dollar annuity. If the contract holder died before retirement or if he surrenders the contract after 10 years, a sum equal to at least all premiums paid would be refunded. If the surrender occurred before the expiration of 10 years, the minimum guaranteed refund would be 50 percent if the surrender occurred after the first year, with an additional 5 percent each year that the surrender is delayed until reaching 100 percent in 10 years.

The SEC claimed that the flexible fund annuity also was a security. Five

---

[40] SEC v. Variable Annuity Life Ins. Co., et al., 359 U.S. 65; 3 L.Ed. (2d) 640.

[41] Justice Douglas, a former SEC chairman, in speaking for the majority, said (p. 71): ". . . we conclude that the concept of 'insurance' involves some investment risk-taking on the part of the company . . . in common understanding 'insurance' involves a guarantee that at least some fraction of the benefits will be payable in fixed amounts."

Justice Brennan's concurring opinion, joined by Mr. Stewart, acknowledged that while these contracts "patently contain a significant annuity feature," "administering them also involves a very substantial and in fact predominant element of the business of an investment company and that in a way totally foreign to the business of a traditional life insurance and annuity company, as traditionally regulated by state law." He then proceeded to view the question from the point of view of the purpose of the insurance exemptions in the two federal statutes. He concluded that, while Congress clearly did not consider the disclosure and other purposes of the Securities Act as relevant or meaningful in so far as traditional insurance and annuity concepts are concerned, it did not intend for this exemption to be extended to this new form of contract which, although labeled annuity, placed so much emphasis on the changing state of the insurer's investment portfolio.

[42] The Securities Act of 1933 and the Investment Company Act of 1940.

years later (1967) the issue reached the U.S. Supreme Court, which ruled in favor of the SEC. The only question to be decided, said the Court, was whether the insurer or the separate account should be required to register as an investment company and remanded the case[43] to the circuit court for a decision on this issue. At this point, United Benefit decided not to continue the litigation and so the flexible fund annuity never left the drawing board.

Thus, it has been firmly established that insurers issuing variable annuities are subject to federal regulation through the SEC: the variable annuity is regulated as a security; the separate account is regulated as an open-end investment company; and the sales organization marketing variable annuities is regulated as a securities broker-dealer.[44]

SPECIAL EXEMPTIONS. The SEC ruled that insurers writing variable annuities but predominantly engaged in insurance operations would be exempt from the Investment Company Act of 1940, but that their separate account used to fund variable annuities would be considered an investment company and subject to federal regulation.[45]

Believing that certain group pension buyers did not need the protection offered under the Investment Company Act of 1940 and the Securities Act of 1933, the SEC agreed to exempt equity funded group annuities from these acts if they were written to fund a plan qualifying under Section 401 of the Internal Revenue Code, covered at least 25 employees when the contract became effective, and restricted the fund to employer contributions only.[46]

Also exempt from the Investment Company Act of 1940 are separate accounts used to fund annuities for self-employed persons and their employees issued under the Keogh Act.[47] However, the exemption does not apply to the Securities Act of 1933. Variable annuities issued under these plans must be registered as securities and a prospectus issued.

---

[43] SEC v. United Benefit Life Insurance Company, 387 U.S. 202, 87 S. Ct. 1557 (1967).

[44] The federal acts involved in the regulation of the variable annuity are the Securities Act of 1933, the Securities Exchange Act of 1934, and the Investment Company Act of 1940. The purposes of these acts are to protect the purchasers of securities by requiring (1) the disclosure of information to the buyers of securities essential for informed decisions, (2) the maintenance of an equitable and honest securities market, (3) that persons associated with the securities business demonstrate knowledge of the business by passing an examination, and (4) that certain ground rules relating to maximum sales charges, distribution of financial reports, and the management of funds be observed.

[45] The SEC was upheld in this ruling by the Third Circuit Court of Appeals. Prudential Insurance Company of America v. SEC, 326 Fed. (2d) 383 (1964). The U.S. Supreme Court refused to hear the case.

[46] Originally, to be exempt the plan had to include a provision for guaranteed future issue of fixed dollar annuities to employees on or after their retirement but this restriction was eliminated one year later (1964). For equity funded group annuity contracts to be exempt from the Securities Act of 1933, in addition to the foregoing restrictions, the plan must result from separate negotiations between the insurer and employer, and the insurer's written advertisements about such plans must be restricted to the name of the insurer, the fact that it writes equity funded plans, and the fact that it invites inquiries.

[47] Self-Employed Individuals Tax Retirement Act, P.L. 87-792. The Keogh Act is discussed in Chapter 17.

Congressional Investigation of State Regulation.   The year 1958 saw the beginning of what may be expected to be periodic congressional appraisals of the regulatory stewardship of the states. An investigation by the Subcommittee on Antitrust and Monopoly of the U.S. Senate Committee on the Judiciary was launched to determine "whether the states have faithfully honored the mandate of the McCarran-Ferguson Act . . . by regulating the insurance industry in the public interest."[48] The subcommittee was not pleased with its findings. It charged that the administrative capacity of many insurance departments is inadequate, and control over many insurance operations is lax and ineffectual. Also, in numerous instances, the subcommittee found state insurance statutes to be too weak to guarantee effective regulation. The subcommittee made 20 recommendations in 20 areas for improving various aspects of state regulation and expressed hope "that these suggestions will not be . . . ignored by the states. It remains to be seen how long such a regulatory structure can stand without substantial improvement in substance and administration."[49]

The subcommittee did not recommend any immediate changes in the McCarran Act. However, it did suggest the possible need of amendments in the future, if, after the states are given further opportunity to improve their systems of regulation, it is conclusively shown that neither the states nor the federal government can prevent or reach abusive practices which otherwise would be construed as violation of the antitrust laws.

Regulation of Private Pension Plans.   In 1958 Congress enacted legislation affecting employee pension and welfare plans. After more than four years of investigation into alleged abuses in both self-administered, including trusteed, plans and those provided by group insurance, Congress passed the Welfare and Pension Plans Disclosure Act amended in 1962. Its purpose is to compel disclosure and reporting of the various details of employee benefit plans providing retirement income, hospital or medical care, disability income, survivorship payments, or unemployment income and covering more than 25 employees.[50] For plans covering 100 or more persons, subsequent filing of detailed annual reports is required.[51] In addition to coverage details, such items as commissions, the persons to whom they are payable, and fees for the installation and administration of the plans are required to be made matters of public record. It also required disclosure of employer and employee contributions, claims, and dividends paid. Its purpose is to compel disclosure of such abuses as mismanagement

---

[48] *The Insurance Industry,* "Aviation, Ocean Marine, and State Regulation" (Report of the Subcommittee on Antitrust and Monopoly, 86th Cong., 1960), p. 2.

[49] *Ibid.,* p. 247.

[50] The employer must be "engaged in (interstate) commerce or in any industry or activity affecting commerce." Or if a union has established the plan, the union must represent "employees engaged in commerce or in any industry affecting commerce."

[51] If the Secretary of Labor upon investigation finds that annual reports should be filed in order to satisfy the Act's purpose, a plan covering less than 100 participants may be required to file them.

of investments or unsound actuarial assumptions in self-administered plans,[52] kickbacks, excessive service fees, switching, contingency commissions,[53] and other drains on the funds available for employees' benefits. The act provides that any person who offers, solicits, or receives any fee, kickback, gift, commission, loan, money, or thing of value to influence the administration of the plan or investment of its funds shall be subject to a fine of $10,000 or three years in prison or both. A fine of $10,000 or five years in prison or both is provided for anyone convicted of embezzlement or theft of a plan's assets. The same penalty is provided for anyone who fraudulently conceals any facts or misrepresents facts that the law requires be revealed. The abuses that were uncovered by the Senate and House investigatory committees were for the most part confined to union-employer, self-administered plans, although some segments of the insurance industry were not wholly blameless.[54]

Six states have passed special legislation to regulate employee benefit plans: Washington, Wisconsin, California, Massachusetts, Connecticut, and New York. The state laws at this time are neither a uniform nor complete answer to the problem.[55]

REAPPRAISAL OF PENSION REGULATION. In his 1962 Economic Report, President Kennedy suggested that legislation governing private pension plans be reappraised, and a reappraisal is now taking place. The reappraisal continues with the objective of determining the answers to a number of questions. Should the federal standards relating to vesting and funding of qualified pension plans be raised; should a federal program of reinsurance for private pension plans be instituted; should there be arrangements developed for portability of private pension plans; and should

---

[52] This danger is particularly acute in self-administered pension plans where large reserves are accumulated for investment and where payments are deferred for several years. Mistakes may not be uncovered until it is too late to correct them. Isaacson, "Employee Welfare and Pension Plans: Regulation and Protection of Employee Rights," 59 *Col.* L.R. 96–124, at 101.

[53] Contingency commissions are those which are paid by an insurer to an administering broker if the claims experience of his policy is good. Since the policyholder may be ignorant of this arrangement, and since it is the broker who processes the claims, the (Senator) Douglas subcommittee characterized this as "a built-in incentive" to limit the number of successful claims and thereby deny benefits to the participants in whose behalf the insurance had been issued. 59 *Col.* L.R. 96, above, 103.

[54] The group insurance industry as a whole, however, is not permeated by such practices. The Douglas subcommittee found that most of the industry was operated "in an efficient manner and in accordance with high standards." 59 *Col.* L.R. 96, above, at p. 104. Cf. also the (Senator) Kennedy Report (S. 2888) pp. 10–11:

"While it should be stressed that from all the evidence the great percentage of these plans is honestly administered and that great credit is due to the vast numbers of employers, union officials, administrators, insurance and banking institutions, consultants, actuaries, and others who have been responsible for the impressive record made by this private social-security system, numerous instances of abuses and deficiencies have been uncovered which drain off countless millions of dollars from their intended purposes and in other ways deprive the employee beneficiaries of these plans of what rightfully belongs to them."

[55] The NAIC Welfare and Pension Funds Blanks Subcommittee succeeded in 1958 in getting agreement among its members on uniform blanks for annual statements and reports to be used by all regulating states.

the federal regulatory authority over the administration of private pension plans be extended?

Recommendations for regulatory changes are embodied in the Report of the President's Committee on Corporate Pension Funds and Other Welfare Programs;[56] the report of the Inter-Agency Staff Committee;[57] a Pension and Employee Benefit bill first introduced in the U.S. Senate in 1967 by Senator Javits, the then ranking minority member of the Senate Committee on Labor and Public Welfare; a pension reinsurance bill first introduced in 1964 and again in 1967 by Senator Hartke;[58] and a set of proposed amendments to the 1958 Welfare and Pension Plans Disclosure Act introduced by Senator Yarborough in 1967.[59] In March of 1970, President Nixon sent to Congress recommendations to tighten the fiduciary responsibilities of pension plan administrators and to broaden the disclosure requirements of the Welfare and Pension Plans Disclosure Act. His recommendations call for increasing the investigatory and enforcement powers of the Secretary of Labor.

A number of hearings on the problems of private pension plans have been conducted by various committees of Congress. The U.S. Senate Subcommittee on Employment and Retirement Income of the Special Committee on Aging held hearings in 1965 to look into the possibilities of encouraging and stimulating the expansion of private pension coverage. Two sets of hearings were conducted in 1966. The Subcommittee on Fiscal Policy of the Joint Economic Committee of the Congress conducted hearings in April and May on private pension plans and subsequently issued a staff document, *Old Age Income Assurance: An Outline of Issues and Alternatives,* which proved to be provocative enough to "elicit statements of positions from various experts and interested parties."[60] In August, hearings were held on the proposal for a pension reinsurance program. Those hearings were conducted by the Senate Committee on Finance. In 1970, the 91st Congress, just as the 90th Congress, had under consideration bills to stiffen funding and vesting requirements for qualified pension plans and for a scheme to provide insurance against the termination

---

[56] *Public Policy and Private Pension Programs, op. cit.* The Committee was appointed by President Kennedy but made its report in 1965 to President Johnson. The report is often referred to as the Cabinet Committee Report.

[57] The Inter-Agency Staff Committee is a committee representative of federal departments and agencies interested in pension legislation. It was reactivated in 1966 to review and comment on the President's Committee report.

[58] The reinsurance proposal would require private pension plans to participate in a reinsurance program to be administered by the Department of Health, Education, and Welfare.

[59] The Yarborough bill would implement the pension and welfare plan recommendations made by President Johnson in his Message on Consumer Protection submitted February 16, 1967, to Congress. The bill sets up criteria for the fiduciary responsibility of persons handling pension funds, establishes civil liability for failure to perform fiduciary duties, places limits on the investment of pension funds in the employer's business, and broadens the disclosure requirements of the Welfare and Pension Plans Disclosure Act.

[60] In January, 1968, three volumes of a compendium of the elicited statements were published.

of private pension plans. "The private pension debate has yet to reach the point of serious Congressional consideration. . . . Legislative observers believe that . . . the debate on the more basic issues is likely to continue for a number of years."[61]

2. STATE VERSUS FEDERAL REGULATION

State regulation of the business of insurance has been put on probation and those who advocate its survival have been put on the defensive. The NAIC's Committee on the Preservation of State Regulation is seeking to meet the challenge. In a comprehensive statement submitted to the U.S. Senate Subcommittee on Antitrust and Monopoly, the NAIC Committee concluded: "There is no doubt that problems exist, and there is equally no doubt that state supervision is coping and will continue to cope with them."[62] Those who favor state supervision over federal supervision hope that these are not the words of a dying institution and seem willing to make an effort to bring about the changes in state regulatory systems necessary to appease those who seek federal control.

Arguments for Federal Regulation.   That there is much to be criticized in the system of individual state regulation is not to be denied. Chief complaints against it have been:

1. Lack of uniformity among insurance codes and conflicts in rulings creating innumerable complications for companies operating in more than one state. For example, an insurer may have difficulty in obtaining approval of a new policy form in all states in which it operates. One state may forbid a clause that another state requires.

2. The additional expense involved in filing financial reports in different states and the cost of maintaining 51 separate insurance departments.

3. Ill-advised legislation proposed and even passed in various states where legislators presumably are not able to devote as many resources to the study of legislation as are those who occupy seats in the U.S. Congress.

4. The political nature of the appointment or election of insurance commissioners, which too often has produced commissioners who have few qualifications for the job and who are subject to local pressures.

5. Conflict with federal regulations and rulings which, while not aimed exclusively at the insurance business, do affect its operations and transactions.

6. Lack of insurer flexibility because of the rigidity imposed by the necessity of meeting the requirements of several states.

7. The business is national in scope. The fact that the vast majority of companies operate in more than one state would seem to call for national

---

[61] *The Debate on Private Pensions* (Washington, D.C.: American Enterprise for Public Policy Research, 1968), p. 1.

[62] *The Insurance Industry, op. cit.*, pp. 4839–4979.

regulation, especially since it is so difficult and many times impossible for states to solve regulatory problems involving out-of-state insurers.

Arguments for State Regulation.   On the other hand, arguments have been advanced for the system of state control:

1. State regulation is better able to give special consideration to local conditions where such consideration is needed.

2. Federal regulation, which would involve a much larger department than required by any single state, would tend to become cumbersome, rigid, arbitrary, and involved in red tape.

3. State regulation is closer to the individual citizen and hence more subject to his observation and control.

4. Conflicts in state law and practices are steadily being reduced by the activities of the National Association of Insurance Commissioners so that today the complications resulting from company operations in several states have been minimized and are less annoying to the companies.

5. The effects of ill-advised insurance legislation are localized rather than national in scope.

6. Federal control would become a great leveling factor in insurance regulation, with the effect of weakening the supervision in those states such as New York, where both the code and its administration are strong.

Attitude of the Industry.   The thinking of the industry itself has not consistently been on the same side of the question of state versus federal control. As previously pointed out, Elizur Wright was a staunch advocate of federal regulation, and most of the cases testing *Paul* v. *Virginia* were attempts by members of the industry to have insurance declared commerce and hence not subject to state regulation. Many writers in the field, even well into the 1930's, indicated belief in federal as opposed to state control.[63] Some have since changed their stand. Moreover, among company executives throughout history, there has been a difference of opinion as to the desirability of federal regulation of insurance. As state legislation became more bothersome, federal regulation gained more and more support. The greatest drives for federal regulation were made during the years immediately preceding the *Paul* v. *Virginia* case. The most opposition to these drives seems to have stemmed from the insurance commissioners of the states. The large companies in the East seem to have favored federal control, whereas the small companies in the South and West seem to have favored state control. Throughout the history of insurance in America, the question of federal supervision of insurance has come up time and time again in the form of proposed congressional measures, suggested constitutional amendments,

---

[63] Cf., for examples, S. S. Huebner, *Life Insurance* (New York: D. Appleton & Co. [now Appleton-Century-Crofts, Inc.], 1915), pp. 364 f.; J. B. Maclean, *Life Insurance* (New York: McGraw-Hill Book Co., 1932), p. 393; C. K. Knight, *Advanced Life Insurance* (New York: John Wiley & Sons, Inc., 1926), p. 26; J. H. Magee, *Life Insurance* (Chicago: Business Publications, Inc. [now Richard D. Irwin, Inc.], 1939), p. 604.

institutional resolutions, and public statements by company executives. Those who opposed the move have always won.[64]

Whether state regulation will survive depends in part on whether "state regulation . . . will maintain a reputation for objectiveness, a capacity for self-criticism, and a receptiveness toward new ideas and concepts,"[65] and in part on the political thinking in the country toward the federal regulation of an industry that is basically national in scope, at the expense of a further sacrifice of states' rights.

3. CHANNELS OF REGULATION

Three channels of regulation of the insurance business are: judicial, legislative, and administrative. In addition, insurers are subject to some degree of self-regulation.

Judicial Regulation. In the American form of government, it is the function of the legislative branch to pass laws, the administrative branch to carry out their provisions, and the judicial branch to interpret legislation when its application to any particular situation is not clear. Consequently, the law of the land originally stemmed from two sources: the legislative bodies and the courts—legislative law and judicial or case law.

The insurance industry is subject to both types of law. For instance, should the court be called upon to rule regarding the powers or the limitations of the power of the insurance commissioner, that decision, at least until overruled, becomes a part of the body of insurance regulation. The same is true when the court decides on the interpretation of a policy contract, the constitutionality or unconstitutionality of insurance legislation, the liability of an insurer, and in all the host of decisions which may be handed down in the cases of litigation directly or indirectly affecting the insurance business.

Legislative Regulation. Another branch of government to have a hand in insurance regulation is the legislative, and this includes the legislatures and assemblies of the 50 states, and the Congress of the United States. Each state has a large body of law—usually referred to as the insurance code—directly pertaining to the operation, administration, and investments of the various companies domiciled or licensed within the state.

Drafting of legislation in the various states has not been left solely in the hands of the legislators. Interested individuals and groups offer proposed bills that they seek to have sponsored by some legislator who will introduce

---

[64] For an interesting discussion of the history of attitudes toward federal regulation of insurance, see R. Carlyle Buley, *A Study in the History of Life Insurance, op. cit.*, selections (see Index). President Theodore Roosevelt exerted strong pressure for federal regulation. History shows companies were lines up on both sides of the fence. Two U.S. senators who were also presidents of life insurance companies were on opposing sides of the issue. Senator Dryden, who was president of Prudential, favored federal control, whereas Senator Bulkeley, president of Aetna, opposed it.

[65] Arthur C. Mertz, *The First Twenty Years* (Chicago: National Association of Independent Insurers, 1965), p. 69.

them for possible passage by the legislature. New legislation or amendments to the insurance code are sponsored by the insurance companies themselves, either directly or through associations, and by the various insurance commissioners. When the state insurance commissioner is considering the sponsorship of legislation hearings are usually held at which interested parties such as the companies, company associations, and agents, as well as the general public, may express their views or make recommendations.

Legislation is also introduced at times by labor unions or other organized lay groups. One of the most bothersome sources of new legislative proposals is "spite bills" introduced by legislators who either have a grudge against insurance companies resulting from some personal experience or who are urged to "do something" by a constituent who has had a bad experience with an insurer.

As a general rule, state legislative bodies lean heavily on the insurance department both for the sponsorship of any needed legislation and for approval or disapproval of proposed legislation. The National Association of Insurance Commissioners is a source of proposed "model" legislation.

Administrative Regulation.   Administrative regulation of the insurance industry is accomplished in the various states by an official or department specifically appointed to oversee the carrying out of the provisions of the law. The official is known as the commissioner, superintendent, or director of insurance and his department, as the department of insurance. (Whatever his official title, he is generally referred to as commissioner.)

The operations of insurance commissioners are an early American example of what is now known as administrative law. Today this type of law has become identified with a multiplicity of agencies concerned with regulation of economic activity. Prominent examples include the activities of the Interstate Commerce Commission, the National Labor Relations Board, state utilities commissions, the Securities and Exchange Commission, and many others. Administrative law evolved out of the necessity for both flexibility and technical understanding inherently impossible in either the normal legislative or judicial processes.

The essence of administrative law has been the granting of authority by the legislative branch to an administrative agency which both makes and enforces rules within the limits of the initial grant and is subject to judicial review. For example, as noted in Chapter 26, insurance commissioners are given the power to establish rules for the valuation of insurance companies' assets. For another example, the commissioner is given the power to revoke an insurer's license whenever in his judgment such action "will best promote the interests of the people of this state. . . ." The insurance commissioners in some states have the power to levy fines after a formal hearing of the charges. In making decisions, the commissioner is setting up rules of conduct; i.e., creating administrative law. Such rules must always lie within the general scope of powers granted by the legislature to the administrator, and the courts stand ready to see that these powers are not exceeded and that neither wilfulness nor arbitrariness appears in their application.[66]

An insurance commissioner combines the functions of an official clerk, judge, legislator, and often prosecutor, judge, and jury. Partly judicial, partly legislative, and partly administrative, he is not confined within any of these areas.

The powers of a commissioner are broad and discretionary. By direct or indirect means he can bring about compliance with nearly any rule he promulgates. In fact, the powers of a state commissioner may even be extraterritorial. For instance, no company has successfully challenged the right of the New York department to require "substantial compliance" with New York law in all other states in which a company operates as a condition of licensing in New York. Thus, a company domiciled in Connecticut, for example, and admitted to do business in New York must observe the maximum commission allowances set by New York in every state in which it operates. This is one reason why some very large insurers choose not to operate in New York.

Self-Regulation. Insurers are faced with restraints imposed on the business from within the industry both through individual company conscience and through group pressure exerted through trade associations. Self-regulation was the first type of insurance regulation in America and is the predominant type in Great Britain.

A sense of trusteeship in the insurance business acts as what might be called the "individual company conscience." The cynic will say that good behavior is a result of necessity, that the business is under such intense public scrutiny in all phases of its operation that it is "the better part of valor" to act in the public interest. However, the source of such operating philosophy matters little.

Through trade associations, business conscience becomes even more important as a foundation for self-regulation. Many associations serve to regulate the business through "codes of ethics" and similar statements and agreements adopted by them. For instance, in 1950 the National Association of Insurance Commissioners took action to approve and adopt a Statement of Principles for Personal Accident & Health Insurance drawn up by an industry committee. It includes principles for the construction of policy forms; principles applying to policy provisions and their uses, particularly exclusions, qualifying and waiting periods, and disability definitions; and principles applying to advertising and soliciting materials. As

---

[66] Some judicial authorities are seriously concerned by the increased reliance on administrative law. One judge in writing a court opinion said: "Concern with the problem of merger of the powers of prosecutor and judge in the same agency springs from the fear that the agency official adjudicating upon private rights cannot wholly free himself from the influences toward partiality inherent in his identification with the prosecuting aspects of the case . . . in a sense the combination of functions violate the ancient tenet of Anglo-American justice that 'No man shall be a judge in his own cause.' " (*In re* Larsen, 86A2D 430, 436.)

another example, in 1954, prior to the release of the FTC complaints, members of both of the then-existing health insurance associations adopted voluntary codes of advertising standards for individual health policies and required members to agree to the codes as a condition of membership. The Code of Ethical Practices with Respect to the Insuring of the Benefits of Union or Union-Management Welfare and Pension Funds was adopted by the NAIC in 1957 and is adhered to voluntarily by many companies.

As further self-regulation, agents' associations such as the National Association of Life Underwriters, the American Society of Chartered Life Underwriters, and the International Association of Health Underwriters have codes of ethics for their members. However, unfortunately as in other business and professional groups, some members of these associations fail to take the codes seriously enough.

4. WHAT IS REGULATED?

A list of duties or powers of an insurance commissioner constitutes a list of those aspects of the business subject to state regulation. At least four of these regulatory areas deserve specific treatment. They are the formation of new companies, company finance, product regulation, and marketing activities.

Organization of New Companies.   The insurance department or commissioner acts upon the formation of new companies, in supervising conformity with the requirements established by the insurance code and interpreting that code whenever such interpretation is needed.

Since the New York code has been widely copied and used as the model in many other states, it will serve to illustrate the details of regulation dealing with the formation of new companies.

The New York law requires those contemplating the formation of a new life insurance company to draw up a charter giving among other data the name of the company, the location, and the kinds of business it plans to write (life, life and annuities, annuities, life and health, or the like); the powers of the company officers and how these powers are to be exercised; methods of internal control, and, if a stock company, details of stock arrangement. Next, the founders must advertise their intention to incorporate as an insurance company and file a certificate of intention and a copy of the charter.

After the charter is approved, and the certificate recorded, a stock company may sell stock or a mutual company may solicit applications for insurance, but neither can yet issue policies. Organization under the New York law is complete, in the case of mutuals, when the premiums on a necessary minimum of insurance have been paid, when the necessary statutory surplus has been cleared with the superintendent of insurance, and when the directors who are elected have authorized the issue of the policies. A stock company organization is complete and policies can be issued when the minimum required amount of capital and surplus has been paid in, when the statutory deposits have been placed with the super-intendent of insurance, and when the directors have been elected and have authorized the issuance of the stock.

Under New York law, it is easier to organize a stock company than a mutual company. Therefore, even if the ultimate goal is to have a mutual insurer, the organizers may form a stock company and later mutualize. When Hyde formed the Equitable Assurance Society of New York, he referred to it as a mutual; but he had to organize it as a stock company.[67]

The laws regulating the formation of an insurer are designed primarily to protect policyholders from promoters whose sole purpose in organizing the company is to profit from the sale of its stock, and to protect the public by prohibiting the birth of inadequately conceived insurers.[68] However, the evidence suggests that the state regulatory birth control policy regarding life insurance companies has not been successful. "From 1950, at which time 611 life insurance companies were domiciled in the United States, to July 1964, 1,570 new companies have been organized and 471 of these have been retired."[69] These 471 insurers were retired either by reinsurance, liquidation, or merger. Of these 471 retired insurers, 89 percent owned assets of less than $5 million, 89 percent had less than $50 million of life insurance in force, and only 11 percent had survived for a period of 10 or more years.[70] "It has been suggested, with some force, that the ultimate retirement rate for these companies will be substantially in excess of 30 percent, perhaps as high as 60 percent to 70 percent. With the passing of several years it is likely that many of the newly organized companies will be unable to withstand the rigors of the insurance business."[71]

Two important characteristics of new life insurers as a group are their high birth rate and their high death rate.[72] Some states are making an effort to reduce both the birth rate and the death rate among new life in-

---

[67] The company has long since been mutualized.

[68] An ancillary effect of state regulation of the formation of insurers (and of other state insurance regulatory activities) is to give some protection to investors holding stock in insurance companies.

[69] J. S. Hanson and D. R. Farney, "New Life Insurance Companies: Their Promotion and Regulation," *Marquette Law Review*, Fall, 1965, p. 176.

[70] *Probe*, January 25, 1965.

[71] Hanson and Farney, *op. cit.*, pp. 176–77. Hanson and Farney cite Phillip Goldberg's observation before the Chicago conference on acquisitions and mergers (October, 1964) that of the life insurers doing business in the United States, more than 25 percent "are probably marginal operations" and note that this appraisal has not been challenged.

[72] *Ibid.*, p. 177. Hanson and Farney observe: "The majority of life insurance company agents and officers are competent, sincere and honest in conducting their business. Their companies may be new or old. . . . On the other hand, there are those life insurance companies whose promoters seem to be motivated by the opportunity for stock speculation; whose achievements are measured not in terms of policyholder benefits but in terms of stock appreciation; whose sales techniques seem designed to confuse or mislead their prospective policyholders; and whose activities have been a source of grave concern both to state and federal regulatory agencies and to the established companies who fear irreparable damage to the industry's hard-won reputation for financial stability, integrity, and continuity of management. . . . Many of the new companies are soundly conceived and competently managed. But some—whose assets and insurance in force are but a small fraction of the industry total—are not." It is this minority which causes concern.

surers by increasing the minimum capital and initial paid-in surplus requirements for insurers, and through various administrative regulations promulgated by the insurance commissioners. For example, an amendatory act of 1965 in Illinois increased the minimum capital requirements applicable to domestic life and health insurance companies organized after the effective date of the act from $300,000 to $600,000. Because an Illinois domestic life and health insurer must have an initial paid-in surplus equal to 50 percent of its required capital, the amendment had the effect of increasing the minimum initial paid-in surplus requirement from $150,000 to $300,000. Effective January 1, 1967, the minimum capital required of life insurance companies organized in New York was increased from $500,000 to $1 million, and the minimum paid-in surplus was increased from $250,000 to $2 million.

In Iowa, the commissioner of insurance issued a ruling requiring promoters of new domestic insurance companies to make a cash investment of their own equal to at least 20 percent of the proposed stock issue for the new company and to neither sell nor hypothecate their stock in the companies for a period of three years from the date of acquisition. The ruling also prohibited the granting of stock options in excess of 10 percent of the issue if there is to be a public offering. Under the ruling, the chief executive officer of the company must be a resident of Iowa, and he must devote full time to his duties. Furthermore, the majority of directors must be bona fide Iowa residents. In Illinois, a rule was issued requiring all persons proposing to form an insurance company to submit to the insurance department its proposed contracts with agents, a detailed five-year actuarial projection, and biographical statements of all promoters, incorporators, directors, trustees, and proposed management personnel of the company. The biographical data required include a number of items: shares subscribed to or owned, amount of funds borrowed to finance the purchase of shares, nature and tenure of employments for the past 10 years, education, convictions for felony, and charges of fraud in any criminal or civil actions. The commissioner may order financial and character reports of persons submitting biographical data.

LICENSING OF AN INSURER. A difference exists between the organization of a company and the *licensing* of a company, and regulations cover both. The control of the insurance business by the state is exercised chiefly through its licensing power. Although the license fee may be sizable, the primary purpose of the licensing requirements today is not revenue raising, as was probably the original intention, but regulation. A license, called a certificate of authority in some states, is a document stating that the company involved has complied with the laws of the state and is authorized to engage in the kind of business or businesses specified.

A license to write life or health insurance may be issued to a domestic company, a foreign company, or an alien company. The state has the right to set up requirements for the issuance of a license to foreign or alien companies which are more stringent than those required of domestic companies. For instance, domestic companies usually are issued licenses on a permanent basis whereas foreign and alien insurers usually are issued licenses for a period of one year, subject to renewal. Moreover, the grounds for the revocation of a domestic company's license are usually more limited than those applied to a foreign or alien company. The law usually requires foreign and alien insurers to deposit a specified amount of securities with the appropriate state official in order to protect local policyholders and creditors. While such discrimination might appear to be local favoritism, it is justified because the assets of a domestic company are more easily subject to the control of the commissioner of insurance of that state through court procedure. The insurance commissioner in any given state has no power to seize assets domiciled in another state, and often he cannot even sue in the other state for that purpose except when acting as a liquidator or receiver.[73]

The commissioner has the power to refuse an insurer a license, to revoke one after it has been issued, and to deny renewal of a license which has expired. When an insurer is denied a license, the presumption is that the commissioner acted within his administrative authority. If the question is taken to court the burden of proof that the commissioner acted otherwise is on the insurer. In general the commissioner will license insurers that meet the statutory requirements if none of the incorporators or proposed directors has a record of fraud or dishonesty and if he believes that the granting of the license does not jeopardize the interest of the people of the state. The licensing power gives the commissioner an effective tool to require insurers to abide by the insurance code and by the department's administrative rulings.

The licensing power is the major instrument for state control of the insurance business. By conducting business through the mails, an insurer may do business in a state without a license. The regulation of unlicensed insurers, also called unauthorized or nonadmitted insurers, creates a special problem for the states. Wisconsin was the first of a number of states to cope with the problem through an unauthorized insurance statute passed in 1961. Under this statute, an unauthorized insurer is not permitted to do business in the state. "Doing business" is broadly defined in the statute as doing any of a number of particular acts in the state whether by mail or otherwise. These acts include all of those essential to soliciting, writing, rating, administering, and servicing of an insurance contract. The statute makes unauthorized insurers subject to the jurisdiction of the Wisconsin courts in suits brought by resident policyholders and their beneficiaries, and in actions brought by the state to enforce compliance with its insurance laws. Unauthorized insurers are subject to fines and to the state premium

---

[73] Because the U.S. Supreme Court has held that corporations are not citizens within the meaning of the 4th and 14th Amendments to the federal Constitution, discrimination between domestic insurers and nondomestic insurers is not illegal.

tax. The constitutionality of the statute was challenged by an unlicensed foreign mail-order insurer in a suit against the insurance commissioner of Wisconsin. The Dane County Circuit Court upheld the constitutionality of the statute and its decision was affirmed by the Wisconsin Supreme Court.[74]

Two uniform acts have been recommended by the NAIC to deal with the problem of unauthorized insurers: (1) the Unauthorized Insurers Service of Process Act passed in 48 jurisdictions under which the insurance commissioner of the state becomes the agent of the foreign insurer for service of processs and (2) the Uniform Reciprocal Licensing Act passed in 14 jurisdictions under which the license of a domestic company may be revoked if it operates without a license in one of the other states having the reciprocal licensing law.

MERGERS, CONSOLIDATIONS, AND HOLDING COMPANIES. Under New York law, a domestic insurance company is allowed to consolidate or merge with another domestic insurance company or with any foreign company licensed in New York as long as the merger or consolidation would not violate the law of the foreign company's home state. In addition, the New York statutes require that the stockholders or members approve the proposed plan by a two-thirds majority. The statutes further stipulate that the merger or consolidation shall not take effect until the insurance superintendent has approved all the provisions of the agreement. If either of the insurance companies so desires, the actions of the superintendent in refusing to accept the agreement can be subject to judicial review. Similar legislation exists in other states.

More recently, the regulatory authorities have had to deal with several new forms of insurance company amalgamations. The formation of holding companies and their subsequent purchase of insurance companies have brought about revision of the insurance statutes. It is the opinion of many legislators and insurance commissioners that the unregulated association of insurance company operations with noninsurance enterprises creates a situation that could be dangerous to the interest of the policyholders and the public. The principal area of concern centers around the possibility that holding companies will shift resources away from insurers. In April of 1969, Governor Rockefeller signed into law a New York statute limiting the ability of a holding company or conglomerate to purchase an insurance subsidiary. The statute permits such an acquisition only with insurance department approval. In addition, the New York law limits the transfer of funds between a holding company and its insurer subsidiary and gives the insurance department extensive rights for examination of any member of a holding company in regard to the insurer subsidiary. Prior to the passage of this statute, New York law had established limita-

---

[74] *Ministers Life and Casualty Union* v. *Haase,* 30 Wis. (2d) 339, 141 N.W. (2d) 287 (1966). The U.S. Supreme Court dismissed the appeal for want of a substantial federal question (December 5, 1966—No. 634).

tions on the ability of a domestic life insurance company to control a company not primarily an insurer.

Insurance regulators oppose any significant shift of life insurance company resources into noninsurance operations. The NAIC has a model bill on holding companies which deals with the insurer's investment in subsidiaries (one provision dealing with investment in subsidiaries engaged in named ancillary activities and another with investment in subsidiaries of any type) and with the acquisition of insurers by conglomerates or other noninsurance business operations.

The merger activity of life insurance companies comes under both state and federal supervision. Federal guidance is exercised by the Securities and Exchange Commission (SEC). Under the Securities Act Amendments of 1964, if the states fail to enact legislation controlling the operations of proxies and inside trading the federal government may do so through the SEC. In order for over-the-counter trading of insurance company stocks to be exempt from the SEC Act, state statutes must follow lines similar to those of the SEC Act of 1934. In addition to this potential power given the SEC by the 1964 Act, the Supreme Court has ruled that the SEC has the right to use the antifraud provisions of the SEC Act of 1934 in connection with insurance company mergers. The SEC may intervene under the 1934 SEC Act when the commission believes that false or misleading proxy solicitations have occurred. The Supreme Court reasoned that the McCarran Act gives the states authority for "insurance" regulation but at the same time this does not exclude the federal government from initiating "securities" regulation with regard to insurance companies. The ruling has not usurped the power of the states, but has made them a partner in overseeing the merger activities of insurance companies. The public could benefit from this dual regulation since one would expect that the SEC is more experienced and better equipped to investigate the complexities of contemporary merger activities.

In addition to their rule in regulating merger activity, the SEC and the appropriate state regulatory bodies are involved in the supervision of the stock distribution of new insurers.

Company Finance.   A second important area of insurance regulation pertains to the financial condition of the company. Regulation in this area may be classified into six categories: (1) standards for the valuation of reserve liabilities, (2) standards for the valuation of assets, (3) regulation of expenses, (4) regulation of rates, (5) regulation of surplus and dividends, and (6) liquidation of insurers.

COMPUTATION OF RESERVE LIABILITY.   The Guertin Standard Valuation and Nonforfeiture legislation, which has become standard in all states, requires that life insurance company reserves on currently issued business must not be less than those calculated according to the CRVM making use of the 1958 Commissioners Standard Ordinary Mortality Table and $3\frac{1}{2}$ percent interest or a method, mortality table, and interest rate producing, in the aggregate, higher reserves. Health insurers must set up unearned premiums, loss reserves, and, in the case of noncancellable contracts, an active life disability reserve.

THE VALUATION OF ASSETS. Any company may be made to appear solvent if its investments are assigned a high enough value. Consequently, state commissioners are empowered to determine the method of valuing investments owned by an insurance company for the purposes of determining whether that company is in a sound condition. Formulas for the valuation of securities are both complicated and lengthy. They are designed to prevent life insurance companies from overvaluing their assets in their financial reports. The interests of the policyholders weigh heavily in the commissioners' decisions concerning the particular valuation method to be used by any specific class of insurers. As a result, a more than ordinary amount of reliance may be placed in the financial statements of insurance companies in determining their financial strength. Without formulas for the valuation of assets, requirements for reserves would be meaningless.

INVESTMENT REGULATION. The types of investments in which an insurance company may place its funds are restricted by statute and regulation. For example, companies doing business in New York are restricted to substantially the following types of investments:

1. Obligations of the federal, state, or municipal governments in the United States or its possessions, which are not in default as to principal or interest.

2. Obligations of solvent U.S. corporations with a prescribed earnings record or secured by specific property.

3. Mortgage loans secured by first liens on real property; bonds or notes insured or guaranteed by the FHA or VA; bonds, notes, and mortgages issued by slum clearance or development corporations.

4. Stock and debt obligations of housing and real estate companies.

5. Stock and debt obligations of mortgage companies.

6. Stock collateral loans.

7. Equipment trust obligations or certificates.

8. Obligations issued by receivers administering the assets of institutions under judicial supervision.

9. Bank and bankers acceptances and other bills of exchange eligible for purchase by federal reserve banks.

10. Federal Home Loan bank stocks.

11. Obligations issued or guaranteed by the International Bank for Reconstruction and Development.

12. Shares of savings and loan associations.

13. Investment in housing projects.

14. Investment in company-occupied real estate; limited investment in income-producing real estate.

15. Limited investment in preferred and common stocks meeting certain qualifications, including an earnings test.

16. Limited investment in Canadian and certain other foreign securities of types and qualities that would qualify as domestic investments for life insurance company holdings.

17. Additional investments, not otherwise qualifying, to the extent of $3\frac{1}{2}$ percent of admitted assets, but without altering the limit placed on the percentage of one institution's issued and outstanding stock that can be loaned upon or purchased.

In general, laws regulating life insurance company investments are designed to restrict the investments not only into specified classes of securities but also to the proportion of funds that may be invested in any single issue in order to assure diversification. Even with the numerous restrictions on the investments of life insurance company funds, insurers have wide latitude for use of discretion in how these funds will be invested among the permissible classes.

Separate Accounts. Life insurers maintain what are known as separate or segregated accounts for assets that are not commingled with general assets. Separate accounts are not subject to the limitations that apply to the general funds of the life insurance companies. To allow these companies an opportunity to perform varying services for their clientele, state statutes established a less stringent set of investment limitations for separate accounts. As a result, insurers are allowed to compete in the market for equity-funded retirement plans. The New York statutes permit unrestricted investment for separate accounts except that the common stock investment in any one institution cannot exceed 2 percent of that institution's total issued and outstanding common stock. Furthermore the commissioner has the power to reject any investment program a life insurance company proposes for a separate account.

Other states have passed similar statutes. The Illinois statute limits investment in common stock and bonds for any one separate account to 10 percent of the voting shares or assets of an individual institution. In addition, not more than 5 percent of any one separate account can be invested in the shares of a single institution. Illinois further restricts separate account stock investment to the common stock of companies that are listed on a U.S. or Canadian securities exchange or are traded on the over-the-counter market.

REGULATION OF EXPENSES. Only two states have laws limiting the expenses of life insurance companies. However, since one of the states is New York, whose regulation has an extraterritorial effect, the limitations imposed have widespread application.[75]

---

[75] The other state is Wisconsin. A maximum allowance for expenses is calculated for each policy according to duration as specified by law. The totals of such allowances for first year only and for total business are compared with corresponding expenses of the calendar year excluding certain items, mainly investment expenses, taxes, licenses, and fees. This Wisconsin law also is extraterritorial in effect. The Wisconsin law does not apply to the nonparticipating insurance operations of stock life insurance companies.

The New York expense limitation requirements grew out of the findings of the Armstrong investigation, which revealed extravagance in amounts spent, especially for the acquisition of new business. The limitation is placed on a specific list of items involving field expenses, the total of which in a calendar year must not exceed a given amount as defined. Insurers other than those writing nonparticipating policies exclusively also are subject to a total expense limit.

Field expenses include seven items among which are commissions for agents, allowances for agency supervision and training, compensation for some home office personnel, premium collection and policy service fees, and a portion of the expenditures for advertising. To discuss the details of these items would serve no useful purpose here. Interested students are referred to Section 213 of the New York Insurance Code.

The total field expenses are limited to an amount which is a function of new business written, renewal premiums collected, insurance in force, the increase in salaries of agency personnel, the age of the insurer, and the length of time the insurer has had an approved training allowance plan.

The total amount of field expenses associated with the obtaining of new business is specifically restricted. Furthermore, the first-year commission rate payable to the agent is limited to 55 percent of the premium. The general agent may be paid 60 percent including the amount paid to the agent.

Total expenses are limited to the sum of the following items:

1. the total field expense limit;

2. a specific amount for each $1,000 of new insurance (and $100 of new annual annuity income) paid for during the year; and

3. a given amount graded down by size of insurer for each $1,000 of insurance (and $100 of annual annuity income) in force.

Also subject to specific maximum limitations are renewal commissions and policy service fees. In addition to the allowances included in compensation, the insurer may pay a reasonable training allowance for new agents under a plan approved by the insurance commissioner subject to a set of statutory limitations.

Insurers are not allowed to pay a bonus, prize, reward, or other additional compensation beyond the maximum first-year limit on remuneration based on the volume of new business or the aggregate number of written and paid-for policies. However, insurers may have contests among agents for recognition but this recognition must be limited to awards of pins, ash trays, medals, ribbon decorations, pats on the back, or other tokens having small intrinsic value given as bona fide recognition of merit and not as additional compensation.

RATE REGULATION.   Life and health insurance rates except for credit insurance are not regulated in the same sense that rates are controlled in certain property and liability insurance lines.[76]

---

[76] The regulation of credit life and health insurance is discussed in Chapter 15.

Unfair price discrimination among buyers of the same policy from the same insurer is prohibited. However, unit prices may vary inversely with the size of the policy and with the degree of insurability of the applicant.

In health insurance, rates and loss ratios sometimes are checked before the department approves policy forms. The majority of states require that health insurance rates and occupational classifications be filed with the commissioner. A number of states provide that the commissioner's approval shall be withdrawn if the benefits payable are unreasonable in relation to the premium charged, but no standards of "reasonableness" are set. In practice, the understaffed insurance departments simply do not have time to check the rates for the vast number of health insurance policies against the benefits they provide. In another small group of states, the filing of a policy form for approval must be accompanied by an estimate of loss ratios expected under the coverage. All states require the filing of an annual statement of loss ratios by policy forms.

Reserve requirements in life insurance are designed to assure the adequacy of rates, whereas the theory has been that competition would assure that the rates will not be excessive. But if it is true that the life insurance buyer is not "generally aware of the price he pays when he buys life insurance" and that he is not "generally aware of the prices of available alternatives," then it is appropriate to raise the question of the effectiveness of competition as a regulator of life insurance prices.[77]

In a study of life insurance prices, data "suggest a large amount of price variation . . . large enough to suggest that price competition . . . has not been effective."[78] One set of reasons for the lack of effectiveness of competition is "the complexities involved in the measurement of life insurance prices and the attendant general lack of buyer sophistication."[79] Another set is "the substantial amount of distortion inherent in the . . . simple methods of price analysis" and the "formidable problems in securing the necessary policy data" for refined price calculations even when computer facilities are available.[80] A U.S. Senator has suggested that a "Truth in Insurance Bill" may become necessary unless the industry makes more price information available to the buyer,[81] and others have suggested that disclosure of price information "possibly should be compelled if a formula can be devised under which it can practically be accomplished."[82]

---

[77] Joseph M. Belth, *The Retail Price Structure in American Life Insurance* (Bloomington: Indiana University Bureau of Business Research, 1966), p. 237. After defining "an excessive price as one at which no sales would be consummated if buyers were aware of both the price in question and the prices of available alternatives," Professor Belth observes that "price analysis of a life insurance policy involves complexities that place such analysis beyond the reach of the average buyer and perhaps even beyond the reach of the fairly sophisticated buyer."

[78] *Ibid.*, p. 238.

[79] *Ibid.*, p. 239.

[80] *Ibid.*

[81] Senator Hart at the 1968 annual meeting of the American Life Convention, Chicago.

[82] Spencer L. Kimball and Jon S. Hanson, "The Regulation of Specialty Policies in Life Insurance," *Michigan Law Review*, Vol. LXII (December, 1963), p. 256. On pages 239 to

SURPLUS AND POLICY DIVIDENDS.   In a number of states, mutual life insurers are prohibited from accumulating a surplus in excess of some given relative amount. For example, the New York law limits surplus to 10 percent of policy reserves. One purpose of the restriction is to discipline the insurers by preventing them from accumulating surpluses so large that they become both lax in controlling expenses and extravagant in their operations. Of greater importance is the requirement that dividends be paid annually rather than left to accumulate over a deferred period to be paid to those policyholders who survive the period and keep their policies in force, as was a practice during the tontine days before the Armstrong investigation of 1905. Annual dividends are required also to assure that policyholders are treated with at least some semblance of equity. However, dividend schedules under which unusually low dividends are paid during the early years of policy duration and unusually high dividends are paid during the later years of the policy duration have the earmarks of a semitontine system.

LIQUIDATION.   Insurance companies are required to file annual reports based on forms developed by the NAIC, called the convention blank. The blank is discussed in Chapter 26. The information filed is subject to review by the state insurance department by direct examination every three years. The examination is conducted under a zone system whereby a group of examiners with not more than one from each of the five zones outside the home zone participating. The insurance department of the insurer's domiciliary state serves as the chairman of the examination and the insurer pays the cost of the examination. For the giant companies, the examination might take three years. Therefore, for some insurers the examination is a continuous process. By the time one examination is completed it is time to start another.

If the examination reveals that the insurer is in trouble, the domiciliary state's insurance commissioner can apply to the court of jurisdiction for an order to take over the assets of the insurer with the objective of conducting the business in the best interest of the insureds, the creditors, and the general public. As soon as the order is granted, the assets of the insurer vest in the insurance commissioner. The commissioner may also seek to take over the in-state assets of a foreign insurer. The insurance code is likely to specify particular grounds for taking over the assets of an insurer and these include such developments as failure to cooperate with examiners, impaired capital or impaired surplus, refusal to remove dishonest officers or directors, willful violation of charter provisions or of state laws, or technical insolvency. Whenever the commissioner has evidence that the continued operation of the insurer in its present condition is contrary to the interests of its policy-

---

250 of his book, *The Retail Price Structure in American Life Insurance, op. cit.*, Professor Belth discusses the role, ramifications, and conceivable effects of price disclosure in life insurance.

holders, he can take over the company. The insurer involved is entitled to a court hearing on the issue, and if there are no supportable grounds for the takeover the insurer is given back the title to its property and may resume the management of the company. In the interim, the assets of the insurer are vested in the insurance commissioner. The task of the commissioner is to conserve the insurer and to turn it back hopefully as a stronger organization.

Instead of seeking a conservation order, the commissioner may seek a reorganization order to preserve certain intangible assets of the insurer such as its agency force. In this case, the commissioner may order a change of name of the insurer before it is turned over to private operations. However, rehabilitation may be impossible and liquidation the only practical solution. In a number of states, the insurance commissioner serves as liquidator and if his state has adopted the Uniform Insurers Liquidation Act, claims are processed uniformly among insureds residing in all states and not just among those residing in the domiciliary state of the insurer. In order to protect the interests of the policyholder an attempt is made to find reasonable reinsurance agreements with insurers willing to assume the obligations of the liquidated insurer. Under such an agreement the insureds of the liquidated insurer would retain their insurance even though a lien may be placed on the amount of insurance. The New York law has created the Life Insurance Guaranty Corporation to assume or reinsure partially or wholly the policies of member domestic insurers. The corporation is financed through assessments on member insurers. Membership is limited to insurers that have been writing insurance for a period of at least six years.

Product Regulation.   In nearly all states, policy forms in both life and health insurance must be filed with the insurance commissioner. In some states, approval is required before the policy can be issued. In others, if not disapproved within a certain period of time, the policy may be issued. In general, the commissioner at his discretion may disapprove a life or health insurance form if it contains provisions that are unjust, unfair, inequitable, misleading, deceptive, or encourage misrepresentation. In addition, both life and health insurance forms must contain a number of standard provisions.[83] Also special product regulation applies to credit life and health insurance as discussed in Chapter 15.

An important new product written by life insurance companies is the variable annuity, and as of late 1968 this product has been subjected to specific regulation either by statutes, administrative rulings, or both in 43 jurisdictions. In addition to these 43 jurisdictions, 6 more have enacted laws allowing separate accounts to be used with pensions and deferred profit sharing plans. In 26 of the 43 jurisdictions, the first law or admin-

---

[83] These standard provisions are discussed in Chapters 10 (for life insurance policies) and 14 (for health policies).

istrative ruling was enacted or promulgated between 1966 and 1968, with the bulk of them occurring in 1967. The first states to promulgate regulations governing the sale of variable annuities were West Virginia in 1956 and New Mexico in 1958. The first states to enact laws permitting the sale of variable annuities and the use of separate accounts in connection with them were Arkansas and New Jersey in 1959.

State laws and regulations relating to the variable annuity vary among the states just as do the regulations affecting nearly every other aspect of insurance company operations. However, the NAIC Subcommittee on Variable Annuities has endorsed a model variable annuity regulation proposal prepared by an industry advisory committee. These regulations require that for an insurer to qualify to write variable annuities it not only be licensed to write annuities but also satisfy the commissioner with its method of operation. Furthermore the insurer must file a description of its variable annuity contract, a copy of the regulations of its domiciliary state, and a statement of the qualifications of its officers and directors. Also, the variable annuity contract must include (1) a description of how the annuity benefits are to be determined, (2) a statement that these benefits may decrease as well as increase, (3) a minimum 30-day grace period, (4) a statement of the nonforfeiture options (cash value and paid-up annuity units), (5) reinstatement provisions, (6) a statement of the assumptions relating to expenses, mortality, and interest used in the initial benefit computation, (7) annuity purchase rates based on mortality rates not in excess of those produced by the Annuity Table for 1949, or on one specifically approved by the commissioner, and (8) an assumed rate of interest used in computing the initial annuity payment not in excess of 5 percent.

The model regulations prohibit insurers from issuing illustrations that either project past performance into the future or predict future performance, but the use of hypothetical investment returns in illustrations is permitted. The variable annuity may be written with or without an expense or mortality guarantee, that is the model regulations permit the variable annuity to offer participation not only in the investment results of the fund but also in mortality and expense experience. The model regulations also require the insurer to disclose fully the activity in the fund, the number of units held by the participant and the dollar value of each unit, and to file an annual report with the commissioner in a form prescribed by the NAIC. Furthermore, the model regulations require that agents intending to sell a registered variable annuity plan, that is, one not exempt by the SEC from registration requirements under the 1933 Securities Act, be specifically licensed for that purpose and pass a written examination on variable annuities and investments as a condition for qualifying for a license.

Regulation in force in the various states does not necessarily follow the model regulation proposal. For example, in some states mortality and expense fluctuations may not be used to affect annuity values adversely—that is, minimum mortality and expense results must be guaranteed. In those states that regulate the mortality and interest assumption for the initial monthly annuity payment, the ceiling on the payment usually is that governed by the 1937 Standard Annuity Table at from 3 to 4 percent.

Group Insurance Regulation. In general, much that has been discussed in regard to rate regulation and policy forms relates to individual policies. In most states, group insurance is regulated by a special set of laws. Laws relating to group insurance usually include: the definition of a group, the minimum size of a group, and the percentage of participation required in contributory plans. In most states special group policy form requirements have been established. They cover such items as the definition of a contract, representations, issuance of certificates to individuals covered, new admissions, remittance of premiums, time limit on notice of claim, proof of loss, time limit on filing proof of loss, payment of claims, physical examination and autopsy, and time limit on legal actions.[84]

In group life insurance, a few states set the minimum first-year premium for group term life insurance because of the fear that competition among insurers for group life insurance business will drive the premium down below a level considered safe for the protection not only of the insurer's group policyholders but also of its other policyholders. The minimum premium also is supposed to prohibit unfair discrimination among groups—that is, it is supposed to restrain the insurer from offering unfair inducements to large and big-name corporations to attract their group life insurance business. The minimum premium law does not apply to group permanent insurance because it is anticipated that the reserve requirement will assure rate adequacy. After the first year, premiums may be adjusted to the loss experience of the particular group. Minimum first-year premiums are not required in group health insurance, although in practice filed rate schedules are usually followed the first year, the rate being adjusted thereafter according to the experience of the group.

Regulation of Marketing Activities. Agents and brokers must be licensed by the state. Qualifications for obtaining a license as an agent or broker vary widely from state to state. Applicants may or may not be subject to any particular qualifications or examination. However, the agent must be authorized by the company. The term "agent" indicates that he has been designated by his principal (the company) to act as its representative in the transactions specified in his contract. In a growing number of states, written examinations are required.[85] In a few of these states the

---

[84] Cf. Chapters 15 and 16 for discussion of group life and health insurance regulation.

[85] Holders of the CLU designation receive special recognition in several of these states. For example, the New York law gives the commissioner the power to waive the agent's written examination in the event that the applicant has been awarded the CLU designation. In Georgia the written examination is waived automatically. This practice follows from the belief that the CLU examinations are a far more demanding and extensive test of insurance knowledge than is the agent's examination.

applicant is required to take formal courses in insurance before he may sit for the examination. In other states, the law assumes quite naïvely that because the agent has extremely broad power to commit his principal, the company can be depended upon to use care in the selection and training of its agents. However, there is a tendency to tighten agents' licensing and qualification requirements, as a result of the activities of state agents' associations.

Agents' licenses may be refused or revoked by the insurance commissioner, but not without cause, such as dishonesty, twisting, rebating, fraud, untrustworthiness, and similar undesirable characteristics or practices.[86] Some few states regard incompetence or ignorance as grounds for rejection of a license. If serious qualification laws ever are adopted or if licenses ever are to mean more to the public than a source of state revenue, these two elements (incompetence and ignorance) will have to be given more recognition and weight than it seems are being given to them today in a number of states.

Penalties are usually provided in state insurance codes for doing business as an agent in the state without a license. In general, these penalties are similar to those applied to a company that operates in a state without a license. They usually are of two types: criminal and civil. Criminal penalties may include both fines and jail sentences. Assessment of these penalties can be made only after due trial as provided for all criminal offenses. Such trials are infrequent. More deterring than criminal penalties are the civil penalties, which may include the refusal of the court to allow the agent to recover against his company for nonpayment of commissions. In most states the license is granted for an indefinite duration and is subject to termination by the commissioner for cause after a hearing.

High among causes considered sufficient for license revocation are *rebating, misrepresentation,* and *twisting.*

Rebating is the practice of returning part of the premium or giving a valuable consideration as an inducement to purchase a policy. Rebating generally takes the form of a refund of part of the commissions on the business. Regulation of rebating is aimed at preventing inequitable treatment among policyholders and at maintaining a fair plane of competition among agents. The prohibition against rebating also is designed to protect the career agent from the avocational agent. The latter, not depending for his living on his life insurance sales, may be more prone to return part of the premium to the applicant as consideration for buying insurance.[87]

Rebating is not clearly defined by law. State laws usually provide that a rebate may consist not only of part of a premium but also any inducement,

---

[86] There is always appeal to the courts from the rulings of a commissioner.

[87] There are those who argue that sophisticated buyers should not be prevented from driving a hard bargain by a rebate law enacted under the guise of protecting the public interest, any more than they are prevented from driving a hard bargain when they purchase things other than life insurance.

favor, or advantage not specified in the policy. In some jurisdictions, it is illegal for an employer to accept a commission for a policy issued to an employee, or for an employee to accept one for insurance on an employer. In some jurisdictions attorneys are prohibited from accepting fees for inducing a client to take insurance. Rebating may extend to an agreement to render certain tangible services, for example, to do a specified amount of work for the applicant in return for his application. The giving of trading stamps with the issuance of an insurance policy is specifically prohibited in several states. However, the acceptance of interest-bearing notes instead of cash has been held not to constitute a rebate.[88] The acceptance of noninterest-bearing notes would be open to question as would the waiving of interest charges on interest-bearing notes, a practice sometimes used especially in connection with student business. As a further precaution, agents are expected to write a reasonable amount of business for people other than themselves and their immediate family so that commission payments do not indirectly become a rebate.

In many states, rebating is a legal offense (usually a misdemeanor) for the agent, and in others it is an offense for both the agent and the person receiving the rebate. Few rebating cases appear in court. A rebating case is difficult to prove, especially in those states where both parties, the buyer and the seller, are held guilty. Neither will desire to testify against the other and hence incriminate himself.

Misrepresentation involves the making of any unfair, misleading, or incomplete comparison of two policies, or any misleading statement about the financial condition or reputation of another company or of any of the relationships between the insured and the company.

Twisting refers in general to misrepresentation in order to induce a policyholder to drop a contract he already has and to replace it with a new one. The practice generally relates to dropping a policy in one company in favor of taking a policy in a different one, although twisting might also consist of inducing a policyholder to drop a policy in the agent's own company in order to take another one in that same company.[89] Twisting is difficult to define; and since there are, on occasion, valid reasons for having a policyholder drop one policy and replace it with another, the definition of twisting must include the notion of a misleading or incomplete comparison. In one state, specific replacement regulations have been promulgated, requiring that a cost comparison between the policy being offered and the policy to be replaced be prepared on the basis of a specified formula and given to the insured in writing. The NAIC has developed a model replacement bill that requires policyholders to be given complete and accurate written information on all aspects of a proposed replacement including a

[88] *Diehl* v. *American Life Insurance Company,* 204 Iowa 706, 213 N.W. 753 (1927).
[89] The fact that the first-year commission on a new policy exceeds the renewal commissions on an old one might tempt an unscrupulous agent to twist his own policies to the disadvantage of his client.

comparison of certain data respecting the existing and proposed coverage, and that the prospective insurer be made responsible to see that this information is provided. Furthermore, each insurer that has a policy in force that is to be affected must be advised that a replacement is contemplated and be given the opportunity to comment on the information pertinent to the sale. Regulations against twisting are fostered and encouraged by the companies because twisting increases the incidence of lapsation and the ratio of acquisition costs to total expenses.

That there are those in the federal government who believe that state regulation does not adequately protect the consumer against deceptive practices of insurance companies and their agents is evidenced by the inclusion of insurance services in the proposed Consumers Protection Act of 1969, a bill setting forth a number of defined unfair or deceptive practices and authorizing the Attorney General to seek injunctions in the U.S. district courts to restrain these practices. When successful government action against any of the specified deceptive practices is concluded, any consumer may institute a civil suit for damages. The proscribed practices spelled out in the proposed legislation are those said to "have substantial effects on consumers" and to "account for some 85 percent of identifiable deceptive practices." Two congressional subcommittees were studying the proposed legislation in 1970, the House Subcommittee on Commerce and Finance and the Senate Subcommittee for Consumers of the Committee on Commerce.[90]

5. TAXATION OF LIFE INSURANCE COMPANIES

The life insurance business is subject to federal, state, and local taxation. Taxes, licenses, and fees take about $4 out of each $100 received by U.S. life insurance companies. Of this amount, nearly 60 percent is paid in federal income taxes and 25 percent in state premium taxes. The rest

---

[90] The National Association of Insurance Commissioners in its testimony before the Senate Commerce Subcommittee opposed the inclusion of insurance in the definition of services because it would result in a "federal regulatory mechanism which impinges upon an area long and comprehensively occupied by state regulation of the insurance business" and would result in duplication of concurrent jurisdiction, a position inconsistent with the McCarran Act. The Association argued that since every state has adopted a law based on the NAIC Model Unfair Trade Practices Act, state regulation "fully covers the field" and is "tailored specifically to the problems in the insurance business."

Professor Belth in his statement prepared for the Senate Commerce Subcommittee "examined one fundamental characteristic of life insurance—the critical importance of the interest factor—that is the basis for a variety of questionable practices," and presented several illustrations taken from sales and advertising practices of life insurance companies that he considers to be deceptive. "All of the practices described . . . have one thing in common—the misallocation of the interest earnings on the savings element of a life insurance contract. Each of the practices involves either an understatement of the price of the protection element or an overstatement of the rate of return on the savings element. In my opinion, such practices are deceptive." He observed that it "is possible that either the industry itself or the state regulatory agencies could correct the situation, but there has been little progress to date."

is for social security taxes, real estate taxes not associated with invest-ments,[91] and licenses, fees, and other taxes.

The Federal Income Tax. Because of the special nature of life insur-ance operations, the federal income tax formulas applied to that branch of the business continually have failed to meet the revenue expectations of the Treasury Department. And, because of the complicated nature of the life insurance business, the tax formulas also have failed to include all the essential modifications and refinements necessary to make them acceptable to all segments of the industry with its wide array of views. Frequent revi-sions of the applicable tax law have resulted.

Prior to 1921, life insurance companies were taxed like commercial corporations. All earnings from whatever source were considered gross income. All expenditures, including charges for reserves, were deductible from gross income. The corporate tax rate was applied to the net taxable income so determined.

The 1921 law set up special tax provisions for life insurance companies. Under these provisions, premium income was treated the same as capital deposits that the insurance company invested for the benefit of policy-holders. Investment income was considered to be the only new income accruing to the life insurance company. Underwriting income was ignored. Net taxable income consisted of gross investment income, minus investment expenses, minus interest necessary to maintain legal reserves. The last de-duction recognized that life insurance companies are contractually obligated to credit a given rate of interest on policyholder reserves, whether or not net investment income is sufficient for this purpose. Gains from sales or redemptions of securities, interest from tax-exempt securities, and dividends received on stocks of corporations subject to federal income taxes were not considered as part of investment income.[92]

From 1921 to 1932 the interest required for maintaining reserves was set at 4 percent. This rate was applied to each company's mean reserves for the year in order to determine the allowable deduction. In 1932 the rate was lowered to 3.75 percent and remained at this level until 1942. During the latter part of this period, companies, because of declining interest earn-ings, began reducing interest assumptions on new policies with the result that the government failed to get what it considered to be a reasonable tax income; so the formula was changed in 1942.

From 1942 to 1948 the interest required for maintaining reserves was computed by applying an industrywide ratio to each company's investment income rather than to the mean of its reserves.[93] This ratio was known as

---

[91] Taxes directly related to investment, such as taxes on real estate held for investment, are charged as investment expenses and are reflected in the net investment earnings of the insurers.

[92] Because this approach assumes that insurance transactions yield no insurance profit, it is patently not suitable for stock life insurers, particularly with respect to their nonpartici-pating business.

[93] The formula assigned a weight of 35 percent to the actual rate assumed by the companies and 65 percent to an arbitrary rate of 3.25 percent.

the secretary's ratio, and, when subtracted from 100 percent, measured that portion of the investment income of each company subject to federal income taxation. For example, the ratio in 1942 was 93 percent; so 7 percent of each company's investment income was subject to taxes at regular corporate rates. The application of this formula provided additional tax income to the government and, at the time, seemed satisfactory. But a continued decline in interest earnings and an increase in deductions resulting from reserve revaluations produced a situation in 1947 in which the secretary's ratio exceeded 100 percent, so that the formula produced no taxable income.

In 1950 a new averaging formula was established, using the 1942 system, except that it discarded the old divided percentage weighting system in favor of the average valuation rate of interest for all companies. To assure the government that the ratio obtained would be less than 100 percent, companies whose assumptions would have produced a negative amount of taxable income were eliminated from the calculation. This formula was applied only during the taxable years 1949 and 1950.

In 1951 a temporary bill was enacted that provided for a tax of $6\frac{1}{2}$ percent of the net investment income of life insurance companies less certain deductions. These deductions were provided for health insurance reserves and for companies not earning sufficient interest to meet their reserve requirements. This law was extended one year at a time through 1954. This change in approach was made because it was simple in its conception and application. It assumed that since the amount of net investment income needed to meet interest requirements on reserves would remain relatively constant, no specific deduction need be allowed. This expectation did not materialize.

In 1955 another temporary measure was passed that provided for a tax at the corporate rate of 52 percent on the net investment income of life insurance companies after allowing for a deduction of about 85 percent for the interest required to meet reserve liabilities.[94] This law gave special tax consideration to those companies failing to earn sufficient investment income to meet their individual reserve requirements. It also taxed income received on cancellable health insurance differently than income received on life insurance operations. This was the first time such a distinction had been made. The 1955 formula was extended through the 1957 taxable year, and produced a tax of about 7.8 percent of net investment income for these years.

All the tax formulas applied after the abandonment of the 1942 approach were on a stopgap basis. In any year in which new tax legislation

---

[94] Under the formula, the amount each company was permitted to deduct to meet interest requirements on reserves was 87.5 percent of the first $1 million of net investment income and 85 percent of the balance. These figures were chosen on the theory that in the long run approximately 85 percent of net investment income is needed to meet interest requirements on policyholder reserves. The 87.5 percent deduction was designed to aid small companies.

had not been enacted or the current formula extended, the 1942 formula would have reapplied.

In 1959 a new tax law was enacted. Its provisions were made retroactive to 1958. This law replaced the 1942 legislation as the permanent method of taxing life insurance companies. Several distinguishing features of the Life Insurance Company Income Tax Act of 1959 are: *First,* stock life insurance companies are taxed on a basis somewhat different from that applying to mutual companies. *Second,* the investment income approach to the taxation of life insurance companies is abandoned and replaced with a total income approach similar to that employed prior to 1921. *Third,* interest required to maintain policyholder reserves is determined on a basis of individual company experience. Formerly, a uniform rate was used by all companies. *Fourth,* interest earnings on funds held by life insurers to offset reserves behind qualified employee benefit plans are given the same tax treatment as interest earnings on funds held by banks or other trustees under qualified pension plans. *Fifth,* more liberal tax provisions are applied to both small and new companies than were embodied in any previous act.

The tax rates applying to corporations generally also apply to life insurance companies. Life insurance company taxable income is defined as the sum of (1) taxable investment income[95] plus (2) 50 percent of the amount by which gain from operations exceeds taxable income[96] plus (3) the amount subtracted from the policyholder's surplus account for the taxable year.[97] A separate alternate tax of 30 percent after 1970 (28 per-

---

[95] Taxable investment income is the net investment income less a deduction for the interest required to maintain reserves. The deduction consists of three elements:

1. A deduction for earnings on reserves at the lower of a company's earnings rate and the five-year average of such rate, as applied to reserves revalued at such rate by an approximate formula known as the 10 for 1 rule.

2. Interest actually paid on funds left on deposit and on indebtedness.

3. A special deduction for interest on reserves for qualified pension plans.

A further deduction is then allowed of a proportion of tax-free interest, partially tax-exempt interest, and the dividends received credit.

[96] Taxable income is designated as net investment income plus premium income, less deductions for required interest, claims, expenses, increases in reserves, and the "life insurance company's share" of wholly and partially tax-exempt interest. There is also an allowance for nonparticipating premiums and for group premiums. This resulting figure can be considered as underwriting income for stock companies only, since the additional deduction for policyholders' dividends generally results in eliminating the tax under this phase for mutual companies.

[97] Under this phase stock companies pay tax on the underwriting income which has not been previously taxed. This is accomplished by considering new surplus as being divided into two accounts:

1. Shareholders' surplus account.

2. Policyholders' surplus account.

The shareholders' account receives all income which has been previously taxed plus capital gains (after taxes). Cash dividends may be paid to shareholders from this account without incurring additional taxes. The policyholders' account receives all income that is not taxed under phases 1 and 2, and all cash dividends paid from this account are first subjected to a 52 percent tax.

cent in 1970) is imposed on capital gains to conform to provisions applicable to other corporations.

Gain from operations will be smaller than taxable investment income if there are underwriting losses. Gain from operations will be greater than taxable investment income if there are underwriting gains. If there are underwriting losses, the full amount of such losses is allowed as a credit against investment income. The tax base in this latter case would be gain from operations plus the amount subtracted from the policyholder's account.

Only 50 percent of apparent underwriting gain is currently taxed, on the theory that true underwriting gain cannot be determined for a 12-month period. In order to prevent that portion of underwriting gain not currently taxed from escaping tax liability altogether, the concept of the policyholders' surplus account was introduced.

Additions to the policyholders' surplus account include (1) underwriting income which has not been currently taxed, (2) the deduction allowed for certain nonparticipating contracts, and (3) the deduction of 2 percent of the premiums for the taxable year attributable to group life insurance contracts and group health insurance contracts. The latter two amounts are deducted in determining gain or loss from operations. These deductions, like the 50 percent deductions of underwriting gains, are allowed because such amounts may be necessary for the protection of policyholders. If distributions are made to stockholders from the policyholders' surplus account, it is evident that management has decided that amounts previously set aside are no longer needed for the protection of the policyholder. Regular corporate rates apply to distributions when they are made.

State Taxes.   The premium tax is the principal tax imposed on life insurers by the states. The tax rate varies among states, ranging from 1.7 percent to 4 percent, with 2 percent being the most common. In a few states a reduction in the premium tax is allowed if a given percentage of the insurer's assets are invested in the state.

Also not uniform among states are the tax base, the tax offsets, and the "in lieu of" provisions. For example, in some states premiums paid for annuity contracts are not included in the tax base; in others, annuity premiums are included and taxed at the full rate; and in still others, annuity premiums are included but taxed at a rate lower than that applied to life insurance premiums. Another important variable found in the tax base among states is the way in which dividends to policyholders are handled. Although in most states the insurer is allowed to take a deduction for policy dividends, unfortunately about one fourth of the states do not allow dividends to be deducted from the tax base, thereby discriminating against insurers issuing participating policies. Where a deduction for life insurance policy dividends is allowed, dividends used to purchase paid-up additions or to shorten the endowment or premium payment period are included in the tax base in all but one state. Where a deduction for dividends is not allowed, dividends used to purchase paid-up additions or to shorten the endowment period need not be added to the tax base except in one state. Other interesting variations are found. In one state cash surrender values paid on life insurance policies are deducted from the base; in another state first-year premiums on life and health insurance are excluded from the tax base, and in another state all health insurance premiums collected by a domestic insurer are excluded.

Several states allow offsets against the premium tax. For example, a few states allow credit for ad valorem taxes paid on domestic real estate. The amounts of the offset and the conditions under which it is allowed vary among the handful of states offering it. One state allows an offset for all property taxes paid for general state purposes. Examination and valuation fees are allowed as a credit in some states. Franchise taxes and income taxes under the state law are offset against the premium tax in a few states. However, premium tax offsets are the exception rather than the rule.

In the majority of states the premium tax is in lieu of some other tax or taxes. It might be in lieu of all other state and local taxes except those on real estate and tangible personal property located within the state or in lieu of all other taxes except those upon real property owned in the state. It might be in lieu of all other taxes except franchise and excise taxes, or in lieu of any franchise tax or capital stock tax. It might be in lieu of all taxes except state income and property taxes or in lieu of personal property and state income taxes.

Thus with four variables (tax rate, tax base, tax offsets, and "in lieu of" provisions) the task of comparing the relative tax burden placed on insurers by the various states becomes Herculean.[98]

Most states levy a retaliatory tax on foreign insurers where such tax applies. The retaliatory tax is a tax designed to equalize the tax rate that one of its domestic insurers would have to pay in another state. If a domestic insurer in state A would have to pay a 3 percent tax in state B then a domestic insurer of state B would be required to pay a 3 percent tax in state A even though state A's tax is set at 2 percent. Retaliatory taxes serve as a damper on the desire of states to increase their premium tax rates on out-of-state insurers. In fact, Connecticut charges a lower premium tax on foreign insurers than is charged domestic insurers. Furthermore, New York City insurers pay a higher voluntary city premium tax to avoid the effect of the retaliatory tax elsewhere.

Originally, the premium tax was a tariff on out-of-state companies designed to protect home companies. Later it became a retaliatory measure against taxes imposed by other states on out-of-state companies. Today some states still make a differential between the rate charged home companies and that charged foreign and alien companies. Some states do not

---

[98] Cf. Robert I. Mehr, "Taxation of Insurance Companies," appearing as chap. XXII in *Report of the Commission on Revenue of the State of Illinois* (Springfield, Illinois: State of Illinois, 1963), pp. 760–94.

impose a premium tax on domestic companies. Once the tax was explained as a source of funds to pay the cost of state insurance regulation. However, the premium tax has developed into a revenue measure and is an important source of state funds in many states. Only a small fraction of the total premium tax collected by states is used to finance the regulation and supervision of the business.

The premium tax levied against life insurance companies is subject to question on the basis of tax theory. However, the question is controversial because there are many different theories regarding taxation, and taxation itself is potentially not only a revenue-raising medium but also a tool for social adjustment. Some economists hold to the theory that taxes should be levied on the ability to pay and that they be levied directly; i.e., that they be recognizable as taxes. If these are the tests of a "good" tax, then premium taxes applied against life insurance are not theoretically acceptable.

If, on the other hand, this theory is cast aside and the question is looked at historically, it becomes clear that throughout history some taxes have been levied with two thoughts in mind: the amount of revenue they will raise and the ease with which they may be collected without objection by voters. If these tests are used to determine what is a fair tax, then the life insurance business is properly taxed. Policyholders have shown no resistance to the premium tax; insurers prefer it over a state income tax because the premium tax can be loaded into the premium rate, and the states prefer it because it is likely to produce a steadily increasing revenue rather than a fluctuating revenue as might be the case under an income tax.

Pennsylvania passed a 6 percent sales tax on all insurance premiums except health coverage written by life companies and travel accident policies, effective March 10, 1970. This tax appeared to be in lieu of an increase in the premium tax from 2 percent to 3 percent. The tax was repealed one week after it was passed following a massive protest. It was argued that such a tax could "virtually destroy the Pennsylvania insurance industry," destroy the insured pension plan business in the state, and subject insurers to retaliatory taxation in other states.

Insurers also may be subject to taxes and fees levied by local communities.

Questions for Discussion

CHAPTER 1

1. (*a*) "The amount of human life value is irrelevant to the study of life insurance." Explain why you agree or disagree with the foregoing statement. (*b*) Do you agree with the late Professor Huebner's assertion that the proper education in life insurance would lead one to believe that a person has absconded if he dies without life insurance?

2. "Whole life insurance is the most expensive form of term insurance and the cheapest form of endowment life insurance." Explain why you agree or disagree with the foregoing statement.

3. Explain the source of savings accumulations to a policyholder in a life insurance policy.

4. "Using the concept of a divided contract, partially protection and partially savings does not do justice to the concept of the level premium and of protection for the whole of life." Explain why you agree or disagree with the foregoing statement.

5. In the "Penny for Your Thoughts" daily radio program over a local station, the officers of the local Association of Life Underwriters appeared as guests on insurance questions day. One of the questions asked was, "What's the optimum amount of life insurance for a person?" The answer given was, "five times annual income." Do you think this thought is worth a penny?

CHAPTER 2

1. For the study of insurance, what is the advantage of defining risk as uncertainty concerning loss? Is there a disadvantage to defining risk in this manner?

2. (*a*) Explain how the chance of loss can affect the degree of risk. (*b*) What factors other than chance of loss affect the degree of risk?

3. Explain how the concept of the expected value of the game can be useful in making decisions about the purchase of insurance.

4. Explain why people might be willing to risk a little for a lot with adverse odds but not willing to risk a lot for a little with favorable odds. Does your answer to this question give any insight into why people purchase insurance? Does it give any insight into why insurance companies cannot write certain kinds of insurance coverage?

5. (*a*) Explain why the purchaser of a health insurance policy should be concerned about the concept of a peril. Should a purchaser of a life insurance policy also be concerned about the concept of a peril? (*b*) Explain why the purchaser of a health insurance policy should be concerned about the concept of a hazard. Should the purchaser of a life insurance policy also be concerned about the concept of a hazard? (*c*) Explain why the purchaser of a health insurance policy should be concerned about the concept of a loss. Should a purchaser of a life insurance policy also be concerned about the concept of a loss?

CHAPTER 3

1. What is the advantage of defining insurance in terms of risk reduction and loss sharing? Is there a disadvantage to defining insurance in this manner?

2. With reference to the law of large numbers, how large must the numbers be?

3. What requisites are necessary to make a risk insurable commercially that are not necessary for the risk to be self-insured? What requisites are necessary for a risk to be both commercially insurable and self-insurable? Explain.

4. Explain why insurance is a particularly attractive technique for handling risk when the loss potential is large and the chance of loss is small. Is it possible for the chance of loss to be too small to make insurance an attractive risk management technique? Explain.

5. How does one go about selecting the appropriate risk management device?

CHAPTER 4

1. Why do you suppose that term insurance is playing an increasing role in the life insurance programs of the American people? What kinds of products can the life insurance companies develop that might compete more favorably with other financial institutions for investable funds?

2. The typical life insurance agent is more inclined to emphasize the limitations rather than the uses of term insurance. Explain why you *agree* or *disagree* with this statement.

3. The following question was printed in a syndicated newspaper column called *"Your Life Insurance"*: "What is all this talk about life insurance, after a number of years, getting to "cost practically nothing"? I have a policy for $20,000, costing me about $430 a year today, just as it did 15 years ago when I bought it. That certainly isn't practically nothing." How do you suppose the question was answered? Do you agree with this answer?

4. Often the advice, "Buy term and invest the difference," is heard. What is this *difference* referred to in the advice? What do you think about the advice?

5. The endowment insurance policy is the ideal insurance contract because you cannot lose with one: the policy pays off whether you live or die. It is the

sure way of beating the company. Explain why you agree or disagree with this concept of endowment insurance.

CHAPTER 5

1. A common objection to continuous premium whole life is summed up in the statement, "I don't want to pay premiums all my life." How would you counsel a young man who has just been sold a continuous premium whole life?

2. It has been said, "When a young man aged 25 buys a 20-payment life policy, it is safe to assume that he has bought the wrong contract." Explain why you agree or disagree with this statement.

3. "It is a common assertion among misinformed commentators on insurance that the premium on a 'cash value' policy includes an extra charge because of the presence of the cash value, implying that the removal of cash values would cheapen the cost of insurance considerably." Does the policyholder "pay for" the cash value in a whole life policy? What concept of pay for are you using in answering this question? Would some other concept of pay for change your answer?

4. Is there any similarity between a minimum deposit life insurance plan and term insurance? If so, why might an insured choose one rather than the other?

5. This text contends that whole life insurance is more flexible than endowment insurance and that a continuous premium whole life insurance policy is the most flexible type of whole life insurance. A distinguished teacher of life insurance with many years of experience has said that he does "not see that any one of these insurance policies is any more flexible than the other." Explain why you agree or disagree with the text.

CHAPTER 6

1. Under what set of family circumstances would you recommend each of the following: (a) immediate annuity, (b) joint and last survivorship annuity, (c) joint annuity, (d) temporary life annuity, (e) annuity certain, and (f) no annuity.

2. How is the variable annuity supposed to offset two of the principal drawbacks of conventional annuities? What are the major criticisms of the variable annuity?

3. Assume that the annuitant does not want to expose himself to the inflation risk, does not want to accept the financial risk associated with the variable annuity, and wants his standard of living to improve with economic growth. Design an annuity contract that will be palatable to him. What limitations do you see to this contract?

4. What is logical and what is not logical in the federal income tax treatment of annuity income? Can you recommend a method that would be totally logical? Why is this method not used?

5. How do you think that the concept of a managed annuity differs from the prototype variable annuity? Develop a case for and a case against the managed annuity.

CHAPTER 7

1. What are the basic elements out of which special purpose policy plans are constructed? Design a special purpose policy plan that you believe will be attractive to an unmarried college graduating senior about to take his first job.

2. In what set of family circumstances would you purchase insurance on the lives of your children? Why? You are looking at two policies: one is a jumping juvenile, which increases protection from $1,000 to $5,000 at age 21; the other is a regular continuous premium whole life written for a level $5,000 throughout life. Your child is one year old. How much would you expect the premium difference to be between these contracts? If you must buy one to please your wife, which one would you buy? Why?

3. What limitations do you see in the guaranteed insurability rider now written with certain forms of life insurance?

4. Why was the return of premium rider developed? Why was the face amount plus cash value policy developed? Would you purchase either one? Why or why not?

5. What new types of life insurance policies do you anticipate will be developed to meet insurable needs not now handled on an efficient or effective basis? Why have such policies not yet been developed?

CHAPTER 8

1. What information do you need in order to determine the "best" life insurance policy? What is your concept of the term "best policy"?

2. What characteristics of the various life insurance plans should be considered in making a purchase decision when the purchase objective is for savings as well as for protection? Would your answer be different if the purchase objective was for protection only? Explain.

3. How does life insurance compare with savings accounts, savings and loan shares, and United States Savings Bonds as a savings medium? How does it compare with mutual funds?

4. Explain and evaluate the Linton technique for computing the rate of return on the cash values of a life insurance policy.

5. In the body of the text, illustrations were given to show how the imputed rates of return on the savings element of cash value life insurance vary among policies according to ages of issues, types of policy, the duration over which the rates are computed, and the insurer from whom the policy is bought. How do you account for the significantly different imputed rates of return based on each of these variables?

CHAPTER 9

1. In what circumstances may an insurer deny liability under a life insurance contract?

2. The insurance company issued a policy to the wife of the insured without notifying the insured. After the wife attempted to murder the insured, he brought suit in tort against the insurer. Could the insurer be liable?

3. The insured failed to disclose a serious blood vessel disorder when he completed his application for insurance. The insurance was issued. The insured was aware that the agent knew of this condition, but believed that the agent would not forward the information to the insurer. The insurer died. Must the insurer pay the proceeds?

4. The beneficiary sued to recover the proceeds of an insurance policy on the life of her husband when the insurer denied the claim on the grounds that the beneficiary had been convicted of second degree murder in her husband's death. Is this a reasonable defense on the part of the insurer? Under what types of circumstances might the court permit the beneficiary to collect the policy proceeds?

5. The widow sued the insurer to recover accidental death benefits under a policy on the life of her husband when the insurer denied liability because the insured had not completed his medical examination and his application had not been acted upon at the time of his death. Is this a reasonable defense on the part of the insurer? Under what types of circumstances might the court permit the widow to collect the policy proceeds?

CHAPTER 10

1. Some of the provisions of the typical life insurance policy are designed to protect the company whereas others are designed to protect the insured. Classify the provisions according to the parties protected.

2. Tom Jones has a $1,000 continuous premium whole life policy. His 10th annual premium is due on July 1. He fails to pay the premium and dies on July 15. How much does his beneficiary collect? Suppose he dies on August 15; how much does his beneficiary collect?

3. If you were a banker to whom a life insurance policyholder is applying for a loan, would you rather have the policy assigned to the bank or have the bank named as the beneficiary of the policy?

4. The insured's policy was issued June 20, 1969 but provided that its effective date was March 14, 1969, to give the insured the benefit of a lower premium rate. It provided that the company would be liable only for return of premiums paid if the insured should commit suicide within "one year from the date of issue of this policy." The insured committed suicide on June 8, 1970 and the company denied liability for the face of the policy and admitted liability only for the return of premiums paid. The beneficiary sued for recovery of the face of policy. What should be the verdict?

5. After the issuance of the policy, the insured had had an operation in which over half of his stomach was removed. Thereafter, he permitted his insurance policy to lapse. In applying for the reinstatement, negative answers were made to the questions inquiring if he had consulted a physician within the last five years or had had a surgical operation or had been hospitalized. The agent testified that he asked the insured the questions in the application; that he inserted the answers as given by the insured; that the insured took the application, appeared to read it over, and then signed it. Is the company liable for payment of policy face?

CHAPTER 11

1. In what set of circumstances would you recommend the selection of each of the following nonforfeiture options: (a) cash surrender payment, (b) paid up at a reduced amount, and (c) extended term insurance?

2. In what set of circumstances would you recommend the selection of each of the following dividend options: (a) cash, (b) paid-up additions, (c) accumulation at interest, (d) the accelerative option, and (e) the one-year term option?

3. In what circumstances would you recommend each of the following methods of settlement of a life insurance contract: (a) life income 20 years certain, (b) life income no years certain, (c) joint and last survivorship income, (d) lump-sum payment, (e) interest only with no withdrawal rights, and (f) interest only with unlimited withdrawal rights?

4. What changes can you suggest for improving the utility of settlement options for the insured and his beneficiaries?

5. The following question appeared in a syndicated newspaper column handling requests for investment advice: "I was recently widowed. Because I knew nothing about investments—I was advised to take $4,500 a year for life from my husband's $70,000 insurance policy instead of drawing out the lump sum and investing it. Now, I fear, I acted hastily. I'm in my early 50's and was entirely unprepared for this tragedy." If you were the author of the column, how would you have replied?

CHAPTER 12

1. In some ways industrial life insurance policies are more liberal than ordinary life insurance policies and in other ways they are less liberal. Why are these two classes of insurance policies not identical in their contractual provisions?

2. Why do you suppose that straight term policies are not written in industrial insurance? Do you think term should be written?

3. If you were called upon to suggest a more appropriate name for what is now called industrial insurance, what name would you suggest? Why?

An economics professor who was commissioned by an insurance trade The Life Insurance Conference) to prepare a study on the future of industrial life insurance concluded, to the delight of the sponsors, that industrial insurance has a bright future, especially in the South. Upon what evidence and line of reasoning do you suspect he reached his conclusions? (b) Suppose an insurance company or group of companies not now writing industrial insurance were to ask you to make a study of the potential growth of industrial life insurance, do you think you would reach the same conclusion as that reached by the economics professor? Explain.

5. (a) Industrial insurance often is severely criticized. Some critics feel it should be outlawed. Can you build a defense for industrial insurance? If so, what would this defense be? (b) What do you suspect the critics of industrial insurance would say in rebuttal? Do you have answers for the rebuttal? (c) If you are unable to build a defense for industrial insurance, what do you suspect the advocates of industrial insurance would say in rebuttal to your reasons for not defending it? Do you have an answer for the rebuttal?

CHAPTER 13

1. How would you distinguish a Blue Shield plan from a group practice prepayment plan? How would you distinguish Blue Cross insurance from coverage written by an insurance company?

2. A man age 25 can purchase $10,000 of continuous premium whole life insurance in one company for an annual premium of $124, nonparticipating. He can add a double indemnity rider to the policy for an additional premium of $9. Should he use this $9 to purchase double indemnity or should he purchase an additional $726 of life insurance?

3. How do disability income riders written with life insurance policies differ from loss of income policies written by the accident and health departments of life insurance companies?

4. How does a business overhead expense policy differ from (1) an ordinary disability income policy; (2) a major medical policy?

5. Design what you believe would be the ideal older age medical care insurance policy.

CHAPTER 14

1. If you were buying a disability income policy, what points would you check in comparing the various policies available to you? If you were buying a basic hospital and surgical expense policy, what points would you check in comparing the various policies available to you? If you were buying a major medical policy, what points would you check in comparing the various policies available to you?

2. The insured's death was caused by asphyxia due to an aspiration of vomitus in the trachea. Would his death be covered under an accidental death policy? What is your reason?

3. In *Prince* v. *United States Life Insurance Co.,* 257 N.Y.S. (2d) 891

(1965), the expenses for the physician's services in treating psychoneurotic re-action resulting from traumatic injury was a covered expense arising from acci-dental bodily injury not from sickness or disease. What difference does it make whether an expense such as the one in this case is treated as one arising from accident or one arising from illness? Explain.

4. The insured suffered from a serious heart condition. He dropped dead after a minor traffic accident. Should his beneficiary be allowed to collect under the insured's accident coverage? What is your reason?

5. The policy defined confining illness as a "confinement within doors." The insured's doctor advised reasonable activity for the insured such as walks, trips to the beach, and reasonable operation of an automobile. The insured followed his doctor's advice. Can he collect disability income benefits. What is your reason?

CHAPTER 15

1. The average rate per $1,000 of group life insurance was computed in the text for a particular group to be $10.24. The average age of that group is 40. The tabular gross premium at age 40 is $5.28. Why is the average rate for the group nearly twice the rate for the average age of the group?

2. What factors are important in underwriting group life insurance? What underwriting safeguards can be used in connection with each of the factors dis-cussed in the first part of this question?

3. What factors should be considered in making a choice between group term insurance and group permanent insurance? If group permanent insurance is chosen, what factors should be considered in making a choice between group paid-up life insurance and level premium group permanent insurance?

4. (a) Distinguish between prospective and retrospective experience rating in group life insurance. (b) What factors affect the credibility of a group's own loss experience and thus the weight given to it in experience rating formulas? (c) How can a group earn a dividend or a retroactive rate credit even when it is carried by the insurer at a loss? Is it fair to pay these loss producing groups a dividend? Justify your position. (d) Explain the purpose of each of the follow-ing charges made against a group in computing dividend allocations: the risk charge, conversion charge, claims charge, and the contingency reserve.

5. Not only state laws but also company underwriting rules restrict the amount of life insurance that can be written on one life in the group. (a) What constraints limit the amount of life insurance that an employer can give to an individual employee under a group life insurance policy? With respect to each constraint identify whether it is a legal constraint or one set up by the insurer. (b) With respect to each legal constraint, explain why it is there and comment on why you believe it to be necessary or unnecesary for the public interest. (c) With respect to the constraints imposed by the insurer, explain the logic behind them. (d) What constraints are imposed upon the amount of life insur-4. (that can be written on the life of an individual debtor? When the amount asse) loan exceeds the amount of insurance available under the group policy,

explain the two formulas that are currently used to relate the coverage to the amount of the debt. Explain the logic behind each formula.

CHAPTER 16

1. Why do you suspect that the laws regulating group health insurance are more lenient than those regulating group life insurance? In what ways are group health insurance statutes less strict than group life insurance statutes?

2. Group health insurance must be underwritten to control cost. With respect to each of the following underwriting factors, show how they affect the cost of each of the various types of group health covers: (*a*) type of group, (*b*) size of group, (*c*) industry, (*d*) composition of employees (sex, race, economic level), (*e*) location of group (residence of employees), (*f*) percentage of temporary and part-time workers, (*g*) personnel practices of the employer, and (*h*) general economic conditions. Why is the first-year claim experience frequently poor? How can the insurer offset this poor first-year experience?

3. "Claim reserves are of considerably greater importance to group health insurance than they are to group life insurance." Explain why you agree or disagree with this statement. How does the claim reserve policy of the insurer affect the retroactive rate credit or dividend to be paid the policyholder under the retrospective experience rating formula?

4. *a*) The manual premium for an employer group life insurance policy is a function of the age distribution among group members, the size of the group, and the type of work to be performed by the members of the group. What variables are considered in developing manual premiums for group major medical coverage that are not considered in developing manual premiums for group life coverage? For each of the additional variables mentioned, explain why it is considered in group major medical coverage but not in group life insurance coverage.

b) Equity in an insurance rating system is attempted by using a classification system based on the factors discussed in part (*a*) of this question, and by giving some weight to the insured's own experience through an experience rate modification. In experience rating formulas, credibility refers to the statistical significance that can be accorded to the loss experience of a given group in establishing the premium for that group. Assume that the group coverage written for employer A has a credibility factor of 0.20 and that the group coverage written for employer B has a credibility factor of 0.75. One or more of five different variables may account for the higher credibility factor for employer A than for employer B. Identify the five variables and explain why each one would affect the size of the credibility factor assigned to the group's own experience.

c) "Sound principles of experience rating are perhaps harder to uphold and to justify to the policyholder for group life insurance than for group hospital expense cover." What do you consider to be sound principles of experience rating? Explain why you agree or disagree with the above statement.

5. The initial rate charged by the insurer is only one of the factors to be considered in the determination of which insurer shall be selected. (*a*) Explain why the above statement is true even when cost is the controlling factor in the deci-

sion. (*b*) Suppose a choice has to be made between an insurer offering a lower premium but a higher retention and one offering a higher premium but a lower retention. What factors should be considered in making the choice? (*c*) Is it possible to negotiate any part of the cost with the insurers? Explain. (*d*) What can the employer do to reduce the cost of his employee benefits program?

CHAPTER 17

1. "The employer using a nonqualified plan is willing to sacrifice the federal tax advantages accorded to qualified plans in exchange for freedom to establish whatever coverage requirements, benefit structures, and financing methods he deems best for the company." (*a*) What tax advantages to employer and employee are sacrificed when a nonqualified plan is used? (*b*) What kinds of coverage requirements, benefit structures, and financing method might the employer establish under a nonqualified plan that would not be possible under a qualified plan?

2. The Black Power and Light Company is in the process of designing a pension plan for its employees and will seek to have it qualified by the Internal Revenue Service. The following are provisions which the company intends to put into the plan. With respect to each provision you are to point out whether it will meet the qualifying requirements of Section 401a of the 1954 Internal Revenue Code and Section 1.401 of the regulations implementing the code. In those instances where you find that a provision *does not* meet a requirement, you are to (1) explain what revision in the provision would be necessary to qualify the plan, (2) explain the logic behind the requirement that would disqualify the provision, and (3) explain why you accept or reject the disqualification as being in the public interest. In those instances where you find that a provision *does* meet the requirements, you are to (1) explain the requirement involved and (2) explain why you accept or reject the requirement as being in the public interest.

a) The plan provides for a $50 a week layoff benefit.

b) The plan provides that upon the death of the employee participant, lifetime income benefits will be paid to his widow commencing when she reaches age 60.

c) The plan covers all full-time employees who have been with the company at least 5 years, and have reached age 28 if females, and age 25 if males. The current thinking is to make the plan noncontributory. The company has 200 employees distributed as follows: 20 part-time employees; 10 seasonal workers; 50 employees with less than 5 years of service; 30 female employees whose husbands have more than adequate pension coverage where they work; and 30 employees with 5 or more years of service who do not meet the age requirement.

d) Someone suggests making the plan contributory and it is learned that 65 employees would participate.

e) The plan will cover only those employees who earn more than the maximum wage subject to social security taxes.

f) Of the eligible employees, 20 percent owned all the stock of the corporation and more than 52 percent of the total employer contributions to the plan over the first 5 years will be on behalf of these owner employees because of their greater ages and higher salaries. These contributions will bear a uniform relation to the basic rate of compensation of the participants.

g) The plan is to be funded through the purchase of life insurance on each participant, these policies to be endowments at age 65. A definite benefit formula is used under which each participating employee who has reached age 65 and has at least 15 years of credited service receives a pension equal to 23 percent of his average annual compensation in excess of $7,800 a year for the 5 highest years.

3. *a*) Assume that the pension plan of the Black Power and Light Corporation has been qualified by the Internal Revenue Service. (1) The corporation paid $800,000 into the pension fund for the first year, but the Internal Revenue Service allowed only $500,000 as a tax deduction for that year. Explain two reasons why the Internal Revenue Service might not have allowed the full $800,-000 deduction. (2) The corporation paid its pension contributions to a qualified pension trust which earned $48,000 on these funds. The Internal Revenue Service claimed that $5,000 of these earnings were subject to income taxes. Why would the Internal Revenue Service tax $5,000 of these earnings and not the other $43,000?

b) The qualified pension plan of the Black Power and Light Company has been in force for a number of years. It is a contributory plan. During January of last year 2 employees retired and were given monthly pensions of $500. One employee was allowed to exclude from gross income for tax purposes the *entire* amount of his pension for that year, whereas the other employee was allowed to exclude only a part of his pension from gross income for that year. What explains the difference between the manner in which these two retired employees were taxed? Do you think that the tax treatment of the two was equitable? Why or why not?

c) One employee terminated his employment during the current year and was paid the full amount credited to his account. How will he be taxed on this amount? Do you think that he is to be taxed equitably? Why or why not?

d) Two active employees died during the year. In one case the death benefits were paid to the employee's widow. In the other case the death benefits were paid to the employee's estate. Explain how these payments were treated for federal estate tax purposes. Do you think that the two estates were treated equitably? Why or why not?

4. (*a*) Explain three provisions that can be put into a qualified deferred profit sharing plan that cannot be included in a qualified pension plan. (*b*) Why are qualified pension plans subject to more constraints than are qualified deferred profit sharing plans? (*c*) Do you think that they should be? Why or why not?

5. (*a*) Explain how retirement plans covering owner employees under the Keogh Act are subject to *more* constraints than are qualified pension or profit sharing plans written for employees of the Black Power and Light Company with respect to establishing eligibility standards for coverage, vesting, employee contributions, distributions, and level of employer contributions. (*b*) Why are Keogh plans subject to more constraints? (*c*) Do you think they should be? Why or why not?

6. (*a*) Explain how retirement plans written under Section 403b of the In-

ternal Revenue Code for Public School employees and employees of 501c(3) Organizations are subject to *less* constraints than are qualified pension and profit sharing plans written for employees of the Black Power and Light Company. (*b*) Why are these plans subject to less constraints? (*c*) Do you think that they should be? Why or why not?

CHAPTER 18

1. *a*) What logical argument can be made for covering part-time workers under a private pension plan? What logical argument can be made to exclude part-time workers from coverage? Which argument has the greater merit?

b) Under what set of conditions would it make no difference either to the employer or to the employees whether or not coverage for a particular class of employees is deferred?

c) Explain why eligibility requirements for participation in deferred profit sharing plans usually are less restrictive than those for pension plans.

2. *a*) What considerations are important in selecting the normal retirement age for a pension plan?

b) When the plan provides for early retirement, the benefits of employees who elect early retirement are usually decreased. What are the justifications for decreased benefits for early retirement?

c) When the plan provides for late retirement, the benefits of employees who elect late retirement usually are not increased. How do you explain what appears to be a discrimination against those who retire late?

d) Under some pension plans, the employee is offered various options in lieu of the normal form of retirement benefit (usually is a pure life annuity). In reaching decisions about options to be offered and conditions to be imposed on their selection, what should the pension designers consider?

3. *a*) With respect to benefits upon termination of employment, the principal variation among pension plans revolves around the disposition of benefit rights not attributable to employee contributions. The question of vesting of benefits in pension plans has become a public policy issue, and various vesting standards have been proposed by federal administrative committees. The case for and the case against compulsory federal vesting standards are based on the arguments of equity and efficiency. Explain the cruxes of the fairness argument and the efficiency argument for and against compulsory federal vesting standards.

b) If, in establishing a pension plan, you find that you have a large number of employees near retirement age, what can you do to handle this problem without increasing the cost of the pension to a prohibitive level?

4. The right to accumulate qualified pension funds for medical care expenses of retired employees, their spouses, and dependents has been effective only since 1962. Explain why a medical expense benefit for retired employees should be included in the pension plan, even if it would mean reducing the amount of the pension benefit by the cost of the medical expense benefit.

5. Explain why the excess plan is more popular than the offset plan of integrating pension benefits.

CHAPTER 19

1. In developing a case for current disbursement financing of pension plans, what types of public policy questions need to be raised? What types of business finance questions need to be raised?

2. *a*) The principal arguments given in favor of the use of trust fund plans as a funding agency for pensions are: flexibility in benefits; flexibility in contributions; flexibility in administration; and greater freedom in the investment of funds. To what extent can life insurance companies match the claims made by competing pension funding agencies?

b) The principal arguments given in favor of insured pension plans are: guaranteed benefits; pooling of investments; pooling of mortality; and the provision of actuarial, legal, financial, and administrative services at low cost. Compare the various types of insured plans (funding instruments) in terms of how they measure up with respect to these advantages cited for insured plans. To what extent can competing pension funding agencies match the claims made by life insurance companies?

3. *a*) Distinguish the various pension actuarial cost methods and explain what might attract the employer to each method.

b) When a pension plan provides for early retirement, the benefit might be scaled down from the normal retirement amount to reflect the difference in the actuarial cost of early retirement. Explain the various actuarial cost assumptions that need to be considered in establishing the benefit adjustment rates for early retirement.

4. What does the funded ratio of a pension plan measure? Assume that at one valuation date the plan has a 100 percent funded ratio but at the next valuation date the ratio is less than (or more than) 100 percent. Summarize the variables that could account for the change in the funded ratio.

5. Federal legislation has been proposed to establish new minimum funding standards for private pension plans. One standard proposed is that vested liabilities be funded within a 25-year period. Another standard proposal is that unfunded liabilities be amortized in not less than 40 years for plans in existence and in not less than 30 years for new plans, and that any experience deficiencies developing be liquidated within 5 years. Evaluate the case for and the case against the proposals for higher minimum funding standards for private pension plans.

CHAPTER 20

You are asked to review the income insurance program of Mr. Richard Knight. He is 35 years old. His wife also is 35 years old. They have an eight-year-old male child and a six-year-old female child.

Mr. K. has an income of $15,000 a year, and is covered under social security for the maximum amount. He owns his home which he purchased five years ago for $31,000. He paid $6,000 down and borrowed the other $25,000 at 6½ percent under an amortized mortgage for 30 years. His property taxes and insurance amount to about $60 a month. Mr. K.'s income taxes amount to about $100 a month.

Mr. K. is covered under a group life insurance policy for $10,000 reducing to $3,000 when he reaches age 65. He is covered also under a group disability income policy paying $100 a week for 26 weeks, after a seven-day waiting period. He is given seven days a year sick leave, noncumulative. He and his family are covered under a group hospitalization policy for full service benefits for the cost of semiprivate accommodations (room and board) for a maximum of 70 days, and for the cost of most hospital extras (drugs, laboratory, operating room, and so forth) incurred during these 70 days. Compulsory retirement age at his company is 65, when he will be retired on a pension of $400 a month. The pension plan is funded, and a reduced pension on a joint and last survivorship annuity may be selected. These employee benefits are noncontributory.

Mr. K. has $1,500 in an insured savings account currently paying 5.25 percent quarterly and owns a 1967 Volkswagen, debt free. He has no debt of any consequences other than the mortgage on his house.

Mr. K. estimates that his family can get along on $750 monthly after his death, provided the mortgage is paid off. He believes that this income can be reduced to $500 a month for his wife after his son graduates from college but he wants to provide an additional $100 a month for each child during the four years the children are in college. Mr. K. estimates that $2,000 would be sufficient to handle expenses associated with the cost of dying.

In the event that Mr. K. becomes disabled, he estimates that an income of $850 a month will be sufficient during his disability until his son reaches age 18; then he wants $750 a month until his daughter reaches age 22. After that he wants $650 a month for life. He wants an additional $158 a month until the mortgage is retired. He also wants some form of catastrophe medical expense coverage for himself and his family. He would like the medical expense coverage to continue for his family upon his death.

In the event that Mr. K. reaches age 65, he would like an income for himself and his wife of $650 a month as long as both are alive and $500 a month to the survivor.

Mr. K. has no health insurance other than that provided by his employer and that provided under social security. He has, in addition to social security and group life insurance, one 20-payment life policy that he purchased 10 years ago, about a year before he was married. This policy is a nonpar policy for $10,000. The premium is $280 a year. The cash value of the policy is now $1,840 and it is worth $3,700 in paid-up insurance. There is no insurance on the lives of his wife and children.

1. *a*) Draw diagrams showing the K. family's post loss resource objectives and point out the gaps that exist based on his current resources for meeting each of these objectives. (You will need to consider premature death, disability, and retirement.)

b) Complete the K. family's preloss plan for the needed post loss resources and point out specifically each of the following: (1) How much life insurance is needed to fill each of the gaps indicated in part (*a*)? (2) What recommendations would you make for filling in the gaps in Mr. K.'s disability income and medical expense coverage? (Be specific as to policies.) (3) How much life insurance cash values are needed at age 65 to complete Mr. K.'s retirement program?

(4) How much additional annual premium would it take to complete the K. family's income insurance objectives? (Include both life and health insurance premiums.)

2. *a*) With respect to Mr. K.'s life insurance, point out with supporting reasons each of the following: (1) What types of life insurance policies are to be purchased. (2) What beneficiary arrangements are to be made. (3) What dividend options are to be selected. (4) What settlement options are to be used.

b) With respect to Mr. K.'s health insurance, point out with supporting reasons each of the following: (1) *For medical care insurance,* who is to be covered, how long and what type of deductible is to be used, how is the maximum benefit to be measured, what charges are to be included, are there to be any internal limits on any of these charges, what restrictions or exclusions are acceptable, and what type of continuation provision is to be used. (2) *For disability income insurance,* who is to be covered, what perils are to be covered, how is disability to be defined in the policy, what restrictions and exclusions are acceptable, is partial disability to be covered, and what type of continuation provision is to be used.

3. What changes would you suggest in the K. family's income insurance program if Mr. K. says he is willing to spend only one half of the additional premium required to put into effect your proposed coverage? Be specific with respect to each section of the program and show the savings involved and coverage depletion resulting from each specific recommendation. What additional coverage would you recommend if Mr. K. says he can spend twice the proposed additional premium?

4. In arranging an income insurance program, what difficulties are encountered in developing a disability income insurance program that are not encountered in developing a life insurance program? What suggestions can you make in terms of product development and underwriting standards that would eliminate these difficulties? What specific arguments can be made in support of your suggestions? What arguments can be made in opposition to your suggestions?

5. Textbooks of life insurance that discuss life insurance programming usually restrict the discussion to traditional or static programming. Professor Belth has developed a concept of dynamic programming as outlined in his paper in the *Journal of Risk and Insurance* (December, 1964, p. 539).

a) What are the principal defects of static programming that led Professor Belth to develop the concept of dynamic programming?

b) What do you perceive to be the principal defects in the use of Professor Belth's dynamic programming concept?

c) What can you offer as an alternative that might not only be an acceptable solution to the defects of traditional programming but also overcome the defects that you perceive in the use of Professor Belth's dynamic programming concept?

CHAPTER 21

1. *a*) Aside from its principal function—that of providing for estate liquidity —life insurance can be used in a number of other ways as an instrument of estate

planning. Describe briefly at least two ways in which life insurance can be used advantageously in estate planning other than that of providing for estate liquidity.

b) Evaluate each of the following instruments of estate planning: (1) *inter vivos* gifts, (2) *inter vivos* trusts, (3) named beneficiaries in life insurance, (4) testamentary life estate for the wife, and (5) joint ownership with right of survivorship.

2. In the process of transferring the estate from the deceased owner to the beneficiaries, the amount available for the beneficiaries is likely to be less than the value of the estate at the time of the estate owner's death. Items said to reduce the value of the estate are administrative expenses, taxes, debts, forced liquidation of assets, and changes in the management of estate assets.

a) What are the variables involved in estimating probable estate administration expenses? Of what value are tables of estimated administration costs?

b) Any debts of the estate owner are charges against the estate whether the owner lives or dies. Therefore, what logic, if any, is there in considering debts as an item that reduces the value of an estate upon the death of the estate owner?

c) Any unpaid taxes incurred by the owner prior to his death are claims against his estate (income and property taxes). Other taxes arise by reason of his death. These later taxes may be classified federal or state. Explain the basic differences and similarities between federal and state death taxes.

d) The state and federal governments recognize the difficulties inherent in any attempt to get large sums of cash out of the estate quickly without serious liquidation losses, and death tax laws usually provide that the period for payment of the tax may be extended under special circumstances. Why, then, does the problem of losses through forced liquidations have to be considered by estate planners?

e) Of what value are credit resources in preventing forced liquidation of estate assets?

f) Of what importance is it to the estate planner to consider possible changes in the character of the estate following the death of the estate owner?

3. Several questions may be raised concerning whether life insurance proceeds are includable in the gross estate for federal estate tax purposes in the estate of the person whose life is insured.

a) Of what importance is the ownership by the insured at the time of his death of the incidents of ownership in the policies on his life in determining whether the proceeds of such policies are includable in his gross estate for federal estate tax purposes?

b) Of what importance is it whether the insured or someone else paid the premiums on his policy in determining whether the proceeds of such policies are includable in his gross estate for federal estate tax purposes?

c) Of what importance is the type of beneficiary arrangement on the policies in determining whether the proceeds of such policies are includable in the gross estate of the insured for federal estate tax purposes?

d) What constitutes incidents of ownership in a life insurance policy? What rights with respect to the policy do not constitute incidents of ownership?

e) Of what importance are the answers to the foregoing questions to estate planning?

4. Several questions may be raised concerning whether the policy values are includable in the estate of a beneficiary.

a) If the beneficiary predeceases the insured and he owns the policy, its value is includable in his estate. How is the value of the policy determined for estate tax purposes?

b) What is the estate tax liability where the primary beneficiary survives the insured and receives proceeds under an optional mode of settlement which includes a *general* power of appointment?

c) Under what circumstances would there be no estate tax liability where the beneficiary survives the insured for proceeds held under an optional mode of settlement?

d) Of what importance are the answers to the foregoing questions to estate planning?

5. Explain the federal income, estate, and gift tax applications, if any, of the following life insurance transactions:

a) "A" who is age 65 purchases a $300 monthly immediate life annuity for the single premium of $39,000. He dies after receiving an annuity income for ten years.

b) "A" purchased a whole life policy of $20,000 for a single premium of $10,574. He surrendered the policy at the end of five years for $10,052.

c) Assume that in the above case, "A" surrendered the policy at the end of ten years for $11,020.

d) "A" dies, leaving the proceeds of a $25,000 policy payable to Mrs. "A" under a life income option.

e) Excess interest is paid on the guaranteed installments under the above policy.

f) "A" dies and leaves the proceeds of his life insurance policy to his widow under the interest-only option subject to full withdrawal. Six years later, the widow asks the company to pay her the proceeds on a life-income option. The company agrees.

g) "A" gives his wife an allowance of $200 a month. She uses part of this money to purchase a $30,000 life insurance policy on "A" 's life. After several years, "A" dies. She has full ownership of the policy.

h) "A" left the dividends on his $20,000 life insurance policy to accumulate at interest. After four years, he drew out the entire dividend accumulation which amounted to $250.

6. Among the following statements, some are true, others are false. Ignore the true statements and explain briefly why you consider the others false.

a) There can be no reportable loss for income tax purposes when a business surrenders a life insurance policy.

b) If a limited payment policy is paid up, and year by year the dividends are taken in cash, no income tax is levied upon the dividends as they are withdrawn.

c) Disability income benefits paid to the insured under a health policy are not subject to income taxes.

d) Premiums on health insurance are deductible as an expense for purposes of computing personal income taxes.

e) If the surrender value of a life insurance or endowment policy is settled under a fixed amount or fixed-period option pursuant to a right contained in the contract to do so, there will be no taxable income until the installments received exceed aggregate premiums paid, after which the full amount received is taxable.

f) The same rule as above would apply if the surrender value of a life insurance or endowment policy is settled under a life-annuity option.

CHAPTER 22

1. *a*) Alec Trician, the sole owner of a large electrical supply house, was shocked to hear of the untimely death of his best friend. When he learned of the shrinkage of his friend's estate, he immediately generated some interest in the problem of estate planning. Alec decided to conduct a study of his own problem and charged you with the responsibility of enlightening him on the avenues of approach to a solution. Since Alec's estate included little more than his business, the problem was simply one of preserving the value of this business interest. Alec, 39 years old, has a wife and two children, a son aged 18 and a daughter aged 16. Assume that Alec's son has his heart set on eventually taking over the business and is studying electrical engineering and business management at the university, and that Alec's daughter is madly in love with a mediocre piano player, and it looks like the real thing. Alec's wife is a good mother without any business sense. With this set of facts, it becomes patent that Alec would want his estate to retain the business interest in the event of his death. What plans, if any, should Alec make to protect his business after his death until his son is ready to take over? Would life and health insurance be helpful in these plans? Discuss.

b) What other problems should Alec consider in his estate plans if he should decide to will the business interest to his son? Would life insurance be helpful in handling any of these problems? Discuss.

2. *a*) Discuss the ways in which life and health insurance can be used effectively by a business in improving employee relations.

b) Aside from the use of business life and health insurance in estate planning and employee relations, what other legitimate needs might a business have for such insurance?

3. Good business management principles dictate the use by many partnerships and close corporations of buy and sell agreements funded by life and disability income insurance. It is important, therefore, that both the philosophical and the technical aspects of buy and sell agreements financed by life insurance be understood by those who use them or advise their use.

a) As to the philosophical aspects: (1) explain briefly why properly financed buy and sell agreements are so important to the surviving partners or stockholders, and (2) explain briefly why life insurance and disability income are useful in funding these buy and sell agreements.

b) As to the technical aspects in arranging insurance to fund a partnership or close corporation buy and sell agreement, several decisions need to be made. For example, questions relating to policy ownership, policy beneficiaries, and premium payments need to be settled. What factors would you consider in a specific situation in reaching an answer to these questions? Explain.

4. A & B have entered into a partnership buy and sell agreement. The insurance was arranged so that A's wife would be the beneficiary on the policy on A's life and B's wife would be the beneficiary on the policy on B's life. Each has signed an agreement to deliver her husband's interest in the partnership to the surviving partner. Assume the partnership is worth $300,000—each partner owning a $150,000 interest and each partner being insured for that amount. A dies and his widow receives $150,000 from his policy and then turns over A's interest in the partnership to B as agreed. Can you see any *possible* income tax disadvantage in this arrangement to B if B subsequently sells the business? If so, what plan could have eliminated this disadvantage? Would the $150,000 life insurance proceeds paid to A's widow upon A's death be subject to the federal estate tax on A's estate?

5. A, B, and C are the stockholders of a close corporation, and own 100 shares of stock each. The corporation purchases $75,000 of life insurance on each stockholder (the value of each stockholder's share) and names itself as beneficiary. It enters into an agreement to purchase the shares of a deceased stockholder. A dies and the corporation purchases A's stock from his widow with the proceeds of the $75,000 life insurance policy. What are the income tax disadvantages of this arrangement to C if he should later sell his stock for $150,000? What plan could have eliminated this disadvantage? Can you see any income tax advantage in having the corporation purchase the life insurance? If so, what?

CHAPTER 23

1. Why is it necessary that an applicant for life and health insurance meet certain underwriting standards, whereas there are no selection standards applied by the government for social security?

2. Why is the physical condition of an applicant important in the underwriting of accident insurance?

3. What information is needed for the underwriting of life insurance that is not needed for the underwriting of health insurance? What information is needed for the underwriting of health insurance that is not needed for the underwriting of life insurance? Why?

4. Your friend Irma has a heart condition so she is not able to buy insurance at standard rates. One agent offers her a policy on a rated-up age plan, whereas a second agent offers a policy on a flat additional premium basis. It so happens that the cost to friend Irma in either case would be $35 per $1,000 of insurance. Which plan would you advise her to take? Would any other method of substandard rating be more beneficial to her than either of these two plans?

5. *a*) What are the objections to an automatic reinsurance treaty on the part of the reinsurance company? What can a reinsurance company do to offset any disadvantages resulting from an automatic treaty?

b) For what purposes other than coverage for excess liability might reinsurance be used?

CHAPTER 24

1. *a*) Construct a mortality table from ages 35 to 39 using the following basic data.

Age	Number of Living	Number Dying
35 40,000		143
36 35,000		129
37 85,000		390
38 73,000		350
39 64,000		395

b) A mortality table has been described as the picture of "a generation of individuals passing through time." Comment on the accuracy of this description.

2. Explain how interest rates enter into life insurance premium calculations.

3. *a*) "Loading is more of a problem in cost accounting than of actuarial science." Explain why you agree or disagree with this statement.
b) If rate-making is a science, how do you account for the fact that all companies do not charge the same rates?

4. What effect will each of the following have upon the premium of a life insurance policy: (*a*) a shift from the 1941 CSO to the 1958 CSO Mortality Table; (*b*) a shift from a 2½ percent to a 3 percent interest assumption. Why?

5. Explain how lapse rates affect the cost of life insurance.

CHAPTER 25

1. Compute the net level annual premium for a five-year term policy issued at age 30. Use either the method developed in the chapter or in Appendix A of the chapter, and explain each step in the computation.

2. Explain why the net level premium for a five-year term policy is not the net single premium divided by five.

3. Explain why the problem of rate making for major medical insurance is more complex than premium rate computation for accidental death benefits.

4. Explain the nature of a continuance table and show how it is used to compute rates for a disability income policy paying $1 daily for a maximum of 70 days after a 3-day waiting period.

5. Explain how the method of premium computation for life insurance illustrated in Appendix B differs from that developed in Chapters 24 and 25. Is one of these methods easier to understand than the other? Explain.

CHAPTER 26

1. Describe the nature and purpose of the *summary of operations* and *allocation of surplus* statements.

2. What problems do policy loans create for life insurance companies? How might these problems be solved?

3. a) Why is it important to have regulatory standards for valuating insurance company assets? What do you consider to be the principal problems in valuing life insurance company assets today?

b) Explain the meaning of the term "admitted assets." Why are some assets admitted whereas other are nonadmitted?

4. a) Explain what you consider to be the important objectives of a life insurance company investment policy.

b) Explain the ways life insurance funds have been and could be invested for a socioeconomic purpose.

5. Check the current issue of the *Life Insurance Fact Book*, note the relative changes over the past 5 years in the percentage distributions among assets held by life insurers, and then explain what you believe to be the factors that fostered these changes.

CHAPTER 27

1. a) Compute the third-year terminal reserve per $1,000 of 5-pay 10-year endowment insurance issued at age 30, using 1958 CSO at $2\frac{1}{2}$ percent. Use the full net level premium reserve, and compute it first using the prospective method and then using the retrospective method. Explain why the answers are the same.

b) Compute the foregoing reserve on the Commissioners Standard Valuation method. Explain the theory behind this method of reserve computation.

c) Compute the minimum surrender value of the foregoing policy at the end of the third year. Why is the nonforfeiture surrender value different from the policy reserve? Trace what you suspect would normally be the size of the policy's asset share in relation to its surrender value and policy reserve over its duration. Why do you expect the relative size of the policy's asset share to be as you indicated?

2. Explain why the size of the reserve for a level premium whole life policy is a function of the steepness of the slope of the mortality curve.

3. a) Explain the problems involved in achieving equity in dividend distribution.

b) Explain why the experience premium method of dividend allocation might be considered less scientific than the contribution system.

4. Why are surrendering policyholders expected to make a permanent contribution to the surplus of the insurer? Would those whose policies terminated as a death claim expected to make a permanent contribution to the insurer's surplus? Explain.

5. a) What problems do the actuaries have in establishing reserves for health insurance that they do not have in developing reserves for life insurance?

b) Why is a two-year preliminary term valuation method permitted in establishing the active life reserve for health insurance but only a one-year preliminary term valuation method permitted in establishing reserves for life insurance?

CHAPTER 28

1. The following is a quotation from a speech given before a group of life insurance agents: "People think most of the time that life insurance costs money, and you want to dissuade them from that erroneous impression. Life insurance is absolutely free." What did the speaker mean by such a statement? Should life insurance agents be allowed much less encouraged to tell policyholders that they can get something for nothing? Explain.

2. Is it better to assume that good companies are represented only by good agents or that good agents represent only good companies? What is your concept of the terms good companies and good agents?

3. *a*) Why might a stock life insurance company choose to mutualize? Why might a mutual insurer choose to convert into a stock insurer?

b) Which do you suspect would be the more difficult (create more problems), the conversion of a mutual insurer into a stock insurer or the conversion of a stock insurer into a mutual insurer? Why?

c) Examine the role that holding companies can be expected to play in the life insurance business.

4. The publication, *Cost Facts on Life Insurance,* presents cost information on a number of life insurance companies. It uses three different bases for measuring cost: (1) the traditional method; (2) the equalized cost method; and (3) the benefits cost method.

a) Explain how an insurer might show a relatively low cost under the traditional cost basis but a relatively high cost under the equalized cost method.

b) Explain how an insurer might show a relatively low cost under the equalized cost basis but a relatively high cost under the benefits cost method.

c) Explain the circumstances under which you think the most appropriate method for the purchaser to use in comparing costs among insurers is: (1) the benefits cost method; (2) the equalized cost method; and (3) the traditional cost method.

5. *a*) If you were assigned the job of designing a system for recruiting, selecting, and training life insurance agents, what questions would you ask in order to identify problems and reach recommended solutions? Explain the purpose of each question.

b) If you were asked to redesign the compensation system for life insurance agents, what changes would you recommend? Why?

c) If you were asked to redesign the job of a life insurance agent, what changes in his functions would you suggest? Why?

d) What do you suspect are the reasons for the high turnover among life insurance agents? Would a reduced rate of agent turnover be in the public interest? Explain.

CHAPTER 29

1. *a*) Explain why the business of insurance is more closely regulated than is the business of manufacturing and marketing of men's clothing.

b) Do you agree with Elizur Wright that the decision in the *Paul* v. *Virginia* case was "a blow to the sound regulation of the business"? Explain the logic behind your position.

2. What do you conceive to be the case for price disclosure laws in life insurance? What do you conceive to be the case against price disclosure laws in life insurance? Are there any reasons why there has been no agitation for price disclosure laws in health insurance? Explain.

3. *a*) Explain why you would support or oppose legislation to allow tontine plans to be written by life insurance companies.

b) How effective are state antitrust laws? Explain the criteria you have used in measuring effectiveness.

4. *a*) "The regulation of unlicensed insurers creates a special problem for the states." Explain three ways in which the problem might be solved. What method do you consider to be the most appropriate? What criteria have you used in reaching this conclusion?

b) Explain the role of the Securities and Exchange Commission in the regulation of life insurance companies. Is this the proper role for the SEC?

5. Are life insurance companies fairly taxed by the federal and state governments? What criteria have you used in measuring fairness?

A) Insurance actually helps. Why? What the decline in the P/E ratio can be traced from to the actual operations of the insurance business, or does not behind your position?

2) What do you consider to be the more Reasonable to the return? What are current. What do you consider to be the more standard your position? At what any circumstances that have a significant impact on business laws which influence its plan.

3) Explain why you would support or oppose a legislative attempt to place the P/E ratio by life insurance companies.

4) How would you as an actual base your business investment in relation to your firm.

5) The regulation of ordinary life insurance types of life policies. Explain the various steps that the ordinary life type of policy the standard by the standard type of the ordinary policy. This affect how do you feel of this institution.

6) Explain the role of the operation and cost. Some more contact for the insurance companies about the type of the type of policies.

7) As has always required or when the case that the standards apply. Do you consider your position on the situation.

Index of Court Cases Cited

Index of Authors
and Sources Cited

Index of Subjects